תנ״ך קורן אביב • בראשית

The Koren Aviv Tanakh • Bereshit

KOREN

THE MAGERMAN EDITION

תנ״ך קורן אביב • בראשית

THE KOREN AVIV TANAKH • BERESHIT

TORAH TRANSLATION BY
Rabbi Lord Jonathan Sacks זצ״ל

DEVELOPED BY
Rabbi Dr. Daniel Rose

MANAGING EDITOR
Caryn Meltz

•

KOREN PUBLISHERS JERUSALEM

The Koren Aviv Tanakh • Bereshit
The Magerman Edition
First Hebrew-English Edition

Koren Publishers Jerusalem Ltd.
POB 4044, Jerusalem 9104001, ISRAEL
POB 8531, New Milford, CT, 06776, USA

www.korenpub.com

ISBN 978-965-7812-62-4, HARDCOVER

Printed in the PRC
First printing
KATB01

The Torah is eternal.

Humanity is ephemeral and dynamic.

The Torah is the cornerstone of the world, of our People, and it forms
the baseline of the Tanakh, the holy writings of God and His prophets.
The changing nature of human society in which our children are growing up
in demands a fresh while remaining rooted in the eternal essence of the Torah.
The Tanakh is a living script, the screenplay of the
history of humanity from Creation to the present.

We pray that this creative and innovative new approach to learning Tanakh will engage and
empower young and old alike to find their own meaning in our ancient wisdom,
uniting us in our traditions, exposing us to new ways of thinking,
and ultimately bringing us closer to the Redemption.

אֲנִי מַאֲמִין בֶּאֱמוּנָה שְׁלֵמָה
בְּבִיאַת הַמָּשִׁיחַ
וְאַף עַל פִּי שֶׁיִּתְמַהְמֵהַּ עִם כָּל זֶה אֲחַכֶּה לּוֹ
בְּכָל יוֹם שֶׁיָּבוֹא.

I believe with perfect faith
in the coming of the Messiah,
and though he may delay,
I wait daily for his coming.

We are pleased that we were able to contribute to this critically important
Tanakh series for young people.

Debra and David Magerman
Philadelphia, Pennsylvania

Contents

לך לך • Lekh Lekha

וירא • Vayera

חיי שרה • Ḥayei Sara

תולדת • Toledot

ויצא • Vayetze

וישלח • Vayishlaḥ

ויֵשֶׁב • Vayeshev

מקץ • Miketz

ויגש • Vayigash

ויחי • Vayeḥi

הפטרות • Haftarot

קריאות והפטרות לשבתות מיוחדות
Readings and Haftarot for Special Shabbatot

Appendices

Publisher's Preface

דור לדור ישבח מעשיך.

One generation will praise Your works to the next.

(Tehillim 145:4)

It is with gratitude and a certain ambition that we introduce this volume of the Magerman Edition of *The Koren Aviv Tanakh*, a multivolume, colorful, and enticing Tanakh designed to encourage connection, reflection, and learning of our foundational text.

The Tanakh is under-studied by our teenagers. The connection between Jewish young adults and the Tanakh is critical, more so today than ever. Students must learn the text of the Tanakh and the classical commentators who have illuminated difficult passages. But it is just as important that young adults engage emotionally and experientially with the text, and all too often, those aspects are neglected.

This project's unique contribution to Tanakh education is that it places the students firmly at the center of the learning experience, allowing them to relate directly to the text and find their own meaning there. While learning Tanakh through the prism of traditional commentaries is undoubtedly important, these volumes empower the next generation to connect to Tanakh in a direct and personal way. Using creative educational resources and approaches, *The Koren Aviv Tanakh* encourages students to analyze the text and find meaning in the verses that is personal and relevant for their own lives.

It is with this ambition that Koren Publishers Jerusalem has created this edition, designed for middle and high school students and young adults in synagogue *minyanim*. Since 1962, the

Koren Tanakh has been recognized for its textual accuracy and innovative graphic design. We have remained committed to these qualities, and we have recently had the privilege of enriching the Tanakh text with the eloquent English translation of one of the most articulate and original Jewish thinkers of our time, Rabbi Lord Jonathan Sacks, *zt"l*.

It is with gratitude that we acknowledge Rabbi Sacks for this exceptional translation of the Torah. And our thanks are no less due to Rabbi Dr. Daniel Rose, Koren's Director of Education, whose vision is executed in these volumes. Caryn Meltz, our Managing Editor, brought it all together into a handsome and useful edition, and Tani Bayer, our art director, created the design for the Tanakh and cover. Finally, thank you to our typesetters, Esther Be'er and Taly Hahn, and to our copyeditors and proofreaders, Efrat Gross, Tali Simon, Avichai Gamdani, and Daniel Safran, who made this volume a reality.

None of this would have been possible without the support and vision of Debra and David Magerman of Philadelphia and Jerusalem, who understood both our ambitions and the methods of this edition.

On behalf of all our rabbis, scholars, editors, and designers, we thank the Magerman family. And on behalf of the many thousands of readers, in this and future generations – we are forever in your debt.

We hope the use of these volumes of Tanakh will bring Jews closer and closer to the Torah and all the good it represents.

Matthew Miller, Publisher
Jerusalem, 5784 (2024)

Introduction

> The text of Torah is our covenant with God, our written constitution as a nation under His sovereignty. The interpretation of this text has been the subject of an ongoing conversation for as long as Jews have studied the divine word, a conversation that began at Sinai thirty-three centuries ago and has not ceased since. Every age has added its commentaries, and so must ours. Participating in that conversation is a major part of what it is to be a Jew. For we are the people who never stopped learning the Book of Life, our most precious gift from the God of life.
>
> Rabbi Lord Jonathan Sacks[1]

Tanakh studies has always been synonymous with Koren as a publishing house. Ever since Eliyahu Koren published the first edition of the Koren Tanakh in 1962, Koren has committed itself to bringing serious Tanakh scholarship to a broader Hebrew-speaking, and more recently, English-speaking audience. In 2013 Koren established an educational department dedicated to the education of young Jews through innovative pedagogical publications. The launch of *The Koren Aviv Tanakh* series heralds a new stage in this journey, utilizing innovative and creative educational approaches to Tanakh study for the young. In the words of Rabbi Sacks, every age has added its own commentaries to the Tanakh, and so must ours. What better time than the teenage years to begin the empowerment of the next generation in this process.

---

1 | *Covenant & Conversation: A Weekly Reading of the Jewish Bible – Genesis: The Book of Beginnings* (Jerusalem: Maggid Books, 2009), 3.

Educational Vision Behind the Series

The wisdom of student-centered learning has been informing the pedagogy of thoughtful educators since the research on how children learn by, among others, John Dewey, Jean Piaget, and Lev Vygotsky, generations before our classrooms became populated by Gen Z and now Gen Alpha. Our students, through no fault of their own, are more focused on their own sense of self and self-worth than young people at any previous point in history.[2] Conventional pedagogic wisdom has for some time encouraged the educator to think about becoming a "guide on the side" rather than a "sage on the stage."

Perhaps influenced by these trends, the field of Tanakh study has also evolved in recent years toward encouraging students to engage directly with the text, rather than only through the prism of classical and modern commentaries. This approach has been pioneered by our friends at Herzog College, as well as other centers of Tanakh scholarship across the world. In the introduction to the Maggid series *Torah MiEtzion,* Rabbi Ezra Bick writes: "Tanakh is meant to be read and understood by the reader, without the absolute necessity of outside interlocutors. The keys to understanding Tanakh are found within Tanakh itself."[3]

This pedagogy forms the foundation and guiding light behind the approach to learning and teaching Tanakh found in *The Koren Aviv Tanakh.* That is not to say that we believe this approach should replace the traditional in-depth study of Tanakh with classical commentaries. There is without doubt a deep value to approaching the text of the Tanakh through the eyes of the classical and modern commentators, who themselves reflect ancient traditions and readings. However, we believe this approach complements that one and, we would argue, should precede it. The brave educator will encourage his or her students to find their own meaning in the text before they then explore the rich library of Jewish commentaries available to navigate our understanding of Tanakh.

Explanation of Educational Elements

The educational elements found in *The Koren Aviv Tanakh* are explained below. Several of these elements contain excerpts from essays written by Tanakh scholars, and in some cases these texts have been slightly modified for the sake of standardization and consistency, or to make the text flow.

---

2 | For fascinating research on this topic, see Jean M. Twenge, *iGen: Why Today's Super-Connected Kids Are Growing Up Less Rebellious, More Tolerant, Less Happy – and Completely Unprepared for Adulthood – and What That Means for the Rest of Us* (New York: Atria Books, 2017).

3 | *Torah MiEtzion: New Readings in Tanach – Volume I: Bereshit* (Jerusalem: Maggid Books and Yeshivat Har Etzion, 2011), xv.

While all of these elements are tools and resources to achieve the educational vision of the project – namely, independent, student-centered learning of Tanakh, allowing for a robust meaning-making process that will encourage connecting to the text in a direct and personal way – each element stands alone. Some of the elements may be more appealing than others to you as an educator and to your students. There is no need to feel that all the segments must be utilized in your classroom. Creative educators will plan their classes and facilitate the learning process in a way that only they can, and this edition can provide an array of educational resources to choose from to achieve their personal educational goals.

Taking an Episodic Approach to Structuring the Narrative

In order to focus the student on the narrative and thematic segments found in the Tanakh, *The Koren Aviv Tanakh* has taken an episodic approach, dividing the text into thematic episodes that aid in the reading and understanding of the text.

Over time, there have been various ways to break up the text of the Tanakh. For example, the division into chapters and verses dates from the thirteenth century and is Christian in origin. The Masoretic text was divided into *parashot,* and although there is some controversy over this tradition, the division of *parashot* used by *soferim* in writing modern-day *sifrei Torah* is based on Rambam's list found in the eighth chapter of *Hilkhot Tefillin UMezuza VeSefer Torah* in his *Mishneh Torah.* These *parashot* are delineated by "open portions" *(parashot petuḥot),* where the line ends with an open space and the next *parasha* begins on the following line), and "closed portions" *(parashot setumot),* where a space is left at the end of the last verse of the *parasha,* and the next *parasha* begins after that space on the same line.

The division of the Torah into weekly readings (somewhat confusingly also called *parashot*) dates from the sixth century BCE as described in the book of Neḥemya, when the weekly system of reading the *parasha* with an annual completion was standardized. These weekly readings of the Torah portion were further divided into seven sections, one for each *aliya*, or person called to the Torah reading, on Shabbat.

It should be noted that while the episodic approach taken in this book maintains the divisions of the weekly readings, these divisions do not always coincide with the Masoretic *(setuma/petuḥa)* divisions. Due to the logistics of layout and design, at times a new episode begins on a new line and may appear to be a *parasha petuḥa*. While this is something to be avoided in general, after consultation with halakhic and educational experts, we decided it was justifiable to further the educational vision of this project.

Parasha Introduction Page

At the beginning of each *parasha*, an introductory page will feature a ***Parasha Overview***, a list of the episodes featured in this *parasha*, and a list of ***Parasha Stats***. The Parasha Overview is generally taken from the introductions to the chapters of *Covenant & Conversation: A Weekly Reading of the Jewish Bible – Genesis: The Book of Beginnings* by Rabbi Jonathan Sacks.

The First Page of Each Episode

Each episode has a title and begins with a ***Summary.*** This is often adapted content from the *Steinsaltz Humash*. On the first page of each episode there is also a list of three underlying ***Themes*** that can be found in the text of the episode. More than twenty-five overarching themes were identified running throughout Tanakh, and through signaling the themes most central to each episode, we can highlight the intertextuality of parts of Tanakh, encouraging the student to identify and reflect on these themes throughout their Tanakh studies.

There are also two categories of reflection and textual analysis questions on this page, which encourage the student to engage directly with the text on their own terms, and become a Tanakh commentator in their own right. ***Unlocking the Text is*** a list of questions that identify the gaps in the text, which close readers of the Tankah would wish to address and explore. Students are encouraged to use these questions (or ask their own questions) to unlock the meaning of the text, or develop their own commentary or creative midrash. ***Finding Yourself in the Text*** asks three questions that encourage the student to relate to the text in a personal way, using their own life as a frame of reference. Reflection on these questions and their own lived experiences could help them to understand the text, and this is the aim of these questions.

In the text of many of the episodes, there are key words and phrases (in Hebrew and English) highlighted in various colors which connect them to the ***Taking a Literary Approach*** sections (see below). This helps the student immediately see the textual analysis of those authors in a visual way.

Bibliodrama

Bibliodrama is a creative educational tool that enables students to deepen their connection to the characters in the text by "stepping into their shoes." It is a form of role-playing in which students are asked to take on the role of the characters in biblical texts. Bibliodrama asks students to imagine what was going on in the minds and hearts of the personalities from the narrative, and in so doing, the students are creating their own midrash (as more often than not, the text keeps the emotions and thoughts of the characters hidden from the reader). The characters that feature in the ***A Question of Bibliodrama*** sections of this volume are largely the human personalities from the text, but in some cases they also include non-humans, such as animals (for example, Bilaam's donkey) or spiritual beings such as angels or God.

Peter A. Pitzele, a pioneer in utilizing bibliodrama in Tanakh study, compares bibliodrama to Midrash in the following way:

> Bibliodrama is a form of interpretive play. To honor it with a venerable Hebrew name, bibliodrama can be called a form of Midrash.…For the rabbis, this interpretive engagement with the Bible manifested itself in word-plays, analogies, and even puns that intensified the active experience of reading texts. Midrash is derived from a Hebrew root that means to investigate or explore. In the Midrash the written text is closely examined for meanings and insights that will enrich our understanding and enhance our relationship to the Bible. In a more generic sense, however, midrash – now in lower case – may extend in time to later ages and to our own. From a more liberal perspective, midrash may include extra-literary acts of interpretation such as movement, song, visual art, and drama, which, like their classical forebears, serve to illuminate meaning in the biblical narrative.[4]

The questions in the Bibliodrama sections lend themselves well to full group role-play simulation, small group discussions, or even *chavruta* conversations, where one student could be an interviewer asking questions of the other, who plays the role of the character. They could then switch roles. You may also wish to invite your students to create their own questions. It is important to let the conversations flow in their own organic and creative directions, even if this may lead to some tricky discussions. While there are no right and wrong answers in bibliodrama, and one can never be sure of the direction the conversations will lead, you can intersperse the conversations with more information about the narrative that the students may not be aware of, using scholarship and other texts in Tanakh. But be careful not to use midrashic sources, as these would compete with the students' own midrashic approach taken during the process of bibliodrama. A period of reflection and discussion after the bibliodrama has ended is always worthwhile so that the process can be framed and reflected on, then brought back to the students and their task to develop understanding of the text.

The Art of Midrash

Using art as a modern form of Midrash has become more and more popular among creative Tanakh teachers. Just as our classical midrashim address the gaps in the text begging to be addressed, so have artists throughout the ages when they create a visual interpretation of the Tanakh text through their art. Rabbi Shlomo Riskin draws similarities between the midrashic processes involved in both ancient midrashim and contemporary art:

---

4 | *Scripture Windows: Toward a Practice of Bibliodrama* (Lewisville, NC: Torah Aura Productions, 1998), 11–12.

> The Midrash expands and builds upon the text in its description of scriptural figures, inviting us to share its thoughts and emotions as it fills gaps left in the biblical account. It suggests conversations, actions, and spiritual quandaries that are not specified in the Bible itself. By describing the qualities and personalities of scriptural figures, the Midrash helps us to visualize the characters more vividly as human individuals.…[Art] opens our eyes to additional interpretations of the text [which] emerge from the world of Torah, Jewish tradition, and from the world of artists from the seventy nations of the world and different cultures. All of them read the Torah and used visual and verbal means to express the particular facet they found there. The artist, like the commentator, has a unique gift, divine inspiration, emanating directly from the ultimate Creator.[5]

Each episode in this volume has an associated piece of art that expresses in some way an approach to the text of the episode. Asking our students to analyze the midrashic process the artists have embarked on, and to evaluate if and how it enlightens our own connection to and understanding of the text, can be a powerful way for students to engage in the text. For this to be most effective, a process of debriefing and reflection facilitated by the teacher is vital. Relating to artwork as midrash can also form the foundation for your students to use their own artistic talents as a midrashic expression of their understanding of text, and this could be a fun and meaningful class activity or assignment.

Integrating Ḥokhma

In his book *Future Tense,* Rabbi Sacks describes a dual epistemology, knowledge of the world, through Torah and *ḥokhma* (which he translates as wisdom). He distinguishes them in the following way:

> *Ḥokhma* is the truth we discover; Torah is the truth we inherit. *Ḥokhma* is the universal heritage of humankind; Torah is the specific heritage of Israel. *Ḥokhma* is what we attain by being in the image of God; Torah is what guides Jews as the people of God. *Ḥokhma* is acquired by seeing and reasoning; Torah is received by listening and responding. *Ḥokhma* tells us what is; Torah tells us what ought to be. *Ḥokhma* is about facts; Torah is about commands. *Ḥokhma* yields descriptive, scientific laws; Torah yields prescriptive, behavioral laws. *Ḥokhma* is about creation; Torah is about revelation.[6]

---

5 | Shlomo Riskin, Yardenna Lubotzky, and Ruth Mark, *Brushes with the Bible: Jewish Commentaries and Biblical Illustrations* (Jerusalem: Maggid Books, 2018), ix.

6 | *Future Tense* (Maggid Books, 2021), 221.

While differentiating between the knowledge of the world that we can gain from the Torah and that which we can gain from the sciences, he also described a conversation between these two worlds in his essays on the weekly *parasha*. In each essay, while drawing insight and understanding from this ancient divine text for our contemporary world, he also drew from scientific wisdom and the best that human culture has to offer, to deepen his and our understanding of the text of the Torah. For Rabbi Sacks, "Torah is a commentary on life, and life is a commentary on Torah. Together they constitute a conversation, each shedding light on the other."[7]

In each episode in this volume, we have brought texts and resources from the world of *ḥokhma* to enlighten and deepen our understanding of the text. More often than not, this scientific wisdom was not available to the medieval and even many of the modern commentators, and this is an opportunity to empower students to engage with the text in a way that previous commentators could not.

Taking a Literary Approach

In the final section in each episode, a literary analysis approach to studying Tanakh is presented by a variety of recognized Tanakh scholars. Rabbi Ezra Bick makes the case for this approach when he writes:

> If we are reading the text directly, then we are reading it as a text is meant to be read, and this introduces the need to read using the tools of literary analysis. Of course, if the Torah is not a book, but a code or a mystery, it would be illegitimate to read it with the same eyes and mind that one reads literature. For this we have the oft-repeated principle, *dibra Torah belashon benei adam* (the Torah speaks in human language). The Torah is literature, divine literature, written not in a special divine language but in the language and the style of man.[8]

Literary analysis tools found in this section include structural analysis, terminology analysis, such as the discovery of a "leading term," textual comparison and intertextuality, plot analysis, and character analysis. Because the understanding of a literary work requires understanding of factors external to its writing, findings from history, archaeology, and Semitics also feature. The focus of these excerpts is on the story, the entire narrative, and in some cases, the whole Tanakh, rather than the traditional verse-by-verse approach taken by many of the classic commentaries.

---

7 | *Covenant & Conversation – Genesis: The Book of Beginnings*, 3.

8 | *Torah MiEtzion: New Readings in Tanach – Volume I: Bereshit*, xvi.

Acknowledgments

Every day I wake with newfound gratitude to God that I found my calling as a Jewish educator and have the privilege to make some small impact on the lives of young Jews around the world with the publications I contribute to.

My thanks and friendship to the publisher, Matthew Miller, who continues to show confidence in my abilities, and has supported my work consistently over many years, even when it means sometimes taking a risk on a radical new approach. He has assembled a world-class team of talented and wonderful people I have the honor to call my colleagues and my friends, without whom a project such as this would never see the light of day. These include Rabbi Reuven Ziegler, Rabbi Avishai Magence, Caryn Meltz, Tali Simon, Taly Hahn, Tani Bayer, Esther Be'er, Dr. Yoel Finkelman, Aryeh Grossman, Efrat Gross, Daniel Safran, and Jenni Menashe.

I would like to take this opportunity to thank David and Debra Magerman once again for their generosity in supporting this project. This is the latest in a long line of projects I have worked on that they have made possible. Their vision and passion for Jewish education and the Jewish people is inspiring.

As always, my love and thanks must go to my loving family who are the foundation upon which anything I have ever achieved is built. To Jacqueline, Orli, Keren, Aryeh, Eliya, and Elisha, for your never-ending love and support, I dedicate this volume to you.

The last stages of this volume were completed during a very dark time for our nation. Rabbi Sacks taught me that just as the Chinese ideogram for "crisis" also means "opportunity," the Hebrew word for crisis, *mashber,* also means "child-birth chair." From pain and darkness comes new life. He writes, "Any civilization that can see the blessing within the curse, the fragment of light within the heart of darkness, has within it the capacity to endure."[9] From one of the darkest periods of our modern history has come forth light and goodness. I wish to dedicate this volume to those we have lost; to their families; to those who have fought, on whose shoulders our state exists; and to the Jewish people, *am hanetzaḥ.*

Rabbi Dr. Daniel Rose
Modi'in, Nisan 5784

9 | *Studies in Spirituality* (Jerusalem: Maggid Books, 2021), 63–64.

בראשית
Bereshit

Parasha Overview

The Book of Books starts with the beginning of beginnings: the creation of the universe and life. The story is told from two different perspectives, first as cosmology (the origins of matter), then as anthropology (the birth of humanity).

The first narrative (Bereshit 1:1–2:3) emphasizes harmony and order. The second narrative (2:4–2:23) focuses on humanity, not as a biological species but as persons-in-relation. First God creates man, and then He creates woman, so humans do not live alone. The serpent tempts them; they sin and are banished from the Garden of Eden.

From then on, the human drama unfolds as tragedy. Kayin murders his brother. By the end of the *parasha*, God sees "how great man's wickedness on the earth had become" and "regrets that He had made man on earth." God creates order; man creates chaos. Which will prevail?

Episodes

1. **The Seven Days of Creation** 1:1–2:3
2. **The Second Account of Creation** 2:4–25
3. **The Fall of Eden** 3:1–24
4. **The Children of Adam and Ḥava** 4:1–26
5. **The First Family Tree** 5:1–32
6. **Humanity Disappoints** 6:1–8

Parasha Stats

- 7,235 letters
- 1,931 words
- 146 verses
- 241 lines in a sefer Torah
- 1 mitzva

1 1 2 When God began creating heaven and earth, the earth was void and desolate, there
3 was darkness on the face of the deep, and the spirit of God moved over the waters. God
4 said, "Let there be light." And there was light. God saw the light: it was good; and God
5 separated the light from the darkness. And God called the light "day," and the darkness
He called "night." There was evening, and there was morning – one day.
6 Then God said, "Let an expanse stretch through the water, let it separate water from
7 water." So God made the expanse, and it separated the water beneath the expanse from
8 the water above. And so it was. God called the expanse "heavens." There was evening,
and there was morning – a second day.
9 Then God said, "Let the water beneath the heavens be gathered to one place, and let
10 dry ground appear." And so it was. God called the dry ground "earth," and the gathered
11 waters He called "seas." And God saw: it was good. Then God said, "Let the earth
produce vegetation: seed-bearing plants and trees of all the kinds on earth that grow
12 seed-bearing fruit." And so it was. The earth produced vegetation: plants bearing seeds,
each of its kind, and trees bearing fruit containing seeds, each of its kind. And God saw:
13 it was good. There was evening, and there was morning – a third day.
14 Then God said, "Let there be lights in the heavens' expanse to separate day from night

UNLOCKING THE TEXT

- Why does each day conclude with the words "There was evening, and there was morning"?
- Why is the first day described as "one day" but the others as a counted number (e.g., "a second day")?
- What does it mean that "God saw...and it was good"?
- Who is God talking to when He says, "Let us make man"?
- What does it mean to be created "in the image of God"?
- Did God create a single human at first or two humans, one of each gender?
- Why does God use the language of "very good" on the sixth day?
- What does it mean that the seventh day is "blessed" and "holy"?
- What does it mean that God "rested"?

FINDING YOURSELF IN THE TEXT

- Have you ever created something you were so proud of that you needed to tell everyone about it?
- Can you see the godliness in all people? Is this sometimes a challenge for you?
- Is your weekly Shabbat "blessed" and "holy"? How?

Consider using these questions as the basis for your own commentary or creative midrash.

How does reflecting on these firsthand experiences help you better understand the text?

א בְּרֵאשִׁ֖ית בָּרָ֣א אֱלֹהִ֑ים אֵ֥ת הַשָּׁמַ֖יִם וְאֵ֥ת הָאָֽרֶץ: וְהָאָ֗רֶץ הָיְתָ֥ה תֹ֙הוּ֙ **א בראשית**

ב וָבֹ֔הוּ וְחֹ֖שֶׁךְ עַל־פְּנֵ֣י תְה֑וֹם וְר֣וּחַ אֱלֹהִ֔ים מְרַחֶ֖פֶת עַל־פְּנֵ֥י הַמָּֽיִם: וַיֹּ֥אמֶר אֱלֹהִ֖ים

ג יְהִי־א֑וֹר וַֽיְהִי־אֽוֹר: וַיַּ֧רְא אֱלֹהִ֛ים אֶת־הָא֖וֹר כִּי־ט֑וֹב וַיַּבְדֵּ֣ל אֱלֹהִ֔ים בֵּ֥ין הָא֖וֹר

ד וּבֵ֥ין הַחֹֽשֶׁךְ: וַיִּקְרָ֨א אֱלֹהִ֤ים ׀ לָאוֹר֙ י֔וֹם וְלַחֹ֖שֶׁךְ קָ֣רָא לָ֑יְלָה וַֽיְהִי־עֶ֥רֶב וַֽיְהִי־בֹ֖קֶר

ה י֥וֹם אֶחָֽד:

ו וַיֹּ֣אמֶר אֱלֹהִ֔ים יְהִ֥י רָקִ֖יעַ בְּת֣וֹךְ הַמָּ֑יִם וִיהִ֣י מַבְדִּ֔יל בֵּ֥ין מַ֖יִם לָמָֽיִם: וַיַּ֣עַשׂ אֱלֹהִים֮ אֶת־הָרָקִיעַ֒ וַיַּבְדֵּ֗ל בֵּ֤ין הַמַּ֙יִם֙ אֲשֶׁר֙ מִתַּ֣חַת לָרָקִ֔יעַ וּבֵ֣ין הַמַּ֔יִם אֲשֶׁ֖ר מֵעַ֣ל לָרָקִ֑יעַ

ז וַֽיְהִי־כֵֽן: וַיִּקְרָ֧א אֱלֹהִ֛ים לָֽרָקִ֖יעַ שָׁמָ֑יִם וַֽיְהִי־עֶ֥רֶב וַֽיְהִי־בֹ֖קֶר י֥וֹם שֵׁנִֽי:

ח וַיֹּ֣אמֶר אֱלֹהִ֗ים יִקָּו֨וּ הַמַּ֜יִם מִתַּ֤חַת הַשָּׁמַ֙יִם֙ אֶל־מָק֣וֹם אֶחָ֔ד וְתֵרָאֶ֖ה הַיַּבָּשָׁ֑ה

ט וַֽיְהִי־כֵֽן: וַיִּקְרָ֨א אֱלֹהִ֤ים ׀ לַיַּבָּשָׁה֙ אֶ֔רֶץ וּלְמִקְוֵ֥ה הַמַּ֖יִם קָרָ֣א יַמִּ֑ים וַיַּ֥רְא אֱלֹהִ֖ים

י כִּי־טֽוֹב: וַיֹּ֣אמֶר אֱלֹהִ֗ים תַּֽדְשֵׁ֤א הָאָ֙רֶץ֙ דֶּ֔שֶׁא עֵ֚שֶׂב מַזְרִ֣יעַ זֶ֔רַע עֵ֣ץ פְּרִ֞י עֹ֤שֶׂה פְּרִי֙

יא לְמִינ֔וֹ אֲשֶׁ֥ר זַרְעוֹ־ב֖וֹ עַל־הָאָ֑רֶץ וַֽיְהִי־כֵֽן: וַתּוֹצֵ֨א הָאָ֜רֶץ דֶּ֠שֶׁא עֵ֣שֶׂב מַזְרִ֤יעַ זֶ֙רַע֙

יב לְמִינֵ֔הוּ וְעֵ֧ץ עֹֽשֶׂה־פְּרִ֛י אֲשֶׁ֥ר זַרְעוֹ־ב֖וֹ לְמִינֵ֑הוּ וַיַּ֥רְא אֱלֹהִ֖ים כִּי־טֽוֹב: וַֽיְהִי־עֶ֥רֶב וַֽיְהִי־בֹ֖קֶר י֥וֹם שְׁלִישִֽׁי:

יג וַיֹּ֣אמֶר אֱלֹהִ֗ים יְהִ֤י מְאֹרֹת֙ בִּרְקִ֣יעַ הַשָּׁמַ֔יִם לְהַבְדִּ֕יל בֵּ֥ין הַיּ֖וֹם וּבֵ֣ין הַלָּ֑יְלָה וְהָי֤וּ

| THEMES | GOD | CREATION | HOLINESS |

Episode 1: *The Seven Days of Creation* – Bereshit 1:1–2:3

SUMMARY

It is commonly thought that the beginning of sefer Bereshit presents a theory of how the universe came to exist. While this is mostly correct, the account of creation appearing in sefer Bereshit diverges from other recorded accounts in that it disregards the question of what was the starting point of existence itself. For this reason, the Torah begins with the word *bereshit,* literally, "in the beginning of." The account marks the start of a specific, unnamed, preexisting process. Had the verse stated *bareshit,* it would have been understood as meaning simply "in the beginning." It appears that a fundamental message lies hidden in this first word: at some early stage in the mysterious process of creating existence, God created the heavens and the earth.

15 and to serve for signs and seasons, days and years. They shall be lights in the heavens'
16 expanse, shining upon the earth." And so it was. God made the two great lights – the
17 greater light to rule by day and the lesser light to rule by night – and the stars. God set
18 them in the heavens' expanse to shine upon the earth, to rule by day and by night and
19 to separate light from darkness. And God saw that it was good. There was evening, and
there was morning – a fourth day.
20 Then God said, "Let the water teem with swarms of living creatures, and let birds fly over
21 the earth across the heavens' expanse." So God created the great sea creatures, and all
the kinds of crawling, living things that swarm in the water, and all the kinds of winged,
22 flying creatures. And God saw that it was good. God blessed them, saying: "Be fertile
and multiply and fill the waters of the seas, and let flying creatures multiply on earth."
23 There was evening, and there was morning – a fifth day.
24 Then God said, "Let the land produce every kind of living thing: all the different
25 species of cattle, crawling things, and wild animals of the earth." And so it was. God
made the different kinds of wild animals of the earth, and cattle, and all the species of
26 creature that creep upon land. And God saw that it was good. Then God said, "Let us
make humankind in our image, our likeness, that they may rule over the fish of the sea
and the flying creatures of the heavens, the cattle and all the earth, and every living
27 creature that moves upon the earth." So God created humankind in His image: in the
28 image of God He created him; male and female He created them. God blessed them,
saying, "Be fertile and multiply. Fill the earth and subdue it. Rule over the fish of the
sea, and the flying creatures of the heavens, and every living thing that moves upon
29 the earth." Then God said, "I give you all these seed-bearing plants on the face of the
30 earth and every tree with seed-bearing fruit. They shall be yours to eat. And to all the
beasts of the earth and birds of the heavens and everything that crawls over the earth
31 and has within it living spirit – I give every green plant for food." And so it was. Then
God saw all that He had made: and it was very good. There was evening, and there was
morning – the sixth day.
2 1 So the heavens and the earth were finished, and all their vast array. On the seventh day
2 God finished the work that He had done, and on the seventh day He rested from all
3 the work that He had done. God blessed the seventh day and sanctified it, because on
it He rested from all His work, from all that God had created and done.

טו לְאֹתֹת וּלְמוֹעֲדִים וּלְיָמִים וְשָׁנִים׃ וְהָיוּ לִמְאוֹרֹת בִּרְקִיעַ הַשָּׁמַיִם לְהָאִיר עַל־
טז הָאָרֶץ וַיְהִי־כֵן׃ וַיַּעַשׂ אֱלֹהִים אֶת־שְׁנֵי הַמְּאֹרֹת הַגְּדֹלִים אֶת־הַמָּאוֹר הַגָּדֹל
יז לְמֶמְשֶׁלֶת הַיּוֹם וְאֶת־הַמָּאוֹר הַקָּטֹן לְמֶמְשֶׁלֶת הַלַּיְלָה וְאֵת הַכּוֹכָבִים׃ וַיִּתֵּן
יח אֹתָם אֱלֹהִים בִּרְקִיעַ הַשָּׁמָיִם לְהָאִיר עַל־הָאָרֶץ׃ וְלִמְשֹׁל בַּיּוֹם וּבַלַּיְלָה
יט וּלֲהַבְדִּיל בֵּין הָאוֹר וּבֵין הַחֹשֶׁךְ וַיַּרְא אֱלֹהִים כִּי־טוֹב׃ וַיְהִי־עֶרֶב וַיְהִי־בֹקֶר יוֹם
רְבִיעִי׃
כ וַיֹּאמֶר אֱלֹהִים יִשְׁרְצוּ הַמַּיִם שֶׁרֶץ נֶפֶשׁ חַיָּה וְעוֹף יְעוֹפֵף עַל־הָאָרֶץ עַל־פְּנֵי רְקִיעַ
כא הַשָּׁמָיִם׃ וַיִּבְרָא אֱלֹהִים אֶת־הַתַּנִּינִם הַגְּדֹלִים וְאֵת כָּל־נֶפֶשׁ הַחַיָּה ׀ הָרֹמֶשֶׂת
אֲשֶׁר שָׁרְצוּ הַמַּיִם לְמִינֵהֶם וְאֵת כָּל־עוֹף כָּנָף לְמִינֵהוּ וַיַּרְא אֱלֹהִים כִּי־טוֹב׃
כב וַיְבָרֶךְ אֹתָם אֱלֹהִים לֵאמֹר פְּרוּ וּרְבוּ וּמִלְאוּ אֶת־הַמַּיִם בַּיַּמִּים וְהָעוֹף יִרֶב בָּאָרֶץ׃
כג וַיְהִי־עֶרֶב וַיְהִי־בֹקֶר יוֹם חֲמִישִׁי׃
כד וַיֹּאמֶר אֱלֹהִים תּוֹצֵא הָאָרֶץ נֶפֶשׁ חַיָּה לְמִינָהּ בְּהֵמָה וָרֶמֶשׂ וְחַיְתוֹ־אֶרֶץ לְמִינָהּ
כה וַיְהִי־כֵן׃ וַיַּעַשׂ אֱלֹהִים אֶת־חַיַּת הָאָרֶץ לְמִינָהּ וְאֶת־הַבְּהֵמָה לְמִינָהּ וְאֵת כָּל־
כו רֶמֶשׂ הָאֲדָמָה לְמִינֵהוּ וַיַּרְא אֱלֹהִים כִּי־טוֹב׃ וַיֹּאמֶר אֱלֹהִים נַעֲשֶׂה אָדָם בְּצַלְמֵנוּ
כִּדְמוּתֵנוּ וְיִרְדּוּ בִדְגַת הַיָּם וּבְעוֹף הַשָּׁמַיִם וּבַבְּהֵמָה וּבְכָל־הָאָרֶץ וּבְכָל־הָרֶמֶשׂ
כז הָרֹמֵשׂ עַל־הָאָרֶץ׃ וַיִּבְרָא אֱלֹהִים ׀ אֶת־הָאָדָם בְּצַלְמוֹ בְּצֶלֶם אֱלֹהִים בָּרָא
כח אֹתוֹ זָכָר וּנְקֵבָה בָּרָא אֹתָם׃ וַיְבָרֶךְ אֹתָם אֱלֹהִים וַיֹּאמֶר לָהֶם אֱלֹהִים פְּרוּ וּרְבוּ
וּמִלְאוּ אֶת־הָאָרֶץ וְכִבְשֻׁהָ וּרְדוּ בִּדְגַת הַיָּם וּבְעוֹף הַשָּׁמַיִם וּבְכָל־חַיָּה הָרֹמֶשֶׂת
כט עַל־הָאָרֶץ׃ וַיֹּאמֶר אֱלֹהִים הִנֵּה נָתַתִּי לָכֶם אֶת־כָּל־עֵשֶׂב ׀ זֹרֵעַ זֶרַע אֲשֶׁר עַל־
פְּנֵי כָל־הָאָרֶץ וְאֶת־כָּל־הָעֵץ אֲשֶׁר־בּוֹ פְרִי־עֵץ זֹרֵעַ זָרַע לָכֶם יִהְיֶה לְאָכְלָה׃
ל וּלְכָל־חַיַּת הָאָרֶץ וּלְכָל־עוֹף הַשָּׁמַיִם וּלְכֹל ׀ רוֹמֵשׂ עַל־הָאָרֶץ אֲשֶׁר־בּוֹ נֶפֶשׁ חַיָּה
לא אֶת־כָּל־יֶרֶק עֵשֶׂב לְאָכְלָה וַיְהִי־כֵן׃ וַיַּרְא אֱלֹהִים אֶת־כָּל־אֲשֶׁר עָשָׂה וְהִנֵּה־טוֹב
מְאֹד וַיְהִי־עֶרֶב וַיְהִי־בֹקֶר יוֹם הַשִּׁשִּׁי׃
ב א ב וַיְכֻלּוּ הַשָּׁמַיִם וְהָאָרֶץ וְכָל־צְבָאָם׃ וַיְכַל אֱלֹהִים בַּיּוֹם הַשְּׁבִיעִי מְלַאכְתּוֹ
ג אֲשֶׁר עָשָׂה וַיִּשְׁבֹּת בַּיּוֹם הַשְּׁבִיעִי מִכָּל־מְלַאכְתּוֹ אֲשֶׁר עָשָׂה׃ וַיְבָרֶךְ אֱלֹהִים
אֶת־יוֹם הַשְּׁבִיעִי וַיְקַדֵּשׁ אֹתוֹ כִּי בוֹ שָׁבַת מִכָּל־מְלַאכְתּוֹ אֲשֶׁר־בָּרָא אֱלֹהִים
לַעֲשׂוֹת׃

THE ART OF MIDRASH

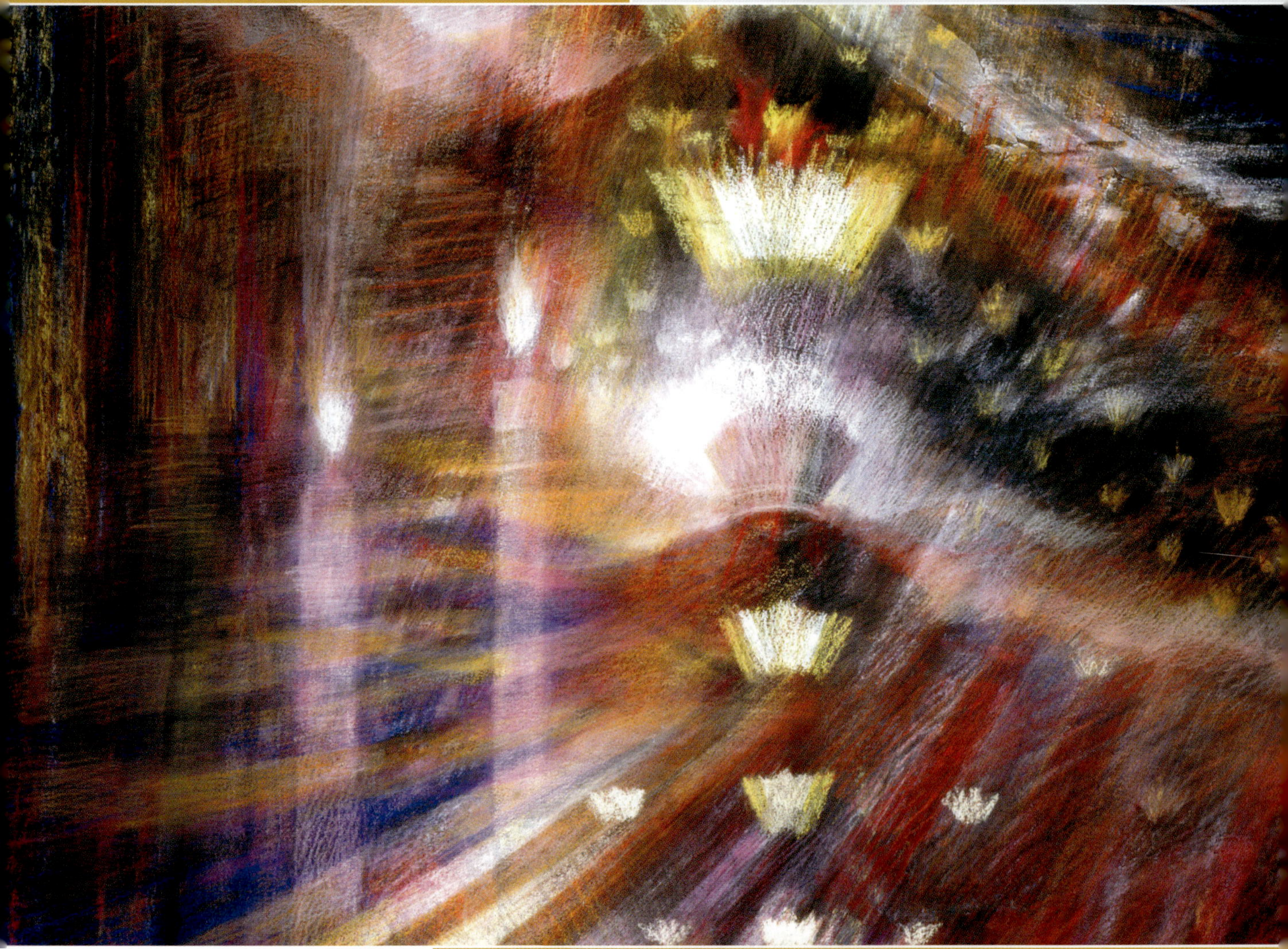

Day 7, Yoram Raanan (2014)

Analysis

- Which elements of this image are directly mentioned in the text?
- Which elements of this image are not found in the text?
- What midrashic interpretation is the artist giving us?

A QUESTION OF BIBLIODRAMA

TO GOD

- What was there before You created the universe?
- Why did You create the universe?
- Why did You choose to create the world in this way?
- Why did You create humankind last?
- Who are You talking to when You say, "Let us make man"?
- In what way is humankind created in Your image?
- Why did You create humanity despite knowing how much evil it will come to do?
- What does it mean for You to rest on Shabbat?

TO ADAM

- What does being created in the image of God mean to you?
- What does it feel like to be the first human being and know the world will be populated from your descendants?
- Do you feel part of the animal kingdom, or the pinnacle of creation?
- What does it feel like to be told by God to "fill the earth and subdue it"?
- What was the first Shabbat in history like?

oranges) in the high-G (or high-V) environment is actually longer than the duration between ticks of a clock (or beats of a heart) in the low-G (or low-V) environment. These differences in time's passage are known as time dilation....

Just as gravity affects the weight of mass, it also affects the flow of time, but at a much less dramatic rate. That is why it took an Einstein to discover this law of nature.

A few years ago at dinner, my family and I discussed the concept of time dilation. We decided to take a mental excursion into the realm of relativistic time to make the effect more clear. We can know how it works even if we can't understand *why* it works.

We conjured an imaginary planet so massive that its gravity slowed time by a factor of 350,000 *relative to Earth's rate of time*. That meant that while we here on Earth live out two years, a mere three minutes would tick by on that imaginary planet. My then eleven-year-old daughter, Hadas, exclaimed, "Dad, this is great! This is just super. Send me to that planet. I'll stay there for three minutes, do two years of homework, come home and no more homework for two years!"

That's not quite correct, is it?

In Hadas's time, three minutes will have passed. But for us on Earth, those three minutes will have taken two years. In those two years Hadas will have done only three minutes of homework and aged only three minutes. Upon return to Earth, all her friends will be thirteen while she will still be eleven. That is the proven nature of time in our awesome universe.

Had I watched Hadas from my low-gravity location, her time (and all her events, including her aging) would have passed v e r y s l o w l y. To me, events in my system were totally normal. From Hadas's perspective, her watch and her actions were normal, but looking across the reaches of space from her high-gravity system into my lower-gravity system, she would have seen my watch and everything else on Earth going very rapidly. Between two beats of her heart, my heart would beat 350,000 times.

There was only one sequence of events, one Hadas. For her, that sequence took three minutes. Three minutes of heartbeats, three minutes of study and homework. For us here on Earth, that identical time span took two years. Two years of heartbeats, two years of life's accomplishments and joys, two years of orange harvests. And both occurred in exactly the same "time." Hadas lived three minutes while we here on Earth lived two years. And which time is correct? Both. It's all relative.

Dr. Gerald L. Schroeder

Analysis

- What specific information do we now have that was unavailable to classical Jewish commentators? How can it aid our understanding of the text?
- How can this small excerpt from our new understanding of the laws of physics help us approach a tricky question facing us in the text?
- What further questions do you have and what else do you need to understand after reading this?

INTEGRATING ḤOKHMA

In 1915, Einstein published a description of nature which revealed an extraordinary and seemingly quite unnatural fact: the rate at which time passes is not the same in all places. Changes in gravity and changes in the velocity at which we travel actually change the rate at which our time flows. At first, such a concept appeared to be highly speculative, and so this aspect of nature was referred to as the theory of relativity. But it is no longer a theory. During the past few decades, the relativity of time has been tested and verified thousands of times. It is now the law of relativity. Einstein had discovered a hitherto overlooked law of nature.

If anything in our life seems constant, it is the flow of time. This perception, or rather this misperception, of time results from the reality that the events with which we are familiar all occur on Earth, or if not exactly on Earth, then quite close to Earth. Huge changes in gravity (G) or velocity (V) are required to produce easily measurable changes in the flow of time. And even with the needed large variations in G or V, the flow of time wherever you happen to be will always appear as normal, just as it does right now. It appears normal because you and your biology are in tune with the local system. Only if we view events across a boundary, looking from one location into another location that has a very different G or V, can we observe the effect of this extraordinary law of nature discovered by Einstein. The relativity of time is encountered only when comparing one system relative to another; hence the name the law of *relativity*.

The law of relativity tells us that the flow of time at a location with high gravity or high velocity is actually slower than at another location with lower gravity or lower velocity. This means that the duration between ticks of a clock (and the beats of a heart, and even the time to ripen

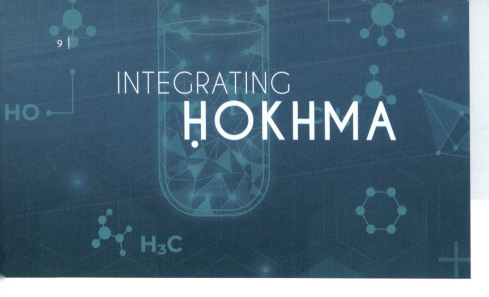

First cycle of creation	*Second cycle of creation*
Day 1 *Or*	**Day 4** *Meorot* (from the same Hebrew root as *or*)
Day 2 Separation of "lower" from "upper" waters	**Day 5** Sea animals to inhabit lower waters Flying creatures to inhabit upper waters
Day 3 Emergence of land Vegetation	**Day 6** Land animals and humans Consumers of vegetation

What emerges is a picture of a creation that is not only orderly and sequential, it is carefully planned and organized. It is not six sequential days of creation but two parallel cycles of three days each, in which the first round lays foundations that are developed or populated in the second.

This sense of structure, pattern, order, and planning is intentional, and stands in stark contrast to many ancient Mesopotamian creation stories in which the world emerges as a result of a clash between gods, is the violent or accidental product of some heavenly conflagration, or came to be to provide the gods with their daily needs. In the Torah there is but a single Creator who plans, decides, controls, and creates everything.

God is not only a Creator, He is intelligent, thoughtful, organized, and powerful, among other adjectives which we can add based on the above observations. These are all part of our emerging "image" of God. It is no wonder that the Hebrew name for God used in this creation story is Elohim, which translated accurately would yield "the All-Powerful" or "Almighty." God as Almighty is an essential thrust of Bereshit 1.

Rabbi Zvi Grumet

TAKING A LITERARY APPROACH

Pervasive throughout Bereshit 1 is a profound sense of order. One example is the five-step format which structures each "day" of creation:

- God said…
- God made/did/created/formed…
- God saw that it was "good"…
- (God named…)
- It was *erev* and it was *boker*, a (number) "day"

The regularity of the structure leaves us with a profound sense that the process has been carefully planned in advance and is methodical. Every stage is introduced by divine thought or speech, and speech is the vehicle through which things are created. At the conclusion of each creative stage, God is reflective about His creations, saying that they are "good." The structure is so reliable that any deviation from it commands our attention and demands explanation. Thus, for example, when *ki tov* ("it was 'good'") is missing on the second "day" but appears twice on the third, or when the first "day" concludes with a cardinal rather than an ordinal number (that is, *one* day rather than a *first* day), or the sixth "day" concludes with the definite article (that is, *the* sixth rather than *a* sixth), a flurry of commentary rushes to explain the anomaly.

The systematic nature of creation expresses itself in yet another remarkable way. The six days of creation are organized so that there are actually two cycles of three days each, with the second cycle paralleling the first; each day in the first cycle has its companion in the second. The first and the fourth discuss creations revolving around *or*; the second and the fifth focus on the separation of the "upper waters" from the "lower waters" (on the fifth day, those two domains – the upper waters and the lower waters – are populated by the water creatures and the flying things); the third and the sixth focus on the emergence of land and vegetation, and the beings which inhabit that land and consume that vegetation. The chart that follows illustrates this succinctly:

4 This is the story of the heavens and the earth when they were created, on the day the LORD
5 God made earth and heaven. No shrub of the field yet grew on earth, and no plant had yet
sprouted, for the LORD God had not yet brought rain upon the earth, and there was no one
6 to work the land. A mist would rise up from the earth and water all the face of the land. Then
7 the LORD God formed man from the dust of the land[1] and breathed the breath of life into
8 his nostrils, and the man became a living being. The LORD God planted a garden in Eden,
9 in the east, and there he put the man He had formed. And from the land, the LORD God
caused all kinds of trees to grow, pleasant to look at and good to eat from, and the Tree of
10 Life stood in the middle of the garden, and the Tree of Knowledge of good and evil. A river
11 flows from Eden to water this garden, and from there divides into four headwaters. The
12 name of the first is Pishon. It surrounds the land of Ḥavila, where there is gold. And the
13 gold of that land is good; bdellium and rock crystal are there also. The name of the second
14 river is Giḥon; it is the one that surrounds the land of Kush. The name of the third river is
15 the Tigris, and it flows to the east of Assyria. The fourth river is the Euphrates. The LORD
16 God took the man and placed him in the Garden of Eden to work it and safeguard it. And
17 the LORD God commanded the man: "You are free to eat from any tree in the garden. But
the Tree of Knowledge of good and evil – you may not eat from that, for on the day you
18 eat of it, you shall die." Then the LORD God said, "It is not good for man to be alone. I will

1 | The Hebrew *adam* ("man") resonates with *adama* ("land").

UNLOCKING THE TEXT

- Why are there two accounts of creation?
- Which aspects of this account of creation are the same as the previous one?
- Which aspects of this account of creation are different from the previous one?
- What do the new aspects in the second account add to our understanding of creation?
- Why did God bring the animals to Adam to name them?
- What specific messages can be learned from the description in this account of the way man and woman are created?

FINDING YOURSELF IN THE TEXT

- Do you connect more to being created "in the image of God" or "from the dust of the land"?
- Do you agree that it is not good to be alone?
- What will your *ezer kenegdo* ("fitting partner") be like?

Consider using these questions as the basis for your own commentary or creative midrash.

How does reflecting on these firsthand experiences help you better understand the text?

ד אֵ֣לֶּה תוֹלְד֧וֹת הַשָּׁמַ֛יִם וְהָאָ֖רֶץ בְּהִבָּֽרְאָ֑ם בְּי֗וֹם עֲשׂ֛וֹת יְהוָ֥ה אֱלֹהִ֖ים אֶ֥רֶץ וְשָׁמָֽיִם׃ ב שני
ה וְכֹ֣ל ׀ שִׂ֣יחַ הַשָּׂדֶ֗ה טֶ֚רֶם יִֽהְיֶ֣ה בָאָ֔רֶץ וְכָל־עֵ֥שֶׂב הַשָּׂדֶ֖ה טֶ֣רֶם יִצְמָ֑ח כִּי֩ לֹ֨א הִמְטִ֜יר
ו יְהוָ֤ה אֱלֹהִים֙ עַל־הָאָ֔רֶץ וְאָדָ֣ם אַ֔יִן לַעֲבֹ֖ד אֶת־הָֽאֲדָמָֽה׃ וְאֵ֖ד יַעֲלֶ֣ה מִן־הָאָ֑רֶץ
ז וְהִשְׁקָ֖ה אֶֽת־כָּל־פְּנֵֽי־הָאֲדָמָֽה׃ וַיִּ֩יצֶר֩ יְהוָ֨ה אֱלֹהִ֜ים אֶת־הָֽאָדָ֗ם עָפָר֙ מִן־הָ֣אֲדָמָ֔ה
ח וַיִּפַּ֥ח בְּאַפָּ֖יו נִשְׁמַ֣ת חַיִּ֑ים וַֽיְהִ֥י הָֽאָדָ֖ם לְנֶ֥פֶשׁ חַיָּֽה׃ וַיִּטַּ֞ע יְהוָ֧ה אֱלֹהִ֛ים גַּ֥ן בְּעֵ֖דֶן
ט מִקֶּ֑דֶם וַיָּ֣שֶׂם שָׁ֔ם אֶת־הָֽאָדָ֖ם אֲשֶׁ֥ר יָצָֽר׃ וַיַּצְמַ֞ח יְהוָ֤ה אֱלֹהִים֙ מִן־הָ֣אֲדָמָ֔ה כָּל־עֵ֛ץ
י נֶחְמָ֥ד לְמַרְאֶ֖ה וְט֣וֹב לְמַאֲכָ֑ל וְעֵ֤ץ הַֽחַיִּים֙ בְּת֣וֹךְ הַגָּ֔ן וְעֵ֕ץ הַדַּ֖עַת ט֥וֹב וָרָֽע׃ וְנָהָר֙
יא יֹצֵ֣א מֵעֵ֔דֶן לְהַשְׁק֖וֹת אֶת־הַגָּ֑ן וּמִשָּׁם֙ יִפָּרֵ֔ד וְהָיָ֖ה לְאַרְבָּעָ֥ה רָאשִֽׁים׃ שֵׁ֥ם הָֽאֶחָ֖ד
יב פִּישׁ֑וֹן ה֣וּא הַסֹּבֵ֗ב אֵ֚ת כָּל־אֶ֣רֶץ הַֽחֲוִילָ֔ה אֲשֶׁר־שָׁ֖ם הַזָּהָֽב׃ וּֽזֲהַ֛ב הָאָ֥רֶץ הַהִ֖וא
יג ט֑וֹב שָׁ֥ם הַבְּדֹ֖לַח וְאֶ֥בֶן הַשֹּֽׁהַם׃ וְשֵֽׁם־הַנָּהָ֥ר הַשֵּׁנִ֖י גִּיח֑וֹן ה֣וּא הַסּוֹבֵ֔ב אֵ֖ת כָּל־אֶ֥רֶץ
יד כּֽוּשׁ׃ וְשֵׁ֨ם הַנָּהָ֤ר הַשְּׁלִישִׁי֙ חִדֶּ֔קֶל ה֥וּא הַהֹלֵ֖ךְ קִדְמַ֣ת אַשּׁ֑וּר וְהַנָּהָ֥ר הָֽרְבִיעִ֖י ה֥וּא
טו טז פְרָֽת׃ וַיִּקַּ֛ח יְהוָ֥ה אֱלֹהִ֖ים אֶת־הָֽאָדָ֑ם וַיַּנִּחֵ֣הוּ בְגַן־עֵ֔דֶן לְעָבְדָ֖הּ וּלְשָׁמְרָֽהּ׃ וַיְצַו֙
יז יְהוָ֣ה אֱלֹהִ֔ים עַל־הָֽאָדָ֖ם לֵאמֹ֑ר מִכֹּ֥ל עֵֽץ־הַגָּ֖ן אָכֹ֥ל תֹּאכֵֽל׃ וּמֵעֵ֗ץ הַדַּ֙עַת֙ ט֣וֹב וָרָ֔ע
יח לֹ֥א תֹאכַ֖ל מִמֶּ֑נּוּ כִּ֗י בְּי֛וֹם אֲכָלְךָ֥ מִמֶּ֖נּוּ מ֥וֹת תָּמֽוּת׃ וַיֹּ֙אמֶר֙ יְהוָ֣ה אֱלֹהִ֔ים לֹא־ט֛וֹב

THEMES	GOD	CREATION	RELATIONSHIPS AND LOVE

Episode 2: *The Second Account of Creation* – Bereshit 2:4–25

SUMMARY

This episode is one of the most dramatic, mystifying, and challenging sections in the entire Torah. Some of its details can be understood only vaguely. Following the sweeping description of creation, which dealt with the universe on a broad scale, the Torah now provides a detailed description of the process of creating all that emerged from nothing (*yesh me'ayin)*. This account is more tangible than the abstract, conceptual depiction of the first chapter. Even the divine name of God differs in this account from the previous one. In the first version, God is called Elohim, a term which on the one hand expresses God's authority and power, and on the other His all-encompassing, impersonal essence. By contrast, here God is called Adonai Elohim, the Lord God, the first word of which is spelled *yod-heh-vav-heh*, the Tetragrammaton, the personal name of God, as it were. In this account, God is not merely an abstract philosophical or theological entity, as He functioned in the first chapter, which focused on the large-scale plan of creation. Rather, God attends to the specific details of the creation process.

19 make a fitting partner for him.” The Lord God formed all the wild animals, and all the
birds of the heavens, out of the land. He brought them to the man to see what he would
20 call them, and whatever he called each living thing, that became its name. So the man
gave names to all the animals, the birds of the heavens, and all the wild creatures. But
21 he found no fitting partner for himself. Then the Lord God made the man fall into a
deep sleep, and while he was sleeping He took one of his ribs and closed the flesh in its
22 place. And the Lord God built the rib He had taken from the man into a woman. He
23 brought her to the man. And the man said: “This, at last is bone of my bones and flesh
24 of my flesh. This shall be called Woman, for from Man was this one taken.”[2] That is why
a man leaves his father and mother and cleaves to his wife and they become one flesh.
25 The man and his wife were both naked, but they were not ashamed.

---

2 | *Isha* (“woman”) resonates with *ish* (“man”).

TO ADAM

- How does it feel to know you were created from the dust of the land?
- How does it feel to know you have the breath of God in you?
- How did it feel to name the animals?
- Why do you think God brought them to you to name?
- What do you think about Ḥava?
- How do you feel knowing she came from your own rib?
- Are you interested, intrigued, or tempted by the two trees at the center of the Garden of Eden?
- Why were you naked? How did it feel?
- How do you feel about God?

TO ḤAVA

- What do you think about Adam?
- How do you feel knowing you came from his rib?
- Are you interested, intrigued, or tempted by the two trees at the center of the Garden of Eden?
- Why were you naked? How did it feel?
- How do you feel about God?

יט הֱיוֹת הָאָדָם לְבַדּוֹ אֶעֱשֶׂה־לּוֹ עֵזֶר כְּנֶגְדּוֹ: וַיִּצֶר יְהוָה אֱלֹהִים מִן־הָאֲדָמָה כָּל־
חַיַּת הַשָּׂדֶה וְאֵת כָּל־עוֹף הַשָּׁמַיִם וַיָּבֵא אֶל־הָאָדָם לִרְאוֹת מַה־יִּקְרָא־לוֹ וְכֹל
כ אֲשֶׁר יִקְרָא־לוֹ הָאָדָם נֶפֶשׁ חַיָּה הוּא שְׁמוֹ: וַיִּקְרָא הָאָדָם שֵׁמוֹת לְכָל־הַבְּהֵמָה שלישי
כא וּלְעוֹף הַשָּׁמַיִם וּלְכֹל חַיַּת הַשָּׂדֶה וּלְאָדָם לֹא־מָצָא עֵזֶר כְּנֶגְדּוֹ: וַיַּפֵּל יְהוָה אֱלֹהִים ׀
כב תַּרְדֵּמָה עַל־הָאָדָם וַיִּישָׁן וַיִּקַּח אַחַת מִצַּלְעֹתָיו וַיִּסְגֹּר בָּשָׂר תַּחְתֶּנָּה: וַיִּבֶן יְהוָה
כג אֱלֹהִים ׀ אֶת־הַצֵּלָע אֲשֶׁר־לָקַח מִן־הָאָדָם לְאִשָּׁה וַיְבִאֶהָ אֶל־הָאָדָם: וַיֹּאמֶר
הָאָדָם זֹאת הַפַּעַם עֶצֶם מֵעֲצָמַי וּבָשָׂר מִבְּשָׂרִי לְזֹאת יִקָּרֵא אִשָּׁה כִּי מֵאִישׁ
כד לֻקֳחָה־זֹּאת: עַל־כֵּן יַעֲזָב־אִישׁ אֶת־אָבִיו וְאֶת־אִמּוֹ וְדָבַק בְּאִשְׁתּוֹ וְהָיוּ לְבָשָׂר
כה אֶחָד: וַיִּהְיוּ שְׁנֵיהֶם עֲרוּמִּים הָאָדָם וְאִשְׁתּוֹ וְלֹא יִתְבֹּשָׁשׁוּ:

A QUESTION OF BIBLIODRAMA

TO GOD

- Why did You write two accounts of creation in the Torah?
- Why do You appear in this second account by the name Adonai Elohim rather than just Elohim (as in the previous account)?
- Why did You create humankind?
- What was the purpose of the Tree of Life and the Tree of Knowledge?
- Why did You start with a single human if "it is not good for humans to be alone"?
- Does giving Adam the right to name the animals mean that humans are masters over them?

In these two chiastically related stories, we have seen:

- **A1.** — Total separation – 1:1
  - **B1.** — Anticipation of interaction – 1:2
    - **C1.** — Vehicle for interaction (the creation of light) – 1:3, 5
      - **D1.** — Establishing boundaries – 1:6, 8
        - **E1.** — Fidelity of the species – 1:11–13
          - **F1.** — Illumination and power – 1:14–19
            - **G1.** — Reptiles – 1:20–22
              - **H1.** — Creation of animals – 1:24–25
                - **I1.** — Uniqueness of Man – 1:26–28
                  - **J1.** — Man's role on earth (Man's responsibility) – 1:29–30
                    - **K.** — Shabbat – 1:31–2:4
                  - **J2.** — Man's role on earth – 2:4–6
                - **I2.** — Uniqueness of humankind – 2:7–16
              - **H2.** — Creation of animals – 2:18–25
            - **G2.** — Reptiles – 3:1–4
          - **F2.** — Illumination and power – 3:5–7
        - **E2.** — Fidelity of the species – 3:8–12
      - **D2.** — Establishing boundaries – 3:14–20
    - **C2.** — Vehicle for interaction (the creation of light) – 3:21
  - **B2.** — Anticipation of interaction – 3:22
- **A2.** — Total separation – 3:23–24

TAKING A LITERARY APPROACH

Although a superficial perusal of the text of the first two chapters of Bereshit leaves the impression that we are dealing with two distinct – and diametrically opposite – stories that demand reconciliation, this is not necessarily the case. If we take a closer look at the literary structure of these two descriptions, we will note an interesting pattern that suggests one integrated presentation.

The Biblical text is often presented in chiastic form. A chiasmus (as with any parallelism) can be identified in one of two manners: 1. common words or phrases are used, or 2. similar ideas are presented. I would like to suggest that if we look at both creation stories, we will find some interesting parallels between them that suggest a chiastic structure.

As in any inverted parallel, the focus point is at the fulcrum, or nexus, of the parallel. The extreme points of each story describe a total and ultimate separation. With each step, interaction and integration are enabled, enhanced, and realized. At the final step, not only are all creatures in place, but they all stand in proper relation to each other. Man, the crown of creation, is charged with implementing God's plan of dynamic growth and synthesis on earth, all within the divine mandate.

The neat symmetry presented here not only renders the challenges raised by the conflicting reports of creation moot, but also serves to reorient our appreciation of the entire presentation of creation in the first three chapters and to see it as one integrated story. This is all fine and good, but what's the lesson here?

The pointing of each story as beginning with a total separation of God from His world, as it were, and culminating in unity, places *teshuva* as the glorious background on the tapestry of the world. All things stem from God's will and all things are profoundly connected to God. All of creation points toward God and yearns to return to its source. However we understand *teshuva* (repentance/return to God in its pure legal sense), as an independent mitzva or one that attaches to all others as a contingency, we see a powerful thread of *teshuva* woven throughout these two stories of creation.

Teshuva is the very life-spirit of all of creation. The separation and isolation, be it heavens from earth or Man from the garden, stand at the polar extremes from the holiness of Shabbat. Shabbat is that singular experience, which we are blessed with each week, where all of creation stands at its perfect place in relation to the Creator – and to itself. Is it any wonder that the Rabbis attributed the "Song of Shabbat" (Tehillim 92) to Adam, after he learned of the power of *teshuva* (Bereshit Rabba 22:13)? "Great is *teshuva*, that it preceded the creation of the world" (Midrash Tehillim 90:12).

Rabbi Yitzchak Etshalom

THE ART OF MIDRASH

Adam and Eve
Michelle Levy (2022)

Analysis

- Which elements of this image are directly mentioned in the text?
- Which elements of this image are not found in the text?
- What midrashic interpretation is the artist giving us?

INTEGRATING ḤOKHMA

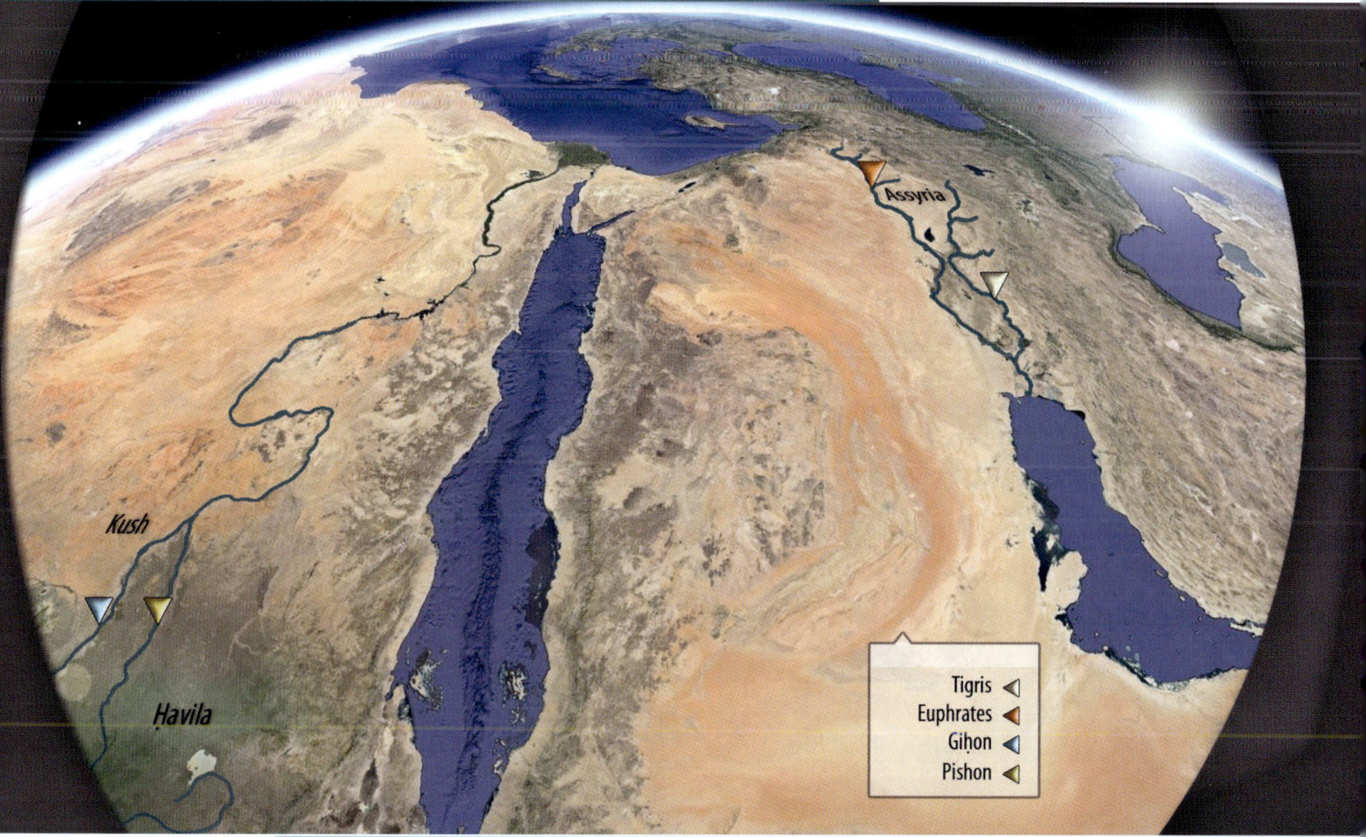

The four rivers

Analysis

- What specific information do we now have that was unavailable to classical Jewish commentators? How can it aid our understanding of the text?
- What can we learn from this map that can help us understand the text?
- What further questions on the text do you have now that you have seen this map?

3 1 The serpent was the slyest of all the wild animals the Lord God had made. "Did God say,"
2 it asked the woman, "that you must not eat from any tree in the garden?" The woman told
3 the serpent, "We may eat the fruit of the trees in the garden, but God did say, 'You must
not eat fruit from the tree in the middle of the garden, and you must not touch it, or you
4 5 will die.'" But the serpent told the woman, "You will not die; God knows that on the day
you eat from it your eyes will be opened, and you will be like God, knowing good and evil."
6 The woman saw that the tree was ripe for eating, enticing to the eyes, and desirable too
for granting insight. She took some of its fruit and ate, and she gave some to her husband
7 and he too ate. The eyes of both of them were opened, and they realized that they were
8 naked. So they sewed fig leaves together and made coverings for themselves. They heard
the sound of the Lord God walking in the garden in the cool of the day, and the man and
9 his wife hid from the Lord God among the trees of the garden. The Lord God called
10 to the man: "Where are you?" He answered, "I heard Your voice in the garden, and I was
11 afraid, because I was naked. So I hid." "Who told you," God asked, "that you were naked?
12 Have you eaten from the tree from which I commanded you not to eat?" The man said,
13 "The woman you put here with me – she gave me fruit from the tree and I ate." Then the
Lord God said to the woman, "What is this you have done?" The woman said, "The
14 serpent beguiled me and I ate." And the Lord God said to the serpent, "Because you have

UNLOCKING THE TEXT

- What role does the serpent play in the story?
- Why does Ḥava add to the command God gave (by saying that they were also forbidden to touch the tree)?
- Was Adam tempted by the tree, the serpent, or his wife?
- What was the knowledge they gained after eating from the tree?
- What does it mean that God was "walking" in the garden? What did this sound like to them?
- Why did they only realize they were naked after eating from the tree, and why were they now embarrassed?
- Who was to blame for this sin?
- What is the nature of the punishments God gave? Are these fitting punishments?
- Why does Adam now name Ḥava? Why does he give her this name?

FINDING YOURSELF IN THE TEXT

- Have you ever been convinced by someone to do something you know you shouldn't? How do you feel about them now?
- Have you ever blamed someone else for your failings even when you knew deep down it was your fault?
- How does it feel to be caught doing something you know is wrong?

Consider using these questions as the basis for your own commentary or creative midrash.

How does reflecting on these firsthand experiences help you better understand the text?

ג א וְהַנָּחָשׁ הָיָה עָרוּם מִכֹּל חַיַּת הַשָּׂדֶה אֲשֶׁר עָשָׂה יהוה אֱלֹהִים וַיֹּאמֶר אֶל־הָאִשָּׁה
ב אַף כִּי־אָמַר אֱלֹהִים לֹא תֹאכְלוּ מִכֹּל עֵץ הַגָּן: וַתֹּאמֶר הָאִשָּׁה אֶל־הַנָּחָשׁ מִפְּרִי
ג עֵץ־הַגָּן נֹאכֵל: וּמִפְּרִי הָעֵץ אֲשֶׁר בְּתוֹךְ־הַגָּן אָמַר אֱלֹהִים לֹא תֹאכְלוּ מִמֶּנּוּ וְלֹא
ד ה תִגְּעוּ בּוֹ פֶּן תְּמֻתוּן: וַיֹּאמֶר הַנָּחָשׁ אֶל־הָאִשָּׁה לֹא־מוֹת תְּמֻתוּן: כִּי יֹדֵעַ אֱלֹהִים
ו כִּי בְּיוֹם אֲכָלְכֶם מִמֶּנּוּ וְנִפְקְחוּ עֵינֵיכֶם וִהְיִיתֶם כֵּאלֹהִים יֹדְעֵי טוֹב וָרָע: וַתֵּרֶא
הָאִשָּׁה כִּי טוֹב הָעֵץ לְמַאֲכָל וְכִי תַאֲוָה־הוּא לָעֵינַיִם וְנֶחְמָד הָעֵץ לְהַשְׂכִּיל וַתִּקַּח
ז מִפִּרְיוֹ וַתֹּאכַל וַתִּתֵּן גַּם־לְאִישָׁהּ עִמָּהּ וַיֹּאכַל: וַתִּפָּקַחְנָה עֵינֵי שְׁנֵיהֶם וַיֵּדְעוּ כִּי
ח עֵירֻמִּם הֵם וַיִּתְפְּרוּ עֲלֵה תְאֵנָה וַיַּעֲשׂוּ לָהֶם חֲגֹרֹת: וַיִּשְׁמְעוּ אֶת־קוֹל יהוה אֱלֹהִים
מִתְהַלֵּךְ בַּגָּן לְרוּחַ הַיּוֹם וַיִּתְחַבֵּא הָאָדָם וְאִשְׁתּוֹ מִפְּנֵי יהוה אֱלֹהִים בְּתוֹךְ עֵץ הַגָּן:
ט י וַיִּקְרָא יהוה אֱלֹהִים אֶל־הָאָדָם וַיֹּאמֶר לוֹ אַיֶּכָּה: וַיֹּאמֶר אֶת־קֹלְךָ שָׁמַעְתִּי בַּגָּן
יא וָאִירָא כִּי־עֵירֹם אָנֹכִי וָאֵחָבֵא: וַיֹּאמֶר מִי הִגִּיד לְךָ כִּי עֵירֹם אָתָּה הֲמִן־הָעֵץ אֲשֶׁר
יב צִוִּיתִיךָ לְבִלְתִּי אֲכָל־מִמֶּנּוּ אָכָלְתָּ: וַיֹּאמֶר הָאָדָם הָאִשָּׁה אֲשֶׁר נָתַתָּה עִמָּדִי הִוא
יג נָתְנָה־לִּי מִן־הָעֵץ וָאֹכֵל: וַיֹּאמֶר יהוה אֱלֹהִים לָאִשָּׁה מַה־זֹּאת עָשִׂית וַתֹּאמֶר
יד הָאִשָּׁה הַנָּחָשׁ הִשִּׁיאַנִי וָאֹכֵל: וַיֹּאמֶר יהוה אֱלֹהִים ׀ אֶל־הַנָּחָשׁ כִּי עָשִׂיתָ זֹּאת

THEMES	GOD	PROPHECY AND REVELATION	FREE WILL, REWARD AND PUNISHMENT

Episode 3: *The Fall of Eden* – Bereshit 3:1–24

SUMMARY

Together in the Garden of Eden, surrounded by the rich panoply of creation, the first human couple have everything they could possibly want – except one thing, a tree from which they are forbidden to eat. The temptation is too great, and they sin by eating from the Tree of Knowledge. Their eyes are opened; they lose their innocence. For the first time, they feel shame. When they hear "the voice of God" they are embarrassed and ashamed, and try to hide, only to discover that one cannot hide from God. Both insist that it was not their fault. Adam blames the woman. The woman blames the serpent. The result is paradise lost: they are both punished and exiled from the Garden of Eden.

done this, you are accursed more than all the animals and all wild beasts. You will creep on
15 your belly and dust will you eat all the days of your life. I will plant hostility between you
and the woman, between your children and hers. And man will strike your head, and you
will strike his heel." To the woman He said, "I will make your pain in pregnancy searingly
great; in sorrow will you bear children. You will long for your husband, but he will rule
17 over you." To Adam[1] he said, "Because you listened to your wife and ate of the
tree from which I commanded you not to eat – cursed will be the land on your account.
18 By painful toil you will eat from it all the days of your life. It will sprout thorns and thistles
19 for you, and you shall eat plants of the field. By the sweat of your brow will you eat bread
until you return to the land, for from there you were taken. You are dust, and you will
20 return to dust." Then the man named his wife Ḥava, for she would become the mother of
21 all life.[2] Then the Lord God made garments of skins for Adam and his wife and clothed
them.
22 The Lord God then said, "Now that man has become like one of us, knowing good and
evil, he must not be allowed to reach out his hand and take also from the Tree of Life,
23 eat, and live forever." So the Lord God sent him away from the Garden of Eden to work
24 the land from which he had been taken. He drove out the man, and east of the Garden
of Eden He placed the cherubim and the flaming, whirling sword to guard the way to the
Tree of Life.

1 | The Hebrew *adam* can be read, depending on usage, as a common noun ("man"; cf. 2:7) or as a proper name.

2 | The name Ḥava resonates with *ḥai* ("life").

parasha setuma is comprised of a break of nine letters in the written text, while the *parasha petuḥa* is a break until the beginning of the next line. The Torah contains 290 *parashot petuḥot* and 379 *parashot setumot.*

The story of the Garden of Eden begins with the new *parasha* in Bereshit 2:4, which begins the second recounting of the creation story, and concludes with the end of chapter 3 and the expulsion of humanity from the Garden of Eden. The implications of this are profound – to understand properly how Adam and Ḥava erred and the purpose of narrating this failure for eternity, we cannot limit our exploration to chapter 3 and begin with the dialogue wherein the serpent successfully convinces Ḥava to eat from the tree. We must also attempt to include what occurs in chapter 2, from the creation of the garden and the rivers within it, the placing of man in the garden and his charge, the naming of the animals, and the creation of woman.

אָרוּר אַתָּה מִכָּל־הַבְּהֵמָה וּמִכֹּל חַיַּת הַשָּׂדֶה עַל־גְּחֹנְךָ תֵלֵךְ וְעָפָר תֹּאכַל כָּל־יְמֵי
טו חַיֶּיךָ: וְאֵיבָה ׀ אָשִׁית בֵּינְךָ וּבֵין הָאִשָּׁה וּבֵין זַרְעֲךָ וּבֵין זַרְעָהּ הוּא יְשׁוּפְךָ רֹאשׁ
טז וְאַתָּה תְּשׁוּפֶנּוּ עָקֵב: אֶל־הָאִשָּׁה אָמַר הַרְבָּה אַרְבֶּה עִצְּבוֹנֵךְ וְהֵרֹנֵךְ
יז בְּעֶצֶב תֵּלְדִי בָנִים וְאֶל־אִישֵׁךְ תְּשׁוּקָתֵךְ וְהוּא יִמְשָׁל־בָּךְ: וּלְאָדָם אָמַר
כִּי שָׁמַעְתָּ לְקוֹל אִשְׁתֶּךָ וַתֹּאכַל מִן־הָעֵץ אֲשֶׁר צִוִּיתִיךָ לֵאמֹר לֹא תֹאכַל מִמֶּנּוּ
יח אֲרוּרָה הָאֲדָמָה בַּעֲבוּרֶךָ בְּעִצָּבוֹן תֹּאכֲלֶנָּה כֹּל יְמֵי חַיֶּיךָ: וְקוֹץ וְדַרְדַּר תַּצְמִיחַ
יט לָךְ וְאָכַלְתָּ אֶת־עֵשֶׂב הַשָּׂדֶה: בְּזֵעַת אַפֶּיךָ תֹּאכַל לֶחֶם עַד שׁוּבְךָ אֶל־הָאֲדָמָה
כ כִּי מִמֶּנָּה לֻקָּחְתָּ כִּי־עָפָר אַתָּה וְאֶל־עָפָר תָּשׁוּב: וַיִּקְרָא הָאָדָם שֵׁם אִשְׁתּוֹ
כא חַוָּה כִּי הִוא הָיְתָה אֵם כָּל־חָי: וַיַּעַשׂ יהוה אֱלֹהִים לְאָדָם וּלְאִשְׁתּוֹ כָּתְנוֹת עוֹר
וַיַּלְבִּשֵׁם:
כב וַיֹּאמֶר ׀ יהוה אֱלֹהִים הֵן הָאָדָם הָיָה כְּאַחַד מִמֶּנּוּ לָדַעַת טוֹב וָרָע וְעַתָּה ׀ פֶּן־ ג רביעי
כג יִשְׁלַח יָדוֹ וְלָקַח גַּם מֵעֵץ הַחַיִּים וְאָכַל וָחַי לְעֹלָם: וַיְשַׁלְּחֵהוּ יהוה אֱלֹהִים מִגַּן־עֵדֶן
כד לַעֲבֹד אֶת־הָאֲדָמָה אֲשֶׁר לֻקַּח מִשָּׁם: וַיְגָרֶשׁ אֶת־הָאָדָם וַיַּשְׁכֵּן מִקֶּדֶם לְגַן־עֵדֶן
אֶת־הַכְּרֻבִים וְאֵת לַהַט הַחֶרֶב הַמִּתְהַפֶּכֶת לִשְׁמֹר אֶת־דֶּרֶךְ עֵץ הַחַיִּים:

TAKING A LITERARY APPROACH

In trying to define the parameters of a particular biblical passage, we find ourselves bereft of the traditional signs and cues that a modern reader takes for granted: headlines and subtitles, punctuation marks, and indentations (let alone the italics, underlines, and fonts available on the word processor). The division of the text into chapters was completed by English bishop Stephen Langton only in the thirteenth century; these divisions were incorporated by scribes in Hebrew manuscripts by 1330. The verse divisions predate the Mishna, but they do not appear in the text of a Torah scroll (and they were not standardized until the text of Ben Asher in the tenth century).

The only visual cue available to a reader are the breaks between large sections of the text, known as *parashot*. There were two forms of breaks, the *parasha petuḥa* (marked by the letter *peh* in *ḥumashim*) and the *parasha setuma* (marked by the letter *samekh*). The

The Torah begins with a description of the four tributaries that flow from the garden. Unexpectedly, we find these lands described by their natural resources: "And the gold of that land was good; there are the bdellium and the onyx stone" (2:11). Precious stones and metals are not mentioned in the first chapter, where the creation of man is part of the creation of the entire natural kingdom. Suddenly, the Torah emphasizes those resources that animals would find useless; only man assigns value to what are ultimately shiny rocks and stones.

The process of differentiating man from the animal kingdom continues when God creates woman. Between God's statement in verse 18 that "it is not good that man is alone; I will create a help-mate for him" and the actual creation of woman in verses 20–22, we find a strange interlude:

And out of the ground the LORD God formed every beast of the field, and every fowl of the air and brought them unto the man to see what he would call them; and whatsoever the man would call every living creature, that was to be the name thereof.

And the man gave names to all cattle, and to the fowl of the air, and to every beast of the field; but for Adam there was not found a help-mate for him.

The act of naming and categorizing reflects a level of contemplation and separation of the namer from the object being named, if not a level of superiority. The midrashic literature is rich with interpretation regarding this interlude. Rashi (on 2:21) chooses the interpretation that connects the act of naming with the creation of woman:

When He [God] brought them [the animals before Adam], He brought before him of every species male and female. He [Adam] said, "For each one there is a mate, but for me there is no mate." Immediately, "He caused a deep sleep to fall upon the man."

Clearly, the Torah contrasts man's relationship with woman with those of the animals. They mate naturally, as part of a biological process. The supernatural creation of man's mate demonstrates that even this relationship, potentially the most "animal-like" of all of man's behaviors, is on a qualitatively different level. If in chapter 1, mankind was part of the animal kingdom, in chapter 2, mankind is commanded to recognize what distinguishes him from the animals around him, as well as the animal in him. This, ultimately, is the test of the garden and of humanity in our attempts to return to that garden.

Rabbi Yaakov Beasley

עֲשֶׂה יְהוָה אֱלֹ
ֹכֹּל עֵץ הַגָּן: וַתֹּאמֶר הָאִשָּׁ
ֲשֶׁר בְּתוֹךְ־הַגָּן אָמַר אֱלֹהִים לֹא
הַנָּחָשׁ אֶל־הָאִשָּׁה לֹא־מוֹת תְּמֻת
חוּ עֵינֵיכֶם וִהְיִיתֶם כֵּאלֹהִים יֹדְעֵי
וְכִי תַאֲוָה־הוּא לָעֵינַיִם וְנֶחְמָד ד
ֹשֶׁה עִמָּהּ וַיֹּאכַל: וַתִּפָּקַחְנָה עֵי
ֵלֶהֶם חֲגֹרֹת: וַיִּשְׁמְ

We can now suggest the following structure to this story:

A1. — CREATION OF MAN (2:4–17) – his placement in a garden where he has unlimited access to food, without effort, and access to the Tree of Life.

B1. — CREATION OF WOMAN (2:18–25) – she begins as an equal helpmate to Adam.

C1. — SERPENT (3:1–5) – able to walk and converse with man, attempts to convince the woman to sin.

D. — SIN AND DISCOVERY (3:6–13) – the woman eats, man eats, *Hashem* confronts them, and they shift the blame.

C2. — SERPENT PUNISHED (3:14–15) – loses ability to walk and relationship with humanity is destroyed.

B2. — WOMAN PUNISHED (3:16) – her equal and happy relationship with man destroyed.

A2. — MAN PUNISHED (3:17–24) – expelled from the garden, must work now for food, loses access to the Tree of Life.

Clearly, within this structure, chapter 2 plays an important role in understanding the penalties that God metes out to the participants. Each punishment reflects the reversal of the idyllic situation that previously existed. In unlocking the meaning of our narrative, we must play close attention to this structure.

We can now see how the theme of the difference between man and animals is prevalent throughout the story. The Torah already highlighted this distinction in chapter 2. From the beginning, we sense that man is separate from the animals that also inhabit the garden.

THE ART OF MIDRASH

Adam and Eve Are Driven out of Eden
Gustave Doré (1866)

Analysis

- Which elements of this image are directly mentioned in the text?
- Which elements of this image are not found in the text?
- What midrashic interpretation is the artist giving us?

A QUESTION OF BIBLIODRAMA

TO ADAM AND ḤAVA

- Why did you eat from the tree?
- What did you feel once you ate the fruit?
- Why did you cover yourselves with fig leaves?
- Why did you hide from God?
- How do you feel about the punishment God gave you?
- Do you regret eating from the tree?

TO ḤAVA

- What was your first thought when the serpent spoke to you? Had any other animals spoken to you previously?
- Did you feel the serpent was trustworthy?
- Why did you add a prohibition (of touch) to God's command when speaking to the serpent?
- Did you find the argument of the serpent convincing? Why?
- Did you need to convince your husband to eat it or was he immediately willing?
- What do you feel about the name your husband gave you?

TO ADAM

- Why did you blame your wife when God challenged you?
- Whose fault do you believe this sin was?
- Why did you name your wife Ḥava?

TO GOD

- Why did You forbid Adam and Ḥava from eating from the Tree of Knowledge?
- Did You know they would? Was this Your plan all along?
- Did You send the serpent to tempt them?
- Why did You choose these punishments?
- Will humans ever find their way back to the Garden of Eden?

TO THE SERPENT

- What is your agenda and motivation in this episode?
- How do you feel about the punishment God gave you?

With this contrast in mind, we can now understand the story of the first sin. It is all about appearances, shame, vision, and the eye. The serpent says to the woman, "God knows that on the day you eat from it, your eyes will be opened, and you will be like God, knowing good and evil" (Bereshit 3:5). That is, in fact, what happens: "The eyes of both of them were opened, and they realized that they were naked" (v. 7). It was the appearance of the tree that the Torah emphasizes: "The woman saw that the tree was good to eat and desirable to the eyes, and that the tree was attractive as a means to gain intelligence" (v. 6). The key emotion in the story is shame. Before eating the fruit, the couple were "naked but unashamed" (2:25). After eating it they feel shame and seek to hide. Every element of the story – the fruit, the tree, the nakedness, the shame – has the visual element typical of a shame culture.

But in Judaism we believe that God is heard not seen. The first humans "heard God's voice moving about in the garden with the wind of the day" (3:8). Replying to God, the man says, "I heard Your voice in the garden and I was afraid because I was naked, so I hid" (v. 10). Note the deliberate, even humorous irony of what the couple did. They heard God's voice in the garden, and they "hid themselves from God among the trees of the garden" (v. 8). But you can't hide from a voice. Hiding means trying not to be seen. It is an immediate, intuitive response to shame. But the Torah is the supreme example of a culture of guilt, not shame, and you cannot escape guilt by hiding. Guilt has nothing to do with appearances and everything to do with conscience, the voice of God in the human heart.

The sin of the first humans in the Garden of Eden was that they followed their eyes, not their ears. Their actions were determined by what they saw, the beauty of the tree, not by what they heard, namely the word of God commanding them not to eat from it. The result was that they did indeed acquire a knowledge of good and evil, but it was the wrong kind. They acquired an ethic of shame, not guilt; of appearances not conscience.

Rabbi Jonathan Sacks

Analysis

- What areas of understanding of human nature and society do we now have that were unavailable to classical Jewish commentators? How can they aid our understanding of the text?
- What can we learn from this essay to help us understand the text?
- What further questions on the text do you have now that you have read this new take on the story?

INTEGRATING ḤOKHMA

After the attack on Pearl Harbor in December 1941, Americans knew they were about to enter a war against a nation, Japan, whose culture they did not understand. So they commissioned one of the great anthropologists of the twentieth century, Ruth Benedict, to explain the Japanese to them, which she did. After the war, she published her ideas in a book, *The Chrysanthemum and the Sword*. One of her central insights was the difference between shame cultures and guilt cultures. In shame cultures the highest value is honor. In guilt cultures it is righteousness. Shame is feeling bad that we have failed to live up to the expectations others have of us. Guilt is what we feel when we fail to live up to what our own conscience demands of us. Shame is other-directed. Guilt is inner-directed.

Philosophers, among them Bernard Williams, have pointed out that shame cultures are usually visual. Shame itself has to do with how you appear (or imagine you appear) in other people's eyes. The instinctive reaction to shame is to wish you were invisible, or somewhere else. Guilt, by contrast, is much more internal. You cannot escape it by becoming invisible or being elsewhere. Your conscience accompanies you wherever you go, regardless of whether you are seen by others. Guilt cultures are cultures of the ear, not the eye.

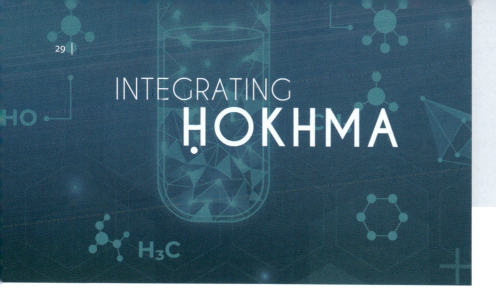

4 1 The man knew[1] his wife Ḥava, and she conceived and gave birth to Kayin. She said, "With
2 the Lord's help I have made a man."[2] Later, she gave birth to his brother Hevel.[3] Hevel
3 became a shepherd, while Kayin was a worker of the land. Time passed, and Kayin brought
4 fruit of the land as an offering to the Lord. Hevel too brought an offering: fat portions from
5 the firstborn of his flock. The Lord looked favorably on Hevel and his offering, but upon
Kayin and his offering He did not look with favor. Kayin became very angry, and his face,
6 7 downcast. The Lord said to Kayin: "Why are you angry; why is your face downcast? If
you act well, will you not be uplifted? If you fail to act well, sin is crouching at the door; it
8 longs to have you, but you must rule over it." Then Kayin said to his brother Hevel[4] – and
9 when they were in the field, Kayin rose up against his brother Hevel and killed him. The
Lord asked Kayin, "Where is your brother, Hevel?" "I do not know," he said. "Am I my
10 brother's keeper?" He said, "What is it you have done? The voice of your brother's blood
11 cries out to Me from the land! Now you are cursed, more so than the land[5] that has opened
12 its mouth to receive your brother's blood from your hand. When you work the land, it
13 will no longer grant you its powers. You will be a fugitive wanderer over the land." Kayin
14 said to the Lord, "My sin is more than I can bear. You have banished me today from the
face of the land, and from Your face too I will be hidden. I will be a fugitive wanderer over

1 | A euphemism for sexual relations.

2 | The name Kayin resonates with *kaniti* ("I have made").

3 | *Hevel* means "breath" and carries connotations of transience.

4 | It is not specified what Kayin told Hevel.

5 | Cf. 3:17.

UNLOCKING THE TEXT

- Why did they name the second child Hevel? Why does the Torah not tell us the meaning of his name?
- Why does Hevel become a shepherd when God has not yet allowed the eating of meat?
- Why did they decide to bring offerings from their produce?
- Why did God favor Hevel's offering over Kayin's?
- What did Kayin say to Hevel in verse 8?
- Why did Kayin kill his brother?
- Why did God ask Kayin where his brother was?
- Why did God choose to punish Hevel in this way?
- Why is Kayin concerned that he may be killed?
- What does the "mark of Kayin" mean?

FINDING YOURSELF IN THE TEXT

- Do you have siblings? Do you ever argue with them? Are you and your siblings sometimes jealous of each other?
- Is it harder being the oldest or youngest or middle child?
- Have you ever been tempted to answer a question in a similar way to "Am I my brother's keeper?" Is this ever justified?

Consider using these questions as the basis for your own commentary or creative midrash.

How does reflecting on these firsthand experiences help you better understand the text?

ד א וְהָ֣אָדָ֔ם יָדַ֖ע אֶת־חַוָּ֣ה אִשְׁתּ֑וֹ וַתַּ֙הַר֙ וַתֵּ֣לֶד אֶת־קַ֔יִן וַתֹּ֕אמֶר קָנִ֥יתִי אִ֖ישׁ אֶת־יְהֹוָֽה:

ב וַתֹּ֣סֶף לָלֶ֔דֶת אֶת־אָחִ֖יו אֶת־הָ֑בֶל וַֽיְהִי־הֶ֙בֶל֙ רֹ֣עֵה צֹ֔אן וְקַ֕יִן הָיָ֖ה עֹבֵ֥ד **אֲדָמָֽה**: ג וַֽיְהִ֖י

ד מִקֵּ֣ץ יָמִ֑ים וַיָּבֵ֨א קַ֜יִן מִפְּרִ֧י **הָֽאֲדָמָ֛ה** מִנְחָ֖ה לַֽיהֹוָֽה: וְהֶ֨בֶל הֵבִ֥יא גַם־ה֛וּא מִבְּכֹר֥וֹת

ה צֹאנ֖וֹ וּמֵֽחֶלְבֵהֶ֑ן וַיִּ֣שַׁע יְהֹוָ֔ה אֶל־הֶ֖בֶל וְאֶל־מִנְחָתֽוֹ: וְאֶל־קַ֥יִן וְאֶל־מִנְחָת֖וֹ לֹ֣א

ו שָׁעָ֑ה וַיִּ֤חַר לְקַ֙יִן֙ מְאֹ֔ד וַֽיִּפְּל֖וּ פָּנָֽיו: וַיֹּ֥אמֶר יְהֹוָ֖ה אֶל־קָ֑יִן לָ֚מָּה חָ֣רָה לָ֔ךְ וְלָ֖מָּה

ז נָֽפְל֥וּ פָנֶֽיךָ: הֲל֤וֹא אִם־תֵּיטִיב֙ שְׂאֵ֔ת וְאִם֙ לֹ֣א תֵיטִ֔יב לַפֶּ֖תַח חַטָּ֣את רֹבֵ֑ץ וְאֵלֶ֙יךָ֙

ח תְּשׁ֣וּקָת֔וֹ וְאַתָּ֖ה תִּמְשָׁל־בּֽוֹ: וַיֹּ֥אמֶר קַ֖יִן אֶל־הֶ֣בֶל אָחִ֑יו וַֽיְהִי֙ בִּֽהְיוֹתָ֣ם **בַּשָּׂדֶ֔ה**

ט וַיָּ֥קׇם קַ֛יִן אֶל־הֶ֥בֶל אָחִ֖יו וַיַּֽהַרְגֵֽהוּ: וַיֹּ֤אמֶר יְהֹוָה֙ אֶל־קַ֔יִן אֵ֖י הֶ֣בֶל אָחִ֑יךָ וַיֹּ֙אמֶר֙

י לֹ֣א יָדַ֔עְתִּי הֲשֹׁמֵ֥ר אָחִ֖י אָנֹֽכִי: וַיֹּ֖אמֶר מֶ֣ה עָשִׂ֑יתָ ק֚וֹל דְּמֵ֣י אָחִ֔יךָ צֹֽעֲקִ֥ים אֵלַ֖י מִן־

יא **הָֽאֲדָמָֽה**: וְעַתָּ֖ה אָר֣וּר אָ֑תָּה מִן־**הָֽאֲדָמָה֙** אֲשֶׁ֣ר פָּֽצְתָ֣ה אֶת־פִּ֔יהָ לָקַ֛חַת אֶת־דְּמֵ֥י

יב אָחִ֖יךָ מִיָּדֶֽךָ: כִּ֤י תַֽעֲבֹד֙ אֶת־**הָ֣אֲדָמָ֔ה** לֹֽא־תֹסֵ֥ף תֵּת־כֹּחָ֖הּ לָ֑ךְ נָ֥ע וָנָ֖ד תִּֽהְיֶ֥ה בָאָֽרֶץ:

יג וַיֹּ֥אמֶר קַ֖יִן אֶל־יְהֹוָ֑ה גָּד֥וֹל עֲוֺנִ֖י מִנְּשֽׂוֹא: הֵן֩ גֵּרַ֨שְׁתָּ אֹתִ֜י הַיּ֗וֹם מֵעַל֙ פְּנֵ֣י **הָֽאֲדָמָ֔ה**

THEMES	ETHICS	FREE WILL, REWARD AND PUNISHMENT	RELATIONSHIPS AND LOVE

Episode 4: *The Children of Adam and Ḥava* – Bereshit 4:1–26

SUMMARY

This chapter marks the beginning of the story of Adam and his family outside the Garden of Eden. After their banishment from the garden, Adam and Ḥava begin a new life with all its complexities. Their family must deal with some of the fundamental issues facing humanity, one of which is relations between siblings. The story opens with two brothers, each living in his own manner and in his own realm. From the outset, they are different from one another, and perhaps there is some friction between them, but each remains in his own world. Eventually, however, their worlds collide.

15 the land, and whoever finds me will kill me." The Lord said to him, "Whoever then kills
Kayin will suffer vengeance seven times over." Then the Lord put a mark on Kayin so
16 that none who found him would kill him. So Kayin departed from the Lord's presence
17 and lived in the land of Nod,[6] east of Eden. Kayin knew his wife, and she conceived and
18 gave birth to Ḥanokh. He built a city, naming it Ḥanokh after his son. Ḥanokh had a son
Irad, and Irad had a son Meḥuyael. Meḥiyael had a son Metushael, and Metushael had
19 20 a son Lemekh. Lemekh married two women, one named Ada and the other Tzila. Ada
21 gave birth to Yaval. He was the ancestor of those who live in tents and raise livestock. His
brother's name was Yuval. He was the ancestor of all who those who play the lyre and the
22 pipe. Tzila, too, had a son, Tuval-Kayin, who forged all kinds of copper and iron tools.
23 Tuval-Kayin's sister was Naama. Lemekh said to his wives: "Ada and Tzila, listen to my
voice; wives of Lemekh, heed my words. I killed a man for wounding me, killed a boy for
24 25 bruising me. If Kayin will be avenged seven times, then Lemekh: seventy-seven." Adam
knew his wife again, and she gave birth to a son and named him Shet, "because God has
26 granted[7] me another child in place of Hevel," for Kayin had killed him. And Shet too had a
son, and named him Enosh. That was when people began to pray in the name of the Lord.

---

6 | "Land of Nod" bears the simultaneous meaning "land of wandering."

7 | The name Shet resonates with *shat* ("granted").

Analysis

- Which elements of this image are directly mentioned in the text?
- Which elements of this image are not found in the text?
- What midrashic interpretation is the artist giving us?

Cain & Abel, Adi Nes (2006)

טו וּמִפָּנֶיךָ אֶסָּתֵר וְהָיִיתִי נָע וָנָד בָּאָרֶץ וְהָיָה כָל־מֹצְאִי יַהַרְגֵנִי׃ וַיֹּאמֶר לוֹ יהוה לָכֵן
כָּל־הֹרֵג קַיִן שִׁבְעָתַיִם יֻקָּם וַיָּשֶׂם יהוה לְקַיִן אוֹת לְבִלְתִּי הַכּוֹת־אֹתוֹ כָּל־מֹצְאוֹ׃
טז יז וַיֵּצֵא קַיִן מִלִּפְנֵי יהוה וַיֵּשֶׁב בְּאֶרֶץ־נוֹד קִדְמַת־עֵדֶן׃ וַיֵּדַע קַיִן אֶת־אִשְׁתּוֹ וַתַּהַר
יח וַתֵּלֶד אֶת־חֲנוֹךְ וַיְהִי בֹּנֶה עִיר וַיִּקְרָא שֵׁם הָעִיר כְּשֵׁם בְּנוֹ חֲנוֹךְ׃ וַיִּוָּלֵד לַחֲנוֹךְ
אֶת־עִירָד וְעִירָד יָלַד אֶת־מְחוּיָאֵל וּמְחִיָּיאֵל יָלַד אֶת־מְתוּשָׁאֵל וּמְתוּשָׁאֵל יָלַד
יט כ אֶת־לָמֶךְ׃ וַיִּקַּח־לוֹ לֶמֶךְ שְׁתֵּי נָשִׁים שֵׁם הָאַחַת עָדָה וְשֵׁם הַשֵּׁנִית צִלָּה׃ וַתֵּלֶד חמישי
כא עָדָה אֶת־יָבָל הוּא הָיָה אֲבִי יֹשֵׁב אֹהֶל וּמִקְנֶה׃ וְשֵׁם אָחִיו יוּבָל הוּא הָיָה אֲבִי
כב כָּל־תֹּפֵשׂ כִּנּוֹר וְעוּגָב׃ וְצִלָּה גַם־הִוא יָלְדָה אֶת־תּוּבַל קַיִן לֹטֵשׁ כָּל־חֹרֵשׁ נְחֹשֶׁת
כג וּבַרְזֶל וַאֲחוֹת תּוּבַל־קַיִן נַעֲמָה׃ וַיֹּאמֶר לֶמֶךְ לְנָשָׁיו עָדָה וְצִלָּה שְׁמַעַן קוֹלִי נְשֵׁי
כד לֶמֶךְ הַאְזֵנָּה אִמְרָתִי כִּי אִישׁ הָרַגְתִּי לְפִצְעִי וְיֶלֶד לְחַבֻּרָתִי׃ כִּי שִׁבְעָתַיִם יֻקַּם־קָיִן
כה וְלֶמֶךְ שִׁבְעִים וְשִׁבְעָה׃ וַיֵּדַע אָדָם עוֹד אֶת־אִשְׁתּוֹ וַתֵּלֶד בֵּן וַתִּקְרָא אֶת־שְׁמוֹ
כו שֵׁת כִּי שָׁת־לִי אֱלֹהִים זֶרַע אַחֵר תַּחַת הֶבֶל כִּי הֲרָגוֹ קָיִן׃ וּלְשֵׁת גַּם־הוּא יֻלַּד־בֵּן
וַיִּקְרָא אֶת־שְׁמוֹ אֱנוֹשׁ אָז הוּחַל לִקְרֹא בְּשֵׁם יהוה׃

THE ART OF MIDRASH

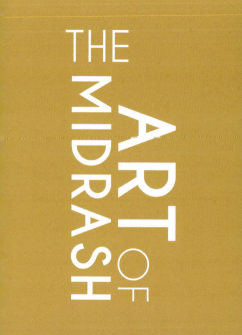

TO HEVEL

- Why did you decide to bring an offering to God?
- How did it feel when God rejected Kayin's offering and accepted yours?
- Were you ever scared of your brother?
- Did you ever imagine he was capable of killing you?

TO GOD

- Did You expect Kayin to murder his brother?
- How could You expect Kayin to know murder was wrong if You hadn't forbidden killing yet?
- Do You regret giving humans free will?
- Is it inevitable that humans will do evil?

A QUESTION OF BIBLIODRAMA

TO ḤAVA

- How does it feel to give birth to a child?
- What are your feelings toward your second-born child?
- How did you react when you heard your son was dead?
- Do you think you and Adam were to blame in any way for what happened?
- How did you feel when Shet was born? Could he really replace Hevel?

TO KAYIN

- Why did you decide to bring an offering to God?
- How did it feel when God rejected your offering? Why did you become angry?
- What did you understand from God's response to your disappointment?
- Did you mean to kill your brother?
- Why did you attack him?
- What did you feel once you realized you had killed him?

INTEGRATING ḤOKHMA

The first religious act, Kayin and Hevel's offerings to God, leads directly to the first murder. God does seem to have favorites. There does seem to be a zero-sumness about the stories. It is no accident that Jews, Christians and Muslims read these stories the way they did.

But what if they do not mean what people have thought them to mean? What if there is another way of reading them? What if this alternative reading turned out, on close analysis, to be how they were written to be read? What if the narratives of Bereshit are deliberately constructed to seem to mean one thing on the surface, but then, in the light of cues or clues within the text, reveal a second level of meaning beneath?

What if the Hebrew Bible understood, as did Freud and Girard, as did Greek and Roman myth, that sibling rivalry is the most primal form of violence? And what if, rather than endorsing it, it set out to undermine it, subvert it, challenge it, and eventually replace it with another, quite different way of understanding our relationship with God and with the human Other? What if Bereshit is a more profound, multi-leveled, transformative text than we have taken it to be? What if it turned out to be God's way of saying to us what He said to Kayin: that violence in a sacred cause is not holy but an act of desecration? What if God were saying: *Not in My name?*

Rabbi Jonathan Sacks

Analysis

- What areas of understanding of human nature and society do we now have that were unavailable to classical Jewish commentators? How can they aid our understanding of the text?
- What can we learn from this passage to help us understand the text?
- What further questions on the text do you have now that you have read this new take on the story?

TAKING A LITERARY APPROACH

The word *adama*, "ground," appears six times during the course of the story, and once the word "field" is used instead (referring to the specific land, owned and worked by Kayin, where the murder takes place). The ground is not merely Kayin's place of work and the source of his income – it is also the scene of the murder. The first half of the story (vv. 1–8) mentions the word "ground" three times, in its description of Kayin's connection with the ground (his tilling of it, his bringing its fruits as an offering, and his murder of Hevel upon it). The next three instances of the word in the second half of the story (vv. 9–16), in God's words to Kayin, parallel the first three in the inverse order:

4–3: In light of the murder of Hevel in the field (it also appears that his blood and corpse were buried there), God says to Kayin, "Your brother's blood calls to Me from the ground." In other words, you cannot hide your deed; the ground will not cooperate in this venture.

5–2: In the past, the ground offered Kayin its fruits (compare further on, verse 12: "It will no longer yield its strength to you"), and Kayin made use of them for the purpose of bringing an offering to God. Now, in light of the murder, the ground has "opened its mouth **to accept (take)** your brother's blood from your hand." The ground will henceforth no longer be a source of divine gifts and blessing; it will now become the source of Kayin's curse: "You are cursed **from the ground**."

6–1: Kayin, who chose to be a "tiller of the ground," will now cut himself off from it. And the ground will no longer respond to his working of it: "When **you till the ground** it will no longer yield its strength to you." As a result: "You will be a wanderer and a vagabond upon the earth" – Kayin will be forced to adapt himself to the lifestyle of Hevel, who, as a shepherd, would wander upon the earth in search of pasture for his flocks.

In the seventh and final mention of the word, we hear from Kayin himself the significance of his punishment: "Behold, You have driven me out today from upon the ground, and I shall be hidden from Your face."

Thus we learn that the tilling of the ground and the relationship between man and ground are at the heart of the story, and they join all of its stages. Both the sin and its punishment are connected with this cultivated ground. The story comes to teach us that the ground cannot tolerate a person who uses it for a negative purpose, and it vomits him out from upon it. This is the relationship that God has set out since the beginning of days to exist between man and ground.

Rabbi Elchanan Samet

5 1 This is the book of Adam's descendants: On the day God created humankind, He made them
2 in the likeness of God. Male and female He created them, and on the day they were created,
3 He blessed them and called them Humankind.[1] Adam lived one hundred and thirty years
4 and then had a son in his own likeness and image, and named him Shet. After Shet was born,
5 Adam lived eight hundred years and had other sons and daughters. Altogether Adam lived
6 nine hundred and thirty years, and then he died. Shet lived one hundred and five
7 years and then had a son, Enosh. After Enosh was born, Shet lived eight hundred and seven
8 years and had other sons and daughters. Altogether, Shet lived nine hundred and twelve years,
9 10 and then he died. Enosh lived ninety years and then had a son, Keinan. After Keinan
was born, Enosh lived eight hundred and fifteen years and had other sons and daughters.
11 12 Altogether, Enosh lived nine hundred and five years, and then he died. Keinan
13 lived seventy years and had a son, Mahalalel. After Mahalalel was born, Keinan lived eight

1 | Hebrew *adam.*

UNLOCKING THE TEXT

- Why does the Torah repeat some of the details of the creation of humankind here?
- How can the extraordinarily long lives of the people in this chapter be explained?
- What is the significance behind the names of these personalities?
- Why does the Torah only list the descendants of Adam through his son Shet and not his other children?
- What is different about Ḥanokh from all the other names in the list and why is it different?
- Why did Lemekh feel the need to name his son Noaḥ?
- Why does this chronology end with the sons of Noaḥ?

FINDING YOURSELF IN THE TEXT

- Do you have a family tree that someone in your family has compiled? Can you see the importance of compiling a family tree?
- What do you know about your direct ancestors?
- Do you ever think about your future descendants and what their lives might be like?

Consider using these questions as the basis for your own commentary or creative midrash.

How does reflecting on these firsthand experiences help you better understand the text?

ה א זֶה סֵפֶר תּוֹלְדֹת אָדָם בְּיוֹם בְּרֹא אֱלֹהִים אָדָם בִּדְמוּת אֱלֹהִים עָשָׂה אֹתוֹ: זָכָר ד ששי

ב וּנְקֵבָה בְּרָאָם וַיְבָרֶךְ אֹתָם וַיִּקְרָא אֶת־שְׁמָם אָדָם בְּיוֹם הִבָּרְאָם: וַיְחִי אָדָם

ג שְׁלֹשִׁים וּמְאַת שָׁנָה וַיּוֹלֶד בִּדְמוּתוֹ כְּצַלְמוֹ וַיִּקְרָא אֶת־שְׁמוֹ שֵׁת: וַיִּהְיוּ יְמֵי־

ד אָדָם אַחֲרֵי הוֹלִידוֹ אֶת־שֵׁת שְׁמֹנֶה מֵאֹת שָׁנָה וַיּוֹלֶד בָּנִים וּבָנוֹת: וַיִּהְיוּ כָּל־יְמֵי

ה אָדָם אֲשֶׁר־חַי תְּשַׁע מֵאוֹת שָׁנָה וּשְׁלֹשִׁים שָׁנָה וַיָּמֹת: וַיְחִי־שֵׁת

ו חָמֵשׁ שָׁנִים וּמְאַת שָׁנָה וַיּוֹלֶד אֶת־אֱנוֹשׁ: וַיְחִי־שֵׁת אַחֲרֵי הוֹלִידוֹ אֶת־אֱנוֹשׁ

ז שֶׁבַע שָׁנִים וּשְׁמֹנֶה מֵאוֹת שָׁנָה וַיּוֹלֶד בָּנִים וּבָנוֹת: וַיִּהְיוּ כָּל־יְמֵי־שֵׁת שְׁתֵּים

ח עֶשְׂרֵה שָׁנָה וּתְשַׁע מֵאוֹת שָׁנָה וַיָּמֹת: וַיְחִי אֱנוֹשׁ תִּשְׁעִים שָׁנָה

ט וַיּוֹלֶד אֶת־קֵינָן: וַיְחִי אֱנוֹשׁ אַחֲרֵי הוֹלִידוֹ אֶת־קֵינָן חֲמֵשׁ עֶשְׂרֵה שָׁנָה וּשְׁמֹנֶה

י מֵאוֹת שָׁנָה וַיּוֹלֶד בָּנִים וּבָנוֹת: וַיִּהְיוּ כָּל־יְמֵי אֱנוֹשׁ חָמֵשׁ שָׁנִים וּתְשַׁע מֵאוֹת שָׁנָה

יא וַיָּמֹת: וַיְחִי קֵינָן שִׁבְעִים שָׁנָה וַיּוֹלֶד אֶת־מַהֲלַלְאֵל: וַיְחִי קֵינָן אַחֲרֵי

THEMES	RELATIONSHIPS AND LOVE	COVENANT	CREATION

Episode 5: *The First Family Tree* – Bereshit 5:1–32

SUMMARY

This episode consists of a brief chronology of the first ten generations of man, descendants of Shet. It encompasses a period of roughly 1,700 years, and outlines the ten generations from Adam through Shet, climaxing with Lemekh, the father of Noaḥ, the main protagonist in the following episodes. Then the birth of Noaḥ is described. Noaḥ's birth stands out in multiple ways, chief among them that he is the first person since Shet whose name is explained.

14 hundred and forty years and had other sons and daughters. Altogether, Keinan lived nine
15 hundred and ten years, and then he died. Mahalalel lived sixty-five years and had a
16 son, Yered. After Yered was born, Mahalalel lived eight hundred and thirty years and
17 had other sons and daughters. Altogether, Mahalalel lived eight hundred and ninety-five
18 years, and then he died. Yered lived one hundred and sixty-two years and
19 had a son, Ḥanokh. After Ḥanokh was born, Yered lived eight hundred years and had
20 other sons and daughters. Altogether, Yered lived nine hundred and sixty-two years,
21 and then he died. Ḥanokh lived sixty-five years and had a son, Metushelaḥ.
22 Ḥanokh walked faithfully with God for three hundred years after Metushelaḥ was born,
23 and had other sons and daughters. Altogether, Ḥanokh lived for three hundred and
24 sixty-five years. Ḥanokh walked faithfully with God and then he was no more, for God
25 took him. Metushelaḥ lived one hundred and eighty-seven years and had a
26 son, Lemekh. After Lemekh was born, Metushelaḥ lived seven hundred and eighty-two
27 years and had other sons and daughters. Altogether, Metushelaḥ lived nine hundred
28 and sixty-nine years, and then he died. Lemekh lived one hundred and eighty-
29 two years and had a son. He named him Noaḥ, saying, "This one will bring us comfort[2]
30 after all our labor and the sorrow of our hands on the land the Lord has cursed." After
Noaḥ was born, Lemekh lived five hundred and ninety-five years and had other sons and
31 daughters. Altogether, Lemekh lived seven hundred and seventy-seven years, and then he
32 died. After Noaḥ was five hundred years old, Noaḥ had three sons: Shem, Ḥam,
and Yefet.

2 | *Noaḥ* resonates with *yenaḥamenu* ("will bring us comfort").

יד הוֹלִיד֖וֹ אֶת־מַהֲלַלְאֵ֑ל אַרְבָּעִ֣ים שָׁנָ֔ה וּשְׁמֹנֶ֥ה מֵא֖וֹת שָׁנָ֑ה וַיּ֥וֹלֶד בָּנִ֖ים וּבָנֽוֹת׃ וַיִּֽהְיוּ֙
טו כָּל־יְמֵ֣י קֵינָ֔ן עֶ֣שֶׂר שָׁנִ֔ים וּתְשַׁ֥ע מֵא֖וֹת שָׁנָ֑ה וַיָּמֹֽת׃ וַיְחִ֣י מַֽהֲלַלְאֵ֔ל
טז חָמֵ֥שׁ שָׁנִ֖ים וְשִׁשִּׁ֣ים שָׁנָ֑ה וַיּ֖וֹלֶד אֶת־יָֽרֶד׃ וַיְחִ֣י מַֽהֲלַלְאֵ֗ל אַֽחֲרֵי֙ הוֹלִיד֣וֹ אֶת־יֶ֔רֶד
יז שְׁלֹשִׁ֣ים שָׁנָ֔ה וּשְׁמֹנֶ֥ה מֵא֖וֹת שָׁנָ֑ה וַיּ֥וֹלֶד בָּנִ֖ים וּבָנֽוֹת׃ וַיִּֽהְיוּ֙ כָּל־יְמֵ֣י מַֽהֲלַלְאֵ֔ל חָמֵ֤שׁ
יח וְתִשְׁעִים֙ שָׁנָ֔ה וּשְׁמֹנֶ֥ה מֵא֖וֹת שָׁנָ֑ה וַיָּמֹֽת׃ וַֽיְחִי־יֶ֕רֶד שְׁתַּ֧יִם וְשִׁשִּׁ֛ים שָׁנָ֖ה
יט וּמְאַ֣ת שָׁנָ֑ה וַיּ֖וֹלֶד אֶת־חֲנֽוֹךְ׃ וַֽיְחִי־יֶ֗רֶד אַֽחֲרֵי֙ הוֹלִיד֣וֹ אֶת־חֲנ֔וֹךְ שְׁמֹנֶ֥ה מֵא֖וֹת
כ שָׁנָ֑ה וַיּ֥וֹלֶד בָּנִ֖ים וּבָנֽוֹת׃ וַיִּֽהְיוּ֙ כָּל־יְמֵי־יֶ֔רֶד שְׁתַּ֤יִם וְשִׁשִּׁים֙ שָׁנָ֔ה וּתְשַׁ֥ע מֵא֖וֹת שָׁנָ֑ה
כא כב וַיָּמֹֽת׃ וַֽיְחִ֣י חֲנ֔וֹךְ חָמֵ֥שׁ וְשִׁשִּׁ֖ים שָׁנָ֑ה וַיּ֖וֹלֶד אֶת־מְתוּשָֽׁלַח׃ וַיִּתְהַלֵּ֨ךְ חֲנ֜וֹךְ
אֶת־הָֽאֱלֹהִ֗ים אַֽחֲרֵי֙ הוֹלִיד֣וֹ אֶת־מְתוּשֶׁ֔לַח שְׁלֹ֥שׁ מֵא֖וֹת שָׁנָ֑ה וַיּ֥וֹלֶד בָּנִ֖ים וּבָנֽוֹת׃
כג כד וַיְהִ֖י כָּל־יְמֵ֣י חֲנ֑וֹךְ חָמֵ֤שׁ וְשִׁשִּׁים֙ שָׁנָ֔ה וּשְׁלֹ֥שׁ מֵא֖וֹת שָׁנָֽה׃ וַיִּתְהַלֵּ֥ךְ חֲנ֖וֹךְ אֶת־
כה הָאֱלֹהִ֑ים וְאֵינֶ֕נּוּ כִּֽי־לָקַ֥ח אֹת֖וֹ אֱלֹהִֽים׃ וַיְחִ֣י מְתוּשֶׁ֔לַח שֶׁ֧בַע וּשְׁמֹנִ֛ים שביעי
כו שָׁנָ֖ה וּמְאַ֣ת שָׁנָ֑ה וַיּ֖וֹלֶד אֶת־לָֽמֶךְ׃ וַיְחִ֣י מְתוּשֶׁ֗לַח אַֽחֲרֵי֙ הוֹלִיד֣וֹ אֶת־לֶ֔מֶךְ שְׁתַּ֤יִם
כז וּשְׁמוֹנִים֙ שָׁנָ֔ה וּשְׁבַ֥ע מֵא֖וֹת שָׁנָ֑ה וַיּ֥וֹלֶד בָּנִ֖ים וּבָנֽוֹת׃ וַיִּֽהְיוּ֙ כָּל־יְמֵ֣י מְתוּשֶׁ֔לַח תֵּ֚שַׁע
כח וְשִׁשִּׁים֙ שָׁנָ֔ה וּתְשַׁ֥ע מֵא֖וֹת שָׁנָ֑ה וַיָּמֹֽת׃ וַֽיְחִי־לֶ֕מֶךְ שְׁתַּ֧יִם וּשְׁמֹנִ֛ים
כט שָׁנָ֖ה וּמְאַ֣ת שָׁנָ֑ה וַיּ֖וֹלֶד בֵּֽן׃ וַיִּקְרָ֧א אֶת־שְׁמ֛וֹ נֹ֖חַ לֵאמֹ֑ר זֶ֞ה יְנַחֲמֵ֤נוּ מִֽמַּעֲשֵׂ֙נוּ֙
ל וּמֵעִצְּב֣וֹן יָדֵ֔ינוּ מִן־הָ֣אֲדָמָ֔ה אֲשֶׁ֥ר אֵרְרָ֖הּ יהוה׃ וַֽיְחִי־לֶ֗מֶךְ אַֽחֲרֵי֙ הוֹלִיד֣וֹ אֶת־נֹ֔חַ
לא חָמֵ֤שׁ וְתִשְׁעִים֙ שָׁנָ֔ה וַחֲמֵ֥שׁ מֵאֹ֖ת שָׁנָ֑ה וַיּ֥וֹלֶד בָּנִ֖ים וּבָנֽוֹת׃ וַֽיְהִי֙ כָּל־יְמֵי־לֶ֔מֶךְ
לב שֶׁ֤בַע וְשִׁבְעִים֙ שָׁנָ֔ה וּשְׁבַ֥ע מֵא֖וֹת שָׁנָ֑ה וַיָּמֹֽת׃ וַֽיְהִי־נֹ֕חַ בֶּן־חֲמֵ֥שׁ
מֵא֖וֹת שָׁנָ֑ה וַיּ֣וֹלֶד נֹ֔חַ אֶת־שֵׁ֖ם אֶת־חָ֥ם וְאֶת־יָֽפֶת׃

THE ART OF MIDRASH

God Appears to Noah
James Jacques Joseph Tissot (c. 1896–1902)

Analysis

- Which elements of this image are directly mentioned in the text?
- Which elements of this image are not found in the text?
- What midrashic interpretation is the artist giving us?

INTEGRATING ḤOKHMA

The genealogical line between Adam and Noaḥ

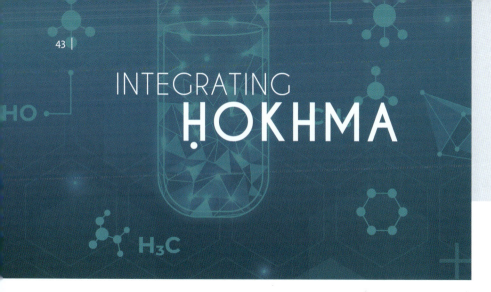

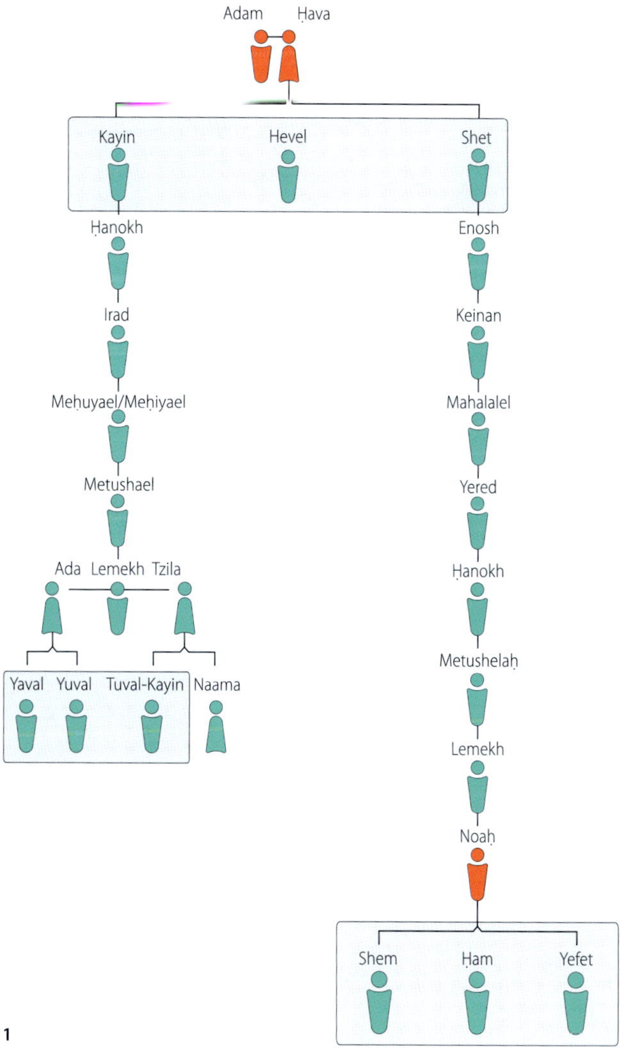

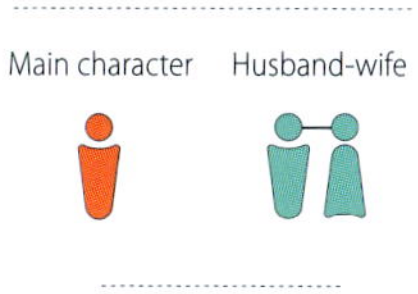

BERESHIT 4–5; I DIVREI HAYAMIM 1

descendants can begin to emerge from the shadow of the curse of Kayin and commence their lives as their own selves. Noaḥ represents their hopes for that life.

Rabbi Zvi Grumet

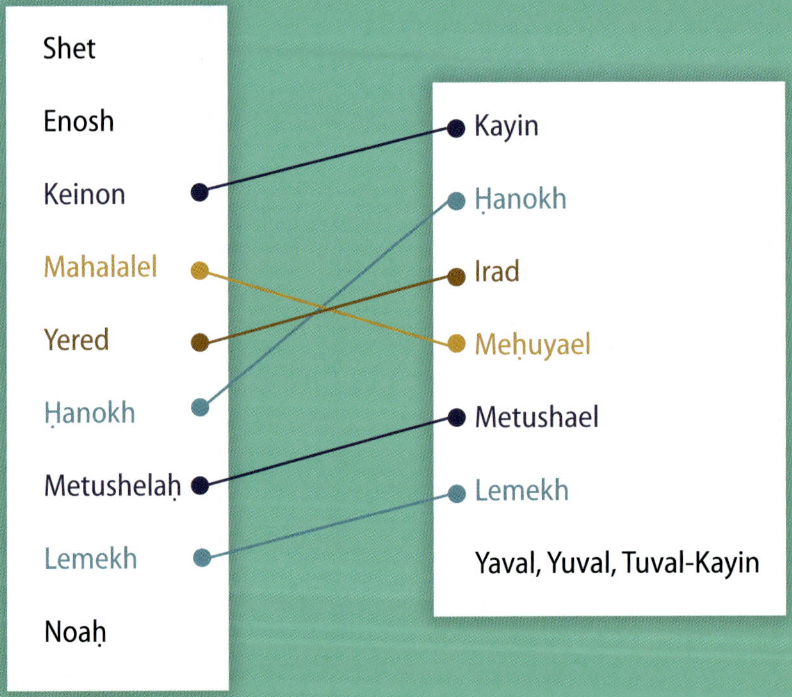

TAKING A LITERARY APPROACH

The genealogy of Shet describes each individual as having lived and having perpetuated himself through his children. There is a sense of celebration with each new generation as it completes a cycle of life. Kayin's descendants are pursued by the dark cloud of God's curse, while Shet's descendants find closure in the completion of their lives.

Despite the dramatic differences in description, a closer look at the two genealogies reveals striking similarities between them. Names that appear in Kayin's line of descendants reappear, albeit with minor changes, in Shet's progeny. In both lines there is a Ḥanokh and a Lemekh, Keinon parallels Kayin, Metushelaḥ matches Metushael, Mahalalel is mirrored by Meḥuyael, and Yered echoes Irad (in the Hebrew they are identical, with the addition of a single letter in Irad's name). The chart that follows demonstrates the remarkable parallels.

It appears that the descendants of Shet are intentionally giving names to their offspring that mirror Kayin and his line. If, as suggested in the previous chapter, there is a concern of some impending curse on Kayin and his descendants, then it seems that Shet's line is determined to preserve their names. This, in fact, likely predated a similar attempt we noticed in the previous chapter, in which the children of Kayin's Lemekh carry variations of Hevel's name, seeking to keep Hevel's name alive. Thus, it is Shet's (or Enosh's) inspiration which prompts Lemekh to redeem Hevel as Shet's descendants were doing for Kayin's line.

The two genealogies paint for us an image of six generations desperately seeking to counteract a divine curse. In this light, two generations stand out. First, there is no one in Shet's line carrying the names of Yaval/Yuval/Tuval-Kayin, Kayin's seventh generation. This is likely because those three are carrying Hevel's name. They do not need redemption because they are redeemers themselves, not only in name but in profession.

The second name that stands out is Noaḥ. He is the first in seven generations to carry his own name, unconnected to Kayin's line. Moreover, we are offered an explanation for it: "This one will console us (*yenaḥamenu* – from the same root as *Noaḥ*) for our deeds and the pain of our labor from the ground which God cursed" (Bereshit 5:29).

The references to the curses of both Adam and Kayin are clear, and so are the implications. After six generations of trying to rescue the line of Kayin, Shet's

6 1 Humans began to multiply on earth, and daughters were born to them. When the sons of
2 God[1] saw that the daughters of man were lovely, they began to take whomever they chose
3 to be wives to them. Then the LORD said, "My spirit will not forever judge man; he is of
4 flesh. His life shall be but one hundred and twenty years." In those days the Nefilim[2] were
on earth, and later also, for the sons of God had gone to the daughters of man and had
children with them. These were the heroes of old, men of legends.
5 The LORD saw how great man's wickedness was upon the earth, and that his thoughts
6 constantly inclined toward evil. Then the LORD regretted that He had made man on
7 earth, and His heart was touched with sorrow. The LORD said, "I will erase My creation,
humankind, from the face of the land – man, even animals and creeping things, even birds
8 of the heavens – for I regret having made them." But Noaḥ found favor in the LORD's sight.

1 | Opinions vary regarding the meaning and proper translation of this phrase.

2 | Apparently giants (see Bemidbar 13:33).

UNLOCKING THE TEXT

- Who are the *benei Elohim* ("sons of God")?
- What does God mean when He says He will "not forever judge humans" because they are "of flesh"?
- What does it mean that human lives will be 120 years? Why 120?
- Who are the Nefilim?
- What evil did God see humans do that made Him regret creating humankind?
- How can God "regret" if He has perfect knowledge?
- Why did God choose to destroy the world, including all the animals?
- Why did Noaḥ "find favor" in the eyes of God?

Consider using these questions as the basis for your own commentary or creative midrash.

FINDING YOURSELF IN THE TEXT

- Have you ever regretted a decision and wished you could start over?
- Have you ever trusted someone who then betrayed your trust?
- Do you think there is something you could ever do that could never be forgiven?

How does reflecting on these firsthand experiences help you better understand the text?

ו א ב וַיְהִי֙ כִּֽי־הֵחֵ֣ל הָֽאָדָ֔ם לָרֹ֖ב עַל־פְּנֵ֣י הָֽאֲדָמָ֑ה וּבָנ֖וֹת יֻלְּד֥וּ לָהֶֽם׃ וַיִּרְא֤וּ בְנֵי־הָֽאֱלֹהִים֙
ג אֶת־בְּנ֣וֹת הָֽאָדָ֔ם כִּ֥י טֹבֹ֖ת הֵ֑נָּה וַיִּקְח֤וּ לָהֶם֙ נָשִׁ֔ים מִכֹּ֖ל אֲשֶׁ֥ר בָּחָֽרוּ׃ וַיֹּ֣אמֶר יְהוָ֗ה
לֹֽא־יָד֨וֹן רוּחִ֤י בָֽאָדָם֙ לְעֹלָ֔ם בְּשַׁגַּ֖ם ה֣וּא בָשָׂ֑ר וְהָי֣וּ יָמָ֔יו מֵאָ֥ה וְעֶשְׂרִ֖ים שָׁנָֽה׃
ד הַנְּפִלִ֞ים הָי֣וּ בָאָרֶץ֮ בַּיָּמִ֣ים הָהֵם֒ וְגַ֣ם אַֽחֲרֵי־כֵ֗ן אֲשֶׁ֨ר יָבֹ֜אוּ בְּנֵ֤י הָֽאֱלֹהִים֙ אֶל־בְּנ֣וֹת
הָֽאָדָ֔ם וְיָלְד֖וּ לָהֶ֑ם הֵ֧מָּה הַגִּבֹּרִ֛ים אֲשֶׁ֥ר מֵעוֹלָ֖ם אַנְשֵׁ֥י הַשֵּֽׁם׃
ה וַיַּ֣רְא יְהוָ֔ה כִּ֥י רַבָּ֛ה רָעַ֥ת הָֽאָדָ֖ם בָּאָ֑רֶץ וְכָל־יֵ֙צֶר֙ מַחְשְׁבֹ֣ת לִבּ֔וֹ רַ֥ק רַ֖ע כָּל־הַיּֽוֹם׃ מפטיר
ו וַיִּנָּ֣חֶם יְהוָ֔ה כִּֽי־עָשָׂ֥ה אֶת־הָֽאָדָ֖ם בָּאָ֑רֶץ וַיִּתְעַצֵּ֖ב אֶל־לִבּֽוֹ׃ וַיֹּ֣אמֶר יְהוָ֗ה אֶמְחֶ֨ה
אֶת־הָאָדָ֤ם אֲשֶׁר־בָּרָ֙אתִי֙ מֵעַל֙ פְּנֵ֣י הָֽאֲדָמָ֔ה מֵֽאָדָם֙ עַד־בְּהֵמָ֔ה עַד־רֶ֖מֶשׂ וְעַד־
ח ע֣וֹף הַשָּׁמָ֑יִם כִּ֥י נִחַ֖מְתִּי כִּ֥י עֲשִׂיתִֽם׃ וְנֹ֕חַ מָ֥צָא חֵ֖ן בְּעֵינֵ֥י יְהוָֽה׃

THEMES | FREE WILL, REWARD AND PUNISHMENT | ETHICS | GOD

Episode 6: *Humanity Disappoints* – Bereshit 6:1–8

SUMMARY

The scene is set for the flood story that follows in the next episodes, as humankind grows as a species, and with it, the evil it performs. God is portrayed as regretting the creation of humankind because, despite being created in the image of God, the thoughts of humans are "constantly inclined toward evil." God therefore decides to erase the human (along with the other animals) from the earth. The exception is Noaḥ, who finds favor in God's eyes.

THE ART OF MIDRASH

The World on Fire
Javier Miranda (2022)

Analysis

- Which elements of this image are directly mentioned in the text?
- Which elements of this image are not found in the text?
- What midrashic interpretation is the artist giving us?

A QUESTION OF BIBLIODRAMA

TO GOD

- Why did You create humankind if they were destined to become evil?
- Can humans overcome their evil nature?
- Why did You cease to judge humankind because of their evil?
- Why do You "regret" creating humankind?
- How can You "regret" something?
- Why did You choose to reboot creation?
- Why does Noaḥ find favor in Your eyes?

us why. We are born to compete and cooperate. On the one hand, life is a competitive struggle for scarce resources – so we fight and kill. On the other hand, we survive only within groups. Without habits of cooperation, altruism, and trust, we would have no groups and we would not survive. That is part of what the Torah means when it says, "It is not good for man to be alone" (Bereshit 2:18).

God Himself recognizes that we are not naturally good. After the flood, He says: "I will never again curse the ground because of humankind, even though the inclination of their minds is evil from childhood on" (8:21). The antidote to the *yetzer*, the inclination to evil, is covenant.

We now know the neuroscience behind this. We have a prefrontal cortex that evolved to allow humans to think and act reflectively, considering the consequences of their deeds. But this is slower and weaker than the amygdala (what the Jewish mystics called the *nefesh habehemit*, "the animal soul"), which produces, even before we have had time to think, the fight-or-flight reactions without which humans before civilization would simply not have survived.

The problem is that these reactions can be deeply destructive. Often they lead to violence – not only the violence between species (predator and prey) that is part of the order of nature, but also to the more gratuitous violence that is a feature of the life of most social animals, not just humans. It is not that we only do evil. Empathy and compassion are as natural to us as are fear and aggression. The problem is that fear lies just beneath the surface of human interaction, and it threatens all else.

Daniel Goleman calls this an *amygdala hijack*. "Emotions make us pay attention right now – this is urgent – and give us an immediate action plan without having to think twice. The emotional component evolved very early: do I eat it, or does it eat me?" Impulsive action is often destructive because it is undertaken without thought of the consequences. That is why Rambam argued that many of the laws of the Torah constitute a training in virtue by making us think before we act.

So the Torah tells us that naturally we are neither good nor bad but have the capacity for both. We have a natural inclination to empathy and sympathy, but we have an even stronger instinct for fear that leads to violence. That is why, in the move from Adam to Noaḥ, the Torah shifts from nature to covenant, from *tov* to *brit*, from power to the moral limits of power. Genes are not enough. We also need the moral law.

Rabbi Jonathan Sacks

Analysis

- What areas of understanding of human nature and society do we now have that were unavailable to classical Jewish commentators? How can they aid our understanding of the text?
- What can we learn from this essay to help us understand the text?
- What further questions on the text do you have now that you have read this new take on the story?

INTEGRATING ḤOKHMA

Are we naturally good or naturally bad? On this great minds have argued for a very long time indeed. Hobbes believed that we have naturally "a perpetual and restless desire of power after power, that ceaseth only in death."[1] We are bad, but governments and police can help limit the harm we do. Rousseau, to the contrary, believed that naturally we are good. It is society and its institutions that make us bad.

The argument continues today among the neo-Darwinians. Some believe that natural selection and the struggle for survival make us, genetically, hawks rather than doves. As Michael T. Ghiselin puts it, "Scratch an 'altruist' and watch a 'hypocrite' bleed." By contrast, naturalist Frans de Waal in a series of delightful books about the primates, including his favorite, the bonobos, shows that they can be empathic, caring, and even altruistic. So by nature are we.

T. E. Hulme called this the fundamental divide between Romantics and Classicists throughout history. Romantics believed that "man was by nature good, that it was only bad laws and customs that had suppressed him. Remove all these and the infinite possibilities of man would have a chance." Classicists believed the opposite, that "man is an extraordinarily fixed and limited animal whose nature is absolutely constant. It is only by tradition and organization that anything decent can be got out of him."

In Judaism, according to the Sages, this was the argument between the angels when God consulted them as to whether He should or should not create humans. The angels were the "us" in "Let us make mankind." The angels of *ḥesed* (mercy) and *tzedek* (righteousness) said, "Let him be created because humans do merciful and righteous deeds." The angels of *shalom* (peace) and *emet* (truth) said, "Let him not be created because he is full of falsehood and never ceases quarreling." What did God do? He created humans anyway and had faith that we would gradually become better and less destructive. That, in secular terms, is what Harvard neuroscientist Steven Pinker argues in *The Better Angels of Our Nature*.

The Torah suggests we are both destructive and constructive, and evolutionary psychology tells

1| *Leviathan*, 48.

verse 3 we find the Tetragrammaton, and therefore the categorization of this verse is clear. Verses 1–2, which represent a single unit which does not continue on to verse 3, would appear to belong to the aspect that is characterized by the name Elohim. Verses 4–5 mention explicitly the events referred to in verses 1–2, and therefore they too belong to the aspect of Elohim.

We shall not discuss here the meaning of the verses belonging to the aspect of Elohim, nor the significance of the merging of the two aspects into a single textual unit. For the purposes of our discussion, we shall focus only on the aspect characterized by the Tetragrammaton.

Verse 3 is the only portion of the unit that falls into this category. Clearly, this verse cannot stand alone; it must be read as the continuation of some previous verse. Hence, we must seek the last preceding verses belonging to the same aspect.

Chapter 5 is devoted to the "generations," as evidenced by its introduction, style, and structure. For various reasons, such genealogical chapters are usually categorized under the name Elohim, even where they contain no divine name at all. In chapter 5, however, there is one verse that deviates from the otherwise fixed structure and which uses the Tetragrammaton. We refer here to the verse cited above, describing how Noaḥ received his name: "And he called his name Noaḥ, saying: This one shall comfort us for our work and the toil of our hands caused by the ground, which God has cursed." Had the Tetragrammaton aspect stood alone here, the Torah would have presented Lemekh and the fact of Noaḥ's birth in accordance with the style of that aspect. However, since the text interweaves both aspects, the fact that a son is born to Lemekh belongs exclusively within the aspect of Elohim. The aspect of the Tetragrammaton covers only his name and its meaning.

Hence, within the Tetragrammaton aspect, verse 3 of chapter 6 should be read as a direct continuation of verse 29 of chapter 5. Thus, the verse must be understood as referring to the curse of Adam. Accordingly, the word *yidon*, "strive," is meant in the sense of judging and punishing, i.e., "I shall not continue to argue with man and punish him by cursing the earth."

TAKING A LITERARY APPROACH

The first two verses of this unit describe two groups: the "distinguished men" and the "daughters of man." Whether the "distinguished men" here are regular mortals or not, it is clear that the "daughters of man" certainly are. In these verses the "distinguished men" are active, while "man" (Adam) and his daughters are the passive victims.

God's words in verse 3 are open to various interpretations. They may be meant as an expression of reconcilement, or the opposite – an expression of punishment or retribution. In any event, it is clear that God is talking here about "man," in the wake of some unworthy behavior on his part. This is puzzling, since in the preceding verses, as pointed out above, mankind is the passive, injured party. Even if, in the formal sense, the "distinguished men" are included within the category of "man," from a literary perspective the differing usages of the word make for very confusing reading, and serve to break the literary flow.

Apparently, this unit combines two separate levels of meaning, or "aspects." We adopt here the exegetical methodology known as the *shitat habeḥinot*, developed by my *rav* and teacher, Rav Mordechai Breuer. According to this approach, God writes the Torah in layers, with narratives or halakhic units that parallel one another – different "aspects" – each of which is able to stand alone and to be read in its own right, such that sometimes they appear to contradict one another. Often, these aspects are intertwined, creating a complex or multilayered unit. This complex unit blurs the points of transition between one aspect and the other, but highlights the difficulties inherent in these transitions. Each story expresses its own independent content, which is important in its own right; however, there is some relationship between them, which justifies their integration into a single text. By delving into the difficulties that arise from the joining together of the two aspects – such as repetitions or contradictions – we are able to expose the two independent "aspects," and thereafter to explore their significance.

The story of the "distinguished men and the daughters of man" is usually categorized under the aspect that uses the Tetragrammaton to refer to God. However, in light of the difficulty that we have indicated above, it may make more sense to divide this unit. In

If this is the case, then the verse is indeed meant in a spirit of appeasement, and the rest of the verse should be understood as proposed by Ramban, in accordance with Tehillim 78:38–39: "For He is compassionate, forgiving sin, and not destroying; often turning away His anger and not stirring up all of His wrath; He remembers that they are mere flesh; a wind that passes and does not return."

Here, in the wake of Lemekh's prayer, God declares that He will indeed turn away His wrath from man and no longer judge him according to the strict demands of the attribute of justice. Man is in need of the attribute of mercy, for he is mere flesh and blood – a mortal who departs from the world after a brief 120 years. According to the exegetical direction that we are now taking, Lemekh's wish does receive due attention. God accepts his prayer, in principle, and declares that through Noaḥ consolation will come to mankind for the curse of the earth.

We must now reread the concluding verses of Parashat Bereshit (6:5–8) which, as noted above, are actually the introduction to the story of the flood:

> And God saw that the wickedness of man [*haadam*] was great in the land, and all the inclination of the thoughts of his heart was only evil all the time. And God repented [*vayinaḥem*] for having made man [*haadam*] in the land, and He was grieved to His heart. And God said: I shall wipe out [*emḥeh*] man [*haadam*] whom I have created from the face of the earth [*haadama*] – both man [*me'adam*] and beast and crawling things and birds of the sky, for I repent [*niḥamti*] that I made them. But Noaḥ found favor [*ḥen*] in God's eyes.

There are repeated expressions involving the Hebrew root *a-d-m*, as well as regret/comfort (*neḥama*), wiping out (*meḥiya*) and favor (*ḥen*), and expressions of action (*a-s-h*) and of melancholy (*itzavon*). These alliterations serve to link these verses to the words of Lemekh: "This one will comfort us [*yenaḥamenu*] for our work *[mimaasenu]* and the toil [*itzavon*, literally, "melancholy"] of our hands, because of the land *[adama]* which God has cursed."

Man is a transitory creature; he passes on and does not return, but his wickedness has already become a matter of enormous scope and proportion. Man's evil inclination admittedly arises from the fact that he is mere flesh, but this inclination of his heart is only evil, all the time. For this reason, corresponding to *zeh yenaḥamenu*, "this one will comfort us," we find *vayinaḥem Hashem*, "God repented," and corresponding to *me'itzvon yadenu*, "for the toil of our hands," we find *vayitatzev el libo*, "He grieved to His heart." God would like to comfort man and relieve him of the melancholy of his heart, but the situation has reached a point where man's wickedness is grieving God and causing Him to regret having created man in the world. This being the case, God decides to wipe man off the face of the earth. Instead of *neḥamat haadam min haadama* (comforting man for the melancholy of the cursed ground), God brings about *meḥiyat haadam min haadama* (wiping man off the face of the earth).

Rabbi Yehuda Rock

נח
Noaḥ

Parasha Overview

Man's wickedness leads God to bring a flood. Noaḥ alone is found righteous. He is commanded to bring his family, and animals, into an ark. Alone, they survive the flood. After the waters subside, Noaḥ emerges and offers a sacrifice to God. God then makes a covenant, through Noaḥ, with all humanity, laying down basic commands and vowing never again to destroy the world by flood. Noaḥ plants a vineyard, makes wine, and becomes drunk. A new generation of humans aspires to build a city whose tower will reach heaven. God frustrates their plan by confusing their language. The *parasha* ends with a genealogy tracing the ten generations between Noaḥ's son Shem and Avraham.

Episodes

Parasha Stats

- 6,907 letters
- 1,861 words
- 153 verses
- 230 lines in a sefer Torah

NOAḤ

9 This is the story of Noaḥ. Noaḥ was a righteous man, a person of integrity in his generation;
10 11 Noaḥ walked with God. And Noaḥ had three sons: Shem, Ḥam, and Yefet. The earth had
12 become corrupt in God's sight, full of violence. And when God saw how corrupt the earth
13 had become, all flesh corrupting its ways upon the earth, God said to Noaḥ, "The
end of all flesh has come before Me, for the earth is full of violence because of them. I am
14 about to destroy them, along with all the earth. So make yourself an ark of cypress wood.
15 Make it with compartments and coat it in pitch inside and out. This is how you shall make
it: the ark shall be three hundred cubits long, fifty cubits wide, and thirty cubits high.
16 Make a window for the ark, and taper the latter to within a cubit of the top.[1] Put a door in
17 the side of the ark and make lower, middle, and upper decks. And I – I am about to bring
floodwaters over the earth to destroy all flesh that has within it the breath of life under the
18 heavens. Everything on earth will die. But I will establish My covenant with you, and you
19 will enter the ark – you, your sons, your wife, and your sons' wives with you. And you shall
20 take two of each living creature, male and female, into the ark to keep alive with you. Of

1 | That is, the ark should slant upward, becoming narrower as it approaches the top.

UNLOCKING THE TEXT

- Why does the Torah give us a second introduction to the flood story?
- What was the "corruption" in the world that justified God destroying it?
- Is there a difference between the description of the evil in the two introductions?
- Who was Noaḥ and why was he chosen by God to save the world?
- Why does the Torah give us so many details about the ark God commanded Noaḥ to build?
- What was God's goal in bringing the flood? Why did God choose a flood to achieve this?
- What are the details of the covenant between God and Noaḥ?
- What qualified an animal to be "pure"? Why did these animals require seven of each rather than the pairs of all other species?
- Did Noaḥ do everything God expected of him?

FINDING YOURSELF IN THE TEXT

- Have you ever given up on someone or something?
- Has anyone ever given up on you?
- Have you ever been chosen for a really important task, where the pressure seemed too great to bear?

Consider using these questions as the basis for your own commentary or creative midrash.

How does reflecting on these firsthand experiences help you better understand the text?

ט אֵ֚לֶּה תּוֹלְדֹ֣ת נֹ֔חַ נֹ֗חַ אִ֥ישׁ צַדִּ֛יק תָּמִ֥ים הָיָ֖ה בְּדֹֽרֹתָ֑יו אֶת־הָֽאֱלֹהִ֖ים הִֽתְהַלֶּךְ־נֹֽחַ׃ ה נח
י יא וַיּ֥וֹלֶד נֹ֖חַ שְׁלֹשָׁ֣ה בָנִ֑ים אֶת־שֵׁ֖ם אֶת־חָ֥ם וְאֶת־יָֽפֶת׃ וַתִּשָּׁחֵ֥ת הָאָ֖רֶץ לִפְנֵ֣י הָֽאֱלֹהִ֑ים
יב וַתִּמָּלֵ֥א הָאָ֖רֶץ חָמָֽס׃ וַיַּ֧רְא אֱלֹהִ֛ים אֶת־הָאָ֖רֶץ וְהִנֵּ֣ה נִשְׁחָ֑תָה כִּֽי־הִשְׁחִ֧ית כָּל־
יג בָּשָׂ֛ר אֶת־דַּרְכּ֖וֹ עַל־הָאָֽרֶץ׃ וַיֹּ֨אמֶר אֱלֹהִ֜ים לְנֹ֗חַ קֵ֤ץ כָּל־בָּשָׂר֙ בָּ֣א
יד לְפָנַ֔י כִּֽי־מָלְאָ֥ה הָאָ֛רֶץ חָמָ֖ס מִפְּנֵיהֶ֑ם וְהִנְנִ֥י מַשְׁחִיתָ֖ם אֶת־הָאָֽרֶץ׃ עֲשֵׂ֤ה לְךָ֙ תֵּבַ֣ת
טו עֲצֵי־גֹ֔פֶר קִנִּ֖ים תַּעֲשֶׂ֣ה אֶת־הַתֵּבָ֑ה וְכָֽפַרְתָּ֥ אֹתָ֛הּ מִבַּ֥יִת וּמִח֖וּץ בַּכֹּֽפֶר׃ וְזֶ֕ה אֲשֶׁ֥ר
תַּעֲשֶׂ֖ה אֹתָ֑הּ שְׁלֹ֨שׁ מֵא֤וֹת אַמָּה֙ אֹ֣רֶךְ הַתֵּבָ֔ה חֲמִשִּׁ֤ים אַמָּה֙ רָחְבָּ֔הּ וּשְׁלֹשִׁ֥ים אַמָּ֖ה
טז קוֹמָתָֽהּ׃ צֹ֣הַר ׀ תַּעֲשֶׂ֣ה לַתֵּבָ֗ה וְאֶל־אַמָּה֙ תְּכַלֶּ֣נָּה מִלְמַ֔עְלָה וּפֶ֥תַח הַתֵּבָ֖ה בְּצִדָּ֣הּ
יז תָּשִׂ֑ים תַּחְתִּיִּ֛ם שְׁנִיִּ֥ם וּשְׁלִשִׁ֖ים תַּעֲשֶֽׂהָ׃ וַאֲנִ֗י הִנְנִי֩ מֵבִ֨יא אֶת־הַמַּבּ֥וּל מַ֙יִם֙ עַל־
הָאָ֔רֶץ לְשַׁחֵ֣ת כָּל־בָּשָׂ֗ר אֲשֶׁר־בּוֹ֙ ר֣וּחַ חַיִּ֔ים מִתַּ֖חַת הַשָּׁמָ֑יִם כֹּ֥ל אֲשֶׁר־בָּאָ֖רֶץ יִגְוָֽע׃
יח וַהֲקִמֹתִ֥י אֶת־בְּרִיתִ֖י אִתָּ֑ךְ וּבָאתָ֙ אֶל־הַתֵּבָ֔ה אַתָּ֕ה וּבָנֶ֛יךָ וְאִשְׁתְּךָ֥ וּנְשֵֽׁי־בָנֶ֖יךָ אִתָּֽךְ׃
יט וּמִכָּל־הָ֠חַי מִֽכָּל־בָּשָׂ֞ר שְׁנַ֧יִם מִכֹּ֛ל תָּבִ֥יא אֶל־הַתֵּבָ֖ה לְהַחֲיֹ֣ת אִתָּ֑ךְ זָכָ֥ר וּנְקֵבָ֖ה יִהְיֽוּ׃
כ מֵהָע֣וֹף לְמִינֵ֗הוּ וּמִן־הַבְּהֵמָה֙ לְמִינָ֔הּ מִכֹּ֛ל רֶ֥מֶשׂ הָאֲדָמָ֖ה לְמִינֵ֑הוּ שְׁנַ֧יִם מִכֹּ֛ל יָבֹ֥אוּ

THEMES | FREE WILL, REWARD AND PUNISHMENT | ETHICS | COVENANT

Episode 7: *The Impending Flood* – Bereshit 6:9–7:6

SUMMARY

In addition to the sin of sexual promiscuity mentioned at the end of the previous section, theft was rampant among humankind as well. For this reason, humans, and along with them all animals living on dry land, were doomed to perish in a flood. Only a few representatives of each species would be saved from the calamity and form the nucleus of a new world.

21 every kind of bird, animal, and wild beast, bring two to keep alive. As for you, take all the
22 food to be eaten and store it: it will be for food for you and for them." Noaḥ did so: all that
7 1 God commanded him, he fulfilled. Then the Lord said to Noaḥ, "Enter the ark, you and
all your household, for I have seen you alone to be righteous before Me in this generation.
2 Take seven and seven of every pure animal, seven pairs, and two of every animal that is not
3 pure, of each kind a pair. Also take seven pairs of each kind of bird, male and female, to keep
4 their kind alive across the earth. For in seven days' time I will send rain on the earth for
forty days and forty nights, and I will wipe from the face of the earth every living creature
5 6 I have made." Noaḥ did all that the Lord commanded him. Noaḥ was six hundred years
old when the floodwaters came upon the earth.

THE ART OF MIDRASH

Noah's Ark
Edward Hicks
(1780–1849)

Analysis

- Which elements of this image are directly mentioned in the text?
- Which elements of this image are not found in the text?
- What midrashic interpretation is the artist giving us?

כא אֵלֶ֖יךָ לְהַחֲיֽוֹת: וְאַתָּ֣ה קַח־לְךָ֗ מִכָּל־מַֽאֲכָל֙ אֲשֶׁ֣ר יֵֽאָכֵ֔ל וְאָֽסַפְתָּ֖ אֵלֶ֑יךָ וְהָיָ֥ה לְךָ֛ וְלָהֶ֖ם
ז כב לְאָכְלָֽה: וַיַּ֖עַשׂ נֹ֑חַ כְּ֠כֹל אֲשֶׁ֨ר צִוָּ֥ה אֹת֛וֹ אֱלֹהִ֖ים כֵּ֥ן עָשָֽׂה: וַיֹּ֤אמֶר יהוה֙ לְנֹ֔חַ בֹּֽא־ שני
ב אַתָּ֥ה וְכָל־בֵּֽיתְךָ֖ אֶל־הַתֵּבָ֑ה כִּֽי־אֹֽתְךָ֥ רָאִ֛יתִי צַדִּ֥יק לְפָנַ֖י בַּדּ֥וֹר הַזֶּֽה: מִכֹּ֣ל ׀ הַבְּהֵמָ֣ה
הַטְּהוֹרָ֗ה תִּֽקַּח־לְךָ֛ שִׁבְעָ֥ה שִׁבְעָ֖ה אִ֣ישׁ וְאִשְׁתּ֑וֹ וּמִן־הַבְּהֵמָ֡ה אֲ֠שֶׁר לֹ֣א טְהֹרָ֥ה
ג הִ֛וא שְׁנַ֖יִם אִ֥ישׁ וְאִשְׁתּֽוֹ: גַּ֣ם מֵע֧וֹף הַשָּׁמַ֛יִם שִׁבְעָ֥ה שִׁבְעָ֖ה זָכָ֣ר וּנְקֵבָ֑ה לְחַיּ֥וֹת
ד זֶ֖רַע עַל־פְּנֵ֥י כָל־הָאָֽרֶץ: כִּי֩ לְיָמִ֨ים ע֜וֹד שִׁבְעָ֗ה אָֽנֹכִי֙ מַמְטִ֣יר עַל־הָאָ֔רֶץ אַרְבָּעִ֣ים
ה י֔וֹם וְאַרְבָּעִ֖ים לָ֑יְלָה וּמָחִ֗יתִי אֶֽת־כָּל־הַיְקוּם֙ אֲשֶׁ֣ר עָשִׂ֔יתִי מֵעַ֖ל פְּנֵ֥י הָֽאֲדָמָֽה: וַיַּ֖עַשׂ
ו נֹ֑חַ כְּכֹ֥ל אֲשֶׁר־צִוָּ֖הוּ יהוה: וְנֹ֕חַ בֶּן־שֵׁ֥שׁ מֵא֖וֹת שָׁנָ֑ה וְהַמַּבּ֣וּל הָיָ֔ה מַ֖יִם עַל־הָאָֽרֶץ:

A QUESTION OF
BIBLIODRAMA

TO GOD

- ◉ What was so evil about the world that meant You had no other choice than to start again?
- ◉ Why did the animal world also deserve to be destroyed?
- ◉ What did You see in Noaḥ that led to You choosing to save the world through him?
- ◉ Did Your creation disappoint You or was this always Your plan?
- ◉ Can You be sure the world won't make the same mistakes again?

TO NOAḤ

- ◉ How did you manage to remain righteous in such an evil generation?
- ◉ Do you agree with God's decision to reboot the world?
- ◉ Did you try to change God's mind? If not, why not?
- ◉ Do you understand why God chose to save the world through you and your family?
- ◉ Are you scared about the impending flood?
- ◉ Are you hopeful for the future?

TO THE FAMILY OF NOAḤ

- ◉ What did you think when Noaḥ told you about what God had told him?
- ◉ Do you think Noaḥ should have responded differently?
- ◉ Are you scared about the impending flood?
- ◉ Are you hopeful for the future?

Would an ark built to the specifications outlined in the Bible, filled with two of every species of animal, be able to actually float? Four physics graduate students at the University of Leicester researched this question in a course that encourages students to apply basic physics principles to more general questions. They calculated that an ark full of animals in those dimensions could theoretically float. They published their research in a peer-reviewed, student-run publication, the *Journal of Physics Special Topics*.

To float, a boat has to exert the same amount of force on the ocean as the weight of the water it displaces. This buoyancy force is essentially the biggest weight the ark could hold and not sink. This means an object with a density greater than water will sink. So, if the volume of the ark can be calculated, and after factoring in the mass of the wood used to build it, how much mass the system could take before it becomes more dense than water and sinks can be calculated.

The students calculated that, by their approximations, the ark would have been 144.6 meters long, 24.1 meters wide, and 14.46 meters tall - the size of a very small cargo ship. Using the density of cypress wood, they calculated the weight of this hypothetical ark: 1,200,000 kilograms. Based on the density of sea water, they figured out that an empty box-shaped ark would float with its hull only dipping 0.34 meters into the water.

Forcing the bulk of the ark down into the water while still keeping it afloat would displace about twenty Olympic-sized swimming pools' worth of sea water. Knowing the volume of displaced sea water, and knowing that an object in water displaces its own weight, they crunched the numbers and found the total mass needed to displace that water. They subtracted the mass of an empty ark and found that the ark could hold 50,540,000 kilograms. The average sheep is about 23.47 kilograms, so the ark could have held about 2.15 million sheep.

Scientists question how many species Noah would have needed to save to produce the modern populations of species that inhabit our planet today. Scientists have characterized about 1.7 million species to date, so if the average mass of species represented on the ark was the average mass of sheep, the ark would theoretically have been able to accommodate them all without capsizing.

Sarah Knapton, *The Daily Telegraph* (April 3, 2014)

Analysis

- What areas of scientific understanding do we now have that were unavailable to classical Jewish commentators? How can they aid our understanding of the text?
- What can we learn from these scientific calculations to help us understand the text?
- What further questions on the text do you have now that you have read this new take on the story?

INTEGRATING ḤOKHMA

The Ark Encounter in Williamstown, Kentucky

Divinity that is prevalent among academic scholars worldwide – the concept of God as experienced generally as creator of the material world, as the active force behind nature, and as the source of life.

2. The name *Y-H-V-H* is used to express Divinity in its "personal" sense, and in direct relationship to people or to nature; the name Elohim is used when the text alludes to Divinity as a transcendental entity, existing absolutely beyond and above material nature.

Cassuto draws a distinction between the name Elohim, expressing God's control over nature and His guiding of the world in accordance with universal laws, and the name *Y-H-V-H*, which denotes God's closeness to man and His intervention in nature in accordance with the needs of those who are close to Him.

If we combine Rabbi Breuer's "perspectives approach" and Cassuto's commentary, we might propose an answer to the question that we posed at the outset. The issue of repentance, developed at such length in the *midrashei Ḥazal*, is hinted at in the two-fold repetition of different parts of the story. One account, narrated with the name Elohim, describes the annihilation of the world in accordance with the laws of morality and nature, with no favoritism shown to anyone. The corruption of creation that is brought about by man's perversions of morality demands a total destruction that leaves only the most minimal natural foundations for the continuity of man and beast in a new world. The story narrated with the name *Y-H-V-H*, on the other hand, describes a process in which there is an attempt to put off the destruction, to enlarge the circle of those who will be delivered from it, and to set down moral laws leading to a renewed closeness between man and his Creator. The doubled storyline highlights the privilege of repentance, which allows for a deviation from the attribute of justice associated with Elohim, "taking advantage," as it were, of God's desire for people to draw close to Him and His transformation of their dire verdict into compassion as a result of their return to Him.

Dr. Brachi Elitzur

TAKING A LITERARY APPROACH

A notable characteristic of the description of the flood is the doubled and even tripled description of the preparations prior to its arrival, of its duration, and of its results:

	A	B
Description of sin	6:5–7	6:11–13
Description of Noaḥ	6:8	6:9
Description of the salvation	7:1–5	6:14–22
Entry into the ark	7:10–15	7:6–9
Results of the flood	7:23	7:21–22
Renewed covenant	8:20–22	9:12–17

The phenomenon of repetition in biblical narratives led to the development of a critical school that cast doubt on the unity of the Torah text and raised different theories as to its origins. The story of the flood, with its many repetitions, provided ample material for this type of analysis. Religious belief in the unity of the Torah and its divine origin demands a satisfying exegetical explanation for all the repetition in this story.

Rabbi Mordechai Breuer laid the foundations for a refutation of the "documentary hypothesis" postulated by Bible critics in the form of his "perspectives approach." This exegetical approach instructs the scholar to take note of the similarities between repetitive or repeated units, but to focus specifically on the fine differences between them, using these to discern the different aims behind each iteration. To this view, repetition is a technique that is meant to broaden the range of messages arising from the unit and to orient it toward different target populations, different outlooks, or different historical periods.

Let us follow Rabbi Breuer's approach and try to clarify the messages arising from the repetition of the details of the story of the flood. If we compare the verses comprising the two parallel columns as set forth above, we find that the systematic difference between them concerns the name of God. Column A brings together the details of the story that are conveyed with the use of the name *Y-H-V-H*, while column B brings together the details that appear in connection with the name Elohim. Cassuto offers the following explanation of the significance behind the use of these different names:

1. The name *Y-H-V-H* is used to express the Divinity that is unique to *am Yisrael*, especially in its moral aspect, while the name Elohim is used to express the abstract idea of

7 Noaḥ, with his sons, his wife, and his sons' wives, came into the ark to escape the waters of
8 the flood. The pure animals, the animals that were not pure, the birds, and all that walked
9 the earth came two by two to Noaḥ into the ark, male and female, as God had commanded
10 11 Noaḥ. Thus after seven days the floodwaters came upon the earth. In the six hundredth
year of Noaḥ's life, in the second month, on the seventeenth of the month – on that day, all
12 the wellsprings of the great deep burst, and heavens' floodgates opened. The rain fell on
13 the earth for forty days and forty nights. On that very day, Noaḥ, his sons Shem, Ḥam, and
14 Yefet, Noaḥ's wife, and his sons' three wives entered the ark. With them came every kind of
wild beast, every kind of animal, every creeping, crawling creature of the land, every kind
15 of flying creature, every bird, and each winged thing. They came to Noaḥ, to the ark, two
16 by two, of all flesh that had within it the breath of life. They came, male and female of all
17 flesh, as God had commanded him. Then the Lord shut him in. For forty days the flood
18 came upon the earth. The waters swelled, lifting the ark so that it rose above the land. The
waters surged, swelling enormously on the earth, and the ark began to drift on the surface
19 of the water. The waters surged ever more, until all the high mountains beneath all the
20 heavens were covered. Fifteen cubits above them the waters surged as the mountains were

UNLOCKING THE TEXT

- Did Noaḥ's family deserve to be saved on their own merits or just through their relationship to him?
- What is the significance of the date given for the start of the flood?
- What is the significance of the number forty?
- Why did God need to shut Noaḥ in?
- Why did the animal kingdom need to be destroyed?

Consider using these questions as the basis for your own commentary or creative midrash.

FINDING YOURSELF IN THE TEXT

- Have you ever felt like you were the only person in the world who really understood something?
- Have you ever had to hide for a length of time or been scared for your life?
- Have you ever felt a tremendous weight of responsibility on your shoulders?

How does reflecting on these firsthand experiences help you better understand the text?

ז ח וַיָּבֹא נֹחַ וּבָנָיו וְאִשְׁתּוֹ וּנְשֵׁי־בָנָיו אִתּוֹ אֶל־הַתֵּבָה מִפְּנֵי מֵי הַמַּבּוּל׃ מִן־הַבְּהֵמָה
הַטְּהוֹרָה וּמִן־הַבְּהֵמָה אֲשֶׁר אֵינֶנָּה טְהֹרָה וּמִן־הָעוֹף וְכֹל אֲשֶׁר־רֹמֵשׂ עַל־
ט הָאֲדָמָה׃ שְׁנַיִם שְׁנַיִם בָּאוּ אֶל־נֹחַ אֶל־הַתֵּבָה זָכָר וּנְקֵבָה כַּאֲשֶׁר צִוָּה אֱלֹהִים
י יא אֶת־נֹחַ׃ וַיְהִי לְשִׁבְעַת הַיָּמִים וּמֵי הַמַּבּוּל הָיוּ עַל־הָאָרֶץ׃ בִּשְׁנַת שֵׁשׁ־מֵאוֹת שָׁנָה
לְחַיֵּי־נֹחַ בַּחֹדֶשׁ הַשֵּׁנִי בְּשִׁבְעָה־עָשָׂר יוֹם לַחֹדֶשׁ בַּיּוֹם הַזֶּה נִבְקְעוּ כָּל־מַעְיְנוֹת
יב תְּהוֹם רַבָּה וַאֲרֻבֹּת הַשָּׁמַיִם נִפְתָּחוּ׃ וַיְהִי הַגֶּשֶׁם עַל־הָאָרֶץ אַרְבָּעִים יוֹם וְאַרְבָּעִים
יג לָיְלָה׃ בְּעֶצֶם הַיּוֹם הַזֶּה בָּא נֹחַ וְשֵׁם־וְחָם וָיֶפֶת בְּנֵי־נֹחַ וְאֵשֶׁת נֹחַ וּשְׁלֹשֶׁת נְשֵׁי־
יד בָנָיו אִתָּם אֶל־הַתֵּבָה׃ הֵמָּה וְכָל־הַחַיָּה לְמִינָהּ וְכָל־הַבְּהֵמָה לְמִינָהּ וְכָל־הָרֶמֶשׂ
טו הָרֹמֵשׂ עַל־הָאָרֶץ לְמִינֵהוּ וְכָל־הָעוֹף לְמִינֵהוּ כֹּל צִפּוֹר כָּל־כָּנָף׃ וַיָּבֹאוּ אֶל־נֹחַ
טז אֶל־הַתֵּבָה שְׁנַיִם שְׁנַיִם מִכָּל־הַבָּשָׂר אֲשֶׁר־בּוֹ רוּחַ חַיִּים׃ וְהַבָּאִים זָכָר וּנְקֵבָה
יז מִכָּל־בָּשָׂר בָּאוּ כַּאֲשֶׁר צִוָּה אֹתוֹ אֱלֹהִים וַיִּסְגֹּר יהוה בַּעֲדוֹ׃ וַיְהִי הַמַּבּוּל אַרְבָּעִים שלישי
יח יוֹם עַל־הָאָרֶץ וַיִּרְבּוּ הַמַּיִם וַיִּשְׂאוּ אֶת־הַתֵּבָה וַתָּרָם מֵעַל הָאָרֶץ׃ וַיִּגְבְּרוּ הַמַּיִם
יט וַיִּרְבּוּ מְאֹד עַל־הָאָרֶץ וַתֵּלֶךְ הַתֵּבָה עַל־פְּנֵי הַמָּיִם׃ וְהַמַּיִם גָּבְרוּ מְאֹד מְאֹד עַל־
כ הָאָרֶץ וַיְכֻסּוּ כָּל־הֶהָרִים הַגְּבֹהִים אֲשֶׁר־תַּחַת כָּל־הַשָּׁמָיִם׃ חֲמֵשׁ עֶשְׂרֵה אַמָּה

THEMES	FREE WILL, REWARD AND PUNISHMENT	GOD	CREATION

Episode 8: *The Flood* – Bereshit 7:7–24

SUMMARY

With the completion of the ark, God instructs Noaḥ to board the ark with his family as the flood begins. As he is commanded, he takes seven pairs of the "pure" animals and one pair of the "impure" ones. Noaḥ is six hundred years old when the flood begins. In contrast to life inside the free-floating ark, disconnected from all information and sense of time and place, the Torah anchors the story of the flood with precise dates and lengths of time.

21 covered. All flesh that moved upon the earth perished – birds, animals, wild beasts, and
22 all the creatures that swarm on the earth, and all humankind. Everything on dry land that
23 had breath of life in its nostrils died. Every living thing on the face of the earth was wiped
out: from humans to animals, from creeping creatures to winged birds of the heavens, all
24 were wiped from the earth. Only Noaḥ and those with him in the ark survived. For one
hundred fifty days, the waters surged over the earth.

THE ART OF MIDRASH

The Deluge
Ivan Konstantinovich Aivazovsky (1864)

Analysis

- Which elements of this image are directly mentioned in the text?
- Which elements of this image are not found in the text?
- What midrashic interpretation is the artist giving us?

כא מִלְמַעְלָה גָּבְרוּ הַמָּיִם וַיְכֻסּוּ הֶהָרִים: וַיִּגְוַע כָּל־בָּשָׂר ׀ הָרֹמֵשׂ עַל־הָאָרֶץ בָּעוֹף
כב וּבַבְּהֵמָה וּבַחַיָּה וּבְכָל־הַשֶּׁרֶץ הַשֹּׁרֵץ עַל־הָאָרֶץ וְכֹל הָאָדָם: כֹּל אֲשֶׁר נִשְׁמַת־
כג רוּחַ חַיִּים בְּאַפָּיו מִכֹּל אֲשֶׁר בֶּחָרָבָה מֵתוּ: וַיִּמַח אֶת־כָּל־הַיְקוּם ׀ אֲשֶׁר ׀ עַל־פְּנֵי
הָאֲדָמָה מֵאָדָם עַד־בְּהֵמָה עַד־רֶמֶשׂ וְעַד־עוֹף הַשָּׁמַיִם וַיִּמָּחוּ מִן־הָאָרֶץ וַיִּשָּׁאֶר
כד אַךְ־נֹחַ וַאֲשֶׁר אִתּוֹ בַּתֵּבָה: וַיִּגְבְּרוּ הַמַּיִם עַל־הָאָרֶץ חֲמִשִּׁים וּמְאַת יוֹם:

A QUESTION OF BIBLIODRAMA

TO GOD

- What did You feel while the flood was destroying Your world?
- How do You feel about rebooting humanity through Noaḥ and his family?

TO NOAḤ AND HIS FAMILY

- What was life like on the ark?
- Did you feel safe on the ark?
- How did it feel to know that the rest of humanity was perishing outside the ark while you were safe inside?
- Do you feel a weight of responsibility as the only humans to survive the flood?

"BRING FLOODWATERS OVER THE EARTH"

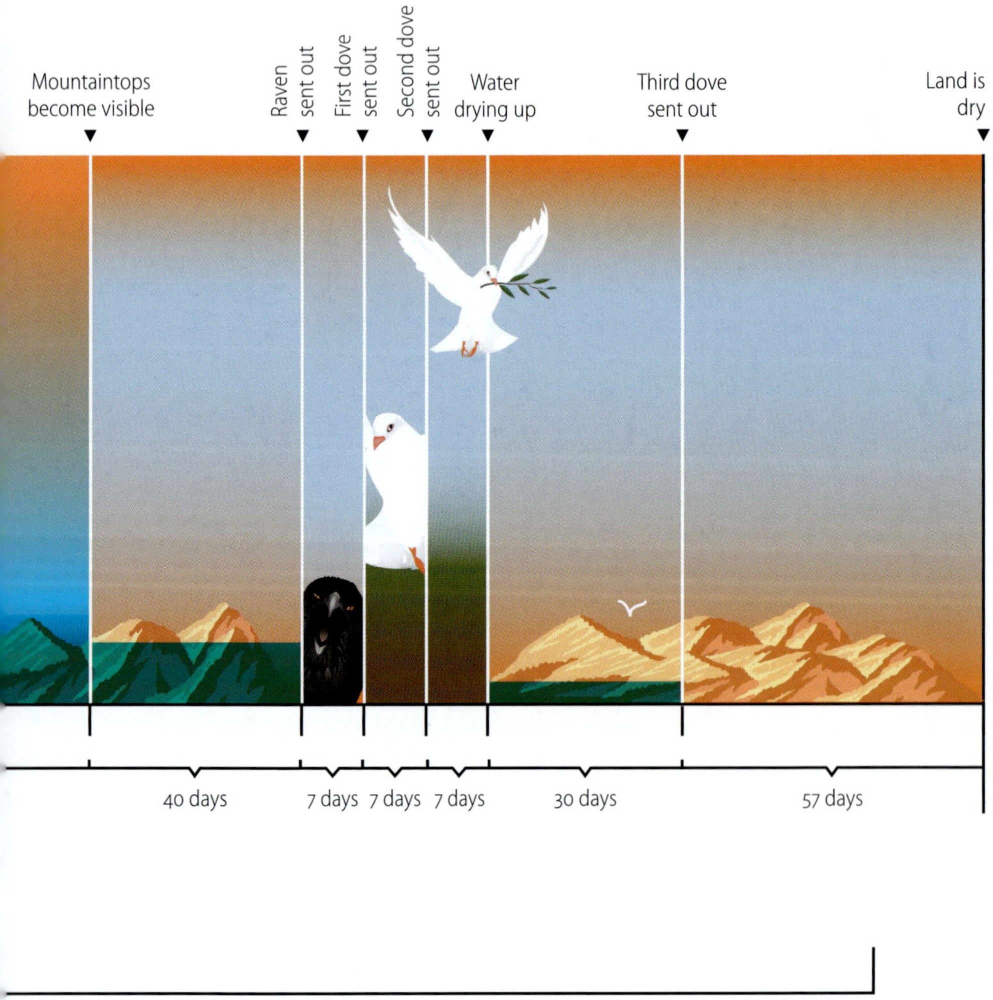

INTEGRATING ḤOKHMA

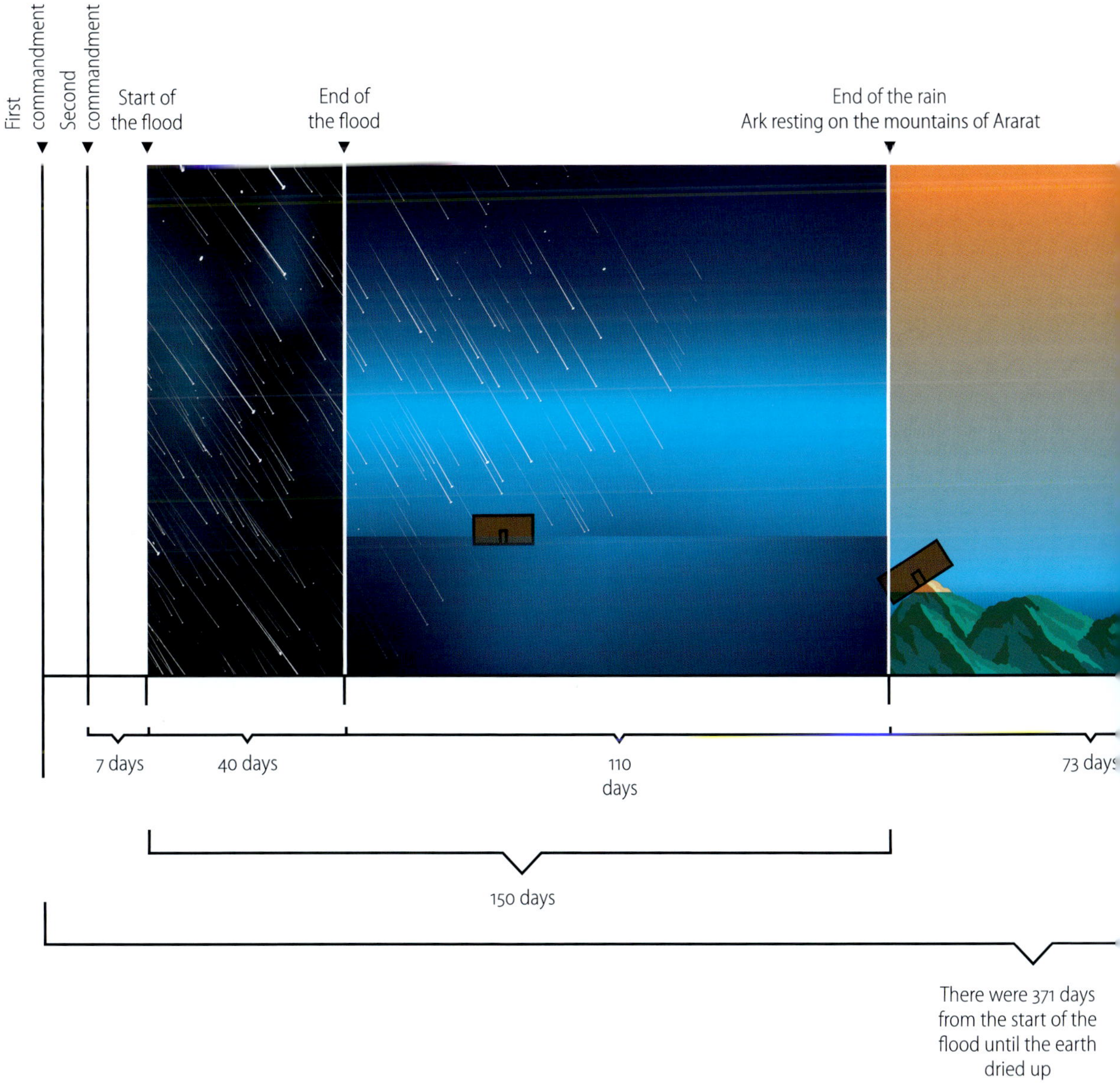
First commandment
Second commandment
Start of the flood
End of the flood
End of the rain
Ark resting on the mountains of Ararat
7 days
40 days
110 days
73 days
150 days
There were 371 days from the start of the flood until the earth dried up

If the first half of the story is un-creation, then we should expect to find evidence in the second half of re-creation and indeed, we do not have to look far. Bereshit 8 begins the second half of the story, and already the first verse gives us a taste of what to expect: "God passed a wind over the *aretz* and the waters eased." This is reminiscent of the second verse of the creation story, in which "God's wind hovers over the face of the water." It is in the second verse of Bereshit 8, however, that we begin to get a clearer picture: "The springs of the deep and the storehouses of the heavens closed," precisely the inverse of the first half of our story in which they opened, beginning the un-creation. Reversing the un-creation is actually the beginning of the re-creation, as the *rakia* separating the upper waters from the lower ones is reconstituted.

If Bereshit 8:2, the restoration of the *rakia*, represents the remaking of day two of creation, then day three follows immediately afterward with the recession of the waters from the land. This is followed in succession by Noaḥ's search for vegetation (8:8), reenacting the second half of day three; reintroducing flying animals into the world (8:12), reenacting day five; and bringing forth the land animals and people (8:18–19), renewing day six.

The idea that God is systematically undoing that which He had created in order to put it back together again is hinted to via the language used in the second introduction to this story: "God saw the land, that it had become ruined" (6:12). The focus is not what anyone or anything is doing but on what the result is – the land is self-destructing. God intervenes to stop that before it's too late. This enables Him to methodically undo the creation in order to allow the possibility for its rebuilding.

Rabbi Zvi Grumet

TAKING A LITERARY APPROACH

The biblical narrative of the story of Noaḥ is complex, filled with repetitions and internal contradictions. Nevertheless, when viewed as a single literary unit, it neatly divides into two sections. There are many textual indicators pointing to this division, and, in fact, the two halves of the story often mirror each other. One simple example of this is the Torah's use of numbers in the story. In the first half of the story there is a seven-day waiting period, followed by a forty-day period of rain, and culminating with a span of 150 days of the waters rising. The mirror image of this is apparent in the second half of the story, in which we have a 150-day period of the waters receding, followed by a forty-day waiting period, and a seven-day span between Noaḥ's sending of the raven and his sending of the dove.

I would identify the first half of the narrative as the un-creation and the second section as the re-creation. The un-creation is summed up in a single verse (Bereshit 7:23): "[It] erased all that existed on the face of the earth, from human to domestic animal to crawling creature to the things that fly in the sky." Notice what is being erased and the order in which it is happening: human, animal, crawling creatures, and birds. This is reminiscent of the creation narrative but in reverse order. Moving backward from humans, the last thing created on day six, to the flying things, created on day five, God is dismantling the initial creation.

Even more striking is the Torah's description of the process. It is not just that the incessant rain inundated everything, but that "the springs of the great deep were split open and the storehouses of the heavens opened up" (6:11). The lower waters rise to meet the upper waters which are crashing down. Once again, the reader is invited to recall Bereshit 1: on day two, God created the *rakia* as a separation between the upper waters and the lower waters, and our story describes the disappearance of the *rakia*/separator. This process continues as the waters cover the mountains (7:19), effectively erasing the separation between water and land that God put in place on day three.

To call this story a "flood" contravenes its central message. It is un-creation. God is dismantling the world He created and restoring it to its initial state of *tohu* and *bohu* – undifferentiated matter brimming with potential that is not actualized. In fact, the term for this event in the Torah is *mabul*, which literally means "confusion" or "mixing up." It is the returning of the world to its state of confusion, *tohu vavohu*, reversing the creative vector in Bereshit which moved the world methodically from chaos to order.

8 1 Then God remembered Noaḥ and all the wild beasts and animals with him in the ark. God
2 sent a wind over the earth, and the waters began to subside. The wellsprings of the deep and
3 heavens' floodgates closed, and the heavens' rains were reined in. The water steadily receded
4 from the earth, and by the end of one hundred fifty days, the water had abated. In the
seventh month, on the seventeenth day of the month, the ark came to rest on the mountains
5 of Ararat. The water continued to abate until the tenth month, and on the first day of the
6 tenth month, the mountaintops became visible. After forty days Noaḥ opened the window
7 he had made in the ark and sent a raven forth. It flew to and fro until the water on the earth
8 had dried. After that he sent forth a dove to see whether the water had subsided from the
9 face of the land. But the dove found no resting place to plant its foot, and so it returned to
him, to the ark, for water still covered the face of the earth completely. He reached out his
10 hand and brought the dove back to him, into the ark. Then he waited another seven days,
11 and again he sent the dove forth from the ark. The dove came back to him in the evening –
and in its beak was a freshly picked olive leaf. Noaḥ knew then that the water had subsided
12 from the earth. He waited another seven days and again sent forth the dove – and it returned
13 to him no more. So it was that, by the first day of the first month of Noaḥ's six hundred and
first year, the water on the earth dried up. Noaḥ removed the covering of the ark and saw

UNLOCKING THE TEXT

- What does it mean for God to "remember" the inhabitants of the ark?
- Why is it important to know the process of how the waters receded and the time it took?
- Why did Noaḥ send the raven out of the ark?
- What was the fate of the raven?
- Why did Noaḥ send the dove out of the ark?
- Why did the dove bring Noaḥ a branch from an olive tree?
- Why did God have to tell Noaḥ and his family to leave the ark?
- What instructions did God give the survivors of the flood and why?

FINDING YOURSELF IN THE TEXT

- Have you ever had to wait impatiently for something really important to happen?
- Have you ever had to have faith that something would happen even when you couldn't be sure it actually would?
- Have you ever been the first of all the people you know to do something or be somewhere?

Consider using these questions as the basis for your own commentary or creative midrash.

How does reflecting on these firsthand experiences help you better understand the text?

ח א וַיִּזְכֹּר אֱלֹהִים אֶת־נֹחַ וְאֵת כָּל־הַחַיָּה וְאֶת־כָּל־הַבְּהֵמָה אֲשֶׁר אִתּוֹ בַּתֵּבָה וַיַּעֲבֵר ו
ב אֱלֹהִים רוּחַ עַל־הָאָרֶץ וַיָּשֹׁכּוּ הַמָּיִם׃ וַיִּסָּכְרוּ מַעְיְנֹת תְּהוֹם וַאֲרֻבֹּת הַשָּׁמָיִם
ג וַיִּכָּלֵא הַגֶּשֶׁם מִן־הַשָּׁמָיִם׃ וַיָּשֻׁבוּ הַמַּיִם מֵעַל הָאָרֶץ הָלוֹךְ וָשׁוֹב וַיַּחְסְרוּ הַמַּיִם
ד מִקְצֵה חֲמִשִּׁים וּמְאַת יוֹם׃ וַתָּנַח הַתֵּבָה בַּחֹדֶשׁ הַשְּׁבִיעִי בְּשִׁבְעָה־עָשָׂר יוֹם
ה לַחֹדֶשׁ עַל הָרֵי אֲרָרָט׃ וְהַמַּיִם הָיוּ הָלוֹךְ וְחָסוֹר עַד הַחֹדֶשׁ הָעֲשִׂירִי בָּעֲשִׂירִי
ו בְּאֶחָד לַחֹדֶשׁ נִרְאוּ רָאשֵׁי הֶהָרִים׃ וַיְהִי מִקֵּץ אַרְבָּעִים יוֹם וַיִּפְתַּח נֹחַ אֶת־חַלּוֹן
ז הַתֵּבָה אֲשֶׁר עָשָׂה׃ וַיְשַׁלַּח אֶת־הָעֹרֵב וַיֵּצֵא יָצוֹא וָשׁוֹב עַד־יְבֹשֶׁת הַמַּיִם מֵעַל
ח ט הָאָרֶץ׃ וַיְשַׁלַּח אֶת־הַיּוֹנָה מֵאִתּוֹ לִרְאוֹת הֲקַלּוּ הַמַּיִם מֵעַל פְּנֵי הָאֲדָמָה׃ וְלֹא־
מָצְאָה הַיּוֹנָה מָנוֹחַ לְכַף־רַגְלָהּ וַתָּשָׁב אֵלָיו אֶל־הַתֵּבָה כִּי־מַיִם עַל־פְּנֵי כָל־הָאָרֶץ
י וַיִּשְׁלַח יָדוֹ וַיִּקָּחֶהָ וַיָּבֵא אֹתָהּ אֵלָיו אֶל־הַתֵּבָה׃ וַיָּחֶל עוֹד שִׁבְעַת יָמִים אֲחֵרִים
יא וַיֹּסֶף שַׁלַּח אֶת־הַיּוֹנָה מִן־הַתֵּבָה׃ וַתָּבֹא אֵלָיו הַיּוֹנָה לְעֵת עֶרֶב וְהִנֵּה עֲלֵה־זַיִת
יב טָרָף בְּפִיהָ וַיֵּדַע נֹחַ כִּי־קַלּוּ הַמַּיִם מֵעַל הָאָרֶץ׃ וַיִּיָּחֶל עוֹד שִׁבְעַת יָמִים אֲחֵרִים
יג וַיְשַׁלַּח אֶת־הַיּוֹנָה וְלֹא־יָסְפָה שׁוּב־אֵלָיו עוֹד׃ וַיְהִי בְּאַחַת וְשֵׁשׁ־מֵאוֹת שָׁנָה
בָּרִאשׁוֹן בְּאֶחָד לַחֹדֶשׁ חָרְבוּ הַמַּיִם מֵעַל הָאָרֶץ וַיָּסַר נֹחַ אֶת־מִכְסֵה הַתֵּבָה

THEMES | FREE WILL, REWARD AND PUNISHMENT | GOD | CREATION

Episode 9: *Exit from the Ark* – Bereshit 8:1–19

SUMMARY

This episode describes the gradual conclusion of the flood and the cautious exit of the ark's inhabitants into the world, after more than a year had passed since they entered it.

14 that the face of the land was dry. By the twenty-seventh day of the second month, the earth
15 16 had dried completely. Then God said to Noaḥ, "Leave the ark – you, and your
17 wife, your sons, and your sons' wives with you. And every living thing with you – birds,
animals, and all wild beasts that walk the earth – bring them out with you. Let them swarm
18 again on the earth and be fertile and multiply upon it." So Noaḥ came out with his sons,
19 his wife, and his sons' wives. Every beast, creeping thing, winged creature, everything that
creeps across the earth, emerged from the ark by families.

THE ART OF MIDRASH

The Dove Sent Forth from the Ark
Gustave Doré (1866)

Analysis

- Which elements of this image are directly mentioned in the text?
- Which elements of this image are not found in the text?
- What midrashic interpretation is the artist giving us?

יד וַיַּרְא וְהִנֵּה חָרְבוּ פְּנֵי הָאֲדָמָה׃ וּבַחֹדֶשׁ הַשֵּׁנִי בְּשִׁבְעָה וְעֶשְׂרִים יוֹם לַחֹדֶשׁ יָבְשָׁה
טו טז הָאָרֶץ׃ וַיְדַבֵּר אֱלֹהִים אֶל־נֹחַ לֵאמֹר׃ צֵא מִן־הַתֵּבָה אַתָּה וְאִשְׁתְּךָ ז רביעי
יז וּבָנֶיךָ וּנְשֵׁי־בָנֶיךָ אִתָּךְ׃ כָּל־הַחַיָּה אֲשֶׁר־אִתְּךָ מִכָּל־בָּשָׂר בָּעוֹף וּבַבְּהֵמָה וּבְכָל־
הָרֶמֶשׂ הָרֹמֵשׂ עַל־הָאָרֶץ הוֹצֵא אִתָּךְ וְשָׁרְצוּ בָאָרֶץ וּפָרוּ וְרָבוּ עַל־הָאָרֶץ׃ הַיְצֵא
יח יט וַיֵּצֵא־נֹחַ וּבָנָיו וְאִשְׁתּוֹ וּנְשֵׁי־בָנָיו אִתּוֹ׃ כָּל־הַחַיָּה כָּל־הָרֶמֶשׂ וְכָל־הָעוֹף כֹּל
רוֹמֵשׂ עַל־הָאָרֶץ לְמִשְׁפְּחֹתֵיהֶם יָצְאוּ מִן־הַתֵּבָה׃

A QUESTION OF BIBLIODRAMA

TO GOD

- Why did You only remember Noaḥ and the inhabitants of the ark now?
- Now that Noaḥ and his family are ready to leave the ark, what are Your expectations for them and the future of humanity?

TO NOAḤ AND HIS FAMILY

- How are you feeling now that you are finally on the verge of gaining your freedom once again?
- Reflecting back on your experience living in the ark for 150 days, what can you say you learned?
- Why did you wait until God told you to leave the ark?
- What are your hopes and dreams for your life post-flood?
- What are your hopes and dreams for humanity post-flood?

INTEGRATING ḤOKHMA

The mountains of Ararat (a dormant volcano), East Turkey

Mountains of Ararat

Analysis

- What specific information do we now have that was unavailable to classical Jewish commentators? How can it aid our understanding of the text?
- What can we learn from this map to help us understand the text?
- What further questions on the text do you have after seeing this map?

TAKING A LITERARY APPROACH

As several commentators have pointed out, the timing scheme in the flood narrative is arranged in a chiasmus, as follows:

- **A1:** 7 days (Bereshit 7:1–4)
  - **B1:** 40 days (Bereshit 7:12)
    - **C1:** 150 days (Bereshit 7:24)
    - **C2:** 150 days (Bereshit 8:3)
  - **B2:** 40 days (Bereshit 8:6)
- **A2:** 7 days (Bereshit 8:12–16)

When the Torah presents a chiastic structure, whether in narrative or legalistic text, it does so in order to highlight the "center." What sits at the center of this "reversed chiasmus"? ("Reversed" because the movements described in the first set of verses – entrance into the ark and the onset of the flood – are reversed in the second.) In other words, what changed to allow Noaḥ to come out and to allow the world to be restored?

One of the significant differences between the "old world" and the postdiluvian world is the introduction of a covenant. Adam had no covenantal relationship with his Creator. God blessed Man, provided him with all of his needs, commanded, chastised, punished, and exiled him – but at no point was Adam a "covenantal partner" with God. Indeed, there is very little (aside from naming animals and siring the next generation) that Adam does that is productive. Adam is presented in the Torah chiefly as the passive recipient of divine favor.

No member of humanity is any different, including Noaḥ. (The one exception may be the offerings brought by Kayin and Hevel.) This is true only up until the time of the flood (I am following Sforno's interpretation of Bereshit 6:18). Note what has changed between the first set of verses, where Noaḥ enters the Ark, and the second set, announcing his impending exit.

Whereas in the first set, we are told that "the Lord shut him in" (7:16), in the aftermath of the flood we read, "And Noaḥ removed the covering of the ark" (8:13). Noaḥ, who had entered the ark not of his own volition (see Rashi on 7:8) and who was sealed in by God, suddenly becomes an active participant in his own rescue, opening the cover of the ark. Note that the Hebrew word used to describe God's sealing him in (*sagar*) is a direct antonym of the word used for Noaḥ's opening of the cover (*pataḥ*). The center of this entire narrative, the highlight of the flood, is Noaḥ's active involvement in the affairs of the world.

Rabbi Yitzchak Etshalom

20 Then Noaḥ built an altar to the LORD and, taking of each of the kinds of pure animals and
21 pure birds, sacrificed burnt offerings on the altar. The LORD smelled the fragrant aroma
and said in His heart, "Never again will I curse the land because of man;[1] the devisings
of the human heart are evil from its youth. And never again will I destroy all life as I have
22 done. As long as earth and time endure – sowing time and harvest, cold and heat, summer,
9 1 winter, day, and night will not cease." Then God blessed Noaḥ and his sons, saying to
2 them, "Be fertile, multiply, fill the earth. Fear and dread of you shall fall upon all beasts
of the earth, upon all winged creatures of the heavens, upon all that creeps upon the land
3 and all fish of the sea. Into your hand they are given. Every moving thing that lives shall
4 be food for you; I allow them all to you, like green plants. But flesh with its lifeblood still
5 in it you may not eat. And for your own lifeblood I will demand account; I will demand
it from every wild beast. For human life I will demand account, of every man toward his
6 fellow man: One who sheds the blood of man – by man shall his blood be shed, for in
7 God's image man was made. As for you, be fertile and multiply, abound on earth and
8 9 become many on it." Then God said to Noaḥ and to his sons with him: "I – I am
10 about to establish My covenant with you and your descendants after you, and with every
living creature that is with you – the birds, the animals, and all the wild beasts of earth that
11 are with you, everything that left the ark, every living creature on earth. I will establish
My covenant with you, that never again may all life be destroyed by the waters of a flood;

1 | Cf. 3:17, 5:29.

UNLOCKING THE TEXT

- What is the connection between "the devisings of the human heart are evil from its youth" and God's promise to "never again destroy all life"?
- What do the seasons of the year have to do with the sacrifices of Noaḥ?
- Why does God repeat the blessings/commands He gave to Adam and to Noaḥ?
- Are there any differences?
- Why does God only now introduce the command not to spill human blood?
- What is the nature of this new covenant, and with whom is it made?
- Why does the covenant need a "sign"?
- What is the meaning behind the sign God chose to remind humanity of the covenant?

FINDING YOURSELF IN THE TEXT

- Is it your experience that "the devisings of the human heart are evil from its youth"?
- Do you think you need to be commanded ethical laws or would you be ethical through intuition and natural law?
- What do you feel when you see a rainbow in the sky?

Consider using these questions as the basis for your own commentary or creative midrash.

How does reflecting on these firsthand experiences help you better understand the text?

כ וַיִּבֶן נֹחַ מִזְבֵּחַ לַיהוָה וַיִּקַּח מִכֹּל ׀ הַבְּהֵמָה הַטְּהֹרָה וּמִכֹּל הָעוֹף הַטָּהֹר וַיַּעַל
כא עֹלֹת בַּמִּזְבֵּחַ: וַיָּרַח יהוה אֶת־רֵיחַ הַנִּיחֹחַ וַיֹּאמֶר יהוה אֶל־לִבּוֹ לֹא אֹסִף
לְקַלֵּל עוֹד אֶת־הָאֲדָמָה בַּעֲבוּר הָאָדָם כִּי יֵצֶר לֵב הָאָדָם רַע מִנְּעֻרָיו וְלֹא־
כב אֹסִף עוֹד לְהַכּוֹת אֶת־כָּל־חַי כַּאֲשֶׁר עָשִׂיתִי: עֹד כָּל־יְמֵי הָאָרֶץ זֶרַע וְקָצִיר
ט א וְקֹר וָחֹם וְקַיִץ וָחֹרֶף וְיוֹם וָלַיְלָה לֹא יִשְׁבֹּתוּ: וַיְבָרֶךְ אֱלֹהִים אֶת־נֹחַ וְאֶת־בָּנָיו
ב וַיֹּאמֶר לָהֶם פְּרוּ וּרְבוּ וּמִלְאוּ אֶת־הָאָרֶץ: וּמוֹרַאֲכֶם וְחִתְּכֶם יִהְיֶה עַל כָּל־
חַיַּת הָאָרֶץ וְעַל כָּל־עוֹף הַשָּׁמָיִם בְּכֹל אֲשֶׁר תִּרְמֹשׂ הָאֲדָמָה וּבְכָל־דְּגֵי הַיָּם
ג בְּיֶדְכֶם נִתָּנוּ: כָּל־רֶמֶשׂ אֲשֶׁר הוּא־חַי לָכֶם יִהְיֶה לְאָכְלָה כְּיֶרֶק עֵשֶׂב נָתַתִּי
ד ה לָכֶם אֶת־כֹּל: אַךְ־בָּשָׂר בְּנַפְשׁוֹ דָמוֹ לֹא תֹאכֵלוּ: וְאַךְ אֶת־דִּמְכֶם לְנַפְשֹׁתֵיכֶם
אֶדְרֹשׁ מִיַּד כָּל־חַיָּה אֶדְרְשֶׁנּוּ וּמִיַּד הָאָדָם מִיַּד אִישׁ אָחִיו אֶדְרֹשׁ אֶת־נֶפֶשׁ
ו הָאָדָם: שֹׁפֵךְ דַּם הָאָדָם בָּאָדָם דָּמוֹ יִשָּׁפֵךְ כִּי בְּצֶלֶם אֱלֹהִים עָשָׂה אֶת־הָאָדָם:
ז ח וְאַתֶּם פְּרוּ וּרְבוּ שִׁרְצוּ בָאָרֶץ וּרְבוּ־בָהּ: וַיֹּאמֶר אֱלֹהִים אֶל־נֹחַ וְאֶל־ חמישי
ט בָּנָיו אִתּוֹ לֵאמֹר: וַאֲנִי הִנְנִי מֵקִים אֶת־בְּרִיתִי אִתְּכֶם וְאֶת־זַרְעֲכֶם אַחֲרֵיכֶם:
י וְאֵת כָּל־נֶפֶשׁ הַחַיָּה אֲשֶׁר אִתְּכֶם בָּעוֹף בַּבְּהֵמָה וּבְכָל־חַיַּת הָאָרֶץ אִתְּכֶם מִכֹּל
יא יֹצְאֵי הַתֵּבָה לְכֹל חַיַּת הָאָרֶץ: וַהֲקִמֹתִי אֶת־בְּרִיתִי אִתְּכֶם וְלֹא־יִכָּרֵת כָּל־בָּשָׂר

THEMES | COVENANT | CREATION | GOD

Episode 10: *A Brave New World* – Bereshit 8:20–9:17

SUMMARY

For the first time, God enacts a covenant between Himself and man, along with all living beings. This covenant includes a promise, as well as a sign of its implementation. God blesses Noaḥ and his sons to be fruitful and multiply and fill the land. After the flood, humans will instill fear in all the other creatures, as they are now permitted to hunt and eat them. There are some restrictions, though – people are not permitted to eat live flesh or to kill other people, as people are created in the image of God.

12 never again will there be a flood to destroy the earth." God said, "This is the sign of the
covenant I am making between Me and you – and every living creature with you – for all
13 generations to come. I have laid down My bow in the clouds to be the sign of the covenant
14 between Me and the earth. Whenever I bring clouds over the earth and the rainbow
15 appears in the clouds, I will remember My covenant that binds Me and you and every
living creature of all flesh so that never again will the waters become a flood to destroy
16 all life. The rainbow will be there in the cloud, and I will see it, remembering the eternal
17 covenant between God and every living creature, all flesh upon the earth." So said God to
Noaḥ: "This is the sign of the covenant that I have established between Me and all flesh
that is on earth."

INTEGRATING ḤOKHMA

We are all in God's image, and we are all different. Another great nineteenth-century thinker, Rabbi Samson Raphael Hirsch, saw this idea already foreshadowed in the symbol of the covenant God made with humanity after the flood, namely the rainbow. Rabbi Hirsch suggests that it represents the white light of God's radiance refracted into the infinite shadings of the spectrum. For Rabbi Hirsch, the division of humanity into many languages and cultures is the necessary precondition of human freedom and dignity until the end of days.

Rabbi Jonathan Sacks

Analysis

- What areas of scientific knowledge do we have now that were unavailable to classical Jewish commentators? How can that aid our understanding of the text?
- What can we learn from this passage to help us understand the text?
- What further questions on the text do you have now that you have read this new take on the story?

יב עוֹד מִמֵּי הַמַּבּוּל וְלֹא־יִהְיֶה עוֹד מַבּוּל לְשַׁחֵת הָאָרֶץ׃ וַיֹּאמֶר אֱלֹהִים זֹאת
אוֹת־הַבְּרִית אֲשֶׁר־אֲנִי נֹתֵן בֵּינִי וּבֵינֵיכֶם וּבֵין כָּל־נֶפֶשׁ חַיָּה אֲשֶׁר אִתְּכֶם לְדֹרֹת
יג יד עוֹלָם׃ אֶת־קַשְׁתִּי נָתַתִּי בֶּעָנָן וְהָיְתָה לְאוֹת בְּרִית בֵּינִי וּבֵין הָאָרֶץ׃ וְהָיָה בְּעַנְנִי
טו עָנָן עַל־הָאָרֶץ וְנִרְאֲתָה הַקֶּשֶׁת בֶּעָנָן׃ וְזָכַרְתִּי אֶת־בְּרִיתִי אֲשֶׁר בֵּינִי וּבֵינֵיכֶם וּבֵין
טז כָּל־נֶפֶשׁ חַיָּה בְּכָל־בָּשָׂר וְלֹא־יִהְיֶה עוֹד הַמַּיִם לְמַבּוּל לְשַׁחֵת כָּל־בָּשָׂר׃ וְהָיְתָה
הַקֶּשֶׁת בֶּעָנָן וּרְאִיתִיהָ לִזְכֹּר בְּרִית עוֹלָם בֵּין אֱלֹהִים וּבֵין כָּל־נֶפֶשׁ חַיָּה בְּכָל־
יז בָּשָׂר אֲשֶׁר עַל־הָאָרֶץ׃ וַיֹּאמֶר אֱלֹהִים אֶל־נֹחַ זֹאת אוֹת־הַבְּרִית אֲשֶׁר הֲקִמֹתִי
בֵּינִי וּבֵין כָּל־בָּשָׂר אֲשֶׁר עַל־הָאָרֶץ׃

A QUESTION OF BIBLIODRAMA

TO GOD

- How did You feel about Noaḥ's offerings?
- How do You feel about the covenant You have made with humanity?
- Why does this covenant need a sign?
- Why did You choose the rainbow as a sign for this covenant?

TO NOAḤ

- How does it feel to be the sole surviving humans on earth?
- Why did you bring sacrifices to God?
- How do you feel about this new set of commands/instructions received from God?
- How does it feel to be part of a covenant with God?
- What did you feel when you saw the rainbow?

Rainbow Landscape
Yoram Raanan (2006–2007)

Analysis

- Which elements of this image are directly mentioned in the text?
- Which elements of this image are not found in the text?
- What midrashic interpretation is the artist giving us?

THE ART OF MIDRASH

> mountains have seen You and they tremble; the rush of water passes over; the deep has sounded its voice and has lifted its hands on high.

Accordingly, Ramban explains that the sign of the bow expresses the "end of hostilities," since the curved side of the rainbow points heavenward, while the open side – opposite the direction in which the arrows are released – points toward the earth:

> For the rainbow is not fashioned with its legs facing upward, so as to appear that it is used for shooting from the heavens.... Rather, it is fashioned in the opposite manner, showing that it will not be used for shooting from the heavens. This is the manner of combatants – to reverse it [the bow] in their hands in this way when they call for peace to their opponents. Furthermore, the rainbow does not have a bowstring upon which to place arrows.

However, it may be that the bow represents a cessation of hostilities in a slightly different sense. The word *kashti*, "My bow," does not appear by itself in our *parasha*; in all three instances in which it is used, it appears along with the word "cloud" – and it is this combination that represents the sign of the covenant:

> I have set My bow in the cloud, that it may be a sign of the covenant between Me and the earth. And it shall be, when I bring clouds over the earth and the bow appears in the cloud, that...the bow will be in the cloud, and I shall see it and remember the eternal covenant.

Hence, it is not the rainbow alone that is the sign of the covenant, but rather its appearance in the cloud. Clouds appear in Tanakh as a screen or covering – for instance, for God's glory, for the covering over the Ark of the Covenant, and for the *Mishkan*. Setting the bow in the cloud therefore symbolizes the act of "covering" or "hiding" the bow, a sign of a ceasefire, like returning a sword to its scabbard. God covers one of His weapons of war and promises not to use it anymore. When clouds fill the sky and the rainbow appears, it is a sign that the bow is still "covered"; it will not be used against all flesh.

Rabbi Amnon Bazak

TAKING A LITERARY APPROACH

Why is it specifically the rainbow that is chosen as the sign that there will not be another flood?

The commentators suggest different directions in interpreting the significance of the rainbow. *Ḥizkuni* refers us to the concluding verse of the unit describing the divine chariot at the beginning of the book of Yeḥezkel, which is the only other place in all of Tanakh where the word *keshet*, "bow," is used in this sense: "Like the appearance of the bow that is in the cloud on the day of rain, so was the appearance of the brightness around; it was the appearance of the likeness of God's glory" (Yeḥezkel 1:28). On the basis of this verse, *Ḥizkuni* argues that the rainbow represents God's manifestation in the world, and this manifestation in and of itself proves that there will not be another flood:

> If it were My intention to destroy them when there is heavy rain, then I would not show them the likeness of My glory, for a king does not show himself among his subjects when they are censured by him.

The problem with this interpretation is that it is theologically complicated; it suggests that God is reminded of His covenant by looking at something that resembles "the appearance of the likeness of God's glory," a problematic assertion.

Most of the commentators maintain that the sign of the rainbow is related to the more common meaning of the word *keshet* in Tanakh – the bow as a weapon. Furthermore, this is no ordinary bow, it is God's own bow: "I have placed My bow in the cloud." What does this mean?

In several places in Tanakh, we find the bow mentioned as a weapon of God. Examples include such verses as "I bend Yehuda for Me as a bow" (Zekharia 9:13), "He has drawn His bow like an enemy" (Eikha 2:4), and others. Arrows, too, are invoked metaphorically to describe God waging war (see Devarim 32:23, 42, among other sources). In the context of our *parasha*, it would therefore seem that the (rain)bow symbolizes the weapon by means of which God brought the flood.

Indeed, it is highly symbolic to liken the rain of the flood to arrows released with great force from a bow. The same idea arises from the prophecy of Ḥabakkuk (3:9–10):

> Your bow is made bare, sworn are the rods of words, Selah; You cleave the earth with rivers. The

18 Noaḥ's sons who came out from the ark were Shem, Ḥam, and Yefet. Ḥam was the father
19 of Kenaan.[1] These three were Noaḥ's sons; and from them all the world branched out.
20 21 Noaḥ began to be a man of the land, and he planted a vineyard. He drank some of the
22 wine, became drunk, and lay uncovered in his tent. Ḥam, father of Kenaan, saw his father's
23 nakedness and told his two brothers who were outside. Shem and Yefet then took a cloak
and put it over both their shoulders. They walked backward and covered their father's
24 nakedness, averting their faces so as not to see the nakedness of their father. Noaḥ woke
25 from his wine and realized what his youngest son had done to him. He said, "Cursed be
26 Kenaan! The lowest of slaves shall he be to his brothers." Then he said, "Blessed be the
27 LORD, God of Shem, Kenaan shall be his slave. May God enlarge Yefet, and let him dwell
28 in the tents of Shem; Kenaan shall be his slave." After the flood Noaḥ lived three hundred
29 and fifty years. Noaḥ lived a total of nine hundred and fifty years, and he died.

---

1 | The ancestor of the Canaanites, whose land would ultimately be given to Israel, descendants of Shem.

UNLOCKING THE TEXT

- Why does the Torah single out Shem as the father of Kenaan?
- Why did Noaḥ only become a "man of the land" now? What was his occupation before the flood?
- Did Noaḥ only plant a vineyard? Why does the Torah focus on this?
- Why did Noaḥ become drunk?
- What was Ḥam's sin that deserved this curse?
- What is the meaning of the blessing Noaḥ gave to Yefet and Shem?
- Why does Noaḥ create a hierarchy among his descendants, with Shem at the top and Ḥam at the bottom?

FINDING YOURSELF IN THE TEXT

- Have you ever had a difficult or traumatic experience, and afterward needed to totally relax or unwind?
- Have you ever been embarrassed in front of your parents or embarrassed your parents?
- Have you ever defended a parent or looked after their interests when they were not there?

Consider using these questions as the basis for your own commentary or creative midrash.

How does reflecting on these firsthand experiences help you better understand the text?

יח יט וַיִּהְיוּ בְנֵי־נֹחַ הַיֹּצְאִים מִן־הַתֵּבָה שֵׁם וְחָם וָיָפֶת וְחָם הוּא אֲבִי כְנָעַן׃ שְׁלֹשָׁה ח ששי
כ אֵלֶּה בְּנֵי־נֹחַ וּמֵאֵלֶּה נָפְצָה כָל־הָאָרֶץ׃ וַיָּחֶל נֹחַ אִישׁ הָאֲדָמָה וַיִּטַּע כָּרֶם׃
כא כב וַיֵּשְׁתְּ מִן־הַיַּיִן וַיִּשְׁכָּר וַיִּתְגַּל בְּתוֹךְ אָהֳלֹה׃ וַיַּרְא חָם אֲבִי כְנַעַן אֵת עֶרְוַת אָבִיו
כג וַיַּגֵּד לִשְׁנֵי־אֶחָיו בַּחוּץ׃ וַיִּקַּח שֵׁם וָיֶפֶת אֶת־הַשִּׂמְלָה וַיָּשִׂימוּ עַל־שְׁכֶם שְׁנֵיהֶם
וַיֵּלְכוּ אֲחֹרַנִּית וַיְכַסּוּ אֵת עֶרְוַת אֲבִיהֶם וּפְנֵיהֶם אֲחֹרַנִּית וְעֶרְוַת אֲבִיהֶם לֹא
כד כה רָאוּ׃ וַיִּיקֶץ נֹחַ מִיֵּינוֹ וַיֵּדַע אֵת אֲשֶׁר־עָשָׂה לוֹ בְּנוֹ הַקָּטָן׃ וַיֹּאמֶר אָרוּר כְּנָעַן
כו עֶבֶד עֲבָדִים יִהְיֶה לְאֶחָיו׃ וַיֹּאמֶר בָּרוּךְ יהוה אֱלֹהֵי שֵׁם וִיהִי כְנַעַן עֶבֶד לָמוֹ׃
כז כח יַפְתְּ אֱלֹהִים לְיֶפֶת וְיִשְׁכֹּן בְּאָהֳלֵי־שֵׁם וִיהִי כְנַעַן עֶבֶד לָמוֹ׃ וַיְחִי־נֹחַ אַחַר הַמַּבּוּל
כט שְׁלֹשׁ מֵאוֹת שָׁנָה וַחֲמִשִּׁים שָׁנָה׃ וַיְהִי כָּל־יְמֵי־נֹחַ תְּשַׁע מֵאוֹת שָׁנָה וַחֲמִשִּׁים
שָׁנָה וַיָּמֹת׃

THEMES | ETHICS | CREATION | RELATIONSHIPS AND LOVE

Episode 11: *Noaḥ in the Post-Flood World* – Bereshit 9:18–29

SUMMARY

The first actions which the survivors of the flood, Noaḥ's family, perform in the new world involve the loss of consciousness caused by drinking wine, and as a result, the exposing and eventual covering of the body. This can be seen as an inverse parallel to the beginning of the old world, where Adam and Ḥava acquired knowledge of good and evil through eating fruit that was forbidden to them, and as a result, they became ashamed of their nakedness and covered themselves up.

THE ART OF MIDRASH

Noah Curses Canaan
Gustave Doré (1865)

Analysis

- Which elements of this image are directly mentioned in the text?
- Which elements of this image are not found in the text?
- What midrashic interpretation is the artist giving us?

A QUESTION OF BIBLIODRAMA

TO NOAḤ

- Why did you try your hand at agriculture after leaving the ark? Why a vine?
- Did you mean to get drunk?
- What did it feel like to be the sole survivors of the destruction of the world?
- How did you know Ḥam had behaved inappropriately?
- How did you feel toward him after this?
- How did you feel toward your other sons?

TO ḤAM

- What did you think when you saw your father lying naked?
- What choices did you have? Why did you choose to react the way you did?
- How did you feel hearing your father curse you?

TO YEFET AND SHEM

- What did you think about your father when you heard Ḥam tell you what he had seen?
- What did you think about Ḥam's behavior?
- Why did you decide to act in the way you did?
- What did you think about the curse your father gave Ḥam and the blessings he gave you?

INTEGRATING ḤOKHMA

Intuitively, the Sages understood that the hero of faith was not Noaḥ but Avraham – Avraham who fought a war to rescue his nephew, who prayed for the people of the plain even though he knew they were wicked; Avraham who challenged Heaven itself in words unrivaled in the history of the human encounter with God: "Shall the judge of all the earth not do justice?"

What might an Avraham not have said when confronted with the possibility of a flood. "What if there are fifty righteous people? What if there are ten? Far be it from You to do such a thing – to kill the righteous with the wicked, treating the righteous and the wicked alike." Avraham might have saved the world. Noaḥ saved only himself and his family. Avraham might have failed, but Noaḥ – at least on the evidence of the text – did not even try (to be sure, there are midrashic traditions that he did try, but most prefer to accept that he did not). Noaḥ's end – drunk, disheveled, an embarrassment to his children – eloquently tells us that if you save yourself while doing nothing to save the world, you do not even save yourself. Noaḥ could not live with the guilt of survival.[1]

Rabbi Jonathan Sacks

1 | Survivor guilt (also called survivor syndrome) is a mental condition that occurs when a person believes they have done something wrong by surviving a traumatic or tragic event when others could not. It is considered a symptom of post-traumatic stress disorder (PTSD).

Analysis

- What areas of understanding of human nature and society do we now have that were unavailable to classical Jewish commentators? How can they aid our understanding of the text?
- What can we learn from this passage to help us understand the text?
- What further questions on the text do you have now that you have read this new take on the story?

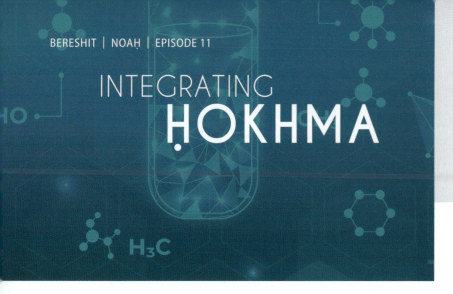

TAKING A LITERARY APPROACH

Of all the plants available, what motivated Noaḥ to plant grapes? Glancing at other stories in Tanakh, we find that the drinking of wine is often accompanied by sexual behavior, often immoral. For example, wine has sexual overtones in Shir HaShirim (1:2, 4; 4:10; 5:1; 7:2, 9; 8:2). Eikha mocks the daughter of Edom: "Rejoice and be glad, O daughter of Edom…you shall be drunken, and shall make yourself naked (4:21). In Bereshit 19, Lot's daughters use wine to repeatedly seduce their aged father, while David uses wine to get Uriya drunk in a vain attempt to induce Uriya to have intercourse with his wife Batsheva, so David's adultery and her pregnancy could be concealed. What does this suggest about Noaḥ's motivations?

We suggest, however, that the planting alludes to another event in Bereshit – the planting by God of the Garden of Eden. Just as God engaged in planting, so too Noaḥ engaged in planting. If so, then we can suggest that Noaḥ's actions after the flood mimic God's actions in creation – an act of *imitatio Dei*. Indeed, the entire section contains many parallels to the creation story, which we will enumerate. This leads one to conclude that just as the flood served as the undoing of the original creation, our story of Noaḥ and the vineyard serves to undo the attempt to start creation again after the flood.

Parallels:

1. Both stories begin with the blessing to "be fruitful and multiply."
2. God planted a garden; Noaḥ planted a vineyard.
3. Both stories take a turn for the worse when the protagonist(s) consumes some fruit.
4. After the eating/drinking of the forbidden fruit, the protagonist's naked state and the efforts to cover it become prominent details in the story.
5. Curses (and blessings) are distributed at the finale of the story (creating the parallel between Ḥam and the snake).

That Shem and Yefet are forced to walk backward to cover their father becomes the symbolic theme of the story: any forward progress made by humanity after the flood has been reversed. Indeed, their act is the pivot of the chiastic structure that frames this story.

wording of "uncover nakedness" is only used in Vayikra to describe heterosexual incest, not the homosexual act. More specifically, Vayikra 18:8 equates "the nakedness of your mother" with the "nakedness of your father." Furthermore, if Ḥam engaged in incestuous sex with his mother, the text's emphasis on his son Canaan becomes clear. Canaan is the product of this incestuous union, as Moav and Amon are the product of Lot and his daughters. That explains why the text consistently identifies Ḥam as the "father of Canaan," and why Noaḥ chooses to curse Canaan upon awakening. The Torah also alludes to the possibility that this occurred in Ḥam's mother's tent. As Rashi notes, the written word (the *ketiv*) "the tent" in verse 21 has the feminine possessive suffix "her tent," although we read (*keri*) the word as "his tent." Ḥam's act of sleeping with his mother would therefore be seen as an act of rebellion against Noaḥ's authority (as seen later with Reuven with Bilha, Avshalom with David's concubines, and Adoniyahu's attempt to claim Avishag as his rightful bride from Shlomo). We could suggest that this was *Ḥazal*'s intention in interpreting his act as castration – the ultimate removal of the father's creative power.

Rabbi Yaakov Beasley

- A. And *Noaḥ drank of the wine* and became drunk
  - B. Ḥam *saw his father's nakedness*
    - C. and told *his two brothers outside [the tent]*
      - D. Then Shem and Yefet took a garment
    - C1. and *[the two brothers] walked backward [into the tent]* and covered the nakedness of their father
  - B1. and *their father's nakedness they did not see*
- A1. And *Noaḥ awoke from his wine*

In this case, the chiasm reflects the text's contrast of the differing reactions of Noaḥ's children to his predicament.

The precise nature of what Ḥam did while in the tent remains obscure. According to Radak, his offense was solely to see his father uncovered (and his willingness to share that information with his brothers). *Ḥazal* in the Talmud went much further than what is explicit in the text: they suggested that in fact, either Ḥam castrated Noaḥ, or that he engaged in homosexual relations with Noaḥ (an alternative form of "uncreation"), and then castrated him. The parallels mentioned above to the incestuous Lot/daughters episode certainly point in this direction. The failure to interpret Ḥam's offense as simple voyeurism (itself a serious misdemeanor) and the interpretation that something more drastic occurred are supported by the verse "And Noaḥ awoke from his wine, and knew what his youngest son had done to him." Clearly, something beyond simple peeking had to have occurred.

We suggest that Ḥam in fact committed an incestuous act with Noaḥ's wife (Ḥam's mother). The rationales for this interpretation are several. First, the

10 1 These are the descendants of Noaḥ's sons, Shem, Ḥam, and Yefet; after the flood, children
2 were born to them.[1] Yefet's sons were Gomer, Magog, Madai, Yavan, Tuval, Meshekh, and
3 4 Tiras. Gomer's sons were Ashkenaz, Rifat, and Togarma. Yavan's sons were Elisha, Tarshish,
5 Kitim, and Dodanim. From these the sea-going nations spread out to their territories, each
6 with its own language, by their clans and their nations. Ḥam's sons were Kush, Mitzrayim,[2]
7 Put, and Kenaan. Kush's sons were Seva, Ḥavila, Savta, Raama, and Savtekha. Raama's sons
8 were Sheva and Dedan. Kush was the father of Nimrod, the first mighty warrior on earth.
9 He was a mighty hunter before the Lord, which is why people still say, "Like Nimrod,
10 a mighty hunter before the Lord." His kingdom began with Babylon, Erekh, Akad, and
11 Kalneh in the land of Shinar. From that land, Ashur went out and built Nineveh, Reḥovot
12 13 Ir, Kalaḥ, and Resen between Nineveh and Kalaḥ; that is the great city. Mitzrayim fathered
14 the Ludim, Anamim, Lehavim and Naftuḥim, Patrusim, Kasluḥim – from whom the
15 16 Philistines descended – and the Kaftorim. Kenaan fathered Tzidon, his firstborn,
17 and Ḥet, and the Jebusites, Amorites, and Girgashites, the Hivites, Arkites, and Sinites, the
18 19 Arvadites, Zemarites, and Hamatites. Later, the Canaanite families were dispersed. The
Canaanite borders were from Sidon toward Gerar near Aza, and toward Sedom, Amora,

1 | The following are the eponymous ancestors of various nations.

2 | In this translation, Ḥam's son is rendered "Mitzrayim," while the nation is called "Egypt."

UNLOCKING THE TEXT

- Why is it important for the Torah to give a detailed list of Noaḥ's descendants and where they settled?
- If Noaḥ and his family spoke one language, how did their descendants develop into different languages?
- Why are the descendants of Yefet listed first?
- Why does the Torah spend less time listing the descendants of Yefet?
- Are you familiar with any of the descendants of Ḥam? What do the names from this list that you have heard often have in common?

Consider using these questions as the basis for your own commentary or creative midrash.

FINDING YOURSELF IN THE TEXT

- Does your family have a family tree?
- Do you think it is important to know about your ancestors?
- Does anyone in your family have a different mother tongue?

How does reflecting on these firsthand experiences help you better understand the text?

‎י ‎א וְאֵ֣לֶּה תּוֹלְדֹ֣ת בְּנֵי־נֹ֗חַ שֵׁ֤ם חָ֣ם וָיָ֔פֶת וַיִּוָּלְד֥וּ לָהֶ֛ם בָּנִ֖ים אַחַ֥ר הַמַּבּֽוּל: בְּנֵ֣י יֶ֔פֶת
‎ב גֹּ֣מֶר וּמָג֔וֹג וּמָדַ֖י וְיָוָ֣ן וְתֻבָ֑ל וּמֶ֖שֶׁךְ וְתִירָֽס: וּבְנֵ֖י גֹּ֑מֶר אַשְׁכְּנַ֥ז וְרִיפַ֖ת וְתֹגַרְמָֽה:
‎ד וּבְנֵ֥י יָוָ֖ן אֱלִישָׁ֣ה וְתַרְשִׁ֑ישׁ כִּתִּ֖ים וְדֹֽדָנִֽים: מֵ֠אֵ֠לֶּה נִפְרְד֞וּ אִיֵּ֤י הַגּוֹיִם֙ בְּאַרְצֹתָ֔ם
‎ה אִ֖ישׁ לִלְשֹׁנ֑וֹ לְמִשְׁפְּחֹתָ֖ם בְּגֽוֹיֵהֶֽם: וּבְנֵ֣י חָ֔ם כּ֥וּשׁ וּמִצְרַ֖יִם וּפ֥וּט וּכְנָֽעַן: וּבְנֵ֣י כ֔וּשׁ
‎ו סְבָ֣א וַֽחֲוִילָ֔ה וְסַבְתָּ֥ה וְרַעְמָ֖ה וְסַבְתְּכָ֑א וּבְנֵ֣י רַעְמָ֔ה שְׁבָ֖א וּדְדָ֑ן: וְכ֖וּשׁ יָלַ֣ד אֶת־
‎ז נִמְרֹ֑ד ה֣וּא הֵחֵ֔ל לִֽהְי֥וֹת גִּבֹּ֖ר בָּאָֽרֶץ: הֽוּא־הָיָ֥ה גִּבֹּֽר־צַ֖יִד לִפְנֵ֣י יהו֑ה עַל־כֵּן֙
‎ח יֵֽאָמַ֔ר כְּנִמְרֹ֛ד גִּבֹּ֥ר צַ֖יִד לִפְנֵ֣י יהוֽה: וַתְּהִ֨י רֵאשִׁ֤ית מַמְלַכְתּוֹ֙ בָּבֶ֔ל וְאֶ֖רֶךְ וְאַכַּ֣ד
‎ט וְכַלְנֵ֑ה בְּאֶ֖רֶץ שִׁנְעָֽר: מִן־הָאָ֥רֶץ הַהִ֖וא יָצָ֣א אַשּׁ֑וּר וַיִּ֨בֶן֙ אֶת־נִ֣ינְוֵ֔ה וְאֶת־רְחֹבֹ֥ת
‎י עִ֖יר וְאֶת־כָּֽלַח: וְאֶת־רֶ֕סֶן בֵּ֥ין נִֽינְוֵ֖ה וּבֵ֣ין כָּ֑לַח הִ֖וא הָעִ֥יר הַגְּדֹלָֽה: וּמִצְרַ֡יִם
‎יא יָלַ֣ד אֶת־לוּדִ֣ים וְאֶת־עֲנָמִ֗ים וְאֶת־לְהָבִ֖ים וְאֶת־נַפְתֻּחִֽים: וְֽאֶת־פַּתְרֻסִ֞ים וְאֶת־
‎יב כַּסְלֻחִ֗ים אֲשֶׁ֨ר יָֽצְא֥וּ מִשָּׁ֛ם פְּלִשְׁתִּ֖ים וְאֶת־כַּפְתֹּרִֽים: וּכְנַ֗עַן יָלַ֛ד
‎יד אֶת־צִידֹ֥ן בְּכֹר֖וֹ וְאֶת־חֵֽת: וְאֶת־הַיְבוּסִי֙ וְאֶת־הָ֣אֱמֹרִ֔י וְאֵ֖ת הַגִּרְגָּשִֽׁי: וְאֶת־הַֽחִוִּ֥י
‎טו וְאֶת־הָֽעַרְקִ֖י וְאֶת־הַסִּינִֽי: וְאֶת־הָֽאַרְוָדִ֥י וְאֶת־הַצְּמָרִ֖י וְאֶת־הַֽחֲמָתִ֑י וְאַחַ֣ר נָפֹ֔צוּ
‎יו מִשְׁפְּח֖וֹת הַֽכְּנַֽעֲנִֽי: וַֽיְהִ֞י גְּב֤וּל הַֽכְּנַֽעֲנִי֙ מִצִּידֹ֔ן בֹּאֲכָ֥ה גְרָ֖רָה עַד־עַזָּ֑ה בֹּאֲכָ֛ה סְדֹ֥מָה

THEMES	CREATION	RELATIONSHIPS AND LOVE	THE LAND OF ISRAEL

Episode 12: *Noaḥ's Family Tree* – Bereshit 10:1–32

SUMMARY

The Torah presents a list of Noaḥ's descendants, including families that developed into nations. These families are divided "after their families, in/after their tongues, in their lands" (10:20, 31), in accordance with familial, linguistic, and national criteria. This chapter is the source of the accepted number of seventy nations. The list consists only of tribes that came directly from the land of Shinar; it does not include other nations, as those were very remote and had no direct contact with the children of Israel.

20 Adma, and Tzevoyim, near Lasha. These were the descendants of Ḥam, by their clans and
21 their languages, with their lands and their nations. Sons were also born to Shem.
22 The older brother of Yefet, he was the ancestor of all the sons of Ever. Shem's sons were
23 Elam, Ashur, Arpakhshad, Lud, and Aram. Aram's sons were Utz, Ḥul, Geter, and Mash.
24 25 Arpakhshad was the father of Shelaḥ, and Shelaḥ was the father of Ever. To Ever, two sons
were born. One was named Peleg, for in his time the earth was divided.[3] His brother was
26 named Yoktan. Yoktan was the father of Almodad, Shelef, Ḥatzarmavet, Yeraḥ, Hadoram,
27 28 Uzal, Dikla, Oval, Avimael, Sheva, Ofir, Ḥavila, and Yovav; all these were Yoktan's sons.
29 30 31 Their settlements extended from Mesha toward Sefar, in the eastern hill country. These
were the descendants of Shem, by their clans and their languages, with their lands and their
32 nations. These, then, are the clans of the sons of Noaḥ, by their lines, in their nations. And
from these, the nations spread out across the earth after the flood.

3 | Peleg evokes the Hebrew *niflega* ("divided"). This is often understood to refer to the dispersion recounted in 11:1–9.

Analysis

- Which elements of this image are directly mentioned in the text?
- Which elements of this image are not found in the text?
- What midrashic interpretation is the artist giving us?

Noah's Family Tree, Tani Bayer (2023)

כ וַעֲמֹרָה וְאַדְמָה וּצְבֹיִם עַד־לָשַׁע׃ אֵלֶּה בְנֵי־חָם לְמִשְׁפְּחֹתָם לִלְשֹׁנֹתָם בְּאַרְצֹתָם
כא בְּגוֹיֵהֶם׃ וּלְשֵׁם יֻלַּד גַּם־הוּא אֲבִי כָּל־בְּנֵי־עֵבֶר אֲחִי יֶפֶת הַגָּדוֹל׃
כב כג בְּנֵי שֵׁם עֵילָם וְאַשּׁוּר וְאַרְפַּכְשַׁד וְלוּד וַאֲרָם׃ וּבְנֵי אֲרָם עוּץ וְחוּל וְגֶתֶר וָמַשׁ׃
כד כה וְאַרְפַּכְשַׁד יָלַד אֶת־שָׁלַח וְשֶׁלַח יָלַד אֶת־עֵבֶר׃ וּלְעֵבֶר יֻלַּד שְׁנֵי בָנִים שֵׁם הָאֶחָד
כו פֶּלֶג כִּי בְיָמָיו נִפְלְגָה הָאָרֶץ וְשֵׁם אָחִיו יָקְטָן׃ וְיָקְטָן יָלַד אֶת־אַלְמוֹדָד וְאֶת־שָׁלֶף
כז כח וְאֶת־חֲצַרְמָוֶת וְאֶת־יָרַח׃ וְאֶת־הֲדוֹרָם וְאֶת־אוּזָל וְאֶת־דִּקְלָה׃ וְאֶת־עוֹבָל וְאֶת־
כט אֲבִימָאֵל וְאֶת־שְׁבָא׃ וְאֶת־אוֹפִר וְאֶת־חֲוִילָה וְאֶת־יוֹבָב כָּל־אֵלֶּה בְּנֵי יָקְטָן׃
ל לא וַיְהִי מוֹשָׁבָם מִמֵּשָׁא בֹּאֲכָה סְפָרָה הַר הַקֶּדֶם׃ אֵלֶּה בְנֵי־שֵׁם לְמִשְׁפְּחֹתָם לִלְשֹׁנֹתָם
לב בְּאַרְצֹתָם לְגוֹיֵהֶם׃ אֵלֶּה מִשְׁפְּחֹת בְּנֵי־נֹחַ לְתוֹלְדֹתָם בְּגוֹיֵהֶם וּמֵאֵלֶּה נִפְרְדוּ
הַגּוֹיִם בָּאָרֶץ אַחַר הַמַּבּוּל׃

THE ART OF MIDRASH

Distribution of Noaḥ's descendants

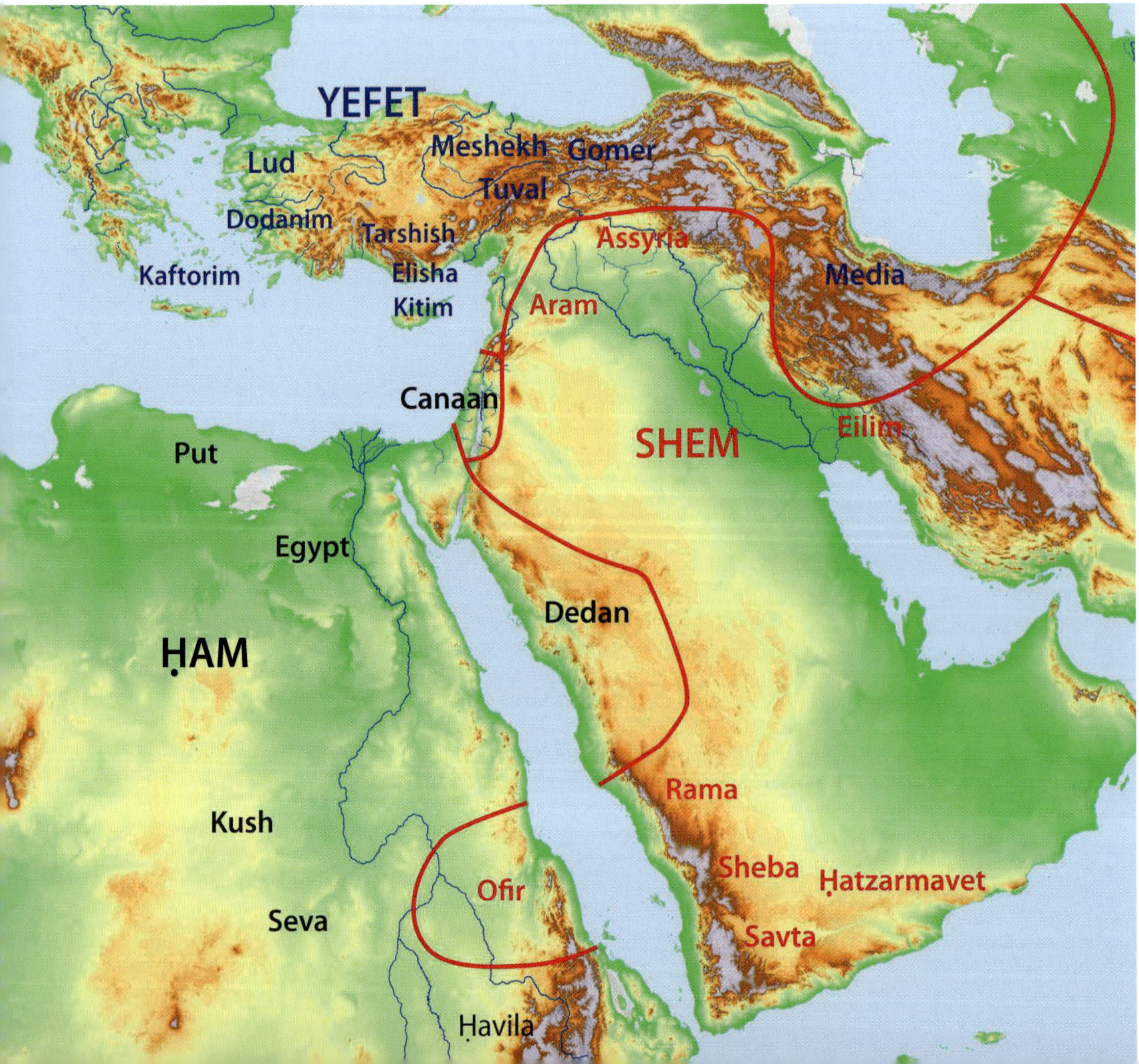

INTEGRATING ḤOKHMA

"Be yourself; everyone else is already taken." - *Oscar Wilde*

What can Parashat Noaḥ teach us about comparing ourselves to others? The opening verse begs interpretation when it states that "Noaḥ was a righteous man… in his generations." How does one understand the phrase "in his generations," which implies his righteousness was relative?

Rashi cites a well-known midrashic debate about whether these words are meant to complement Noaḥ or discredit his righteousness. Rashi Comments that some of our Rabbis interpret this to his credit - had he lived in a righteous generation Noaḥ would have been even more righteous. Others, however, explain it to his discredit - in his own generation Noaḥ was a tzadik, but had he lived in Avraham's generation he would have been considered insignificant. The second opinion seems to harshly contrast Noaḥ with Avraham. However, Rashi is incredibly specific with his words. The opinion which praises Noaḥ by comparing him positively is in the name of "our rabbis," while the negative comparison to Avraham is brought only in the name of "others." While Rashi does not explicitly take a position on this debate, the language he uses implies he prefers the opinion which makes a positive comparison. Additionally, he brings the positive comparison first.

The business of comparing ourselves to others has become amplified in our time through social media use. Research has found that social media has a negative impact on the mental health of teenagers, especially girls, due to their tendency to compare themselves to others. Rashi on Parashat Noaḥ teaches that positive comparison can be useful and inspiring. Yet, it is important to be aware of comparisons which lead to negative thoughts and a decline in emotional wellbeing, and to foster ways to guard against this.

Rabbanit Karen Miller Jackson

Analysis

- What specific information do we now have that was unavailable to classical Jewish commentators? How can it aid our understanding of the text?
- What can we learn from this map that can help us understand the text?
- What further questions on the text do you have now that you have seen this map?

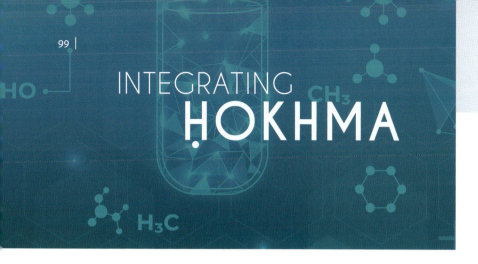

The word *toladot* stems from the Hebrew word *velad*, "child" or "offspring." Therefore, *Eleh toledot* should be translated "These are the children of...." For example: *Eleh toledot Adam* (Bereshit 5:1) means "These are the children of Adam" – and thus introduces the story of Adam's children, i.e., Shet, Enosh, Kenan, etc. Similarly, *Eleh toledot Noaḥ* introduces the story of Noaḥ's children – Shem, Ḥam, and Yefet. (See Rashbam on Bereshit 37:2 for a more complete explanation.)

This pattern of *toladot* that introduce stories continues all the way until the very end of Bereshit. Therefore, we conclude that these *sifrei toladot* do more than "keep the book together"; they also help develop the theme of Bereshit. We will now show how these *toladot* create not only a framework for Bereshit; they can also help us identify its two distinct sections that create its primary theme.

Despite this successive nature of the *toladot* in Bereshit, they clearly divide into two distinct sections: God's creation of mankind (ch. 1–11) and the stories of our forefathers (ch. 12–50).

Though the majority of Bereshit focuses on the family of Avraham Avinu (section two), in the first eleven chapters (section one), the Torah's focus is on mankind as a whole. Even when the Torah includes special details about Noaḥ, it is not because he is designated to become a special nation – rather, it is because it is through Noaḥ that mankind will be preserved. After the flood, the Torah tells us how Noaḥ's offspring evolve into nations (ch. 10). Even though we find that Noaḥ blesses Shem and Yefet (9:25–27), the concept of a special nation with a special covenant does not begin until the story of Avraham Avinu.

In contrast, chapters 11–50 focus on the story of *am Yisrael* – God's special nation. In this section, Bereshit is no longer universalistic; rather, it becomes particularistic. Therefore, this section begins with *toledot Shem* till Teraḥ (11:10–24) to introduce the story of Avraham Avinu, whom God chooses in chapter 12 to become the forefather of His special nation. The remainder of Bereshit explains which of Avraham's offspring are chosen (= *beḥira*, e.g., Yitzḥak and Yaakov), and which are rejected (= *deḥiya*, e.g., Yishmael and Esav). This explains why Bereshit concludes precisely when this complicated *beḥira* process reaches its completion – i.e., when all twelve sons of Yaakov have been chosen, and none of his offspring will ever again be rejected.

Rabbi Menachem Leibtag

TAKING A LITERARY APPROACH

Bereshit moves quickly from one topic to another. The creation of the world is followed by the stories of the Garden of Eden and Kayin and Hevel. A description of the sorry state of mankind is followed quickly by the flood. The attempts to rebuild the world led to the building of the Tower of Bavel. Finally, God turns to Avram to assist His overall plan. We note that all of these stories relate in one form or other to God's *hashgaḥa* (providence), i.e., His intervention in the history of mankind as He punishes man (or mankind) for wayward behavior.

However, within this progression of topics, we find a very interesting phenomenon. The Torah introduces each of the general stories with a set of *toladot* (genealogies). The following table summarizes this pattern and illustrates how *toladot* introduce each of the main topics in Bereshit.

Although this pattern is rarely noticed, these *sifrei toladot* actually create a framework for the entire book of Bereshit! In this manner, the *toladot* introduce each and every story in Bereshit. To explain why, we must first take a minute to explain what the word "*toladot*" means.

Chapters	Topic
2	*Toledot shamayim vaaretz*
2–4	Man in (and out of) the Garden of Eden
5	*Toledot* Adam to Noaḥ
6–9	*HaMabul* – the story of the flood
10	*Toledot Benei Noaḥ* – Shem, Ḥam, and Yefet
11:1–9	*Migdal Bavel* – the Tower of Bavel
11	*Toledot* Shem to Teraḥ
12–25	God's choice of Avraham
25–35	*Toledot* Yitzḥak – the story of Yaakov and Esav
36	*Toledot* Esav – the story of Esav's children
37–50	*Toledot* Yaakov – the story of Yosef and his brothers

11 1 2 The whole world spoke the same language, the same words. And as the people migrated
3 from the east they found a valley in the land of Shinar and settled there. They said to each
other, "Come, let us make bricks, let us bake them thoroughly." They used bricks for stone
4 and tar for mortar. And they said, "Come, let us build ourselves a city and a tower that
reaches the heavens, and make a name for ourselves. Otherwise we will be scattered across
5 the face of the earth." But the LORD came down to see the city and the tower being built
6 by the children of men. The LORD said, "If, as one people with one language, they have
7 begun to do this, nothing they plan to do will be impossible for them. Let us go down and
8 confuse their language so that one will not understand the speech of another." From there
the LORD scattered them all over the earth, and they abandoned the building of the city.
9 That is why it was called Bavel, because it was there that the LORD confused[1] the language
of all the earth; and from there the LORD scattered them all across the face of the earth.

1 | The name Bavel ("Babylon") resonates with *balal* ("confused").

UNLOCKING THE TEXT

- Does "the whole world spoke the same language" contradict the previous section that spoke of seagoing nations each having its "own language"?
- What is the difference between speaking "the same language" and "the same words"?
- Why were the people migrating eastward?
- Why does the Torah go into detail about how they created the bricks for building?
- What was the motivation behind the building project?
- How will this project prevent them from being "scattered across the face of the earth"?
- Why was God fearful of their unity?
- Who is the us of "Let us go down and confuse their language"?
- Why did God disperse them and confuse their languages?
- What was the sin of the builders of the Tower of Bavel?

FINDING YOURSELF IN THE TEXT

- Do you speak any other languages apart from your mother tongue? Do you see a value in this?
- Do you enjoy interacting with people culturally different from you or do you find it stressful?
- Do you think the world would be a better or worse place if everyone spoke the same language?

Consider using these questions as the basis for your own commentary or creative midrash.

How does reflecting on these firsthand experiences help you better understand the text?

יא א ב וַיְהִי כָל־הָאָרֶץ שָׂפָה אֶחָת וּדְבָרִים אֲחָדִים: וַיְהִי בְּנָסְעָם מִקֶּדֶם וַיִּמְצְאוּ ט שביעי
ג בִקְעָה בְּאֶרֶץ שִׁנְעָר וַיֵּשְׁבוּ שָׁם: וַיֹּאמְרוּ אִישׁ אֶל־רֵעֵהוּ הָבָה נִלְבְּנָה לְבֵנִים
ד וְנִשְׂרְפָה לִשְׂרֵפָה וַתְּהִי לָהֶם הַלְּבֵנָה לְאָבֶן וְהַחֵמָר הָיָה לָהֶם לַחֹמֶר: וַיֹּאמְרוּ
הָבָה ׀ נִבְנֶה־לָּנוּ עִיר וּמִגְדָּל וְרֹאשׁוֹ בַשָּׁמַיִם וְנַעֲשֶׂה־לָּנוּ שֵׁם פֶּן־נָפוּץ עַל־פְּנֵי
ה כָל־הָאָרֶץ: וַיֵּרֶד יהוה לִרְאֹת אֶת־הָעִיר וְאֶת־הַמִּגְדָּל אֲשֶׁר בָּנוּ בְּנֵי הָאָדָם:
ו וַיֹּאמֶר יהוה הֵן עַם אֶחָד וְשָׂפָה אַחַת לְכֻלָּם וְזֶה הַחִלָּם לַעֲשׂוֹת וְעַתָּה לֹא־יִבָּצֵר
ז מֵהֶם כֹּל אֲשֶׁר יָזְמוּ לַעֲשׂוֹת: הָבָה נֵרְדָה וְנָבְלָה שָׁם שְׂפָתָם אֲשֶׁר לֹא יִשְׁמְעוּ
ח אִישׁ שְׂפַת רֵעֵהוּ: וַיָּפֶץ יהוה אֹתָם מִשָּׁם עַל־פְּנֵי כָל־הָאָרֶץ וַיַּחְדְּלוּ לִבְנֹת הָעִיר:
ט עַל־כֵּן קָרָא שְׁמָהּ בָּבֶל כִּי־שָׁם בָּלַל יהוה שְׂפַת כָּל־הָאָרֶץ וּמִשָּׁם הֱפִיצָם יהוה
עַל־פְּנֵי כָּל־הָאָרֶץ:

THEMES | ETHICS | GOD | FREE WILL, REWARD AND PUNISHMENT

Episode 13: *The Tower of Bavel* – Bereshit 11:1–9

SUMMARY

By this time, most of the world is filled with plants and animals, but it remains empty of humans. Since people can settle wherever they please, there is no need for wars. There is still no conceptual distance or sense of alienation between cultures, and unfettered collaboration leads to swift technological progress. God responds to this effort by dispersing humankind all over the earth.

THE ART OF MIDRASH

The Tower of Babel
Pieter Bruegel the Elder (1563)

Analysis

- Which elements of this image are directly mentioned in the text?
- Which elements of this image are not found in the text?
- What midrashic interpretation is the artist giving us?

A QUESTION OF BIBLIODRAMA

THE BUILDERS OF THE TOWER OF BAVEL

- How did you know how to make bricks and build?
- What was your purpose in building this tower?
- Was there unanimous agreement to initiate this building project and how to achieve it?
- Why were you worried about being scattered across the face of the earth?
- How did it feel when you could no longer understand the people around you?

TO GOD

- What were Your fears from this building project?
- Could You see any positives in this initiative?
- Why did You choose to disperse humanity and diversify its languages?

The tower or ziggurat was the great symbol of the ancient Mesopotamian city-states of the lower Tigris-Euphrates valley, the cradle of civilization. It was there that human beings first settled, established agriculture, and built cities.

As the Torah makes clear with unusual attention to what seems like a peripheral fact, one of the great discoveries of Mesopotamia (along with the wheel, the arch, and the calendar) was the ability to manufacture building materials, especially bricks made by pouring clay into molds, drying it in the sun, and eventually firing it in kilns. This made possible the construction of buildings on a larger scale and reaching greater heights than hitherto. From this grew the ziggurat, a stepped building of many stories, which came to have profound religious significance.

Essentially these towers – of which the remains of at least thirty have been discovered – were man-made "holy mountains," the mountain being the place where heaven and earth most visibly meet. Inscriptions on several of these buildings, decoded by archaeologists, refer, as does the Torah, to the idea that their top "reaches heaven": "And they said: 'Come, let us build us a city, and a tower, with its top in heaven'" (Bereshit 11:4). The largest – the great ziggurat of Babylon to which the Torah refers – was a structure of seven stories, three hundred feet high, on a base of roughly the same dimensions.

Rabbi Jonathan Sacks

Analysis

- What areas of understanding of human nature and society do we now have that were unavailable to classical Jewish commentators? How can they aid our understanding of the text?
- What can we learn from this passage to help us understand the text?
- What further questions on the text do you have now that you have read this new take on the story?

INTEGRATING
ḤOKHMA

An ancient ziggurat in Iraq

the heart of the passage. The people's enduring "name" depends on their staying "there," in the city that they intend to build.

As we continue to follow the trail of these guiding words, we find that curiously, the word "city," *ir*, recurs more often than the word "tower" (*migdal*), despite the title frequently bestowed on this passage, "The Tower of Bavel." Later events support the primacy of the city in this tale. For one thing, God obstructs the building of the city, but makes no reference at all to the tower (11:8). For another, the narrative affixes a pejorative name to the city, even as the tower escapes a negative label: "Therefore He called its name Bavel, because there the Lord confused the language of all the earth" (v. 9). The passage's emphasis on the city suggests a preference by the builders, later repudiated by God, for horizontal rather than vertical construction. It is primarily the city, and not the tower, that acts as a central component in their effort to achieve geographic consolidation.

The passage's guiding words suggest a stylistic foundation for a basic plot line, in which a group of people seek unity and permanence through the building of a city. In addition, these words assure readers that a sin has, in fact, been committed. Traditional biblical commentators detect an elaborate quid pro quo, in which each of the people's words and actions are met with divine retorts.

The people, referred to in the passage's opening as all the earth, *kol haaretz*, are of one language, *safa*; God later confuses the language of all the earth, *sefat kol haaretz*. The people call to one another, *ish el re'ehu*, to begin building; God confuses them so that they may not understand one another's speech, *ish sefat re'ehu*. The people summon each other to action with the words "Come let us make bricks," *Hava nilbena*; God's call for reaction is "Come let us go down," *Hava nereda*, and confuse their language there. The people's greatest fear is "lest we be scattered over the face of the whole earth," *p-v-tz al penei kol haaretz*; God responds as He scatters them over the face of all the earth, *p-v-tz al penei kol haaretz*. Finally, this literary action and reaction reaches its crescendo in the passage's stinging conclusion, which offers a literary response to the people's desire to make a name for themselves.

A structural analysis of this passage, then, makes a compelling case for reading it as a tale of cause and effect, misdeed and punishment. Yet, as we have seen, a reading that takes its cues from the guiding words suggests that the people of Bavel enjoyed an unusual degree of unity. These two notions seem to be at odds. If the people lived in such great harmony, where is the sin? Should God not congratulate humanity on its rare state of oneness rather than condemn it? On the road to the subversive sequel, we must find a nexus between humanity's unity and God's anger. In search of this meeting point, we turn to the classical biblical exegetes.

Judy Klitsner

TAKING A LITERARY APPROACH

With a close reading of the Bavel narrative, paying keen attention to its structure and style, we can appreciate the linguistic artistry of this passage. Terse in its narration, this passage omits descriptive adjectives and even the names of its characters. Its most basic premise shrouds itself in ambiguous brevity; God has been affronted, but the text withholds the details of the offense.

Yet along with this stylistic economy, the passage indulges in lavish redundancy, repeating specific words and phrases with remarkable frequency. The phrase *kol haaretz*, "all the earth," appears five times; the word *safa*, "language," appears five times; the root *b-n-h*, "to build," appears three times; the word *ir*, "city," appears three times; the root *p-v-tz*, "to spread out," appears three times; the word *shem*, "name," appears twice, with the identical consonantal construct *sham*, "there," appearing five times, for a total of seven. The feminine and masculine forms for "one," *eḥad* and *aḥat*, appear four times.

These repetitions might be taken to reveal unimaginative writing that could be easily remedied with a sprinkling of synonyms. For instance, the Hebrew root *p-v-tz*, "to scatter," recurs three times in these nine verses, even though a reasonable alternative appears in the verse immediately preceding the passage: *ume'ela nifredu hagoyim*, "from these the nations branched out" (Bereshit 10:32). The Bible frequently employs diversified language; why here does it fail to do so?

In this case, repetition is not an absence of style but a style in itself. The Bible frequently appoints and repeats a particular "guiding word," or *leitwort*, to use Martin Buber's term, by means of which it conveys its perspectives in subtle ways, "making a meaning available without articulating it explicitly." The many guiding words in this passage combine to suggest a strong focus on the human drive for indivisibility. The people begin as one, and invest enormous efforts in safeguarding their unity, fearing that if they do not do so, they will be scattered throughout the earth. A closer look at the repeated words and phrases reveals the ways in which language encodes the people's goals:

Kol haaretz, safa, eḥad (aḥat), p-v-tz ("all the earth," "language," "one," "scatter"): The people's oneness in speech and geography contributes to an unusual degree of unity. The people are referred to as the singular unit "all the earth," whose greatest fear is falling into the antithetical mode of being scattered "over the face of all the earth."

Ir, b-n-h ("city," "build"): These words further highlight the people's belief that their geographic consolidation guarantees their unity. In their desperation to remain together, the people build a city – using the building materials *ḥomer* and *leveinim*, mortar and bricks – hoping that doing so will shield them from dispersal.

Hava ("come let us"): *Hava* is a public call to action. In this story, no one acts alone. These unnamed, undifferentiated people call out for a cooperative effort. The adjunct *pen*, "lest," makes the threat emphatic: we had better unite, *lest* the dreaded dispersal occur.

Shem, sham ("name," "there"): By their act of collective building, the people hope to prevent their scattering, and to create a "name," a sense of permanence, perhaps even immortality. Together, these identically constructed words are the passage's most oft-repeated, and, as such, have particular power to guide toward

10 These are the descendants of Shem. When Shem was one hundred years old, he had a
11 son, Arpakhshad, two years after the flood. After Arpakhshad was born, Shem lived five
12 hundred years and had other sons and daughters. When Arpakhshad was thirty-
13 five years old, he had a son, Shelaḥ. After Shelaḥ was born, Arpakhshad lived four hundred
14 and three years and had other sons and daughters. When Shelaḥ was thirty years
15 old, he had a son, Ever. After Ever was born, Shelaḥ lived four hundred and three years and
16 had other sons and daughters. Ever lived thirty-four years and then had a son,
17 Peleg. After Peleg was born, Ever lived four hundred and thirty years and had other sons and
18 19 daughters. Peleg lived thirty years and then had a son, Reu. After Reu was born,
20 Peleg lived two hundred and nine years and had other sons and daughters. Reu
21 lived thirty-two years and then had a son, Serug. After Serug was born, Reu lived two
22 hundred and seven years and had other sons and daughters. Serug lived thirty
23 years and then had a son, Naḥor. After Naḥor was born, Serug lived two hundred years
24 and had other sons and daughters. Naḥor lived twenty-nine years and then had
25 a son, Teraḥ. After Teraḥ was born, Naḥor lived one hundred and nineteen years and had

UNLOCKING THE TEXT

- Why does the Torah revisit the list of Noaḥ's descendants?
- Why does this list only focus on the descendants of Noaḥ's son Shem?
- Why does this list focus on the life spans and age when the next-in-line is born?
- Why does the list end with Teraḥ?
- Why does the Torah include here some narrative details about the lives of Teraḥ and his children?
- How and why did Haran die?
- Why was Sarai barren?
- Why did Teraḥ leave with his family toward the land of Canaan?
- Why did they stop their journey short in Ḥaran?
- Is this the same journey we read about in the next episode? If so, was it initiated by Teraḥ, Avram, or God?

FINDING YOURSELF IN THE TEXT

- Have you continued (or do you intend to continue) in the path of your parents?
- Can you imagine a time when your children will continue what you started?
- How important is family to you?

Consider using these questions as the basis for your own commentary or creative midrash.

How does reflecting on these firsthand experiences help you better understand the text?

אֵ֣לֶּה תּֽוֹלְדֹ֣ת שֵׁ֔ם שֵׁ֚ם בֶּן־מְאַ֣ת שָׁנָ֔ה וַיּ֖וֹלֶד אֶת־אַרְפַּכְשָׁ֑ד שְׁנָתַ֖יִם אַחַ֥ר י

הַמַּבּֽוּל: וַֽיְחִי־שֵׁ֗ם אַֽחֲרֵי֙ הֽוֹלִיד֣וֹ אֶת־אַרְפַּכְשָׁ֔ד חֲמֵ֥שׁ מֵא֖וֹת שָׁנָ֑ה וַיּ֥וֹלֶד בָּנִ֖ים יא

וּבָנֽוֹת: וְאַרְפַּכְשַׁ֣ד חַ֔י חָמֵ֥שׁ וּשְׁלֹשִׁ֖ים שָׁנָ֑ה וַיּ֖וֹלֶד אֶת־שָֽׁלַח: וַֽיְחִ֣י יב יג

אַרְפַּכְשַׁ֗ד אַֽחֲרֵי֙ הֽוֹלִיד֣וֹ אֶת־שֶׁ֔לַח שָׁלֹ֣שׁ שָׁנִ֔ים וְאַרְבַּ֥ע מֵא֖וֹת שָׁנָ֑ה וַיּ֥וֹלֶד

בָּנִ֖ים וּבָנֽוֹת: וְשֶׁ֥לַח חַ֖י שְׁלֹשִׁ֣ים שָׁנָ֑ה וַיּ֖וֹלֶד אֶת־עֵֽבֶר: וַֽיְחִי־ יד טו

שֶׁ֗לַח אַֽחֲרֵי֙ הֽוֹלִיד֣וֹ אֶת־עֵ֔בֶר שָׁלֹ֣שׁ שָׁנִ֔ים וְאַרְבַּ֥ע מֵא֖וֹת שָׁנָ֑ה וַיּ֥וֹלֶד בָּנִ֖ים

וּבָנֽוֹת: וַֽיְחִי־עֵ֕בֶר אַרְבַּ֥ע וּשְׁלֹשִׁ֖ים שָׁנָ֑ה וַיּ֖וֹלֶד אֶת־פָּֽלֶג: וַֽיְחִי־ טז יז

עֵ֗בֶר אַֽחֲרֵי֙ הֽוֹלִיד֣וֹ אֶת־פֶּ֔לֶג שְׁלֹשִׁ֣ים שָׁנָ֔ה וְאַרְבַּ֥ע מֵא֖וֹת שָׁנָ֑ה וַיּ֥וֹלֶד בָּנִ֖ים

וּבָנֽוֹת: וַֽיְחִי־פֶ֕לֶג שְׁלֹשִׁ֖ים שָׁנָ֑ה וַיּ֖וֹלֶד אֶת־רְעֽוּ: וַֽיְחִי־פֶ֗לֶג אַֽחֲרֵי֙ הֽוֹלִיד֣וֹ יח יט

אֶת־רְע֔וּ תֵּ֥שַׁע שָׁנִ֖ים וּמָאתַ֣יִם שָׁנָ֑ה וַיּ֥וֹלֶד בָּנִ֖ים וּבָנֽוֹת: וַֽיְחִ֣י רְע֔וּ כ

שְׁתַּ֥יִם וּשְׁלֹשִׁ֖ים שָׁנָ֑ה וַיּ֖וֹלֶד אֶת־שְׂרֽוּג: וַֽיְחִ֣י רְע֗וּ אַֽחֲרֵי֙ הֽוֹלִיד֣וֹ אֶת־שְׂר֔וּג כא

שֶׁ֥בַע שָׁנִ֖ים וּמָאתַ֣יִם שָׁנָ֑ה וַיּ֥וֹלֶד בָּנִ֖ים וּבָנֽוֹת: וַֽיְחִ֣י שְׂר֔וּג שְׁלֹשִׁ֖ים כב

שָׁנָ֑ה וַיּ֖וֹלֶד אֶת־נָחֽוֹר: וַֽיְחִ֣י שְׂר֗וּג אַֽחֲרֵי֙ הֽוֹלִיד֣וֹ אֶת־נָחוֹר֙ מָאתַ֣יִם שָׁנָ֑ה וַיּ֥וֹלֶד כג

בָּנִ֖ים וּבָנֽוֹת: וַֽיְחִ֣י נָח֔וֹר תֵּ֥שַׁע וְעֶשְׂרִ֖ים שָׁנָ֑ה וַיּ֖וֹלֶד אֶת־תָּֽרַח: וַֽיְחִ֣י כד כה

נָח֗וֹר אַֽחֲרֵי֙ הֽוֹלִיד֣וֹ אֶת־תֶּ֔רַח תְּשַֽׁע־עֶשְׂרֵ֥ה שָׁנָ֖ה וּמְאַ֣ת שָׁנָ֑ה וַיּ֥וֹלֶד בָּנִ֖ים

| THEMES | RELATIONSHIPS AND LOVE | THE JEWISH NATIONAL MISSION | THE LAND OF ISRAEL |

Episode 14: *Noaḥ's Family Tree, Continued* – Bereshit 11:10–32

SUMMARY

This section provides a brief historical account covering many generations, which leads to the heroes of the biblical narrative. Within nine generations the Torah describes the transition from Shem to Teraḥ. Teraḥ has three sons, Avram, Naḥor, and Haran. Haran dies, leaving behind Lot, Milka, and Yiska as orphans. Avram marries Sarai, who is barren, and Naḥor marries Milka. Teraḥ moves the family from Ur Kasdim intending to go to Canaan, but ends up in Ḥaran, where he eventually dies.

26 other sons and daughters. Teraḥ lived seventy years and fathered Avram, Naḥor,
27 and Haran. These are the descendants of Teraḥ. Teraḥ was the father of Avram, Naḥor, and
28 Haran, and Haran had a son, Lot. While his father Teraḥ was still alive, Haran died in the
29 land of his birth, Ur Kasdim. Avram and Naḥor married; the name of Avram's wife was
Sarai, and the name of Naḥor's wife was Milka. She was the daughter of Haran, father of
30 31 Milka and Yiska. And Sarai was barren – she had no child. Teraḥ took his son Avram, and
his grandson Lot, son of Haran, and his daughter-in-law Sarai, his son Avram's wife, and
together they set out from Ur Kasdim to go to the land of Canaan. But when they arrived
32 at Ḥaran, they settled there. Teraḥ lived two hundred and five years, and he died in Ḥaran.

THE ART OF MIDRASH

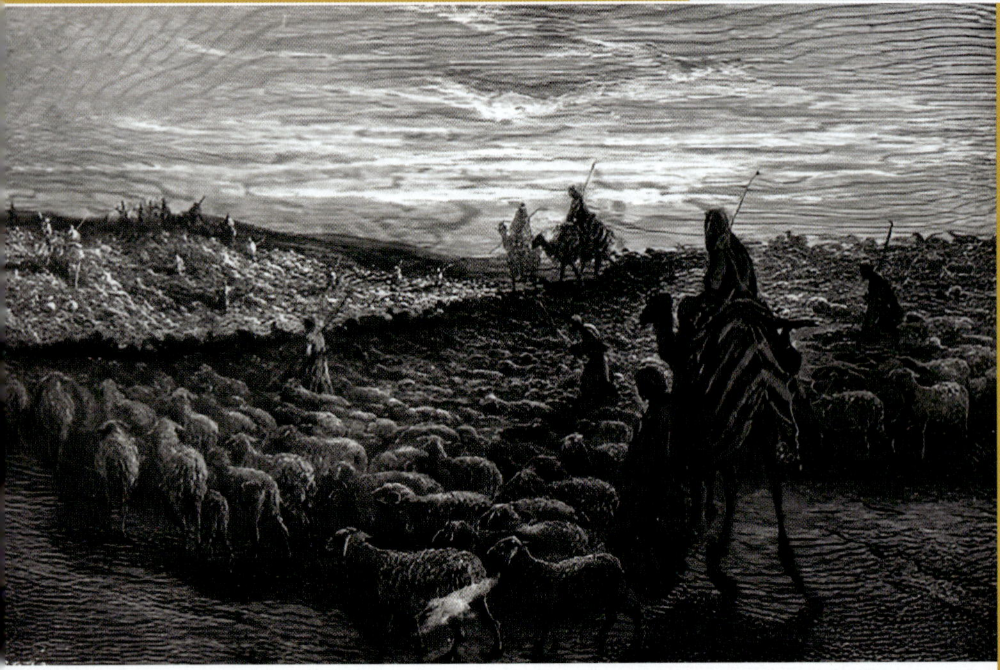

Abraham Journeying into the Land of Canaan
Gustave Doré (1866)

Analysis

- Which elements of this image are directly mentioned in the text?
- Which elements of this image are not found in the text?
- What midrashic interpretation is the artist giving us?

כו וַיְחִי־תֶ֗רַח שִׁבְעִ֣ים שָׁנָ֔ה וַיּ֙וֹלֶד֙ אֶת־אַבְרָ֔ם אֶת־נָח֖וֹר וְאֶת־
     וּבָנֽוֹת:
כז הָרָֽן: וְאֵ֙לֶּה֙ תּוֹלְדֹ֣ת תֶּ֔רַח תֶּ֚רַח הוֹלִ֣יד אֶת־אַבְרָ֔ם אֶת־נָח֖וֹר וְאֶת־הָרָ֑ן
כח הוֹלִ֥יד אֶת־לֽוֹט: וַיָּ֣מָת הָרָ֗ן עַל־פְּנֵי֙ תֶּ֣רַח אָבִ֔יו בְּאֶ֖רֶץ מוֹלַדְתּ֑וֹ בְּא֖וּר כַּשְׂדִּֽים:
כט וַיִּקַּ֨ח אַבְרָ֧ם וְנָח֛וֹר לָהֶ֖ם נָשִׁ֑ים שֵׁ֤ם אֵֽשֶׁת־אַבְרָם֙ שָׂרָ֔י וְשֵׁ֤ם אֵֽשֶׁת־נָחוֹר֙ מִלְכָּ֔ה   מפטיר
ל בַּת־הָרָ֥ן אֲבִֽי־מִלְכָּ֖ה וַאֲבִ֥י יִסְכָּֽה: וַתְּהִ֥י שָׂרַ֖י עֲקָרָ֑ה אֵ֥ין לָ֖הּ וָלָֽד: וַיִּקַּ֨ח תֶּ֜רַח
לא אֶת־אַבְרָ֣ם בְּנ֗וֹ וְאֶת־ל֤וֹט בֶּן־הָרָן֙ בֶּן־בְּנ֔וֹ וְאֵת֙ שָׂרַ֣י כַּלָּת֔וֹ אֵ֖שֶׁת אַבְרָ֣ם בְּנ֑וֹ
לב וַיֵּצְא֙וּ אִתָּ֜ם מֵא֣וּר כַּשְׂדִּ֗ים לָלֶ֙כֶת֙ אַ֣רְצָה כְּנַ֔עַן וַיָּבֹ֥אוּ עַד־חָרָ֖ן וַיֵּ֥שְׁבוּ שָֽׁם: וַיִּהְי֣וּ
     יְמֵי־תֶ֗רַח חָמֵ֥שׁ שָׁנִ֛ים וּמָאתַ֖יִם שָׁנָ֑ה וַיָּ֥מָת תֶּ֖רַח בְּחָרָֽן:

INTEGRATING
ḤOKHMA

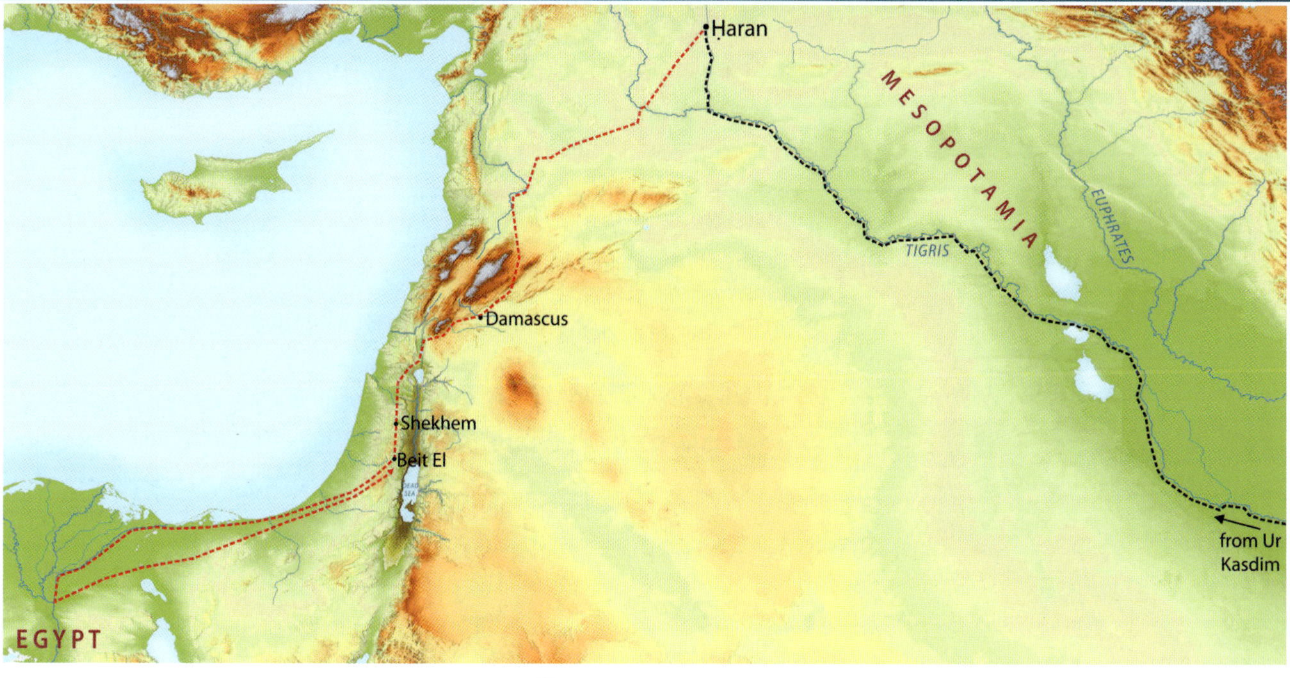

Avraham's journey to the land

TAKING A LITERARY APPROACH

The lineage of Shem is chronicled twice. The first time it is included in the listing commonly known as the Table of Nations. Like his brothers, Shem also has descendants from whom emerge many of the families of Man. The second iteration of Shem's line, however, is quite different. It is headlined by its own *toledot*, it provides us with ten generations of descendants (as opposed to a maximum of four generations for his two brothers), and most significantly, the Torah lists the life spans of each central figure as well as his age when the next-in-line is born. Cross-referencing the two genealogical listings of Shem provides clues for the timing of the Great Dispersion in Bavel.

In the first manifest of Shem we are told that Peleg, the fourth generation from Shem, received his name because "in his days the land was divided (*niflega*)." This is a reference to none other than the central event of the second ten generations of humanity, the division of the people into distinct nations and languages. Why did Peleg, of all people, bear this name? There are two likely possibilities: the event coincided with his birth or it coincided with his death. It is highly unlikely that a mere four generations after the *mabul* there would be enough people to be split into seventy nations. Most likely, then, is that the event is coterminous with Peleg's death.

The second genealogy of Shem puts Peleg's death at 340 years after the *mabul*. Peleg's place in the parallel description of the descendants of Shem contributes a chronological reference to the story. The significance of that chronology, however, is not merely for establishing a biblical version of history. The Bible is not concerned with history as a record of events, it is interested in understanding what those events mean in the larger scheme of man's relationship with God, and how any story interacts with the rest of the biblical narrative – that is, how other stories affect our understanding of this one, and how this one impacts on our understanding of other biblical narratives. If indeed the dispersion occurs with Peleg's death, then according to that chronology Avram is alive at that time! In fact, he would have been forty-eight years old, and fully aware of the events.

The genealogical lists provide a rich picture of the Bible's conceptual presentation of the pre-history of humanity. With the interpolation of the story of Bavel, that pre-history is infused with even greater meaning. God's initial attempt to establish a relationship with humanity falls short because there are insufficient guidelines. Absent a code to direct their behavior, people degenerate into chaos, and take the rest of the world with them. When God starts again, He provides them with the basic protocols, but in their overreaction to the chaos which reigned pre-flood, they establish so much order that they crush the very humanity they were trying to protect.

With the boundaries of abuse clearly established on both ends of the spectrum, God is prepared to try again. Perhaps the third attempt, with the new modifications God will make, will yield a better result.

Rabbi Zvi Grumet

לך לך
Lekh Lekha

Parasha Overview

In response to the call of God, Avram and Sarai begin their journey to a new land and a new kind of faith, which will become the context of the entire Jewish drama thereafter. There are initial setbacks. There is a famine, and they have to leave. There is a quarrel between Avram and his nephew Lot, and they part. Lot is captured in a local war, and Avram has to fight a battle to free him. God makes a covenant with Avram, who remains childless. He has a son by Sarai's handmaid Hagar, but God tells him this is not the heir to the covenant. The sign of the covenant is circumcision.

Episodes

15.	**Avram's Journey**	12:1–9
16.	**Avram's Time in Egypt**	12:10–20
17.	**Avram and Lot in Canaan**	13:1–18
18.	**Avram Goes to War**	14:1–24
19.	**Brit bein HaBetarim**	15:1–21
20.	**The Birth of Yishmael**	16:1–16
21.	**Brit Mila**	17:1–27

Parasha Stats

- 6,336 letters
- 1,686 words
- 126 verses
- 208 lines in a sefer Torah
- 1 mitzva

12 1 The Lord said to Avram, "Go – from your land, your birthplace, and your father's house LEKH LEKHA
2 – to the land that I will show you. I will make you a great nation, and I will bless you
3 and make your name great. You will become a blessing. And I will bless those who bless
you, and those who curse you I will curse. And through you, all the families of the earth
4 will be blessed." So Avram went, as the Lord had told him, and with him went Lot.
5 Avram was seventy-five years old when he left Ḥaran. Avram took Sarai his wife, and
Lot his nephew, and all the wealth they had acquired and the people they had gathered
6 in Ḥaran. They set out to go to the land of Canaan, and they entered the land of Canaan.
Avram traveled through the land to the region of Shekhem, to the Oak of Moreh. The
7 Canaanites were then in the land. Then the Lord appeared to Avram and said, "To
your descendants I will give this land." There he built an altar to the Lord, who had
8 appeared to him. And from there he moved on to the hills east of Beit El, and pitched
his tent with Beit El to the west and Ai to the east. There he built an altar to the Lord
9 and called on the name of the Lord. Then Avram journeyed on, traveling toward the
Negev.

UNLOCKING THE TEXT

- Who is Avram? Why is he chosen for this task?
- How will the world be blessed through Avram?
- Who is Sarai? What role will she play?
- Who is Lot? Why did he come along? Where is the rest of the family?
- Who else was in the entourage? Where did they come from?
- Where did Avram's wealth come from?
- Why this route? What was Avram's destination?

Consider using these questions as the basis for your own commentary or creative midrash.

FINDING YOURSELF IN THE TEXT

- Have you ever had to make a new start and leave everything you knew before behind? How did this feel? What was most challenging?
- Have you ever had to trust someone else as they made a decision about your life? Was this difficult? What did you learn from this experience?
- Has anyone ever promised you that something will happen in the future, and you weren't convinced? How did you manage your expectations and deal with the potential for disappointment?

How does reflecting on these firsthand experiences help you better understand the text?

יב א וַיֹּאמֶר יהוה אֶל־אַבְרָם לֶךְ־לְךָ מֵאַרְצְךָ וּמִמּוֹלַדְתְּךָ וּמִבֵּית אָבִיךָ אֶל־הָאָרֶץ י לך לך
ב ג אֲשֶׁר אַרְאֶךָּ׃ וְאֶעֶשְׂךָ לְגוֹי גָּדוֹל וַאֲבָרֶכְךָ וַאֲגַדְּלָה שְׁמֶךָ וֶהְיֵה בְּרָכָה׃ וַאֲבָרְכָה
ד מְבָרְכֶיךָ וּמְקַלֶּלְךָ אָאֹר וְנִבְרְכוּ בְךָ כֹּל מִשְׁפְּחֹת הָאֲדָמָה׃ וַיֵּלֶךְ אַבְרָם כַּאֲשֶׁר
דִּבֶּר אֵלָיו יהוה וַיֵּלֶךְ אִתּוֹ לוֹט וְאַבְרָם בֶּן־חָמֵשׁ שָׁנִים וְשִׁבְעִים שָׁנָה בְּצֵאתוֹ
ה מֵחָרָן׃ וַיִּקַּח אַבְרָם אֶת־שָׂרַי אִשְׁתּוֹ וְאֶת־לוֹט בֶּן־אָחִיו וְאֶת־כָּל־רְכוּשָׁם אֲשֶׁר
רָכָשׁוּ וְאֶת־הַנֶּפֶשׁ אֲשֶׁר־עָשׂוּ בְחָרָן וַיֵּצְאוּ לָלֶכֶת אַרְצָה כְּנַעַן וַיָּבֹאוּ אַרְצָה כְּנָעַן׃
ו ז וַיַּעֲבֹר אַבְרָם בָּאָרֶץ עַד מְקוֹם שְׁכֶם עַד אֵלוֹן מוֹרֶה וְהַכְּנַעֲנִי אָז בָּאָרֶץ׃ וַיֵּרָא יהוה
אֶל־אַבְרָם וַיֹּאמֶר לְזַרְעֲךָ אֶתֵּן אֶת־הָאָרֶץ הַזֹּאת וַיִּבֶן שָׁם מִזְבֵּחַ לַיהוה הַנִּרְאֶה
ח אֵלָיו׃ וַיַּעְתֵּק מִשָּׁם הָהָרָה מִקֶּדֶם לְבֵית־אֵל וַיֵּט אָהֳלֹה בֵּית־אֵל מִיָּם וְהָעַי מִקֶּדֶם
ט וַיִּבֶן־שָׁם מִזְבֵּחַ לַיהוה וַיִּקְרָא בְּשֵׁם יהוה׃ וַיִּסַּע אַבְרָם הָלוֹךְ וְנָסוֹעַ הַנֶּגְבָּה׃

THEMES	THE JEWISH NATIONAL MISSION	THE LAND OF ISRAEL	COVENANT

Episode 15: *Avram's Journey* – Bereshit 12:1–9

SUMMARY

In this episode, we see Avram continue his journey away from his birthplace, Ur Kasdim, this time at the command of God, who tells him to go to an unnamed land that he will be shown. The Torah reveals almost nothing about Avram's youth and early life, other than a few basic details such as the names of his father and family members, his place of birth, and the fact that his family set out in the direction of Canaan before stopping in Ḥaran. In fact, the account of Avram's selection by God appears with absolutely no description of his character. This stands in sharp contrast to Noaḥ, who is defined as "righteous" and "wholehearted" (6:9), explaining why he was chosen to continue the human race.

THE ART OF MIDRASH

Lech Lecha, Yoram Raanan (2014)

Analysis

- Which elements of this image are directly mentioned in the text?
- Which elements of this image are not found in the text?
- What midrashic interpretation is the artist giving us?

A QUESTION OF BIBLIODRAMA

TO AVRAM

- Is this the first time God has spoken to you?
- If not, can you tell me about previous occasions?
- If so, were you ready for it or did you find it overwhelming?
- Was God as you had imagined?
- What emotions did you experience...
  - when you heard the command to leave your birthplace to an unknown destination?
  - after many days of travel?
  - when you finally arrived in Canaan?

TO SARAI

- Why are you on this journey? What did Avram say to convince you to join him?
- How did you respond when Avram told you about this plan?
- What emotions did you experience when you reached the land?

TO GOD

- Why did You choose Avram for this role?
- What is this role?
- What role do You foresee Sarai playing in Your plan?

TO LOT

- Why are you on this journey?
- How do you feel about your uncle and aunt?
- How do you feel about the God that spoke to Avram?

TO THE SOULS MADE IN ḤARAN

- Why did you make this journey?
- What did Avram and Sarai say to convince you?

TAKING A LITERARY APPROACH

The source of the term "the land of Israel" (*Eretz Yisrael*) as it is used today – as the land that was promised, consecrated, and designated for the people of Israel – is in the words of *Ḥazal*. Nowhere is it used in this sense in the Torah. In those places where the term is found in the Torah, it means "the land of the people of Israel," the land in which Israel actually dwells. As such, the term "the land of Israel" in Biblical Hebrew has no special religious, moral, or conceptual weight – it is equivalent to "the land of Moav," "the land of Edom," "the land of the Philistines," and the like. In the Torah, this expression is not found at all, not even in the sense of the land in which the Israelites live, because the Israelites did not yet live there. In the meantime, it is the land of the Canaanites and the other nations who actually lived there.

On the other hand, we find in Biblical Hebrew, and especially in the Torah, another term, which indeed bears the special weight that would later be borne by the term "the land of Israel" in the wording of *Ḥazal* and in Modern Hebrew, in the sense of its special sanctity. I refer here to the term "the land" (*haaretz*) – with the definite article (the letter *heh*) – the land that is known, chosen, designated, and promised to Israel.

What is more, the term "the land" – the Promised Land – represents in miniature "the land" in the sense of the entire earth. Originally "the land" referred to the entire earth (Bereshit 1:1); man in general was created to inherit it, and to fulfill his mission in it (1:28). Eventually, "this land" was chosen from the entire earth, and Avraham was chosen from among all of mankind. As soon as Avraham was chosen, he was sent to the Promised Land to fulfill the mission of "the way of the Lord, to do justice and judgment" (18:19). Therefore, when *Ḥazal* used the term "the land of Israel," they referred to what the Torah called "the land" or "this land" – "To your seed I will give this land" (12:7).

"The land of Canaan" which was mentioned in verse 5 is not the natural and absolute possession of the Canaanites living there; rather, like "the land"/the whole earth, it is in God's hands to give away, and the Canaanites' settlement in the land is only temporary, only as long as God wishes it to be theirs. When we re-examine the verse, we immediately see the importance of this distinction: Indeed, Avraham goes to the land "as the Lord had spoken to him" (12:4), and thus begins the special chapter of Avraham and his descendants, whose spiritual mission is connected to this land and its role in the world. But the journey to "the land of Canaan" in the natural-human sense began with Teraḥ, rather than with Avraham (11:31).

Rabbi Yoel Bin-Nun

INTEGRATING ḤOKHMA

Avraham's journeys

Analysis

- What specific information do we now have that was unavailable to classical Jewish commentators? How can it aid our understanding of the text?
- What can we learn from this map that can help us understand the text?
- What further questions on the text do you have now that you have seen this map?

10 There was a famine in the land. Avram went down to Egypt to stay there for a while
11 because the famine in the land was severe. And as his arrival in Egypt drew close, he said
12 to Sarai his wife, "I know what a beautiful woman you are. When the Egyptians see you,
13 they will say, 'She is his wife'; they will kill me and keep you alive. Please: say you are my
sister. Then I will be treated well for your sake, and because of you my life will be spared."
14 When Avram came to Egypt, the Egyptians saw the woman, saw that she was very beautiful
15 indeed. And when Pharaoh's officials saw her, they praised her to Pharaoh, and the woman
16 was taken into Pharaoh's palace. He treated Avram well for her sake: he acquired flocks,
17 herds, donkeys, male and female servants, she-donkeys, and camels. But the Lord struck
18 Pharaoh and his household with terrible afflictions because of Avram's wife Sarai. Pharaoh
summoned Avram and said, "What have you done to me? Why did you not tell me she
19 was your wife? Why did you say 'She is my sister,' so that I took her as a wife? Now – here
20 is your wife. Take her. Go." Pharaoh gave orders to his men about him, and they sent him
on his way, together with his wife and all that he had.

UNLOCKING THE TEXT

- If God wanted Avram to be in the land of Israel, why was there a famine in the land when he arrived, forcing him to leave?
- Did Avram have a plan to keep Sarai safe or was he only concerned with his own safety?
- Why did Avram accept the gifts?
- Is Pharaoh good or bad in this story?
- Why is this story included in the narrative in the Torah?

Consider using these questions as the basis for your own commentary or creative midrash.

FINDING YOURSELF IN THE TEXT

- Have you ever had to adjust your plans because your first plans did not work out the way you had hoped? How did you manage this?
- Have you ever had a dilemma over whether to prioritize your own needs over someone else's? Did you make the right decision? Did Avram?
- Can you think of a time in your life when you feel like God saved the day?

How does reflecting on these firsthand experiences help you better understand the text?

יא וַיְהִ֥י רָעָ֖ב בָּאָ֑רֶץ וַיֵּ֨רֶד אַבְרָ֤ם מִצְרַ֙יְמָה֙ לָג֣וּר שָׁ֔ם כִּֽי־כָבֵ֥ד הָרָעָ֖ב בָּאָֽרֶץ: וַיְהִ֕י כַּאֲשֶׁ֥ר הִקְרִ֖יב לָב֣וֹא מִצְרָ֑יְמָה וַיֹּ֙אמֶר֙ אֶל־שָׂרַ֣י **אִשְׁתּ֔וֹ** הִנֵּה־נָ֣א יָדַ֔עְתִּי כִּ֛י אִשָּׁ֥ה

יב יְפַת־מַרְאֶ֖ה אָֽתְּ: וְהָיָ֗ה כִּֽי־יִרְא֤וּ אֹתָךְ֙ הַמִּצְרִ֔ים וְאָמְר֖וּ **אִשְׁתּ֣וֹ** זֹ֑את וְהָרְג֥וּ אֹתִ֖י

יג וְאֹתָ֥ךְ יְחַיּֽוּ: אִמְרִי־נָ֖א אֲחֹ֣תִי אָ֑תְּ לְמַ֙עַן֙ **יִֽיטַב־לִ֣י** בַעֲבוּרֵ֔ךְ וְחָיְתָ֥ה נַפְשִׁ֖י בִּגְלָלֵֽךְ:

יד שני וַיְהִ֕י כְּב֥וֹא אַבְרָ֖ם מִצְרָ֑יְמָה **וַיִּרְא֤וּ** הַמִּצְרִים֙ אֶת־**הָֽאִשָּׁ֔ה** כִּֽי־יָפָ֥ה הִ֖וא מְאֹֽד: **וַיִּרְא֙וּ**

טו אֹתָ֜הּ שָׂרֵ֣י פַרְעֹ֗ה וַיְהַֽלְל֤וּ אֹתָהּ֙ אֶל־פַּרְעֹ֔ה **וַתֻּקַּ֥ח** **הָֽאִשָּׁ֖ה** בֵּ֥ית פַּרְעֹֽה: וּלְאַבְרָ֖ם

טז הֵיטִ֣יב בַּעֲבוּרָ֑הּ וַֽיְהִי־ל֤וֹ צֹאן־וּבָקָר֙ וַחֲמֹרִ֔ים וַעֲבָדִים֙ וּשְׁפָחֹ֔ת וַאֲתֹנֹ֖ת וּגְמַלִּֽים:

יז וַיְנַגַּ֨ע יְהֹוָ֧ה ׀ אֶת־פַּרְעֹ֛ה נְגָעִ֥ים גְּדֹלִ֖ים וְאֶת־בֵּית֑וֹ עַל־דְּבַ֥ר שָׂרַ֖י **אֵ֥שֶׁת** אַבְרָֽם:

יח וַיִּקְרָ֤א פַרְעֹה֙ לְאַבְרָ֔ם וַיֹּ֕אמֶר מַה־זֹּ֖את עָשִׂ֣יתָ לִּ֑י לָ֚מָּה לֹא־הִגַּ֣דְתָּ לִּ֔י כִּ֥י **אִשְׁתְּךָ֖**

יט הִֽוא: לָמָ֤ה אָמַ֙רְתָּ֙ אֲחֹ֣תִי הִ֔וא וָאֶקַּ֥ח אֹתָ֛הּ לִ֖י לְאִשָּׁ֑ה וְעַתָּ֗ה הִנֵּ֤ה אִשְׁתְּךָ֙ קַ֥ח **וָלֵֽךְ**:

כ וַיְצַ֥ו עָלָ֛יו פַּרְעֹ֖ה אֲנָשִׁ֑ים **וַֽיְשַׁלְּח֥וּ** אֹת֛וֹ וְאֶת־**אִשְׁתּ֖וֹ** וְאֶת־כָּל־אֲשֶׁר־לֽוֹ:

THEMES	EXILE	FREE WILL, REWARD AND PUNISHMENT	RELATIONSHIPS AND LOVE

Episode 16: *Avram in Egypt* – Bereshit 12:10–20

SUMMARY

Although he had received a blessing upon his departure from Ḥaran, Avram encounters many difficulties and challenges when he arrives. He was promised the land of Canaan but cannot continue living there due to famine. Likewise, God had assured him that all the nations would be blessed through him, but then he has to cope with his wife being taken against her will to the house of the king of Egypt.

THE ART OF MIDRASH

Abraham and Sarah at the Court of the Pharaohs
Giovanni Muzzioli (1875)

Analysis

- Which elements of this image are directly mentioned in the text?
- Which elements of this image are not found in the text?
- What midrashic interpretation is the artist giving us?

A QUESTION OF BIBLIODRAMA

TO AVRAM AND SARAI

- What went through your minds when, having finally arrived at the land God had brought you to, you had to immediately leave because of famine? Were you worried you wouldn't return? Did you question God?

TO AVRAM

- What were you feeling when you asked Sarai to hide her relationship with you?
- Were you worried she would be unwilling to do this for you?
- What were you thinking about God at this point?
- Why didn't you ask God what to do?
- How did it feel when Sarai was taken away from you?
- What did you say to Sarai when the episode was over?
- In hindsight, do you regret any of the choices you made in this episode?

TO SARAI

- How did you feel when Avram made this request of you?
- How did you feel toward Avram and God when you were put in this situation?
- What was it like to pretend to be your husband's sister?
- How did it feel to be "seen" by the Egyptians and their princes?
- What would you like to say now to Avram, Pharaoh, and God?

TO GOD

- Why did You create famine in the land of Israel?
- Was the episode with Sarai and Pharaoh part of a bigger plan?
- Why did You punish Pharaoh's house rather than communicate with him in a dream to warn him off Sarai?

TO PHARAOH

- Why did you take Sarai in this way?
- What did you learn from this experience?
- Were you upset at how the story unfolded? Why? Who were you upset with?

else had done so. Such is the power of the pressure to conform: it can lead us to say what we know is untrue.

More frightening still was the Stanford experiment carried out in the early 1970s by Philip Zimbardo. The participants were randomly assigned roles as guards or prisoners in a mock prison. Within days the students cast as guards were behaving abusively, some of them subjecting the "prisoners" to psychological torture. The students cast as prisoners put up with this passively, even siding with the guards against those who resisted. The experiment was called off after six days, by which time even Zimbardo had found himself drawn into the artificial reality he had created. The pressure to conform to assigned roles is strong enough to lead people into doing what they know is wrong.

That is why Avraham, at the start of his mission, was told to leave "his land, his birthplace, and his father's house," to free himself from the pressure to conform. Leaders must be prepared not to follow the consensus. One of the great writers on leadership, Warren Bennis, writes: "By the time we reach puberty, the world has shaped us to a greater extent than we realize. Our family, friends, and society in general have told us – by word and example – how to be. But people begin to become leaders at that moment when they decide for themselves how to be."

One reason why Jews have become, out of all proportion to their numbers, leaders in almost every sphere of human endeavor, is precisely this willingness to be different. Throughout the centuries, Jews have been the most striking example of a group that refused to assimilate to the dominant culture or convert to the dominant faith.

Judaism is the counter-voice in the conversation of humankind. As Jews, we do not follow the majority merely because it is the majority. In age after age, century after century, Jews were prepared to do what the poet Robert Frost immortalized: *Two roads diverged in a wood, and I, I took the one less traveled by, And that has made all the difference.*

Rabbi Jonathan Sacks

Analysis

- What areas of understanding of human nature and society do we now have that were unavailable to classical Jewish commentators? How can they aid our understanding of the text?
- What can we learn from this essay to help us understand the text?
- What further questions on the text do you have now that you have read this new take on the story?

INTEGRATING ḤOKHMA

Avraham is without doubt the most influential person who ever lived. Today he is claimed as the spiritual ancestor of 2.3 billion Christians, 1.8 billion Muslims, and 14 million Jews, more than half the people alive today. Yet he ruled no empire, commanded no great army, performed no miracles, and proclaimed no prophecy. He is the supreme example in all of history of *influence without power*.

Why? Because he was prepared to be different. As the Sages say, he was called *haIvri*, "the Hebrew," because "all the world was on one side (*be'ever eḥad*) and he was on the other."

After the Holocaust, some social scientists were haunted by the question of why so many people were prepared, whether by active participation or silent consent, to go along with a regime that was committing one of the great crimes against humanity. One key experiment was conducted by Solomon Asch. He assembled a group of people, asking them to perform a series of simple cognitive tasks. They were shown two cards, one with a line on it, the other with three lines of different lengths, and asked which was the same size as the line on the first. Unbeknown to one participant, all the others had been briefed by Asch to give the correct answer for the first few cards, and then to answer incorrectly for most of the rest. On a significant number of occasions the experimental subject gave an answer he could see was wrong, because everyone

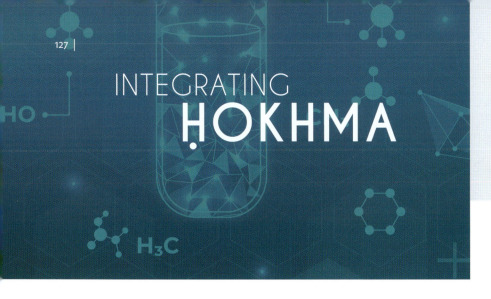

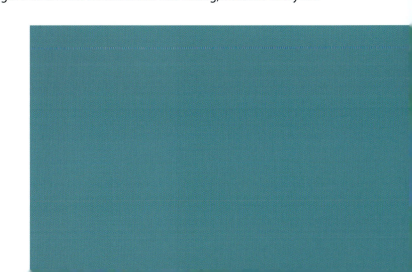

> And Pharaoh put men in charge of him, and they sent him off [*vayeshaleḥu oto*] with his wife and all that he possessed. (12:20)

Why does the text cast Pharaoh in the role of God? This unscrupulous character, who forcibly takes another man's wife into his home (12:15), now assumes the position of Avraham's accuser, judge, and moral superior. It seems that through this act of subtle literary association, the text equates Avraham with Adam, a fellow errant who is banished from a naturally fertile land (13:10). But Avraham receives an extra sting. Perhaps because he upset God's desired balance of *tov* by giving up Sara, Avraham faces eviction not by God, but by the evil Pharaoh.

Pharaoh's words then carry the insult even further. While expelling Avraham, Pharaoh makes sure to correct Avraham's misrepresentation of Sara as his sister by proclaiming, "Now here is your *wife*, *ishtekha*; take her and be gone!" (12:19). In fact, the word for "wife," *isha*, appears ten times in this one passage, lending a tone of sardonic criticism to Avraham's actions. We are reminded time and again of the couple's true relationship, one that Avraham has denied. In addition, the repetition of the word *isha* serves as an ironic reminder of the hoped-for relations between the original *Ish* and *Isha* of the Garden of Eden. Rather than clinging to Sara "as one flesh" (2:24), Avraham's actions lead to their separation.

By the story's end, Avraham has traveled a long and troubling distance. He began by following God's order of *Lekh lekha*, "Go forth" (12:1), "taking" (*l-k-ḥ*) Sara his wife on the divine journey (12:5). Yet along the road, Avraham has denied Sara's identity as his wife, contributing, albeit unintentionally, to her being taken by others. It is now Pharaoh, the Bible's quintessentially evil king, who orders Avraham to "take" (*l-k-ḥ*) Sara and "go," *lekh*, not for any godly purpose, but in the shame of banishment.

The story of Avraham and Sara's sojourn in Egypt ends on a familiar and regrettable note. Old patterns continue as man exercises control over his wife, man and woman are alienated from each other, and both are banished from a land of plenty. Yet, rather than following the expected script, the story begins to veer in a surprising and subversive new direction. Instead of objectively reporting its tale, assuming that, in light of Eden's conclusions, man must naturally rule over woman, the text *attacks* that assumption through well-crafted literary substitution. First, woman replaces Eden's fruit as object, as *she* is now the beautiful object that is inappropriately "seen" and "taken." Then Pharaoh replaces God as man's judge, as suggested by his echoing of God's language when he cries: *Ma zot asita li*, "What have you done to me!" and when he banishes, *sh-l-ḥ*, Avraham from his land. Through the similarities in language, the two stories are drawn together. Then, by the substitutions, their differences come to light. These differences whisper to the reader that it is one thing for fruit to be objectified and inappropriately taken. But it is far worse for a woman to be treated in this way. When man allows for this to happen, he is rebuked and expelled not by God, but by a morally debased mortal being.

Judy Klitsner

TAKING A LITERARY APPROACH

Throughout the story of Sara's abduction, Avraham's failures are highlighted by the passage's unexpected use of Eden-like language. Such similarities invite us to draw parallels between the two stories, and consequently to view Avraham's behavior as deserving of the Bible's subtle literary reproach. The first example, which will only indirectly implicate Avraham, is the verb combination of *seeing* and *taking*. In the garden, the forbidden fruit was a beautiful object of desire, to be inappropriately *seen* and *taken*:

> When the woman saw that the tree was good for eating and a delight to the eyes, and that the tree was desirable as a source for wisdom, she took of its fruit and ate. (Bereshit 3:6)

In Egypt, Sara is the beautiful object to be *seen* and *taken*:

> When Avram entered Egypt, the Egyptians saw how very beautiful the woman was. Pharaoh's courtiers *saw* her and praised her to Pharaoh, and the woman was *taken* into Pharaoh's palace. (12:14–15)

The text's choice of language suggests that the Egyptians view Sara not as a human being, but, like Eden's fruit, as a commodity to be desired and seized. But the text hints at something more. In assessing their situation at the portal to dangerous territory, Avraham, like the unscrupulous Egyptians, sees only one thing: Sara's physical beauty: "I know what a beautiful woman you are" (12:11).

It would appear that in devising his plan for their survival, Avraham considers Sara's beauty, but not her indispensability to him. In his assessment of the potential dangers facing them, he mentions only the risks of having Sara by his side, but not those inherent in claiming she is his sister. As a result of his incomplete analysis of the situation, he adopts a strategy that will likely separate them, possibly forever. Instead of doing everything possible to keep Sara at his side, Avraham's actions lead to Sara's being "seen" and "taken" like Eden's fruit.

In what is perhaps another nod to Eden, the narrative makes ironic use of the word *tov*, "good." At the start of the biblical record, all of God's creations were pronounced *tov* (1:12, 18, 21, 25, 31). Yet as we have seen, Bereshit 2 introduces a state of *lo tov* by stating, "It is not good for man to be alone" (2:18). God rectifies that situation by creating woman, in essence declaring that only man and woman together could bring a sense of *tov* into the world. In Egypt, Avraham turns God's sentiment on its head with his words *Imri na aḥoti at lemaan yitav li*, "Please say you are my sister so that it will be *good* for me." Although Avraham's plan would result in the separation of husband and wife and would return him to a lone existence, he mistakenly thinks that his actions will lead him to *tov*.

In a very strange and surprising turn, God's role in the story of the Garden of Eden is performed here by Pharaoh, the morally tainted king of Egypt. In rebuking the woman after her disobedience in Eden, God asks rhetorically, "What is this you have done!" – *Ma zot asit!* (3:13). Pharaoh now echoes these words in chastising Avraham, *Ma zot asita li!* – "What is this you have done to me!" (12:18). Moreover, when God drives humanity from His garden, the text says:

> So the Lord God sent him off [*vayeshaleḥehu*] from the Garden of Eden, to till the soil from which he was taken. (3:23)

Similarly, Pharaoh "sends off" the recalcitrant man and his wife, away from his land of plenty:

13 1 Then Avram went up from Egypt to the Negev with his wife and all he had, and with him
2 3 went Lot. And Avram had become very wealthy in cattle, silver, and gold. From the Negev
he continued on his journey to Beit El, to the site between Beit El and Ai where his tent
4 had previously been, and where he had first made an altar. There Avram called on the name
5 6 of the Lord. Lot, who went with Avram, had flocks, herds, and tents as well, and the land
could not support them living together; so many were their possessions that they were
7 unable to live side by side. A dispute broke out between Avram's herdsmen and those of
8 Lot; and the Canaanites and the Perizzites were then too living in the land. Avram said to
Lot, "Please, let there be no friction between me and you, and between my herdsmen and
9 yours, for we are brothers. The whole land lies before you; please separate yourself from
10 me. If you go to the left, I will go to the right; if you go to the right, I will go to the left." Lot
raised his eyes and saw that the whole plain of the Jordan up to Tzoar was well watered. It
was like the garden of the Lord, like the land of Egypt; this was before the Lord destroyed
11 Sedom and Amora.[1] So Lot chose for himself the entire plain of the Jordan. He traveled
12 eastward, and the two men separated. Avram settled in the land of Canaan while Lot settled
13 in the cities of the plain, pitching his tent near Sedom. But the people of Sedom were evil,
14 great sinners against the Lord. After Lot had separated from him, the Lord said to Avram,

1 | See chapter 19.

UNLOCKING THE TEXT

- Why does Avram return now to the land of Canaan?
- What term does the Torah use for this migration and why?
- Why was there tension between Avram and Lot and their camps?
- Why did Avram choose to settle in Eilon Mamre?
- Why does the Torah hint here at the story (that will follow later) of the destruction of Sedom and Amora?
- Why does God reaffirm the promise of the land to Avram now?

FINDING YOURSELF IN THE TEXT

- Do you have any relationships in your life that work better with a little distance?
- Do you find it a challenge to live side by side with people who have different values and a different lifestyle than you?
- Is it important to be grateful for what you have right now, even if it isn't everything you dream of? Why?

Consider using these questions as the basis for your own commentary or creative midrash.

How does reflecting on these firsthand experiences help you better understand the text?

יג וַיַּ֩עַל֩ אַבְרָ֨ם מִמִּצְרַ֜יִם ה֣וּא וְאִשְׁתּ֣וֹ וְכָל־אֲשֶׁר־ל֗וֹ וְל֥וֹט עִמּ֖וֹ הַנֶּֽגְבָּה: וְאַבְרָ֖ם כָּבֵ֣ד א

מְאֹ֑ד בַּמִּקְנֶ֕ה בַּכֶּ֖סֶף וּבַזָּהָֽב: וַיֵּ֙לֶךְ֙ לְמַסָּעָ֔יו מִנֶּ֖גֶב וְעַד־בֵּֽית־אֵ֑ל עַד־הַמָּק֗וֹם אֲשֶׁר־ ג

הָ֨יָה שָׁ֤ם אׇֽהֳלֹה֙ בַּתְּחִלָּ֔ה בֵּ֥ין בֵּֽית־אֵ֖ל וּבֵ֥ין הָעָֽי: אֶל־מְקוֹם֙ הַמִּזְבֵּ֔חַ אֲשֶׁר־עָ֥שָׂה ד

שָׁ֖ם בָּרִֽאשֹׁנָ֑ה וַיִּקְרָ֥א שָׁ֛ם אַבְרָ֖ם בְּשֵׁ֥ם יְהֹוָֽה: וְגַ֨ם־לְל֔וֹט הַהֹלֵ֖ךְ אֶת־אַבְרָ֑ם הָ֥יָה ה   שלישי

צֹֽאן־וּבָקָ֖ר וְאֹהָלִֽים: וְלֹֽא־נָשָׂ֥א אֹתָ֛ם הָאָ֖רֶץ לָשֶׁ֣בֶת יַחְדָּ֑ו כִּֽי־הָיָ֤ה רְכוּשָׁם֙ רָ֔ב וְלֹ֥א ו

יָֽכְל֖וּ לָשֶׁ֥בֶת יַחְדָּֽו: וַֽיְהִי־רִ֗יב בֵּ֚ין רֹעֵ֣י מִקְנֵֽה־אַבְרָ֔ם וּבֵ֖ין רֹעֵ֣י מִקְנֵה־ל֑וֹט וְהַֽכְּנַעֲנִי֙ ז

וְהַ֨פְּרִזִּ֔י אָ֖ז יֹשֵׁ֥ב בָּאָֽרֶץ: וַיֹּ֨אמֶר אַבְרָ֜ם אֶל־ל֗וֹט אַל־נָ֨א תְהִ֤י מְרִיבָה֙ בֵּינִ֣י וּבֵינֶ֔ךָ ח

וּבֵ֥ין רֹעַ֖י וּבֵ֣ין רֹעֶ֑יךָ כִּֽי־אֲנָשִׁ֥ים אַחִ֖ים אֲנָֽחְנוּ: הֲלֹ֤א כׇל־הָאָ֨רֶץ֙ לְפָנֶ֔יךָ הִפָּ֥רֶד נָ֖א ט

מֵֽעָלָ֑י אִם־הַשְּׂמֹ֣אל וְאֵימִ֔נָה וְאִם־הַיָּמִ֖ין וְאַשְׂמְאִֽילָה: וַיִּשָּׂא־ל֣וֹט אֶת־עֵינָ֗יו וַיַּרְא֙ י

אֶת־כׇּל־כִּכַּ֣ר הַיַּרְדֵּ֔ן כִּ֥י כֻלָּ֖הּ מַשְׁקֶ֑ה לִפְנֵ֣י ׀ שַׁחֵ֣ת יְהֹוָ֗ה אֶת־סְדֹם֙ וְאֶת־עֲמֹרָ֔ה

כְּגַן־יְהֹוָה֙ כְּאֶ֣רֶץ מִצְרַ֔יִם בֹּֽאֲכָ֖ה צֹ֑עַר: וַיִּבְחַר־ל֣וֹ ל֗וֹט אֵ֚ת כׇּל־כִּכַּ֣ר הַיַּרְדֵּ֔ן וַיִּסַּ֥ע יא

ל֖וֹט מִקֶּ֑דֶם וַיִּפָּ֣רְד֔וּ אִ֖ישׁ מֵעַ֥ל אָחִֽיו: אַבְרָ֖ם יָשַׁ֣ב בְּאֶֽרֶץ־כְּנָ֑עַן וְל֗וֹט יָשַׁב֙ בְּעָרֵ֣י יב

הַכִּכָּ֔ר וַיֶּאֱהַ֖ל עַד־סְדֹֽם: וְאַנְשֵׁ֣י סְדֹ֔ם רָעִ֖ים וְחַטָּאִ֑ים לַיהֹוָ֖ה מְאֹֽד: וַֽיהֹוָ֣ה אָמַ֣ר יג

| THEMES | THE LAND OF ISRAEL | RELATIONSHIPS AND LOVE | COVENANT |

Episode 17: *Avram and Lot in Canaan* – Bereshit 13:1–18

SUMMARY

After some tension between their respective camps, Avram separates from his nephew Lot, who has accompanied him until this point. Together they decide that it makes more economic sense to find different geographic locations to make their respective camps. Lot chooses the Jordan valley to the south, as it has rich pastural lands, and Avram initially stays at Beit El in the northern Judean hills. However, he soon follows Lot southward, while still keeping his distance, settling in Ḥevron (perhaps so he can continue to fulfill his duty to family, and keep an eye on his nephew). God then reminds Avram that this land is promised to his descendants as an eternal inheritance.

"Raise your eyes and look around from where you are to the north, south, east, and west.
15 16 All the land you see I will give to you and your descendants forever. I will make your
descendants like the dust of the earth: if anyone could count the dust of the earth, then
17 could your descendants be counted. Get up and walk through the length and breadth of
18 the land, for to you shall I give it." So Avram took his tent and came to settle by the Oaks
of Mamre, in Ḥevron. There he built an altar to the Lord.

well watered everywhere, like the garden of the Lord, like the land of Egypt." But he did not understand that all this was only temporary – "before the Lord destroyed Sedom and Amora" – because he did not pay attention to the fact that "the men of Sedom were wicked and sinners before the Lord exceedingly" (v. 13). Avram – his very *aliya* was "as the Lord had spoken to him." For this reason he did not choose his land on his own, but rather God said to him: "Lift up now your eyes, and look…northward, and southward, and eastward, and westward," and it is God who promises to give him "all the land which you see." In this way Avram merited to dwell in Ḥevron that looked out upon Sedom; and from there he would later see the smoke rising from Sedom at the time of its destruction.

Rabbi Mordechai Breuer

אֶל־אַבְרָ֗ם אַחֲרֵי֙ הִפָּֽרֶד־ל֣וֹט מֵעִמּ֔וֹ שָׂא־נָ֣א עֵינֶ֗יךָ וּרְאֵ֗ה מִן־הַמָּק֛וֹם אֲשֶׁר־
טו אַתָּ֥ה שָׁ֖ם צָפֹ֥נָה וָנֶ֖גְבָּה וָקֵ֥דְמָה וָיָֽמָּה׃ כִּ֧י אֶת־כָּל־הָאָ֛רֶץ אֲשֶׁר־אַתָּ֥ה רֹאֶ֖ה לְךָ֣
טז אֶתְּנֶ֑נָּה וּֽלְזַרְעֲךָ֖ עַד־עוֹלָֽם׃ וְשַׂמְתִּ֥י אֶֽת־זַרְעֲךָ֖ כַּעֲפַ֣ר הָאָ֑רֶץ אֲשֶׁ֣ר ׀ אִם־יוּכַ֣ל אִ֗ישׁ
יז לִמְנוֹת֙ אֶת־עֲפַ֣ר הָאָ֔רֶץ גַּֽם־זַרְעֲךָ֖ יִמָּנֶֽה׃ ק֚וּם הִתְהַלֵּ֣ךְ בָּאָ֔רֶץ לְאָרְכָּ֖הּ וּלְרָחְבָּ֑הּ
יח כִּ֥י לְךָ֖ אֶתְּנֶֽנָּה׃ וַיֶּאֱהַ֣ל אַבְרָ֗ם וַיָּבֹ֛א וַיֵּ֛שֶׁב בְּאֵלֹנֵ֥י מַמְרֵ֖א אֲשֶׁ֣ר בְּחֶבְר֑וֹן וַיִּֽבֶן־שָׁ֥ם
מִזְבֵּ֖חַ לַֽיהוָֽה׃

TAKING A LITERARY APPROACH

In Bereshit 13:14–17, God repeats the promise that had already been given to Avram in Shekhem, only there the promise was worded in brief: "To your seed will I give this land," whereas here it is explained at length, and it includes both a promise about the land and about seed, and also the command to rise up and walk through the land. Furthermore, in Shekhem the Promised Land is referred to as "this land," whereas here Avram is commanded to lift up his eyes and look "northward, and southward, and eastward, and westward," and he is told that God will give him "all the land which you see." Only here does God fulfill the promise included in the words "the land that I will show you" (12:1), for only now does He show him the land, in the literal sense.

Of special significance is God's address to Avram: "Lift up now your eyes, and look from the place where you are" (13:14); these words parallel what was said earlier regarding Lot: "And Lot lifted up his eyes, and beheld all the plain of the Jordan" (v. 10). The meaning seems to be as follows: Lot chose his land on his own; he "lifted up his eyes" and beheld all the plain of the Jordan, "that it was

THE ART OF MIDRASH

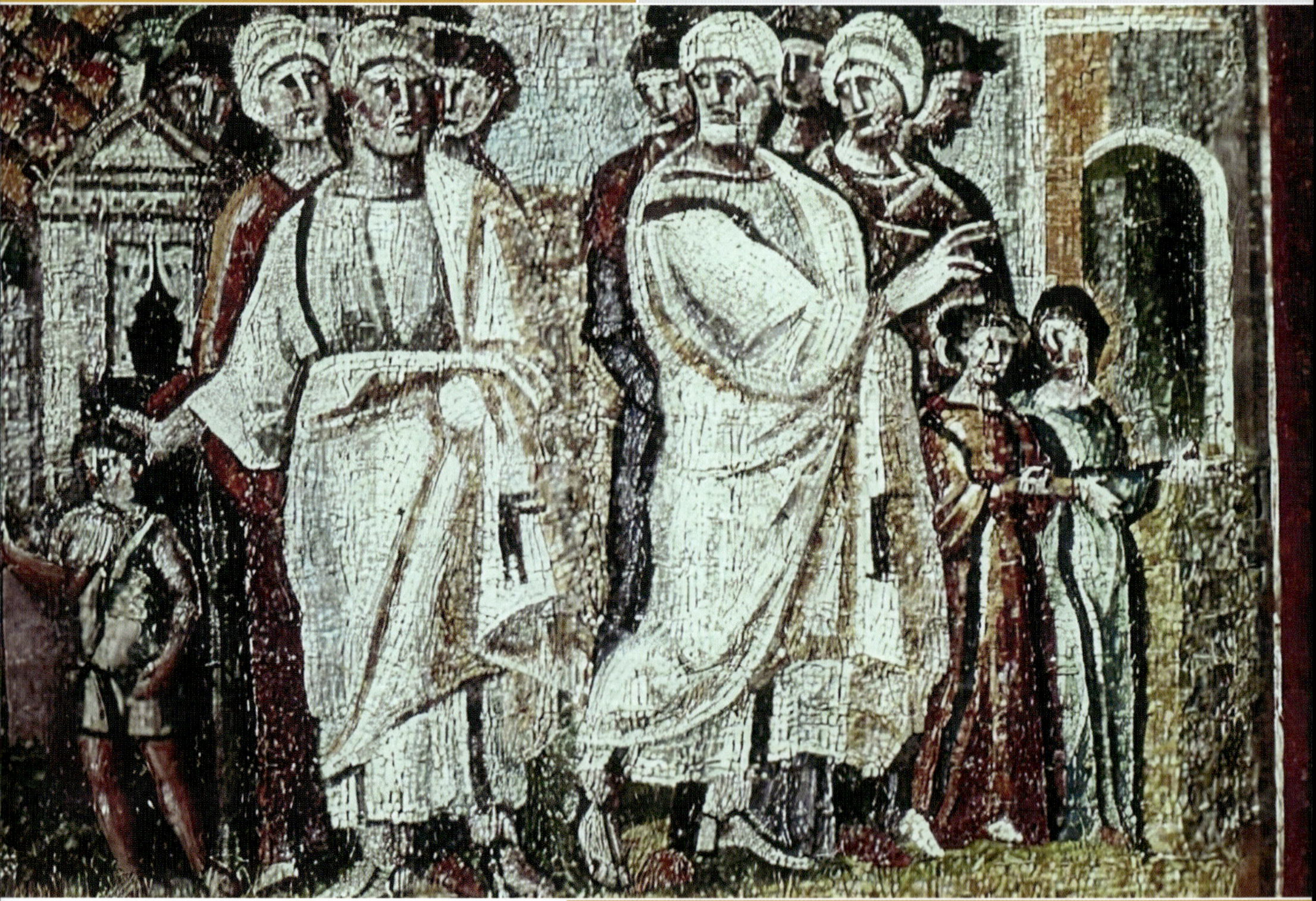

The Parting of Lot and Abraham
Mosaic in the Santa Maria Maggiore (432–440 CE)

Analysis

- Which elements of this image are directly mentioned in the text?
- Which elements of this image are not found in the text?
- What midrashic interpretation is the artist giving us?

A QUESTION OF BIBLIODRAMA

TO AVRAM AND SARAI

- Share something you said to your spouse on the journey home.
- What went through your mind on the journey? What were your concerns and dreams?

TO AVRAM

- How does it feel to be able to return to the land God promised you?
- What do you think of Lot?
- What was the tension between you and Lot really about?
- Why did you suggest parting ways as a solution to the problem?
- Is this a painful parting for you?
- How do you feel about Lot's choice?
- How did it feel to hear God reaffirm His promise of the land to you?
- Why did you choose to build an altar to God at the conclusion of this episode?

TO LOT

- How was the experience of Egypt for you?
- Why have you shown such loyalty to Avram until now?
- Do you believe in the God of Avram and Sarai?
- How did you feel when Avram suggested parting ways?
- Why did you choose the Jordan Valley?

TO A SHEPHERD

- What were you quarreling about?
- What do you think of your master?

TO A CANAANITE OR A PERIZZITE

- What do you think of these foreigners in your land?

TO GOD

- Why is this the right time for Avram to return to the land of Canaan?
- Why do You take this opportunity to reaffirm the promise You made to give this land to Avram's descendants?
- Why do You tell Avram to walk through the length and breadth of the land?

עָרֵי הַכִּכָּר
CITIES OF THE PLAIN

"The plain" refers to the Dead Sea Valley, mentioned thirteen times, often as "the plain of the Jordan." These "cities of the plain" are a cluster of five cities: Sedom (mentioned about forty times); Amora (nineteen times), always together with Sedom; Adma and Tzevoyim are mentioned four times together with Sedom and Amora, and once as a lone pair. Tzoar is mentioned ten times, and is sometimes called "Bela" or "Mitzar."

As early as the Second Temple era, the Sages tried to determine where the "cities of the plain" were. Their precise location remains a mystery, as no remains of major cities have been found in the Dead Sea area from this ancient era. The remains of two large cemeteries from the early Bronze Age have been found on the southeast shore of the Dead Sea: one along the road descending from the Moav Mountains to the Dead Sea (south of Arnon), and the other at Ghor es-Safi, which some identify with Tzoar. These graves testify to populations of large settlements that are no more; their remains could theoretically be deep below the water. The destruction of Sedom might resemble a volcanic eruption, an earthquake, or a flood, although these sites predate the biblical dating of Sedom's destruction.

Some hold that the "cities of the plain," associated with "the Jordan plain," is located north of the Dead Sea, in the Ḥirbat el-Ḥamam area east of the Jordan, opposite Yeriḥo where the Jordan River empties into the sea. This area is a fertile oasis, consistent with Lot's,[1] Avraham's,[2] and Moshe's views of "the plain – the Valley of Yeriḥo, city of palm trees – as far as Tzoar."[3] All three men gaze down upon the northern area of the Dead Sea.

"Mount Sedom" is a mound of salt to the southwest of the Dead Sea; some of its formations resemble the figure of a woman and are associated, of course, with Lot's wife. It is not clear, however, when this name came into use, and it is not sufficient proof of biblical Sedom's location.

1| Bereshit 13:3, 10.

2| Bereshit 18:1.

3| Devarim 34:3.

Analysis

- What specific information do we now have that was unavailable to classical Jewish commentators? How can it aid our understanding of the text?
- What can we learn from this photo that can help us understand the text?
- What further questions on the text do you have now that you have seen this photo?

INTEGRATING ḤOKHMA

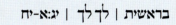

Dead Sea valley at sunrise

14 1 In the days of Amrafel, king of Shinar, Aryokh, king of Elasar, Kedorlaomer, king of Eilam,
2 and Tidal, king of Goyim, they all waged war against Bera, king of Sedom, Birsha, king of
Amora, Shinav, king of Adma, and Shemever, king of Tzevoyim, and the king of Bela – that
3 4 is, Tzoar. These had all come together in Siddim Valley – now the Dead Sea; for twelve
5 years they had served Kedorlaomer, but in the thirteenth year they had rebelled. In the
fourteenth year Kedorlaomer and his allied kings came and defeated the Refaim in Ashterot
6 Karnayim, the Zuzim in Ham, the Eimim in Shaveh Kiryatayim,[1] and the Horites in the
7 hill country of Se'ir as far as Eil Paran by the wilderness. Then they swung back and came
to Ein Mishpat – that is, Kadesh – conquering the whole territory of the Amalekites, as
8 well as the Amorites living in Ḥatzetzon Tamar. Then the kings of Sedom, Amora, Adma,
Tzevoyim, and Bela – that is, Tzoar – marched out and drew up their battle lines in Siddim
9 Valley against Kedorlaomer, king of Eilam, Tidal, king of Goyim, Amrafel, king of Shinar,

1 | Concerning these peoples, see Devarim 2:10–11, 20.

UNLOCKING THE TEXT

- Why does the Torah spend so much time giving us the context for this story?
- Why does Avram allow himself to become involved in a local conflict?
- How does this story contribute to the overall narrative of Avram, his covenant with God, and the destiny of his descendants?
- What was the agenda of all the people involved in these battles, including the four kings, the five kings, Lot the "fugitive," and Avram?
- How did Avram relate to Malki Tzedek, the king of Shalem?
- How did Avram relate to the king of Sedom?

FINDING YOURSELF IN THE TEXT

- Have you ever been dragged into a conflict that you did not start and had no previous involvement in?
- Have you ever exposed yourself to any kind of risk for a loved one?
- Have you ever done anything for someone who wanted to pay you, but you refused? Why did you refuse payment?

Consider using these questions as the basis for your own commentary or creative midrash.

How does reflecting on these firsthand experiences help you better understand the text?

יד א וַיְהִי בִּימֵי אַמְרָפֶל מֶלֶךְ־שִׁנְעָר אַרְיוֹךְ מֶלֶךְ אֶלָּסָר כְּדָרְלָעֹמֶר מֶלֶךְ עֵילָם וְתִדְעָל יא רביעי
ב מֶלֶךְ גּוֹיִם׃ עָשׂוּ מִלְחָמָה אֶת־בֶּרַע מֶלֶךְ סְדֹם וְאֶת־בִּרְשַׁע מֶלֶךְ עֲמֹרָה שִׁנְאָב ׀
ג מֶלֶךְ אַדְמָה וְשֶׁמְאֵבֶר מֶלֶךְ צביים וּמֶלֶךְ בֶּלַע הִיא־צֹעַר׃ כָּל־אֵלֶּה חָבְרוּ אֶל־ צְבוֹיִם
ד עֵמֶק הַשִּׂדִּים הוּא יָם הַמֶּלַח׃ שְׁתֵּים עֶשְׂרֵה שָׁנָה עָבְדוּ אֶת־כְּדָרְלָעֹמֶר וּשְׁלֹשׁ־
ה עֶשְׂרֵה שָׁנָה מָרָדוּ׃ וּבְאַרְבַּע עֶשְׂרֵה שָׁנָה בָּא כְדָרְלָעֹמֶר וְהַמְּלָכִים אֲשֶׁר אִתּוֹ וַיַּכּוּ
אֶת־רְפָאִים בְּעַשְׁתְּרֹת קַרְנַיִם וְאֶת־הַזּוּזִים בְּהָם וְאֵת הָאֵימִים בְּשָׁוֵה קִרְיָתָיִם׃
ו ז וְאֶת־הַחֹרִי בְּהַרְרָם שֵׂעִיר עַד אֵיל פָּארָן אֲשֶׁר עַל־הַמִּדְבָּר׃ וַיָּשֻׁבוּ וַיָּבֹאוּ אֶל־
עֵין מִשְׁפָּט הִוא קָדֵשׁ וַיַּכּוּ אֶת־כָּל־שְׂדֵה הָעֲמָלֵקִי וְגַם אֶת־הָאֱמֹרִי הַיֹּשֵׁב
ח בְּחַצְצֹן תָּמָר׃ וַיֵּצֵא מֶלֶךְ־סְדֹם וּמֶלֶךְ עֲמֹרָה וּמֶלֶךְ אַדְמָה וּמֶלֶךְ צביים וּמֶלֶךְ צְבוֹיִם
ט בֶּלַע הִוא־צֹעַר וַיַּעַרְכוּ אִתָּם מִלְחָמָה בְּעֵמֶק הַשִּׂדִּים׃ אֵת כְּדָרְלָעֹמֶר מֶלֶךְ עֵילָם
וְתִדְעָל מֶלֶךְ גּוֹיִם וְאַמְרָפֶל מֶלֶךְ שִׁנְעָר וְאַרְיוֹךְ מֶלֶךְ אֶלָּסָר אַרְבָּעָה מְלָכִים אֶת־

THEMES	RELATIONSHIPS AND LOVE	ETHICS	THE LAND OF ISRAEL

Episode 18: *Avram Goes to War* – Bereshit 14:1–24

SUMMARY

The story of the great war in the area known today as the Dead Sea reveals additional aspects of Avram's character. Whereas until now he has been portrayed as a simple shepherd who preached and taught during his wanderings, this chapter shows a different side to him – a warrior and military leader. However, his daring attack against the powerful kings is not motivated by political interest or hope of personal gain. Rather, it is a further expression of his familial duty and sense of responsibility for his nephew Lot. When Avram hears that Lot been captured, he organizes a rescue party of 318 people, including three allies from Ḥevron with whom he had made a treaty. They chase the four kings and catch up to them in the north, where Avram splits his camp and launches a surprise nighttime attack from two different sides; the enemy flees and Avram pursues them past Damascus. In the process, Avram rescues Lot along with many others and their looted wealth. On the way back from the battle, Avram is greeted by the king of Sedom and later by Malki Tzedek, the king of Shalem. The king of Sedom offers Avram to keep all the property Avram recovered. Avram refuses to take anything from the king of Sedom, lest he claim that it was he who made Avram wealthy, but he does insist that his allies be allowed to take their fair share of the spoils.

10 and Aryokh, king of Elasar: four kings battling five. The Siddim Valley was riddled with
tar pits, and when the kings of Sedom and Amora tried to flee, they fell into them. The
11 others fled to the mountains. The victors seized all the possessions of Sedom and Amora
12 and all the food, and they left, taking with them – since he had been living in Sedom –
13 Avram's nephew, Lot, and his possessions. A fugitive came and reported this to Avram the
Hebrew, who was then living near the Oaks of Mamre the Amorite, a kinsman of Avram's
14 allies, Eshkol and Aner. When Avram heard that his own kinsman had been taken captive,
he marshaled the three hundred eighteen trained men born in his household, and went in
15 pursuit as far as Dan. He divided his forces against the captors at night and defeated them,
16 pursuing them to Ḥova, north of Damascus. He recovered all the plunder, as well as his
17 kinsman Lot and his possessions, the women, and the other survivors as well. When he
returned from defeating Kedorlaomer and the kings with him, the king of Sedom came out
18 to greet him at Shaveh Valley – that is, the Valley of the King. And Malki Tzedek, king of
19 Shalem, offered bread and wine. He was a priest of God Most High, and he blessed Avram,
20 saying: "Blessed be Avram by God Most High, Maker of heaven and earth, and blessed be
God Most High who delivered your foes into your hand." Then Avram gave him a tenth
21 of everything. And the king of Sedom said to Avram, "Give me the people, and keep the
22 possessions for yourself." But Avram said to the king of Sedom, "I raise my hand in oath to
23 the Lord, God Most High, Maker of heaven and earth, that I will not accept anything of
24 yours, not even a thread or a shoe strap, so that you never shall say, 'I made Avram rich.' I
will accept nothing but what my young men have eaten and the share that belongs to the
men who went with me – Aner, Eshkol, and Mamre; let them have their share."

י הַחֲמִשָּֽׁה׃ וְעֵ֨מֶק הַשִּׂדִּ֜ים בֶּֽאֱרֹ֤ת בֶּאֱרֹת֙ חֵמָ֔ר וַיָּנֻ֛סוּ מֶֽלֶךְ־סְדֹ֥ם וַעֲמֹרָ֖ה וַיִּפְּלוּ־שָׁ֑מָּה
יא וְהַנִּשְׁאָרִ֖ים הֶ֥רָה נָּֽסוּ׃ וַ֠יִּקְחוּ אֶת־כָּל־רְכֻ֨שׁ סְדֹ֧ם וַעֲמֹרָ֛ה וְאֶת־כָּל־אָכְלָ֖ם וַיֵּלֵֽכוּ׃
יב יג וַיִּקְח֨וּ אֶת־ל֧וֹט וְאֶת־רְכֻשׁ֛וֹ בֶּן־אֲחִ֥י אַבְרָ֖ם וַיֵּלֵ֑כוּ וְה֥וּא יֹשֵׁ֖ב בִּסְדֹֽם׃ וַיָּבֹא֙ הַפָּלִ֔יט
וַיַּגֵּ֖ד לְאַבְרָ֣ם הָעִבְרִ֑י וְהוּא֩ שֹׁכֵ֨ן בְּאֵלֹנֵ֜י מַמְרֵ֣א הָאֱמֹרִ֗י אֲחִ֤י אֶשְׁכֹּל֙ וַאֲחִ֣י עָנֵ֔ר וְהֵ֖ם
יד בַּעֲלֵ֥י בְרִית־אַבְרָֽם׃ וַיִּשְׁמַ֣ע אַבְרָ֔ם כִּ֥י נִשְׁבָּ֖ה אָחִ֑יו וַיָּ֨רֶק אֶת־חֲנִיכָ֜יו יְלִידֵ֣י בֵית֗וֹ
טו שְׁמֹנָ֤ה עָשָׂר֙ וּשְׁלֹ֣שׁ מֵא֔וֹת וַיִּרְדֹּ֖ף עַד־דָּֽן׃ וַיֵּחָלֵ֨ק עֲלֵיהֶ֧ם ׀ לַ֛יְלָה ה֥וּא וַעֲבָדָ֖יו וַיַּכֵּ֑ם
טז וַֽיִּרְדְּפֵם֙ עַד־חוֹבָ֔ה אֲשֶׁ֥ר מִשְּׂמֹ֖אל לְדַמָּֽשֶׂק׃ וַיָּ֕שֶׁב אֵ֖ת כָּל־הָרְכֻ֑שׁ וְגַם֩ אֶת־ל֨וֹט
יז אָחִ֤יו וּרְכֻשׁוֹ֙ הֵשִׁ֔יב וְגַ֥ם אֶת־הַנָּשִׁ֖ים וְאֶת־הָעָֽם׃ וַיֵּצֵ֣א מֶֽלֶךְ־סְדֹם֮ לִקְרָאתוֹ֒ אַחֲרֵ֣י
שׁוּב֗וֹ מֵֽהַכּוֹת֙ אֶת־כְּדָרְלָעֹ֔מֶר וְאֶת־הַמְּלָכִ֖ים אֲשֶׁ֣ר אִתּ֑וֹ אֶל־עֵ֣מֶק שָׁוֵ֔ה ה֖וּא עֵ֥מֶק
יח יט הַמֶּֽלֶךְ׃ וּמַלְכִּי־צֶ֙דֶק֙ מֶ֣לֶךְ שָׁלֵ֔ם הוֹצִ֖יא לֶ֣חֶם וָיָ֑יִן וְה֥וּא כֹהֵ֖ן לְאֵ֥ל עֶלְיֽוֹן׃ וַֽיְבָרְכֵ֖הוּ
כ וַיֹּאמַ֑ר בָּר֤וּךְ אַבְרָם֙ לְאֵ֣ל עֶלְי֔וֹן קֹנֵ֖ה שָׁמַ֥יִם וָאָֽרֶץ׃ וּבָרוּךְ֙ אֵ֣ל עֶלְי֔וֹן אֲשֶׁר־מִגֵּ֥ן
כא צָרֶ֖יךָ בְּיָדֶ֑ךָ וַיִּתֶּן־ל֥וֹ מַעֲשֵׂ֖ר מִכֹּֽל׃ וַיֹּ֥אמֶר מֶֽלֶךְ־סְדֹ֖ם אֶל־אַבְרָ֑ם תֶּן־לִ֣י הַנֶּ֔פֶשׁ חמישי
כב וְהָרְכֻ֖שׁ קַח־לָֽךְ׃ וַיֹּ֥אמֶר אַבְרָ֖ם אֶל־מֶ֣לֶךְ סְדֹ֑ם הֲרִמֹ֨תִי יָדִ֤י אֶל־יהוה אֵ֣ל עֶלְי֔וֹן
כג קֹנֵ֖ה שָׁמַ֥יִם וָאָֽרֶץ׃ אִם־מִחוּט֙ וְעַ֣ד שְׂרֽוֹךְ־נַ֔עַל וְאִם־אֶקַּ֖ח מִכָּל־אֲשֶׁר־לָ֑ךְ וְלֹ֣א
כד תֹאמַ֔ר אֲנִ֖י הֶעֱשַׁ֥רְתִּי אֶת־אַבְרָֽם׃ בִּלְעָדַ֗י רַ֚ק אֲשֶׁ֣ר אָֽכְל֣וּ הַנְּעָרִ֔ים וְחֵ֙לֶק֙ הָאֲנָשִׁ֔ים
אֲשֶׁ֥ר הָלְכ֖וּ אִתִּ֑י עָנֵר֙ אֶשְׁכֹּ֣ל וּמַמְרֵ֔א הֵ֖ם יִקְח֥וּ חֶלְקָֽם׃

THE ART OF MIDRASH

The Meeting of Abraham and Melchizedek
Dieric Bouts (1464–1467)

Analysis

- Which elements of this image are directly mentioned in the text?
- Which elements of this image are not found in the text?
- What midrashic interpretation is the artist giving us?

A QUESTION OF BIBLIODRAMA

TO KEDORLAOMER AND THE OTHER INVADING KINGS

- Why have you traveled so far to wage war on these local kings?
- What was your goal in taking captives (such as Lot)?
- Did you notice anything different about him?
- What did you think when the foreigner Avram became involved in this battle?

TO LOT

- Did you take an active role in this conflict before you were taken captive? Had you taken sides?
- What went through your mind when you were taken captive?
- Did you send the messenger to Avram, or were you surprised when he came to your rescue?
- Did you have any idea Avram was also a warrior, or was this a surprise to you?
- Were you surprised he won the war and was successful in rescuing you?
- How did it feel when Avram came to your rescue and interceded in the conflict?
- Did you speak with your uncle on the way home? What about?
- Has your relationship with him changed since he rescued you?

TO MALKI TZEDEK

- What is your impression of this foreigner, Avram?

TO THE KING OF SEDOM

- What is your impression of this foreigner, Avram?
- Do you understand why he helped you?
- What did you think when he refused to accept payment for his role in the battle?

TO AVRAM

- Were you aware of this war before you were told that Lot had been taken captive?
- What did you feel and think when you heard this?
- Did it come naturally to you to lead a military force into battle? Did you have any previous experience?
- Did you expect to win?
- Why did you put yourself in harm's way for Lot?
- Did you seek counsel from God? If so, what were you told? If not, why not?
- What was your impression of Malki Tzedek? How did this impact your interaction with him?
- What was your impression of the king of Sedom? How did this impact your interaction with him?
- What did you learn from this whole experience?

INTEGRATING ḤOKHMA

If my friend is gracious enough to give me a twenty-dollar bill as a present, my gratitude would appropriately be directed at him. Yet, if I happen to find a twenty-dollar bill on the street, to whom should I direct my gratitude?

For those who aren't particularly spiritual or religious, finding money on the street may engender positive emotions, but gratitude would likely be absent, as there is nobody to thank. For those who are religious, however, such fortunate experiences could lend themselves to being grateful to God.

Dr. David Rosmarin hypothesized that since religious individuals have more opportunities to feel and express gratitude, they consequentially are able to reap the positive benefits associated with gratitude – such as increased feelings of happiness and life satisfaction – above and beyond the advantages associated with gratitude in general.

Taking the twenty-dollar bill example one step further, we can add an additional layer of reflection. From a religious perspective, even if my friend gives me a gift, my gratitude to him should be supplemented with an additional gratitude toward God. Meaning, every benefit accrued socially should also be attributed to God's providence and beneficence.

After Avram helped the five kings defeat the four kings, Malki Tzedek, king of Shalem, who was also the "priest of God Most High," brings out bread and water for Avram and his soldiers (Bereshit 14:18). As an expression of gratitude, Malki Tzedek blesses Avram to "God Most High, Creator of heaven and earth" (14:19) and afterward blesses God, "Who has delivered your foes into your hand" (14:20).

When others do us a kindness, we should not limit our gratitude to the interpersonal realm. We must expand our expression of gratitude to God as well. The person doing the *ḥesed* is acting as an emissary of God, making His name great and revealed in this world. In addition, we must acknowledge that it is God's providence that allowed for the kindness to happen.

By incorporating a divine element into all of our interpersonal gratitude experiences, may we merit additional spiritual and psychological well-being, above and beyond what is generally associated with being grateful people.

Rabbi Mordechai Schiffman

Analysis

- What specific information do we now have that was unavailable to classical Jewish commentators? How can it aid our understanding of the text?
- What can we learn from this passage that can help us understand the text?
- What further questions on the text do you have now that you have read this passage?

TAKING A LITERARY APPROACH

The route taken by the Babylonian coalition, described in painful detail, is quite unusual. Rather than choosing one of the well-traveled, direct routes to Sedom, they instead follow a circuitous route, wasting precious time and energy on their way to crushing a rebellion. Moreover, the Refaim, Zuzim, Eimim, and Horites with whom they chose to engage in warfare were known as mighty and fierce fighters. Why do the invaders from the east intentionally get involved with difficult, unnecessary battles which could tire out their soldiers? Why would they choose a route which circumnavigates Sedom rather than a more direct one?

One of the fascinating things about the route the Babylonian coalition takes is that it is familiar to careful readers of the Torah. It is essentially the same route later traveled by the Israelites in their fortieth year in the wilderness, but in reverse. Bemidbar 20–21 and Devarim 2–3 describe their departure from Kadesh, swinging around toward Eilat to circumnavigate Edom, Amon, and Moav, and finally the battles with Siḥon and Og. This route is as bizarre as the one in our own story. Given that the Israelites begin their trek at Kadesh, on the southern border, we must wonder why it is necessary for them to travel on a circuitous route and enter from the east, with all the attendant problems. Can God not help them defeat the Canaanite in the south just as He helps them defeat the mighty Emorite kings in the east?

Apparently the Israelite journey is designed to serve the same function as that of the Babylonian invaders. When the Israelites first leave Egypt they strike fear in the hearts of the Canaanite nations: "Peoples heard, they quaked; trembling seized Philistia's dwellers. Then the chieftains of Edom were shaken, shuddering seized the mighty of Moav, all the dwellers of Canaan melted. Terror and fear fell upon them" (Shemot 15.14–16). Word of the nation that humbles the mighty Egyptian Empire and whose God splits the Reed Sea brings great fear to the entire region. That fear serves an essential function – it obviates the need to fight for every inch of the land: "I shall send My terror before you and I shall panic the whole people among whom you shall come, and I shall make all your enemies turn tail to you. I shall the send the wasp before you and it will drive out the Hivite and the Canaanite and Hittite before you" (23:27–28). Under God's initial plan, the conquest of the Promised Land will be a quick, bloodless enterprise.

Rabbi Zvi Grumet

15 1 After these events the word of the LORD came to Avram in a vision, saying: "Do not be
2 afraid, Avram. I am your Shield. Your reward shall be very great." But Avram said, "My
Lord GOD, what will You have given me if I remain childless and the one who will take
3 charge of my household is Eliezer of Damascus?"[1] Avram said, "You have given me no
4 children. A man of my household will be my heir." Then the word of the LORD came to
him: "That man will not be your heir; one who comes forth from your own loins will be
5 your heir." He took him outside and said, "Look at the heavens and count the stars – if
indeed you can count them." He said to him, "That is how your descendants will be."
6 And because Avram put his trust in the LORD, He reckoned it to him as righteousness.[2]
7 And He told him, "I am the LORD who brought you out from Ur Kasdim to give you this
8 land to possess it." And he said, "My Lord GOD, how shall I know that I will possess it?"
9 And He said to him, "Take for Me a three-year-old heifer, and a three-year-old goat, and a
10 three-year-old ram, and a turtledove, and a young pigeon." And he took all these and cut
11 them in two and put each half opposite its other half, but the birds he did not cut.[3] Birds
12 of prey descended on the carcasses, but Avram drove them away. And so it was that, as the
13 sun went down, a deep sleep fell upon Avram and a deep, dark dread came upon him. And
God said to Avram, "Know with certainty that your descendants will be migrants in a land

1 | Eliezer is understood to have been a prominent servant of Avram.

2 | Alternatively, Avram recognized the righteousness of God.

3 | This was a covenant ceremony (cf., e.g., Yirmeya 34:18).

UNLOCKING THE TEXT

- Why does this vision happen to Avram at this point? Is this a response to something?
- Is there anything new in these promises, or are they merely reaffirming previous promises?
- Why would Avram need them reaffirmed?
- Have the promises God made in this vision come true in history?
- If a covenant has two parties with two sets of responsibilities, who and what are these here?
- What do all the separate elements of the enactment of this covenant symbolize?

FINDING YOURSELF IN THE TEXT

- Can you think of a time when you needed reassurance that a promise made to you would be fulfilled?
- Are you a visual person? Does it help you to see things visually represented?
- Where in your life are relationships navigated by a form of covenant?

Consider using these questions as the basis for your own commentary or creative midrash.

How does reflecting on these firsthand experiences help you better understand the text?

טו א אַחַר ׀ הַדְּבָרִים הָאֵלֶּה הָיָה דְבַר־יהוה אֶל־אַבְרָם בַּמַּחֲזֶה לֵאמֹר אַל־תִּירָא אַבְרָם יב
ב אָנֹכִי מָגֵן לָךְ שְׂכָרְךָ הַרְבֵּה מְאֹד: וַיֹּאמֶר אַבְרָם אֲדֹנָי יֱהוִה מַה־תִּתֶּן־לִי וְאָנֹכִי
ג הוֹלֵךְ עֲרִירִי וּבֶן־מֶשֶׁק בֵּיתִי הוּא דַּמֶּשֶׂק אֱלִיעֶזֶר: וַיֹּאמֶר אַבְרָם הֵן לִי לֹא נָתַתָּה
ד זָרַע וְהִנֵּה בֶן־בֵּיתִי יוֹרֵשׁ אֹתִי: וְהִנֵּה דְבַר־יהוה אֵלָיו לֵאמֹר לֹא יִירָשְׁךָ זֶה כִּי־אִם
ה אֲשֶׁר יֵצֵא מִמֵּעֶיךָ הוּא יִירָשֶׁךָ: וַיּוֹצֵא אֹתוֹ הַחוּצָה וַיֹּאמֶר הַבֶּט־נָא הַשָּׁמַיְמָה
ו וּסְפֹר הַכּוֹכָבִים אִם־תּוּכַל לִסְפֹּר אֹתָם וַיֹּאמֶר לוֹ כֹּה יִהְיֶה זַרְעֶךָ: וְהֶאֱמִן בַּיהוה
ז וַיַּחְשְׁבֶהָ לּוֹ צְדָקָה: וַיֹּאמֶר אֵלָיו אֲנִי יהוה אֲשֶׁר הוֹצֵאתִיךָ מֵאוּר כַּשְׂדִּים לָתֶת לְךָ ששי
ח ט אֶת־הָאָרֶץ הַזֹּאת לְרִשְׁתָּהּ: וַיֹּאמַר אֲדֹנָי יֱהוִה בַּמָּה אֵדַע כִּי אִירָשֶׁנָּה: וַיֹּאמֶר אֵלָיו
י קְחָה לִי עֶגְלָה מְשֻׁלֶּשֶׁת וְעֵז מְשֻׁלֶּשֶׁת וְאַיִל מְשֻׁלָּשׁ וְתֹר וְגוֹזָל: וַיִּקַּח־לוֹ אֶת־כָּל־
אֵלֶּה וַיְבַתֵּר אֹתָם בַּתָּוֶךְ וַיִּתֵּן אִישׁ־בִּתְרוֹ לִקְרַאת רֵעֵהוּ וְאֶת־הַצִּפֹּר לֹא בָתָר:
יא יב וַיֵּרֶד הָעַיִט עַל־הַפְּגָרִים וַיַּשֵּׁב אֹתָם אַבְרָם: וַיְהִי הַשֶּׁמֶשׁ לָבוֹא וְתַרְדֵּמָה נָפְלָה
יג עַל־אַבְרָם וְהִנֵּה אֵימָה חֲשֵׁכָה גְדֹלָה נֹפֶלֶת עָלָיו: וַיֹּאמֶר לְאַבְרָם יָדֹעַ תֵּדַע

THEMES | COVENANT | THE LAND OF ISRAEL | PROPHECY AND REVELATION

Episode 19: *The Brit bein HaBetarim* – Bereshit 15:1–21

SUMMARY

In this episode, Avram's relationship with God as well as the form of communication between them gets an upgrade, with an intense vision that leads to a covenant between Avram and God. The two promises that form the essence of this covenant have already been promised to Avram but are now reaffirmed to him. First, he is promised that he will have descendants to continue after him. Then, in a symbolic enactment of a covenant, God provides him with some details regarding the future of those descendants and promises him that they will ultimately inherit the land of Canaan.

14 not their own, and there they will be enslaved and oppressed for four hundred years. But
I will bring judgment on the nation they will serve, and afterward they will go free with
15 great wealth. As for you, you will join your ancestors in peace; you will be buried in ripe
16 old age. And the fourth generation will return here, for the guilt of the Amorites is not
17 yet resolved."[4] And when the sun set and it was very dark, a smoking furnace appeared
18 and a blazing torch passed between these pieces. On that day the Lord made a covenant
with Avram: "To your descendants I will give this land, from the River of Egypt to the
19 20 great river Euphrates, the land of the Kenites, the Kenizzites, the Kadmonites, the Hittites,
21 the Perizzites, the Refaim, the Amorites, the Canaanites, the Girgashites, and the Jebusites."

4 | The accumulated guilt of the indigenous people does not yet warrant their displacement.

In the *brit bein habetarim*, we find the answer to Avraham's question: God informs Avraham Avinu that indeed his offspring will one day conquer (*yerusha*) the land. However, this conquest will take place only after several generations of bondage in a foreign land, after which they will gain their independence and their oppressor shall be punished (Bereshit 15:13–16).

Therefore, in the aftermath of the war of the kings, an additional promise of *zera ve'aretz* (descendants and land) must be made, one which explains how the process of Avraham's offspring becoming a nation will unfold.

Rabbi Menachem Leibtag

יד כִּי־גֵר ׀ יִהְיֶ֣ה זַרְעֲךָ֗ בְּאֶ֙רֶץ֙ לֹ֣א לָהֶ֔ם וַעֲבָד֖וּם וְעִנּ֣וּ אֹתָ֑ם אַרְבַּ֥ע מֵא֖וֹת שָׁנָֽה: וְגַ֧ם
טו אֶת־הַגּ֛וֹי אֲשֶׁ֥ר יַעֲבֹ֖דוּ דָּ֣ן אָנֹ֑כִי וְאַחֲרֵי־כֵ֥ן יֵצְא֖וּ בִּרְכֻ֥שׁ גָּדֽוֹל: וְאַתָּ֛ה תָּב֥וֹא אֶל־
טז אֲבֹתֶ֖יךָ בְּשָׁל֑וֹם תִּקָּבֵ֖ר בְּשֵׂיבָ֥ה טוֹבָֽה: וְד֥וֹר רְבִיעִ֖י יָשׁ֣וּבוּ הֵ֑נָּה כִּ֧י לֹא־שָׁלֵ֛ם עֲוֹ֥ן
יז הָאֱמֹרִ֖י עַד־הֵֽנָּה: וַיְהִ֤י הַשֶּׁ֙מֶשׁ֙ בָּ֔אָה וַעֲלָטָ֖ה הָיָ֑ה וְהִנֵּ֨ה תַנּ֤וּר עָשָׁן֙ וְלַפִּ֣יד אֵ֔שׁ אֲשֶׁ֣ר
יח עָבַ֔ר בֵּ֖ין הַגְּזָרִ֥ים הָאֵֽלֶּה: בַּיּ֣וֹם הַה֗וּא כָּרַ֧ת יְהוָֹ֛ה אֶת־אַבְרָ֖ם בְּרִ֣ית לֵאמֹ֑ר לְזַרְעֲךָ֗
יט נָתַ֙תִּי֙ אֶת־הָאָ֣רֶץ הַזֹּ֔את מִנְּהַ֣ר מִצְרַ֔יִם עַד־הַנָּהָ֥ר הַגָּדֹ֖ל נְהַר־פְּרָֽת: אֶת־הַקֵּינִ֥י
כא וְאֶת־הַקְּנִזִּ֖י וְאֵ֣ת הַקַּדְמֹנִֽי: וְאֶת־הַחִתִּ֥י וְאֶת־הַפְּרִזִּ֖י וְאֶת־הָרְפָאִֽים: וְאֶת־הָֽאֱמֹרִי֙
וְאֶת־הַֽכְּנַעֲנִ֔י וְאֶת־הַגִּרְגָּשִׁ֖י וְאֶת־הַיְבוּסִֽי:

TAKING A LITERARY APPROACH

Now there are numerous opinions among the commentators explaining why Avraham was fearful (and these opinions are not all mutually exclusive). However, there is one point that Avraham raises over and over again in his ensuing conversation that definitely relates to his military conquest, as well as his lack of a son.

Avraham realizes that without a son, everything that he has acquired will be taken over by his servant Eliezer.

But note the use of the verb *yorash* (which is usually understood simply as to "inherit") in Bereshit 15:3–8.

There can be no doubt that *yerusha* is the keyword in this conversation, but what does it mean?

Throughout Ḥumash, *yerusha* almost always implies military conquest, usually by (or to become) a sovereign nation. (See, for example, Bemidbar 33:50–54.) Here too, after his military victory, Avraham wants to know how his offspring will one day gain sovereignty over this land.

THE ART OF MIDRASH

The Covenant of the Pieces
Moshe Castel (2021)

Analysis

- Which elements of this image are directly mentioned in the text?
- Which elements of this image are not found in the text?
- What midrashic interpretation is the artist giving us?

A QUESTION OF BIBLIODRAMA

TO GOD

- Why do You choose now to appear to Avram in a vision?
- What are the responsibilities of Avram (or his descendants) in this covenant?
- Why did You choose to use these visual and experiential ways to enact this covenant?
- Why will Avram's descendants have to start their national journey in slavery?

TO AVRAM

- How did this vision compare to the way God spoke to you previously?
- Was this vision awe-inspiring and dramatic, or was it intimate and quiet?
- Were you scared?
- Did the message of the vision impact your faith?
- Did this vision address any particular concerns you were having?
- Why did you ask God for a sign? Were you struggling with your faith in God's promises?
- Did you understand the symbolism behind the vision and the things God showed you?
- How do you feel after this experience and after receiving this message?
- Did you share this experience with Sarai or Lot or anyone else? If so, how did they respond?

Pigeon

Heifer

Turtledove

Analysis

- What specific information do we now have that was unavailable to classical Jewish commentators? How can it aid our understanding of the text?
- How can these images help us understand the text?
- What further questions on the text do you have after seeing these images?

INTEGRATING ḤOKHMA

Ram

Goat

16 1 Sarai, Avraham's wife, had borne him no children; but she had an Egyptian maidservant
2 named Hagar. Sarai said to Avram, "The LORD has kept me from having children. Come
now to my maid. Perhaps through her I might build a family." And Avram listened to
3 Sarai. So it was that, after living in Canaan for ten years, Avram's wife Sarai took Hagar,
4 her Egyptian maidservant, and gave her to her husband Avram to be his wife. He came to
Hagar and she conceived. And when she realized that she was pregnant, she began to look
5 upon her mistress with contempt. Sarai said to Avram, "The abuse I suffer is your fault. I
laid my servant in your arms and now that she knows she is pregnant, she looks upon me
6 with contempt. Let the LORD judge between me and you!" Avram said to Sarai, "Your maid
is in your own hands. Do with her whatever you think best." Sarai treated her harshly – and
7 Hagar ran away from her. An angel of the LORD found her near a spring of water in the
8 desert, the spring by the road to Shur. He said, "Hagar, maidservant of Sarai, where have
you come from and where are you going?" She said, "I am running away from my mistress
9 Sarai." The angel of the LORD said to her, "Go back to your mistress; submit yourself under
10 her hand." And the angel of the LORD added: "I will greatly multiply your descendants;
11 they will be too many to count." Said the angel of the LORD: "You are pregnant and will
give birth to a son. You shall name him Yishmael, for the LORD has heard your affliction.[1]

1 | The name Yishmael means "God hears."

UNLOCKING THE TEXT

- Why does Sarai suggest Avram take Hagar?
- Why is it important to know that Hagar was Egyptian?
- Why did Avram listen to Sarai?
- Why was Sarai barren?
- Why did Hagar become pregnant immediately?
- Why did Sarai blame Avram for the abuse she received at the hand of Hagar?
- Why did Avram respond in this way to Sarai's claim?
- Why did Hagar flee?
- Why did the angel instruct her to return?
- What is the meaning behind Yishmael's name?

FINDING YOURSELF IN THE TEXT

- Can you think of a time when the phrase "be careful what you wish for" came back to haunt you in a similar way to Sarai in this episode?
- Who do you relate to more in this story, Sarai or Avram?
- If you were Sarai, what would you have done differently here? If you were Avram, what would you have done differently here?

Consider using these questions as the basis for your own commentary or creative midrash.

How does reflecting on these firsthand experiences help you better understand the text?

טז וְשָׂרַי֙ אֵ֣שֶׁת אַבְרָ֔ם לֹ֥א יָלְדָ֖ה ל֑וֹ וְלָ֛הּ שִׁפְחָ֥ה מִצְרִ֖ית וּשְׁמָ֥הּ הָגָֽר: וַתֹּ֨אמֶר שָׂרַ֜י יג
אֶל־אַבְרָ֗ם הִנֵּה־נָ֞א עֲצָרַ֤נִי יְהֹוָה֙ מִלֶּ֔דֶת בֹּא־נָא֙ אֶל־שִׁפְחָתִ֔י אוּלַ֖י אִבָּנֶ֣ה מִמֶּ֑נָּה
וַיִּשְׁמַ֥ע אַבְרָ֖ם לְק֥וֹל שָׂרָֽי: וַתִּקַּ֞ח שָׂרַ֣י | אֵֽשֶׁת־אַבְרָ֗ם אֶת־הָגָ֤ר הַמִּצְרִית֙ שִׁפְחָתָ֔הּ ג
מִקֵּץ֙ עֶ֣שֶׂר שָׁנִ֔ים לְשֶׁ֥בֶת אַבְרָ֖ם בְּאֶ֣רֶץ כְּנָ֑עַן וַתִּתֵּ֥ן אֹתָ֛הּ לְאַבְרָ֥ם אִישָׁ֖הּ ל֥וֹ לְאִשָּֽׁה:
וַיָּבֹ֥א אֶל־הָגָ֖ר וַתַּ֑הַר וַתֵּ֨רֶא֙ כִּ֣י הָרָ֔תָה וַתֵּקַ֥ל גְּבִרְתָּ֖הּ בְּעֵינֶֽיהָ: וַתֹּ֨אמֶר שָׂרַ֣י אֶל־ ה
אַבְרָ֗ם חֲמָסִ֣י עָלֶ֘יךָ֘ אָנֹכִ֣י נָתַ֣תִּי שִׁפְחָתִי֙ בְּחֵיקֶ֔ךָ וַתֵּ֨רֶא֙ כִּ֣י הָרָ֔תָה וָאֵקַ֖ל בְּעֵינֶ֑יהָ
יִשְׁפֹּ֥ט יְהֹוָ֖ה בֵּינִ֥י וּבֵינֶֽיךָ: וַיֹּ֨אמֶר אַבְרָ֜ם אֶל־שָׂרַ֗י הִנֵּ֤ה שִׁפְחָתֵךְ֙ בְּיָדֵ֔ךְ עֲשִׂי־לָ֖הּ ו
הַטּ֣וֹב בְּעֵינָ֑יִךְ וַתְּעַנֶּ֣הָ שָׂרַ֔י וַתִּבְרַ֖ח מִפָּנֶֽיהָ: וַֽיִּמְצָאָ֞הּ מַלְאַ֧ךְ יְהֹוָ֛ה עַל־עֵ֥ין הַמַּ֖יִם ז
בַּמִּדְבָּ֑ר עַל־הָעַ֖יִן בְּדֶ֥רֶךְ שֽׁוּר: וַיֹּאמַ֗ר הָגָ֞ר שִׁפְחַ֥ת שָׂרַ֛י אֵֽי־מִזֶּ֥ה בָ֖את וְאָ֣נָה תֵלֵ֑כִי ח
וַתֹּ֕אמֶר מִפְּנֵי֙ שָׂרַ֣י גְּבִרְתִּ֔י אָנֹכִ֖י בֹּרַֽחַת: וַיֹּ֤אמֶר לָהּ֙ מַלְאַ֣ךְ יְהֹוָ֔ה שׁ֖וּבִי אֶל־גְּבִרְתֵּ֑ךְ ט
וְהִתְעַנִּ֖י תַּ֥חַת יָדֶֽיהָ: וַיֹּ֤אמֶר לָהּ֙ מַלְאַ֣ךְ יְהֹוָ֔ה הַרְבָּ֥ה אַרְבֶּ֖ה אֶת־זַרְעֵ֑ךְ וְלֹ֥א יִסָּפֵ֖ר י
מֵרֹֽב: וַיֹּ֤אמֶר לָהּ֙ מַלְאַ֣ךְ יְהֹוָ֔ה הִנָּ֥ךְ הָרָ֖ה וְיֹלַ֣דְתְּ בֵּ֑ן וְקָרָ֤את שְׁמוֹ֙ יִשְׁמָעֵ֔אל כִּֽי־ יא

| THEMES | COVENANT | RELATIONSHIPS AND LOVE | ETHICS |

Episode 20: *The Birth of Yishmael* – Bereshit 16:1–16

SUMMARY

This story can be seen as a continuation of part of the previous dialogue between Avram and God, which focused mainly on the problem of Avram's succession and his progeny. Despite Sarai's barrenness, Avram continues to have faith in the promises God has given of an heir and legacy. But Sarai focuses on the logistics of this and convinces him to take her maidservant Hagar as a surrogate. Hagar's pregnancy causes tension and Hagar flees. An angel then promises Hagar that the baby she will birth will achieve greatness (despite not being the heir of Avram) and instructs her to return to Avram's household.

12 He will become a wild donkey of a man; his hand will be against everyone, and everyone's
13 hand against him. He will live up against all his brothers." She gave a name to the Lord
who had spoken to her: "You are the God who sees me," for she said: "Have I not here seen
14 Him who sees me?" That is why the well is called Be'er Laḥai Ro'i.[2] It is still there between
15 Kadesh and Bered. So Hagar bore Avram a son, and Avram gave the name Yishmael to the
16 son that she had borne. Avram was eighty-six years old when Hagar bore him Yishmael.

2 | Meaning "Well of the Living One Who Sees Me."

Yishmael qualify as one who emerged from Avram's loins? Is his divinely ordained name, which Avram gives him as well (Bereshit 16:15), not Yishmael – literally, "God hears"? Hagar and Avram have every reason to believe that Yishmael is the promised heir, fulfilling Sarai's initial plan – despite the personal difficulties between Sarai and Hagar.

Indeed, were we to read only the angel's first two messages to Hagar we would likely draw the same conclusion. But despite the uncanny parallels between Avram's and Hagar's respective destinies, there is one dramatic – and fundamental – difference between them. The climax of the promise to Avram is rootedness in a particular land: "The fourth generation will return here" (15:16), while the climax of the promise to Hagar is the rootlessness of her "wild donkey" of a child, free to the extent of being untamable. The promises of progeny are parallel, but the relationships to the land point in opposite directions. Yishmael's descendants will be nomads, while Avram's children will forever be rooted in their land.

Rabbi Zvi Grumet

יב שָׁמַ֥ע יהוה אֶל־עָנְיֵֽךְ׃ וְה֤וּא יִהְיֶה֙ פֶּ֣רֶא אָדָ֔ם יָד֣וֹ בַכֹּ֔ל וְיַ֥ד כֹּ֖ל בּ֑וֹ וְעַל־פְּנֵ֥י כָל־אֶחָ֖יו
יג יִשְׁכֹּֽן׃ וַתִּקְרָ֤א שֵׁם־יהוה֙ הַדֹּבֵ֣ר אֵלֶ֔יהָ אַתָּ֖ה אֵ֣ל רֳאִ֑י כִּ֣י אָֽמְרָ֗ה הֲגַ֥ם הֲלֹ֛ם רָאִ֖יתִי
יד טו אַחֲרֵ֥י רֹאִֽי׃ עַל־כֵּן֙ קָרָ֣א לַבְּאֵ֔ר בְּאֵ֥ר לַחַ֖י רֹאִ֑י הִנֵּ֥ה בֵין־קָדֵ֖שׁ וּבֵ֥ין בָּֽרֶד׃ וַתֵּ֨לֶד
טז הָגָ֛ר לְאַבְרָ֖ם בֵּ֑ן וַיִּקְרָ֨א אַבְרָ֧ם שֶׁם־בְּנ֛וֹ אֲשֶׁר־יָלְדָ֥ה הָגָ֖ר יִשְׁמָעֵֽאל׃ וְאַבְרָ֕ם בֶּן־
שְׁמֹנִ֥ים שָׁנָ֖ה וְשֵׁ֣שׁ שָׁנִ֑ים בְּלֶֽדֶת־הָגָ֥ר אֶת־יִשְׁמָעֵ֖אל לְאַבְרָֽם׃

TAKING A LITERARY APPROACH

The three messages delivered to Hagar by the angel outline a dramatic moment. The second message, informing her of the multitude of her progeny, echoes God's promise to Avram. In the covenant between the pieces, God tells Avram that he will not get to see that promise fulfilled in his lifetime, nor will his children. There will first be an extended period of trials and suffering, and only after the suffering of the parents will the promise come true for the children. Based on the message she hears form the angel, Hagar can easily draw the conclusion that she is the parent of the covenantal child promised to Avram, as she will also endure suffering to bring God's promise to her child. In fact, there are three key prerequisites for the fulfillment of God's promise to Avram: being a stranger (*ger*) in a foreign land, being enslaved, and being oppressed (*inui*), and all three are used to describe Hagar's experience – in the exact same language. She is a servant to Sarai, she suffers *inui* inflicted by Sarai, and her name, Hagar, in the unvocalized text of the Torah, could easily be read as *hager*, "the stranger."

When Hagar hears the angel's second utterance promising bountiful progeny, the first of the angel's pronouncements demanding that she suffer takes on new meaning. For Hagar, Yishmael is the heir promised to Avram, and like Avram, she will endure so that her child can receive that divine reward. Even Avram might believe that Yishmael is the promised heir; didn't Yishmael fit all the criteria spelled out earlier? Doesn't

THE ART OF MIDRASH

Hagar and Ishmael
Dikla Laor (2015)

Analysis

- Which elements of this image are directly mentioned in the text?
- Which elements of this image are not found in the text?
- What midrashic interpretations could be inferred from this image?

A QUESTION OF BIBLIODRAMA

TO SARAI

- How is being childless impacting you emotionally?
- How do you feel about the covenant between Avram and God in this light?
- Why did you give Hagar to Avram? Why now?
- How did it feel to give Hagar over to your husband?
- How did it feel when you found out she became pregnant?
- Did your feelings toward Avram or your relationship with him change after this?
- Are you angry with Avram? Why?
- How do you feel about his response to you?
- How do you feel toward Yishmael and toward Hagar now that he has been born?
- If you could ask or say anything to God at this point, what would it be?

TO GOD

- Was this part of Your master plan?
- What lessons do You hope we learn from this story?

TO AVRAM

- How do you think Sarai was doing before this episode?
- Did her suggestion surprise you? Why did you go along with it?
- How do you feel when Hagar becomes pregnant?
- Do you understand why Sarai is angry? How do you feel toward her now?
- Why did you respond to Sarai in the way you did?
- How do you feel when you hear that Sarai treated Hagar harshly?
- How do you feel when Hagar runs away?
- How do you feel when Yishmael is born?
- Why do you name him Yishmael?

HAGAR

- What was your life like in the household of Avram and Sarai? How was your relationship with Sarai before this episode?
- How did you feel when you heard that Avram would take you as a wife?
- Did your feelings toward Sarai change when you became Avram's wife? And when you became pregnant?
- Why did you flee?
- How did you feel about the baby in your womb before you met the angel? And after?
- How do you feel about the message and instruction from the angel?

On the way to Shur: Shur is located between Kadesh Barnea and Bered, and is identified with Bir el-Hasana in central Sinai. It is also the name of a desert east of Egypt (Bereshit 25:18; Shemot 15:22). The road mentioned here is assumed to be the route through central Sinai, which extends from Be'er Sheva through Kadesh Barnea, Bered, and Refidim, all the way to present-day Ismailia in Egypt. In Aramaic, *shur* means "wall" or "fortification." The route was called by this name due to the fortresses on the eastern border of Egypt, along the line of today's Suez Canal.

Bered: According to Targum Yonatan, this is Ḥalutza, north of Kadesh Barnea. However, contemporary researchers identify it with Bir el-Hasana, in the center of the Sinai Peninsula.

Aerial photo of the Desert of Shur in the northern Sinai Peninsula

Analysis

- What specific information do we now have that was unavailable to classical Jewish commentators? How can it aid our understanding of the text?
- What can we learn from these images that can help us understand the text?
- What further questions on the text do you have now that you have seen these images?

INTEGRATING ḤOKHMA

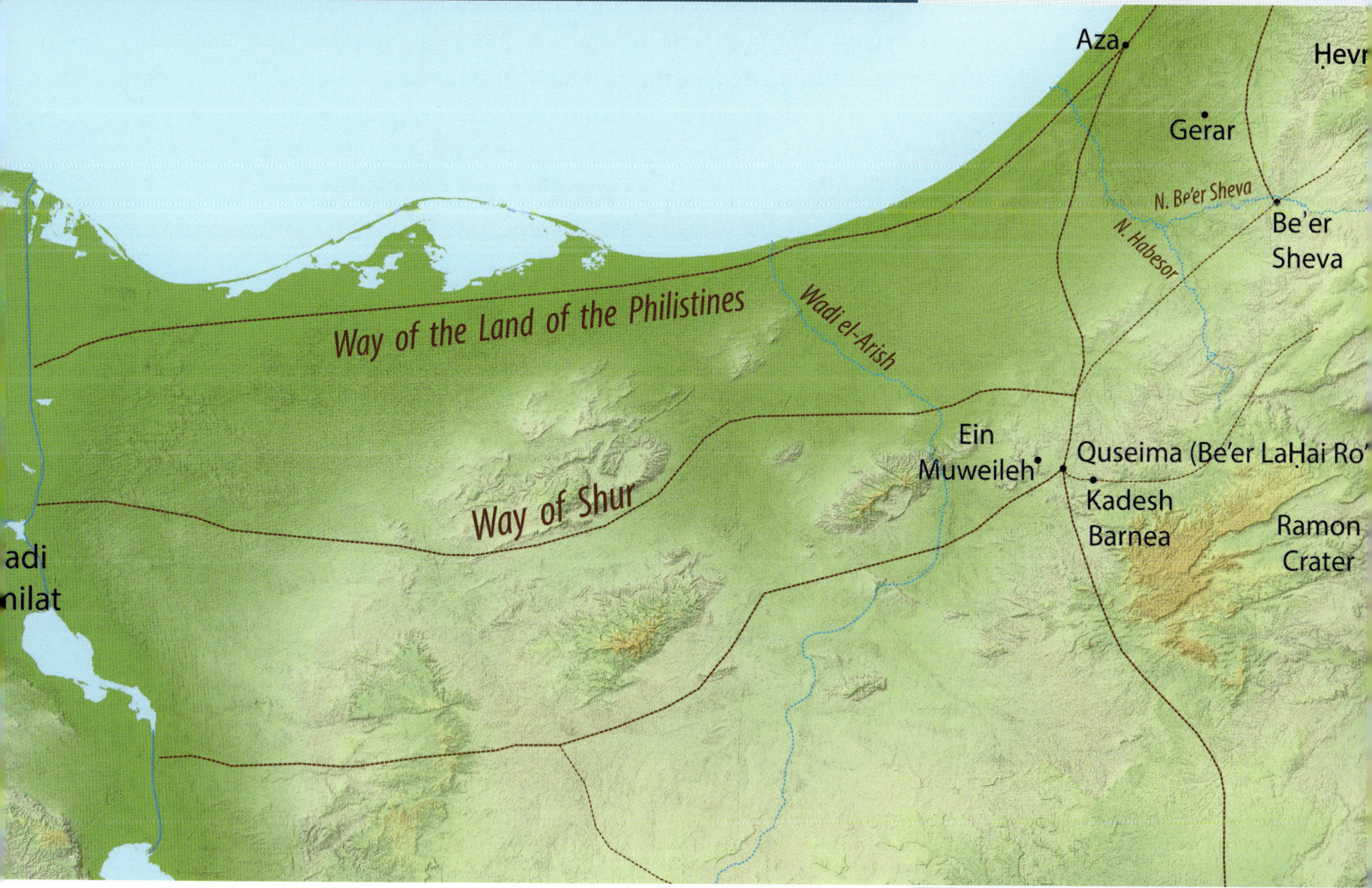

Hagar's journey

17 1 When Avram was ninety-nine years old, the LORD appeared to him and said, "I am El
2 Shaddai. Walk before Me in integrity, and I will establish My covenant between Me and
3 you, and make you exceedingly numerous." Avram fell facedown. And God said to him,
4 "As for Me – this is My covenant with you: you shall be father to a multitude of nations.
5 No longer shall you be called Avram. Your name will be Avraham, for I have made you
6 father to a multitude of nations.[1] I will make you exceptionally fertile, I will turn you into
7 nations; kings will come from you. I will establish My covenant between Me and you
and your descendants after you throughout the generations: an eternal covenant. I will
8 be God to you and your descendants after you, and I will give you and your descendants
after you the land where you now live as strangers, the whole land of Canaan, an everlasting
9 possession, and I will be their God." Then God said to Avraham, "As for you, you shall keep
10 My covenant, you and your descendants after you throughout their generations. This is My
covenant, kept between Me and you and your descendants after you: every male among
11 you shall be circumcised. You must circumcise the flesh of your foreskin – this shall be
12 the sign of the covenant between Me and you. Throughout the generations, every male
among you shall be circumcised at the age of eight days, including the slave born in your

1 | The name Avraham resonates with *av hamon* ("father of a multitude").

UNLOCKING THE TEXT

- What is the significance of the name God uses here?
- What does it mean to walk before God? How is this different from Bereshit 6:9?
- How is this covenant different from the previous one?
- If a covenant has two parties with two sets of responsibilities, who and what would those be in this covenant?
- What is the significance of changing one's name?
- What is the significance of Avram's new name?
- What is the significance of Sarai's new name?
- What is significant about the sign of this covenant? Compare to previous covenants including Bereshit 9 and 15.
- Why does Avraham mention Yishmael to God?
- Why does God respond in this way?

FINDING YOURSELF IN THE TEXT

- Have you ever committed to anything that resembled a covenant? What was it? How was it "signed"?
- Have you ever been promised something that you deeply wanted but thought was impossible? What emotions did you experience?
- Do you know what your name means? Do you know how your parents chose it?

Consider using these questions as the basis for your own commentary or creative midrash.

How does reflecting on these firsthand experiences help you better understand the text?

יז א וַיְהִי אַבְרָם בֶּן־תִּשְׁעִים שָׁנָה וְתֵשַׁע שָׁנִים וַיֵּרָא יהוה אֶל־אַבְרָם וַיֹּאמֶר אֵלָיו יד
ב אֲנִי־אֵל שַׁדַּי הִתְהַלֵּךְ לְפָנַי וֶהְיֵה תָמִים: וְאֶתְּנָה בְרִיתִי בֵּינִי וּבֵינֶךָ וְאַרְבֶּה אוֹתְךָ
ג ד בִּמְאֹד מְאֹד: וַיִּפֹּל אַבְרָם עַל־פָּנָיו וַיְדַבֵּר אִתּוֹ אֱלֹהִים לֵאמֹר: אֲנִי הִנֵּה בְרִיתִי
ה אִתָּךְ וְהָיִיתָ לְאַב הֲמוֹן גּוֹיִם: וְלֹא־יִקָּרֵא עוֹד אֶת־שִׁמְךָ אַבְרָם וְהָיָה שִׁמְךָ אַבְרָהָם
ו כִּי אַב־הֲמוֹן גּוֹיִם נְתַתִּיךָ: וְהִפְרֵתִי אֹתְךָ בִּמְאֹד מְאֹד וּנְתַתִּיךָ לְגוֹיִם וּמְלָכִים
ז מִמְּךָ יֵצֵאוּ: וַהֲקִמֹתִי אֶת־בְּרִיתִי בֵּינִי וּבֵינֶךָ וּבֵין זַרְעֲךָ אַחֲרֶיךָ לְדֹרֹתָם לִבְרִית שביעי
ח עוֹלָם לִהְיוֹת לְךָ לֵאלֹהִים וּלְזַרְעֲךָ אַחֲרֶיךָ: וְנָתַתִּי לְךָ וּלְזַרְעֲךָ אַחֲרֶיךָ אֵת | אֶרֶץ
ט מְגֻרֶיךָ אֵת כָּל־אֶרֶץ כְּנַעַן לַאֲחֻזַּת עוֹלָם וְהָיִיתִי לָהֶם לֵאלֹהִים: וַיֹּאמֶר אֱלֹהִים
י אֶל־אַבְרָהָם וְאַתָּה אֶת־בְּרִיתִי תִשְׁמֹר אַתָּה וְזַרְעֲךָ אַחֲרֶיךָ לְדֹרֹתָם: זֹאת בְּרִיתִי
יא אֲשֶׁר תִּשְׁמְרוּ בֵּינִי וּבֵינֵיכֶם וּבֵין זַרְעֲךָ אַחֲרֶיךָ הִמּוֹל לָכֶם כָּל־זָכָר: וּנְמַלְתֶּם אֵת
יב בְּשַׂר עָרְלַתְכֶם וְהָיָה לְאוֹת בְּרִית בֵּינִי וּבֵינֵיכֶם: וּבֶן־שְׁמֹנַת יָמִים יִמּוֹל לָכֶם
כָּל־זָכָר לְדֹרֹתֵיכֶם יְלִיד בָּיִת וּמִקְנַת־כֶּסֶף מִכֹּל בֶּן־נֵכָר אֲשֶׁר לֹא מִזַּרְעֲךָ הוּא:

THEMES | COVENANT | PROPHECY AND REVELATION | THE LAND OF ISRAEL

Episode 21: *Brit Mila* – Bereshit 17:1–27

SUMMARY

This episode, which discusses another significant incident in Avram's history, can been seen as a major turning point in his life. God changes his name and establishes a second covenant with him whose signs would be etched onto the flesh of his offspring, in the form of circumcision. Sarai's name is also changed, to Sara, and God promises them a son. Despite Avraham's protest that Yishmael could be heir to the covenant between God and Avraham, God makes it clear that Sara will be the mother of this heir, who will be called Yitzḥak. When God departs following this interaction with him, Avraham circumcises Yishmael, the other members of his household, and himself.

13 household, including one acquired from a stranger not descended from you. All must be
circumcised – those born in your household, those acquired with your money – and My
14 covenant in your flesh will be a covenant everlasting. Any uncircumcised male, whose
foreskin has not been circumcised, shall be severed from his people; he has broken My
15 covenant." God then said to Avraham, "As for Sarai your wife, you shall no
16 longer call her Sarai. Her name will be Sara.[2] I will bless her and give you a son by her. I will
17 bless her so that she shall birth nations; kings of peoples shall descend from her." Avraham
fell on his face and laughed. "Can a hundred-year-old man become a father?" he said to
18 himself. "Can Sara, at ninety, bear a child?" To God Avraham said, "If only Yishmael might
19 live before you!" God said, "Nonetheless: Sara your wife will bear you a son, and you shall
name him Yitzḥak.[3] I will establish My covenant with him as an everlasting covenant for his
20 descendants after him. As for Yishmael – I have heard you.[4] I will bless him and make him
fertile and multiply him exceedingly. He will become father of twelve princes, and I will
21 make of him a great nation. But I will establish My covenant[5] with Yitzḥak, whom Sara will
22 bear to you this time next year." When He finished speaking with him, God went up from
23 Avraham. On that very day, Avraham took his son Yishmael, along with all those born in
his house or acquired with money, every male in Avraham's household, and circumcised
24 the flesh of their foreskins as God had instructed him. Avraham was ninety-nine years old
25 26 when he was circumcised, and his son Yishmael was thirteen. That very day, Avraham and
27 his son Yishmael were circumcised; and all the men of his household, whether home-born
or acquired from strangers, were circumcised together with him.

2 | Meaning "noblewoman."

3 | The name Yitzḥak derives from the verb *vayitzḥak,* "to laugh," referring to Avraham's mirth in verse 17.

4 | The name Yishmael means "God hears" (cf. 16:10).

5 | The covenant affirming that Avraham's progeny will take possession of the land of Canaan.

יג הִמּ֧וֹל ׀ יִמּ֛וֹל יְלִ֥יד בֵּֽיתְךָ֖ וּמִקְנַ֣ת כַּסְפֶּ֑ךָ וְהָיְתָ֧ה בְרִיתִ֛י בִּבְשַׂרְכֶ֖ם לִבְרִ֥ית עוֹלָֽם׃
יד וְעָרֵ֣ל ׀ זָכָ֗ר אֲשֶׁ֤ר לֹֽא־יִמּוֹל֙ אֶת־בְּשַׂ֣ר עָרְלָת֔וֹ וְנִכְרְתָ֛ה הַנֶּ֥פֶשׁ הַהִ֖וא מֵעַמֶּ֑יהָ
טו אֶת־בְּרִיתִ֖י הֵפַֽר׃ וַיֹּ֤אמֶר אֱלֹהִים֙ אֶל־אַבְרָהָ֔ם שָׂרַ֣י אִשְׁתְּךָ֔ לֹא־תִקְרָ֥א
טז אֶת־שְׁמָ֖הּ שָׂרָ֑י כִּ֥י שָׂרָ֖ה שְׁמָֽהּ׃ וּבֵרַכְתִּ֣י אֹתָ֔הּ וְגַ֨ם נָתַ֧תִּי מִמֶּ֛נָּה לְךָ֖ בֵּ֑ן וּבֵֽרַכְתִּ֙יהָ֙
יז וְהָֽיְתָ֣ה לְגוֹיִ֔ם מַלְכֵ֥י עַמִּ֖ים מִמֶּ֥נָּה יִהְיֽוּ׃ וַיִּפֹּ֧ל אַבְרָהָ֛ם עַל־פָּנָ֖יו וַיִּצְחָ֑ק וַיֹּ֣אמֶר בְּלִבּ֗וֹ
יח הַלְּבֶ֤ן מֵאָֽה־שָׁנָה֙ יִוָּלֵ֔ד וְאִ֨ם־שָׂרָ֔ה הֲבַת־תִּשְׁעִ֥ים שָׁנָ֖ה תֵּלֵֽד׃ וַיֹּ֥אמֶר אַבְרָהָ֖ם אֶל־
יט הָאֱלֹהִ֑ים ל֥וּ יִשְׁמָעֵ֖אל יִחְיֶ֥ה לְפָנֶֽיךָ׃ וַיֹּ֣אמֶר אֱלֹהִ֗ים אֲבָל֙ שָׂרָ֣ה אִשְׁתְּךָ֗ יֹלֶ֤דֶת לְךָ֙
בֵּ֔ן וְקָרָ֥אתָ אֶת־שְׁמ֖וֹ יִצְחָ֑ק וַהֲקִמֹתִ֨י אֶת־בְּרִיתִ֥י אִתּ֛וֹ לִבְרִ֥ית עוֹלָ֖ם לְזַרְע֥וֹ אַחֲרָֽיו׃
כ וּֽלְיִשְׁמָעֵאל֮ שְׁמַעְתִּיךָ֒ הִנֵּ֣ה ׀ בֵּרַ֣כְתִּי אֹת֗וֹ וְהִפְרֵיתִ֥י אֹת֛וֹ וְהִרְבֵּיתִ֥י אֹת֖וֹ בִּמְאֹ֣ד
כא מְאֹ֑ד שְׁנֵים־עָשָׂ֤ר נְשִׂיאִם֙ יוֹלִ֔יד וּנְתַתִּ֖יו לְג֥וֹי גָּדֽוֹל׃ וְאֶת־בְּרִיתִ֖י אָקִ֣ים אֶת־יִצְחָ֑ק
כב אֲשֶׁר֩ תֵּלֵ֨ד לְךָ֤ שָׂרָה֙ לַמּוֹעֵ֣ד הַזֶּ֔ה בַּשָּׁנָ֖ה הָאַחֶֽרֶת׃ וַיְכַ֖ל לְדַבֵּ֣ר אִתּ֑וֹ וַיַּ֣עַל אֱלֹהִ֔ים
כג מֵעַ֖ל אַבְרָהָֽם׃ וַיִּקַּ֨ח אַבְרָהָ֜ם אֶת־יִשְׁמָעֵ֣אל בְּנ֗וֹ וְאֵ֨ת כָּל־יְלִידֵ֤י בֵיתוֹ֙ וְאֵת֙ כָּל־
מִקְנַ֣ת כַּסְפּ֔וֹ כָּל־זָכָ֕ר בְּאַנְשֵׁ֖י בֵּ֣ית אַבְרָהָ֑ם וַיָּ֜מָל אֶת־בְּשַׂ֣ר עָרְלָתָ֗ם בְּעֶ֙צֶם֙ הַיּ֣וֹם
כד הַזֶּ֔ה כַּאֲשֶׁ֛ר דִּבֶּ֥ר אִתּ֖וֹ אֱלֹהִֽים׃ וְאַ֨בְרָהָ֔ם בֶּן־תִּשְׁעִ֥ים וָתֵ֖שַׁע שָׁנָ֑ה בְּהִמֹּל֖וֹ בְּשַׂ֥ר מפטיר
כה כו עָרְלָתֽוֹ׃ וְיִשְׁמָעֵ֣אל בְּנ֔וֹ בֶּן־שְׁלֹ֥שׁ עֶשְׂרֵ֖ה שָׁנָ֑ה בְּהִ֨מֹּל֔וֹ אֵ֖ת בְּשַׂ֥ר עָרְלָתֽוֹ׃ בְּעֶ֙צֶם֙
כז הַיּ֣וֹם הַזֶּ֔ה נִמּ֖וֹל אַבְרָהָ֑ם וְיִשְׁמָעֵ֖אל בְּנֽוֹ׃ וְכָל־אַנְשֵׁ֤י בֵיתוֹ֙ יְלִ֣יד בָּ֔יִת וּמִקְנַת־כֶּ֖סֶף
מֵאֵ֣ת בֶּן־נֵכָ֑ר נִמֹּ֖לוּ אִתּֽוֹ׃

THE ART OF MIDRASH

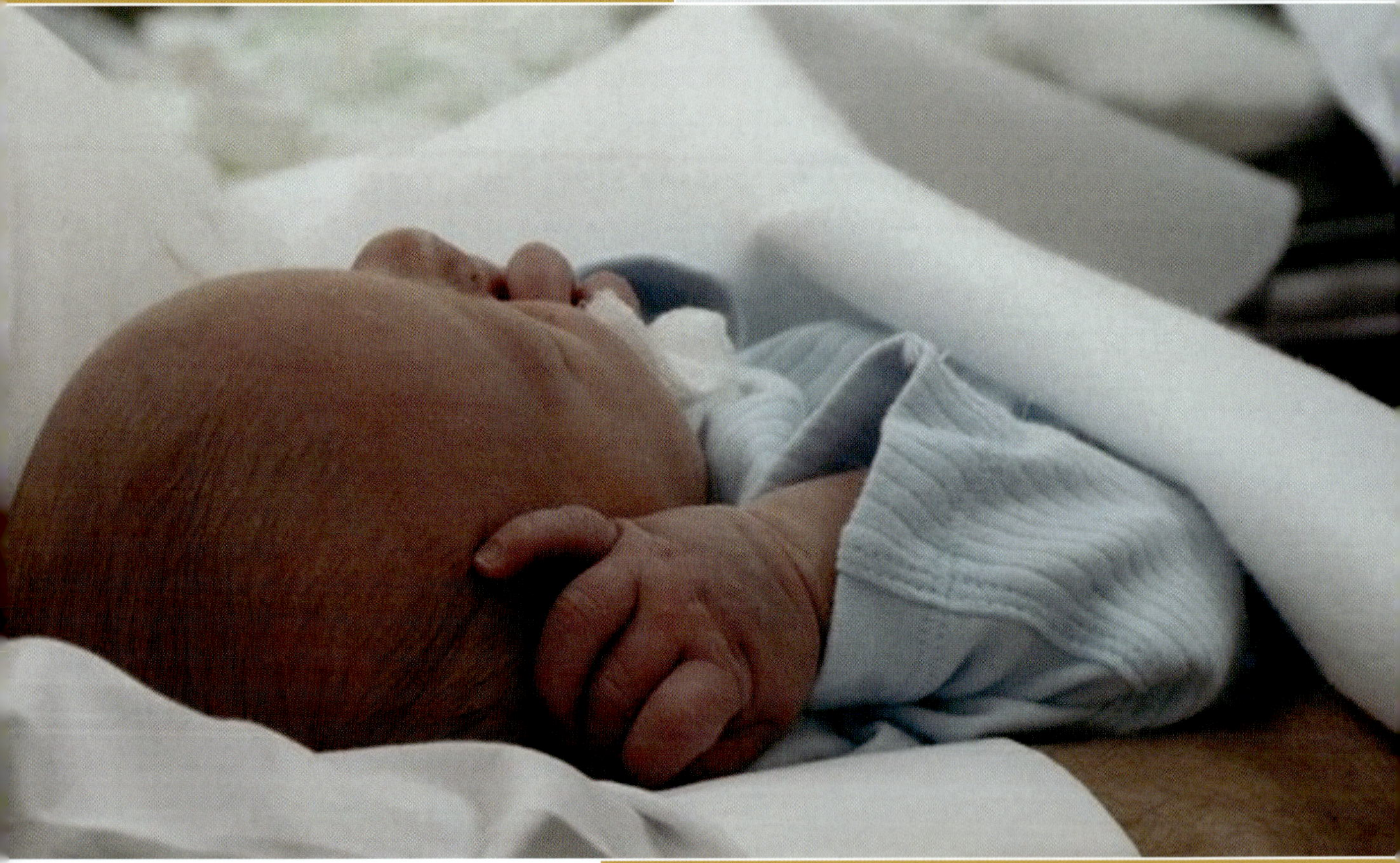

Blessed are You who has commanded us to bring our son into the covenant of Avraham Our Father
Zena Behrman (2013)

Analysis

- Which elements of this image are directly mentioned in the text?
- Which elements of this image are not found in the text?
- What midrashic interpretation could be inferred from this image?

A QUESTION OF BIBLIODRAMA

TO AVRAHAM

- How did it feel to once again hear God promise you these blessings in another covenant?
- Why did you fall on your face this time?
- What did you understand from the new name that God gave you?
- How did it feel for God to change your name?
- Why did you laugh when God promised that you will have a son with Sara? Why did you challenge God over this?
- Why did you mention Yishmael to God in response to this news?
- How did you feel when you heard God's plan for Yishmael?

TO SARA

- What did you understand from the new name that God gave you?
- How did it feel for God to change your name?
- How did it feel to hear you will "birth nations" and that kings will descend from you?
- Did you hear God promise Avraham that you would give birth to a baby boy? What did you feel when you heard this?
- Did you hear Avraham laugh when God told him? How did that feel?
- Did you hear Avraham mention Yishmael to God? How did that feel?
- Did you hear God's plan for Yishmael? How did that make you feel?

TO GOD

- What is different about this covenant from the previous one You gave Avraham?
- Why did You choose this method of signing this covenant?
- Why is Yishmael not the heir to this covenant?
- What is Your plan for Yishmael? Why?

INTEGRATING ḤOKHMA

The Romans found circumcision strange because it was unnatural. Why not celebrate the human body as God made it? God, said R. Akiva to the Roman governor, values culture, not just nature, the work of humans not just the work of God. It was this cluster of ideas – that God left creation unfinished so that we could become partners in its completion; that by responding to God's commands we become refined; that God delights in our creativity and helped us along the way by teaching the first humans how to make light – that made Judaism unique in its faith in God's faith in humankind. All of this is implicit in the idea of the eighth day as the day on which God sent humans out into the world to become His partners in the work of creation.

Why is this symbolized in the act of circumcision? Because if Darwin was right, then the most primal of all human instincts is to seek to pass on one's genes to the next generation. That is the strongest force of nature within us. Circumcision symbolizes the idea that there is something higher than nature. Passing on our genes to the next generation should not simply be a blind instinct, a Darwinian drive. The Abrahamic covenant was based on sexual fidelity, the sanctity of marriage, and the consecration of the love that brings new life into the world. It is a rejection of the ethic of the alpha male.

God created physical nature: the nature charted by science. But He asks us to be co-creators – with Him – of human nature. As Rabbi Avraham Mordechai Alter of Ger said, "When God said, 'Let us make man in our image,' to whom was He speaking? To man himself. God said to man, 'Let us – you and I – make man together.'" The symbol of that co-creation is the eighth day, the day He helps us begin to create a world of light and love.

Rabbi Jonathan Sacks

Analysis

- What specific information do we now have that was unavailable to classical Jewish commentators? How can it aid our understanding of the text?
- What can we learn from this passage that can help us understand the text?
- What further questions on the text do you have now that you have read this passage?

TAKING A LITERARY APPROACH

In Parashat Lekh Lekha, Avraham Avinu enters into two covenants with God concerning his future. Both covenants precisely define the Promised Land, but each covenantconsists of an entirely different piece of land. In the *brit bein habetarim*, "HaAretz" is promised (Bereshit 15:18–21) and in the *brit mila*, "Eretz Canaan" is promised (17:8).

The land defined by "HaAretz" is expansive. To the northeast, the border extends to the Euphrates River, which flows from northern Syria to the Persian Gulf, and to the southwest, it runs from the sources of the Nile River in Ethiopia down to the port city of Alexandria. However, "Eretz Canaan" is much smaller. The geographic definition of this area is outlined in Parashat Noaḥ:

> The Canaanite borders were from Sidon [the Litani valley in Lebanon] toward Gerar near Aza, [and from Sidon, down the Syrian-African Rift] toward Sedom, Amora... [the Dead Sea area]. (10:19)

In the *brit bein habetarim*, God promises Avraham that his offspring will one day conquer (*yerusha*) the land (*HaAretz*), just as Avraham himself had just done. However, this conquest will take place only after several generations of bondage in a foreign land, after which they will gain their independence and their oppressor will be punished. This covenant with Avraham Avinu reflects the historical/national aspect of *am Yisrael*'s relationship with God, as it focuses on the long-term, historical process required for Avraham's offspring to achieve their sovereignty

In the *brit mila* covenant, God first changes Avram's name to Avraham, in anticipation of the birth of a child from Sara. God then promises Avraham that He will establish and maintain a special relationship between Himself and Avraham's descendants and be a close, intimate God for them (17:3–9). This covenant reflects the religious/personal aspect of *am Yisrael*'s relationship with God, as it emphasizes a unique, intimate relationship with the Divine. In this covenant, the Promised Land is referred to as "Eretz Canaan" and its inheritance is referred to as *aḥuza*.

Hence, there are two aspects latent in the *kedusha* (sanctity) of *Eretz Yisrael*:

The national aspect – the *kedushat haaretz* of *brit bein habetarim* relates to the conquest of the land (*yerushat haaretz*) and the establishment of a national entity – a sovereign state. This *kedusha* is achieved once *Benei Yisrael* gain sovereignty, upon Yehoshua's conquest of the land.

The personal aspect – the *kedushat Eretz Canaan* of *brit mila* already existed in the time of the *avot* and remains eternal. This *kedusha* reflects God's special providence over this land, even while inhabited by other nations. This intrinsic *kedusha* is forever present regardless of who seizes control over the land.

Rabbi Menachem Leibtag

וירא

Vayera

Parasha Overview

God appears to Avraham. Three strangers pass by, and Avraham offers them hospitality. One of them tells Avraham that Sara will have a child. Sara, overhearing, laughs in disbelief. God then tells Avraham of the judgment He is about to visit on the people of Sedom. Avraham engages in a momentous dialogue with God about justice. God agrees that if there are ten innocent men in the city He will spare it. Two of the visitors, by now identified as angels, go to Avraham's nephew, Lot, in Sedom and rescue him, his wife, and two of their daughters from the destruction. Eventually, the promised child, Yitzḥak, is born to Sara. The *parasha* ends with the great test of the binding of Yitzḥak.

Episodes

Parasha Stats

- 7,862 letters
- 2,085 words
- 147 verses
- 252 lines in a sefer Torah

18 1 The LORD appeared to him by the Oaks of Mamre as he was sitting at the entrance to his
2 tent in the heat of the day. Avraham looked up and saw three men standing nearby. The
moment he saw them, he ran from the opening of his tent to greet them, and bowed down
3 low to the ground. He said, "My lords, if I have found favor in your sight, please do not
4 pass your servant by. Let a little water be brought so that you can wash your feet and rest
5 under the tree. Since you are passing by your servant, let me bring a morsel of bread so
that you can be refreshed before you go on your way." They replied, "Do just as you say."
6 Avraham rushed to Sara in the tent and said, "Hurry – three measures of fine flour: knead
7 it and bake bread." Avraham himself ran to the herd and took a tender choice calf and gave
8 it to the young man, who hurried to prepare it. He brought curds and milk and the calf
that had been prepared, and set them before them, standing by them as they ate, under
9 10 the tree. They asked him, "Where is your wife Sara?" "There, in the tent," he replied. Then
one of them said, "I will return to you this time next year, and your wife Sara will have a
11 son." Sara was listening at the opening of the tent behind him. Avraham and Sara were
12 already old, advanced in years; the way of women no longer visited Sara. So Sara laughed
to herself, saying, "Now that I am worn out, can I have this pleasure? With my lord an old
13 man?" Then the LORD said to Avraham, "Why did Sara laugh and say, 'Can I really have

UNLOCKING THE TEXT

- Why does God appear but not speak to Avraham?
- Who are the three men?
- If the men were messengers of God, why did God send them when He was already present?
- Is it troubling that Avraham prepared the men a meal of dairy and meat?
- Why do they inform Avraham again about the birth of a son when he has already heard it previously, directly from God?
- Why is God angered by Sara's laughter here but not by Avraham's laughter at the same news in the previous chapter?
- Why did God inform Avraham about His plans to destroy Sedom and Amora?
- What is the connection between God informing Avraham and Avraham's role as parent-educator?
- Was Avraham disrespectful to challenge God in this way?
- Why did Avraham stop negotiating at ten people?

FINDING YOURSELF IN THE TEXT

- Do you find it challenging to act on the value of hospitality and showing kindness to strangers?
- Have you ever laughed at something nice or good that someone said about you because you felt it wasn't true or possible?
- Have you ever taken a stand for something you believed in?

Consider using these questions as the basis for your own commentary or creative midrash.

How does reflecting on these firsthand experiences help you better understand the text?

וַיֵּרָ֤א אֵלָיו֙ יְהוָ֔ה בְּאֵלֹנֵ֖י מַמְרֵ֑א וְה֛וּא יֹשֵׁ֥ב פֶּֽתַח־הָאֹ֖הֶל כְּחֹ֥ם הַיּֽוֹם: וַיִּשָּׂ֤א עֵינָיו֙ טו וירא
וַיַּ֔רְא וְהִנֵּה֙ שְׁלֹשָׁ֣ה אֲנָשִׁ֔ים נִצָּבִ֖ים עָלָ֑יו וַיַּ֗רְא וַיָּ֤רָץ לִקְרָאתָם֙ מִפֶּ֣תַח הָאֹ֔הֶל וַיִּשְׁתַּ֖חוּ
אָֽרְצָה: וַיֹּאמַ֑ר אֲדֹנָ֗י אִם־נָ֨א מָצָ֤אתִי חֵן֙ בְּעֵינֶ֔יךָ אַל־נָ֥א תַעֲבֹ֖ר מֵעַ֥ל עַבְדֶּֽךָ: יֻקַּֽח־נָ֣א
מְעַט־מַ֔יִם וְרַחֲצ֖וּ רַגְלֵיכֶ֑ם וְהִֽשָּׁעֲנ֖וּ תַּ֥חַת הָעֵֽץ: וְאֶקְחָ֨ה פַת־לֶ֜חֶם וְסַעֲד֤וּ לִבְּכֶם֙ אַחַ֣ר
תַּעֲבֹ֔רוּ כִּֽי־עַל־כֵּ֥ן עֲבַרְתֶּ֖ם עַל־עַבְדְּכֶ֑ם וַיֹּ֣אמְר֔וּ כֵּ֥ן תַּעֲשֶׂ֖ה כַּאֲשֶׁ֥ר דִּבַּֽרְתָּ: וַיְמַהֵ֧ר
אַבְרָהָ֛ם הָאֹ֖הֱלָה אֶל־שָׂרָ֑ה וַיֹּ֗אמֶר מַהֲרִ֞י שְׁלֹ֤שׁ סְאִים֙ קֶ֣מַח סֹ֔לֶת ל֖וּשִׁי וַעֲשִׂ֥י עֻגֽוֹת:
וְאֶל־הַבָּקָ֖ר רָ֣ץ אַבְרָהָ֑ם וַיִּקַּ֨ח בֶּן־בָּקָ֜ר רַ֤ךְ וָטוֹב֙ וַיִּתֵּ֣ן אֶל־הַנַּ֔עַר וַיְמַהֵ֖ר לַעֲשׂ֥וֹת
אֹתֽוֹ: וַיִּקַּ֨ח חֶמְאָ֜ה וְחָלָ֗ב וּבֶן־הַבָּקָר֙ אֲשֶׁ֣ר עָשָׂ֔ה וַיִּתֵּ֖ן לִפְנֵיהֶ֑ם וְהֽוּא־עֹמֵ֧ד עֲלֵיהֶ֛ם
תַּ֥חַת הָעֵ֖ץ וַיֹּאכֵֽלוּ: וַיֹּאמְר֣וּ אֵלָ֔יו אַיֵּ֖ה שָׂרָ֣ה אִשְׁתֶּ֑ךָ וַיֹּ֖אמֶר הִנֵּ֥ה בָאֹֽהֶל: וַיֹּ֗אמֶר
שׁ֣וֹב אָשׁ֤וּב אֵלֶ֙יךָ֙ כָּעֵ֣ת חַיָּ֔ה וְהִנֵּה־בֵ֖ן לְשָׂרָ֣ה אִשְׁתֶּ֑ךָ וְשָׂרָ֥ה שֹׁמַ֛עַת פֶּ֥תַח הָאֹ֖הֶל
וְה֥וּא אַחֲרָֽיו: וְאַבְרָהָ֤ם וְשָׂרָה֙ זְקֵנִ֔ים בָּאִ֖ים בַּיָּמִ֑ים חָדַל֙ לִהְי֣וֹת לְשָׂרָ֔ה אֹ֖רַח כַּנָּשִֽׁים:
וַתִּצְחַ֥ק שָׂרָ֖ה בְּקִרְבָּ֣הּ לֵאמֹ֑ר אַחֲרֵ֤י בְלֹתִי֙ הָֽיְתָה־לִּ֣י עֶדְנָ֔ה וַֽאדֹנִ֖י זָקֵֽן: וַיֹּ֥אמֶר יְהוָ֖ה

| THEMES | LEADERSHIP | FREE WILL, REWARD AND PUNISHMENT | PROPHECY AND REVELATION |

Episode 22: *Avraham's Tent* – Bereshit 18:1–33

SUMMARY

In this episode, two parallel events occur: God reveals Himself to Avraham and visitors arrive at Avraham's tent. The passage begins with a detailed description of Avraham's generous conduct with his guests, despite the fact that he is apparently leaving the Divine Presence in favor of earthly pursuits. But when the guests foretell the birth of Avraham and Sara's son, it becomes apparent that God Himself is participating in the conversation. When the visitors move on toward Sedom, God reveals to Avraham His intention of destroying the city. By now it is clear that the guests are in fact angels, messengers of God sent to Avraham to bring him news of a child and to bring an end to Sedom. Avraham's traits of kindness and alacrity are highlighted in this story, both in his treatment of the guests and in his subsequent effort to convince God to spare the inhabitants of the city of Sedom. The text does not specify the time of year when the circumcision of Avraham and his household occurred, but there is a tradition that it took place at the time of the festival of Passover.

14 a child, now that I am old?' Is anything beyond the LORD's powers? At the due time next
15 year I will return to you and Sara will have a son." Sara, because she was afraid, denied it:
16 "I did not laugh," she said. But He said, "Not so. You laughed." The men got up to leave and
17 looked down toward Sedom. Avraham accompanied them to see them on their way. The
18 LORD said, "Shall I hide from Avraham what I am about to do? Avraham is about to become
19 a great and mighty nation, and through him all the nations on earth will be blessed. For
I have chosen him so that he may direct his children and his household after him to keep
the way of the LORD by doing what is right and just, that the LORD may bring about for
20 Avraham what He spoke of for him." Then the LORD said, "The outcry against Sedom and
21 Amora is great, and their sin is very grave. I shall go down now and see if they have really
22 done as much as the outcry that has reached Me. If not, I will know." The men turned from
23 there and went toward Sedom, while Avraham still stood before the LORD. Then Avraham
stepped forward and said: "Would You really sweep away the righteous with the wicked?
24 What if there are fifty righteous people in the city? Would You really sweep it away and
25 not spare the place for the sake of the fifty righteous people in it? Far be it from You to do
such a thing – to kill the righteous with the wicked, treating the righteous like the wicked.
26 Far be it from You! Shall the Judge of all the earth not do justice?" The LORD said, "If I find
27 fifty righteous people in the city of Sedom, I will spare the whole place for their sake." Then
Avraham spoke up again and said, "Now that I have dared to speak to the Lord, though I
28 am mere dust and ashes, what if the righteous are five less than fifty? Will You destroy the
whole city for the lack of five people?" He said, "If I find forty-five there, I will not destroy
29 it." He spoke to Him yet again, saying, "What if only forty are found there?" He said, "I will
30 refrain for the sake of the forty." Then he said, "Please: may the Lord not be angry, but let
me speak. What if only thirty are found there?" He answered, "I will refrain if I find thirty
31 there." "Now that I have dared to speak to the Lord," he said, "what if only twenty are found
32 there?" He said, "I will not destroy, for the sake of the twenty." Then he said, "Please: may
the Lord not be angry, but let me speak just once more. What if only ten are found there?"
33 He said, "I will not destroy, for the sake of the ten." When the LORD had finished speaking
with Avraham, He left. And Avraham went back to his place.

יד אֶל־אַבְרָהָ֑ם לָ֣מָּה זֶּ֜ה צָחֲקָ֣ה שָׂרָ֗ה לֵאמֹ֔ר הַאַ֥ף אֻמְנָ֛ם אֵלֵ֖ד וַאֲנִ֥י זָקַֽנְתִּי׃ הֲיִפָּלֵ֥א
טו מֵיהו֖ה דָּבָ֑ר לַמּוֹעֵ֞ד אָשׁ֥וּב אֵלֶ֛יךָ כָּעֵ֥ת חַיָּ֖ה וּלְשָׂרָ֥ה בֵֽן׃ וַתְּכַחֵ֨שׁ שָׂרָ֧ה ׀ לֵאמֹ֛ר לֹ֥א שני
טז צָחַ֖קְתִּי כִּ֣י ׀ יָרֵ֑אָה וַיֹּ֥אמֶר ׀ לֹ֖א כִּ֥י צָחָֽקְתְּ׃ וַיָּקֻ֤מוּ מִשָּׁם֙ הָֽאֲנָשִׁ֔ים וַיַּשְׁקִ֖פוּ עַל־פְּנֵ֣י
יז סְדֹ֑ם וְאַ֨בְרָהָ֔ם הֹלֵ֥ךְ עִמָּ֖ם לְשַׁלְּחָֽם׃ וַיהו֖ה אָמָ֑ר הַֽמְכַסֶּ֤ה אֲנִי֙ מֵֽאַבְרָהָ֔ם אֲשֶׁ֖ר אֲנִ֥י
יח יט עֹשֶֽׂה׃ וְאַ֨בְרָהָ֔ם הָי֧וֹ יִהְיֶ֛ה לְג֥וֹי גָּד֖וֹל וְעָצ֑וּם וְנִ֨בְרְכוּ־ב֔וֹ כֹּ֖ל גּוֹיֵ֥י הָאָֽרֶץ׃ כִּ֣י יְדַעְתִּ֗יו
לְמַ֩עַן֩ אֲשֶׁ֨ר יְצַוֶּ֜ה אֶת־בָּנָ֣יו וְאֶת־בֵּיתוֹ֮ אַחֲרָיו֒ וְשָֽׁמְרוּ֙ דֶּ֣רֶךְ יהו֔ה לַעֲשׂ֥וֹת צְדָקָ֖ה
כ וּמִשְׁפָּ֑ט לְמַ֗עַן הָבִ֤יא יהוה֙ עַל־אַבְרָהָ֔ם אֵ֥ת אֲשֶׁר־דִּבֶּ֖ר עָלָֽיו׃ וַיֹּ֣אמֶר יהו֔ה זַעֲקַ֛ת
כא סְדֹ֥ם וַעֲמֹרָ֖ה כִּי־רָ֑בָּה וְחַ֨טָּאתָ֔ם כִּ֥י כָבְדָ֖ה מְאֹֽד׃ אֵֽרְדָה־נָּ֣א וְאֶרְאֶ֔ה הַכְּצַעֲקָתָ֛הּ
כב הַבָּ֥אָה אֵלַ֖י עָשׂ֣וּ ׀ כָּלָ֑ה וְאִם־לֹ֖א אֵדָֽעָה׃ וַיִּפְנ֤וּ מִשָּׁם֙ הָֽאֲנָשִׁ֔ים וַיֵּלְכ֖וּ סְדֹ֑מָה וְאַ֨בְרָהָ֔ם
כג כד עוֹדֶ֥נּוּ עֹמֵ֖ד לִפְנֵ֥י יהוֽה׃ וַיִּגַּ֥שׁ אַבְרָהָ֖ם וַיֹּאמַ֑ר הַאַ֣ף תִּסְפֶּ֔ה צַדִּ֖יק עִם־רָשָֽׁע׃ אוּלַ֥י
יֵ֛שׁ חֲמִשִּׁ֥ים צַדִּיקִ֖ם בְּת֣וֹךְ הָעִ֑יר הַאַ֤ף תִּסְפֶּה֙ וְלֹא־תִשָּׂ֣א לַמָּק֔וֹם לְמַ֛עַן חֲמִשִּׁ֥ים
כה הַצַּדִּיקִ֖ם אֲשֶׁ֥ר בְּקִרְבָּֽהּ׃ חָלִ֨לָה לְּךָ֜ מֵעֲשֹׂ֣ת ׀ כַּדָּבָ֣ר הַזֶּ֗ה לְהָמִ֤ית צַדִּיק֙ עִם־רָשָׁ֔ע
כו וְהָיָ֥ה כַצַּדִּ֖יק כָּרָשָׁ֑ע חָלִ֣לָה לָּ֔ךְ הֲשֹׁפֵט֙ כָּל־הָאָ֔רֶץ לֹ֥א יַעֲשֶׂ֖ה מִשְׁפָּֽט׃ וַיֹּ֣אמֶר יהו֔ה
אִם־אֶמְצָ֥א בִסְדֹ֛ם חֲמִשִּׁ֥ים צַדִּיקִ֖ם בְּת֣וֹךְ הָעִ֑יר וְנָשָׂ֥אתִי לְכָל־הַמָּק֖וֹם בַּעֲבוּרָֽם׃
כז כח וַיַּ֥עַן אַבְרָהָ֖ם וַיֹּאמַ֑ר הִנֵּה־נָ֤א הוֹאַ֙לְתִּי֙ לְדַבֵּ֣ר אֶל־אֲדֹנָ֔י וְאָנֹכִ֖י עָפָ֥ר וָאֵֽפֶר׃ א֠וּלַי
יַחְסְר֞וּן חֲמִשִּׁ֤ים הַצַּדִּיקִם֙ חֲמִשָּׁ֔ה הֲתַשְׁחִ֥ית בַּחֲמִשָּׁ֖ה אֶת־כָּל־הָעִ֑יר וַיֹּ֙אמֶר֙ לֹ֣א
כט אַשְׁחִ֔ית אִם־אֶמְצָ֣א שָׁ֔ם אַרְבָּעִ֖ים וַחֲמִשָּֽׁה׃ וַיֹּ֨סֶף ע֜וֹד לְדַבֵּ֤ר אֵלָיו֙ וַיֹּאמַ֔ר אוּלַ֛י
ל יִמָּצְא֥וּן שָׁ֖ם אַרְבָּעִ֑ים וַיֹּ֙אמֶר֙ לֹ֣א אֶֽעֱשֶׂ֔ה בַּעֲב֖וּר הָֽאַרְבָּעִֽים׃ וַ֠יֹּאמֶר אַל־נָ֞א יִ֤חַר
לַֽאדֹנָי֙ וַאֲדַבֵּ֔רָה אוּלַ֛י יִמָּצְא֥וּן שָׁ֖ם שְׁלֹשִׁ֑ים וַיֹּ֙אמֶר֙ לֹ֣א אֶֽעֱשֶׂ֔ה אִם־אֶמְצָ֥א שָׁ֖ם
לא שְׁלֹשִֽׁים׃ וַיֹּ֗אמֶר הִנֵּה־נָ֤א הוֹאַ֙לְתִּי֙ לְדַבֵּ֣ר אֶל־אֲדֹנָ֔י אוּלַ֛י יִמָּצְא֥וּן שָׁ֖ם עֶשְׂרִ֑ים
לב וַיֹּ֙אמֶר֙ לֹ֣א אַשְׁחִ֔ית בַּעֲב֖וּר הָֽעֶשְׂרִֽים׃ וַ֠יֹּאמֶר אַל־נָ֨א יִ֤חַר לַֽאדֹנָי֙ וַאֲדַבְּרָ֣ה אַךְ־
לג הַפַּ֔עַם אוּלַ֛י יִמָּצְא֥וּן שָׁ֖ם עֲשָׂרָ֑ה וַיֹּ֙אמֶר֙ לֹ֣א אַשְׁחִ֔ית בַּעֲב֖וּר הָעֲשָׂרָֽה׃ וַיֵּ֣לֶךְ יהו֔ה
כַּאֲשֶׁ֣ר כִּלָּ֔ה לְדַבֵּ֖ר אֶל־אַבְרָהָ֑ם וְאַבְרָהָ֖ם שָׁ֥ב לִמְקֹמֽוֹ׃

THE ART OF MIDRASH

Les Hotes d'Abraham
Abel Pann (1930)

Analysis

- Which elements of this image are directly mentioned in the text?
- Which elements of this image are not found in the text?
- What midrashic interpretation could be inferred from this image?

A QUESTION OF BIBLIODRAMA

TO AVRAHAM

- How does it feel that God makes a personal visit to you?
- Why did you rush to greet these men?
- Did you turn your back on God? Why?
- Did you hear Sara laugh? What did you think when she laughed at the news?
- Were you scared to challenge God in the way that you did?
- Why did you challenge God over His plans to destroy Sedom and Amora?

TO SARA

- What emotions did you experience when you overheard the men give Avraham the news?
- Why did you laugh at the news?
- Why did you deny you laughed when you were confronted by God over this?

TO GOD

- Why did You send the messengers to Avraham and Sara if You were already in their presence?
- Why did you tell them about giving birth again, seeing as You had already told Avraham?
- Why did Sara laughing anger You?
- Why were You not angry when Avraham laughed when you told him previously?
- Why did You want to destroy Sedom and Amora?
- Why did You inform Avraham about these plans?
- What do you think about the way Avraham challenged You over these plans?
- If You knew there was no one to save in these cities, why did You continue to negotiate with Avraham?

household full of servants who could have done the work on his behalf. Avraham teaches us the importance of doing the mitzva with alacrity (*zerizut*), and making sure to do most of the mitzva on one's own (*mitzva bo yoter mi'beshluḥo*).

In his elucidation of Avraham's behavior in the story, Alshikh prefaces his analysis by explaining that there are several reasons a guest may feel uncomfortable accepting an invitation. Primarily, guests do not want to impose on their hosts. This could be related to the financial burden incurred by hosting, or to the time and energy necessary to clean the house and tend to the guests' needs. In addition, the guests themselves may be in a rush and do not want to get caught up in a long layover at the host's home.

To perform acts of *ḥesed* properly, we need a degree of social intelligence so we can behave in a way that is more beneficial to those around us. Avraham uses strategic language when speaking to allay the fears his guests might be experiencing. He tells them that he has people who can help, so it will not be such a burden, and that they can stay under the tree, so they do not have to worry about intruding inside the house. He also tells them that he will just bring out a little water and a slice of bread so that they do not feel that they are imposing, but then brings out an entire meal so they can be satiated. Finally, Avraham himself moves quickly, so the guests would not feel uncomfortable in case they were rushing to leave.

Rabbi Eliezer Ashkenazi (*Maasei Hashem*) mentions the midrash wherein one of the angels came on a mission to heal Avraham. While the *pesukim* do not explicitly indicate when or how that occurred, Rabbi Ashkenazi suggests that the healing was a blessing that came as a direct consequence of the *ḥesed* that Avraham performed. By commencing and performing an act of kindness, his pain decreased, and his speed, alacrity, and vitality improved. Avraham – old, frail, and pained – was healed.

May we all learn from Avraham, the paradigm of *ḥesed*, and personally commit to passionately perform acts of kindness, with nuanced social awareness and sensitivity. Even when we are tired, down, weak, or frail, when we visit the sick, comfort the mourner, host guests, or perform other acts of kindness, it will add energy and vigor to our lives. By so doing, may we merit living long lives infused with health, happiness, and vitality.

Rabbi Mordechai Schiffman

Analysis

- What areas of understanding of human nature and society do we now have that were unavailable to classical Jewish commentators? How can they aid our understanding of the text?
- What can we learn from this essay to help us understand the text?
- What further questions on the text do you have now that you have read this new take on the story?

INTEGRATING ḤOKHMA

A common and logical response to the experience of intense or chronic pain is to decrease activity and focus on the self. However, research indicates that people in pain who focus outside of themselves by, for example, volunteering, reap benefits such as a decrease in both physical pain and negative emotional symptoms, such as depression. The same is true when it comes to aging. As people age, they tend to focus on their own needs and decrease their activity, while research suggests that even (or especially) for the elderly, volunteering is correlated with improved well-being, lower mortality rates, and a decrease in general functional decline. In one fascinating study, researchers measured how quickly older adults walked and climbed stairs both before and after a year's worth of volunteering, and found that those who volunteered had improved walking and stair climbing speeds.

The Torah portrays the scene of Avraham welcoming the angels (who were disguised as unidentified nomads) by providing a detailed account of how Avraham prepared and executed the mitzva of *hakhnasat orḥim*. In fact, Radak suggests that the primary purpose of the entire story is to provide us with a paradigm for how to perform acts of kindness. Even a cursory reading of the *pesukim* leaves the reader in awe of the speed with which Avraham exhibited hospitality. When performing each task, Avraham doesn't just walk; he runs. The preparations are done with zest and vitality. His actions are even more impressive, as Ramban points out, since he was old, and weakened from the pain of his recent *brit mila*, and because he had a

"for their sake" (i.e., so that they not suffer the hardships mentioned above). The negotiations end at ten because the last group of innocents that was spared totaled just under ten (Noaḥ, his wife, his three sons and their wives, all evidently innocent as they were saved) and their place (the world) was not spared for their sake.

The word *tzaddik* is the keyword of this section because it is the possibility of there existing a community of innocents that is the linchpin of Avraham's pleas.

There is another *leitwort* in this section – *matza*, "to find." It should be clear why this word also appears exactly seven times – the entire enterprise of the divine investigation into Sedom depends on "finding" a group of innocent people.

Rabbi Yitzchak Etshalom

TAKING A LITERARY APPROACH

In this section, there is a *leitwort* (*mila manḥa*) that appears seven times: *tzaddik*. Note how cleverly this word is elided in the "lower numbers" in order to preserve the sevenfold repetition.

In Rabbinic and Modern Hebrew, a *tzaddik* is a "righteous person, that is, someone whose behavior is exemplary and whose piety is unquestioned. This is not the case in Biblical Hebrew, where the word, simply put, means "innocent." For example, the passage introducing court procedures and "lashes" states "by justifying the *tzaddik* and condemning the wicked" (Devarim 2:1), clearly meaning "innocent."

What, then, was Avraham using as his argument against the destruction of Sedom? The notion that God, as "judge of the earth" (whom Avraham had been publicizing these many years) would violate His own reputation by destroying those who were innocent along with the guilty? Why didn't he then point to the possibility of there being one innocent person in Sedom, thereby saving the town?

There was a history to the destruction of the place in spite of innocent people being there. Noaḥ is told by God that "I have found you to be a *tzaddik* before Me in this generation" (Bereshit 7:1); again, the *peshat* is that Noaḥ is simply innocent of the crimes of the generation and, as such, does not merit their fate. His ignominious end seems to testify to his being less than pious; but he is not deserving of the destruction rained upon the generation of the flood.

How did God serve His justice here? He destroyed the place and rescued the innocent. He "plucked" the innocent from the doomed place and kept him (and his family) safe while destruction rained down.

As such, Avraham, who may have harbored hopes that after these many years in Sedom, his nephew and former apprentice Lot may have influenced some of the sinning citizenry to give up their evil ways, raises that very possibility with God. If there is a large group of innocent folks, justice will be better served by punishing the wicked alone and leaving the innocent in their place. The reputation of justice (as opposed to the capricious judgment accorded to the pagan) will not be served if a town with a sizeable population innocent of the crimes leading to the "terrible cry" that is emanating from the town is utterly destroyed and its innocent residents are displaced and made into refugees.

God allows for the possibility that there are fifty innocent people there, and that He will spare the town

19 1 The two angels arrived at Sedom in the evening, while Lot was sitting in the city gate. Lot
2 saw them, and rose to greet them, bowing with his face to the ground. He said, "Please,
my lords, turn aside to your servant's house, stay the night, wash your feet, and then go on
your way early in the morning." "No," they said, "we will spend the night in the square."
3 But he was so insistent that they followed him to his house and came in. He made a feast
4 for them and baked unleavened bread, and they ate. They had not yet gone to bed when
all the townsmen, the men of Sedom – young and old, all the people from every quarter
5 – surrounded the house. They called to Lot, "Where are the men who came to you
6 tonight? Bring them out to us so that we may know them."[1] Lot went out to speak to them,
7 8 shutting the door behind him, and said, "My brothers, please do not do this evil. I have
two daughters who have never known a man. Let me bring them out to you; you may do
what you like with them. But do not do anything to these men, for they have come under
9 the protection of my roof." "Get out of our way," they replied. "This fellow came here as a
migrant and now he is setting himself up as a judge! We will treat you worse than them."
10 They pressed hard against Lot and moved forward to break down the door. But the men

1 | That is, violate them.

UNLOCKING THE TEXT

- Are the two angels from the group of three "men" who visited Avraham in the previous chapter? If so, why are they called angels here and men when they approach Avraham?
- What happened to the third man?
- Why was Lot sitting in the gateway to the city?
- How does Lot's hospitality compare to Avraham's?
- What do the people of the city want with Lot's guests?
- Is Lot's offer to hand over his daughters instead of the guests a moral act or an evil one?
- Why did Lot hesitate when the men instructed him to flee?
- Why does Lot not want to escape to the mountains?
- What was so wrong about looking back on the destruction?
- Was the act of Lot's daughters considered a moral one by the Torah?

FINDING YOURSELF IN THE TEXT

- Have you ever found yourself begging someone not to do something wrong?
- Are you proud of the positive influence you have been on someone?
- Have you ever had to rescue someone?

Consider using these questions as the basis for your own commentary or creative midrash.

How does reflecting on these firsthand experiences help you better understand the text?

יט א וַיָּבֹאוּ שְׁנֵי הַמַּלְאָכִים סְדֹמָה בָּעֶרֶב וְלוֹט יֹשֵׁב בְּשַׁעַר־סְדֹם וַיַּרְא־לוֹט וַיָּקָם טז שלישי
ב לִקְרָאתָם וַיִּשְׁתַּחוּ אַפַּיִם אָרְצָה: וַיֹּאמֶר הִנֶּה נָּא־אֲדֹנַי סוּרוּ נָא אֶל־בֵּית עַבְדְּכֶם
וְלִינוּ וְרַחֲצוּ רַגְלֵיכֶם וְהִשְׁכַּמְתֶּם וַהֲלַכְתֶּם לְדַרְכְּכֶם וַיֹּאמְרוּ לֹּא כִּי בָרְחוֹב נָלִין:
ג וַיִּפְצַר־בָּם מְאֹד וַיָּסֻרוּ אֵלָיו וַיָּבֹאוּ אֶל־בֵּיתוֹ וַיַּעַשׂ לָהֶם מִשְׁתֶּה וּמַצּוֹת אָפָה
ד וַיֹּאכֵלוּ: טֶרֶם יִשְׁכָּבוּ וְאַנְשֵׁי הָעִיר אַנְשֵׁי סְדֹם נָסַבּוּ עַל־הַבַּיִת מִנַּעַר וְעַד־זָקֵן
ה כָּל־הָעָם מִקָּצֶה: וַיִּקְרְאוּ אֶל־לוֹט וַיֹּאמְרוּ לוֹ אַיֵּה הָאֲנָשִׁים אֲשֶׁר־בָּאוּ אֵלֶיךָ
ו הַלָּיְלָה הוֹצִיאֵם אֵלֵינוּ וְנֵדְעָה אֹתָם: וַיֵּצֵא אֲלֵהֶם לוֹט הַפֶּתְחָה וְהַדֶּלֶת סָגַר
ז ח אַחֲרָיו: וַיֹּאמַר אַל־נָא אַחַי תָּרֵעוּ: הִנֵּה־נָא לִי שְׁתֵּי בָנוֹת אֲשֶׁר לֹא־יָדְעוּ אִישׁ
אוֹצִיאָה־נָּא אֶתְהֶן אֲלֵיכֶם וַעֲשׂוּ לָהֶן כַּטּוֹב בְּעֵינֵיכֶם רַק לָאֲנָשִׁים הָאֵל אַל־תַּעֲשׂוּ
ט דָבָר כִּי־עַל־כֵּן בָּאוּ בְּצֵל קֹרָתִי: וַיֹּאמְרוּ ׀ גֶּשׁ־הָלְאָה וַיֹּאמְרוּ הָאֶחָד בָּא־לָגוּר
וַיִּשְׁפֹּט שָׁפוֹט עַתָּה נָרַע לְךָ מֵהֶם וַיִּפְצְרוּ בָאִישׁ בְּלוֹט מְאֹד וַיִּגְּשׁוּ לִשְׁבֹּר הַדָּלֶת:
י וַיִּשְׁלְחוּ הָאֲנָשִׁים אֶת־יָדָם וַיָּבִיאוּ אֶת־לוֹט אֲלֵיהֶם הַבָּיְתָה וְאֶת־הַדֶּלֶת סָגָרוּ:

THEMES	FREE WILL, REWARD AND PUNISHMENT	RELATIONSHIPS AND LOVE	ETHICS

Episode 23: *The Destruction of Sedom* – Bereshit 19:1–38

SUMMARY

Two of the angels who visited Avraham come to Lot in Sedom. Since the two stories of their visits are presented consecutively, the characters of Avraham and his nephew, Lot, may be compared and contrasted in stark detail. Once the complex natures of Lot and his family have been revealed, it can be concluded that their relationship to Avraham was the primary reason they merited rescue from Sedom.

11 inside reached out and pulled Lot back into the house and shut the door behind him. Then
they struck the men at the door, young and old, with blindness so that they wore themselves
12 out trying in vain to find the door. The visitors said to Lot, "Who else do you have here –
13 children-in-law, sons, daughters, or anyone else in the city? Bring them out of here, because
we are about to destroy this place. So great is the outcry against them before the LORD that
14 He has sent us to destroy it." Lot went out and spoke to his sons-in-law, the men who were
betrothed to his daughters, and told them, "Get up and leave this place: the LORD is about
15 to destroy the city!" But his sons-in-law thought him laughable. As dawn was breaking, the
angels hurried Lot. "Get up," they said. "Take your wife and your two daughters here, or
16 you will be swept away amid the city's sin." Still he hesitated. So the men seized him, his
wife, and his two daughters by the hand and led them safely outside the city, for the LORD
17 had mercy upon him. As soon as they had brought them out, one said, "Run for your life.
Do not look back. Do not stop anywhere in the plain. Flee to the mountains or you will be
18 19 swept away." But Lot said to them, "No, my lords, please. Your servant has found favor in
your eyes, and you have done me great kindness in saving my life. But I cannot flee to the
20 mountains; the disaster would overtake me, and I would die.[2] There is a town here close
enough for refuge. It is small. Let me flee there – is it not small? – so that I might survive."
21 "Very well," he said, "I will grant this request also; I will not overthrow the town of which
22 you speak. But hurry. Flee there, because I cannot do anything until you reach it." That
23 is why the town is called Tzoar.[3] By the time Lot reached Tzoar, the sun had risen over
24 the land. Then the LORD rained down sulfur and fire on Sedom and Amora. Out of the
25 heavens it came from the LORD. He overthrew those cities, and the whole plain, and all
26 the cities' inhabitants, and the vegetation on the land. But Lot's wife looked back – and she
27 was turned into a pillar of salt. Avraham rose early the next morning and returned to the
28 place where he had stood before the LORD. He looked down toward Sedom and Amora
and all the land of the plain, and he saw thick smoke rising from the land like smoke from
29 a kiln. So it was that, when God destroyed the cities of the plain, He remembered Avraham
30 and brought Lot out of the overthrow that overturned the cities where Lot had lived. Lot
went up from Tzoar and settled in the hills together with his two daughters because he
31 was afraid to stay in Tzoar. He and his two daughters settled in a cave. The elder said to the
younger, "Our father is old, and there is no man left on earth to come to us in the normal
32 way of the world. Let us get our father drunk with wine and then sleep with him, so that we
may raise a new generation through our father." That night they gave their father wine to

2 | Lot does not regard the mountains as a safe haven from the impending source of destruction.

3 | Tzoar resonates with *mitzar* ("small" in v. 20).

יא וְֽאֶת־הָאֲנָשִׁ֞ים אֲשֶׁר־פֶּ֣תַח הַבַּ֗יִת הִכּוּ֙ בַּסַּנְוֵרִ֔ים מִקָּטֹ֖ן וְעַד־גָּד֑וֹל וַיִּלְא֖וּ לִמְצֹ֥א
יב הַפָּֽתַח׃ וַיֹּאמְר֨וּ הָאֲנָשִׁ֜ים אֶל־ל֗וֹט עֹ֚ד מִֽי־לְךָ֣ פֹ֔ה חָתָן֙ וּבָנֶ֣יךָ וּבְנֹתֶ֔יךָ וְכֹ֥ל אֲשֶׁר־
יג לְךָ֖ בָּעִ֑יר הוֹצֵ֖א מִן־הַמָּקֽוֹם׃ כִּֽי־מַשְׁחִתִ֣ים אֲנַ֔חְנוּ אֶת־הַמָּק֖וֹם הַזֶּ֑ה כִּֽי־גָדְלָ֤ה
יד צַעֲקָתָם֙ אֶת־פְּנֵ֣י יְהוָ֔ה וַיְשַׁלְּחֵ֥נוּ יְהוָ֖ה לְשַֽׁחֲתָֽהּ׃ וַיֵּצֵ֨א ל֜וֹט וַיְדַבֵּ֣ר ׀ אֶל־חֲתָנָ֣יו ׀
לֹקְחֵ֣י בְנֹתָ֗יו וַיֹּ֙אמֶר֙ ק֤וּמוּ צְּאוּ֙ מִן־הַמָּק֣וֹם הַזֶּ֔ה כִּֽי־מַשְׁחִ֥ית יְהוָ֖ה אֶת־הָעִ֑יר וַיְהִ֥י
טו כִמְצַחֵ֖ק בְּעֵינֵ֥י חֲתָנָֽיו׃ וּכְמוֹ֙ הַשַּׁ֣חַר עָלָ֔ה וַיָּאִ֥יצוּ הַמַּלְאָכִ֖ים בְּל֣וֹט לֵאמֹ֑ר קוּם֩ קַ֨ח
טז אֶֽת־אִשְׁתְּךָ֜ וְאֶת־שְׁתֵּ֤י בְנֹתֶ֙יךָ֙ הַנִּמְצָאֹ֔ת פֶּן־תִּסָּפֶ֖ה בַּעֲוֺ֥ן הָעִֽיר׃ וַיִּתְמַהְמָ֓הּ ׀ וַיַּחֲזִ֨קוּ
הָאֲנָשִׁ֜ים בְּיָד֣וֹ וּבְֽיַד־אִשְׁתּ֗וֹ וּבְיַד֙ שְׁתֵּ֣י בְנֹתָ֔יו בְּחֶמְלַ֥ת יְהוָ֖ה עָלָ֑יו וַיֹּצִאֻ֥הוּ וַיַּנִּחֻ֖הוּ
יז מִח֥וּץ לָעִֽיר׃ וַיְהִי֩ כְהוֹצִיאָ֨ם אֹתָ֜ם הַח֗וּצָה וַיֹּ֙אמֶר֙ הִמָּלֵ֣ט עַל־נַפְשֶׁ֔ךָ אַל־תַּבִּ֣יט
יח אַחֲרֶ֔יךָ וְאַל־תַּעֲמֹ֖ד בְּכָל־הַכִּכָּ֑ר הָהָ֥רָה הִמָּלֵ֖ט פֶּן־תִּסָּפֶֽה׃ וַיֹּ֥אמֶר ל֖וֹט אֲלֵהֶ֑ם
יט אַל־נָ֖א אֲדֹנָֽי׃ הִנֵּה־נָ֠א מָצָ֨א עַבְדְּךָ֜ חֵ֗ן בְּעֵינֶ֘יךָ֮ וַתַּגְדֵּ֣ל חַסְדְּךָ֗ אֲשֶׁ֤ר עָשִׂ֙יתָ֙ עִמָּדִ֔י
לְהַחֲי֖וֹת אֶת־נַפְשִׁ֑י וְאָנֹכִ֗י לֹ֤א אוּכַל֙ לְהִמָּלֵ֣ט הָהָ֔רָה פֶּן־תִּדְבָּקַ֥נִי הָרָעָ֖ה וָמַֽתִּי׃
כ הִנֵּה־נָ֠א הָעִ֨יר הַזֹּ֜את קְרֹבָ֥ה לָנ֛וּס שָׁ֖מָּה וְהִ֣וא מִצְעָ֑ר אִמָּלְטָ֨ה נָּ֜א שָׁ֗מָּה הֲלֹ֥א
כא מִצְעָ֛ר הִ֖וא וּתְחִ֥י נַפְשִֽׁי׃ וַיֹּ֣אמֶר אֵלָ֔יו הִנֵּה֙ נָשָׂ֣אתִי פָנֶ֔יךָ גַּ֖ם לַדָּבָ֣ר הַזֶּ֑ה לְבִלְתִּ֛י הָפְכִּ֥י רביעי
כב אֶת־הָעִ֖יר אֲשֶׁ֥ר דִּבַּֽרְתָּ׃ מַהֵר֙ הִמָּלֵ֣ט שָׁ֔מָּה כִּ֣י לֹ֤א אוּכַל֙ לַעֲשׂ֣וֹת דָּבָ֔ר עַד־בֹּאֲךָ֖
כג שָׁ֑מָּה עַל־כֵּ֛ן קָרָ֥א שֵׁם־הָעִ֖יר צֽוֹעַר׃ הַשֶּׁ֖מֶשׁ יָצָ֣א עַל־הָאָ֑רֶץ וְל֖וֹט בָּ֥א צֹֽעֲרָה׃
כד כה וַֽיהוָ֗ה הִמְטִ֧יר עַל־סְדֹ֛ם וְעַל־עֲמֹרָ֖ה גָּפְרִ֣ית וָאֵ֑שׁ מֵאֵ֥ת יְהוָ֖ה מִן־הַשָּׁמָֽיִם׃ וַיַּהֲפֹךְ֙
כו אֶת־הֶֽעָרִ֣ים הָאֵ֔ל וְאֵ֖ת כָּל־הַכִּכָּ֑ר וְאֵת֙ כָּל־יֹשְׁבֵ֣י הֶעָרִ֔ים וְצֶ֖מַח הָאֲדָמָֽה׃ וַתַּבֵּ֥ט
כז אִשְׁתּ֖וֹ מֵאַחֲרָ֑יו וַתְּהִ֖י נְצִ֥יב מֶֽלַח׃ וַיַּשְׁכֵּ֥ם אַבְרָהָ֖ם בַּבֹּ֑קֶר אֶל־הַ֨מָּק֔וֹם אֲשֶׁר־עָ֥מַד
כח שָׁ֖ם אֶת־פְּנֵ֥י יְהוָֽה׃ וַיַּשְׁקֵ֗ף עַל־פְּנֵ֤י סְדֹם֙ וַעֲמֹרָ֔ה וְעַ֖ל כָּל־פְּנֵ֣י אֶ֣רֶץ הַכִּכָּ֑ר וַיַּ֗רְא
כט וְהִנֵּ֤ה עָלָה֙ קִיטֹ֣ר הָאָ֔רֶץ כְּקִיטֹ֖ר הַכִּבְשָֽׁן׃ וַיְהִ֗י בְּשַׁחֵ֤ת אֱלֹהִים֙ אֶת־עָרֵ֣י הַכִּכָּ֔ר
וַיִּזְכֹּ֥ר אֱלֹהִ֖ים אֶת־אַבְרָהָ֑ם וַיְשַׁלַּ֤ח אֶת־לוֹט֙ מִתּ֣וֹךְ הַהֲפֵכָ֔ה בַּהֲפֹךְ֙ אֶת־הֶ֣עָרִ֔ים
ל אֲשֶׁר־יָשַׁ֥ב בָּהֵ֖ן לֽוֹט׃ וַיַּעַל֩ ל֨וֹט מִצּ֜וֹעַר וַיֵּ֣שֶׁב בָּהָ֗ר וּשְׁתֵּ֤י בְנֹתָיו֙ עִמּ֔וֹ כִּ֥י יָרֵ֖א לָשֶׁ֣בֶת
לא בְּצ֑וֹעַר וַיֵּ֙שֶׁב֙ בַּמְּעָרָ֔ה ה֖וּא וּשְׁתֵּ֥י בְנֹתָֽיו׃ וַתֹּ֧אמֶר הַבְּכִירָ֛ה אֶל־הַצְּעִירָ֖ה אָבִ֣ינוּ זָקֵ֑ן
לב וְאִ֨ישׁ אֵ֤ין בָּאָ֙רֶץ֙ לָב֣וֹא עָלֵ֔ינוּ כְּדֶ֖רֶךְ כָּל־הָאָֽרֶץ׃ לְכָ֨ה נַשְׁקֶ֧ה אֶת־אָבִ֛ינוּ יַ֖יִן וְנִשְׁכְּבָ֣ה

33 drink. Then the elder daughter went in and slept with him. He was unaware when she lay
down and when she arose. The next day, the elder said to the younger, "Last night I slept
34 with my father. Let us get him to drink wine again tonight, then you go in and sleep with
him. So may we preserve our family line through our father." So that night they got their
35 father to drink wine again, and the younger went and slept with him. And he was unaware
when she lay down and when she arose. And so both of Lot's daughters became pregnant
36 by their father. The elder had a son, whom she named Moav.[4] He is the ancestor of the
37 Moabites of today. The younger also had a son, whom she named Ben Ami.[5] And he is the
38 ancestor of the Amonites of today.

---

4 | The name Moav resonates with *me'av* ("from father").

5 | Literally, "son of my kin."

note the stark differences between the two scenes, drawn together to show us how very different they are.

Avraham receives his three visitors during the day, in the open, with a meal that consists of everything but wine, in a state of total consciousness. (According to Rambam, this visitation was a prophecy and never took place in the real world, and there is no higher state of consciousness than prophecy.) The astounding birth of this child will be the source of blessing to the world (see 12:2 and 17:21).

The three refugees act at night, in a cave, with a meal that consists (as far as we are told) only of wine, in a state of such total unconsciousness that Lot is able to be "fooled" again the next night.

I would like to propose that this is the purpose of the angelic visit to Avraham. There is no need to inform him of that which he already knows; rather, that visit is presented to contrast it with the horrible and abominable mirror scene at the end of the narrative.

This is also the reason for the gratuitous addition of the phrase *Ve'avinu zaken*, "Our father is old," spoken by the older daughter – it serves to bolster the parallel with the annunciation in Ḥevron where Sara accurately and pointedly reacts to the glad tidings with "My lord being old...."

Rabbi Yitzchak Etshalom

לג עִמּוֹ וּנְחַיֶּה מֵאָבִינוּ זָרַע׃ וַתַּשְׁקֶיןָ אֶת־אֲבִיהֶן יַיִן בַּלַּיְלָה הוּא וַתָּבֹא הַבְּכִירָה
לד וַתִּשְׁכַּב אֶת־אָבִיהָ וְלֹא־יָדַע בְּשִׁכְבָהּ וּבְקוּמָהּ׃ וַיְהִי מִמָּחֳרָת וַתֹּאמֶר הַבְּכִירָה
אֶל־הַצְּעִירָה הֵן־שָׁכַבְתִּי אֶמֶשׁ אֶת־אָבִי נַשְׁקֶנּוּ יַיִן גַּם־הַלַּיְלָה וּבֹאִי שִׁכְבִי עִמּוֹ
לה וּנְחַיֶּה מֵאָבִינוּ זָרַע׃ וַתַּשְׁקֶיןָ גַּם בַּלַּיְלָה הַהוּא אֶת־אֲבִיהֶן יָיִן וַתָּקָם הַצְּעִירָה
לו לז וַתִּשְׁכַּב עִמּוֹ וְלֹא־יָדַע בְּשִׁכְבָהּ וּבְקֻמָהּ׃ וַתַּהֲרֶיןָ שְׁתֵּי בְנוֹת־לוֹט מֵאֲבִיהֶן׃ וַתֵּלֶד
לח הַבְּכִירָה בֵּן וַתִּקְרָא שְׁמוֹ מוֹאָב הוּא אֲבִי־מוֹאָב עַד־הַיּוֹם׃ וְהַצְּעִירָה גַם־הִוא
יָלְדָה בֵּן וַתִּקְרָא שְׁמוֹ בֶּן־עַמִּי הוּא אֲבִי בְנֵי־עַמּוֹן עַד־הַיּוֹם׃

TAKING A LITERARY APPROACH

Even though the seventy-one verses that comprise Bereshit 18 and 19 make up two full chapters and are conventionally broken into more than three separate readings (*aliyot*), they are one paragraph in the Masoretic text. In other words, the only division that is inherent in the text – the breakdown into *parashot* – defines this sequence of scenes, a veritable travelogue that begins and ends in the mountain country but descends to the topographical and moral abyss of Sedom, as one literary unit.

Although the story begins in Ḥevron and ends in Tzoar, there is a circle that nearly becomes closed by the end of the passages. The narrative begins in the mountainous region of Judea, abruptly descends (in more ways than one) to the lowest point of human civilization, and then returns up to the mountainous area overlooking the formerly fertile plain of Sedom. A close look at the unit reveals that there are two sequences here that mirror each other in an inverted manner.

(18:1–15) The story begins with the arrival of three people (= angels), to a place (Ḥevron) where there will be the birth of a child, whose name (Yitzḥak) will be a deliberate play on words (*midrash shem*) associated with the events related to his conception (Avraham and Sara's laughter), and a repast (food) is served at that place.

(19:30–38) The story ends with the arrival of three people (Lot and his two daughters) to a place (the cave above Tzoar) where there will be the birth of two children, whose names (Moav, Ben Ami) are a deliberate play on words associated with the events related to their conception (Moav as in *me'av*, "from the father"; Ben Ami means "son of my kin"), and a repast (wine) is served there.

I would like to propose that this is why the text credits the daughter with the seemingly superfluous statement "Our father is old"; it further strengthens the parallel with the annunciation at Avraham's tent, where Sara thinks "my lord (husband) being old..." (18:12). Yet

THE ART OF MIDRASH

The Destruction of Sodom and Gomorrah
John Martin (1852)

Analysis

- Which elements of this image are directly mentioned in the text?
- Which elements of this image are not found in the text?
- What midrashic interpretation could be inferred from this image?

A QUESTION OF BIBLIODRAMA

TO LOT

- Why did you give the angels refuge, even though it put your life at risk?
- Were you scared of the townspeople?
- Why did you choose to live in such a place?
- How could you have offered your own daughters to the townspeople?
- What did you think when the angels announced God's plans and told you to flee?
- What did you think when your sons-in-law mocked you?
- Why did you choose to go to Tzoar instead of the mountains?

TO AVRAHAM

- Are you proud of the way Lot behaved in Sedom?
- Do you consider your influence on him a success or a failure?

TO LOT'S DAUGHTERS

- What did you think when Lot took the angels' advice and fled, taking you with him?
- How do you feel knowing that your husbands perished in the destruction?
- Why did you act like this with your father after the destruction?

"I'm being considerate of others" is a catch-all statement of avoidance. Leaders put off decisions because morale is low, yet it usually gets lower when those in charge evade honest conversations; this only leads to greater dysfunction. Ignoring problems to avoid disappointing people also means putting off creative solutions and leaving those very people "demoralized and confused by their leader's deceit."

"I'm committed to quality and accuracy." Some leaders have difficulty making decisions that have a long-term impact because not knowing outcomes generates high levels of anxiety. They fear looking stupid, Carucci observes, so they ask for more data or seek prolonged consultations. They often ask too many people. "Taking action in the face of incomplete data," Carucci writes, "is an executive's job. You sometimes won't know if the decision was 'right' until long after it's made." When leaders avoid hard decisions because of these factors, they communicate that looking right is more important than doing what's right.

"I want to be seen as fair." It's not hard to understand why leaders want to be seen as caring and just. To avoid playing favorites, however, they risk creating environments where everyone is praised equally or no one is. This, Carucci argues, is also unfair and disrespectful. High performers need acknowledgement if you want great organizations. People who underperform also need to know, even if some difficult decisions and conversations follow.

When leaders repeatedly make excuses for inaction, they are, in effect, telling others that self-interest and self-protection are more important than the organization, the family, or others in their orbit. When Lot and his family were forcibly brought outside Sedom, they were not subtle in their demand: "'Flee for your life! Do not look behind you, nor stop anywhere in the plain; flee to the hills, lest you be swept away.' But Lot said to them, 'Oh no, my lord! You have been so gracious to your servant and have already shown me so much kindness in order to save my life; but I cannot flee to the hills, lest the disaster overtake me, and I die'" (19:17–19).

Avraham picked up his life, changed it for the good, and changed the known world as a result. Lot, however, ended his life in ignominy. Ambivalence is rarely neutral. Indecision is also a decision. It's a decision to abdicate responsibility. It does make us feel lost. Yet every day, we wake up to a new dawn and the new decisions dawn brings. With each rising sun, we have another chance to rise, to shine, and to make better choices.

Dr. Erica Brown

Analysis

- What areas of understanding of human nature and society do we now have that were unavailable to classical Jewish commentators? How can they aid our understanding of the text?
- What can we learn from this essay to help us understand the text?
- What further questions on the text do you have now that you have read this new take on the story?

INTEGRATING ḤOKHMA

"He who hesitates is lost," goes the well-known proverb. I heard this as a teenager for the first time and wondered what it meant.

There's an incredible moment in Parashat Vayera that explains why he who hesitates is lost. Tentativeness can make us unsure of who we are. Our indecision can make us feel untethered. It is at this liminal hour when Lot was approached by an angel with an important message. He told Lot to save himself and his family from the catastrophe about to plague Sedom and Amora: "As dawn broke, the angels urged Lot on, saying, 'Arise, take your wife and your two remaining daughters, lest you be swept away because of the iniquity of the city.' Still he delayed" (Bereshit 19:15–16).

Lot ignored the metaphor of the dawn. With doom on the horizon but the glimmer of light that this day could be different for him and those he loved, "still he delayed." Rashi writes that Lot delayed to save his property, putting money above his life and that of his family. As time passed, every hour became increasingly consequential. Lot was forced to forego his possessions and leave at dawn with only the clothing on his back. Hesitation has its costs. Still Lot wasn't ready.

The Hebrew word used for "delay" in the verse is *vayitmameha*. The root of this word is *ma* – which sounds like the Hebrew for "what." It is as if in delaying, we are asking what, what, what shall I do? The word itself sounds like the hesitation that it represents. It only appears in Tanakh nine times. Strong's Exhaustive Concordance also defines this word as to question, to be reluctant, to linger, to stay, or to tarry.

Several years ago, management consultant and bestselling writer Ron Carucci wrote that "too many leaders avoid making tough calls." He conducted a ten-year longitudinal study of more than 2,700 leaders and found that 57 percent of new executives confronted decisions that were "more complicated and difficult than they expected." As a result, many leaders make excuses for not making hard decisions because they don't want to lose status with followers. Carucci boils down these excuses into three common phrases:

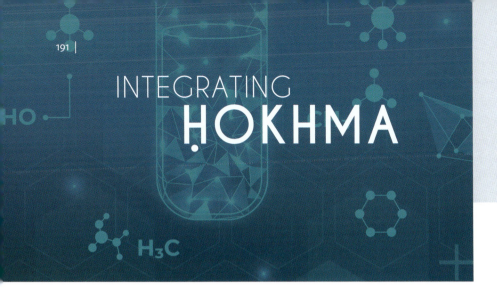

20 1 Avraham then journeyed on to the Negev region, settling between Kadesh and Shur. For
2 a while he lived as a stranger in Gerar. There Avraham said of his wife Sara, "She is my
3 sister." Avimelekh, king of Gerar, sent for Sara and took her as his own. But God came to
Avimelekh in a dream one night and told him, "You will die because of the woman you
4 have taken. She is already married." Avimelekh had not gone near her, so he said, "Lord,
5 would You destroy an innocent nation? Did he not tell me, 'She is my sister'? Did she not
6 say, 'He is my brother'? I have acted from an innocent heart, with clean hands." Then, in the
dream, God said to him, "I too knew you that acted from an innocent heart, and so I kept
7 you from sinning against Me. That is why I did not let you touch her. But now, give back
the man's wife. He is a prophet. He will pray for you and you will live. But if you do not give
8 her back, know that you and all your people are to die." Early the next morning, Avimelekh
9 summoned all his servants and told them all this – they were very afraid. Then Avimelekh
summoned Avraham and said, "What have you done to us? What wrong have I done you?
Why have you brought such onerous guilt upon me and my kingdom? You have done to
10 me that which should never be done. What were you thinking of," asked Avimelekh, "that
11 you did such a thing?" Avraham replied, "I thought, 'There is no fear of God in this place.
12 They will kill me because of my wife.' Besides, she really is my sister. She is the daughter

UNLOCKING THE TEXT

- Why is Avraham on the move again?
- What does it mean that he was a "stranger" in Gerar?
- How is this story different from that of Avraham and Sara in Egypt? What new lesson can be learned?
- Why would it be a "sin against God" if Avimelekh took Sara?
- Why did Avraham choose to come to this place if there was "no fear of God" there?
- Why did Avimelekh give Avraham so much wealth?
- Why had God caused the women to become barren?

FINDING YOURSELF IN THE TEXT

- Have you ever been in a place you felt was unsafe?
- Have you ever told a lie to protect yourself?
- Have you ever bene surprised by the goodness of people?

Consider using these questions as the basis for your own commentary or creative midrash.

How does reflecting on these firsthand experiences help you better understand the text?

כ א ב וַיִּסַּע מִשָּׁם אַבְרָהָם אַרְצָה הַנֶּגֶב וַיֵּשֶׁב בֵּין־קָדֵשׁ וּבֵין שׁוּר וַיָּגָר בִּגְרָר׃ וַיֹּאמֶר יז
אַבְרָהָם אֶל־שָׂרָה אִשְׁתּוֹ אֲחֹתִי הִוא וַיִּשְׁלַח אֲבִימֶלֶךְ מֶלֶךְ גְּרָר וַיִּקַּח אֶת־שָׂרָה׃
ג וַיָּבֹא אֱלֹהִים אֶל־אֲבִימֶלֶךְ בַּחֲלוֹם הַלָּיְלָה וַיֹּאמֶר לוֹ הִנְּךָ מֵת עַל־הָאִשָּׁה אֲשֶׁר־
ד לָקַחְתָּ וְהִוא בְּעֻלַת בָּעַל׃ וַאֲבִימֶלֶךְ לֹא קָרַב אֵלֶיהָ וַיֹּאמַר אֲדֹנָי הֲגוֹי גַּם־צַדִּיק
ה תַּהֲרֹג׃ הֲלֹא הוּא אָמַר־לִי אֲחֹתִי הִוא וְהִיא־גַם־הִוא אָמְרָה אָחִי הוּא בְּתָם־לְבָבִי
ו וּבְנִקְיֹן כַּפַּי עָשִׂיתִי זֹאת׃ וַיֹּאמֶר אֵלָיו הָאֱלֹהִים בַּחֲלֹם גַּם אָנֹכִי יָדַעְתִּי כִּי בְתָם־
לְבָבְךָ עָשִׂיתָ זֹּאת וָאֶחְשֹׂךְ גַּם־אָנֹכִי אוֹתְךָ מֵחֲטוֹ־לִי עַל־כֵּן לֹא־נְתַתִּיךָ לִנְגֹּעַ
ז אֵלֶיהָ׃ וְעַתָּה הָשֵׁב אֵשֶׁת־הָאִישׁ כִּי־נָבִיא הוּא וְיִתְפַּלֵּל בַּעַדְךָ וֶחְיֵה וְאִם־אֵינְךָ
ח מֵשִׁיב דַּע כִּי־מוֹת תָּמוּת אַתָּה וְכָל־אֲשֶׁר־לָךְ׃ וַיַּשְׁכֵּם אֲבִימֶלֶךְ בַּבֹּקֶר וַיִּקְרָא
לְכָל־עֲבָדָיו וַיְדַבֵּר אֶת־כָּל־הַדְּבָרִים הָאֵלֶּה בְּאָזְנֵיהֶם וַיִּירְאוּ הָאֲנָשִׁים מְאֹד׃
ט וַיִּקְרָא אֲבִימֶלֶךְ לְאַבְרָהָם וַיֹּאמֶר לוֹ מֶה־עָשִׂיתָ לָּנוּ וּמֶה־חָטָאתִי לָךְ כִּי־הֵבֵאתָ
י עָלַי וְעַל־מַמְלַכְתִּי חֲטָאָה גְדֹלָה מַעֲשִׂים אֲשֶׁר לֹא־יֵעָשׂוּ עָשִׂיתָ עִמָּדִי׃ וַיֹּאמֶר
יא אֲבִימֶלֶךְ אֶל־אַבְרָהָם מָה רָאִיתָ כִּי עָשִׂיתָ אֶת־הַדָּבָר הַזֶּה׃ וַיֹּאמֶר אַבְרָהָם כִּי
יב אָמַרְתִּי רַק אֵין־יִרְאַת אֱלֹהִים בַּמָּקוֹם הַזֶּה וַהֲרָגוּנִי עַל־דְּבַר אִשְׁתִּי׃ וְגַם־אָמְנָה

THEMES	RELATIONSHIPS AND LOVE	GOD	FREE WILL, REWARD AND PUNISHMENT

Episode 24: *Avraham and Sara in Gerar* – Bereshit 20:1–18

SUMMARY

The Torah returns to the story of Avraham and Sara, whose journey to Gerar brings them into a situation similar to the one they experienced earlier in Egypt. The Sages note the juxtaposition of this episode to the destruction of Sedom, and suggest that Avraham may have left Ḥevron due to the effects of the calamity on the surrounding area. If the actions of Lot and his daughters had become widely known, the rumors alone could have prompted Avraham to migrate.

13 of my father though not of my mother, and she became my wife. When God made me
wander from my father's house, I said to her, 'Do me this kindness: wherever we go, say
14 of me, "He is my brother."'" Avimelekh gave Avraham sheep, cattle, and male and female
15 slaves, and returned his wife Sara to him. Avimelekh said, "Here is my land. Live wherever
16 you wish." To Sara he said, "I am giving your brother a thousand pieces of silver. This will
17 allay the suspicions of everyone who is with you. You are fully vindicated." Then Avraham
prayed to God, and God healed Avimelekh, his wife, and his female slaves so they could
18 again have children, for the LORD had prevented all the women in Avimelekh's household
from bearing children, because of Sara, Avraham's wife.

THE ART OF MIDRASH

Sarah and Abimelech
Marc Chagall (1960)

Analysis

- Which elements of this image are directly mentioned in the text?
- Which elements of this image are not found in the text?
- What midrashic interpretation could be inferred from this image?

יג אֲחֹתִ֤י בַת־אָבִי֙ הִ֔וא אַ֖ךְ לֹ֣א בַת־אִמִּ֑י וַתְּהִי־לִ֖י לְאִשָּֽׁה׃ וַיְהִ֞י כַּאֲשֶׁ֨ר הִתְע֣וּ אֹתִ֗י
אֱלֹהִים֮ מִבֵּ֣ית אָבִי֒ וָאֹמַ֣ר לָ֔הּ זֶ֣ה חַסְדֵּ֔ךְ אֲשֶׁ֥ר תַּעֲשִׂ֖י עִמָּדִ֑י אֶ֤ל כָּל־הַמָּקוֹם֙ אֲשֶׁ֣ר
יד נָב֣וֹא שָׁ֔מָּה אִמְרִי־לִ֖י אָחִ֥י הֽוּא׃ וַיִּקַּ֨ח אֲבִימֶ֜לֶךְ צֹ֣אן וּבָקָ֗ר וַעֲבָדִים֙ וּשְׁפָחֹ֔ת וַיִּתֵּ֖ן
טו לְאַבְרָהָ֑ם וַיָּ֣שֶׁב ל֔וֹ אֵ֖ת שָׂרָ֥ה אִשְׁתּֽוֹ׃ וַיֹּ֣אמֶר אֲבִימֶ֔לֶךְ הִנֵּ֥ה אַרְצִ֖י לְפָנֶ֑יךָ בַּטּ֥וֹב
טז בְּעֵינֶ֖יךָ שֵֽׁב׃ וּלְשָׂרָ֣ה אָמַ֗ר הִנֵּ֨ה נָתַ֜תִּי אֶ֤לֶף כֶּ֙סֶף֙ לְאָחִ֔יךְ הִנֵּ֤ה הוּא־לָךְ֙ כְּס֣וּת עֵינַ֔יִם
יז לְכֹ֖ל אֲשֶׁ֣ר אִתָּ֑ךְ וְאֵ֥ת כֹּ֖ל וְנֹכָֽחַת׃ וַיִּתְפַּלֵּ֥ל אַבְרָהָ֖ם אֶל־הָאֱלֹהִ֑ים וַיִּרְפָּ֨א אֱלֹהִ֜ים
יח אֶת־אֲבִימֶ֧לֶךְ וְאֶת־אִשְׁתּ֛וֹ וְאַמְהֹתָ֖יו וַיֵּלֵֽדוּ׃ כִּֽי־עָצֹ֤ר עָצַר֙ יהוה בְּעַ֥ד כָּל־רֶ֖חֶם
לְבֵ֣ית אֲבִימֶ֑לֶךְ עַל־דְּבַ֥ר שָׂרָ֖ה אֵ֥שֶׁת אַבְרָהָֽם׃

A QUESTION OF BIBLIODRAMA

TO AVRAHAM

- Why are you on the move again?
- Why did you not trust that God would protect you and Sara?
- Were you surprised by Avimelekh's response to this episode?

TO SARA

- After your experiences in Egypt, why did you agree again to this arrangement?
- Were you scared when Avimelekh took you?
- Did you have faith that God would protect you?

TO AVIMELEKH

- Why did you take Sara?
- Were you angry when God appeared to you and told you who she was?
- Why did you give Avraham so much wealth?

INTEGRATING ḤOKHMA

Avraham's journeys in the land of Israel

Analysis

- What specific information do we now have that was unavailable to classical Jewish commentators? How can it aid our understanding of the text?
- What can we learn from this map that can help us understand the text?
- What further questions on the text do you have now that you have seen this map?

TAKING A LITERARY APPROACH

After having become entangled in Egypt, Avraham should have considered the possibility that Sara would once again be taken to the house of the king when he arrives in Gerar. Nevertheless, he uses the same trick, which, as expected, proves itself ineffective in such a case. Thus, Sara finds herself once again in the king's house, and once again God is forced to come to her aid. This time, however, the story is more complex. This time, Scripture reveals to us the dialogue that God conducts with Avimelekh, to whom He reveals Himself in order to save him from the sin that Avraham had brought to his door (Bereshit 20:3–4).

As a result, he summons Avraham and reproaches him for abandoning him to sin, but this time Scripture spells out Avraham's answer in detail (20:9–13).

There are two striking differences in the details of the stories, and the common denominator of those differences lies in the dialogue. God reveals Himself to Avimelekh with the goal of dissuading him from sinning, and a dialogue develops between them, something that did not happen with Pharaoh. In the continuation, after Avimelekh rebukes Avraham, the text details Avraham's justification of his decision to present Sara as his sister.

It seems that these two details seek to create an impression that is different from that left by the case in Egypt. In that context, Scripture wishes to allude that the sole culprit is Pharaoh, and he is therefore not worthy of God's revelation, which would explain the situation to him, but he is rather immediately punished. In addition, Scripture does not bother to bring Avraham's explanation. The impression is that the explanation for his conduct was already given earlier. Exposing the fact that Sara is his wife could have cost Avraham his life, and no cry on the part of Pharaoh would change that, and therefore there is no point or need to repeat the explanation from Avraham's side.

In any event, we understand that in Avimelekh's case, things are different. He receives a divine revelation because he does not deserve to fall into sin. In order to emphasize his innocence, Scripture even puts into his mouth the moral argument that Avraham had put forward when he petitioned on behalf of the people of Sedom (18:23).

But this time, this argument is sounded by Avimelekh, who is the victim of that very same Avraham (20:4). In addition, the text "demands" that Avraham explain his action, and therefore cites his words in response to Avimelekh's rebuke. There is even a hint of criticism of Avraham's explanation (20:11). This follows the text that had already noted that this is not so (20:8). The understanding that is shown for Avimelekh's claim is expressed even in the words of God (20:6).

At the end of the story, even though he had been misled by him, Avimelekh allows Avraham to remain in Gerar, whereas Pharaoh had sent him away. This fact too is credited to Avimelekh.

Rabbi Gad Eldad

21 1 The Lord remembered Sara as He had said He would, and acted for Sara as He
2 had promised. Sara became pregnant and bore a son to Avraham in his old age
3 at the very time God had promised. Avraham named his newborn son, whom Sara had
4 borne him, Yitzḥak. And when Yitzḥak his son was eight days old, Avraham circumcised
5 him as God had commanded. Avraham was one hundred years old when his son Yitzḥak
6 was born to him. Sara said, "God has brought me laughter; all those who hear will laugh
7 with me."[1] Then she said, "Who would have told Avraham, 'Sara will nurse children'? Yet
8 I have borne a son in his old age." The child grew and was weaned; on the day Yitzḥak was
weaned, Avraham held a great feast.

---

1 | The name Yitzḥak derives from the verb denoting laughter (cf. 17:17–19, 18:12–14).

UNLOCKING THE TEXT

- What does it mean that God "remembered" (*pakad*) Sara?
- Why did Avraham choose Yitzḥak's name alone?
- Why did Avraham choose the name Yitzḥak?
- Is this command to circumcise Yitzḥak included in the original command of *brit mila* given to Avraham previously, or is it something new?
- Is Sara changing the previous meaning of the "laughter" surrounding the promised birth of Yitzḥak?
- Why did Avraham throw a party for the weaning of Yitzḥak (is there a precedent for this)?

FINDING YOURSELF IN THE TEXT

- Have you ever had something you had always dreamed of happen to you?
- Who chose your name?
- What does your name mean and why was it chosen?

Consider using these questions as the basis for your own commentary or creative midrash.

How does reflecting on these firsthand experiences help you better understand the text?

כא א ב וַיהוָה פָּקַד אֶת־שָׂרָה כַּאֲשֶׁר אָמָר וַיַּעַשׂ יְהוָה לְשָׂרָה כַּאֲשֶׁר דִּבֵּר׃ וַתַּהַר וַתֵּלֶד יח
ג שָׂרָה לְאַבְרָהָם בֵּן לִזְקֻנָיו לַמּוֹעֵד אֲשֶׁר־דִּבֶּר אֹתוֹ אֱלֹהִים׃ וַיִּקְרָא אַבְרָהָם אֶת־
ד שֶׁם־בְּנוֹ הַנּוֹלַד־לוֹ אֲשֶׁר־יָלְדָה־לּוֹ שָׂרָה יִצְחָק׃ וַיָּמָל אַבְרָהָם אֶת־יִצְחָק בְּנוֹ
ה בֶּן־שְׁמֹנַת יָמִים כַּאֲשֶׁר צִוָּה אֹתוֹ אֱלֹהִים׃ וְאַבְרָהָם בֶּן־מְאַת שָׁנָה בְּהִוָּלֶד לוֹ אֵת חמישי
ו ז יִצְחָק בְּנוֹ׃ וַתֹּאמֶר שָׂרָה צְחֹק עָשָׂה לִי אֱלֹהִים כָּל־הַשֹּׁמֵעַ יִצְחַק־לִי׃ וַתֹּאמֶר
ח מִי מִלֵּל לְאַבְרָהָם הֵינִיקָה בָנִים שָׂרָה כִּי־יָלַדְתִּי בֵן לִזְקֻנָיו׃ וַיִּגְדַּל הַיֶּלֶד וַיִּגָּמַל
וַיַּעַשׂ אַבְרָהָם מִשְׁתֶּה גָדוֹל בְּיוֹם הִגָּמֵל אֶת־יִצְחָק׃

THEMES	COVENANT	RELATIONSHIPS AND LOVE	PEOPLEHOOD

Episode 25: *The Birth of Yitzḥak* – Bereshit 21:1–8

SUMMARY

God fulfills His promise; Sara bears a child to Avraham when Avraham is one hundred years old. Sara is overjoyed – nobody would have ever said that at her age, Sara would be nursing a child. Avraham names his son Yitzḥak, circumcises him as he was commanded, and throws a great feast when he is weaned.

Surrounded by prose sections, which describe the sequence of events, the celebratory first verse of the next passage, and likewise Sara's joyous comments in verses 6–7, stand out for their poetry, employing parallelism. They emphasize the dramatic importance of the birth of Sara's promised son, heir to the House of Avraham.

THE ART OF MIDRASH

A Mother's Joy
Tani Bayer (2023)

Analysis

- Which elements of this image are directly mentioned in the text?
- Which elements of this image are not found in the text?
- What midrashic interpretation could be inferred from this image?

A QUESTION OF BIBLIODRAMA

TO AVRAHAM

- What emotions did you experience when Sara gave birth to Yitzḥak?
- Why did you give the baby the name Yitzḥak?
- How do you imagine Yishmael feels after the birth of Yitzḥak, and how does that make you feel?

TO SARA

- What emotions did you experience when God fulfilled His promise to you and you gave birth to Yitzḥak?
- What did you feel about Avraham's choice of name for Yitzḥak?
- What message was behind your statement after the birth of Yitzḥak and who was the intended audience?

INTEGRATING ḤOKHMA

Judaism, more than any other faith, sees parenthood as the highest challenge of all. On the first day of Rosh Hashana – the anniversary of creation – we read of two mothers, Sara and Ḥana, and the births of their sons, as if to say: Every life is a universe. Therefore, if you wish to understand the creation of the universe, think about the birth of a child.

Avraham, the hero of faith, is simply a father. Stephen Hawking famously wrote at the end of *A Brief History of Time* that if we had a unified field theory, a scientific "theory of everything," we would "know the mind of God." We believe otherwise. To know the mind of God we do not need theoretical physics. We simply need to know what it is to be a parent. The miracle of childbirth is as close as we come to understanding the-love-that-brings-new-life-into-the-world that is God's creativity.

Judaism takes what is natural and sanctifies it; what is physical and invests it with spirituality; what is elsewhere considered normal and sees it as a miracle. What Darwin saw as the urge to reproduce, what Richard Dawkins calls "the selfish gene," is for Judaism high religious art, full of drama and beauty. Avraham the father, and Sara the mother, are our enduring role models of parenthood as God's gift and our highest vocation.

Rabbi Jonathan Sacks

Analysis

- What areas of scientific understanding do we now have that were unavailable to classical Jewish commentators? How can they aid our understanding of the text?
- What can we learn from this passage to help us understand the text?
- What further questions on the text do you have now that you have read this new take on the story?

TAKING A LITERARY APPROACH

After decades of barrenness, Sara conceives and bears Avraham a son, as God promised. If there is any chapter in the Torah which belongs to Sara, it is this. It opens with a glorious "God remembered Sara as He had spoken" (Bereshit 21:1) and continues with Sara's exultation, "God has made me joyous; anyone who hears will rejoice for me" (21:6). Sara is the one who sees Yishmael's actions and demands that Avraham banish him, and when that displeases Avraham, God intervenes: "Whatever Sara says to you, obey her voice" (21:12). For some Sara is the villain, for others she is the heroine. Regardless, this is her moment. Despite Avraham's unpreparedness, Sara becomes the covenantal mother. God redeems Sara, and she quickly takes her place of prominence in the family.

With Sara at the center of the narrative, Avraham fades into the background, and this is not surprising. We recall Avraham's reaction to hearing that Sara will bear him a child: "No," he says, "that is unnecessary; I have Yishmael" (17:18). He is so ambivalent about this new prospect that he doesn't even tell Sara. Even more extraordinary, he allows the future mother of the covenantal child – his child – to be taken to Avimelekh's palace in Gerar!

Yet Avraham quickly moves from out of the background. Already by the third verse he takes charge and pushes Sara out of the limelight:

> Avraham named *his* son, the one born to *him*, which Sara had birthed to *him*, Yitzḥak. Avraham circumcised Yitzḥak, *his* son, at the age of eight days, as God had commanded *him*. Avraham was one hundred years old when Yitzḥak, *his* son, was born to *him*. (21:3–5)

Notice how prominent Avraham becomes in Sara's story – seven times in the span of just three verses, the text emphasizes that Yitzḥak belongs to *him*. Avraham seeks to own Yitzḥak, the son he only begrudgingly accepts, lest he, or his mother, disrupt the life Avraham has carefully constructed with Yishmael.

If this were not enough, Avraham throws a lavish party on the day Yitzḥak is weaned. Nowhere in the Bible do we hear of a party for the weaning of a child, and even the brief description of the party as being "large" is *sui generis* in the Torah. It is worth taking a moment to look at the verse describing that party: "The child grew (*g-d-l*) and was weaned, and Avraham made a large (*g-d-l*) party on the day Yitzḥak was weaned" (21:8).

The verse has a parallel structure within it. The opening phrase has three elements: the child, growing up (*g-d-l*), and weaning. Those same three elements appear in the latter phrase of the verse. At the very center of this verse is Avraham. He takes center stage, and his great moment of celebration arrives when he can begin to separate Yitzḥak from his mother.

Avraham's exclusion of Sara stands in stark contrast to Sara's inclusion of Avraham. Sara bears a child *to Avraham* (21:2), and when Sara sings her poem praising God she includes Avraham in it: "Who would have said *to Avraham*, 'Sara is nursing children!' For I have borne a son in *his* old age" (21:7). Sara's nobility of soul is marked by her understanding that her redemption is not only personal; it redeems Avraham too, and is strikingly contrasted with Avraham's inability to let Sara stand by his side.

Rabbi Zvi Grumet

9 10 But Sara saw the son whom Hagar the Egyptian had borne Avraham mocking.[1] She said
to Avraham, "Drive out that slave woman and her son, for the son of that slave woman
11 must not share the inheritance with my son, with Yitzḥak." This distressed Avraham
12 greatly because of his son. But God told Avraham, "Do not be distressed about the boy or
about your slave. Listen to whatever Sara tells you, because it is through Yitzḥak that your
13 descendants will be reckoned. But I will make the slave's son too into a nation, because he is
14 your child." Early the next morning Avraham took bread and a skin of water and gave them
to Hagar. He placed them on her shoulder, and together with the child, he sent her away.
15 She went wandering in the Be'er Sheva desert. When the water in the skin was all gone, she
16 cast the child away under one of the bushes and went and sat down at a distance, about a
bowshot away, saying, "I cannot watch the child die." Sitting there, at a distance, she raised
17 her voice and wept. God heard the boy crying, and an angel of God called to Hagar from
the heavens and said to her, "Hagar, what is wrong? Fear not. God has heard the boy's cry
18 there, where he is. Go, raise up the boy and take him by the hand, for I will make of him a
19 great nation." Then God opened her eyes and she saw a well of water. She went and filled

1 | Hebrew *metzaḥek* – again bearing a connection to the name Yitzḥak.

UNLOCKING THE TEXT

- What was Yishmael "mocking" (*metzaḥek*)?
- What was Sara's motivation for demanding Avraham send Hagar and Yishmael away, and was she justified?
- Why was Avraham distressed?
- Did God agree with Sara?
- Why did God command that Avraham listen to Sara's request?
- Why did God also promise that Yishmael would become a nation?
- Why did Hagar behave in this way?
- Why does the Torah say Hagar wept, but God heard Yishmael crying?
- Was the well always there or was it miraculous?
- What does it mean that God was with the boy as he grew? Why?

FINDING YOURSELF IN THE TEXT

- Have you ever had to do something you knew was right but would cause someone else pain?
- Can you imagine how your parents feel when they know you are in pain?
- Have you ever questioned God?

Consider using these questions as the basis for your own commentary or creative midrash.

How does reflecting on these firsthand experiences help you better understand the text?

ט וַתֵּ֨רֶא שָׂרָ֜ה אֶֽת־בֶּן־הָגָ֧ר הַמִּצְרִ֛ית אֲשֶׁר־יָלְדָ֥ה לְאַבְרָהָ֖ם מְצַחֵֽק׃ וַתֹּ֙אמֶר֙
לְאַבְרָהָ֔ם גָּרֵ֛שׁ הָאָמָ֥ה הַזֹּ֖את וְאֶת־בְּנָ֑הּ כִּ֣י לֹ֤א יִירַשׁ֙ בֶּן־הָאָמָ֣ה הַזֹּ֔את עִם־בְּנִ֖י
יא עִם־יִצְחָֽק׃ וַיֵּ֧רַע הַדָּבָ֛ר מְאֹ֖ד בְּעֵינֵ֣י אַבְרָהָ֑ם עַ֖ל אוֹדֹ֥ת בְּנֽוֹ׃ וַיֹּ֨אמֶר אֱלֹהִ֜ים אֶל־
אַבְרָהָ֗ם אַל־יֵרַ֤ע בְּעֵינֶ֙יךָ֙ עַל־הַנַּ֣עַר וְעַל־אֲמָתֶ֔ךָ כֹּל֩ אֲשֶׁ֨ר תֹּאמַ֤ר אֵלֶ֙יךָ֙ שָׂרָ֔ה שְׁמַ֣ע
יג בְּקֹלָ֔הּ כִּ֣י בְיִצְחָ֔ק יִקָּרֵ֥א לְךָ֖ זָֽרַע׃ וְגַ֥ם אֶת־בֶּן־הָאָמָ֖ה לְג֣וֹי אֲשִׂימֶ֑נּוּ כִּ֥י זַרְעֲךָ֖ הֽוּא׃
יד וַיַּשְׁכֵּ֣ם אַבְרָהָ֣ם ׀ בַּבֹּ֡קֶר וַיִּֽקַּֽח־לֶ֩חֶם֩ וְחֵ֨מַת מַ֜יִם וַיִּתֵּ֣ן אֶל־הָ֠גָר שָׂ֧ם עַל־שִׁכְמָ֛הּ
וְאֶת־הַיֶּ֖לֶד וַֽיְשַׁלְּחֶ֑הָ וַתֵּ֣לֶךְ וַתֵּ֔תַע בְּמִדְבַּ֖ר בְּאֵ֥ר שָֽׁבַע׃ וַיִּכְל֥וּ הַמַּ֖יִם מִן־הַחֵ֑מֶת
טז וַתַּשְׁלֵ֣ךְ אֶת־הַיֶּ֔לֶד תַּ֖חַת אַחַ֣ד הַשִּׂיחִֽם׃ וַתֵּ֡לֶךְ וַתֵּשֶׁב֩ לָ֨הּ מִנֶּ֜גֶד הַרְחֵ֣ק כִּמְטַחֲוֵ֣י
קֶ֗שֶׁת כִּ֤י אָֽמְרָה֙ אַל־אֶרְאֶ֖ה בְּמ֣וֹת הַיָּ֑לֶד וַתֵּ֣שֶׁב מִנֶּ֔גֶד וַתִּשָּׂ֥א אֶת־קֹלָ֖הּ וַתֵּֽבְךְּ׃
יז וַיִּשְׁמַ֣ע אֱלֹהִים֮ אֶת־ק֣וֹל הַנַּעַר֒ וַיִּקְרָא֩ מַלְאַ֨ךְ אֱלֹהִ֤ים ׀ אֶל־הָגָר֙ מִן־הַשָּׁמַ֔יִם וַיֹּ֥אמֶר
לָ֖הּ מַה־לָּ֣ךְ הָגָ֑ר אַל־תִּ֣ירְאִ֔י כִּֽי־שָׁמַ֧ע אֱלֹהִ֛ים אֶל־ק֥וֹל הַנַּ֖עַר בַּאֲשֶׁ֥ר הוּא־שָֽׁם׃
יח ק֚וּמִי שְׂאִ֣י אֶת־הַנַּ֔עַר וְהַחֲזִ֥יקִי אֶת־יָדֵ֖ךְ בּ֑וֹ כִּֽי־לְג֥וֹי גָּד֖וֹל אֲשִׂימֶֽנּוּ׃ וַיִּפְקַ֤ח אֱלֹהִים֙
אֶת־עֵינֶ֔יהָ וַתֵּ֖רֶא בְּאֵ֣ר מָ֑יִם וַתֵּ֜לֶךְ וַתְּמַלֵּ֤א אֶת־הַחֵ֙מֶת֙ מַ֔יִם וַתַּ֖שְׁקְ אֶת־הַנָּֽעַר׃

THEMES | COVENANT | RELATIONSHIPS AND LOVE | PEOPLEHOOD

Episode 26: *The Banishment of Hagar and Yishmael* – Bereshit 21:9–21

SUMMARY

The proper development of Yitzḥak, Avraham's heir and successor, necessitates the banishment of Avraham's firstborn son, Yishmael. Sara is the driving force behind the exile of Yishmael and his mother Hagar in response to the boy's problematic conduct, which she fears will adversely affect Yitzḥak. Wandering in the desert, her water exhausted, Hagar sits down to cry after tossing Yishmael under a bush where she can no longer see or hear him. But God does hear him. An angel calls out to Hagar, telling her that God has heard the child's cries, and that she should pick the child up, for his destiny is to become a great nation. God opens her eyes so that she sees a well from which she gives the child to drink. God watches over that child as he grows up in the wilderness and becomes an archer. His mother finds him an Egyptian bride.

20 the skin with water and gave the boy to drink. God was with the boy as he grew. He lived
21 in the desert and became an expert with the bow. In the Paran desert he lived, and his
mother took him a wife from Egypt.

THE ART OF MIDRASH

Hagar and Ishmael in the Wilderness
Gustave Doré (1860)

Analysis

- Which elements of this image are directly mentioned in the text?
- Which elements of this image are not found in the text?
- What midrashic interpretation could be inferred from this image?

כ כא וַיְהִ֧י אֱלֹהִ֛ים אֶת־הַנַּ֖עַר וַיִּגְדָּ֑ל וַיֵּ֙שֶׁב֙ בַּמִּדְבָּ֔ר וַיְהִ֖י רֹבֶ֥ה קַשָּֽׁת׃ וַיֵּ֖שֶׁב בְּמִדְבַּ֣ר פָּארָ֑ן
וַתִּֽקַּֽח־ל֥וֹ אִמּ֛וֹ אִשָּׁ֖ה מֵאֶ֥רֶץ מִצְרָֽיִם׃

A QUESTION OF BIBLIODRAMA

TO SARA

- Why did you behave in this way to Hagar and her son?
- Did you feel threatened by them?
- Did you feel any guilt toward them?

TO HAGAR

- How do you feel about Sara?
- How do you feel about Avraham?
- How do you feel about God?
- Why did you abandon your child under the bush?

TO AVRAHAM

- Why did Sara's request distress you?
- Why did you do it anyway?
- Do you think Sara was justified?
- Do you understand God's justification for sending Hagar and Yishmael away?

TO YISHMAEL

- What are your feelings toward your father?
- What are your feelings toward your mother?
- What are your feelings toward Yitzḥak?
- What are your feelings toward God?

INTEGRATING ḤOKHMA

Par. 170: If a man's chief wife bears him children and his maidservant [also] bears him children, and the father, while he still lives, tells the children whom the maidservant bore him, "[You are] my children," then he counts them among the children of his chief wife. After the father dies, the children of the chief wife and the children of the maidservant divide the property of the father's estate between them equally. The son of the chief wife is first to choose and take his portion of the inheritance.

Par. 171: If the father, while still alive, does not say to the children whom the maidservant bore him, "[You are] my children," then after the father dies, the children of the maidservant do not receive a portion of the father's estate with the children of the chief wife. The release of the maidservant and her children is assured; the children of the chief wife shall not demand servitude of the children of the maidservant.

The Code of Hammurabi

Analysis

- What areas of understanding of human nature, society, and history do we have now that were unavailable to classical Jewish commentators? How can they aid our understanding of the text?
- What can we learn from the Code of Hammurabi to help us understand the text?
- What further questions on the text do you have now that you have read this new take on the story?

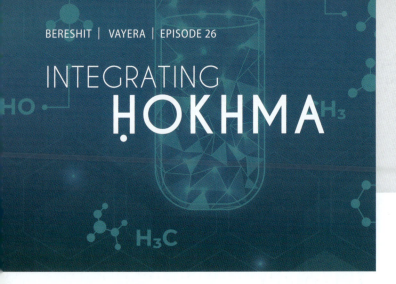

TAKING A LITERARY APPROACH

Upon close analysis, the ordeal of Hagar and Yishmael bears a striking resemblance to another story in Parashat Vayera. The narrative opens with the phrase "And Avraham got up early in the morning" and depicts him as "taking" (Bereshit 21:14). No reader of the Bible can miss the echo. This is Avraham's first action in the *akeda*, the story of the binding of Yitzḥak. In the *akeda*, the Torah utilizes the exact same phrase: "And Avraham got up early in the morning," and likewise depicts him as "taking" (22:3). This parallel is not just linguistic. In both cases Avraham rises early to accomplish a divine command. In both cases, the divine command involves a final parting from a son, the expulsion of Yishmael and the sacrifice of Yitzḥak (21:11–12; 22:1–2).

All of this is just the tip of the iceberg. In both cases, a young lad, referred to by the term *hanaar* (21:17–20; 22:5, 12), is endangered in the course of a journey. The respective journeys are described by a term comprising a variation on the Hebrew root *h-l-kh*, meaning "go" (21:14; 22:2–3). Furthermore, in both cases the danger threatens the lad as a result of the action of a parent. Hagar wanders aimlessly in the desert, and when dehydration consequently threatens, she casts her son away, leaving him to die under one of the shrubs (21:15–17). The danger to Yitzḥak also stems from a parent. It is the hand and knife of Avraham that threaten Yitzḥak's life (22:10).

More strikingly, in the respective climaxes of the stories, the endangered lad is saved by the call of an angel of God sounding from heaven (21:17; 22:11). In each case, the heavenly intervention is followed by "seeing," a vision that provides the solution to the problem of imminent death: water in the case of Yishmael (21:19), and the ram (as an alternate sacrifice) in the case of Yitzḥak (22:13). Furthermore, in both cases the angel reiterates the promise of future nationhood before departing (21:18; 22:17–18).

Finally, after depicting the young man as having survived his life-threatening ordeal, both narratives turn toward marriage. Chapter 21, the story of Yishmael, informs us of Yishmael's marriage (21:21). On a similar note, chapter 22, the story of Yitzḥak, closes with the genealogy of Naḥor, focusing on the birth of Rivka, the future wife of our once endangered and now saved youth.

Rabbi Chanoch Waxman

22 At that time, Avimelekh and Pikhol, commander of his troops, said to Avraham, “God is
23 with you in all you do. Now swear to me here before God that you will not deal falsely
with me or with my children or grandchildren. Show me and the land where you have
24 25 lived as a stranger the same kindness I have shown to you.”[1] Avraham said, “I swear.” Then
26 Avraham rebuked Avimelekh for the well of water that Avimelekh’s servants had seized. But
Avimelekh said, “I do not know who has done this. You did not tell me; I had not heard
27 about it until today.” Avraham then brought sheep and cattle and gave them to Avimelekh,
28 and the two of them forged a covenant. Avraham set apart seven ewe lambs from the flock.
29 Avimelekh asked him, “What is the meaning of these seven ewe lambs you have set apart?”
30 31 He replied, “Accept these seven lambs from me as testimony that I dug this well.” That is
32 why that place is called Be’er Sheva, because there the two men swore an oath.[2] Thus they
made a pact at Be’er Sheva. And then Avimelekh and Pikhol, commander of his troops,
33 returned to the land of the Philistines. Avraham planted a tamarisk tree in Be’er Sheva, and
34 there he called on the name of the Lord, the Everlasting God. Avraham stayed on in the
land of the Philistines for many days.

---

1 | See 20:14–16.

2 | The name Be’er Sheva resonates with both *sheva* (“seven”) and *nishbe’u* (“swore”).

UNLOCKING THE TEXT

- What led to Avimelekh approaching Avraham at this point in time?
- Why does the Torah include this episode at this point in Avraham’s narrative?
- Why was Avraham interested in entering into a covenant with Avimelekh?
- Why did Avimelekh bring Pikhol, the commander of his army, with him to negotiate with Avraham?
- Why did the issue of the well almost derail the covenant?
- What is the significance of the seven lambs?
- Why did Avraham plant a tamarisk tree in Be’er Sheva?

FINDING YOURSELF IN THE TEXT

- Have you ever entered into a deal with someone that protected both party’s interests?
- Have you ever challenged someone over a wrong and accepted their explanation?
- Have you ever been to Be’er Sheva? How does it feel to know that Be’er Sheva is a city in the modern State of Israel?

Consider using these questions as the basis for your own commentary or creative midrash.

How does reflecting on these firsthand experiences help you better understand the text?

כב וַיְהִי בָּעֵת הַהִוא וַיֹּאמֶר אֲבִימֶלֶךְ וּפִיכֹל שַׂר־צְבָאוֹ אֶל־אַבְרָהָם לֵאמֹר אֱלֹהִים ששי
כג עִמְּךָ בְּכֹל אֲשֶׁר־אַתָּה עֹשֶׂה: וְעַתָּה הִשָּׁבְעָה לִּי בֵאלֹהִים הֵנָּה אִם־תִּשְׁקֹר לִי
וּלְנִינִי וּלְנֶכְדִּי כַּחֶסֶד אֲשֶׁר־עָשִׂיתִי עִמְּךָ תַּעֲשֶׂה עִמָּדִי וְעִם־הָאָרֶץ אֲשֶׁר־גַּרְתָּה
כד כה בָּהּ: וַיֹּאמֶר אַבְרָהָם אָנֹכִי אִשָּׁבֵעַ: וְהוֹכִחַ אַבְרָהָם אֶת־אֲבִימֶלֶךְ עַל־אֹדוֹת
כו בְּאֵר הַמַּיִם אֲשֶׁר גָּזְלוּ עַבְדֵי אֲבִימֶלֶךְ: וַיֹּאמֶר אֲבִימֶלֶךְ לֹא יָדַעְתִּי מִי עָשָׂה אֶת־
כז הַדָּבָר הַזֶּה וְגַם־אַתָּה לֹא־הִגַּדְתָּ לִּי וְגַם אָנֹכִי לֹא שָׁמַעְתִּי בִּלְתִּי הַיּוֹם: וַיִּקַּח
כח אַבְרָהָם צֹאן וּבָקָר וַיִּתֵּן לַאֲבִימֶלֶךְ וַיִּכְרְתוּ שְׁנֵיהֶם בְּרִית: וַיַּצֵּב אַבְרָהָם אֶת־שֶׁבַע
כט כִּבְשֹׂת הַצֹּאן לְבַדְּהֶן: וַיֹּאמֶר אֲבִימֶלֶךְ אֶל־אַבְרָהָם מָה הֵנָּה שֶׁבַע כְּבָשֹׂת הָאֵלֶּה
ל אֲשֶׁר הִצַּבְתָּ לְבַדָּנָה: וַיֹּאמֶר כִּי אֶת־שֶׁבַע כְּבָשֹׂת תִּקַּח מִיָּדִי בַּעֲבוּר תִּהְיֶה־לִּי
לא לְעֵדָה כִּי חָפַרְתִּי אֶת־הַבְּאֵר הַזֹּאת: עַל־כֵּן קָרָא לַמָּקוֹם הַהוּא בְּאֵר שָׁבַע כִּי
לב שָׁם נִשְׁבְּעוּ שְׁנֵיהֶם: וַיִּכְרְתוּ בְרִית בִּבְאֵר שָׁבַע וַיָּקָם אֲבִימֶלֶךְ וּפִיכֹל שַׂר־צְבָאוֹ
לג וַיָּשֻׁבוּ אֶל־אֶרֶץ פְּלִשְׁתִּים: וַיִּטַּע אֶשֶׁל בִּבְאֵר שָׁבַע וַיִּקְרָא־שָׁם בְּשֵׁם יְהוָה אֵל
לד עוֹלָם: וַיָּגָר אַבְרָהָם בְּאֶרֶץ פְּלִשְׁתִּים יָמִים רַבִּים:

THEMES | COVENANT | THE LAND OF ISRAEL | PRAYER

Episode 27 : *The Covenant between Avraham and Avimelekh –* Bereshit 21:22–34

SUMMARY

Before Avraham fathered children, he was considered an individual who would eventually die and leave the world much as he found it. Now that he has an heir, those around him realize that he cannot be disregarded. Even after he dies, the tribe that he establishes will remain.

THE ART OF MIDRASH

Abraham and Abimelech
Jan de Herdt (1658)

Analysis

- Which elements of this image are directly mentioned in the text?
- Which elements of this image are not found in the text?
- What midrashic interpretation could be inferred from this image?

A QUESTION OF BIBLIODRAMA

TO AVRAHAM

- Do you trust Avimelekh?
- What were your interests in this covenant and were they sufficiently protected?
- Were you distracted during this episode because of the strife in your family that preceded it?

TO AVIMELEKH

- Why were you motivated to make this covenant with Avraham?
- Why now?
- Why did you bring Pikhol?

בְּאֵר שֶׁבַע
BE'ER SHEVA

Be'er Sheva, mentioned thirty-four times, is a central city in the Negev; in the patriarchal narratives it is portrayed as a desert campsite for nomadic shepherds, with a well at its center.

Be'er Sheva is part of the territory within Yehuda designated for Shimon. In biblical times, Be'er Sheva marked the southern edge of the settled part of the land, as reflected in the expression "from Dan until Be'er Sheva" (which appears nine times in Tanakh).

Biblical Be'er Sheva is generally identified with the site known as Tel as-Saba (today Tel Be'er Sheva National Park), on the banks of Naḥal Be'er Sheva, one of the main tributaries of Naḥal Besor. Artifacts found on-site date back to prehistoric times. The archaeological strata include a small village from the time of the Judges; during the monarchic period, this village was expanded into a large, well-planned, fortified city with strong mud-brick walls that offered protection from desert raiders. The city contained large storehouses and an impressive underground water system that provided access to water in the event of a siege. Excavations also revealed a four-horned stone altar that had been dismantled and repurposed; some ascribe this to King Ḥizkiyahu's religious reforms.[1]

At the site known as Bir Saba, near the modern city's central bus station, remains of a different First Temple-era settlement were discovered. Some believe the city relocated to that spot after the earlier site was destroyed by Sanḥeriv, while others surmise that this location was the actual site of Be'er Sheva, whereas Tel as-Saba was once the biblical city Sheva.[2]

---

1 | II Melakhim 18:4.

2 | Yehoshua 19:2.

Analysis

- What areas of archaeological, geographical, and historical knowledge do we have now that were unavailable to classical Jewish commentators? How can they aid our understanding of the text?
- How can this information about Be'er Sheva help us understand the text?
- What further questions on the text do you have now that you have read this new information and research?

INTEGRATING ḤOKHMA

Excavations at Tel Be'er Sheva

predicating their mutual trust upon the matter of oaths and pledges, responsibilities and obligations, constancy and dependability, it really serves as a foil for the ongoing story of the interaction of God with Avraham. Had not that interaction been consistently framed in the same terms? Hadn't God extended oaths and pledges, communicated responsibilities and obligations, demonstrated constancy and dependability, all of it revolving around the axis of Yitzḥak's birth and then his growth and maturation into the progenitor of the nation? Avimelekh looks toward the future, thinking of his son and his grandson after him, and for the very first time in his long and eventful life, Avraham is able to do the same. And while Avimelekh fears treachery and betrayal, therefore insisting upon a formal treaty, Avraham fears neither, for his God, the eternal Lord, the transcendent God who champions and demands moral conduct from His adherents, neither deceives nor acts with duplicity.

In the end, the seven sheep are accepted and the treaty is sealed. There will be no disputes about the ownership of the well and Avimelekh's descendants will be safe. The Philistine king, his mind at ease, departs with his enforcer, and Avraham turns toward his God in gratitude. He plants a tree, often (because of its great longevity) a potent symbol of the future, in His honor, and he turns to Him in prayer. We can imagine his silent words to God as his aged heart overflows with gratitude and appreciation: "Thank You God for granting me a son, thank You for fulfilling Your pledge, and thank You for being dependable and worthy of my undying trust. While Avimelekh may have wronged me, You never have. And while the treaty that we just now concluded with such fanfare may in the future, after my demise, be breached, You will never abrogate Your treaty with me, for You are eternal, Your essence is compassion, and Your seal is truth!"

Rabbi Michael Hattin

TAKING A LITERARY APPROACH

Underlying this entire passage is the matter of treaty or covenant, namely that people who swear an oath to each other must obligate themselves to fulfill the provisions of the pledge. How else can trust be built and fostered between different parties with diverse but overlapping interests, if not by each one of those parties being prepared to abide by the agreed-upon terms? If Avimelekh cannot depend upon Avraham and vice versa, then any treaty concluded between them, no matter how lofty their respective compliments and how noble their good wishes, is utterly ineffectual and worthless.

Having thus analyzed the elements of this passage, we may now be in a better position to appreciate the significance of its location in the Torah. In a short textual moment (though after the chronological lapse of many years), God is about to call upon Avraham to take his beloved son to the land of Moriah. This is the same God who had pledged to Avraham that a) He would provide him with offspring, and b) He would grant him the land of Canaan, so that the nation of Israel could be crafted from that offspring. The divine pledge of children and land had been repeated with great frequency throughout the parashot of Lekh Lekha and Vayera, and though we had all (Avraham, Sara, and the reader) been anxious about its fulfillment, God did not disappoint and in the end Sara had a son that they joyously called Yitzḥak, at divine behest.

That son rightfully represented in their minds the future, the very same future that Avimelekh foresees when he approaches Avraham and demands the conclusion of a treaty. "Do not betray me," he insists, "and do not deal treacherously with my son or grandson either." But then Avraham introduced the matter of the wells, emphasizing that for there to be trust there must be mutual respect, for Avimelekh can scarcely be a signatory to a treaty if he or his servants are in breach of its provisions. Can one rely upon his fellow if that fellow is undependable? The implication of this unsettling and rhetorical query is pronounced. "What makes my God so reliable," Avraham seems to suggest, "is that I know that He will not fail to uphold His side of OUR covenant, of the pledge that He extended to me when I left the land of Ḥaran. God's word is unassailable and His commitment to His pledge is forever, for He is 'God, the eternal Lord.'"

Thus it is that although the passage relates the story of the interaction of Avimelekh with Avraham,

22 1 After these things, God tested Avraham. "Avraham!" He said. And Avraham replied, "Here I
2 am." Then God said, "Take your son, your only one, the one whom you love – Yitzḥak – and
go to the land of Moria. There, offer him up as a burnt offering on one of the mountains, the
3 one that I will show you." Early the next morning Avraham rose and saddled his donkey. With
him he took two of his young men and Yitzḥak his son. He cut wood for the offering and set
4 out toward the place of which God had told him. On the third day Avraham looked up and,
5 in the distance, he saw the place. He told his young men, "Stay here with the donkey. I and
6 the boy will go there and worship. Then we will come back to you." Avraham took the wood
for the offering and placed it on Yitzḥak his son. He himself took the fire and the knife. The
7 two of them walked together. Then Yitzḥak said to his father, Avraham, "Father?" Avraham
said, "Here I am, my son." Yitzḥak said, "Here is the fire and the wood, but where is the lamb
8 for the burnt offering?" And Avraham replied, "God will see to a lamb for an offering, my
9 son." The two of them walked on together. They came to the place of which God had spoken.
There Avraham built an altar and arranged the wood. Then he bound Yitzḥak his son and
10 laid him on the altar on top of the wood. Avraham reached out his hand
11 and took hold of the knife to slay his son. But an angel of the Lord called out to him from the

UNLOCKING THE TEXT

- What was the test for Avraham? Did he pass?
- Was this also a test for Yitzḥak? Did he pass?
- Why did God use so many different words to describe Yitzḥak?
- Did Yitzḥak know what was going on during the test?
- How could God have commanded Avraham to do this act?
- How could Avraham follow God's command to do this?
- Why does the Torah immediately list the children of Avraham's brother Naḥor at this point in the narrative?

FINDING YOURSELF IN THE TEXT

- Has someone in authority ever told you to do something that you knew was wrong?
- Do you ever struggle with your faith that God always does the right thing?
- Does this story weaken or strengthen that faith?

Consider using these questions as the basis for your own commentary or creative midrash.

How does reflecting on these firsthand experiences help you better understand the text?

כב א וַיְהִי אַחַר הַדְּבָרִים הָאֵלֶּה וְהָאֱלֹהִים נִסָּה אֶת־אַבְרָהָם וַיֹּאמֶר אֵלָיו אַבְרָהָם יט שביעי
ב וַיֹּאמֶר הִנֵּנִי: וַיֹּאמֶר קַח־נָא אֶת־בִּנְךָ אֶת־יְחִידְךָ אֲשֶׁר־אָהַבְתָּ אֶת־יִצְחָק וְלֶךְ־
לְךָ אֶל־אֶרֶץ הַמֹּרִיָּה וְהַעֲלֵהוּ שָׁם לְעֹלָה עַל אַחַד הֶהָרִים אֲשֶׁר אֹמַר אֵלֶיךָ:
ג וַיַּשְׁכֵּם אַבְרָהָם בַּבֹּקֶר וַיַּחֲבֹשׁ אֶת־חֲמֹרוֹ וַיִּקַּח אֶת־שְׁנֵי נְעָרָיו אִתּוֹ וְאֵת יִצְחָק
ד בְּנוֹ וַיְבַקַּע עֲצֵי עֹלָה וַיָּקָם וַיֵּלֶךְ אֶל־הַמָּקוֹם אֲשֶׁר־אָמַר־לוֹ הָאֱלֹהִים: בַּיּוֹם
ה הַשְּׁלִישִׁי וַיִּשָּׂא אַבְרָהָם אֶת־עֵינָיו וַיַּרְא אֶת־הַמָּקוֹם מֵרָחֹק: וַיֹּאמֶר אַבְרָהָם
אֶל־נְעָרָיו שְׁבוּ־לָכֶם פֹּה עִם־הַחֲמוֹר וַאֲנִי וְהַנַּעַר נֵלְכָה עַד־כֹּה וְנִשְׁתַּחֲוֶה וְנָשׁוּבָה
ו אֲלֵיכֶם: וַיִּקַּח אַבְרָהָם אֶת־עֲצֵי הָעֹלָה וַיָּשֶׂם עַל־יִצְחָק בְּנוֹ וַיִּקַּח בְּיָדוֹ אֶת־הָאֵשׁ
ז וְאֶת־הַמַּאֲכֶלֶת וַיֵּלְכוּ שְׁנֵיהֶם יַחְדָּו: וַיֹּאמֶר יִצְחָק אֶל־אַבְרָהָם אָבִיו וַיֹּאמֶר אָבִי
ח וַיֹּאמֶר הִנֶּנִּי בְנִי וַיֹּאמֶר הִנֵּה הָאֵשׁ וְהָעֵצִים וְאַיֵּה הַשֶּׂה לְעֹלָה: וַיֹּאמֶר אַבְרָהָם
ט אֱלֹהִים יִרְאֶה־לּוֹ הַשֶּׂה לְעֹלָה בְּנִי וַיֵּלְכוּ שְׁנֵיהֶם יַחְדָּו: וַיָּבֹאוּ אֶל־הַמָּקוֹם אֲשֶׁר
אָמַר־לוֹ הָאֱלֹהִים וַיִּבֶן שָׁם אַבְרָהָם אֶת־הַמִּזְבֵּחַ וַיַּעֲרֹךְ אֶת־הָעֵצִים וַיַּעֲקֹד אֶת־
י יִצְחָק בְּנוֹ וַיָּשֶׂם אֹתוֹ עַל־הַמִּזְבֵּחַ מִמַּעַל לָעֵצִים: וַיִּשְׁלַח אַבְרָהָם אֶת־יָדוֹ וַיִּקַּח
יא אֶת־הַמַּאֲכֶלֶת לִשְׁחֹט אֶת־בְּנוֹ: וַיִּקְרָא אֵלָיו מַלְאַךְ יהוה מִן־הַשָּׁמַיִם וַיֹּאמֶר

THEMES	COVENANT	RELATIONSHIPS AND LOVE	GOD

Episode 28: *Akedat Yitzḥak* – Bereshit 22:1–24

SUMMARY

The binding of Yitzḥak is one of the most dramatic episodes in the Bible. It occurs shortly after the events recounted above, suggesting a connection between the stories. Avraham has achieved a measure of stability. After sending Yishmael away, there is quiet in his household, his heir is growing to maturity, and he has made peace with the neighboring kingdom. It is now, when his life has finally stabilized, that the test of the binding of Yitzḥak will shake the very foundations of his existence.

Immediately following the binding of Yitzḥak, the Torah presents the family tree of Naḥor, Avraham's brother. At first glance this appears unrelated to the preceding story, but the information is important for Yitzḥak's future. The episode at Mount Moriah is not an ending, but the beginning of a new stage of life, which also has roots in a faraway land. Avraham's descendants survive and will multiply through Yitzḥak, whom he had bound on the altar, and Rivka, Yitzḥak's future wife, born meanwhile in Ḥaran.

12 heavens, "Avraham! Avraham!" He said, "Here I am." "Do not lift your hand against the boy;
do nothing to him, for now I know that you fear God: for you have not withheld from Me
13 your son, your only one." Avraham looked up and saw a ram caught in a thicket by its horns.
Avraham went, took hold of the ram, and offered it up as a burnt offering in place of his son.
14 And Avraham named the place The Lord Will See.[1] To this day it is said, "On the mountain
15 of the Lord, He will be seen." Then the angel of the LORD called to Avraham from the
16 heavens a second time and said, "By My own Self I swear, says the LORD, that because you
17 have done this and have not withheld your son, your only one, I will bless you greatly and
make your descendants as many as the stars of the heavens, as the sand on the seashore. Your
18 descendants will possess their enemies' gate,[2] and through your descendants will all nations
19 of the earth be blessed, because you have listened to My voice." Avraham returned to his
young men, and together they set out and went to Be'er Sheva, and Avraham stayed on in
Be'er Sheva.

20 Some time later, Avraham was told, "Milka too has had children with your brother Naḥor:
21 22 Utz, his firstborn, his brother Buz, Kemuel, father of Aram, Kesed, Ḥazo, Pildash, Yidlaf,
23 and Betuel." Betuel had a daughter Rivka. Milka bore these eight sons to Avraham's brother
24 Naḥor. His concubine, named Reuma, also had children: Tevaḥ, Gaḥam, Taḥash, and
Maakha.

1 | Cf. verse 8: "God will see to a lamb for an offering."

2 | That is, their cities.

יב אַבְרָהָ֣ם ׀ אַבְרָהָ֑ם וַיֹּ֖אמֶר הִנֵּֽנִי׃ וַיֹּ֗אמֶר אַל־תִּשְׁלַ֤ח יָֽדְךָ֙ אֶל־הַנַּ֔עַר וְאַל־תַּ֥עַשׂ
ל֖וֹ מְא֑וּמָה כִּ֣י ׀ עַתָּ֣ה יָדַ֗עְתִּי כִּֽי־יְרֵ֤א אֱלֹהִים֙ אַ֔תָּה וְלֹ֥א חָשַׂ֛כְתָּ אֶת־בִּנְךָ֥ אֶת־
יג יְחִידְךָ֖ מִמֶּֽנִּי׃ וַיִּשָּׂ֨א אַבְרָהָ֜ם אֶת־עֵינָ֗יו וַיַּרְא֙ וְהִנֵּה־אַ֔יִל אַחַ֕ר נֶאֱחַ֥ז בַּסְּבַ֖ךְ בְּקַרְנָ֑יו
יד וַיֵּ֤לֶךְ אַבְרָהָם֙ וַיִּקַּ֣ח אֶת־הָאַ֔יִל וַיַּעֲלֵ֥הוּ לְעֹלָ֖ה תַּ֥חַת בְּנֽוֹ׃ וַיִּקְרָ֧א אַבְרָהָ֛ם שֵֽׁם־
טו הַמָּק֥וֹם הַה֖וּא יְהוָ֣ה ׀ יִרְאֶ֑ה אֲשֶׁר֙ יֵאָמֵ֣ר הַיּ֔וֹם בְּהַ֥ר יְהוָ֖ה יֵרָאֶֽה׃ וַיִּקְרָ֛א מַלְאַ֥ךְ
טז יְהוָ֖ה אֶל־אַבְרָהָ֑ם שֵׁנִ֖ית מִן־הַשָּׁמָֽיִם׃ וַיֹּ֕אמֶר בִּ֥י נִשְׁבַּ֖עְתִּי נְאֻם־יְהוָ֑ה כִּ֗י יַ֚עַן אֲשֶׁ֤ר
יז עָשִׂ֨יתָ֙ אֶת־הַדָּבָ֣ר הַזֶּ֔ה וְלֹ֥א חָשַׂ֖כְתָּ אֶת־בִּנְךָ֥ אֶת־יְחִידֶֽךָ׃ כִּֽי־בָרֵ֣ךְ אֲבָרֶכְךָ֗ וְהַרְבָּ֨ה
אַרְבֶּ֤ה אֶֽת־זַרְעֲךָ֙ כְּכוֹכְבֵ֣י הַשָּׁמַ֔יִם וְכַח֕וֹל אֲשֶׁ֖ר עַל־שְׂפַ֣ת הַיָּ֑ם וְיִרַ֣שׁ זַרְעֲךָ֔ אֵ֖ת
יח יט שַׁ֥עַר אֹיְבָֽיו׃ וְהִתְבָּרְכ֣וּ בְזַרְעֲךָ֔ כֹּ֖ל גּוֹיֵ֣י הָאָ֑רֶץ עֵ֕קֶב אֲשֶׁ֥ר שָׁמַ֖עְתָּ בְּקֹלִֽי׃ וַיָּ֤שָׁב
אַבְרָהָם֙ אֶל־נְעָרָ֔יו וַיָּקֻ֛מוּ וַיֵּלְכ֥וּ יַחְדָּ֖ו אֶל־בְּאֵ֣ר שָׁ֑בַע וַיֵּ֥שֶׁב אַבְרָהָ֖ם בִּבְאֵ֥ר
שָֽׁבַע׃
כ וַיְהִ֗י אַחֲרֵי֙ הַדְּבָרִ֣ים הָאֵ֔לֶּה וַיֻּגַּ֥ד לְאַבְרָהָ֖ם לֵאמֹ֑ר הִ֠נֵּה יָלְדָ֨ה מִלְכָּ֥ה גַם־הִ֛וא בָּנִ֖ים מפטיר
כא כב לְנָח֥וֹר אָחִֽיךָ׃ אֶת־ע֥וּץ בְּכֹר֖וֹ וְאֶת־בּ֣וּז אָחִ֑יו וְאֶת־קְמוּאֵ֖ל אֲבִ֥י אֲרָֽם׃ וְאֶת־כֶּ֣שֶׂד
כג וְאֶת־חֲז֔וֹ וְאֶת־פִּלְדָּ֖שׁ וְאֶת־יִדְלָ֑ף וְאֵ֖ת בְּתוּאֵֽל׃ וּבְתוּאֵ֖ל יָלַ֣ד אֶת־רִבְקָ֑ה שְׁמֹנָ֥ה
כד אֵ֨לֶּה֙ יָלְדָ֣ה מִלְכָּ֔ה לְנָח֖וֹר אֲחִ֥י אַבְרָהָֽם׃ וּפִֽילַגְשׁ֖וֹ וּשְׁמָ֣הּ רְאוּמָ֑ה וַתֵּ֤לֶד גַּם־הִוא֙
אֶת־טֶ֣בַח וְאֶת־גַּ֔חַם וְאֶת־תַּ֖חַשׁ וְאֶת־מַעֲכָֽה׃

THE ART OF MIDRASH

Sacrifice of Isaac
Rembrandt Harmensz
van Rijn (1635)

Analysis

- Which elements of this image are directly mentioned in the text?
- Which elements of this image are not found in the text?
- What midrashic interpretation could be inferred from this image?

A QUESTION OF BIBLIODRAMA

TO AVRAHAM

- What were your thoughts and emotions when you first heard the command from God to take your son and offer him as a sacrifice?
- Why did you not argue with God here like you did when He informed you of His plans for the cities of Sedom and Amora?
- What did you learn from this test from God?
- How do you feel toward God now?
- How has this event affected your relationship with your son?

TO YITZḤAK

- Did you know where your father was leading you and for what purpose?
- When you realized what your father was doing at the command of God, did you try and resist, or did you cooperate?
- How do you feel toward your father now?
- How do you feel toward God?

TO GOD

- Why did You test Avraham in this way that contradicted morality and Your covenant with him?
- Did Avraham pass Your test?
- What do You want future generations to learn from this episode?

ancestors. Seeking the spirits of the dead is explicitly forbidden. Equally noteworthy is the fact that in the early narratives, succession does *not* pass to the firstborn: not to Yishmael but Yitzḥak, not to Esav but Yaakov, not to the tribe of Reuven but to Levi (priesthood) and Yehuda (kingship), not to Aharon but to Moshe.

What God was doing when He asked Avraham to offer up his son was not requesting a child sacrifice but something quite different. He wanted Avraham to *renounce ownership* of his son. He wanted to establish as a non-negotiable principle of Jewish law that *children are not the property of their parents*.

If the analysis of Fustel de Colanges and Larry Siedentop is correct, it follows that something fundamental was at stake. *As long as parents believed they owned their children, the concept of the individual could not yet be born.* The fundamental unit was the family. The Torah represents the birth of the individual as the central figure in the moral life. Because children – all children – belong to God, parenthood is not ownership but guardianship. As soon as they reach the age of maturity (traditionally twelve for girls, thirteen for boys) children become independent moral agents with their own dignity and freedom.

Rabbi Jonathan Sacks

Analysis

- What areas of understanding of human nature, society, and history do we have now that were unavailable to classical Jewish commentators? How can they aid our understanding of the text?
- What can we learn from this passage to help us understand the text?
- What further questions on the text do you have now that you have read this new take on the story?

INTEGRATING ḤOKHMA

To understand the binding of Yitzḥak we have to realize that much of the Torah, Bereshit in particular, is a polemic against worldviews the Torah considers pagan, inhuman, and wrong. One institution to which Bereshit is opposed is the ancient family as described by Fustel de Coulanges in *The Ancient City* (1864) and recently restated by Larry Siedentop in *Inventing the Individual: The Origins of Western Liberalism*.

Before the emergence of the first cities and civilizations, the fundamental social and religious unit was the family. As Coulanges puts it, in ancient times there was an intrinsic connection between three things: the domestic religion, the family, and the right to property. Each family had its own gods, among them the spirits of dead ancestors, from whom it sought protection and to whom it offered sacrifices. The authority of the head of the family, the paterfamilias, was absolute. He had the power of life and death over his wife and children. Authority invariably passed, on the death of the father, to his firstborn son. Meanwhile, as long as the father lived, children had the status of property rather than the status of persons in their own right. This idea persisted even beyond the biblical era in the Roman law principle of *patria potestas*.

The Torah is opposed to every element of this worldview. As anthropologist Mary Douglas notes, one of the most striking features of the Torah is that it includes no sacrifices to dead

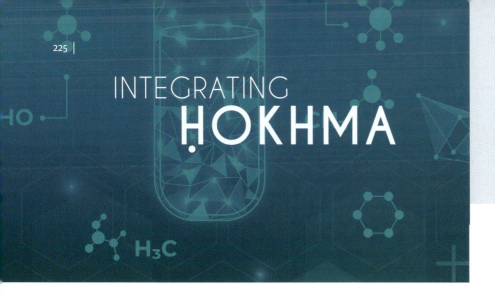

Burning bush (Shemot 3)	Akedat Yitzḥak (Bereshit 21)
(3:1) Now Moshe shepherded the sheep of Yitro, his father-in-law, priest of Midyan, and he led the flock far into the desert, And he came to the mountain of God, to Ḥorev.	(21:8) And Avraham said, "God will provide Himself with a lamb for a burnt offering, my son." And the two of them walked together. (21:9) And they came to the place which God had told him.
(3:2) And an angel of God appeared to him in a flame of fire from the midst of the bush, and he saw, and behold – the bush was burning with fire, But the bush was not consumed (*ukal*).	(21:13) And Avraham lifted his eyes and he saw, and behold, a ram behind [him], caught by its horns in the thicket.
(3:3) And Moshe said, "Let me turn aside and see *(er'eh)* this great sight *(mar'eh)*, why the bush is not burning."	(21:10) And Avraham stretched out his hand and he took the knife *(maakhelet)*
(3:4) And God saw that he had turned aside to see, and God called to him from amidst the bush, and He said, "Moshe, Moshe," and he said, "Here I am."	(21:14) And Avraham called the name of that place *Hashem yir'eh*, of which it is said [to] this day, "In the mount shall the Lord appear *(yera'eh)*."
(3:5) And He said, "Do not come near; remove your shoes from upon your feet, for the place upon which you stand is holy ground."	
(3:6) And He said, "I am the God of your fathers, the God of Avraham, the God of Yitzḥak, and the God of Yaakov." And Moshe hid his face, for he feared to look at God.	(21:11) And an angel of God called to him from the heavens, and he said, "Avraham, Avraham," and he said, "Here I am."

The revelation at the burning bush reinforces the idea of the covenant between the nation and God and God's commitment to save the nation from the "knife" that threatens to destroy them. The location of the burning bush, the smell of fire, and the voice of the angel are all meant to arouse recollections in Moshe's mind of Avraham's obedience and readiness to bind his son, as well as the angel's command, "Do not lay your hand upon the boy," and thereby to hint to Moshe, by a sort of *kal vaḥomer*, that he must obey this divine mission to save the nation from its *akeda*.

A contrast to fractured family connections: The sale of Yosef

TAKING A LITERARY APPROACH

The story of the *akeda*, the binding of Yitzḥak, is one of the core narratives in the history of *am Yisrael*, but surprisingly, there is no mention of it at any later stage in Tanakh. However, we do find several narratives that allude to it. Some specific expressions and motifs that are used in the text to describe Avraham's test are interwoven in other units whose connection to the story of the *akeda* is not immediately apparent.

There are some ten stories in Tanakh that interweave allusions to the *akeda* narrative, and it would seem that by means of this sophisticated device, the text manages to highlight the important messages of parts of the story without becoming entangled in the theological paradox of the *akeda* narrative in its entirety. We will present two of these "mirror stories" and try to discern the messages that the text extracts from the paralleling of a given situation with that of Avraham and Yitzḥak in the *akeda* story.

The *akeda* story as an expression of a renewed bond between the nation and God: The burning bush

The binding of Yitzḥak heralds a special connection between man and his Creator. In this story, Avraham indicates the pinnacle of man's closeness to God, as well as its boundary. It would appear that employing the literary devices and special expressions belonging to the story of the *akeda* in describing later events is meant to imbue the latter with something of the atmosphere of upliftment and holiness of the former and to present it as a new way of the nation drawing closer to God.

The story of Moshe's induction into the position of leader of *am Yisrael* maintains strong allusions to the story of the *akeda*, as we see in the corresponding verses as presented below:

and to merit receiving his son back again, leads – in the story of Yosef – to the brothers' hatred and to the casting of the most profound grief upon Yaakov, owing to the news that his son is lost to him forever.

The story of the *akeda* in its later incarnations has served as an archetype of devotion to God and sanctification of His name. Avraham's willingness to sacrifice his son upon the altar of his values has served as a model for generations of parents who have been required to sacrifice their children upon the altar of the Jewish nation and the land of Israel and who have answered with their own cry of "Here I am."

Dr. Brachi Elitzur

Four separate biblical narratives describing problematic family relations contain allusions to the story of the *akeda*. The characters in these narratives "carry out an *akeda*," as it were, motivated by personal revenge, pride, or ignorance. These narratives bemoan the characters' ignoring of the angel's cry, "Do not lay your hand upon the boy, nor do anything to him," and distort Avraham's words: "A lamb for a burnt offering, my son."

The fatherly love for a son which elevated Avraham in the story of the *akeda* to the ultimate level of loving God

The sale of Yosef (Bereshit 37)	*Akedat Yitzḥak* (Bereshit 21)
(37:3) And Yisrael loved Yosef more than all his children, because he was the son of his old age, and he made him a striped coat.	(21:2) He said, "Take, I pray you, your son, your only son, whom you love – Yitzḥak...."
(37:13) And Yisrael said to Yosef, "Are your brothers not tending the flocks in Shekhem? Come now, I will send you to them"; and he said to him, "Here I am."	(21:1) And it came to pass after these things that God tested Avraham; and He said to him, "Avraham, Avraham," and he said, "Here I am."
(37:18) And they saw him from afar, and before he came close to them, they conspired against him to kill him.	(21:4) On the third day, Avraham lifted his eyes and he saw the place from afar.
(37:20) "Come now, therefore; let us kill him and cast him into one of the pits, and we shall say, 'A wild animal devoured him (*akhalatehu*)' – and we shall see what will become of his dreams."	(21:10) And Avraham stretched forth his hand and he took the knife (*maakhelet*), to slay his son.
(37:22) And Reuven said to them, "Do not shed blood; cast him into this pit that is in the wilderness, but lay no hand upon him" – [intending] that he might save him from their hand, to bring him back to his father.	(21:12) And he said, "Do not lay your hand upon the boy, nor do anything to him, for now I know that you fear God; you have not spared your only son from Me."
(37:25) And they sat to eat bread, and they lifted their eyes and saw, and behold, a caravan of Ishmaelites was coming from the Gilad.	(21:13) And Avraham lifted his eyes and he saw, and behold, a ram behind [him], caught by its horns in the thicket.
(37:29) And Reuven returned to the pit, but behold – Yosef was not in the pit; and he tore his garments.	(21:19) And Avraham returned to his young men, and the arose and they went together to Be'er Sheva, and Avraham dwelled in Be'er Sheva.

חיי שרה
Ḥayei Sara

Parasha Overview

Ḥayei Sara contains three narratives: the death of Sara and Avraham's purchase of a burial plot for her, the first part of the holy land to be owned by the people of the covenant; the search for a wife for Yitzḥak, the first Jewish child; and the last period of Avraham's life, and his death.

Episodes

29. **Sara's Death**	23:1–20
30. **Finding Yitzḥak a Wife**	24:1–31
31. **The Arrangements Are Made**	24:32–60
32. **Yitzḥak and Rivka Meet**	24:61–67
33. **Avraham's Other Children**	25:1–6
34. **Avraham's Death**	25:7–18

Parasha Stats

- 5,314 letters
- 1,402 words
- 105 verses
- 171 lines in a sefer Torah

23 1 2 Sara's lifetime – the years of Sara's life – were one hundred and twenty-seven. Sara died ḤAYEI SARA
in Kiryat Arba – that is, Ḥevron – in the land of Canaan. And Avraham came to mourn
3 for Sara and to weep for her. Then Avraham rose from beside his dead and spoke to the
4 Hittites. He said, "I am a migrant and a visitor among you. Sell me a burial site here so
5 6 that I can bury my dead." The Hittites answered Avraham, "Hear us, my lord. You are a
prince of God in our midst. Bury your dead in the choicest of our tombs. None of us will
7 refuse you his tomb to bury your dead." Avraham rose and bowed down to the Hittites, the
8 people of the land, and said to them, "If you are willing to allow me to bury the dead that
9 lies before me, then hear me and intercede on my behalf with Efron son of Tzoḥar. Let him
sell me the cave of Makhpela that he owns, at the edge of his field. Ask him to sell it to me
10 at the full price as a burial site in your midst." Efron was sitting among the Hittites. Efron
the Hittite answered Avraham in the hearing of all the Hittites who had come to the city
11 gate. He said, "No, my lord, hear me. I give you the field and I give you the cave that is in
12 it. In the presence of my people, I give it to you. Bury your dead." Avraham bowed down
13 again before the people of the land and said to Efron in their hearing, "Please, would that
you would hear me. I give you the money for the field. Take it from me so that I can bury
14 15 my dead there." Efron answered Avraham and said to him, "My lord, hear me. A piece

UNLOCKING THE TEXT

- Is there a connection between Sara's death and the previous episode?
- Why did Avraham feel the need to buy a burial plot?
- Are the terms *ger* and *toshav* (translated here as "migrant" and "visitor") opposites?
- Why did Avraham refuse the offer of the Hittites to take the plot for free?
- Why did Avraham choose the cave of Makhpela?
- Why was it important to Avraham that he pay the full price?
- Why did Efron mention the price of the field if he wanted to give it to Avraham for free?

FINDING YOURSELF IN THE TEXT

- Do you have a valuable possession that you can prove belongs to your family?
- Have you ever had a discussion with someone who you knew was not being completely truthful about their position?
- Have you ever been to the cave of Makhpela? How did it feel to be there?

Consider using these questions as the basis for your own commentary or creative midrash.

How does reflecting on these firsthand experiences help you better understand the text?

כג א וַיִּהְיוּ חַיֵּי שָׂרָה מֵאָה שָׁנָה וְעֶשְׂרִים שָׁנָה וְשֶׁבַע שָׁנִים שְׁנֵי חַיֵּי שָׂרָה: וַתָּמָת שָׂרָה
ב בְּקִרְיַת אַרְבַּע הִוא חֶבְרוֹן בְּאֶרֶץ כְּנָעַן וַיָּבֹא אַבְרָהָם לִסְפֹּד לְשָׂרָה וְלִבְכֹּתָהּ: וַיָּקָם
ג אַבְרָהָם מֵעַל פְּנֵי מֵתוֹ וַיְדַבֵּר אֶל־בְּנֵי־חֵת לֵאמֹר: גֵּר־וְתוֹשָׁב אָנֹכִי עִמָּכֶם תְּנוּ
ד לִי אֲחֻזַּת־קֶבֶר עִמָּכֶם וְאֶקְבְּרָה מֵתִי מִלְּפָנָי: וַיַּעֲנוּ בְנֵי־חֵת אֶת־אַבְרָהָם לֵאמֹר
ה לוֹ: שְׁמָעֵנוּ | אֲדֹנִי נְשִׂיא אֱלֹהִים אַתָּה בְּתוֹכֵנוּ בְּמִבְחַר קְבָרֵינוּ קְבֹר אֶת־מֵתֶךָ
ו אִישׁ מִמֶּנּוּ אֶת־קִבְרוֹ לֹא־יִכְלֶה מִמְּךָ מִקְּבֹר מֵתֶךָ: וַיָּקָם אַבְרָהָם וַיִּשְׁתַּחוּ לְעַם־
ז הָאָרֶץ לִבְנֵי־חֵת: וַיְדַבֵּר אִתָּם לֵאמֹר אִם־יֵשׁ אֶת־נַפְשְׁכֶם לִקְבֹּר אֶת־מֵתִי מִלְּפָנַי
ח שְׁמָעוּנִי וּפִגְעוּ־לִי בְּעֶפְרוֹן בֶּן־צֹחַר: וְיִתֶּן־לִי אֶת־מְעָרַת הַמַּכְפֵּלָה אֲשֶׁר־לוֹ
ט אֲשֶׁר בִּקְצֵה שָׂדֵהוּ בְּכֶסֶף מָלֵא יִתְּנֶנָּה לִּי בְּתוֹכְכֶם לַאֲחֻזַּת־קָבֶר: וְעֶפְרוֹן יֹשֵׁב
י בְּתוֹךְ בְּנֵי־חֵת וַיַּעַן עֶפְרוֹן הַחִתִּי אֶת־אַבְרָהָם בְּאָזְנֵי בְנֵי־חֵת לְכֹל בָּאֵי שַׁעַר־
יא עִירוֹ לֵאמֹר: לֹא־אֲדֹנִי שְׁמָעֵנִי הַשָּׂדֶה נָתַתִּי לָךְ וְהַמְּעָרָה אֲשֶׁר־בּוֹ לְךָ נְתַתִּיהָ
יב לְעֵינֵי בְנֵי־עַמִּי נְתַתִּיהָ לָךְ קְבֹר מֵתֶךָ: וַיִּשְׁתַּחוּ אַבְרָהָם לִפְנֵי עַם־הָאָרֶץ: וַיְדַבֵּר
יג אֶל־עֶפְרוֹן בְּאָזְנֵי עַם־הָאָרֶץ לֵאמֹר אַךְ אִם־אַתָּה לוּ שְׁמָעֵנִי נָתַתִּי כֶּסֶף הַשָּׂדֶה
יד קַח מִמֶּנִּי וְאֶקְבְּרָה אֶת־מֵתִי שָׁמָּה: וַיַּעַן עֶפְרוֹן אֶת־אַבְרָהָם לֵאמֹר לוֹ: אֲדֹנִי

| THEMES | THE LAND OF ISRAEL | COVENANT | RELATIONSHIPS AND LOVE |

Episode 29: *Sara's Death* – Bereshit 23:1–20

SUMMARY

It might be inferred from the juxtaposition of the death of Sara to the story of the binding of Yitzḥak that Sara's death immediately followed the binding of her son. The Sages maintain that this was indeed the case. However, a straightforward reading of the verses indicates that Yitzḥak was a young boy at the time of the binding. If so, a long time passed from then until his mother's death. Although nothing is stated about the events of Sara's life after the birth of Yitzḥak, one can assume that she was busy raising him. During this period, Sara likely lived in Ḥevron, where she died, while Avraham wandered between several locations.

This episode relates Avraham's initial purchase of property in the land of Canaan, the very first example of ownership of the land by the Jewish people. The Torah provides precise details about the transaction (including the location of the property purchased for the burial of Sara, where future generations of the family would also be buried), the person from whom it was purchased, and the public and ceremonious nature of the event.

of land worth four hundred silver shekel – what is that between you and me? Bury your
16 dead." Avraham heard Efron.[1] He weighed out for him the price he had mentioned in the
17 Hittites' hearing: four hundred silver shekel at the merchants' standard rate. So Efron's field
in Makhpela near Mamre – the field, its cave, and all the trees within the field's borders –
18 passed to Avraham as his possession, in the presence of all the Hittites who had come to
19 the city gate. Avraham then buried Sara his wife in the cave in the field of Makhpela near
20 Mamre – that is, Ḥevron – in the land of Canaan. Thus the field and its cave passed from
the Hittites to Avraham as a burial site.

1 | Avraham discerned Efron's real intention: that he be paid the specified amount.

THE ART OF MIDRASH

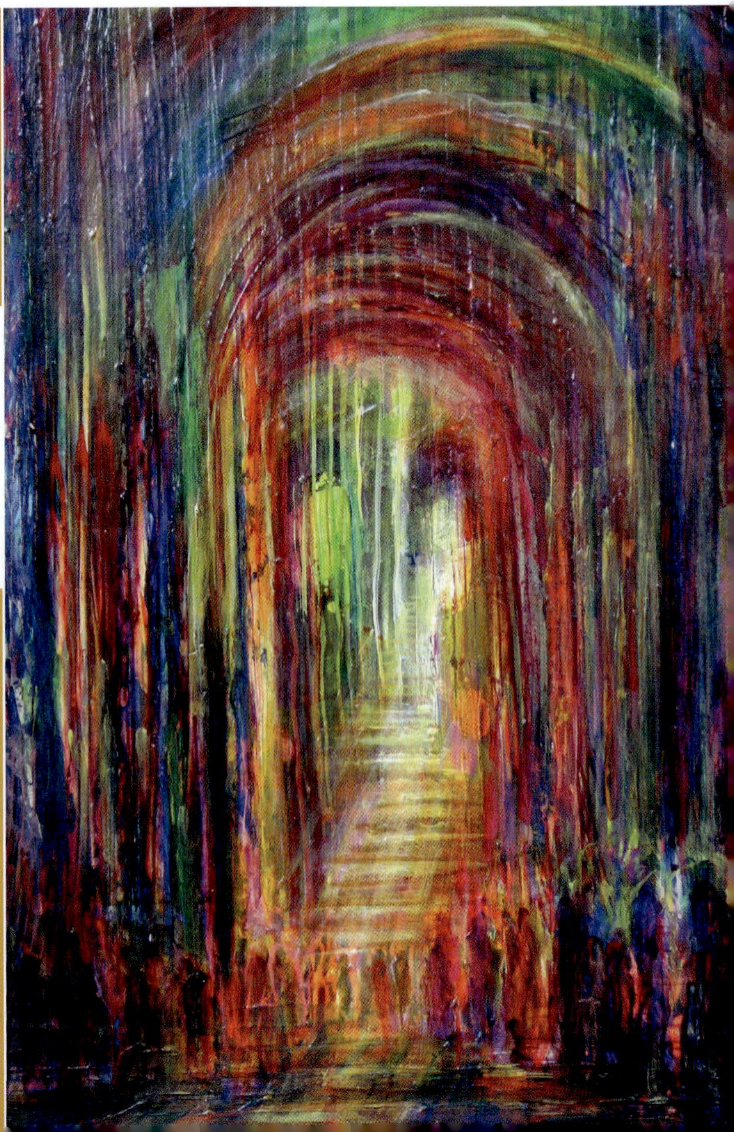

Cave of the patriarchs
Yoram Raanan (2013)

Analysis

- Which elements of this image are directly mentioned in the text?
- Which elements of this image are not found in the text?
- What midrashic interpretation could be inferred from this image?

שְׁמָעֵ֔נִי אֶ֠רֶץ אַרְבַּ֨ע מֵאֹ֧ת שֶֽׁקֶל־כֶּ֛סֶף בֵּינִ֥י וּבֵינְךָ֖ מַה־הִ֑וא וְאֶת־מֵתְךָ֖ קְבֹֽר׃
טז וַיִּשְׁמַ֣ע אַבְרָהָם֮ אֶל־עֶפְרוֹן֒ וַיִּשְׁקֹ֤ל אַבְרָהָם֙ לְעֶפְרֹ֔ן אֶת־הַכֶּ֕סֶף אֲשֶׁ֥ר דִּבֶּ֖ר בְּאָזְנֵ֣י
יז בְנֵי־חֵ֑ת אַרְבַּ֤ע מֵאוֹת֙ שֶׁ֣קֶל כֶּ֔סֶף עֹבֵ֖ר לַסֹּחֵֽר׃ וַיָּ֣קָם ׀ שְׂדֵ֣ה עֶפְרֹ֗ון אֲשֶׁר֙ בַּמַּכְפֵּלָ֔ה שני
אֲשֶׁ֖ר לִפְנֵ֣י מַמְרֵ֑א הַשָּׂדֶה֙ וְהַמְּעָרָ֣ה אֲשֶׁר־בּ֔וֹ וְכָל־הָעֵץ֙ אֲשֶׁ֣ר בַּשָּׂדֶ֔ה אֲשֶׁ֥ר בְּכָל־
יח יט גְּבֻל֖וֹ סָבִֽיב׃ לְאַבְרָהָ֥ם לְמִקְנָ֖ה לְעֵינֵ֣י בְנֵי־חֵ֑ת בְּכֹ֖ל בָּאֵ֥י שַֽׁעַר־עִירֽוֹ׃ וְאַחֲרֵי־כֵ֡ן
קָבַ֨ר אַבְרָהָ֜ם אֶת־שָׂרָ֣ה אִשְׁתּ֗וֹ אֶל־מְעָרַ֞ת שְׂדֵ֧ה הַמַּכְפֵּלָ֛ה עַל־פְּנֵ֥י מַמְרֵ֖א הִ֣וא
כ חֶבְר֑וֹן בְּאֶ֖רֶץ כְּנָֽעַן׃ וַיָּ֨קָם הַשָּׂדֶ֜ה וְהַמְּעָרָ֧ה אֲשֶׁר־בּ֛וֹ לְאַבְרָהָ֖ם לַאֲחֻזַּת־קָ֑בֶר
מֵאֵ֖ת בְּנֵי־חֵֽת׃

A QUESTION OF BIBLIODRAMA

TO AVRAHAM

- Can you articulate the emotions you experienced when Sara died?
- Why was it so important for you to buy a burial plot and not use one offered to you by the Hittites?
- How do you feel about Efron and the negotiations with him?

TO EFRON AND THE HITTITES

- How do you feel about Avraham?
- Why do you at first offer Avraham to bury his wife in one of your own burial plots for free?
- Do you think four hundred silver shekel is a fair price?

חֶבְרוֹן
ḤEVRON

Ḥevron is mentioned over sixty times in Tanakh, in addition to the names Kiryat Arba (nine times), Mamre (six), and Makhpela (six). Ḥevron was also the name of one of Kehat son of Levi's sons.[1]

The city's original name was Kiryat Arba, named for Arba, "the mightiest of giants,"[2] and the father of Sheshai, Aḥiman, and Talmai.[3]

Mamre was the name of one of Avraham's allies;[4] the "Oaks of Mamre" seems to have been an oak grove he owned in the area.

"The field of Makhpela" or "the cave of Makhpela" was an area around the city that was perhaps named for its size or for the folds of earth it contained; *kiflei*, "folds," comes from the same root as "Makhpela." The Sages explain that it was a double cave, a cave within a cave. Indeed, in the 1980s, a double cave was discovered at the site, a cave within a cave, typical of burial caves from the Middle Bronze Age – that is, the time of the patriarchs.

The city referred to in Arabic as El-Ḥalil (meaning "the friend") after Avraham is unquestionably identified with Ḥevron, and excavations at Tel Rumeida, where today's Ḥevron stands, uncovered a fortified city from the Bronze Age. A cuneiform stone tablet discovered there lists the sacrifices brought to the city's king, showing that in the patriarchs' time, the city was a center of government, and perhaps a center of worship as well. Excavations show that the city was also an important residential area in the early Iron Age. Pitchers with the phrase *lemelekh Ḥevron* engraved on their handles were discovered there and in other places in the land, testifying to the city's importance throughout the monarchic period. In the Second Temple era, Ḥevron was considered part of Idomea until it was conquered by the Hasmoneans. The building over the cave of Makhpela is ascribed to King Herod.

---

1 | Shemot 6:18.

2 | Yehoshua 14:15.

3 | Yehoshua 15:13–14.

4 | Bereshit 14:13, 24.

Analysis

- What areas of archaeological, geographical, and historical knowledge do we have now that were unavailable to classical Jewish commentators? How can they aid our understanding of the text?
- How can this information about Ḥevron help us understand the text?
- What further questions on the text do you have now that you have read this new information and research?

INTEGRATING ḤOKHMA

Cave of Makhpela in Ḥevron

capital after the death of Sha'ul, when David asks God where to have his capital (I Shmuel 1:11). Shekhem became the first capital of the kingdom of Israel: Reḥavam arrived in Shekhem for his coronation (I Melakhim 12:1), but as a result of the "counsel of the children" to increase the people's burden, the kingdom split, and eventually Yorovam was crowned at Shekhem, which became his capital. Jerusalem was the capital of the united kingdom of Israel: after the death of Avner and Ishboshet, the elders decide to accept upon themselves, as did their brethren in Judea, the kingship of David. His first step is the capture of Jerusalem and its establishment as his capital (II Shmuel 5:5). Shomron was the capital of the dynasty of Omri, which, despite its corruption, was the strongest and most central to rule over the tribes of Israel. *Ḥazal* noted this (Sanhedrin 102b): "Why did Omri deserve kingship? Because he added a major city to the land of Israel, as it says: 'He bought Mount Shomron.'"

The common element to these four purchases was that they were bought not privately, but by the common entity representing the nation. In the case of the forefathers this is true by definition, once we accept that a forefather represents *klal Yisrael*. In the latter two cases, the king bought the area for a national purpose – the place of the altar (and ultimately the Temple), and the capital of the kingdom of Israel. This is presumably the reason why they served as capital cities. The purchase gave them a status of national property rather than private or tribal property.

Rabbi Amnon Bazak

TAKING A LITERARY APPROACH

The Torah describes at length the refusal of Avraham to accept the field for free; he demands to pay Efron its full value. The Torah emphasizes that the purchase is "before the eyes of the sons of Ḥet amid all who came within the gates of the city," and repeats – twice – that the field "was upheld" (*vayakam*) as Avraham's possession and burial ground. Interestingly, whenever the Torah hereafter refers to the cave of Makhpela, it proceeds to describe at uncharacteristic length the way in which the field was bought (e.g., Bereshit 25:9, 49:29–32, 50:13).

The same phenomenon is evident in other cases as well. Yaakov buys a field in Shekhem from Ḥamor, and again the Torah spells out the price: "And he bought the field where he pitched his tent from Ḥamor, the father of Shekhem, for one hundred kesita." Later, when Yosef is buried there, the transaction is again described in detail (Yehoshua 24:32).

The book of Shmuel concludes, as the backdrop for Melakhim, with the purchase of the granary of Aravna the Jebusite. The story of the purchase is quite reminiscent of the acquisition of the field by Avraham: in both narratives, a highly esteemed figure (Avraham – "a prince of God in our midst"; David, the king of Israel) initiates contact with a gentile (Efron, Aravna) in order to buy a plot of land. In both cases we read of socially correct dialogue, replete with prostrations, in which the seller offers the land free of charge ("I have given you the field, and I have given you the cave therein"; "My lord the king may take and go up as he sees fit"). In both instances the buyer insists on paying the full price in silver (II Shmuel 24).

There is one more place whose acquisition is recorded (I Melakhim 16:23–24). "In the thirty-first year of Asa the king of Judea, Omri reigned over Israel.... He bought Mount Shomron from Shemer for two talents of silver. And he built the mountain, and called the city which he built Shomron, after Shemer the master of the mountain."

Here, too, the verses spell out the exact price paid for the city. There are four places, then, where land in *Eretz Yisrael* was bought for a price: Ḥevron, Shekhem, Jerusalem, and Shomron. The four have something else in common. These cities were the four which served as capitals during different periods: Ḥevron was made

24 1 2 Avraham was old, advanced in years, and the Lord had blessed him in all things. And
Avraham said to the senior servant of his household, who was in charge of all he had,
3 "Place your hand under my thigh.[1] I want you to swear by the Lord, God of heaven and
earth, that you will not take a wife for my son from among the daughters of the Canaanites
4 among whom I live. Instead, go to my land and birthplace, and there find a wife for Yitzḥak
5 my son." The servant asked, "What if the woman does not want to come back with me to
6 this land? Shall I bring your son back to the land from which you came?" Avraham said
7 to him, "Be sure not to take my son back there. The Lord, God of the heavens, took me
from my father's house and from the land of my birth. He spoke to me and swore to me,
'To your descendants I will give this land.' He will send His angel before you, and there
8 you will find a wife for my son. But if the woman does not want to come back with you,
9 then you will be released from this oath to me. Just do not take my son back there." So the
servant placed his hand under his master Avraham's thigh and swore this by an oath to
10 him. The servant then took ten of his master's camels, laden with all his master's bounty,
11 and set out to Aram Naharayim, to the city of Naḥor. By the well outside the city, he had
the camels kneel. It was evening, the time when the women came out to draw water.

1 | An act sometimes performed in conjunction with an oath.

UNLOCKING THE TEXT

- Why wasn't Yitzḥak involved in the finding of his wife?
- Why would Avraham only accept a wife for Yitzḥak from his birthplace and not Canaan?
- Why did Avraham's servant choose this sign to determine he had found a wife for Yitzḥak?
- Why is Lavan mentioned here and what role does he play in this story?
- Why is Avraham so adamant that Yitzḥak should not leave the land of Israel?
- The Torah gives various reasons for why Rivka is an appropriate wife for Yitzḥak. Which are the most important for Eliezer and why?

FINDING YOURSELF IN THE TEXT

- Have you ever entrusted a vitally important task to someone you trusted? How did that feel?
- Did you ever pray to God that something should happen, and then it did? How did that feel?
- Do you know how your parents or grandparents met? Do you think God was involved in the story?

Consider using these questions as the basis for your own commentary or creative midrash.

How does reflecting on these firsthand experiences help you better understand the text?

כד ‏א וְאַבְרָהָ֣ם זָקֵ֔ן בָּ֖א בַּיָּמִ֑ים וַֽיהוָ֛ה בֵּרַ֥ךְ אֶת־אַבְרָהָ֖ם בַּכֹּֽל: וַיֹּ֣אמֶר אַבְרָהָ֗ם אֶל־עַבְדּ֤וֹ ‏ב

‏ג זְקַ֣ן בֵּית֔וֹ הַמֹּשֵׁ֖ל בְּכָל־אֲשֶׁר־ל֑וֹ שִֽׂים־נָ֥א יָדְךָ֖ תַּ֥חַת יְרֵכִֽי: וְאַשְׁבִּ֣יעֲךָ֔ בַּֽיהוָה֙

אֱלֹהֵ֣י הַשָּׁמַ֔יִם וֵֽאלֹהֵ֖י הָאָ֑רֶץ אֲשֶׁ֨ר לֹֽא־תִקַּ֤ח אִשָּׁה֙ לִבְנִ֔י מִבְּנוֹת֙ הַֽכְּנַעֲנִ֔י אֲשֶׁ֥ר

‏ד אָנֹכִ֖י יוֹשֵׁ֥ב בְּקִרְבּֽוֹ: כִּ֧י אֶל־אַרְצִ֛י וְאֶל־מֽוֹלַדְתִּ֖י תֵּלֵ֑ךְ וְלָֽקַחְתָּ֥ אִשָּׁ֖ה לִבְנִ֥י לְיִצְחָֽק:

‏ה וַיֹּ֤אמֶר אֵלָיו֙ הָעֶ֔בֶד אוּלַי֙ לֹֽא־תֹאבֶ֣ה הָֽאִשָּׁ֔ה לָלֶ֥כֶת אַֽחֲרַ֖י אֶל־הָאָ֣רֶץ הַזֹּ֑את

‏ו הֶֽהָשֵׁ֤ב אָשִׁיב֙ אֶת־בִּנְךָ֔ אֶל־הָאָ֖רֶץ אֲשֶׁר־יָצָ֣אתָ מִשָּֽׁם: וַיֹּ֥אמֶר אֵלָ֖יו אַבְרָהָ֑ם

‏ז הִשָּׁ֣מֶר לְךָ֔ פֶּן־תָּשִׁ֥יב אֶת־בְּנִ֖י שָֽׁמָּה: יְהוָ֣ה ׀ אֱלֹהֵ֣י הַשָּׁמַ֗יִם אֲשֶׁ֨ר לְקָחַ֜נִי מִבֵּ֣ית

אָבִי֮ וּמֵאֶ֣רֶץ מֽוֹלַדְתִּי֒ וַֽאֲשֶׁ֨ר דִּבֶּר־לִ֜י וַֽאֲשֶׁ֤ר נִֽשְׁבַּֽע־לִי֙ לֵאמֹ֔ר לְזַ֨רְעֲךָ֔ אֶתֵּ֖ן אֶת־

‏ח הָאָ֣רֶץ הַזֹּ֑את ה֗וּא יִשְׁלַ֤ח מַלְאָכוֹ֙ לְפָנֶ֔יךָ וְלָֽקַחְתָּ֥ אִשָּׁ֖ה לִבְנִ֥י מִשָּֽׁם: וְאִם־לֹ֨א

תֹאבֶ֤ה הָֽאִשָּׁה֙ לָלֶ֣כֶת אַֽחֲרֶ֔יךָ וְנִקִּ֕יתָ מִשְּׁבֻֽעָתִ֖י זֹ֑את רַ֣ק אֶת־בְּנִ֔י לֹ֥א תָשֵׁ֖ב שָֽׁמָּה:

שלישי ‏ט וַיָּ֤שֶׂם הָעֶ֨בֶד֙ אֶת־יָד֔וֹ תַּ֛חַת יֶ֥רֶךְ אַבְרָהָ֖ם אֲדֹנָ֑יו וַיִּשָּׁ֣בַֽע ל֔וֹ עַל־הַדָּבָ֖ר הַזֶּֽה: וַיִּקַּ֣ח ‏י

הָעֶ֡בֶד עֲשָׂרָה֩ גְמַלִּ֨ים מִגְּמַלֵּ֤י אֲדֹנָיו֙ וַיֵּ֔לֶךְ וְכָל־ט֥וּב אֲדֹנָ֖יו בְּיָד֑וֹ וַיָּ֗קָם וַיֵּ֛לֶךְ אֶל־אֲרַ֥ם

‏יא נַֽהֲרַ֖יִם אֶל־עִ֥יר נָחֽוֹר: וַיַּבְרֵ֧ךְ הַגְּמַלִּ֛ים מִח֥וּץ לָעִ֖יר אֶל־בְּאֵ֣ר הַמָּ֑יִם לְעֵ֣ת עֶ֔רֶב

THEMES	RELATIONSHIPS AND LOVE	COVENANT	ETHICS

Episode 30: *Finding Yitzḥak a Wife* – Bereshit 24:1–31

SUMMARY

The story of how a wife is found for Yitzḥak is related in this and the following episodes in greater detail than any comparable account in the Torah. In this regard, the Sages said that the ordinary conversation of the servants of the patriarchs is more beloved before God than the Torah of their sons, as the section dealing with Eliezer is repeated in the Torah, whereas many fundamentals of the Torah are taught only through allusion. In this episode, the chain of events is described down to the smallest detail: The precise conversations between the parties are recorded, as well as the journey and the lodging, the care given to the camels, the hospitality granted to Avraham's servant, and other such matters. All of these events are accompanied by divine assistance, as their occurrence is miraculously arranged in the most advantageous manner. This story includes a large element of human initiative and kindness, but it also highlights the crucial role of divine providence in achieving the goal of finding a wife for Yitzḥak.

12 "LORD, God of my master Avraham," he said, "please: grant me success today and show
13 kindness to my master Avraham. I am standing here by the spring and the daughters of
14 the townspeople are coming out to draw water. If I say to a young woman, 'Please lower
your jar so that I can drink,' and she replies, 'Drink, and I will water your camels also,' let
her be the one You have chosen for Your servant Yitzḥak. By this I will know that You have
15 shown kindness to my master." Before he had even finished speaking, Rivka, daughter
of Betuel son of Milka, the wife of Avraham's brother Naḥor, came out with her jar on
16 her shoulder. The young woman was very beautiful, a virgin whom no man had known.
17 She went down to the spring, filled her jar, and came up. The servant ran to meet her
18 and said, "Please let me sip a little water from your jar." She said, "Drink, my lord," and
19 quickly lowered her jar to her hand and let him drink. When she had let him drink his
fill, she said, "I will draw water for your camels, too, until they have had enough to drink."
20 Quickly she emptied her jar into the trough and ran back to the well to draw more water;
21 she drew for all his camels. The man stood gazing at her, silently wondering whether the
22 LORD had made his journey successful. When the camels had finished drinking, the man
took a gold ring weighing a half-shekel and two gold bracelets for her arms weighing ten
23 shekels, and he asked, "Whose daughter are you? Please tell me, is there room in your
24 father's house for us to spend the night?" She answered him, "I am the daughter of Betuel,
25 the son Milka bore to Naḥor." She added, "We have plenty of straw and fodder, as well as
26 room for you to spend the night." The man bowed low, prostrating himself to the LORD.
27 He said, "Blessed be the LORD, God of my master Avraham, who has not withheld His
kindness and faithfulness from my master. As for me – the LORD has guided me on the
28 way to the house of my master's close family." The young woman ran and told all this to
29 her mother's household. Rivka had a brother named Lavan; he ran outside to the man
30 at the spring. He had seen the ring, and the bracelets on his sister's arms, and had heard
his sister Rivka tell what the man had said to her. He came up to the man who was still
31 standing by the camels at the spring, and said, "Come. The LORD bless you! Why are you
standing outside? I have made room in the house and prepared a place for the camels."

יב לְעֵת צֵאת הַשֹּׁאֲבֹת׃ וַיֹּאמַר ׀ יְהוָה אֱלֹהֵי אֲדֹנִי אַבְרָהָם הַקְרֵה־נָא לְפָנַי הַיּוֹם
יג וַעֲשֵׂה־חֶסֶד עִם אֲדֹנִי אַבְרָהָם׃ הִנֵּה אָנֹכִי נִצָּב עַל־עֵין הַמָּיִם וּבְנוֹת אַנְשֵׁי הָעִיר
יד יֹצְאֹת לִשְׁאֹב מָיִם׃ וְהָיָה הַנַּעֲרָ אֲשֶׁר אֹמַר אֵלֶיהָ הַטִּי־נָא כַדֵּךְ וְאֶשְׁתֶּה וְאָמְרָה
שְׁתֵה וְגַם־גְּמַלֶּיךָ אַשְׁקֶה אֹתָהּ הֹכַחְתָּ לְעַבְדְּךָ לְיִצְחָק וּבָהּ אֵדַע כִּי־עָשִׂיתָ חֶסֶד
טו עִם־אֲדֹנִי׃ וַיְהִי־הוּא טֶרֶם כִּלָּה לְדַבֵּר וְהִנֵּה רִבְקָה יֹצֵאת אֲשֶׁר יֻלְּדָה לִבְתוּאֵל
טז בֶּן־מִלְכָּה אֵשֶׁת נָחוֹר אֲחִי אַבְרָהָם וְכַדָּהּ עַל־שִׁכְמָהּ׃ וְהַנַּעֲרָ טֹבַת מַרְאֶה
יז מְאֹד בְּתוּלָה וְאִישׁ לֹא יְדָעָהּ וַתֵּרֶד הָעַיְנָה וַתְּמַלֵּא כַדָּהּ וַתָּעַל׃ וַיָּרָץ הָעֶבֶד
יח לִקְרָאתָהּ וַיֹּאמֶר הַגְמִיאִינִי נָא מְעַט־מַיִם מִכַּדֵּךְ׃ וַתֹּאמֶר שְׁתֵה אֲדֹנִי וַתְּמַהֵר
יט וַתֹּרֶד כַּדָּהּ עַל־יָדָהּ וַתַּשְׁקֵהוּ׃ וַתְּכַל לְהַשְׁקֹתוֹ וַתֹּאמֶר גַּם לִגְמַלֶּיךָ אֶשְׁאָב עַד
כ אִם־כִּלּוּ לִשְׁתֹּת׃ וַתְּמַהֵר וַתְּעַר כַּדָּהּ אֶל־הַשֹּׁקֶת וַתָּרָץ עוֹד אֶל־הַבְּאֵר לִשְׁאֹב
כא וַתִּשְׁאַב לְכָל־גְּמַלָּיו׃ וְהָאִישׁ מִשְׁתָּאֵה לָהּ מַחֲרִישׁ לָדַעַת הַהִצְלִיחַ יְהוָה דַּרְכּוֹ
כב אִם־לֹא׃ וַיְהִי כַּאֲשֶׁר כִּלּוּ הַגְּמַלִּים לִשְׁתּוֹת וַיִּקַּח הָאִישׁ נֶזֶם זָהָב בֶּקַע מִשְׁקָלוֹ
כג וּשְׁנֵי צְמִידִים עַל־יָדֶיהָ עֲשָׂרָה זָהָב מִשְׁקָלָם׃ וַיֹּאמֶר בַּת־מִי אַתְּ הַגִּידִי נָא לִי
כד הֲיֵשׁ בֵּית־אָבִיךְ מָקוֹם לָנוּ לָלִין׃ וַתֹּאמֶר אֵלָיו בַּת־בְּתוּאֵל אָנֹכִי בֶּן־מִלְכָּה אֲשֶׁר
כה כו יָלְדָה לְנָחוֹר׃ וַתֹּאמֶר אֵלָיו גַּם־תֶּבֶן גַּם־מִסְפּוֹא רַב עִמָּנוּ גַּם־מָקוֹם לָלוּן׃ וַיִּקֹּד
כז הָאִישׁ וַיִּשְׁתַּחוּ לַיהוָה׃ וַיֹּאמֶר בָּרוּךְ יְהוָה אֱלֹהֵי אֲדֹנִי אַבְרָהָם אֲשֶׁר לֹא־עָזַב רביעי
כח חַסְדּוֹ וַאֲמִתּוֹ מֵעִם אֲדֹנִי אָנֹכִי בַּדֶּרֶךְ נָחַנִי יְהוָה בֵּית אֲחֵי אֲדֹנִי׃ וַתָּרָץ הַנַּעֲרָ
כט וַתַּגֵּד לְבֵית אִמָּהּ כַּדְּבָרִים הָאֵלֶּה׃ וּלְרִבְקָה אָח וּשְׁמוֹ לָבָן וַיָּרָץ לָבָן אֶל־הָאִישׁ
ל הַחוּצָה אֶל־הָעָיִן׃ וַיְהִי ׀ כִּרְאֹת אֶת־הַנֶּזֶם וְאֶת־הַצְּמִדִים עַל־יְדֵי אֲחֹתוֹ וּכְשָׁמְעוֹ
אֶת־דִּבְרֵי רִבְקָה אֲחֹתוֹ לֵאמֹר כֹּה־דִבֶּר אֵלַי הָאִישׁ וַיָּבֹא אֶל־הָאִישׁ וְהִנֵּה עֹמֵד
לא עַל־הַגְּמַלִּים עַל־הָעָיִן׃ וַיֹּאמֶר בּוֹא בְּרוּךְ יְהוָה לָמָּה תַעֲמֹד בַּחוּץ וְאָנֹכִי פִּנִּיתִי
הַבַּיִת וּמָקוֹם לַגְּמַלִּים׃

THE ART OF MIDRASH

Rebecca
Dikla Laor (2017)

Analysis

- Which elements of this image are directly mentioned in the text?
- Which elements of this image are not found in the text?
- What midrashic interpretation could be inferred from this image?

A QUESTION OF BIBLIODRAMA

TO AVRAHAM

- Why did you entrust this important task to Eliezer your servant?
- Were you optimistic that he would succeed?

RIVKA

- What did you think when you first saw Eliezer and heard his request for water?
- Why did you respond in the way that you did?
- What did you tell your family, and what were you feeling about what had happened?

TO ELIEZER, AVRAHAM'S SERVANT

- Did you feel pressure to be successful in this task?
- Were you optimistic that you would be successful?
- How did you feel when you saw Rivka approach? How did you feel when she offered you and your camels water?

TO LAVAN

- What do you think about Eliezer at this stage?
- What is your angle? What are you thinking?

חָרָן (פַּדַּן אֲרָם)
ḤARAN (PADAN ARAM)

This city in Aram Naharayim is mentioned ten times by this name, mostly in Bereshit, and eleven times more by the name Padan Aram. The name Ḥaran was preserved in the site Tel Haran by the Khabur River in southern Turkey, not far from the Syrian border.

Ḥaran means "way" or "convoy," and ancient inscriptions indeed imply that it was once an economic center along the road between Assyria, Aram, and Canaan. The name Padan Aram seems to mean "the field of Aram," based on Hoshea's description that "Yaakov fled to the field of Aram,"[1] although the Akkadian meaning of the word "Padan" is also "way" – that is, synonymous with the name Ḥaran.

The city was known as the northern cultic center for the Mesopotamian moon god Sin.

1 | Hoshea 12:13.

Analysis

- What areas of archaeological, geographical, and historical knowledge do we have now that were unavailable to classical Jewish commentators? How can they aid our understanding of the text?
- How can this information about Ḥaran help us understand the text?
- What further questions on the text do you have now that you have read this new information and research?

INTEGRATING ḤOKHMA

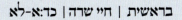

Ancient ruins in Ḥaran

The similarities between Rivka and Avraham in character and in the description of their journey frame another resemblance: Avraham was chosen by God, and his first test is to leave his homeland and journey to an unknown land. Rivka engages in a similar journey, from Avraham's homeland, which is also her own, and his family, which is also her own. In fact, God's first words to Avraham in Bereshit 12:1 – "Go unto you" – are echoed in Rivka's own departure (24:58–61):

> And they called Rivka and said to her, "**Will you go with this man?**" She said, "**I will.**" [...] Then Rivka and her maids **rose up**, mounted the camels, and **went after** the man, and the servant **took** Rivka and **went**.

It seems that Rivka's family would have preferred for her to stay – but when asked, she is committed to go toward the unknown, just like Avraham.

This comparison sheds new light on the story of choosing Rivka, and indicates that Rivka, just like Avraham, was chosen directly by God. Both persevered through clear tests of character: Avraham proved that he was God-fearing (through the binding of his son); Rivka proves herself as worthy (through her acts of ḥesed), and both show their devotion to God by leaving their past behind them to go to the Promised Land.

While Avraham follows a direct commandment from God, Rivka follows in Avraham's ways (practically, she follows his servant). Rivka knows little about the servant (other than his apparent wealth), except that he is filled with thanks and praise for God, and is part of Avraham's household – which is known as a God-fearing clan. She will later learn from the servant – who often mentions God's name and bows down to Him, and who was sent by the God-fearing Avraham – that it was an angel messenger who picked Rivka. Based on all this information she decides to take action and follow – but while Rivka's stated intent is to follow the servant and marry Yitzḥak, all signs indicate that she is truly following God. The servant's test proved that Rivka is worthy of marrying Yitzḥak, but this perspective indicates that Rivka was, in fact, directly chosen by God, to be a matriarch of the Jewish people.

Rabbanit Dr. Adina Sternberg

רְעֶה וַתֵּרֶד הָעַ
גְמִיאִינִי נָא מְעַט־מַיִם מִכַּ
רָה וַתַּשְׁקֵהוּ: וַתְּכַל לְהַשְׁקֹתוֹ וַ
וַתְּמַהֵר וַתְּעַר כַּדָּהּ אֶל־הַשֹּׁקֶת וַ
מַלָּיו: וְהָאִישׁ מִשְׁתָּאֵה לָהּ מַחֲרִישׁ
אֲשֶׁר כִּלּוּ הַגְּמַלִּים לִשְׁתּוֹת וַיִּקַּח
דִיהָ עֲשָׂרָה זָהָב מִשְׁקָלָם: וַ
לָנוּ לָלִין: וַתֹּאמֶר אֵלָ

TAKING A LITERARY APPROACH

While Avraham's instructions concentrate on Rivka's background, his servant applies a test that relates to other facets. There are two major approaches among commentators regarding this test. Some (e.g., Rashi, Ibn Ezra, Rabbi Samson Raphael Hirsch, and others) view the test as an assessment of character. The servant searches for a quality of *ḥesed* in Rivka, which she expresses through her initiative to act with kindness, the extent of her investment, and her haste.

Rivka's *ḥesed* and hospitality are reminiscent of Avraham's marked character traits. The connection between Rivka and Avraham is illustrated through lexical similarities, with an emphasis on haste and running:

Avraham (Bereshit 18:6–8)

And Avraham hastened into the tent to Sara and said, "Make ready quickly three measures of choice flour, knead it, and make cakes." Avraham ran to the herd and took a calf, tender and good, and gave it to the servant, who hastened to prepare it. Then he took curds and milk and the calf that he had prepared and set it before them, and he stood by them under the tree while they ate.

Rivka (Bereshit 24:17–20)

Then the servant ran to meet her and said, "Please let me sip a little water from your jar." "Drink, my lord," she said and hastily lowered her jar upon her hand and gave him a drink. When she had finished giving him a drink, she said, "I will draw for your camels also, until they have finished drinking." So she hastily emptied her jar into the trough and ran again to the well to draw, and she drew for all his camels.

The verbs *ratz*, "run," and *maher*, "quickly," appear in both texts – and furthermore, both Avraham and Rivka are described as people whose actions speak louder than words, since their minimal offer does not reflect their extensive action, emulating the rabbinic idiom "Say little and do much." Like Avraham, Rivka also shows hospitality toward a stranger, who ultimately turns out to be a faithful messenger.

Seemingly, the test was intended to find an appropriate wife for Yitzḥak, a woman who has the right personality traits and who might fit in with Avraham's family. She may have been raised among idolaters, as Avraham was, but if her character is similar to Avraham's, she is worthy of joining his family

32 So the man entered the house, the camels were unloaded, straw and fodder were brought
33 for the camels, and water was brought for him and his men to wash their feet. Food was
set before him to eat, but he said, "I will not eat until I have said what I have to say." "Speak,
34 35 then," said Lavan. "I am Avraham's servant," he said. "The LORD has blessed my master
greatly, and he has prospered. He has given him sheep and cattle, silver and gold, male and
36 female servants, camels and donkeys. My master's wife Sara bore my master a son in her
37 old age, and he committed to his son all that is his. My master made me swear, saying, 'You
must not take a wife for my son from among the daughters of the Canaanites in whose land I
38 39 live. Instead you must go to my father's house and family and there find a wife for my son.' I
40 asked my master, 'What if the woman does not want to come back with me?' He answered,
'The LORD before whom I have walked will send His angel with you to make your journey
41 a success, so that you may find a wife for my son from my family and father's house. You
are released from this vow only if you come to my family and they refuse to give her to you.
42 Then you are released from my vow.' Today, when I came to the spring, I said, 'LORD, God
of my master Avraham, if You will, please grant success to this journey on which I have
43 come. I am standing here by a spring of water. The woman who comes out to draw water,

UNLOCKING THE TEXT

- Why did Eliezer refuse to eat until he had explained his mission and received an answer?
- Why is Avraham's wealth an important detail to share?
- Why did Eliezer give so much detail of the story that led him there?
- There are several discrepancies between the two versions of the story. Why?
  - The word "kindness" is missing from the second version.
  - At the well, Rivka went beyond Eliezer's expectations, but he doesn't relay this to her family.
  - In his retelling of the story, Eliezer reverses the order of the giving of the jewelry and his inquiries about Rivka's family.
  - Eliezer leaves out Rivka's offer of hospitality.
  - In his retelling, Eliezer adds details of Yitzḥak's miraculous birth to Sara in her old age.
- Why is so much jewelry changing hands?
- Why did Lavan ask for Rivka to stay another year before departing?
- Why did Rivka agree to go on such short notice?
- Who ultimately decided whether Rivka would go with Eliezer to return to Avraham and marry Yitzḥak?

FINDING YOURSELF IN THE TEXT

- Do you believe that God decides who you are destined to marry?
- Do you think your parents will be involved in deciding who you marry?
- Can you imagine agreeing to marry someone you have never met, or only met a few times?

Consider using these questions as the basis for your own commentary or creative midrash.

How does reflecting on these firsthand experiences help you better understand the text?

לב וַיָּבֹא הָאִישׁ הַבַּיְתָה וַיְפַתַּח הַגְּמַלִּים וַיִּתֵּן תֶּבֶן וּמִסְפּוֹא לַגְּמַלִּים וּמַיִם לִרְחֹץ
לג רַגְלָיו וְרַגְלֵי הָאֲנָשִׁים אֲשֶׁר אִתּוֹ: ויישם לְפָנָיו לֶאֱכֹל וַיֹּאמֶר לֹא אֹכַל עַד וַיּוּשַׂם
לד לה אִם־דִּבַּרְתִּי דְּבָרָי וַיֹּאמֶר דַּבֵּר: וַיֹּאמַר עֶבֶד אַבְרָהָם אָנֹכִי: וַיהוָה בֵּרַךְ אֶת־
אֲדֹנִי מְאֹד וַיִּגְדָּל וַיִּתֶּן־לוֹ צֹאן וּבָקָר וְכֶסֶף וְזָהָב וַעֲבָדִם וּשְׁפָחֹת וּגְמַלִּים
לו וַחֲמֹרִים: וַתֵּלֶד שָׂרָה אֵשֶׁת אֲדֹנִי בֵן לַאדֹנִי אַחֲרֵי זִקְנָתָהּ וַיִּתֶּן־לוֹ אֶת־כָּל־
לז אֲשֶׁר־לוֹ: וַיַּשְׁבִּעֵנִי אֲדֹנִי לֵאמֹר לֹא־תִקַּח אִשָּׁה לִבְנִי מִבְּנוֹת הַכְּנַעֲנִי אֲשֶׁר
לח אָנֹכִי יֹשֵׁב בְּאַרְצוֹ: אִם־לֹא אֶל־בֵּית־אָבִי תֵּלֵךְ וְאֶל־מִשְׁפַּחְתִּי וְלָקַחְתָּ אִשָּׁה
לט מ לִבְנִי: וָאֹמַר אֶל־אֲדֹנִי אֻלַי לֹא־תֵלֵךְ הָאִשָּׁה אַחֲרָי: וַיֹּאמֶר אֵלָי יְהוָה אֲשֶׁר־
הִתְהַלַּכְתִּי לְפָנָיו יִשְׁלַח מַלְאָכוֹ אִתָּךְ וְהִצְלִיחַ דַּרְכֶּךָ וְלָקַחְתָּ אִשָּׁה לִבְנִי
מא מִמִּשְׁפַּחְתִּי וּמִבֵּית אָבִי: אָז תִּנָּקֶה מֵאָלָתִי כִּי תָבוֹא אֶל־מִשְׁפַּחְתִּי וְאִם־לֹא
מב יִתְּנוּ לָךְ וְהָיִיתָ נָקִי מֵאָלָתִי: וָאָבֹא הַיּוֹם אֶל־הָעָיִן וָאֹמַר יְהוָה אֱלֹהֵי אֲדֹנִי כא
מג אַבְרָהָם אִם־יֶשְׁךָ־נָּא מַצְלִיחַ דַּרְכִּי אֲשֶׁר אָנֹכִי הֹלֵךְ עָלֶיהָ: הִנֵּה אָנֹכִי נִצָּב עַל־

THEMES	RELATIONSHIPS AND LOVE	COVENANT	ETHICS

Episode 31: *The Arrangements Are Made* – Bereshit 24:32–60

SUMMARY

Lavan offers Eliezer a meal, but he refuses to eat until he says what he needs to say. He identifies himself as Avraham's servant, and proceeds to recount the entire story, beginning with God blessing Avraham with extraordinary wealth, the miracle birth of the heir, and his sacred mission to find a bride for the wealthy, blessed child. He continues by describing his journey, the sign he requested from God, and how Rivka fulfilled the conditions of his test. Finally, he concludes by requesting that Rivka accompany him home to marry his master's son.

Lavan and Betuel are initially overwhelmed by Eliezer's description of the divine hand in the saga, and so they feel compelled to immediately agree to send Rivka. The next morning, however, after receiving gifts from the servant, they suggest delaying for a while before she leaves. When Eliezer pushes back, they suggest asking Rivka what she wants to do. To their surprise, Rivka agrees to go immediately. They send Rivka and her nursemaid with Eliezer and bless her to have numerous descendants.

44 to whom I say, "Please let me sip a little water from your jar," and who says to me, "Drink,
and I will also draw for your camels" – let her be the one the Lord has chosen for my
45 master's son.' Before I had even finished speaking to myself, Rivka came out with her jar on
her shoulder. She went down to the spring and drew water, and I asked her, 'Please, let me
46 drink.' She immediately lowered her jar and said, 'Drink, and I will also water your camels.'
47 So I drank, and she gave the camels water too. I asked her, 'Whose daughter are you?' She
said, 'The daughter of Betuel son of Naḥor, whom Milka bore to him.' So I placed a ring on
48 her nose and bracelets on her arms. I bowed low and prostrated myself to the Lord, and
blessed the Lord, God of my master Avraham, who led me on the right way to take the
49 daughter of my master's brother for his son. Now, if you are willing to show kindness and
faithfulness to my master, tell me; and if not, tell me that, so that I may move on, right or
50 left." Lavan and Betuel answered, "This is surely from the Lord: there is nothing for us to
51 say to you, bad or good. Here is Rivka in front of you. Take her: go. Let her be the wife of
52 your master's son, as the Lord has spoken." When Avraham's servant heard these words,
53 he bowed down to the ground before the Lord. The servant brought out gold and silver
jewelry and clothes and gave them to Rivka. He also gave costly gifts to her brother and
54 her mother. Then he and his men ate and drank and spent the night there. When they got
55 up the next morning he said, "Send me on my way to my master." But her brother and her
mother replied, "Let the young woman stay with us a year or ten months. Then she may
56 go." "Do not delay me," he said, "now that the Lord has made my journey a success. Let
57 me leave so that I may go back to my master." They replied, "Let us call the young woman
58 and ask her." So they called Rivka and asked her, "Will you go with this man?" She replied,
59 "I will." So they sent their sister Rivka on her way, together with her nurse and Avraham's
60 servant and his men. They blessed Rivka and said to her, "Our sister, may you grow into
thousands of myriads, and may your descendants possess their enemies' gates."

עֵ֣ין הַמַּ֔יִם וְהָיָ֤ה הָֽעַלְמָה֙ הַיֹּצֵ֣את לִשְׁאֹ֔ב וְאָמַרְתִּ֣י אֵלֶ֔יהָ הַשְׁקִֽינִי־נָ֥א מְעַט־מַ֖יִם

מד מִכַּדֵּֽךְ: וְאָמְרָ֤ה אֵלַי֙ גַּם־אַתָּ֣ה שְׁתֵ֔ה וְגַ֥ם לִגְמַלֶּ֖יךָ אֶשְׁאָ֑ב הִ֣וא הָֽאִשָּׁ֔ה אֲשֶׁר־הֹכִ֥יחַ

מה יְהוָ֖ה לְבֶן־אֲדֹנִֽי: אֲנִי֩ טֶ֨רֶם אֲכַלֶּ֜ה לְדַבֵּ֣ר אֶל־לִבִּ֗י וְהִנֵּ֨ה רִבְקָ֤ה יֹצֵאת֙ וְכַדָּ֣הּ עַל־

מו שִׁכְמָ֔הּ וַתֵּ֥רֶד הָעַ֖יְנָה וַתִּשְׁאָ֑ב וָאֹמַ֥ר אֵלֶ֖יהָ הַשְׁקִ֥ינִי נָֽא: וַתְּמַהֵ֗ר וַתּ֤וֹרֶד כַּדָּהּ֙ מֵֽעָלֶ֔יהָ

מז וַתֹּ֣אמֶר שְׁתֵ֔ה וְגַם־גְּמַלֶּ֖יךָ אַשְׁקֶ֑ה וָאֵ֕שְׁתְּ וְגַ֥ם הַגְּמַלִּ֖ים הִשְׁקָֽתָה: וָאֶשְׁאַ֣ל אֹתָ֗הּ וָֽאֹמַר֮ בַּת־מִ֣י אַתְּ֒ וַתֹּ֗אמֶר בַּת־בְּתוּאֵל֙ בֶּן־נָח֔וֹר אֲשֶׁ֥ר יָֽלְדָה־לּ֖וֹ מִלְכָּ֑ה וָאָשִׂ֤ם הַנֶּ֨זֶם֙

מח עַל־אַפָּ֔הּ וְהַצְּמִידִ֖ים עַל־יָדֶֽיהָ: וָאֶקֹּ֥ד וָֽאֶשְׁתַּחֲוֶ֖ה לַֽיהוָ֑ה וָֽאֲבָרֵ֗ךְ אֶת־יְהוָה֙ אֱלֹהֵי֙

מט אֲדֹנִ֣י אַבְרָהָ֔ם אֲשֶׁ֤ר הִנְחַ֨נִי֙ בְּדֶ֣רֶךְ אֱמֶ֔ת לָקַ֛חַת אֶת־בַּת־אֲחִ֥י אֲדֹנִ֖י לִבְנֽוֹ: וְ֠עַתָּה אִם־יֶשְׁכֶ֨ם עֹשִׂ֜ים חֶ֧סֶד וֶֽאֱמֶ֛ת אֶת־אֲדֹנִ֖י הַגִּ֣ידוּ לִ֑י וְאִם־לֹ֕א הַגִּ֣ידוּ לִ֔י וְאֶפְנֶ֥ה עַל־

נ יָמִ֖ין א֥וֹ עַל־שְׂמֹֽאל: וַיַּ֨עַן לָבָ֤ן וּבְתוּאֵל֙ וַיֹּ֣אמְר֔וּ מֵֽיְהוָ֖ה יָצָ֣א הַדָּבָ֑ר לֹ֥א נוּכַ֛ל דַּבֵּ֥ר

נא אֵלֶ֖יךָ רַ֥ע אוֹ־טֽוֹב: הִנֵּֽה־רִבְקָ֥ה לְפָנֶ֖יךָ קַ֣ח וָלֵ֑ךְ וּתְהִ֤י אִשָּׁה֙ לְבֶן־אֲדֹנֶ֔יךָ כַּאֲשֶׁ֖ר

נב דִּבֶּ֥ר יְהוָֽה: וַיְהִ֕י כַּאֲשֶׁ֥ר שָׁמַ֛ע עֶ֥בֶד אַבְרָהָ֖ם אֶת־דִּבְרֵיהֶ֑ם וַיִּשְׁתַּ֥חוּ אַ֖רְצָה לַֽיהוָֽה:

נג וַיּוֹצֵ֨א הָעֶ֜בֶד כְּלֵי־כֶ֨סֶף וּכְלֵ֤י זָהָב֙ וּבְגָדִ֔ים וַיִּתֵּ֖ן לְרִבְקָ֑ה וּמִ֨גְדָּנֹ֔ת נָתַ֖ן לְאָחִ֥יהָ חמישי

נד וּלְאִמָּֽהּ: וַיֹּֽאכְל֣וּ וַיִּשְׁתּ֗וּ ה֛וּא וְהָאֲנָשִׁ֥ים אֲשֶׁר־עִמּ֖וֹ וַיָּלִ֑ינוּ וַיָּק֣וּמוּ בַבֹּ֔קֶר וַיֹּ֖אמֶר

נה שַׁלְּחֻ֣נִי לַֽאדֹנִֽי: וַיֹּ֤אמֶר אָחִ֨יהָ֙ וְאִמָּ֔הּ תֵּשֵׁ֨ב הַנַּעֲרָ֥ אִתָּ֛נוּ יָמִ֖ים א֣וֹ עָשׂ֑וֹר אַחַ֖ר תֵּלֵֽךְ:

נו וַיֹּ֤אמֶר אֲלֵהֶם֙ אַל־תְּאַחֲר֣וּ אֹתִ֔י וַֽיהוָ֖ה הִצְלִ֣יחַ דַּרְכִּ֑י שַׁלְּח֕וּנִי וְאֵלְכָ֖ה לַֽאדֹנִֽי:

נז וַיֹּאמְר֖וּ נִקְרָ֣א לַֽנַּעֲרָ֑ וְנִשְׁאֲלָ֖ה אֶת־פִּֽיהָ: וַיִּקְרְא֤וּ לְרִבְקָה֙ וַיֹּאמְר֣וּ אֵלֶ֔יהָ הֲתֵלְכִ֖י

נח עִם־הָאִ֣ישׁ הַזֶּ֑ה וַתֹּ֖אמֶר אֵלֵֽךְ: וַֽיְשַׁלְּח֛וּ אֶת־רִבְקָ֥ה אֲחֹתָ֖ם וְאֶת־מֵנִקְתָּ֑הּ וְאֶת־

ס עֶ֥בֶד אַבְרָהָ֖ם וְאֶת־אֲנָשָֽׁיו: וַיְבָרֲכ֤וּ אֶת־רִבְקָה֙ וַיֹּ֣אמְרוּ לָ֔הּ אֲחֹתֵ֕נוּ אַ֥תְּ הֲיִ֖י לְאַלְפֵ֣י

רְבָבָ֑ה וְיִירַ֣שׁ זַרְעֵ֔ךְ אֵ֖ת שַׁ֥עַר שֹׂנְאָֽיו:

THE ART OF MIDRASH

Isaac's Servant Tying the Bracelet on Rebecca's Arm
Benjamin West (1775)

Analysis

- Which elements of this image are directly mentioned in the text?
- Which elements of this image are not found in the text?
- What midrashic interpretation could be inferred from this image?

A QUESTION OF BIBLIODRAMA

TO ELIEZER, AVRAHAM'S SERVANT

- What emotions were you experiencing when you went into the house?
- How did you feel when you heard the response of Lavan and Betuel?

TO LAVAN AND BETUEL

- What did you think when you first met Eliezer?
- What did you think after you heard his story?
- Why did you respond in the way that you did?

TO RIVKA

- How did you think your family would respond to Eliezer? How did you want them to respond?
- How are you feeling now that the have accepted Eliezer's proposal?

to giving other prisoners the will to live. He tells the story in several books, most famously in *Man's Search for Meaning*. He did this by finding for each of them a task that was calling to them, something they had not yet done but that only they could do. In effect, he gave them a future. This allowed them to survive the present and turn their minds away from the past.

Frankl lived his teachings. After the liberation of Auschwitz he built a school of psychotherapy called Logotherapy, based on the human search for meaning. It was almost an inversion of the work of Freud. Freudian psychoanalysis had encouraged people to think about their very early past. Frankl taught people to build a future, or more precisely, to hear the future calling to them. Like Avraham, Frankl lived a long and good life, gaining worldwide recognition and dying at the age of 92.

Rabbi Jonathan Sacks

Analysis

- What areas of understanding of human nature and society do we now have that were unavailable to classical Jewish commentators? How can they aid our understanding of the text?
- What can we learn from this passage to help us understand the text?
- What further questions on the text do you have now that you have read this new take on the story?

INTEGRATING ḤOKHMA

He was 137 years old. He had been through two traumatic events involving the people most precious to him in the world. What does a man of 137 do – the Torah calls him "old and advanced in years" – after such a trauma and such a bereavement? We would not be surprised to find that he spent the rest of his days in sadness and memory.

Yet he did not. In one of the most extraordinary sequences of words in the Torah, his grief is described in a mere five Hebrew words: in English, "Avraham came to mourn for Sara and to weep for her." Then immediately we read, "And Avraham rose from his grief." From then on, he engaged in a flurry of activity with two aims in mind: first to buy a plot of land in which to bury Sara, second to find a wife for his son. Note that these correspond precisely to the two divine blessings: of land and descendants. Avraham did not wait for God to act. He understood one of the profoundest truths of Judaism: that God is waiting for us to act.

How did Avraham overcome the trauma and the grief? How do you survive almost losing your child and actually losing your life partner and still have the energy to keep going? What gave Avraham his resilience, his ability to survive, his spirit intact? He set the precedent: first build the future, and only then can you mourn the past. If you reverse the order, you will be held captive by the past. You will be unable to move on.

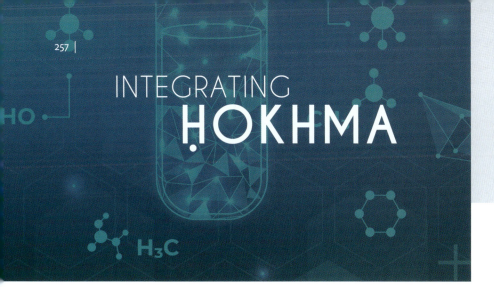

Something of this deep truth drove the work of one of the most remarkable survivors of the Holocaust, the psychotherapist Viktor Frankl. Frankl lived through Auschwitz, dedicating himself

tent to Betuel's house, locating on the way the woman worthy of Yitzḥak, and half of his mission has been accomplished. In this half, Eliezer is mentioned by the various titles a total of fourteen times, with the servant undergoing a strange metamorphosis: from "servant of Avraham" he has become a "master" in Rivka's words. But "master" is the unchanging title of Avraham throughout the story (nine times during the first half). Likewise, he is called "blessed one of God" by Lavan – and this title, too, is more appropriate for Avraham, about whom we read in the introduction to the story: "And God blessed Avraham with everything." In seven other places, he is called "the man" – a title also generally not used for a servant, but only for a free man.

This is not difficult to understand: the change in the servant's title results from Rivka's and Lavan's new perspectives as they arise. After all, they are not aware that the elderly and dignified man leading a train of ten camels laden with all kinds of good things and overseeing others as well (v. 32) is in fact a servant. From their point of view, Eliezer appears to be a rich merchant who happens to pass through their city. Therefore they address him as "master" and "blessed one of God" – titles of honor appropriate for a dignified stranger. Hence the Torah, too, adapts its language and calls him "the man," in keeping with Rivka's and Lavan's perception of him. This is what an important and unfamiliar person is called.

During the course of his long speech (vv. 35–49), Eliezer's title of "servant" is missing, simply because he is speaking about himself in the first person. However, he betrays a constant awareness of his status through his continual references to Avraham as his "master" (ten times).

The next time he is referred to as a "servant" is in verse 52, "And when Avraham's servant heard their words, he prostrated himself on the ground before God," and immediately thereafter in verse 53, "And the servant took out vessels of silver...." Both are parts of the narrative; now that his identity has become clear, the text also returns to referring to him by his true identity.

Rabbi Elchanan Samet

TAKING A LITERARY APPROACH

"Avraham's servant," the "elder of his household, in charge of all that was his," who stands at the center of the story of Yitzḥak's betrothal – is not identified by name! It seems that he is not an anonymous character whom we have not yet encountered; rather, it is someone who was mentioned many years ago in a conversation between Avraham and God, prior to the *brit bein habetarim*: "And Avram said: My Lord God, what will You give me, for I go childless, and the steward of my house is Eliezer of Damascus?" (Bereshit 15:2).

It is Eliezer who ran Avaham's household then (and he would therefore have been the natural heir, had Avraham not later had a son), and after this lengthy period he is called "the elder" of Avraham's house, "in charge of all that was his." This was the understanding of *Ḥazal* (Bereshit Rabba 59:9), and Rashi interprets 24:39 in the same vein. Why, then, does the *parasha* hide the identity of the servant throughout the story?

The absence of Eliezer's name allows us to follow the exchange of his titles throughout the course of the story, in order that we may learn from this how the servant functions in fulfilling his assignment in accordance with the changing circumstances. The change of circumstances includes a change in Eliezer's perspective as well as a change in the attitude toward him on the part of the characters in the story.

He is first mentioned here in 24:2, by a long and impressive title appropriate to his introduction at the story's beginning as its central hero: "And Avraham said to his servant, the elder of his household, in charge of all that was his...." From here onward, he is called "the servant" four more times by the text – in verses 5 and 9, which describe him in relation to Avraham his master, who makes him swear to fulfill his mission, and also in verses 10 and 17, which describe his efforts to do so.

Thereafter, Rivka becomes the active character in the story, until verse 28. Then the focus of action moves to Lavan, Rivka's brother. From verse 18 until verse 33 he is not called "servant" even once. Instead, other unexpected titles are used: Rivka refers to him as "my master" (v. 18), and then the text refers to him as "the man" a total of seven times until verse 33. Finally, an additional title is mentioned by Lavan: "blessed one of God" (v. 31).

Verse 33 concludes the first half of the story, during the course of which Eliezer has come from Avraham's

61 Then Rivka set off with her maids, riding on camels and following the man. The servant
62 took Rivka and went. Yitzḥak was just coming back from the direction of Be'er Laḥai
63 Ro'i, for he was then living in the Negev. He had gone out in the field toward evening to
64 meditate. Looking up, he saw – there were camels approaching. Rivka too looked up – and
65 saw Yitzḥak. She jumped down from the camel and asked the servant, "Who is that man
walking in the field toward us?" The servant replied, "That is my master." And she took her
66 67 veil and covered herself. The servant told Yitzḥak all he had done. And Yitzḥak brought her
into the tent of his mother Sara. He took Rivka as his wife, and he loved her. And Yitzḥak
was comforted after his mother's death.

UNLOCKING THE TEXT

- Where was Yitzḥak traveling?
- What was he doing in the field at evening time and why is that important for the narrative?
- Why did Rivka jump (or fall) off her camel when they first saw Yitzḥak?
- Why did she cover herself with a veil?
- Why did Yitzḥak bring Rivka into the tent of his mother Sara?
- Why does the Torah mention Yitzḥak's love for Rivka?
- How did Rivka bring comfort to Yitzḥak after the loss of his mother?

FINDING YOURSELF IN THE TEXT

- Do you believe in love at first sight?
- Have you ever met someone after hearing a lot about them? How did it feel?
- Do you ever think about what it will feel like to introduce your future spouse to your parents?

Consider using these questions as the basis for your own commentary or creative midrash.

How does reflecting on these firsthand experiences help you better understand the text?

סא וַתָּ֨קָם רִבְקָ֜ה וְנַעֲרֹתֶ֗יהָ וַתִּרְכַּ֙בְנָה֙ עַל־הַגְּמַלִּ֔ים וַתֵּלַ֖כְנָה אַחֲרֵ֣י הָאִ֑ישׁ וַיִּקַּ֥ח הָעֶ֛בֶד
סב סג אֶת־רִבְקָ֖ה וַיֵּלַֽךְ׃ וְיִצְחָק֙ בָּ֣א מִבּ֔וֹא בְּאֵ֥ר לַחַ֖י רֹאִ֑י וְה֥וּא יוֹשֵׁ֖ב בְּאֶ֥רֶץ הַנֶּֽגֶב׃ וַיֵּצֵ֥א
סד יִצְחָ֛ק לָשׂ֥וּחַ בַּשָּׂדֶ֖ה לִפְנ֣וֹת עָ֑רֶב וַיִּשָּׂ֤א עֵינָיו֙ וַיַּ֔רְא וְהִנֵּ֥ה גְמַלִּ֖ים בָּאִֽים׃ וַתִּשָּׂ֤א
סה רִבְקָה֙ אֶת־עֵינֶ֔יהָ וַתֵּ֖רֶא אֶת־יִצְחָ֑ק וַתִּפֹּ֖ל מֵעַ֥ל הַגָּמָֽל׃ וַתֹּ֣אמֶר אֶל־הָעֶ֗בֶד מִֽי־
הָאִ֤ישׁ הַלָּזֶה֙ הַהֹלֵ֤ךְ בַּשָּׂדֶה֙ לִקְרָאתֵ֔נוּ וַיֹּ֥אמֶר הָעֶ֖בֶד ה֣וּא אֲדֹנִ֑י וַתִּקַּ֥ח הַצָּעִ֖יף
סו סז וַתִּתְכָּֽס׃ וַיְסַפֵּ֥ר הָעֶ֖בֶד לְיִצְחָ֑ק אֵ֥ת כָּל־הַדְּבָרִ֖ים אֲשֶׁ֥ר עָשָֽׂה׃ וַיְבִאֶ֣הָ יִצְחָ֗ק
הָאֹ֙הֱלָה֙ שָׂרָ֣ה אִמּ֔וֹ וַיִּקַּ֧ח אֶת־רִבְקָ֛ה וַתְּהִי־ל֥וֹ לְאִשָּׁ֖ה וַיֶּאֱהָבֶ֑הָ וַיִּנָּחֵ֥ם יִצְחָ֖ק
אַחֲרֵ֥י אִמּֽוֹ׃

THEMES	RELATIONSHIPS AND LOVE	COVENANT	PRAYER

Episode 32: *Yitzḥak and Rivka Meet* – Bereshit 24:61–67

SUMMARY

Rivka and her entourage leave with the servant; Yitzḥak is on his way back from Be'er Laḥai Ro'i. When Yitzḥak is in the field he sees a caravan of camels coming his way; when Rivka sees Yitzḥak she dismounts her camel. Rivka asks the servant who the man in the field is, the servant identifies him as his master, and Rivka covers herself with a scarf. The servant tells Yitzḥak all that he did; Yitzḥak marries Rivka and loves her. It is only then that Yitzḥak is comforted following the death of his mother. With this, the potential for the continuity of the covenantal family is achieved for another generation, and the fulfillment of the promise God made to Avraham of future descendants becomes closer to a reality.

THE ART OF MIDRASH

The Meeting of Isaac and Rebecca
James Tissot (1896–1902)

Analysis

- Which elements of this image are directly mentioned in the text?
- Which elements of this image are not found in the text?
- What midrashic interpretation could be inferred from this image?

A QUESTION OF BIBLIODRAMA

TO RIVKA

- What was going through your mind as you left your home for the long journey to Canaan?
- What was your first impression of Yitzḥak?
- Did this change by the time you were married?
- How did it feel when Yitzḥak took you into Sara's tent?

TO YITZḤAK

- What was your first impression of Rivka?
- Did this change by the time you were married?
- How did it feel to take Rivka into your mother Sara's tent?
- Can you articulate the comfort you felt from Rivka after the death of your mother Sara?

TO ELIEZER, AVRAHAM'S SERVANT

- How did it feel to see Yitzḥak and Rivka meet and marry?

INTEGRATING ḤOKHMA

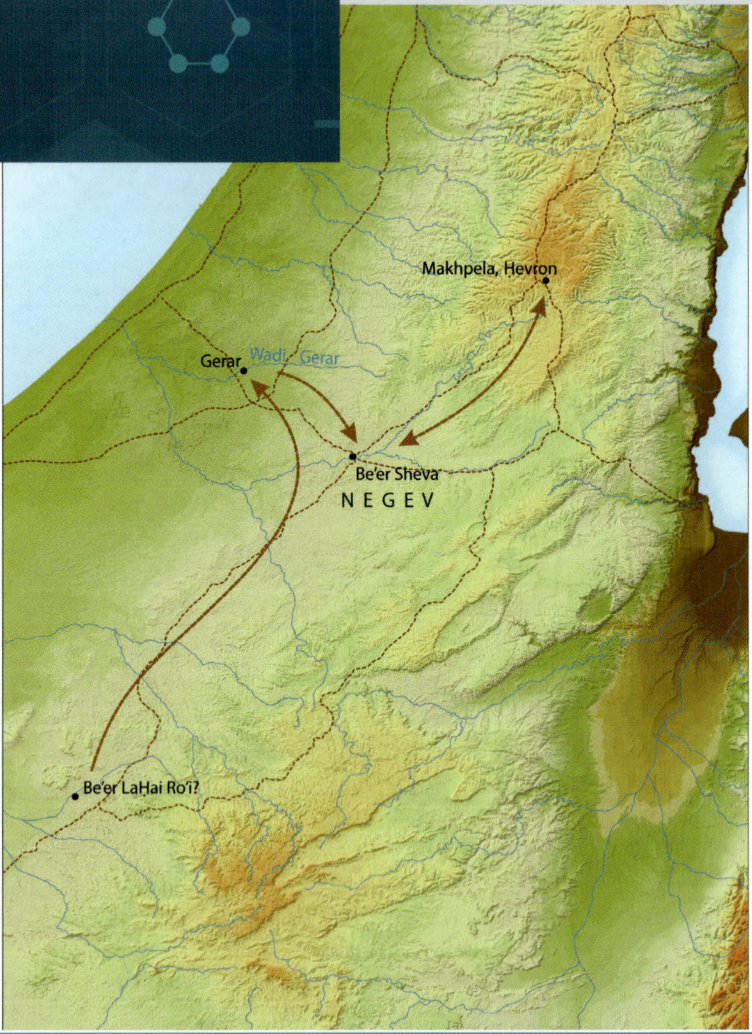

Yitzḥak's journeys in the land of Israel

Analysis

- What specific information do we now have that was unavailable to classical Jewish commentators? How can it aid our understanding of the text?
- What can we learn from this map that can help us understand the text?
- What further questions on the text do you have now that you have seen this map?

TAKING A LITERARY APPROACH

Of all the matriarchs in Bereshit, only Rivka is introduced as a full-fledged character outside the context of her relationship with her husband. Her bold, authoritative actions evoke the autonomous woman of Bereshit 1, the female half of the masterful *HaAdam*. But as Yitzḥak enters the narrative, there are hints that in the presence of a bonafide patriarch, Rivka will be recast in more traditional terms, as tent-dwelling wife and mother. In a narrative sequence that is similar to the complex portrayal of primordial woman, we now meet a second Rivka. This matriarch behaves in ways that are similar to the *Isha* of Bereshit 2. Like her, Rivka will be greatly valued by her husband. Yet at the same time she will be overshadowed by him, as he becomes God's – and the text's – primary focus.

In Rivka's initial encounter with Yitzḥak he has "gone out" (*y-tz-a*) to the *sadeh*, the field. In "going out" to the field, Yitzḥak follows the patriarchal model set down by Avraham who stood at the doorway to his tent, waiting to engage with the world around him. Previously, it was Rivka who "went out" to meet others (Bereshit 24:15, 45). But now, upon meeting Yitzḥak, she is "brought in" to the more circumscribed – and traditionally matriarchal – environment, the tent (24:67).

In going out to the field, Yitzḥak assumes two traditionally patriarchal roles: engaging with the outside world and with God. It appears that as Yitzḥak asserts himself as patriarch, Rivka grows more matriarchal. Not only will Rivka physically move from the public domain to the interior spaces of the tent, we will soon discover that she will assume a background position in matters of the spirit as well.

We may detect subtle literary hints of Rivka's changing stature in a close reading of her first encounter with Yitzḥak. Whereas Rivka first "arose" to mount her camel (24:61), now, in meeting Yitzḥak, she "falls down" from her camel (24:64). Perhaps there is special significance in her ascent to, and fall from, this particular animal. In her first appearance, Rivka's patriarchal qualities are demonstrated by her alacrity and determination in attending to the servant's camels. Now, upon meeting Yitzḥak, Rivka can no longer maintain her bearings atop the camel. Her fall symbolizes a shift away from the bold independence of her early narrative.

Rivka's veil may present yet another symbol of her changing status. Until now, Rivka has been a visible and vocal presence in her family and in the public sphere. Now, upon learning Yitzḥak's identity, Rivka covers herself with a veil. Like Sara, who was frequently unseen (18:9) and unheard (12:13–14) by her husband and by others, Rivka now engages in a symbolic act of self-effacement in the presence of the patriarch.

intimacy between her and Yitzḥak.

It is noteworthy that Rivka's trajectory parallels that of the Bible's first woman. In Rivka's first appearance, she is capable and authoritative, like *HaAdam* in Bereshit 1. But then Rivka begins to resemble the *Isha* of Bereshit 2. Like the *Isha*, Rivka is dependent on her husband for communication with God. Yet like her forebear in the Garden of Eden, Rivka is appreciated by her husband in profound ways.

Perhaps encouraged by Yitzḥak's love and by his inclusion of her in his prayers, Rivka initiates an encounter with God that breaks the mold of godly exclusion cast by both Sara and the *Isha* of the Garden of Eden. When her twin sons struggle within her womb, a distraught Rivka goes to "inquire of the Lord" (25:22–23). In an even more astonishing development, "the Lord answered her." For the first and only time in the annals of Bereshit, God delivers a verbal response to a woman in need.

Judy Klitsner

With time, as Rivka inhabits her mother-in-law's tent, she will come to resemble her more and more. Like Sara, Rivka will be barren (24:67). And like Sara, she will defer to her husband when it becomes necessary to appeal to God:

> Yitzḥak was forty years old when he married Rivka, daughter of Betuel the Aramean of Padan Aram, sister of Lavan the Aramean. Yitzḥak pleaded with the Lord opposite his wife, because she was barren; and the Lord responded to his plea, and his wife Rivka conceived. (25:20–21)

In this passage, a new word for the patriarch's prayer appears: *vaye'etar*. This word is then echoed in God's response, *vaye'ater*, from the same root *a-t-r*. The verb repetition suggests a common language and natural communication between God and His male prophet, in which Yitzḥak alone pleads with God and he alone is answered. These verses mark the continuation of early patterns, in which biblical woman is silent while communication with the Divine is carried out exclusively by the patriarch.

Yet despite Rivka's retreat to the more limited role of the traditional matriarch, she enjoys greater devotion from her husband than we have previously seen. Unlike Avraham who never prayed for Sara, Yitzḥak uses his status as mediator between God and woman in an inclusive way, in this case praying for a child in Rivka's presence (25:21). In addition, Rivka is twice called *ishto*, "his wife," suggesting Yitzḥak's exclusive attachment to her. Of all three patriarchs, only Yitzḥak is monogamous, despite the couple's twenty infertile years together (25:20, 26). Yitzḥak's commitment is accompanied by the first biblical statement of affection by a man for a woman: Yitzḥak "loves" Rivka (24:67).

In this context, we may revisit Yitzḥak's escorting Rivka into Sara's tent, an act that in some ways signals a constricting of Rivka's role. In addition to connoting limitation, this act suggests a deepening of the emotional bond between husband and wife. When Yitzḥak ushers Rivka into Sara's tent he finds "comfort after his mother's death" (24:67). By replacing Sara with Rivka as the primary woman in his life, Yitzḥak enacts the promise of Bereshit 2. "Hence a man leaves his father and mother and clings to his wife, so that they become one flesh" (2:24). Seen this way, Rivka's entry into the tent is an expression of

25 1 2 Avraham took another wife, whose name was Ketura. She bore him Zimran, Yokshan,
3 Medan, Midyan, Yishbak, and Shuaḥ; Yokshan was the father of Sheva and Dedan. The
4 sons of Dedan were Ashurim, Letushim, and Leumim. The sons of Midyan were Eifa, Efer,
5 Ḥanokh, Avida, and Eldaa: all these were descendants of Ketura. Avraham left all that was
6 his to Yitzḥak – while he was still living he gave gifts to the sons of his concubines and sent
them eastward, away from his son Yitzḥak, to the land of the East.

UNLOCKING THE TEXT

- Why did Avraham feel the need to remarry after the death of Sara?
- Who was Ketura?
- Why did Yitzḥak alone inherit Avraham's wealth?
- What is the difference between Yitzḥak inheriting wealth after the death of Avraham, and his other sons receiving gifts while he was still alive?
- Why does the Torah emphasize that these were the sons of concubines?
- Why did Avraham send these children away to the land of the East?

FINDING YOURSELF IN THE TEXT

- Have you ever thought about what you will inherit from your parents? Is that important to you?
- Is an inheritance only financial or do we inherit other things from our parents?
- Does your family have a family tree? Do you think having one is important?

Consider using these questions as the basis for your own commentary or creative midrash.

How does reflecting on these firsthand experiences help you better understand the text?

כה א ב וַיֹּסֶף אַבְרָהָם וַיִּקַּח אִשָּׁה וּשְׁמָהּ קְטוּרָה׃ וַתֵּלֶד לוֹ אֶת־זִמְרָן וְאֶת־יָקְשָׁן וְאֶת־ כב ששי
ג מְדָן וְאֶת־מִדְיָן וְאֶת־יִשְׁבָּק וְאֶת־שׁוּחַ׃ וְיָקְשָׁן יָלַד אֶת־שְׁבָא וְאֶת־דְּדָן וּבְנֵי דְדָן
ד הָיוּ אַשּׁוּרִם וּלְטוּשִׁם וּלְאֻמִּים׃ וּבְנֵי מִדְיָן עֵיפָה וָעֵפֶר וַחֲנֹךְ וַאֲבִידָע וְאֶלְדָּעָה
ה ו כָּל־אֵלֶּה בְּנֵי קְטוּרָה׃ וַיִּתֵּן אַבְרָהָם אֶת־כָּל־אֲשֶׁר־לוֹ לְיִצְחָק׃ וְלִבְנֵי הַפִּילַגְשִׁים
אֲשֶׁר לְאַבְרָהָם נָתַן אַבְרָהָם מַתָּנֹת וַיְשַׁלְּחֵם מֵעַל יִצְחָק בְּנוֹ בְּעוֹדֶנּוּ חַי קֵדְמָה
אֶל־אֶרֶץ קֶדֶם׃

THEMES	RELATIONSHIPS AND LOVE	COVENANT	PEOPLEHOOD

Episode 33: *Avraham's Other Children* – Bereshit 25:1–6

SUMMARY

Following the marriage of Yitzḥak and Rivka, before the Torah discusses their descendants at length, it provides a short summary of the last years of Avraham's life. Although he continued to live for more than thirty years after Yitzḥak's marriage, few details are related about those years, as the focus of the narrative switches to Yitzḥak. The stage of Avraham's life in which he built the foundation for the Jewish people is complete. He now establishes many additional families, and thereby begins to fulfill his destiny as the father of many nations. Avraham then sends his many sons, who will become heads of nations, to the east, together with gifts, while everything else in his possession he gives to Yitzḥak.

THE ART OF MIDRASH

Family of Abraham
Venice Haggadah (1609)

Analysis

- Which elements of this image are directly mentioned in the text?
- Which elements of this image are not found in the text?
- What midrashic interpretation could be inferred from this image?

A QUESTION OF BIBLIODRAMA

TO AVRAHAM

- Why did you take another wife after the death of Sara?
- Do you love the children Ketura gave you?
- Why did you send them away to the land of the East?
- Why did you give your entire inheritance to Yitzḥak?

TO KETURA

- How do you know Avraham?
- How does it feel to become part of Avraham's life at this late stage in his story?
- How do you feel about his decision to give Yitzḥak his inheritance?

TO YITZḤAK

- How do you feel about Avraham taking another wife after the death of your mother Sara?
- How do you feel about your new half-siblings?

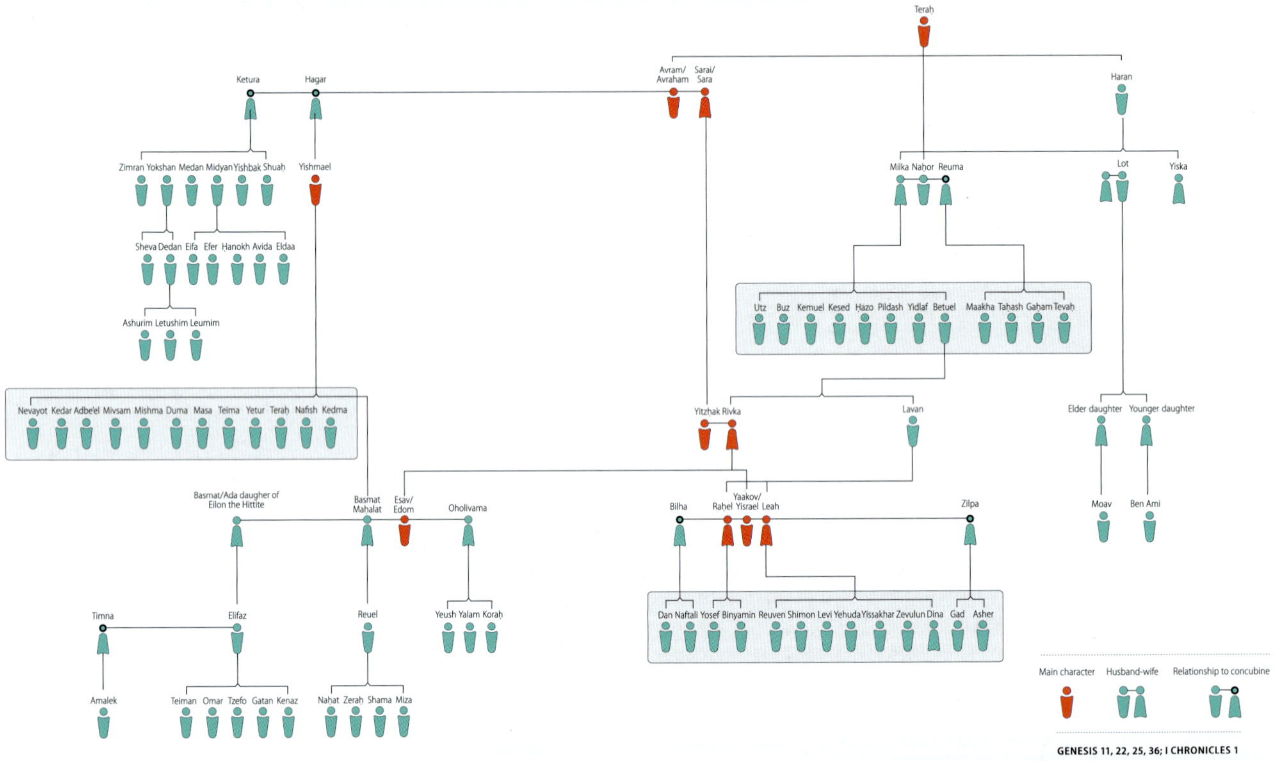

Teraḥ, Avraham, and Yitzḥak's descendants

influence is also strongly felt – it is she who demands the expulsion of Yishmael and it is her potent memory that serves as the backdrop for the sending away of Ketura's children. And in both episodes, it is a coming-of-age event in the life of Yitzḥak that precipitates the expulsion: first Yitzḥak's weaning as he leaves infanthood behind and begins his formal induction into the teachings of his parents, and later his marriage to Rivka, as he prepares to take on Avraham's role as progenitor of the nation that will make God's service their banner.

Rabbi Michael Hattin

TAKING A LITERARY APPROACH

Though Avraham still has many good years of life ahead of him (thirty-five to be exact), the Torah now proleptically records his death in order to allow the focus of the narrative to shift to the story of Yitzḥak. But prior to that premature death notice, the Torah indicates that Avraham remarries and (unexpectedly?) fathers a brood of children. While it is not unusual for a widow/widower to remarry in order to preclude the loneliness and helplessness that old age often confers, it is unusual that the patriarch has six more sons and ten grandchildren in quick succession, whereas in all of his previous 140 or so years he had but two sons, and each of those by a separate wife.

The Torah is unusually silent concerning the marriage of Avraham to Ketura. The text tells us nothing about her origins and nothing about her descendants, and while some of her children and grandchildren father nations that are known to us from later passages in the Tanakh, here there is only reticence. But this much we do know: the offspring from Avraham's marriage to Ketura were numerous. Perhaps then, the intent of the Torah is to indicate that God's earlier promise to the patriarch, vouchsafed to him at the time that the command of circumcision was introduced, was eminently fulfilled: "As for Me, behold My covenant is with you and you shall become the father of a multitude of nations. Your name shall no longer be called Avram; rather your name shall be Avraham, for I have made you into the father of a multitude of nations" (Bereshit 17:4–5).

Of course, here we assume that this "multitude of nations" is not a reference to the diverse tribes of Israel (as indeed some of the commentaries maintain), but rather to the related families that together constitute the offspring

of Avraham from his children other than Yitzḥak. What is perhaps more significant, however, is not the report of Avraham's remarriage and numerous new offspring but rather what transpires next: "Avraham gave all that he possessed to Yitzḥak. As for the children of his concubines, Avraham gave gifts, and he sent them away from Yitzḥak his son toward the east, to the land of the nations of the east" (25:5–6). This dual act of appointing Yitzḥak as sole heir while simultaneously sending away his half-siblings constitutes the last reported deed of Avraham during his lifetime.

There is a parallel to the story of Hagar and Yishmael in chapter 21. In both episodes, the former from Yitzḥak's early years and the latter from his adulthood, half-siblings are banished or otherwise sent away by Avraham. Yishmael, his son from Hagar, and the numerous children from Ketura are all sent away, the one to the west and the others to the east. In both cases, Avraham seeks in so doing to solidify the supremacy of Yitzḥak as true heir and successor. In both events, there is a statement of divine approval appended to the proceedings – in the case of Yishmael that approval is communicated on the eve of his banishment, and in the case of the children of Ketura it is communicated in the form of a "divine blessing" that, although it takes place much later temporally (after the death of Avraham), is nevertheless mentioned by the Torah in the context of the episode. In both cases, Sara's

וִשְׁמָהּ קְטוּרָה: וַתֵּלֶד לוֹ אֶת
בָּק וְאֶת־שׁוּחַ: וְיָקְשָׁן יָלַד אֶת־שְׁבָ
לְאֻמִּים: וּבְנֵי מִדְיָן עֵיפָה וָעֵפֶר וַחֲנֹ
תֵּן אַבְרָהָם אֶת־כָּל־אֲשֶׁר־לוֹ לְיִצְ
הֶם מַתָּנֹת וַיְשַׁלְּחֵם מֵעַל יִצְחָק

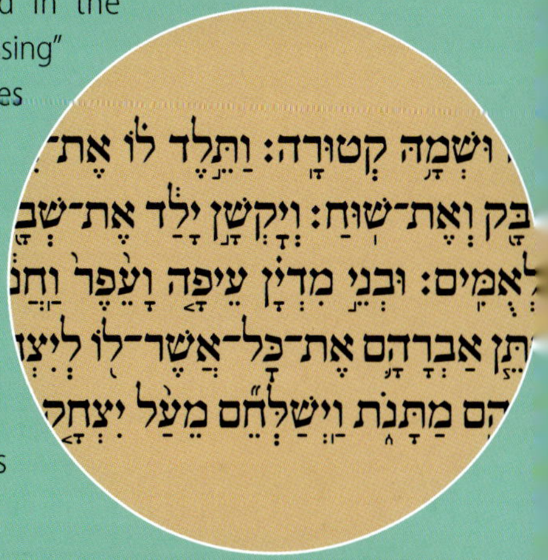

7 These are the days, the years of Avraham's life: he lived one hundred and seventy-five years.
8 Avraham breathed his last and died in his ripe old age, aged and satisfied, and was gathered
9 to his people. His sons, Yitzḥak and Yishmael, buried him in the cave of Makhpela, near
10 Mamre, in the field of Efron son of Tzoḥar the Hittite – the field Avraham had bought from
11 the Hittites. There Avraham was buried with Sara his wife. After Avraham's death, God
blessed Yitzḥak his son, who was then living near Be'er Laḥai Ro'i.
12 These are the descendants of Avraham's son Yishmael, whom Sara's maidservant, Hagar the
13 Egyptian, bore to Avraham. The names of Yishmael's sons, in the order of their birth, are:
14 15 Nevayot – Yishmael's firstborn, Kedar, Adbe'el, Mivsam, Mishma, Duma, Massa, Ḥadad,
16 Teima, Yetur, Nafish, and Kedma. These were Yishmael's sons, and these are their names
17 by their villages and encampments: twelve princes and their tribes. These were the years
of Yishmael's life: he lived one hundred and thirty-seven years. He breathed his last and
18 died, and was gathered to his people. The Ishmaelites dwelt from Ḥavila to Shur, up against
Egypt, all the way to Assyria, settling up against all their brothers.

UNLOCKING THE TEXT

- What does the Torah want us to understand by telling us that Avraham dies in his ripe old age?
- What was Avraham satisfied about?
- Where has Yishmael been during this time?
- Why does Yishmael join Yitzḥak in burying Avraham? What about Avraham's other children?
- Why does the Torah remind us about the story when Avraham bought the cave of Makhpela?
- What did God bless Yitzḥak with?
- Why does the Torah list the descendants of Yishmael?

FINDING YOURSELF IN THE TEXT

- Have you ever argued with your sibling and not spoken to them for a while?
- Did you make up eventually? How did it feel?
- Does love and concern for your parents bring you closer to your siblings?

Consider using these questions as the basis for your own commentary or creative midrash.

How does reflecting on these firsthand experiences help you better understand the text?

ז וְאֵ֗לֶּה יְמֵ֛י שְׁנֵֽי־חַיֵּ֥י אַבְרָהָ֖ם אֲשֶׁר־חָ֑י מְאַ֥ת שָׁנָ֛ה וְשִׁבְעִ֥ים שָׁנָ֖ה וְחָמֵ֥שׁ שָׁנִֽים׃
ח ט וַיִּגְוַ֨ע וַיָּ֧מָת אַבְרָהָ֛ם בְּשֵׂיבָ֥ה טוֹבָ֖ה זָקֵ֣ן וְשָׂבֵ֑עַ וַיֵּאָ֖סֶף אֶל־עַמָּֽיו׃ וַיִּקְבְּר֨וּ אֹת֜וֹ
יִצְחָ֤ק וְיִשְׁמָעֵאל֙ בָּנָ֔יו אֶל־מְעָרַ֖ת הַמַּכְפֵּלָ֑ה אֶל־שְׂדֵ֞ה עֶפְרֹ֤ן בֶּן־צֹ֙חַר֙ הַֽחִתִּ֔י אֲשֶׁ֖ר
י עַל־פְּנֵ֥י מַמְרֵֽא׃ הַשָּׂדֶ֛ה אֲשֶׁר־קָנָ֥ה אַבְרָהָ֖ם מֵאֵ֣ת בְּנֵי־חֵ֑ת שָׁ֛מָּה קֻבַּ֥ר אַבְרָהָ֖ם
יא וְשָׂרָ֥ה אִשְׁתּֽוֹ׃ וַיְהִ֗י אַחֲרֵי֙ מ֣וֹת אַבְרָהָ֔ם וַיְבָ֥רֶךְ אֱלֹהִ֖ים אֶת־יִצְחָ֣ק בְּנ֑וֹ וַיֵּ֣שֶׁב יִצְחָ֔ק
עִם־בְּאֵ֥ר לַחַ֖י רֹאִֽי׃
יב וְאֵ֛לֶּה תֹּלְדֹ֥ת יִשְׁמָעֵ֖אל בֶּן־אַבְרָהָ֑ם אֲשֶׁ֨ר יָלְדָ֜ה הָגָ֧ר הַמִּצְרִ֛ית שִׁפְחַ֥ת שָׂרָ֖ה שביעי
יג לְאַבְרָהָֽם׃ וְאֵ֗לֶּה שְׁמוֹת֙ בְּנֵ֣י יִשְׁמָעֵ֔אל בִּשְׁמֹתָ֖ם לְתוֹלְדֹתָ֑ם בְּכֹ֤ר יִשְׁמָעֵאל֙ נְבָיֹ֔ת
יד טו וְקֵדָ֥ר וְאַדְבְּאֵ֖ל וּמִבְשָֽׂם׃ וּמִשְׁמָ֥ע וְדוּמָ֖ה וּמַשָּֽׂא׃ חֲדַ֣ד וְתֵימָ֔א יְט֥וּר נָפִ֖ישׁ וָקֵֽדְמָה׃
טז אֵ֣לֶּה הֵ֞ם בְּנֵ֣י יִשְׁמָעֵאל֮ וְאֵ֣לֶּה שְׁמֹתָם֒ בְּחַצְרֵיהֶ֖ם וּבְטִֽירֹתָ֑ם שְׁנֵים־עָשָׂ֥ר נְשִׂיאִ֖ם מפטיר
יז לְאֻמֹּתָֽם׃ וְאֵ֗לֶּה שְׁנֵי֙ חַיֵּ֣י יִשְׁמָעֵ֔אל מְאַ֥ת שָׁנָ֛ה וּשְׁלֹשִׁ֥ים שָׁנָ֖ה וְשֶׁ֣בַע שָׁנִ֑ים וַיִּגְוַ֣ע
יח וַיָּ֔מָת וַיֵּאָ֖סֶף אֶל־עַמָּֽיו׃ וַיִּשְׁכְּנ֨וּ מֵֽחֲוִילָ֜ה עַד־שׁ֗וּר אֲשֶׁר֙ עַל־פְּנֵ֣י מִצְרַ֔יִם בֹּאֲכָ֖ה
אַשּׁ֑וּרָה עַל־פְּנֵ֥י כָל־אֶחָ֖יו נָפָֽל׃

THEMES	RELATIONSHIPS AND LOVE	COVENANT	PEOPLEHOOD

Episode 34: *Avraham's Death* – Bereshit 25:7–18

SUMMARY

In the final episode of this *parasha*, the Torah relates the death of Avraham at the age of 175, and his burial by Yitzḥak and Yishmael in the cave of Makhpela. Following Avraham's death Yitzḥak goes to live in Be'er Laḥai Ro'i and is blessed by God. Yishmael, Hagar's son, has twelve children who become princes with palaces and courts. He dies at the age of 137 and his descendants spread out over the wilderness of the south.

THE ART OF MIDRASH

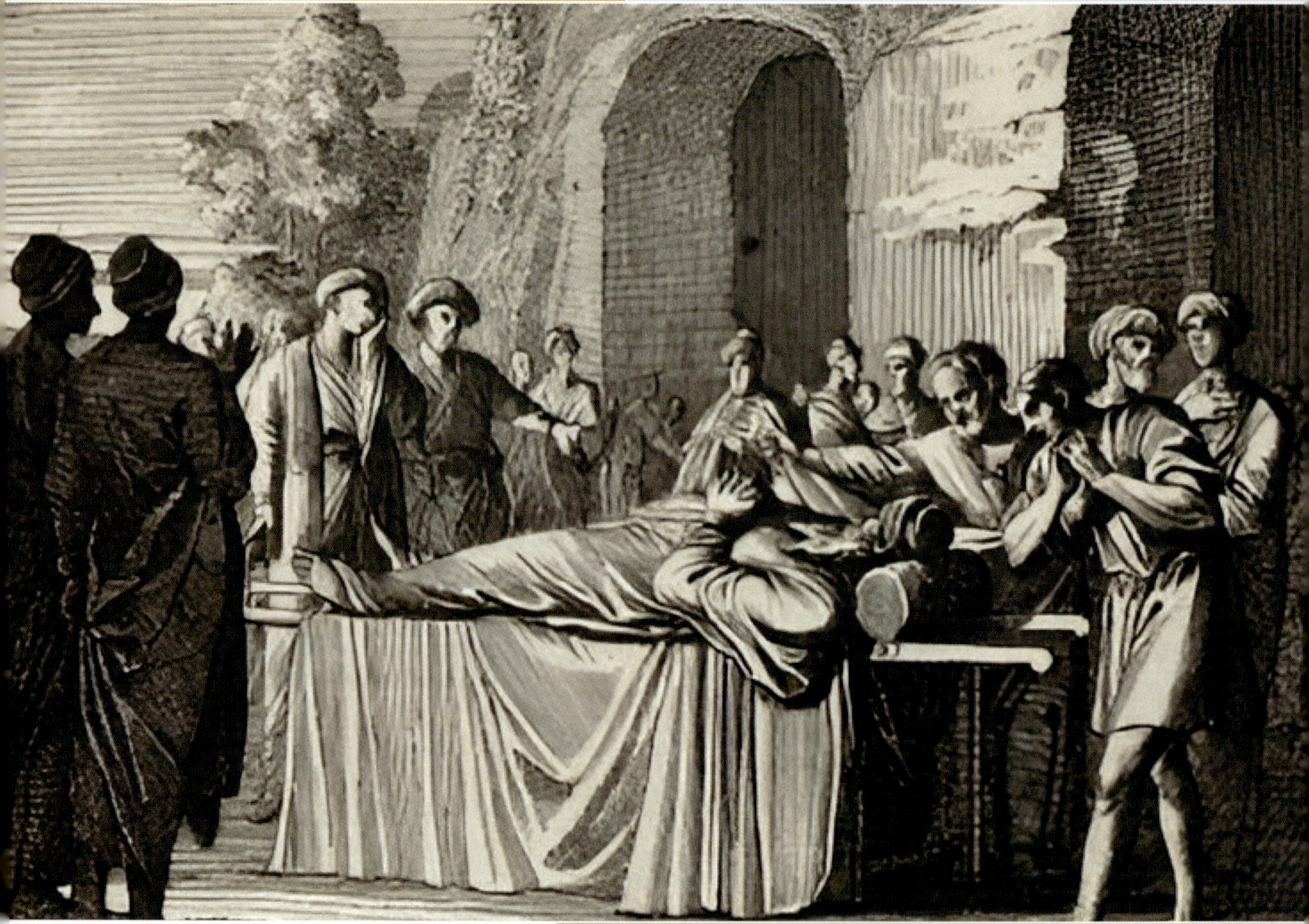

Burial of Abraham
Jan Luyken (1712)

Analysis

- Which elements of this image are directly mentioned in the text?
- Which elements of this image are not found in the text?
- What midrashic interpretation could be inferred from this image?

A QUESTION OF BIBLIODRAMA

TO YITZḤAK

- What are you feeling as you bury your father Avraham?
- How does it feel to see Yishmael again? What are your feelings toward him?
- Was it difficult or did it feel natural to bury your father together with him?

TO YISHMAEL

- What are you feeling as you bury your father Avraham?
- How does it feel to see Yitzḥak again? What are your feelings toward him?
- Was it difficult or did it feel natural to bury your father together with him?

בְּאֵר לַחַי רֹאִי

BE'ER LAḤAI RO'I

Be'er Laḥai Ro'i is an oasis in the western Negev on the way to Egypt, "near a spring of water in the desert, the spring by the road to Shur… between Kadesh and Bered."[1] It appears three times in Bereshit.

Some identify this site with the spring Ein Ovdat, while others connect it to the place known in Arabic as Bir Asluj, where Kibbutz Revivim was established.

1 | Bereshit 16:7, 14.

Analysis

- What areas of archaeological, geographical, and historical knowledge do we have now that were unavailable to classical Jewish commentators? How can they aid our understanding of the text?
- How can this information about Be'er Laḥai Ro'i help us understand the text?
- What further questions on the text do you have now that you have read this new information and research?

INTEGRATING ḤOKHMA

Ein Ovdat

TAKING A LITERARY APPROACH

After the binding of Yitzḥak, Avraham returned to Be'er Sheva. The death and burial of Sara take place at Ḥevron. We would expect to find Yitzḥak at one or other of these two places. However, two episodes locate him elsewhere. When Avraham's servant returns, bringing Rivka to become Yitzḥak's wife, we read: "Yitzḥak had just come from Be'er Laḥai Ro'i, for he was living in the Negev" (Bereshit 24:62). After Avraham's funeral we read again: "After the death of Avraham, God blessed his son Yitzḥak. At that time, Yitzḥak was living near Be'er Laḥai Ro'i" (25:11). What is this place and what was Yitzḥak doing there?

Looking back, we discover that Be'er Laḥai Ro'i appears in Bereshit 16 when Hagar first fled into the desert. Having been met and blessed by an angel, she gave the place a name: "So she called the name of the Lord who spoke to her 'You are the God of seeing,' for she said, 'Did I not have a vision after He saw me?' That is why the well was called Be'er Laḥai Ro'i ['the well of the living One who sees me']; it is still there, between Kadesh and Bered (16:13–14). Be'er Laḥai Ro'i is *the place of Hagar*. Teasing out the implications of this unexpected turn in the plot, the Sages said: "On seeing that his father had sent to fetch him a wife, Yitzḥak said, 'Can I live with her while my father lives alone? I will go and return Hagar to him.'" Yitzḥak had been on a mission of reconciliation to reunite Hagar and Avraham.

The Rabbis made a further interpretive leap. One device of Midrash is to identify unknown with known biblical characters. Who then was Ketura? Said the Rabbis: Hagar herself! Why then was she called Ketura? Because, said the Sages, "her acts were as fragrant as incense [*ketoret*]."

A complete counter-narrative is taking shape. Whether of his own accord or at the prompting of Yitzḥak, Avraham took Hagar back and gave her a place of honor in his household. What does this midrash tell us about how the Rabbis read the text? It tells us that they felt there was something morally amiss about the story as it stood. Hagar, obedient to her mistress's wishes, was sent away. So too was Yishmael, the child born at Sara's request.

The story beneath the story, hinted at by these three discrepant details, is that neither Avraham nor Yitzḥak made their peace with the banishment of handmaid and child. As long as Sara was alive, they could do nothing about it, respecting her feelings as God had commanded Avraham to do. But once Sara was no longer alive, they could engage in an act of reconciliation. That is how Yitzḥak and Yishmael came to be together when Avraham died.

Rabbi Jonathan Sacks

תולדת

Toledot

Parasha Overview

Toledot tells the story of Yitzḥak and Rivka's twin sons, Yaakov and Esav, who struggle in the womb and seem destined to clash throughout their lives and those of their descendants. It contains two great passages: the birth and childhood of the boys, and the scene in which Yaakov, at Rivka's behest, dresses in Esav's clothes and takes his blessing from their father Yitzḥak, now blind. Between them is a narrative about Yitzḥak and Rivka going to Gerar because of famine, very similar to that told about Avraham and Sara in Bereshit 20.

Episodes

35.	**The Birth of Esav and Yaakov and the Selling of the Birthright**	25:19–34
36.	**Yitzḥak Stays in Canaan**	26:1–33
37.	**Yaakov Tricks Yitzḥak for the Blessing**	26:34–27:29
38.	**Esav Mourns His Lost Birthright**	27:30–40
39.	**Yaakov Flees and Esav Marries**	27:41–28:9

Parasha Stats

- 5,426 letters
- 1,432 words
- 106 verses
- 173 lines in a sefer Torah

19 20 This is the story of Yitzḥak, son of Avraham: Avraham was Yitzḥak's father. When Yitzḥak
was forty he married Rivka, daughter of Betuel the Aramean of Padan Aram, sister of
21 Lavan the Aramean. And Yitzḥak pleaded with the LORD on behalf of his wife, for she was
22 childless. The LORD granted his plea and Rivka became pregnant. But the children clashed
within her. She said, "If this is so, why am I living?" So she went to inquire of the LORD.
23 The LORD said to her, "Two nations are inside your womb; two peoples are to part from
24 you. People will overpower people, and the greater shall the younger serve."[1] When the
25 time came for her to give birth, there were twins in her womb. The first came out red. His
26 whole body was like a hairy cloak, so they named him Esav.[2] Then his brother emerged,
his hand grasping Esav's heel, so he named him Yaakov.[3] Yitzḥak was sixty years old when
27 they were born. The boys grew up. Esav became a skilled hunter, a man of the field, while
28 Yaakov was an innocent man who stayed among the tents. Yitzḥak loved Esav because he
29 ate of his game, but Rivka loved Yaakov. Once when Yaakov was cooking a stew, Esav came

1 | The ambiguity as to who will serve whom reflects the Hebrew.

2 | The name Esav may bear the sense of "covered" or "concealed" (cf. Ovadya 1:6). The word *se'ar* ("hair") resonates with Se'ir, the land inhabited by Esav's descendants.

3 | The name Yaakov resonates with *akev* ("heel").

UNLOCKING THE TEXT

- Why does the Torah remind us who Yitzḥak and Rivka's fathers were?
- How does Yitzḥak's prayer for children compare to Avraham's prayer in Bereshit 15:2–3? What might explain the differences?
- Rivka asks, "If this is so, why am I living?" What does she mean?
- What is the meaning of the prediction Rivka received? Who will serve whom?
- Why were the boys' given names connected to their births?
- What does it mean that Yaakov was "innocent and stayed among the tents"?
- Did Yitzḥak not love Yaakov? Did Rivka not love Esav?
- Why did they have favorites? Why these favorites?
- When was Esav called Edom, by whom, and why?
- What does the "birthright" refer to?

FINDING YOURSELF IN THE TEXT

- Are there favorites in your family? How does that make you feel?
- Are you different from your siblings? How so, if you have the same genes and upbringing?
- Do you know any twins (or are you a twin)? How is it different from being a regular sibling?

Consider using these questions as the basis for your own commentary or creative midrash.

How does reflecting on these firsthand experiences help you better understand the text?

יט כ וְאֵ֛לֶּה תּוֹלְדֹ֥ת יִצְחָ֖ק בֶּן־אַבְרָהָ֑ם אַבְרָהָ֖ם הוֹלִ֥יד אֶת־יִצְחָֽק׃ וַיְהִ֤י יִצְחָק֙ בֶּן־ כג תולדת
אַרְבָּעִ֣ים שָׁנָ֔ה בְּקַחְתּ֣וֹ אֶת־רִבְקָ֗ה בַּת־בְּתוּאֵל֙ הָאֲרַמִּ֔י מִפַּדַּ֖ן אֲרָ֑ם אֲח֛וֹת לָבָ֥ן
כא הָאֲרַמִּ֖י ל֥וֹ לְאִשָּֽׁה׃ וַיֶּעְתַּ֨ר יִצְחָ֤ק לַֽיהוה֙ לְנֹ֣כַח אִשְׁתּ֔וֹ כִּ֥י עֲקָרָ֖ה הִ֑וא וַיֵּעָ֤תֶר לוֹ֙
כב יהוה֔ וַתַּ֖הַר רִבְקָ֥ה אִשְׁתּֽוֹ׃ וַיִּתְרֹֽצְצ֤וּ הַבָּנִים֙ בְּקִרְבָּ֔הּ וַתֹּ֣אמֶר אִם־כֵּ֔ן לָ֥מָּה זֶּ֖ה אָנֹ֑כִי
כג וַתֵּ֖לֶךְ לִדְרֹ֥שׁ אֶת־יהוה׃ וַיֹּאמֶר֩ יהוה֨ לָ֜הּ שְׁנֵ֤י גיים֙ בְּבִטְנֵ֔ךְ וּשְׁנֵ֣י לְאֻמִּ֔ים מִמֵּעַ֖יִךְ גּוֹיִם֙
כד יִפָּרֵ֑דוּ וּלְאֹם֙ מִלְאֹ֣ם יֶֽאֱמָ֔ץ וְרַ֖ב יַעֲבֹ֥ד צָעִֽיר׃ וַיִּמְלְא֥וּ יָמֶ֖יהָ לָלֶ֑דֶת וְהִנֵּ֥ה תוֹמִ֖ם
כה כו בְּבִטְנָֽהּ׃ וַיֵּצֵ֤א הָרִאשׁוֹן֙ אַדְמוֹנִ֔י כֻּלּ֖וֹ כְּאַדֶּ֣רֶת שֵׂעָ֑ר וַיִּקְרְא֥וּ שְׁמ֖וֹ עֵשָֽׂו׃ וְאַֽחֲרֵי־
כֵ֞ן יָצָ֣א אָחִ֗יו וְיָד֤וֹ אֹחֶ֙זֶת֙ בַּעֲקֵ֣ב עֵשָׂ֔ו וַיִּקְרָ֥א שְׁמ֖וֹ יַעֲקֹ֑ב וְיִצְחָ֛ק בֶּן־שִׁשִּׁ֥ים שָׁנָ֖ה
כז בְּלֶ֥דֶת אֹתָֽם׃ וַֽיִּגְדְּלוּ֙ הַנְּעָרִ֔ים וַיְהִ֣י עֵשָׂ֗ו אִ֛ישׁ יֹדֵ֥עַ צַ֖יִד אִ֣ישׁ שָׂדֶ֑ה וְיַעֲקֹב֙ אִ֣ישׁ תָּ֔ם
כח כט יֹשֵׁ֖ב אֹהָלִֽים׃ וַיֶּאֱהַ֥ב יִצְחָ֛ק אֶת־עֵשָׂ֖ו כִּי־צַ֣יִד בְּפִ֑יו וְרִבְקָ֖ה אֹהֶ֥בֶת אֶת־יַעֲקֹֽב׃ וַיָּ֥זֶד

THEMES | COVENANT | RELATIONSHIPS AND LOVE | PRAYER

Episode 35: *The Birth of Esav and Yaakov and the Selling of the Birthright* – Bereshit 25:19–34

SUMMARY

After enumerating Yishmael's descendants in brief, the Torah focuses at length on the generations of Yitzḥak. Here, the description is not merely a list of descendants but the story of Yitzḥak's life, especially the issue of which of his two sons, Yaakov or Esav, will be his successor. Although the incident depicted in this chapter involving the sale of the birthright is of little importance to Esav, Yaakov considers it a matter of great significance, as it signals his position as the future leader of the family after Yitzḥak's death.

As the boys grow, their differences become clear – Esav is a man of the field, a hunter, while Yaakov is a simple shepherd. Yitzḥak prefers Esav because he provides fresh meat; Rivka prefers Yaakov. One day, as Yaakov is preparing lentil stew, Esav returns exhausted from the hunt. He asks Yaakov for some of the reddish food, and Yaakov asks him to sell the birthright. Esav mocks the birthright as meaningless, and when pressed by Yaakov, swears to affirm the transfer. Yaakov provides Esav with bread and stew, which Esav eats in haste. He then leaves.

30 in exhausted from the field. He said to Yaakov, "Let me gulp down some of that red stuff.
31 I am starved!" – that is how he came to be named Edom.[4] Yaakov said, "First sell me your
32 33 birthright." And Esav said, "Look, I am about to die. What use to me is a birthright?" But
34 Yaakov said, "Swear to me first." So he swore, and sold Yaakov his birthright. Yaakov then
gave Esav bread and lentil stew. He ate, drank, got up, and left. Thus – Esav disdained his
birthright.

4 | The name Edom resonates with *adom* ("red") here, as well as with *admoni* ("red") in verse 25.

THE ART OF MIDRASH

Jacob and Esau
Adi Nes (2017)

Analysis

- Which elements of this image are directly mentioned in the text?
- Which elements of this image are not found in the text?
- What midrashic interpretation could be inferred from this image?

ל יַעֲקֹב נָזִיד וַיָּבֹא עֵשָׂו מִן־הַשָּׂדֶה וְהוּא עָיֵף׃ וַיֹּאמֶר עֵשָׂו אֶל־יַעֲקֹב הַלְעִיטֵנִי נָא
לא מִן־הָאָדֹם הָאָדֹם הַזֶּה כִּי עָיֵף אָנֹכִי עַל־כֵּן קָרָא־שְׁמוֹ אֱדוֹם׃ וַיֹּאמֶר יַעֲקֹב מִכְרָה
לב כַיּוֹם אֶת־בְּכֹרָתְךָ לִי׃ וַיֹּאמֶר עֵשָׂו הִנֵּה אָנֹכִי הוֹלֵךְ לָמוּת וְלָמָּה־זֶּה לִי בְּכֹרָה׃
לג לד וַיֹּאמֶר יַעֲקֹב הִשָּׁבְעָה לִּי כַּיּוֹם וַיִּשָּׁבַע לוֹ וַיִּמְכֹּר אֶת־בְּכֹרָתוֹ לְיַעֲקֹב׃ וְיַעֲקֹב נָתַן
לְעֵשָׂו לֶחֶם וּנְזִיד עֲדָשִׁים וַיֹּאכַל וַיֵּשְׁתְּ וַיָּקָם וַיֵּלַךְ וַיִּבֶז עֵשָׂו אֶת־הַבְּכֹרָה׃

A QUESTION OF BIBLIODRAMA

TO YITZḤAK

- Why was Rivka the focus of your prayer (rather than yourself and/or the covenant with God)?
- How did you feel when you heard the news that Rivka was pregnant with twins?
- Did you love Esav more than Yaakov? Why?

TO RIVKA

- What emotions did you experience when you heard you were having twins?
- What did you think about the prophecy you received on the future of your boys?
- Did you love Yaakov more than Esav? Why?

TO ESAV

- How are you different from your brother?
- Do you love your brother?
- Do you feel more loved by your father than your mother? How does that make you feel?
- Why was your birthright unimportant to you?

TO YAAKOV

- How are you different from your brother?
- Do you love your brother?
- Do you feel more loved by your mother than your father? How does this make you feel?
- Why did you want Esav's birthright?
- Were you surprised he gave it to you so easily

Rivka's strong sense of self was suddenly altered by her pregnancy. The first biblical character who acknowledged a personal identity had to negotiate, with twins in her belly, the transformation within from one to three. Children shifted her from an "I" to a "we"; it is a joyful transition but one that can also be untethering. Dr. Avivah Gottleib Zornberg, in her book *The Murmuring Deep: Reflections on the Biblical Unconscious*, contends that Rivka "was the first biblical character to speak the word *anokhi* as a term of identity.... With total assurance she had initiated the construction of the human subject as *anokhi*.... What has eroded her confident subjectivity?"

In their article "Managing Yourself: Stop Holding Yourself Back," Anne Morriss, Robin J. Ely, and Frances X. Frei speak to the personal identity of leaders. Those who construct a false identity for the public may find themselves tottering: a "common impediment to leadership is being overly distracted by your image – that ideal self you've created in your mind. Sticking to the script that goes along with that image takes a lot of energy, leaving little left over for the real work of leadership" (*Harvard Business Review*, Jan.–Feb. 2011). Maintaining an inauthentic identity has genuine psychic costs: "Once you've crafted your persona and determined not to veer from it, your effectiveness often suffers. The need to be seen as intelligent can inhibit learning and risk taking, for instance. The need to be seen as likable can keep you from asking tough questions or challenging existing norms. The need to be seen as decisive can cause you to shut down critical feedback loops."

These authors argue that the difference between image and impact, between looking powerful and empowering others, forces a terrible choice "between impersonating a leader and being one." Rivka offers us a model of authenticity. She impersonated no one. She was determined to help, determined to chart her future, and determined to understand why she suffered. All of this came out of her I-awareness. God honored this in her by responding to her directness. God made her the mother of not one nation but two.

Reading about Rivka's fierce courage prompts us to ask our own identity questions. In leadership and in life, when has betraying who you are led to loss and shame? When has honoring and articulating who you are helped you have greater impact?

Dr. Erica Brown

Analysis

- What areas of understanding of human nature and society do we now have that were unavailable to classical Jewish commentators? How can they aid our understanding of the text?
- What can we learn from this essay to help us understand the text?
- What further questions on the text do you have now that you have read this new take on the story?

INTEGRATING ḤOKHMA

When Eliezer encountered Rivka at the well, he asked for a little water for himself. Then she gave him water. Then she watered his camels. Then Eliezer checked if Rivka was a relative of Avraham's. Then he asked if there was room in her father's house for guests. With each request, Eliezer asked more of Rivka. This, too, may have been part of Eliezer's test.

Rivka's reply was full of self-assurance: "'I am (*anokhi*) the daughter of Betuel the son of Milka, whom she bore to Naḥor.' And she went on, 'There is plenty of straw and feed at home, and also room to spend the night'" (Bereshit 24:24–25). Rivka invited Eliezer to join her family of her own accord. She did not wait for her father's permission. It is this that Eliezer noticed immediately. He suddenly bowed and thanked God for making his job so easy: "Blessed be the Lord, the God of my master Avraham, who has not withheld His steadfast faithfulness from my master. For I have been guided on my errand by the Lord to the house of my master's kinsmen" (24:28).

Later, after negotiating with the family, Eliezer wanted to take Rivka back to his people. The group sought out Rivka's opinion, and with that same confidence and clarity she displayed earlier, Rivka responded. "'Will you go with this man?' and she said, 'I will'" (24:58).

Rashi explains Rivka's assertion; she would go of her own accord even if her family did not consent. Rivka knew her own mind. In saying "I will," Rivka was confirming her desire to make her future happen rather than waiting for it. Rivka looked forward. Rabbi Jonathan Sacks advises us to always do the right thing. Period. "Don't wait for the world to get better. Take the initiative yourself. The world is waiting for you" (*Covenant and Conversation,* "The World Is Waiting for You"). When you have lucidity on the course of action before you, don't wait another minute. And Rivka didn't.

In these two scenes, Rivka took charge of her destiny. It is only in Bereshit 25, when her pregnancy proved painful and mysterious, that she questioned her existence. When twins struggled in her womb, she said, "If so, why do I (*anokhi*) exist?" (25:22). So, she marched up to God with her characteristic curiosity and directness, and God answered her. There is an authenticity to Rivka because of her I-awareness that is both profound and disarming.

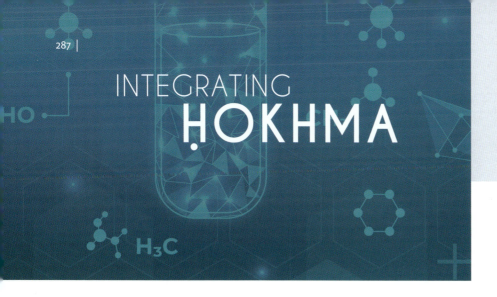

Yefet, because Yefet was the eldest. Once again, the chosen son was not the eldest.

Avraham, likewise, was not the firstborn. While the Torah mentions him before the other sons of Teraḥ – "These are the generations of Teraḥ; Teraḥ bore Avram and Naḥor and Haran" – the Talmud (Sanhedrin 69b) explains that Avraham was the youngest son, and is mentioned first only because of his importance.

The story of Avraham being chosen by God is not the last time that there is a choice. Bereshit continues to address the issue of chosenness, and in a much clearer and more overt manner. Avraham's eldest son is Yishmael. While Yishmael is not born of Sara, he is still Avraham's firstborn. He is banished from Avraham's house (Bereshit 21) in the wake of Sara's demand. Sara understands that what is involved is a significant battle over the inheritance. The conflict is not an economic one, but rather a fundamental, essential one. Sara, observing Yishmael's base behavior, demands that the handmaid's son should not be one of Avraham's inheritors. He is unworthy of it. He is a "wild man, whose hand is against everyone, and everyone's hand is against him" (16:12); he cannot succeed Avraham. God agrees with Sara, and tells Avraham, "Your seed shall be called through Yitzḥak."

The next instance of chosenness involves Yaakov and Esav. Both are sons of Yitzḥak and Rivka; they are twins, but even while still in the womb it is clear that there is a difference between them. It is clear that one of them will be chosen, and the one who is chosen will be the younger brother, as Rivka is told through prophecy: "The elder shall serve the younger" (25:23). Indeed, further on, Yaakov buys the birthright from Esav, and eventually also receives Yitzḥak's blessing.

In Yaakov's family, once again, the firstborn son – Reuven – is not the one who is chosen. Yehuda and Yosef receive the blessing and the leadership of *Benei Yisrael*. And in Yosef's own family, the younger son is once again chosen: Yaakov deliberately crosses his arms so that his right hand rests upon the head of Efrayim, the younger brother, and he gives him the more important blessing (48:13–20).

One of the most important themes of Bereshit is the matter of divine chosenness. Throughout the book we grapple with the question of who is chosen. Who is God choosing to represent God's way in the world? And throughout the book, the one who is chosen is not the firstborn. The entire book teaches that the physical fact of being the eldest does not automatically ensure the right to the firstborn blessing. God chooses the person who is worthy of receiving the blessing. God's blessing is given on the basis of merit, not chronology.

Rabbanit Sharon Rimon

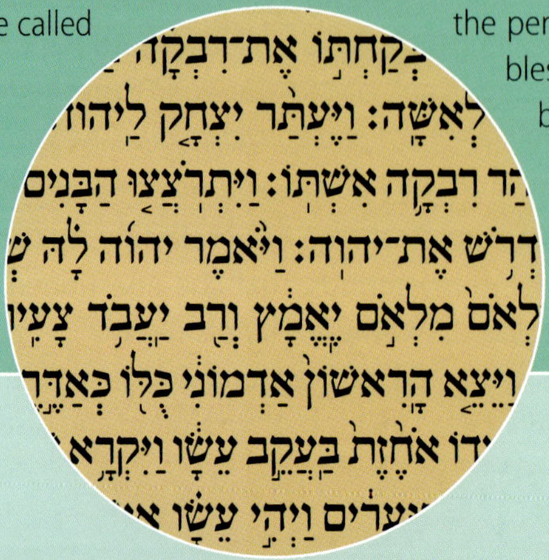

TAKING A LITERARY APPROACH

The birthright that Yaakov wants to receive is the one that involves the right to receive the blessing of Avraham. This blessing is not material, but rather spiritual: special closeness to God and the inheritance of the land, which is God's land. Yaakov was aware of the spiritual importance of the blessing, and therefore he sought to receive it. Esav, in contrast, was not worthy of this blessing, nor was he at all interested in it, because he did not follow the path of his forefathers.

The transfer of the birthright from Esav to Yaakov was a process arising from the actions of both brothers. Yaakov bought the birthright: not for lentil stew, but with his actions – by being a "simple man, dwelling in tents," continuing the path of his forefathers, Avraham and Yitzḥak. Esav sold the birthright by choosing to be a hunter, a man of the field, a person unworthy of inheriting the blessing of Avraham. The sale described in our *parasha* is not a sudden, unexpected act, but rather the final development in a process, expressing all that has happened thus far.

It is possible that, in fact, Yaakov had no need to buy the birthright at all. It would have come to him naturally, by virtue of his actions, and because of Esav's unsuitability. Even though Yaakov is not the firstborn, his actions – and those of his elder brother – bring about a situation in which he will receive the blessing of Avraham. This conclusion, arising from our analysis here of the story of Yaakov and Esav, also arises from a review of all the stories of the firstborns in the book of Bereshit.

The first story reflecting this theme is that of Kayin and Hevel. Kayin was the firstborn, but Hevel – his younger brother – is the one whose sacrifice is accepted by God. Apparently, this sacrifice and its acceptance were significant in God's eyes – and therefore in the eyes of Kayin and Hevel, too: "God responded to Hevel and to his offering, but to Kayin and to his sacrifice He did not respond." The verse emphasizes that what was involved here was not only the acceptance of the sacrifice, but something much deeper: an indication of which path is acceptable to God. It is for this reason that it pains Kayin so deeply that Hevel's sacrifice is accepted while his own is not. Kayin is certain that he, as the firstborn, is more worthy, but it turns out that God does not endorse his path. Even after Hevel's death, the meaningful continuation of the world is not through Kayin, but rather through a different son – Shet.

After the flood, the world continues through Noaḥ. Noaḥ has three sons – Shem, Ḥam, and Yefet. Clearly, Shem is the chosen son: he receives from Noaḥ the blessing of closeness to God (see Bereshit 9:18–29), and it is his dynasty that produces Avraham, who is chosen by God. But was Shem the firstborn? While all of the genealogical lists mention Shem first, and hence it would appear that he was in fact the eldest son, in 10:21 we read: "To Shem, too, were children born…he, the brother of Yefet, the elder." Rashi explains that Yefet was the eldest brother. Ramban, too (on 10:1), explains that the list of Noaḥ's descendants begins with the descendants of

26 1 Another famine afflicted the land, apart from the earlier famine in Avraham's days, and
2 Yitzḥak went to Avimelekh, king of the Philistines, in Gerar. The Lord had appeared to
3 him: "Do not go down to Egypt," He had said. "Stay in the land I tell you of. Bide in this
land and I will be with you and bless you, for I am going to give all these lands to you and
4 your descendants, fulfilling the oath I swore to Avraham your father. I will make your
descendants as many as the stars of the heavens, and I will give them all these lands. All
5 the nations of the earth will bless themselves by your descendants, because Avraham
listened to My voice and kept My charge: My commandments, My statutes, and My laws."
6 7 So Yitzḥak now settled in Gerar. The men of the place inquired after his wife; "She is my
sister," he said. He was terrified to say "She is my wife." "The men of the place might kill me
8 for Rivka," he thought, "she is so beautiful." When he had already been there for some time,
Avimelekh, king of the Philistines, looked down from a window and saw Yitzḥak enjoying
9 himself with his wife Rivka. Avimelekh summoned Yitzḥak. "She is your wife," he said.
"Why did you say, 'She is my sister'?" Yitzḥak replied, "I thought I might die because of
10 her." "What is this you have done to us?" said Avimelekh. "One of the people might have
11 slept with your wife, and you would have brought guilt upon us." Avimelekh then issued
an order to all the people: "Whoever touches this man or his wife shall be put to death."

UNLOCKING THE TEXT

- Why did Yitzḥak go to Avimelekh in Gerar?
- Is this the same Avimelekh from the story with his parents?
- Why did God prevent Yitzḥak from going down to Egypt, but allow Avraham to go there?
- Why did Yitzḥak decide to plant crops in a time of famine?
- Why did Yitzḥak take the same approach as his father in this situation?
- Why did the Philistines stop up the wells that Avraham dug? Didn't this disadvantage them also?
- Why was Avimelekh threatened by Yitzḥak?
- What is the significance of Yitzḥak reopening the wells of his father and renaming them with the same names?
- What is the significance of Yitzḥak's men digging new wells?
- What similarities and differences are there between the stories in this episode and the stories that happened to Avraham here?

FINDING YOURSELF IN THE TEXT

- How do you feel when people compare you to your parents?
- Do you feel pressure to make life decisions similar to those made by your parents?
- Do you plan to lead a life that is very different from your parents?

Consider using these questions as the basis for your own commentary or creative midrash.

How does reflecting on these firsthand experiences help you better understand the text?

כו א וַיְהִי רָעָב בָּאָרֶץ מִלְּבַד הָרָעָב הָרִאשׁוֹן אֲשֶׁר הָיָה בִּימֵי אַבְרָהָם וַיֵּלֶךְ יִצְחָק אֶל־
ב אֲבִימֶלֶךְ מֶלֶךְ־פְּלִשְׁתִּים גְּרָרָה׃ וַיֵּרָא אֵלָיו יהוה וַיֹּאמֶר אַל־תֵּרֵד מִצְרָיְמָה שְׁכֹן
ג בָּאָרֶץ אֲשֶׁר אֹמַר אֵלֶיךָ׃ גּוּר בָּאָרֶץ הַזֹּאת וְאֶהְיֶה עִמְּךָ וַאֲבָרְכֶךָּ כִּי־לְךָ וּלְזַרְעֲךָ
אֶתֵּן אֶת־כָּל־הָאֲרָצֹת הָאֵל וַהֲקִמֹתִי אֶת־הַשְּׁבֻעָה אֲשֶׁר נִשְׁבַּעְתִּי לְאַבְרָהָם אָבִיךָ׃
ד וְהִרְבֵּיתִי אֶת־זַרְעֲךָ כְּכוֹכְבֵי הַשָּׁמַיִם וְנָתַתִּי לְזַרְעֲךָ אֵת כָּל־הָאֲרָצֹת הָאֵל וְהִתְבָּרְכוּ
ה בְזַרְעֲךָ כֹּל גּוֹיֵי הָאָרֶץ׃ עֵקֶב אֲשֶׁר־שָׁמַע אַבְרָהָם בְּקֹלִי וַיִּשְׁמֹר מִשְׁמַרְתִּי מִצְוֺתַי
ו ז חֻקּוֹתַי וְתוֹרֹתָי׃ וַיֵּשֶׁב יִצְחָק בִּגְרָר׃ וַיִּשְׁאֲלוּ אַנְשֵׁי הַמָּקוֹם לְאִשְׁתּוֹ וַיֹּאמֶר אֲחֹתִי שני
הִוא כִּי יָרֵא לֵאמֹר אִשְׁתִּי פֶּן־יַהַרְגֻנִי אַנְשֵׁי הַמָּקוֹם עַל־רִבְקָה כִּי־טוֹבַת מַרְאֶה
ח הִוא׃ וַיְהִי כִּי־אָרְכוּ־לוֹ שָׁם הַיָּמִים וַיַּשְׁקֵף אֲבִימֶלֶךְ מֶלֶךְ פְּלִשְׁתִּים בְּעַד הַחַלּוֹן
ט וַיַּרְא וְהִנֵּה יִצְחָק מְצַחֵק אֵת רִבְקָה אִשְׁתּוֹ׃ וַיִּקְרָא אֲבִימֶלֶךְ לְיִצְחָק וַיֹּאמֶר אַךְ הִנֵּה
אִשְׁתְּךָ הִוא וְאֵיךְ אָמַרְתָּ אֲחֹתִי הִוא וַיֹּאמֶר אֵלָיו יִצְחָק כִּי אָמַרְתִּי פֶּן־אָמוּת עָלֶיהָ׃
י וַיֹּאמֶר אֲבִימֶלֶךְ מַה־זֹּאת עָשִׂיתָ לָּנוּ כִּמְעַט שָׁכַב אַחַד הָעָם אֶת־אִשְׁתֶּךָ וְהֵבֵאתָ
יא עָלֵינוּ אָשָׁם׃ וַיְצַו אֲבִימֶלֶךְ אֶת־כָּל־הָעָם לֵאמֹר הַנֹּגֵעַ בָּאִישׁ הַזֶּה וּבְאִשְׁתּוֹ מוֹת

THEMES	THE LAND OF ISRAEL	GOD	RELATIONSHIPS AND LOVE

Episode 36: *Yitzḥak Stays in Canaan* – Bereshit 26:1–33

SUMMARY

After the previous story, which dealt with the initial tension between the two brothers and the sale of the birthright, the Torah focuses on Yitzḥak. Up to this point, the verses have provided mostly factual information about Yitzḥak: where he lived, whom he married, and the like. However, almost nothing has been stated about his personality. Here God appears to Yitzḥak for the first time, and Yitzḥak's special relationship with the land of Canaan is also presented. In contrast to his father Avraham and his son Yaakov, Yitzḥak remained in the land of Canaan his entire life. This chapter describes how he gained a foothold in the land, his success in finding water, and his cultivation of its produce. Yitzḥak advances in economic and social status, as he establishes his family's settlement in the land promised to his father.

12 Yitzḥak planted crops in that land, and that year he reaped a hundredfold because the Lord
13 had blessed him. The man became rich; he prospered more and more until he became
14 very wealthy. He had flocks and herds and a large retinue of servants, and the Philistines
15 envied him. So the Philistines stopped up all the wells that his father's servants had dug in
16 the time of his father Avraham, filling them with earth. Avimelekh said to Yitzḥak, "Move
17 away from us. You have become much too powerful for us." So Yitzḥak left and camped in
18 the valley of Gerar and settled there. And he reopened the wells that had been dug in the
time of his father Avraham, which the Philistines had stopped up after Avraham died, and
19 gave them the same names his father had given them. Yitzḥak's servants dug in the valley
20 and discovered a well of fresh water, but the shepherds of Gerar quarreled with Yitzḥak's
shepherds, claiming that the water was theirs. So he called the well Esek,[1] because they
21 contended with him there. They dug another well, and there was a quarrel about that too;
22 so he called it Sitna.[2] He moved on from there and dug another well, and this time they did
not quarrel over it; so he named this one Reḥovot.[3] "Now the Lord has given us space," he
23 24 said, "and we will flourish in the land." From there he went up to Be'er Sheva. That night the
Lord appeared to him and said, "I am the God of your father Avraham. Do not be afraid,
for I am with you. I will bless you and multiply your descendants for the sake of Avraham
25 My servant." Yitzḥak built an altar there and called on the name of the Lord. There he
26 pitched his tent, and there his servants dug a well. Avimelekh came to him from Gerar,
27 with Aḥuzat his advisor and Pikhol the commander of his troops. Yitzḥak said to them,
28 "Why have you come to me? You hate me; you sent me away from you." They said, "We
have seen clearly that the Lord is with you, so we say: let there be a pact between you and
29 us. Let us make a covenant with you that you will do us no harm, just as we did not touch
you, just as we have done you nothing but good and we sent you on your way in peace.
30 31 And now – the Lord bless you." Yitzḥak made them a feast, and they ate and drank. Early
in the morning they rose and exchanged oaths, and Yitzḥak sent them on their way. They
32 parted from him in peace. That day, Yitzḥak's servants came and told him about the well
33 that they had dug; they said, "We have found water." He named it Shiva,[4] which is why the
town is called Be'er Sheva to this day.[5]

1 | Meaning "contention."

2 | Meaning "hostility."

3 | Meaning "wide spaces."

4 | The name Shiva resonates with *vayishave'u* ("exchanged oaths") in verse 31.

5 | Be'er denotes a well, and Sheva resonates with Shiva and *vayishave'u*.

יב יוּמָת: וַיִּזְרַע יִצְחָק בָּאָרֶץ הַהִוא וַיִּמְצָא בַּשָּׁנָה הַהִוא מֵאָה שְׁעָרִים וַיְבָרְכֵהוּ יְהוָה:
יג יד וַיִּגְדַּל הָאִישׁ וַיֵּלֶךְ הָלוֹךְ וְגָדֵל עַד כִּי־גָדַל מְאֹד: וַיְהִי־לוֹ מִקְנֵה־צֹאן וּמִקְנֵה בָקָר שלישי
טו וַעֲבֻדָּה רַבָּה וַיְקַנְאוּ אֹתוֹ פְּלִשְׁתִּים: וְכָל־הַבְּאֵרֹת אֲשֶׁר חָפְרוּ עַבְדֵי אָבִיו בִּימֵי
טז אַבְרָהָם אָבִיו סִתְּמוּם פְּלִשְׁתִּים וַיְמַלְאוּם עָפָר: וַיֹּאמֶר אֲבִימֶלֶךְ אֶל־יִצְחָק לֵךְ
יז יח מֵעִמָּנוּ כִּי־עָצַמְתָּ מִמֶּנּוּ מְאֹד: וַיֵּלֶךְ מִשָּׁם יִצְחָק וַיִּחַן בְּנַחַל־גְּרָר וַיֵּשֶׁב שָׁם: וַיָּשָׁב
יִצְחָק וַיַּחְפֹּר ׀ אֶת־בְּאֵרֹת הַמַּיִם אֲשֶׁר חָפְרוּ בִּימֵי אַבְרָהָם אָבִיו וַיְסַתְּמוּם פְּלִשְׁתִּים
יט אַחֲרֵי מוֹת אַבְרָהָם וַיִּקְרָא לָהֶן שֵׁמוֹת כַּשֵּׁמֹת אֲשֶׁר־קָרָא לָהֶן אָבִיו: וַיַּחְפְּרוּ
כ עַבְדֵי־יִצְחָק בַּנָּחַל וַיִּמְצְאוּ־שָׁם בְּאֵר מַיִם חַיִּים: וַיָּרִיבוּ רֹעֵי גְרָר עִם־רֹעֵי יִצְחָק
כא לֵאמֹר לָנוּ הַמָּיִם וַיִּקְרָא שֵׁם־הַבְּאֵר עֵשֶׂק כִּי הִתְעַשְּׂקוּ עִמּוֹ: וַיַּחְפְּרוּ בְּאֵר אַחֶרֶת
כב וַיָּרִיבוּ גַּם־עָלֶיהָ וַיִּקְרָא שְׁמָהּ שִׂטְנָה: וַיַּעְתֵּק מִשָּׁם וַיַּחְפֹּר בְּאֵר אַחֶרֶת וְלֹא רָבוּ
כג עָלֶיהָ וַיִּקְרָא שְׁמָהּ רְחֹבוֹת וַיֹּאמֶר כִּי־עַתָּה הִרְחִיב יְהוָה לָנוּ וּפָרִינוּ בָאָרֶץ: וַיַּעַל רביעי
כד מִשָּׁם בְּאֵר שָׁבַע: וַיֵּרָא אֵלָיו יְהוָה בַּלַּיְלָה הַהוּא וַיֹּאמֶר אָנֹכִי אֱלֹהֵי אַבְרָהָם אָבִיךָ
אַל־תִּירָא כִּי־אִתְּךָ אָנֹכִי וּבֵרַכְתִּיךָ וְהִרְבֵּיתִי אֶת־זַרְעֲךָ בַּעֲבוּר אַבְרָהָם עַבְדִּי:
כה וַיִּבֶן שָׁם מִזְבֵּחַ וַיִּקְרָא בְּשֵׁם יְהוָה וַיֶּט־שָׁם אָהֳלוֹ וַיִּכְרוּ־שָׁם עַבְדֵי־יִצְחָק בְּאֵר:
כו כז וַאֲבִימֶלֶךְ הָלַךְ אֵלָיו מִגְּרָר וַאֲחֻזַּת מֵרֵעֵהוּ וּפִיכֹל שַׂר־צְבָאוֹ: וַיֹּאמֶר אֲלֵהֶם יִצְחָק
כח מַדּוּעַ בָּאתֶם אֵלָי וְאַתֶּם שְׂנֵאתֶם אֹתִי וַתְּשַׁלְּחוּנִי מֵאִתְּכֶם: וַיֹּאמְרוּ רָאוֹ רָאִינוּ
כִּי־הָיָה יְהוָה ׀ עִמָּךְ וַנֹּאמֶר תְּהִי נָא אָלָה בֵּינוֹתֵינוּ בֵּינֵינוּ וּבֵינֶךָ וְנִכְרְתָה בְרִית
כט עִמָּךְ: אִם־תַּעֲשֵׂה עִמָּנוּ רָעָה כַּאֲשֶׁר לֹא נְגַעֲנוּךָ וְכַאֲשֶׁר עָשִׂינוּ עִמְּךָ רַק־טוֹב
ל וַנְּשַׁלֵּחֲךָ בְּשָׁלוֹם אַתָּה עַתָּה בְּרוּךְ יְהוָה: וַיַּעַשׂ לָהֶם מִשְׁתֶּה וַיֹּאכְלוּ וַיִּשְׁתּוּ: חמישי
לא לב וַיַּשְׁכִּימוּ בַבֹּקֶר וַיִּשָּׁבְעוּ אִישׁ לְאָחִיו וַיְשַׁלְּחֵם יִצְחָק וַיֵּלְכוּ מֵאִתּוֹ בְּשָׁלוֹם: וַיְהִי ׀
בַּיּוֹם הַהוּא וַיָּבֹאוּ עַבְדֵי יִצְחָק וַיַּגִּדוּ לוֹ עַל־אֹדוֹת הַבְּאֵר אֲשֶׁר חָפָרוּ וַיֹּאמְרוּ לוֹ
לג מָצָאנוּ מָיִם: וַיִּקְרָא אֹתָהּ שִׁבְעָה עַל־כֵּן שֵׁם־הָעִיר בְּאֵר שֶׁבַע עַד הַיּוֹם הַזֶּה:

THE ART OF MIDRASH

The Jewish Bride (Isaac and Rebecca)
Rembrandt Harmensz van Rijn (1665)

Analysis

- Which elements of this image are directly mentioned in the text?
- Which elements of this image are not found in the text?
- What midrashic interpretation could be inferred from this image?

A QUESTION OF BIBLIODRAMA

TO YITZḤAK

- Why did you take the same approach to your wife in Gerar as did your father?
- Do you think Avraham made the right decision when he did it?
- Why did you plant crops (something your father never did), especially at a time of famine?
- How do you feel about the wealth you generated?
- Why did you give the wells you reopened the same names your father gave them?
- Was it important to find new wells of your own? Why?

TO AVIMELEKH AND THE PHILISTINES

- Why did you stop up the wells that Avraham had dug?
- Why did you feel threatened by Yitzḥak?
- Why did your feelings toward Yitzḥak change?

TO RIVKA

- How did it feel when Yitzḥak told people you were his sister?
- Did you know the similar story about Avraham and Sara? Did that influence the way you felt?

published separately as *Antisemitism*). Hostility to Jews becomes dangerous, she argued, not when Jews are strong, but when they are weak.

This is deeply paradoxical because, on the face of it, the opposite is true. A single thread runs from the Philistines' reaction to Yitzḥak and Pharaoh's to the Israelites, to the myth concocted in the late nineteenth century known as *The Protocols of the Elders of Zion*. It says that Jews are powerful, too powerful. They control resources. They are a threat. They must be removed.

Yet, says Arendt, antisemitism did not become dangerous until they had lost the power they had once had: "When Hitler came to power, the German banks were already almost *Judenrein* (and it was here that Jews had held key positions for more than a hundred years) and German Jewry as a whole, after a long steady growth in social status and numbers, was declining so rapidly that statisticians predicted its disappearance in a few decades."

The same was true in France: "The Dreyfus affair exploded not under the Second Empire, when French Jewry was at the height of its prosperity and influence, but under the Third Republic when Jews had all but vanished from important positions."

Antisemitism is a complex, protean phenomenon because antisemites must be able to hold together two beliefs that seem to contradict one another: Jews are so powerful that they should be feared, and at the same time so powerless that they can be attacked without fear.

It would seem that no one could be so irrational as to believe both of these things simultaneously. But emotions are not rational, despite the fact that they are often rationalized, for there is a world of difference between *rationality* and *rationalization* (the attempt to give rational justification for irrational beliefs).

So, for example, in the twenty-first century we can find that (a) the Western media is almost universally hostile to Israel, and (b) otherwise intelligent people claim that the media is controlled by Jews who support Israel: the same inner contradiction of perceived powerlessness and ascribed power.

Arendt summarizes her thesis in a single, telling phrase which links her analysis to that of Amy Chua. What gives rise to antisemitism is, she says, the phenomenon of "wealth without power." That was precisely the position of Yitzḥak among the Philistines.

Rabbi Jonathan Sacks

Analysis

- What specific information do we now have that was unavailable to classical Jewish commentators? How can it aid our understanding of the text?
- What can we learn from this essay that can help us understand the text?
- What further questions on the text do you have now that you have read this essay?

INTEGRATING ḤOKHMA

This passage in Bereshit intimates what will later be the turning point of the fate of the Israelites in Egypt. Avimelekh says, "You have become *too powerful* for us." Centuries later, Pharaoh says, at the beginning of the book of Shemot, "Behold, the people of the children of Israel are greater in number and *power* than we are. Come on, let us deal wisely with them, lest they multiply and it come to pass, when there befall any war, that they join also with our enemies and fight against us, and so get them up out of the land" (Shemot 1:9–10). The same word, *atzum*, "power/powerful," appears in both cases. Our passage signals the birth of one of the deadliest of human phenomena, antisemitism.

Antisemitism is in some respects unique. It is, in Robert Wistrich's phrase, the world's longest hatred. No other prejudice has lasted so long, mutated so persistently, attracted such demonic myths, or had such devastating effects. But in other respects it is not unique, and we must try to understand it as best we can.

One of the best books about antisemitism is in fact not about antisemitism at all, but about similar phenomena in other contexts, Amy Chua's *World on Fire*. Her thesis is that any conspicuously successful minority will attract envy that may deepen into hate and provoke violence. All three conditions are essential. The hated group must be conspicuous, for otherwise it would not be singled out. It must be *successful*, for otherwise it would not be envied. And it must be a *minority*, for otherwise it would not be attacked.

All three conditions were present in the case of Yitzḥak. He was conspicuous: he was not a Philistine; he was different from the local population as an outsider, a stranger, someone with a different faith. He was successful: his crops had succeeded a hundredfold, his flocks and herds were large, and the people envied him. And he was a minority: a single family in the midst of the local population. All the ingredients were present for the distillation of hostility and hate.

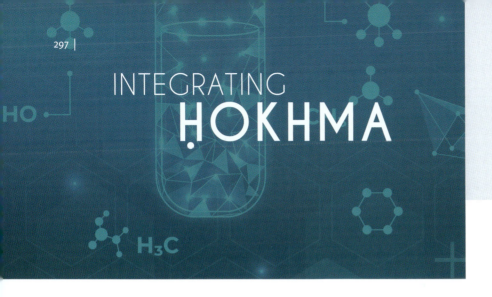

There is more. Another profound insight into the conditions that give rise to antisemitism was given by Hannah Arendt in her book *The Origins of Totalitarianism* (the section has been

rejection of Esav – and the favoring of Yaakov – as part of the *toledot* schema.

Now we understand why the sequence of chapters 25–27 is not true to the chronology of events: Yishmael's *toledot* could not be left "unanswered." Once Yitzḥak's children are mentioned, the process of the selection of Yaakov and the rejection of Esav must be introduced. This is the overriding concern that mitigates the text's usual loyalty to chronological sequence and is why the births of Yaakov and Esav were recorded before the story of Yitzḥak's descent to Gerar.

Rabbi Yitzchak Etshalom

TAKING A LITERARY APPROACH

How could Yitzḥak pass Rivka off as his sister if they had two grown children living with them there? Remember, the earlier wife/sister stories (both involving Avraham and Sara, one in Egypt and the other right here in Gerar) occurred when Sara was still childless. Following that model – and the inherent difficulty in pulling off such a ruse with children as contradictory evidence – it is hard to read the wife/sister story here as taking place with Esav and Yaakov nearby.

The most evident and reasonable solution to these questions is for us to reconsider the sequence of events. We approach all biblical texts with a number of standard assumptions, including the notion that the sequence of the story is chronologically consistent, save when overriding considerations render that impossible. Ramban is the staunchest supporter of the chronological sequencing known as *yesh mukdam ume'uḥar baTorah* (see his comments on Shemot 18:1; see also the Talmud's discussion at Pesaḥim 6b); yet even he admits to occasions where the text is clearly and blatantly in violation of chronological sequencing (the clearest example is Bemidbar 9:1 in light of Bemidbar 1:1).

When juxtaposition, completing one biography before moving on to the next generation (see Ramban's comments on Bereshit 35:28), or other similar textual concerns are present, time sequence may suffer. A survey of the listings of *toledot* (generations) in Bereshit suggests an answer. Every time there is a mention of *toledot*, there is a process of rejection and selection. When the Torah lists the *toledot* of Teraḥ, for instance (11:27), we are immediately informed of the selection of Avraham (and the rejection of his brothers). When we are introduced to the *toledot* of Yaakov, that entire narrative is about the (aborted) selection of Yosef as Yaakov's heir to the patriarchate (see Ramban on 37:3).

Hence, it was important not only to list the *toledot* of Yitzḥak, but also to present the first steps of the

34 When Esav was forty years old, he married Yehudit daughter of Be'eri the Hittite, and
35 Basmat daughter of Eilon the Hittite. These were a source of bitter sorrow to Yitzḥak and
27 1 Rivka. When Yitzḥak had grown old, when his eyes had grown so dim that he
could not see, he summoned his elder son Esav. "My son," he said. Esav replied, "Here I
2 3 am." He said, "I am old, and I do not know when I will die. So now, take your weapons, your
4 quiver and bow, and go out into the field and hunt me some game. Then make me delicious
food, prepared in the way that I love, and bring it to me to eat so that my soul may bless you
5 before I die." When Yitzḥak was speaking to Esav his son, Rivka was listening. Esav went out
6 into the field to hunt game to bring back. And Rivka said to her son Yaakov, "I overheard
7 your father say to your brother Esav, 'Fetch me some game and make me delicious food
8 so that I may eat and give you my blessing before the Lord before I die.' Now, my son,
9 listen carefully to my instructions. Go to the flock and bring me two choice young goats.
10 I will make them into delicious food, in the way he loves. Then take it to your father to eat
11 so that he may give you his blessing before he dies." Yaakov said to Rivka his mother, "My

UNLOCKING THE TEXT

- If Yitzḥak was disappointed with Esav's choice of wife, why does he still favor him for the blessing?
- Is this blessing the same as or different from the birthright that Esav sold to Yaakov?
- Why did Yitzḥak ask Esav to prepare his favorite food so he could bless him?
- What is the connection between the food and the blessing?
- Who is to blame for the deception of Yitzḥak?
- Did Yaakov have reservations, and if so, what were they?
- Did Rivka think Yitzḥak could really be tricked? Was Yitzḥak really tricked?
- Why did he bless Yaakov anyway after voicing doubt over his true identity?
- Why did Yitzḥak ignore the fact that the voice he heard was Yaakov's and not Esav's?
- What is the nature of the blessing?

FINDING YOURSELF IN THE TEXT

- Have you ever lied to your parents because you felt it was justifiable?
- Were you found out?
- Did your parents accept your explanation?

Consider using these questions as the basis for your own commentary or creative midrash.

How does reflecting on these firsthand experiences help you better understand the text?

לד וַיְהִי עֵשָׂו בֶּן־אַרְבָּעִים שָׁנָה וַיִּקַּח אִשָּׁה אֶת־יְהוּדִית בַּת־בְּאֵרִי הַחִתִּי וְאֶת־
לה כז א בָּשְׂמַת בַּת־אֵילֹן הַחִתִּי: וַתִּהְיֶיןָ מֹרַת רוּחַ לְיִצְחָק וּלְרִבְקָה: וַיְהִי כד
כִּי־זָקֵן יִצְחָק וַתִּכְהֶיןָ עֵינָיו מֵרְאֹת וַיִּקְרָא אֶת־עֵשָׂו | בְּנוֹ הַגָּדֹל וַיֹּאמֶר אֵלָיו בְּנִי
ב ג וַיֹּאמֶר אֵלָיו הִנֵּנִי: וַיֹּאמֶר הִנֵּה־נָא זָקַנְתִּי לֹא יָדַעְתִּי יוֹם מוֹתִי: וְעַתָּה שָׂא־נָא
ד כֵלֶיךָ תֶּלְיְךָ וְקַשְׁתֶּךָ וְצֵא הַשָּׂדֶה וְצוּדָה לִּי צידה: וַעֲשֵׂה־לִי מַטְעַמִּים כַּאֲשֶׁר צָיִד
ה אָהַבְתִּי וְהָבִיאָה לִּי וְאֹכֵלָה בַּעֲבוּר תְּבָרֶכְךָ נַפְשִׁי בְּטֶרֶם אָמוּת: וְרִבְקָה שֹׁמַעַת
ו בְּדַבֵּר יִצְחָק אֶל־עֵשָׂו בְּנוֹ וַיֵּלֶךְ עֵשָׂו הַשָּׂדֶה לָצוּד צַיִד לְהָבִיא: וְרִבְקָה אָמְרָה
אֶל־יַעֲקֹב בְּנָהּ לֵאמֹר הִנֵּה שָׁמַעְתִּי אֶת־אָבִיךָ מְדַבֵּר אֶל־עֵשָׂו אָחִיךָ לֵאמֹר:
ז הָבִיאָה לִּי צַיִד וַעֲשֵׂה־לִי מַטְעַמִּים וְאֹכֵלָה וַאֲבָרֶכְכָה לִפְנֵי יהוה לִפְנֵי מוֹתִי:
ח ט וְעַתָּה בְנִי שְׁמַע בְּקֹלִי לַאֲשֶׁר אֲנִי מְצַוָּה אֹתָךְ: לֶךְ־נָא אֶל־הַצֹּאן וְקַח־לִי מִשָּׁם
י שְׁנֵי גְּדָיֵי עִזִּים טֹבִים וְאֶעֱשֶׂה אֹתָם מַטְעַמִּים לְאָבִיךָ כַּאֲשֶׁר אָהֵב: וְהֵבֵאתָ לְאָבִיךָ
יא וְאָכָל בַּעֲבֻר אֲשֶׁר יְבָרֶכְךָ לִפְנֵי מוֹתוֹ: וַיֹּאמֶר יַעֲקֹב אֶל־רִבְקָה אִמּוֹ הֵן עֵשָׂו אָחִי

THEMES	COVENANT	THE LAND OF ISRAEL	RELATIONSHIPS AND LOVE

Episode 37: *Yaakov Tricks Yitzḥak for the Blessing* – Bereshit 26:34–27:29

SUMMARY

This episode, which deals with Yitzḥak's blessings, begins by mentioning Esav's marriage to Hittite women. In his choice of wives Esav strays from Avraham's path, as Avraham instructed his servant not to take a wife for his son from the women of Canaan (24:3).

The central issue in this episode is who will merit the blessings of Yitzḥak, and to whom the blessing of Avraham will pass. In contrast to the uniformity of Yitzḥak and Rivka's negative response to Esav's wives, they disagree over who should be the recipient of the blessings. Despite Yaakov's use of deception to receive the blessings that Yitzḥak intended to give to Esav, Yitzḥak initiates granting the blessing of Avraham to Yaakov before he leaves for Ḥaran.

12 brother Esav is hairy, but I have smooth skin. What if my father touches me? I will look to
13 him like a fraud and bring upon myself not a blessing but a curse." But his mother replied,
14 "Your curse will be on me, my son. Do as I say. Go: fetch them for me." So he went, took
the goats, and brought them to his mother, and his mother prepared delicious food in the
15 way his father loved. Then Rivka took her elder son Esav's best clothes, which were with
16 her in the house, and put them on Yaakov, her younger son. She put the goatskins on his
17 hands and the smooth part of his neck. She then handed her son Yaakov the delicious
18 food and bread that she had prepared. He went in to his father; "My father," he said. His
19 father replied, "Here I am. Who are you, my son?" Yaakov said to his father, "I am Esav
your firstborn. I have done as you asked. Please sit up and eat some of my game so that
20 your soul may bless me." Yitzḥak asked his son, "How did you find it so quickly, my son?"
21 He replied, "The Lord your God brought it about for me." Then Yitzḥak said to Yaakov,
22 "Come close and let me feel you, my son, to know – are you really my son Esav?" Yaakov
came close to Yitzḥak his father, who felt him and said, "The voice is the voice of Yaakov, but
23 the hands are the hands of Esav." He did not recognize him, because his hands were hairy
24 like those of his brother Esav. And he blessed him. "Are you really my son Esav?" he asked.
25 He replied, "I am." "Then serve me and let me eat some of my son's game so that my soul
26 may bless you." He served him food and he ate, he brought him wine and he drank. Then
27 Yaakov's father Yitzḥak said to him, "Come close and kiss me, my son." So he came close
and kissed him, and Yitzḥak smelled the smell of his clothes and blessed him, saying: "The
28 smell of my son is the smell of a field the Lord has blessed. God endow you with dew of
29 heaven, the cream of the land, much grain and wine. May peoples serve you; may nations
bow down to you. Be lord over your brothers, and may your mother's sons bow down to
you. A curse on those who curse you; on those who bless you, blessing."

יב אִ֣ישׁ שָׂעִ֔ר וְאָנֹכִ֖י אִ֥ישׁ חָלָֽק׃ אוּלַ֤י יְמֻשֵּׁ֙נִי֙ אָבִ֔י וְהָיִ֥יתִי בְעֵינָ֖יו כִּמְתַעְתֵּ֑עַ וְהֵבֵאתִ֥י
יג עָלַ֛י קְלָלָ֖ה וְלֹ֥א בְרָכָֽה׃ וַתֹּ֤אמֶר לוֹ֙ אִמּ֔וֹ עָלַ֥י קִלְלָתְךָ֖ בְּנִ֑י אַ֛ךְ שְׁמַ֥ע בְּקֹלִ֖י וְלֵ֥ךְ
יד טו קַח־לִֽי׃ וַיֵּ֙לֶךְ֙ וַיִּקַּ֔ח וַיָּבֵ֖א לְאִמּ֑וֹ וַתַּ֤עַשׂ אִמּוֹ֙ מַטְעַמִּ֔ים כַּאֲשֶׁ֖ר אָהֵ֥ב אָבִֽיו׃ וַתִּקַּ֨ח
רִבְקָ֜ה אֶת־בִּגְדֵ֨י עֵשָׂ֜ו בְּנָ֤הּ הַגָּדֹל֙ הַחֲמֻדֹ֔ת אֲשֶׁ֥ר אִתָּ֖הּ בַּבָּ֑יִת וַתַּלְבֵּ֥שׁ אֶֽת־יַעֲקֹ֖ב
טז יז בְּנָ֥הּ הַקָּטָֽן׃ וְאֵ֗ת עֹרֹת֙ גְּדָיֵ֣י הָֽעִזִּ֔ים הִלְבִּ֖ישָׁה עַל־יָדָ֑יו וְעַ֖ל חֶלְקַ֥ת צַוָּארָֽיו׃ וַתִּתֵּ֧ן
יח אֶת־הַמַּטְעַמִּ֛ים וְאֶת־הַלֶּ֖חֶם אֲשֶׁ֣ר עָשָׂ֑תָה בְּיַ֖ד יַעֲקֹ֥ב בְּנָֽהּ׃ וַיָּבֹ֥א אֶל־אָבִ֖יו
יט וַיֹּ֣אמֶר אָבִ֑י וַיֹּ֣אמֶר הִנֶּ֔נִּי מִ֥י אַתָּ֖ה בְּנִֽי׃ וַיֹּ֨אמֶר יַעֲקֹ֜ב אֶל־אָבִ֗יו אָנֹכִי֙ עֵשָׂ֣ו בְּכֹרֶ֔ךָ
עָשִׂ֕יתִי כַּאֲשֶׁ֖ר דִּבַּ֣רְתָּ אֵלָ֑י קוּם־נָ֣א שְׁבָ֗ה וְאָכְלָה֙ מִצֵּידִ֔י בַּעֲב֖וּר תְּבָרְכַ֥נִּי נַפְשֶֽׁךָ׃
כ וַיֹּ֤אמֶר יִצְחָק֙ אֶל־בְּנ֔וֹ מַה־זֶּ֛ה מִהַ֥רְתָּ לִמְצֹ֖א בְּנִ֑י וַיֹּ֕אמֶר כִּ֥י הִקְרָ֛ה יְהוָ֥ה אֱלֹהֶ֖יךָ
כא לְפָנָֽי׃ וַיֹּ֤אמֶר יִצְחָק֙ אֶֽל־יַעֲקֹ֔ב גְּשָׁה־נָּ֥א וַאֲמֻֽשְׁךָ֖ בְּנִ֑י הַאַתָּ֥ה זֶ֛ה בְּנִ֥י עֵשָׂ֖ו אִם־לֹֽא׃
כב וַיִּגַּ֧שׁ יַעֲקֹ֛ב אֶל־יִצְחָ֥ק אָבִ֖יו וַיְמֻשֵּׁ֑הוּ וַיֹּ֗אמֶר הַקֹּל֙ ק֣וֹל יַעֲקֹ֔ב וְהַיָּדַ֖יִם יְדֵ֥י עֵשָֽׂו׃
כג כד וְלֹ֣א הִכִּיר֔וֹ כִּֽי־הָי֣וּ יָדָ֗יו כִּידֵ֛י עֵשָׂ֥ו אָחִ֖יו שְׂעִרֹ֑ת וַֽיְבָרְכֵֽהוּ׃ וַיֹּ֕אמֶר אַתָּ֥ה זֶ֖ה בְּנִ֣י
כה עֵשָׂ֑ו וַיֹּ֖אמֶר אָֽנִי׃ וַיֹּ֗אמֶר הַגִּ֤שָׁה לִּי֙ וְאֹֽכְלָה֙ מִצֵּ֣יד בְּנִ֔י לְמַ֥עַן תְּבָרֶכְךָ֖ נַפְשִׁ֑י וַיַּגֶּשׁ־
כו לוֹ֙ וַיֹּאכַ֔ל וַיָּ֧בֵא ל֛וֹ יַ֖יִן וַיֵּֽשְׁתְּ׃ וַיֹּ֥אמֶר אֵלָ֖יו יִצְחָ֣ק אָבִ֑יו גְּשָׁה־נָּ֥א וּשְׁקָה־לִּ֖י בְּנִֽי׃
כז וַיִּגַּשׁ֙ וַיִּשַּׁק־ל֔וֹ וַיָּ֛רַח אֶת־רֵ֥יחַ בְּגָדָ֖יו וַֽיְבָרְכֵ֑הוּ וַיֹּ֗אמֶר רְאֵה֙ רֵ֣יחַ בְּנִ֔י כְּרֵ֣יחַ שָׂדֶ֔ה
כח אֲשֶׁ֥ר בֵּרֲכ֖וֹ יְהוָֽה׃ וְיִתֶּן־לְךָ֙ הָאֱלֹהִ֔ים מִטַּל֙ הַשָּׁמַ֔יִם וּמִשְׁמַנֵּ֖י הָאָ֑רֶץ וְרֹ֥ב דָּגָ֖ן כה ששי
כט וְתִירֹֽשׁ׃ יַֽעַבְד֣וּךָ עַמִּ֗ים וְיִשְׁתַּחֲוֻ֤ לְךָ֙ לְאֻמִּ֔ים הֱוֵ֤ה גְבִיר֙ לְאַחֶ֔יךָ וְיִשְׁתַּחֲוּ֥וּ לְךָ֖ בְּנֵ֣י
אִמֶּ֑ךָ אֹרְרֶ֣יךָ אָר֔וּר וּמְבָרְכֶ֖יךָ בָּרֽוּךְ׃

THE ART OF MIDRASH

Isaac Blessing Jacob
Yoram Raanan (2014)

Analysis

- Which elements of this image are directly mentioned in the text?
- Which elements of this image are not found in the text?
- What midrashic interpretation could be inferred from this image?

A QUESTION OF BIBLIODRAMA

TO YITZḤAK

- When Esav took a Hittite wife, did this affect your love for him?
- Why did you choose now to give your sons blessings?
- What blessing had you intended to give Esav?
- Were you aware that God had promised the birthright and covenant to Yaakov?
- Who did you really think was standing before you when you blessed Yaakov?

TO RIVKA

- Why was it so important to you that Yaakov received the blessing from his father?
- How did you justify the deception you convinced Yaakov to carry out?
- Why didn't you speak to Yitzḥak about the blessing instead of helping Yaakov to deceive him?

TO YAAKOV

- You had already taken the birthright from Esav – why was it important for you to also have the blessing from Yitzḥak?
- What did you think when your mother shared the plan with you to deceive your father? Did you have any reservations?
- Did you think your father would fall for the deception? Were you surprised when he did?
- What do you think of the blessing you received? Was it the blessing you were hoping for?
- Now that you have succeeded in tricking your father, how do you feel? Have you experienced any feelings of guilt or regret?

favored Esav because he had a taste for game, but Rivka favored Yaakov" (25:28). Commentators fill in the gaps trying to explain these loves. Haamek Davar suggests that Rivka's love was based on the higher vision she had for Yaakov that God placed in her mind during her pregnancy.

We lie most often for personal benefit, what Ariely calls "rational economic motivation." Sometimes we lie "to view ourselves as wonderful human beings" (this is the psychological motivation). This explains many of the lies that leaders tell. They lie or fudge the truth to protect themselves or others, to maintain morale when it's low, or to facilitate a better bottom-line. Lies make life easier in the short-term but dissipate trust in the long-term. Yaakov understood this all too well.

Rivka's motivation, of course, was never for personal gain. After all, Esav was her son also. No matter how different children are, mothers want every child to thrive. Rivka had a different agenda; she needed to make good on God's prediction. Yet every time I read this story, I wonder why Rivka never reported to Yitzḥak what God said about the fate of their twins. Perhaps the two could have found a way as parents to grow Yaakov into his leadership role without having to snatch a birthright from Esav. It could have spared heartache for all four of them.

Trust could not be more critical now in leadership or more absent in our everyday discourse. "A world of truth is a world of trust," writes Rabbi Sacks in *Morality*. "In it, there is something larger than individuals seeking their own interest. Truth becomes the intellectual equivalent of a public space that we can all inhabit, whatever our desires and predilections." It's our responsibility to instill and restore trust so that it fills a public space we can all inhabit.

Dr. Erica Brown

Analysis

- What areas of understanding of human nature and society do we now have that were unavailable to classical Jewish commentators? How can they aid our understanding of the text?
- What can we learn from this essay to help us understand the text?
- What further questions on the text do you have now that you have read this new take on the story?

INTEGRATING ḤOKHMA

Although Yaakov was a necessary actor in the story, it was Rivka who hatched this deception and carried it out in detail. She demanded that Yaakov hunt for meat to make Yitzḥak his favorite dish from his favorite son. "Rivka then took the best clothes of her older son Esav, which were there in the house, and had her younger son Yaakov put them on; and she covered his hands and the hairless part of his neck with the skins of the kids. Then she put in the hands of her son Yaakov the dish and the bread that she had prepared." Rivka took the meat. She brought the coat. She put gloves on Yaakov's hands and placed the food in his arms. Yaakov was an adult who could have dressed himself, but in his stiff, unyielding gestures, it is as if Yaakov communicated he wanted no part in his mother's plan. Why else would the Torah have gone into this level of detail to inform us what was happening backstage?

Behavioral economist Dan Ariely, in *The (Honest) Truth About Dishonesty: How We Lie to Everyone—Especially Ourselves* believes that the will to lie touches us all: "Our sense of our own morality is connected to the amount of cheating we feel comfortable with. Essentially, we cheat up to the level that allows us to retain our self-image as reasonably honest individuals."

Yaakov did not willingly participate in his mother's plan because his own self-image was not as a deceiver. Rivka, however, was comfortable with this lie because God told her while she was pregnant that her younger twin would be the rightful heir: "Two nations are in your womb. Two separate peoples shall issue from your body; one people shall be mightier than the other, *and the older shall serve the younger*" (Bereshit 25:23). A few verses later, we read that "Yitzḥak

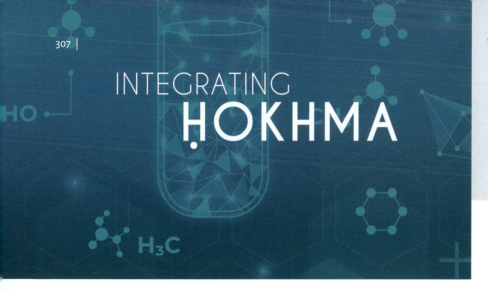

E2: Esav enters with the food his father loves, with coarse garments and hairy arms.

F1: The nexus of the selection: Yaakov's direct meeting with Yitzḥak, when he receives the prized blessing. There is no parallel to this subsection, nor can there be (if there were, Yitzḥak's answer to Esav in v. 38 would have been dramatically different).

For our purposes, the significant sections of the chiasmus that may shed light on Rivka's favoring of Yaakov are B and D.

In B1, Yitzḥak speaks to Esav about his death, but we hear no reaction from the loyal son, save to go a-hunting. The eerie similarity to Rivka's command to Yaakov in B2 highlights the difference – Yaakov flees without protest because it is his own life he is saving; it is the prudent thing to do and protesting would be of no avail. That is certainly not the case with Esav's obeisance to his father's command. The later development of the story demonstrates that his zealous exit to the hunt was motivated by his desire to attain his father's blessing, not to bring pleasure to his father or to fulfill his command.

In D1, Yaakov's protests to Rivka fall into two categories, ethical and pragmatic. He is concerned that the blessing will backfire because his father will discover the ruse, and he is concerned that he will fail in his father's eyes. When Rivka accepts responsibility for these potential troubles, his concerns are assuaged and he protests no further.

In D2, Esav continues to whine and complain about Yaakov's "theft"; nothing that his father can do will calm him down. He is, remember, the stronger one, the brother to be feared, yet he cannot be placated.

When we compare the way each of these sons responded to challenges and potential troubles, we can readily understand why Rivka favored Yaakov over Esav and why, as the prophet Malakhi indicates (1:2), God Himself validated her favoritism. The mature person, worthy of God's grace and favor, accepts the obstacles that face him and understands that his own shortcomings are the ultimate cause of his external obstacles. Once he changes that which is alterable and the terrain has been leveled to the extent possible, he faces his challenge head-on. His realization of his own power is, counterintuitively, the source of his humility, which allows him to look inward for the solution. That which needs to be confronted is faced and that which needs to be repaired is attended to. Once his own internal work has been done, he is ready to face the external challenges. The immature, impetuous Esav is unable to overcome his anger to sense which way the wind blows and to adjust accordingly. He looks for devils outside of his heart and, as such, never solves the problem that lies deep inside.

Rabbi Yitzchak Etshalom

TAKING A LITERARY APPROACH

This story has the following chiastic structure:

- **A1:** — Esav marries Hittite women
  - **B1:** — Yitzḥak speaks with Esav
    - **C1:** — Rivka overhears Yitzḥak's request of Esav
      - **D1:** — Rivka speaks with Yaakov
        - **E1:** — Yaakov prepares to enter his father's tent
          - **F:** — Yaakov and Yitzḥak
        - **E2:** — Esav and Yitzḥak
      - **D2:** — Esav's reaction to Yaakov's "theft"
    - **C2:** — Rivka overhears Esav's plans
  - **B2:** — Rivka and Yaakov
- **A2:** — Rivka speaks with Yitzḥak about Yaakov marrying Hittite women

A1: Esav marries two Hittite women. They are a source of bitterness to Rivka and Yitzḥak – the only time that Rivka and Yitzḥak are presented as having one common reaction to anything.

A2: Rivka speaks to Yitzḥak – the only time in the text that either of them speaks to the other – complaining about the Hittite women.

B1: Yitzḥak speaks to Esav about his impending death, and using the transitional word *ve'ata* ("and now"), commands Esav to go bring venison. Esav obeys without question.

B2: Rivka speaks to Yaakov about his impending death, and using the transitional word *ve'ata*, commands him to run away to Lavan. Yaakov obeys without question.

C1: Rivka hears about Yitzḥak's request of Esav: she introduces her report of the information with the word *hineni* ("behold").

C2: Rivka hears about Esav's plot to kill Yaakov; she introduces her report of the information with the word *hineni*.

D1: Rivka commands Yaakov to bring the goats that she will prepare; Yaakov expresses concern that he will bring a curse upon himself instead of a blessing.

D2: Esav reacts to Yaakov's "theft" of the blessing by plotting to kill him – the ultimate curse.

E1: Yaakov takes on the guise of Esav, bringing the food his father loves, with coarse garments and hairy arms.

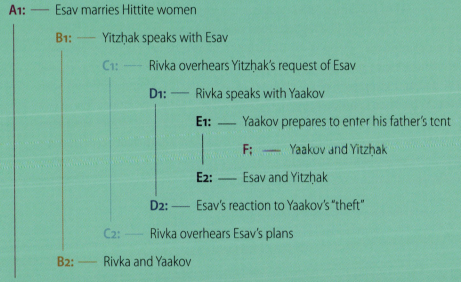

30 Yitzḥak had finished blessing Yaakov, and Yaakov had just left his father Yitzḥak, when his
31 brother Esav came back from the hunt. He too had prepared delicious food and brought it
to his father. And he said to his father, "Let my father sit up and eat some of his son's game
32 so that your soul may bless me." "Who are you?" asked his father Yitzḥak. "I am your son,
33 your firstborn, Esav," he replied. Yitzḥak was seized with a violent fit of trembling. "Who
then was it that hunted game and brought it to me? I ate it all before you came, and I blessed
34 him – and he will be blessed." When Esav heard his father's words, he burst into a loud
35 and bitter cry. He said to his father, "Bless me, me too, my father!" "Your brother came
36 in deceit and took your blessing," he replied. Esav said, "Is he not rightly named Yaakov?
Twice he has supplanted me.[1] He took my birthright and now he has taken my blessing."
37 And then, "Do you not have any blessing left for me?" Yitzḥak answered Esav, "I have made
him lord over you and given him all his brothers as servants. I have endowed him with
38 grain and wine. What then can I do for you, my son?" Esav said to his father, "Have you
39 only one blessing, father? Bless me, me too, my father!" And Esav wept aloud. His father
Yitzḥak answered him and said: "Of the cream of the land your home shall be, of the dew
40 of heaven above. By your sword you will live, and your brother you will serve; but when
you break loose, you will throw off his yoke from your neck."

---

1 | Hebrew *vayakeveni*, resonating with the name Yaakov.

UNLOCKING THE TEXT

- Does Yitzḥak really not know who has returned from the field?
- Why does Esav introduce himself to his father with so many descriptors, rather than just with his name?
- Is there a meaningful difference between Yitzḥak's "violent trembling" and Esav's "loud and bitter cry"?
- According to Esav, what is the connection between the name Yaakov and deceit?
- Did Yitzḥak already know about Esav selling his birthright to Yaakov? Why did he not react to that?
- Why can Yitzḥak not also bless Esav?
- How then does he suddenly find a blessing for Esav?
- How do the two blessings compare?
- Is the blessing a prediction/prophecy, or is it a blessing for a potential future that Esav must achieve?

FINDING YOURSELF IN THE TEXT

- Do you argue with your siblings?
- How do you think your parents feel when that happens?
- Have you ever been deceived or let down by a sibling? How did it feel?
- Have you ever tricked your sibling? Why did you do it? How did you feel afterward?

Consider using these questions as the basis for your own commentary or creative midrash.

How does reflecting on these firsthand experiences help you better understand the text?

ל וַיְהִ֗י כַּאֲשֶׁ֨ר כִּלָּ֣ה יִצְחָק֮ לְבָרֵ֣ךְ אֶֽת־יַעֲקֹב֒ וַיְהִ֗י אַ֣ךְ יָצֹ֤א יָצָא֙ יַעֲקֹ֔ב מֵאֵ֥ת פְּנֵ֖י יִצְחָ֣ק אָבִ֑יו
לא וְעֵשָׂ֣ו אָחִ֔יו בָּ֖א מִצֵּידֽוֹ׃ וַיַּ֤עַשׂ גַּם־הוּא֙ מַטְעַמִּ֔ים וַיָּבֵ֖א לְאָבִ֑יו וַיֹּ֣אמֶר לְאָבִ֗יו יָקֻ֤ם אָבִי֙
לב וְיֹאכַל֙ מִצֵּ֣יד בְּנ֔וֹ בַּעֲב֖וּר תְּבָרְכַ֥נִּי נַפְשֶֽׁךָ׃ וַיֹּ֥אמֶר ל֛וֹ יִצְחָ֥ק אָבִ֖יו מִי־אָ֑תָּה וַיֹּ֗אמֶר אֲנִ֛י
לג בִּנְךָ֥ בְכֹרְךָ֖ עֵשָֽׂו׃ וַיֶּחֱרַ֨ד יִצְחָ֣ק חֲרָדָה֮ גְּדֹלָ֣ה עַד־מְאֹד֒ וַיֹּ֡אמֶר מִֽי־אֵפוֹא֩ ה֨וּא הַצָּֽד־
לד צַ֜יִד וַיָּ֣בֵא לִ֗י וָאֹכַ֥ל מִכֹּ֛ל בְּטֶ֥רֶם תָּב֖וֹא וָאֲבָרֲכֵ֑הוּ גַּם־בָּר֖וּךְ יִהְיֶֽה׃ כִּשְׁמֹ֤עַ עֵשָׂו֙ אֶת־
דִּבְרֵ֣י אָבִ֔יו וַיִּצְעַ֣ק צְעָקָ֔ה גְּדֹלָ֥ה וּמָרָ֖ה עַד־מְאֹ֑ד וַיֹּ֣אמֶר לְאָבִ֔יו בָּרְכֵ֥נִי גַם־אָ֖נִי אָבִֽי׃
לה לו וַיֹּ֕אמֶר בָּ֥א אָחִ֖יךָ בְּמִרְמָ֑ה וַיִּקַּ֖ח בִּרְכָתֶֽךָ׃ וַיֹּ֡אמֶר הֲכִי֩ קָרָ֨א שְׁמ֜וֹ יַעֲקֹ֗ב וַֽיַּעְקְבֵ֙נִי֙ זֶ֣ה
פַעֲמַ֔יִם אֶת־בְּכֹרָתִ֣י לָקָ֔ח וְהִנֵּ֥ה עַתָּ֖ה לָקַ֣ח בִּרְכָתִ֑י וַיֹּאמַ֕ר הֲלֹא־אָצַ֥לְתָּ לִּ֖י בְּרָכָֽה׃
לז וַיַּ֨עַן יִצְחָ֜ק וַיֹּ֣אמֶר לְעֵשָׂ֗ו הֵ֣ן גְּבִ֞יר שַׂמְתִּ֤יו לָךְ֙ וְאֶת־כָּל־אֶחָ֗יו נָתַ֤תִּי לוֹ֙ לַעֲבָדִ֔ים
לח וְדָגָ֥ן וְתִירֹ֖שׁ סְמַכְתִּ֑יו וּלְכָ֣ה אֵפ֔וֹא מָ֥ה אֶעֱשֶׂ֖ה בְּנִֽי׃ וַיֹּ֨אמֶר עֵשָׂ֜ו אֶל־אָבִ֗יו הַֽבְרָכָ֨ה
לט אַחַ֤ת הִוא־לְךָ֙ אָבִ֔י בָּרְכֵ֥נִי גַם־אָ֖נִי אָבִ֑י וַיִּשָּׂ֥א עֵשָׂ֛ו קֹל֖וֹ וַיֵּֽבְךְּ׃ וַיַּ֛עַן יִצְחָ֥ק אָבִ֖יו
מ וַיֹּ֣אמֶר אֵלָ֑יו הִנֵּ֞ה מִשְׁמַנֵּ֤י הָאָ֙רֶץ֙ יִהְיֶ֣ה מֽוֹשָׁבֶ֔ךָ וּמִטַּ֥ל הַשָּׁמַ֖יִם מֵעָֽל׃ וְעַל־חַרְבְּךָ֣
תִֽחְיֶ֔ה וְאֶת־אָחִ֖יךָ תַּעֲבֹ֑ד וְהָיָה֙ כַּאֲשֶׁ֣ר תָּרִ֔יד וּפָרַקְתָּ֥ עֻלּ֖וֹ מֵעַ֥ל צַוָּארֶֽךָ׃

THEMES	COVENANT	RELATIONSHIPS/LOVE	ETHICS

Episode 38: *Esav Mourns His Lost Birthright* – Bereshit 27:30–40

SUMMARY

In this episode, the drama of the story reaches a climax when Esav returns from hunting to bring his father the meal he requested and to receive his blessing. Upon realizing that Yaakov has deceived Yitzḥak, both Esav and Yitzḥak are gripped by shock and despair.

THE ART OF MIDRASH

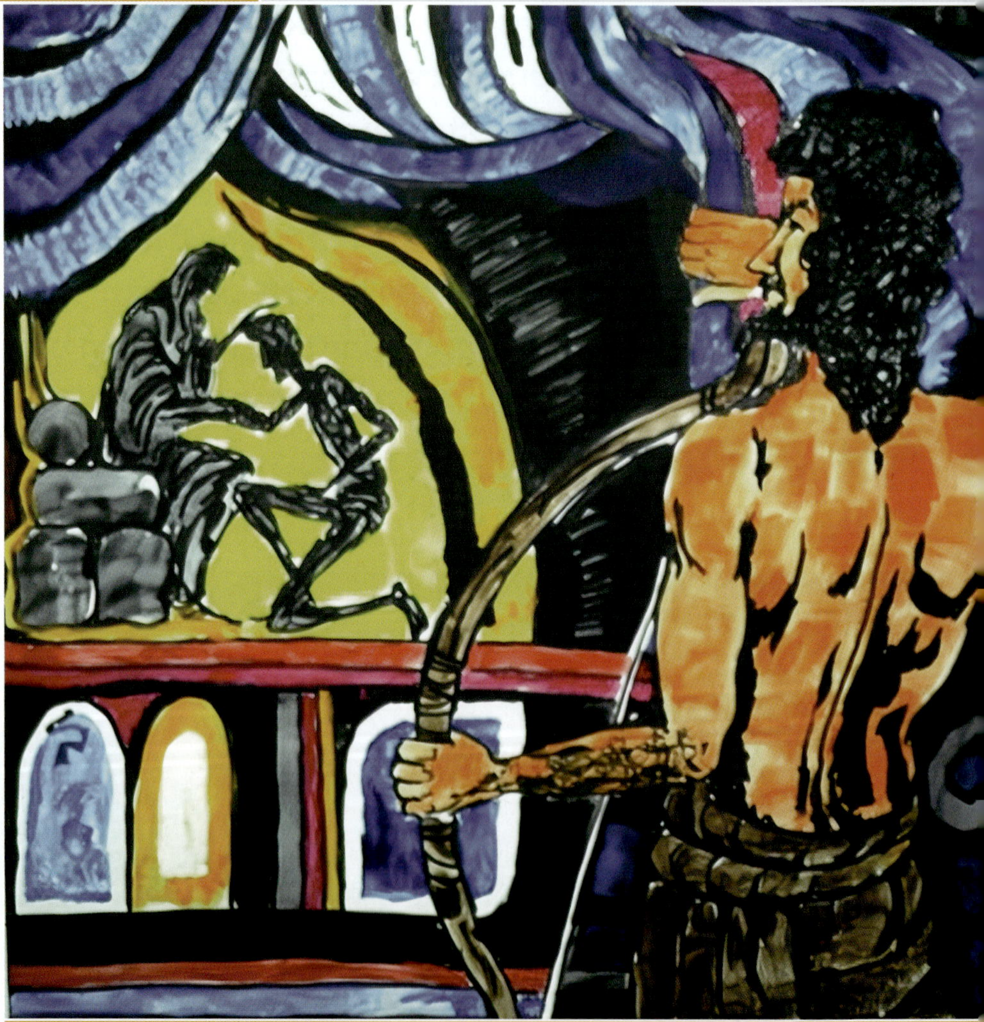

The Eighth Commandment: "Thou shalt not steal"
Phillip Ratner (1984)

Analysis

- Which elements of this image are directly mentioned in the text?
- Which elements of this image are not found in the text?
- What midrashic interpretation could be inferred from this image?

A QUESTION OF BIBLIODRAMA

TO YITZḤAK

- What went through your mind as Esav came through the door and gave you the food he had prepared?
- Can you describe what emotions you were feeling that caused your "violent fit of trembling"?
- Were you aware that Esav had exchanged his birthright with Yaakov for a pot of soup? How do you feel about that?
- Why could you not see a way to bless Esav also?
- What changed in your mind allowing you to give him a blessing after all?

TO ESAV

- What were you feeling when you realized what Yaakov had done?
- Why were you so desperate to receive a blessing from your father?
- Why was the blessing more important to you than the birthright?
- What do you think about the blessing your father gave to you?

Nor is this unexpected. In a unique scene, the theme of sibling rivalry is announced even before the children are born. Rivka, hitherto infertile, becomes pregnant but suffers agonizing pain. She goes "to inquire of the Lord," who tells her that she is carrying twins already contending for dominance: "Two nations are in your womb, and two peoples will separate from within you. One people will be mightier than the other, and the elder will serve the younger" (25:23). The brothers' fate is to clash, their destiny to conflict. Nowhere else does the Bible come so close to Greek tragedy. The scene reminds us of the Delphic oracle in *Oedipus Rex* who tells Laius that he will be killed by his son. The story begins with the end, and the tension lies in waiting to see how it comes to pass. Fate and tragedy belong together, which is what makes this passage so unexpected, so *unbiblical*. The Hebrew Bible rejects the idea of inescapable fate, a pre-ordained future. Yet the verse sets up an expectation, shaping the way we interpret all that follows. The story begins with the words "The elder will serve the younger" and ends with Yitzḥak's blessing to Yaakov: "Rule over your brothers, and may your mother's sons bow down to you." The prediction has come true. Yaakov has been granted dominance, his apparently predestined fate. A simple tale.

Yet something is amiss. Reading the passage in which Yaakov takes the blessing, it is impossible not to notice how often Yitzḥak doubts that the son in front of him is really Esav. Three times, Yitzḥak expresses doubts – giving Yaakov three opportunities to admit the truth. He does not. Far from glossing over the morally ambiguous nature of Yaakov's conduct, the text goes out of its way to emphasize it.

Yaakov leaves. Esav enters. The power in this scene is not just what happens, but how the Bible describes it (27:30–38). *Reading this passage, we cannot but identify with Yitzḥak and Esav, not Yaakov*. We feel the father's shock – "Yitzḥak trembled violently" – as he realizes that his younger son has deceived him. We empathize with Esav, whose first thought is not anger against his brother but simple love for Yitzḥak: "Bless me – me too, my father." Then comes Yitzḥak's helplessness – "So what can I possibly do for you, my son?" – and Esav's weeping, all the more poignant given what we know of him, that he is strong, a hunter, a man not given to tears. The scene of the two together, robbed of what should have been a moment of tenderness and intimacy – son feeding father, father blessing son – is deeply affecting. There is only one other scene like it in the Pentateuch: Hagar and Yishmael, alone in the heat of the desert, without water, about to die. The comparison is deliberate. Just as there, so here, our sympathies are being enlisted on behalf of the elder son.

Rabbi Jonathan Sacks

Analysis

- What areas of understanding of human nature, society, and history do we have now that were unavailable to classical Jewish commentators? How can they aid our understanding of the text?
- What can we learn from this essay to help us understand the text?
- What further questions on the text do you have now that you have read this new take on the story?

INTEGRATING ḤOKHMA

Nowhere are narrative and counter-narrative more subtly interwoven than in the story of Yaakov and Esav. It is a work of awesome brilliance, so surprising in its effect that we cannot doubt, once we have understood its hidden message, that it is intended as *the* refutation of sibling rivalry in the Bible. Its significance, set at the very center of Bereshit, is unmistakable. Once we have decoded the mystery of Yaakov, our understanding of covenant and identity will be changed forever.

The surface narrative is a paradigm – almost a caricature – of displacement. The first time we see the twins, at their birth, the younger Yaakov is already clinging to the heels of the firstborn Esav. They are different types, Esav a hunter, Yaakov "a plain man staying with the tents" (Bereshit 25:27). The tension is heightened by parental attachment. Yitzḥak loves Esav; Rivka favors Yaakov. In the first dramatic scene between the two brothers, Esav comes in exhausted from the hunt, smells the stew Yaakov is making, and asks for some. Yaakov drives a hard bargain: my stew for your birthright. Esav agrees and in a staccato succession of five consecutive verbs – "he ate, drank, rose, left, and despised his birthright" – reveals his character: mercurial, impetuous, no match for the subtle Yaakov.

The story rises to a crescendo in the great scene of the deception. Yitzḥak, by now old and blind, asks Esav to hunt him some venison and prepare a meal so that "my soul may bless you before I die" (27:2–4). Rivka, overhearing, decides that Yaakov must take the blessing. Yaakov has his doubts. What if Yitzḥak feels him to check his identity? Esav is hairy, Yaakov smooth-skinned. Rivka, ever resourceful, has an answer. She takes Esav's goatskin clothes and puts them on Yaakov, covering his hands and neck. The disguise works, despite Yitzḥak's repeatedly expressed doubts and misgivings. The blessing is bestowed.

Yaakov leaves. Soon after, Esav arrives with the food he has prepared. Father and son slowly realize what has happened. Yitzḥak trembles. Esav lets out "a long and bitter cry," adding, "Is he not rightly called Yaakov seeing that *he has supplanted me* these two times" (27:36). Here, displacement is explicit. The younger has usurped the place of the elder. Conflict has yielded tragedy – a blind man misled, a son robbed of his blessing, a trust betrayed, a family divided, and violence waiting in the wings: "Esav said in his heart: 'The days of mourning for my father are approaching. Then I will kill my brother Yaakov'" (27:41).

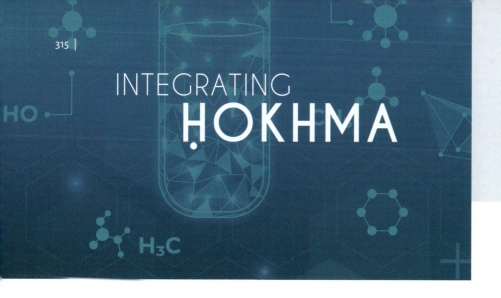

1. The second and third blessings are relatively similar to one another; at the center of both lies the promise of a multiplicity of descendants and of the land. The first blessing is an exception: it contains no promise as to dominion in the land or its inheritance; it speaks only of general abundance, with no mention of the classic element of descendants.

2. There are considerable differences in style between the second and third blessings, with additions and elaborations of one as opposed to the other and vice versa.

3. The first blessing is preceded by a process apparently aimed not only at arousing Yitzḥak's affection for his son, but also at arousing a serene and joyful atmosphere conducive to divine inspiration. The meat and wine give Yitzḥak vitality, causing him to want to convey his blessing. The character of the blessing is entirely mortal and worldly. While it does contain a prominently religious element, ultimately it lacks any transcendental foundation.

4. Formulations of blessings are usually based on the pattern of previous blessings. The first blessing fits the general mold of a father's blessing to his son. In the third blessing it is easy to identify the elements of the various blessings to Avraham. Below we shall trace the exact sources.

5. The blessings invoke different names of God. In this context, a general principle should be pointed out: In the Torah we find frequent interchanges of God's names. The three most dominant names are the ones mentioned here: Elohim, the Tetragrammaton, and El Shaddai (less common than the other two). God's different names represent different aspects of His appearance and involvement in reality. *Ḥazal* set forth the following distinction: the name Elohim reflects divine justice, while the Tetragrammaton represents the trait of divine mercy. Since the etymology of both of these

TAKING A LITERARY APPROACH

Yaakov received, within a very short period of time (both chronologically and textually), three blessings, on three different occasions:

1. Yitzḥak blesses him, believing him to be Esav (Bereshit 27:27–29).
2. Yitzḥak blesses him as he sends him off to Ḥaran to find a wife (28:1–4).
3. God blesses him in Beit El, in the dream of the ladder (28:12–15).

Our question is: why does Yaakov need three blessings; why will one not suffice? Let us now focus on the differences between these blessings:

1. Preparation for and context of the blessing: Yitzḥak utters the first blessing in the midst of eating his meal and drinking wine; this implies a mortal blessing. The second blessing relates to the purpose of sending Yaakov away: marriage. The third blessing is unexpected; it offers Yaakov support and encouragement.
2. God's name in the blessing: The first blessing includes the words "May God (Elohim) give you"; in the second, Yitzḥak says, "May the Almighty God (El Shaddai) bless you"; in the third, we read, "Behold, God (*Y-H-V-H*) stood over him."
3. Content of the blessing: Yitzḥak's first blessing to Yaakov invokes material abundance of the land, dominion over nations and brethren, a curse to those who curse him, and a blessing to those who bless him. His second blessing to him speaks of being fruitful and multiplying, the blessing of Avraham, and the inheritance of the land of his sojourning – Canaan. God's blessing starts off with an identification: "I am the Lord God of your fathers," there is the promise of the land – "to you I shall give it," there are descendants like the dust of the earth, expansion beyond the geographical limitations, and a blessing to all the families of the earth through him.

Examining the three blessings leads us to the following conclusions:

story of Avraham's circumcision, where God identifies Himself to Avraham using this name. Hence, we must seek the reason for this name in that context.

In the third blessing, God appears with the text referring to Him as *Y-H-V-H*. From the context of this blessing and its purpose, the reason is clear: this is a private revelation, a substantial part of which reflects the divine will to encourage Yaakov and promise him support. God reveals Himself to Yaakov for the first time, and, understandably, presents Himself using the name by which He was known to the forefathers: "I am *Y-H-V-H*, the God of your father Avraham." As we mentioned concerning the second blessing, here, too, it should be noted that the use of this name takes us back to a previous blessing – one or more of the blessings to Avraham.

Rabbi Tamir Granot

names is unclear, and since both cases represent unique grammatical forms, we have no way of understanding the names on their own; we can only arrive at their significance based on their respective contexts. In this regard, the first appearance of each, in the first two chapters of creation, is of particular importance. The name Elohim is used in the first chapter, which recounts the story of the creation of nature in general, in a process of orderly development and fixed laws. The name is connected to the fact that God is the source of nature, the source of natural law and regularity in the world, and this is also a context for what *Ḥazal* refer to as the "trait of strict justice" or the "trait of law."

The second section of the creation story (ch. 2–3) is recounted using the name *Y-H-V-H*. The greater part of this section describes the creation of man and woman. It contains much of what is absent from the first section – particularly concerning the personal connection between God and man and the closeness between them, as manifest in God's concern for him, His placement of him in the Garden of Eden, the commandment He gives him, etc. Hence, we deduce that the use of the name *Y-H-V-H* should be regarded as a private, personal name – or, as arises from God's words to Moshe at the burning bush, where Moshe asks: "They shall say to me, what is His name?" and God's answer is "Ehyeh" and *Y-H-V-H* (we shall not elaborate here on the difference between these two names). Thus it appears that the name Elohim expresses God's relationship with the world in terms of function and rule, while *Y-H-V-H* is His "private" name.

In light of the above analysis, we can better understand the different blessings:

In the first blessing, the divine name that is used is Elohim – a general name, referring to the Creator of nature; this name relates to all humans on the same level. It is therefore natural that Yitzḥak uses it in a blessing whose source is human and whose character and content are universal.

In his second blessing, Yitzḥak uses the name El Shaddai. The source of this name is to be found in the

41 Esav resented Yaakov because of the blessing his father had given him. "The days of
mourning for my father are approaching," he said to himself, "and then I will kill my
42 brother Yaakov." When Rivka was told what her elder son Esav had said, she summoned
her younger son Yaakov and said, "Your brother Esav is consoling himself with the thought
43 44 of killing you. Now, my son, listen to me. Flee at once to my brother Lavan in Ḥaran. Stay
45 with him a while, until your brother's rage subsides. When your brother is no longer angry
with you and has forgotten what you did to him, I will send word to you to come back. Why
46 should I lose you both in one day?" Rivka then said to Yitzḥak, "I loathe my life because
of these Hittite women. If Yaakov marries a Hittite woman like them, one of the women of
28 1 the land, why should I go on living?" So Yitzḥak called Yaakov to him. He blessed him and
2 charged him: "You are not to marry a Canaanite woman. Go at once to Padan Aram, to the
house of your mother's father Betuel, and there marry a daughter of your mother's brother
Lavan. May El Shaddai bless you, make you fertile, and multiply you so that you become
4 a community of peoples. May He grant Avraham's blessing to you and your descendants,
that you may possess the land where of your wayfaring you live as a stranger, which God
5 gave to Avraham." Then Yitzḥak sent Yaakov on his way. He went toward Padan Aram, to
6 Lavan son of Betuel the Aramean, brother of Rivka, Yaakov and Esav's mother. Esav learned
that Yitzḥak had blessed Yaakov and sent him to Padan Aram to find a wife, and that when

UNLOCKING THE TEXT

- Is killing Yaakov a just or understandable reaction to what had happened?
- Who did Esav tell of his plans, and how did Rivka find out?
- How was Rivka so sure Esav's rage would subside?
- Why was Rivka worried about losing both her sons "in one day"?
- Why does Yitzḥak give Yaakov yet another blessing?
- How is this blessing different from the previous one Yaakov received?
- Why did Esav only realize now that taking a wife from the local of women of Canaan was distressing for his parents?
- Were the Ishmaelites acceptable to Rivka and Yitzḥak?

FINDING YOURSELF IN THE TEXT

- Has anyone ever said they wanted to kill you? Do you think they meant it?
- Have you ever run away from a difficult situation? In retrospect, was there a better response you could have chosen?
- Do you think your parents should have a say in choosing who you marry?

Consider using these questions as the basis for your own commentary or creative midrash.

How does reflecting on these firsthand experiences help you better understand the text?

מא וַיִּשְׂטֹ֤ם עֵשָׂו֙ אֶֽת־יַעֲקֹ֔ב עַל־הַ֨בְּרָכָ֔ה אֲשֶׁ֥ר בֵּרְכ֖וֹ אָבִ֑יו וַיֹּ֨אמֶר עֵשָׂ֜ו בְּלִבּ֗וֹ יִקְרְבוּ֙ יְמֵי֙

מב אֵ֣בֶל אָבִ֔י וְאַֽהַרְגָ֖ה אֶת־יַעֲקֹ֥ב אָחִֽי׃ וַיֻּגַּ֣ד לְרִבְקָ֔ה אֶת־דִּבְרֵ֖י עֵשָׂ֣ו בְּנָ֣הּ הַגָּדֹ֑ל וַתִּשְׁלַ֞ח

וַתִּקְרָ֤א לְיַעֲקֹב֙ בְּנָ֣הּ הַקָּטָ֔ן וַתֹּ֣אמֶר אֵלָ֔יו הִנֵּה֙ עֵשָׂ֣ו אָחִ֔יךָ מִתְנַחֵ֥ם לְךָ֖ לְהׇרְגֶֽךָ׃

מג מד וְעַתָּ֥ה בְנִ֖י שְׁמַ֣ע בְּקֹלִ֑י וְק֧וּם בְּרַח־לְךָ֛ אֶל־לָבָ֥ן אָחִ֖י חָרָֽנָה׃ וְיָשַׁבְתָּ֥ עִמּ֖וֹ יָמִ֣ים אֲחָדִ֑ים

מה עַ֥ד אֲשֶׁר־תָּשׁ֖וּב חֲמַ֣ת אָחִ֑יךָ עַד־שׁ֨וּב אַף־אָחִ֜יךָ מִמְּךָ֗ וְשָׁכַח֙ אֵ֣ת אֲשֶׁר־עָשִׂ֣יתָ לּ֔וֹ

מו וְשָׁלַחְתִּ֖י וּלְקַחְתִּ֣יךָ מִשָּׁ֑ם לָמָ֥ה אֶשְׁכַּ֛ל גַּם־שְׁנֵיכֶ֖ם י֥וֹם אֶחָֽד׃ וַתֹּ֤אמֶר רִבְקָה֙ אֶל־

יִצְחָ֔ק קַ֣צְתִּי בְחַיַּ֔י מִפְּנֵ֖י בְּנ֣וֹת חֵ֑ת אִם־לֹקֵ֣חַ יַ֠עֲקֹ֠ב אִשָּׁ֨ה מִבְּנֽוֹת־חֵ֤ת כָּאֵ֙לֶּה֙ מִבְּנ֣וֹת

כח א הָאָ֔רֶץ לָ֥מָּה לִּ֖י חַיִּֽים׃ וַיִּקְרָ֥א יִצְחָ֛ק אֶֽל־יַעֲקֹ֖ב וַיְבָ֣רֶךְ אֹת֑וֹ וַיְצַוֵּ֙הוּ֙ וַיֹּ֣אמֶר ל֔וֹ לֹֽא־תִקַּ֥ח

ב אִשָּׁ֖ה מִבְּנ֥וֹת כְּנָֽעַן׃ ק֥וּם לֵךְ֙ פַּדֶּ֣נָֽה אֲרָ֔ם בֵּ֥יתָה בְתוּאֵ֖ל אֲבִ֣י אִמֶּ֑ךָ וְקַח־לְךָ֤ מִשָּׁם֙

ג אִשָּׁ֔ה מִבְּנ֥וֹת לָבָ֖ן אֲחִ֣י אִמֶּֽךָ׃ וְאֵ֤ל שַׁדַּי֙ יְבָרֵ֣ךְ אֹֽתְךָ֔ וְיַפְרְךָ֖ וְיַרְבֶּ֑ךָ וְהָיִ֖יתָ לִקְהַ֥ל

ד עַמִּֽים׃ וְיִֽתֶּן־לְךָ֙ אֶת־בִּרְכַּ֣ת אַבְרָהָ֔ם לְךָ֖ וּלְזַרְעֲךָ֣ אִתָּ֑ךְ לְרִשְׁתְּךָ֙ אֶת־אֶ֣רֶץ מְגֻרֶ֔יךָ

ה אֲשֶׁר־נָתַ֥ן אֱלֹהִ֖ים לְאַבְרָהָֽם׃ וַיִּשְׁלַ֤ח יִצְחָק֙ אֶֽת־יַעֲקֹ֔ב וַיֵּ֖לֶךְ פַּדֶּ֣נָֽה אֲרָ֑ם אֶל־לָבָ֤ן

ו בֶּן־בְּתוּאֵל֙ הָֽאֲרַמִּ֔י אֲחִ֥י רִבְקָ֖ה אֵ֣ם יַעֲקֹ֥ב וְעֵשָֽׂו׃ וַיַּ֣רְא עֵשָׂ֗ו כִּֽי־בֵרַ֣ךְ יִצְחָק֮ אֶֽת־

יַעֲקֹב֒ וְשִׁלַּ֤ח אֹתוֹ֙ פַּדֶּ֣נָֽה אֲרָ֔ם לָקַֽחַת־ל֥וֹ מִשָּׁ֖ם אִשָּׁ֑ה בְּבָרֲכ֣וֹ אֹת֔וֹ וַיְצַ֤ו עָלָיו֙ לֵאמֹ֔ר

THEMES	COVENANT	RELATIONSHIPS AND LOVE	THE LAND OF ISRAEL

Episode 39: *Yaakov Flees* – Bereshit 27:41–28:9

SUMMARY

In this episode, Rivka instructs Yaakov to flee to her brother Lavan's house in Ḥaran after she hears of Esav's plan to murder Yaakov in retribution for the deception in the previous episode. Yaakov obeys his mother's wish and flees. Esav then takes more wives, this time from the Ishmaelites, in addition to the Hittite wives he had previously taken.

7 he blessed him, he commanded him not to marry a Canaanite woman, and that Yaakov
8 had obeyed his father and mother and had gone to Padan Aram. Esav realized then that
9 the Canaanite women displeased his father Yitzḥak. So Esav went to Yishmael and took
Maḥalat, daughter of Avraham's son Yishmael, a sister of Nevayot, to be his wife, with his
other wives.

THE ART OF MIDRASH

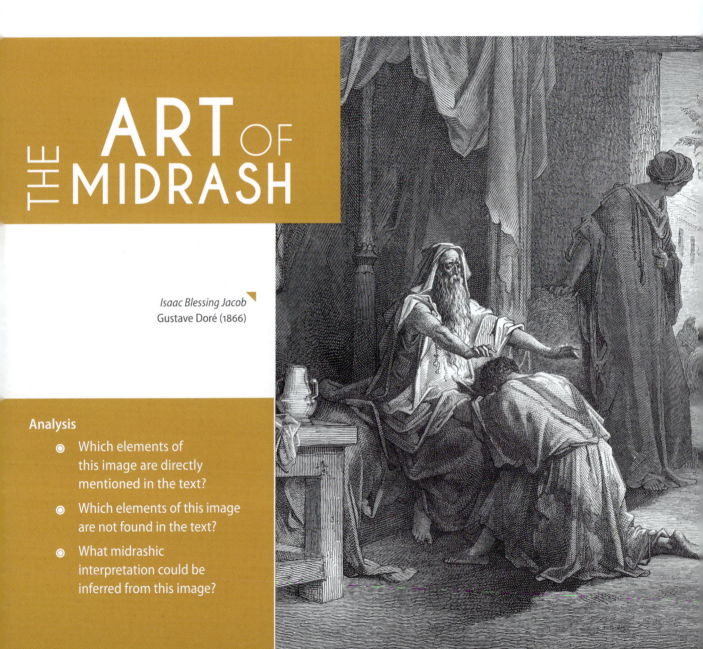

Isaac Blessing Jacob
Gustave Doré (1866)

Analysis

- Which elements of this image are directly mentioned in the text?
- Which elements of this image are not found in the text?
- What midrashic interpretation could be inferred from this image?

ז לֹֽא־תִקַּ֥ח אִשָּׁ֖ה מִבְּנ֣וֹת כְּנָ֑עַן: וַיִּשְׁמַ֣ע יַעֲקֹ֔ב אֶל־אָבִ֖יו וְאֶל־אִמּ֑וֹ וַיֵּ֖לֶךְ פַּדֶּ֥נָֽה אֲרָֽם: מפטיר
ט וַיַּ֣רְא עֵשָׂ֔ו כִּ֥י רָע֖וֹת בְּנ֣וֹת כְּנָ֑עַן בְּעֵינֵ֖י יִצְחָ֥ק אָבִֽיו: וַיֵּ֥לֶךְ עֵשָׂ֖ו אֶל־יִשְׁמָעֵ֑אל וַיִּקַּ֡ח
אֶת־מָחֲלַ֣ת ׀ בַּת־יִשְׁמָעֵ֣אל בֶּן־אַבְרָהָ֗ם אֲח֛וֹת נְבָי֖וֹת עַל־נָשָׁ֑יו ל֥וֹ לְאִשָּֽׁה:

A QUESTION OF
BIBLIODRAMA

TO ESAV

◉ What are your current feelings toward your brother Yaakov?

◉ How do you feel about your parents right now?

◉ Do you still care what your parents think about who you marry? Both your parents, or just your father?

◉ How could you not have known this previously? What does that tell you about your relationship with them/him?

TO RIVKA

◉ What are your worst fears when to comes to your sons?

◉ Why didn't you confront Esav about his plans rather than encourage Yaakov to flee?

◉ How do you feel about Esav's choice of new wives?

TO YAAKOV

◉ Are you scared of your brother Esav?

◉ Do you understand his rage? Do you think it is justified?

◉ Why are you fleeing to Ḥaran?

חֵת, חִתִּי
ḤET – HITTITE

The Hittites were one of the Canaanite nations, mentioned about seventy times, usually as part of a list of Canaanite nations. In the second half of the nineteenth century, scholars of the ancient Near East began to understand that a large kingdom called Ḥati existed from the mid-seventeenth century BCE in what is today central Turkey, and in the fourteenth century BCE, it became a large empire whose domain spread all the way to northern Syria. The residents of this kingdom were of Indo-European descent, and after their kingdom was destroyed at the end of the thirteenth century BCE, a number of small kingdoms remained in the area of northern Syria, which scholars refer to as "neo-Hittites." In the ninth century BCE, these kingdoms were annexed by the kingdom of Aram Damesek, and in the eighth century BCE the area came under Assyrian control. With the discovery of the Hattite culture, many scholars began to assume that the Hattites in Canaan were part of a group that emigrated south to Canaan, and to this day, it is acceptable to refer to the kingdom, culture, religion, and language of the Hattites by their biblical name, the Hittites. Today, however, most scholars believe that there is no direct connection between the biblical Hittites and the Hattite kingdom in the north.

Analysis

- What areas of archaeological, geographical, and historical knowledge do we have now that were unavailable to classical Jewish commentators? How can they aid our understanding of the text?
- How can this information about the Hittite nation help us understand the text?
- What further questions on the text do you have now that you have read this new information and research?

INTEGRATING ḤOKHMA

Foundations of the cave of Makhpela in Ḥevron

Gat, not telling him of the massacre that he had wrought among the Gizrites and Geshurites, inhabitants of the land. Like Esav, the man of the sword who protected his father, a man of the land, David too forged a covenant with the people of Yehuda who dwelled in the Kenite and Jerahmeelite Negev, to protect their fields and their flocks. He lived by the sword, and that was how he made his living. Like Esav, picked out by his father for kingship ("You shall be a lord to your brethren"), David was anointed for kingship by Shmuel. Like Esav, who lost his right to rule when he exchanged the sword of defensive battle for the sword of the murderer, David almost lost his right to rule – but only "almost."

On one occasion, Esav the redhead did have the merit of resembling King David. The valiant fighter indeed became, for just one moment, a true hero, who conquered his evil inclination. The conqueror of the city became the master of his own spirit. The man whose hand never let go of his sword discovered the secret of its boundaries. For one moment, the murderer once again – rightfully – assumed the features of a fighter in defense. This was when Esav lifted his sword against his competitor, the one who stole his blessing, his birthright, and his future – Yaakov – but returned it to its sheath out of honor for his father.

No moral consideration, in my eyes, can take this merit away from Esav. This merit was greater than that of the brothers, the tribes of God, in their conflict with Yosef. It was a moment in which Esav was truly worthy of the kingship that his father had wanted to bestow upon him.

Esav was indeed awarded this kingship when the king of Yehuda, Yehoram ben Yehoshafat, the eldest son, killed all his brothers in order to become king (II Divrei HaYamim 21). Then Edom revolted, and appointed themselves a king.

He was awarded kingship again when the two sons of Shlomtzion – Hyrcanus and Aristobulus – fought over the kingdom and were ready to kill one another. At that time, the merit of Esav – who had refrained from killing his brother in similar circumstances – stood firm for his descendants. And it was then that Antipater and Herod inherited the royal throne of Israel – may it be rebuilt and restored speedily in our days, amen.

Rabbi Yaakov Medan

TAKING A LITERARY APPROACH

If Esav was a rotten murderer from the start, how are we to explain Yitzḥak's love for him? Was Yitzḥak so completely cut off from his surroundings? Was he blind from the day that Esav was born? Can we imagine a blind father who is so acutely out of touch with his son? Why did Rivka not report Yitzḥak's son's doings?

To my mind, the red-haired Esav did not grow up as a murderer. He grew up as a warrior. He took with him into battle the brave spirit and military heritage of his grandfather Avraham, and the band of fighters that he commanded was only slightly greater than that headed by Avraham: he had four hundred men as opposed to Avraham's 318.

It is precisely for this reason that Yitzḥak loves Esav. The blind Yitzḥak, sitting in his tent and communing with the *Shekhina*, is not the only Yitzḥak that we know. Yitzḥak was a "man of the field," who held onto his land tenaciously, sowed it, and reaped a hundredfold. He achieved this in the Negev region during a drought (Rashi on Bereshit 26:12)! Yitzḥak owned much property and vast flocks. Owing to his extensive property and his stubborn attachment to the land, he earned himself many enemies. In contrast to Avraham, Yitzḥak's solitary nature did not allow him to lead an army of soldiers.

It is reasonable to assume that even after Yitzḥak settled in Reḥovot, in the Negev, he was open to raids by lawless desert bandits. It seems that here, too, Esav was required to rely on his sword and bow, and not just to hunt for food.

A covenant of blood was forged between Yitzḥak – a man of the field, the land, and hard labor – and his son Esav, who maintained his legion on Yitzḥak's land, with its wells and the flocks grazing in the wilderness. It was a covenant between the scythe and the sword, between the farmer and the guard. Because of these qualities in Esav, Yitzḥak wanted to eventually bestow the kingship upon him, since "a king is appointed in order to effect justice and to wage war." When the plan was thwarted, his blessing to Esav was "You shall live by the sword, and you shall serve your brother." Yaakov was to be the lord of the land, while Esav and his army would be the mercenaries who would protect it.

It is the Esav who plots to kill Yaakov, who gives rise to the midrashic image of Esav the murderer, the spiller of blood – an image that, to my mind, is as far removed from the literal text as a soldier from a murderer. And since we can neither abandon the literal text nor ignore the image depicted by the midrash, we seem to have no choice but to describe a character comprised of both sides of the sword: defensive war on the one hand, and murder on the other.

Still, we must ask: can we really judge a warrior, whose sensitivity to blood is dulled as a result of his occupation, by the same standards that we apply to a person who sits engaged in study in the *beit midrash*? The key to answering our question lies with Esav's biblical "double" – none other than King David.

Like Esav, he too was a red-haired hunter, who killed a lion and a bear with his bare hands. Like Esav, he gathered a band of four hundred embittered fighters under his leadership, and went off with them to the northern Negev in order to engage the desert bandits in battle. Like Esav, who managed to paint a deceptive picture of himself in the eyes of his father, David deceived Akhish, king of

ויצא
Vayetze

Parasha Overview

Yaakov leaves home in flight from Esav who had sworn to kill him, only to find himself in a fraught relationship with Lavan, his uncle, with whom he takes refuge. He falls in love with Lavan's younger daughter Raḥel and agrees to work the seven years to earn her hand in marriage. When the wedding eventually takes place, Yaakov wakes the next morning to discover that Lavan has substituted the elder, Leah, in place of Raḥel. Yaakov later marries Raḥel as well, but there is tension between the sisters. Leah, unloved, is blessed with children; Raḥel, loved, is not. Interwoven with this is another tension between Yaakov and Lavan – about flocks, wages, and ownership – which eventually leads Yaakov to flee again, this time homeward. The *parasha* is framed by these two journeys.

Episodes

40.	**Yaakov's Dream**	28:10–22
41.	**Yaakov Marries Raḥel and Leah**	29:1–30
42.	**The Birth of Yaakov's Children**	29:31–30:24
43.	**Yaakov Negotiates an Exit Settlement**	30:25–43
44.	**Yaakov Escapes Lavan**	31:1–21
45.	**Lavan Pursues Yaakov and They Reconcile**	31:22–32:2

Parasha Stats

- 5,512 letters
- 2,021 words
- 148 verses
- 235 lines in a sefer Torah

10 11 Yaakov left Be'er Sheva and journeyed toward Ḥaran. In time he chanced upon a certain
place and decided to spend the night there, because the sun had set. He took some stones
12 of the place and put them under his head, and in that place lay down to sleep. And he
dreamed: he saw a ladder set upon the ground, whose top reached the heavens. On it,
13 angels of God went up and came down. The LORD stood over him there and said, "I am
the LORD, the God of Avraham your father, and the God of Yitzḥak. The land on which
14 you lie I will give to you and your descendants. Your descendants shall be like the dust of
the earth, and you will spread out to the west, the east, the north, and the south. Through
15 you and your descendants, all the families of the earth will be blessed. I am with you. I
will protect you wherever you go and I will bring you back to this land, for I will not leave
16 you until I have done what I have spoken of to you." Then Yaakov awoke from his sleep
17 and said, "Truly, the LORD is in this place – and I did not know it!" He was afraid and said,
"How full of awe is this place! This is none other than the House of God, and this the gate
18 of the heavens!" Yaakov rose early the next morning, took the stone he had placed under

UNLOCKING THE TEXT

- What do the ladder and the angels in Yaakov's dream represent?
- Are the same angels going up and down the ladder?
- Why is Avraham – but not Yitzḥak – described as "your father"?
- How do the promises God gives here to Yaakov compare to those given to Avraham and Yitzḥak?
- Why does this episode happen now?
- Why did Yaakov become afraid?
- What does it mean that this place was the "House of God" and the "gate of heaven"? How does Yaakov know this?
- Why does Yaakov make a conditional commitment to God?

FINDING YOURSELF IN THE TEXT

- Have you ever woken up from a dream and wondered if it was real?
- Do you think dreams have meaning beyond what they tell you about what is going on in your head?
- Have you ever felt God was sending you a message of some kind through a dream or other medium?

Consider using these questions as the basis for your own commentary or creative midrash.

How does reflecting on these firsthand experiences help you better understand the text?

י יא וַיֵּצֵא יַעֲקֹב מִבְּאֵר שָׁבַע וַיֵּלֶךְ חָרָנָה: וַיִּפְגַּע בַּמָּקוֹם וַיָּלֶן שָׁם כִּי־בָא הַשֶּׁמֶשׁ כו ויצא
יב וַיִּקַּח מֵאַבְנֵי הַמָּקוֹם וַיָּשֶׂם מְרַאֲשֹׁתָיו וַיִּשְׁכַּב בַּמָּקוֹם הַהוּא: וַיַּחֲלֹם וְהִנֵּה סֻלָּם
יג מֻצָּב אַרְצָה וְרֹאשׁוֹ מַגִּיעַ הַשָּׁמָיְמָה וְהִנֵּה מַלְאֲכֵי אֱלֹהִים עֹלִים וְיֹרְדִים בּוֹ: וְהִנֵּה
יהוה נִצָּב עָלָיו וַיֹּאמַר אֲנִי יהוה אֱלֹהֵי אַבְרָהָם אָבִיךָ וֵאלֹהֵי יִצְחָק הָאָרֶץ אֲשֶׁר
יד אַתָּה שֹׁכֵב עָלֶיהָ לְךָ אֶתְּנֶנָּה וּלְזַרְעֶךָ: וְהָיָה זַרְעֲךָ כַּעֲפַר הָאָרֶץ וּפָרַצְתָּ יָמָּה
טו וָקֵדְמָה וְצָפֹנָה וָנֶגְבָּה וְנִבְרְכוּ בְךָ כָּל־מִשְׁפְּחֹת הָאֲדָמָה וּבְזַרְעֶךָ: וְהִנֵּה אָנֹכִי
עִמָּךְ וּשְׁמַרְתִּיךָ בְּכֹל אֲשֶׁר־תֵּלֵךְ וַהֲשִׁבֹתִיךָ אֶל־הָאֲדָמָה הַזֹּאת כִּי לֹא אֶעֱזָבְךָ
טז עַד אֲשֶׁר אִם־עָשִׂיתִי אֵת אֲשֶׁר־דִּבַּרְתִּי לָךְ: וַיִּיקַץ יַעֲקֹב מִשְּׁנָתוֹ וַיֹּאמֶר אָכֵן יֵשׁ
יז יהוה בַּמָּקוֹם הַזֶּה וְאָנֹכִי לֹא יָדָעְתִּי: וַיִּירָא וַיֹּאמַר מַה־נּוֹרָא הַמָּקוֹם הַזֶּה אֵין זֶה
יח כִּי אִם־בֵּית אֱלֹהִים וְזֶה שַׁעַר הַשָּׁמָיִם: וַיַּשְׁכֵּם יַעֲקֹב בַּבֹּקֶר וַיִּקַּח אֶת־הָאֶבֶן אֲשֶׁר־

THEMES | THE LAND OF ISRAEL | COVENANT | PROPHECY AND REVELATION

Episode 40: *Yaakov's Dream* – Bereshit 28:10–22

SUMMARY

Yaakov flees from his brother, leaves his parents, and ventures alone, exiled from the land he was to inherit. Only now does his independent adult life begin. During his stay overnight in Beit El he is granted a vision that will strengthen him on his path to a new life in a foreign place. Although it is an opaque night vision rather than a clear prophecy, this unique revelation symbolizes the start of his making his own way in the world and his ability to hear the word of God.

19 his head, set it up as a pillar, and poured oil on top of it. He named the place Beit El;[1] the
20 town was originally called Luz. Yaakov then made a vow. "If God will be with me," he said,
"protecting me on this journey I am taking, giving me bread to eat and clothes to wear,
21 22 and if I return in peace to my father's house, then the Lord will be my God. This stone I
set up as a pillar will become a house of God, and of all that You give me I will dedicate a
tenth to You."

---

1 | Meaning "House of God."

THE ART OF MIDRASH

Jacob's Ladder
Marc Chagall (1973)

Analysis

- Which elements of this image are directly mentioned in the text?
- Which elements of this image are not found in the text?
- What midrashic interpretation could be inferred from this image?

יט שָׁם מְרַאֲשֹׁתָיו וַיָּשֶׂם אֹתָהּ מַצֵּבָה וַיִּצֹק שֶׁמֶן עַל־רֹאשָׁהּ: וַיִּקְרָא אֶת־שֵׁם־הַמָּקוֹם
כ הַהוּא בֵּית־אֵל וְאוּלָם לוּז שֵׁם־הָעִיר לָרִאשֹׁנָה: וַיִּדַּר יַעֲקֹב נֶדֶר לֵאמֹר אִם־יִהְיֶה
אֱלֹהִים עִמָּדִי וּשְׁמָרַנִי בַּדֶּרֶךְ הַזֶּה אֲשֶׁר אָנֹכִי הוֹלֵךְ וְנָתַן־לִי לֶחֶם לֶאֱכֹל וּבֶגֶד
כא כב לִלְבֹּשׁ: וְשַׁבְתִּי בְשָׁלוֹם אֶל־בֵּית אָבִי וְהָיָה יְהוָה לִי לֵאלֹהִים: וְהָאֶבֶן הַזֹּאת
אֲשֶׁר־שַׂמְתִּי מַצֵּבָה יִהְיֶה בֵּית אֱלֹהִים וְכֹל אֲשֶׁר תִּתֶּן־לִי עַשֵּׂר אֲעַשְּׂרֶנּוּ לָךְ:

A QUESTION OF BIBLIODRAMA

TO YAAKOV

- Describe your emotions as you left your home for Ḥaran.
- What do you think this dream means?
- Are the promises and blessings that God gave you here what you needed to hear? Why?
- Describe your emotions when you woke from your dream.
- Why did you declare a conditional commitment to God after this experience?

In his vision of God's throne, Yeḥezkel (10:14) describes seeing four faces: a cherub, a lion, an eagle, and a human. The Gemara in Ḥullin (91b) elaborates on Yaakov's dream and suggests that the angels were going up and down, looking at the picture of the human face by the throne and comparing it to Yaakov's face. Seeing the resemblance, they became jealous of his presence on the throne and wanted to harm him, so God had to protect Yaakov.

Rabbi Shimshon of Ostropoli suggests that Yaakov was previously aware that there were creatures that could reach elevated spiritual heights. He knew that the cherub, lion, and eagle had their place by God's throne, but he was not aware that his image was there as well. It was not until the dream, when he saw the angels comparing the image on the throne with his face, that he realized his true potential. In a brilliantly creative rereading of the *pasuk*, Rabbi Shimshon suggests that Yaakov's word choice alludes to self-efficacy. He already knew the spiritual potential of *akhen*, in Hebrew spelled *alef-kaf-nun,* representing the lion (*aryeh*), cherub, and eagle (*nesher*). Yet, until this dream, he was unaware of the spiritual potential of *anokhi*, literally, "myself," spelled *alef-nun-kaf-yod*, representing the three images from *akhen* with the addition of the *yod* – for Yaakov.

This newfound self-efficacy was not domain specific. It was not just limited to spiritual pursuits. Yaakov's new attitude pervaded all his interactions, as is clear from the very next episode regarding the shepherds by the well. In a powerful *derasha* ("The Stone on the Well – Boulder or Pebble?"), Rabbi Norman Lamm contrasts the attitude of the shepherds with that of Yaakov. When Yaakov asks the shepherds why they do not water their herds, they respond that there is a giant stone covering the well, and until more people come to help push it off, *lo nuchal* – they just can't do it (29:8). They don't believe in their ability, so they don't even try. Yaakov, believing in his ability to accomplish, walks over to the stone and succeeds in removing it from the well. He believes in his ability to effect change, puts in the effort, and succeeds.

How many areas of life – spiritual or otherwise – do we write off as being too hard or not within our abilities? Perhaps if we learn this lesson from Yaakov, we can work on boosting our self-efficacy by realizing our potential, putting in the effort, and increasing our chances of success and accomplishment.

Rabbi Mordechai Schiffman

Analysis

- What areas of understanding of human nature and society do we now have that were unavailable to classical Jewish commentators? How can they aid our understanding of the text?
- What can we learn from this essay to help us understand the text?
- What further questions on the text do you have now that you have read this new take on the story?

INTEGRATING ḤOKHMA

One of the best predictors of success is the belief that our actions can bring about the desired results. Believing in our ability to accomplish something specific will help boost our motivation and make it more likely that we will succeed in attaining that goal. This power of believing in our own abilities, referred to as "self-efficacy" in the psychological literature, was first formulated by Albert Bandura. Bandura understood self-efficacy to be domain specific, meaning that we have different beliefs regarding the different types of ability in question. For example, I may have high self-efficacy for writing but low self-efficacy for calculus. Later researchers suggested that there can also be a general self-efficacy that is not domain specific. This means that I can have a general belief in my ability to accomplish tasks and overcome barriers, regardless of what type of task it may be.

As Yaakov makes his way to Ḥaran he dreams of angels ascending and descending on a ladder that reaches the heavens (Bereshit 28:12). Through this vision, he realizes that God was present in that place (*Akhen, yesh Hashem bamakom hazeh*), of which he seemed previously unaware (*ve'anokhi lo yadati*) (28:16). Rabbi Shimshon of Ostropoli, perhaps bothered by the assumption that Yaakov did not perceive God's presence before the dream, rereads this *pasuk* with a message related to self-efficacy. To fully understand his point, we first need some background.

Yaakov's vow is deeply problematic. How can he take what God just promised and make that the condition for his belief and worship? Does he not trust that God will fulfill His promise? Is he, like Avraham, seeking some kind of heavenly sign?

It seems to me that we are once again privy to a window into the soul of a budding prophet. Let us return to the opening scene. Alone and terrified, Yaakov dreams of reaching up to the heavens for safety and succor. His dream moves from the ground to the heavens and from angels to God. God's message is comforting, reassuring, and even elevating. (Indeed, Yaakov later "lifts up his legs" as though he were walking on air as he continues his journey.) The drama of his nocturnal vision awakens him in the middle of night, and the startling appearance of God jolts Yaakov into a state of fear, as he confronts coming to a holy place unaware and unprepared.

In the morning, however, it seems that Yaakov is not quite sure of what happened during the night. Was it actually a prophetic message, or does Yaakov want so much to hear from God that he imagines the whole thing? Was it just the ladder or the entire divine oration that was a product of his imagination?

Some dreams are so vivid that we wake in the middle of the night and check our surroundings to verify our reality. But in the morning, what was so real in the middle of the night is just a blurry memory. Yaakov has no way to verify his dream-prophecy, so he takes a vow: "If, indeed, it is God who came to me.... If God really did promise to protect and care for me.... If the God of my fathers indeed chose me to be their successor and will hence be my God, then I vow to reciprocate." Yaakov does not doubt whether God will fulfill His promise; he doubts whether God ever made such a promise. And only time will tell.

Rabbi Zvi Grumet

TAKING A LITERARY APPROACH

Yaakov's startled reaction to the dream and the divine message notwithstanding, he is exhausted from his travels and falls back asleep. When he awakens in the morning he sees the rock of his protection and, recognizing that it is no longer necessary (as God has promised to be his protector), he anoints it and dedicates it to God. The presence of God, who is *nitzav*, "standing" over him in his dream, is now represented by a *matzeva*, an upright stone monument. God is now Yaakov's Rock.

What comes next, however, is particularly troubling. Yaakov makes a conditional vow to God, and his conditions seem to refer to the very things God has just promised in the dream:

God's nocturnal promise (28:15)	***Yaakov's vow (28:20–22)***
I will be with you,	If God is with me,
I will protect you wherever you go,	and protects me on this path which I take,
	and gives me food to eat and clothes to wear,
and return you to this land	and returns me peacefully to my home,
until I do what I told you.	and He will be God to me
	then this stone which I set as a *matzeva* will become a house for God,
	and from all that You give me, I will tithe to You.

29 1 2 Yaakov began traveling again and came to the land of the people of the East. There he saw
a well in a field. Three flocks of sheep were lying beside it because this was the well from
3 which the flocks were watered. The top of it was covered with a large stone. When all the
flocks were gathered there, the stone would be rolled from the mouth of the well and the
4 sheep watered. The stone would then be put back in place on top of the well. Yaakov asked
5 the shepherds, "Brothers, where are you from?" "We are from Ḥaran," they replied. He
6 asked, "Do you know Lavan son of Naḥor?" "We know him," they said. He asked, "Is he
well?" "He is well," they said, "and look, here is his daughter Raḥel coming with the sheep."
7 "Look," he said, "it is still broad daylight. It is not yet time to gather in the animals. Water
8 the flocks and take them back to pasture." But they said, "We cannot do that until all the
flocks are gathered and the stone is rolled from the top of the well. Only then can we water
9 the flocks." While he was still talking with them, Raḥel came with her father's sheep; she
10 was a shepherdess. When Yaakov saw Raḥel, daughter of his mother's brother Lavan, with
Lavan's sheep, he stepped forward, rolled the stone from the top of the well, and watered his
11 12 uncle's sheep. And Yaakov kissed Raḥel – and wept aloud. And Yaakov told Raḥel that he
13 was related to her father: he was Rivka's son. She ran to tell her father. When Lavan heard

UNLOCKING THE TEXT

- Where is the land of the people of the East?
- What are the similarities and differences between this narrative and the story of the marriage of Yitzḥak and Rivka?
- Why does the well have a large stone on it?
- How did Yaakov manage to roll the stone off the well? Why is this an important detail for the Torah to share?
- Why did Yaakov weep?
- What does it mean to have sensitive eyes?
- What is the basis of Yaakov's love for Raḥel?
- Why does Yaakov need to work for seven years to marry Raḥel?
- Why did Lavan trick Yaakov into marrying Leah?
- Why did Yaakov agree to remain married to Leah?

FINDING YOURSELF IN THE TEXT

- Have you ever managed a difficult feat you thought you couldn't, because you wanted to impress someone?
- Can you think of something in your life worth working seven years for?
- Have you ever been tricked by someone in public? How did it feel?

Consider using these questions as the basis for your own commentary or creative midrash.

How does reflecting on these firsthand experiences help you better understand the text?

כט א ב וַיִּשָּׂא יַעֲקֹב רַגְלָיו וַיֵּלֶךְ אַרְצָה בְנֵי־קֶדֶם: וַיַּרְא וְהִנֵּה בְאֵר בַּשָּׂדֶה וְהִנֵּה־שָׁם שני
שְׁלֹשָׁה עֶדְרֵי־צֹאן רֹבְצִים עָלֶיהָ כִּי מִן־הַבְּאֵר הַהִוא יַשְׁקוּ הָעֲדָרִים וְהָאֶבֶן
ג גְּדֹלָה עַל־פִּי הַבְּאֵר: וְנֶאֶסְפוּ־שָׁמָּה כָל־הָעֲדָרִים וְגָלְלוּ אֶת־הָאֶבֶן מֵעַל פִּי הַבְּאֵר
ד וְהִשְׁקוּ אֶת־הַצֹּאן וְהֵשִׁיבוּ אֶת־הָאֶבֶן עַל־פִּי הַבְּאֵר לִמְקֹמָהּ: וַיֹּאמֶר לָהֶם יַעֲקֹב
ה אַחַי מֵאַיִן אַתֶּם וַיֹּאמְרוּ מֵחָרָן אֲנָחְנוּ: וַיֹּאמֶר לָהֶם הַיְדַעְתֶּם אֶת־לָבָן בֶּן־נָחוֹר
ו וַיֹּאמְרוּ יָדָעְנוּ: וַיֹּאמֶר לָהֶם הֲשָׁלוֹם לוֹ וַיֹּאמְרוּ שָׁלוֹם וְהִנֵּה רָחֵל בִּתּוֹ בָּאָה עִם־
ז הַצֹּאן: וַיֹּאמֶר הֵן עוֹד הַיּוֹם גָּדוֹל לֹא־עֵת הֵאָסֵף הַמִּקְנֶה הַשְׁקוּ הַצֹּאן וּלְכוּ רְעוּ:
ח וַיֹּאמְרוּ לֹא נוּכַל עַד אֲשֶׁר יֵאָסְפוּ כָּל־הָעֲדָרִים וְגָלְלוּ אֶת־הָאֶבֶן מֵעַל פִּי הַבְּאֵר
ט וְהִשְׁקִינוּ הַצֹּאן: עוֹדֶנּוּ מְדַבֵּר עִמָּם וְרָחֵל ׀ בָּאָה עִם־הַצֹּאן אֲשֶׁר לְאָבִיהָ כִּי
י רֹעָה הִוא: וַיְהִי כַּאֲשֶׁר רָאָה יַעֲקֹב אֶת־רָחֵל בַּת־לָבָן אֲחִי אִמּוֹ וְאֶת־צֹאן לָבָן
אֲחִי אִמּוֹ וַיִּגַּשׁ יַעֲקֹב וַיָּגֶל אֶת־הָאֶבֶן מֵעַל פִּי הַבְּאֵר וַיַּשְׁקְ אֶת־צֹאן לָבָן אֲחִי
יא יב אִמּוֹ: וַיִּשַּׁק יַעֲקֹב לְרָחֵל וַיִּשָּׂא אֶת־קֹלוֹ וַיֵּבְךְּ: וַיַּגֵּד יַעֲקֹב לְרָחֵל כִּי אֲחִי אָבִיהָ
יג הוּא וְכִי בֶן־רִבְקָה הוּא וַתָּרָץ וַתַּגֵּד לְאָבִיהָ: וַיְהִי כִשְׁמֹעַ לָבָן אֶת־שֵׁמַע ׀ יַעֲקֹב

THEMES | RELATIONSHIPS AND LOVE | THE LAND OF ISRAEL | COVENANT

Episode 41: *Yaakov Marries Raḥel and Leah* – Bereshit 29:1–30

SUMMARY

The Torah does not relate Yaakov's precise route to Ḥaran, but it can be assumed that he followed a similar path to the one he would later use upon his return to Canaan, crossing the Jordan River and then heading northward. Like Avraham's servant, who sought a wife for Yaakov's father Yitzḥak, Yaakov will find a wife near a well in Ḥaran. However, this similarity only serves to highlight Yaakov's more complicated situation. Unlike his grandfather's servant, he is on the run with nowhere else to go, and he must deal with Lavan's deceit equipped with only his wits.

the news about Yaakov, his sister's son, he ran to meet him. He embraced and kissed him
14 and brought him to his house. Yaakov told Lavan all that had happened. Lavan said to him,
"You are truly of my own bones, my own flesh." And Yaakov stayed with him for a month.
15 Then Lavan said to him, "If you are my brother, does that mean you should work for me
16 for nothing? Tell me what your hire should be." Lavan had two daughters. The elder was
17 called Leah and the younger Raḥel. Leah had sensitive eyes; Raḥel was beautiful and lovely.
18 And Yaakov was in love with Raḥel, so he said, "I will work for you seven years for your
19 younger daughter Raḥel." Lavan replied, "Better that I give her to you than to some other
20 man. Stay on with me." So Yaakov worked for Raḥel seven years. But so great was his love
21 for her that they seemed to him but a few days. Then Yaakov said to Lavan, "Give me my
22 wife – my time is done, let me come to her." So Lavan brought together all the local people
23 and made a feast. In the evening he took his daughter Leah and brought her in to him, and
24 25 he came to her. Lavan also gave his servant Zilpa to his daughter Leah as her maid. Then
came morning – and it was Leah. Yaakov said to Lavan, "What is this you have done to
26 me? I served you for Raḥel, did I not? Why did you deceive me?" Lavan said, "This is not
27 done in our country – to marry off the younger before the firstborn. Wait until the bridal
week of this one is over and then we will give you the other one also, in return for your
28 serving me another seven years." Yaakov did so. He completed Leah's bridal week; then
29 Lavan gave him his daughter Raḥel as a wife. Lavan gave his servant Bilha to his daughter
30 Raḥel as her maid. And Yaakov came also to Raḥel; and he loved Raḥel more than Leah.
And he served him for another seven years.

בֶּן־אֲחֹתוֹ וַיָּ֣רָץ לִקְרָאתוֹ֘ וַיְחַבֶּק־לוֹ֙ וַיְנַשֶּׁק־לוֹ֙ וַיְבִיאֵ֖הוּ אֶל־בֵּיתוֹ֑ וַיְסַפֵּ֣ר לְלָבָ֔ן

אֵ֖ת כָּל־הַדְּבָרִ֥ים הָאֵֽלֶּה: וַיֹּ֤אמֶר לוֹ֙ לָבָ֔ן אַ֛ךְ עַצְמִ֥י וּבְשָׂרִ֖י אָ֑תָּה וַיֵּ֥שֶׁב עִמּ֖וֹ חֹ֥דֶשׁ

יד

יָמִֽים: וַיֹּ֤אמֶר לָבָן֙ לְיַעֲקֹ֔ב הֲכִי־אָחִ֣י אַ֔תָּה וַעֲבַדְתַּ֖נִי חִנָּ֑ם הַגִּ֥ידָה לִּ֖י מַה־מַּשְׂכֻּרְתֶּֽךָ:

טו

וּלְלָבָ֖ן שְׁתֵּ֣י בָנ֑וֹת שֵׁ֤ם הַגְּדֹלָה֙ לֵאָ֔ה וְשֵׁ֥ם הַקְּטַנָּ֖ה רָחֵֽל: וְעֵינֵ֥י לֵאָ֖ה רַכּ֑וֹת וְרָחֵל֙

טז

הָֽיְתָ֔ה יְפַת־תֹּ֖אַר וִיפַ֥ת מַרְאֶֽה: וַיֶּאֱהַ֥ב יַעֲקֹ֖ב אֶת־רָחֵ֑ל וַיֹּ֗אמֶר אֶֽעֱבָדְךָ֙ שֶׁ֣בַע שָׁנִ֔ים

שלישי

יח

בְּרָחֵ֥ל בִּתְּךָ֖ הַקְּטַנָּֽה: וַיֹּ֣אמֶר לָבָ֗ן ט֚וֹב תִּתִּ֣י אֹתָ֣הּ לָ֔ךְ מִתִּתִּ֥י אֹתָ֖הּ לְאִ֣ישׁ אַחֵ֑ר

יט

שְׁבָ֖ה עִמָּדִֽי: וַיַּעֲבֹ֧ד יַעֲקֹ֛ב בְּרָחֵ֖ל שֶׁ֣בַע שָׁנִ֑ים וַיִּהְי֤וּ בְעֵינָיו֙ כְּיָמִ֣ים אֲחָדִ֔ים בְּאַהֲבָת֖וֹ

כ

אֹתָֽהּ: וַיֹּ֨אמֶר יַעֲקֹ֤ב אֶל־לָבָן֙ הָבָ֣ה אֶת־אִשְׁתִּ֔י כִּ֥י מָלְא֖וּ יָמָ֑י וְאָב֖וֹאָה אֵלֶֽיהָ: וַיֶּאֱסֹ֥ף

כא

לָבָ֛ן אֶת־כָּל־אַנְשֵׁ֥י הַמָּק֖וֹם וַיַּ֥עַשׂ מִשְׁתֶּֽה: וַיְהִ֣י בָעֶ֔רֶב וַיִּקַּח֙ אֶת־לֵאָ֣ה בִתּ֔וֹ וַיָּבֵ֥א

כב

כג

אֹתָ֖הּ אֵלָ֑יו וַיָּבֹ֖א אֵלֶֽיהָ: וַיִּתֵּ֤ן לָבָן֙ לָ֔הּ אֶת־זִלְפָּ֖ה שִׁפְחָת֑וֹ לְלֵאָ֥ה בִתּ֖וֹ שִׁפְחָֽה: וַיְהִ֣י

כד

כה

בַבֹּ֗קֶר וְהִנֵּה־הִ֣וא לֵאָ֔ה וַיֹּ֣אמֶר אֶל־לָבָ֗ן מַה־זֹּאת֙ עָשִׂ֣יתָ לִּ֔י הֲלֹ֤א בְרָחֵל֙ עָבַ֣דְתִּי

עִמָּ֔ךְ וְלָ֖מָּה רִמִּיתָֽנִי: וַיֹּ֣אמֶר לָבָ֔ן לֹא־יֵעָשֶׂ֥ה כֵ֖ן בִּמְקוֹמֵ֑נוּ לָתֵ֥ת הַצְּעִירָ֖ה לִפְנֵ֥י

כו

הַבְּכִירָֽה: מַלֵּ֖א שְׁבֻ֣עַ זֹ֑את וְנִתְּנָ֨ה לְךָ֜ גַּם־אֶת־זֹ֗את בַּעֲבֹדָה֙ אֲשֶׁ֣ר תַּעֲבֹ֣ד עִמָּדִ֔י

כז

ע֖וֹד שֶֽׁבַע־שָׁנִ֥ים אֲחֵרֽוֹת: וַיַּ֤עַשׂ יַעֲקֹב֙ כֵּ֔ן וַיְמַלֵּ֖א שְׁבֻ֣עַ זֹ֑את וַיִּתֶּן־ל֛וֹ אֶת־רָחֵ֥ל

כח

בִּתּ֖וֹ ל֥וֹ לְאִשָּֽׁה: וַיִּתֵּ֨ן לָבָ֜ן לְרָחֵ֣ל בִּתּ֗וֹ אֶת־בִּלְהָ֛ה שִׁפְחָת֖וֹ לָ֥הּ לְשִׁפְחָֽה: וַיָּבֹא֙ גַּ֣ם

כט

ל

אֶל־רָחֵ֔ל וַיֶּאֱהַ֥ב גַּֽם־אֶת־רָחֵ֖ל מִלֵּאָ֑ה וַיַּעֲבֹ֣ד עִמּ֔וֹ ע֖וֹד שֶֽׁבַע־שָׁנִ֥ים אֲחֵרֽוֹת:

THE ART OF MIDRASH

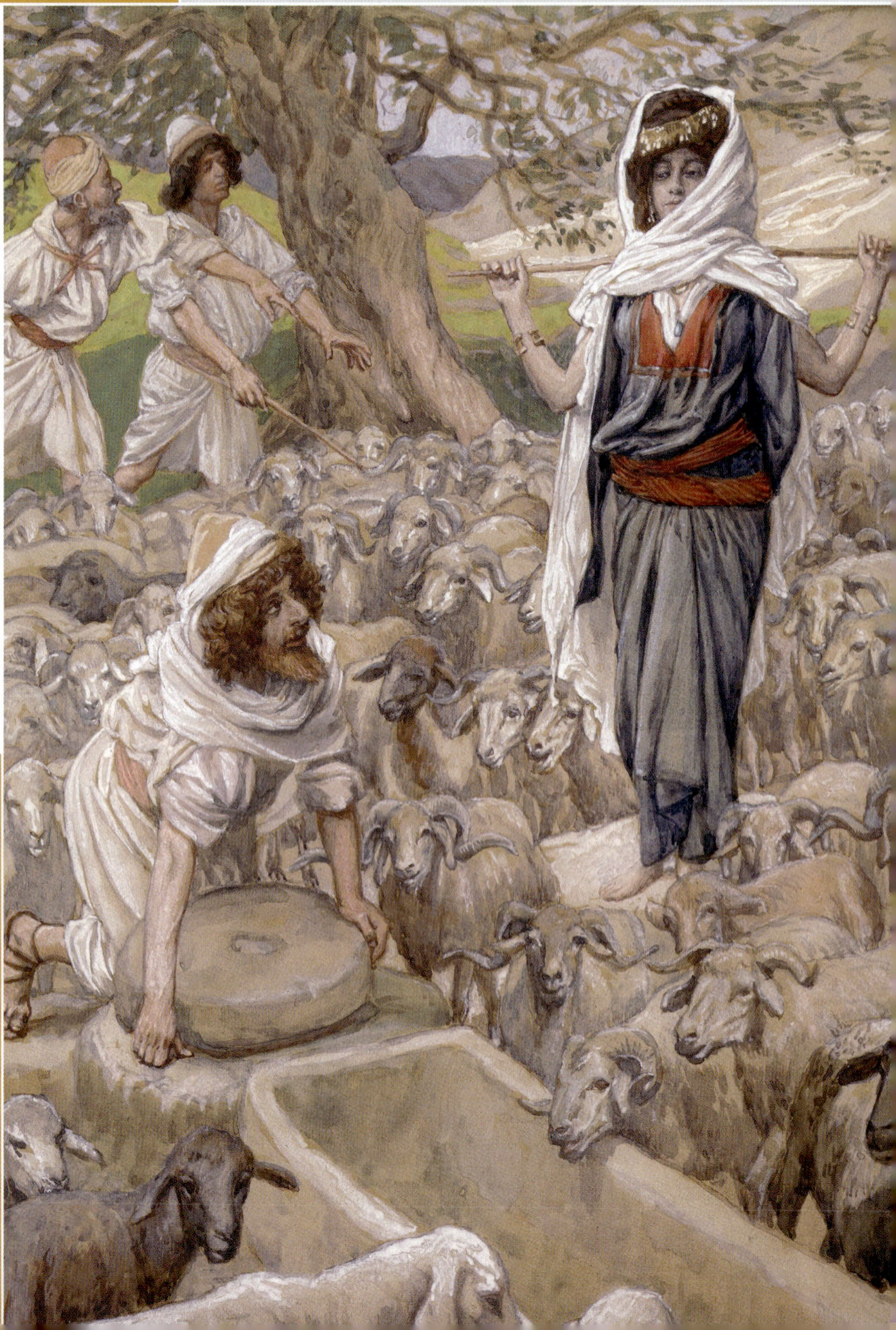

Jacob and Rachel at the Well
James Jacques Joseph Tissot
(1896–1902)

Analysis

- Which elements of this image are directly mentioned in the text?
- Which elements of this image are not found in the text?
- What midrashic interpretation could be inferred from this image?

A QUESTION OF BIBLIODRAMA

TO YAAKOV

- What were your hopes and fears as you drew close to Ḥaran?
- What puzzled you at the well?
- What emotions did you experience as you saw Raḥel approaching the well?
- What did you think when Lavan offered to pay you for your work?
- Why did you choose Raḥel and not Leah to be your wife?
- What were you feeling the next morning when you realized what Lavan had done?
- How do you feel toward Leah?

TO LAVAN

- What did you think when you heard that your nephew Yaakov was in town?
- What was your motivation to offer him payment for his work?
- Were you happy to have Yaakov as a son-in-law?
- Why did you trick him into marrying Leah first?

TO RAḤEL

- What were your thoughts and feelings when you first met Yaakov?
- Were you happy to marry him?
- Did you know your father was planning to trick Yaakov into marrying Leah first?
- Did you help him?
- Why didn't you tell Yaakov?
- Were you close to Leah before your marriage to Yaakov?
- How do you feel toward Leah now that you are both married to Yaakov?

TO LEAH

- What did you think about your father's plan to trick Yaakov?
- Were you complicit in the plan? Did you have any choice?
- What are your feelings toward your father?
- What are your feelings toward your sister?
- What are your feelings toward your husband?

about whether to act in accordance with personal, narrow interests or to cooperate with the other players is impacted by the critical consideration of "the next game." In other words, the player who betrays in the first game will likely be betrayed the next round, and the cycle will continue.

The shepherds in Ḥaran faced an iterated Prisoner's Dilemma. A shepherd could take all of the water for himself, only to discover a day or two later that a different shepherd beat him to the well, leaving him and his flock with an empty trough. The shepherds' collective fear of a bad (or selfish) actor – who would not only undermine economic stability and security but potentially send the entire system spiraling out of control – led them to institute a measure that protected the interests of the locals. This defense mechanism included three layers of protection: technological, legal, and social.

The stone was a basic technological solution. The next layer of protection was strict obedience to the rules that provided security to everyone, so that no individual intruded on another person's water supply. The third level of protection was the threat of ostracization; thus, even three flocks would not dare form a cartel. Consequently, the defense mechanism was successful, and the shepherds patiently awaited the arrival of the rest.

Such protective measures preserve stability, barring the arrival of a new player who has not been playing the game continuously and who is therefore not worried about counter-betrayal on the next day. (This is also true of a player who decides to disobey the rules for a different reason.) When Yaakov approached the well to roll off the stone, he was acting like any other player who has not been playing an iterated game; he maximized his profit at the expense of the other players, namely, the shepherds. Yaakov, who was not bound by their stipulations, did not fear their betrayal because he did not have his own flocks that he would need to water the next day. Unlike the shepherds gathered there, Yaakov had no reason to wait. When he saw Raḥel and her sheep, he had what economists call a "trembling hand." Yaakov looked only at the short-term benefits and maximized his (and his cousin's) profits immediately.

Yaakov's critique of the shepherds' misuse of resources – they waited to open the well together instead of using the time more effectively by grazing the flocks – is the classic price paid by a society that lacks interpersonal trust. That is, the entire protective mechanism, even when it is warranted and necessary, comes at a price. In the words of Francis Fukuyama:

> People who do not trust one another will end up cooperating only under a system of formal rules and regulations, which have to be negotiated, agreed to, litigated, and enforced, sometimes by coercive means. This legal apparatus, serving as a substitute for trust, entails what economists call "transaction costs." Widespread distrust in a society, in other words, imposes a kind of tax on all forms of economic activity, a tax that high-trust societies do not have to pay.

Michael A. Eisenberg

Analysis

- What areas of understanding of human nature and society do we now have that were unavailable to classical Jewish commentators? How can they aid our understanding of the text?
- What can we learn from this essay to help us understand the text?
- What further questions on the text do you have now that you have read this new take on the story?

INTEGRATING ḤOKHMA

Yaakov left his father's home and traveled to Padan Aram. There, at the edge of the well, he met his cousin Raḥel. Yaakov, perhaps aided by a rush of adrenaline, removed the stone that covered the well in a display of superhuman strength. This is how most of the commentators understand the narrative.

The verses state that "the stone on the mouth of the well was large" and that it was necessary to wait for all the flocks to gather at the well to roll off the stone. However, the verses do not explain what prevented the shepherds from removing the stone. They do not indicate that the shepherds were weak, nor do they specify that Yaakov, "a mild man who stayed in the camp," was any stronger than the shepherds of the three flocks. In his commentary on Bereshit 29:3, Rabbi Avraham ben HaRambam (Avraham son of Maimonides) offers a different explanation for the shepherds' delay:

> "But they said, 'We cannot'" – Not because they were not strong enough to lift the stone. If that were the case, Yaakov too would not have been able to lift it. Rather, they could not violate the agreement that they had reached among themselves.

According to Rabbi Avraham ben HaRambam, the shepherds did not trust one another. In the absence of the stone that blocked access to the well and mutual supervision, the shepherds suspected that one of the shepherds would take all the water for himself. Because the people of Ḥaran did not trust one another, they covered the well and stipulated that the shepherds needed to wait for everyone to reach the well. Only after that would they be able to draw water. In the words of Rabbi Avraham, the shepherds' solution or "the agreement" was the classic cooperative solution to resolving the Prisoner's Dilemma, thus preventing a tragedy of the commons.

The Prisoner's Dilemma is a paradoxical problem in game theory first publicized in 1950 by Merrill Flood and Melvin Dresher of the RAND Corporation. The dilemma presents a situation where completely rational behavior, from the perspective of the individual who is looking to maximize his personal success, will lead to a non-optimal aggregate benefit for all the players in the game. The paradox derives from the fact that each player stands to gain more by not cooperating with the others. However, in order to reach the optimum result for all the players, they actually need to cooperate with one another.

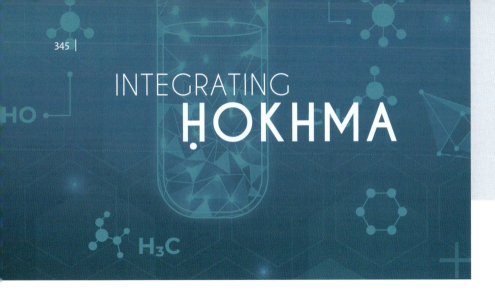

One factor that can influence the players to cooperate is the iteration of the game (or " repeated Prisoner's Dilemma"), wherein the game is played many times. In an iterated game, the decision

again emphasizes that it is God who had made his mission successful.

6. How is the woman chosen? For Yitzḥak there is a "character test," accompanied by divine assistance. For Yaakov, there is no test. He sees Raḥel and decides on his own that he wants to marry her.

7. Eliezer announces the purpose of his visit immediately upon arrival at Betuel's home; he will not eat with the family until he has made it clear why he has come, at Avraham's command. Yaakov, in his first meeting with Lavan, makes no mention of marriage at all. A month later, when he does talk about marriage, he says nothing about his father's command, but rather asks simply to marry Raḥel.

8. In Yitzḥak's case, there is a return journey to Canaan immediately upon finding the woman. For Yaakov, the return takes much longer; he remains in Ḥaran for many years.

What is the essential difference between the story of the match for Yitzḥak and the story of the match for Yaakov? In Yitzḥak's case, there are two great ideals that guide the search. The practical difficulties are set aside; it is clear that God will help to overcome them. Additionally, Yitzḥak has no personal involvement in the match. The marriage is directed from Above; the choice is explicitly left in the hands of God.

For Yaakov, the entire episode reflects an altogether human plot. A man is fleeing from his brother; he reaches some relatives and stays with them. In the natural course of events he falls in love with one of the daughters, and asks to marry her in return for his labor. There is no appeal by Yaakov for divine aid in finding a wife, nor does there seem to be any divine intervention in the course of events.

Rabbanit Sharon Rimon

TAKING A LITERARY APPROACH

There are some obvious parallels between the story of Eliezer's quest for a wife for Yitzḥak and Yaakov's path to Raḥel. In both cases, the father commands that no Canaanite woman be considered; the woman chosen for marriage should be from Ḥaran. In both stories, the journey to Ḥaran ends at the well, where the first encounter with the woman takes place, and in both cases, the woman turns out to be from the family of Naḥor. Following the meeting with the woman, there is a meeting with the family.

Based on the above outline, the two stories appear to be quite similar. Nevertheless, it is specifically the similarities between them that serve to highlight the significant differences between them.

1. Yitzḥak does not go out to seek a wife for himself. The quest for his wife is initiated by Avraham, and it is Eliezer who is dispatched to bring the woman. Yitzḥak is involved in neither the choice of the woman nor the decision. Yaakov, in contrast, is sent himself to Ḥaran to find a wife, and he decides on his own whom to choose.
2. Yitzḥak is forbidden from leaving the land and going to Ḥaran; Yaakov goes to Ḥaran.
3. For Yitzḥak, the journey to Ḥaran has only one purpose: to find a wife for him. For Yaakov, the journey is also a flight from Esav.
4. Yaakov experiences a divine revelation on the way.
5. In the case of Yitzḥak, throughout the narrative there is an emphasis on divine signs that Rivka is the right woman to choose. In Avraham's directive to his servant, he says: "The Lord God of the heavens...He will send His angel before you, that you may take a wife from there for my son" (Bereshit 24:7). Eliezer in turn does not rely on his own discretion, but asks for God's help in finding the right woman. When he finds Rivka and understands that she is the one, he once

31 When the LORD saw that Leah was unloved, He opened her womb; but Raḥel was barren.
32 Leah became pregnant and had a son. She named him Reuven, saying, "The LORD has seen
33 my affliction. Now my husband will love me."[1] She became pregnant again and had a son.
She said, "The LORD has heard that I am unloved, so He has given me this son also"; and
34 she named him Shimon.[2] She became pregnant again and had a son and said, "Now that
I have borne him three sons, my husband will walk with me." That is why he was named
35 Levi.[3] She became pregnant again and had a son. She said, "This time I will praise the
30 1 LORD," so she named him Yehuda.[4] Then she ceased having children. Aware that she had
borne Yaakov no children, Raḥel became envious of her sister. To Yaakov she said, "Give
2 me children! If not, let me die!" Yaakov grew angry with Raḥel, and said, "Am I in place of
3 God, who has kept you from having children?" "Here is Bilha my slave –" she said, "come
4 to her. Let her give birth on my knees[5] so that I too can build a family through her." So she
5 gave him her maid Bilha as a wife. Yaakov came to her, and she became pregnant and bore
6 Yaakov a son. Then Raḥel said, "God has vindicated me. He has listened to my voice and

1 | The name Reuven resonates with *raa* ("has seen") and *ben* ("son").
2 | The name Shimon resonates with *shama* ("has heard").
3 | The name Levi resonates with *yillaveh* ("will walk with").
4 | The name Yehuda resonates with *odeh* ("I will praise").
5 | Meaning, I will raise the child as my own.

UNLOCKING THE TEXT

- Why did Leah deserve a child just because she was unloved?
- Why did Raḥel deserve to be barren because Yaakov loved her more than Leah?
- Why is there such an importance placed on the meaning of the names given to the children?
- Did Bilha's pregnancy make Raḥel feel better or worse?
- Why does Leah feel the need to have more children through her maid Zilpa?
- Why does Yaakov agree to have so many children?
- Did Leah not spend any nights with Yaakov?
- Why did Yaakov allow Raḥel to decide who he slept with?
- What role does Yaakov play in this whole episode?
- Why did Leah deserve to have half of Yaakov's children?
- Why did God only "remember" Raḥel now?

FINDING YOURSELF IN THE TEXT

- What are your names? What do they mean? Why were they chosen?
- Do you think it is important to have meaningful names?
- What would you call your child if you were naming them today?

Consider using these questions as the basis for your own commentary or creative midrash.

How does reflecting on these firsthand experiences help you better understand the text?

כט לא לב וַיַּרְא יהוה כִּי־שְׂנוּאָה לֵאָה וַיִּפְתַּח אֶת־רַחְמָהּ וְרָחֵל עֲקָרָה: וַתַּהַר לֵאָה וַתֵּלֶד
בֵּן וַתִּקְרָא שְׁמוֹ רְאוּבֵן כִּי אָמְרָה כִּי־רָאָה יהוה בְּעָנְיִי כִּי עַתָּה יֶאֱהָבַנִי אִישִׁי:
לג וַתַּהַר עוֹד וַתֵּלֶד בֵּן וַתֹּאמֶר כִּי־שָׁמַע יהוה כִּי־שְׂנוּאָה אָנֹכִי וַיִּתֶּן־לִי גַּם־אֶת־
לד זֶה וַתִּקְרָא שְׁמוֹ שִׁמְעוֹן: וַתַּהַר עוֹד וַתֵּלֶד בֵּן וַתֹּאמֶר עַתָּה הַפַּעַם יִלָּוֶה אִישִׁי
לה אֵלַי כִּי־יָלַדְתִּי לוֹ שְׁלֹשָׁה בָנִים עַל־כֵּן קָרָא־שְׁמוֹ לֵוִי: וַתַּהַר עוֹד וַתֵּלֶד בֵּן
וַתֹּאמֶר הַפַּעַם אוֹדֶה אֶת־יהוה עַל־כֵּן קָרְאָה שְׁמוֹ יְהוּדָה וַתַּעֲמֹד מִלֶּדֶת:
ל א וַתֵּרֶא רָחֵל כִּי לֹא יָלְדָה לְיַעֲקֹב וַתְּקַנֵּא רָחֵל בַּאֲחֹתָהּ וַתֹּאמֶר אֶל־יַעֲקֹב הָבָה־
ב לִּי בָנִים וְאִם־אַיִן מֵתָה אָנֹכִי: וַיִּחַר־אַף יַעֲקֹב בְּרָחֵל וַיֹּאמֶר הֲתַחַת אֱלֹהִים אָנֹכִי
ג אֲשֶׁר־מָנַע מִמֵּךְ פְּרִי־בָטֶן: וַתֹּאמֶר הִנֵּה אֲמָתִי בִלְהָה בֹּא אֵלֶיהָ וְתֵלֵד עַל־בִּרְכַּי
ד וְאִבָּנֶה גַם־אָנֹכִי מִמֶּנָּה: וַתִּתֶּן־לוֹ אֶת־בִּלְהָה שִׁפְחָתָהּ לְאִשָּׁה וַיָּבֹא אֵלֶיהָ יַעֲקֹב:
ה ו וַתַּהַר בִּלְהָה וַתֵּלֶד לְיַעֲקֹב בֵּן: וַתֹּאמֶר רָחֵל דָּנַנִּי אֱלֹהִים וְגַם שָׁמַע בְּקֹלִי וַיִּתֶּן־לִי

THEMES	RELATIONSHIPS AND LOVE	PEOPLEHOOD	COVENANT

Episode 42: *The Birth of Yaakov's Children* – Bereshit 29:31–30:24

SUMMARY

The overwhelming majority of Yaakov's descendants, during his lifetime, were born outside the land of Canaan. Through his two wives and their maidservants he established the twelve tribes. The names given to his sons, and the explanations for these names, reveal the internal world of the mothers.

7 given me a son." So she named him Dan.[6] Bilha, Raḥel's maid, became pregnant again and
8 bore Yaakov a second son. And Raḥel said, "I have struggled hard with my sister and I have
9 won." So she named him Naftali.[7] Leah realized that she was no longer having children,
10 so she took her maid Zilpa and gave her to Yaakov as a wife. And Leah's maid Zilpa bore
11 12 Yaakov a son. Leah said, "Good fortune has come!" So she named him Gad.[8] Then Zilpa,
13 Leah's maid, bore Yaakov a second son. Leah said, "How blessed I am; young girls will
14 call me blessed." So she named him Asher.[9] During the wheat harvest, Reuven went for a
walk and found mandrakes in the field. He brought them to his mother Leah. Raḥel said
15 to Leah, "Please give me some of your son's mandrakes." She replied, "Is it not enough that
you have taken away my husband? Now you want to take my son's mandrakes too!" "Very
well," said Raḥel, "Let him sleep with you tonight in exchange for your son's mandrakes."
16 When Yaakov came back from the field that evening, Leah went out to meet him and said,
"You are to come to me, for I have hired you with my son's mandrakes." So that night he
17 slept with her. God listened to Leah, and she became pregnant and bore Yaakov a fifth son.
18 Leah said, "God has rewarded me for giving my maid to my husband," so she named him
19 20 Yissakhar.[10] Leah became pregnant again and bore Yaakov a sixth son. "God has given me
a precious gift," said Leah. "This time my husband will honor me, for I have borne him
21 six sons," so she named him Zevulun.[11] Later she gave birth to a daughter and named her
22 23 Dina. Then God remembered Raḥel and listened to her and enabled her to conceive. She
24 became pregnant and gave birth to a son. She said, "God has taken away my shame," and
she named him Yosef, saying, "May the Lord grant me another son also."[12]

---

6 | The name Dan resonates with *dananni* ("has vindicated me").

7 | The name Naftali resonates with *niftalti* ("I have struggled hard").

8 | *Gad* is the word used to denote "good fortune."

9 | The name Asher resonates with *be'oshri* ("How blessed I am").

10 | The name Yissakhar resonates with *natan sekhari* ("has rewarded me").

11 | The name Zevulun resonates with *zeved* ("gift") and *yizbeleni* ("will honor me").

12 | *Yosef* is the word used by Raḥel to denote "grant." The name also resonates with *asaf* ("has taken away," v. 23).

ז בֵּ֛ן עַל־כֵּ֥ן קָֽרְאָ֖ה שְׁמ֣וֹ דָּ֑ן: וַתַּ֣הַר ע֗וֹד וַתֵּ֙לֶד֙ בִּלְהָ֔ה שִׁפְחַ֣ת רָחֵ֔ל בֵּ֥ן שֵׁנִ֖י לְיַעֲקֹֽב:

ח וַתֹּ֣אמֶר רָחֵ֗ל נַפְתּוּלֵ֨י אֱלֹהִ֧ים ׀ נִפְתַּ֛לְתִּי עִם־אֲחֹתִ֖י גַּם־יָכֹ֑לְתִּי וַתִּקְרָ֥א שְׁמ֖וֹ נַפְתָּלִֽי:

ט וַתֵּ֣רֶא לֵאָ֔ה כִּ֥י עָֽמְדָ֖ה מִלֶּ֑דֶת וַתִּקַּח֙ אֶת־זִלְפָּ֣ה שִׁפְחָתָ֔הּ וַתִּתֵּ֥ן אֹתָ֛הּ לְיַעֲקֹ֖ב לְאִשָּֽׁה:

י וַתֵּ֗לֶד זִלְפָּ֛ה שִׁפְחַ֥ת לֵאָ֖ה לְיַעֲקֹ֥ב בֵּֽן: וַתֹּ֥אמֶר לֵאָ֖ה בְּגָ֑ד וַתִּקְרָ֥א אֶת־שְׁמ֖וֹ גָּֽד: בָּ֣א גָ֖ד

יא יב וַתֵּ֗לֶד זִלְפָּה֙ שִׁפְחַ֣ת לֵאָ֔ה בֵּ֥ן שֵׁנִ֖י לְיַעֲקֹֽב: וַתֹּ֣אמֶר לֵאָ֔ה בְּאָשְׁרִ֕י כִּ֥י אִשְּׁר֖וּנִי בָּנ֑וֹת

יג יד וַתִּקְרָ֥א אֶת־שְׁמ֖וֹ אָשֵֽׁר: וַיֵּ֨לֶךְ רְאוּבֵ֜ן בִּימֵ֣י קְצִיר־חִטִּ֗ים וַיִּמְצָ֤א דֽוּדָאִים֙ בַּשָּׂדֶ֔ה רביעי

טו וַיָּבֵ֣א אֹתָ֔ם אֶל־לֵאָ֖ה אִמּ֑וֹ וַתֹּ֨אמֶר רָחֵ֜ל אֶל־לֵאָ֗ה תְּנִי־נָ֣א לִ֔י מִדּֽוּדָאֵ֖י בְּנֵ֑ךְ: וַתֹּ֣אמֶר לָ֗הּ הַמְעַט֙ קַחְתֵּ֣ךְ אֶת־אִישִׁ֔י וְלָקַ֕חַת גַּ֥ם אֶת־דּֽוּדָאֵ֖י בְּנִ֑י וַתֹּ֣אמֶר רָחֵ֗ל לָכֵן֙ יִשְׁכַּ֤ב

טז עִמָּךְ֙ הַלַּ֔יְלָה תַּ֖חַת דּוּדָאֵ֥י בְנֵֽךְ: וַיָּבֹ֨א יַעֲקֹ֣ב מִן־הַשָּׂדֶה֮ בָּעֶרֶב֒ וַתֵּצֵ֨א לֵאָ֜ה לִקְרָאת֗וֹ

יז וַתֹּ֙אמֶר֙ אֵלַ֣י תָּב֔וֹא כִּ֚י שָׂכֹ֣ר שְׂכַרְתִּ֔יךָ בְּדוּדָאֵ֖י בְּנִ֑י וַיִּשְׁכַּ֥ב עִמָּ֖הּ בַּלַּ֥יְלָה הֽוּא: וַיִּשְׁמַ֤ע

יח אֱלֹהִים֙ אֶל־לֵאָ֔ה וַתַּ֛הַר וַתֵּ֥לֶד לְיַעֲקֹ֖ב בֵּ֣ן חֲמִישִֽׁי: וַתֹּ֣אמֶר לֵאָ֗ה נָתַ֤ן אֱלֹהִים֙ שְׂכָרִ֔י

יט אֲשֶׁר־נָתַ֥תִּי שִׁפְחָתִ֖י לְאִישִׁ֑י וַתִּקְרָ֥א שְׁמ֖וֹ יִשָּׂשכָֽר: וַתַּ֤הַר עוֹד֙ לֵאָ֔ה וַתֵּ֥לֶד בֵּן־שִׁשִּׁ֖י

כ לְיַעֲקֹֽב: וַתֹּ֣אמֶר לֵאָ֗ה זְבָדַ֨נִי אֱלֹהִ֥ים ׀ אֹתִי֮ זֵ֣בֶד טוֹב֒ הַפַּ֙עַם֙ יִזְבְּלֵ֣נִי אִישִׁ֔י כִּֽי־יָלַ֥דְתִּי

כא ל֖וֹ שִׁשָּׁ֣ה בָנִ֑ים וַתִּקְרָ֥א אֶת־שְׁמ֖וֹ זְבֻלֽוּן: וְאַחַ֖ר יָ֣לְדָה בַּ֑ת וַתִּקְרָ֥א אֶת־שְׁמָ֖הּ דִּינָֽה:

כב כג וַיִּזְכֹּ֥ר אֱלֹהִ֖ים אֶת־רָחֵ֑ל וַיִּשְׁמַ֤ע אֵלֶ֙יהָ֙ אֱלֹהִ֔ים וַיִּפְתַּ֖ח אֶת־רַחְמָֽהּ: וַתַּ֖הַר וַתֵּ֣לֶד כח

כד בֵּ֑ן וַתֹּ֕אמֶר אָסַ֥ף אֱלֹהִ֖ים אֶת־חֶרְפָּתִֽי: וַתִּקְרָ֧א אֶת־שְׁמ֛וֹ יוֹסֵ֖ף לֵאמֹ֑ר יֹסֵ֧ף יְהוָ֛ה לִ֖י בֵּ֥ן אַחֵֽר:

THE ART OF MIDRASH

And God Remembered Rachel
Abel Pann (1950)

Analysis

- Which elements of this image are directly mentioned in the text?
- Which elements of this image are not found in the text?
- What midrashic interpretation could be inferred from this image?

A QUESTION OF BIBLIODRAMA

TO LEAH

- Why do you feel that you are unloved by Yaakov?
- What are your feelings toward Yaakov?
- How do you feel about your sister Raḥel?
- Does the birth of children mitigate these feelings?
- Why did you choose the names you did for your children?
- Why did you give Zilpa to Yaakov? Did you not have enough children already?

TO RAḤEL

- Describe how you felt while Leah was having her children and you were barren.
- How did you feel toward Leah during this time?
- How did you feel toward Yaakov during this time?
- Why did you give your maid Bilha to Yaakov as a wife?
- How did it feel when she also gave birth?
- How did it feel to finally have a child of your own?

TO BILHA AND ZILPA

- How do you feel toward your mistresses?
- How do you feel toward your husband Yaakov?

TO YAAKOV

- Why did you agree to marry Bilha and Zilpa?
- How do you feel toward Raḥel?
- Why did you become angry with Raḥel after her plea to you?
- How did it feel when Raḥel and Leah gave their maids to you to marry? How did it feel when they negotiated over who would spend the night with you?
- Do you feel any responsibility for the breakdown in relationship between Leah and Raḥel?

Judaism is a religion of love. So many of our texts express that love: the paragraph before the *Shema* with its talk of "great" and "eternal" love; the *Shema* itself with its command of love; the priestly blessings to be uttered in love; Shir HaShirim, the Song of Songs, the great poem of love; Shlomo Albaketz's *Lekha Dodi*, "Come, My Beloved"; Eliezer Azikri's *Yedid Nefesh*, "Beloved of the Soul." If you want to live well, love. If you seek to be close to God, love. If you want your home to be filled with the light of the Divine Presence, love. Love is where God lives.

But love is not enough. You cannot build a family, let alone a society, on love alone. For that you need justice also. Love is partial; justice is impartial. Love is particular; justice is universal. Love is for this person, not that; justice is for all. Much of the moral life is generated by this tension between love and justice. It is no accident that this is the theme of many of the narratives of Bereshit. Bereshit is about people and their relationships while the rest of the Torah is predominantly about society.

Justice without love is harsh. Love without justice is unfair, or so it will seem to the less-loved. Yet to experience both at the same time is virtually impossible. As Niels Bohr, the Nobel Prize-winning physicist, put it when he discovered that his son had stolen an object from a local shop: he could look at him from the perspective of a judge (justice) and as his father (love), but not both simultaneously.

At the heart of the moral life is a conflict with no simple resolution. There is no general rule to tell us when love is the right reaction and when justice is. In the 1960s the Beatles sang "All you need is love." Would that it were so, but it is not. Let us love, but let us never forget those who feel unloved. They too are people. They too have feelings. They too are in the image of God.

Rabbi Jonathan Sacks

Analysis

- What areas of understanding of human nature and society do we now have that were unavailable to classical Jewish commentators? How can they aid our understanding of the text?
- What can we learn from this essay to help us understand the text?
- What further questions on the text do you have now that you have read this new take on the story?

INTEGRATING ḤOKHMA

These are the words we hear: "And he [Yaakov] loved also Raḥel" (Bereshit 29:30). This is what we expected and hoped for. Yaakov now has two wives, sisters, something that will be forbidden in later Jewish law. It is a situation fraught with tension. But our first impression is that all will be well. He loves them both.

That expectation is dashed by the next word, *miLeah*, "more than Leah." This is not merely unexpected. It is also grammatically impossible. You cannot have a sentence that says, "X also loved Y more than Z." "Also" and "more than" contradict one another. This is one of those rare and powerful instances in which the Torah deliberately uses fractured syntax to indicate a fractured relationship.

Then comes the next phrase and it is shocking: "The Lord saw that Leah was hated" (29:31). Was Leah hated? No. The previous sentence has just told us she was loved. What then does the Torah mean by "hated"? It means that is how Leah felt. Yes, she was loved, but less than her sister. Leah knew, and had known for seven years, that Yaakov was passionately in love with her younger sister Raḥel. The Torah says that he worked for her for seven years "but they seemed to him like a few days because he was so in love with her" (29:20).

Leah was not hated. She was less loved. But someone in that situation cannot but feel rejected. The Torah forces us to hear Leah's pain in the names she gives her children. Her first she calls Reuven, saying, "It is because the Lord has seen my misery. Surely my husband will love me now." The second she calls Shimon "because the Lord heard that I am not loved." The third she calls Levi, saying, "Now at last my husband will become attached to me" (29:32–35). There is sustained anguish in these words.

If we look at the eleven times the word "love," *ahava*, is mentioned in the book of Bereshit, we make an extraordinary discovery. Every time love is mentioned, it generates conflict. Yitzḥak loved Esav but Rivka loved Yaakov. Yaakov loved Yosef, Raḥel's firstborn, more than his other sons. From these came two of the most fateful sibling rivalries in Jewish history. Even these pale into insignificance when we reflect on the first time the word love appears in the Torah, in the opening words of the trial of the binding of Yitzḥak: "Take now your son, your only one, the one you love" (22:2).

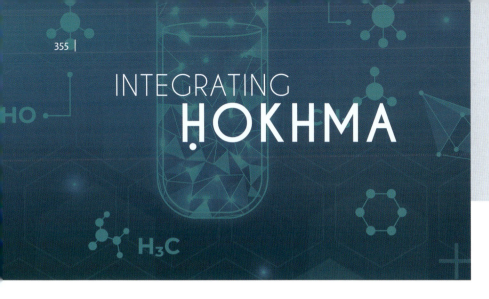

depiction seems, at first glance, surprising. What is the source of these signs that Raḥel reveals to Leah? More to the point, where does the Midrash come up with this halcyon portrayal, which emerges in direct opposition to the plain meaning of the story?

To answer this, we turn to Raḥel's posthumous appearance:

> A voice is heard on high, wailing, bitter weeping; Raḥel is weeping over her children. She refuses to be consoled over her children, for they are gone. So says the LORD, "Prevent your voice from crying and your eyes from tears, for there is reward for your exertions," says the LORD, "and they will return from the land of the enemy. And there is hope for your future," says the LORD, "and your children will return to their borders." (Yirmeya 31:14–16)

A rare biblical phenomenon, those who make posthumous appearances – Shmuel, Eliyahu, Raḥel – appear to have left unfinished business. Shmuel failed to inform Sha'ul that David is the next designated king and Eliyahu was unable to offer Israel a gentler prophetic message. These men must return after their death (I Shmuel 28:17; Malakhi 3:23–24) to complete their unfulfilled task. In her lifetime, Raḥel's relentless, self-absorbed pursuit of a child has negative and far-reaching repercussions. Her rivalry with Leah continues in the next generation, where both "hatred" (Bereshit 37:8) and "jealousy" (37:11) govern relations between Leah's sons and her own. Divisiveness and animosity continue to hold sway throughout the generations, finding expression in the rivalry between the house of Sha'ul (Raḥel's descendant) and the House of David (Leah's descendant), as well as the eventual division of the kingdoms (into the Judean southern dynasty – led by Leah's son – and the Efraimite, northern dynasty – led initially by Raḥel's son, the tribe of Efrayim, and bearing his name thereafter.) Correctives to these divisions are short-term (as, for example, when David unites the tribes into one kingdom, which lasts two generations). The roots of the problem remain in place; perhaps only Raḥel can fix this explosive situation.

Raḥel surfaces from the stillness of the afterlife, just as the Judean kingdom is going into exile. The poignant tears she sheds over "her" absent children recall Raḥel's life-long passion to procure children, filling the void created by their absence. Yet, these refugees are not precisely Raḥel's descendants! The Judean kingdom is governed by the Davidic dynasty; this kingdom represents the power of Leah's descendants. In this scenario, Raḥel weeps bitterly over the fate of her sister's dynasty, illustrating that she has overcome her self-absorbed ambition and used her considerable strength to the benefit of the kingdom led by Leah's descendant. It is in Yirmeya 31 that *Ḥazal* find evidence for Raḥel's selflessness toward Leah, and perhaps the midrash extrapolates from here the extra-biblical story about the signs. The phrase used to describe Raḥel's tears is *bekhi tamrurim*, generally translated as "bitter weeping," based on the assumption that the word *tamrurim* is related to the word *mar*, meaning "bitter." Yet, a few verses later (in Yirmeya 31:20) the word *tamrurim* appears in parallel to the word *tziyunim*, which means "signs." The Midrash interprets Raḥel's tears – the *bekhi tamrurim* – as tears associated with the signs, laying the groundwork for the elaborate story cited above.

Dr. Yael Ziegler

TAKING A LITERARY APPROACH

Yaakov has two wives: one is beloved and barren and the other fecund yet shunned. Raḥel, however, refuses to accept her barren state. Her first words in the story illustrate her determination to have a child: "And she said to Yaakov: 'Give me children (*banim*), for if not (*ayin*) I am dead' (Bereshit 30:1). Her words will prove to contain a tragic irony; in fact, her life ends while she births her second – and last – child, Binyamin. Raḥel's final words echo her first words as she names her child "Ben Oni," or "the son of my grief" (35:18). Raḥel's passion for a child frames her story, as do the words that express her heartfelt desire: *banim/ben* and *ayin/oni*.

Raḥel's death is not her final biblical appearance. In a rare posthumous cameo, Raḥel's voice intrudes upon Yirmeya's prophecy, alerting us that she remains on active duty even after her departure from this world. The nature of Raḥel's role in Yirmeya 31:14 is consistent with her lifelong ambition; she weeps over her children who are absent, in exile. Raḥel refuses to be consoled over these children (*baneha*), for they are no longer (*aneinu*). This tireless pursuit of children – who are elusive – girds Raḥel with rare resolve. And she is successful in this quest. During Raḥel's lifetime, she births Yosef and Binyamin. And the bitter tears Raḥel sheds over her absent sons also accomplish their goal. In 31:15–16, God instructs Raḥel to cease her weeping, promising her due reward for her exertions: These children of hers will return from the land of the enemies. They will be duly restored to their rightful inheritance.

Linguistic connections notwithstanding, Raḥel's posthumous appearance turns out to be quite different from her lifetime labors, as we shall see. Raḥel's single-minded goal while she was alive was to have children for herself. Raḥel candidly expresses her bitter envy of Leah, prompting her demand that Yaakov give her a child: "And Raḥel was jealous of her sister, and she said to Yaakov, 'Give me children, for if not, I am dead'" (Bereshit 30:1). Competition is fierce: Each sister desires that which the other has. Leah desires her husband's love and Raḥel desires children. This finds expression in the brief but poignant incident where Raḥel barters for Leah's mandrakes (30:14–15).

However one interprets the details of this incident, one thing seems clear: these sisters are locked in an intense rivalry; the above anecdote records no empathy, compassion, or sisterly affection. Worse yet, the situation produces emotions such as envy (30:1) and hate (29:31).

In a bewildering twist, a midrash posits an opposite scenario, in which Raḥel displays heroic sympathy for her elder sister, causing her to collaborate with Leah to deceive Yaakov into marrying her:

> [Yaakov] said to Raḥel: "Marry me!" She answered: "Very well. However, my father is a deceiver, and you will not be able to overcome him." He said to her: "What is [the nature of] his deceit?" She told him: "I have a sister older than me, and he will not marry me off before her." [Yaakov] said: "I am his brother in deceit…." [Yaakov] gave Raḥel signs [so that he would know it was she on the wedding night]. When Leah was brought [to Yaakov], [Raḥel] thought: "Now my sister will be humiliated…." [Thus] the signs that Yaakov had given to Raḥel, she gave to Leah. (Bava Batra 123a)

This midrash reverses the narrative, arriving at an opposite portrayal of the relationship between Raḥel and Leah. Perhaps this midrash means to suggest that this empathetic sisterly collusion constitutes the initial phase of the story. Only later does the relationship turn competitive and bitter. Yet, the overall picture of the midrash seems designed to sketch an idyllic portrait of sisterly love, one that defies expectation and involves heroic selflessness on Raḥel's side. This midrashic

25 After Raḥel had given birth to Yosef, Yaakov said to Lavan, "Release me to go home
26 to my own land. Give me my wives and my children for whom I have worked for you,
27 and let me go. You know very well how much work I have done for you." But Lavan said
to him, "If you will allow me to say so, I have learned by divination that it is because
28 of you that the Lord has blessed me." He added, "Name your hire and I will pay it."
29 Yaakov said, "You know well how I have worked for you and how your livestock have fared
30 under my care. You had little before I came, but it has swelled into much. The Lord has
blessed you wherever I have been. Now, when can I do likewise for my own household?"
31 Lavan asked, "What shall I give you?" Yaakov replied, "Do not give me anything. If you
32 do this one thing for me, I will continue to shepherd and guard your flocks. Let me
go through all your flocks today and remove every speckled or spotted sheep, every
33 dark-colored lamb and every spotted or speckled goat. They shall be my hire. Let my
honesty testify for me in the future, whenever you come to check the wages you have
paid me. Any goat not speckled or spotted or any lamb not dark colored in my possession
34 35 shall be considered stolen." Lavan said, "Agreed. Let it be as you have said." That day Lavan
removed the streaked or spotted goats, all the speckled or spotted female goats – every
one that had a trace of white – and every dark-colored lamb. These he placed in the care
36 of his sons. Then he put a three-day journey's distance between him and Yaakov. Yaakov
37 tended the rest of Lavan's flock. Yaakov took fresh shoots of poplar, almond, and plane trees
38 and peeled white strips in them, exposing the white of the shoots. Then he set the peeled

UNLOCKING THE TEXT

- Why does Yaakov need Lavan's permission to leave?
- Why does Yaakov need to ask permission to take his own wives and children?
- Why does Lavan not want Yaakov to leave?
- Is Lavan being dishonest in his dealings with Yaakov?
- Is Yaakov being dishonest in his dealings with Lavan?
- Why does Yaakov accept Lavan's offer if what he really wants is to leave?
- What is the significance of the practice employed by Yaakov with the sticks? Did it really work?

FINDING YOURSELF IN THE TEXT

- Do you always know when it is the right time to leave?
- Have you ever made a decision to leave, and then been convinced by someone to stay?
- Do you ever get FOMO (Fear of Missing Out)? Is FOMO more likely when you stay or when you leave a place?

Consider using these questions as the basis for your own commentary or creative midrash.

How does reflecting on these firsthand experiences help you better understand the text?

כה וַיְהִ֕י כַּאֲשֶׁ֛ר יָלְדָ֥ה רָחֵ֖ל אֶת־יוֹסֵ֑ף וַיֹּ֤אמֶר יַעֲקֹב֙ אֶל־לָבָ֔ן שַׁלְּחֵ֙נִי֙ וְאֵ֣לְכָ֔ה אֶל־מְקוֹמִ֖י
כו וּלְאַרְצִֽי׃ תְּנָ֞ה אֶת־נָשַׁ֣י וְאֶת־יְלָדַ֗י אֲשֶׁ֨ר עָבַ֧דְתִּי אֹֽתְךָ֛ בָּהֵ֖ן וְאֵלֵ֑כָה כִּ֚י אַתָּ֣ה יָדַ֔עְתָּ
כז אֶת־עֲבֹדָתִ֖י אֲשֶׁ֥ר עֲבַדְתִּֽיךָ׃ וַיֹּ֤אמֶר אֵלָיו֙ לָבָ֔ן אִם־נָ֛א מָצָ֥אתִי חֵ֖ן בְּעֵינֶ֑יךָ נִחַ֕שְׁתִּי
כח כט וַיְבָרְכֵ֥נִי יְהוָ֖ה בִּגְלָלֶֽךָ׃ וַיֹּאמַ֑ר נָקְבָ֧ה שְׂכָרְךָ֛ עָלַ֖י וְאֶתֵּֽנָה׃ וַיֹּ֣אמֶר אֵלָ֔יו אַתָּ֣ה יָדַ֔עְתָּ חמישי
ל אֵ֖ת אֲשֶׁ֣ר עֲבַדְתִּ֑יךָ וְאֵ֛ת אֲשֶׁר־הָיָ֥ה מִקְנְךָ֖ אִתִּֽי׃ כִּ֡י מְעַט֩ אֲשֶׁר־הָיָ֨ה לְךָ֤ לְפָנַי֙ וַיִּפְרֹ֣ץ
לא לָרֹ֔ב וַיְבָ֧רֶךְ יְהוָ֛ה אֹתְךָ֖ לְרַגְלִ֑י וְעַתָּ֗ה מָתַ֛י אֶֽעֱשֶׂ֥ה גַם־אָנֹכִ֖י לְבֵיתִֽי׃ וַיֹּ֖אמֶר מָ֣ה
אֶתֶּן־לָ֑ךְ וַיֹּ֤אמֶר יַעֲקֹב֙ לֹא־תִתֶּן־לִ֣י מְא֔וּמָה אִם־תַּֽעֲשֶׂה־לִּי֙ הַדָּבָ֣ר הַזֶּ֔ה אָשׁ֛וּבָה
לב אֶרְעֶ֥ה צֹאנְךָ֖ אֶשְׁמֹֽר׃ אֶֽעֱבֹ֨ר בְּכָל־צֹאנְךָ֜ הַיּ֗וֹם הָסֵ֨ר מִשָּׁ֜ם כָּל־שֶׂ֣ה ׀ נָקֹ֣ד וְטָל֗וּא
לג וְכָל־שֶׂה־חוּם֙ בַּכְּשָׂבִ֔ים וְטָל֥וּא וְנָקֹ֖ד בָּעִזִּ֑ים וְהָיָ֖ה שְׂכָרִֽי׃ וְעָֽנְתָה־בִּ֤י צִדְקָתִי֙
בְּי֣וֹם מָחָ֔ר כִּֽי־תָב֥וֹא עַל־שְׂכָרִ֖י לְפָנֶ֑יךָ כֹּ֣ל אֲשֶׁר־אֵינֶנּוּ֩ נָקֹ֨ד וְטָל֜וּא בָּֽעִזִּ֗ים וְחוּם֙
לד לה בַּכְּשָׂבִ֔ים גָּנ֥וּב ה֖וּא אִתִּֽי׃ וַיֹּ֥אמֶר לָבָ֖ן הֵ֑ן ל֖וּ יְהִ֥י כִדְבָרֶֽךָ׃ וַיָּ֣סַר בַּיּוֹם֩ הַה֨וּא אֶת־
הַתְּיָשִׁ֜ים הָעֲקֻדִּ֣ים וְהַטְּלֻאִ֗ים וְאֵ֤ת כָּל־הָֽעִזִּים֙ הַנְּקֻדּ֣וֹת וְהַטְּלֻאֹ֔ת כֹּ֤ל אֲשֶׁר־לָבָן֙
לו בּ֔וֹ וְכָל־ח֖וּם בַּכְּשָׂבִ֑ים וַיִּתֵּ֖ן בְּיַד־בָּנָֽיו׃ וַיָּ֗שֶׂם דֶּ֚רֶךְ שְׁלֹ֣שֶׁת יָמִ֔ים בֵּינ֖וֹ וּבֵ֣ין יַעֲקֹ֑ב
לז וְיַעֲקֹ֗ב רֹעֶ֛ה אֶת־צֹ֥אן לָבָ֖ן הַנּוֹתָרֹֽת׃ וַיִּֽקַּֽח־ל֤וֹ יַעֲקֹב֙ מַקַּ֥ל לִבְנֶ֛ה לַ֖ח וְל֣וּז וְעַרְמ֑וֹן
לח וַיְפַצֵּ֤ל בָּהֵן֙ פְּצָל֣וֹת לְבָנ֔וֹת מַחְשֹׂף֙ הַלָּבָ֔ן אֲשֶׁ֖ר עַל־הַמַּקְלֽוֹת׃ וַיַּצֵּ֗ג אֶת־הַמַּקְלוֹת֙

THEMES | RELATIONSHIPS AND LOVE | COVENANT | PEOPLEHOOD

Episode 43: *Yaakov Negotiates an Exit Settlement* – Bereshit 30:25–43

SUMMARY

It is likely that Yaakov has wanted to return home for a long time, but he waits until he has completed the fourteen years of service he owes Lavan, and perhaps also until Raḥel has had a child of her own. Perhaps he thought that it would be easier for his favorite wife to become pregnant in familiar surroundings. Now, with the birth of Yosef, Yaakov seeks to leave Lavan. He negotiates a settlement, under which he amasses great wealth at Lavan's expense.

shoots in all the water troughs so that they would be in front of the flocks when they came
39 to drink. They would mate when they came to drink, and since they mated by the shoots,
40 they bore streaked, speckled, and spotted young.[1] Yaakov set apart the young of the flock,
and he made the others belonging to Lavan face the streaked and dark-colored animals.
Thus he bred separate flocks for himself, and he did not let them breed with Lavan's
41 flocks. Whenever the stronger animals were mating, Yaakov would place the shoots in
42 the troughs facing them so that they mated facing the shoots. But the weaker animals he
43 did not put there, so the weaker went to Lavan and the stronger to Yaakov. Thus the man's
wealth swelled into a fortune. He had large flocks, female and male servants, and camels
and donkeys.

---

1 | The animals produced offspring that exhibited the designs seen during the mating process.

THE ART OF MIDRASH

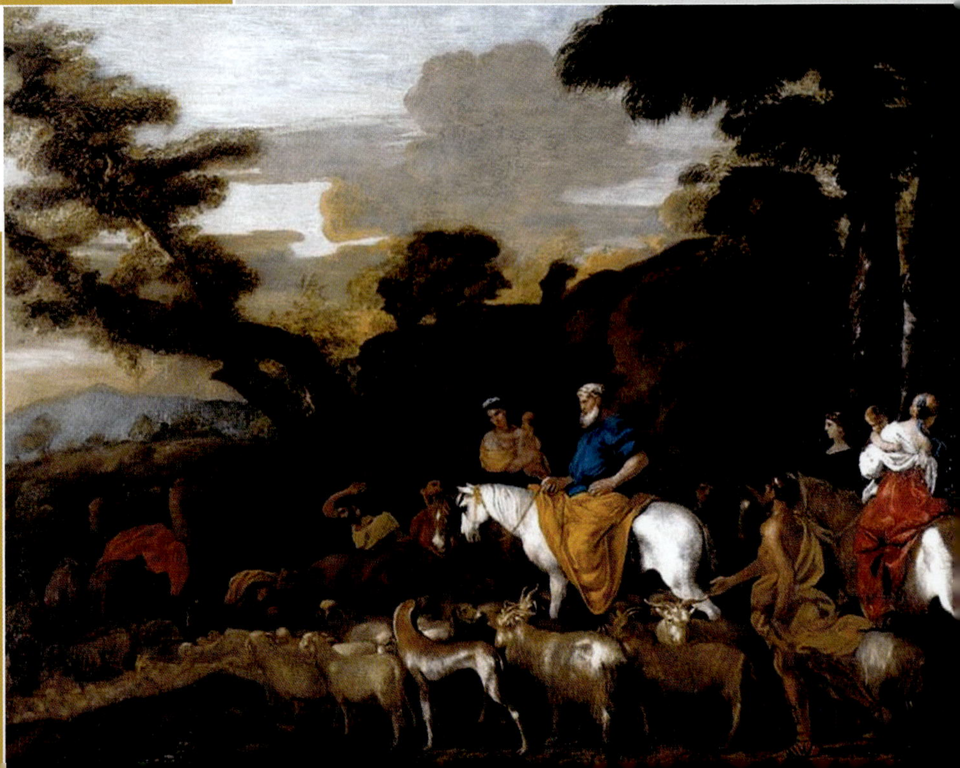

Jacob Leading the Flocks of Laban
Giovanni Benedetto Castiglione
(1632)

Analysis

- Which elements of this image are directly mentioned in the text?
- Which elements of this image are not found in the text?
- What midrashic interpretation could be inferred from this image?

אֲשֶׁ֣ר פִּצֵּ֗ל בָּרְהָטִ֤ים בְּשִֽׁקֲתֹ֣ות הַמַּ֔יִם אֲשֶׁר֩ תָּבֹ֨אןָ הַצֹּ֤אן לִשְׁתֹּות֙ לְנֹ֣כַח הַצֹּ֔אן

לט וַיֵּחַ֖מְנָה בְּבֹאָ֥ן לִשְׁתּֽוֹת: וַיֵּֽחֲמ֥וּ הַצֹּ֖אן אֶל־הַמַּקְלֹ֑ות וַתֵּלַ֣דְןָ הַצֹּ֔אן עֲקֻדִּ֥ים נְקֻדִּ֖ים

מ וּטְלֻאִֽים: וְהַכְּשָׂבִים֘ הִפְרִ֣יד יַעֲקֹב֒ וַ֠יִּתֵּ֠ן פְּנֵ֨י הַצֹּ֧אן אֶל־עָקֹ֛ד וְכָל־ח֖וּם בְּצֹ֣אן לָבָ֑ן

מא וַיָּֽשֶׁת־ל֤וֹ עֲדָרִים֙ לְבַדֹּ֔ו וְלֹ֥א שָׁתָ֖ם עַל־צֹ֥אן לָבָֽן: וְהָיָ֗ה בְּכָל־יַחֵ֞ם הַצֹּ֤אן הַֽמְקֻשָּׁרֹות֙

מב וְשָׂ֧ם יַעֲקֹ֛ב אֶת־הַמַּקְלֹ֖ות לְעֵינֵ֣י הַצֹּ֑אן בָּרְהָטִ֖ים לְיַחְמֵ֥נָּה בַּמַּקְלֹֽות: וּבְהַעֲטִ֥יף

מג הַצֹּ֖אן לֹ֣א יָשִׂ֑ים וְהָיָ֤ה הָעֲטֻפִים֙ לְלָבָ֔ן וְהַקְּשֻׁרִ֖ים לְיַעֲקֹֽב: וַיִּפְרֹ֥ץ הָאִ֖ישׁ מְאֹ֣ד מְאֹ֑ד וַֽיְהִי־לֹו֙ צֹ֣אן רַבֹּ֔ות וּשְׁפָחֹות֙ וַעֲבָדִ֔ים וּגְמַלִּ֖ים וַחֲמֹרִֽים:

A QUESTION OF
BIBLIODRAMA

TO YAAKOV

- Why did you decide it was time to leave Ḥaran now?

- Why did you feel you needed to ask Lavan's permission?

- Why did you change your mind and not leave?

- Where did you learn the breeding technique you used, and do you think it really worked?

TO LAVAN

- Why didn't you want Yaakov to leave?

- Would you really have given Yaakov whatever he asked for?

- Did it surprise you that Yaakov became wealthy while he worked with you?

Analysis

- What areas of understanding of human nature and society do we now have that were unavailable to classical Jewish commentators? How can they aid our understanding of the text?
- What can we learn from this passage to help us understand the text?
- What further questions on the text do you have now that you have read this new take on the story?

TAKING A LITERARY APPROACH

After the birth of twelve children over the second seven-year period, specifically the birth of Yosef, and what by now must seem an eternity of servitude, Yaakov decides it is time to leave. He summons the courage to request permission from his father-in-law: "Send me away, so that I may go to my place and my land" (Bereshit 30:25). Notice how little of the Abrahamic language remains – the word "my place" replaces the more dramatic identity phrases used for Avraham. Yaakov understands that it is time to go, but he can barely remember why or to where. He must simply get away: "Give me my wives and my children for whom I served you; you know how I served you" (30:26). For Yaakov to ask permission to leave may be understandable, but to ask permission for his wives and children betrays his inability to assert himself and demand what is rightfully his. So crushed is his spirit that he doesn't even assert his right to his own family. In the Hebrew, this is even more striking, as the root *a-v-d* ("to serve" or "to be a servant") appears three times in a single verse of Yaakov's request. Just as a servant owns nothing, as Lavan's servant, whatever Yaakov owns is Lavan's.

Lavan's dual response reveals both his method and his true motives. He begins with flattery, seemingly ceding control of the situation to Yaakov: "If I find favor in your eyes…I have engaged in divination, and God has blessed me on account of you." Lavan is, and has been, interested in the prosperity Yaakov brings as the blessed one. Once he has Yaakov's attention he speaks again: "Name your wages, and I will pay it." Handing Yaakov a blank check is both intensely empowering and a masterful ploy; Lavan makes Yaakov an offer he cannot refuse. Since, for Lavan, controlling Yaakov is of paramount importance, the pay is irrelevant. It will all come back to him eventually anyway. As for Yaakov, how can he turn down Lavan's seemingly unlimited generosity and the opportunity to become independently wealthy?

The reader of the Hebrew text is alerted not only to Lavan's methods and motives, but also to a powerful wordplay. The last time Yaakov was invited to name his price he ended up serving Lavan for fourteen years in order to marry Raḥel. In Lavan's present proposal, he says *nakva sekharkha*. The word *nakva* is a play on the word *nekeva*, meaning "female." Even as Lavan puts Yaakov in the driver's seat he reminds Yaakov of his previous request and how, blinded by his desire for a woman, he lost himself to Lavan. Yaakov will never be able to leave; he might as well make the best of his situation.

Rabbi Zvi Grumet

INTEGRATING ḤOKHMA

There were two ways for Yaakov to pay Lavan back for his aggressive behavior. The Torah tells us that part of the separation agreement between Yaakov and Lavan was that Yaakov was entitled to the speckled and spotted lambs. Since this agreement was outcome based, Yaakov took advantage of a loophole in the deal and placed spotted sticks in the sheep's troughs. This resulted in the birth of only spotted and speckled sheep, which meant all the sheep belonged to him. As recounted in the Torah, this was a "small blow" to Lavan.

The bigger blow that Yaakov dealt to Lavan was in setting the time of the "endgame." As we previously noted, players' behavior in a given game is directly influenced by their concern about revenge and betrayal in the game's next iteration. This fear encourages cooperating to reap long-term profits instead of achieving short-term profits through betrayal. A long-term vision builds stability and routine, a good reputation, and the expectation of a steady and predictable pattern of conduct. Strict adherence to the rules lends confidence and enables the same strategy to be used again and again. In the endgame, however, both players could have a vested interest in betraying because they know they will not be facing their opponent again.

Raḥel, herself a victim of her father's deceit, understood that she would never see her father again. Before she left, she stole his household idols. This may have been her symbolic way of breaking the dishes of her father's home and burning the bridges to her birthplace.

With that, the Torah seems to emphasize that though he lost his daughters, grandchildren, camels, cattle, household idols, and other property, Lavan was most wounded and felt cheated by Yaakov's failure to tell him he was leaving: "Yaakov kept Lavan the Aramean in the dark, not telling him that he was fleeing." Keeping Lavan "in the dark" or sneaking away under the cover of night or some other ruse defines a disengagement strategy based on mistrust. We can say that Yaakov used Lavan's own strategy against him; he repaid Lavan tit for tat. Ultimately, Lavan – who had not engaged in confidence-building measures for twenty years and had continuously violated Yaakov's trust – was forced to pay the highest price of all. Yaakov and his own daughters betrayed him while he was "in the dark" about their plans.

The story of Yaakov's flight to Ḥaran, his experiences there, and his return home, is devoted entirely to the importance of cultivating interpersonal trust, as well as the factors that lead to its violation and the price exacted by its absence. The Bible is teaching us the price of the lack of interpersonal trust in business and family.

Michael A. Eisenberg

31 1 Yaakov heard that Lavan's sons were saying, "Yaakov has taken everything our father owned;
2 of what belonged to our father, he has made all these riches." And Yaakov saw that Lavan's
3 manner toward him was not what it had been. The LORD said to Yaakov, "Go back to the
4 land of your fathers where you were born; I will be with you." So Yaakov sent word to Raḥel
5 and Leah to come out to the field where his flock was. He said to them, "I see that your
father's manner toward me is not what it used to be. But the God of my father has been
6 7 with me. You well know how I have worked for your father with all my strength. Your father
8 cheated me, changing my wages ten times, but God has not let him harm me. If he said,
'The speckled animals shall be your hire,' then all the flock would give birth to speckled
young. If he said, 'The streaked animals shall be your hire,' then all the flock would give birth
9 10 to streaked young. God has taken your father's livestock and given it to me. Once, during
the breeding season, I had a dream: I saw that the rams mounting the flock were streaked,
11 speckled, or spotted. And in the dream an angel of God said to me, 'Yaakov.' I replied, 'Here
12 I am.' He said, 'Look up and see that all the rams mounting the flock are streaked, speckled,
13 or spotted, for I have seen all that Lavan is doing to you. I am the God of Beit El, where you
anointed a pillar and made a vow to Me. Now – leave this land at once and return to the
14 land where you were born.'" Raḥel and Leah answered him, "Do we still have a share in the

UNLOCKING THE TEXT

- Which is the real reason why Yaakov decided to escape: the way Lavan's sons behaved toward him; the way Lavan behaved toward him; or the prophecy he received from God?
- Why did the Torah need to mention all three?
- How had Lavan's manner changed toward Yaakov?
- Why did God decide now to instruct Yaakov to return to the land of Israel?
- Who was really responsible for Yaakov increasing his wealth?
- Why did Yaakov give such a long speech to Raḥel and Leah rather than just informing them they were leaving?
- Why did Raḥel steal her father's idols?
- Why did Yaakov sneak away without telling Lavan he was leaving?

FINDING YOURSELF IN THE TEXT

- Have you ever sensed God influencing you to make a decision?
- Have you ever left a place without saying goodbye so no one would notice?
- Is it ever ethical to steal something from someone?

Consider using these questions as the basis for your own commentary or creative midrash.

How does reflecting on these firsthand experiences help you better understand the text?

לא א וַיִּשְׁמַע אֶת־דִּבְרֵי בְנֵי־לָבָן לֵאמֹר לָקַח יַעֲקֹב אֵת כָּל־אֲשֶׁר לְאָבִינוּ וּמֵאֲשֶׁר
ב לְאָבִינוּ עָשָׂה אֵת כָּל־הַכָּבֹד הַזֶּה: וַיַּרְא יַעֲקֹב אֶת־פְּנֵי לָבָן וְהִנֵּה אֵינֶנּוּ עִמּוֹ
ג כִּתְמוֹל שִׁלְשׁוֹם: וַיֹּאמֶר יהוה אֶל־יַעֲקֹב שׁוּב אֶל־אֶרֶץ אֲבוֹתֶיךָ וּלְמוֹלַדְתֶּךָ כט
ד ה וְאֶהְיֶה עִמָּךְ: וַיִּשְׁלַח יַעֲקֹב וַיִּקְרָא לְרָחֵל וּלְלֵאָה הַשָּׂדֶה אֶל־צֹאנוֹ: וַיֹּאמֶר לָהֶן
רֹאֶה אָנֹכִי אֶת־פְּנֵי אֲבִיכֶן כִּי־אֵינֶנּוּ אֵלַי כִּתְמֹל שִׁלְשֹׁם וֵאלֹהֵי אָבִי הָיָה עִמָּדִי:
ו ז וְאַתֵּנָה יְדַעְתֶּן כִּי בְּכָל־כֹּחִי עָבַדְתִּי אֶת־אֲבִיכֶן: וַאֲבִיכֶן הֵתֶל בִּי וְהֶחֱלִף אֶת־
ח מַשְׂכֻּרְתִּי עֲשֶׂרֶת מֹנִים וְלֹא־נְתָנוֹ אֱלֹהִים לְהָרַע עִמָּדִי: אִם־כֹּה יֹאמַר נְקֻדִּים
יִהְיֶה שְׂכָרֶךָ וְיָלְדוּ כָל־הַצֹּאן נְקֻדִּים וְאִם־כֹּה יֹאמַר עֲקֻדִּים יִהְיֶה שְׂכָרֶךָ וְיָלְדוּ
ט י כָל־הַצֹּאן עֲקֻדִּים: וַיַּצֵּל אֱלֹהִים אֶת־מִקְנֵה אֲבִיכֶם וַיִּתֶּן־לִי: וַיְהִי בְּעֵת יַחֵם
הַצֹּאן וָאֶשָּׂא עֵינַי וָאֵרֶא בַּחֲלוֹם וְהִנֵּה הָעַתֻּדִים הָעֹלִים עַל־הַצֹּאן עֲקֻדִּים נְקֻדִּים
יא יב וּבְרֻדִּים: וַיֹּאמֶר אֵלַי מַלְאַךְ הָאֱלֹהִים בַּחֲלוֹם יַעֲקֹב וָאֹמַר הִנֵּנִי: וַיֹּאמֶר שָׂא־נָא
עֵינֶיךָ וּרְאֵה כָּל־הָעַתֻּדִים הָעֹלִים עַל־הַצֹּאן עֲקֻדִּים נְקֻדִּים וּבְרֻדִּים כִּי רָאִיתִי אֵת
יג כָּל־אֲשֶׁר לָבָן עֹשֶׂה לָּךְ: אָנֹכִי הָאֵל בֵּית־אֵל אֲשֶׁר מָשַׁחְתָּ שָּׁם מַצֵּבָה אֲשֶׁר נָדַרְתָּ
יד לִּי שָׁם נֶדֶר עַתָּה קוּם צֵא מִן־הָאָרֶץ הַזֹּאת וְשׁוּב אֶל־אֶרֶץ מוֹלַדְתֶּךָ: וַתַּעַן רָחֵל

THEMES | RELATIONSHIPS AND LOVE | COVENANT | LAND OF ISRAEL

Episode 44: *Yaakov Escapes Lavan* – Bereshit 31:1–21

SUMMARY

Extricating himself from his father-in-law and employer is no simple task. Along with settling financial arrangements between them, many complex emotional issues have to be addressed. Even after the property has been divided between them, they cannot come to an agreement in Ḥaran for Yaakov's departure, and he ends up taking flight.

15 inheritance of our father's estate? He treats us like strangers. He has sold us and spent the
16 money. All the wealth that God has taken from our father belongs to us and our children.
17 18 So do whatever God has told you." So Yaakov put his children and wives on camels and
drove all the livestock and wealth he had accumulated – the livestock he had acquired in
19 Padan Aram – heading for his father Yitzhak in the land of Canaan. Meanwhile, when
20 Lavan had gone to shear his sheep, Rahel had stolen her father's household gods. Yaakov
21 deceived Lavan the Aramean by not telling him that he was running away. He fled with all
he had, crossed the Euphrates, and headed for the hill country of Gilad.

THE ART OF MIDRASH

Jacob persuades Leah and Rachel to flee
Pieter Potter (1638)

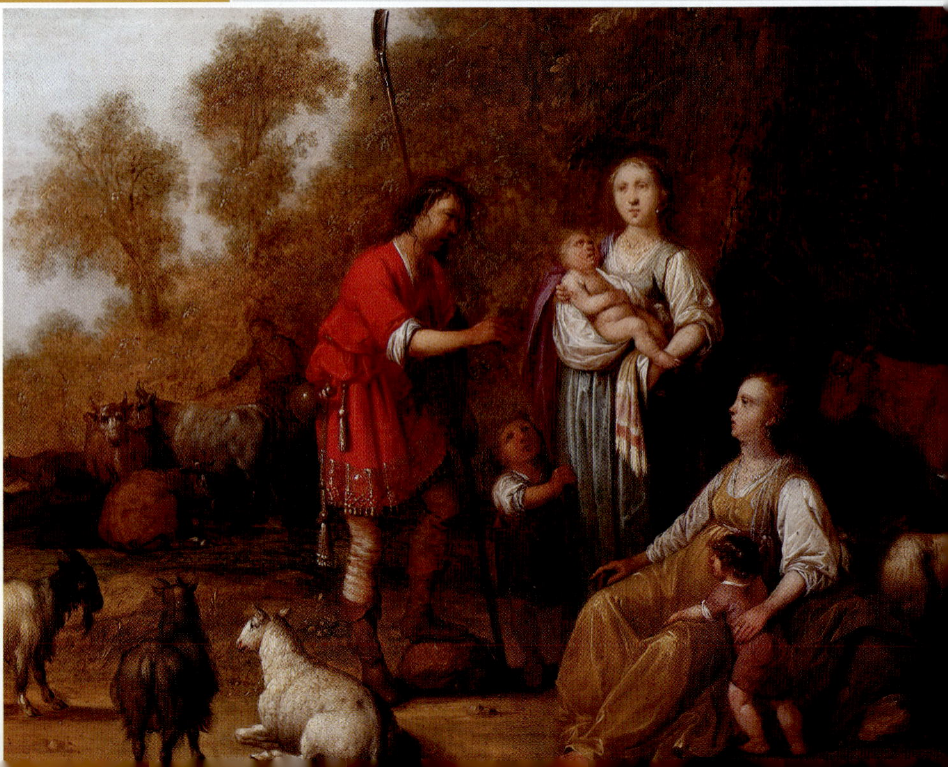

Analysis

- Which elements of this image are directly mentioned in the text?
- Which elements of this image are not found in the text?
- What midrashic interpretation could be inferred from this image?

טו וְלֵאָ֖ה וַתֹּאמַ֣רְנָה לֹּ֑ו הַעֹ֥וד לָ֛נוּ חֵ֥לֶק וְנַחֲלָ֖ה בְּבֵ֣ית אָבִ֑ינוּ: הֲלֹ֧וא נָכְרִיֹּ֛ות נֶחְשַׁ֥בְנוּ

טז לֹ֖ו כִּ֣י מְכָרָ֑נוּ וַיֹּ֥אכַל גַּם־אָכֹ֖ול אֶת־כַּסְפֵּֽנוּ: כִּ֣י כָל־הָעֹ֗שֶׁר אֲשֶׁ֨ר הִצִּ֤יל אֱלֹהִים֙

יז מֵאָבִ֔ינוּ לָ֥נוּ ה֖וּא וּלְבָנֵ֑ינוּ וְעַתָּ֗ה כֹּל֩ אֲשֶׁ֨ר אָמַ֧ר אֱלֹהִ֛ים אֵלֶ֖יךָ עֲשֵֽׂה: וַיָּ֖קָם יַעֲקֹ֑ב

יח וַיִּשָּׂ֛א אֶת־בָּנָ֥יו וְאֶת־נָשָׁ֖יו עַל־הַגְּמַלִּֽים: וַיִּנְהַ֣ג אֶת־כָּל־מִקְנֵ֗הוּ וְאֶת־כָּל־רְכֻשֹׁו֙

אֲשֶׁ֣ר רָכָ֔שׁ מִקְנֵה֙ קִנְיָנֹ֔ו אֲשֶׁ֥ר רָכַ֖שׁ בְּפַדַּ֣ן אֲרָ֑ם לָבֹ֛וא אֶל־יִצְחָ֥ק אָבִ֖יו אַ֥רְצָה כְּנָֽעַן:

יט וְלָבָ֣ן הָלַ֔ךְ לִגְזֹ֖ז אֶת־צֹאנֹ֑ו וַתִּגְנֹ֣ב רָחֵ֔ל אֶת־הַתְּרָפִ֖ים אֲשֶׁ֥ר לְאָבִֽיהָ: וַיִּגְנֹ֣ב יַעֲקֹ֗ב

כא אֶת־לֵ֥ב לָבָ֖ן הָֽאֲרַמִּ֑י עַל־בְּלִ֕י הִגִּ֣יד לֹ֔ו כִּ֥י בֹרֵ֖חַ הֽוּא: וַיִּבְרַ֥ח הוּא֙ וְכָל־אֲשֶׁר־לֹ֔ו

וַיָּ֖קָם וַיַּעֲבֹ֣ר אֶת־הַנָּהָ֑ר וַיָּ֥שֶׂם אֶת־פָּנָ֖יו הַ֥ר הַגִּלְעָֽד:

A QUESTION OF
BIBLIODRAMA

TO YAAKOV

- What have you noticed about the way Lavan and his sons are relating to you?

- How do you feel toward them now?

- Were you expecting your wives to respond differently to your explanation of why you should leave?

- What did you learn from the dreams where God appeared to you?

- Did you know Raḥel took Lavan's idols?

TO RAḤEL AND LEAH

- What did you think of Yaakov's plans to leave?

- Did you both agree on this?

- How do you each feel toward your father?

What arouses his anger, his rage, is that Yaakov maintains his dignity and independence. Faced with an impossible existence as his father-in-law's slave, Yaakov always finds a way of carrying on. Yes, he has been cheated of his beloved Raḥel, but he works so that he can marry her too. Yes, he has been forced to work for nothing, but he uses his superior knowledge of animal husbandry to propose a deal which will allow him to build flocks of his own so that he can maintain what is now a large family. Yaakov refuses to be defeated. Hemmed in on all sides, he finds a way out. That is Yaakov's greatness. His methods are not those he would have chosen in other circumstances. He has to outwit an extremely cunning adversary. But Yaakov refuses to be defeated, or crushed and demoralized. In a seemingly impossible situation Yaakov retains his dignity, independence, and freedom. Yaakov is no man's slave.

Lavan is, in effect, the first antisemite. In age after age, Jews sought refuge from those, like Esav, who sought to kill them. The nations who gave them refuge seemed at first to be benefactors. But they demanded a price. They saw, in Jews, people who would make them rich. Wherever Jews went they brought prosperity to their hosts. Yet they refused to be mere chattels. They refused to be owned. They had their own identity and way of life; they insisted on the basic human right to be free. The host society then eventually turned against them. They claimed that Jews were exploiting them rather than what was in fact the case, that they were exploiting the Jews. And when Jews succeeded, they accused them of theft: "The flocks are my flocks! All that you see is mine!" They forgot that Jews had contributed massively to national prosperity. The fact that Jews had salvaged some self-respect, some independence, that they too had prospered, made them not just envious but angry. That was when it became dangerous to be a Jew.

Lavan was the first to display this syndrome but not the last. It happened again in Egypt after the death of Yosef. It happened under the Greeks and Romans, the Christian and Muslim empires of the Middle Ages, the European nations of the nineteenth and early twentieth centuries, and after the Russian Revolution.

In her fascinating book *World on Fire*, Amy Chua argues that ethnic hatred will always be directed by the host society against any conspicuously successful minority. All three conditions must be present.

INTEGRATING ḤOKHMA

Lavan's behavior is the paradigm of antisemites through the ages. Lavan begins by seeming like a friend. He offers Yaakov refuge when he is in flight from Esav who has vowed to kill him. Yet it turns out that his behavior is less generous than self-interested and calculating. Yaakov works for him for seven years for Raḥel. Then on the wedding night Lavan substitutes Leah for Raḥel, so that to marry Raḥel, Yaakov has to work another seven years. When Yosef is born to Raḥel, Yaakov tries to leave. Lavan protests. Yaakov works another six years, and then realizes that the situation is untenable. Lavan's sons are accusing him of getting rich at Lavan's expense. Yaakov senses that Lavan himself is becoming hostile. Raḥel and Leah agree, saying, "He treats us like strangers! He has sold us and spent the money!" (Bereshit 31:14–15).

Yaakov realizes that there is nothing he can do or say that will persuade Lavan to let him leave. He has no choice but to escape. Lavan then pursues him, and were it not for God's warning the night before he catches up with him, there is little doubt that he would have forced Yaakov to return and live out the rest of his life as his unpaid laborer. As he says to Yaakov the next day: "The daughters are my daughters! The sons are my sons! The flocks are my flocks! All that you see is mine!" (31:43). It turns out that everything he had ostensibly given Yaakov, in his own mind he had not given at all.

Lavan treats Yaakov as his property, his slave. He is a non-person. In his eyes Yaakov has no rights, no independent existence. He has given Yaakov his daughters in marriage but still claims that they and their children belong to him, not Yaakov. He has given Yaakov an agreement as to the animals that will be his as his wages, yet he still insists that "the flocks are my flocks."

1. The hated group must be a minority or people will fear to attack it.
2. It must be successful or people will not envy it, merely feel contempt for it.
3. It must be conspicuous or people will not notice it.

Jews tended to fit all three. That is why they were hated. And it began with Yaakov during his stay with Lavan. He was a minority, outnumbered by Lavan's family. He was successful, and it was conspicuous: you could see it by looking at his flocks.

The syndrome still exists today. As Amy Chua notes, Israel in the context of the Middle East is a conspicuously successful minority. It is a small country, a minority; it is successful and it is conspicuously so. Somehow, in a tiny country with few natural resources, it has outshone its neighbors. The result is envy that becomes anger that becomes hate. Where did it begin? With Lavan.

Put this way, we begin to see Yaakov in a new light. Yaakov stands for minorities and small nations everywhere. Yaakov is the refusal to let large powers crush the few, the weak, the refugee. Yaakov refuses to define himself as a slave, someone else's property. He maintains his inner dignity and freedom. He contributes to other people's prosperity but he defeats every attempt to be exploited. Yaakov is the voice that says: I too am human. I too have rights. I too am free.

If Lavan is the eternal paradigm of hatred of conspicuously successful minorities, then Yaakov is the eternal paradigm of the human capacity to survive the hatred of others. In this strange way Yaakov becomes the voice of hope in the conversation of humankind, the living proof that hate never wins the final victory; freedom does.

Rabbi Jonathan Sacks

Analysis

- What areas of understanding of human nature and society do we now have that were unavailable to classical Jewish commentators? How can they aid our understanding of the text?
- What can we learn from this essay to help us understand the text?
- What further questions on the text do you have now that you have read this new take on the story?

TAKING A LITERARY APPROACH

Yaakov's increasing wealth impacts not only him but his adopted family and their relationship with him. He overhears his brothers-in-law complaining about how he has stripped their father's wealth and become rich at their expense. Even Lavan, who wanted Yaakov around for the blessing he brought, no longer looks at him the same way. Despite the signs that he needs to move on, Yaakov does not. He is too caught up with increasing his flocks. Ironically, what initially draws Yaakov into Lavan's house is the promise of joining a family to replace the one he lost. Now, despite being rejected by that very family, Yaakov cannot bring himself to leave. Were it not for a divine directive, Yaakov would have ignored his adopted family's rejection and stayed to further increase his wealth.

Using the same terms that moved Avraham from this very place two generations earlier, God tells Yaakov that he must uproot himself and return to his true family and identity: "Return to the land of your fathers and your *moledet*; I will be with you" (Bereshit 31:3). As with Avraham, the journey involves more than a geographic relocation; it demands a shift in identity. Yaakov, who has become an Aramean, needs to restore himself within the Abrahamic tradition.

Avraham is told to find himself a new home; Yaakov undoes Avraham's *lekh lekha*, returning to Avraham's origins in Ḥaran, where he loses the ability to find his way back home. Like Avraham at his lowest point, Yaakov is lost. He accepts two seven-year cycles of servitude to Lavan, and just one year before completing a third cycle – ensuring his permanent enslavement – God pushes him to leave.

While Yaakov gets the message that he needs to leave Lavan's house and return home, he seems to miss the bigger point – his orientation needs to change. He needs to change, to seek out his selfhood, his *anokhi*. His entire presentation to his wives is one of victimhood. He takes no responsibility for allowing himself to become victimized or for the things he did earlier in life which set him up for victimization. It is all Lavan's fault, and the only solution Yaakov can envision is to get away from him.

Rather than learning from his mistakes, Yaakov repeats them, but without the subsequent soul-searching. Twenty years after he runs away from Esav, he deceitfully sneaks away from Lavan. Packing his things hastily in the middle of the night, Yaakov takes his family and flees. The language used in the Torah is unmistakable: "Yaakov stole the heart of Lavan the Aramean" (31:20). He arrived in Aram as an unwilling thief; he leaves Aram as a willing one.

And it is not just his family that he takes. Three times in a single verse (31:18), the Torah uses the root *k-n-h*, alternately meaning "flocks" or "acquisitions," to describe what he takes with him. Just as Yaakov dreams of sheep (31:10), what concerns him now are his many acquisitions. We shudder to imagine what Yaakov would have become were it not for God's push.

Yaakov's midnight flight raises the terrifying thought that he has learned nothing from his twenty years in Ḥaran, or worse – that he learned only the wrong things there, becoming completely absorbed into Lavan's culture. Yaakov is a son who jeopardizes the covenant into which he is born.

Earlier, when Yaakov awoke from his divine vision in Beit El, he was unsure of whether God had really spoken with him. As we saw then, whether God will be with Yaakov is very much dependent on Yaakov himself. And at this point, it does not look good.

Rabbi Zvi Grumet

22 23 On the third day, Lavan was told that Yaakov had fled. Taking his kinsmen with him, he
24 pursued him for seven days, catching up with him in the hill country of Gilad. That night
God came to Lavan the Aramean in a dream and said to him, "Take care not to say anything
25 to Yaakov for good or for bad." When Lavan overtook him, Yaakov had pitched his tent
in the hill country, and Lavan and his kinsmen too encamped in the hill country of Gilad.
26 Lavan said to Yaakov, "What have you done? You have deceived me, and carried off my
27 daughters like captives of the sword. Why did you leave secretly? Why did you deceive me
by not telling me? I would have sent you off with celebration and song, with tambourines
28 and harps. You did not even let me kiss my grandchildren and daughters goodbye. You have
29 behaved foolishly. I have the power to harm you, but last night your father's God spoke
30 to me and said, 'Take care not to say anything to Yaakov for good or for bad.' I realize you
left because you longed so much for your father's house. But why did you steal my gods?"
31 Yaakov answered Lavan, saying, "I was afraid; I thought you would take your daughters
32 away from me by force. But if you find your gods with anyone here, they shall not live. In
the presence of our kinsmen, see if there is anything of yours here, and take it." Yaakov

UNLOCKING THE TEXT

- Why did it take three days until Lavan became aware that Yaakov had left?
- Did Lavan have a point? Was he being truthful in how he expressed his feelings?
- What power does Lavan have to hurt Yaakov?
- Why is God described as the God of Yaakov's father, rather than the God of Yaakov?
- Why was Yaakov afraid of Lavan?
- Why did Yaakov condemn to death whoever hid the idols?
- What message does the Torah want us to take from the story of Raḥel hiding the idols?
- What was Yaakov's reason behind the speech he delivered to Lavan?
- On what basis can Lavan claim that all that Yaakov has belongs to him?
- Why does Yaakov call the angels "God's own camp"?
- What is the meaning of "Maḥanayim"?
- How is the dream at the end of the *parasha* connected to the dream at the beginning of the *parasha*?

FINDING YOURSELF IN THE TEXT

- Have you ever experienced someone accusing you of things you didn't do or are not to blame for?
- Have you found yourself exploding with emotion as you described a long list of injustices that you have experienced?
- Do you find it hard to assert your independence from those who have previously had a senior role in your life?

Consider using these questions as the basis for your own commentary or creative midrash.

How does reflecting on these firsthand experiences help you better understand the text?

כב כג וַיֻּגַּד לְלָבָן בַּיּוֹם הַשְּׁלִישִׁי כִּי בָרַח יַעֲקֹב: וַיִּקַּח אֶת־אֶחָיו עִמּוֹ וַיִּרְדֹּף אַחֲרָיו
כד דֶּרֶךְ שִׁבְעַת יָמִים וַיַּדְבֵּק אֹתוֹ בְּהַר הַגִּלְעָד: וַיָּבֹא אֱלֹהִים אֶל־לָבָן הָאֲרַמִּי
כה בַּחֲלֹם הַלָּיְלָה וַיֹּאמֶר לוֹ הִשָּׁמֶר לְךָ פֶּן־תְּדַבֵּר עִם־יַעֲקֹב מִטּוֹב עַד־רָע: וַיַּשֵּׂג
לָבָן אֶת־יַעֲקֹב וְיַעֲקֹב תָּקַע אֶת־אָהֳלוֹ בָּהָר וְלָבָן תָּקַע אֶת־אֶחָיו בְּהַר הַגִּלְעָד:
כו וַיֹּאמֶר לָבָן לְיַעֲקֹב מֶה עָשִׂיתָ וַתִּגְנֹב אֶת־לְבָבִי וַתְּנַהֵג אֶת־בְּנֹתַי כִּשְׁבֻיוֹת חָרֶב:
כז לָמָּה נַחְבֵּאתָ לִבְרֹחַ וַתִּגְנֹב אֹתִי וְלֹא־הִגַּדְתָּ לִּי וָאֲשַׁלֵּחֲךָ בְּשִׂמְחָה וּבְשִׁרִים
כח כט בְּתֹף וּבְכִנּוֹר: וְלֹא נְטַשְׁתַּנִי לְנַשֵּׁק לְבָנַי וְלִבְנֹתָי עַתָּה הִסְכַּלְתָּ עֲשׂוֹ: יֶשׁ־לְאֵל
יָדִי לַעֲשׂוֹת עִמָּכֶם רָע וֵאלֹהֵי אֲבִיכֶם אֶמֶשׁ ׀ אָמַר אֵלַי לֵאמֹר הִשָּׁמֶר לְךָ מִדַּבֵּר
ל עִם־יַעֲקֹב מִטּוֹב עַד־רָע: וְעַתָּה הָלֹךְ הָלַכְתָּ כִּי־נִכְסֹף נִכְסַפְתָּה לְבֵית אָבִיךָ
לא לָמָּה גָנַבְתָּ אֶת־אֱלֹהָי: וַיַּעַן יַעֲקֹב וַיֹּאמֶר לְלָבָן כִּי יָרֵאתִי כִּי אָמַרְתִּי פֶּן־תִּגְזֹל
לב אֶת־בְּנוֹתֶיךָ מֵעִמִּי: עִם אֲשֶׁר תִּמְצָא אֶת־אֱלֹהֶיךָ לֹא יִחְיֶה נֶגֶד אַחֵינוּ הַכֶּר־לְךָ

THEMES	RELATIONSHIPS AND LOVE	COVENANT	LAND OF ISRAEL

Episode 45: *Lavan Pursues Yaakov and They Reconcile* – Bereshit 31:22–32:2

SUMMARY

In this episode, as Yaakov flees with his family, Lavan pursues them, accusing Yaakov of deceit in sneaking away without a farewell, and also of stealing his household idols, which Raḥel hid in the cushion on her camel. The final parting between them, which includes a covenant between Yaakov's family and that of Lavan, occurs far from Ḥaran, at Mount Gilad.

At the end of this episode, a short account is found which deals entirely with Yaakov's first exile. Just as he had a vision of angels upon his departure from Canaan, ascending and descending a ladder, so too on his return he encounters angels. One can see that Yaakov was strengthened by his travels, as initially he merely dreamed of angels but now, and later on as well, he sees them with his waking eyes. As in his dream, his meeting with the angels reminds him that God is accompanying him on his journey, emboldening him for the upcoming encounter with his brother Esav.

33 did not know that Raḥel was the one who had stolen them. So Lavan went into Yaakov's
tent, Leah's tent, and the tents of the two female slaves, but found nothing. Leaving Leah's
34 tent, he entered Raḥel's. But Raḥel had taken the household gods and put them inside a
camel cushion, and was sitting on them; and Lavan rummaged through the tent but found
35 nothing. She said to her father, "Do not be angry, my lord, but I cannot get up for you, for
the way of women is with me now." So he searched but did not find his household gods.
36 Yaakov became indignant and confronted Lavan. "What is my crime?" he asked Lavan.
37 "What wrong did I do that you come chasing after me? You have rummaged through all
my possessions. What have you found that belongs to your house? Put it here in front of
38 my kinsmen and yours and let them decide between the two of us! For the twenty years I
was with you, your sheep and goats did not miscarry. Not once did I take a ram from your
39 flock as food. I never brought you an animal torn by wild beasts. I bore the loss myself.
40 Whether it was stolen by day or by night you demanded payment from me. By day I was
41 ravaged by the heat; at night by the freezing cold. Sleep fled from my eyes. Twenty years I
spent working in your household – fourteen for your two daughters and six for your flock –
42 and ten times you changed my wages. Had the God of my father – the God of Avraham, the
Fear of Yitzḥak – not been with me, you would have sent me away empty-handed. But God
43 saw my plight and the toil of my hands, and He rebuked you last night." Then Lavan spoke
up and said to Yaakov, "The daughters are my daughters. The children are my children. The
flocks are my flocks. All that you see is mine. But what can I do now about my daughters
44 or the children they have borne? Come now, let us make a covenant, you and I, and let it
45 46 be a witness between us." So Yaakov took a stone and set it up as a pillar. Yaakov said to his
kinsmen, "Gather stones." They took stones and made a mound, and there by the mound
47 48 they ate. Lavan called it Yegar Sahaduta, while Yaakov called it Galed.[1] Lavan said, "This
49 mound is a witness between me and you this day." That is why it is called Galed. It is also
called Mitzpa because he said, "May the Lord keep watch between me and you when we
50 are out of each other's sight.[2] If you mistreat my daughters or take other wives besides my
daughters, even though no one else is present, remember that God is the witness between
51 me and you." Lavan said to Yaakov, "Here is the mound and here is the pillar I have set up
52 between us. This mound is a witness, and the pillar is a witness, that I will not go past this
mound on your side and that you will not go past this mound and pillar on my side with

1 | Both names mean "mound of testimony," the former in Aramaic, the latter in Hebrew (cf. also the name Gilad in v. 25).

2 | The name Mitzpa derives from the same root as *yitzef* ("keep watch").

מַה עִמָּדִ֔י וְקַח־לָ֑ךְ וְלֹֽא־יָדַ֣ע יַעֲקֹ֔ב כִּ֥י רָחֵ֖ל גְּנָבָֽתַם: וַיָּבֹ֨א לָבָ֜ן בְּאֹֽהֶל־יַעֲקֹ֣ב ׀ לג

וּבְאֹ֣הֶל לֵאָ֗ה וּבְאֹ֛הֶל שְׁתֵּ֥י הָאֲמָהֹ֖ת וְלֹ֣א מָצָ֑א וַיֵּצֵא֙ מֵאֹ֣הֶל לֵאָ֔ה וַיָּבֹ֖א בְּאֹ֥הֶל

רָחֵֽל: וְרָחֵ֞ל לָקְחָ֣ה אֶת־הַתְּרָפִ֗ים וַתְּשִׂמֵ֛ם בְּכַ֥ר הַגָּמָ֖ל וַתֵּ֣שֶׁב עֲלֵיהֶ֑ם וַיְמַשֵּׁ֥שׁ לד

לָבָ֛ן אֶת־כׇּל־הָאֹ֖הֶל וְלֹ֥א מָצָֽא: וַתֹּ֣אמֶר אֶל־אָבִ֗יהָ אַל־יִ֙חַר֙ בְּעֵינֵ֣י אֲדֹנִ֔י כִּ֣י ל֤וֹא לה

אוּכַל֙ לָק֣וּם מִפָּנֶ֔יךָ כִּי־דֶ֥רֶךְ נָשִׁ֖ים לִ֑י וַיְחַפֵּ֕שׂ וְלֹ֥א מָצָ֖א אֶת־הַתְּרָפִֽים: וַיִּ֥חַר לְיַעֲקֹ֖ב לו

וַיָּ֣רֶב בְּלָבָ֑ן וַיַּ֤עַן יַעֲקֹב֙ וַיֹּ֣אמֶר לְלָבָ֔ן מַה־פִּשְׁעִי֙ מַ֣ה חַטָּאתִ֔י כִּ֥י דָלַ֖קְתָּ אַחֲרָֽי:

כִּֽי־מִשַּׁ֣שְׁתָּ אֶת־כׇּל־כֵּלַ֗י מַה־מָּצָ֙אתָ֙ מִכֹּ֣ל כְּלֵי־בֵיתֶ֔ךָ שִׂ֣ים כֹּ֔ה נֶ֥גֶד אַחַ֖י וְאַחֶ֑יךָ לז

וְיוֹכִ֖יחוּ בֵּ֥ין שְׁנֵֽינוּ: זֶה֩ עֶשְׂרִ֨ים שָׁנָ֤ה אָנֹכִי֙ עִמָּ֔ךְ רְחֵלֶ֥יךָ וְעִזֶּ֖יךָ לֹ֣א שִׁכֵּ֑לוּ וְאֵילֵ֥י לח

צֹאנְךָ֖ לֹ֥א אָכָֽלְתִּי: טְרֵפָה֙ לֹא־הֵבֵ֣אתִי אֵלֶ֔יךָ אָנֹכִ֣י אֲחַטֶּ֔נָּה מִיָּדִ֖י תְּבַקְשֶׁ֑נָּה גְּנֻֽבְתִ֣י לט

י֔וֹם וּגְנֻבְתִ֖י לָֽיְלָה: הָיִ֧יתִי בַיּ֛וֹם אֲכָלַ֥נִי חֹ֖רֶב וְקֶ֣רַח בַּלָּ֑יְלָה וַתִּדַּ֥ד שְׁנָתִ֖י מֵֽעֵינָֽי: מא

זֶה־לִּ֞י עֶשְׂרִ֣ים שָׁנָה֮ בְּבֵיתֶ֒ךָ֒ עֲבַדְתִּ֜יךָ אַרְבַּֽע־עֶשְׂרֵ֤ה שָׁנָה֙ בִּשְׁתֵּ֣י בְנֹתֶ֔יךָ וְשֵׁ֥שׁ

שָׁנִ֖ים בְּצֹאנֶ֑ךָ וַתַּחֲלֵ֥ף אֶת־מַשְׂכֻּרְתִּ֖י עֲשֶׂ֥רֶת מֹנִֽים: לוּלֵ֡י אֱלֹהֵ֣י אָבִ֩י אֱלֹהֵ֨י אַבְרָהָ֜ם מב

וּפַ֤חַד יִצְחָק֙ הָ֣יָה לִ֔י כִּ֥י עַתָּ֖ה רֵיקָ֣ם שִׁלַּחְתָּ֑נִי אֶת־עׇנְיִ֞י וְאֶת־יְגִ֧יעַ כַּפַּ֛י רָאָ֥ה אֱלֹהִ֖ים

וַיּ֥וֹכַח אָֽמֶשׁ: וַיַּ֨עַן לָבָ֜ן וַיֹּ֣אמֶר אֶֽל־יַעֲקֹ֗ב הַבָּנ֨וֹת בְּנֹתַ֜י וְהַבָּנִ֤ים בָּנַי֙ וְהַצֹּ֣אן צֹאנִ֔י מג שביעי

וְכֹ֛ל אֲשֶׁר־אַתָּ֥ה רֹאֶ֖ה לִי־ה֑וּא וְלִבְנֹתַ֞י מָֽה־אֶעֱשֶׂ֤ה לָאֵ֙לֶּה֙ הַיּ֔וֹם א֥וֹ לִבְנֵיהֶ֖ן אֲשֶׁ֥ר

יָלָֽדוּ: וְעַתָּ֗ה לְכָ֛ה נִכְרְתָ֥ה בְרִ֖ית אֲנִ֣י וָאָ֑תָּה וְהָיָ֥ה לְעֵ֖ד בֵּינִ֥י וּבֵינֶֽךָ: וַיִּקַּ֥ח יַעֲקֹ֖ב מד מה

אָ֑בֶן וַיְרִימֶ֖הָ מַצֵּבָֽה: וַיֹּ֨אמֶר יַעֲקֹ֤ב לְאֶחָיו֙ לִקְט֣וּ אֲבָנִ֔ים וַיִּקְח֥וּ אֲבָנִ֖ים וַיַּֽעֲשׂוּ־גָ֑ל מו

וַיֹּ֥אכְלוּ שָׁ֖ם עַל־הַגָּֽל: וַיִּקְרָא־ל֣וֹ לָבָ֔ן יְגַ֖ר שָׂהֲדוּתָ֑א וְיַ֣עֲקֹ֔ב קָ֥רָא ל֖וֹ גַּלְעֵֽד: וַיֹּ֣אמֶר מז מח

לָבָ֔ן הַגַּ֨ל הַזֶּ֥ה עֵ֛ד בֵּינִ֥י וּבֵֽינְךָ֖ הַיּ֑וֹם עַל־כֵּ֥ן קָרָֽא־שְׁמ֖וֹ גַּלְעֵֽד: וְהַמִּצְפָּה֙ אֲשֶׁ֣ר אָמַ֔ר מט

יִ֥צֶף יְהֹוָ֖ה בֵּינִ֣י וּבֵינֶ֑ךָ כִּ֥י נִסָּתֵ֖ר אִ֥ישׁ מֵרֵעֵֽהוּ: אִם־תְּעַנֶּ֣ה אֶת־בְּנֹתַ֗י וְאִם־תִּקַּ֤ח נ

נָשִׁים֙ עַל־בְּנֹתַ֔י אֵ֥ין אִ֖ישׁ עִמָּ֑נוּ רְאֵ֕ה אֱלֹהִ֛ים עֵ֥ד בֵּינִ֖י וּבֵינֶֽךָ: וַיֹּ֥אמֶר לָבָ֖ן לְיַעֲקֹ֑ב נא

הִנֵּ֣ה ׀ הַגַּ֣ל הַזֶּ֗ה וְהִנֵּה֙ הַמַּצֵּבָ֔ה אֲשֶׁ֥ר יָרִ֖יתִי בֵּינִ֣י וּבֵינֶֽךָ: עֵ֚ד הַגַּ֣ל הַזֶּ֔ה וְעֵדָ֖ה נב

הַמַּצֵּבָ֑ה אִם־אָ֗נִי לֹֽא־אֶֽעֱבֹ֤ר אֵלֶ֙יךָ֙ אֶת־הַגַּ֣ל הַזֶּ֔ה וְאִם־אַ֠תָּ֠ה לֹא־תַעֲבֹ֨ר אֵלַ֜י אֶת־

53 intent to do harm. May the God of Avraham, the god of Naḥor and the god of their father
54 be our judge." Yaakov swore by the Fear of his father Yitzḥak. He offered a sacrifice on
the hill and invited his kinsmen to break bread. And they ate and spent the night upon
55 that hill. Lavan rose early the next morning. He kissed his grandchildren and daughters
32 1 goodbye and blessed them. Lavan then left to return home. Yaakov continued on his way –
2 and angels of God encountered him. When he saw them, Yaakov said, "This is God's own camp,"
and he named the place Maḥanayim.[3]

3 | Literally, "two camps."

THE ART OF MIDRASH

Rachel Hides Her Father's Household Gods
Marc Chagall (1956)

Analysis

- Which elements of this image are directly mentioned in the text?
- Which elements of this image are not found in the text?
- What midrashic interpretation could be inferred from this image?

נג הַגַּל הַזֶּה וְאֶת־הַמַּצֵּבָה הַזֹּאת לְרָעָה׃ אֱלֹהֵי אַבְרָהָם וֵאלֹהֵי נָחוֹר יִשְׁפְּטוּ בֵינֵינוּ
נד אֱלֹהֵי אֲבִיהֶם וַיִּשָּׁבַע יַעֲקֹב בְּפַחַד אָבִיו יִצְחָק׃ וַיִּזְבַּח יַעֲקֹב זֶבַח בָּהָר וַיִּקְרָא
נה לְאֶחָיו לֶאֱכָל־לָחֶם וַיֹּאכְלוּ לֶחֶם וַיָּלִינוּ בָּהָר׃ וַיַּשְׁכֵּם לָבָן בַּבֹּקֶר וַיְנַשֵּׁק לְבָנָיו מפטיר
לב א וְלִבְנוֹתָיו וַיְבָרֶךְ אֶתְהֶם וַיֵּלֶךְ וַיָּשָׁב לָבָן לִמְקֹמוֹ׃ וְיַעֲקֹב הָלַךְ לְדַרְכּוֹ וַיִּפְגְּעוּ־בוֹ
ב מַלְאֲכֵי אֱלֹהִים׃ וַיֹּאמֶר יַעֲקֹב כַּאֲשֶׁר רָאָם מַחֲנֵה אֱלֹהִים זֶה וַיִּקְרָא שֵׁם־הַמָּקוֹם
הַהוּא מַחֲנָיִם׃

A QUESTION OF BIBLIODRAMA

TO LAVAN

- Why are you so angry that Yaakov escaped with his family?
- Why do you think God came to you in a dream to warn you not to harm Yaakov?
- What were you hoping to achieve when you caught up with Yaakov and his camp?
- How do you feel toward Yaakov at the beginning of this encounter?
- How do you feel about Yaakov after you make a treaty with him?
- What impact did Yaakov's speech make on you?
- What is your aim regarding the treaty you make with Yaakov?

TO YAAKOV

- Why did you flee without allowing Lavan to say goodbye to his children and grandchildren?
- What are your fears as Lavan catches up to you?
- Do you know where Lavan's idols are?
- What do you hope to achieve with the speech you gave to Lavan?
- What do you hope to achieve with the treaty you make with Lavan?
- How do you feel about Lavan at the beginning of this encounter?
- How do you feel about Lavan after you make a treaty with him?

INTEGRATING ḤOKHMA

גִּלְעָד - GILAD

Gilad is a region in northern Transjordan. Mentioned eighty times, "Mount Gilad" first appears in Bereshit when Lavan chases Yaakov, and its name is explained thus: "They took stones and made a mound, and there by the mound they ate. Lavan called it Yegar Sahaduta, while Yaakov called it Galed (literally, 'mound of testimony')."

The Gilad's precise boundaries shifted over time, but it generally refers to the area between Madaba in the south and the Yarmouk River in the north. When Moshe first led the Israelites through the area, Amon and Moav inhabited the southern part of the Gilad, and Canaanites inhabited the northern part. However, after Siḥon of the Amorites and Og of Bashan conquered the land from Amon and Moav, the Israelites conquered it from them.

The Gilad is a very fertile area, rich in natural resources and medicinal herbs. Due to its excellent pastureland, the tribes of Reuven and Gad ask to settle there, and are granted the territory between the Arnon and Yabok streams, including the southern "half" of "the hill country of Gilad," while "the rest of Gilad and all of Bashan, Og's kingdom" – the northern part of the Gilad, from the Yabok to the Yarmouk – was granted to half the tribe of Menashe.

Analysis

- What specific information do we now have that was unavailable to classical Jewish commentators? How can it aid our understanding of the text?
- How can this information about Gilad help us understand the text?
- What further questions on the text do you have now that you have learned this information?

TAKING A LITERARY APPROACH

No chapter in the Torah is to be read in a vacuum. As we search for stylistic, linguistic, and thematic similarities to the story of Raḥel and the *terafim*, we find ourselves drawn to a strikingly similar episode that occurs, not coincidentally, in the lives of Raḥel's sons. Although it occurs many years after Raḥel's death and many miles from Ḥaran, Bereshit 34 similarly depicts a long-brewing intra-familial confrontation sparked by a false charge of theft.

Yosef, the then-viceroy of Egypt, has his royal goblet secretly planted in Binyamin's sack of provisions. Like his mother's act of stealing the *terafim*, Yosef's act of planting the goblet is recorded by the text with no explicit motive attached. Yosef's agents pursue his brothers and accuse them of stealing the goblet – just as Lavan pursued Yaakov and accused him of stealing the *terafim*. Like their father before them (Bereshit 31:32), Yosef's brothers steadfastly proclaim their innocence, in the process uttering a curse condemning the unidentified thief to death (44:9). Like Lavan searching through Yaakov's camp, Yosef's agents conduct a systematic search of the brothers' belongings. This search proceeds in order of the brothers' ages culminating with the search of the youngest brother's sack (44:12), just as Lavan's search culminated in the tent of his younger daughter (31:33). When the goblet is ultimately "found" in Binyamin's sack, the brothers are led back to the city, setting the stage for the climactic confrontation between Yosef and Yehuda echoing, of course, the confrontation between Yaakov and Lavan.

What was the state of Yaakov's family prior to this confrontation between Yosef and his brothers? If not dysfunctional, then certainly deteriorating. Fathers appeared to be shirking paternal responsibilities, sons were lying to their fathers, and, most importantly for this discussion, brothers were figuratively if not literally at each other's throats. At the center of this turmoil stands Yosef, arguably the greatest victim of the family's breakdown, who has been struggling throughout his years in exile to understand the dynamics that tore his family apart.

With this in mind, we return to the account of the *terafim* and notice that the long-awaited confrontation between Yaakov and Lavan, like the confrontation between Yosef and his brothers, is the climax of a dysfunctional family drama.

For twenty years, Yaakov is kept off balance by the manipulative Lavan, and this disequilibrium, these feelings of guilt, resentment, and repressed anger,

found of all your household objects? Set it here, before my kinsmen and yours, and let them decide between us two" (31:37). Pushed beyond the brink, Yaakov angrily confronts Lavan about the abuses and exploitations he has suffered at his hands (31:38–42). At long last, Yaakov reclaims the side of himself that has for so long been smothered by Lavan's manipulations and by his own guilty conscience.

Like her son Yosef and his goblet, Raḥel uses her father's *terafim* to engineer a situation designed to achieve a specific goal. Knowing the significance of the *terafim* and the value her father placed upon them, and painfully aware of Lavan's relationship with Yaakov, Raḥel steals the *terafim* in order to manipulate the context of the inevitable and final confrontation between the two men. Raḥel's machinations set the tone for that confrontation, and Yaakov's response at that critical juncture sets the trajectory of his future. As Raḥel planned, Lavan's "false" accusation becomes the proverbial straw that breaks the camel's back. That Lavan has capitalized on, and taken advantage of, Yaakov's guilt is one thing. But his accusation that Yaakov is a thief is unbearable (31:42). As a result, Yaakov's long-suppressed rage and indignation come pouring forth, creating a final break between the two men, a break concretized by the construction of a physical boundary between the two families (32:45–51). Lavan's influence is at an end, no longer serving to manipulate Yaakov or destabilize his family life.

Yael Leibowitz

poison every facet of his life. When Yaakov finally leaves, he packs up his family and flees Lavan's house without notice (31:17–21). Raḥel, knowing of Yaakov's plans to flee (31:5–16), steals Lavan's *terafim*. Lavan pursues Yaakov, catches up with him, and proceeds to hurl a series of accusations at him, accusing him of "stealing his heart," treating his daughters as "captives of the sword," and denying him an opportunity to bid them a proper farewell (31:26). Given the history between these two men, these accusations are disingenuous and no doubt infuriating. But they are not totally without merit.

Absent Raḥel's theft of the *terafim*, it is hard to imagine Yaakov articulating his anger and frustration any more in this instance than when Lavan switched brides on him. After all, Yaakov *was* sneaking out, and his wives had *not*, in fact, taken the kids to say goodbye to their grandfather. Cognizant of his own culpability, Yaakov would not have had the wherewithal to defend himself and Lavan's accusations would have remained unanswered. It is Yaakov who would have been remembered as perpetrating the final scam in a long cycle of trickery and deceit. The emotional consequences of their final confrontation might have continued to preclude Yaakov from fully being the husband and father that he should be. But Raḥel saw to it that the scene played out differently.

There is little doubt that Lavan would have pursued Yaakov whether or not he discovered that his *terafim* were gone. But Raḥel's theft altered the ensuing confrontation in one crucial respect. It ensured that Yaakov would find at least of one of Lavan's accusations to be completely baseless. For the first time since meeting his father-in-law, Yaakov demonstrably holds the moral high ground. He denies the charge of theft and, as Lavan makes his way slowly and deliberately through each tent in Yaakov's camp, we sense Yaakov's rising indignation. In a revealing juxtaposition of verses, Lavan's failure to find the *terafim* (31:35) is immediately followed by Yaakov's forceful reiteration of his innocence. Raḥel's stratagem has sparked the tinderbox that was Yaakov and Lavan's relationship. The Torah tells us that Yaakov "became incensed" (31:36), lambasting Lavan for his accusations. In a verse dripping with bitter sarcasm, Yaakov taunts Lavan: "You rummaged through all my things; what have you

וישלח
Vayishlaḥ

Parasha Overview

Vayishlaḥ tells the story of the meeting, after an estrangement that lasted twenty-two years, between Yaakov and Esav. Hearing that his brother is coming to meet him with a force of four hundred men, Yaakov is "greatly afraid and distressed." He divides his camp into two, sends gifts to Esav, and prays. That night he wrestles with a mysterious stranger, in an incident that ends with his being given a new name, Yisrael, meaning "one who struggles with God and men and prevails." The next day the two brothers meet, not in violence but in peace. They embrace and then go their separate ways. The *parasha* ends with the death of Yitzḥak and a genealogy of the descendants of Esav.

Episodes

46. **Yaakov Prepares for His Encounter with Esav** 32:3–21
47. **Yaakov Fights the Stranger Until Dawn** 32:22–32
48. **The Encounter Between Yaakov and Esav** 33:1–20
49. **The Violation of Dina** 34:1–31
50. **Yaakov in Beit El** 35:1–15
51. **Raḥel Dies Giving Birth to Binyamin** 35:16–22
52. **Family Trees** 35:23–36:43

Parasha Stats

- 7,458 letters
- 1,976 words
- 153 verses
- 237 lines in a sefer Torah
- 1 mitzva

3 Yaakov sent messengers ahead of him to his brother Esav in the land of Se'ir, the country
4 of Edom. He instructed them, "Say the following to my lord Esav: 'Your servant Yaakov
5 says, "I have been staying with Lavan; until now I have remained there. And I have acquired
cattle, donkeys, sheep, and male and female servants. I am sending this message to my
6 lord to find favor in your eyes."'" And when the messengers returned to Yaakov, they said,
"We came to your brother Esav. He is on his way to meet you, and with him, four hundred
7 men." Yaakov was acutely afraid and distressed. He divided the people with him into two
8 camps,[1] along with the flocks, the cattle, and the camels; "If Esav comes and attacks one
9 camp," he thought, "the other camp may still survive." Then Yaakov prayed, "God of my
father Avraham and God of my father Yitzḥak, LORD, You who said to me, 'Go back to the
10 land where you were born and I will deal well with you,' I am unworthy of all the kindnesses and the faithfulness that You have bestowed upon Your servant. When I crossed the
11 Jordan I had only my staff, and now I have become two camps. Rescue me, I pray, from
my brother's hand, from the hand of Esav. I am afraid he will come and kill us all, mothers
12 and children alike. Yet You said, 'I will deal well with you and make your descendants

1 | Cf. previous note.

UNLOCKING THE TEXT

- Is Yaakov really interested in reconciliation or is he just afraid for his life?
- Why does Yaakov make a point to emphasize to Esav how wealthy he is now?
- Was Esav journeying to Ḥaran to find Yaakov, or did he only come to meet him after he had received word that Yaakov was on his way to him?
- Why is Esav bringing four hundred men with him? What is the significance of the number four hundred?
- When Yaakov cries out in prayer, is he demonstrating strong faith or a lack of faith?
- Why does Yaakov mention his father and grandfather in his prayer?
- Does God respond to his prayer?
- What does Yaakov hope to achieve by sending gifts to Esav?
- Why does Yaakov split the gifts into three waves?

FINDING YOURSELF IN THE TEXT

- Have you ever been convinced that someone is still angry with you when they were not?
- Have you ever given someone a gift to help repair a relationship?
- Have you ever cried out to God in fear of something you were anxious was going to happen?

Consider using these questions as the basis for your own commentary or creative midrash.

How does reflecting on these firsthand experiences help you better understand the text?

ל וישלח

ג וַיִּשְׁלַ֨ח יַעֲקֹ֤ב מַלְאָכִים֙ לְפָנָ֔יו אֶל־עֵשָׂ֖ו אָחִ֑יו אַ֥רְצָה שֵׂעִ֖יר שְׂדֵ֥ה אֱדֽוֹם: וַיְצַ֤ו אֹתָם֙

ד לֵאמֹ֔ר כֹּ֣ה תֹֽאמְר֔וּן לַֽאדֹנִ֖י לְעֵשָׂ֑ו כֹּ֤ה אָמַר֙ עַבְדְּךָ֣ יַֽעֲקֹ֔ב עִם־לָבָ֣ן גַּ֔רְתִּי וָֽאֵחַ֖ר עַד־

ה עָֽתָּה: וַֽיְהִי־לִי֙ שׁ֣וֹר וַֽחֲמ֔וֹר צֹ֥אן וְעֶ֖בֶד וְשִׁפְחָ֑ה וָֽאֶשְׁלְחָה֙ לְהַגִּ֣יד לַֽאדֹנִ֔י לִמְצֹא־חֵ֖ן

ו בְּעֵינֶֽיךָ: וַיָּשֻׁ֨בוּ֙ הַמַּלְאָכִ֔ים אֶֽל־יַעֲקֹ֖ב לֵאמֹ֑ר בָּ֤אנוּ אֶל־אָחִ֨יךָ֙ אֶל־עֵשָׂ֔ו וְגַם֙ הֹלֵ֣ךְ

ז לִקְרָֽאתְךָ֔ וְאַרְבַּע־מֵא֥וֹת אִ֖ישׁ עִמּֽוֹ: וַיִּירָ֧א יַעֲקֹ֛ב מְאֹ֖ד וַיֵּ֣צֶר ל֑וֹ וַיַּ֜חַץ אֶת־הָעָ֣ם

ח אֲשֶׁר־אִתּ֗וֹ וְאֶת־הַצֹּ֧אן וְאֶת־הַבָּקָ֛ר וְהַגְּמַלִּ֖ים לִשְׁנֵ֥י מַֽחֲנֽוֹת: וַיֹּ֕אמֶר אִם־יָב֥וֹא

ט עֵשָׂ֛ו אֶל־הַמַּֽחֲנֶ֥ה הָאַחַ֖ת וְהִכָּ֑הוּ וְהָיָ֛ה הַמַּֽחֲנֶ֥ה הַנִּשְׁאָ֖ר לִפְלֵיטָֽה: וַיֹּאמֶר֮ יַעֲקֹב֒

י אֱלֹהֵי֙ אָבִ֣י אַבְרָהָ֔ם וֵֽאלֹהֵ֖י אָבִ֣י יִצְחָ֑ק יְהֹוָ֞ה הָֽאֹמֵ֣ר אֵלַ֗י שׁ֧וּב לְאַרְצְךָ֛ וּלְמֽוֹלַדְתְּךָ֖

יא וְאֵיטִ֥יבָה עִמָּֽךְ: קָטֹ֜נְתִּי מִכֹּ֤ל הַֽחֲסָדִים֙ וּמִכׇּל־הָ֣אֱמֶ֔ת אֲשֶׁ֥ר עָשִׂ֖יתָ אֶת־עַבְדֶּ֑ךָ כִּ֣י

יב בְמַקְלִ֗י עָבַ֨רְתִּי֙ אֶת־הַיַּרְדֵּ֣ן הַזֶּ֔ה וְעַתָּ֥ה הָיִ֖יתִי לִשְׁנֵ֥י מַֽחֲנֽוֹת: הַצִּילֵ֥נִי נָ֛א מִיַּ֥ד אָחִ֖י

יג מִיַּ֣ד עֵשָׂ֑ו כִּֽי־יָרֵ֤א אָֽנֹכִי֙ אֹת֔וֹ פֶּן־יָב֣וֹא וְהִכַּ֔נִי אֵ֖ם עַל־בָּנִֽים: וְאַתָּ֣ה אָמַ֔רְתָּ הֵיטֵ֣ב

THEMES   THE LAND OF ISRAEL   COVENANT   RELATIONSHIPS AND LOVE

Episode 46: *Yaakov Prepares for His Encounter with Esav* – Bereshit 32:3–21

SUMMARY

Yaakov, upon returning from exile in Ḥaran, readies himself for a charged encounter with his brother Esav, from whom he had fled years before in fear of his life. In anticipation of this confrontation, Yaakov prays to God. He also takes practical measures, as he attempts to placate his brother while at the same time prepares for a possible armed conflict.

13 countless, like the sand of the sea.'" He spent the night there. Then, from what he had
14 at hand, he selected a gift for his brother Esav: two hundred female goats, twenty male
15 goats, two hundred ewes, twenty rams, thirty milk camels and their young, forty cows,
16 ten bulls, twenty female donkeys, and ten male donkeys. He put them in the care of his
servants, each herd by itself, and he told the servants, "Go on ahead of me. Keep a space
17 between the herds." He instructed the first, "When my brother Esav meets you and asks,
'To whom do you belong? Where are you going? Who owns all these animals ahead of
18 you?' you must say, 'They belong to your servant Yaakov; they are a gift sent to my lord
19 Esav – and he is coming behind us.'" He likewise instructed the second and third and
all the others who followed the herds, "You shall say the same thing to Esav when you
20 meet him. Also say, 'Your servant Yaakov is coming behind us.'" He thought, "I will pacify
him with these gifts I am sending on ahead. Then I will face him. Perhaps he will accept
21 me." So the gifts went on ahead of him, while he remained in the camp that night. hip
socket at the sciatic nerve.

THE ART OF MIDRASH

Analysis

- Which elements of this image are directly mentioned in the text?
- Which elements of this image are not found in the text?
- What midrashic interpretation could be inferred from this image?

The Prayer of Jacob
Gustave Doré (1866)

יג אֵיטִיב עִמָּךְ וְשַׂמְתִּי אֶת־זַרְעֲךָ כְּחוֹל הַיָּם אֲשֶׁר לֹא־יִסָּפֵר מֵרֹב׃ וַיָּלֶן שָׁם בַּלַּיְלָה שני
יד הַהוּא וַיִּקַּח מִן־הַבָּא בְיָדוֹ מִנְחָה לְעֵשָׂו אָחִיו׃ עִזִּים מָאתַיִם וּתְיָשִׁים עֶשְׂרִים
טו רְחֵלִים מָאתַיִם וְאֵילִים עֶשְׂרִים׃ גְּמַלִּים מֵינִיקוֹת וּבְנֵיהֶם שְׁלֹשִׁים פָּרוֹת אַרְבָּעִים
טז וּפָרִים עֲשָׂרָה אֲתֹנֹת עֶשְׂרִים וַעְיָרִם עֲשָׂרָה׃ וַיִּתֵּן בְּיַד־עֲבָדָיו עֵדֶר עֵדֶר לְבַדּוֹ
יז וַיֹּאמֶר אֶל־עֲבָדָיו עִבְרוּ לְפָנַי וְרֶוַח תָּשִׂימוּ בֵּין עֵדֶר וּבֵין עֵדֶר׃ וַיְצַו אֶת־הָרִאשׁוֹן
לֵאמֹר כִּי יִפְגָשְׁךָ עֵשָׂו אָחִי וּשְׁאֵלְךָ לֵאמֹר לְמִי־אַתָּה וְאָנָה תֵלֵךְ וּלְמִי אֵלֶּה
יח לְפָנֶיךָ׃ וְאָמַרְתָּ לְעַבְדְּךָ לְיַעֲקֹב מִנְחָה הִוא שְׁלוּחָה לַאדֹנִי לְעֵשָׂו וְהִנֵּה גַם־הוּא
יט אַחֲרֵינוּ׃ וַיְצַו גַּם אֶת־הַשֵּׁנִי גַּם אֶת־הַשְּׁלִישִׁי גַּם אֶת־כָּל־הַהֹלְכִים אַחֲרֵי הָעֲדָרִים
כ לֵאמֹר כַּדָּבָר הַזֶּה תְּדַבְּרוּן אֶל־עֵשָׂו בְּמֹצַאֲכֶם אֹתוֹ׃ וַאֲמַרְתֶּם גַּם הִנֵּה עַבְדְּךָ
יַעֲקֹב אַחֲרֵינוּ כִּי־אָמַר אֲכַפְּרָה פָנָיו בַּמִּנְחָה הַהֹלֶכֶת לְפָנָי וְאַחֲרֵי־כֵן אֶרְאֶה
כא פָנָיו אוּלַי יִשָּׂא פָנָי׃ וַתַּעֲבֹר הַמִּנְחָה עַל־פָּנָיו וְהוּא לָן בַּלַּיְלָה־הַהוּא בַּמַּחֲנֶה׃

A QUESTION OF BIBLIODRAMA

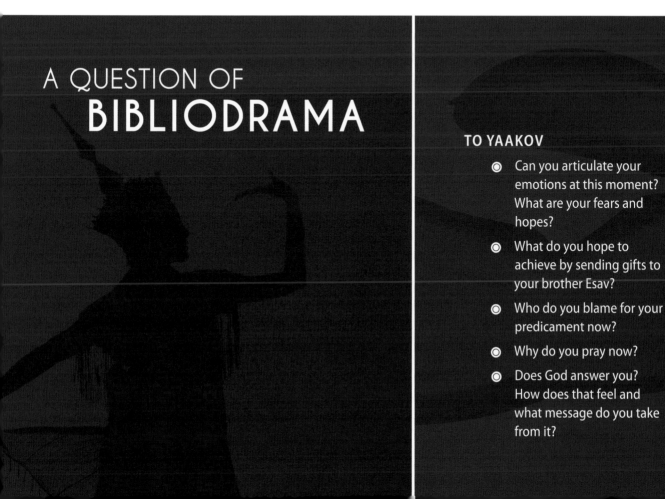

TO YAAKOV

- Can you articulate your emotions at this moment? What are your fears and hopes?
- What do you hope to achieve by sending gifts to your brother Esav?
- Who do you blame for your predicament now?
- Why do you pray now?
- Does God answer you? How does that feel and what message do you take from it?

The principle at stake, according to the *Siftei Ḥakhamim*, is the minimum use of force. The rules of defense and self-defense are not an open-ended permission to kill. There are laws restricting what is nowadays called "collateral damage," the killing of innocent civilians even if undertaken in the course of self-defense. Yaakov was distressed at the possibility that in the heat of conflict he might kill some of the combatants when injury alone might have been all that was necessary to defend the lives of those – including himself – who were under attack.

There is, however, a second possible explanation for Yaakov's fear – namely that the Midrash means what it says, no more, no less: Yaakov was distressed at the possibility of being forced to kill even if it were entirely justified.

What we are encountering here is the concept of a moral dilemma. (See *Moral Dilemmas* edited by Christopher Gowans for a collection of philosophical essays on this subject.) This phrase is often used imprecisely, to mean a moral problem, a difficult ethical decision. But a dilemma is not simply a conflict. There are many moral conflicts. May we perform an abortion to save the life of the mother? Should we obey a parent when he or she asks us to do something forbidden in Jewish law? May we desecrate the Shabbat to extend the life of a terminally ill patient? These questions have answers. There is a right course of action and a wrong one. Two duties conflict and we have meta-halakhic principles to tell us which takes priority. There are some systems in which all moral conflicts are of this kind. There is always a decision procedure and thus a determinate answer to the question, "What should I do?"

A dilemma, however, is a situation in which there is no right answer. It arises in cases of conflict between right and right, or between wrong and wrong – where, whatever we do, we are doing something that in other circumstances we ought not to do.

Rabbi Jonathan Sacks

Analysis

- What areas of understanding of human nature and society do we now have that were unavailable to classical Jewish commentators? How can they aid our understanding of the text?
- What can we learn from this essay to help us understand the text?
- What further questions on the text do you have now that you have read this new take on the story?

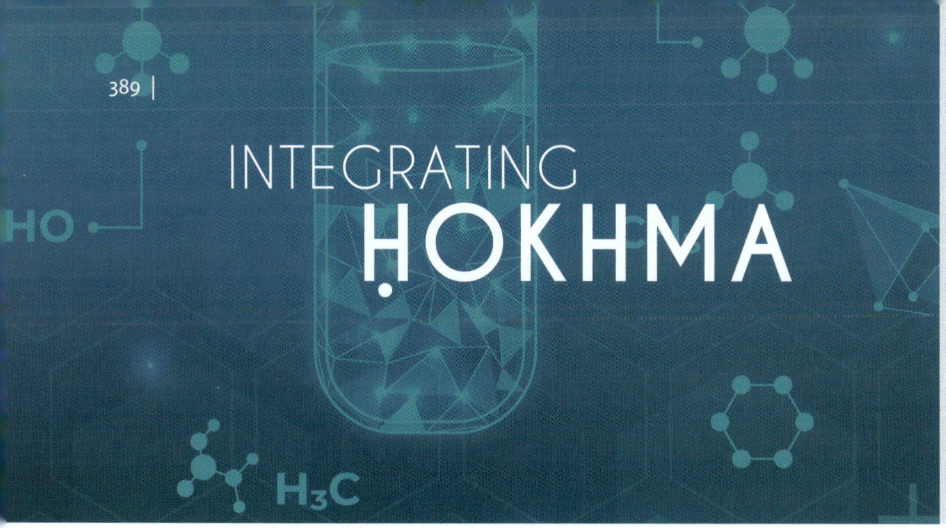

INTEGRATING ḤOKHMA

Twenty-two years have passed since Yaakov fled his brother, penniless and alone; twenty-two years have passed since Esav swore his revenge for what he saw as the theft of his blessing. Now the brothers are about to meet again. It is a fraught encounter. Once, Esav had sworn to kill Yaakov. Will he do so now – or has time healed the wound? Yaakov sends messengers to let his brother know he is coming. They return, saying that Esav is coming to meet Yaakov with a force of four hundred men – a contingent so large it suggests to Yaakov that Esav is intent on violence.

Yaakov's response is immediate and intense: "Then Yaakov was greatly afraid and distressed" (Bereshit 32:8).

The fear is understandable, but his response contains an enigma. Why the duplication of verbs? What is the difference between fear and distress? To this a midrash gives a profound answer: R. Yehuda bar Ilai said: Are not fear and distress identical? The meaning, however, is that "he was afraid" that he might be killed; "he was distressed" that he might kill. For Yaakov thought: If he prevails against me, will he not kill me; while if I prevail against him, will I not kill him? That is the meaning of "he was afraid" – lest he should be killed, "and distressed" – lest he should kill (Bereshit Rabba 76:2).

> which He then fulfilled. He is saying that he is not worthy that He should have promised him and done all those good things that He had promised him, or the many other good things that He had done for him. (Ramban on 32:11)

According to both of these approaches, the basic idea is the same: Yaakov lives his life with the sense that everything is a gift from God. He is not entitled to anything by his merits; whatever he has is purely by the grace of God.

It seems that we can learn from Yaakov what we too should feel: We should not think that there are things we deserve by right, but rather we should live with a consciousness of gratitude for all the kindnesses that God has performed for us.

Rabbi Mosheh Lichtenstein

TAKING A LITERARY APPROACH

The first obligation learned from our *parasha* is that of humility and gratitude. Despite God's promises to Avraham and Yitzḥak, and to Yaakov himself, when Yaakov finds himself in trouble he does not demand on that basis that God come to his rescue. On the contrary, he thanks God for what he has and begs to be saved:

> I am not worthy of all the mercies, and of all the truth, which You have shown to Your servant; for with my staff I passed over this Jordan; and now I have become two camps. Deliver me, I pray You, from the hand of my brother, from the hand of Esav; for I fear him, lest he come and smite me, the mother with the children. (Bereshit 32:11–12)

Only after this introduction does Yaakov mention the promises: "And You said: I will surely do you good, and make your seed as the sand of the sea, which cannot be numbered for multitude" (32:13).

There are two approaches to interpreting this passage. According to one, Yaakov was afraid of his upcoming meeting with Esav because he feared that his merits had diminished and that his sins would cause him to be delivered into the hands of Esav. Rashi formulates this idea:

> "I am not worthy [*katonti*, literally 'I am small because'] of all the mercies" – My merits are diminished in consequence of all the kindness and truth which You have already shown me. For this reason I am afraid: Perhaps, since You made these promises to me, I have become deprived by sin and this may cause me to be delivered into Esav's hand. (Rashi on 32:11)

On the other hand, some understand that Yaakov's saying *katonti* does not express concern about the diminishing of his merits, but rather Yaakov's opinion that he is not worthy of all the promises and good given him by God:

> Rather, *katonti* comes to say that he is too small to be worthy of all the kindnesses that [God] performed for him. And similarly: "How shall Yaakov stand? For he is small" (Amos 7:2), [too small] to be able to bear all that was decreed against him. And similarly they said in Bereshit Rabba (76:8): "'*Katonti*' – R. Abba said: I am not worthy." The "kindness" refers to the good things that He performed for him without an oath, and "the truth" is the good that He had promised and

22 That night Yaakov got up and took his two wives, two maidservants, and eleven sons and
23 crossed the ford of the Yabok. He took them and crossed the stream with them and then
24 brought across all that he had. And Yaakov was left alone. And a man wrestled with him until
25 dawn. When he saw that he could not overpower him, the man wrenched Yaakov's hip in
its socket so that the socket of Yaakov's hip was strained as he wrestled with the man. "Let
26 me go," said the man, "for dawn is breaking." But he replied, "I will not let you go unless you
27 28 bless me." "What is your name?" asked the man. "Yaakov," he replied. "No longer will your
name be Yaakov, but Yisrael," said the man, "for you have struggled with God and with men
29 and have prevailed."[1] Yaakov asked, "Please tell me your name." But he said, "Why do you
30 ask my name?" and he blessed him there.[2] Yaakov named the place Peniel, "for I have seen
31 God face-to-face and yet my life has been spared."[3] The sun was rising on him as he moved
32 on from Penuel, limping on his thigh. That is why, to this day, the Israelites do not eat the
sciatic nerve by the hip socket: because he wrenched Yaakov's hip socket at the sciatic nerve.

1 | The first part of the name Yisrael resonates with *sarita* ("you have struggled"). The ending "el" is a divine name.

2 | This response implies that the "man" is an angel; cf. Shofetim 13:18.

3 | The first part of the name Peniel resonates with *panim* ("face"). The ending "el" is a reference to God.

UNLOCKING THE TEXT

- Why did Yaakov cross the river with his family at night?
- Why was Yaakov "left alone"?
- Who is the man? Why did they wrestle?
- What is the significance of there being no winner in this contest?
- What is the significance of the injury to Yaakov's hip?
- Why did Yaakov demand a blessing from the man?
- Why did the man give Yaakov a new name? Is this the same as a blessing?
- What does it mean that Yaakov has "struggled with God and with men and prevailed"?
- Why did Yaakov want to know the man's name? Why did he refuse to tell him?
- When Yaakov named the place Peniel, was he saying that the man was a manifestation (or a messenger) of God?

FINDING YOURSELF IN THE TEXT

- Have you ever battled (an angel/God/yourself) in the middle of the night?
- Can you articulate the feeling of night versus the feeling of a new dawn?
- If you could change your name, what would you change it to?

Consider using these questions as the basis for your own commentary or creative midrash.

How does reflecting on these firsthand experiences help you better understand the text?

כב וַיָּקָם ׀ בַּלַּיְלָה הוּא וַיִּקַּח אֶת־שְׁתֵּי נָשָׁיו וְאֶת־שְׁתֵּי שִׁפְחֹתָיו וְאֶת־אַחַד עָשָׂר יְלָדָיו
כג כד וַיַּעֲבֹר אֵת מַעֲבַר יַבֹּק׃ וַיִּקָּחֵם וַיַּעֲבִרֵם אֶת־הַנָּחַל וַיַּעֲבֵר אֶת־אֲשֶׁר־לוֹ׃ וַיִּוָּתֵר
כה יַעֲקֹב לְבַדּוֹ וַיֵּאָבֵק אִישׁ עִמּוֹ עַד עֲלוֹת הַשָּׁחַר׃ וַיַּרְא כִּי לֹא יָכֹל לוֹ וַיִּגַּע בְּכַף־
כו יְרֵכוֹ וַתֵּקַע כַּף־יֶרֶךְ יַעֲקֹב בְּהֵאָבְקוֹ עִמּוֹ׃ וַיֹּאמֶר שַׁלְּחֵנִי כִּי עָלָה הַשָּׁחַר וַיֹּאמֶר
כז כח לֹא אֲשַׁלֵּחֲךָ כִּי אִם־בֵּרַכְתָּנִי׃ וַיֹּאמֶר אֵלָיו מַה־שְּׁמֶךָ וַיֹּאמֶר יַעֲקֹב׃ וַיֹּאמֶר לֹא
יַעֲקֹב יֵאָמֵר עוֹד שִׁמְךָ כִּי אִם־יִשְׂרָאֵל כִּי־שָׂרִיתָ עִם־אֱלֹהִים וְעִם־אֲנָשִׁים וַתּוּכָל׃
כט וַיִּשְׁאַל יַעֲקֹב וַיֹּאמֶר הַגִּידָה־נָּא שְׁמֶךָ וַיֹּאמֶר לָמָּה זֶּה תִּשְׁאַל לִשְׁמִי וַיְבָרֶךְ אֹתוֹ
ל שָׁם׃ וַיִּקְרָא יַעֲקֹב שֵׁם הַמָּקוֹם פְּנִיאֵל כִּי־רָאִיתִי אֱלֹהִים פָּנִים אֶל־פָּנִים וַתִּנָּצֵל שלישי
לא לב נַפְשִׁי׃ וַיִּזְרַח־לוֹ הַשֶּׁמֶשׁ כַּאֲשֶׁר עָבַר אֶת־פְּנוּאֵל וְהוּא צֹלֵעַ עַל־יְרֵכוֹ׃ עַל־כֵּן
לֹא־יֹאכְלוּ בְנֵי־יִשְׂרָאֵל אֶת־גִּיד הַנָּשֶׁה אֲשֶׁר עַל־כַּף הַיָּרֵךְ עַד הַיּוֹם הַזֶּה כִּי נָגַע
בְּכַף־יֶרֶךְ יַעֲקֹב בְּגִיד הַנָּשֶׁה׃

THEMES | GOD | PEOPLEHOOD | SPIRITUALITY

Episode 47: *Yaakov Fights the Stranger Until Dawn* – Bereshit 32:22–32

SUMMARY

Between his preparations for the meeting with his brother and the encounter itself, Yaakov is confronted alone by a mysterious figure who fights him. This struggle, which unfolds in the darkness of the night, is clearly meant to prepare Yaakov for his meeting with Esav. The Sages consider it symbolic of the perpetual spiritual clash between Yaakov and Esav; they refer to the figure as Esav's angel.

Just as Yaakov met angels in his dream when he left Canaan, he now encounters metaphysical forces at night upon his return to the land. In fact, Yaakov had already met angels at an earlier station on his approach to Canaan, in Maḥanayim (32:2). When he sees this lone man at night, Yaakov realizes that he possesses metaphysical powers. However, as opposed to the angels in Maḥanayim, this angelic being fights and injures Yaakov. Ultimately, Yaakov subdues his adversary and compels him to grant him a blessing. As in Maḥanayim, Yaakov names the location after the encounter.

THE ART OF MIDRASH

Jacob Wrestling with the Angel
Rembrandt Harmensz van Rijn (1660)

Analysis

- Which elements of this image are directly mentioned in the text?
- Which elements of this image are not found in the text?
- What midrashic interpretation could be inferred from this image?

A QUESTION OF BIBLIODRAMA

TO YAAKOV

- Why did you get up in the middle of the night?
- Why were you on your own when the man came? What were you doing?
- Who do you think the man was?
- Why did you wrestle him? Why couldn't you overcome him?
- Why did you refuse to let him go until he blessed you?
- Do you consider a new name the same as a blessing?
- What do you think of your new name?
- Why did you name the place where this happened? Why this name?

TO THE MAN

- Who are you?
- What do you want with Yaakov?
- Why could you not defeat Yaakov?
- Why did you refuse to tell Yaakov your name?
- Why did you give Yaakov a new name? Why this name?

ZARQA RIVER

Zarqa River

One of the most important streams on the eastern side of the Jordan, the Yabok – mentioned seven times – divides the Gilad into two parts. The only way to cross from the northern part of the Jordan to the south was through the Yabok; this led to the establishment of major cities such as Penuel, Maḥanayim, and Sukkot in the area.

The Yabok is identified with the Zarqa River, which flows northeast from Amman, curves west next to the city of Jerash, crosses through the Gilad mountains, flows down southwest in the Sukkot Valley – the Yabok crossing is there – and finally empties into the Jordan near Adam. The river marks the border between the Amorites on the west, the Amonites on the east, and the Bashan on the north.

Analysis

- What areas of archaeological, geographical, and historical knowledge do we have now that were unavailable to classical Jewish commentators? How can they aid our understanding of the text?
- How can this information about the Zarqa River help us understand the text?
- What further questions on the text do you have now that you have read this new information and research?

INTEGRATING ḤOKHMA

upcoming confrontation (31:8–9). In pointed contrast to the previous splitting of his camp, he gathers together all of his people and possessions. He is breaking camp and initiating a journey. The sense of reversal of Yaakov's previous preparations is further emphasized by the image of "getting up that night" (32:23), the precise opposite of the "sleeping there that night" (32:22) that closes out Yaakov's preparations. Yaakov seems to have undergone a last-minute change of plans.

To put all of this together, something has changed during the night. Whether out of fear, despair, habit, shame, or a sense of not deserving divine protection, Yaakov has decided to slip away into the dark.

From this reading of the context of the struggle, Rashbam reaches the obvious conclusion – and so should we – that God sends the angel to prevent Yaakov from fleeing. The angel grasps Yaakov at the last minute, after all have crossed over, and Yaakov alone remains. They wrestle and thrash about in the dirt (Rashi and Ibn Ezra on 32:25), thus physically preventing Yaakov from running away. When the angel realizes that he cannot prevail and Yaakov seems on the verge of breaking away, he "touches" Yaakov on his thigh, apparently dislocating his leg and thereby preventing Yaakov from slipping away.

If so, we may conclude that the story of the struggle really constitutes a story of frustrated flight. At the last minute, Yaakov wavers. God sends the angel, seizes Yaakov, and forces him to meet Esav. Yaakov can no longer flee.

Rabbi Chanoch Waxman

TAKING A LITERARY APPROACH

In grappling with this story, I have become convinced that a key to interpreting it can be found in Rashbam's comments. Rashbam notes a parallel between the textual context of Yaakov's wrestling match and the story of David's river crossing (II Shmuel 17:21–24). Immediately preceding the story of the struggle, the Torah informs us that Yaakov got up in the middle of the night, took his wives, children, and possessions, and crossed the Yabok. This closely parallels the later story of David. Just as Yaakov "got up," so too David "got up" (17:22). Just as the Hebrew root for crossing (*a-v-r*) appears three times in the Yaakov story to describe a middle-of-the-night event, so too the root appears three times in the David story, and likewise describes a middle-of-the-night water traversal (17:21–22). Finally, as Rashbam notes, the two crossings happen in geographic proximity one to the other. Immediately after the river crossing, David arrives at Maḥanayim (17:24). This, of course, is the place Yaakov has last been located (Bereshit 32:3), the approximate geographic locale of his crossing.

Rashbam concludes that just as David crosses to flee Avshalom, so too Yaakov crosses to flee. The two are both stories of avoidance and flight. Yaakov's nocturnal crossing constitutes an attempt to run away, to avoid meeting his brother the next morning.

A careful reading of the larger context of the struggle story provides further support for Rashbam's revolutionary claim. The beginning of Parashat Vayishlaḥ describes Yaakov's preparations for meeting Esav. After receiving word from his emissaries that Esav, accompanied by four hundred men, already marches to greet him, Yaakov is gripped by fear and anxiety (32:7–8). He divides his camp into two and prays for divine help (32:9–13). Nevertheless, despite his fear, he apparently remains steadfast in his intention to meet with Esav. At this point, Yaakov has but one more preparation to make. As night begins, either just before or just after going to sleep (32:14), Yaakov engages in a final activity. He gathers together an offering for his brother and sends it off in the hands of his servants (32:14–22). His threefold preparation complete, Yaakov goes to sleep, as ready as he can be (32:22).

Surprisingly, immediately after being informed of Yaakov's lying down for the night, and right before the story of the struggle, we find Yaakov up and about, crossing the Yabok (32:23–24). Is this some new preparation for meeting Esav? I think not. Yaakov has already arranged his camp in preparation for the

33 1 Yaakov looked up – and saw Esav coming with his four hundred men. So he divided the chil-
2 dren among Leah, Raḥel, and the two maidservants. He put the maidservants and their chil-
3 dren first, Leah and her children behind, and Raḥel and Yosef at the rear. And he went ahead
4 of them, bowing down to the ground seven times until he came close to his brother. Esav
ran to meet him and embraced him. He threw his arms around his neck and kissed him, and
5 they wept. Esav looked up and saw the women and children. He asked, "Who are these with
6 you?" Yaakov answered, "They are the children God has graciously given your servant." Then
7 the maidservants and their children came forward and bowed down. Leah and her children
came forward and bowed down. And last, Yosef and Raḥel approached and bowed down.
8 Esav asked, "What did you mean by all the procession that I met before?" He said, "To find fa-
9 vor in your eyes, my lord." But Esav said, "I have plenty, my brother. Let what is yours remain
10 yours." "No, please," said Yaakov. "If I have found favor in your eyes, accept this gift from me,
11 for seeing your face is like seeing the face of God, and you have shown me favor. Please accept
my blessing that was brought to you, for God has been gracious to me, and I have everything."
12 Yaakov pressed him, and he accepted. Then Esav said, "Let us be on our way. I will go beside
13 you." But Yaakov said, "My lord knows that the children are fragile, and I must care for the
14 nursing sheep and cattle. If they are driven hard even for one day, all the flocks will die. Let my
lord go on ahead of his servant, and I will go slowly at the pace of the livestock before

UNLOCKING THE TEXT

- Why did Yaakov choose this order to present his family?
- Why did he bow and ask his family to bow to Esav?
- Why did he bow seven times?
- Why did the brothers weep?
- Why did Yaakov insist that Esav accept the gifts?
- What did Yaakov mean by comparing Esav's face to the face of God?
- What does Yaakov refer to when he tells Yaakov to accept his "blessing"?
- Why did Yaakov refuse to accept Esav's offer to accompany him?

FINDING YOURSELF IN THE TEXT

- When was the last time you argued and then made up with your sibling? How did it feel?
- Have you ever been fearful of a confrontation with someone only to find out that there was nothing to worry about after all?
- Do you think you will want to live near your siblings, or will you need space from them?

Consider using these questions as the basis for your own commentary or creative midrash.

How does reflecting on these firsthand experiences help you better understand the text?

לג א וַיִּשָּׂא יַעֲקֹב עֵינָיו וַיַּרְא וְהִנֵּה עֵשָׂו בָּא וְעִמּוֹ אַרְבַּע מֵאוֹת אִישׁ וַיַּחַץ אֶת־
ב הַיְלָדִים עַל־לֵאָה וְעַל־רָחֵל וְעַל שְׁתֵּי הַשְּׁפָחוֹת׃ וַיָּשֶׂם אֶת הַשְּׁפָחוֹת וְאֶת־
יַלְדֵיהֶן רִאשֹׁנָה וְאֶת־לֵאָה וִילָדֶיהָ אַחֲרֹנִים וְאֶת־רָחֵל וְאֶת־יוֹסֵף אַחֲרֹנִים׃
ג ד וְהוּא עָבַר לִפְנֵיהֶם וַיִּשְׁתַּחוּ אַרְצָה שֶׁבַע פְּעָמִים עַד־גִּשְׁתּוֹ עַד־אָחִיו׃ וַיָּרָץ
ה עֵשָׂו לִקְרָאתוֹ וַיְחַבְּקֵהוּ וַיִּפֹּל עַל־צַוָּארָו וַיִּשָּׁקֵהוּ וַיִּבְכּוּ׃ וַיִּשָּׂא אֶת־עֵינָיו
וַיַּרְא אֶת־הַנָּשִׁים וְאֶת־הַיְלָדִים וַיֹּאמֶר מִי־אֵלֶּה לָּךְ וַיֹּאמַר הַיְלָדִים אֲשֶׁר־חָנַן
רביעי ו ז אֱלֹהִים אֶת־עַבְדֶּךָ׃ וַתִּגַּשְׁןָ הַשְּׁפָחוֹת הֵנָּה וְיַלְדֵיהֶן וַתִּשְׁתַּחֲוֶיןָ׃ וַתִּגַּשׁ גַּם־
ח לֵאָה וִילָדֶיהָ וַיִּשְׁתַּחֲווּ וְאַחַר נִגַּשׁ יוֹסֵף וְרָחֵל וַיִּשְׁתַּחֲווּ׃ וַיֹּאמֶר מִי לְךָ כָּל־
ט הַמַּחֲנֶה הַזֶּה אֲשֶׁר פָּגָשְׁתִּי וַיֹּאמֶר לִמְצֹא־חֵן בְּעֵינֵי אֲדֹנִי׃ וַיֹּאמֶר עֵשָׂו יֶשׁ־לִי
י רָב אָחִי יְהִי לְךָ אֲשֶׁר־לָךְ׃ וַיֹּאמֶר יַעֲקֹב אַל־נָא אִם־נָא מָצָאתִי חֵן בְּעֵינֶיךָ
יא וְלָקַחְתָּ מִנְחָתִי מִיָּדִי כִּי עַל־כֵּן רָאִיתִי פָנֶיךָ כִּרְאֹת פְּנֵי אֱלֹהִים וַתִּרְצֵנִי׃ קַח־נָא
אֶת־בִּרְכָתִי אֲשֶׁר הֻבָאת לָךְ כִּי־חַנַּנִי אֱלֹהִים וְכִי יֶשׁ־לִי־כֹל וַיִּפְצַר־בּוֹ וַיִּקָּח׃
יב יג וַיֹּאמֶר נִסְעָה וְנֵלֵכָה וְאֵלְכָה לְנֶגְדֶּךָ׃ וַיֹּאמֶר אֵלָיו אֲדֹנִי יֹדֵעַ כִּי־הַיְלָדִים רַכִּים
יד וְהַצֹּאן וְהַבָּקָר עָלוֹת עָלָי וּדְפָקוּם יוֹם אֶחָד וָמֵתוּ כָּל־הַצֹּאן׃ יַעֲבָר־נָא אֲדֹנִי

THEMES	RELATIONSHIPS AND LOVE	PEOPLEHOOD	COVENANT

Episode 48: *The Encounter Between Yaakov and Esav* – Bereshit 33:1–20

SUMMARY

After all of Yaakov's preparations, on the diplomatic, military, and spiritual planes, by day and by night, the encounter he had feared for so many years finally arrives.

15 me and the pace of the children until I come to my lord in Se'ir." Esav said, "Let me leave
some of my people with you." "Why do that?" he said, "Just let me find favor in the eyes of
16 17 my lord." So that day Esav started back on his way to Se'ir, and Yaakov journeyed on to Sukkot. There he built himself a house and made huts for his livestock; that is why he named the
18 place Sukkot.[1] Thus Yaakov, having come from Padan Aram, arrived safely at the
19 town of Shekhem in Canaan, and he set up camp within sight of the town. He bought the
plot of ground where he pitched his tent from the sons of Ḥamor, father of Shekhem, for one
20 hundred *kesita*[2] of silver. There he erected an altar and named it El Elohei Yisrael.[3]

---

1 | Meaning "huts."

2 | Apparently a unit of silver.

3 | Meaning "God, the God of Yisrael."

TO YAAKOV

- How do you feel when you see Esav approaching with his four hundred men?
- Were you surprised when Esav ran to hug you?
- How did you feel toward Esav at this time?
- Why do you insist that Esav accepts the gifts?
- Why do you refuse Esav's offer to accompany you?

TO ESAV

- How do you feel when you see Yaakov with his family?
- Was your intention always to show love to Yaakov during this reunion?
- Why do you refuse to accept the gifts from Yaakov?
- Why do you eventually accept them?
- How do you feel when Yaakov refuses your offer to accompany him?
- As you depart from your brother, how do you feel toward him now? Have you forgiven him for stealing the blessing from your father?

לִפְנֵי עַבְדּוֹ וַאֲנִי אֶתְנָהֲלָה לְאִטִּי לְרֶגֶל הַמְּלָאכָה אֲשֶׁר־לְפָנַי וּלְרֶגֶל הַיְלָדִים עַד
טו אֲשֶׁר־אָבֹא אֶל־אֲדֹנִי שֵׂעִירָה׃ וַיֹּאמֶר עֵשָׂו אַצִּיגָה־נָּא עִמְּךָ מִן־הָעָם אֲשֶׁר אִתִּי
טז וַיֹּאמֶר לָמָּה זֶּה אֶמְצָא־חֵן בְּעֵינֵי אֲדֹנִי׃ וַיָּשָׁב בַּיּוֹם הַהוּא עֵשָׂו לְדַרְכּוֹ שֵׂעִירָה׃
יז וְיַעֲקֹב נָסַע סֻכֹּתָה וַיִּבֶן לוֹ בָּיִת וּלְמִקְנֵהוּ עָשָׂה סֻכֹּת עַל־כֵּן קָרָא שֵׁם־הַמָּקוֹם
יח סֻכּוֹת׃ וַיָּבֹא יַעֲקֹב שָׁלֵם עִיר שְׁכֶם אֲשֶׁר בְּאֶרֶץ כְּנַעַן בְּבֹאוֹ מִפַּדַּן לא
יט אֲרָם וַיִּחַן אֶת־פְּנֵי הָעִיר׃ וַיִּקֶן אֶת־חֶלְקַת הַשָּׂדֶה אֲשֶׁר נָטָה־שָׁם אָהֳלוֹ מִיַּד בְּנֵי־
כ חֲמוֹר אֲבִי שְׁכֶם בְּמֵאָה קְשִׂיטָה׃ וַיַּצֶּב־שָׁם מִזְבֵּחַ וַיִּקְרָא־לוֹ אֵל אֱלֹהֵי יִשְׂרָאֵל׃

A QUESTION OF BIBLIODRAMA

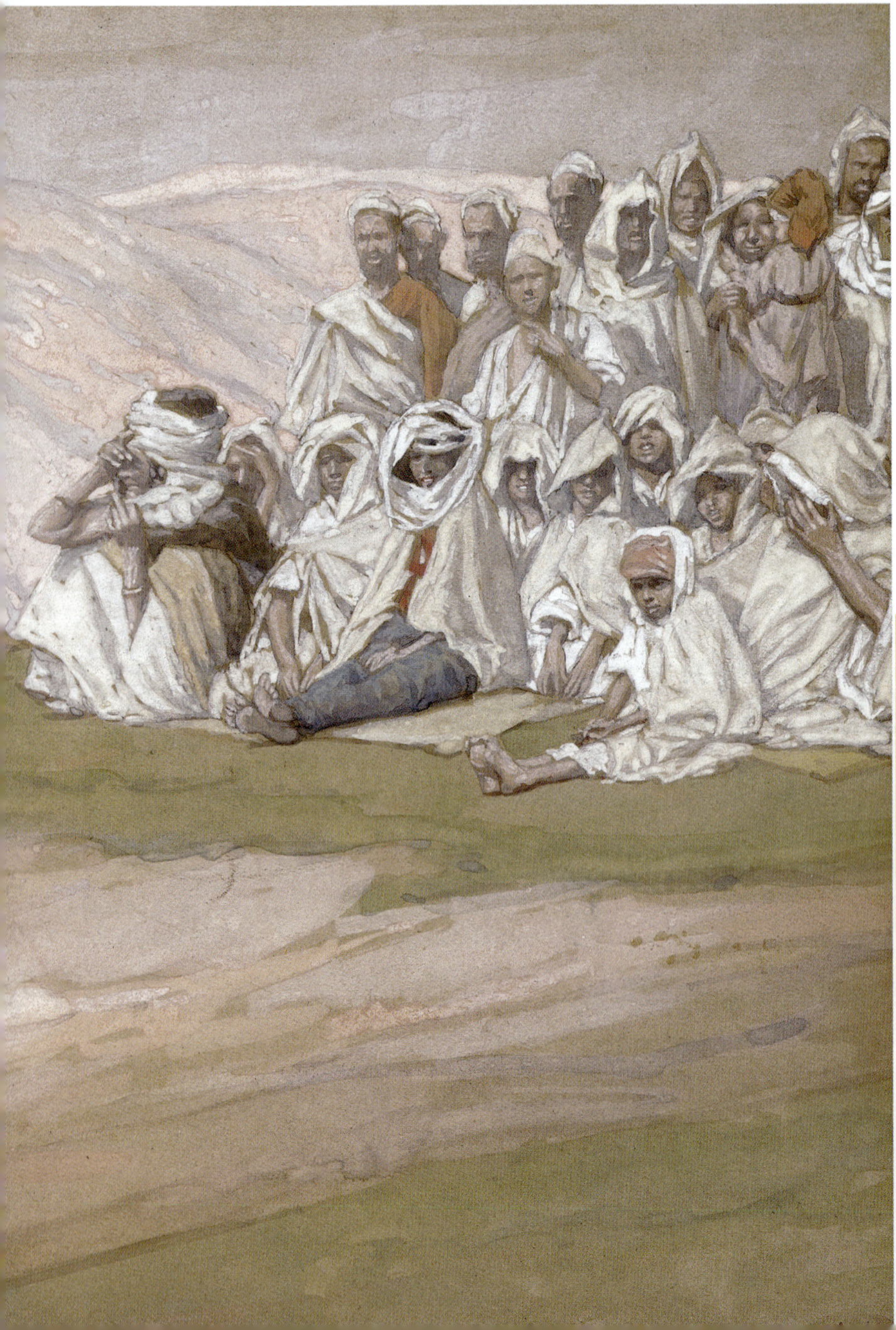

Analysis

- Which elements of this image are directly mentioned in the text?
- Which elements of this image are not found in the text?
- What midrashic interpretation could be inferred from this image?

THE ART OF MIDRASH

The meeting of Esau and Jacob
James Tissot (1896–1902)

Rashi suggests that he was "frightened" of being killed by Esav and "distressed" that he may have to kill Esav. Even though killing Esav in self-defense would be morally justified, it does not mitigate the anxiety beforehand nor necessarily the trauma afterward (had it played out that way). Others suggest that he was "frightened" for his own life, but "distressed" about the welfare of his family or the loss of his property (Shmuel ben Ḥofni Gaon). Alternatively, he may have been anxious as he was uncertain of Esav's intentions. Yes, he was "frightened" that Esav was coming to kill him, but if he knew that for sure, at least he could prepare militarily. However, it was also possible that Esav was coming in peace. Consequently, he was reticent to show military strength, which could accidentally provoke Esav (Bekhor Shor).

An additional layer that complicates Yaakov's emotional experience is the fact that God previously promised that He would protect him. If so, then why was Yaakov afraid in the first place? The Talmud answers that Yaakov was afraid that his sins may have caused an annulment of God's promise. Particularly, his lack of being able to honor his parents while he was away for so many years (see *Ḥizkuni*), in stark contrast to Esav's virtue in this realm, may have swayed the merits in Esav's favor (see Bereshit Rabba 76:2). Taking a different approach, other commentators suggest that Yaakov's "distress" was actually a direct result of being "frightened." Since God promised him security, in his mind, he shouldn't have been anxious (*Daat Zekenim*). He was anxious about the fact that he was anxious!

Despite being both "frightened" and "distressed," and despite the plethora of anxiety-provoking stimuli, Yaakov's emotional experience was healthy. As Abarbanel points out, Yaakov clearly believed in God's promise – otherwise he would have hid or avoided going back home. Yaakov trusted in God, and his anxiety was a normal emotional reaction. Knowing things rationally doesn't cause our anxiety to disappear. The essential question is not whether we feel any anxiety, but whether we act according to our goals and values, despite the anxiety.

Yaakov serves as a paradigm for how to deal with anxiety. Despite feeling anxious he took charge of the situation, and functionally prepared for several different possibilities. He planned the diplomatic route of gifts and appeasement, set up his camp for fighting should that have proved necessary, and engaged in heartfelt prayer (Rashi on 32:9). We would do well to learn from his example when we are anxious, effectively preparing for different realistic outcomes, and praying to God for help and guidance through our challenges.

Rabbi Mordechai Schiffman

Analysis

- What areas of understanding of human nature and society do we now have that were unavailable to classical Jewish commentators? How can they aid our understanding of the text?
- What can we learn from this essay to help us understand the text?
- What further questions on the text do you have now that you have read this new take on the story?

INTEGRATING ḤOKHMA

Anxiety is a normal, healthy emotion that we all experience. Anxiety disorders, however, are not. Where do we draw the line between healthy and disordered anxiety? Dr. David Myers defines a psychological disorder as being deviant (different from the norm), distressful (to self and/or others), and dysfunctional. This last point is especially important in distinguishing healthy versus unhealthy anxiety. If the anxiety is based on a real threat and motivates us to prepare effectively for that threat, then it is probably healthy. However, anxiety is probably disordered under the following circumstances: it causes us to avoid, instead of confront, whatever is causing it; the anxiety interferes with trying to solve the problem that initiated it; it negatively impacts other important values or goals, such as our relationships with others.

Yaakov experiences his share of anxiety, perhaps setting the stage for his Jewish descendants throughout the millennia. His last interaction with his brother Esav left Yaakov fleeing for his life. As he is about to engage with Esav again, Yaakov is unsure how Esav will react. Did Esav move on and forgive, or does he still want to kill Yaakov for stealing the blessings? Yaakov sends envoys with an appeasing message, and finds out that Esav is coming to greet him with four hundred men. When Yaakov hears this, we are told that "Yaakov was very frightened [*vayira Yaakov me'od*] and distressed [*vayeitzer lo*]" (Bereshit 32:8). The fact that Yaakov was afraid for his life is self-evident from the context. However, the verse adds that he was also distressed, causing commentators to speculate about a host of secondary triggers that may have contributed to Yaakov's anxiety.

merciful to me (33:11)." If we choose merely to scratch the surface of Yaakov's statement, the term "blessing" here means only the offering being proffered to Esav. But this would be naive. The language of "taking" and "blessing" is the exact language found in the aftermath of the theft in Parashat Toledot. Yitzḥak informs Esav that Yaakov has "come in trickery and taken [*velakaḥ*] your blessing" (27:35). Esav responds that he now finally understands the true meaning of the name Yaakov: "He has supplanted me (*vayaakveni*) twice; he took (*lakaḥ*) my birthright and now he has taken (*lakaḥ*) my blessing!" (27:36). Flash ahead twenty years to the meeting of Parashat Vayishlaḥ, the first conversation between Esav and Yaakov since that fateful day. On the level of subtext, at the very least, Yaakov symbolically offers to give back the blessing he has taken.

Rabbi Chanoch Waxman

אֶת־עַבְדְּךָ: וַתִּגַּ

ה וִילָדֶיהָ וַיִּשְׁתַּחֲווּ וְאַחַר

מַחֲנֶה הַזֶּה אֲשֶׁר פָּגָשְׁתִּי וַיֹּאמֶ

רַב אָחִי יְהִי לְךָ אֲשֶׁר־לָךְ: וַיֹּאמֶ

וְלָקַחְתָּ מִנְחָתִי מִיָּדִי כִּי עַל־כֵּן רָא

אֶת־בִּרְכָתִי אֲשֶׁר הֻבָאת לָךְ כִּי

מַר נִסְעָה וְנֵלֵכָה וְאֵלְכָה לְ

הַבָּקָר עָלוֹת עָלָי

TAKING A LITERARY APPROACH

The bowing of Yaakov's family to Esav occurs after Esav and Yaakov have embraced, kissed, and cried (Bereshit 33:4). Offhand, there seems no reason to doubt the apparent mutual sincerity. At the very least, Yaakov must already realize that Esav has no intention of killing him. If Esav intended to kill him, he already would have done the deed. If it is a false front, a mask worn over the fear, why keep it up?

Moreover, at this point, after the threat has evaporated, a crucial conversation occurs between Yaakov and Esav (33:8–11). Yaakov continues to employ the "servant-master" language and insists that Esav accept his offering. Esav declines and replies, "I have much [*rav*], my brother" (33:9). While Esav only means to tell his brother Yaakov that he has enough possessions, he manages to conjoin the word *rav,* also meaning "older," with the word "brother." This linkage creates an unmistakable echo of *verav yaavod tza'ir,* "and the older shall serve the younger," the phrase appearing in the oracle of Rivka and the genesis of the entire Yaakov-Esav conflict (25:23). While Yaakov, the younger, now proclaims himself Esav's servant, Esav defines himself as *rav* (possessing much/older) versus Yaakov. On the level of subtext, Esav's refusal of Yaakov's offering subversively contains the acknowledgement that it is the younger brother who serves the older, and not the reverse. Once again, we see another reversal of the supposed superiority and lordship of Yaakov over Esav. But once again, if it is all a false front and Esav no longer threatens Yaakov, why are they talking about something that happened before they were born?

Let us go on. Yaakov refuses to accept no for an answer. Twice using the word for "please," he practically begs Esav to accept the offering (33:10). Moreover, he compares the experience of having his face seen and accepted by Esav with that of being seen and accepted by God (33:10). As if this were not enough, Yaakov describes Esav's actions until this point as *vatirtzeni*, a term normally referring to divine acceptance of sacrifices (Vayikra 1:3). Is this a bluff? Rather, Yaakov insists upon concrete acceptance of his offering because it is about far more than augmenting Esav's wealth. For Yaakov, it is about a very real and concrete act of atonement, a way to physically correct his previous treatment of Esav.

If any doubts remain, let us take a look at the very next verse. Yaakov beseeches Esav: "Please take [*kaḥ*] my blessing that has been brought to you, for God has been

34 1 Dina, the daughter whom Leah had borne to Yaakov, went out to see the daugh-
2 ters of the land. When Shekhem son of Ḥamor the Hivite, prince of the land, saw
3 her, he took hold of her, lay with her, and violated her. He became deeply drawn to Dina,
4 Yaakov's daughter, and, in love with the young woman, he spoke to her heart. Shekhem
5 said to his father Ḥamor, "Take this girl as a wife for me." When Yaakov heard that he had
defiled his daughter Dina, his sons were in the field with his livestock, and so he stayed
6 silent until they came home. Shekhem's father Ḥamor came to Yaakov to speak with him.
7 Meanwhile, Yaakov's sons, having heard what had happened, came back from the field.
They were shocked and furious, for Shekhem had committed an outrage in Israel by sleep-
8 ing with Yaakov's daughter. Such a thing cannot be done! But Ḥamor spoke with them
and said, "My son Shekhem has his heart set upon your daughter. Please give her to him
9 as his wife. Intermarry with us. Give us your daughters and take our daughters for your-
10 selves. Settle with us. The land is open to you. Live here, trade here, acquire property here."
11 Then Shekhem said to Dina's father and brothers, "Let me but find favor in your eyes and I

UNLOCKING THE TEXT

- Why did Dina want to go out to see the daughters of the land?
- Did Shekhem try to seduce her first? Was Dina totally passive in the story?
- Why did Shekhem rape her first, rather than try to marry her instead?
- Why was Yaakov initially silent when he heard the news?
- Did Shekhem or Ḥamor show any regret or remorse for this episode?
- Was Ḥamor being genuine in offering a treaty with Yaakov and his sons? What was his incentive?
- Was the slaughter of the people of Shekhem an act of revenge or rescue?
- Were Shimon and Levi morally justified in this act?
- Why was it necessary to also plunder the town?
- Was the basis of Yaakov's rebuke of Shimon and Levi on moral grounds or purely pragmatic?

FINDING YOURSELF IN THE TEXT

- Have you ever been so enraged by an injustice that you couldn't control your anger?
- Was there someone at the time who had a calmer, more controlled voice that you found hard to hear?
- Now looking back, can you understand their perspective more?

Consider using these questions as the basis for your own commentary or creative midrash.

How does reflecting on these firsthand experiences help you better understand the text?

לד א ב וַתֵּצֵא דִינָה בַּת־לֵאָה אֲשֶׁר יָלְדָה לְיַעֲקֹב לִרְאוֹת בִּבְנוֹת הָאָרֶץ׃ וַיַּרְא אֹתָהּ חמישי
ג שְׁכֶם בֶּן־חֲמוֹר הַחִוִּי נְשִׂיא הָאָרֶץ וַיִּקַּח אֹתָהּ וַיִּשְׁכַּב אֹתָהּ וַיְעַנֶּהָ׃ וַתִּדְבַּק
ד נַפְשׁוֹ בְּדִינָה בַּת־יַעֲקֹב וַיֶּאֱהַב אֶת־הַנַּעֲרָ וַיְדַבֵּר עַל־לֵב הַנַּעֲרָ׃ וַיֹּאמֶר שְׁכֶם
ה אֶל־חֲמוֹר אָבִיו לֵאמֹר קַח־לִי אֶת־הַיַּלְדָּה הַזֹּאת לְאִשָּׁה׃ וְיַעֲקֹב שָׁמַע כִּי טִמֵּא
ו אֶת־דִּינָה בִתּוֹ וּבָנָיו הָיוּ אֶת־מִקְנֵהוּ בַּשָּׂדֶה וְהֶחֱרִשׁ יַעֲקֹב עַד־בֹּאָם׃ וַיֵּצֵא חֲמוֹר
ז אֲבִי־שְׁכֶם אֶל־יַעֲקֹב לְדַבֵּר אִתּוֹ׃ וּבְנֵי יַעֲקֹב בָּאוּ מִן־הַשָּׂדֶה כְּשָׁמְעָם וַיִּתְעַצְּבוּ
הָאֲנָשִׁים וַיִּחַר לָהֶם מְאֹד כִּי נְבָלָה עָשָׂה בְיִשְׂרָאֵל לִשְׁכַּב אֶת־בַּת־יַעֲקֹב וְכֵן לֹא
ח יֵעָשֶׂה׃ וַיְדַבֵּר חֲמוֹר אִתָּם לֵאמֹר שְׁכֶם בְּנִי חָשְׁקָה נַפְשׁוֹ בְּבִתְּכֶם תְּנוּ נָא אֹתָהּ
ט י לוֹ לְאִשָּׁה׃ וְהִתְחַתְּנוּ אֹתָנוּ בְּנֹתֵיכֶם תִּתְּנוּ־לָנוּ וְאֶת־בְּנֹתֵינוּ תִּקְחוּ לָכֶם׃ וְאִתָּנוּ
יא תֵּשֵׁבוּ וְהָאָרֶץ תִּהְיֶה לִפְנֵיכֶם שְׁבוּ וּסְחָרוּהָ וְהֵאָחֲזוּ בָּהּ׃ וַיֹּאמֶר שְׁכֶם אֶל־אָבִיהָ

THEMES | ETHICS | RELATIONSHIPS AND LOVE | COVENANT

Episode 49: *The Violation of Dina* – Bereshit 34:1–31

SUMMARY

The travails of Yaakov's family have not ended. After an extended exile, feuds with the extended family, wanderings, struggles, and fear, Yaakov and his family finally return to the land of Canaan. However, they do not merit to dwell there in tranquility, as Yaakov's only daughter, Dina, is raped in Shekhem by the prince of the city. For the first time, two of Yaakov's sons, Shimon and Levi, initiate a bold move. Their zealous response to the rape of their sister provokes criticism from their father. There is a renewed sense of danger threatening the household that has been created with great hardships.

12 will give whatever you ask. Set the bridal price and gifts as high as you like. I will give what-
13 ever you ask of me; only give me the young woman as my wife." Yaakov's sons responded
to Shekhem and his father Ḥamor, and they spoke deceptively: he had, after all, defiled
14 their sister Dina. They told them, "We cannot do this. To give our sister to an uncircum-
15 cised man would be a disgrace to us. Only on one condition will we agree with you: if you
16 become like us, circumcising all your males, then we will give you our daughters and take
17 your daughters for ourselves. We will live with you and become one people. If you do not
18 agree to be circumcised, we will take our daughter and go." Their words gratified Ḥamor
19 and his son Shekhem. The young man, the most honored of his father's family, lost no time
20 in doing it, because he longed for Yaakov's daughter. Ḥamor and his son Shekhem came to
21 the town gate and spoke to their fellow townsmen. "These people are friendly toward us,"
they said. "Let them live in the land and trade in it. We have space enough for them. We
22 can marry their daughters and they can marry ours. But only on one condition will they
agree to dwell with us as one people. Every male among us must be circumcised as they
23 are. Will not their livestock, property, and all their animals be ours? Let us, then, agree to
24 their terms and let them settle among us." All the people who went out by the town gate
listened to Ḥamor and his son Shekhem, and all the males who went out by the town gate
25 were circumcised. On the third day, when the people were weak from pain, two of Yaakov's
sons, Shimon and Levi, Dina's brothers, took their swords, entered the unsuspecting town,
26 and killed every single male. They killed Ḥamor and his son Shekhem by the sword, took
27 Dina from Shekhem's house and left. Yaakov's sons came upon the dead and plundered
28 the town that had defiled their sister. They took their flocks, their cattle, their donkeys, and
29 everything else of theirs in the town and out in the field. Their wealth, their children, and
30 their women they took captive and looted, and all that was in the houses. Yaakov said to
Shimon and Levi, "You have brought trouble upon me – you have made me odious to the
inhabitants of the land, the Canaanites and Perizzites. I am few in number, and if they join
31 forces and attack me, I and my household will be destroyed." But they said, "Should our
sister be treated like a whore?"

יב וְאֶל־אַחֶ֔יהָ אֶמְצָא־חֵ֖ן בְּעֵינֵיכֶ֑ם וַאֲשֶׁ֥ר תֹּאמְר֛וּ אֵלַ֖י אֶתֵּֽן׃ הַרְבּ֨וּ עָלַ֤י מְאֹד֙ מֹ֣הַר
יג וּמַתָּ֔ן וְאֶ֨תְּנָ֔ה כַּאֲשֶׁ֥ר תֹּאמְר֖וּ אֵלָ֑י וּתְנוּ־לִ֥י אֶת־הַֽנַּעֲרָ֖ לְאִשָּֽׁה׃ וַיַּעֲנ֨וּ בְנֵֽי־יַעֲקֹ֜ב
יד אֶת־שְׁכֶ֨ם וְאֶת־חֲמ֥וֹר אָבִ֛יו בְּמִרְמָ֖ה וַיְדַבֵּ֑רוּ אֲשֶׁ֣ר טִמֵּ֔א אֵ֖ת דִּינָ֥ה אֲחֹתָֽם׃ וַיֹּאמְר֣וּ
אֲלֵיהֶ֗ם לֹ֤א נוּכַל֙ לַעֲשׂוֹת֙ הַדָּבָ֣ר הַזֶּ֔ה לָתֵת֙ אֶת־אֲחֹתֵ֔נוּ לְאִ֖ישׁ אֲשֶׁר־ל֣וֹ עָרְלָ֑ה
טו כִּי־חֶרְפָּ֥ה הִ֖וא לָֽנוּ׃ אַךְ־בְּזֹ֖את נֵא֣וֹת לָכֶ֑ם אִ֚ם תִּהְי֣וּ כָמֹ֔נוּ לְהִמֹּ֥ל לָכֶ֖ם כָּל־זָכָֽר׃
טז וְנָתַ֤נּוּ אֶת־בְּנֹתֵ֙ינוּ֙ לָכֶ֔ם וְאֶת־בְּנֹתֵיכֶ֖ם נִֽקַּֽח־לָ֑נוּ וְיָשַׁ֣בְנוּ אִתְּכֶ֔ם וְהָיִ֖ינוּ לְעַ֥ם אֶחָֽד׃
יז יח וְאִם־לֹ֧א תִשְׁמְע֛וּ אֵלֵ֖ינוּ לְהִמּ֑וֹל וְלָקַ֥חְנוּ אֶת־בִּתֵּ֖נוּ וְהָלָֽכְנוּ׃ וַיִּיטְב֥וּ דִבְרֵיהֶ֖ם בְּעֵינֵ֣י
יט חֲמ֑וֹר וּבְעֵינֵ֖י שְׁכֶ֥ם בֶּן־חֲמֽוֹר׃ וְלֹֽא־אֵחַ֤ר הַנַּ֙עַר֙ לַעֲשׂ֣וֹת הַדָּבָ֔ר כִּ֥י חָפֵ֖ץ בְּבַֽת־יַעֲקֹ֑ב
כ וְה֣וּא נִכְבָּ֔ד מִכֹּ֖ל בֵּ֥ית אָבִֽיו׃ וַיָּבֹ֥א חֲמ֛וֹר וּשְׁכֶ֥ם בְּנ֖וֹ אֶל־שַׁ֣עַר עִירָ֑ם וַיְדַבְּר֛וּ אֶל־
כא אַנְשֵׁ֥י עִירָ֖ם לֵאמֹֽר׃ הָאֲנָשִׁ֨ים הָאֵ֜לֶּה שְׁלֵמִ֧ים הֵ֣ם אִתָּ֗נוּ וְיֵשְׁב֤וּ בָאָ֙רֶץ֙ וְיִסְחֲר֣וּ
אֹתָ֔הּ וְהָאָ֛רֶץ הִנֵּ֥ה רַחֲבַת־יָדַ֖יִם לִפְנֵיהֶ֑ם אֶת־בְּנֹתָם֙ נִקַּֽח־לָ֣נוּ לְנָשִׁ֔ים וְאֶת־בְּנֹתֵ֖ינוּ
כב נִתֵּ֥ן לָהֶֽם׃ אַךְ־בְּ֠זֹאת יֵאֹ֨תוּ לָ֤נוּ הָֽאֲנָשִׁים֙ לָשֶׁ֣בֶת אִתָּ֔נוּ לִהְי֖וֹת לְעַ֣ם אֶחָ֑ד בְּהִמּ֥וֹל
כג לָ֙נוּ֙ כָּל־זָכָ֔ר כַּאֲשֶׁ֖ר הֵ֥ם נִמֹּלִֽים׃ מִקְנֵהֶ֤ם וְקִנְיָנָם֙ וְכָל־בְּהֶמְתָּ֔ם הֲל֥וֹא לָ֖נוּ הֵ֑ם אַ֚ךְ
כד נֵא֣וֹתָה לָהֶ֔ם וְיֵשְׁב֖וּ אִתָּֽנוּ׃ וַיִּשְׁמְע֤וּ אֶל־חֲמוֹר֙ וְאֶל־שְׁכֶ֣ם בְּנ֔וֹ כָּל־יֹצְאֵ֖י שַׁ֣עַר עִיר֑וֹ
כה וַיִּמֹּ֙לוּ֙ כָּל־זָכָ֔ר כָּל־יֹצְאֵ֖י שַׁ֥עַר עִירֽוֹ׃ וַיְהִי֩ בַיּ֨וֹם הַשְּׁלִישִׁ֜י בִּֽהְיוֹתָ֣ם כֹּאֲבִ֗ים וַיִּקְח֣וּ
שְׁנֵֽי־בְנֵי־יַ֠עֲקֹב שִׁמְע֨וֹן וְלֵוִ֜י אֲחֵ֤י דִינָה֙ אִ֣ישׁ חַרְבּ֔וֹ וַיָּבֹ֥אוּ עַל־הָעִ֖יר בֶּ֑טַח וַיַּֽהַרְג֖וּ
כו כָּל־זָכָֽר׃ וְאֶת־חֲמוֹר֙ וְאֶת־שְׁכֶ֣ם בְּנ֔וֹ הָרְג֖וּ לְפִי־חָ֑רֶב וַיִּקְח֧וּ אֶת־דִּינָ֛ה מִבֵּ֥ית שְׁכֶ֖ם
כז כח וַיֵּצֵֽאוּ׃ בְּנֵ֣י יַעֲקֹ֗ב בָּ֚אוּ עַל־הַֽחֲלָלִ֔ים וַיָּבֹ֖זּוּ הָעִ֑יר אֲשֶׁ֥ר טִמְּא֖וּ אֲחוֹתָֽם׃ אֶת־צֹאנָ֥ם
כט וְאֶת־בְּקָרָ֖ם וְאֶת־חֲמֹרֵיהֶ֑ם וְאֵ֧ת אֲשֶׁר־בָּעִ֛יר וְאֶת־אֲשֶׁ֥ר בַּשָּׂדֶ֖ה לָקָֽחוּ׃ וְאֶת־כָּל־
ל חֵילָ֤ם וְאֶת־כָּל־טַפָּם֙ וְאֶת־נְשֵׁיהֶ֔ם שָׁב֖וּ וַיָּבֹ֑זּוּ וְאֵ֖ת כָּל־אֲשֶׁ֥ר בַּבָּֽיִת׃ וַיֹּ֨אמֶר יַעֲקֹ֜ב
אֶל־שִׁמְע֣וֹן וְאֶל־לֵוִי֮ עֲכַרְתֶּ֣ם אֹתִי֒ לְהַבְאִישֵׁ֙נִי֙ בְּיֹשֵׁ֣ב הָאָ֔רֶץ בַּֽכְּנַעֲנִ֖י וּבַפְּרִזִּ֑י וַאֲנִי֙
לא מְתֵ֣י מִסְפָּ֔ר וְנֶאֶסְפ֤וּ עָלַי֙ וְהִכּ֔וּנִי וְנִשְׁמַדְתִּ֖י אֲנִ֥י וּבֵיתִֽי׃ וַיֹּאמְר֑וּ הַכְזוֹנָ֕ה יַעֲשֶׂ֖ה
אֶת־אֲחוֹתֵֽנוּ׃

A QUESTION OF BIBLIODRAMA

TO DINA

- What were you looking for when you went out to see the daughters of the land?
- What were your thoughts about Shekhem when you first met him?
- How do you feel about him now?
- How do you feel about your brothers' response to this episode?
- How do you feel about your father's response to this whole episode?

TO SHEKHEM

- When you first set eyes on Dina, what were your thoughts?
- Why did you rape Dina?
- Why did you want to subsequently marry her?

TO YAAKOV

- What did you think when you first heard about the rape of your daughter?
- Why did you remain silent at first?
- Do you understand Shimon and Levi's response?
- Why were you so angered by it?

TO SHIMON AND LEVI

- Why did you respond to the rape of Dina in the way that you did?
- What do you think of your father's rebuke of your behavior?

TO ḤAMOR

- What do you think of your son's actions and behavior during this episode?
- Was your offer of a treaty with Yaakov genuine?

THE ART OF MIDRASH

Dina, Dikla Laor (2018)

Analysis

- Which elements of this image are directly mentioned in the text?
- Which elements of this image are not found in the text?
- What midrashic interpretation could be inferred from this image?

that *kesita* is a form of currency, while Onkelos and Rav Se'adya Gaon explain that *kesita* is an animal. The explanation advanced by Onkelos and Rav Se'adya Gaon fits better with the general framework of the story: Yaakov, who had just repopulated his herds in Sukkot, traded his livestock for a parcel of land on the outskirts of Shekhem. Exchanging his animal herds for real estate symbolizes the transition from wandering and moveable wealth to permanence in the land of Israel. Yaakov's message was that to hold the land firmly, one must buy real estate, while to build an exemplary society, one must build wealth honestly, observing the highest standards of transparency and trust.

Accordingly, purchasing real estate from the sons of Ḥamor was a transaction designed to cultivate good neighborly relations and build trust. In Sukkot, Yaakov was a homesteader; he raised cattle and built a temporary shelter. In the land of Israel, he bought land. His actions thus cultivated upright and trustworthy neighborly relations.

Harvard Business School professor Rosabeth Moss Kanter argues that individuals and leaders are more successful in achieving cooperation when they are present, frame the discussion, espouse values, and generally cultivate an atmosphere of generous reciprocal relations. Building an enchanted circle where the giver will receive more than is put out strengthens trust between strategic players.

Upon entering the land, Yaakov appeared before the people of the city, spoke clearly, and conducted an important business deal with obvious benefits for the townsfolk, thus successfully cultivating a spirit of cooperation and reciprocity. By camping near Shekhem, whose leaders were apparently the princes of a large region of the land of Israel, Yaakov positioned himself as a person who was ready to conduct business honestly and transparently in the most central, influential region of ancient Canaan.

Michael A. Eisenberg

Analysis

- What areas of understanding of human nature and society do we now have that were unavailable to classical Jewish commentators? How can they aid our understanding of the text?
- What can we learn from this essay to help us understand the text?
- What further questions on the text do you have now that you have read this new take on the story?

INTEGRATING ḤOKHMA

Great leaders understand that trust matters. They understand that power and fear have their limits. More deeply, they understand that societies that are founded on fear and rules are fragile. The ties that bind different populations or tribes in a given land or country must be erected on a bedrock of trust. If not, they are easily frayed.

Like Abraham Lincoln, who sought to avoid a civil war and pleaded for friendship between North and South, our forefathers stood for good neighborly relations in the land of Israel. They understood that the successful foundation of a people on its land must be built on the foundation of an exemplary society and achieved through trust, integrity, and cooperation. Avraham's family forged alliances with the Canaanites Aner, Eshkol, and Mamrei; King Malki Tzedek of Shalem; and Abimelech (at least after the latter came to his senses and accepted their reproach). Against this backdrop, Yaakov arrived in the city of Shekhem financially whole or intact (through wholesome means) and purchased a parcel of land within the city limits: "The parcel of land where he pitched his tent he purchased from the children of Ḥamor, Shekhem's father, for one hundred *kesita.* He set up an altar there, and called it God, the God of Israel" (33:18–20).

The commentators suggest two alternate explanations for the word *kesita*. Rashi contends

4. Yonatan's accusation of Sha'ul as issuing a decree that might not reach everyone, such that there is a threat of the land being sullied: "And Yonatan said, 'My father has sullied (*akhar*) the land; see, now, how my eyes have brightened because I tasted a little of this honey'" (I Shmuel 14:29).
5. The argument between Eliyahu and Aḥav as to who answers to the definition of *okher Yisrael*, "one who sullies Israel": "And it was, when Aḥav saw Eliyahu, then Aḥav said to him: 'Is that you, O sullier (*okhar*) of Israel?' And he said, 'It is not I who have sullied (*akharti*) Israel, but rather you and your father's house, by abandoning God's commandments and going after the Baal'" (I Melakhim 18:17–18).

More than the honor of his own family, Yaakov is concerned for the ramifications of the massacre on the project of calling in God's name throughout the land. In not fulfilling the obligations of the covenant, his sons have caused damage to the national cause of the forefathers, and this may have a fateful effect on the continued enterprise of inculcating moral values in the land.

Yaakov is not apathetic as to what is happening to his daughter. On the contrary, his choice not to negotiate with Shekhem and Ḥamor may perhaps arise from his emotional involvement and the concern lest this override his better judgment and harm his family's image. Yaakov behaves as his fathers did when their wives were taken from them – he waits for divine intervention, which indeed comes swiftly: "And they journeyed, and the fear of God was upon the cities that were around them, and they did not pursue after Yaakov's sons" (Bereshit 35:5). However, he is forced to deal with the possible fallout of his sons' strong family emotions, and instead of maintaining his land holdings in Shekhem and continued inculcation of religious and moral values among his neighbors, he is forced to abandon his inheritance and seek a place of refuge until the storm passes.

Dr. Brachi Elitzur

TAKING A LITERARY APPROACH

The story of Dina is recorded at great length and seems to place the question of a positive or negative evaluation of the actions of Yaakov's sons at center stage. However, despite the value of the discussion as to the justice of killing the men of Shekhem, Yaakov's conduct is actually the main message of the story.

First, his conduct raises some questions:

1. What is the meaning of Yaakov's forgiving attitude toward Shekhem and Ḥamor, while his daughter is still captive in her rapist's house?
2. Why does Yaakov display no involvement in the drawing up of the conditions of the covenant with Shekhem and Ḥamor?
3. What is the meaning of Yaakov's rebuke of his sons following their attack on the city?

A close examination of Yaakov's angry rebuke addressed to his sons may teach us something about the circumstances of his actions:

> And Yaakov said to Shimon and to Levi, "You have sullied (*akhartem*) me, making me odious to the inhabitants of the land, the Canaani and the Perizi. For I am but few in number, and they will gather against me and strike me, and I shall be destroyed, me and my household." (Bereshit 34:30)

In Tanakh the root *"a-kh-r"* is used to denote a situation of real or potential desecration of God's name caused by a public violation of a religious or moral law. Examples include:

1. Yehoshua's command concerning the spoils of the city of Yeriḥo: "As for you – keep away from the devoted things, lest you make yourselves accursed in taking from the devoted things and making the camp of Israel a curse, and sullying (*vaakhartem*) it" (Yehoshua 6:18).
2. Akhan's appropriation of some of the spoils: "And Yehoshua said: 'Why have you sullied us (*akhartanu*)? God will sully you (*yakerkha*) this day.' And all of Israel stoned him with stones, and they burned them with fire after they had stoned them with stones" (Yehoshua 7:25).
3. Yiftaḥ's mourning and his concern as to the potential outcome if he fails to fulfill his vow to sacrifice his daughter: "And it was, when he saw her, that he tore his garments and said, 'Alas, my daughter, you have brought me low, and you have sullied me (*at hayit be'okhrai*), for I opened my mouth to God and I cannot go back'" (Shofetim 11:35).

35 1 God said to Yaakov, "Arise, go up to Beit El. Stay there and there build an altar to God, who
2 appeared to you as you fled your brother Esav." Yaakov told his household and everyone
with him, "Be rid of the alien gods you have with you. Purify yourselves and change your
3 clothes. Then come, let us go up to Beit El, and there I will make an altar to God, who
4 answered me in my time of trouble and who has been with me wherever I have gone."
They gave Yaakov all the alien gods they had, and even the rings in their ears,[1] and Yaakov
5 buried them under a terebinth near Shekhem. As they set out, the terror of God fell on the
6 surrounding towns so that no one pursued Yaakov's sons. Yaakov and all the people with
7 him came to Luz – that is, Beit El – in the land of Canaan. There he built an altar and called
the place El Beit El,[2] because it was there that God had revealed Himself to him as he fled
8 his brother. Devora, Rivka's nurse, died and was buried under the oak outside Beit El. And
so it was named Oak of Weeping.
9 After Yaakov had returned from Padan Aram God appeared to him again and blessed him. God
10 said to him, "Your name is Yaakov; no longer shall you be called Yaakov: Yisrael shall be your

1 | Earrings may have been associated with idol worship (cf. Shemot 32:2–4).
2 | Literally, "God, the House of God."

UNLOCKING THE TEXT

- What is significant about Beit El such that God told Yaakov to go there?
- Why does God describe Himself in this way?
- Who would have idols and why?
- What process of purification is Yaakov referring to and why is it necessary now?
- Why did Yaakov rename Beit El to El Beit El?
- Who is Devora and why is she only mentioned now, at her death?
- Why does God need to reaffirm Yaakov's change of name to Yisrael?
- Why does God use a new name, El Shaddai, to refer to Himself?
- Why does God give Yaakov this blessing now?

FINDING YOURSELF IN THE TEXT

- Have you ever lost something that reminds you of your childhood?
- Have you ever had to say goodbye to someone from your childhood?
- How did these experiences make you feel?

Consider using these questions as the basis for your own commentary or creative midrash.

How does reflecting on these firsthand experiences help you better understand the text?

לה א וַיֹּאמֶר אֱלֹהִים אֶל־יַעֲקֹב קוּם עֲלֵה בֵית־אֵל וְשֶׁב־שָׁם וַעֲשֵׂה־שָׁם מִזְבֵּחַ לָאֵל
ב הַנִּרְאֶה אֵלֶיךָ בְּבָרְחֲךָ מִפְּנֵי עֵשָׂו אָחִיךָ׃ וַיֹּאמֶר יַעֲקֹב אֶל־בֵּיתוֹ וְאֶל כָּל־אֲשֶׁר
ג עִמּוֹ הָסִרוּ אֶת־אֱלֹהֵי הַנֵּכָר אֲשֶׁר בְּתֹכְכֶם וְהִטַּהֲרוּ וְהַחֲלִיפוּ שִׂמְלֹתֵיכֶם׃ וְנָקוּמָה
וְנַעֲלֶה בֵּית־אֵל וְאֶעֱשֶׂה־שָּׁם מִזְבֵּחַ לָאֵל הָעֹנֶה אֹתִי בְּיוֹם צָרָתִי וַיְהִי עִמָּדִי בַּדֶּרֶךְ
ד אֲשֶׁר הָלָכְתִּי׃ וַיִּתְּנוּ אֶל־יַעֲקֹב אֵת כָּל־אֱלֹהֵי הַנֵּכָר אֲשֶׁר בְּיָדָם וְאֶת־הַנְּזָמִים
ה אֲשֶׁר בְּאָזְנֵיהֶם וַיִּטְמֹן אֹתָם יַעֲקֹב תַּחַת הָאֵלָה אֲשֶׁר עִם־שְׁכֶם׃ וַיִּסָּעוּ וַיְהִי ׀
ו חִתַּת אֱלֹהִים עַל־הֶעָרִים אֲשֶׁר סְבִיבוֹתֵיהֶם וְלֹא רָדְפוּ אַחֲרֵי בְּנֵי יַעֲקֹב׃ וַיָּבֹא
ז יַעֲקֹב לוּזָה אֲשֶׁר בְּאֶרֶץ כְּנַעַן הִוא בֵּית־אֵל הוּא וְכָל־הָעָם אֲשֶׁר־עִמּוֹ׃ וַיִּבֶן שָׁם
מִזְבֵּחַ וַיִּקְרָא לַמָּקוֹם אֵל בֵּית־אֵל כִּי שָׁם נִגְלוּ אֵלָיו הָאֱלֹהִים בְּבָרְחוֹ מִפְּנֵי אָחִיו׃
ח וַתָּמָת דְּבֹרָה מֵינֶקֶת רִבְקָה וַתִּקָּבֵר מִתַּחַת לְבֵית־אֵל תַּחַת הָאַלּוֹן וַיִּקְרָא שְׁמוֹ
אַלּוֹן בָּכוּת׃
ט וַיֵּרָא אֱלֹהִים אֶל־יַעֲקֹב עוֹד בְּבֹאוֹ מִפַּדַּן אֲרָם וַיְבָרֶךְ אֹתוֹ׃ וַיֹּאמֶר־לוֹ אֱלֹהִים לב
י שִׁמְךָ יַעֲקֹב לֹא־יִקָּרֵא שִׁמְךָ עוֹד יַעֲקֹב כִּי אִם־יִשְׂרָאֵל יִהְיֶה שְׁמֶךָ וַיִּקְרָא אֶת־

THEMES	COVENANT	THE LAND OF ISRAEL	GOD

Episode 50: *Yaakov in Beit El* – Bereshit 35:1–15

SUMMARY

Beit El was a significant stop in Yaakov's journey to Ḥaran, as he experienced the dream of the ladder there when God promised to protect him on his journey. He subsequently vowed that the stone he established there as a monument would become a house of God (28:22). Now that Yaakov has returned to Canaan, he fulfills his vow. God appears to him again in Beit El, changes his name to Yisrael, and bestows upon him the blessing of offspring and the inheritance of the land.

11 name." Thus He named him Yisrael. God said to him: "I am El Shaddai. Be fertile and multiply.
A nation, a community of nations will come to be from you. Of your loins, kings shall come
12 forth. The land I gave to Avraham and Yitzḥak I surely give to you; to your descendants after
13 you I will give the land." God went up from him at the place where He had spoken with him.
14 Yaakov set up a stone pillar at the place where God had talked with him, and on it he offered a
15 libation and poured oil. And Yaakov named the place where God had spoken to him Beit El.[3]

3 | Meaning "House of God."

THE ART OF MIDRASH

Deborah, the Nurse of Rebecca
Dikla Laor (2013)

Analysis

- Which elements of this image are directly mentioned in the text?
- Which elements of this image are not found in the text?
- What midrashic interpretation could be inferred from this image?

יא שְׁמוֹ יִשְׂרָאֵל: וַיֹּאמֶר לוֹ אֱלֹהִים אֲנִי אֵל שַׁדַּי פְּרֵה וּרְבֵה גּוֹי וּקְהַל גּוֹיִם יִהְיֶה מִמֶּךָּ
יב וּמְלָכִים מֵחֲלָצֶיךָ יֵצֵאוּ: וְאֶת־הָאָרֶץ אֲשֶׁר נָתַתִּי לְאַבְרָהָם וּלְיִצְחָק לְךָ אֶתְּנֶנָּה ששי
יג וּלְזַרְעֲךָ אַחֲרֶיךָ אֶתֵּן אֶת־הָאָרֶץ: וַיַּעַל מֵעָלָיו אֱלֹהִים בַּמָּקוֹם אֲשֶׁר־דִּבֶּר אִתּוֹ:
יד וַיַּצֵּב יַעֲקֹב מַצֵּבָה בַּמָּקוֹם אֲשֶׁר־דִּבֶּר אִתּוֹ מַצֶּבֶת אָבֶן וַיַּסֵּךְ עָלֶיהָ נֶסֶךְ וַיִּצֹק
טו עָלֶיהָ שָׁמֶן: וַיִּקְרָא יַעֲקֹב אֶת־שֵׁם הַמָּקוֹם אֲשֶׁר דִּבֶּר אִתּוֹ שָׁם אֱלֹהִים בֵּית־אֵל:

A QUESTION OF BIBLIODRAMA

TO YAAKOV

- Why had you not returned to Beit El until now?
- Do you now feel ready to return?
- How do you feel about the death of your mother's nurse, Devora?
- Did you need to hear the covenantal blessings again now?

Analysis

- What areas of archaeological, geographical, and historical knowledge do we have now that were unavailable to classical Jewish commentators? How can they aid our understanding of the text?
- How can this information about Beit El help us understand the text?
- What further questions on the text do you have now that you have read this new information and research?

INTEGRATING ḤOKHMA

בֵּית אֵל - BEIT EL / לוּז - LUZ

Beit El, a city in Binyamin mentioned seventy times, was a cultic center throughout the biblical period. Beit El is located near the main highway across the top of the central mountain range, northward toward Shekhem.[1] In the description of the tribal inheritances, Beit El is mentioned both as part of Yosef's southern border[2] and as part of Binyamin's northern border.[3]

Based on biblical and later traditions, Edward Robinson suggests identifying Beit El with the tel located in the village of Beitin, east of Ramallah, which preserves the ancient name, or with the adjacent site Burj Beitin, which is generally accepted in research.

The site was excavated several times during the twentieth century, but only partially, as the homes of the village cover much of the tel. These excavations revealed that the site was a fortified city in the Middle Bronze Age, and was inhabited throughout the Late Bronze Age and the entire Iron Age. However, no definitive indications of a cultic site during the Israelite period have been discovered to date. Some surmise that a different place named Beit El was located on the site of the village Baytillu, north of Ramallah, which is in the territory of Efrayim.

The modern Israeli town Beit El was built two kilometers northwest of Beitin.

Remains of a Canaanite cultic site at Tel Beit El

1 | Shofetim 20:31, 21:19.

2 | Yehoshua 16:1–2; I Divrei HaYamim 7:28.

3 | Yehoshua 18:13.

Avraham is intended to mark a significant milestone in a journey which begins with *lekh lekha*. Avraham's journey is distinguished by leaving his past behind to build for himself new personal, national, and religious identities.

By contrast, Yaakov's new identity does not erase his old one. Yaakov and Israel coexist; God affirms his old identity ("Your name is Yaakov") just prior to conferring upon him a new one, and throughout the rest of the narrative he is referred to alternately as Yaakov and Israel. Sometimes, in fact, the Torah refers to him using both names in the same or adjacent verses, yielding a complex and multifaceted character, Yaakov-Israel. Yaakov is not supposed to become a completely new person. Rather, his identity as Israel is meant to complement the preexisting character. Avraham's covenant of circumcision seals the distinction between himself and the rest of his ancestral family; Yaakov's "covenant" binds him to his ancestral family. Avraham's destiny is to permanently leave home, while Yaakov's is to return home as a new person.

Rabbi Zvi Grumet

TAKING A LITERARY APPROACH

Were Yaakov to have immediately returned to fulfill his promise in Beit El and then continue home to his mother and father, he would likely have been judged a dramatic failure, as he would have learned nothing from his extended exile. The Yaakov who is exiled from his home, his land, and his family is in dire need of repair; a return without self-reflection and change would leave him unfit to continue as God's covenantal partner. By contrast, the Yaakov who struggles with Lavan, reaches out to Esav, fights to recover his integrity, refuses to stand by idly when his children cross the line, and declares himself to be Israel – with its multiple meanings – is a redeemed Yaakov.

When he ultimately does arrive in Beit El, God finally confirms what Yaakov has been trying to achieve: "God said to him: 'Your name is Yaakov; you will no longer be called Yaakov. Rather, your name will be Israel. And He called his name Israel'" (Bereshit 34:10). God doesn't need to explain the name Israel; Yaakov already knows what it means to be Israel: to confront both the external and internal devils, to stand up for himself while maintaining his dignity and integrity, to stand firm even against his own children without chasing them away, and to do all of the above while accepting a partnership with God. From the time of his nocturnal struggle until his return to Beit El, he calls himself Israel and his children think of him as Israel, but the Torah does not refer to him as such until now, when God confers that new name upon him.

Yaakov is not the first biblical character to have his name changed. His grandfather Avraham's name is changed by God as well. A careful look reveals striking similarities between those two events, resulting in what appears to be a formula. For both Avraham and Yaakov, God introduces Himself as El Shaddai (17:1; 35:11), both Avraham and Yaakov are informed that they will become a nation and a community of nations (17:5; 35:11), both are promised the land for their descendants (17:8; 35:12), and both are promised that among their descendants will be kings (17:6; 35:11). For Avraham, this formula is part of his induction into the covenant of circumcision; we have every reason to believe that it has parallel significance for Yaakov.

The strong similarities between the two name changes, however, invite an exploration of the differences between them. For Avraham, once his name is changed from Avram, he is never again referred to by his former name. The change of Avram's name to

16 From Beit El they moved on. While they were still some distance from Efrat, Raḥel began
17 to give birth; her labor pains were intense. When her labor was at its worst, the midwife said
18 to her, "Don't be afraid. You have another son." But she was dying. With her last breath, she
19 named him Ben Oni;[1] but his father called him Binyamin.[2] So Raḥel died and was buried
20 on the road to Efrat – that is, Beit Leḥem. Yaakov erected a pillar at her grave. To this day,
21 that pillar marks Raḥel's grave. Yisrael traveled on, pitching his tent beyond Migdal Eder.
22 While Yisrael was staying in that region, Reuven went and lay with his father's concubine
Bilha. And Yisrael heard –[3]

Yaakov had twelve sons.

---

1 | Meaning "son of my sorrow," but it may also denote "son of my strength."

2 | Meaning "son of the right side." The right side signifies strength.

3 | A break appears here in the middle of the verse, implying that the ensuing passage bears a connection to the present one.

UNLOCKING THE TEXT

- Why is Efrat used as a geographic marker?
- What did the midwife hope to achieve by telling Raḥel she had given birth to a son?
- What is the meaning of the name Ben Oni?
- Why did Yaakov name him something different?
- What is the meaning of the name Binyamin?
- Why is Binyamin the only child Yaakov names?
- Why did Yaakov bury Raḥel on the side of the road, and not in the cave of Makhpela?
- Why is Yaakov referred to as Yisrael at the end of this episode?
- What is the significance of Reuven sleeping with Bilha? Why is it included in the narrative here?
- Did Yaakov respond? If he did, why does the Torah not report it?

FINDING YOURSELF IN THE TEXT

- Do different members of your family call you by different names?
- Have you ever visited any of the places mentioned in this episode, including Kever Raḥel (Raḥel's tomb)?
- Have you ever been to a cemetery, and seen the gravestones? What is normally written on them? What would you like written on yours?

Consider using these questions as the basis for your own commentary or creative midrash.

How does reflecting on these firsthand experiences help you better understand the text?

טז וַיִּסְעוּ֙ מִבֵּ֣ית אֵ֔ל וַֽיְהִי־ע֥וֹד כִּבְרַת־הָאָ֖רֶץ לָב֣וֹא אֶפְרָ֑תָה וַתֵּ֥לֶד רָחֵ֖ל וַתְּקַ֥שׁ בְּלִדְתָּֽהּ׃
יז יח וַיְהִ֥י בְהַקְשֹׁתָ֖הּ בְּלִדְתָּ֑הּ וַתֹּ֨אמֶר לָ֤הּ הַמְיַלֶּ֙דֶת֙ אַל־תִּ֣ירְאִ֔י כִּֽי־גַם־זֶ֥ה לָ֖ךְ בֵּֽן׃ וַיְהִ֞י
יט בְּצֵ֤את נַפְשָׁהּ֙ כִּ֣י מֵ֔תָה וַתִּקְרָ֥א שְׁמ֖וֹ בֶּן־אוֹנִ֑י וְאָבִ֖יו קָֽרָא־ל֥וֹ בִנְיָמִֽין׃ וַתָּ֖מָת רָחֵ֑ל
כ וַתִּקָּבֵר֙ בְּדֶ֣רֶךְ אֶפְרָ֔תָה ה֖וּא בֵּ֥ית לָֽחֶם׃ וַיַּצֵּ֧ב יַעֲקֹ֛ב מַצֵּבָ֖ה עַל־קְבֻרָתָ֑הּ הִ֛וא
כא מַצֶּ֥בֶת קְבֻֽרַת־רָחֵ֖ל עַד־הַיּֽוֹם׃ וַיִּסַּ֖ע יִשְׂרָאֵ֑ל וַיֵּ֣ט אָהֳלֹ֔ה מֵהָ֖לְאָה לְמִגְדַּל־עֵֽדֶר׃
כב וַיְהִ֗י בִּשְׁכֹּ֤ן יִשְׂרָאֵל֙ בָּאָ֣רֶץ הַהִ֔וא וַיֵּ֣לֶךְ רְאוּבֵ֗ן וַיִּשְׁכַּב֙ אֶת־בִּלְהָה֙ פִּילֶ֣גֶשׁ אָבִ֔יו
וַיִּשְׁמַ֖ע יִשְׂרָאֵ֑ל
וַיִּהְי֥וּ בְנֵֽי־יַעֲקֹ֖ב שְׁנֵ֥ים עָשָֽׂר׃

THEMES	RELATIONSHIPS AND LOVE	ETHICS	THE LAND OF ISRAEL

Episode 51: *Raḥel Dies Giving Birth to Binyamin* – Bereshit 35:16–22

SUMMARY

Raḥel is the only matriarch not buried in the family burial plot in the cave of Makhpela in Ḥevron. Tragically, Raḥel, who had said to Yaakov: "Give me children, and if not, I am dead" (30:1), passes away while giving birth to her second child.

The Sages, with their keen powers of observation, associate Raḥel's death with the fulfillment of the unwitting curse that Yaakov uttered while Lavan was searching for his idols in Yaakov's camp. In complete faith that no one from his family could have stolen the idols, Yaakov declared: "With whomever you find your gods, he shall not live" (31:32). Alas, it was Raḥel who stole them, and due to this mistaken curse she dies prematurely.

THE ART OF MIDRASH

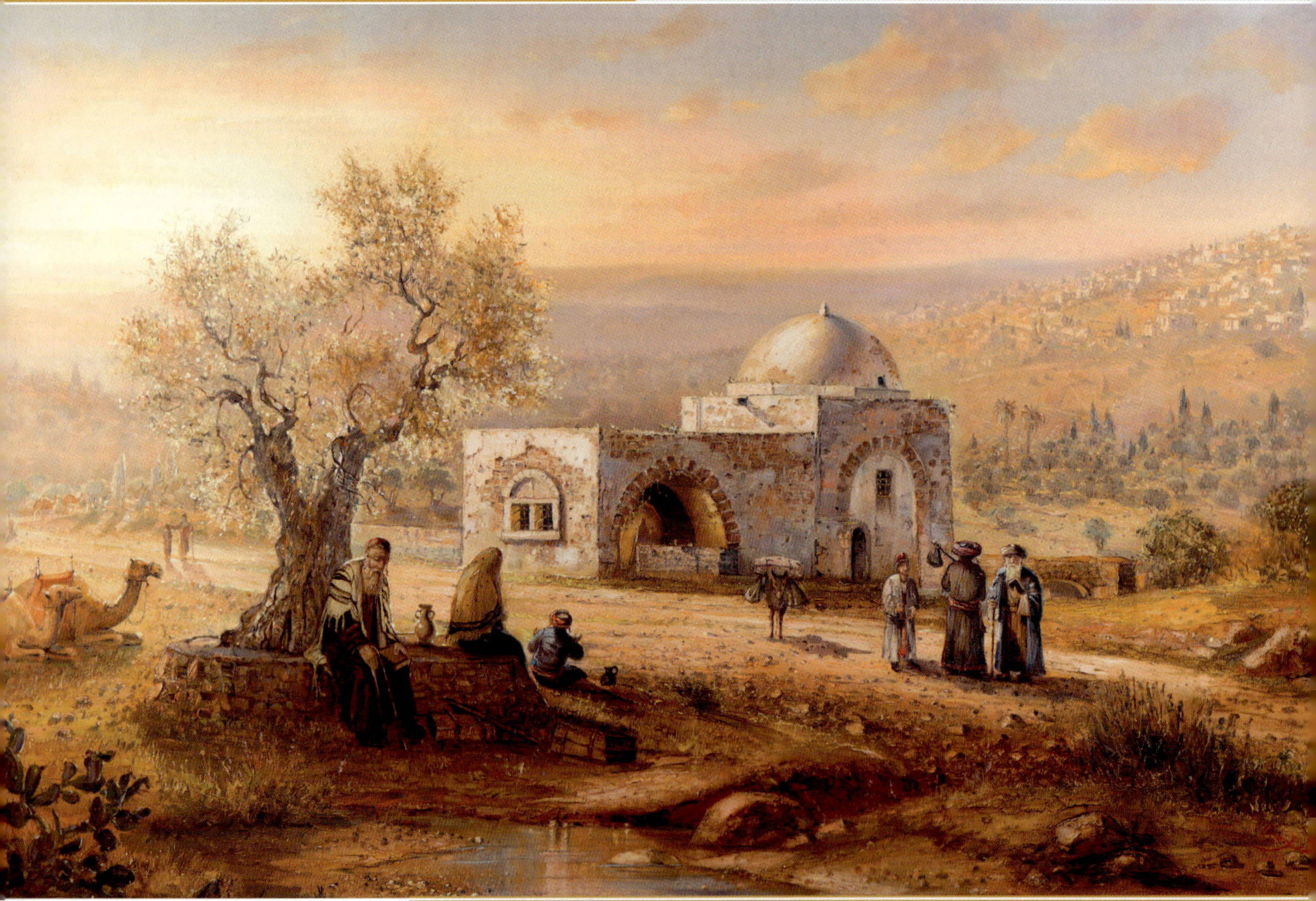

Journey to Pray with Rachel
Alex Levin (2017)

Analysis

- Which elements of this image are directly mentioned in the text?
- Which elements of this image are not found in the text?
- What midrashic interpretation could be inferred from this image?

A QUESTION OF BIBLIODRAMA

TO YAAKOV

- Can you describe your feelings after the death of Raḥel?
- Did this create a crisis of faith for you?
- Why did you change the name that Raḥel had given the child?
- What are your feelings toward this child?
- How did it make you feel when Reuven slept with Bilha?

TO REUVEN

- Why did you sleep with Bilha?
- How did you feel about Yaakov's lack of response to this?

TO BILHA

- How do you feel about Reuven?
- How do you feel about Yaakov?

INTEGRATING ḤOKHMA

Raḥel's tomb today and in 1900

TAKING A LITERARY APPROACH

The best-known interpretation of Raḥel's burial is that of Rashi:

> "And I buried her there" – and I did not take her even to Beit Leḥem to bring her into the land of Israel, and I knew that in your heart you bear ill will toward me. But know that according to God's will I buried her there, so that she will be of help to her sons when Nevuzaradan exiles them and they take the same road where Raḥel leaves her grave and weeps and asks for mercy on their behalf. As it is written: "A voice is heard in Rama... Raḥel weeps for her children" (Yirmeya 31:14). (Rashi on Bereshit 48:7)

According to Rashi (based on a midrash), Yaakov's words to Yosef attach the greatest significance to Raḥel's burial place. Yaakov explains that he buried Raḥel on the way neither because of the unavoidable circumstances nor because of her inferior status compared to Leah. Rather, Raḥel was buried there to pray for her children as they were exiled.

The source for the idea expressed in the midrash that Raḥel is destined to pray for her exiled children comes from the Bible itself:

> Thus says God: "A voice is heard in Rama, mourning and great weeping. Raḥel weeps for her children; she refuses to be comforted over her children, for they are gone." So says God: "Restrain your voice from weeping and your eyes from tears, for your actions will be rewarded," says God, "and they shall return from the land of their enemies. And there is hope for your future," says God, "and your children shall return to their borders." (Yirmeya 31:10–16)

Yirmeya describes Raḥel's prayer for her children as they are exiled and God's promise to her that they will return. Why is it specifically Raḥel who prays for her children?

Raḥel, who was barren, understands particularly well the value of children. Therefore, her love for them is greater, and when they are exiled she weeps and shouts to the heavens, refusing to be comforted. She is the matriarch who prays for her children until her prayers are answered.

Raḥel is also the matriarch who learned the importance of prayer through personal experience. Through the trials she endured, she ultimately understood that only addressing God in prayer can bring relief. This understanding through experience makes her prayers so powerful that God cannot help but listen.

Exile can be understood as the end of the process: The covenant between the Jewish people and God was broken, which led to a disconnect between God and the Jewish people. When the nation was exiled, it faced the danger of assimilating into the surrounding peoples. Raḥel, who symbolizes the journey, gives the nation hope that exile is only one part of a larger progression, which will ultimately conclude with redemption. This is Raḥel's prayer – she begs God not to allow the exile to be the end of the journey, but only one part of it.

Raḥel's death during the journey is no coincidence – it represents the essence of her life. Her death and burial on the road symbolize her entire life, a life in progress, constantly moving forward. Her burial during the journey reminds her children, as they are expelled from the land of Israel, that exile is only one stage of a process. Through Raḥel, they understand the power of prayer to lead them through even the most difficult of journeys – and that ultimately, their prayers will be answered.

Rabbanit Sharon Rimon

23 The sons of Leah were Reuven, Yaakov's firstborn, Shimon, Levi, Yehuda, Yissakhar, and
24 25 Zevulun. The sons of Raḥel were Yosef and Binyamin. The sons of Raḥel's maid Bilha were
26 Dan and Naftali. The sons of Leah's maid Zilpa were Gad and Asher. These were the sons
27 of Yaakov, born to him in Padan Aram. Yaakov came home to his father Yitzḥak at Mamre,
near Kiryat Arba – that is, Ḥevron – where Avraham and Yitzḥak had lived as strangers.
28 29 Yitzḥak lived one hundred and eighty years. Then he breathed his last, and died, and was
gathered to his people, aged, satisfied with his years. His sons Esav and Yaakov buried him.
36 1 2 These are the descendants of Esav – that is, Edom. Esav took wives from among the
daughters of Canaan: Ada daughter of Eilon the Hittite, and Oholivama daughter of Ana,
3 granddaughter of Tzivon the Hivite – and also Basmat, daughter of Yishmael and sister of
4 5 Nevayot. Ada bore Elifaz to Esav, and Basmat bore Reuel. Oholivama bore Yeush, Yalam,
6 and Koraḥ. These were the sons of Esav, born in the land of Canaan. Esav took his wives,
sons and daughters, and all the members of his household, together with his livestock, his
other animals, and all the possessions he had acquired in Canaan, and he moved to another
7 region, away from his brother Yaakov, for their possessions were too great for them to
remain together; because of all their livestock, the land where they were living could not

UNLOCKING THE TEXT

- Why does the Torah list Yaakov's children again here?
- What does Esav's presence at the burial of Yitzḥak tell us about his relationship with both his father and brother?
- Why does the Torah list the descendants of Esav?
- Was the separation of Esav and Yaakov only due to economic reasons?
- What does "Esav is Edom" mean?

Consider using these questions as the basis for your own commentary or creative midrash.

FINDING YOURSELF IN THE TEXT

- Do you have a lot of cousins? Do you know who they all are?
- Do you consider your cousins to be part of your immediate family?
- Do you feel that your cousins are an important part of your life?

How does reflecting on these firsthand experiences help you better understand the text?

כג כד בְּנֵי לֵאָה בְּכוֹר יַעֲקֹב רְאוּבֵן וְשִׁמְעוֹן וְלֵוִי וִיהוּדָה וְיִשָּׂשכָר וּזְבֻלוּן: בְּנֵי רָחֵל יוֹסֵף
כה כו וּבִנְיָמִן: וּבְנֵי בִלְהָה שִׁפְחַת רָחֵל דָּן וְנַפְתָּלִי: וּבְנֵי זִלְפָּה שִׁפְחַת לֵאָה גָּד וְאָשֵׁר
כז אֵלֶּה בְּנֵי יַעֲקֹב אֲשֶׁר יֻלַּד־לוֹ בְּפַדַּן אֲרָם: וַיָּבֹא יַעֲקֹב אֶל־יִצְחָק אָבִיו מַמְרֵא
כח קִרְיַת הָאַרְבַּע הִוא חֶבְרוֹן אֲשֶׁר־גָּר־שָׁם אַבְרָהָם וְיִצְחָק: וַיִּהְיוּ יְמֵי יִצְחָק מְאַת
כט שָׁנָה וּשְׁמֹנִים שָׁנָה: וַיִּגְוַע יִצְחָק וַיָּמָת וַיֵּאָסֶף אֶל־עַמָּיו זָקֵן וּשְׂבַע יָמִים וַיִּקְבְּרוּ
אֹתוֹ עֵשָׂו וְיַעֲקֹב בָּנָיו:

לו א ב וְאֵלֶּה תֹּלְדוֹת עֵשָׂו הוּא אֱדוֹם: עֵשָׂו לָקַח אֶת־נָשָׁיו מִבְּנוֹת כְּנָעַן אֶת־עָדָה
ג בַּת־אֵילוֹן הַחִתִּי וְאֶת־אָהֳלִיבָמָה בַּת־עֲנָה בַּת־צִבְעוֹן הַחִוִּי: וְאֶת־בָּשְׂמַת בַּת־
ד יִשְׁמָעֵאל אֲחוֹת נְבָיוֹת: וַתֵּלֶד עָדָה לְעֵשָׂו אֶת־אֱלִיפָז וּבָשְׂמַת יָלְדָה אֶת־רְעוּאֵל:
ה וְאָהֳלִיבָמָה יָלְדָה אֶת־יעיש וְאֶת־יַעְלָם וְאֶת־קֹרַח אֵלֶּה בְּנֵי עֵשָׂו אֲשֶׁר יֻלְּדוּ־לוֹ יְעוּשׁ
ו בְּאֶרֶץ כְּנָעַן: וַיִּקַּח עֵשָׂו אֶת־נָשָׁיו וְאֶת־בָּנָיו וְאֶת־בְּנֹתָיו וְאֶת־כָּל־נַפְשׁוֹת בֵּיתוֹ
וְאֶת־מִקְנֵהוּ וְאֶת־כָּל־בְּהֶמְתּוֹ וְאֵת כָּל־קִנְיָנוֹ אֲשֶׁר רָכַשׁ בְּאֶרֶץ כְּנָעַן וַיֵּלֶךְ אֶל־
ז אֶרֶץ מִפְּנֵי יַעֲקֹב אָחִיו: כִּי־הָיָה רְכוּשָׁם רָב מִשֶּׁבֶת יַחְדָּו וְלֹא יָכְלָה אֶרֶץ מְגוּרֵיהֶם

THEMES | RELATIONSHIPS AND LOVE | PEOPLEHOOD | COVENANT

Episode 52: *Family Trees* – Bereshit 35:23–36:43

SUMMARY

A major chapter in the life of Yaakov, which incorporated his departure to Ḥaran and his return to Canaan, has ended. This section, which lists the chieftains of Esav's family, separates the accounts of Yaakov's two exiles: his first exile, during which he established his family until his return to Canaan, and the events that will ultimately lead to his second exile, together with his family, to Egypt.

The death of Yitzḥak is reported, and just as when the Torah finishes telling the story of Avraham's life, a short passage is devoted to Yishmael's family (25:12–18), following the description of Yitzḥak's death, whose burial is attended by both his sons, this section lists Esav's descendants and relates their history. Before continuing with its primary narrative, which follows Yaakov and his family, the Torah digresses and focuses on Esav's descendants. Esav had also received a blessing from his father, and this section describes its fulfillment, as his descendants rule over a land of their own through an independent government. It is notable that the history of Esav's children is intertwined with that of Yaakov's descendants for many generations, alternating between the roles of allies and adversaries.

8 9 support them both. So Esav settled in the hill country of Se'ir. Esav is Edom. These, then, are
10 the descendants of Esav, ancestor of the Edomites, in the hill country of Se'ir. These are the
names of Esav's sons: Elifaz, son of Esav's wife Ada, and Reuel, son of Esav's wife Basmat.
11 12 The sons of Elifaz were Teiman, Omar, Tzefo, Gatam, and Kenaz. Timna, a concubine of
13 Esav's son Elifaz, bore him Amalek. These are the descendants of Esav's wife Ada. The
sons of Reuel were Naḥat, Zeraḥ, Shama, and Miza. These were the descendants of Esav's
14 wife Basmat. The sons of Oholivama, daughter of Ana and granddaughter of Esav's wife
15 Tzivon, whom she bore to Esav, were Yeush, Yalam, and Koraḥ. These were the tribal chiefs
among Esav's descendants. The sons of Elifaz, Esav's firstborn, were the chiefs Teiman,
16 Omar, Tzefo, Kenaz, Koraḥ, Gatam, and Amalek. These were the chiefs descended from
17 Elifaz in Edom; they were grandsons of Ada. The sons of Esav's son Reuel were the chiefs
Naḥat, Zeraḥ, Shama, and Miza. These were the chiefs descended from Reuel in Edom; they
18 were grandsons of Esav's wife Basmat. The sons of Esav's wife Oholivama were the chiefs
Yeush, Yalam, and Koraḥ. These were the chiefs descended from Esav's wife Oholivama
19 daughter of Ana. These were the sons of Esav – that is, Edom – and these were their
20 chiefs. These are the sons of Se'ir the Horite who were settled in the land: Lotan,
21 Shoval, Tzivon, Ana, Dishon, Etzer, and Dishan. These were the chiefs of the Horites,
22 descendants of Se'ir in the land of Edom. Lotan's sons were Ḥori and Heimam. Timna was
23 24 Lotan's sister. Shoval's sons were Alvan, Manaḥat, Eival, Shefo, and Onam. Tzivon's sons
were Aya and Ana. This is the Ana who discovered hot springs in the desert while pasturing
25 the donkeys of his father Tzivon. Ana's children were Dishon and Oholivama daughter of
26 27 Ana. Dishon's sons were Ḥemdan, Eshban, Yitran, and Keran. Etzer's sons were Bilhan,
28 29 Zaavan, and Akan. Dishan's sons were Utz and Aran. These were the tribal chiefs of the
30 Horites: chiefs Lotan, Shoval, Tzivon, Ana, Dishon, Etzer, and Dishan. These were the
Horite chiefs by their divisions in the land of Se'ir.
31 32 These were the kings who reigned in Edom before any king reigned over the Israelites. Bela
33 son of Beor became king in Edom. His city was named Dinhava. When Bela died, Yovav
34 son of Zeraḥ from Botzra succeeded him as king. When Yovav died, Ḥusham from the
35 land of the Temanites succeeded him as king. When Ḥusham died, Hadad son of Bedad,
who defeated Midyan in the country of Moav, succeeded him as king. His city was named
36 37 Avit. When Hadad died, Samla from Masreka succeeded him as king. When Samla died,
38 Sha'ul from Reḥovot HaNahar succeeded him as king. When Sha'ul died, Baal Ḥanan son
39 of Akhbor succeeded him as king. When Baal Ḥanan son of Akhbor died, Hadar succeeded
him as king. His city was named Pa'u, and his wife's name was Meheitavel, daughter of

ח ט לָשֵׂאת אֹתָם מִפְּנֵי מִקְנֵיהֶם: וַיֵּשֶׁב עֵשָׂו בְּהַר שֵׂעִיר עֵשָׂו הוּא אֱדוֹם: וְאֵלֶּה תֹּלְדוֹת
י עֵשָׂו אֲבִי אֱדוֹם בְּהַר שֵׂעִיר: אֵלֶּה שְׁמוֹת בְּנֵי־עֵשָׂו אֱלִיפַז בֶּן־עָדָה אֵשֶׁת עֵשָׂו
יא רְעוּאֵל בֶּן־בָּשְׂמַת אֵשֶׁת עֵשָׂו: וַיִּהְיוּ בְּנֵי אֱלִיפָז תֵּימָן אוֹמָר צְפוֹ וְגַעְתָּם וּקְנַז:
יב וְתִמְנַע ׀ הָיְתָה פִילֶגֶשׁ לֶאֱלִיפַז בֶּן־עֵשָׂו וַתֵּלֶד לֶאֱלִיפַז אֶת־עֲמָלֵק אֵלֶּה בְּנֵי עָדָה
יג אֵשֶׁת עֵשָׂו: וְאֵלֶּה בְּנֵי רְעוּאֵל נַחַת וָזֶרַח שַׁמָּה וּמִזָּה אֵלֶּה הָיוּ בְּנֵי בָשְׂמַת אֵשֶׁת
יד עֵשָׂו: וְאֵלֶּה הָיוּ בְּנֵי אָהֳלִיבָמָה בַת־עֲנָה בַּת־צִבְעוֹן אֵשֶׁת עֵשָׂו וַתֵּלֶד לְעֵשָׂו
טו אֶת־יעיש וְאֶת־יַעְלָם וְאֶת־קֹרַח: אֵלֶּה אַלּוּפֵי בְנֵי־עֵשָׂו בְּנֵי אֱלִיפַז בְּכוֹר עֵשָׂו יְעוּשׁ
טז אַלּוּף תֵּימָן אַלּוּף אוֹמָר אַלּוּף צְפוֹ אַלּוּף קְנַז: אַלּוּף־קֹרַח אַלּוּף גַּעְתָּם אַלּוּף
יז עֲמָלֵק אֵלֶּה אַלּוּפֵי אֱלִיפַז בְּאֶרֶץ אֱדוֹם אֵלֶּה בְּנֵי עָדָה: וְאֵלֶּה בְּנֵי רְעוּאֵל בֶּן־עֵשָׂו
אַלּוּף נַחַת אַלּוּף זֶרַח אַלּוּף שַׁמָּה אַלּוּף מִזָּה אֵלֶּה אַלּוּפֵי רְעוּאֵל בְּאֶרֶץ אֱדוֹם
יח אֵלֶּה בְּנֵי בָשְׂמַת אֵשֶׁת עֵשָׂו: וְאֵלֶּה בְּנֵי אָהֳלִיבָמָה אֵשֶׁת עֵשָׂו אַלּוּף יְעוּשׁ אַלּוּף
יט יַעְלָם אַלּוּף קֹרַח אֵלֶּה אַלּוּפֵי אָהֳלִיבָמָה בַּת־עֲנָה אֵשֶׁת עֵשָׂו: אֵלֶּה בְנֵי־עֵשָׂו
כ וְאֵלֶּה אַלּוּפֵיהֶם הוּא אֱדוֹם: אֵלֶּה בְנֵי־שֵׂעִיר הַחֹרִי יֹשְׁבֵי הָאָרֶץ לוֹטָן שביעי
כא וְשׁוֹבָל וְצִבְעוֹן וַעֲנָה: וְדִשׁוֹן וְאֵצֶר וְדִישָׁן אֵלֶּה אַלּוּפֵי הַחֹרִי בְּנֵי שֵׂעִיר בְּאֶרֶץ
כב כג אֱדוֹם: וַיִּהְיוּ בְנֵי־לוֹטָן חֹרִי וְהֵימָם וַאֲחוֹת לוֹטָן תִּמְנָע: וְאֵלֶּה בְּנֵי שׁוֹבָל עַלְוָן
כד וּמָנַחַת וְעֵיבָל שְׁפוֹ וְאוֹנָם: וְאֵלֶּה בְנֵי־צִבְעוֹן וְאַיָּה וַעֲנָה הוּא עֲנָה אֲשֶׁר מָצָא
כה אֶת־הַיֵּמִם בַּמִּדְבָּר בִּרְעֹתוֹ אֶת־הַחֲמֹרִים לְצִבְעוֹן אָבִיו: וְאֵלֶּה בְנֵי־עֲנָה דִּשֹׁן
כו כז וְאָהֳלִיבָמָה בַּת־עֲנָה: וְאֵלֶּה בְּנֵי דִישָׁן חֶמְדָּן וְאֶשְׁבָּן וְיִתְרָן וּכְרָן: אֵלֶּה בְּנֵי־אֵצֶר
כח כט בִּלְהָן וְזַעֲוָן וַעֲקָן: אֵלֶּה בְנֵי־דִישָׁן עוּץ וַאֲרָן: אֵלֶּה אַלּוּפֵי הַחֹרִי אַלּוּף לוֹטָן אַלּוּף
ל שׁוֹבָל אַלּוּף צִבְעוֹן אַלּוּף עֲנָה: אַלּוּף דִּשֹׁן אַלּוּף אֵצֶר אַלּוּף דִּישָׁן אֵלֶּה אַלּוּפֵי
הַחֹרִי לְאַלֻּפֵיהֶם בְּאֶרֶץ שֵׂעִיר:
לא לב וְאֵלֶּה הַמְּלָכִים אֲשֶׁר מָלְכוּ בְּאֶרֶץ אֱדוֹם לִפְנֵי מְלָךְ־מֶלֶךְ לִבְנֵי יִשְׂרָאֵל: וַיִּמְלֹךְ
לג בֶּאֱדוֹם בֶּלַע בֶּן־בְּעוֹר וְשֵׁם עִירוֹ דִּנְהָבָה: וַיָּמָת בָּלַע וַיִּמְלֹךְ תַּחְתָּיו יוֹבָב בֶּן־
לד לה זֶרַח מִבָּצְרָה: וַיָּמָת יוֹבָב וַיִּמְלֹךְ תַּחְתָּיו חֻשָׁם מֵאֶרֶץ הַתֵּימָנִי: וַיָּמָת חֻשָׁם
וַיִּמְלֹךְ תַּחְתָּיו הֲדַד בֶּן־בְּדַד הַמַּכֶּה אֶת־מִדְיָן בִּשְׂדֵה מוֹאָב וְשֵׁם עִירוֹ עֲוִית:
לו לז וַיָּמָת הֲדָד וַיִּמְלֹךְ תַּחְתָּיו שַׂמְלָה מִמַּשְׂרֵקָה: וַיָּמָת שַׂמְלָה וַיִּמְלֹךְ תַּחְתָּיו שָׁאוּל
לח לט מֵרְחֹבוֹת הַנָּהָר: וַיָּמָת שָׁאוּל וַיִּמְלֹךְ תַּחְתָּיו בַּעַל חָנָן בֶּן־עַכְבּוֹר: וַיָּמָת בַּעַל
חָנָן בֶּן־עַכְבּוֹר וַיִּמְלֹךְ תַּחְתָּיו הֲדַר וְשֵׁם עִירוֹ פָּעוּ וְשֵׁם אִשְׁתּוֹ מְהֵיטַבְאֵל

40 Matred, daughter of Mei Zahav. These were the chiefs descended from Esav, by their
41 clans, localities, and names: the chiefs Timna, Alva, Yetet, Oholivama, Ela, Pinon, Kenaz,
42
43 Teiman, Mivtzar, Magdiel, and Iram. These were the chiefs of Edom – of Esav, ancestor of
the Edomites – each with their own settlements in the land that they held.

THE ART OF MIDRASH

The Families of Jacob
Phillip Ratner (1984)

Analysis

- Which elements of this image are directly mentioned in the text?
- Which elements of this image are not found in the text?
- What midrashic interpretation could be inferred from this image?

מ בַּת־מַטְרֵד בַּת מֵי זָהָב: וְאֵלֶּה שְׁמוֹת אַלּוּפֵי עֵשָׂו לְמִשְׁפְּחֹתָם לִמְקֹמֹתָם מפטיר
מא בִּשְׁמֹתָם אַלּוּף תִּמְנָע אַלּוּף עַלְוָה אַלּוּף יְתֵת: אַלּוּף אָהֳלִיבָמָה אַלּוּף אֵלָה
מב מג אַלּוּף פִּינֹן: אַלּוּף קְנַז אַלּוּף תֵּימָן אַלּוּף מִבְצָר: אַלּוּף מַגְדִּיאֵל אַלּוּף עִירָם אֵלֶּה ו
אַלּוּפֵי אֱדוֹם לְמֹשְׁבֹתָם בְּאֶרֶץ אֲחֻזָּתָם הוּא עֵשָׂו אֲבִי אֱדוֹם:

INTEGRATING ḤOKHMAH

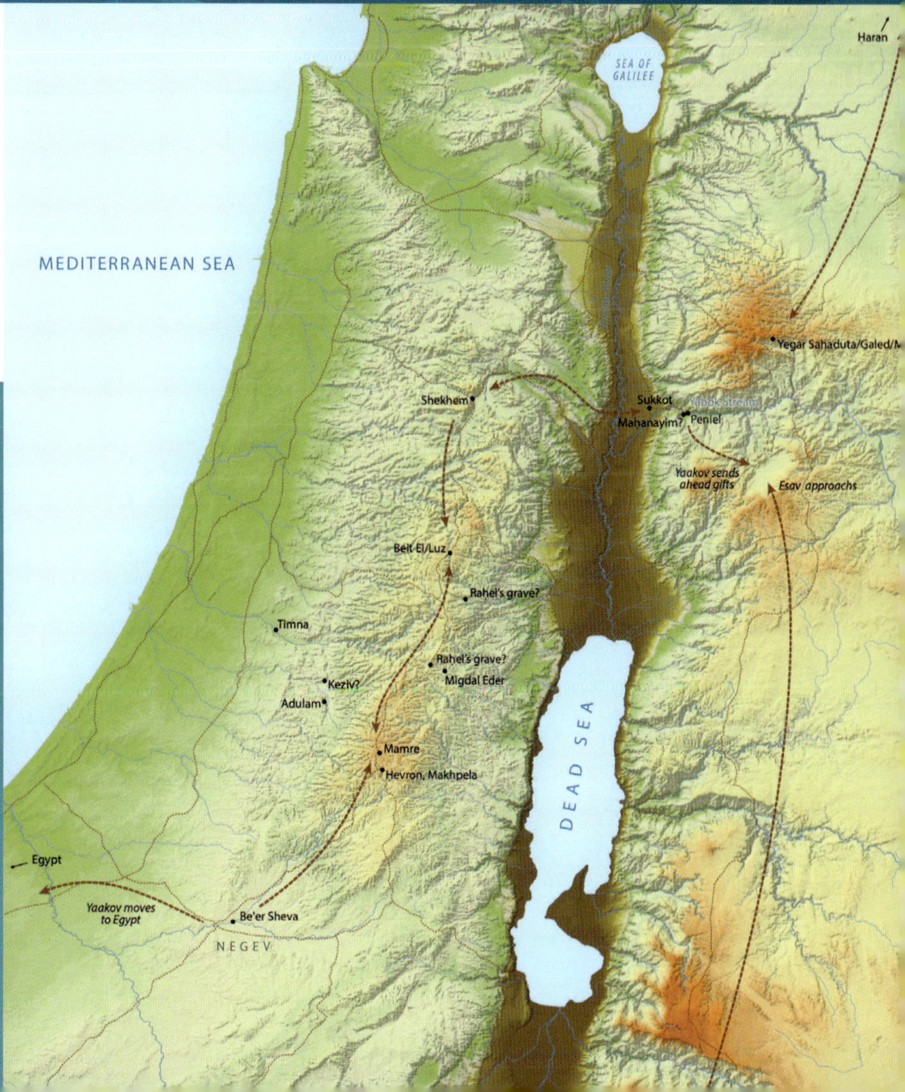

Yaakov's journeys in the land of Israel

Analysis

- What specific information do we now have that was unavailable to classical Jewish commentators? How can it aid our understanding of the text?
- What can we learn from this map that can help us understand the text?
- What further questions on the text do you have now that you have seen this map?

A single line at the close of the legacy of Esav-Se'ir captures the distinction powerfully. While Esav merges with Se'ir and builds himself a powerful nation, Yaakov dwells in the land of Canaan, the land of his father's sojourn (37:1). Three times Yaakov narrowly escapes the kind of merger (with Lavan, Shekhem, and Esav) that propels his elder brother to instant success, following instead the slow, arduous, covenantal path. It is the same kind of path Yaakov chooses years earlier, prepared to wait as long as necessary to cash in on the birthright. Esav finds his fortunes in the immediate; Yaakov returns to the land of his promise.

Rabbi Zvi Grumet

TAKING A LITERARY APPROACH

If the nation of Israel is the product of slow and careful nurturing, Esav's emergence as a nation follows a profoundly different path. Esav is the only figure in the Bible described with two books of *toledot*, or legacies. The first is the legacy of Esav, otherwise known as Edom (Bereshit 36:1). Using imagery evocative of Avraham's nephew Lot, after building a family with five sons in Canaan, Esav travels eastward, crossing the Jordan, because his ancestral land of Canaan "could not support" both him and his brother, Yaakov. Leaving the land to go eastward in search of better grazing follows the model of those seeking to leave the covenant for more immediate material gains.

But there is a second *toledot* of Esav presented immediately afterward: Esav the father of the Edomite nation, in the mountains of Se'ir (36:9). The legacy of Esav presented here is far more complex and involves Esav marrying into and eventually merging with the people of Se'ir. The family relationships in this account are intertwined and complicated, with more than a hint of incest. The merged family defies the Bereshit model of twelve sons (Esav has thirteen), as well as the model of the proto-nation, and with the merger Esav flourishes into a nation almost immediately. Let us recall that when he comes to greet Yaakov he already has four hundred men.

And not only does Esav become a nation right away, his nation has kings – long before there are kings in Israel (36:31). The Torah lists a long line of kings (although lacking any line of succession; each generation sports a king from a different region). Esav emerges from the womb complete, and he later emerges as a complete nation even before Yaakov has his twelve sons.

Esav receives the divine blessings as promised to Avraham and Yitzḥak. His children are numerous and they become a nation – even nations – adorned by royalty. Yet fulfillment of the promise is quite different from fulfillment of the covenant. As we've seen, being part of the covenant entails patience and endurance: four hundred years of servitude, oppression, and slow development. Impetuous Esav, who sells his birthright because he cannot imagine waiting for it to become valuable, is incompatible with God's covenant. He gets his nation, complete with kings, even as Yaakov struggles to establish his fledgling clan.

ויישב

Vayeshev

Parasha Overview

With Parashat Vayeshev, the story shifts from Yaakov to his children. The tension we have already sensed between Leah and Raḥel is transferred to the next generation in the form of the rivalry between Yosef and his brothers, the story whose twists and turns take us to the end of sefer Bereshit. Yosef is Yaakov's favorite son, firstborn of his beloved Raḥel. The envy and antagonism of his brothers leads them to sell Yosef into slavery in Egypt, an act that will many years later result in the enslavement of the entire family, by then a nation.

Episodes

53.	**Yosef's Dreams**	37:1–11
54.	**The Sale of Yosef**	37:12–36
55.	**Yehuda and Tamar**	38:1–30
56.	**Yosef in the House of Potifar**	39:1–20
57.	**Yosef in Prison**	39:21–40:23

Parasha Stats

- 5,972 letters
- 1,558 words
- 112 verses
- 237 lines in a sefer Torah

37 1 2 Yaakov settled where his father had lived as a stranger, in the land of Canaan. This is the
story of Yaakov. Yosef, seventeen years old, was shepherding the flock with his brothers, an
assistant to the sons of his father's wives Bilha and Zilpa. And Yosef brought his father bad
3 reports of them. Now, Yisrael loved Yosef more than all his other sons, for he was a child
4 of his old age; he made him an ornately colored robe. But when his brothers saw that their
father loved him more than any of them, they hated him and could not say a peaceful word
5 to him. Then Yosef had a dream, and when he told it to his brothers, they hated him still
6 7 more. "Listen to this dream I had," he said. "We were binding sheaves in the field when my
sheaf rose and stood upright and your sheaves gathered around mine and bowed down to
8 it." His brothers said to him, "Do you mean to be king over us? Do you mean to rule over
9 us?" Then they hated him even more for his dreams and for what he said. Then he had
another dream and told it to his brothers. "I had another dream," he said. "This time, the
10 sun, moon, and eleven stars were bowing down to me." When he told his father as well as
his brothers, his father rebuked him and said, "What kind of dream is this that you have
had? Shall we really come, I and your mother and your brothers, to bow to the ground
11 before you?" His brothers were jealous of him; but his father kept the matter in mind.

UNLOCKING THE TEXT

- Why does the Torah use the word *toledot* here but not list generations (as it does in other places)?
- Why does the Torah consider Yosef's age important to know?
- Where were the sons of Leah?
- What was the "bad report" Yosef brought about the sons of Bilha and Zilpa?
- Why did Yaakov love Yosef more than his brothers?
- Were the brothers justified in their hatred?
- How did Yaakov and the brothers interpret Yosef's dreams? Was there room for a different interpretation?
- Did Yaakov see the hatred of the brothers? Why did he hold his peace?
- Why did Yosef share his dreams with them? What was his motivation and goal?

FINDING YOURSELF IN THE TEXT

- Do you dream? Do you wonder about the meaning behind your dreams?
- Does one of your siblings (or you!) think they are superior?
- How do you, your siblings, and your parents deal with that?

Consider using these questions as the basis for your own commentary or creative midrash.

How does reflecting on these firsthand experiences help you better understand the text?

לז א וַיֵּ֣שֶׁב יַעֲקֹ֔ב בְּאֶ֖רֶץ מְגוּרֵ֣י אָבִ֑יו בְּאֶ֖רֶץ כְּנָֽעַן: ב אֵ֣לֶּה ׀ תֹּלְד֣וֹת יַעֲקֹ֗ב יוֹסֵ֞ף בֶּן־   לג וישב

שְׁבַֽע־עֶשְׂרֵ֤ה שָׁנָה֙ הָיָ֨ה רֹעֶ֤ה אֶת־אֶחָיו֙ בַּצֹּ֔אן וְה֣וּא נַ֗עַר אֶת־בְּנֵ֥י בִלְהָ֛ה וְאֶת־בְּנֵ֥י

זִלְפָּ֖ה נְשֵׁ֣י אָבִ֑יו וַיָּבֵ֥א יוֹסֵ֛ף אֶת־דִּבָּתָ֥ם רָעָ֖ה אֶל־אֲבִיהֶֽם: ג וְיִשְׂרָאֵ֗ל אָהַ֤ב אֶת־

ד יוֹסֵף֙ מִכָּל־בָּנָ֔יו כִּֽי־בֶן־זְקֻנִ֥ים ה֖וּא ל֑וֹ וְעָ֥שָׂה ל֖וֹ כְּתֹ֥נֶת פַּסִּֽים: וַיִּרְא֣וּ אֶחָ֗יו כִּֽי־אֹת֞וֹ

ה אָהַ֤ב אֲבִיהֶם֙ מִכָּל־אֶחָ֔יו וַֽיִּשְׂנְא֖וּ אֹת֑וֹ וְלֹ֥א יָכְל֖וּ דַּבְּר֥וֹ לְשָׁלֹֽם: וַיַּחֲלֹ֤ם יוֹסֵף֙ חֲל֔וֹם

ו וַיַּגֵּ֖ד לְאֶחָ֑יו וַיּוֹסִ֥פוּ ע֖וֹד שְׂנֹ֥א אֹתֽוֹ: וַיֹּ֖אמֶר אֲלֵיהֶ֑ם שִׁמְעוּ־נָ֕א הַחֲל֥וֹם הַזֶּ֖ה אֲשֶׁ֥ר

ז חָלָֽמְתִּי: וְ֠הִנֵּ֠ה אֲנַ֜חְנוּ מְאַלְּמִ֤ים אֲלֻמִּים֙ בְּת֣וֹךְ הַשָּׂדֶ֔ה וְהִנֵּ֛ה קָ֥מָה אֲלֻמָּתִ֖י וְגַם־

ח נִצָּ֑בָה וְהִנֵּ֤ה תְסֻבֶּ֨ינָה֙ אֲלֻמֹּ֣תֵיכֶ֔ם וַתִּֽשְׁתַּחֲוֶ֖יןָ לַאֲלֻמָּתִֽי: וַיֹּ֤אמְרוּ לוֹ֙ אֶחָ֔יו הֲמָלֹ֤ךְ

תִּמְלֹךְ֙ עָלֵ֔ינוּ אִם־מָשׁ֥וֹל תִּמְשֹׁ֖ל בָּ֑נוּ וַיּוֹסִ֤פוּ עוֹד֙ שְׂנֹ֣א אֹת֔וֹ עַל־חֲלֹמֹתָ֖יו וְעַל־

ט דְּבָרָֽיו: וַיַּחֲלֹ֥ם עוֹד֙ חֲל֣וֹם אַחֵ֔ר וַיְסַפֵּ֥ר אֹת֖וֹ לְאֶחָ֑יו וַיֹּ֗אמֶר הִנֵּ֨ה חָלַ֤מְתִּי חֲלוֹם֙ ע֔וֹד

י וְהִנֵּ֧ה הַשֶּׁ֣מֶשׁ וְהַיָּרֵ֗חַ וְאַחַ֤ד עָשָׂר֙ כּֽוֹכָבִ֔ים מִֽשְׁתַּחֲוִ֖ים לִֽי: וַיְסַפֵּ֣ר אֶל־אָבִיו֮ וְאֶל־

אֶחָיו֒ וַיִּגְעַר־בּ֣וֹ אָבִ֔יו וַיֹּ֣אמֶר ל֔וֹ מָ֛ה הַחֲל֥וֹם הַזֶּ֖ה אֲשֶׁ֣ר חָלָ֑מְתָּ הֲב֣וֹא נָב֗וֹא אֲנִ֤י

יא וְאִמְּךָ֙ וְאַחֶ֔יךָ לְהִשְׁתַּחֲוֹ֥ת לְךָ֖ אָֽרְצָה: וַיְקַנְאוּ־ב֖וֹ אֶחָ֑יו וְאָבִ֖יו שָׁמַ֥ר אֶת־הַדָּבָֽר:

THEMES	RELATIONSHIPS AND LOVE	LEADERSHIP	PROPHECY AND REVELATION

Episode 53: *Yosef's Dreams* – Bereshit 37:1–11

SUMMARY

After concluding the narrative of Yitzhak's life, and after briefly listing the descendants of Esav, the Torah returns its focus to Yaakov and the events of his life. The seeds of Yaakov's eventual second exile from Canaan lie in his relationships with his wives and his twelve sons. His preference for Yosef son of Rahel sets in motion the events that ultimately lead to the family's exile in Egypt.

THE ART OF MIDRASH

Joseph Tells His Dreams to Jacob
Rembrandt Harmensz van Rijn
(1633)

Analysis

- Which elements of this image are directly mentioned in the text?
- Which elements of this image are not found in the text?
- What midrashic interpretation could be inferred from this image?

A QUESTION OF BIBLIODRAMA

TO YOSEF

- What was the bad report about your brothers that you brought to your father?
- Why did you do it?
- How did it feel when your father gave you the multicolored robe?
- Did you feel he loved you more than your brothers?
- Could you sense your brothers' jealousy and hatred?
- What do you think your dreams meant?
- Why did you share them with your brothers and your father?

TO THE BROTHERS

- What did you think of Yosef before he shared his dreams?
- Did this episode change anything in your relationship with Yosef?
- Do you think your father favors Yosef? Why do you think this is?
- What do you think Yosef's dreams meant?

TO YAAKOV

- How does it feel to return home to the land of your fathers?
- Do you feel that God has now fulfilled His side of the covenant with you and your fathers?
- Why did you love Yosef more than your other sons?
- Did you love him to the exclusion of the others?
- Didn't the experiences of your childhood and of your father's childhood influence you to avoid this?
- Why did you give Yosef a multicolored robe?
- Why did you rebuke Yosef for his dreams?

Judaism is about the God who cannot be seen, who can only be heard; about the God who created the universe with words and whose first act of kindness to the first human being was to teach him how to use words. Jews, even highly secular Jews, have often been preoccupied with language. Wittgenstein understood that philosophy is about language.

Levi Strauss saw cultures as forms of language. Noam Chomsky and Steven Pinker pioneered study of the language instinct. George Steiner has written about translation and the limits of language.

The Sages were eloquent in speaking about the dangers of *lashon hara*, "evil speech," the power of language to fracture relationships and destroy trust and goodwill. But there is evil silence as well as evil speech. It is no accident that at the very beginning of the most fateful tale of sibling rivalry in Bereshit, the role – specifically the failure – of language is alluded to, in a way missed by virtually all translations. Yosef's brothers might have "spoken him to peace" had they been open, candid, and willing to communicate. Speech broke down at the very point where it was needed most.

Words create; words reveal; words command; words redeem. Judaism is a religion of holy words. For words are the narrow bridge across the abyss between soul and soul, between two human beings, and between humanity and God.

Language is the redemption of solitude, and the mender of broken relationships. However painful it is to speak about our hurt, it is more dangerous not to do so. Yosef and his brothers might have been reconciled early on in their lives, and thus spared themselves, their father, and their descendants, much grief. Revealing pain is the first step to healing pain.

Speech is a path to peace.

Rabbi Jonathan Sacks

Analysis

- What areas of understanding of human nature and society do we now have that were unavailable to classical Jewish commentators? How can they aid our understanding of the text?
- What can we learn from this essay to help us understand the text?
- What further questions on the text do you have now that you have read this new take on the story?

INTEGRATING ḤOKHMA

"When his brothers saw that their father loved him more than any of them, they hated him. *Velo yakhlu dabro leshalom*" (Bereshit 37:4).

What is the meaning of this last phrase? Rabbi Yonatan Eybeshutz recognized that the Hebrew construction is strange. Literally, it means "They could not speak him to peace." What might this mean? Rabbi Eybeshutz refers us to the command in Vayikra 19:17: "You shall not hate your brother in your heart. You shall surely reprimand your neighbor and not bear sin because of him."

Had the brothers been able to speak to Yosef they might have told him of their anger at his talebearing, and of their distress at seeing the many-colored coat. They might have spoken frankly about their sense of humiliation at the way their father favored Raḥel over their mother Leah, a favoritism that was now being carried through into a second generation. Yosef might have come to understand their feelings. It might have made him more modest or at least more thoughtful. But *lo yakhlu dabro leshalom.* They simply couldn't bring themselves to speak.

We have here an instance of one of the Torah's great insights, that conversation is a form of conflict resolution, whereas the breakdown of speech is often a prelude to violent revenge.

Conversation does not, in and of itself, resolve conflict. Two people who are open with one another may still have clashing desires or competing claims. They may simply not like one another. There is no law of predetermined harmony in the human domain. But conversation means that we recognize one another's humanity. At its best it allows us to engage in role reversal, seeing the world from the other's point of view. Think of how many real and intractable conflicts, whether in the personal or political domain, might be transformed if we could do that.

In the end Yosef and his brothers had to live through real trauma before they were able to recognize one another's humanity, and much of the rest of their story – the longest single narrative in the Torah – is about just that.

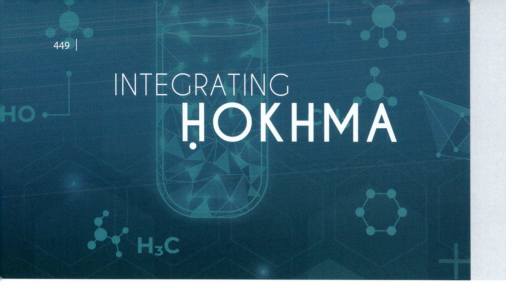

to prevent Yaakov from passing on the leadership of the family to Yosef.

The brothers' hatred of Yosef and their decision to sell him has two levels of motivation: on the natural, human level, Yaakov's preference of Yosef over his brothers caused intense enmity and jealousy between them to the point that they were willing to kill him. But on a fundamental level, Yosef is truly unfit to be the leader of Yaakov's household. The brothers sold him in order to prevent Yaakov from making the mistake of appointing Yosef to lead.

This explanation may be difficult to accept. Some might still prefer to see the brothers' sale of Yosef as resulting from simple human hatred and jealousy rather than more lofty considerations. Even so, this incident can be read as an act of temporarily distancing Yosef from Yaakov's house and rejecting him for leadership – but as a result of God's will. God causes the entire chain of events to take place under the cover of the brothers' jealousy and competitiveness. When Yosef is sold, he becomes aware of his true role; this episode also allows Yehuda to display his leadership abilities.

Yaakov's twelve sons, who eventually produce the twelve tribes of Israel, each possess different strengths. Together, these gifts are used to found the nation of Israel. For this to happen, each tribe must become fully aware of its unique strengths and its proper role.

Among the brothers remaining in Yaakov's house, Yehuda emerges as the leader (see 37:26; 43:1–14; 44:18–34; 46:28). Yosef's special gift comes to light precisely because he loses his special status and is distanced from his family. In this situation his true nature reveals itself. After all of Yosef's trials, he understands his role in the family: he is revealed to be particularly gifted in effecting material blessings, and he has become "the governor over the entire nation of the land." In this sense, the brothers bow to him – they are dependent on him.

At first, Yosef's dreams seemed to be expression of his misplaced desire to rule, which did not come true. In fact, the dreams do come true – the brothers are now bowing down to Yosef! Yosef's dreams were indeed prophetic – God showed Yosef his future, but He did not explicitly tell Yosef the meaning of his dreams. Yosef and his brothers attempted to interpret the dreams themselves, but just as Yosef had misunderstood his role in Yaakov's house, so too he misinterpreted his dreams and assumed they were signs of his future ruling position in Yaakov's family. The dreams were actually a prophecy that Yosef would lead his family financially, not that he would rule over them.

After many years in Egypt, cut off from his family, Yosef finally understands the message imparted by his dreams. His true place in Yaakov's family is sustaining the family by channeling material blessing and bounty from God.

Rabbanit Sharon Rimon

TAKING A LITERARY APPROACH

Yosef has two dreams; in both of them, he sees objects that represent his family bowing down to him. How are these dreams understood? Both Yaakov and his sons interpret Yosef's dreams as reflecting Yosef's ambitions and his desire to rule. Yosef seems to interpret them this way as well; he aspires to become the leader of the House of Yaakov.

Yosef's brothers do not accept his dream. Apparently, the brothers did not see Yosef's dreams as prophetic; rather, they were simply expressions of his subconscious desires. They do not consider him fit for leadership. Why?

First, their hatred of him, as described at the beginning of the *parasha* – "And they hated him, and they could not speak peacefully to him" – could certainly have caused them to doubt his leadership abilities. But beyond their natural jealousy and competitiveness, the brothers might have sensed that a grave error was set to occur. Yaakov loved Yosef very much – he was the son of Yaakov's beloved, barren wife – and Yosef dreamed of greatness. The brothers, however, know Yosef's nature. They feel that Yosef's rising importance in Yaakov's house is inappropriate, and that he should not be allowed to rule over them.

Why did the brothers feel that Yosef was not worthy of leading them?

Before we answer this question, it should be noted that Yaakov, too, ultimately concluded that Yosef was not suitable for leadership; as mentioned above, this role was later given to Yehuda (see Bereshit 49:8–10). However, the brothers, who grew up with Yosef, already perceived during his youth that he was not fit to lead them.

The Torah foreshadows this conclusion in a number of places: Yosef chooses to inform his father of his brothers' misdeeds, rather than rebuke them and attempt to resolve the issue. This demonstrates his inability to influence his brothers positively and his ineffectiveness as a leader in his own right. Yosef, "the young man, was with the sons of Bilha and the sons of Zilpa" (37:2), the sons of the maidservants. To his other brothers, this may have indicated that Yosef could not handle leading more powerful elements, and instead preferred to associate with marginal groups in society.

In addition, the special treatment that Yosef received from his father led to his isolation from his brothers, further harming his chances of being able to lead them. These signs can be interpreted in a number of ways – they are not absolute proof that Yosef was unfit to lead. At the same time, as Yosef is ultimately not chosen to lead the House of Yaakov, these details can be interpreted as the first signs that Yosef is not suited for leadership.

This perspective may offer some insight into the brothers' cruel behavior in selling Yosef. Their decision to sell him was not motivated by anger or jealousy alone, but by a feeling of responsibility toward their family. They were aware of the episodes in their father's and grandfather's families in which the unsuitable son was rejected completely and banished from the house (as was done to Yishmael and Esav). The brothers feel that it is their responsibility to act, and they banish Yosef, having judged him unfit to rule.

The brothers decide to act because they feel that Yaakov cannot see what they see. In selling Yosef, the brothers perceive themselves as emulating their father – Yaakov deceived Yitzḥak in order to take Esav's blessing, so as to prevent Yitzḥak from giving the blessing to someone unworthy of it. The brothers were attempting

12 When his brothers had gone to pasture their father's flock near Shekhem, Yisrael said to
13 Yosef, "Come, your brothers are pasturing the flocks near Shekhem; I will send you to
14 them." Yosef said, "Here I am." He said to him, "Go and see how your brothers and the
flocks are doing, and bring me back word," and he sent him from the Ḥevron Valley, from
15 where he walked to Shekhem. A man found him wandering lost among the fields and asked
16 him, "What are you looking for?" He replied, "I'm looking for my brothers. Can you tell
17 me where they are pasturing the sheep?" "They have moved on from here," said the man.
"I heard them say, 'Let us go to Dotan.'" So Yosef went after his brothers and found them
18 at Dotan. They saw him in the distance, and by the time he reached them, they had plotted
19 to kill him. "Here comes the dreamer!" they said to one another. "Now let us kill him and
20 throw him into one of the pits – we can say that a wild animal ate him – then we shall see
21 what will come of his dreams!" When Reuven heard this, he tried to save him from them;

UNLOCKING THE TEXT

- Why wasn't Yosef with the brothers in Shekhem?
- Who is the man and why does the Torah include this detail in the story?
- Why didn't Reuven stand up to the brothers and save him on the spot?
- Why does the Torah not record Yosef's voice in this story?
- If the pit was empty, why is it necessary to also state that there was no water? And why include this detail in the narrative at all?
- What caused Yehuda's change of mind? If his objection was on moral grounds, why did he not fully save Yosef?
- Who are all the people mentioned in the sale of Yosef, what role did each play, and why is the text so unclear about the role that each had?
- Why is it important to state what the Ishmaelites were carrying in their caravan?
- Why does the Torah only state the price the Midianites paid for Yosef (and not the other transactions that took place in the story)?
- Why did Yaakov refuse to be comforted?

FINDING YOURSELF IN THE TEXT

- Have you ever stood up to your friends when they were doing something you felt was wrong?
- Have you ever had to deliver bad news to someone you cared about?
- Have you ever experienced grief that felt like it would never go away?

Consider using these questions as the basis for your own commentary or creative midrash.

How does reflecting on these firsthand experiences help you better understand the text?

יב יג וַיֵּלְכוּ אֶחָיו לִרְעוֹת אֶת־צֹאן אֲבִיהֶם בִּשְׁכֶם׃ וַיֹּאמֶר יִשְׂרָאֵל אֶל־יוֹסֵף הֲלוֹא אַחֶיךָ שני
יד רֹעִים בִּשְׁכֶם לְכָה וְאֶשְׁלָחֲךָ אֲלֵיהֶם וַיֹּאמֶר לוֹ הִנֵּנִי׃ וַיֹּאמֶר לוֹ לֶךְ־נָא רְאֵה אֶת־
שְׁלוֹם אַחֶיךָ וְאֶת־שְׁלוֹם הַצֹּאן וַהֲשִׁבֵנִי דָּבָר וַיִּשְׁלָחֵהוּ מֵעֵמֶק חֶבְרוֹן וַיָּבֹא שְׁכֶמָה׃
טו טז וַיִּמְצָאֵהוּ אִישׁ וְהִנֵּה תֹעֶה בַּשָּׂדֶה וַיִּשְׁאָלֵהוּ הָאִישׁ לֵאמֹר מַה־תְּבַקֵּשׁ׃ וַיֹּאמֶר
יז אֶת־אַחַי אָנֹכִי מְבַקֵּשׁ הַגִּידָה־נָּא לִי אֵיפֹה הֵם רֹעִים׃ וַיֹּאמֶר הָאִישׁ נָסְעוּ מִזֶּה
יח כִּי שָׁמַעְתִּי אֹמְרִים נֵלְכָה דֹּתָיְנָה וַיֵּלֶךְ יוֹסֵף אַחַר אֶחָיו וַיִּמְצָאֵם בְּדֹתָן׃ וַיִּרְאוּ אֹתוֹ
יט מֵרָחֹק וּבְטֶרֶם יִקְרַב אֲלֵיהֶם וַיִּתְנַכְּלוּ אֹתוֹ לַהֲמִיתוֹ׃ וַיֹּאמְרוּ אִישׁ אֶל־אָחִיו הִנֵּה
כ בַּעַל הַחֲלֹמוֹת הַלָּזֶה בָּא׃ וְעַתָּה ׀ לְכוּ וְנַהַרְגֵהוּ וְנַשְׁלִכֵהוּ בְּאַחַד הַבֹּרוֹת וְאָמַרְנוּ
כא חַיָּה רָעָה אֲכָלָתְהוּ וְנִרְאֶה מַה־יִּהְיוּ חֲלֹמֹתָיו׃ וַיִּשְׁמַע רְאוּבֵן וַיַּצִּלֵהוּ מִיָּדָם וַיֹּאמֶר

THEMES | RELATIONSHIPS AND LOVE | LEADERSHIP | ETHICS

Episode 54: *The Sale of Yosef* – Bereshit 37:12–36

SUMMARY

One day, as Yosef's brothers are tending the flocks far from home, Yaakov sends Yosef to see how they are doing. The entire future of the children of Israel depends on this encounter. The brothers see Yosef from afar, and the sight of the cloak enrages them. They realize that, alone, with no one to witness, they can kill Yosef and concoct a tale that will be impossible to refute. Only Reuven protests. While Reuven is somewhere else, Yosef is taken from the pit and sold to a passing caravan of merchants who carry him to Egypt to be sold as a slave. Reuven, unaware of all this, returns to the pit to rescue Yosef but finds him gone. The brothers dip Yosef's coat in blood. They bring it back to their father and ask him to identify it as Yosef's. Yaakov recognizes it and mourns his son.

22 "Let us not kill him," he said. "Do not shed blood," said Reuven. "Throw him into this pit in
the desert, but do not lay hands on him." His plan was to rescue him and bring him back to
23 his father. So when Yosef came to his brothers, they stripped him of his robe, the ornately
24 colored robe he was wearing, and they took him and threw him into the pit. The pit was
25 empty; there was no water in it. And they sat down and ate their meal. Looking up, they
saw a caravan of Ishmaelites coming from Gilad, their camels laden with spices, balm, and
26 myrrh, to be taken to Egypt. Yehuda said to his brothers, "What do we gain by killing our
27 brother and covering his blood? Let's sell him to the Ishmaelites and not harm him with
our own hands. After all, he is our brother, our own flesh and blood." His brothers agreed.
28 Some Midianite traders passed by and they pulled Yosef up out of the pit, and they sold him
29 to the Ishmaelites for twenty pieces of silver. They then brought Yosef to Egypt. Reuven
30 returned to the pit – and Yosef was not there. He tore his clothes, went back to his brothers,
31 and said, "The boy is gone, and I – where can I turn?" They took Yosef's robe, slaughtered
32 a goat, and dipped the robe in the blood. They had the ornately colored robe brought to
their father, and they said, "We found this. Try to identify it. Is it your son's robe or not?"
33 He recognized it and said, "It is my son's robe! A wild animal must have eaten him! Yosef
34 has been torn limb from limb!" Yaakov tore his clothes, put sackcloth on his loins, and
35 mourned for his son for many days. All his sons and daughters tried to comfort him, but
he refused to be comforted and said, "I will go down to Sheol[1] mourning for my son." His
36 father wept for him. Meanwhile, the Medanites had sold him in Egypt to Potifar, one of
Pharaoh's officials, captain of the guard.

1 | The netherworld.

TO YAAKOV

- What were your concerns regarding your sons that led you to send Yosef on this mission?
- Did you believe your sons when they informed you that Yosef was dead?
- Why did you refuse to be comforted?

TO THE BROTHERS

- Did you really want to kill Yosef? Why?
- Why did you agree to Reuven and Yehuda's change of plan?
- How did it feel when you told your father that Yosef was dead?
- Do you have any regrets?

TO REUVEN AND YEHUDA

- Why did you not want to kill Yosef?
- Why didn't you stand up to your brothers and stop them?
- What was your real motivation behind the plan you hatched?

כב לֹא נַכֶּנּוּ נָפֶשׁ׃ וַיֹּאמֶר אֲלֵהֶם ׀ רְאוּבֵן אַל־תִּשְׁפְּכוּ־דָם הַשְׁלִיכוּ אֹתוֹ אֶל־הַבּוֹר
הַזֶּה אֲשֶׁר בַּמִּדְבָּר וְיָד אַל־תִּשְׁלְחוּ־בוֹ לְמַעַן הַצִּיל אֹתוֹ מִיָּדָם לַהֲשִׁיבוֹ אֶל־אָבִיו׃
כג וַיְהִי כַּאֲשֶׁר־בָּא יוֹסֵף אֶל־אֶחָיו וַיַּפְשִׁיטוּ אֶת־יוֹסֵף אֶת־כֻּתָּנְתּוֹ אֶת־כְּתֹנֶת הַפַּסִּים שלישי
כד כה אֲשֶׁר עָלָיו׃ וַיִּקָּחֻהוּ וַיַּשְׁלִכוּ אֹתוֹ הַבֹּרָה וְהַבּוֹר רֵק אֵין בּוֹ מָיִם׃ וַיֵּשְׁבוּ לֶאֱכָל־לֶחֶם
וַיִּשְׂאוּ עֵינֵיהֶם וַיִּרְאוּ וְהִנֵּה אֹרְחַת יִשְׁמְעֵאלִים בָּאָה מִגִּלְעָד וּגְמַלֵּיהֶם נֹשְׂאִים
כו נְכֹאת וּצְרִי וָלֹט הוֹלְכִים לְהוֹרִיד מִצְרָיְמָה׃ וַיֹּאמֶר יְהוּדָה אֶל־אֶחָיו מַה־בֶּצַע כִּי
כז נַהֲרֹג אֶת־אָחִינוּ וְכִסִּינוּ אֶת־דָּמוֹ׃ לְכוּ וְנִמְכְּרֶנּוּ לַיִּשְׁמְעֵאלִים וְיָדֵנוּ אַל־תְּהִי־בוֹ
כח כִּי־אָחִינוּ בְשָׂרֵנוּ הוּא וַיִּשְׁמְעוּ אֶחָיו׃ וַיַּעַבְרוּ אֲנָשִׁים מִדְיָנִים סֹחֲרִים וַיִּמְשְׁכוּ וַיַּעֲלוּ
אֶת־יוֹסֵף מִן־הַבּוֹר וַיִּמְכְּרוּ אֶת־יוֹסֵף לַיִּשְׁמְעֵאלִים בְּעֶשְׂרִים כָּסֶף וַיָּבִיאוּ אֶת־יוֹסֵף
כט ל מִצְרָיְמָה׃ וַיָּשָׁב רְאוּבֵן אֶל־הַבּוֹר וְהִנֵּה אֵין־יוֹסֵף בַּבּוֹר וַיִּקְרַע אֶת־בְּגָדָיו׃ וַיָּשָׁב
לא אֶל־אֶחָיו וַיֹּאמַר הַיֶּלֶד אֵינֶנּוּ וַאֲנִי אָנָה אֲנִי־בָא׃ וַיִּקְחוּ אֶת־כְּתֹנֶת יוֹסֵף וַיִּשְׁחֲטוּ
לב שְׂעִיר עִזִּים וַיִּטְבְּלוּ אֶת־הַכֻּתֹּנֶת בַּדָּם׃ וַיְשַׁלְּחוּ אֶת־כְּתֹנֶת הַפַּסִּים וַיָּבִיאוּ אֶל־
לג אֲבִיהֶם וַיֹּאמְרוּ זֹאת מָצָאנוּ הַכֶּר־נָא הַכְּתֹנֶת בִּנְךָ הִוא אִם־לֹא׃ וַיַּכִּירָהּ וַיֹּאמֶר
לד כְּתֹנֶת בְּנִי חַיָּה רָעָה אֲכָלָתְהוּ טָרֹף טֹרַף יוֹסֵף׃ וַיִּקְרַע יַעֲקֹב שִׂמְלֹתָיו וַיָּשֶׂם שַׂק
לה בְּמָתְנָיו וַיִּתְאַבֵּל עַל־בְּנוֹ יָמִים רַבִּים׃ וַיָּקֻמוּ כָל־בָּנָיו וְכָל־בְּנֹתָיו לְנַחֲמוֹ וַיְמָאֵן
לו לְהִתְנַחֵם וַיֹּאמֶר כִּי־אֵרֵד אֶל־בְּנִי אָבֵל שְׁאֹלָה וַיֵּבְךְּ אֹתוֹ אָבִיו׃ וְהַמְּדָנִים מָכְרוּ
אֹתוֹ אֶל־מִצְרָיִם לְפוֹטִיפַר סְרִיס פַּרְעֹה שַׂר הַטַּבָּחִים׃

A QUESTION OF BIBLIODRAMA

TO YOSEF

- How did you feel when your father gave you the task to report on your brothers' welfare?
- Can you tell us anything about the man you met along the way? How did you feel toward him?
- What were your thoughts about your brothers as you approached them?
- Did you know the extent of their hatred toward you? Did you think they were capable of killing you?
- What was going through your head as they lowered you into the pit?

THE ART OF MIDRASH

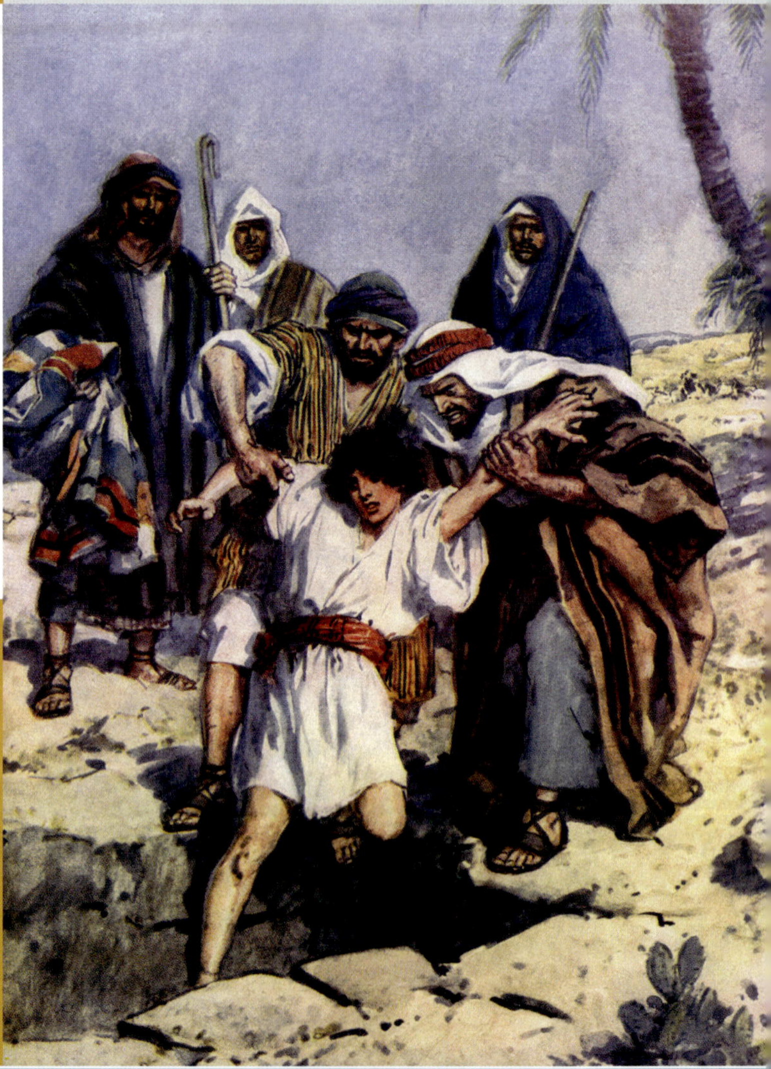

Joseph's Brothers Throw Him in the Pit
C. E. Brock (1928)

Analysis

- Which elements of this image are directly mentioned in the text?
- Which elements of this image are not found in the text?
- What midrashic interpretation could be inferred from this image?

Analysis

- What areas of archaeological, geographical, and historical knowledge do we have now that were unavailable to classical Jewish commentators? How can they aid our understanding of the text?
- What can we learn from this essay to help us understand the text?
- What further questions on the text do you have now that you have read this essay?

INTEGRATING ḤOKHMA

Recall that Yosef met his brothers while they were grazing their sheep in the hilly area of Dotan (Bereshit 37:17), north of Shekhem. During their meal, the brothers "lifted up their eyes" and noticed a caravan of Ishmaelites traveling down from the Gilad (the northern mountain range in Jordan), on its way to Egypt (37:25). Most assume that this convoy will soon pass near the spot where the brothers are eating. However, when we consider the geography involved, it is more probable to arrive at a very different conclusion.

This caravan of Ishmaelites (camels et al.) most likely should be traveling along the ancient trade route (better known as the Via Maris), which crosses through Emek Yizrael (the Jezreel Valley) on its way toward the Mediterranean coast. Therefore, this convoy, now sighted by the brothers as it descends from the Gilad Mountains in Transjordan, must first pass through the Beit She'an valley, continuing on toward Afula and Megiddo in Emek Yizrael, on its way toward the coast. Certainly, it would not pass the hilly area of Dotan, for it would make no sense for the caravan to climb the Gilboa mountain range to cross through the Dotan area to reach the coast.

Dotan, today the area of Jenin (about twenty kilometers north of Shekhem) lies about ten kilometers south of this main highway (the Via Maris) as it crosses Emek Yizrael. In altitude, Dotan sits about three hundred to four hundred meters above Emek Yizrael. Hence, from the hills of the Dotan/Gilboa area (where the brothers are eating lunch), one has a nice view of both the Gilad and parts of the Jezreel Valley. However, the trade route itself follows through a valley that cuts between the mountains.

This explains why the brothers are able to see an Ishmaelite caravan as it was descending from the Gilad toward Beit She'an on its way to Emek Yizrael. Even though it was in sight, it was still far enough away to allow the brothers at least several hours to meet it, when it would pass some ten kilometers to the north. Therefore, in order to sell Yosef to that caravan, the brothers would have to first fetch Yosef from the pit, and carry him on a short trip till they met the caravan in Emek Yizrael. They have ample time to first "finish their meal," go fetch Yosef from the pit in the *midbar* (on their way to the valley), and then meet the convoy to sell Yosef.

Rabbi Menachem Leibtag

Note the word *vayashov*, "and Reuven returned," in both verse 29 and verse 30. This proves that the brothers could not have been eating near the pit, for if so, Reuven would not need to "return" to them. Since Reuven and his brothers are eating away from the pit, Reuven must first return to the pit, then he must return back to his brothers to tell them the news – hence twice the verb *vayashov*.

Rabbi Menachem Leibtag

וַיְשַׁלְחוּ־בוֹ לְמַעַן הַ

לְ־אֶחָיו וַיַּפְשִׁיטוּ אֶת־יוֹסֵף אֶ

יַּשְׁלִכוּ אֹתוֹ הַבֹּרָה וְהַבּוֹר רֵק אֵין נ

וּ וְהִנֵּה אֹרְחַת יִשְׁמְעֵאלִים בָּאָה נ

לְכִים לְהוֹרִיד מִצְרָיְמָה: וַיֹּאמֶר יְהוּ

זִינוּ אֶת־דָּמוֹ: לְכוּ וְנִמְכְּרֶנּוּ לַיִּשְׁמ

יִשְׁמְעוּ אֶחָיו: וַיַּעַבְרוּ אֲנָשִׁים

אֶת־יוֹסֵף לַיִּשְׁמְעֵאל

TAKING A LITERARY APPROACH

Let's take a careful look at the next verse, noting its grammar:

> And a group of Midianite traders passed by, and they pulled, and they lifted Yosef out of the pit, and they sold Yosef to the Ishmaelites for twenty pieces of silver, and brought Yosef to Egypt. (Bereshit 37:28)

Based on the wording of this verse, it's quite clear that the Midianites and the Ishmaelites are two different groups of people. To support this, note how the Torah describes the Midianites as local "traders" (*soḥarim*), while the Ishmaelites are described as international "movers" (*orḥat Yishmaelim* – a transport caravan). A simple reading of this verse implies that a group of Midianite traders happened to pass by the pit (they most probably heard Yosef screaming), and pulled him out. As these Midianites are "traders," they were probably on their way to sell their wares (now including Yosef) to the Ishmaelite caravan.

If this explanation is correct, then the Midianites themselves pulled Yosef out of the pit and sold him. Where were the brothers during all of this? Most probably, still eating! Recall our explanation above: The brothers had thrown Yosef into a pit out in the *midbar* and returned to their grazing area to eat. They are far enough away that they do not see or hear what transpired between Yosef and the Midianites!

And where was Reuven? Again, as we explained above, he must have been eating with his brothers. However, as soon as he heard Yehuda's new plan (and the brothers' agreement) to sell Yosef, he would have to get back to the pit (before his brothers) to save Yosef – and that's exactly what he does! But it's too late. Note how this explanation fits perfectly into the next verse: "And Reuven returned [*vayashov*] to the pit, and behold, Yosef was no longer in the pit! Then he tore his clothes" (37:29).

Reuven is not the last brother to find out that Yosef was sold (as is commonly assumed). Rather, he is the first brother to recognize that Yosef is missing!

What can Reuven do? Shocked, he immediately returns to his brothers (probably eating dessert by now) with the terrible news: "And he returned [*vayashov*] to his brothers and said, 'The boy is gone! And as for myself, what am I going to do?'" (37:30).

38 1 Around that time, Yehuda left his brothers and camped near an Adulamite named Ḥira.
2 There, Yehuda met the daughter of Shua, a Canaanite, and he married her and came to
3 4 her. She became pregnant and had a son, whom he named Er. She became pregnant again
5 and had another son, and she named him Onan. She had yet another son and named him
6 Shela; Yehuda was in Keziv when she gave birth to him. Yehuda took a wife for his firstborn,
7 Er; her name was Tamar. But Er, Yehuda's firstborn, was wicked in the Lord's sight, and
8 the Lord took his life. Yehuda then said to Onan, "Go in to your brother's wife and fulfill
9 your duty as her brother-in-law.[1] Provide children for your brother." But Onan knew that
the children would not be considered his. Whenever he came to his brother's wife, he let
his seed go to waste on the ground so as not to have children in his brother's name. What
10 11 he did was wicked in the Lord's sight, and so He took his life also. Then Yehuda said to
his daughter-in-law Tamar, "Live as a widow in your father's house until my son Shela
grows up" – for he thought he too might die like his brothers. So Tamar went to live in
12 her father's house. A long time passed, and Yehuda's wife, Shua's daughter, died. When
he had completed his time of mourning, he and his neighbor Ḥira the Adulamite went to

1 | On levirate marriage, see Devarim 25:5–10.

UNLOCKING THE TEXT

- Why does the Torah break with the narrative of Yosef to tell this story?
- Why did Yehuda leave his brothers at this time?
- What is the significance of Yehuda marrying a Canaanite woman?
- What was Er's sin?
- Why did Onan not want to fulfill this duty?
- Why was Tamar so driven to marry Shela?
- What was the end goal of Tamar's plan?
- What is a "cult prostitute"?
- Why did Yehuda not marry Tamar after he found out about the pregnancy?
- What is the significance of the birthing story of Peretz and Zeraḥ?

FINDING YOURSELF IN THE TEXT

- Have you ever hurt someone in order to protect someone else?
- Have you ever felt that you were destined for something despite it feeling like a distant possibility at the time?
- Have you ever been proven wrong when you were convinced you were right? How did that feel?

Consider using these questions as the basis for your own commentary or creative midrash.

How does reflecting on these firsthand experiences help you better understand the text?

לח א וַיְהִי בָּעֵת הַהִוא וַיֵּרֶד יְהוּדָה מֵאֵת אֶחָיו וַיֵּט עַד־אִישׁ עֲדֻלָּמִי וּשְׁמוֹ חִירָה׃ לד רביעי
ב ג וַיַּרְא־שָׁם יְהוּדָה בַּת־אִישׁ כְּנַעֲנִי וּשְׁמוֹ שׁוּעַ וַיִּקָּחֶהָ וַיָּבֹא אֵלֶיהָ׃ וַתַּהַר וַתֵּלֶד
ד ה בֵּן וַיִּקְרָא אֶת־שְׁמוֹ עֵר׃ וַתַּהַר עוֹד וַתֵּלֶד בֵּן וַתִּקְרָא אֶת־שְׁמוֹ אוֹנָן׃ וַתֹּסֶף עוֹד
ו וַתֵּלֶד בֵּן וַתִּקְרָא אֶת־שְׁמוֹ שֵׁלָה וְהָיָה בִכְזִיב בְּלִדְתָּהּ אֹתוֹ׃ וַיִּקַּח יְהוּדָה אִשָּׁה
ז לְעֵר בְּכוֹרוֹ וּשְׁמָהּ תָּמָר׃ וַיְהִי עֵר בְּכוֹר יְהוּדָה רַע בְּעֵינֵי יְהוָה וַיְמִתֵהוּ יְהוָה׃
ח ט וַיֹּאמֶר יְהוּדָה לְאוֹנָן בֹּא אֶל־אֵשֶׁת אָחִיךָ וְיַבֵּם אֹתָהּ וְהָקֵם זֶרַע לְאָחִיךָ׃ וַיֵּדַע
אוֹנָן כִּי לֹּא לוֹ יִהְיֶה הַזָּרַע וְהָיָה אִם־בָּא אֶל־אֵשֶׁת אָחִיו וְשִׁחֵת אַרְצָה לְבִלְתִּי
יא נְתָן־זֶרַע לְאָחִיו׃ וַיֵּרַע בְּעֵינֵי יְהוָה אֲשֶׁר עָשָׂה וַיָּמֶת גַּם־אֹתוֹ׃ וַיֹּאמֶר יְהוּדָה
לְתָמָר כַּלָּתוֹ שְׁבִי אַלְמָנָה בֵית־אָבִיךְ עַד־יִגְדַּל שֵׁלָה בְנִי כִּי אָמַר פֶּן־יָמוּת גַּם־
יב הוּא כְּאֶחָיו וַתֵּלֶךְ תָּמָר וַתֵּשֶׁב בֵּית אָבִיהָ׃ וַיִּרְבּוּ הַיָּמִים וַתָּמָת בַּת־שׁוּעַ אֵשֶׁת־
יְהוּדָה וַיִּנָּחֶם יְהוּדָה וַיַּעַל עַל־גֹּזְזֵי צֹאנוֹ הוּא וְחִירָה רֵעֵהוּ הָעֲדֻלָּמִי תִּמְנָתָה׃

THEMES	RELATIONSHIPS AND LOVE	LEADERSHIP	ETHICS

Episode 55: *Yehuda and Tamar* – Bereshit 38:1–30

SUMMARY

The Torah interrupts its narrative of Yosef's life to focus on an entirely unrelated story involving Yehuda, one of Yosef's older brothers, who will eventually emerge as the most dominant of the brothers. This chapter, which describes the unique circumstances that lead to the births of Yehuda's primary successors, also reveals his character. Yehuda does not initially act with perfect righteousness; however, when faced with a difficult situation, he accepts responsibility for his actions and displays true greatness. As the narrative continues, this behavior will emerge as a common feature of Yehuda's personality. Although Yehuda errs, he knows how to rectify and correct his failures. This quality will eventually become the hallmark of the tribe that descends from him.

The details of this seemingly tangential episode underscore an important principle concerning the great characters of the Torah: The Torah does not seek to cover up imperfections; it tells the truth, even though it may be unpleasant. An individual's successes and failures are each related in their entirety, without omission or bias. Consequently, the complete story of Yehuda is recorded in the Torah: his descent, the details of his unseemly actions, and ultimately, the rectification of those actions.

13 join his sheepshearers in Timna. Tamar was told, "Your father-in-law is going to Timna
14 to shear his sheep." And she took off her widow's clothes and covered herself with a veil.
Disguised, she sat at the entrance to Einayim on the road to Timna, for she had seen that
15 Shela was now grown up and yet she had not been given to him as a wife. Yehuda saw her
16 and thought she was a prostitute, because she had covered her face. Not realizing that she
was his daughter-in-law, he turned aside to her on the road and said, "Come, let me sleep
17 with you." She said, "What will you give me to sleep with you?" He said, "I will send you a
young goat from my flock." "Only if you give me something as a pledge until you send it,"
18 she said. "What pledge should I give you?" he asked. She answered, "Your seal and cord, and
the staff in your hand." He gave them to her and went in to her – and she became pregnant
19 by him. She got up and left, removed her veil, and put on her widow's clothes again. And
20 Yehuda sent the young goat by his neighbor the Adulamite, to recover the pledge from the
21 woman, but he could not find her. He asked the local men, "Where is the cult prostitute,[2]
the one by the roadside at Einayim?" They said, "No cult prostitute has been here." So he
22 went back to Yehuda and said, "I could not find her. Besides, the local men said that there
23 was no cult prostitute there." Yehuda said, "Let her keep what she has or we will become a
laughingstock. I tried to send her this young goat, but you could not find her." About three
24 months later, Yehuda was told, "Your daughter-in-law Tamar has behaved as a loose woman;
in fact she has become pregnant by her harlotry." "Take her out and let her be burned,"
25 Yehuda said. As she was being brought out, she sent her father-in-law a message: "I am
pregnant by the man to whom these belong." She added, "Please identify to whom this
26 seal and cord and staff belong." Yehuda recognized them and said, "She is more righteous
than I. It was because I did not give her to Shela my son." He did not know her intimately
27 again. When the time came for her to give birth: there were twins in her womb. As she was
28 in labor one child put out a hand, so the midwife took a crimson thread and tied it to his
29 wrist, saying, "This one came out first." But he pulled his hand back and then his brother
came out. She said, "How you have burst through!" So he was named Peretz.[3] Then his
30 brother came out with the crimson thread on his wrist. He was named Zeraḥ.[4]

---

2 | A type of prostitute associated with religious worship.

3 | Meaning "bursting through."

4 | The term *zeraḥ* means "shining," an apparent reference to the color of the thread.

יג יד וַיֻּגַּ֥ד לְתָמָ֖ר לֵאמֹ֑ר הִנֵּ֥ה חָמִ֛יךְ עֹלֶ֥ה תִמְנָ֖תָה לָגֹ֥ז צֹאנֽוֹ׃ וַתָּסַר֩ בִּגְדֵ֨י אַלְמְנוּתָ֜הּ
מֵעָלֶ֗יהָ וַתְּכַ֤ס בַּצָּעִיף֙ וַתִּתְעַלָּ֔ף וַתֵּ֙שֶׁב֙ בְּפֶ֣תַח עֵינַ֔יִם אֲשֶׁ֖ר עַל־דֶּ֣רֶךְ תִּמְנָ֑תָה כִּ֤י
טו רָאֲתָה֙ כִּֽי־גָדַ֣ל שֵׁלָ֔ה וְהִ֕וא לֹֽא־נִתְּנָ֥ה ל֖וֹ לְאִשָּֽׁה׃ וַיִּרְאֶ֣הָ יְהוּדָ֔ה וַֽיַּחְשְׁבֶ֖הָ לְזוֹנָ֑ה
טז כִּ֥י כִסְּתָ֖ה פָּנֶֽיהָ׃ וַיֵּ֨ט אֵלֶ֜יהָ אֶל־הַדֶּ֗רֶךְ וַיֹּ֙אמֶר֙ הָֽבָה נָּא֙ אָב֣וֹא אֵלַ֔יִךְ כִּ֚י לֹ֣א יָדַ֔ע
יז כִּ֥י כַלָּת֖וֹ הִ֑וא וַתֹּ֙אמֶר֙ מַה־תִּתֶּן־לִּ֔י כִּ֥י תָב֖וֹא אֵלָֽי׃ וַיֹּ֕אמֶר אָנֹכִ֛י אֲשַׁלַּ֥ח גְּדִֽי־עִזִּ֖ים
יח מִן־הַצֹּ֑אן וַתֹּ֕אמֶר אִם־תִּתֵּ֥ן עֵרָב֖וֹן עַ֥ד שָׁלְחֶֽךָ׃ וַיֹּ֗אמֶר מָ֣ה הָעֵרָבוֹן֮ אֲשֶׁ֣ר אֶתֶּן־לָּךְ֒
יט וַתֹּ֗אמֶר חֹתָֽמְךָ֙ וּפְתִילֶ֔ךָ וּמַטְּךָ֖ אֲשֶׁ֣ר בְּיָדֶ֑ךָ וַיִּתֶּן־לָ֛הּ וַיָּבֹ֥א אֵלֶ֖יהָ וַתַּ֥הַר לֽוֹ׃ וַתָּ֣קָם
כ וַתֵּ֔לֶךְ וַתָּ֥סַר צְעִיפָ֖הּ מֵעָלֶ֑יהָ וַתִּלְבַּ֖שׁ בִּגְדֵ֥י אַלְמְנוּתָֽהּ׃ וַיִּשְׁלַ֨ח יְהוּדָ֜ה אֶת־גְּדִ֣י
כא הָֽעִזִּ֗ים בְּיַד֙ רֵעֵ֣הוּ הָֽעֲדֻלָּמִ֔י לָקַ֥חַת הָעֵרָב֖וֹן מִיַּ֣ד הָאִשָּׁ֑ה וְלֹ֖א מְצָאָֽהּ׃ וַיִּשְׁאַ֞ל
אֶת־אַנְשֵׁ֤י מְקֹמָהּ֙ לֵאמֹ֔ר אַיֵּ֧ה הַקְּדֵשָׁ֛ה הִ֥וא בָעֵינַ֖יִם עַל־הַדָּ֑רֶךְ וַיֹּ֣אמְר֔וּ לֹא־הָיְתָ֥ה
כב בָזֶ֖ה קְדֵשָֽׁה׃ וַיָּ֙שָׁב֙ אֶל־יְהוּדָ֔ה וַיֹּ֖אמֶר לֹ֣א מְצָאתִ֑יהָ וְגַ֨ם אַנְשֵׁ֤י הַמָּקוֹם֙ אָֽמְר֔וּ לֹא־
כג הָיְתָ֥ה בָזֶ֖ה קְדֵשָֽׁה׃ וַיֹּ֤אמֶר יְהוּדָה֙ תִּֽקַּח־לָ֔הּ פֶּ֖ן נִהְיֶ֣ה לָב֑וּז הִנֵּ֤ה שָׁלַ֙חְתִּי֙ הַגְּדִ֣י
כד הַזֶּ֔ה וְאַתָּ֖ה לֹ֥א מְצָאתָֽהּ׃ וַיְהִ֣י ׀ כְּמִשְׁלֹ֣שׁ חֳדָשִׁ֗ים וַיֻּגַּ֨ד לִֽיהוּדָ֤ה לֵאמֹר֙ זָֽנְתָה֙ תָּמָ֣ר
כה כַּלָּתֶ֔ךָ וְגַ֛ם הִנֵּ֥ה הָרָ֖ה לִזְנוּנִ֑ים וַיֹּ֣אמֶר יְהוּדָ֔ה הוֹצִיא֖וּהָ וְתִשָּׂרֵֽף׃ הִ֣וא מוּצֵ֗את וְהִ֨יא
שָׁלְחָ֤ה אֶל־חָמִ֙יהָ֙ לֵאמֹ֔ר לְאִישׁ֙ אֲשֶׁר־אֵ֣לֶּה לּ֔וֹ אָנֹכִ֖י הָרָ֑ה וַתֹּ֙אמֶר֙ הַכֶּר־נָ֔א לְמִ֞י
כו הַחֹתֶ֧מֶת וְהַפְּתִילִ֛ים וְהַמַּטֶּ֖ה הָאֵֽלֶּה׃ וַיַּכֵּ֣ר יְהוּדָ֗ה וַיֹּ֙אמֶר֙ צָֽדְקָ֣ה מִמֶּ֔נִּי כִּֽי־עַל־כֵּ֥ן
כז לֹא־נְתַתִּ֖יהָ לְשֵׁלָ֣ה בְנִ֑י וְלֹֽא־יָסַ֥ף ע֖וֹד לְדַעְתָּֽהּ׃ וַיְהִ֖י בְּעֵ֣ת לִדְתָּ֑הּ וְהִנֵּ֥ה תְאוֹמִ֖ים
כח בְּבִטְנָֽהּ׃ וַיְהִ֥י בְלִדְתָּ֖הּ וַיִּתֶּן־יָ֑ד וַתִּקַּ֣ח הַמְיַלֶּ֗דֶת וַתִּקְשֹׁ֨ר עַל־יָד֤וֹ שָׁנִי֙ לֵאמֹ֔ר זֶ֖ה
כט יָצָ֥א רִאשֹׁנָֽה׃ וַיְהִ֣י ׀ כְּמֵשִׁ֣יב יָד֗וֹ וְהִנֵּה֙ יָצָ֣א אָחִ֔יו וַתֹּ֕אמֶר מַה־פָּרַ֖צְתָּ עָלֶ֣יךָ פָּ֑רֶץ
ל וַיִּקְרָ֥א שְׁמ֖וֹ פָּֽרֶץ׃ וְאַחַר֙ יָצָ֣א אָחִ֔יו אֲשֶׁ֥ר עַל־יָד֖וֹ הַשָּׁנִ֑י וַיִּקְרָ֥א שְׁמ֖וֹ זָֽרַח׃

THE ART OF MIDRASH

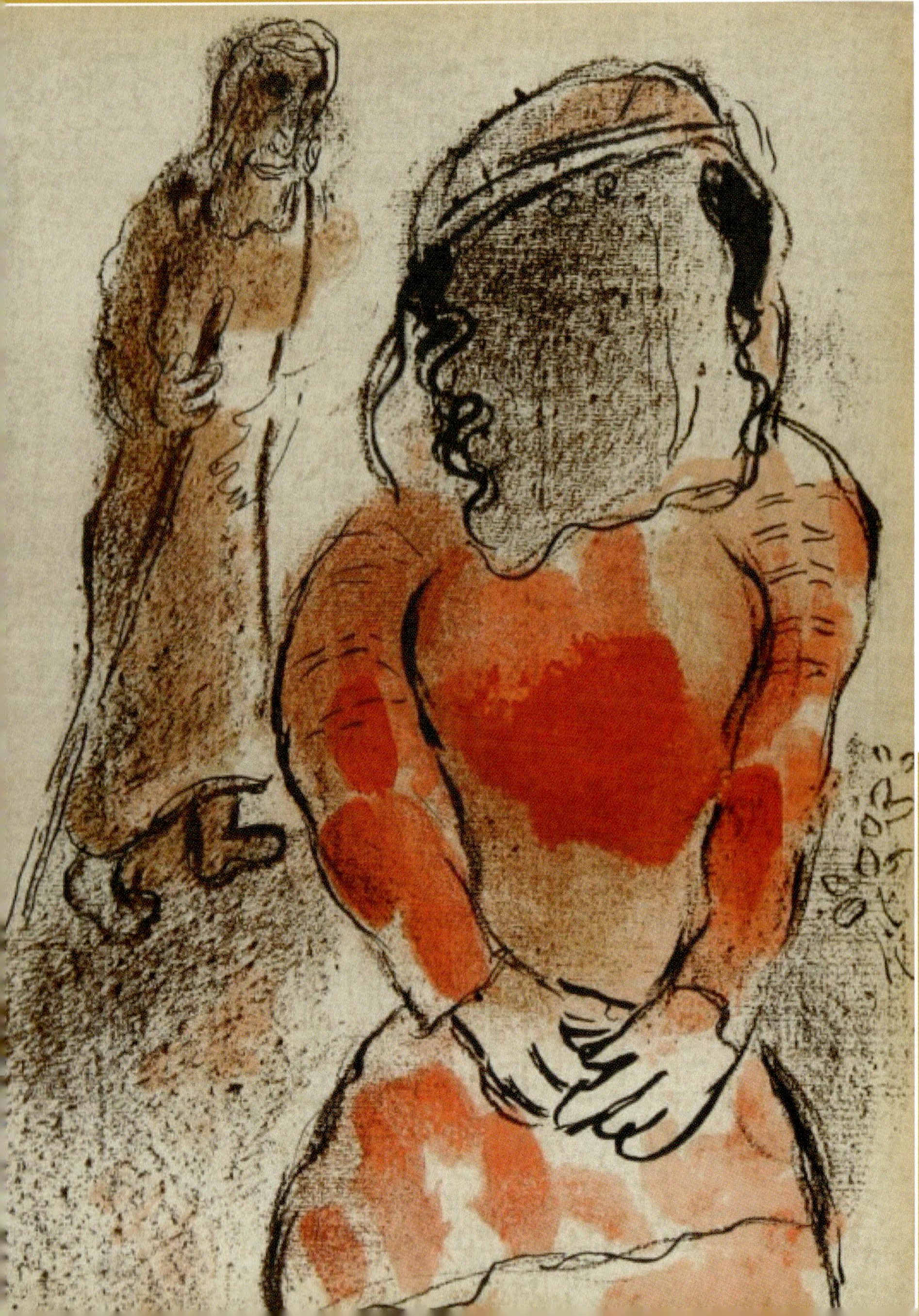

Tamar, Daughter-in-Law of Judah
Marc Chagall (1960)

Analysis

- Which elements of this image are directly mentioned in the text?
- Which elements of this image are not found in the text?
- What midrashic interpretation could be inferred from this image?

A QUESTION OF BIBLIODRAMA

TO YEHUDA

- Why did you leave your brothers at this time?
- Why do you think your sons died?
- Why did you prevent Tamar from marrying Shela?
- Why did you sleep with a prostitute instead of remarrying?
- How did it feel when Tamar proved herself more righteous than you?
- Did you have any other option to respond differently? Why did you choose to respond in this way?

TO TAMAR

- Do you think you were cursed that all your husbands would die?
- Why were you so adamant about marrying Shela?
- What was your goal in tricking Yehuda into sleeping with you?
- Did you fear for your life when you were brought to trial in front of Yehuda?
- Why did you protect Yehuda's identity?

Analysis

- What areas of archaeological, geographical, and historical knowledge do we have now that were unavailable to classical Jewish commentators? How can they aid our understanding of the text?
- How can this information about Timna help us understand the text?
- What further questions on the text do you have now that you have read this new information and research?

INTEGRATING ḤOKHMA

תִּמְנָה - TIMNA

A town in the northern Judean lowlands, Timna is mentioned twelve times. It is identified at Tel Batash in the Valley of Sorek, west of Tzora, about two kilometers south of the modern-day towns of Tzalfon and Tel Shaḥar, between ancient Ekron and Beit Shemesh. Excavations there revealed remains of a fortified city that was settled from the Middle Bronze Age until the Hellenistic era. Archaeological evidence is consistent with the biblical account: during the settlement period, the city was Philistine; during the tenth century BCE, it was an unwalled Israelite town; and from the ninth century BCE until its destruction by Sanḥeriv in 701 BCE, Timna was a walled, fortified city.[1]

View of Tel Batash

1| Yehoshua 15:57.

part with his youngest son, but to no avail. Yehuda, like Tamar, waits for the perfect time to make his move. He waits months, until the sacks run out of food, the children's bellies are empty, and their eyes are sad. He waits until the prospect of Yaakov watching his grandchildren starve to death is a palpable reality, and then he speaks. He speaks words laden with experience and empathy, for only Yehuda could empathize with the desire to protect a son who is all that remains of a bygone life. When Yehuda speaks to Yaakov, he speaks not as son to father, but as father to father. His words carry a depth of understanding that is both personal and profound. By trying to protect his youngest son, Yehuda explained, Yaakov was ensuring the certain death of all his offspring. Yaakov understood, because Yehuda understood, and eventually Yaakov acquiesced. And we come to realize that the admission of guilt that Tamar extracted from Yehuda set in motion a chain of events that culminated in the reunion of the budding nation of Israel.

Readers of Bereshit are struck by the fact that Tamar's impact continues to reverberate long after her name disappears from the page, but Tamar's story is not unique in that sense. Tanakh's influential women are exceptional, but they are not exceptions to Tanakh's rules. While Tanakh reflects a concrete historical reality, it simultaneously challenges that backdrop. Its chapters take place in a time when women were outranked by men, but Tanakh consistently undermines the notion that subordination implies inferiority. In Tanakh there are no uniquely male attributes that account for their dominance, and no uniquely female traits that could ever be used to justify their subservience. As Tikva Frymer-Kensky noted, contrasting the portrayal of biblical women from their Ancient Near Eastern literary counterparts, Tanakh doesn't resort to chauvinism to rationalize powerlessness. The Tanakh speaks matter-of-factly about female prophets, warriors, and leaders, and their eligibility is always taken as a given. Tanakh's protagonists are the products of a broader culture, but as Tamar's story demonstrates on several levels, the Tanakh implicitly condemns the suppositions underlying that culture, and in doing so, ensures that women earn a prominent place in our people's history.

Yael Leibowitz

TAKING A LITERARY APPROACH

Tamar stands at the center of a male-dominated drama about fathers and sons, brothers and viceroys. It is a drama that traces the elevation of Yehuda's eminence among his brothers, and accounts for his tribe's eventual leadership on the national scale. Tamar is the hinge on which that history hangs, but her actions, to be fully appreciated, need to be contextualized.

Years before Tamar steps onto the Biblical stage, Yehuda had already made a calamitous decision. The brothers, jealous of Yosef's favored position, hatched a plan to do away with the person who threatened their status. Yehuda had steered the sale of Yosef down to Egypt and then presented a misleadingly bloody cloak to his father. The brothers, hovering around their aging father, asked Yaakov to "please examine" the tattered garment, conjuring a nightmarish scene. Examine it he did, and with a broken heart he began mourning the imagined death of his favored son.

The brothers' disregard for the value of Yosef's life, and the prioritizing of their ego and pride over and above the cohesion and welfare of their family, fractured the household. So we are not surprised when we are told, in the aftermath of the sale, that Yehuda "left his brothers." Perhaps he was attempting to distance himself from the memories, and the grief, that in his father's home must have been all-consuming. But suppressing trauma doesn't make it disappear and disengaging from co-conspirators doesn't undo damage wrought. When Tamar asked Yehuda to "examine" his staff and seal, employing the identical words the brothers used when they handed their father the bloody cloak, she was doing more than just evoking a painful memory. Tamar was impelling him to realize that he was in the same position that he was all those years ago, and while it was too late for Yosef, it was not too late to do right by her. Tamar was asking Yehuda, *this time*, to prioritize the life of another over concern for his standing. With two hauntingly familiar words, she was imploring him, *this time*, to sacrifice his repute and save her life.

And that's exactly what he did. Yehuda's encounter with Tamar left him a changed person. And individuals who believe in the human ability to repent, and to change, and to grow from their mistakes, are those that are most ripe to lead.

Fast-forward to a time when Yehuda's twins are likely grown men themselves. Yosef, incognito, is ruling Egypt, and has sent the brothers home with the threat that if Binyamin does not join their next descent, Shimon will remain in prison. Reuven, the eldest, and default spokesperson, tries his hardest to persuade Yaakov to

39 1 Meanwhile, Yosef had been brought down to Egypt. Potifar, an Egyptian, one of
Pharaoh's officials and captain of the guard, had bought him from the Ishmaelites who
2 had brought him there. The LORD was with Yosef, and he became a successful man.
3 He lived in the house of his Egyptian master. And his master saw that the LORD was
4 with him and that the LORD granted him success in all he did; Yosef found favor in his
eyes and became his personal attendant. Potifar put him in charge of his household, giving
5 him responsibility for all he owned. From the moment he put him in charge of his household and all he owned, the LORD blessed the Egyptian because of Yosef. The LORD's
6 blessing was in all he owned, in house and field. And so he left all he had in Yosef's hands
and, with him there, he had no concern for anything but the food he ate.[1] Now, Yosef
7 was well built and handsome, and after a while, his master's wife cast her eyes on Yosef.
8 "Lie with me," she said. But he refused. "With me here," he told her, "my master does
not concern himself with the running of the house; he has entrusted me with all that he
9 owns. No one in this house has greater authority than I. He has withheld nothing from
me except you, because you are his wife. How could I do so great a wrong? It would be a
10 sin against God!" And though she spoke to Yosef day after day, he would not consent to
11 lie with her or be with her. One day he came into the house to do his work and none of
12 the other servants were there. She caught him by his cloak and said, "Lie with me!" He ran
away from her and fled outside. When she saw that he had left his cloak in her hand and

1 | Possibly a euphemism for his wife (cf. v. 9).

UNLOCKING THE TEXT

- What led to Poitifar, a senior official in the court of Pharaoh, buying Yosef as a slave?
- What were Yosef's responsibilities that he excelled at fulfilling that made it obvious to Potifar that God was with him?
- What does "the food he ate" refer to and why did Yosef not have responsibility for that also?
- Why is Yosef's physical appearance important to know?
- Why doesn't Yosef allow himself to be seduced?
- What does Potifar's wife mean when she says Yosef was "mocking" them?

FINDING YOURSELF IN THE TEXT

- Have you ever been so successful at something that it seemed obvious that God was helping you out?
- Have you ever been accused of something you did not do? How did that feel?
- Have your plans and progress in life ever been derailed through no fault of your own? How did you cope?

Consider using these questions as the basis for your own commentary or creative midrash.

How does reflecting on these firsthand experiences help you better understand the text?

לט א וְיוֹסֵף הוּרַד מִצְרָיְמָה וַיִּקְנֵהוּ פּוֹטִיפַר סְרִיס פַּרְעֹה שַׂר הַטַּבָּחִים אִישׁ מִצְרִי לה חמישי
ב מִיַּד הַיִּשְׁמְעֵאלִים אֲשֶׁר הוֹרִדֻהוּ שָׁמָּה: וַיְהִי יהוה אֶת־יוֹסֵף וַיְהִי אִישׁ מַצְלִיחַ
ג וַיְהִי בְּבֵית אֲדֹנָיו הַמִּצְרִי: וַיַּרְא אֲדֹנָיו כִּי יהוה אִתּוֹ וְכֹל אֲשֶׁר־הוּא עֹשֶׂה יהוה
ד מַצְלִיחַ בְּיָדוֹ: וַיִּמְצָא יוֹסֵף חֵן בְּעֵינָיו וַיְשָׁרֶת אֹתוֹ וַיַּפְקִדֵהוּ עַל־בֵּיתוֹ וְכָל־
ה יֶשׁ־לוֹ נָתַן בְּיָדוֹ: וַיְהִי מֵאָז הִפְקִיד אֹתוֹ בְּבֵיתוֹ וְעַל כָּל־אֲשֶׁר יֶשׁ־לוֹ וַיְבָרֶךְ
יהוה אֶת־בֵּית הַמִּצְרִי בִּגְלַל יוֹסֵף וַיְהִי בִּרְכַּת יהוה בְּכָל־אֲשֶׁר יֶשׁ־לוֹ בַּבַּיִת
ו וּבַשָּׂדֶה: וַיַּעֲזֹב כָּל־אֲשֶׁר־לוֹ בְּיַד־יוֹסֵף וְלֹא־יָדַע אִתּוֹ מְאוּמָה כִּי אִם־הַלֶּחֶם
ז אֲשֶׁר־הוּא אוֹכֵל וַיְהִי יוֹסֵף יְפֵה־תֹאַר וִיפֵה מַרְאֶה: וַיְהִי אַחַר הַדְּבָרִים הָאֵלֶּה ששי
ח וַתִּשָּׂא אֵשֶׁת־אֲדֹנָיו אֶת־עֵינֶיהָ אֶל־יוֹסֵף וַתֹּאמֶר שִׁכְבָה עִמִּי: וַיְמָאֵן ׀ וַיֹּאמֶר
אֶל־אֵשֶׁת אֲדֹנָיו הֵן אֲדֹנִי לֹא־יָדַע אִתִּי מַה־בַּבָּיִת וְכֹל אֲשֶׁר־יֶשׁ־לוֹ נָתַן בְּיָדִי:
ט אֵינֶנּוּ גָדוֹל בַּבַּיִת הַזֶּה מִמֶּנִּי וְלֹא־חָשַׂךְ מִמֶּנִּי מְאוּמָה כִּי אִם־אוֹתָךְ בַּאֲשֶׁר
י אַתְּ־אִשְׁתּוֹ וְאֵיךְ אֶעֱשֶׂה הָרָעָה הַגְּדֹלָה הַזֹּאת וְחָטָאתִי לֵאלֹהִים: וַיְהִי כְּדַבְּרָהּ
יא אֶל־יוֹסֵף יוֹם ׀ יוֹם וְלֹא־שָׁמַע אֵלֶיהָ לִשְׁכַּב אֶצְלָהּ לִהְיוֹת עִמָּהּ: וַיְהִי כְּהַיּוֹם הַזֶּה
יב וַיָּבֹא הַבַּיְתָה לַעֲשׂוֹת מְלַאכְתּוֹ וְאֵין אִישׁ מֵאַנְשֵׁי הַבַּיִת שָׁם בַּבָּיִת: וַתִּתְפְּשֵׂהוּ

THEMES | EXILE | GOD | ETHICS

Episode 56: *Yosef in the House of Potifar* – Bereshit 39:1–20

SUMMARY

The previous passage followed the path of Yehuda, the most prominent of Leah's sons, interrupting the main plot focusing on Yosef, Raḥel's firstborn. At this point in the narrative, the Torah continues Yosef's story from the time of his arrival in Egypt. Yosef is bought as a slave by Potifar, the chief executioner. With God's help, Yosef is successful at everything he does, so successful that Potifar recognizes his talents and puts him in charge of his household. Yosef's success brings great wealth to Potifar, so he trusts Yosef with everything. Potifar's wife attempts to seduce Yosef and when he resists, she accuses him of rape. When Potifar returns home, his wife tells him her story and he is enraged. Yosef is put into the prison where the royal prisoners are kept.

had run out of the house, she called out to her servants and said to them, "Look! He brought us a Hebrew to mock[2] us! He came to me to lie with me, but I screamed. And when he heard me scream and cry for help, he left his cloak with me and ran outside." She kept his cloak beside her until his master came home. Then she told him the same story: "The Hebrew slave you brought us came to me mock me. I screamed and called for help, and he left his cloak with me and ran outside." When his master heard the story his wife told him – "This is what your servant did to me!" – he was incensed. Yosef's master had him put in prison, where the king's prisoners were confined. He remained there in prison.

2 | This verb (*letzaḥek*) can have sexual connotations (cf., e.g., v. 17, 21:9, 26:8; Shemot 32:6).

A QUESTION OF BIBLIODRAMA

TO YOSEF

- What do you think is the source of your success in Potifar's house?
- What is the real reason that you resisted the advances of Potifar's wife?
- Does this experience, which ends in prison, feel similar to the story with your brothers? Why do you think these things are happening to you?

TO POTIFAR'S WIFE

- Why do you want to sleep with Yosef?
- How does his rejection feel?
- Why do you respond in this way?

TO POTIFAR

- Do you believe your wife?
- How do you feel about Yosef now?
- Why don't you execute Yosef rather than incarcerate him?

יג בִּבְגְדוֹ לֵאמֹר שִׁכְבָה עִמִּי וַיַּעֲזֹב בִּגְדוֹ בְּיָדָהּ וַיָּנׇס וַיֵּצֵא הַחוּצָה: וַיְהִי כִּרְאוֹתָהּ
יד כִּי־עָזַב בִּגְדוֹ בְּיָדָהּ וַיָּנׇס הַחוּצָה: וַתִּקְרָא לְאַנְשֵׁי בֵיתָהּ וַתֹּאמֶר לָהֶם לֵאמֹר רְאוּ
טו הֵבִיא לָנוּ אִישׁ עִבְרִי לְצַחֶק בָּנוּ בָּא אֵלַי לִשְׁכַּב עִמִּי וָאֶקְרָא בְּקוֹל גָּדוֹל: וַיְהִי
טז כְשׇׁמְעוֹ כִּי־הֲרִימֹתִי קוֹלִי וָאֶקְרָא וַיַּעֲזֹב בִּגְדוֹ אֶצְלִי וַיָּנׇס וַיֵּצֵא הַחוּצָה: וַתַּנַּח
יז בִּגְדוֹ אֶצְלָהּ עַד־בּוֹא אֲדֹנָיו אֶל־בֵּיתוֹ: וַתְּדַבֵּר אֵלָיו כַּדְּבָרִים הָאֵלֶּה לֵאמֹר בָּא
יח אֵלַי הָעֶבֶד הָעִבְרִי אֲשֶׁר־הֵבֵאתָ לָּנוּ לְצַחֶק בִּי: וַיְהִי כַּהֲרִימִי קוֹלִי וָאֶקְרָא וַיַּעֲזֹב
יט בִּגְדוֹ אֶצְלִי וַיָּנׇס הַחוּצָה: וַיְהִי כִשְׁמֹעַ אֲדֹנָיו אֶת־דִּבְרֵי אִשְׁתּוֹ אֲשֶׁר דִּבְּרָה אֵלָיו
כ לֵאמֹר כַּדְּבָרִים הָאֵלֶּה עָשָׂה לִי עַבְדֶּךָ וַיִּחַר אַפּוֹ: וַיִּקַּח אֲדֹנֵי יוֹסֵף אֹתוֹ וַיִּתְּנֵהוּ
אֶל־בֵּית הַסֹּהַר מְקוֹם אֲשֶׁר־אֲסוּרֵי הַמֶּלֶךְ אֲסוּרִים וַיְהִי־שָׁם בְּבֵית הַסֹּהַר: אֲסִירֵי

THE ART OF MIDRASH

Joseph Accused by Potiphar's wife
Rembrandt Harmensz van Rijn (1655)

Analysis

- Which elements of this image are directly mentioned in the text?
- Which elements of this image are not found in the text?
- What midrashic interpretation could be inferred from this image?

head of household to one of its prominent citizens, Potifar. Left alone with his master's wife, he finds himself propositioned by her: "Now Yosef was well built and handsome, and after a while his master's wife took notice of Yosef and said, 'Come to bed with me.'" The text continues: "But he refused" (39:8). Over this verb, tradition has placed a *shalshelet*.

We can imagine the conflict in Yosef's mind at that moment. On the one hand, his entire moral sense said no. It would be a betrayal of everything his family stood for: their ethic of sexual propriety and their strong sense of identity as children of the covenant. It would also be, as Yosef himself says, a betrayal of Potifar himself:

> With me in charge, my master does not concern himself with anything in the house; everything he owns he has entrusted to my care. No one is greater in this house then I am. My master has withheld nothing from me except you, because you are his wife. How then could I do such a wicked thing and sin against God? (39:8–9).

And yet, the temptation must have been intense. He was in an urban civilization of a kind he had not seen before. It was his first experience of "bright lights, big city." He was far from home. No one could see him. After all the hostility he had suffered in his childhood, being propositioned by Potifar's wife must have been flattering as well as seductive. It was a decisive moment. A slave, with no realistic hope of rescue – was he to become an Egyptian, with all the sexual laissez faire that implied? Or would he remain faithful to his past, his conscience, his identity?

The *shalshelet* is an elegant commentary on Yosef's crise de conscience. In the end, Yosef refuses, but not without deep inner struggle.

This is an example of what Leon Festinger called cognitive dissonance. According to Festinger, the need to avoid dissonance is fundamental to human beings; otherwise it creates unbearable tension. It is this tension which is signaled by the *shalshelet* over "he refused." It was the ultimate existential question, "Who am I?"

Rabbi Jonathan Sacks

Analysis

- What areas of understanding of human nature and society do we now have that were unavailable to classical Jewish commentators? How can they aid our understanding of the text?
- What can we learn from this essay to help us understand the text?
- What further questions on the text do you have now that you have read this new take on the story?

INTEGRATING ḤOKHMA

The Torah does not have a word for ambivalence (the nearest is Eliyahu's question to the Baal-worshipping Israelites: "How long will you waver between two opinions?"). It does, however, have a tune for it. This is the rare note known as the *shalshelet*. It appears three times in Bereshit, each time at a moment of crisis for the individual concerned. In each case it signifies an existential crisis. The agent is called on to make a choice, one on which his whole future will depend, but he finds that he cannot. He is torn between two alternatives, both of which exercise a powerful sway on him. He must resolve the dilemma one way or another, but either way will involve letting go of deeply felt temptations or deeply held aspirations. It is a moment of high psychological drama.

The *shalshelet* is an unusual note. It goes up and down, up and down, as if unable to move forward to the next note. It was the sixteenth-century commentator Rabbi Yosef Ibn Kaspi (in his commentary on Bereshit 19:16) who best understood what it was meant to convey, namely a psychological state of uncertainty and indecision. The graphic notation of the *shalshelet* itself looks like a streak of lightning, a "zigzag movement" (*tenua meuvetet*), a mark that goes repeatedly backward and forward. It conveys frozen motion – what Hamlet called "the native hue of resolution sicklied o'er by the pale cast of thought" – in which the agent is torn by inner conflict. The *shalshelet* is the music of ambivalence.

One instance occurs with Yosef in Bereshit 39:8. Child of a shepherd (Yaakov), an almost youngest son, hated by his brothers and sold by them into slavery, he finds himself in Egypt as

assistance: "God has solutions, tell [your dreams] to me" (40:8). It appears that his time in prison has afforded him some time to think, as Yosef credits God for the interpretation. Yet his crediting of God is once again tinged with arrogance, as he assumes that God, who holds the keys to reading dreams, will share those keys with him. What gives Yosef the right to assume access to divine knowledge?

Beyond battling his own arrogance, Yosef needs to recognize his own contribution to his misfortunes. Indeed, after he interprets the butler's dream positively, Yosef asks that the butler remember him and help him to be raised from his imprisonment. Listen carefully, though, to Yosef's words: "For I was kidnapped from the land of the Hebrews and here, too, I did nothing wrong that they placed me in this pit" (40:15). God may know how to solve the mystery of the dreams and Yosef can take little credit for that, but he also takes no responsibility for his own downfalls. In his own eyes he remains a blameless victim. None of his fate is his fault.

The need for Yosef to recognize both God's role in his success and his own responsibility for the calamities that befall him mirrors Yaakov's need to accept responsibility for his own actions in dealing with Esav. Yaakov does so only hesitantly, after a night of intense struggle, and even then only partially. Yosef, the wonder boy, struggles similarly. When he fails to recognize his own role in antagonizing his brothers leading up to his sale or his own arrogance in Potifar's house, he needs more time to consider his life's path: "The butler did not remember Yosef; he forgot him" (40:23). Yosef must wait – and contemplate – for another two years.

Rabbi Zvi Grumet

TAKING A LITERARY APPROACH

Yosef is successful at everything he does because God makes him successful, and everyone responsible for him recognizes his divine gift. The great irony is that the only one unaware of the source of his success is Yosef himself.

The pattern of Yosef being thrown into the pit only to emerge more popular than before marks his life until now and continues until he ends up as second-in-command to Pharaoh himself. Each down-phase of Yosef's cycle is preceded by his arrogance, believing that his success is his own. God tries to get Yosef to recognize what everyone else already knows, that it is He who is responsible for Yosef's impossible success, but Yosef has a hard time getting there. In his father's house it is those self-centered dreams, with himself as a god figure, which necessitate his being stripped of his position and his cloak. In Potifar's house it is his hesitating recognition of God's role in his success which again requires that he lose his cloak (by Potifar's wife) and be tossed into a pit (the prison he is in is called a pit in Bereshit 40:15). Note Yosef's response to Potifar's wife:

> Behold, my master knows nothing about what is with me in the house and all which he has placed in my hands, and he has held nothing back from me except for you, as you are his wife. How could I do such a great evil? It would be a sin to God. (39:8–9)

Yosef's primary argument is his loyalty to Potifar and his refusal to violate the trust placed in him; he brings in God only at the very conclusion of his refusal. Even then, it is not clear whether the violation against God is bedding a married woman or violating the trust Potifar has placed in him. Furthermore, it is unclear whether he is referring to a particular God or to the generic gods, or even if the phrase "to God" (*le'Elohim*) might not refer to God at all but may be an expression meaning "greatly."

It seems as if the main obstacle preventing Yosef from succumbing to Potifar's wife is the consequence from Potifar himself. And buried in Yosef's words is his own inflated sense of self ("There is none greater in this house than I"); were it not for practical exigencies he would welcome her advances. It is no wonder she keeps trying. Yosef's words are not a principled objection but a form of flirting, and it is that selfish, reckless playing with danger that brings him crashing down from his successful rise.

Yosef experiences yet another round of this cycle. When he interprets the dreams of the royal butler and baker he sees his light of redemption – the butler is indebted to him and Yosef finally acknowledges God's

21 But the Lord was with Yosef and showed him kindness, granting him favor in the eyes of
22 the prison warden. The warden put Yosef in charge of all the prisoners in the jail. Everything
23 done there was under his direction. The warden did not need to pay attention to anything
he had entrusted to him, because the Lord was with him, giving him success in all he
did.
40 1 Some time later, the Egyptian king's cupbearer and baker gave offense to their master, the
2 king of Egypt. Pharaoh was angry with the two officials, his chief cupbearer, and his chief
3 baker, and he placed them in custody in the house of the captain of the guard, in the very
4 place where Yosef was confined. The captain of the guard assigned them to Yosef and it
5 was he who attended them. When they had been in custody for some time, the two of
them – the imprisoned cupbearer and baker of the king of Egypt – each had a dream on
6 the same night, each dream seeming to carry its own meaning. When Yosef came to them
7 the next morning, he saw that they were both distressed. He asked Pharaoh's officials
who were in custody with him in his master's house, "Why are you looking so troubled
8 today?" "We both had dreams," they told him, "but there is no one to interpret them." Yosef
9 replied, "Interpretation belongs to God. Tell me your dreams." So the chief cupbearer told
10 his dream to Yosef and said to him, "In my dream I saw a vine in front of me. The vine had
three branches. As soon as it budded, it blossomed, and its clusters ripened into grapes.

UNLOCKING THE TEXT

- Why did the prison warden show favor to Yosef?
- What offenses did the cupbearer and baker commit that caused Pharaoh to be angry with them?
- Why were they assigned to Yosef's care?
- What are the similarities and differences with the two dreams?
- What is the significance of the number three in both dreams?
- If interpretations belong to God, how did Yosef understand the interpretations of these dreams?
- Is Yosef's explanation of how he ended up in prison accurate and fair?
- Why did Yosef not also ask the baker to mention him to Pharaoh?

FINDING YOURSELF IN THE TEXT

- Have you ever thrived despite the difficult hand you were dealt?
- Did you ever despair of your situation, only for an opportunity to then present itself?
- Did you ever meet someone, and then in retrospect, recognize that your interaction with them changed the path of your life?

Consider using these questions as the basis for your own commentary or creative midrash.

How does reflecting on these firsthand experiences help you better understand the text?

כא כב וַיְהִי יְהוָה אֶת־יוֹסֵף וַיֵּט אֵלָיו חָסֶד וַיִּתֵּן חִנּוֹ בְּעֵינֵי שַׂר בֵּית־הַסֹּהַר: וַיִּתֵּן שַׂר
בֵּית־הַסֹּהַר בְּיַד־יוֹסֵף אֵת כָּל־הָאֲסִירִם אֲשֶׁר בְּבֵית הַסֹּהַר וְאֵת כָּל־אֲשֶׁר עֹשִׂים
כג שָׁם הוּא הָיָה עֹשֶׂה: אֵין שַׂר בֵּית־הַסֹּהַר רֹאֶה אֶת־כָּל־מְאוּמָה בְּיָדוֹ בַּאֲשֶׁר
יְהוָה אִתּוֹ וַאֲשֶׁר־הוּא עֹשֶׂה יְהוָה מַצְלִיחַ:
מ א וַיְהִי אַחַר הַדְּבָרִים הָאֵלֶּה חָטְאוּ מַשְׁקֵה מֶלֶךְ־מִצְרַיִם וְהָאֹפֶה לַאֲדֹנֵיהֶם לְמֶלֶךְ שביעי
ב ג מִצְרָיִם: וַיִּקְצֹף פַּרְעֹה עַל שְׁנֵי סָרִיסָיו עַל שַׂר הַמַּשְׁקִים וְעַל שַׂר הָאוֹפִים: וַיִּתֵּן
אֹתָם בְּמִשְׁמַר בֵּית שַׂר הַטַּבָּחִים אֶל־בֵּית הַסֹּהַר מְקוֹם אֲשֶׁר יוֹסֵף אָסוּר שָׁם:
ד ה וַיִּפְקֹד שַׂר הַטַּבָּחִים אֶת־יוֹסֵף אִתָּם וַיְשָׁרֶת אֹתָם וַיִּהְיוּ יָמִים בְּמִשְׁמָר: וַיַּחַלְמוּ
חֲלוֹם שְׁנֵיהֶם אִישׁ חֲלֹמוֹ בְּלַיְלָה אֶחָד אִישׁ כְּפִתְרוֹן חֲלֹמוֹ הַמַּשְׁקֶה וְהָאֹפֶה אֲשֶׁר
ו לְמֶלֶךְ מִצְרַיִם אֲשֶׁר אֲסוּרִים בְּבֵית הַסֹּהַר: וַיָּבֹא אֲלֵיהֶם יוֹסֵף בַּבֹּקֶר וַיַּרְא אֹתָם
ז וְהִנָּם זֹעֲפִים: וַיִּשְׁאַל אֶת־סְרִיסֵי פַרְעֹה אֲשֶׁר אִתּוֹ בְמִשְׁמַר בֵּית אֲדֹנָיו לֵאמֹר
ח מַדּוּעַ פְּנֵיכֶם רָעִים הַיּוֹם: וַיֹּאמְרוּ אֵלָיו חֲלוֹם חָלַמְנוּ וּפֹתֵר אֵין אֹתוֹ וַיֹּאמֶר אֲלֵהֶם
ט יוֹסֵף הֲלוֹא לֵאלֹהִים פִּתְרֹנִים סַפְּרוּ־נָא לִי: וַיְסַפֵּר שַׂר־הַמַּשְׁקִים אֶת־חֲלֹמוֹ לְיוֹסֵף
י וַיֹּאמֶר לוֹ בַּחֲלוֹמִי וְהִנֵּה־גֶפֶן לְפָנָי: וּבַגֶּפֶן שְׁלֹשָׁה שָׂרִיגִם וְהִוא כְפֹרַחַת עָלְתָה

THEMES | LEADERSHIP | EXILE | PROPHECY AND REVELATION

Episode 57: *Yosef in Prison* – Bereshit 39:21–40:23

SUMMARY

Once again, God grants grace to Yosef, and he finds himself in charge of all the other prisoners. Pharaoh's baker and cupbearer are also in the prison where Yosef is held, and Potifar puts Yosef in charge of their care. One night they both have similar dreams, and in the morning Yosef notices that they are distraught. When they tell him about their dreams, he offers to interpret them.

Yosef interprets the cupbearer's dream to indicate that in three days Pharaoh will call him back from prison and restore him to his position. Yosef then adds a request: that when he returns to his position he remember Yosef and help free him from his unjust punishment, as he was kidnapped from his homeland. Yosef then interprets the baker's dream with a contrasting interpretation, predicting the demise of the baker. Yosef's success in accurately interpreting their dreams will eventually pave the way to a meeting with Pharaoh, who will require an interpreter for his own dreams.

11 Pharaoh's cup was in my hand; I took the grapes and squeezed them into Pharaoh's cup, and
12 I placed the cup in his hand." "This is what it means," Yosef said. "The three branches are
13 three days. In three days Pharaoh will lift your head and restore you to your position. You
14 will place Pharaoh's cup in his hand again, as you did when you were his cupbearer. When
it goes well with you, remember me and do me this kindness: mention me to Pharaoh so as
15 to free me from this place. The truth is that I was kidnapped from the land of the Hebrews.
16 Here too, I have done nothing to deserve being placed in this pit." The chief baker saw that
he had given a favorable interpretation, so he said to Yosef, "I too had a dream. There were
17 three baskets of white bread on my head. In the top basket were all sorts of baked food
18 that Pharaoh eats, but birds were eating them out of the basket above my head." "This is
19 what it means," Yosef said. "The three baskets are three days. In three days Pharaoh will
lift your head from your body; he will hang you from a stake, and birds will eat your flesh."
20 The third day was Pharaoh's birthday. He made a feast for all his servants, and from among
21 them he singled out his chief cupbearer and chief baker. He restored the chief cupbearer
22 to his position so that, as before, he placed the cup in Pharaoh's hand. But he hung up the
23 chief baker, as Yosef had predicted. Still, the chief cupbearer did not remember Yosef; he
forgot him.

Joseph in Prison
Gerbrand van den Eeckhout
(c. 17th century)

THE ART OF MIDRASH

Analysis

- Which elements of this image are directly mentioned in the text?
- Which elements of this image are not found in the text?
- What midrashic interpretation could be inferred from this image?

יא נָצָּ֣הּ הִבְשִׁ֣ילוּ אַשְׁכְּלֹתֶ֖יהָ עֲנָבִֽים: וְכ֤וֹס פַּרְעֹה֙ בְּיָדִ֔י וָאֶקַּ֣ח אֶת־הָֽעֲנָבִ֗ים וָֽאֶשְׂחַ֤ט

יב אֹתָם֙ אֶל־כּ֣וֹס פַּרְעֹ֔ה וָֽאֶתֵּ֥ן אֶת־הַכּ֖וֹס עַל־כַּ֣ף פַּרְעֹֽה: וַיֹּ֤אמֶר לוֹ֙ יוֹסֵ֔ף זֶ֖ה פִּתְרֹנ֑וֹ

יג שְׁלֹ֙שֶׁת֙ הַשָּׂ֣רִגִ֔ים שְׁלֹ֥שֶׁת יָמִ֖ים הֵ֑ם: בְּע֣וֹד ׀ שְׁלֹ֣שֶׁת יָמִ֗ים יִשָּׂ֤א פַרְעֹה֙ אֶת־רֹאשֶׁ֔ךָ וַֽהֲשִֽׁיבְךָ֖ עַל־כַּנֶּ֑ךָ וְנָֽתַתָּ֤ כוֹס־פַּרְעֹה֙ בְּיָד֔וֹ כַּמִּשְׁפָּט֙ הָֽרִאשׁ֔וֹן אֲשֶׁ֥ר הָיִ֖יתָ מַשְׁקֵֽהוּ:

יד כִּ֣י אִם־זְכַרְתַּ֤נִי אִתְּךָ֙ כַּֽאֲשֶׁר֙ יִ֣יטַב לָ֔ךְ וְעָשִֽׂיתָ־נָּ֥א עִמָּדִ֖י חָ֑סֶד וְהִזְכַּרְתַּ֙נִי֙ אֶל־פַּרְעֹ֔ה

טו וְהֽוֹצֵאתַ֖נִי מִן־הַבַּ֥יִת הַזֶּֽה: כִּֽי־גֻנֹּ֣ב גֻּנַּ֔בְתִּי מֵאֶ֖רֶץ הָֽעִבְרִ֑ים וְגַם־פֹּה֙ לֹֽא־עָשִׂ֣יתִי מְא֔וּמָה כִּֽי־שָׂמ֥וּ אֹתִ֖י בַּבּֽוֹר:

טז וַיַּ֥רְא שַׂר־הָֽאֹפִ֖ים כִּ֣י ט֣וֹב פָּתָ֑ר וַיֹּ֙אמֶר֙ אֶל־יוֹסֵ֔ף אַף־אֲנִי֙ בַּֽחֲלוֹמִ֔י וְהִנֵּ֗ה שְׁלֹשָׁ֛ה סַלֵּ֥י חֹרִ֖י עַל־רֹאשִֽׁי:

יז וּבַסַּ֣ל הָֽעֶלְי֗וֹן מִכֹּ֛ל מַֽאֲכַ֥ל פַּרְעֹ֖ה מַֽעֲשֵׂ֣ה אֹפֶ֑ה וְהָע֗וֹף אֹכֵ֥ל אֹתָ֛ם מִן־הַסַּ֖ל מֵעַ֥ל רֹאשִֽׁי:

יח וַיַּ֤עַן יוֹסֵף֙ וַיֹּ֔אמֶר זֶ֖ה פִּתְרֹנ֑וֹ שְׁלֹ֙שֶׁת֙ הַסַּלִּ֔ים שְׁלֹ֥שֶׁת יָמִ֖ים הֵֽם:

יט בְּע֣וֹד ׀ שְׁלֹ֣שֶׁת יָמִ֗ים יִשָּׂ֙א פַרְעֹ֤ה אֶת־רֹֽאשְׁךָ֙ מֵֽעָלֶ֔יךָ וְתָלָ֥ה אֽוֹתְךָ֖ עַל־עֵ֑ץ וְאָכַ֥ל הָע֛וֹף אֶת־בְּשָֽׂרְךָ֖ מֵֽעָלֶֽיךָ:

כ וַיְהִ֣י ׀ בַּיּ֣וֹם הַשְּׁלִישִׁ֗י י֚וֹם הֻלֶּ֣דֶת אֶת־פַּרְעֹ֔ה וַיַּ֥עַשׂ מִשְׁתֶּ֖ה לְכָל־עֲבָדָ֑יו וַיִּשָּׂ֞א אֶת־רֹ֣אשׁ ׀ שַׂ֣ר הַמַּשְׁקִ֗ים

מפטיר

כא וְאֶת־רֹ֛אשׁ שַׂ֥ר הָֽאֹפִ֖ים בְּת֣וֹךְ עֲבָדָֽיו: וַיָּ֛שֶׁב אֶת־שַׂ֥ר הַמַּשְׁקִ֖ים עַל־מַשְׁקֵ֑הוּ וַיִּתֵּ֥ן

כב הַכּ֖וֹס עַל־כַּ֥ף פַּרְעֹֽה: וְאֵ֛ת שַׂ֥ר הָֽאֹפִ֖ים תָּלָ֑ה כַּֽאֲשֶׁ֥ר פָּתַ֛ר לָהֶ֖ם יוֹסֵֽף: וְלֹֽא־זָכַ֧ר

כג שַׂר־הַמַּשְׁקִ֛ים אֶת־יוֹסֵ֖ף וַיִּשְׁכָּחֵֽהוּ:

A QUESTION OF BIBLIODRAMA

TO THE PRISON WARDEN

- ◉ What did you think of Yosef when he arrived in your prison?
- ◉ What did you see in Yosef that made you want to give him so much responsibility?

TO YOSEF

- ◉ Did you ever despair when you were in prison?
- ◉ What do you think was the explanation behind your latest success in this new situation in which you found yourself?
- ◉ How do you know the meaning of the dreams of the cupbearer and the baker?

TO THE CUPBEARER AND THE BAKER

- ◉ What did you do to offend Pharaoh?
- ◉ What do you think of Yosef?
- ◉ What do you think of his interpretation of your dreams?

What is stunning about the way this story is told in the Torah is that it is constructed to lead us, as readers, in precisely the wrong direction. Parashat Vayeshev has the form of a Greek tragedy. Parashat Miketz then comes and shows us that the Torah embodies another worldview altogether. Judaism is not Athens. The Torah is not Sophocles. The human condition is not inherently tragic. Heroes are not fated to fall.

The reason is fundamental. Ancient Israel and the Greece of antiquity – the two great influences on Western civilization – had profoundly different understandings of time and circumstance. The Greeks believed in *moira*, fate, or *ananke*, blind fate. They thought that the gods were hostile, or at best indifferent, to humankind, so there was no way of avoiding tragedy if that is what fate had decreed. Jews believed, and still believe, that God is with us as we travel through time. Sometimes we feel as if we are lost, but then we discover, as Yosef did, that He has been guiding our steps all along.

Yosef's story is a precise reversal of the narrative structure of Sophocles's *Oedipus*. Everything Laius and his son Oedipus do to *avert* the tragic fate announced by the oracle in fact brings it closer to fulfillment, whereas in the story of Yosef, every episode that seems to be leading to tragedy turns out in retrospect to be a necessary step to saving lives and fulfilling Yosef's dreams.

Judaism is the opposite of tragedy. It tells us that every bad fate can be averted (hence our prayer on the High Holy Days that "penitence, prayer, and charity avert the evil decree") – while every positive promise made by God will never be undone.

Hence the life-changing idea: Despair is never justified. Even if your life has been scarred by misfortune, lacerated by pain, and your chances of happiness seem gone forever, there is still hope. The next chapter of your life can be full of blessings. You can be, in Wordsworth's lovely phrase, "surprised by joy."

Rabbi Jonathan Sacks

Analysis

- What areas of understanding of human nature, society, and history do we have now that were unavailable to classical Jewish commentators? How can they aid our understanding of the text?
- What can we learn from this essay to help us understand the text?
- What further questions on the text do you have now that you have read this new take on the story?

INTEGRATING ḤOKHMA

We live life looking forward but we understand it only looking back.

As we live from day to day, our life can seem like a meaningless sequence of random events, a series of accidents and happenstances that have no shape or inner logic. A traffic jam makes us late for an important meeting. A stray remark we make offends someone in a way we never intended. By a hair's breadth we fail to get the job we so sought. Life as we experience it can sometimes feel like Joseph Heller's definition of history: "a trashbag of random coincidences blown open in a wind."

Yet looking back, it begins to make sense. The opportunity we missed here led to an even better one there. The shame we felt at our unintentionally offensive remark makes us more careful about what we say in the future. Our failures, seen in retrospect many years later, turn out to have been our deepest learning experiences. Our hindsight is always more perceptive than our foresight. We live life facing the future, but we understand life only when it has become our past. Nowhere is this set out more clearly than in the story of Yosef in this *parasha.*

The last line of the *parasha* is one of the cruelest blows of fate in the Torah: "The chief cupbearer did not remember Yosef; he forgot him" (Bereshit 40:23). Seemingly his one chance of escape to freedom is now lost. Yosef, the beloved son in his magnificent robe has become Yosef, the prisoner bereft of hope. This is as near the Torah gets to Greek tragedy. It is a tale of Yosef's hubris leading, step after step, to his nemesis. Every good thing that happens to him turns out to be only the prelude to some new and unforeseen misfortune.

Yet a mere two years later, at the beginning of the next *parasha*, we discover that all this has been leading to Yosef's supreme elevation. Pharaoh makes him viceroy over Egypt, the greatest empire of the ancient world. He gives him his own signet ring, has him dressed in royal robes and a gold chain, and has him paraded in a chariot to the acclaim of the crowds. A mere thirty years old, he has become the second most powerful man in the world. From the lowest pit he has risen to dizzying heights. He has gone from zero to hero overnight.

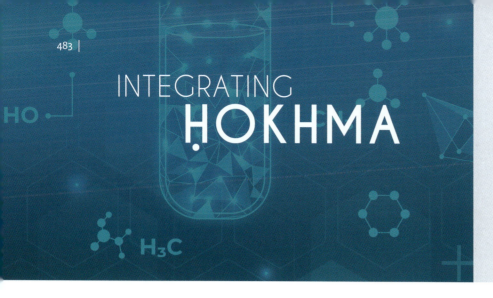

Rather than resorting to the obvious answers, let us complicate things a bit. Yosef plays the role of headman not twice, but in fact three times in Parashat Vayeshev. Parashat Vayeshev opens with another story of Yosef's success and meteoric rise to headman. Yosef is special to his father. Yaakov elevates Yosef above his brothers and gives him a long-sleeved coat (37:3), a garment worn by the children of kings (II Shmuel 13:18). Furthermore, Yosef enjoys special access to his father. While his brothers are away with the sheep in Shekhem, Yosef remains home with his father (Bereshit 37:12–13; Ramban on 37:3).

Finally, Yosef serves as Yaakov's supervisory agent. Yaakov sends Yosef to check on his brothers and the sheep out in the fields of Shekhem (37:14). While Yaakov might not have asked for the slanderous reports (*dibatam raa*) brought home by Yosef about his brothers (37:2), the surprise is the slander, not the report. Yosef, as the preferred son, acts as supervisor and *charge d'affaires*. As befits his role as second-in-command, he reports to the chief. Needless to say, Yosef's dreams reflect his headman role and, together with his coat and his supervisory role, constitute the cause of his brothers' animosity.

If so, Parashat Vayeshev turns out to possess an interesting structure. Yosef starts out as the assistant to Yaakov, the headman of the family fated to form God's chosen nation and to realize the blessings of Avraham. But he falls fast and falls hard. We next find him as headman in Potifar's house, albeit in exile, but in a position of power, prominence, and prestige.

But even this is not to be. Yosef descends again, this time to prison. In stage three of the headman structure, we find Yosef supervising a prison. He is far from his family, far from blessing, and far from his dreams.

Once again, all of this is part of God's plan. But then again, there are infinite ways that God could have arranged Yosef's eventual control over Egypt. Why this way? Why the threefold headman structure for Parashat Vayeshev? In other words, what is the meaning and message of Yosef's descent?

The seam between Parashat Vayishlaḥ and Parashat Vayeshev, the transition between the second part of the book (12:1–36:43) and the third part of the book (37:1–50:26), consists of the symbols of royalty and the topics of leadership and kingship. This is no accident. As pointed out previously, the thematic shift consists of a move from the stage of covenant transaction and transmission to a stage of fulfillment and realization. This means that the future is no longer the inchoate destiny of a single individual. The future now belongs to a group, a nascent nation. Already now, there exists a group, bound up concretely with the historical reality of the unfolding divine plan. But every group that functions in the real world, that navigates the stormy seas of history,

TAKING A LITERARY APPROACH

Jail is not the first place where Yosef rose to prominence. Before prison, Yosef had done some time in the house of Potifar. Before his entanglement with Potifar's wife, Yosef's career had progressed along the servant fast track. He quickly found a position in the house of Potifar (Bereshit 39:2), bypassing the more common slave occupation of field hand, a short and nasty existence consisting of back-breaking hard labor. He "found favor" in his master's eyes (39:4), and just a few short verses after Potifar purchases him, Potifar appoints Yosef as head servant/slave. He places everything he has in "the hand" of Yosef and leaves him completely in charge (39:4–5). Like the officer of the prisons later on, Potifar is now oblivious to the goings-on in his domain (39:6).

As in the prison later on, Yosef constitutes the real power in the house and fields of Potifar. As the headman, the *charge d'affaires* of Potifar, Yosef does all that needs doing. Except for the slightly mysterious bread, Yosef wields total control.

To outline this logically, the headman parallel that emerges from the sketch above consists of three fundamental components. In both the house of Potifar and in prison, we can note "finding favor" in the eyes of the ruling authority (39:4; 39:21), the "placing" of authority into the "hand" of Yosef (39:4, 6; 39:22), and the oblivious, know-nothing attitude of the real chief (39:6; 39:23). In addition, we can add a fourth element. In both cases, the Torah informs us that Yosef was successful, and it attributes his success to God's assistance (39:3; 39:23).

Given the tight parallel above between Yosef's two headman positions, we should pay very careful attention to a set of crucial differences between the two stories. In the first, Yosef serves a man of great importance in the Egyptian kingdom. He acts as assistant to Pharaoh's captain of the guard (*sar hatabaḥim*), a man defined as *seris Paro*, a chamberlain of Pharaoh (39:1). He is in charge of Potifar's entire estate (39:4–5), works in Potifar's house, and is even privileged with private access to the lady of the house (39:7–11). In contrast, in the second story, Yosef is no more than the headman of an ancient Near Eastern jail, a miserable pit (40:15). He serves no important minister, inhabits no luxurious offices, and enjoys no company except that of his fellow prisoners. His kingdom is a prison and his subjects are the wretched and condemned. Yosef has fallen fast and hard.

But if, in fact, God is "with Yosef" both in the house of Potifar and in prison (39:3, 21, 23), why has God done this to him? What mysterious divine imperative propels Yosef downward?

Let us take a look at the bare-bones but significant characterizations of Yosef in the second and third headman stories.

In protesting the advances of Potifar's wife, Yosef manages to refer to the fact that "there is none greater in the house than me" (39:9), twice mentions the fact that everything has been entrusted to his control (39:8–9), and once refers to his master's ignorance. While this is all part of a profession of loyalty on Yosef's part (39:8–9), Yosef is acutely aware of his status and position. He then tumbles once again.

The final headman story, Yosef's ruling of the prison, presents a different picture. Although the disgraced ministers of Pharaoh have been placed in Yosef's hands along with all of the other prisoners (39:22; 40:4), the Torah describes Yosef as "serving them" (40:4). He inquires after their welfare and sad moods (40:5). He serves, rather than rules, those placed in his charge.

Finally, this new humility may also be discerned in Yosef's offer to interpret their dreams. He ascribes the power of interpretation to God (40:8). While this may not seem surprising to us, it is shocking in the context of ancient Egypt, a land abounding in sorcerers and magicians. Even Yosef himself lauds his sorcerer's powers when playing the Egyptian viceroy for his brothers (44:15). Lauding his magical powers would certainly have gotten him out of the pit much faster. Needless to say, Pharaoh's cupbearer forgets the powerless youth and his humble request for help (40:23).

In sum, we have here the same humble Yosef who, when ascribed the power of dream interpretation by Pharaoh, responds that it is God and not he who possesses answers (41:16). We have here the very same Yosef who later humbly tells his brothers that it was all God's plan, that his entire position in Egypt exists for the sake of saving lives and providing for his family (44:5–8). We have here someone suitable for leadership, who acts with humility, whose heart is with his brothers.

Rabbi Zvi Grumet

requires leaders. By no surprise, the topic of leadership becomes paramount in Bereshit. By no surprise, the topic is formulated in the symbolism of kingship, foreshadowing the future of the family's descendants, the nation of Israel.

All of this should help us with the structure of Vayeshev. In keeping with the theme of leadership and kingship, the stories are primarily about Yosef and Yehuda, the two once and future leaders. Reading Parashat Vayeshev as also concerned with marking the leaders/kings and as interested in emphasizing the leadership criterion of humility helped resolve the inclusion of the Yehuda and Tamar story

Now let us turn back to Yosef and the problem of his descent. Does Yosef possess the virtue of humility necessary for leadership and royalty? A quick review of the first headman story should determine the answer.

Yosef is the favored son. Whether due to virtue and ability, his being almost the youngest, or his being the firstborn of the beloved Raḥel, Yaakov loves Yosef more than he loves his other sons (37:3). The brothers resent it. They resent the favoritism and its future implications. They hate Yosef and cannot even speak peaceably to him. But what is Yosef's attitude to the family dynamic? While the text gives us no explicit information, we may glean quite a bit by reading between the lines. At the very least, he seems to feel no qualms about speaking ill of his brothers to their father (37:2), a move which seems to reinforce his claim to superiority. He is above them, sits in judgment upon them, and reports on them.

Moreover, immediately after informing us of the brothers' resentment of Yosef's status and their hatred of him, the Torah tells us about Yosef's dreams (37:5–10). Despite the obvious implications of the dreams and the fact that his brothers are already not talking to him, Yosef insists on telling his dreams to his brothers. Yosef naively glories in his position and visions. Without regard to his brothers' response, he acts the prince, certain of his position and convinced of his destiny. He is not humble.

If so, this may be the meaning of the descent pattern in Parashat Vayeshev. In structuring this pattern, both the *parasha* and divine providence provide an ironic comment on Yosef's pretensions. Yosef viewed himself as a prince, a ruler now and in the future. He prides himself on his talent, his position, and his destiny. But how the mighty have fallen. Yes, he is a headman. Yes, he is a ruler – but not of his family, and not of the future nation of Israel. He who elevated his heart above his brothers rules not even the house of Potifar. He rules only a prison.

But there is more to it than this. I would argue that this very pattern of descent, the providential mocking of his pretensions and pride, effects a change in Yosef.

מקץ
Miketz

Parasha Overview

Parashat Miketz is dominated by two of the great encounters in the Torah. The first is the reversal in Yosef's fortunes. Forgotten and abandoned in prison, he is brought out to interpret Pharaoh's dreams, which he does with ease. Having told Pharaoh that the dreams portend eventual drought and famine, he then articulates a solution to the problem. Pharaoh, impressed, appoints Yosef to high office in Egypt, second only to himself. The second encounter occurs when Yosef's brothers, driven by famine in Canaan, come to Egypt to buy food. They come before Yosef, but fail to recognize him as their brother, though he recognizes them. Yosef, without disclosing his identity, sets in motion a complex scenario, designed to test his brothers, that reaches a climax in the next *parasha.*

Episodes

58.	**Pharaoh's Dreams**	41:1–37
59.	**Yosef's Rise to Power**	41:38–57
60.	**The Brothers' First Encounter with Yosef**	42:1–28
61.	**The Brothers Return to Yaakov**	42:29–43:14
62.	**The Brothers' Second Encounter with Yosef**	43:15–34
63.	**The Brothers' Third Encounter with Yosef**	44:1–17

Parasha Stats

- 7,914 letters
- 2,022 words
- 146 verses
- 255 lines in a sefer Torah

41 1 2 Two years passed. Then Pharaoh had a dream: he was standing by the Nile when seven
3 handsome, healthy cows came up out of the river and grazed among the reeds. Then seven
other cows came up from the river after them, ugly and gaunt, and stood beside them by
4 the riverbank. The ugly, gaunt cows ate up the seven handsome, healthy cows. Pharaoh
5 awoke. Falling back to sleep, he had a second dream: he saw seven ears of grain, ripe and
6 robust, growing on a single stalk. Suddenly, seven other ears sprouted after them, thin and
7 scorched by the east wind. The thin ears swallowed up the seven ripe, full ears. Pharaoh
8 awoke – and realized it had been a dream. In the morning his mind was troubled, so he
sent for all the magicians and sages of Egypt. Pharaoh told them his dream, but no one
9 could offer an interpretation that satisfied him. Then the chief cupbearer said to Pharaoh,
10 "I must recall my sins today. Once, Pharaoh was angry with his servants and placed me
11 and the chief baker in custody in the house of the captain of the guard. One night he and I
12 each had a dream, and each dream seemed to have its own meaning. With us was a young
Hebrew, a slave of the captain of the guard. We told him our dreams and he interpreted

UNLOCKING THE TEXT

- Why did Yosef need to wait two years for his freedom?
- Why didn't the interpretations Pharaoh's magicians and sages gave satisfy him?
- What similarities and differences are there between the two dreams?
- What role does Pharaoh himself play in the dreams?
- Why does Pharaoh dream of livestock, which is not an Egyptian trade? (Compare this to Yosef's dream of wheat, which is not an Israelite trade.)
- Why does Yosef refuse to take any credit for his gift for dream interpretation?
- Why does the Torah repeat Pharaoh's dreams in detail?
- If Egypt has the Nile as a continuous source of water, how can it have a famine?
- Why does Yosef go beyond the dream interpretation to give Pharaoh economic leadership advice?

FINDING YOURSELF IN THE TEXT

- Have you ever been asked advice from someone very important? How did it feel?
- Have you ever understood something about someone that they couldn't see?
- Have you ever given unsolicited advice? How was it received?

Consider using these questions as the basis for your own commentary or creative midrash.

How does reflecting on these firsthand experiences help you better understand the text?

מא וַיְהִי מִקֵּץ שְׁנָתַיִם יָמִים וּפַרְעֹה חֹלֵם וְהִנֵּה עֹמֵד עַל־הַיְאֹר: וְהִנֵּה מִן־הַיְאֹר עֹלֹת לו מקץ
שֶׁבַע פָּרוֹת יְפוֹת מַרְאֶה וּבְרִיאֹת בָּשָׂר וַתִּרְעֶינָה בָּאָחוּ: וְהִנֵּה שֶׁבַע פָּרוֹת אֲחֵרוֹת
עֹלוֹת אַחֲרֵיהֶן מִן־הַיְאֹר רָעוֹת מַרְאֶה וְדַקּוֹת בָּשָׂר וַתַּעֲמֹדְנָה אֵצֶל הַפָּרוֹת עַל־
שְׂפַת הַיְאֹר: וַתֹּאכַלְנָה הַפָּרוֹת רָעוֹת הַמַּרְאֶה וְדַקֹּת הַבָּשָׂר אֵת שֶׁבַע הַפָּרוֹת
יְפֹת הַמַּרְאֶה וְהַבְּרִיאֹת וַיִּיקַץ פַּרְעֹה: וַיִּישָׁן וַיַּחֲלֹם שֵׁנִית וְהִנֵּה ׀ שֶׁבַע שִׁבֳּלִים
עֹלוֹת בְּקָנֶה אֶחָד בְּרִיאוֹת וְטֹבוֹת: וְהִנֵּה שֶׁבַע שִׁבֳּלִים דַּקּוֹת וּשְׁדוּפֹת קָדִים
צֹמְחוֹת אַחֲרֵיהֶן: וַתִּבְלַעְנָה הַשִּׁבֳּלִים הַדַּקּוֹת אֵת שֶׁבַע הַשִּׁבֳּלִים הַבְּרִיאוֹת
וְהַמְּלֵאוֹת וַיִּיקַץ פַּרְעֹה וְהִנֵּה חֲלוֹם: וַיְהִי בַבֹּקֶר וַתִּפָּעֶם רוּחוֹ וַיִּשְׁלַח וַיִּקְרָא
אֶת־כָּל־חַרְטֻמֵּי מִצְרַיִם וְאֶת־כָּל־חֲכָמֶיהָ וַיְסַפֵּר פַּרְעֹה לָהֶם אֶת־חֲלֹמוֹ וְאֵין־
פּוֹתֵר אוֹתָם לְפַרְעֹה: וַיְדַבֵּר שַׂר הַמַּשְׁקִים אֶת־פַּרְעֹה לֵאמֹר אֶת־חֲטָאַי אֲנִי
מַזְכִּיר הַיּוֹם: פַּרְעֹה קָצַף עַל־עֲבָדָיו וַיִּתֵּן אֹתִי בְּמִשְׁמַר בֵּית שַׂר הַטַּבָּחִים אֹתִי
וְאֵת שַׂר הָאֹפִים: וַנַּחַלְמָה חֲלוֹם בְּלַיְלָה אֶחָד אֲנִי וָהוּא אִישׁ כְּפִתְרוֹן חֲלֹמוֹ
חָלָמְנוּ: וְשָׁם אִתָּנוּ נַעַר עִבְרִי עֶבֶד לְשַׂר הַטַּבָּחִים וַנְּסַפֶּר־לוֹ וַיִּפְתָּר־לָנוּ אֶת־

| THEMES | PROPHECY AND REVELATION | LEADERSHIP | GOD |

Episode 58: *Pharaoh's Dreams* – Bereshit 41:1–37

SUMMARY

The upheavals in Yosef's life have taken him from the pit into which he was cast by his brothers to the dungeon in Egypt. Yosef has placed his trust in the chief butler, requesting that he put in a good word for him to Pharaoh, after Yosef correctly interpreted the butler's dream. In this manner he hoped to be rescued from his plight. However, as is common with powerful officials, as soon as the chief butler is restored to his post, he forgets about Yosef. Yosef's release from the dark prison will occur in a different manner.

13 them for us, telling each of us the meaning of his dream. Things turned out exactly as he
14 interpreted them to us. I was restored to my position, and the baker was hung up." So
Pharaoh sent for Yosef. He was rushed from the dungeon, had his hair cut, changed his
15 clothes, and came before Pharaoh. Pharaoh said to Yosef, "I had a dream and no one can
16 interpret it; I have heard that when you hear a dream you can interpret it." "Not I," replied
17 Yosef to Pharaoh. "God will give Pharaoh the answer that he needs." Pharaoh told Yosef:
18 "In my dream, I was standing by the bank of the Nile when seven handsome, healthy
19 cows came up out of the river and grazed among the reeds. Then after them came seven
20 other cows, scrawny, very sickly, and thin – I never saw such sickly cows in all Egypt. Then
21 the thin, sickly cows ate up the first seven healthy cows. But when they had eaten them
you could not tell that they had eaten them, for they still looked as bad as before. Then
22 I awoke. In my dream I then saw seven ears of grain, ripe and full, growing on a single
23 stalk. Suddenly, seven other ears sprouted after them, shriveled, thin, and scorched by
24 the east wind, and the thin ears swallowed the seven good ears. I told this to the magicians,
25 but none could explain it to me." Yosef said to Pharaoh, "The two dreams of Pharaoh are
26 one and the same. God has told Pharaoh what He is about to do. The seven good cows
are seven years, and so too the seven good ears are seven years. It is one and the same dream.
27 The seven thin, sickly cows that came up after them are seven years, as are the seven empty
28 ears scorched by the east wind. They are seven years of famine. It is as I have told Pharaoh:
29 God has shown Pharaoh what He is about to do. Seven years are coming when there
30 will be great abundance throughout the land of Egypt. But after them will come seven
years of famine, when all the abundance in Egypt will be forgotten. Famine will ravage the
31 land. So devastating will the famine be that no one in the land will know anything of
32 abundance any more. As for Pharaoh having the same dream twice, this means that the
33 matter has already been decided by God, and He is soon to bring it about. So now let
34 Pharaoh seek out an astute, wise man and set him over the land of Egypt. Let Pharaoh
appoint overseers across the land and take a fifth of Egypt's harvest during the seven years
35 of abundance. Let them gather all that food in these coming good years, storing the grain
36 under Pharaoh's aegis so that there is food under guard in all the cities. The food should
be held in reserve for the land when the seven years of famine come to Egypt, so that the
37 country is not ruined by the famine." The plan seemed good to Pharaoh and all his officials.

יג חֲלֹמֹתֵ֑ינוּ אִ֥ישׁ כַּחֲלֹמ֖וֹ פָּתָֽר׃ וַיְהִ֛י כַּאֲשֶׁ֥ר פָּֽתַר־לָ֖נוּ כֵּ֣ן הָיָ֑ה אֹתִ֛י הֵשִׁ֥יב עַל־כַּנִּ֖י
יד וְאֹת֥וֹ תָלָֽה׃ וַיִּשְׁלַ֤ח פַּרְעֹה֙ וַיִּקְרָ֣א אֶת־יוֹסֵ֔ף וַיְרִיצֻ֖הוּ מִן־הַבּ֑וֹר וַיְגַלַּח֙ וַיְחַלֵּ֣ף
טו שִׂמְלֹתָ֔יו וַיָּבֹ֖א אֶל־פַּרְעֹֽה׃ וַיֹּ֤אמֶר פַּרְעֹה֙ אֶל־יוֹסֵ֔ף חֲל֣וֹם חָלַ֔מְתִּי וּפֹתֵ֖ר אֵ֣ין שני
טז אֹת֑וֹ וַאֲנִ֗י שָׁמַ֤עְתִּי עָלֶ֙יךָ֙ לֵאמֹ֔ר תִּשְׁמַ֥ע חֲל֖וֹם לִפְתֹּ֥ר אֹתֽוֹ׃ וַיַּ֨עַן יוֹסֵ֧ף אֶת־פַּרְעֹ֛ה
יז לֵאמֹ֖ר בִּלְעָדָ֑י אֱלֹהִ֕ים יַעֲנֶ֖ה אֶת־שְׁל֥וֹם פַּרְעֹֽה׃ וַיְדַבֵּ֥ר פַּרְעֹ֖ה אֶל־יוֹסֵ֑ף בַּחֲלֹמִ֕י
יח הִנְנִ֥י עֹמֵ֖ד עַל־שְׂפַ֥ת הַיְאֹֽר׃ וְהִנֵּ֣ה מִן־הַיְאֹ֗ר עֹלֹת֙ שֶׁ֣בַע פָּר֔וֹת בְּרִיא֥וֹת בָּשָׂ֖ר
יט וִיפֹ֣ת תֹּ֑אַר וַתִּרְעֶ֖ינָה בָּאָֽחוּ׃ וְהִנֵּ֞ה שֶֽׁבַע פָּר֤וֹת אֲחֵרוֹת֙ עֹל֣וֹת אַחֲרֵיהֶ֔ן דַּלּ֨וֹת
וְרָע֥וֹת תֹּ֛אַר מְאֹ֖ד וְרַקּ֣וֹת בָּשָׂ֑ר לֹֽא־רָאִ֧יתִי כָהֵ֛נָּה בְּכָל־אֶ֥רֶץ מִצְרַ֖יִם לָרֹֽעַ׃
כ וַתֹּאכַ֙לְנָה֙ הַפָּר֔וֹת הָֽרַקּ֖וֹת וְהָֽרָע֑וֹת אֵ֣ת שֶׁ֧בַע הַפָּר֛וֹת הָרִאשֹׁנ֖וֹת הַבְּרִיאֹֽת׃
כא וַתָּבֹ֣אנָה אֶל־קִרְבֶּ֗נָה וְלֹ֤א נוֹדַע֙ כִּי־בָ֣אוּ אֶל־קִרְבֶּ֔נָה וּמַרְאֵיהֶ֣ן רַ֔ע כַּאֲשֶׁ֖ר בַּתְּחִלָּ֑ה
כב וָאִיקָֽץ׃ וָאֵ֖רֶא בַּחֲלֹמִ֑י וְהִנֵּ֣ה ׀ שֶׁ֣בַע שִׁבֳּלִ֗ים עֹלֹ֛ת בְּקָנֶ֥ה אֶחָ֖ד מְלֵאֹ֥ת וְטֹבֽוֹת׃
כג כד וְהִנֵּה֙ שֶׁ֣בַע שִׁבֳּלִ֔ים צְנֻמ֥וֹת דַּקּ֖וֹת שְׁדֻפ֣וֹת קָדִ֑ים צֹמְח֖וֹת אַחֲרֵיהֶֽם׃ וַתִּבְלַ֙עְןָ֙
הַשִּׁבֳּלִ֣ים הַדַּקֹּ֔ת אֵ֖ת שֶׁ֣בַע הַשִּׁבֳּלִ֣ים הַטֹּב֑וֹת וָאֹמַר֙ אֶל־הַֽחַרְטֻמִּ֔ים וְאֵ֥ין מַגִּ֖יד
כה לִֽי׃ וַיֹּ֤אמֶר יוֹסֵף֙ אֶל־פַּרְעֹ֔ה חֲל֥וֹם פַּרְעֹ֖ה אֶחָ֣ד ה֑וּא אֵ֣ת אֲשֶׁ֧ר הָאֱלֹהִ֛ים עֹשֶׂ֖ה
כו הִגִּ֥יד לְפַרְעֹֽה׃ שֶׁ֧בַע פָּרֹ֣ת הַטֹּבֹ֗ת שֶׁ֤בַע שָׁנִים֙ הֵ֔נָּה וְשֶׁ֤בַע הַשִּׁבֳּלִים֙ הַטֹּבֹ֔ת שֶׁ֥בַע
כז שָׁנִ֖ים הֵ֑נָּה חֲל֖וֹם אֶחָ֥ד הֽוּא׃ וְשֶׁ֣בַע הַ֠פָּרוֹת הָֽרַקּ֨וֹת וְהָרָעֹ֜ת הָעֹלֹ֣ת אַחֲרֵיהֶ֗ן שֶׁ֤בַע
כח שָׁנִים֙ הֵ֔נָּה וְשֶׁ֤בַע הַשִּׁבֳּלִים֙ הָרֵק֔וֹת שְׁדֻפ֖וֹת הַקָּדִ֑ים יִֽהְי֔וּ שֶׁ֖בַע שְׁנֵ֥י רָעָֽב׃ ה֣וּא
כט הַדָּבָ֔ר אֲשֶׁ֥ר דִּבַּ֖רְתִּי אֶל־פַּרְעֹ֑ה אֲשֶׁ֧ר הָאֱלֹהִ֛ים עֹשֶׂ֖ה הֶרְאָ֥ה אֶת־פַּרְעֹֽה׃ הִנֵּ֛ה
ל שֶׁ֥בַע שָׁנִ֖ים בָּא֑וֹת שָׂבָ֥ע גָּד֖וֹל בְּכָל־אֶ֥רֶץ מִצְרָֽיִם׃ וְ֠קָמוּ שֶׁ֨בַע שְׁנֵ֤י רָעָב֙ אַחֲרֵיהֶ֔ן
לא וְנִשְׁכַּ֥ח כָּל־הַשָּׂבָ֖ע בְּאֶ֣רֶץ מִצְרָ֑יִם וְכִלָּ֥ה הָרָעָ֖ב אֶת־הָאָֽרֶץ׃ וְלֹֽא־יִוָּדַ֤ע הַשָּׂבָע֙
לב בָּאָ֔רֶץ מִפְּנֵ֛י הָרָעָ֥ב הַה֖וּא אַחֲרֵי־כֵ֑ן כִּֽי־כָבֵ֥ד ה֖וּא מְאֹֽד׃ וְעַ֨ל הִשָּׁנ֧וֹת הַחֲל֛וֹם
אֶל־פַּרְעֹ֖ה פַּעֲמָ֑יִם כִּֽי־נָכ֤וֹן הַדָּבָר֙ מֵעִ֣ם הָאֱלֹהִ֔ים וּמְמַהֵ֥ר הָאֱלֹהִ֖ים לַעֲשֹׂתֽוֹ׃
לג לד וְעַתָּה֙ יֵרֶ֣א פַרְעֹ֔ה אִ֖ישׁ נָב֣וֹן וְחָכָ֑ם וִישִׁיתֵ֖הוּ עַל־אֶ֥רֶץ מִצְרָֽיִם׃ יַעֲשֶׂ֣ה פַרְעֹ֔ה
לה וְיַפְקֵ֥ד פְּקִדִ֖ים עַל־הָאָ֑רֶץ וְחִמֵּשׁ֙ אֶת־אֶ֣רֶץ מִצְרַ֔יִם בְּשֶׁ֖בַע שְׁנֵ֥י הַשָּׂבָֽע׃ וְיִקְבְּצ֗וּ
אֶת־כָּל־אֹ֙כֶל֙ הַשָּׁנִ֣ים הַטֹּבֹ֔ת הַבָּאֹ֖ת הָאֵ֑לֶּה וְיִצְבְּרוּ־בָ֞ר תַּ֧חַת יַד־פַּרְעֹ֛ה אֹ֖כֶל
לו בֶּעָרִ֥ים וְשָׁמָֽרוּ׃ וְהָיָ֨ה הָאֹ֤כֶל לְפִקָּדוֹן֙ לָאָ֔רֶץ לְשֶׁ֙בַע֙ שְׁנֵ֣י הָֽרָעָ֔ב אֲשֶׁ֥ר תִּהְיֶ֖יןָ בְּאֶ֣רֶץ
לז מִצְרָ֑יִם וְלֹֽא־תִכָּרֵ֥ת הָאָ֖רֶץ בָּרָעָֽב׃ וַיִּיטַ֥ב הַדָּבָ֖ר בְּעֵינֵ֣י פַרְעֹ֑ה וּבְעֵינֵ֖י כָּל־עֲבָדָֽיו׃

THE ART OF MIDRASH

Joseph Explains the Dreams of Pharaoh
Marc Chagall (1931)

Analysis

- Which elements of this image are directly mentioned in the text?
- Which elements of this image are not found in the text?
- What midrashic interpretation could be inferred from this image?

A QUESTION OF BIBLIODRAMA

TO PHARAOH

- What did you think the dreams might mean?
- Why did you not believe the dream interpretations given to you by your magicians and sages?
- What did you think when your cupbearer suggested there was a young Hebrew slave who could interpret dreams?
- What was your first impression of Yosef?
- Why did his interpretations speak to you immediately?
- Did you ask his advice on how to respond to the dreams? What did you think when he gave you the advice?

TO YOSEF

- What was it like waiting for two years for the cupbearer to remember you?
- Did you make any other efforts to gain your freedom?
- How did it feel when he did remember you and you were summoned to the court of Pharaoh?
- Were you worried that you might not be able to interpret Pharaoh's dreams? Did their interpretations come easily to you?
- Why did you also give Pharaoh advice on how to deal with the dreams? Were you worried about how he would accept this advice?

Similarly, Rabbi Joseph B. Soloveitchik (*Shiurei HaRav, HaDarom* 61) assumes that *ayin hara* represents the negative social dynamics between two people. When one person disagrees, criticizes, or opposes another, he is putting an *ayin hara* on them. If a person's sense of self is too intertwined with what other people think of him, then when he receives any indication that others do not approve of him, he will be devastated. However, someone who has a developed and independent sense of self, and does not desperately require the approval of others, is immune to the *ayin hara*.

Taking a similar rational approach, Rabbi Immanuel Bernstein (*Aggadah: Sages, Stories & Secrets*) argues that Yosef was immune to the *ayin hara* because he was self-confident and not swayed by the opinions or negative influences of others. For instance, he told his brothers about his dreams even though they might not like him as a result (Bereshit 37:5–11). He resisted the solicitation from Potifar's wife, even though he knew he might be punished, because it was morally and spiritually wrong (39:7–16). Additionally, when Pharaoh tells Yosef that he has heard that he can interpret dreams, Yosef brazenly corrects Pharaoh's mistake in public, saying that it is God who interprets the dreams (41:16). Yosef says and does what he believes God wants him to do, despite social pressure to do otherwise. This is what it means to be above the *ayin hara*.

From this perspective, we can all be immune to the *ayin hara*. We can stay firm in our sense of self, not needing the approval of others for our self-worth. When confronted by peer pressure to gossip or to cause undue pain to a third party, we can confidently refuse. When others try to influence us to sway us from following the Torah or performing certain *mitzvot*, we can stay firm and resist the strong pull to seek their approval. By doing so, we can be like Yosef, and rise above the *ayin hara*.

Rabbi Mordechai Schiffman

Analysis

- What areas of understanding of human nature and society do we now have that were unavailable to classical Jewish commentators? How can they aid our understanding of the text?
- What can we learn from this essay to help us understand the text?
- What further questions on the text do you have now that you have read this new take on the story?

INTEGRATING ḤOKHMA

How much do you care about what other people think of you?

On one level, it is natural and healthy to want the approval of others. If someone doesn't care what others think of him, he may do things that are harmful or immoral and end up being isolated from social groups, which in itself is not healthy. Yet the desire to be liked by others can easily become unhealthy if taken to an extreme. People who strongly need to gain approval or admiration from others determinedly seek ways to do so, sometimes at a high cost to their own goals. They tend to be more anxious and depressed, and to have lower self-esteem, which is contingent on what they think other people think of them.

The Talmud (Berakhot 20a) relates that Yosef and his descendants are immune to the destructive power of the "evil eye." Before we understand why they are immune, we first need to understand this mysterious and controversial concept. Broadly speaking, as it is presented in the Talmud, when one person looks upon another with envy or jealousy, the act of looking alone can cause actual damage. There have been several explanations of this concept throughout the ages, including (subsequently disproven) scientific explanations of the eye's ability to emit a dangerous vapor or fire. An alternative explanation is the theological proposal that the first person's negative emotions toward the other provoke God to be extra meticulous toward the second person, an explanation which has its own set of controversial ramifications. Those who view the evil eye as a supernatural phenomenon either try not to draw too much attention to themselves, or else they use various mystical procedures to try and counteract it.

Others, however, provide a more rational, psychological explanation of the concept. Rabbi Avraham Yitzchak HaKohen Kook understands the evil eye to refer to general social influence. We can be easily swayed by other people's beliefs, opinions, and practices; *ayin hara* is the term used to indicate being negatively impacted by others (see *Ein Aya* on *Berakhot*, p. 102). Someone who has self-confidence and is sure that they are doing what is right in God's eyes won't be swayed by the negative influence of others, and would therefore be immune to the evil eye.

got better by engaging in increasingly complicated work.

Yosef's skill at dream interpretation later spilled over into governance, where many of the same tools were required: careful observation, listening, analysis, strategic vision, and execution. These bundled talents could easily have led Yosef to tout his own abilities. But as Yosef matured and his influence grew, he did not take credit for his problem-solving abilities: "Yosef answered Pharaoh, saying, 'Not I! God will see to Pharaoh's welfare'" (Bereshit 41:16). Rashi on this verse explains that Yosef was telling Pharaoh, "The wisdom to interpret dreams is not my own, but God will answer. He will put in my mouth an answer that will be for Pharaoh's welfare."

Yosef answered to a higher authority than Pharaoh and, thereby, felt confident in summoning the God of the Hebrews into his conversation. In *Not in God's Name*, Rabbi Jonathan Sacks writes, "Every text needs interpretation. Every interpretation needs wisdom. Every wisdom needs careful negotiation between the timeless and time." Yosef brought wisdom into his interpretation, and, because of his intimacy with God, his insights became timeless. Yosef became more than a shrewd and capable vizier; he eventually became, in the court's eyes, a widely respected man of conviction because he was more than a problem solver. He was a problem solver who gave God the credit.

Dr. Erica Brown

TAKING A LITERARY APPROACH

Word traveled quickly about Yosef's abilities. Just hearing a dream revealed its significance. Rashi focuses on the verb "to hear" or "to listen," translating it as "to pay attention." The word implies more than simple hearing; it suggests listening for understanding. Rashi cites two other prooftexts to support his reading, Bereshit 42:23 and Devarim 28:49. Sforno suggests that Yosef did not guess or speculate but thought carefully about Pharaoh's words, the context in which they were said, and their larger import and significance. Yosef interpreted Pharaoh's dream on a national economic scale, thinking about the dream politically rather than personally.

Yosef's talent makes an appearance in another story about the ruler of a large empire and a Jewish courtier: Nevukhadnetzar and Daniel. Chapter 4 of the book of Daniel opens with Nevukhadnetzar in a state of confusion and fear, similar to Pharaoh:

> I had a dream that frightened me, and my thoughts in bed and the vision of my mind alarmed me. I gave an order to bring all the wise men of Babylon before me to let me know the meaning of the dream. (Daniel 4:2–3)

Nevukhadnetzar was desperate to have someone explain his own mind to him. When none of his own dream interpreters, magicians, or exorcists could help, he turned to Daniel, regarding him as a person of deep intelligence and intuition. He said to him, "Tell me the meaning of my dream vision that I have seen" and said of Daniel that "the spirit of the holy gods" rested in him and that "no mystery baffles him" (4:6). Daniel was able to explain the dream successfully.

Deborah Ancona and Hal Gregersen in their article, "The Power of Leaders Who Focus on Solving Problems" (*Harvard Business Review*, April 16, 2018) studied leaders who were problem solvers to identify common threads in their behaviors and dispositions. "Most striking," they conclude,

> is that none of these leaders has any expectation that they will attract "followers" personally – by dint of their charisma, status in a hierarchy, or access to resources. Instead, their method is to get others excited about whatever problem they have identified as ripe for a novel solution.

These leaders pursue "their own deep expertise" and bring others along for the ride, seeking out talent and the kind of team that can take on complex issues. They

38 Pharaoh said to them, "Could we find another like him, a man who has within him the spirit
39 of God?" So Pharaoh said to Yosef, "Since God has made all this known to you, there can
40 be no one else as astute or as wise as you. You shall be in charge of my court, and by your
command shall all my people be directed. Only the throne itself will make me greater than
41 you." Then Pharaoh said to Yosef, "I hereby place you in charge of all the land of Egypt."
42 Pharaoh removed his signet ring from his hand and placed it on Yosef's. He had him robed
43 in garments of the finest linen, and placed a gold chain around his neck. He had him ride
in the chariot of his second-in-command, and ahead of him people proclaimed, "*Avrekh*."[1]
44 Thus was he given authority over all Egypt. Pharaoh told Yosef, "I am Pharaoh, but without
45 your consent no one will lift hand or foot in all Egypt." And Pharaoh gave Yosef the name
Tzafenat Pane'aḥ[2] and gave him Asnat, daughter of Potifera, priest of On, as his wife. Thus
46 Yosef went out to oversee Egypt. When he entered the service of Pharaoh, king of Egypt,
Yosef was thirty years old. Leaving Pharaoh's presence, Yosef traveled throughout the land
47 48 of Egypt. During the seven years of plenty the land produced in profusion. He gathered all
the grain produced during the seven years of plenty in Egypt and stored it in the cities. In
49 each city he stored the grain grown in the surrounding fields. Yosef stored so much grain
that it was like the sand of the sea. They had to stop keeping records because it was beyond
50 measure. Before the years of famine came, two sons were born to Yosef by Asnat daughter

1 | Possibly meaning "bow" or "kneel," or in Egyptian "make way."
2 | Possibly "interpreter of secrets," or in Egyptian related to a word meaning "life."

UNLOCKING THE TEXT

- If Pharaoh saw the "spirit of God" in Yosef, did he believe in the same God?
- Why did Pharaoh immediately trust Yosef with this great responsibility?
- Why did Yosef need an Egyptian name?
- What is the significance of Yosef's new robes and jewelry?
- What does the name Tzafenat Paneaḥ mean?
- Why did Pharaoh choose Asnat to be Yosef's wife?
- What statement did Yosef make with the names he chose for his sons?
- How could Yosef take the grain from the people of Egypt and then sell it back to them during the famine?
- Does Yosef's plan save Egypt, or does it just save Pharaoh? Is the plan moral?

FINDING YOURSELF IN THE TEXT

- Have you ever been given a lot of responsibility you didn't feel prepared for?
- Have you ever had "imposter syndrome"?
- Do the leaders of your country have your best interests at heart or their own?

Consider using these questions as the basis for your own commentary or creative midrash.

How does reflecting on these firsthand experiences help you better understand the text?

לח וַיֹּ֤אמֶר פַּרְעֹה֙ אֶל־עֲבָדָ֔יו הֲנִמְצָ֥א כָזֶ֖ה אִ֑ישׁ אֲשֶׁ֛ר ר֥וּחַ אֱלֹהִ֖ים בּֽוֹ׃ וַיֹּ֣אמֶר פַּרְעֹה֮   לז שלישי

מ אֶל־יוֹסֵ֗ף אַחֲרֵ֨י הוֹדִ֧יעַ אֱלֹהִ֛ים אוֹתְךָ֖ אֶת־כָּל־זֹ֑את אֵין־נָב֥וֹן וְחָכָ֖ם כָּמֽוֹךָ׃ אַתָּה֙

מא תִּהְיֶ֣ה עַל־בֵּיתִ֔י וְעַל־פִּ֖יךָ יִשַּׁ֣ק כָּל־עַמִּ֑י רַ֥ק הַכִּסֵּ֖א אֶגְדַּ֥ל מִמֶּֽךָּ׃ וַיֹּ֥אמֶר פַּרְעֹ֖ה

מב אֶל־יוֹסֵ֑ף רְאֵה֙ נָתַ֣תִּי אֹֽתְךָ֔ עַ֖ל כָּל־אֶ֥רֶץ מִצְרָֽיִם׃ וַיָּ֨סַר פַּרְעֹ֤ה אֶת־טַבַּעְתּוֹ֙ מֵעַ֣ל
יָד֔וֹ וַיִּתֵּ֥ן אֹתָ֖הּ עַל־יַ֣ד יוֹסֵ֑ף וַיַּלְבֵּ֤שׁ אֹתוֹ֙ בִּגְדֵי־שֵׁ֔שׁ וַיָּ֛שֶׂם רְבִ֥ד הַזָּהָ֖ב עַל־צַוָּארֽוֹ׃

מג וַיַּרְכֵּ֣ב אֹת֗וֹ בְּמִרְכֶּ֤בֶת הַמִּשְׁנֶה֙ אֲשֶׁר־ל֔וֹ וַיִּקְרְא֥וּ לְפָנָ֖יו אַבְרֵ֑ךְ וְנָת֣וֹן אֹת֔וֹ עַ֖ל

מד כָּל־אֶ֥רֶץ מִצְרָֽיִם׃ וַיֹּ֧אמֶר פַּרְעֹ֛ה אֶל־יוֹסֵ֖ף אֲנִ֣י פַרְעֹ֑ה וּבִלְעָדֶ֗יךָ לֹֽא־יָרִ֨ים אִ֜ישׁ

מה אֶת־יָד֛וֹ וְאֶת־רַגְל֖וֹ בְּכָל־אֶ֥רֶץ מִצְרָֽיִם׃ וַיִּקְרָ֨א פַרְעֹ֥ה שֵׁם־יוֹסֵף֮ צָֽפְנַ֣ת פַּעְנֵ֒חַ֒
וַיִּתֶּן־ל֣וֹ אֶת־אָֽסְנַ֗ת בַּת־פּ֥וֹטִי פֶ֛רַע כֹּהֵ֥ן אֹ֖ן לְאִשָּׁ֑ה וַיֵּצֵ֥א יוֹסֵ֖ף עַל־אֶ֥רֶץ מִצְרָֽיִם׃

מו וְיוֹסֵף֙ בֶּן־שְׁלֹשִׁ֣ים שָׁנָ֔ה בְּעָמְד֕וֹ לִפְנֵ֖י פַּרְעֹ֣ה מֶֽלֶךְ־מִצְרָ֑יִם וַיֵּצֵ֤א יוֹסֵף֙ מִלִּפְנֵ֣י פַרְעֹ֔ה

מז וַֽיַּעֲבֹ֖ר בְּכָל־אֶ֥רֶץ מִצְרָֽיִם׃ וַתַּ֣עַשׂ הָאָ֔רֶץ בְּשֶׁ֖בַע שְׁנֵ֣י הַשָּׂבָ֑ע לִקְמָצִֽים׃ וַיִּקְבֹּ֞ץ
מח אֶת־כָּל־אֹ֣כֶל ׀ שֶׁ֣בַע שָׁנִ֗ים אֲשֶׁ֤ר הָיוּ֙ בְּאֶ֣רֶץ מִצְרַ֔יִם וַיִּתֶּן־אֹ֖כֶל בֶּעָרִ֑ים אֹ֧כֶל שְׂדֵֽה־

מט הָעִ֛יר אֲשֶׁ֥ר סְבִֽיבֹתֶ֖יהָ נָתַ֥ן בְּתוֹכָֽהּ׃ וַיִּצְבֹּ֨ר יוֹסֵ֥ף בָּ֛ר כְּח֥וֹל הַיָּ֖ם הַרְבֵּ֣ה מְאֹ֑ד עַ֛ד

נ כִּֽי־חָדַ֥ל לִסְפֹּ֖ר כִּי־אֵ֥ין מִסְפָּֽר׃ וּלְיוֹסֵ֗ף יֻלַּד֙ שְׁנֵ֣י בָנִ֔ים בְּטֶ֥רֶם תָּב֖וֹא שְׁנַ֣ת הָרָעָ֑ב דוד

| THEMES | PROPHECY AND REVELATION | LEADERSHIP | ETHICS |

Episode 59: *Yosef's Rise to Power* – Bereshit 41:38–57

SUMMARY

This episode records the meteoric rise of Yosef from a prison pit to the second most powerful man in Egypt, and the implementation of the plan he pitched to Pharaoh.

51 of Potifera, priest of On. Yosef named his firstborn Menashe, saying, "God has made me
52 forget all my troubles and all my father's family."[3] The second son he named Efrayim, saying,
53 "God has made me fruitful in the land of my affliction."[4] The seven years of abundance in
54 Egypt came to an end, and the seven years of famine began, just as Yosef had said they
would. There was famine in all the other lands, but throughout Egypt there was food.
55 When all Egypt began to feel the famine, the people cried to Pharaoh for food. Pharaoh
56 told all the Egyptians, "Go to Yosef. Whatever he tells you – do." The famine spread over
the entire country. Yosef then opened all the storehouses and sold grain to the Egyptians,
57 for the famine was worsening throughout Egypt. People from all over the region came
to Egypt to buy grain from Yosef, because all across the land the famine was devastating.

---

3 | The name Menashe resonates with *nashani* ("made me forget").

4 | The name Efrayim resonates with *hifrani* ("made me fruitful").

THE ART OF MIDRASH

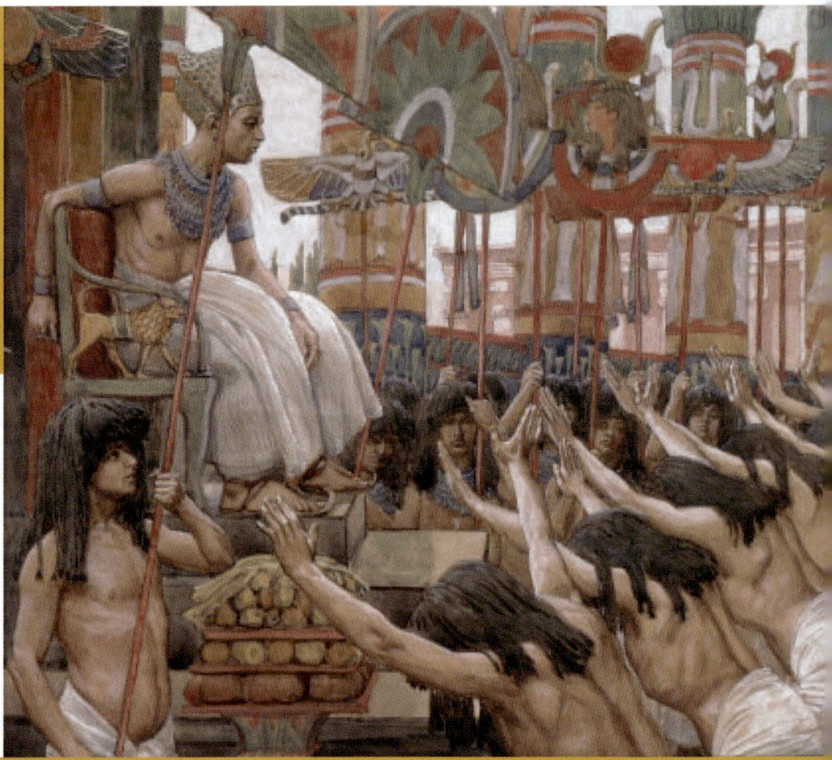

Joseph Dwelt in Egypt
James Tissot (1896–1902)

Analysis

- Which elements of this image are directly mentioned in the text?
- Which elements of this image are not found in the text?
- What midrashic interpretation could be inferred from this image?

נא אֲשֶׁר יָלְדָה־לּוֹ אָסְנַת בַּת־פּוֹטִי פֶרַע כֹּהֵן אוֹן׃ וַיִּקְרָא יוֹסֵף אֶת־שֵׁם הַבְּכוֹר
נב מְנַשֶּׁה כִּי־נַשַּׁנִי אֱלֹהִים אֶת־כָּל־עֲמָלִי וְאֵת כָּל־בֵּית אָבִי׃ וְאֵת שֵׁם הַשֵּׁנִי קָרָא
נג אֶפְרָיִם כִּי־הִפְרַנִי אֱלֹהִים בְּאֶרֶץ עָנְיִי׃ וַתִּכְלֶינָה שֶׁבַע שְׁנֵי הַשָּׂבָע אֲשֶׁר הָיָה רביעי
נד בְּאֶרֶץ מִצְרָיִם׃ וַתְּחִלֶּינָה שֶׁבַע שְׁנֵי הָרָעָב לָבוֹא כַּאֲשֶׁר אָמַר יוֹסֵף וַיְהִי רָעָב
נה בְּכָל־הָאֲרָצוֹת וּבְכָל־אֶרֶץ מִצְרַיִם הָיָה לָחֶם׃ וַתִּרְעַב כָּל־אֶרֶץ מִצְרַיִם וַיִּצְעַק
הָעָם אֶל־פַּרְעֹה לַלָּחֶם וַיֹּאמֶר פַּרְעֹה לְכָל־מִצְרַיִם לְכוּ אֶל־יוֹסֵף אֲשֶׁר־יֹאמַר
נו לָכֶם תַּעֲשׂוּ׃ וְהָרָעָב הָיָה עַל כָּל־פְּנֵי הָאָרֶץ וַיִּפְתַּח יוֹסֵף אֶת־כָּל־אֲשֶׁר בָּהֶם
נז וַיִּשְׁבֹּר לְמִצְרַיִם וַיֶּחֱזַק הָרָעָב בְּאֶרֶץ מִצְרָיִם׃ וְכָל־הָאָרֶץ בָּאוּ מִצְרַיְמָה לִשְׁבֹּר
אֶל־יוֹסֵף כִּי־חָזַק הָרָעָב בְּכָל־הָאָרֶץ׃

A QUESTION OF BIBLIODRAMA

TO PHARAOH

- What did you see in Yosef that led you to give him so much power and responsibility?
- Do you have any concerns or reservations about giving Yosef so much power and responsibility?
- Why do you trust this young man who you have only just met?

TO YOSEF

- How do you feel about your new role?
- Do you have "imposter syndrome"?
- Do you have any reservations about the morality of your plan for Egypt?

have I wronged any one of them" (Bemidbar 16:15). Likewise, the prophet Shmuel rhetorically asks the people who have come asking for a king: "Whose ox have I taken, or whose ass have I taken?" (I Shmuel 12:3). Landes says that these remarks set the Israelites apart from any other culture of the time. Elsewhere, the king's right to appropriate other people's property was taken for granted. The philosopher John Locke understood that private property rights are an essential element of a free society.

A second feature was Judaism's respect for the dignity of labor. God saved Noaḥ from the flood, but Noaḥ had to build the ark. Third was the Judaic sense of linear time: time not as a series of cycles in which everything eventually returns to the way it was, but rather as an arena of change, development, and progress. We are so familiar with these ideas – they form the bedrock of Western culture – that we are not always aware that they are not human universals. Jonathan Haidt calls them weird: that is, they belong to societies that are Western, Educated, Industrialised, Rich, and Democratic.

To my mind, the most decisive single factor – the great break of Judaism from the ancient world of magic, mystery, and myth – was the deconsecration of nature that followed from the fact that God created nature by an act of will, and by making us in His image, gave us too the creative power of will. That meant that for Jews, holiness lies not in the way the world is but in the way it ought to be. Poverty, disease, famine, injustice, and the exploitation of the powerless by the powerful are not the will of God. They may be part of human nature, but we have the power to rise above nature. God wants us not to accept but to heal, to cure, to prevent. So Jews have tended to become, out of all proportion to their numbers, lawyers fighting injustice, doctors fighting disease, teachers fighting ignorance, economists fighting poverty, and (especially in modern Israel) agricultural technologists finding new ways to grow food in environments where it has never grown before.

All of this is brilliantly portrayed in this *parasha*. First Yosef diagnoses the problem. There will be a famine lasting seven years. It is what he does next that is world-changing. He sees this not as a fate to be endured but as a problem to be solved. Then, without fuss, he solves it, saving a whole region from death by starvation.

What can be changed need not be endured. Human suffering is not a fate to be borne, but a challenge to be overcome. This is Yosef's life-changing idea. What can be healed is not holy. God does not want us to accept poverty and pain, but to cure them.

Rabbi Jonathan Sacks

Analysis

- What areas of understanding of human nature, society, and history do we have now that were unavailable to classical Jewish commentators? How can they aid our understanding of the text?
- What can we learn from this essay to help us understand the text?
- What further questions on the text do you have now that you have read this new take on the story?

INTEGRATING ḤOKHMA

In this *parasha*, Yosef became the world's first economist. Interpreting Pharaoh's dreams, he develops a theory of trade cycles – seven fat years followed by seven lean years – a cycle that still seems approximately to hold. Yosef also intuited that when a head of state dreams about cows and ears of corn, he is probably unconsciously thinking about macro-economics. The disturbing nature of the dreams suggested that God was sending an advance warning of a "black swan," a rare phenomenon for which conventional economics is unprepared.

So, having diagnosed the problem, he immediately proceeds to a solution: use the good years to build up resources for the lean times, a sound instance of long-term economic planning.

This turned out to be life-saving advice. His later economic policies, narrated in Parashat Vayigash (Bereshit 47:11–26), are more questionable. When the people ran out of money during the lean years, Yosef told them to trade their livestock. When this too ran out, he arranged for them to sell their land to Pharaoh with the sole exception of the land belonging to the priests. The Egyptians were now, in essence, Pharaoh's serfs, paying him a tax of 20 percent of their produce each year.

This nationalization of livestock, labor, and land meant that power was now concentrated in the hands of Pharaoh, and the people themselves reduced to serfdom. Both of these developments would eventually be used against Yosef's own people, when a new Pharaoh arose and enslaved the Israelites. It cannot be by accident that the Torah twice uses the same phrase about the Egyptians that it will later use about the Israelites: *avadim lePharo*, they have become "Pharaoh's slaves" (47:19, 25). There is already here a hint that too much economic power in the hands of the state leads to what Friedrich Hayek called "the road to serfdom" and the eclipse of liberty.

So a reasonable case could be made that Yosef was the first economist. But why the predominance of Jews in economics in the modern age? There is a strong affinity between the market economy and what is broadly known as the Judaeo-Christian ethic, because it was only in such cultures that it emerged. China, for example, led the West in almost every aspect of technology until the seventeenth century, yet it failed to generate science, a free economy, or an industrial revolution, and fell far behind until recent times. What was it about biblical values that proved so fruitful for economic thought, institutions, and growth?

The Harvard historian and economist David Landes offered insight in his magisterial work *The Wealth and Poverty of Nations*. First is the biblical insistence on property rights. He quotes Moshe's words during the Koraḥ revolt: "I have not taken so much as a donkey from them, nor

minimum – a minimum which was enough to raise them above the level of constant worry about their purely physical needs – would it then be possible to deal with spiritual thirsts and hungers.

Now we can return to our original question. What was Yosef's intention in laying out a complex socio-economic plan to Pharaoh?

What Yosef planned here, with regard to Egypt's economy, was not simply part of the scheme to raise him to greatness. It was *maaseh avot siman labanim* – an event that happens to a forefather foreshadows what will happen to *am Yisrael*. Yosef is teaching something that *am Yisrael* must never forget: Before the Jewish people tries to change the world spiritually, it has to make sure that people are alright on a simple physical level. In the language of *Ḥazal*, "If there is no flour, there is no Torah" (Avot 3:21).

Rabbi Yehuda Amital

TAKING A LITERARY APPROACH

When Yosef finally stands before Pharaoh and interprets his dreams, we encounter a very strange section of the story. All of a sudden, Yosef begins to give Pharaoh all sorts of advice, when not asked to do so. In his position, a slave recalled from the depths of the prison, one would expect him to be taciturn, timid, afraid even to interpret the dream; instead, he presumes to plan Pharaoh's internal policy for the next fourteen years! Abarbanel's explanation is that a "spirit of prophecy" rested upon him and he could not stop himself from speaking.

To understand Yosef's actions, we must examine the tactics which Avraham, Yitzḥak, and Yaakov used in spreading the ideas of monotheism and morality.

Until Avraham arrived on the scene, there was a very small group of people who were trying to spread the ideas of monotheism, morality, and ethics. These few individuals, however, did not seem to be able to reach a wider audience – if anything, we see a decrease in the number of people (percentage-wise) who ascribed to such a belief system from the time of Adam to that of Noaḥ, and again from Noaḥ to Avraham. Many midrashim, for example, speak of the yeshiva of Shem and Ever, which attempted to preach these beliefs during the period between Noaḥ and Avraham. It would seem that this yeshiva failed in its attempt.

Thus, Avraham decided (and he was the first to hit upon the idea) to establish a nation, an entire functioning political entity, which would live out these ideals in day-to-day life; by setting an outstanding example, they would encourage other peoples to adopt these standards. Yitzḥak continued this idea. However, the moment we reach Yaakov Avinu, it appears that the tactic has crumbled. Yaakov's sons go down to Egypt and are enslaved there. Even before that, the internal structure of his family (which was to become the Jewish nation) seems to be crumbling – the problems between Yosef and his brothers are testament to this.

Despite these seeming reversals, the goals of nation-building and spreading monotheism were still there. Yosef (and at the root, God) saw that it was fundamentally impossible to preach monotheism to the nations of the time, or to expect Judaism to influence them. Yosef saw that a religion consisting of rituals and spiritual beliefs alone would never have an overwhelming effect. Rather, the very first thirst which humanity needed to have quenched, and the very first hunger which had to be stilled, were the physical ones.

Yosef understood that only by creating a stable economic system wherein everyone received a

42 1 Knowing that there was grain in Egypt, Yaakov said to his sons, "Why do you keep looking
2 at one another?" He said, "I have heard that there is grain in Egypt. Go down there and buy
3 some for us so that we may live and not die." So ten of Yosef's brothers went down to buy
4 grain in Egypt. But Yaakov did not send Yosef's brother Binyamin with them, for he was
5 afraid that harm might come to him. So Yisrael's sons were among those who came to buy
6 grain, the famine having reached as far as the land of Canaan. Yosef was the governor of the
land; it was he who dispensed food to all its people. When Yosef's brothers arrived, they
7 bowed down to him, their faces to the ground. Yosef recognized his brothers as soon as he
saw them, but he acted like a stranger and spoke harshly to them. "Where have you come
8 from?" he asked. They replied, "From the land of Canaan – to buy food." Yosef recognized
9 his brothers, but they did not recognize him. Then Yosef remembered the dreams he had
dreamed about them. "You are spies!" he said. "You have come to see where our land is
10 11 exposed." "No, my lord," they said. "Your servants have come to buy food. We all are sons
12 of the same man. We are honest men. Your servants are not spies." "Lies," he said. "You have
13 come to see where our land is exposed." "We were once twelve brothers," they replied, "sons

UNLOCKING THE TEXT

- Why does Yaakov sound angry with his sons?
- Why didn't the brothers recognize Yosef?
- Why does Yosef remember his dreams at this point? Wouldn't it make more sense that he remember what his brothers did to him?
- Why did Yosef accuse the brothers of being spies? What is his plan and motivation?
- Why did the brothers volunteer more information on the siblings who were not there?
- Was it strange that an Egyptian leader would describe himself as "God-fearing"?
- Why did Yosef change his demands, from one of the brothers returning to Canaan to bring Binyamin, to one of them staying while the rest return to bring Binyamin to Egypt?
- Why was Shimon chosen to remain?
- What does Yosef hope to achieve by returning their money to them?

FINDING YOURSELF IN THE TEXT

- Have you ever recognized someone who did not recognize you? How did it feel?
- Have you ever been accused of something you did not do? How did it feel?
- Have you ever had a series of bad things happen to you and wondered why?

Consider using these questions as the basis for your own commentary or creative midrash.

How does reflecting on these firsthand experiences help you better understand the text?

מב א וַיַּ֣רְא יַעֲקֹ֔ב כִּ֥י יֶשׁ־שֶׁ֖בֶר בְּמִצְרָ֑יִם וַיֹּ֤אמֶר יַעֲקֹב֙ לְבָנָ֔יו לָ֖מָּה תִּתְרָאֽוּ׃ וַיֹּ֕אמֶר הִנֵּ֣ה
שָׁמַ֔עְתִּי כִּ֥י יֶשׁ־שֶׁ֖בֶר בְּמִצְרָ֑יִם רְדוּ־שָׁ֨מָּה֙ וְשִׁבְרוּ־לָ֣נוּ מִשָּׁ֔ם וְנִחְיֶ֖ה וְלֹ֥א נָמֽוּת׃
ג וַיֵּֽרְד֥וּ אֲחֵֽי־יוֹסֵ֖ף עֲשָׂרָ֑ה לִשְׁבֹּ֥ר בָּ֖ר מִמִּצְרָֽיִם׃ וְאֶת־בִּנְיָמִין֙ אֲחִ֣י יוֹסֵ֔ף לֹא־שָׁלַ֥ח
ה יַעֲקֹ֖ב אֶת־אֶחָ֑יו כִּ֣י אָמַ֔ר פֶּן־יִקְרָאֶ֖נּוּ אָסֽוֹן׃ וַיָּבֹ֨אוּ֙ בְּנֵ֣י יִשְׂרָאֵ֔ל לִשְׁבֹּ֖ר בְּת֣וֹךְ
ו הַבָּאִ֑ים כִּֽי־הָיָ֥ה הָרָעָ֖ב בְּאֶ֣רֶץ כְּנָ֑עַן׃ וְיוֹסֵ֗ף ה֚וּא הַשַּׁלִּ֣יט עַל־הָאָ֔רֶץ ה֥וּא הַמַּשְׁבִּ֖יר
לְכָל־עַ֣ם הָאָ֑רֶץ וַיָּבֹ֨אוּ֙ אֲחֵ֣י יוֹסֵ֔ף וַיִּשְׁתַּֽחֲווּ־ל֥וֹ אַפַּ֖יִם אָֽרְצָה׃ ז וַיַּ֥רְא יוֹסֵ֖ף אֶת־אֶחָ֑יו
וַיַּכִּרֵ֗ם וַיִּתְנַכֵּ֤ר אֲלֵיהֶם֙ וַיְדַבֵּ֨ר אִתָּ֜ם קָשׁ֗וֹת וַיֹּ֤אמֶר אֲלֵהֶם֙ מֵאַ֣יִן בָּאתֶ֔ם וַיֹּ֣אמְר֔וּ
ח מֵאֶ֥רֶץ כְּנַ֖עַן לִשְׁבָּר־אֹֽכֶל׃ וַיַּכֵּ֥ר יוֹסֵ֖ף אֶת־אֶחָ֑יו וְהֵ֖ם לֹ֥א הִכִּרֻֽהוּ׃ ט וַיִּזְכֹּ֣ר יוֹסֵ֔ף אֵ֚ת
הַחֲלֹמ֔וֹת אֲשֶׁ֥ר חָלַ֖ם לָהֶ֑ם וַיֹּ֤אמֶר אֲלֵהֶם֙ מְרַגְּלִ֣ים אַתֶּ֔ם לִרְא֛וֹת אֶת־עֶרְוַ֥ת הָאָ֖רֶץ
י בָּאתֶֽם׃ וַיֹּֽאמְר֥וּ אֵלָ֖יו לֹ֣א אֲדֹנִ֑י וַעֲבָדֶ֥יךָ בָּ֖אוּ לִשְׁבָּר־אֹֽכֶל׃ יא כֻּלָּ֗נוּ בְּנֵ֤י אִישׁ־אֶחָד֙
נַ֔חְנוּ כֵּנִ֣ים אֲנַ֔חְנוּ לֹא־הָי֥וּ עֲבָדֶ֖יךָ מְרַגְּלִֽים׃ יב וַיֹּ֖אמֶר אֲלֵהֶ֑ם לֹ֕א כִּֽי־עֶרְוַ֥ת הָאָ֖רֶץ
יג בָּאתֶ֥ם לִרְאֽוֹת׃ וַיֹּֽאמְר֗וּ שְׁנֵ֣ים עָשָׂר֩ עֲבָדֶ֨יךָ אַחִ֥ים ׀ אֲנַ֛חְנוּ בְּנֵ֥י אִישׁ־אֶחָ֖ד בְּאֶ֣רֶץ

THEMES	RELATIONSHIPS AND LOVE	LEADERSHIP	GOD

Episode 60: *The Brothers' First Encounter with Yosef* – Bereshit 42:1–28

SUMMARY

When Yosef interprets Pharaoh's dream, plans a solution for the grave problems posed by his interpretation, and puts these ideas into practice, he unknowingly, through hidden divine providence, prepares the way for his reencounter with his brothers. The famine, which affects the entire region, reaches the land of Canaan as well, and the family of Yaakov seeks to assuage its hunger by purchasing some of the produce that Yosef has stored in Egypt.

14 of one man in Canaan. The youngest is now with our father, and one is gone." But Yosef
15 said, "It is as I said to you – you are spies. This is how you will be tested. By Pharaoh's life,
16 you will not leave this place unless your youngest brother comes here. Let one of you go
and fetch your brother. The rest of you will remain confined here. This will test whether or
17 not you are telling the truth. If not, by Pharaoh's life, you are spies." He had them placed in
18 custody for three days. On the third day, Yosef said to them, "If you do this you will live,
19 for I am a God-fearing man. If you are honest, let one of your brothers stay here in prison
20 while the rest of you go and take back grain for your starving households. Then bring your
youngest brother to me so that your words can be verified and you will not die." They
21 agreed. And they said to one another, "We are guilty, guilty because of what we did to our
brother. We saw his suffering when he pleaded with us but we did not listen. That is why
22 this trouble has come upon us." Then Reuven spoke up: "Did I not tell you not to sin against
23 the boy? But you would not listen. Now comes the reckoning for his blood." They did not
24 realize that Yosef could understand them, for a translator stood between them. And Yosef
turned away from them and wept. Then he turned back to them and spoke again. He had
25 Shimon taken from them and placed in chains before their eyes. Yosef gave orders to fill
their bags with grain and put each man's money back in his sack. They were to be given
26 provisions for the journey. After this was done for them, they loaded their grain on their
27 donkeys and left. As one of them was opening his sack to feed his donkey at the place
28 where they stopped for the night, he saw his money right there at the top of his pack. "My
money has been returned!" he told his brothers. "There it is in my pack!" Their hearts sank.
Trembling, they turned to one another, saying, "What is this that God has done to us?"

TO THE BROTHERS

- How did it feel to be accused of being spies?
- What were your initial thoughts about the Egyptian leader accusing you?
- Why do you immediately link what is happening to you with your previous sins regarding Yosef?
- Did you have any inkling as to the real identity of the Egyptian ruler in front of you?
- Why did you choose Shimon to remain?
- Can you explain how your money ended up being returned to you?
- How are you going to explain all of this to your father?

יד כְּנַעַן וְהִנֵּה הַקָּטֹן אֶת־אָבִינוּ הַיּוֹם וְהָאֶחָד אֵינֶנּוּ: וַיֹּאמֶר אֲלֵהֶם יוֹסֵף הוּא אֲשֶׁר

טו דִּבַּרְתִּי אֲלֵכֶם לֵאמֹר מְרַגְּלִים אַתֶּם: בְּזֹאת תִּבָּחֵנוּ חֵי פַרְעֹה אִם־תֵּצְאוּ מִזֶּה כִּי

טז אִם־בְּבוֹא אֲחִיכֶם הַקָּטֹן הֵנָּה: שִׁלְחוּ מִכֶּם אֶחָד וְיִקַּח אֶת־אֲחִיכֶם וְאַתֶּם הֵאָסְרוּ

יז וְיִבָּחֲנוּ דִּבְרֵיכֶם הַאֱמֶת אִתְּכֶם וְאִם־לֹא חֵי פַרְעֹה כִּי מְרַגְּלִים אַתֶּם: וַיֶּאֱסֹף אֹתָם

יח אֶל־מִשְׁמָר שְׁלֹשֶׁת יָמִים: וַיֹּאמֶר אֲלֵהֶם יוֹסֵף בַּיּוֹם הַשְּׁלִישִׁי זֹאת עֲשׂוּ וִחְיוּ אֶת־

לח חמישי יט הָאֱלֹהִים אֲנִי יָרֵא: אִם־כֵּנִים אַתֶּם אֲחִיכֶם אֶחָד יֵאָסֵר בְּבֵית מִשְׁמַרְכֶם וְאַתֶּם

כ לְכוּ הָבִיאוּ שֶׁבֶר רַעֲבוֹן בָּתֵּיכֶם: וְאֶת־אֲחִיכֶם הַקָּטֹן תָּבִיאוּ אֵלַי וְיֵאָמְנוּ דִבְרֵיכֶם

כא וְלֹא תָמוּתוּ וַיַּעֲשׂוּ־כֵן: וַיֹּאמְרוּ אִישׁ אֶל־אָחִיו אֲבָל אֲשֵׁמִים ׀ אֲנַחְנוּ עַל־אָחִינוּ

אֲשֶׁר רָאִינוּ צָרַת נַפְשׁוֹ בְּהִתְחַנְנוֹ אֵלֵינוּ וְלֹא שָׁמָעְנוּ עַל־כֵּן בָּאָה אֵלֵינוּ הַצָּרָה

כב הַזֹּאת: וַיַּעַן רְאוּבֵן אֹתָם לֵאמֹר הֲלוֹא אָמַרְתִּי אֲלֵיכֶם ׀ לֵאמֹר אַל־תֶּחֶטְאוּ

כג בַיֶּלֶד וְלֹא שְׁמַעְתֶּם וְגַם־דָּמוֹ הִנֵּה נִדְרָשׁ: וְהֵם לֹא יָדְעוּ כִּי שֹׁמֵעַ יוֹסֵף כִּי הַמֵּלִיץ

כד בֵּינֹתָם: וַיִּסֹּב מֵעֲלֵיהֶם וַיֵּבְךְּ וַיָּשָׁב אֲלֵהֶם וַיְדַבֵּר אֲלֵהֶם וַיִּקַּח מֵאִתָּם אֶת־שִׁמְעוֹן

כה וַיֶּאֱסֹר אֹתוֹ לְעֵינֵיהֶם: וַיְצַו יוֹסֵף וַיְמַלְאוּ אֶת־כְּלֵיהֶם בָּר וּלְהָשִׁיב כַּסְפֵּיהֶם אִישׁ

כו אֶל־שַׂקּוֹ וְלָתֵת לָהֶם צֵדָה לַדָּרֶךְ וַיַּעַשׂ לָהֶם כֵּן: וַיִּשְׂאוּ אֶת־שִׁבְרָם עַל־חֲמֹרֵיהֶם

כז וַיֵּלְכוּ מִשָּׁם: וַיִּפְתַּח הָאֶחָד אֶת־שַׂקּוֹ לָתֵת מִסְפּוֹא לַחֲמֹרוֹ בַּמָּלוֹן וַיַּרְא אֶת־כַּסְפּוֹ

כח וְהִנֵּה־הוּא בְּפִי אַמְתַּחְתּוֹ: וַיֹּאמֶר אֶל־אֶחָיו הוּשַׁב כַּסְפִּי וְגַם הִנֵּה בְאַמְתַּחְתִּי

וַיֵּצֵא לִבָּם וַיֶּחֶרְדוּ אִישׁ אֶל־אָחִיו לֵאמֹר מַה־זֹּאת עָשָׂה אֱלֹהִים לָנוּ:

A QUESTION OF BIBLIODRAMA

TO YOSEF

- What did you feel when you realized who these men from Canaan were?

- What did you think about as you remembered your dreams from your youth?

- Did you have a plan in place from the beginning, or did you change your plan as you thought things through?

- What is your endgame here?

TO YAAKOV

- Were you angry at your sons for not being proactive in the face of famine?

- Why did you keep Binyamin back? Why are you more protective of him than your other sons?

THE ART OF MIDRASH

Joseph and His Brothers in Egypt
Salvador Dalí (1967)

as that will endanger everything he has accomplished. Remembering his dream suddenly puts his Egyptian life into a context which Yosef hasn't considered: that his new life need not be a radical departure from the old but, in fact, a fulfillment of it. Yosef needs some time to think.

Rabbi Zvi Grumet

Analysis

- Which elements of this image are directly mentioned in the text?
- Which elements of this image are not found in the text?
- What midrashic interpretation could be inferred from this image?

TAKING A LITERARY APPROACH

Four times in the span of two verses, the Torah plays on the word which in one form means to recognize and in another means to be a stranger: "Yosef saw his brothers and recognized (*h-k-r*) them, but made himself a stranger (*n-k-r*) to them.... Yosef recognized (*h-k-r*) his brothers but they did not recognize (*h-k-r*) him" (Bereshit 42:7–8). This is the same root used to describe Yitzḥak's inability to recognize Yaakov dressed in Esav's clothes, Yaakov's demand that Lavan identify any stolen possessions, the brothers asking Yaakov to identify Yosef's bloodied *ketonet*, and Tamar's private challenge that Yehuda identify the staff and cloth (38:25). Yaakov's deception of his father keeps coming back to haunt him and his children, and now it is Yosef's turn. He hides behind his Egyptian clothes and presents himself as a stranger to his brothers.

We can only imagine what is happening in Yosef's head at that moment. Anger? Vengeance? Possibly. Is he simply taunting them to watch them squirm? It is impossible to know. What is likely, though, is that seeing his brothers rattles him. He has made it so far in building his new life and has worked so hard to put his past behind him, and he is now forced to contend with that past. Their arrival in Egypt presents him with essentially three options: one, to give them their wheat and hope that they never return; two, to exact some kind of vengeance and live with the knowledge that he is no better than they; and three, to figure out a third option.

What does seem clear is that despite his best efforts to forget his past, Yosef now knows that he cannot forget. He cannot simply give his brothers food and send them on their way. Their very presence forces him to face his buried past. Fascinatingly, the Torah does not describe Yosef as remembering that they had sold him. Rather, it tells us that he remembers his dreams. The former would lead us to expect vengeance, but the latter directs our thinking differently. Ramban (on 42:9) is so taken by this description that he understands everything Yosef does as an attempt to ensure that his prophetic dreams come true, including that all eleven brothers bow before him. That is why, Ramban asserts, Yosef insists that the brothers bring Binyamin, using a ruse to hide his real intentions.

This interpretation is appealing, especially since Yosef's first demand is that one brother return to Canaan to bring Binyamin, but it is built on many assumptions, including Yosef's unerring righteousness and his belief that the dreams are prophetic. It also pits Yosef's righteous intentions against his cruel behavior toward his brothers and father in the attempt to fulfill that prophecy. Perhaps the greatest difficulty with this interpretation is that Yosef continues the ruse against his brothers even after that dream is eventually fulfilled with the arrival of Binyamin, drawing them back in and forcing a confrontation with Yehuda.

Rabbi Yoel Bin-Nun suggests a dramatically different approach. According to him, Yosef is under the impression that his sale is a premeditated plot to remove him from the covenantal family, just as Yishmael and Esav were removed. Moreover, Rabbi Bin-Nun suggests that Yosef suspects Yaakov is complicit – or even the architect of this plot. Yosef's actions are his attempt to discern the truth of his own hypothesis.

Both Ramban and Rabbi Bin-Nun assume that Yosef is still deeply rooted in his past, whether in his dreams (Ramban) or in the covenant (Bin-Nun). I'd like to suggest an alternative to both interpretations, based on the assumption that Yosef long ago abandoned his past identity and is now struggling with the question of how to resolve his past with his present and to figure out how to navigate this new complication. Ignoring his past is no longer possible but neither is fully embracing it,

word for garment, *b-g-d*, is also the Hebrew word for "betrayal," as in the confession formula, *ashamnu*, *bagadnu*, "We have been guilty, we have betrayed."

Is this a mere literary conceit, a way of linking a series of otherwise unconnected stories? Or is there something more fundamental at stake?

It was the nineteenth-century Jewish historian Heinrich Graetz who pointed out a crucial difference between other ancient cultures and Judaism:

> The pagan perceives the Divine in nature through the medium of the eye, and he becomes conscious of it as something to be looked at. On the other hand, to the Jew who conceives God as being outside of nature and prior to it, the Divine manifests itself through the will and through the medium of the ear.... The pagan beholds his god, the Jew hears Him; that is, apprehends His will.

In the twentieth century, literary theorist Erich Auerbach contrasted the literary style of Homer with that of the Hebrew Bible. In Homer's prose we see the play of light on surfaces. *The Odyssey* and *The Iliad* are full of visual descriptions. By contrast, biblical narrative has very few such descriptions. We do not know how tall Avraham was, the color of Yitzḥak's hair, or what Moshe looked like. Visual details are minimal, and are present only when necessary to understand what follows. We are told for example that Yosef was good-looking (Bereshit 39:6) only to explain why Potifar's wife conceived a desire for him.

"Yosef recognized his brothers, but they did not recognize him." The reason they did not recognize him is that, from the start, they allowed their feelings to be guided by what they saw, the "coat of many colors" that inflamed their envy of their younger brother. Judge by appearances and you will miss the deeper truth about situations and people. You will even miss God Himself, for God cannot be seen, only heard. That is why the primary imperative in Judaism is *Shema Yisrael*, "Listen, O Israel," and why, when we say the first line of the *Shema*, we place our hand over our eyes so that we cannot see.

Appearances deceive. Clothes betray. Deep understanding, whether of God or of human beings, needs the ability to listen. In order to choose between right and wrong, between good and bad – in order to live the moral life – we must make sure not only to look, but also to listen.

Rabbi Jonathan Sacks

Analysis

- What areas of understanding of human nature, society, and history do we have now that were unavailable to classical Jewish commentators? How can they aid our understanding of the text?
- What can we learn from this essay to help us understand the text?
- What further questions on the text do you have now that you have read this new take on the story?

INTEGRATING ḤOKHMAH

There were many reasons they did not recognize him. They did not know he was in Egypt. They believed he was still a slave while the man before whom they bowed was a viceroy. Besides which, he looked like an Egyptian, spoke Egyptian, and had an Egyptian name, Tzafenat Paneaḥ. Most importantly, though, he was wearing the uniform of an Egyptian of high rank. That had been the sign of Yosef's elevation at the hand of Pharaoh when he interpreted his dreams.

We know from Egyptian wall paintings and from archaeological discoveries like Tutankhamen's tomb how stylized and elaborate were Egyptian robes of office. Different ranks wore different clothes. Early pharaohs had two headdresses, a white one to mark the fact that they were kings of Upper Egypt, and a red one to signal that they were kings of Lower Egypt. Like all uniforms, clothes told a story, or as we say nowadays, "made a statement." They proclaimed a person's status. Someone dressed like the Egyptian before whom the brothers had just bowed could not possibly be their long-lost brother Yosef. Except that he was.

This seems like a minor matter. I want to argue the opposite. It turns out to be a very major matter indeed. The first thing we need to note is that the Torah as a whole, and Bereshit in particular, has a way of focusing our attention on a major theme: It presents us with recurring episodes. Robert Alter calls them "type scenes." There is, for example, the theme of sibling rivalry that appears four times in Bereshit: Kayin and Hevel, Yitzḥak and Yishmael, Yaakov and Esav, and Yosef and his brothers. There is the theme that occurs three times: the patriarch forced to leave home because of famine, and then realizing that he will have to ask his wife to pretend she is his sister for fear that he will be murdered so that she can be taken into the royal harem. And there is the theme of finding-future-wife-at-well, which also occurs three times: Rivka, Raḥel, and Yitro's daughter Tzipora.

The encounter between Yosef and his brothers is the fifth in a series of stories in which clothes play a key role. The first is Yaakov who dresses in Esav's clothes while bringing his father a meal so that he can take his brother's blessing. The second is Yosef's finely embroidered robe or "coat of many colors," which the brothers bring back to their father stained in blood, saying that a wild animal must have seized him. The third is the story of Tamar taking off her widow's dress, covering herself with a veil, and making herself look as if she were a prostitute. The fourth is the robe Yosef leaves in the hands of Potifar's wife while escaping her attempt to seduce him. The fifth is the one in Parashat Miketz in which Pharaoh dresses Yosef as a high-ranking Egyptian, with clothes of linen, a gold chain, and the royal signet ring. What all five cases have in common is that they facilitate deception.

So the five stories about garments tell a single story: things are not necessarily as they seem. Appearances deceive. It is therefore with a frisson of discovery that we realize that the Hebrew

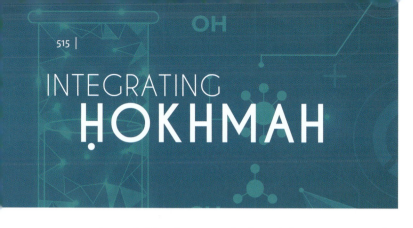

29 When they came to their father Yaakov in the land of Canaan, they told him all that had
30 happened to them. They said, "The man who is the lord of the land spoke to us harshly. He
31 accused us of spying on the land. We said to him, 'We are honest men; we are not spies.
32 We were twelve brothers, sons of the same father. One is gone, and the youngest is now
33 with our father in Canaan.' Then the man who is lord of the land said to us, 'This is how I
will know that you are honest men. Leave one of your brothers with me, take something
34 for your starving households, and go. Then bring your youngest brother to me. Then I will
know that you are not spies but honest men. And then I will give you back your brother,
35 and you can trade in the land.'" They began emptying their sacks, and there in each one's
sack was his money bag. When they and their father saw the money bags, they were afraid.
36 Their father Yaakov said to them, "You have taken my children away from me. Yosef is
37 gone. Shimon is gone. Now you want to take Binyamin? All this I must suffer!" Reuven
said to his father, "You may kill my two sons if I do not bring him back to you; entrust him
38 to my care and I will bring him back to you." "My son will not go down with you," said

UNLOCKING THE TEXT

- Does Yaakov blame the brothers for Yosef's disappearance?
- Why does Yaakov blame the brothers for Shimon's incarceration?
- Why does Reuven think offering his own sons to be killed will compensate for Yaakov's loss?
- What is Sheol?
- Do the brothers lie about Yosef questioning them about their father and brother?
- Is Yaakov comfortable with abandoning Shimon in a jail in Egypt?
- How is Yehuda's proposal reassuring to Yaakov?
- Why does Yaakov suggest taking gifts and doubling the money back to Yosef?
- What is the significance of these particular gifts? (Have we seen them before?)

FINDING YOURSELF IN THE TEXT

- Have you ever tried to tell a story in a way that captures the essence of the experience, but find the person you are telling isn't fully understanding?
- Have you ever been in a situation where you have considered cutting your losses and accepting a compromised situation?
- Have you ever entrusted something very dear to someone you didn't fully trust?

Consider using these questions as the basis for your own commentary or creative midrash.

How does reflecting on these firsthand experiences help you better understand the text?

כט וַיָּבֹ֙אוּ֙ אֶֽל־יַעֲקֹ֣ב אֲבִיהֶ֔ם אַ֖רְצָה כְּנָ֑עַן וַיַּגִּ֣ידוּ ל֔וֹ אֵ֥ת כָּל־הַקֹּרֹ֖ת אֹתָ֥ם לֵאמֹֽר:

ל דִּ֠בֶּר הָאִ֨ישׁ אֲדֹנֵ֤י הָאָ֙רֶץ֙ אִתָּ֖נוּ קָשׁ֑וֹת וַיִּתֵּ֣ן אֹתָ֔נוּ כִּֽמְרַגְּלִ֖ים אֶת־הָאָֽרֶץ: וַנֹּ֣אמֶר

לא אֵלָ֖יו כֵּנִ֣ים אֲנָ֑חְנוּ לֹ֥א הָיִ֖ינוּ מְרַגְּלִֽים: שְׁנֵים־עָשָׂ֧ר אֲנַ֛חְנוּ אַחִ֖ים בְּנֵ֣י אָבִ֑ינוּ הָאֶחָ֣ד

לב אֵינֶ֔נּוּ וְהַקָּטֹ֥ן הַיּ֛וֹם אֶת־אָבִ֖ינוּ בְּאֶ֥רֶץ כְּנָֽעַן: וַיֹּ֣אמֶר אֵלֵ֗ינוּ הָאִישׁ֙ אֲדֹנֵ֣י הָאָ֔רֶץ

לג בְּזֹ֣את אֵדַ֗ע כִּ֣י כֵנִים֮ אַתֶּם֒ אֲחִיכֶ֤ם הָֽאֶחָד֙ הַנִּ֣יחוּ אִתִּ֔י וְאֶת־רַעֲב֥וֹן בָּתֵּיכֶ֖ם קְח֥וּ

לד וָלֵֽכוּ: וְֽ֠הָבִ֠יאוּ אֶת־אֲחִיכֶ֣ם הַקָּטֹן֮ אֵלַי֒ וְאֵֽדְעָ֗ה כִּ֣י לֹ֤א מְרַגְּלִים֙ אַתֶּ֔ם כִּ֥י כֵנִ֖ים אַתֶּ֑ם

לה אֶת־אֲחִיכֶם֙ אֶתֵּ֣ן לָכֶ֔ם וְאֶת־הָאָ֖רֶץ תִּסְחָֽרוּ: וַיְהִ֗י הֵ֚ם מְרִיקִ֣ים שַׂקֵּיהֶ֔ם וְהִנֵּה־אִ֥ישׁ

לו צְרֽוֹר־כַּסְפּ֖וֹ בְּשַׂקּ֑וֹ וַיִּרְא֞וּ אֶת־צְרֹר֧וֹת כַּסְפֵּיהֶ֛ם הֵ֥מָּה וַאֲבִיהֶ֖ם וַיִּירָֽאוּ: וַיֹּ֣אמֶר

לז אֲלֵהֶ֗ם יַעֲקֹ֣ב אֲבִיהֶם֮ אֹתִ֣י שִׁכַּלְתֶּם֒ יוֹסֵ֣ף אֵינֶ֗נּוּ וְשִׁמְעוֹן֙ אֵינֶ֔נּוּ וְאֶת־בִּנְיָמִ֣ן תִּקָּ֔חוּ

לח עָלַ֖י הָי֥וּ כֻלָּֽנָה: וַיֹּ֤אמֶר רְאוּבֵן֙ אֶל־אָבִ֣יו לֵאמֹ֔ר אֶת־שְׁנֵ֤י בָנַי֙ תָּמִ֔ית אִם־לֹ֥א אֲבִיאֶ֖נּוּ

אֵלֶ֑יךָ תְּנָ֤ה אֹתוֹ֙ עַל־יָדִ֔י וַאֲנִ֖י אֲשִׁיבֶ֥נּוּ אֵלֶֽיךָ: וַיֹּ֕אמֶר לֹֽא־יֵרֵ֥ד בְּנִ֖י עִמָּכֶ֑ם כִּֽי־אָחִ֨יו

THEMES	RELATIONSHIPS AND LOVE	LEADERSHIP	EXILE

Episode 61: *The Brothers Return to Yaakov* – Bereshit 42:29–43:14

SUMMARY

The return of Yaakov's sons to their home is marred by the difficulties they faced in Egypt: the demand of the Egyptian ruler that they bring their younger brother, whom their father had refused to send, in order to substantiate their claims; the incarceration of Shimon as a hostage in Egypt; and finally, the mystery of the money restored to their sacks.

The tension between Yaakov and his sons rises. They were already separated by the dark secret that his sons shared with regard to Yosef's fate, and now they are driven further apart by the strange events they experienced in Egypt, with all the accusations and the mistreatment they suffered while their father waited for them in Canaan. Neither Yaakov nor his sons understand the meaning of what has happened, but there is a significant difference between the direct experience of those who have been falsely accused and mistreated and one who has merely heard the report of these events, even if he hears it from his own sons.

Just as Reuven and Yehuda tried to mitigate their brothers' designs in the fateful encounter with Yosef in Dotan, here too the pair acts responsibly in order to soften their father's objections to sending Binyamin back with them to Egypt. Eventually, it is the famine that will compel Yaakov to comply with the Egyptian viceroy's request, as the future of the family depends on their ability to purchase food.

Yaakov. "His brother is dead, and he is all I have left. If any harm comes to him on the way,
43 1 you will bring down my gray head in grief to Sheol." The famine in the land continued to
2 be severe. When they had eaten all the grain they had brought from Egypt, their father
3 said to them, "Go back and buy us some more food." But Yehuda said to him, "The man
4 warned us, 'Do not appear before me unless your brother is with you.' If you agree to send
5 our brother with us, we will go and buy you food. But if you will not send him, we cannot
6 go: the man told us, 'Do not appear before me unless your brother is with you.'" Yisrael
said, "Why did you bring this trouble on me by telling the man you had another brother?"
7 They replied, "The man kept asking about us and our family: 'Is your father still alive?' he
asked. 'Do you have a brother?' We simply answered his questions. How could we know
8 that he would say, 'Bring your brother here'?" And Yehuda said to his father Yisrael, "Send
the boy with me. Let us be on our way so that we, you, and our children may live and not
9 die. I myself am the guarantee for his safety: you may hold me personally responsible. If I
do not bring him back and set him before you, I will have sinned against you for all time.
10 11 We could have been there and back twice if we had not hesitated so long." And then their
father Yisrael said to them, "If that is how it must be, then do this. Take some of the best
produce of the land in your bags, and bring them to the man as a gift – a little balm and a
12 little honey, some spices and myrrh, pistachio nuts and almonds. Take with you double the
13 money. Return the money that was put back into your sacks. Perhaps it was a mistake. And
14 take your brother. Go back to the man at once. May El Shaddai grant you mercy before the
man, that he may send your other brother forth to you, and Binyamin. And as for me, if I
am to be bereaved, I will be bereaved."

TO YAAKOV

- Does the news your sons bring you confirm your greatest fear?
- Do you really accept leaving Shimon behind in Egypt to protect Binyamin?
- Do you feel you need to protect Binyamin more than his brothers? Why?
- Do you love Binyamin more than his brothers?
- Why do you eventually allow your sons to leave with Binyamin?

TO THE BROTHERS

- Do you think you will convince your father to let you return to Egypt with Binyamin?
- What do you think of his plan to take gifts and money back with you?
- Are you scared this story will not end well?

מֵת וְהוּא לְבַדּוֹ נִשְׁאָר וּקְרָאָהוּ אָסוֹן בַּדֶּרֶךְ אֲשֶׁר תֵּלְכוּ־בָהּ וְהוֹרַדְתֶּם אֶת־שֵׂיבָתִי
מג א ב בְּיָגוֹן שְׁאוֹלָה׃ וְהָרָעָב כָּבֵד בָּאָרֶץ׃ וַיְהִי כַּאֲשֶׁר כִּלּוּ לֶאֱכֹל אֶת־הַשֶּׁבֶר אֲשֶׁר
ג הֵבִיאוּ מִמִּצְרָיִם וַיֹּאמֶר אֲלֵיהֶם אֲבִיהֶם שֻׁבוּ שִׁבְרוּ־לָנוּ מְעַט־אֹכֶל׃ וַיֹּאמֶר אֵלָיו
יְהוּדָה לֵאמֹר הָעֵד הֵעִד בָּנוּ הָאִישׁ לֵאמֹר לֹא־תִרְאוּ פָנַי בִּלְתִּי אֲחִיכֶם אִתְּכֶם׃
ד ה אִם־יֶשְׁךָ מְשַׁלֵּחַ אֶת־אָחִינוּ אִתָּנוּ נֵרְדָה וְנִשְׁבְּרָה לְךָ אֹכֶל׃ וְאִם־אֵינְךָ מְשַׁלֵּחַ
ו לֹא נֵרֵד כִּי־הָאִישׁ אָמַר אֵלֵינוּ לֹא־תִרְאוּ פָנַי בִּלְתִּי אֲחִיכֶם אִתְּכֶם׃ וַיֹּאמֶר יִשְׂרָאֵל
ז לָמָה הֲרֵעֹתֶם לִי לְהַגִּיד לָאִישׁ הַעוֹד לָכֶם אָח׃ וַיֹּאמְרוּ שָׁאוֹל שָׁאַל־הָאִישׁ לָנוּ
וּלְמוֹלַדְתֵּנוּ לֵאמֹר הַעוֹד אֲבִיכֶם חַי הֲיֵשׁ לָכֶם אָח וַנַּגֶּד־לוֹ עַל־פִּי הַדְּבָרִים הָאֵלֶּה
ח הֲיָדוֹעַ נֵדַע כִּי יֹאמַר הוֹרִידוּ אֶת־אֲחִיכֶם׃ וַיֹּאמֶר יְהוּדָה אֶל־יִשְׂרָאֵל אָבִיו שִׁלְחָה
ט הַנַּעַר אִתִּי וְנָקוּמָה וְנֵלֵכָה וְנִחְיֶה וְלֹא נָמוּת גַּם־אֲנַחְנוּ גַם־אַתָּה גַּם־טַפֵּנוּ׃ אָנֹכִי
אֶעֶרְבֶנּוּ מִיָּדִי תְּבַקְשֶׁנּוּ אִם־לֹא הֲבִיאֹתִיו אֵלֶיךָ וְהִצַּגְתִּיו לְפָנֶיךָ וְחָטָאתִי לְךָ
י יא כָּל־הַיָּמִים׃ כִּי לוּלֵא הִתְמַהְמָהְנוּ כִּי־עַתָּה שַׁבְנוּ זֶה פַעֲמָיִם׃ וַיֹּאמֶר אֲלֵהֶם
יִשְׂרָאֵל אֲבִיהֶם אִם־כֵּן ׀ אֵפוֹא זֹאת עֲשׂוּ קְחוּ מִזִּמְרַת הָאָרֶץ בִּכְלֵיכֶם וְהוֹרִידוּ
יב לָאִישׁ מִנְחָה מְעַט צֳרִי וּמְעַט דְּבַשׁ נְכֹאת וָלֹט בָּטְנִים וּשְׁקֵדִים׃ וְכֶסֶף מִשְׁנֶה
קְחוּ בְיֶדְכֶם וְאֶת־הַכֶּסֶף הַמּוּשָׁב בְּפִי אַמְתְּחֹתֵיכֶם תָּשִׁיבוּ בְיֶדְכֶם אוּלַי מִשְׁגֶּה
יג יד הוּא׃ וְאֶת־אֲחִיכֶם קָחוּ וְקוּמוּ שׁוּבוּ אֶל־הָאִישׁ׃ וְאֵל שַׁדַּי יִתֵּן לָכֶם רַחֲמִים לִפְנֵי לט
הָאִישׁ וְשִׁלַּח לָכֶם אֶת־אֲחִיכֶם אַחֵר וְאֶת־בִּנְיָמִין וַאֲנִי כַּאֲשֶׁר שָׁכֹלְתִּי שָׁכָלְתִּי׃

A QUESTION OF BIBLIODRAMA

THE ART OF MIDRASH

Drought
Tani Bayer (2024)

Analysis

- Which elements of this image are directly mentioned in the text?
- Which elements of this image are not found in the text?
- What midrashic interpretation could be inferred from this image?

TAKING A LITERARY APPROACH

On the way back home, when one of the brothers discovers the silver in his saddlebag, they all become agitated: "They trembled one before the other and exclaimed, 'What is this which God has done to us?'" (Bereshit 42:28). Imagine the terror magnified ten times when they open their bags at home and discover that all their silver has been returned. Reflecting their angst, it is not surprising that as they retell their saga to Yaakov they omit any mention of Shimon being left behind.

Unwittingly, they press precisely the buttons that Yosef intends, as Yaakov bursts forth, saying: "You have bereaved me of my children! Yosef is not here and Shimon is not here" (42:36). Their omission of Shimon's absence along with the discovery of the silver raises Yaakov's suspicions as he links the disappearances of both his sons. Moreover, in their rendition of the story, the brothers add a line about Yosef assuring them that upon bringing the youngest brother they will be able to conduct their business in the land – which Yosef did not say. That addition not only conjures up for Yaakov the possibility that the brothers are involved in Shimon's absence (is that also a "business" transaction?), but also seems reminiscent of the story of Dina in Shekhem, where Ḥamor promises they can do business in the land in return for Dina. It is no wonder, then, that when the brothers ask to take Binyamin, Yaakov refuses. He does not trust them.

Reuven, the eldest, is of no assistance. Reuven, who loses his father's trust when he violates Bilha, who tries to deceive his brothers and secret Yosef back to Yaakov, is the same Reuven who, when the brothers speak among themselves about their failure to heed Yosef's cries from the pit, can only muster up his version of "I told you so." Reuven, who repeatedly proves himself as a non-leader, offers Yaakov to kill two of his children (presumably in "payment" for Yaakov's lost sons) if he does not bring Binyamin back. Reuven is completely unaware of the absurdity of his offer. He is clueless about what it means to lose a child and apparently does not understand how ridiculous it is to suggest that Yaakov kill his own grandchildren if Reuven does not return Binyamin. His offer convinces Yaakov even further of Reuven's unworthiness. Yaakov is less likely to release Binyamin than ever before.

It is not until many months later, when they finish all the food they brought from Egypt, that Yehuda intervenes, and only after his presentation does Yaakov agree to send Binyamin. The irony in the story continues as Yaakov sends some delicacies to the Egyptian master – including balm, gum, and labdanum – the very items carried by the Ishmaelite traders who bring Yosef to Egypt (37:25). Yosef's gift of the silver sends a powerful message to Yaakov; we can only imagine Yosef's reaction upon receiving a gift from Yaakov containing the potent scents of his own kidnapping.

Rabbi Zvi Grumet

שָׁקֵד / *SHAKED* – ALMOND

The *shaked* is mentioned four times in Tanakh. It is the almond (*Amygdalus communis*), which was eaten, and whose oil was used for cosmetic and medicinal purposes. The almond tree survives and bears fruit even in times of drought; for this reason, perhaps, Yaakov is able to send almonds as part of a gift to the Egyptian ruler (Yosef).

The word *shaked* means "alertness" and "alacrity," and indeed, the almond blooms earlier than other trees, while it is still winter. Therefore, it symbolizes diligence and perseverance, and is a harbinger of a process that will soon be completed: "The almond blossoms...but man is departing for his final home, and the mourners turn and turn about the streets;"[2] "I see the branch of an almond tree.... You have seen well, for I am watchful about keeping My word."[3] Aharon's staff, made of almond wood, blossoms and produces fruit overnight as a sign that God Himself has chosen Aharon as the people's spiritual leader.

The *luz*, which Yaakov uses in his manipulation of Lavan's flock,[4] seems to be a synonym for *shaked*.

Analysis

- What areas of archaeological, geographical, and historical knowledge do we have now that were unavailable to classical Jewish commentators? How can they aid our understanding of the text?
- How can this information about the pistachio, rockrose, and almond plants help us understand the text?
- What further questions on the text do you have now that you have read this new information and research?

Almond branch

---

2 | Kohelet 12:5.

3 | Yirmeya 1:11–12.

4 | Bereshit 30:37.

INTEGRATING ḤOKHMA

בָּטְנִים / *BOTNIM* – PISTACHIO

Botnim are mentioned once in Tanakh, as part of the list of the "best produce of the land" that Yaakov sends to Yosef in Egypt. Traditional commentators unanimously agree that it refers to the fruit of the terebinth tree (*Pistacia*). The Aramaic translations and Rav Se'adya Gaon specify that it refers to the *Pistacia palaestina* variety, known in Arabic as *but'm*. This is a wild tree found readily in Mediterranean woodlands, and which does not grow in Egypt. Its fruit can be eaten roasted, and in ancient times its oil was also considered a delicacy.

The tree known today as pistachio (*Pistacia vera*) did not yet grow in this region in biblical times; the peanut (*Arachis hypogaea*), known erroneously in Modern Hebrew as *botnim*, is a New World plant.

Pistachio nuts

לֹט / *LOT* – ROCKROSE

This plant appears twice in Bereshit in a list of luxury goods brought from the land of Israel to Egypt – once by a caravan of Ishmaelites, and once by Yaakov's sons: "Take some of the best produce of the land in your bags, and bring them to the man as a gift – a little balm and a little honey, some spices and *lot, pistachio nuts and almonds.*"[1] The most commonly accepted (albeit still speculative) suggestion of this item's identification is the fragrant sap of the pink rockrose (*Cistus creticus*).

Pink rockrose

1 | Bereshit 43:11.

15 So the men took the gift and double the money and set out with Binyamin. They went to
16 Egypt and presented themselves to Yosef. When Yosef saw Binyamin with them, he said to
his house steward, "Take these men to my house. Slaughter an animal and prepare a meal,
17 for they will dine with me at noon." The man did as Yosef said and brought them to Yosef's
18 house. The men were frightened that they were being brought to Yosef's house. They said,
"We have been brought here because of the money that was put back in our sacks the first
19 time. He wants to attack us, seize us as slaves, and take our donkeys." So they went up to
20 Yosef's steward and spoke to him at the entrance to the house. "If you please, my lord,"
21 they said, "We came here once before to buy food. But at the place where we stopped for
the night, we opened our bags and each of us found his money, in its exact weight, in the
22 mouth of his bag. So we have brought it back with us. We have also brought additional
23 money to buy food. We do not know who put our money in our bags." He replied, "All
is well. Do not be afraid. Your God, the God of your father, must have placed a hidden
gift in your bags. I received the money you paid." Then he brought Shimon out to them.
24 He brought the brothers into Yosef's house, gave them water to bathe their feet, and had

UNLOCKING THE TEXT

- Was it normal that an Egyptian prince would invite strangers from a foreign land to dine with him in his house?
- Why did this cause the brothers fear?
- Why did the brothers tell their story to the steward of Yosef's house?
- How did the steward know how to respond?
- Does Yosef's emotional reaction mean he has forgiven his brothers and wished to be reconciled with them?
- Why was it considered abhorrent for Egyptians to eat with Hebrews?
- Why did Yosef eat apart from both the Egyptians and the Hebrews?
- Why are the brothers seated in order of age? Why does this amaze them?
- Why did Yosef give Binyamin five times as much as anyone else?

FINDING YOURSELF IN THE TEXT

- Have you ever felt out of place in a foreign environment?
- Have you ever been stressed at trying to explain yourself after a misunderstanding?
- Have you ever had to hide a strong emotion you were feeling inside?

Consider using these questions as the basis for your own commentary or creative midrash.

How does reflecting on these firsthand experiences help you better understand the text?

טו וַיִּקְחוּ הָאֲנָשִׁים אֶת־הַמִּנְחָה הַזֹּאת וּמִשְׁנֶה־כֶּסֶף לָקְחוּ בְיָדָם וְאֶת־בִּנְיָמִן וַיָּקֻמוּ
טז וַיֵּרְדוּ מִצְרַיִם וַיַּעַמְדוּ לִפְנֵי יוֹסֵף׃ וַיַּרְא יוֹסֵף אִתָּם אֶת־בִּנְיָמִין וַיֹּאמֶר לַאֲשֶׁר עַל־ ששי
בֵּיתוֹ הָבֵא אֶת־הָאֲנָשִׁים הַבָּיְתָה וּטְבֹחַ טֶבַח וְהָכֵן כִּי אִתִּי יֹאכְלוּ הָאֲנָשִׁים
יז בַּצָּהֳרָיִם׃ וַיַּעַשׂ הָאִישׁ כַּאֲשֶׁר אָמַר יוֹסֵף וַיָּבֵא הָאִישׁ אֶת־הָאֲנָשִׁים בֵּיתָה יוֹסֵף׃
יח וַיִּירְאוּ הָאֲנָשִׁים כִּי הוּבְאוּ בֵּית יוֹסֵף וַיֹּאמְרוּ עַל־דְּבַר הַכֶּסֶף הַשָּׁב בְּאַמְתְּחֹתֵינוּ
בַּתְּחִלָּה אֲנַחְנוּ מוּבָאִים לְהִתְגֹּלֵל עָלֵינוּ וּלְהִתְנַפֵּל עָלֵינוּ וְלָקַחַת אֹתָנוּ לַעֲבָדִים
יט וְאֶת־חֲמֹרֵינוּ׃ וַיִּגְּשׁוּ אֶל־הָאִישׁ אֲשֶׁר עַל־בֵּית יוֹסֵף וַיְדַבְּרוּ אֵלָיו פֶּתַח הַבָּיִת׃
כ כא וַיֹּאמְרוּ בִּי אֲדֹנִי יָרֹד יָרַדְנוּ בַּתְּחִלָּה לִשְׁבָּר־אֹכֶל׃ וַיְהִי כִּי־בָאנוּ אֶל־הַמָּלוֹן
וַנִּפְתְּחָה אֶת־אַמְתְּחֹתֵינוּ וְהִנֵּה כֶסֶף־אִישׁ בְּפִי אַמְתַּחְתּוֹ כַּסְפֵּנוּ בְּמִשְׁקָלוֹ
כב וַנָּשֶׁב אֹתוֹ בְּיָדֵנוּ׃ וְכֶסֶף אַחֵר הוֹרַדְנוּ בְיָדֵנוּ לִשְׁבָּר־אֹכֶל לֹא יָדַעְנוּ מִי־שָׂם
כג כַּסְפֵּנוּ בְּאַמְתְּחֹתֵינוּ׃ וַיֹּאמֶר שָׁלוֹם לָכֶם אַל־תִּירָאוּ אֱלֹהֵיכֶם וֵאלֹהֵי אֲבִיכֶם נָתַן
כד לָכֶם מַטְמוֹן בְּאַמְתְּחֹתֵיכֶם כַּסְפְּכֶם בָּא אֵלָי וַיּוֹצֵא אֲלֵהֶם אֶת־שִׁמְעוֹן׃ וַיָּבֵא

THEMES | RELATIONSHIPS AND LOVE | LEADERSHIP | EXILE

Episode 62: *The Brothers' Second Encounter with Yosef* – Bereshit 43:15–34

SUMMARY

When Yosef accused his brothers of being spies during their first visit to Egypt, he caused them great consternation. When they come a second time, the brothers are once again confronted with perplexing events. Their treatment as distinguished guests only increases their astonishment. Furthermore, their discomfort is likely increased by a troublesome, subconscious thought: Although they are dealing with the viceroy of Egypt, they have a vague sense that he is familiar to them from somewhere. Yet, the idea that they have met Pharaoh's viceroy on some past occasion seems logically untenable.

25 fodder brought for their donkeys. They set out their gifts in preparation for Yosef's arrival
26 at noon, because they had heard that they were going to eat there. When Yosef entered
the house, they presented him with the gifts they had brought and bowed low to the
27 ground before him. He asked them how they were. Then he asked, "How is the elderly
28 father about whom you spoke? Is he still alive?" They said, "Your servant our father is alive
29 and well." They bowed down and prostrated themselves. Then he looked up and saw his
brother Binyamin, his mother's son, and asked, "Is this your youngest brother, the one
30 you mentioned to me?" And he said, "God be gracious to you, my son." At that, he hurried
out, for he was overcome with feeling toward his brother and was on the verge of tears. He
31 went into a private room and there he wept. He washed his face and came out, controlling
32 himself. "Serve the food," he said. They served him apart, them apart, and the Egyptians
who ate with him apart, for the Egyptians could not eat with Hebrews, since to Egyptians
33 that was considered abhorrent. Seated by his direction in order of age, oldest to youngest,
34 they looked at one another in amazement. He sent them portions from his table, giving
Binyamin five times as much as anyone else. And they drank and grew merry with him.

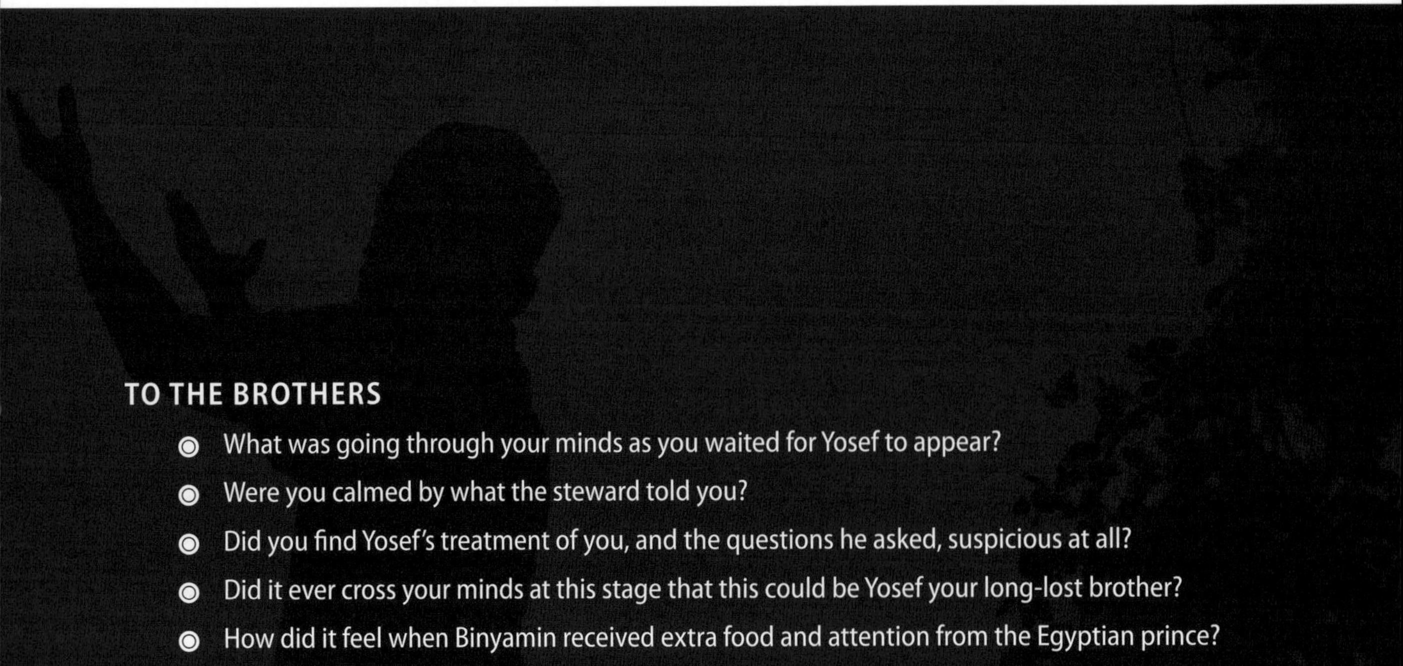

TO THE BROTHERS

- What was going through your minds as you waited for Yosef to appear?
- Were you calmed by what the steward told you?
- Did you find Yosef's treatment of you, and the questions he asked, suspicious at all?
- Did it ever cross your minds at this stage that this could be Yosef your long-lost brother?
- How did it feel when Binyamin received extra food and attention from the Egyptian prince?

הָאִישׁ אֶת־הָאֲנָשִׁים בֵּיתָה יוֹסֵף וַיִּתֶּן־מַיִם וַיִּרְחֲצוּ רַגְלֵיהֶם וַיִּתֵּן מִסְפּוֹא לַחֲמֹרֵיהֶם׃
כה כו וַיָּכִינוּ אֶת־הַמִּנְחָה עַד־בּוֹא יוֹסֵף בַּצָּהֳרָיִם כִּי שָׁמְעוּ כִּי־שָׁם יֹאכְלוּ לָחֶם׃ וַיָּבֹא
יוֹסֵף הַבַּיְתָה וַיָּבִיאוּ לוֹ אֶת־הַמִּנְחָה אֲשֶׁר־בְּיָדָם הַבָּיְתָה וַיִּשְׁתַּחֲווּ־לוֹ אָרְצָה׃
כז וַיִּשְׁאַל לָהֶם לְשָׁלוֹם וַיֹּאמֶר הֲשָׁלוֹם אֲבִיכֶם הַזָּקֵן אֲשֶׁר אֲמַרְתֶּם הַעוֹדֶנּוּ חָי׃
כח כט וַיֹּאמְרוּ שָׁלוֹם לְעַבְדְּךָ לְאָבִינוּ עוֹדֶנּוּ חָי וַיִּקְּדוּ וַיִּשְׁתַּחֲוֻ׃ וַיִּשָּׂא עֵינָיו וַיַּרְא אֶת־
בִּנְיָמִין אָחִיו בֶּן־אִמּוֹ וַיֹּאמֶר הֲזֶה אֲחִיכֶם הַקָּטֹן אֲשֶׁר אֲמַרְתֶּם אֵלָי וַיֹּאמַר אֱלֹהִים
ל יָחְנְךָ בְּנִי׃ וַיְמַהֵר יוֹסֵף כִּי־נִכְמְרוּ רַחֲמָיו אֶל־אָחִיו וַיְבַקֵּשׁ לִבְכּוֹת וַיָּבֹא הַחַדְרָה שביעי
לא לב וַיֵּבְךְּ שָׁמָּה׃ וַיִּרְחַץ פָּנָיו וַיֵּצֵא וַיִּתְאַפַּק וַיֹּאמֶר שִׂימוּ לָחֶם׃ וַיָּשִׂימוּ לוֹ לְבַדּוֹ
וְלָהֶם לְבַדָּם וְלַמִּצְרִים הָאֹכְלִים אִתּוֹ לְבַדָּם כִּי לֹא יוּכְלוּן הַמִּצְרִים לֶאֱכֹל
לג אֶת־הָעִבְרִים לֶחֶם כִּי־תוֹעֵבָה הִוא לְמִצְרָיִם׃ וַיֵּשְׁבוּ לְפָנָיו הַבְּכֹר כִּבְכֹרָתוֹ
לד וְהַצָּעִיר כִּצְעִרָתוֹ וַיִּתְמְהוּ הָאֲנָשִׁים אִישׁ אֶל־רֵעֵהוּ׃ וַיִּשָּׂא מַשְׂאֹת מֵאֵת פָּנָיו
אֲלֵהֶם וַתֵּרֶב מַשְׂאַת בִּנְיָמִן מִמַּשְׂאֹת כֻּלָּם חָמֵשׁ יָדוֹת וַיִּשְׁתּוּ וַיִּשְׁכְּרוּ עִמּוֹ׃

A QUESTION OF BIBLIODRAMA

TO YOSEF

- Why did you wine and dine your brothers in your palace?
- Why did you find it so hard to contain your emotions at this time?
- How did it feel to see Binyamin, your only brother from your mother, after all these years?
- Why did you sit and eat apart from both your brothers and the Egyptians in the room?
- Why did you send Binyamin extra food?

empathy, thinking of all the anguish that his father and brothers had endured throughout the years. Alternatively, Netziv suggests that he was distressed by the fact that he could not yet tell them who he was, and that he knew that his upcoming plan would cause them anguish (see Rashi for an alternative explanation).

Regardless of the precise reason, the verses make it clear that Yosef's feelings were intense. He turns away from his brothers, unable to fight back tears, and weeps in a different room. However, being overwhelmed with emotion threatened to ruin his overall plan. He needed to continue to act as the viceroy at the feast, and set the stage to frame Binyamin for stealing the silver goblet. How could Yosef shift from being overwhelmed with emotion to being calm, cool, and collected?

Although incredibly difficult, Yosef made a strong effort (*vayitapak*), exerting control over his emotions and stopping himself from crying. As part of that process, we are told *vayirḥatz panav* – that he washed his face. Rabbi Yosef Bekhor Shor explains that the reason he washed his face was to remove the traces of the tears, ensuring that his brothers wouldn't know he was crying. However, Shmuel ben Ḥofni Gaon, as understood by *Otzar Mefarshei HaTorah*, suggests that washing his face also served to remove the pain and change his emotional experience, allowing him to now have a meal with his brothers.

While we cannot know the temperature of the water Yosef used to wash his face, we nonetheless see traces of the DBT technique at work. Yosef was able to quickly control his strong emotional experience by washing his face, which then allowed him to proceed. When we are overwhelmed with an emotion that is getting in the way of our goals, we can utilize the cold water technique. This will lead to lower heart rate, blood pressure, and body temperature, helping us to focus on what we need to do to cope effectively.

Rabbi Mordechai Schiffman

Analysis

- What areas of understanding of human nature and society do we now have that were unavailable to classical Jewish commentators? How can they aid our understanding of the text?
- What can we learn from this essay to help us understand the text?
- What further questions on the text do you have now that you have read this new take on the story?

INTEGRATING ḤOKHMA

Managing intense emotions can be difficult. In moments of distress, the body's sympathetic nervous system (SNS) is activated, which increases heart rate, blood pressure, and body temperature. In such a state, feelings may seem overwhelming and difficult to change. In order to calm down and take control, the parasympathetic nervous system (PNS) – which decreases heart rate, blood pressure, and body temperature – needs to be activated. The good news is that there are strategies which can help shift the physiological system from distress to calm, or from the SNS to the PNS. One such strategy, utilized in dialectical behavior therapy (DBT), is to use cold water to alter body temperature. While there are several permutations of the exercise, the crux of the concept is to temporarily immerse your head in cold water while holding your breath. By doing so, your heart rate, blood pressure, and body temperature will decrease, "freezing" the emotion so that you can better handle the challenge.

Yosef, upon seeing his brother Binyamin for the first time in over twenty years, becomes overwhelmed with emotion (Bereshit 45:14). While we probably have a sense of how Yosef felt in the moment, the *pesukim* do not relate the exact thoughts and emotions he experienced. There are several suggestions in the commentaries. Sforno and Alshikh suggest that he was feeling

THE ART OF MIDRASH

The Banquet
Yoram Raanan (2014)

Analysis

- Which elements of this image are directly mentioned in the text?
- Which elements of this image are not found in the text?
- What midrashic interpretation could be inferred from this image?

TAKING A LITERARY APPROACH

The books of the prophets are filled with mercy. In the book of Bereshit, there is no mercy, or at least not the word "mercy" until Yaakov's prayer to his sons before their second time going down to Egypt: "And may El Shaddai dispose the man to mercy toward you" (Bereshit 43:14). Where is the mercy? Why is it being revealed only now? Without mercy, is it possible for the world to exist?

It seems that the Tanakh is teaching that it is not enough for God's mercy or mercy in general to remain only with God (a paraphrase of Yehuda Amichai's poem "God Full of Mercy," where he accuses God of hogging all the available mercy for Himself). Mercy must be embodied on the human level and must be taught from someone whose soul vacillates between mercy and justice, someone who, throughout his life, grapples with real-life dilemmas that range from kindness to heroism. Someone who has not experienced personally the terror of justice can neither appreciate mercy nor bestow it on someone else.

Yaakov, the innocent tent-dwelling man, inherited his sharp senses from his mother Rivka and uncle Lavan. He understands correctly that his sons are not innocent and that they will not survive in Egypt based on justice alone, and therefore his prayer is that mercy will be found in the Egyptian tyrant's heart. And Yosef does not disappoint. He, too, as someone who moves from justice to mercy, understands that without mercy the story cannot continue, that justice can often deeply engrain the pain and injustice and even aggravate them. "With that, Yosef hurried out, for he was overcome with feeling [alternatively, mercy] toward his brother" (43:3). Yosef has mercy, and thanks to his mercy, the story continues.

Only those who have mercy in their heart, even though they have experienced harsh justice, will continue the story of humanity where the image of God resides, God who responds to Moshe's question about God's presence saying: "And I will proclaim before you the name Lord, and the grace that I grant and the compassion [mercy] that I show" (Shemot 33:19).

Rabbanit Yafit Clymer

44 1 Then Yosef instructed his steward, "Fill the men's bags with as much food as they can carry,
2 and put each one's money in the mouth of his bag. Then put my chalice – the silver chalice
– in the mouth of the youngest one's bag, along with the money for his grain." He did as
3 Yosef told him. As morning showed its first light, the men were sent on their way with their
4 donkeys. They had not gone far from the city when Yosef said to his steward, "Go after the
men at once. When you catch up with them, say to them, 'Why have you repaid good with
5 evil? Is it not from this that my master drinks and that he uses for divination? It is a wicked
6 7 thing you have done.'" He caught up with them and repeated those words to them. But
they said to him, "How can my lord say such things? Heaven forbid that we should do such
8 a thing! Look, we brought back to you from Canaan the money we found in the mouths
9 of our bags. Why would we steal silver or gold from your master's house? If any of your
10 servants is found with it, he shall die, and the rest of us will become my lord's slaves." "Let it
be as you say," he replied, "but only the one with whom it is found shall be my slave. The rest
11 of you can go free." Each of them quickly lowered his bag to the ground, and each opened
12 his bag. He searched, beginning with the oldest and ending with the youngest. The chalice
13 was found in Binyamin's bag. The brothers tore their clothes. Each loaded his donkey again,

UNLOCKING THE TEXT

- Why did Yosef frame the brothers once again?
- Why did Yosef single out Binyamin and place the silver chalice in his bag?
- Why did the brothers offer death as a punishment if any of them were found with the chalice?
- Why were the brothers searched in order of age?
- Why did the brothers tear their clothes when the chalice was found in Binyamin's bag?
- Why did they all return to the city if Yosef said he would only take the culprit as his slave?
- Why does the Torah single out Yehuda as the one leading the brothers back to the house of Yosef?
- Why does Yosef claim to know the truth through divine prophecy?
- Why do the brothers confess to a crime they did not commit?

FINDING YOURSELF IN THE TEXT

- Have you ever had so many things go wrong that you felt the universe was out to get you?
- Have you ever set a trap (or a test) for someone, hoping they would pass?
- Have you ever witnessed the anguish of your loved ones from afar? Have you ever been the source of this anguish?

Consider using these questions as the basis for your own commentary or creative midrash.

How does reflecting on these firsthand experiences help you better understand the text?

מד א וַיְצַו אֶת־אֲשֶׁר עַל־בֵּיתוֹ לֵאמֹר מַלֵּא אֶת־אַמְתְּחֹת הָאֲנָשִׁים אֹכֶל כַּאֲשֶׁר יוּכְלוּן
ב שְׂאֵת וְשִׂים כֶּסֶף־אִישׁ בְּפִי אַמְתַּחְתּוֹ: וְאֶת־גְּבִיעִי גְּבִיעַ הַכֶּסֶף תָּשִׂים בְּפִי אַמְתַּחַת
ג הַקָּטֹן וְאֵת כֶּסֶף שִׁבְרוֹ וַיַּעַשׂ כִּדְבַר יוֹסֵף אֲשֶׁר דִּבֵּר: הַבֹּקֶר אוֹר וְהָאֲנָשִׁים שֻׁלְּחוּ
ד הֵמָּה וַחֲמֹרֵיהֶם: הֵם יָצְאוּ אֶת־הָעִיר לֹא הִרְחִיקוּ וְיוֹסֵף אָמַר לַאֲשֶׁר עַל־בֵּיתוֹ
קוּם רְדֹף אַחֲרֵי הָאֲנָשִׁים וְהִשַּׂגְתָּם וְאָמַרְתָּ אֲלֵהֶם לָמָּה שִׁלַּמְתֶּם רָעָה תַּחַת
ה טוֹבָה: הֲלוֹא זֶה אֲשֶׁר יִשְׁתֶּה אֲדֹנִי בּוֹ וְהוּא נַחֵשׁ יְנַחֵשׁ בּוֹ הֲרֵעֹתֶם אֲשֶׁר עֲשִׂיתֶם:
ו ז וַיַּשִּׂגֵם וַיְדַבֵּר אֲלֵהֶם אֶת־הַדְּבָרִים הָאֵלֶּה: וַיֹּאמְרוּ אֵלָיו לָמָּה יְדַבֵּר אֲדֹנִי כַּדְּבָרִים
ח הָאֵלֶּה חָלִילָה לַעֲבָדֶיךָ מֵעֲשׂוֹת כַּדָּבָר הַזֶּה: הֵן כֶּסֶף אֲשֶׁר מָצָאנוּ בְּפִי אַמְתְּחֹתֵינוּ
ט הֱשִׁיבֹנוּ אֵלֶיךָ מֵאֶרֶץ כְּנָעַן וְאֵיךְ נִגְנֹב מִבֵּית אֲדֹנֶיךָ כֶּסֶף אוֹ זָהָב: אֲשֶׁר יִמָּצֵא
י אִתּוֹ מֵעֲבָדֶיךָ וָמֵת וְגַם־אֲנַחְנוּ נִהְיֶה לַאדֹנִי לַעֲבָדִים: וַיֹּאמֶר גַּם־עַתָּה כְדִבְרֵיכֶם
יא כֶּן־הוּא אֲשֶׁר יִמָּצֵא אִתּוֹ יִהְיֶה־לִּי עָבֶד וְאַתֶּם תִּהְיוּ נְקִיִּם: וַיְמַהֲרוּ וַיּוֹרִדוּ אִישׁ
יב אֶת־אַמְתַּחְתּוֹ אָרְצָה וַיִּפְתְּחוּ אִישׁ אַמְתַּחְתּוֹ: וַיְחַפֵּשׂ בַּגָּדוֹל הֵחֵל וּבַקָּטֹן כִּלָּה
יג וַיִּמָּצֵא הַגָּבִיעַ בְּאַמְתַּחַת בִּנְיָמִן: וַיִּקְרְעוּ שִׂמְלֹתָם וַיַּעֲמֹס אִישׁ עַל־חֲמֹרוֹ וַיָּשֻׁבוּ

THEMES | RELATIONSHIPS AND LOVE | LEADERSHIP | EXILE

Episode 63: *The Brothers' Third Encounter with Yosef* – Bereshit 44:1–17

SUMMARY

Here the brothers' distress reaches its climax as Yosef's fresh accusations center on none other than Binyamin, after their father expressed his fears for his youngest son's fate in such a powerful and poignant manner.

In the customary division of weekly Torah readings, this passage is interrupted in the middle, heightening the drama even further just before Yehuda's eloquent speech, which will profoundly move Yosef. Similarly, with regard to the ancient division of chapters in Torah scrolls, indicated by a space between each passage, the portion of Miketz is unusual in that it does not contain any breaks at all until there is a break at the conclusion of the portion. It is as though the entire chain of events, with the gradual increase of drama and tension, should be read in a single breath, and right at the pinnacle of the brothers' woes, the story pauses.

14 and they returned to the city. Yehuda and his brothers came to Yosef's house – he was still
15 there – and they threw themselves on the ground before him. Yosef said to them, "What
is this thing you have done? Do you not know that a man like me can find out the truth by
16 divination?" Yehuda replied, "What can we say to my lord? What can we speak? How can
we prove our innocence? God has uncovered your servants' guilt! We are now my lord's
17 slaves – we and the one in whose possession the chalice was found." "Heaven forbid that I
should do such a thing," he said. "The man in whose possession the chalice was found will
become my slave. As for the rest of you, go back to your father in peace."

THE ART OF MIDRASH

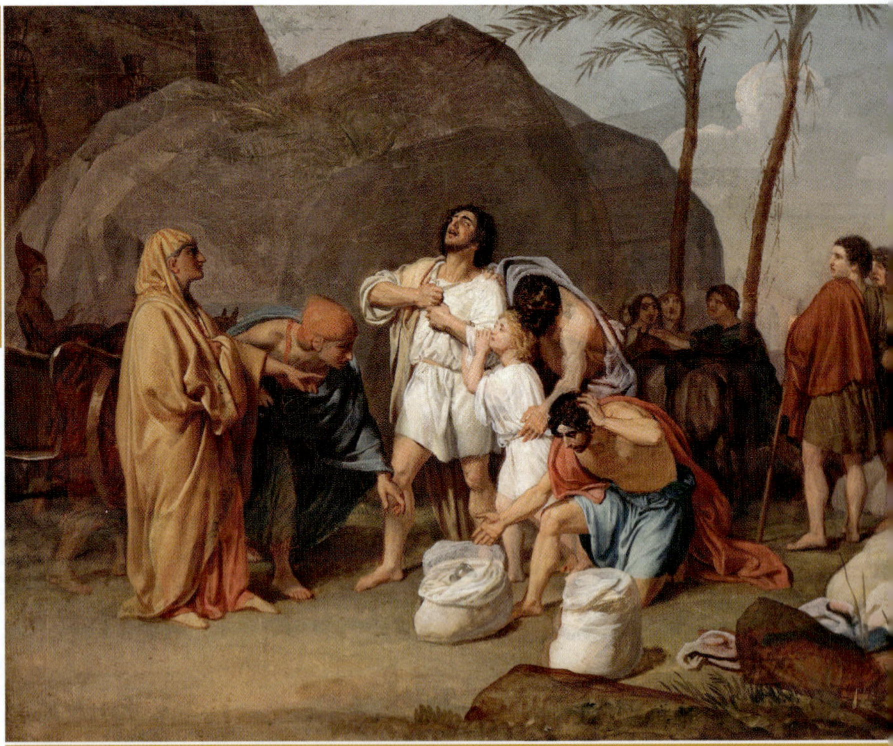

The Silver Goblet Is Found in Benjamin's Sack
Alexander Ivanov (1831–1833)

Analysis

- Which elements of this image are directly mentioned in the text?
- Which elements of this image are not found in the text?
- What midrashic interpretation could be inferred from this image?

יד הָעִירָה: וַיָּבֹא יְהוּדָה וְאֶחָיו בֵּיתָה יוֹסֵף וְהוּא עוֹדֶנּוּ שָׁם וַיִּפְּלוּ לְפָנָיו אָרְצָה: מפטיר
טו וַיֹּאמֶר לָהֶם יוֹסֵף מָה־הַמַּעֲשֶׂה הַזֶּה אֲשֶׁר עֲשִׂיתֶם הֲלוֹא יְדַעְתֶּם כִּי־נַחֵשׁ יְנַחֵשׁ
טז אִישׁ אֲשֶׁר כָּמֹנִי: וַיֹּאמֶר יְהוּדָה מַה־נֹּאמַר לַאדֹנִי מַה־נְּדַבֵּר וּמַה־נִּצְטַדָּק הָאֱלֹהִים
מָצָא אֶת־עֲוֺן עֲבָדֶיךָ הִנֶּנּוּ עֲבָדִים לַאדֹנִי גַּם־אֲנַחְנוּ גַּם אֲשֶׁר־נִמְצָא הַגָּבִיעַ
יז בְּיָדוֹ: וַיֹּאמֶר חָלִילָה לִּי מֵעֲשׂוֹת זֹאת הָאִישׁ אֲשֶׁר נִמְצָא הַגָּבִיעַ בְּיָדוֹ הוּא יִהְיֶה־
לִּי עָבֶד וְאַתֶּם עֲלוּ לְשָׁלוֹם אֶל־אֲבִיכֶם:

A QUESTION OF BIBLIODRAMA

TO YOSEF

- What are you trying to prove by framing Binyamin this time?
- Do you feel guilt over putting your brothers through this ordeal?
- Is your motivation revenge or something else?

TO THE BROTHERS

- What is going through your mind now?
- Why do you so readily exclaim that if one of you has stolen the chalice he deserves death, and the rest of you, enslavement?
- Is there a difference in your minds between leaving Shimon behind and leaving Binyamin behind?

litmus test. Would the brothers act as they had toward him, saying, "Let Binyamin stay here. This is a good way for us to be free of his favoritism," and again be indifferent to their father's feelings as they were when they sold him into slavery? Or had they realized and repented their mistake, and were ready to sacrifice themselves to return Binyamin to their father?

When Yehuda said that he must return Binyamin to his father and offered to stay as a slave in his place, Yosef saw that the brothers had thereby corrected their behavior and had done proper *teshuva.* They had redeemed themselves and would no longer have to bear the guilt and shame for their sin. Yosef was now prepared to reveal his identity to them. Far from being a vengeful torment, Yosef's actions were in their interest, enabling them to redeem themselves and walk with their heads raised high.

What about Yaakov's agony? Yosef knew his father well. He knew that, painful as the ordeal was, Yaakov would gladly accept years of suffering in order to provide his children with the opportunity to gain self-respect. This could not have been achieved in any other way, and Yosef was certain that he was doing what his father wished.

This interpretation shows us the overriding importance of self-esteem. One psychologist writes, "If you have given your child self-esteem, you have given him everything. If you have not given him self-esteem, then whatever else you gave him is of little value." Self-esteem is *the* major component of a healthy personality.

We should be aware of this. Sometimes we say or do things to another person that may depress his self-esteem. We should be aware that this is a kind of psycho-logical homicide. The Torah repeatedly emphasizes the importance of upholding every person's dignity. The saga of Yosef and his brothers teaches us to what extent we must go to preserve a person's feelings of self-respect and dignity.

Rabbi Abraham J. Twerski

Analysis

- What areas of understanding of human nature and society do we now have that were unavailable to classical Jewish commentators? How can they aid our understanding of the text?
- What can we learn from this essay to help us understand the text?
- What further questions on the text do you have now that you have read this new take on the story?

INTEGRATING ḤOKHMA

Yaakov grieved relentlessly over the loss of his beloved son whom he assumed to be dead, and he refused to be consoled. "I will go down to the grave mourning for my son" (Bereshit 37:35). Yosef knew what kind of agony his father was suffering. Even if he was not able to communicate to him when he was a slave of Potifar or when he was in prison, he was certainly able to do so once he became viceroy of Egypt. Why did he not inform his father that he was alive and alleviate his profound grief?

Furthermore, Yosef is referred to in Torah writings as "Yosef the *tzaddik*." Is it characteristic of a *tzaddik* to wreak vengeance and torment his brothers the way Yosef did? We would expect that as a *tzaddik,* he would not harbor a grudge and would forgive them.

The explanation I heard from my late brother, R' Shlomo, addresses these questions and provides an answer that is both ethically and psychologically sound.

If Yosef had forgiven his brothers for their shameful act, he would have been the magnanimous person who, from the goodness of his heart, forgave his offenders. The brothers would have forever been the groveling penitents who would have to eternally bear the guilt of their behavior. There would be no opportunity for them to make any amends. They would never again be able to face Yosef or their father. Their spirits would have been totally crushed.

Yosef wished to avoid this. He wished to give his brothers an opportunity to redeem themselves and retain their self-esteem.

The Talmud says that true and effective *teshuva* is achieved only if the person is placed in the same circumstances of his sin and under the same temptation. Yosef, therefore, designed it so that this would occur. After his absence, Binyamin, the youngest of Yaakov's sons and the only other child of his beloved Raḥel, had now become Yaakov's favorite child. Yosef arranged to have Binyamin brought to him, and he singled out Binyamin for special treatment, giving him five times as much as he gave the brothers. He then engineered it so that Binyamin was suspected of thievery, and said that he was going to keep Binyamin as a slave. He had set the stage for the

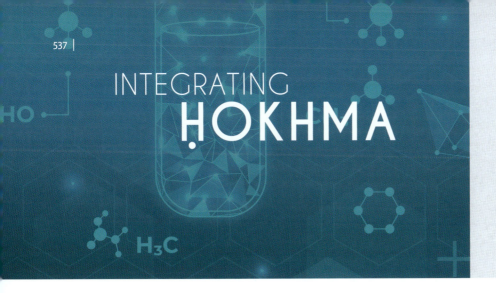

TAKING A LITERARY APPROACH

Yosef decides to press his brothers one more time, this time switching Binyamin for Shimon by arranging to have his special goblet planted in Binyamin's pack. The significance of this is clear. While the brothers do not abandon Shimon, that may be because he is one of "them." Second only to Reuven, co-leader of the rebellion against Yaakov in Shekhem, and son of Leah, he is closely allied with the power brokers in the group. But how will they relate to a son of Raḥel, Yaakov's beloved and the object of Leah's jealousy? Will they stand by him as they do for Shimon, or will they welcome his disposal as they had done so cavalierly with Yosef himself?

Yosef plays on the collective memory of the family encounter with Lavan. When the brothers are accused of theft by Yosef's emissary they are as horrified as Yaakov is by Lavan's accusation, offering death for the thief (as Yaakov does with Lavan) and themselves as slaves to Yosef (which they understand would have been their fate with Lavan). Like Yaakov, they expose themselves to an invasive search to clear their names. How dare this Egyptian accuse the sons of Israel of theft!

Also similar to Lavan is the invocation of divination, *naḥesh*. Lavan claims to use divination to explain his reason for holding on to Yaakov, knowing that Yaakov will bring him success. Some commentaries suggest that Raḥel takes the *terafim* to prevent Lavan from using those same powers of divination to track their escape route. That same word, *naḥesh*, appears four times in this scene to describe Yosef using divination to discover the thief.

While we the readers, or even Yaakov himself, may have understood Raḥel taking her father's *terafim* as a way to provoke Yaakov into confronting Lavan, the rest of the family is likely scandalized when they discover Raḥel's theft – her pettiness nearly cost all of them their freedom. In our present situation Yosef has made sure that his special goblet is secreted in none other than Binyamin's pack: Binyamin, son of Raḥel, the thief. Unlike in Yaakov's confrontation with Lavan, one of them is caught. Binyamin, Raḥel's son, the child thief who must have learned well from his mother, is exposed.

The die is thus cast. The test is in place. The brothers have an easy excuse to rid themselves of Yaakov's other child from Raḥel. But the brothers offer themselves, in toto, to Yosef as slaves. They will all serve Yosef; none will abandon Binyamin, son of Raḥel. Yet Yosef is still not satisfied and he refuses their offer, insisting that only the guilty party remain. What is missing? What else can he want from them before being prepared to reintegrate his past life into his present one?

Rabbi Zvi Grumet

וַיִּגַּשׁ
Vayigash

Parasha Overview

Vayigash begins with the climactic scene in which Yosef finally reveals himself to his brothers. Moved by Yehuda's impassioned plea for Binyamin's freedom, in return for which Yehuda declares himself ready to take Binyamin's place as a slave, Yosef discloses his identity and the estrangement of the brothers comes to an end. On Yosef's instructions, they return to Yaakov with the news that his beloved son is still alive, and the family is reunited.

Episodes

64.	**Yehuda's Speech**	44:18–34
65.	**Yosef Reveals Himself to His Brothers**	45:1–15
66.	**Pharaoh Welcomes Yosef's Brothers**	45:16–24
67.	**Yaakov and His Family Descend to Egypt**	45:25–46:27
68.	**Yaakov and Yosef Reunite**	46:28–47:12
69.	**Yosef Implements His Economic Plan for Egypt**	47:13–27

Parasha Stats

- 5,680 letters
- 1,480 words
- 106 verses
- 178 lines in a sefer Torah

18 But Yehuda stepped forward to him. "If you please, my lord," he said, "let your servant
speak a word in my lord's hearing. Do not be angry with me, you who are the equal of
19 20 Pharaoh. My lord asked his servants, 'Do you have a father or a brother?' And we told
my lord, 'We have an elderly father and there is a young son, a child of his old age. When
21 his brother died, he was the only one of his mother's sons left, and his father loves him.'
22 Then you said to your servants, 'Bring him to me that I may set eyes on him.' But we said
23 to my lord, 'The boy cannot leave his father. If he left him, his father would die.' Then you
told your servants, 'Unless your youngest brother comes with you, you shall not see my
24 face again.' When we went back to your servant my father, we told him what my lord had
25 26 said. Then our father said, 'Go back and buy a little more food.' We said, 'We cannot go.
We can go only if our youngest brother is with us. If he is not with us, we cannot see the
27 man's face.' Then your servant, my father, said to us, 'You know that my wife bore me two
28 sons. One is gone from me, and I said, "He must have been torn to pieces." I have not
29 seen him since. If you take this one from me and harm befalls him, you will bring down
30 my gray head in grief to Sheol.' So now, if the boy is not with us when I go back to your
31 servant my father, so bound together are their lives that when he sees that the boy is not
with us, he will die. Your servants will have brought down the gray head of your servant,
32 our father, in grief to Sheol. Your servant offered himself to my father as a guarantee for
the boy. I said, 'If I do not bring him back to you, I will have sinned against my father for all
33 time.' So, please, let your servant stay as my lord's slave in place of the boy, and let the boy
34 go back with his brothers. For how can I go back to my father if the boy is not with me?
I could not bear to see the misery that would overwhelm my father!"

UNLOCKING THE TEXT

- Why does Yehuda take on a leadership role now?
- Why does Yehuda retell the story to Yosef in full detail?
- Why does Yehuda mention the "death" of Yosef and its impact on Yaakov?
- If Binyamin had stolen the chalice, would Yehuda's speech have been a good defense?
- Why would Yehuda think that taking the place of Binyamin would placate Yosef?

FINDING YOURSELF IN THE TEXT

- Have you ever stood up to take responsibility in public?
- Have you ever made a speech on something you were passionate about?
- Do you know the story of your family?

Consider using these questions as the basis for your own commentary or creative midrash.

How does reflecting on these firsthand experiences help you better understand the text?

יח וַיִּגַּשׁ אֵלָיו יְהוּדָה וַיֹּאמֶר בִּי אֲדֹנִי יְדַבֶּר־נָא עַבְדְּךָ דָבָר בְּאָזְנֵי אֲדֹנִי וְאַל־יִחַר מ ויגש
יט אַפְּךָ בְּעַבְדֶּךָ כִּי כָמוֹךָ כְּפַרְעֹה: אֲדֹנִי שָׁאַל אֶת־עֲבָדָיו לֵאמֹר הֲיֵשׁ־לָכֶם
כ אָב אוֹ־אָח: וַנֹּאמֶר אֶל־אֲדֹנִי יֶשׁ־לָנוּ אָב זָקֵן וְיֶלֶד זְקֻנִים קָטָן וְאָחִיו מֵת
כא וַיִּוָּתֵר הוּא לְבַדּוֹ לְאִמּוֹ וְאָבִיו אֲהֵבוֹ: וַתֹּאמֶר אֶל־עֲבָדֶיךָ הוֹרִדֻהוּ אֵלָי וְאָשִׂימָה
כב עֵינִי עָלָיו: וַנֹּאמֶר אֶל־אֲדֹנִי לֹא־יוּכַל הַנַּעַר לַעֲזֹב אֶת־אָבִיו וְעָזַב אֶת־אָבִיו
כג וָמֵת: וַתֹּאמֶר אֶל־עֲבָדֶיךָ אִם־לֹא יֵרֵד אֲחִיכֶם הַקָּטֹן אִתְּכֶם לֹא תֹסִפוּן לִרְאוֹת
כד כה פָּנָי: וַיְהִי כִּי עָלִינוּ אֶל־עַבְדְּךָ אָבִי וַנַּגֶּד־לוֹ אֵת דִּבְרֵי אֲדֹנִי: וַיֹּאמֶר אָבִינוּ שֻׁבוּ
כו שִׁבְרוּ־לָנוּ מְעַט־אֹכֶל: וַנֹּאמֶר לֹא נוּכַל לָרֶדֶת אִם־יֵשׁ אָחִינוּ הַקָּטֹן אִתָּנוּ
כז וְיָרַדְנוּ כִּי־לֹא נוּכַל לִרְאוֹת פְּנֵי הָאִישׁ וְאָחִינוּ הַקָּטֹן אֵינֶנּוּ אִתָּנוּ: וַיֹּאמֶר עַבְדְּךָ
כח אָבִי אֵלֵינוּ אַתֶּם יְדַעְתֶּם כִּי שְׁנַיִם יָלְדָה־לִּי אִשְׁתִּי: וַיֵּצֵא הָאֶחָד מֵאִתִּי
כט וָאֹמַר אַךְ טָרֹף טֹרָף וְלֹא רְאִיתִיו עַד־הֵנָּה: וּלְקַחְתֶּם גַּם־אֶת־זֶה מֵעִם פָּנַי
ל וְקָרָהוּ אָסוֹן וְהוֹרַדְתֶּם אֶת־שֵׂיבָתִי בְּרָעָה שְׁאֹלָה: וְעַתָּה כְּבֹאִי אֶל־עַבְדְּךָ
לא אָבִי וְהַנַּעַר אֵינֶנּוּ אִתָּנוּ וְנַפְשׁוֹ קְשׁוּרָה בְנַפְשׁוֹ: וְהָיָה כִּרְאוֹתוֹ כִּי־אֵין הַנַּעַר שני
לב וָמֵת וְהוֹרִידוּ עֲבָדֶיךָ אֶת־שֵׂיבַת עַבְדְּךָ אָבִינוּ בְּיָגוֹן שְׁאֹלָה: כִּי עַבְדְּךָ עָרַב
אֶת־הַנַּעַר מֵעִם אָבִי לֵאמֹר אִם־לֹא אֲבִיאֶנּוּ אֵלֶיךָ וְחָטָאתִי לְאָבִי כָּל־הַיָּמִים:
לג לד וְעַתָּה יֵשֶׁב־נָא עַבְדְּךָ תַּחַת הַנַּעַר עֶבֶד לַאדֹנִי וְהַנַּעַר יַעַל עִם־אֶחָיו: כִּי־
אֵיךְ אֶעֱלֶה אֶל־אָבִי וְהַנַּעַר אֵינֶנּוּ אִתִּי פֶּן אֶרְאֶה בָרָע אֲשֶׁר יִמְצָא אֶת־אָבִי:

THEMES	RELATIONSHIPS AND LOVE	LEADERSHIP	REDEMPTION

Episode 64: *Yehuda's Speech* – Bereshit 44:18–34

SUMMARY

Parashat Vayigash continues where Parashat Miketz left off, with Yosef's threat to separate Binyamin from his brothers. Now Yehuda makes an impassioned plea for the sake of their father, causing Yosef to finally reveal his true identity. Yehuda concludes his speech to Yosef by describing how Yaakov would die in anguish if Binyamin did not return. Even more, he tells Yosef that he took personal responsibility for Binyamin and would be unable to return to Yaakov without him (as Yosef had earlier suggested). He offers himself as a slave to Yosef in place of Binyamin.

THE ART OF MIDRASH

Yehuda
Tani Bayer (2023)

Analysis

- Which elements of this image are directly mentioned in the text?
- Which elements of this image are not found in the text?
- What midrashic interpretation could be inferred from this image?

A QUESTION OF BIBLIODRAMA

TO YEHUDA

- What motivated you to take on this leadership role and give this speech to the Egyptian prince?
- Were you being genuine when you offered to be taken prisoner instead of Binyamin?
- Did you think for even an instant that he would accept your offer? If not, why did you even suggest it?

TO YOSEF

- What were you feeling when Yehuda gave this speech to convince you to release Binyamin?

TO BINYAMIN

- Were you scared that you would be imprisoned in Egypt and abandoned by your brothers?
- How did it feel to have Yehuda stand up for you?

think the brothers would be angry? Perhaps Yosef thought they would be angry at themselves because their plan backfired. Anger generally surfaces when our goals are obstructed, and there is little that is more anger-inducing than having our goals thwarted by the very actions we took to achieve them. The brothers sold Yosef as a slave so that he wouldn't rise to greatness, yet that act precipitated his greatness.

If this is correct, then how could they also feel regret and pain? They should either feel regret for what they had done to him, or angry that their plan failed. Malbim maintains that Yosef was not sure what his brothers were feeling, so he addressed both possibilities. Similarly, Netziv writes that Yosef was targeting his statement to two subsets of his brothers. While some of the brothers probably regretted their actions, others may have felt no remorse but instead were angry that their plan didn't work. Addressing both these concerns, whether they felt remorse or anger, Yosef argued that they should realize that this was all done by God for the sake of their survival.

However, there is another possibility. One of the core principles of dialectical behavior therapy (DBT) is that, while it may be difficult, people could hold two seemingly opposite perspectives at the same time. We often run into emotional difficulties when we engage in all-or-nothing thinking. Once we accept that our emotions are complex and often contradictory, we can learn to accept these competing perspectives and work on changing to improve our situation.

Based on this, perhaps our original assumption was wrong. Maybe the brothers could feel *both* remorse *and* anger, and not *either* remorse *or* anger. They could simultaneously regret what they did to Yosef *and* be frustrated that their plan didn't work out. By acknowledging both the moral sentiments of regret and the darker parts of their anger, they would better be able to move forward with repentance and reconciliation.

While sometimes our emotions are clear and straightforward, at other points they are confusing and contradictory. If we allow ourselves to identify and accept competing emotions, we will be better able to both understand and manage our emotional experiences.

Rabbi Mordechai Schiffman

Analysis

- What areas of understanding of human nature and society do we now have that were unavailable to classical Jewish commentators? How can they aid our understanding of the text?
- What can we learn from this essay to help us understand the text?
- What further questions on the text do you have now that you have read this new take on the story?

INTEGRATING ḤOKHMA

After Yehuda passionately pleads to take Binyamin's place to stay in Egypt, Yosef could no longer maintain his ruse. In what is perhaps the most emotion-laden scene in all of Ḥumash, Yosef bursts out crying and reveals his identity. "I am Yosef! Is my father still alive?" (Bereshit 45:3). His brothers are shocked, although it is unclear what emotions they are experiencing. Some commentators assume that they are ashamed and embarrassed. Others argue that they fear retaliation. Yosef attempts to comfort them, although since they are speechless, he is forced to speculate as to the cause of their negative reaction. He tells them, "Do not be pained [*al te'atzvu*] and do not be angry in your eyes [*al yiḥar be'eineikhem*] that you sold me here," because it was all orchestrated by God for the purpose of being able to provide sustenance (45:5).

Yosef assumes that they are pained and angry, but it is not clear what the pain is, nor what they would be angry about. Several commentators assume that the pain refers to the constellation of self-referential negative emotions they may be feeling as it relates to the wrongdoing of the sale, such as regret, shame, anxiety, or sadness. The nature of the anger, however, is less clear. Why would Yosef assume that they would be angry?

Additionally, Rabbi Ḥayyim Ibn Attar asks: Anger is rooted in the ego, while regret and sadness are rooted in the opposite place – not the ego, but in a broken spirit. If so, how could Yosef

Third, Yehuda consciously stresses one issue which is significant to his plea for Binyamin, but significant to Yosef in a profoundly different way – his own personal responsibility. The lack of responsibility is Yehuda's greatest weakness before Tamar presents him with his fateful choice, and his preparedness to accept responsibility is what convinces Yaakov to send Binyamin with him. Yosef never heard any of his brothers take personal responsibility. Even recently, he has heard Reuven absolve himself of the communal responsibility which the others accepted. Yehuda's cavalier "Let us sell him" has rung in his ears for decades, and is now replaced by Yehuda declaring himself Binyamin's personal guarantor. Even beyond this, the flip side of Yosef's suspicions regarding his father's role in his disappearance is the possibility that his father is not involved, and if so, then how could his brothers have so cruelly tortured his father, their father? Yehuda's personal commitment is not only to Binyamin but to Yaakov.

Rabbi Zvi Grumet

TAKING A LITERARY APPROACH

At the end of the previous chapter we wondered what Yosef is waiting for. After all, haven't the brothers cast their fate together with Binyamin, insisting that they will all remain as Yosef's slaves? It seems that the answer is embedded in Yehuda's speech as he confronts Yosef, one which touches a number of core areas, including Yehuda's own transformation.

A number of critical elements make this speech so powerful. First, Yehuda retells the events with extraordinary pathos, righteous indignation, and artful reshaping of those events; his oration likely reminds Yosef of Yaakov's impassioned soliloquy of injustice to Lavan. In Yehuda's carefully crafted version, Yosef never accuses the brothers of wrongdoing – neither of being spies nor of theft. In fact, Yehuda subtly suggests that it is not the brothers who did anything wrong but Yosef himself, first by inquiring about their family and then by wanting to unjustly and cruelly keep behind the most special of them. Finally, with all the above, Yehuda remains respectful, seven times calling Yosef "my master" and thirteen times referring to himself or his family (including Yosef's father) as Yosef's servants.

Second, Yehuda inadvertently touches on numerous issues sensitive to Yosef. For the first time, Yosef hears one of the brothers speak about him. From their perspective he is simply "gone," but in Yaakov's eyes he was torn apart by a wild beast. Yosef must have spent countless hours wondering about his father's role in his sale. Aside from knowing that his father deliberately sends him into a dangerous operation, Yosef is likely plagued by a simple question: why does his father, a wealthy clan leader from a respected family, never try to find him? Yosef now hears that his father thinks him long dead, perhaps stirring his own guilt for not reaching out to his father once he gained the ability to do so. And he now hears that his father is aged and fragile – even the removal of his youngest son could bring about his untimely death. Yosef wonders: can his insistence on bringing Binyamin have already killed Yaakov?

Most powerful, however, is Yehuda's description of Yaakov's comment: "You know that my wife bore me two children." To hear one of Leah's children describe Yaakov referring to Raḥel as his wife, meaning his ***only*** wife, yet remain committed to the father who regards their mother as someone less beloved, is profoundly moving. It means that the jealousy of the brothers for their mother has passed, that they accept their father's preference for Raḥel without rejecting him. It is that preference which began Yosef's domestic troubles. Their ability to move beyond it challenges Yosef to move beyond his hesitation to bring his past life into his present one.

45 1 Yosef could no longer control himself in the company of all his attendants. He cried out,
"Have everyone leave my presence!" So no one else was with Yosef when he revealed himself
2 to his brothers. He wept so loudly that the Egyptians could hear him, and the news reached
3 Pharaoh's palace. Yosef said to his brothers, "I am Yosef. Is my father really still alive?"
4 His brothers were so bewildered at his presence that they could not answer him. "Come
close to me, please," said Yosef to his brothers. They came close, and he said, "I am your
5 brother Yosef, whom you sold into Egypt. And now, do not be distressed or angry with
6 yourselves that you sold me here, for God sent me ahead of you to save lives. For two years
now there has been famine in the land, and for another five years there will be no plowing
7 or reaping. So God sent me ahead of you to ensure your survival in the land, and to save
8 your lives by a great deliverance. So then, it was not you who sent me here, but God.
He has made me a father to Pharaoh, lord of his whole household and ruler of all Egypt.
9 Hurry back to my father and tell him, 'This is what your son Yosef says: God has made
10 me lord of all Egypt. Come down to me without delay. You may live in the region of
Goshen where you will be close to me, you, your children, and your grandchildren, your
11 flocks and herds and all that is yours. I will provide for you there, for there are still five
years of famine to come. Otherwise you, your household, and all who belong to you will
12 be destitute.' You and my brother Binyamin can see with your own eyes that it is I who
13 am speaking to you. Tell my father about all the honor accorded to me in Egypt and
14 about everything you have seen. Hurry now – bring my father here." Then he threw his
15 arms around his brother Binyamin's neck and wept, and Binyamin wept on his neck; he
kissed all his brothers and wept over them. Only after that could his brothers speak to him.

UNLOCKING THE TEXT

- What caused Yosef to break down now?
- Why did he dismiss his staff before revealing his identity to his brothers?
- Why was "Is my father alive?" the first thing he said after the reveal?
- Why did he beckon them closer?
- Why did he repeatedly state that God sent him to Egypt?
- Why was it important to him that they tell Yaakov about the honor he received in Egypt?
- Why did he embrace and weep over Binyamin?
- Why did Binyamin also weep?

FINDING YOURSELF IN THE TEXT

- Have you ever had an emotional reunion with someone you love?
- Did you ever have to reassure someone that you were not upset with them?
- What would be the first thing you would say to a sibling you hadn't seen for many years?

Consider using these questions as the basis for your own commentary or creative midrash.

How does reflecting on these firsthand experiences help you better understand the text?

מה א וְלֹא־יָכֹל יוֹסֵף לְהִתְאַפֵּק לְכֹל הַנִּצָּבִים עָלָיו וַיִּקְרָא הוֹצִיאוּ כָל־אִישׁ מֵעָלָי וְלֹא־
ב עָמַד אִישׁ אִתּוֹ בְּהִתְוַדַּע יוֹסֵף אֶל־אֶחָיו׃ וַיִּתֵּן אֶת־קֹלוֹ בִּבְכִי וַיִּשְׁמְעוּ מִצְרַיִם
ג וַיִּשְׁמַע בֵּית פַּרְעֹה׃ וַיֹּאמֶר יוֹסֵף אֶל־אֶחָיו אֲנִי יוֹסֵף הַעוֹד אָבִי חָי וְלֹא־יָכְלוּ
ד אֶחָיו לַעֲנוֹת אֹתוֹ כִּי נִבְהֲלוּ מִפָּנָיו׃ וַיֹּאמֶר יוֹסֵף אֶל־אֶחָיו גְּשׁוּ־נָא אֵלַי וַיִּגָּשׁוּ
ה וַיֹּאמֶר אֲנִי יוֹסֵף אֲחִיכֶם אֲשֶׁר־מְכַרְתֶּם אֹתִי מִצְרָיְמָה׃ וְעַתָּה ׀ אַל־תֵּעָצְבוּ
וְאַל־יִחַר בְּעֵינֵיכֶם כִּי־מְכַרְתֶּם אֹתִי הֵנָּה כִּי לְמִחְיָה שְׁלָחַנִי אֱלֹהִים לִפְנֵיכֶם׃
ו כִּי־זֶה שְׁנָתַיִם הָרָעָב בְּקֶרֶב הָאָרֶץ וְעוֹד חָמֵשׁ שָׁנִים אֲשֶׁר אֵין־חָרִישׁ וְקָצִיר׃
ז וַיִּשְׁלָחֵנִי אֱלֹהִים לִפְנֵיכֶם לָשׂוּם לָכֶם שְׁאֵרִית בָּאָרֶץ וּלְהַחֲיוֹת לָכֶם לִפְלֵיטָה
ח גְּדֹלָה׃ וְעַתָּה לֹא־אַתֶּם שְׁלַחְתֶּם אֹתִי הֵנָּה כִּי הָאֱלֹהִים וַיְשִׂימֵנִי לְאָב לְפַרְעֹה שלישי
ט וּלְאָדוֹן לְכָל־בֵּיתוֹ וּמֹשֵׁל בְּכָל־אֶרֶץ מִצְרָיִם׃ מַהֲרוּ וַעֲלוּ אֶל־אָבִי וַאֲמַרְתֶּם
אֵלָיו כֹּה אָמַר בִּנְךָ יוֹסֵף שָׂמַנִי אֱלֹהִים לְאָדוֹן לְכָל־מִצְרָיִם רְדָה אֵלַי אַל־
י תַּעֲמֹד׃ וְיָשַׁבְתָּ בְאֶרֶץ־גֹּשֶׁן וְהָיִיתָ קָרוֹב אֵלַי אַתָּה וּבָנֶיךָ וּבְנֵי בָנֶיךָ וְצֹאנְךָ
יא וּבְקָרְךָ וְכָל־אֲשֶׁר־לָךְ׃ וְכִלְכַּלְתִּי אֹתְךָ שָׁם כִּי־עוֹד חָמֵשׁ שָׁנִים רָעָב פֶּן־
יב תִּוָּרֵשׁ אַתָּה וּבֵיתְךָ וְכָל־אֲשֶׁר־לָךְ׃ וְהִנֵּה עֵינֵיכֶם רֹאוֹת וְעֵינֵי אָחִי בִנְיָמִין כִּי־פִי
יג הַמְדַבֵּר אֲלֵיכֶם׃ וְהִגַּדְתֶּם לְאָבִי אֶת־כָּל־כְּבוֹדִי בְּמִצְרַיִם וְאֵת כָּל־אֲשֶׁר רְאִיתֶם
יד וּמִהַרְתֶּם וְהוֹרַדְתֶּם אֶת־אָבִי הֵנָּה׃ וַיִּפֹּל עַל־צַוְּארֵי בִנְיָמִן־אָחִיו וַיֵּבְךְּ וּבִנְיָמִן
טו בָּכָה עַל־צַוָּארָיו׃ וַיְנַשֵּׁק לְכָל־אֶחָיו וַיֵּבְךְּ עֲלֵהֶם וְאַחֲרֵי כֵן דִּבְּרוּ אֶחָיו אִתּוֹ׃

THEMES	RELATIONSHIPS AND LOVE	LEADERSHIP	REDEMPTION

Episode 65: *Yosef Reveals Himself to His Brothers* – Bereshit 45:1–15

SUMMARY

Yosef reveals his identity to his brothers. Sensitive to the shock and guilt they would suffer when recalling the events that led to their brother's place in Egypt, he reinterprets the narrative. Instead of focusing on their role in his odyssey, Yosef emphasizes that this was all part of the divine plan.

THE ART OF MIDRASH

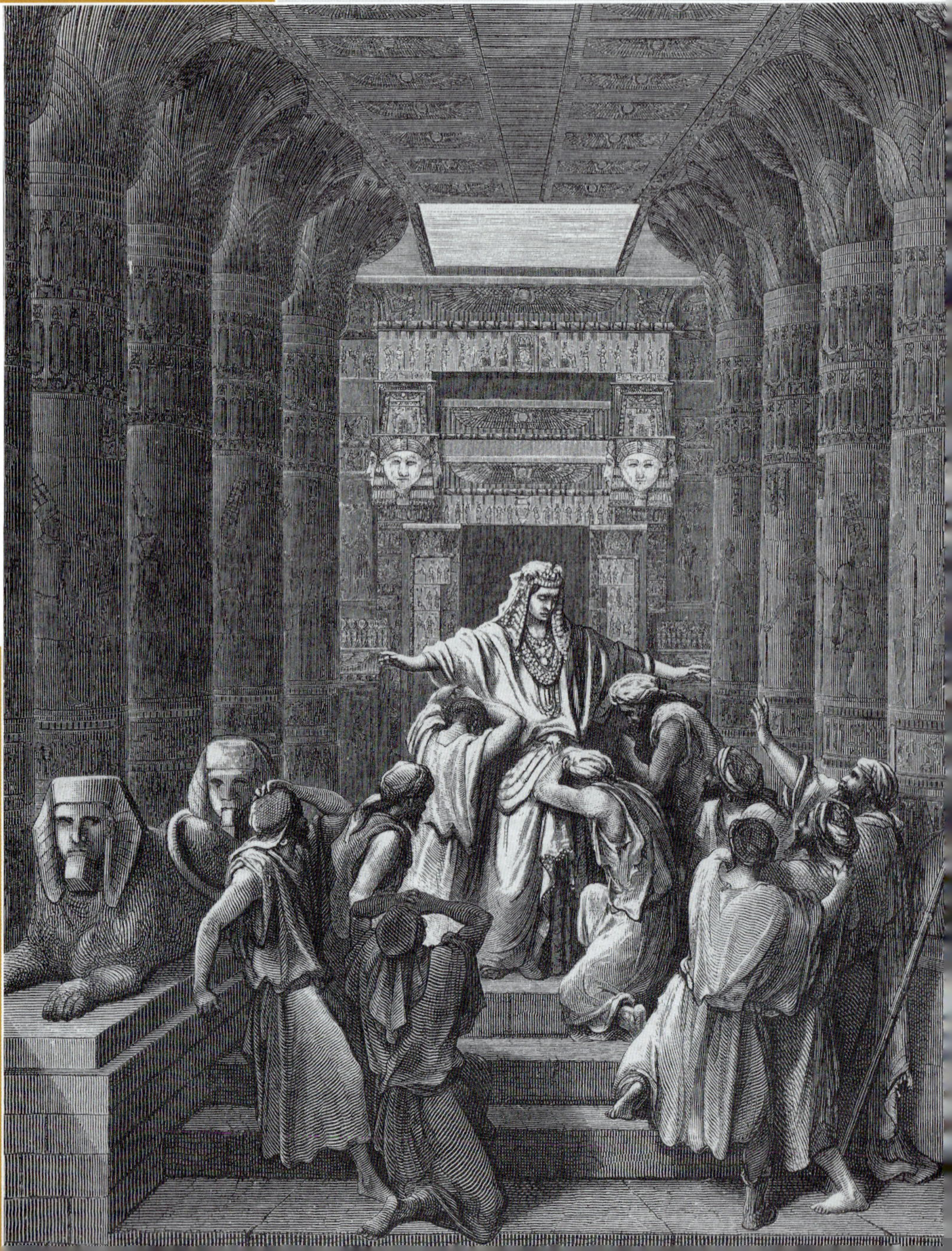

Joseph Reveals Himself to His Brothers
Gustave Doré (1866)

Analysis

- Which elements of this image are directly mentioned in the text?
- Which elements of this image are not found in the text?
- What midrashic interpretation could be inferred from this image?

A QUESTION OF BIBLIODRAMA

TO YOSEF

- What triggered your uncontrollable emotion?
- Had you rehearsed this moment? Did it go as you had planned?
- What was the most important message you wanted your brothers to know once you had revealed your identity to them?
- What are your feelings toward your brothers at this time?
- Why did you weep so intensely over Binyamin?

TO THE BROTHERS

- What questions did you have for Yosef after he dropped this bombshell on you?
- What emotions did you experience after Yosef revealed himself?
- What are your feelings toward Yosef at this time?

INTEGRATING ḤOKHMA

גֹּשֶׁן - GOSHEN

Goshen is a region in eastern Egypt, mentioned twelve times in Bereshit and Shemot. It is generally accepted that Goshen was located in the Wadi Tumilat area east of the Delta, near Ramesses and Sukkot. This region is good pastureland, but lacks enough water for agriculture.

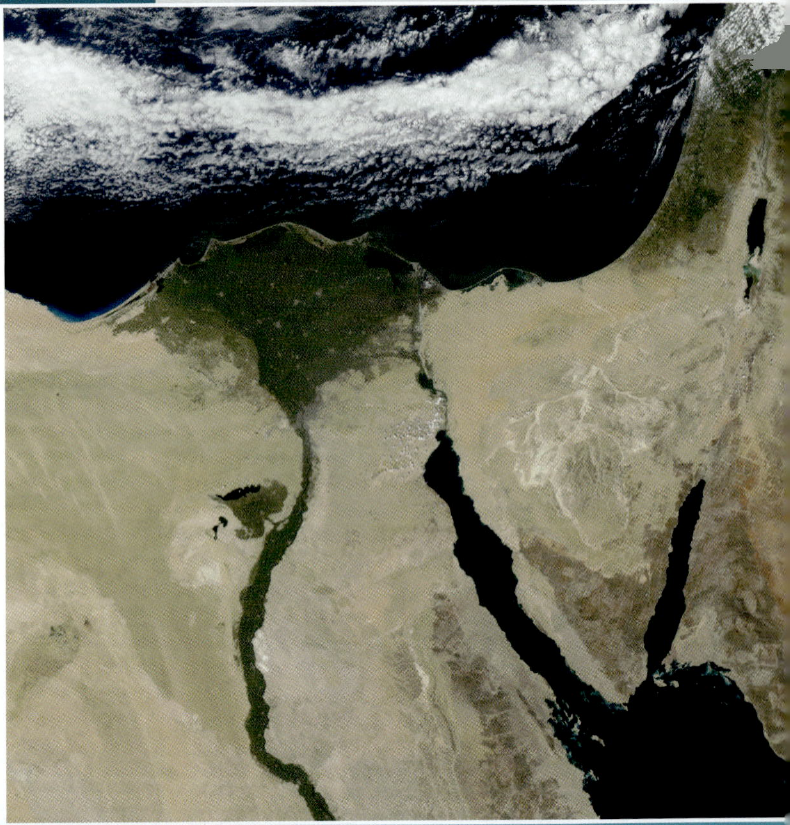

Nile Delta

Analysis

- What areas of archaeological, geographical, and historical understanding do we now have that were unavailable to classical Jewish commentators? How can they aid our understanding of the text?
- How can this information about Goshen help us understand the text?
- What further questions on the text do you have now that you have read this new information and research?

TAKING A LITERARY APPROACH

All of the brothers' actions – particularly those of the two leaders, Reuven and Yehuda – are influenced and dictated by the sin of selling Yosef and the need to atone for it. Our impression is that the ultimate structure of the family and the fate of the brothers depend on their repentance being accepted. Yosef knows this, and regards himself as a partner in this process – both because of his close (passive) connection with the sin, and because of his constant feeling, especially because of his dreams, that he is responsible for the future of Yaakov's family.

Perhaps Yosef was troubled by the brothers' terrible sin and the prospects for the future of Yaakov's household no less than he was concerned for his own personal fate. From the time he is sold, he begins to build – along with his own personal life – the process of reunification of the family. It is preferable that this reunification not be forced upon the brothers, but rather that it be brought about through good will and love. If Yosef would send a messenger to his father, letting him know that he was still alive, Yaakov would admittedly have redeemed him from Egypt and restored him to the family as a free person, but he would still be hated by his brothers, the sons of Leah, and there would be no guarantee that they would not make further attempts to rid themselves of him. Yosef did not want such a situation; he wanted a reunification based on the brothers' regret for their sin and arising from their complete repentance.

Yosef had commanded his brothers to bring Binyamin to Egypt. When the brothers actually brought Binyamin to Egypt, despite the danger, in order to redeem Shimon and to buy food, Yosef, who was unaware of Yehuda's assumption of guardianship and its importance, presumably saw the brothers' action as yet another failure to meet the test and challenge that he had set before them.

Yosef cries three times. The first two times he cries in private, and then restrains himself. The third time he breaks down totally and cries, openly and without control. Rabbi Yoel Bin-Nun cites the third episode as proof that Yosef was taken by surprise by the developments, and therefore concludes that this outcome had not been planned by Yosef. However, Rabbi Bin-Nun ignores the obvious connection between the three instances. Let us examine these three episodes.

1. First Tears

The brothers are subjected to an intensive interrogation

is to test their reaction to the prospect of Binyamin's permanent enslavement in Egypt.

The brothers rend their garments (parallel to Yosef's torn coat). Yehuda says, "God has revealed the sin of your servants" and then offers himself into permanent slavery as atonement for his lifelong sin toward his father (44:32–45:2).

At this point, Yosef is convinced of their total repentance. Yehuda's act combines two kinds of repentance. The first form of repentance is that required by the early mystics (foremost, Rabbi Eliezer of Worms, author of the *Sefer HaRokeaḥ*), whereby penance must counterbalance the crime. Yehuda, in a torn garment as a permanent slave in Egypt, is in the exact position he had placed Yosef. Secondly, we have the repentance as defined by Rambam: "What is complete repentance? When a person is confronted with the opportunity to repeat his sin but restrains himself because of repentance, and not because of fear or weakness (*Hilkhot Teshuva* 2:1).

Yehuda is now prepared to give his life to save Binyamin. Yosef comes to realize his mistake in crying for pity over Binyamin. He understands that Binyamin being brought down to Egypt was not the result of the brothers' disdain for Binyamin but rather the result of Yehuda becoming Binyamin's guarantor. Yehuda's repentance, including his attempt to amend the past, is a continuation and completion of Reuven's atonement. Yosef's weeping for the third time is a continuation of his weeping the first time, when Reuven submitted to the divine punishment.

Yosef is no longer capable of restraining himself, and he weeps openly. At this stage, the brothers' repentance for selling Yosef into slavery is complete, and Yosef can reveal himself to them.

Rabbi Yaakov Medan

during three days of imprisonment, inducing them to repent for their sin and accept the punishment and suffering, with Reuven in the lead (Bereshit 42:18–24). We have previously defined this kind of repentance as "Reuven's repentance," a repentance which involves submission and acceptance of the verdict, but lacks a program for improvement and change. Yosef is prepared to accept his brothers' confession and their submission. He witnesses the beginning of the ten brothers' reconnection to the sons of Raḥel, and he cries (42:24). But this is not sufficient for him. He requires a fuller, deeper repentance.

2. Second Tears

Yosef expected that the brothers would return to him empty-handed, placing themselves in danger by explaining to him that they had decided not to endanger Binyamin for the sake of Shimon and were willing to suffer the shame of hunger. This is what would have happened, had Yaakov had his way. Thus Yosef was disappointed when it became clear to him that the brothers had brought Binyamin in order to redeem Shimon, despite the danger to their youngest brother (43:29–30).

Yosef is still unaware of Yehuda's assumption of responsibility for Binyamin. His mercy is aroused when he realizes that his younger brother's fate is to be no better than his own – Yosef views Binyamin's being brought to Egypt as a recurrence of his own sale. True, in this case it is brought on by hunger and is not the outcome of jealousy or hatred. Nonetheless, this was not the total repentance that was expected in the wake of the confessions he had heard from the brothers and Reuven previously. The verse tells us that Yosef feels compassion toward Binyamin, and weeps in private. Yosef believes that Yehuda, the man who had proposed his sale, had prevailed over Reuven, the man who had tried to save him. This is the only possible explanation of Yosef's crying over Binyamin, his tears being tears of mercy for Binyamin and not tears of happiness at the event of their meeting. Why else should the exiled brother, who had spent a third of his life in prison, have pitied his thirty-year-old brother, who had remained with his father and raised a large family?

3. Third Tears

Yosef decided to test his brothers once more. This time, however, the test would be more difficult. He makes his brothers jealous of Binyamin in the same way that they had once been jealous of him. He displays more outward affection for Binyamin than for them and increases his portion five times over, as well as giving him a striped coat (and five other garments [43:34]). He also attempts to arouse the brothers' hatred toward Binyamin for having stolen his goblet, an act that re-implicated them for the crime of espionage. Yosef's aim

16 When the news reached Pharaoh's palace that Yosef's brothers had come, Pharaoh and
17 his officials were gratified. Pharaoh said to Yosef, "Tell your brothers, 'Do this: Load your
18 animals and go back to Canaan. Bring your father and your families and come to me. I
19 will give you the best of the land of Egypt; you shall live off the cream of the land. You
are also instructed to do this: Take wagons from Egypt for your children and wives. Bring
20 your father and come. Do not trouble yourselves about your belongings, for the best of
21 all Egypt will be yours.'" Yisrael's sons did so. Yosef gave them wagons as Pharaoh had
22 ordered, and gave them provisions for the journey. To each he gave new clothes, but to
23 Binyamin he gave three hundred pieces of silver and five sets of clothes. To his father
he sent the following: ten donkeys loaded with the best things of Egypt and ten female
24 donkeys loaded with grain, bread, and food for his father's journey. He sent his brothers
on their way; and as they were leaving, he said to them, "Do not quarrel on the way."

UNLOCKING THE TEXT

- Why were Pharaoh and his officials pleased about the news that Yosef's brothers were there?
- Why was Pharaoh interested in Yosef's family moving to Egypt?
- Why did he instruct them to leave their belongings behind?
- Why is Yosef still favoring Binyamin?
- Why did he send donkeys as a present to his father?
- Why would Yosef think the brothers may quarrel on the way to Canaan?

Consider using these questions as the basis for your own commentary or creative midrash.

FINDING YOURSELF IN THE TEXT

- Are you excited to meet the family of a new friend?
- Have you ever had to move homes?
- Have you ever experienced great anticipation to see a loved one who you haven't seen for a long time?

How does reflecting on these firsthand experiences help you better understand the text?

טז וְהַקֹּל נִשְׁמַע בֵּית פַּרְעֹה לֵאמֹר בָּאוּ אֲחֵי יוֹסֵף וַיִּיטַב בְּעֵינֵי פַרְעֹה וּבְעֵינֵי עֲבָדָיו׃
יז וַיֹּאמֶר פַּרְעֹה אֶל־יוֹסֵף אֱמֹר אֶל־אַחֶיךָ זֹאת עֲשׂוּ טַעֲנוּ אֶת־בְּעִירְכֶם וּלְכוּ־
יח בֹאוּ אַרְצָה כְּנָעַן׃ וּקְחוּ אֶת־אֲבִיכֶם וְאֶת־בָּתֵּיכֶם וּבֹאוּ אֵלָי **וְאֶתְּנָה לָכֶם אֶת־**
יט **טוּב אֶרֶץ מִצְרַיִם** וְאִכְלוּ אֶת־חֵלֶב הָאָרֶץ׃ וְאַתָּה צֻוֵּיתָה זֹאת עֲשׂוּ קְחוּ־לָכֶם רביעי
כ מֵאֶרֶץ מִצְרַיִם עֲגָלוֹת לְטַפְּכֶם וְלִנְשֵׁיכֶם וּנְשָׂאתֶם אֶת־אֲבִיכֶם וּבָאתֶם׃ וְעֵינְכֶם
כא אַל־תָּחֹס עַל־כְּלֵיכֶם כִּי־טוּב כָּל־אֶרֶץ מִצְרַיִם לָכֶם הוּא׃ וַיַּעֲשׂוּ־כֵן בְּנֵי יִשְׂרָאֵל
כב וַיִּתֵּן לָהֶם יוֹסֵף עֲגָלוֹת עַל־פִּי פַרְעֹה וַיִּתֵּן לָהֶם צֵדָה לַדָּרֶךְ׃ לְכֻלָּם נָתַן לָאִישׁ
כג חֲלִפוֹת שְׂמָלֹת וּלְבִנְיָמִן נָתַן שְׁלֹשׁ מֵאוֹת כֶּסֶף וְחָמֵשׁ חֲלִפֹת שְׂמָלֹת׃ וּלְאָבִיו
שָׁלַח כְּזֹאת עֲשָׂרָה חֲמֹרִים נֹשְׂאִים מִטּוּב מִצְרָיִם וְעֶשֶׂר אֲתֹנֹת נֹשְׂאֹת בָּר וָלֶחֶם
כד וּמָזוֹן לְאָבִיו לַדָּרֶךְ׃ וַיְשַׁלַּח אֶת־אֶחָיו וַיֵּלֵכוּ וַיֹּאמֶר אֲלֵהֶם אַל־תִּרְגְּזוּ בַּדָּרֶךְ׃

THEMES	RELATIONSHIPS AND LOVE	LEADERSHIP	REDEMPTION

Episode 66: *Pharaoh Welcomes Yosef's Brothers* – Bereshit 45:16–24

SUMMARY

When Pharaoh hears that Yosef's brothers have arrived, there is noticeable relief. Pharaoh had apparently been apprehensive all along about Yosef's mysterious origins and whether he would one day return to them. Pharaoh invites Yosef's entire family to settle in Egypt and suggests that they leave their Canaanite belongings behind, as he will provide them with the finest that Egypt has to offer. Pharaoh's plan is clear; Yosef's family will merge into Egypt.

THE ART OF MIDRASH

The land of Goshen

Analysis

- Which elements of this image are directly mentioned in the text?
- Which elements of this image are not found in the text?
- What midrashic interpretation could be inferred from this image?

A QUESTION OF BIBLIODRAMA

TO PHARAOH

- Why are you so happy to hear that Yosef's brothers are in Egypt?
- Why are you so interested in showing them generosity and encouraging them to move with their father to Egypt?
- What did you think when you heard that Yosef was in fact a Hebrew?

TO YOSEF

- Were you nervous for Pharaoh to find out that you are a Hebrew?
- What do you think of Pharaoh's idea to bring your family to Egypt?
- Why did you give Binyamin more gifts than the other brothers?
- How do you think your father will receive the news that you are still alive?

would be able to recognize him among a large population. Yet here, standing directly before him, they are unable to recognize him! Strange!

At the dinner table, Yosef seats them, announcing, "Reuven, Shimon, Levi, etc., sons of one mother, sit here. Dan and Naftali, sons of one mother, sit here," etc. How obvious can you get? Yet, even when Yosef revealed himself to his brothers, they had difficulty in believing it was him!

I believe that what was operative here is the phenomenon of denial. Denial is a psychological defense mechanism that operates subconsciously, so that the person is not aware of it. It is a mechanism that causes a person to be oblivious of something, the knowledge of which would be extremely distressful. To defend a person from the distress, denial renders the person essentially blind to what is right before his eyes, and he is no more capable of seeing it than a blind person is capable of seeing a rainbow.

The brothers believed that Yosef's dreams were his grandiose fantasies rather than prophesies, and it was their hatred of what they felt was his wish to rule over them that led to their selling him into slavery. Had they found Yosef working as someone's slave, they would have had no difficulty in recognizing him. Their subconscious defense, protecting them from realizing that they were wrong in thinking that the dreams were nothing but his grandiose fantasies, threw them into denial, so that when they prostrated themselves to him, like the sheaves in the dream, they could not afford to recognize that his dreams had been prophetic and had come true. The Torah has thus given us a clear case of denial.

Rabbi Abraham J. Twerski

Analysis

- What areas of understanding of human nature and society do we now have that were unavailable to classical Jewish commentators? How can they aid our understanding of the text?
- What can we learn from this passage to help us understand the text?
- What further questions on the text do you have now that you have read this new take on the story?

INTEGRATING ḤOKHMA

Few stories in the Torah are as laden with emotion and psychological teachings as the epic of Yosef and his brothers. First, we see how the minds of great men, the sons of Yaakov, could be so distorted by envy and hatred that they were able to justify committing so dastardly an act, initially plotting to kill their brother, then selling him into slavery. Year after year we read this story, but it has never lost its emotional impact. I have now heard this story repeated for more than seventy years, yet when I hear the Torah reader say, "And Yosef could no longer restrain himself and called out, 'Let everyone leave this room!' and then said, 'I am your brother Yosef, whom you sold into slavery in Egypt'" (Bereshit 45:1–3), I choke up as if this were the first time I heard it.

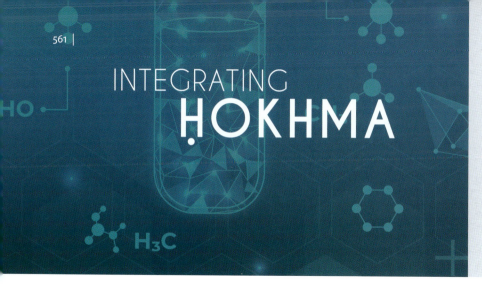

There are several psychological messages in this epic. We are told (Rashi on 37:3) that Yosef bore a striking resemblance to Yaakov. True, when he left his brothers at age seventeen he was beardless and now had a beard. But Yaakov, too, had a beard. Could they not see the resemblance? The Midrash states that they entered the city through ten separate gates, because they were going to disperse throughout the city, looking for Yosef. Obviously, they felt that they

to his court. Even after the change of plan, Pharaoh considered the family of Yaakov as Egyptian nobility, as evidenced by his offer that Yosef's brothers serve as ministers in charge of Pharaoh's own flock. Yosef had to act manipulatively to prevent this from occurring. It is likely that Yosef was concerned with the continued development of the family as a covenantal community. He wanted to avert the threat of assimilation in a situation in which they would be forced to change their names and dress and act as Egyptians in Pharaoh's court. The alternative – that they would openly retain their traditions in Pharaoh's court – would have been totally unacceptable and might have undermined Yosef's status.

Rabbi Yair Kahn

TAKING A LITERARY APPROACH

Pharaoh, in an additional display of liberal tendencies, invited Yosef's family to Egypt and offered them "the good of the land of Egypt" (Bereshit 45:18). According to Rashi, this refers to the land of Goshen. This interpretation is quite difficult, however. Consider how carefully Yosef acted upon the arrival of his family. He met his father and brothers in Goshen, and took only his father and some of his brothers to the capital city to meet Pharaoh. Before they went to meet Pharaoh, Yosef told his brothers what he would tell Pharaoh and how they should respond:

> And Yosef said to his brothers and his father's household, "I will go up and inform Pharaoh and I will say to him: 'My brothers and my father's household from the land of Canaan have come to me. The men are shepherds, for men of flock they have been from their youth till now, and they have brought their sheep and cattle and all their possessions.' And you will say: 'Your servants were men of flock from our youth till now, we and our ancestors.'" (46:31–34)

Why did Yosef prepare a speech for his brothers, and why does the Torah trouble to inform us of this detail? Yosef himself explained his motive: "In order that you shall dwell in the land of Goshen, for shepherds are an abomination to Egypt." If Pharaoh had already invited Yosef's family to Goshen, why would this manipulation have been necessary?

Let's take a closer look at Pharaoh's invitation: "And take your father and your household and come to me" (45:18). In other words, Pharaoh invited Yosef's family to the Egyptian capital – to join the royal court. Yosef took pains to thwart that plan and to ensure that his father's household remained in Goshen, far away from Pharaoh's court. It is instructive that Yosef told his brothers that he would say to Pharaoh, "My brothers and my father's house, who were in the land of Canaan, have come to me" (46:31). But what he actually said to Pharaoh was that they had arrived from Canaan and were currently in Goshen (47:1). Yosef could not tell Pharaoh that they had come to him, contrary to Pharaoh's explicit invitation. It was only after the brothers delivered to Pharaoh the speech that Yosef had prepared for them, saying that they were shepherds (considered an abomination in Egypt), that Pharaoh conceded: "And Pharaoh spoke to Yosef saying: 'Your father and your brothers have come to you'" (47:6). Only at this point did Pharaoh offer them Goshen, which was also considered the "good of the land of Egypt" (47:7).

Pharaoh intended to invite Yaakov and his family

25 26 So they went up out of Egypt and came to their father Yaakov in Canaan. They told him,
"Yosef is still alive; in fact, he is ruler over all Egypt." His heart stood still; he did not believe
27 them. But when they told him everything Yosef had said to them, and when he saw the
28 wagons that Yosef had sent to carry him back, Yaakov's spirit was filled with new life. Yisrael
46 1 said, "It is enough: Yosef my son is still alive. I must go and see him before I die." So Yisrael
set out with all he had. When he reached Be'er Sheva, he offered up sacrifices to the God of
2 his father Yitzḥak. And God spoke to Yisrael in a night vision: "Yaakov, Yaakov." He replied,
3 "Here I am." "I am God, the God of your father," He said. "Do not be afraid to go down
4 to Egypt, for there I will make of you a great nation. I Myself will go down to Egypt with
5 you, and I Myself will also bring you back; and Yosef's hand will close your eyes." Then
Yaakov left Be'er Sheva. Yisrael's sons took their father Yaakov and their children and wives

UNLOCKING THE TEXT

- What does it mean that Yaakov's heart stood still when he heard the news?
- Why did he not believe his sons?
- Why did the wagons help Yaakov to believe what the brothers were saying?
- What is the significance of Yaakov's spirit being filled with new life?
- Why did he choose to stop and connect to God at Be'er Sheva?
- Why does God need to reassure Yaakov he is making the right decision to go down to Egypt?
- What does "Yosef's hand will close your eyes" mean?
- Why does the Torah list the names of all the people in Yaakov's family who accompanied him to Egypt?

Consider using these questions as the basis for your own commentary or creative midrash.

FINDING YOURSELF IN THE TEXT

- Have you ever received news that was so good it was hard to believe?
- Have you ever been on a journey with your entire extended family?
- Can you name everyone in your extended family? Can your parents or grandparents?

How does reflecting on these firsthand experiences help you better understand the text?

כה כו וַֽיַּעֲל֖וּ מִמִּצְרָ֑יִם וַיָּבֹ֙אוּ֙ אֶ֣רֶץ כְּנַ֔עַן אֶֽל־יַעֲקֹ֖ב אֲבִיהֶֽם׃ וַיַּגִּ֨דוּ ל֜וֹ לֵאמֹ֗ר ע֚וֹד יוֹסֵ֣ף
כז חַ֔י וְכִֽי־ה֥וּא מֹשֵׁ֖ל בְּכָל־אֶ֣רֶץ מִצְרָ֑יִם וַיָּ֣פָג לִבּ֔וֹ כִּ֥י לֹא־הֶאֱמִ֖ין לָהֶֽם׃ וַיְדַבְּר֣וּ
אֵלָ֗יו אֵ֣ת כָּל־דִּבְרֵ֤י יוֹסֵף֙ אֲשֶׁ֣ר דִּבֶּ֣ר אֲלֵהֶ֔ם וַיַּרְא֙ אֶת־הָ֣עֲגָל֔וֹת אֲשֶׁר־שָׁלַ֥ח יוֹסֵ֖ף
כח לָשֵׂ֣את אֹת֑וֹ וַתְּחִ֕י ר֖וּחַ יַעֲקֹ֥ב אֲבִיהֶֽם׃ וַיֹּ֙אמֶר֙ יִשְׂרָאֵ֔ל רַ֖ב עוֹד־יוֹסֵ֣ף בְּנִ֣י חָ֑י אֵֽלְכָ֥ה חמישי
מו א וְאֶרְאֶ֖נּוּ בְּטֶ֥רֶם אָמֽוּת׃ וַיִּסַּ֤ע יִשְׂרָאֵל֙ וְכָל־אֲשֶׁר־ל֔וֹ וַיָּבֹ֖א בְּאֵ֣רָה שָּׁ֑בַע וַיִּזְבַּ֣ח זְבָחִ֔ים
ב לֵאלֹהֵ֖י אָבִ֥יו יִצְחָֽק׃ וַיֹּ֨אמֶר אֱלֹהִ֤ים ׀ לְיִשְׂרָאֵל֙ בְּמַרְאֹ֣ת הַלַּ֔יְלָה וַיֹּ֖אמֶר יַעֲקֹ֣ב ׀
ג יַעֲקֹ֑ב וַיֹּ֖אמֶר הִנֵּֽנִי׃ וַיֹּ֕אמֶר אָנֹכִ֥י הָאֵ֖ל אֱלֹהֵ֣י אָבִ֑יךָ אַל־תִּירָא֙ מֵרְדָ֣ה מִצְרַ֔יְמָה
ד כִּֽי־לְג֥וֹי גָּד֖וֹל אֲשִֽׂימְךָ֥ שָֽׁם׃ אָנֹכִ֗י אֵרֵ֤ד עִמְּךָ֙ מִצְרַ֔יְמָה וְאָנֹכִ֖י אַֽעַלְךָ֣ גַם־עָלֹ֑ה וְיוֹסֵ֕ף
ה יָשִׁ֥ית יָד֖וֹ עַל־עֵינֶֽיךָ׃ וַיָּ֥קָם יַעֲקֹ֖ב מִבְּאֵ֣ר שָׁ֑בַע וַיִּשְׂא֨וּ בְנֵֽי־יִשְׂרָאֵ֜ל אֶת־יַעֲקֹ֣ב
אֲבִיהֶ֗ם וְאֶת־טַפָּם֙ וְאֶת־נְשֵׁיהֶ֔ם בָּעֲגָל֕וֹת אֲשֶׁר־שָׁלַ֥ח פַּרְעֹ֖ה לָשֵׂ֥את אֹתֽוֹ׃

THEMES | RELATIONSHIPS AND LOVE | GOD | REDEMPTION

Episode 67: *Yaakov and His Family Descend to Egypt* – Bereshit 45:25–46:27

SUMMARY

For many years, Yaakov's mourning for his son differed from that of one whose loved one died under ordinary circumstances. Generally, the deceased is slowly forgotten over time, whereas Yaakov refused to be consoled even as the years passed, perhaps due to some small hope that Yosef may not have died. It is unknown how much this mourning affected his physical and mental capabilities and whether it impaired his daily functioning. However, from his statement in the continuation of the narrative (47:9), it can be inferred that Yaakov's later years were more difficult than those of his ancestors.

Somewhat spontaneously, Yaakov decides to leave the land of Canaan to see his beloved son. His decision to descend to Egypt without delay attests to his determination to see the son for whom he had mourned so many years. Many years earlier, Yaakov was forced to leave the land of Canaan and travel to Aram out of fear of his brother Esav. He now chooses to leave the land of his own accord in order to see his son. This departure will certainly be accompanied with serious reservations, such as his uncertainty with regard to whether, and when, he will return, and if his family will be able to preserve their unique character. Although the Torah does not describe his concerns about the journey, they can be inferred from the calming statements of God, who reveals Himself to Yaakov at this juncture.

6 in the wagons that Pharaoh had sent to carry him. They took their livestock and all the
possessions they had acquired in Canaan. So Yaakov and all his descendants came to Egypt.
7 He brought with him to Egypt his sons and grandsons, daughters and granddaughters, and
8 all his descendants. These are the names of the children of Israel – Yaakov and his
9 descendants – who came to Egypt: Reuven, Yaakov's firstborn, and Reuven's sons, Ḥanokh,
10 Palu, Ḥetzron, and Karmi. Shimon's sons were Yemuel, Yamin, Ohad, Yakhin, Tzoḥar, and
11 12 Sha'ul, son of the Canaanite woman. Levi's sons were Gershon, Kehat, and Merari. Yehuda's
sons were Er, Onan, Shela, Peretz, and Zeraḥ – but Er and Onan had died in Canaan.[1]
13 Peretz's sons were Ḥetzron and Ḥamul. Yissakhar's sons were Tola, Puva, Yov, and Shimron.
14 15 Zevulun's sons were Sered, Elon, and Yaḥliel. These were the sons whom Leah bore to
Yaakov in Padan Aram, besides his daughter Dina. In all, male and female, they numbered
16 17 thirty-three. Gad's sons were Tzifyon, Ḥagi, Shuni, Etzbon, Eri, Arodi, and Areli. Asher's
sons were Yimna, Yishva, Yishvi, and Beria. Their sister was Seraḥ. Beria's sons were Ḥever
18 and Malkiel. These were the children of Zilpa, whom Lavan had given to his daughter Leah;
19 these she bore to Yaakov – sixteen in all. The sons of Yaakov's wife Raḥel were Yosef and
20 Binyamin. In Egypt Menashe and Efrayim were born to Yosef; Asnat, daughter of Potifera
21 priest of On, bore them to him. Binyamin's sons were Bela, Bekher, Ashbel, Gera, Naaman,
22 Eḥi, Rosh, Mupim, Ḥupim, and Ard. These are the children Raḥel bore to Yaakov – fourteen
23 24 in all. Dan's son was Ḥushim. Naftali's sons were Yaḥtze'el, Guni, Yetzer, and Shilem. These
25 were the sons born to Yaakov by Bilha, whom Lavan had given to his daughter Raḥel – seven
26 in all. So the number of people who came to Egypt with Yaakov – his direct descendants,
27 not including his sons' wives – were sixty-six in all. Yosef's sons, born to him in Egypt, were
two in number. Thus the total number of Yaakov's family who came to Egypt was seventy.

1 | See 38:7–10.

TO YAAKOV

- What went through your mind as you saw your sons approach?
- What did you immediately think and feel when they told you the news?
- What questions do you have at this moment for Yosef?
- Did you have reservations about accepting Yosef's invitation to come to Egypt?
- Why did you stop at Be'er Sheva to worship God?
- Did God's message to you reassure you?

וַיִּקְח֣וּ אֶת־מִקְנֵיהֶ֗ם וְאֶת־רְכוּשָׁם֙ אֲשֶׁ֤ר רָֽכְשׁוּ֙ בְּאֶ֣רֶץ כְּנַ֔עַן וַיָּבֹ֖אוּ מִצְרָ֑יְמָה יַעֲקֹ֖ב ו

וְכָל־זַרְע֖וֹ אִתּֽוֹ: בָּנָ֞יו וּבְנֵ֤י בָנָיו֙ אִתּ֔וֹ בְּנֹתָ֛יו וּבְנ֥וֹת בָּנָ֖יו וְכָל־זַרְע֑וֹ הֵבִ֥יא אִתּ֖וֹ ז

מִצְרָֽיְמָה: וְאֵ֨לֶּה שְׁמ֧וֹת בְּנֵֽי־יִשְׂרָאֵ֛ל הַבָּאִ֥ים מִצְרַ֖יְמָה יַעֲקֹ֥ב וּבָנָ֑יו ח

בְּכֹ֥ר יַעֲקֹ֖ב רְאוּבֵֽן: וּבְנֵ֖י רְאוּבֵ֑ן חֲנ֥וֹךְ וּפַלּ֖וּא וְחֶצְרֹ֥ן וְכַרְמִֽי: וּבְנֵ֣י שִׁמְע֗וֹן יְמוּאֵ֧ל ט

וְיָמִ֣ין וְאֹ֔הַד וְיָכִ֥ין וְצֹ֖חַר וְשָׁא֣וּל בֶּן־הַכְּנַעֲנִ֑ית: וּבְנֵ֣י לֵוִ֔י גֵּרְשׁ֕וֹן קְהָ֖ת וּמְרָרִֽי: וּבְנֵ֣י יא

יְהוּדָ֗ה עֵ֧ר וְאוֹנָ֛ן וְשֵׁלָ֖ה וָפֶ֣רֶץ וָזָ֑רַח וַיָּ֨מָת עֵ֤ר וְאוֹנָן֙ בְּאֶ֣רֶץ כְּנַ֔עַן וַיִּהְי֥וּ בְנֵֽי־ יב

פֶ֖רֶץ חֶצְרֹ֥ן וְחָמֽוּל: וּבְנֵ֣י יִשָּׂשכָ֔ר תּוֹלָ֥ע וּפֻוָּ֖ה וְי֥וֹב וְשִׁמְרֹֽן: וּבְנֵ֣י זְבֻל֔וּן סֶ֖רֶד וְאֵל֥וֹן יג

וְיַחְלְאֵֽל: אֵ֣לֶּה ׀ בְּנֵ֣י לֵאָ֗ה אֲשֶׁ֨ר יָֽלְדָ֤ה לְיַעֲקֹב֙ בְּפַדַּ֣ן אֲרָ֔ם וְאֵ֖ת דִּינָ֣ה בִתּ֑וֹ כָּל־ טו

נֶ֧פֶשׁ בָּנָ֛יו וּבְנוֹתָ֖יו שְׁלֹשִׁ֥ים וְשָׁלֹֽשׁ: וּבְנֵ֣י גָ֔ד צִפְי֥וֹן וְחַגִּ֖י שׁוּנִ֣י וְאֶצְבֹּ֑ן עֵרִ֥י וַֽאֲרוֹדִ֖י טז

וְאַרְאֵלִֽי: וּבְנֵ֣י אָשֵׁ֗ר יִמְנָ֧ה וְיִשְׁוָ֛ה וְיִשְׁוִ֥י וּבְרִיעָ֖ה וְשֶׂ֣רַח אֲחֹתָ֑ם וּבְנֵ֣י בְרִיעָ֔ה יז

חֶ֖בֶר וּמַלְכִּיאֵֽל: אֵ֚לֶּה בְּנֵ֣י זִלְפָּ֔ה אֲשֶׁר־נָתַ֥ן לָבָ֖ן לְלֵאָ֣ה בִתּ֑וֹ וַתֵּ֤לֶד אֶת־אֵ֙לֶּה֙ יח

לְיַעֲקֹ֔ב שֵׁ֥שׁ עֶשְׂרֵ֖ה נָֽפֶשׁ: בְּנֵ֤י רָחֵל֙ אֵ֣שֶׁת יַעֲקֹ֔ב יוֹסֵ֖ף וּבִנְיָמִֽן: וַיִּוָּלֵ֣ד לְיוֹסֵ֗ף יט כ

בְּאֶ֣רֶץ מִצְרַ֔יִם אֲשֶׁ֤ר יָֽלְדָה־לּוֹ֙ אָֽסְנַ֔ת בַּת־פּ֥וֹטִי פֶ֖רַע כֹּהֵ֣ן אֹ֑ן אֶת־מְנַשֶּׁ֖ה וְאֶת־

אֶפְרָֽיִם: וּבְנֵ֣י בִנְיָמִ֗ן בֶּ֤לַע וָבֶ֙כֶר֙ וְאַשְׁבֵּ֔ל גֵּרָ֥א וְנַעֲמָ֖ן אֵחִ֣י וָרֹ֑אשׁ מֻפִּ֥ים וְחֻפִּ֖ים כא

וָאָֽרְדְּ: אֵ֚לֶּה בְּנֵ֣י רָחֵ֔ל אֲשֶׁ֥ר יֻלַּ֖ד לְיַעֲקֹ֑ב כָּל־נֶ֖פֶשׁ אַרְבָּעָ֥ה עָשָֽׂר: וּבְנֵי־דָ֖ן חֻשִֽׁים: כב כג

וּבְנֵ֣י נַפְתָּלִ֔י יַחְצְאֵ֥ל וְגוּנִ֖י וְיֵ֥צֶר וְשִׁלֵּֽם: אֵ֚לֶּה בְּנֵ֣י בִלְהָ֔ה אֲשֶׁר־נָתַ֥ן לָבָ֖ן לְרָחֵ֣ל כד כה

בִּתּ֑וֹ וַתֵּ֧לֶד אֶת־אֵ֛לֶּה לְיַעֲקֹ֖ב כָּל־נֶ֥פֶשׁ שִׁבְעָֽה: כָּל־הַ֠נֶּ֠פֶשׁ הַבָּאָ֨ה לְיַעֲקֹ֜ב כו

מִצְרַ֗יְמָה יֹצְאֵ֤י יְרֵכוֹ֙ מִלְּבַ֔ד נְשֵׁ֖י בְנֵֽי־יַעֲקֹ֑ב כָּל־נֶ֖פֶשׁ שִׁשִּׁ֥ים וָשֵֽׁשׁ: וּבְנֵ֥י יוֹסֵ֛ף כז

אֲשֶׁר־יֻלַּד־ל֥וֹ בְמִצְרַ֖יִם נֶ֣פֶשׁ שְׁנָ֑יִם כָּל־הַנֶּ֧פֶשׁ לְבֵֽית־יַעֲקֹ֛ב הַבָּ֥אָה מִצְרַ֖יְמָה שִׁבְעִֽים:

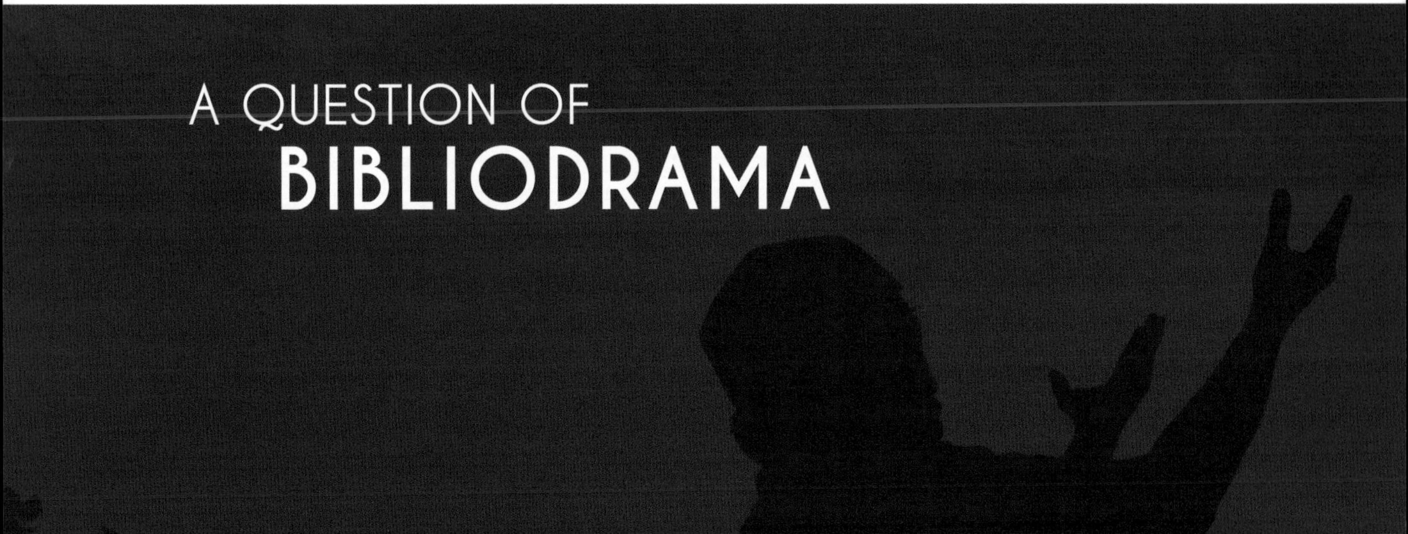

A QUESTION OF
BIBLIODRAMA

THE ART OF MIDRASH

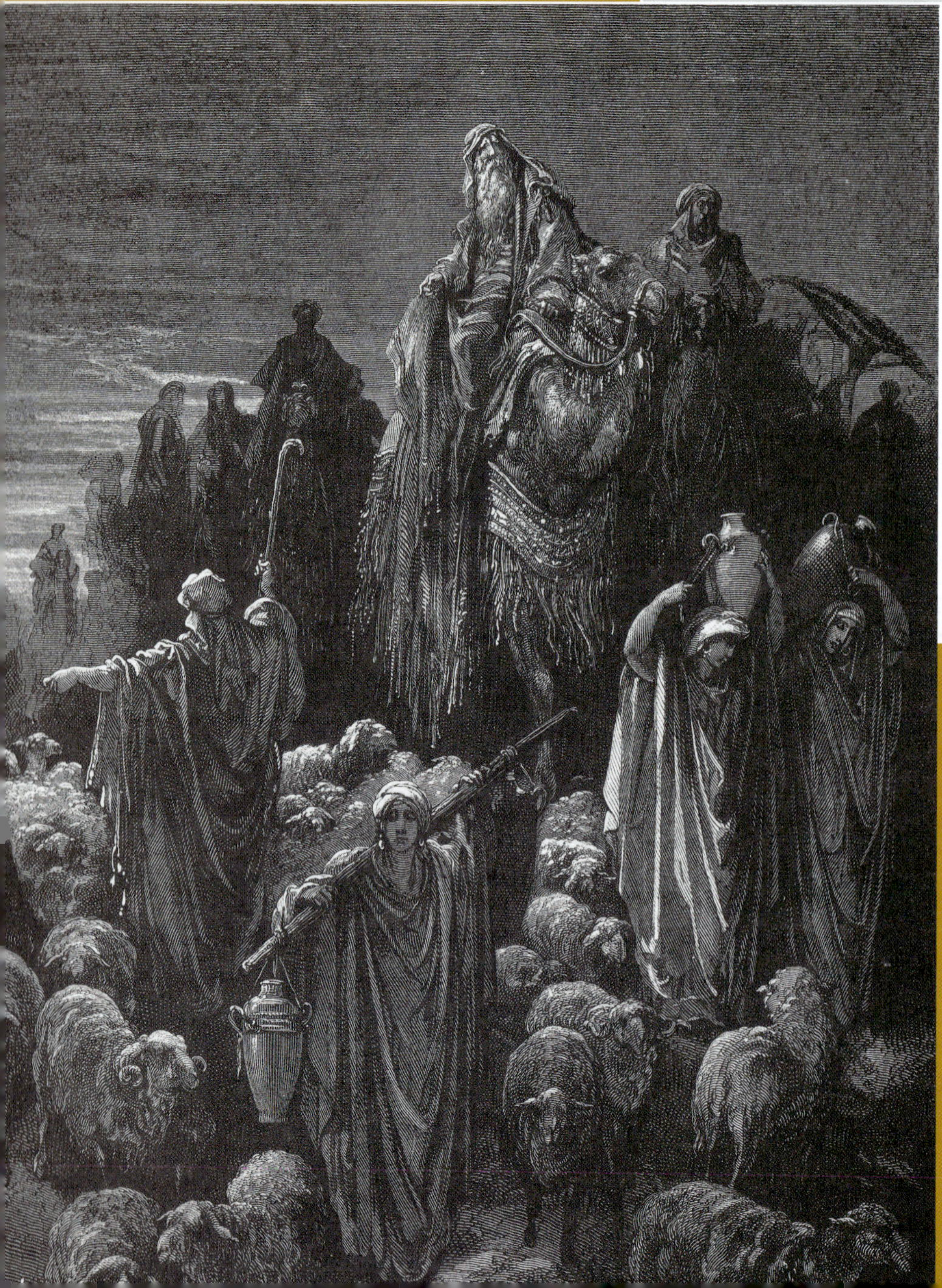

Jacob Goes to Egypt
Gustave Doré (1866)

Analysis

- Which elements of this image are directly mentioned in the text?
- Which elements of this image are not found in the text?
- What midrashic interpretation could be inferred from this image?

INTEGRATING ḤOKHMA

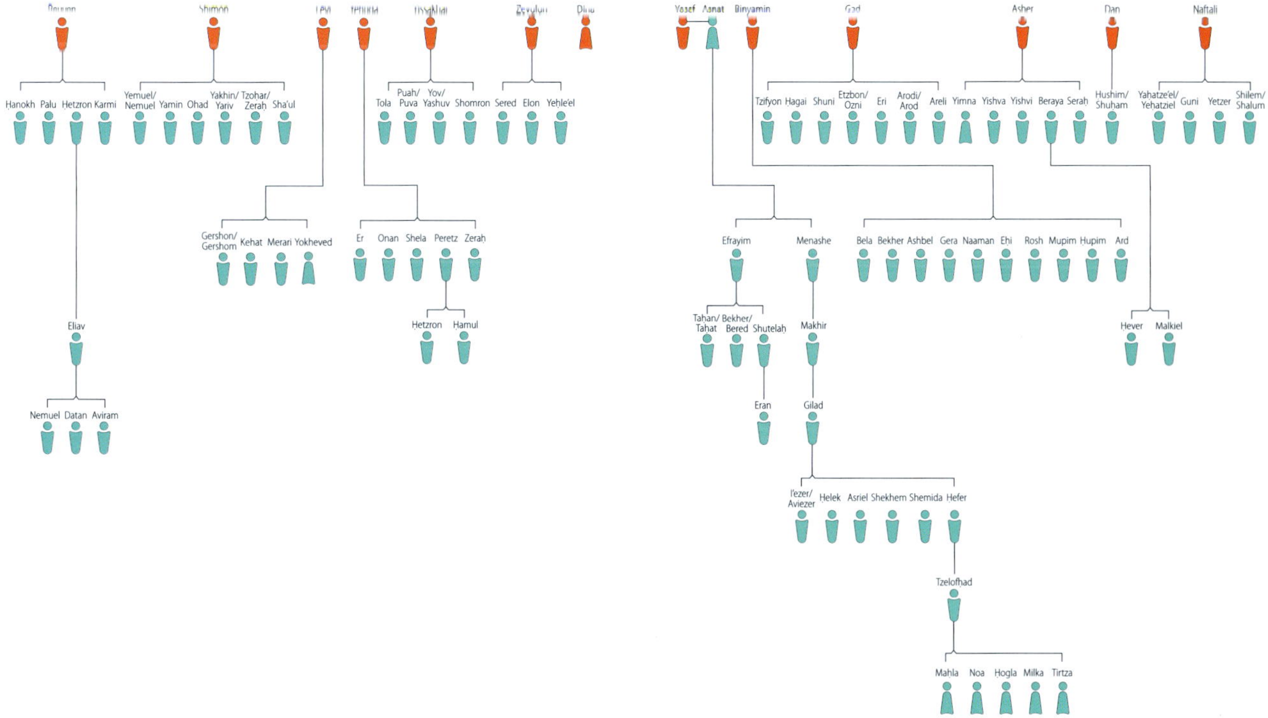

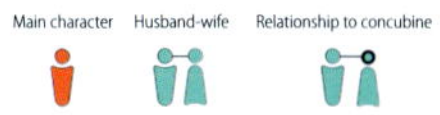

Yaakov's descendants

BERESHIT 46; BEMIDBAR 26

Egypt after settling in *Eretz Yisrael*, and after having built his house there (*vayeshev Yaakov be'eretz megurei aviv*) is exile, in a sense that it is not for his children (who, as Ramban points out, are called *Benei Yisrael* in the very same verse where Yaakov is called Yaakov).

Netziv has a similar interpretation. He disagrees with Ramban concerning the appropriateness of the name Israel in exile – on the contrary, Netziv argues that this name is especially relevant to exile, as there will be a need there to struggle with God and man in order to survive. He ascribes the name change more to the personal life of Yaakov, arguing that the name Israel refers to a miraculous supernatural existence, whereas the name Yaakov refers to existing within the natural order. God is telling Yaakov that the descent to Egypt involves being subject to the natural order, and hence, he reverts to being Yaakov.

I think that the *peshat* of the name change is along the lines of Netziv, but I would like to suggest that it should be understood in relation to the inner spirit of Yaakov. The difference in the names Yaakov and Israel can be seen in the response to Yehuda's demand that he send Binyamin to Egypt (in Parashat Miketz). Israel agrees and takes responsibility and initiative (43:11). Before that scene, Yaakov was passive, not in command of his destiny. Yehuda succeeded in rousing Yaakov from his lethargy, and that was immediately indicated by the use, albeit only for a short time, of the name Israel. The emphasis is, I suggest, on the meaning of the name Israel as "you have struggled with God and man," and less on the "prevailed"; or, if you will, "prevailed" (*vatukhal*) should be understood more as "you have succeeded to struggle" rather than "you have overcome." (After all, Yaakov did not overcome the man with whom he wrestled, but only managed to keep wrestling all night.)

The news of Yosef restores Yaakov's spirit and he rises to the status of Israel, one who will contend with his destiny, with man, and with God. He sets out for Egypt thinking that there is indeed a need to contend with what is waiting for him there, and he is planning to assume once again the leadership of the emerging *am Yisrael*. The fact that Egypt is exile does not imply that there is no need for struggle and leadership. But God informs him that that is not what will be. The experience of Egypt is indeed one of passivity, of suffering, and not one of reaction.

Rabbi Ezra Bick

TAKING A LITERARY APPROACH

In Parashat Vayigash, there is an exact point where Yaakov is finally transformed, almost "reborn," as it were. The verse states, *"Vateḥi ruaḥ Yaakov avihem"* – the spirit of Yaakov their father was revived. This is clearly and dramatically indicated not merely by the plain meaning of the verse, but by the startling juxtaposition of the names of the chief actor in this verse with the following one: "The spirit of Yaakov their father was revived. Israel said: 'It is much; my son Yosef is alive – I shall go and see him before I die'" (Bereshit 45:27)

The significance of the sudden change in Yaakov's name is irresistible, and nearly all commentators who remarked on it interpret it to mean that Yaakov's personality was transformed, with the name Yaakov referring to a lower, diminished level, and the name Israel signifying the higher, inspired manifestation of Yaakov, not merely the individual with his personal problems, but the forefather, the protagonist of Jewish history, the divinely inspired manifestation of Jewish destiny itself.

In light of this, it is noteworthy that the Torah does not continue to refer to Yaakov as Israel, and in fact there is a rather sudden reversion to the name Yaakov: "Israel traveled with all that was his, and he came to Be'er Sheva, and he sacrificed sacrifices to the God of his father Yitzḥak. And God said to Israel in a vision of night, and He said: 'Yaakov, Yaakov.' And he said: 'I am here.' He said: 'Do not fear to descend to Egypt, for I will make you a great nation there.' And Yaakov rose from Be'er Sheva, and the children of Israel bore Yaakov their father and their infants and wives on the wagons which Pharaoh had sent to bear him" (46:1–5).

Israel begins the journey and reaches Be'er Sheva; from there Yaakov continues the rest of the way to Egypt. What has taken place in Be'er Sheva? God appears to Israel and speaks to him, calling him Yaakov. It seems almost as though God has taken Yaakov down a peg, changing his name back to the old one, the one he bore the entire time that Yosef had been missing. What is taking place here?

Ramban (on 46:2) explains that God calls Yaakov by the name Yaakov to tell him that this descent to Egypt is the beginning of the exile. The name Israel means "for you have struggled with God and man and have prevailed," and in Egypt he will "be in the house of bondage until God will raise him, for now the exile begins for him." The obvious problem with this explanation is that the slavery does not begin immediately, but Ramban has, I think, warded off this critique by stating that the "exile begins for him." For Yaakov, or rather for Israel, to have to go to

28 He sent Yehuda ahead of him to Yosef to show him the way to Goshen. When they came
29 to the region of Goshen, Yosef harnessed his chariot and rode to Goshen to greet his
father Yisrael. He presented himself to him, threw his arms around his neck, and wept
30 on his shoulder for a long time. "Now I can die," said Yisrael to Yosef. "I have seen your
31 face! You are still alive!" Yosef said to his brothers and his father's household, "I will go
and speak to Pharaoh. I will tell him, 'My brothers and my father's household have come
32 to me from Canaan. The men are shepherds. They tend livestock. They have brought
33 their sheep and cattle and all they have.' When Pharaoh summons you and asks, 'What
34 is your occupation?' you should say, 'We and our fathers have tended livestock all our
lives.' Then you will be allowed to settle in the region of Goshen, because the Egyptians
47 1 abominate all who keep sheep."[1] So Yosef went and told Pharaoh. He said, "My father and
brothers, together with their flocks, herds, and all they have, have come from Canaan and
2 are now in the region of Goshen." He chose five of his brothers and presented them to
3 Pharaoh. Pharaoh asked the brothers, "What is your occupation?" They replied, "Your
4 servants are shepherds, as our fathers were before." And they said to Pharaoh, "We
have come to stay for a while in your land because the famine is severe in Canaan and
5 there is no pasture for your servants' flocks. Please, then, let your servants settle in the
region of Goshen." Pharaoh said to Yosef, "Your father and brothers have come to you.

---

1 | In other words, because of this consideration, Pharaoh will agree to have you live in a peripheral location such as Goshen.

UNLOCKING THE TEXT

- For what purpose did Yaakov send Yehuda ahead? Why Yehuda?
- Why does Yosef travel to meet his family in Goshen instead of summoning them to the palace?
- Why does Yosef need to prepare his father and brothers for their meeting with Pharaoh?
- Why did he present only five brothers to Pharaoh? Which five?
- Why did Yaakov present his life to Pharaoh in this way?
- How did he know he would not live as long as his fathers?

FINDING YOURSELF IN THE TEXT

- Have you ever been reunited with someone you love who you haven't seen for many years?
- Do you know anyone very important? How does it feel to be associated with them?
- Have you ever met the ruler of a country?

Consider using these questions as the basis for your own commentary or creative midrash.

How does reflecting on these firsthand experiences help you better understand the text?

כח כט וְאֶת־יְהוּדָה שָׁלַח לְפָנָיו אֶל־יוֹסֵף לְהוֹרֹת לְפָנָיו גֹּשְׁנָה וַיָּבֹאוּ אַרְצָה גֹּשֶׁן: וַיֶּאְסֹר מא ששי
יוֹסֵף מֶרְכַּבְתּוֹ וַיַּעַל לִקְרַאת־יִשְׂרָאֵל אָבִיו גֹּשְׁנָה וַיֵּרָא אֵלָיו וַיִּפֹּל עַל־צַוָּארָיו
ל וַיֵּבְךְּ עַל־צַוָּארָיו עוֹד: וַיֹּאמֶר יִשְׂרָאֵל אֶל־יוֹסֵף אָמוּתָה הַפָּעַם אַחֲרֵי רְאוֹתִי
לא אֶת־פָּנֶיךָ כִּי עוֹדְךָ חָי: וַיֹּאמֶר יוֹסֵף אֶל־אֶחָיו וְאֶל־בֵּית אָבִיו אֶעֱלֶה וְאַגִּידָה
לב לְפַרְעֹה וְאֹמְרָה אֵלָיו אַחַי וּבֵית־אָבִי אֲשֶׁר בְּאֶרֶץ־כְּנַעַן בָּאוּ אֵלָי: וְהָאֲנָשִׁים רֹעֵי
לג צֹאן כִּי־אַנְשֵׁי מִקְנֶה הָיוּ וְצֹאנָם וּבְקָרָם וְכָל־אֲשֶׁר לָהֶם הֵבִיאוּ: וְהָיָה כִּי־יִקְרָא
לד לָכֶם פַּרְעֹה וְאָמַר מַה־מַּעֲשֵׂיכֶם: וַאֲמַרְתֶּם אַנְשֵׁי מִקְנֶה הָיוּ עֲבָדֶיךָ מִנְּעוּרֵינוּ
וְעַד־עַתָּה גַּם־אֲנַחְנוּ גַּם־אֲבֹתֵינוּ בַּעֲבוּר תֵּשְׁבוּ בְּאֶרֶץ גֹּשֶׁן כִּי־תוֹעֲבַת מִצְרַיִם
מז א כָּל־רֹעֵה צֹאן: וַיָּבֹא יוֹסֵף וַיַּגֵּד לְפַרְעֹה וַיֹּאמֶר אָבִי וְאַחַי וְצֹאנָם וּבְקָרָם וְכָל־אֲשֶׁר
ב לָהֶם בָּאוּ מֵאֶרֶץ כְּנָעַן וְהִנָּם בְּאֶרֶץ גֹּשֶׁן: וּמִקְצֵה אֶחָיו לָקַח חֲמִשָּׁה אֲנָשִׁים וַיַּצִּגֵם
ג לִפְנֵי פַרְעֹה: וַיֹּאמֶר פַּרְעֹה אֶל־אֶחָיו מַה־מַּעֲשֵׂיכֶם וַיֹּאמְרוּ אֶל־פַּרְעֹה רֹעֵה
ד צֹאן עֲבָדֶיךָ גַּם־אֲנַחְנוּ גַּם־אֲבוֹתֵינוּ: וַיֹּאמְרוּ אֶל־פַּרְעֹה לָגוּר בָּאָרֶץ בָּאנוּ כִּי־
אֵין מִרְעֶה לַצֹּאן אֲשֶׁר לַעֲבָדֶיךָ כִּי־כָבֵד הָרָעָב בְּאֶרֶץ כְּנָעַן וְעַתָּה יֵשְׁבוּ־נָא
ה עֲבָדֶיךָ בְּאֶרֶץ גֹּשֶׁן: וַיֹּאמֶר פַּרְעֹה אֶל־יוֹסֵף לֵאמֹר אָבִיךָ וְאַחֶיךָ בָּאוּ אֵלֶיךָ:

THEMES	RELATIONSHIPS AND LOVE	LEADERSHIP	REDEMPTION

Episode 68: *Yaakov and Yosef Reunite* – Bereshit 46:28–47:12

SUMMARY

Yosef plans to settle his family in the land of Goshen. To accomplish this goal, he prepares them for their initial meeting with Pharaoh by stressing that they should present themselves as shepherds, not farmers. Egypt's economy was largely farming-based, and the Egyptians tended to look down on shepherds. These factors made it more likely that Pharaoh would agree to settle them in the peripheral land of Goshen, which was suitable for tending flocks. Establishing the family in a separate region with governmental approval would give them the opportunity to grow and develop without interference. It also suited Yosef's plans for reorganizing the Egyptian economy, which will be soon be recounted.

6 The land of Egypt is open before you. Settle your father and brothers in the best part of
the land. Let them live in the region of Goshen, and if there are able men among them,
7 you may give them charge of my own livestock." Then Yosef brought his father Yaakov
8 and presented him before Pharaoh. Yaakov blessed Pharaoh, and Pharaoh asked Yaakov,
9 "How old are you?" Yaakov said to Pharaoh, "The years of my wandering are one hundred
and thirty. Few and hard have been the years of my life, and I have not reached the age my
10 fathers reached in their own wanderings." Yaakov blessed Pharaoh and left his presence.
11 Yosef settled his father and brothers, giving them holdings in the best part of Egypt, in
12 the region of Ramesses,[2] as Pharaoh had instructed. And Yosef provided his father, his
brothers, and all his father's household with food, befitting the numbers of their dependents.

2 | Ramesses evidently comprised all or part of Goshen.

THE ART OF MIDRASH

Analysis

- Which elements of this image are directly mentioned in the text?
- Which elements of this image are not found in the text?
- What midrashic interpretation could be inferred from this image?

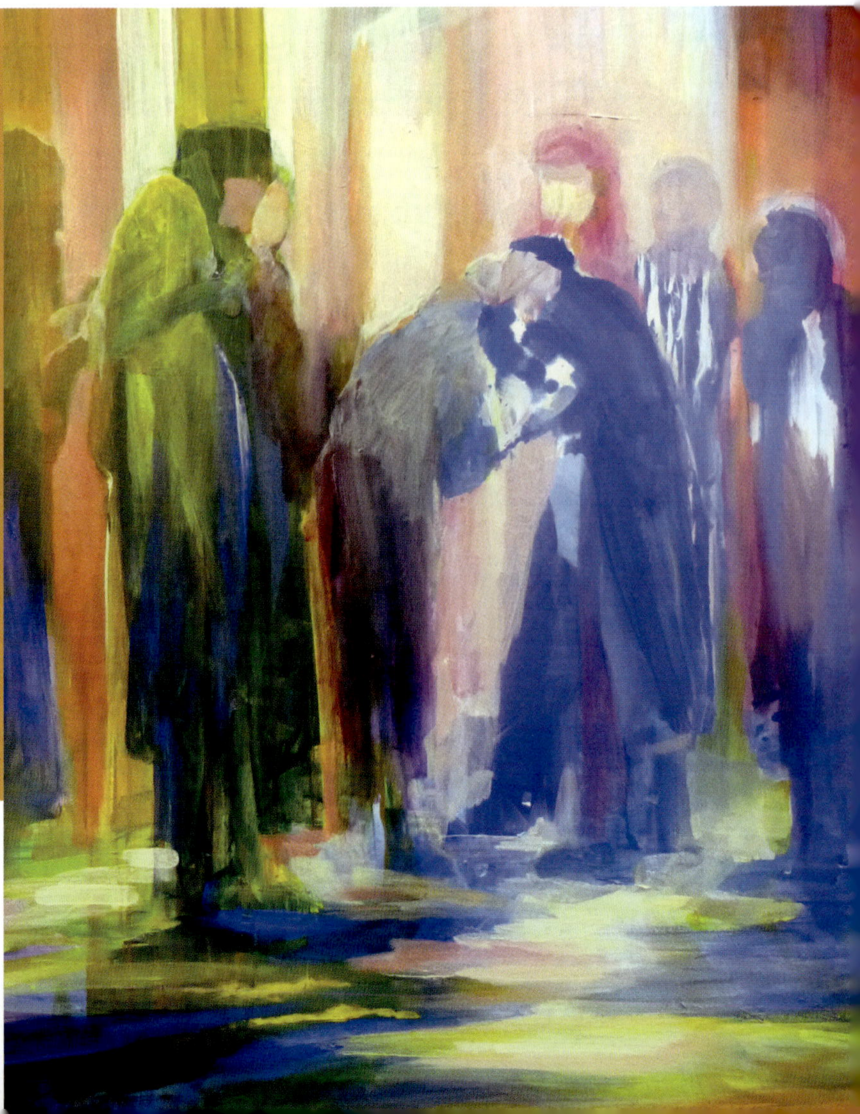

The Reunion
Yoram Raanan (2014)

ו אֶ֣רֶץ מִצְרַ֙יִם֙ לְפָנֶ֣יךָ הִ֔וא בְּמֵיטַ֣ב הָאָ֔רֶץ הוֹשֵׁ֥ב אֶת־אָבִ֖יךָ וְאֶת־אַחֶ֑יךָ יֵשְׁבוּ֙ בְּאֶ֣רֶץ
ז גֹּ֔שֶׁן וְאִם־יָדַ֗עְתָּ וְיֶשׁ־בָּם֙ אַנְשֵׁי־חַ֔יִל וְשַׂמְתָּ֛ם שָׂרֵ֥י מִקְנֶ֖ה עַל־אֲשֶׁר־לִֽי׃ וַיָּבֵ֤א יוֹסֵף֙
ח אֶת־יַעֲקֹ֣ב אָבִ֔יו וַיַּֽעֲמִדֵ֖הוּ לִפְנֵ֣י פַרְעֹ֑ה וַיְבָ֥רֶךְ יַעֲקֹ֖ב אֶת־פַּרְעֹֽה׃ וַיֹּ֥אמֶר פַּרְעֹ֖ה
ט אֶל־יַעֲקֹ֑ב כַּמָּ֕ה יְמֵ֖י שְׁנֵ֥י חַיֶּֽיךָ׃ וַיֹּ֤אמֶר יַעֲקֹב֙ אֶל־פַּרְעֹ֔ה יְמֵי֙ שְׁנֵ֣י מְגוּרַ֔י שְׁלֹשִׁ֥ים
וּמְאַ֖ת שָׁנָ֑ה מְעַ֣ט וְרָעִ֗ים הָיוּ֙ יְמֵי֙ שְׁנֵ֣י חַיַּ֔י וְלֹ֣א הִשִּׂ֗יגוּ אֶת־יְמֵי֙ שְׁנֵ֣י חַיֵּ֣י אֲבֹתַ֔י בִּימֵ֖י
י יא מְגוּרֵיהֶֽם׃ וַיְבָ֥רֶךְ יַעֲקֹ֖ב אֶת־פַּרְעֹ֑ה וַיֵּצֵ֖א מִלִּפְנֵ֥י פַרְעֹֽה׃ וַיּוֹשֵׁ֣ב יוֹסֵף֮ אֶת־אָבִ֣יו שביעי
וְאֶת־אֶחָיו֒ וַיִּתֵּ֨ן לָהֶ֤ם אֲחֻזָּה֙ בְּאֶ֣רֶץ מִצְרַ֔יִם בְּמֵיטַ֥ב הָאָ֖רֶץ בְּאֶ֣רֶץ רַעְמְסֵ֑ס כַּאֲשֶׁ֖ר
יב צִוָּ֥ה פַרְעֹֽה׃ וַיְכַלְכֵּ֤ל יוֹסֵף֙ אֶת־אָבִ֣יו וְאֶת־אֶחָ֔יו וְאֵ֖ת כָּל־בֵּ֣ית אָבִ֑יו לֶ֖חֶם לְפִ֥י
הַטָּֽף׃

A QUESTION OF BIBLIODRAMA

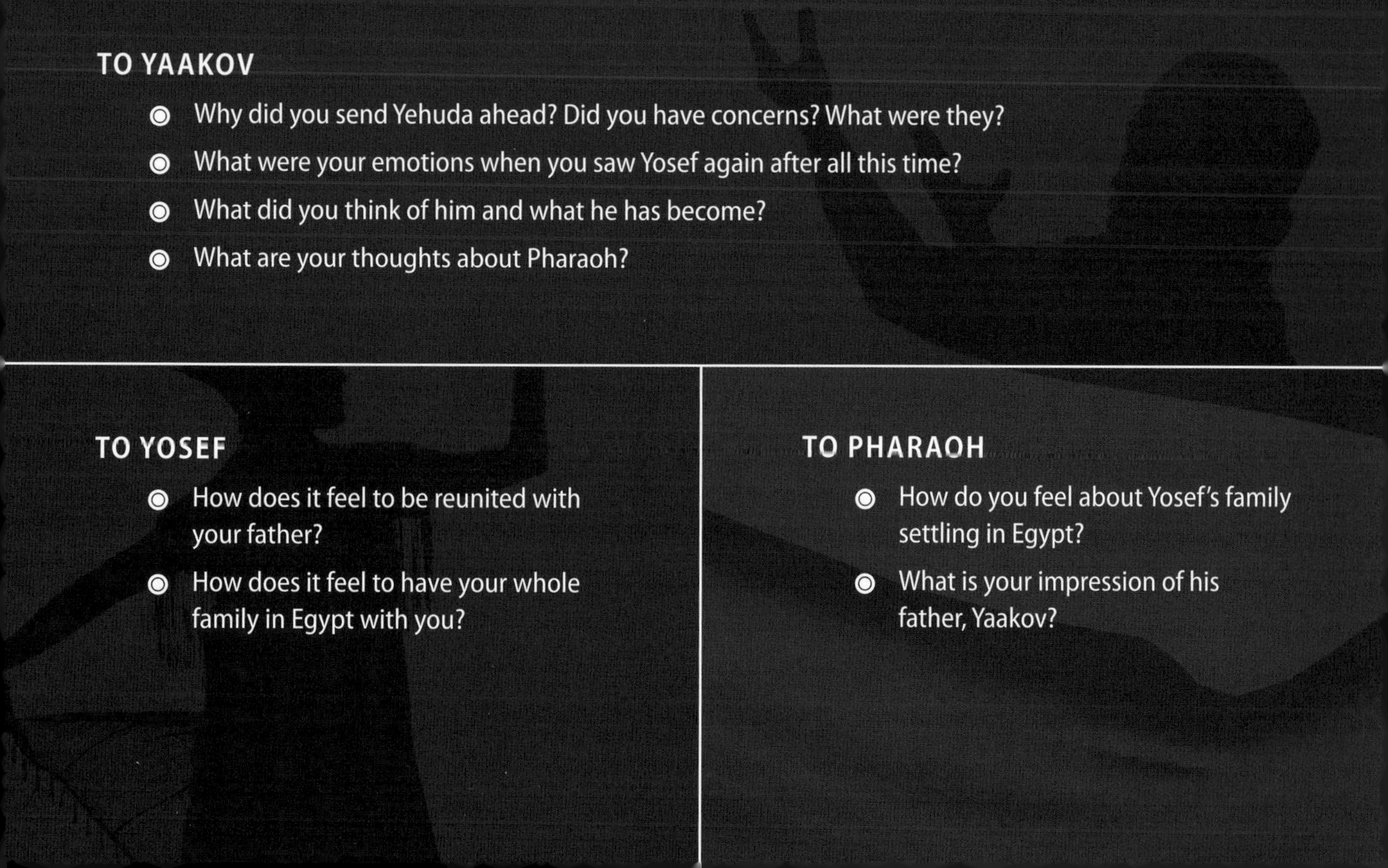

TO YAAKOV

- Why did you send Yehuda ahead? Did you have concerns? What were they?
- What were your emotions when you saw Yosef again after all this time?
- What did you think of him and what he has become?
- What are your thoughts about Pharaoh?

TO YOSEF

- How does it feel to be reunited with your father?
- How does it feel to have your whole family in Egypt with you?

TO PHARAOH

- How do you feel about Yosef's family settling in Egypt?
- What is your impression of his father, Yaakov?

Rabbi Ḥizkiya ben Manoaḥ takes this view when he explains Pharaoh's intake of Yaakov: "You look old and at the end of your days." Life has worn Yaakov down. On the expression Yaakov uses in response – that the years of his life did not achieve that of his ancestors during their sojourns – Rashi explains Yaakov's confession: "All my life I've lived in the country of others." He did not want to spend his old age in someone else's land.

All leaders have dark days, even dark years. Two great leaders in more recent world history – Abraham Lincoln and Winston Churchill – suffered terrible depression. Lincoln called it melancholy. But rather than seeing these difficult periods as obstructions, they may have held the key to their respective greatness. They were able to harness the darkness they experienced to become more empathic to the suffering of others and more willing to take risks to solve problems than others. J. Shenk, in his article "Lincoln's Great Depression" (*The Atlantic*, Oct. 2005) writes:

> Whatever greatness Lincoln achieved cannot be explained as a triumph over personal suffering. Rather, it must be accounted as an outgrowth of the same system that produced that suffering.... Lincoln didn't do great work because he solved the problem of his melancholy; the problem of his melancholy was all the more fuel for the fire of his great work.

Churchill called his dark days the "black dog." A black dog is an interesting image – a hovering, gloomy shadow that stays close but can walk away. In a letter to his wife Clementine in 1911, Churchill wrote that he heard about a German doctor who treated depression: "I think this man might be useful to me – if my black dog returns. He seems quite away from me now – it is such a relief. All the colors come back into the picture." Yaakov struggled in this melancholic moment here, but there is a small, redeeming detail that is often ignored in this conversation. It is bookended by Yaakov blessing Pharaoh on his way in and on his way out. Sforno regards the blessing as a small act of defiance. Yaakov "did not bow to him [Pharaoh], neither when he arrived nor when he departed." Rashi deems the blessing a "greeting of peace, as is usual in the case of all who are granted an interview with kings at long intervals." We find a similar usage in II Shmuel 16:16.

Ramban disagrees with Rashi. This was not a polite, inconsequential gesture, the ancient equivalent of a curtsy or bow before royalty. Ramban believes that Yaakov was truly blessing Pharaoh. Yaakov may not have had bread. He may have been far from home, and his last years were characterized by difficulty, but Yaakov always carried with him the capacity to bless. Even when he struggled with an angel, Yaakov was injured but asked for a blessing. More than any other biblical leader, Yaakov understood the secret of Jewish continuity and leadership: the ability to find the blessing in the struggle.

Dr. Erica Brown

Analysis

- What areas of understanding of human nature and society do we now have that were unavailable to classical Jewish commentators? How can they aid our understanding of the text?
- What can we learn from this essay to help us understand the text?
- What further questions on the text do you have now that you have read this new take on the story?

INTEGRATING ḤOKHMA

A summation of Yaakov's last years emerges in a conversation he has with Pharaoh. This is one of the strangest conversations in all of Tanakh. Yaakov speaks to Pharaoh and tells this powerful leader and stranger of his woes. "Yosef then brought his father Yaakov and presented him to Pharaoh, and Yaakov greeted Pharaoh. Pharaoh asked Yaakov, 'How many are the years of your life?' And Yaakov answered Pharaoh, 'The years of my sojourn [on earth] are one hundred and thirty. Few and hard have been the years of my life, nor do they come up to the life spans of my ancestors during their sojourns.' Then Yaakov bade Pharaoh farewell, and left Pharaoh's presence" (Bereshit 47:7–10).

Pharaoh asks an odd question about Yaakov's age. Yaakov responds by telling Pharaoh something he never revealed to his sons. His life has been punishingly hard and is soon to be over. How Yaakov knows this is never explained. After this upsetting download of misery, Pharaoh says nothing. He offers not a word of solace or consolation. Yaakov then exits the scene. The story progresses with no further mention of the encounter.

Before we look at the content of this dialogue, there is an important context for this conversation that appears a few verses later: "Yosef sustained his father, and his brothers, and all his father's household with bread, down to the little ones. Now there was no bread in all the world, for the famine was very severe; both the land of Egypt and the land of Canaan languished because of the famine" (47:12–13). Yaakov, the inheritor of Avraham and Yitzḥak's legacy, had to be supported by his son, in a land not his own, at the point of starvation. Any leader would be humiliated and ashamed in this desperate situation. How could it be that Yaakov began his leadership with a magnificent dream of a ladder covered with angels and many divine promises, and now he was bereft, untethered from his homeland, and virtually penniless?

Ramban explains that it was Pharaoh who requested the meeting, not Yosef. Pharaoh was so impressed by Yosef's many talents that he, understandably, wanted to meet Yosef's father. Pharaoh then asked Yaakov a puzzling question, one that sounds out of place, even rude: why have you lived so long? Yet some understand this as a question that emerges out of respect. Many pharaohs were young on the throne. This Pharaoh may have been shocked by Yaakov's longevity and regarded it as a blessing. Pharaoh was asking Yaakov to tell him the secret to a long life.

But if this was Pharaoh's intent, why did Yaakov answer that his life was actually short and soon to end? Yaakov was 130 at this time, but his grandfather Avraham died at 175. His father Yitzḥak died at 180. Because of Yaakov's many disappointments – the theft of his brother's blessing, the switching of wives on the marriage alter, Lavan's exploitation, the disappearance of Yosef, the rape of Dina, the famine in Canaan – he felt that death was fast approaching, even if he was unable to predict it.

by the juxtaposition of the description of Yosef's role in providing for his family with the long and detailed account of how Yosef nourished the entire Egyptian population (47:13–26). The family is actually leaderless, for they are dependents on the house of Pharaoh and on his viceroy, who happens to be their brother. This is only one step above slavery. The point is not the oppression, but the passivity. Events will affect them, but they have no opportunity to affect events. Their fate is not in their hands, and they make no attempt to change that.

Like his fathers before him, Yaakov's career as a forefather, as one who is building *am Yisrael*, ends many years before he dies. Avraham's career effectively ended when he arranged for Yitzḥak's marriage, some thirty-five years before he dies. The Torah tells us nothing of those years, other than that he had other children. Yitzḥak's career effectively ended when he arranged for Yaakov's marriage and sent him to Aram. According to the account advanced by Rashi at the end of Toledot, that was seventy-seven years before he died. In fact, the Torah gives the impression that Yitzḥak died shortly after Yaakov returned to *Eretz Yisrael*, years before the Yosef narratives, although he actually only died ten years before Yaakov went to Egypt. Yaakov's career ends when he sees the reunion of his family – in other words, when he guarantees the existence of the House of Yaakov, which now begins to be called by the title *Benei Yisrael*.

Rabbi Ezra Bick

TAKING A LITERARY APPROACH

How did Yaakov know that his life would be shorter than that of his fathers? After all, he still can live many years. I think Yaakov's answer indicates that he did not expect to live much longer, or, more accurately, that the vital part of his life is already over. This I think is the meaning of the curious phrase "the days of the life of my fathers in their dwelling." It means not the total number of years, but the number of years of active vital living, what we might call the years of his career. While the exact years of Yaakov's life are not spelled out in the Torah, we know that he arrived in *Eretz Yisrael* shortly after the birth of Yosef, who was thirty when he became viceroy of Egypt. Hence, Yaakov's total career in *Eretz Yisrael* was only about thirty-nine years (of which twenty-two were spent after Yosef disappeared). Yaakov is convinced that his "career" is over, which is why he has become Yaakov again, even though he has the spirit to be Israel.

In fact, it is not only Yaakov who retires from his leadership role in Parashat Vayigash. One of the important themes of the previous two *parashot* was the coming of Yehuda into leadership – his developing the necessary leadership qualities and his subsequent assumption of the leadership role. Yet, immediately after his success in the opening scene of the *parasha*, whereby he brings Yosef to acknowledge his true character and relationship (parallel to what he has accomplished in the previous *parasha* in regard to Yaakov), he disappears as a leader. Whereas when the brothers return for the final confrontation with Pharaoh, they are described as "Yehuda and his brothers" (Bereshit 44:14) – what could be a clearer indication of his leadership! – when they leave Yosef to go get their father, they are merely described as *Benei Yisrael* (45:21). The *parasha* continues to refer to the brothers as a nameless group. Although Yehuda is sent by his father ahead of the others to learn the route (46:28), he does not actually lead them to the land of Goshen. Yehuda's leadership will not actually have any role before the Jews arrive in *Eretz Yisrael* some 250 years later.

The actual leader of the family in Egypt is Yosef, who provides them with safety and food. But it is a mistake to view Yosef as the leader of the House of Yaakov. Yosef does not act as the head of the House of Yaakov, but as an Egyptian. He is able to take care of his brothers precisely because he is not one of them, not their leader, but because he is viceroy of Egypt. He is their protector, not their leader. This is clearly indicated

13 And there was no food across the land, because the famine was so severe. Egypt and Canaan
14 languished because of the famine. Yosef collected all the money that was to be found in
Egypt and Canaan in payment for the grain the people were buying, and he brought it into
15 Pharaoh's palace. When the money in Egypt and Canaan was gone, all the Egyptians came
to Yosef, saying, "Give us food. Why should we die before your eyes just because there is no
16 more money left?" "Bring your livestock," said Yosef, "and I will sell you food in exchange
17 for your livestock since there is no more money left." So they brought their livestock to
Yosef, and he gave them food in exchange for horses, sheep, cattle, and donkeys. He supplied
18 them with food that year in exchange for all their livestock. That year passed, and they came
to him the following year and said, "We cannot hide from my lord that the money is gone
and the livestock belongs to you. There is nothing left for my lord except our bodies and
19 our land. Why should we and our land die before your eyes? Acquire us and our land in
exchange for food, and we with our land will be slaves to Pharaoh. Give us seed so that we
20 can live and not die and so that the land does not become desolate." Thus Yosef acquired all
the land of Egypt for Pharaoh. Each Egyptian sold his field, because the famine had become
21 too much for them. So the land became Pharaoh's. As for the people, he transferred them

UNLOCKING THE TEXT

- Why does the Torah include Canaan in its description of Egypt's famine? What about other surrounding lands?
- Why did the Egyptians think they had a right to food if they had no money left?
- Why didn't Yosef and Pharaoh feel obligated to protect the people of Egypt?
- Did this harsh economic plan for the Egyptian people originate with Yosef or Pharaoh?
- Why did the priests maintain their own land and receive food directly from Pharaoh?
- If there was a famine, how would they be able to plant and harvest the seeds Yosef gave them?
- Is this system of taxation (one-fifth to Pharaoh and four-fifths to the farmers) fair?

FINDING YOURSELF IN THE TEXT

- Have you ever experienced national economic hardship?
- Do you understand the system of taxation in your country?
- Do you think taxation is fair in general? Is taxation fair in your country?

Consider using these questions as the basis for your own commentary or creative midrash.

How does reflecting on these firsthand experiences help you better understand the text?

יג וְלֶחֶם אֵין בְּכָל־הָאָרֶץ כִּי־כָבֵד הָרָעָב מְאֹד וַתֵּלַהּ אֶרֶץ מִצְרַיִם וְאֶרֶץ כְּנַעַן מִפְּנֵי

יד הָרָעָב: וַיְלַקֵּט יוֹסֵף אֶת־כָּל־הַכֶּסֶף הַנִּמְצָא בְּאֶרֶץ־מִצְרַיִם וּבְאֶרֶץ כְּנַעַן בַּשֶּׁבֶר

טו אֲשֶׁר־הֵם שֹׁבְרִים וַיָּבֵא יוֹסֵף אֶת־הַכֶּסֶף בֵּיתָה פַרְעֹה: וַיִּתֹּם הַכֶּסֶף מֵאֶרֶץ מִצְרַיִם

וּמֵאֶרֶץ כְּנַעַן וַיָּבֹאוּ כָל־מִצְרַיִם אֶל־יוֹסֵף לֵאמֹר הָבָה־לָּנוּ לֶחֶם וְלָמָּה נָמוּת

טז נֶגְדֶּךָ כִּי אָפֵס כָּסֶף: וַיֹּאמֶר יוֹסֵף הָבוּ מִקְנֵיכֶם וְאֶתְּנָה לָכֶם בְּמִקְנֵיכֶם אִם־אָפֵס

יז כָּסֶף: וַיָּבִיאוּ אֶת־מִקְנֵיהֶם אֶל־יוֹסֵף וַיִּתֵּן לָהֶם יוֹסֵף לֶחֶם בַּסּוּסִים וּבְמִקְנֵה הַצֹּאן

יח וּבְמִקְנֵה הַבָּקָר וּבַחֲמֹרִים וַיְנַהֲלֵם בַּלֶּחֶם בְּכָל־מִקְנֵהֶם בַּשָּׁנָה הַהִוא: וַתִּתֹּם הַשָּׁנָה

הַהִוא וַיָּבֹאוּ אֵלָיו בַּשָּׁנָה הַשֵּׁנִית וַיֹּאמְרוּ לוֹ לֹא־נְכַחֵד מֵאֲדֹנִי כִּי אִם־תַּם הַכֶּסֶף

וּמִקְנֵה הַבְּהֵמָה אֶל־אֲדֹנִי לֹא נִשְׁאַר לִפְנֵי אֲדֹנִי בִּלְתִּי אִם־גְּוִיָּתֵנוּ וְאַדְמָתֵנוּ:

יט לָמָּה נָמוּת לְעֵינֶיךָ גַּם־אֲנַחְנוּ גַּם־אַדְמָתֵנוּ קְנֵה־אֹתָנוּ וְאֶת־אַדְמָתֵנוּ בַּלָּחֶם

וְנִהְיֶה אֲנַחְנוּ וְאַדְמָתֵנוּ עֲבָדִים לְפַרְעֹה וְתֶן־זֶרַע וְנִחְיֶה וְלֹא נָמוּת וְהָאֲדָמָה לֹא

כ תֵשָׁם: וַיִּקֶן יוֹסֵף אֶת־כָּל־אַדְמַת מִצְרַיִם לְפַרְעֹה כִּי־מָכְרוּ מִצְרַיִם אִישׁ שָׂדֵהוּ כִּי־

כא חָזַק עֲלֵהֶם הָרָעָב וַתְּהִי הָאָרֶץ לְפַרְעֹה: וְאֶת־הָעָם הֶעֱבִיר אֹתוֹ לֶעָרִים מִקְצֵה

| THEMES | RELATIONSHIPS AND LOVE | LEADERSHIP | ETHICS |

Episode 69: *Yosef Implements His Economic Plan for Egypt* – Bereshit 47:13–27

SUMMARY

Following the reunification and settlement of Yaakov's family in Goshen, the Torah briefly leaves them aside and turns its focus to the repercussions of the ongoing famine. It is evident from this account that Yosef's earlier interpretation of Pharaoh's dreams coincides with what actually occurred. Here the chapter describes how Yosef deals with the task entrusted to him. On the one hand, he increases Pharaoh's absolute authority by means of the taxes paid to him by the Egyptians. On the other hand, he provides the people with reasonable living conditions to ensure they have no reason to rebel against their king.

22 town by town from one end of Egypt to the other.[1] The only land he did not acquire was
that of the priests, because they received an allotment of food from Pharaoh; they were able
to live on the allotment that Pharaoh gave them, and so they did not sell their land. Yosef
23 said to the people, "Today I have acquired you and your land for Pharaoh. Here is seed for
24 you to sow the land. When the harvest comes, give one-fifth to Pharaoh. Four-fifths shall be
yours as seed for your fields and as food for you, your households, and your children." "You
25 have saved our lives," they said. "May we find favor in the eyes of my lord – we shall be slaves
26 to Pharaoh." So Yosef made it a law, as it is to this day, governing land in Egypt, that one-fifth
of all produce belongs to Pharaoh. Only the land of the priests did not become Pharaoh's.
27 Thus Yisrael settled in the land of Egypt, in the region of Goshen. They acquired holdings
in it and were fertile and greatly increased in number.

1 | To help ensure that the people would not try to reclaim their land.

THE ART OF MIDRASH

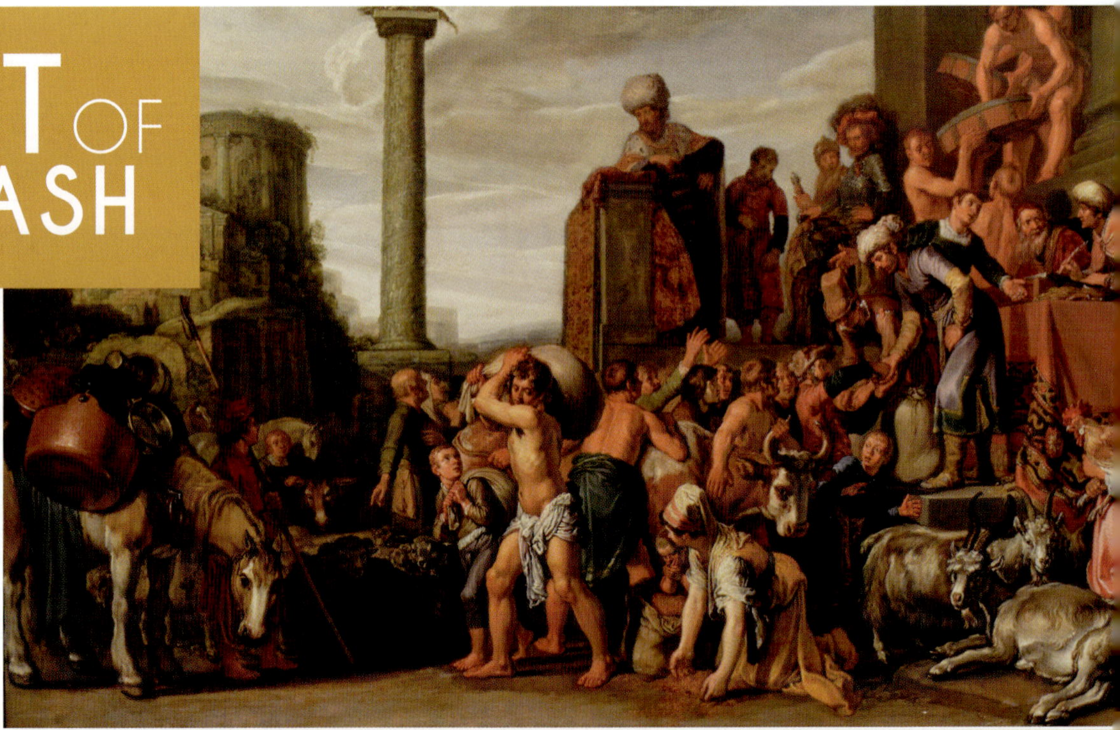

Joseph Selling Corn in Egypt
Pieter Lastman (1612)

Analysis

- Which elements of this image are directly mentioned in the text?
- Which elements of this image are not found in the text?
- What midrashic interpretation could be inferred from this image?

כב גְּב֥וּל־מִצְרַ֖יִם וְעַד־קָצֵֽהוּ׃ רַ֛ק אַדְמַ֥ת הַכֹּהֲנִ֖ים לֹ֣א קָנָ֑ה כִּי֩ חֹ֨ק לַכֹּהֲנִ֜ים מֵאֵ֣ת
פַּרְעֹ֗ה וְאָֽכְל֤וּ אֶת־חֻקָּם֙ אֲשֶׁ֨ר נָתַ֤ן לָהֶם֙ פַּרְעֹ֔ה עַל־כֵּ֕ן לֹ֥א מָכְר֖וּ אֶת־אַדְמָתָֽם׃
כג וַיֹּ֤אמֶר יוֹסֵף֙ אֶל־הָעָ֔ם הֵן֩ קָנִ֨יתִי אֶתְכֶ֥ם הַיּ֛וֹם וְאֶת־אַדְמַתְכֶ֖ם לְפַרְעֹ֑ה הֵֽא־לָכֶ֣ם
כד זֶ֔רַע וּזְרַעְתֶּ֖ם אֶת־הָֽאֲדָמָֽה׃ וְהָיָה֙ בַּתְּבוּאֹ֔ת וּנְתַתֶּ֥ם חֲמִישִׁ֖ית לְפַרְעֹ֑ה וְאַרְבַּ֣ע
הַיָּדֹ֡ת יִהְיֶ֣ה לָכֶם֩ לְזֶ֨רַע הַשָּׂדֶ֧ה וּֽלְאָכְלְכֶ֛ם וְלַאֲשֶׁ֥ר בְּבָתֵּיכֶ֖ם וְלֶאֱכֹ֥ל לְטַפְּכֶֽם׃
כה כו וַיֹּאמְר֖וּ הֶחֱיִתָ֑נוּ נִמְצָא־חֵן֙ בְּעֵינֵ֣י אֲדֹנִ֔י וְהָיִ֥ינוּ עֲבָדִ֖ים לְפַרְעֹֽה׃ וַיָּ֣שֶׂם אֹתָ֣הּ יוֹסֵ֡ף מפטיר
לְחֹק֩ עַד־הַיּ֨וֹם הַזֶּ֜ה עַל־אַדְמַ֥ת מִצְרַ֛יִם לְפַרְעֹ֖ה לַחֹ֑מֶשׁ רַ֞ק אַדְמַ֤ת הַכֹּהֲנִים֙
כז לְבַדָּ֔ם לֹ֥א הָיְתָ֖ה לְפַרְעֹֽה׃ וַיֵּ֧שֶׁב יִשְׂרָאֵ֛ל בְּאֶ֥רֶץ מִצְרַ֖יִם בְּאֶ֣רֶץ גֹּ֑שֶׁן וַיֵּאָחֲז֣וּ בָ֔הּ
וַיִּפְר֥וּ וַיִּרְבּ֖וּ מְאֹֽד׃

A QUESTION OF BIBLIODRAMA

TO YOSEF

- Whose interests were primary in your economic plan for Egypt?
- Do you think your management of the famine was cruel or just?
- Did you have any moral reservations when implementing it?
- Were you worried what your brothers and father would think of you as viceroy of Egypt?

TO PHARAOH

- What do you think of Yosef's implementation of his economic plan for Egypt?
- Do you have any concerns for the people of Egypt?

TO THE PEOPLE OF EGYPT

- Do you feel that Yosef saved your lives, as you said to him?
- Do you think he could have managed the famine in a different way that was fairer?
- What do you think of Yosef and Pharaoh as rulers of Egypt?

There are two approaches to evaluating Yosef's economic activities in Egypt. In both, it is necessary to compare the personal story of Yaakov's sons and their settling in Egypt with the story of the Egyptian economy and how it was managed during the famine years. As noted, the two stories inform and influence one another and are critical in understanding the broad meaning of Yosef's stories.

The first approach sees Yosef as an economic and political genius who presided over the Egyptian economy with ultimate authority. The length of the episode is meant to demonstrate that Yosef was a good person, who benefitted both the Egyptians and his family. Ralbag, known as Gersonides, a late thirteenth- and fourteenth-century French talmudist, mathematician, philosopher, physician, and astronomer, who takes this approach, further elaborates that Yosef managed public funds with integrity and only gave his family per capita rations despite his powerful position. Yosef also transferred all of the accumulated wealth to its proper owner, Pharaoh, and kept nothing for himself. Due to his excellent planning and supervision, his agricultural and economic rescue plan was carried out with probity and wisdom. Although he collected all of Egypt's wealth from its inhabitants, the populace thanked him, proclaiming he had saved them. At the same time, he kept the political and religious elites at bay. By appeasing them at this challenging economic time, he prevented an uprising that would undermine his authority.

Rabbi Samson Raphael Hirsch presents a similar approach. He suggested that Yosef's wisdom tempered the results of the edict. By organizing the people so that the residents of each city would always stay together and be relocated as a unit, their social and communal structures would remain largely intact. Therefore, this change did not lead to complete overhaul.

The second approach maintains that Yosef's economic policies led to the later enslavement of the Israelites. The first commentator to adopt this approach was Rabbi Yosef Bekhor Shor of Orléans, France. In his commentary on Shemot (1:11), he avers that the pharaoh who enslaved the Israelites needed many repositories, since a fifth of all the Egyptian produce belonged to him per Yosef's edict. However, the Israelites did not need to hand over one-fifth of their produce because Yosef had given them ownership of an estate in the choicest part of the land and sustained them without demanding payment. Bekhor Shor suggests that the Egyptians started a libel against the Israelites and claimed that all the Egyptians served the king. They worked the land and turned over one-fifth of their produce and handed over half of their flocks' and herds' offspring to him. Effectively, all of the native Egyptians were sharecroppers. But since the Israelites did not serve him in the same way and the Egyptians gave them grain, the Israelites were required to build the repositories in which to store it.

A socioeconomic analysis of the episode indicates a third approach. By its very nature, the economy is dynamic. Even visionary economists and ministers, equipped with the best forecasts, sometimes adopt policies that cause risk to accumulate to the point of critical mass. It is difficult to anticipate the behavior of the citizenry or the economy when both are changed simultaneously. This is especially true of a centralized and planned economy.

INTEGRATING ḤOKHMA

The Torah painstakingly details all the stages of the famine and the corresponding interventions. Over time, through liquidity, trade-ins, back-to-work programs, and seed money investments, Yosef's government intervention acquired more control over the economy, slowly atrophying its actors and dampening the freedom and vigor of the Egyptian citizenry and economy.

Why does the narrative return to the famine years and describe at length what happened in Egypt at that time? As Abarbanel points out, this section seems to belong in the chronicles of Egypt.

I would like to suggest a different way to analyze the structure of these episodes. The Torah does not begin with the general, geopolitical background of the story and then focus inward on Yaakov and his sons. Rather, it weaves together two stories that happened at the same time and inform one another. In fact, on four different occasions, the Torah jumps back and forth between three different story pairs. After Yosef's dreams, the conflict with his brothers, and his sale into slavery, we jump to the Egyptian story, which describes Yosef interpreting the dreams of the chief butler and the chief baker, as well as the dreams of Pharaoh himself. The Egyptian story continues with a discussion of Yosef's activities in the years of abundance and at the outset of the famine. The narrative then returns to the personal story of Yosef and his brothers, which includes them confronting each other and Yosef revealing his identity.

Earlier, we expounded on the close connection between Yosef's dreams and the plan that he outlined to Pharaoh (the first story pair) and the connection between the steps that Yosef took to save Egypt and the brothers' descent to buy food supplies in Egypt (the second). The verses now move to the third story pair: the continuation of the sons' personal story as they descended to Egypt and settled in their new homestead and the political and economic events that transpired at the same time in Egypt. Finally, the narrative returns to the personal story of Yaakov's sons and concludes the book of Bereshit with the blessings that Yaakov bestowed upon his sons and the deaths of Yaakov, Yosef, and the entire generation.

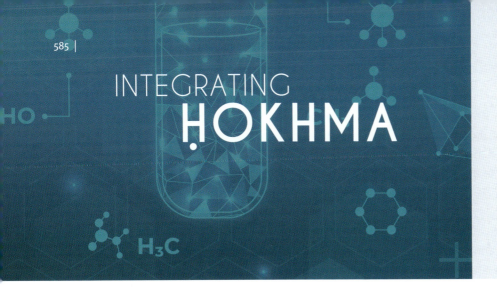

For example, out of millions of economists and investors across the globe, very few foresaw the impending financial crisis of 2008. The interdependencies, counterparty risk, and opaque nature of leverage and the housing market were the results of a complex system – because by their nature, economies and finance are complex.

In complex systems, when one thing is changed, it is nearly impossible to predict the impact that it will have, directly or indirectly. Economies are extremely complicated systems comprised of fiscal activity, both national and international, as well as impulses, psychology, and government intervention. Hidden risks suddenly appear in unpredictable ways. While it is true that Yosef successfully adapted Egypt's foreign, security, and economic policies continuously, he did not anticipate the greatest risk of all: the internal disintegration of Egyptian society.

This third approach combines Yosef's good intentions, presented in the complimentary interpretation (the first approach), with the de facto results noted in more critical interpretations (the second approach). This third approach understands Yosef as a person who tried to act for the benefit of the Egyptian people, not only for the benefit of his brothers. However, he ultimately missed something along the way, leading to bleak results. Yosef's economic reforms did not yield positive results for Egyptian society at the end of the famine, and these results may have been a significant factor in the ensuing enslavement and persecution of the Israelites.

Yosef acted with integrity, skill, and alacrity. He saved the Egyptian people, and perhaps the entire region from famine. However, even the best intentions can be foiled by complex systems, whose outcomes can be hard to anticipate. The centralized control Yosef exerted over the economy meant there was one person to blame when the complex system did not function as everyone had hoped. When things did not end well for the native Egyptians, it might have led to persecution of Yosef's family, the Israelites. The displaced and somewhat impoverished Egyptians took out their anger by enslaving the Israelites. In retrospect, we often forget how dire the original situation was.

Michael A. Eisenberg

Analysis

- What areas of understanding of human nature and society do we now have that were unavailable to classical Jewish commentators? How can they aid our understanding of the text?
- What can we learn from this essay to help us understand the text?
- What further questions on the text do you have now that you have read this new take on the story?

TAKING A LITERARY APPROACH

Yosef purchases the lands of Egypt and transfers the population between cities inside Egypt. No Egyptian owns property in his country, not even a fixed place of residence. Why does Yosef introduce this law and – even more surprising – why does the Torah describe the economic measures enacted in Egypt? It would certainly seem that this pertains more to Egyptian history than to the Torah.

The verse clarifies the matter: "And Yosef made it a law until this day for the land of Egypt to be a fifth part unto Pharaoh; only the land of the priests was not Pharaoh's. And Israel dwelt in the land of Egypt, in the land of Goshen, and they held onto it, and they were fruitful and multiplied exceedingly" (Bereshit 47:26–27).

The Torah itself draws the obvious comparison: the Egyptians have no land ("I have bought you today and your land"), while Israel holds onto their portion and settles in the land of Egypt: "And Israel dwelt in the land of Egypt in the land of Goshen, and they held onto it." The former wander from place to place while the latter, newcomers to the land, settle with some degree of permanence.

Yosef creates differences in status within Egyptian society: there is the general population which has no land or fixed abode, and the Hebrew family which owns land. Even if it has been decreed that Israel will dwell in a strange land for a lengthy period of time, Yosef ensures that the Egyptian masses will not be able to oppress them and may even need them because of their economic power.

However, "many are the thoughts in a man's heart, but God's counsel is what prevails." As is only too familiar to us from Jewish history, it is specifically this preferential economic status that arouses the jealousy of the local population. When Yosef and his generation die out, a new king will arise over Egypt and not only will the differences in status between the Egyptian and Hebrew nations not prevent him from enslaving the latter, but he will in fact succeed in gaining the support of his entire nation in the battle against the Hebrews. The economic issue may even serve as the most convincing argument regarding the danger represented by the Hebrews. (Similar examples are unfortunately found throughout Jewish history – it is sufficient to examine the process which took place in Germany and which led to the most terrible tragedy of our century.)

The irony of what ultimately took place as opposed to Yosef's plan is sharpened by the form of enslavement chosen: Pharaoh decrees that the Hebrews must build him "treasure cities." "And they built treasure cities (*miskenot*) for Pharaoh; Pitom and Raamses" (Shemot 1:11). What are treasure cities? The answer is to be found in the description of Ḥizkiyahu's kingdom in II Divrei HaYamim: "And Ḥizkiyahu had very great riches and honor: he made himself store houses for silver and for gold and for precious stones and for spices and for shields and for all types of beautiful vessels, and treasuries (*miskenot*) for the harvest of corn and wine and oil, and stables for all types of beasts, and folds for sheep" (32:27–28).

Three different types of storage buildings are mentioned: "storehouses" – for silver, gold, etc., "stables" – for the animals, and *miskenot* – for the harvested grain, etc. We learn from this that *miskenot* refers to a place for storing produce. When we read of the Israelite slavery in Egypt and how they are forced to build *arei miskenot* – in other words, cities for the storage of produce – we are immediately reminded of the last time that produce was collected and stored in Egypt – when Yosef bought the entire Egyptian nation as slaves and took their land from them. Now the Hebrews – who were still landowners during the previous gathering of the produce – are enslaved to the Egyptians and are forced to build them cities for storing their produce!

Rabbi Yonatan Grossman

ויחי
Vayeḥi

Parasha Overview

Parashat Vayeḥi brings sefer Bereshit, which is full of family conflicts, to a serene end. Yaakov, reunited with his beloved Yosef, meets and blesses his grandsons, the only such scene in the Torah. He blesses them, and then, on his deathbed, blesses his twelve sons. He dies and is buried in the cave of Makhpela with his parents and grandparents. Yosef forgives his brothers a second time, and he himself dies, having assured his brothers that God will eventually bring the family back to the Promised Land. The long patriarchal narrative concludes, and a new period – the birth of Israel as a nation – is about to begin.

Episodes

70. **Yaakov's Final Days** 47:28–31
71. **Yaakov Blesses Efrayim and Menashe** 48:1–22
72. **Yaakov Blesses His Sons** 49:1–33
73. **Yaakov's Death and Burial** 50:1–21
74. **Yosef's Death** 50:22–26

Parasha Stats

- 4,448 letters
- 1,158 words
- 85 verses
- 148 lines in a sefer Torah

28 Yaakov lived in Egypt for seventeen years; the years of his life were one hundred and forty-
29 seven. As the time of his death drew near, he summoned his son Yosef and said to him, "If I
have found favor in your eyes, place your hand under my thigh[1] and promise to deal kindly
30 and truly with me: do not bury me in Egypt. Let me lie with my fathers. Carry me from
31 Egypt and bury me where they are buried." "I will do as you say," he replied. Yaakov said,
"Swear to me," and Yosef swore. Then, at the head of the bed, Yisrael bowed.

1 | Sometimes performed in conjunction with an oath (cf. 24:2).

UNLOCKING THE TEXT

- Why does Yaakov ask Yosef specifically to carry out this final wish?
- Why does Yaakov make Yosef take an oath to do it?
- Why does Yaakov link this request with kindness and truth?
- Why is it so important for Yaakov to be buried in the land of Israel and in the cave of Makhpela?
- Why does Yaakov ask that Yosef take an oath even after he has agreed to fulfill Yaakov's request?
- Why is it significant that Yaakov "bowed at the head of the bed"?

FINDING YOURSELF IN THE TEXT

- Have you ever made someone swear an oath of some kind to do something that was really important to you?
- What do you think your last request to your children would be?
- Have you thought about where you would wish to be buried?

Consider using these questions as the basis for your own commentary or creative midrash.

How does reflecting on these firsthand experiences help you better understand the text?

כח וַיְחִי יַעֲקֹב בְּאֶרֶץ מִצְרַיִם שְׁבַע עֶשְׂרֵה שָׁנָה וַיְהִי יְמֵי־יַעֲקֹב שְׁנֵי חַיָּיו שֶׁבַע שָׁנִים ויחי
כט וְאַרְבָּעִים וּמְאַת שָׁנָה: וַיִּקְרְבוּ יְמֵי־יִשְׂרָאֵל לָמוּת וַיִּקְרָא ׀ לִבְנוֹ לְיוֹסֵף וַיֹּאמֶר לוֹ
אִם־נָא מָצָאתִי חֵן בְּעֵינֶיךָ שִׂים־נָא יָדְךָ תַּחַת יְרֵכִי וְעָשִׂיתָ עִמָּדִי חֶסֶד וֶאֱמֶת
ל אַל־נָא תִקְבְּרֵנִי בְּמִצְרָיִם: וְשָׁכַבְתִּי עִם־אֲבֹתַי וּנְשָׂאתַנִי מִמִּצְרַיִם וּקְבַרְתַּנִי
לא בִּקְבֻרָתָם וַיֹּאמַר אָנֹכִי אֶעֱשֶׂה כִדְבָרֶךָ: וַיֹּאמֶר הִשָּׁבְעָה לִי וַיִּשָּׁבַע לוֹ וַיִּשְׁתַּחוּ
יִשְׂרָאֵל עַל־רֹאשׁ הַמִּטָּה:

THEMES	RELATIONSHIPS AND LOVE	LEADERSHIP	LAND OF ISRAEL

Episode 70: *Yaakov's Final Days* – Bereshit 47:28–31

SUMMARY

Yaakov takes gradual leave of his family in several stages, in which he gives instructions for his burial and provides spiritual directives for his descendants' future. In this episode, Yaakov asks Yosef not to bury him in Egypt, and the *parasha* concludes with him requesting that his sons ensure he is buried in the cave of Makhpela in Canaan. Between these two stages, Yaakov delivers poetic, prophetic blessings.

THE ART OF MIDRASH

Pilgrims by the Cave of Machpelah
Alex Levin (2018)

Analysis

- Which elements of this image are directly mentioned in the text?
- Which elements of this image are not found in the text?
- What midrashic interpretation could be inferred from this image?

A QUESTION OF BIBLIODRAMA

TO YAAKOV

- Why do you ask Yosef to carry out this request and not one or all of your other sons?
- Why do you make him take an oath to do it?
- Why is it so important to be buried in the land of Israel, in the cave of Makhpela?

TO YOSEF

- What do you think when your father summons you to make this request?
- Do you intend to fulfill it?
- Have you considered where you would wish to be buried?

and they would have been the groveling penitents, doomed to bear the shame of their deed forever. Yosef had heard their expression of remorse (Bereshit 42:21), but what he wanted was to give them the opportunity to redeem themselves so that they could have a feeling of dignity and self-esteem and walk upright with their heads high.

In order to achieve this, Yosef orchestrated the events so that Binyamin, who had now become Yaakov's favorite, would be suspected of thievery and would be kept as a slave. How would the brothers react? This was their opportunity to repeat their sin. "Good! Father's new favorite is a thief. We can get along perfectly well without him. We got rid of Yosef, who was father's favorite, and now we can get rid of Binyamin."

But this time the brothers acted differently. Yehuda said, "Spare Binyamin. Send him back to his father. I will be a slave in his place." Seeing that the brothers had indeed redeemed themselves, Yosef could now reveal himself to them. He had saved their pride.

Yosef could have sent a message to Yaakov, but that would have exposed everything and the brothers would never have the opportunity to redeem themselves. Yosef knew the dreams would come true, and he engineered things to simulate the original sin.

But why did he let his father suffer? This is the powerful message. Yosef knew his father well, and he knew *that Yaakov would gladly accept twenty-two years of suffering in order to allow his children to have self-esteem and not be crushed by guilt for the rest of their lives.*

That is a major teaching of the Yosef epic, and it tells us how important self-esteem is to life.

Rabbi Abraham J. Twerski

Analysis

- What areas of understanding of human nature and society do we now have that were unavailable to classical Jewish commentators? How can they aid our understanding of the text?
- What can we learn from this passage to help us understand the text?
- What further questions on the text do you have now that you have read this new take on the story?

INTEGRATING ḤOKHMA

Another aspect in the Yosef episode is the question raised by a number of Torah commentaries. Knowing how deeply his father must be grieving, why did Yosef not send a message to his father: "Don't grieve for me – I am alive"?

My late brother Rav Shloime *zt"l* provided an answer which must be carefully thought through.

Rambam (*Hilkhot Teshuva* 2:4) says that true *teshuva* requires more than just remorse. *Teshuva* requires a total character overhaul, so that the person can say, "I am no longer the person who committed that sin. I am a different person." When this is achieved, the "new person" is not held culpable for what the previous person did.

One way of demonstrating that one has become a different person, Rambam says (2:1), is that if the person finds himself in similar circumstances to those of the sin, but this time acts differently rather than repeating the sin, that is an indication that one has truly changed and is a different person.

If Yosef had simply forgiven his brothers, he would have been the magnanimous saint,

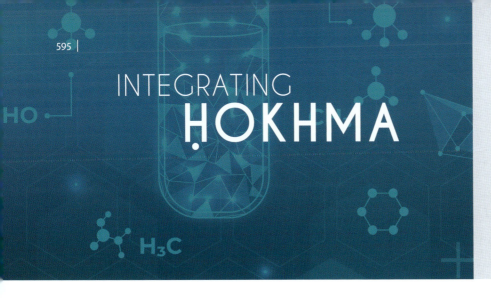

The phrases "do not bury me in Egypt" and "carry me from Egypt," which Yaakov could have omitted, point to his rejection of Egypt and compound his mistrust of Yosef (evident in his request to Yosef to "place your hand under my thigh"). Even the request that Yosef do for him "a kindness and truth" suggests that from Yaakov's perspective the burial in Canaan is a truth; its necessity is clear. But Yaakov understands that Yosef fundamentally disagrees with Yaakov's assumptions about Egypt and Canaan, and therefore frames it as a request for kindness from Yosef.

Yosef and Yaakov understand each other, and recognize that each sees the future of the clan differently. Yosef sees it in Egypt, with Canaan being the primitive old country left behind. Yaakov believes that Yosef's infatuation with Egypt is misguided and that the future is in the land of his fathers, the land of the covenant. Were Yaakov's concern merely about his burial place he would likely have summoned Yehuda, the son he trusts more than any other. It is clear that he is more interested in confronting Yosef than on ensuring his appropriate burial.

Yaakov asks for an oath and Yosef obliges. That seems to be enough to allay Yaakov's concerns, and so he bows to Yosef.

Rabbi Zvi Grumet

ֵי יְמֵי־יַעֲקֹב֮ שְׁנֵ֣י חַיָּ֔יו שֶׁ֖בַע שָׁ
מוֹת וַיִּקְרָ֣א ׀ לִבְנ֣וֹ לְיוֹסֵ֗ף וַיֹּ֤אמֶר ל
ַ֣חַת יְרֵכִ֑י וְעָשִׂ֤יתָ עִמָּדִי֙ חֶ֣סֶד וֶאֱמֶ֔ת
ּבְתִּי֙ וּנְשָׂאתַ֣נִי מִמִּצְרַ֔יִם וּקְבַרְתַּ֖נִי
ר הִשָּׁ֥בְעָה לִ֖י וַיִּשָּׁבַ֣ע ל֑וֹ וַיִּשְׁתַּ֛ח

TAKING A LITERARY APPROACH

After an extended stay in Egypt, Yaakov is familiar with its culture, and particularly its culture of death. In Egypt, death is merely a passageway into a new form of embodied life. The body is preserved and entombed in an elaborate structure with the many provisions it needs in the next world. The more important the deceased, the grander the structure. Yaakov wants no part of that.

Moreover, like Avraham, who understands that a final resting place designates permanence, Yaakov understands that Egypt cannot be his final resting place. Egypt is but a stop on his long and complex journey, and that journey must end back in the land promised to his ancestors and enshrined in the covenant. No foreign land can provide the anchor for the future of Yaakov's clan. He must be buried in the only place he can call home.

The parallel to Avraham is strengthened by a bizarre symbolic act, placing the hand under the thigh. While it may be difficult to decipher the specific symbolism of that act, it appears only twice in the Bible, once as Avraham asks his servant to find a wife for Yitzḥak from his homeland and another as Yaakov asks Yosef to bury him in Canaan. Like Avraham, Yaakov is worried about his future and believes that the request is essential for ensuring that future. And, like Avraham, Yaakov insists on an oath.

Yet this is where the two differ. Avraham demands an oath as an integral part of the request that his servant place his hand under his thigh, while Yaakov demands the oath even *after* Yosef agrees to fulfill his father's request (Bereshit 47:31). Why would an oath be necessary over and above the symbolic act, especially when the son responds, "I will do as you said"?

It seems that Yaakov does not fully trust that Yosef will follow through, even after the symbolic commitment. In hindsight, Yaakov's initial request of Yosef indicates that he is not expressing merely a preference for burial in Canaan, he is rejecting Egypt as a possibility. Look at what he could have said and what he actually does say:

What Yaakov could have said	What Yaakov said
If, please, I find favor in your eyes,	If, please, I find favor in your eyes,
	place your hand under my thigh and do for me a kindness and truth – do not bury me in Egypt.
when I rest with my fathers, bury me in their burial place	When I rest with my fathers, *carry me from Egypt and* bury me in their burial place.

48 1 Some time later, Yosef was told, "Your father is ill." He brought with him his two sons,
2 Menashe and Efrayim. And when Yaakov was told, "Your son Yosef has come to see you,"
3 Yisrael summoned his strength and sat up in the bed. Yaakov said to Yosef, "El Shaddai
4 appeared to me in Luz in the land of Canaan. He blessed me and said to me, 'I will make
you fruitful and increase your numbers. I will make you a community of peoples, and I
5 will give this land to your descendants as an everlasting possession.' Now, the two sons
who were born to you in Egypt before I came here shall be considered mine: Efrayim
6 and Menashe will be like Reuven and Shimon to me. Any child born to you after shall be
7 yours; in any inheritance they will be reckoned under the names of their brothers.[1] For
I – as I was returning from Padan, Raḥel died beside me in Canaan while we were still on
the way, a short distance from Efrat. And I buried her there beside the road to Efrat – that
8 9 is, Beit Leḥem." Then Yisrael looked at Yosef's sons and said, "Who are these?" Yosef told

1 | Descendants of Yosef through any other sons would thus be incorporated into the tribes of Efrayim and Menashe.

UNLOCKING THE TEXT

- Why did Yosef bring his sons along to visit his ailing father, Yaakov?
- Why does Yaakov recap for Yosef the covenant with God?
- What does he mean when he says his grandsons Efrayim and Menashe will be "like sons to him"?
- What does it mean that future sons born will be "reckoned under the names of their brothers" when it comes to inheritance?
- Why does Yaakov mention the death of Yosef's mother Raḥel?
- Why does Yaakov ask who the boys are?
- Does Yosef intentionally place Efrayim on the left of Yaakov and Menashe on his right? Why?
- Why does Yaakov cross his hands so his right hand is on Efrayim when he blesses them?
- Why does Yaakov first bless Yosef?
- Why was it so important to Yosef that Menashe was blessed as a firstborn?

FINDING YOURSELF IN THE TEXT

- Do your parents bless you on Friday nights? Do they use these words to bless the boys in the family?
- What number child in your family are you? Does it make a difference to you?
- Do you have a close relationship with any of your grandparents?

Consider using these questions as the basis for your own commentary or creative midrash.

How does reflecting on these firsthand experiences help you better understand the text?

מח א וַיְהִי אַחֲרֵי הַדְּבָרִים הָאֵלֶּה וַיֹּאמֶר לְיוֹסֵף הִנֵּה אָבִיךָ חֹלֶה וַיִּקַּח אֶת־שְׁנֵי בָנָיו עִמּוֹ מב
ב עִמּוֹ אֶת־מְנַשֶּׁה וְאֶת־אֶפְרָיִם: וַיַּגֵּד לְיַעֲקֹב וַיֹּאמֶר הִנֵּה בִנְךָ יוֹסֵף בָּא אֵלֶיךָ
ג וַיִּתְחַזֵּק יִשְׂרָאֵל וַיֵּשֶׁב עַל־הַמִּטָּה: וַיֹּאמֶר יַעֲקֹב אֶל־יוֹסֵף אֵל שַׁדַּי נִרְאָה־אֵלַי
ד בְּלוּז בְּאֶרֶץ כְּנָעַן וַיְבָרֶךְ אֹתִי: וַיֹּאמֶר אֵלַי הִנְנִי מַפְרְךָ וְהִרְבִּיתִךָ וּנְתַתִּיךָ לִקְהַל
ה עַמִּים וְנָתַתִּי אֶת־הָאָרֶץ הַזֹּאת לְזַרְעֲךָ אַחֲרֶיךָ אֲחֻזַּת עוֹלָם: וְעַתָּה שְׁנֵי־בָנֶיךָ
הַנּוֹלָדִים לְךָ בְּאֶרֶץ מִצְרַיִם עַד־בֹּאִי אֵלֶיךָ מִצְרַיְמָה לִי־הֵם אֶפְרַיִם וּמְנַשֶּׁה
ו כִּרְאוּבֵן וְשִׁמְעוֹן יִהְיוּ־לִי: וּמוֹלַדְתְּךָ אֲשֶׁר־הוֹלַדְתָּ אַחֲרֵיהֶם לְךָ יִהְיוּ עַל שֵׁם
ז אֲחֵיהֶם יִקָּרְאוּ בְּנַחֲלָתָם: וַאֲנִי | בְּבֹאִי מִפַּדָּן מֵתָה עָלַי רָחֵל בְּאֶרֶץ כְּנַעַן בַּדֶּרֶךְ
בְּעוֹד כִּבְרַת־אֶרֶץ לָבֹא אֶפְרָתָה וָאֶקְבְּרֶהָ שָּׁם בְּדֶרֶךְ אֶפְרָת הִוא בֵּית לָחֶם:
ח ט וַיַּרְא יִשְׂרָאֵל אֶת־בְּנֵי יוֹסֵף וַיֹּאמֶר מִי־אֵלֶּה: וַיֹּאמֶר יוֹסֵף אֶל־אָבִיו בָּנַי הֵם אֲשֶׁר־

THEMES | RELATIONSHIPS AND LOVE | LEADERSHIP | LAND OF ISRAEL

Episode 71: *Yaakov Blesses Efrayim and Menashe* – Bereshit 48:1–22

SUMMARY

Yaakov, reunited with Yosef, is ill. Yosef comes to visit him, bringing with him his two sons, Menashe and Efrayim. Yaakov blesses Yosef, and then he places his hands on the heads of the two boys and blesses them with the words that he predicts will be used by the people of Israel to bless their sons. Despite Yosef's protest, Yaakov blesses the younger son, Efrayim, before Menashe, the firstborn.

his father, "They are my sons God has given me here." "Please bring them to me," Yaakov
10 said, "so that I can bless them." Yisrael's eyes were heavy with age and he could not see. So
11 Yosef brought them close to him, and he kissed and embraced them. Yisrael said to Yosef,
"I never expected to see you again, and now God has shown me your children as well."
12 13 Yosef then took them from between his knees and bowed low, his face to the ground. Yosef
took both of them, Efrayim on his right to Yisrael's left, and Menashe on his left to Yisrael's
14 right, and brought them close. Yisrael reached out his right hand and put it on Efrayim's
head, even though he was the younger. And, crossing his hands, he put his left hand on
15 Menashe's head even though he was the firstborn. He blessed Yosef and said, "God before
whom my fathers walked – Avraham and Yitzḥak – God who has been my shepherd all my
16 life to now, the angel who has delivered me from all harm, may He bless the boys. Through
them may my name be recalled, and the names of my fathers, Avraham and Yitzḥak. May
17 they grow to a multitude upon the land." When Yosef saw that his father had placed his
right hand on Efrayim's head, he was displeased. He took hold of his father's hand to move
18 it from Efrayim's head to Menashe's head. Yosef said to his father, "Not so, father. This is
19 the firstborn. Put your right hand on his head." But his father refused: "I know, my son, I
know. He too will be a people, and he too will become great, but his younger brother will
20 become even greater, and his descendants will become an abundance of nations." On that
day, he blessed them: "By you shall Israel bless,[2] saying: May God make you like Efrayim
21 and Menashe." He put Efrayim before Menashe. Then Yisrael said to Yosef, "I am about
22 to die, but God will be with you and will bring you back to the land of your fathers. And
to you I give one portion more than your brothers, which I took from the Amorites by my
sword and my bow."

2 | When the Israelites offer blessings, they will invoke Efrayim and Menashe.

TO YAAKOV

- Why is it important that you bless these grandchildren now?
- Why do you elevate Efrayim over Menashe?
- What are your priorities now as you approach the end of your life?

TO YOSEF

- Why are you reticent to allow your father to bless Efrayim before Menashe?
- How do you feel about your family history when it comes to elevating younger children over older ones (including your own story)?
- Did this influence your position on your father's blessings to your sons?

י נָתַן־לִי אֱלֹהִים בָּזֶה וַיֹּאמַר קָחֶם־נָא אֵלַי וַאֲבָרְכֵם׃ וְעֵינֵי יִשְׂרָאֵל כָּבְדוּ מִזֹּקֶן לֹא שני
יא יוּכַל לִרְאוֹת וַיַּגֵּשׁ אֹתָם אֵלָיו וַיִּשַּׁק לָהֶם וַיְחַבֵּק לָהֶם׃ וַיֹּאמֶר יִשְׂרָאֵל אֶל־יוֹסֵף
יב רְאֹה פָנֶיךָ לֹא פִלָּלְתִּי וְהִנֵּה הֶרְאָה אֹתִי אֱלֹהִים גַּם אֶת־זַרְעֶךָ׃ וַיּוֹצֵא יוֹסֵף אֹתָם
יג מֵעִם בִּרְכָּיו וַיִּשְׁתַּחוּ לְאַפָּיו אָרְצָה׃ וַיִּקַּח יוֹסֵף אֶת־שְׁנֵיהֶם אֶת־אֶפְרַיִם בִּימִינוֹ
יד מִשְּׂמֹאל יִשְׂרָאֵל וְאֶת־מְנַשֶּׁה בִשְׂמֹאלוֹ מִימִין יִשְׂרָאֵל וַיַּגֵּשׁ אֵלָיו׃ וַיִּשְׁלַח יִשְׂרָאֵל
אֶת־יְמִינוֹ וַיָּשֶׁת עַל־רֹאשׁ אֶפְרַיִם וְהוּא הַצָּעִיר וְאֶת־שְׂמֹאלוֹ עַל־רֹאשׁ מְנַשֶּׁה
טו שִׂכֵּל אֶת־יָדָיו כִּי מְנַשֶּׁה הַבְּכוֹר׃ וַיְבָרֶךְ אֶת־יוֹסֵף וַיֹּאמַר הָאֱלֹהִים אֲשֶׁר הִתְהַלְּכוּ
טז אֲבֹתַי לְפָנָיו אַבְרָהָם וְיִצְחָק הָאֱלֹהִים הָרֹעֶה אֹתִי מֵעוֹדִי עַד־הַיּוֹם הַזֶּה׃ הַמַּלְאָךְ
הַגֹּאֵל אֹתִי מִכָּל־רָע יְבָרֵךְ אֶת־הַנְּעָרִים וְיִקָּרֵא בָהֶם שְׁמִי וְשֵׁם אֲבֹתַי אַבְרָהָם
יז וְיִצְחָק וְיִדְגּוּ לָרֹב בְּקֶרֶב הָאָרֶץ׃ וַיַּרְא יוֹסֵף כִּי־יָשִׁית אָבִיו יַד־יְמִינוֹ עַל־רֹאשׁ שלישי
אֶפְרַיִם וַיֵּרַע בְּעֵינָיו וַיִּתְמֹךְ יַד־אָבִיו לְהָסִיר אֹתָהּ מֵעַל רֹאשׁ־אֶפְרַיִם עַל־רֹאשׁ
יח מְנַשֶּׁה׃ וַיֹּאמֶר יוֹסֵף אֶל־אָבִיו לֹא־כֵן אָבִי כִּי־זֶה הַבְּכֹר שִׂים יְמִינְךָ עַל־רֹאשׁוֹ׃
יט וַיְמָאֵן אָבִיו וַיֹּאמֶר יָדַעְתִּי בְנִי יָדַעְתִּי גַּם־הוּא יִהְיֶה־לְּעָם וְגַם־הוּא יִגְדָּל וְאוּלָם
כ אָחִיו הַקָּטֹן יִגְדַּל מִמֶּנּוּ וְזַרְעוֹ יִהְיֶה מְלֹא־הַגּוֹיִם׃ וַיְבָרְכֵם בַּיּוֹם הַהוּא לֵאמוֹר בְּךָ
יְבָרֵךְ יִשְׂרָאֵל לֵאמֹר יְשִׂמְךָ אֱלֹהִים כְּאֶפְרַיִם וְכִמְנַשֶּׁה וַיָּשֶׂם אֶת־אֶפְרַיִם לִפְנֵי
כא מְנַשֶּׁה׃ וַיֹּאמֶר יִשְׂרָאֵל אֶל־יוֹסֵף הִנֵּה אָנֹכִי מֵת וְהָיָה אֱלֹהִים עִמָּכֶם וְהֵשִׁיב
כב אֶתְכֶם אֶל־אֶרֶץ אֲבֹתֵיכֶם׃ וַאֲנִי נָתַתִּי לְךָ שְׁכֶם אַחַד עַל־אַחֶיךָ אֲשֶׁר לָקַחְתִּי
מִיַּד הָאֱמֹרִי בְּחַרְבִּי וּבְקַשְׁתִּי׃

A QUESTION OF BIBLIODRAMA

THE ART OF MIDRASH

Jacob Blessing the Children of Joseph
Rembrandt Harmensz van Rijn (1656)

Analysis

- Which elements of this image are directly mentioned in the text?
- Which elements of this image are not found in the text?
- What midrashic interpretation could be inferred from this image?

TAKING A LITERARY APPROACH

Yaakov's speech appears to be a jumbled collection of disconnected thoughts without a coherent message. What is the connection between God's promise and Yaakov taking Efrayim and Menashe as his own? What does it even mean for Yaakov to take the two boys as his own, and how does that connect with Raḥel's untimely death?

When we look further we realize that Yaakov has conveniently conflated two separate divine messages connected only by the location of their delivery. God's promise to make Yaakov numerous, particularly as he formulates it here, is given only upon Yaakov's return *from* Lavan's house (Bereshit 35:11), while the promise of the land is first given on his way *to* Lavan's house (28:13). It is precisely in this blending of messages that we have a clue regarding the structure of Yaakov's speech. He opens recalling the divine message on his way to Ḥaran, that he will be numerous, and closes with how that message is challenged by the death of Raḥel upon his return. Since, in Yaakov's eyes, Raḥel is his primary wife and the only one whose children can be considered a fulfillment of the divine promise, according to Yaakov, then, God's promise has yet to be fulfilled. As such, in order to fulfill the divine promise, Raḥel's grandchildren – Yosef's sons – need to be surrogates for the additional children Yaakov never has from Raḥel.

Further examination of the passage, however, reveals an additional layer Yaakov has carefully interwoven. In his opening line, he references Canaan as the land of revelation, in the following verse he notes that God promises *that* land to him, and in his closing line he goes to great lengths to describe the geographical location of Raḥel's death and burial – *not* in Padan Aram but in the land of Canaan, just shy of Efrat, on the road to Efrat which is Beit Leḥem. Yaakov's message is clear: the land of the family's past and future, the land of divine revelation and promise, is Canaan. If that were not enough, his identification of Menashe and Efrayim is also geographically linked. They are the two sons born to Yosef *in Egypt*.

When we put the entire speech together it becomes clear that Yaakov wants to transform Menashe and Efrayim from Egyptian children born to an Egyptian lord into Hebrew children tied to their ancestral land of Canaan. Making these children his own means leapfrogging Yosef in the chain of inheritance: they get their inheritance, their portion in the Promised Land, directly from Yaakov.

The conversation which follows now actually makes sense and is quite meaningful. After speaking about Menashe and Efrayim, who have been standing at Yaakov's bedside, and co-opting them as his own, Yaakov asks, "Who are these?" The question is not like Yitzḥak's question trying to identify the son awaiting his blessing, but an existential one. Now that Yaakov has claimed the boys for himself, he challenges Yosef to acknowledge his decision: "Who are they, your Egyptian children or my Hebrew ones?" Observe carefully Yosef's response: "They are *my* children, which God gave *me, here*" (48:9). Yosef refuses Yaakov's request, insisting that the boys are his – Egyptians, not Hebrews. They belong to the future of the clan, in Egypt, not to its humble beginnings in the backwater of Canaan.

Yaakov does not give up easily in the tug-of-war between himself and Yosef regarding the custody of the boys. Yosef presents them to Yaakov for his blessing, but they remain "between his knees" (48:12). Ultimately, Yosef bows before his father, reversing the earlier scene, ceding the children to Yaakov's blessing.

Rabbi Zvi Grumet

To the chagrin of his older children, Yaakov, the youngest child, favored his two youngest children, Yosef and Binyamin. This contributed to the eventual sale of Yosef and set the stage for the reunification of the family in Egypt. While in retrospect the culmination of the plot was fortuitous, the tragedy and trauma of the years of separation took a toll on all the parties involved, especially Yaakov. It is therefore surprising that when blessing Yosef's two sons, Menashe and Efrayim, Yaakov switches his hands and gives the better blessing to the younger son, Efrayim. Yosef, having experienced the dangers inherent in favoring one child over the other, especially a younger child over an older one, tries to intervene, and tells his father that he has the order wrong. Yaakov, however, responds that his preference for Efrayim is intentional. He, after all, will become greater than Menashe, and is thus deserving of the greater blessing.

Does Yaakov not realize the dangers of his decision? Why does he insist on favoring one over the other at the end of his life?

Perhaps Yaakov is communicating to his children, grandchildren, and to all subsequent generations, that success in life should have nothing to do with birth order. While being born first may have advantages, it does not determine one's future accomplishments. Being born second, third, or twelfth may have some disadvantages, but birth order does not dictate one's place in the world. The youngest child can succeed more than the oldest child, and for that matter, the oldest child can succeed more than the younger ones. Starting with Kayin and Hevel and culminating with Efrayim and Menashe, sefer Bereshit subverts the accepted norm in which the oldest is automatically endowed with greatness and privilege. This sets the stage for sefer Shemot, where a younger brother, Moshe, surpasses his older siblings, and everyone graciously accepts that their roles are based on merit alone.

As the scientific community continues to debate whether birth order statistically impacts personality, perhaps the message of sefer Bereshit is that, either way, we should not let it impact our accomplishments. Success should be based on merit, not birth order.

Rabbi Mordechai Schiffman

Analysis

- What areas of understanding of human nature and society do we now have that were unavailable to classical Jewish commentators? How can they aid our understanding of the text?
- What can we learn from this passage to help us understand the text?
- What further questions on the text do you have now that you have read this new take on the story?

INTEGRATING ḤOKHMA

In a fascinating analysis of seven hundred brothers who played Major League Baseball, psychologist Frank Sulloway found that younger brothers were 10.6 times more likely to try and steal a base, and 3.2 times more likely to be successful at stealing one than their older counterparts. This study aligns with previous research which indicates that sibling birth order influences personality development. The oldest sibling is generally more intellectual, responsible, and conforming. To carve out a space for themselves, younger siblings take more risks, are more creative, and tend to be non-conforming. Despite the supporting evidence, these findings are hotly debated. Subsequent studies showed that utilizing more robust research methods yielded no significant personality differences among siblings based on their birth order.

Without taking a stand on which side of this debate is more convincing, the topic of birth order is clearly central to the entire sefer Bereshit, reaching its full development in Parashat Vayeḥi. This theme begins with the deathly rivalry between Kayin and Hevel, and continues with the contentious relationships of Yishmael and Yitzḥak, Esav and Yaakov, Leah and Raḥel, and Yosef and his brothers. While each relationship had its own dynamic that added to the drama, having a younger sibling take the spotlight away from an older one is a theme that cuts through each episode. This is particularly accentuated in the story of Esav and Yaakov, where Esav sells his firstborn rights and the brothers contend for their father's blessing of the firstborn.

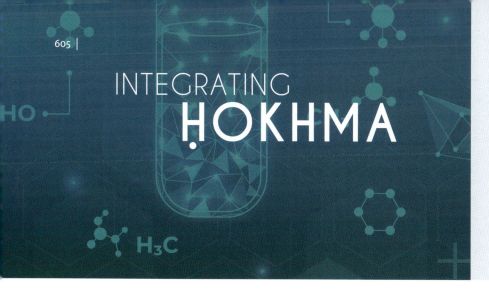

49 1 Then Yaakov called for his sons and said, "Gather together so that I can tell you what will
2 happen to you in the days to come. Assemble and listen, Yaakov's sons. Listen to your father
3 Yisrael. Reuven, you are my firstborn, my strength, first fruit of my manhood, excelling in
4 rank, excelling in power. Unstable as water, you shall not excel, for you went up onto your
father's bed and defiled it – went up onto my couch.[1]
5 6 Shimon and Levi are brothers; weapons of violence their wares.[2] Let me never join their
council, nor my honor be of their assembly. For in their anger they killed men; at their
7 whim they hamstrung oxen. Cursed be their anger, for it is most fierce, and their fury, for
it is most cruel. I will divide them up in Yaakov, and scatter them in Israel.[3]
8 Yehuda, your brothers shall praise you. Your hand will be on the neck of your foes. To you
9 will your father's sons bow.[4] Yehuda is a lion's cub. From the prey, my son, you have risen.
10 Like a lion he crouches, lies down, like a lioness: who dares to rouse him? The scepter shall
not pass from Yehuda, nor the staff from between his feet, so that tribute will come to him
11 and the homage of nations be his. He tethers his donkey to vines, to the vine-bough his

1 | See 35:22.
2 | See 34:25–26.
3 | Neither tribe would receive a contiguous portion of territory in the land of Israel.
4 | The tribe of Yehuda would later give rise to King David and his dynasty.

UNLOCKING THE TEXT

- How can Yaakov be sure he can prophesize his son's futures?
- The "blessings" of Reuven, Shimon, and Levi sound more like curses. Why would this be Yaakov's message to them on his deathbed?
- Why does Yehuda receive such a long and bountiful blessing?
- Why does Yaakov use so much animal imagery in his blessings?
- Who receives the better blessing, Yehuda or Yosef?
- Why does Yaakov repeat his request to be buried in the land of Israel to all of his sons, and make Yosef swear an oath to do this?
- What is the significance of the phrase "he drew his feet back onto the bed"?

FINDING YOURSELF IN THE TEXT

- Are all the siblings in your family very different from each other? Do you think your parents are aware of this?
- Do your parents think they have an idea of what the future of all their children will look like?
- Do you know of anyone who died surrounded by their family?

Consider using these questions as the basis for your own commentary or creative midrash.

How does reflecting on these firsthand experiences help you better understand the text?

מט א וַיִּקְרָ֥א יַעֲקֹ֖ב אֶל־בָּנָ֑יו וַיֹּ֗אמֶר הֵאָֽסְפוּ֙ וְאַגִּ֣ידָה לָכֶ֔ם אֵ֛ת אֲשֶׁר־יִקְרָ֥א אֶתְכֶ֖ם מג רביעי
ב ג בְּאַחֲרִ֥ית הַיָּמִֽים׃ הִקָּבְצ֥וּ וְשִׁמְע֖וּ בְּנֵ֣י יַעֲקֹ֑ב וְשִׁמְע֖וּ אֶל־יִשְׂרָאֵ֥ל אֲבִיכֶֽם׃ רְאוּבֵן֙
ד בְּכֹ֣רִי אַ֔תָּה כֹּחִ֖י וְרֵאשִׁ֣ית אוֹנִ֑י יֶ֥תֶר שְׂאֵ֖ת וְיֶ֥תֶר עָֽז׃ פַּ֤חַז כַּמַּ֙יִם֙ אַל־תּוֹתַ֔ר כִּ֥י עָלִ֖יתָ
מִשְׁכְּבֵ֣י אָבִ֑יךָ אָ֥ז חִלַּ֖לְתָּ יְצוּעִ֥י עָלָֽה׃
ה ו שִׁמְע֥וֹן וְלֵוִ֖י אַחִ֑ים כְּלֵ֥י חָמָ֖ס מְכֵרֹתֵיהֶֽם׃ בְּסֹדָם֙ אַל־תָּבֹ֣א נַפְשִׁ֔י בִּקְהָלָ֖ם אַל־תֵּחַ֣ד
ז כְּבֹדִ֑י כִּ֤י בְאַפָּם֙ הָ֣רְגוּ אִ֔ישׁ וּבִרְצֹנָ֖ם עִקְּרוּ־שֽׁוֹר׃ אָר֤וּר אַפָּם֙ כִּ֣י עָ֔ז וְעֶבְרָתָ֖ם כִּ֣י
קָשָׁ֑תָה אֲחַלְּקֵ֣ם בְּיַעֲקֹ֔ב וַאֲפִיצֵ֖ם בְּיִשְׂרָאֵֽל׃
ח ט יְהוּדָ֗ה אַתָּה֙ יוֹד֣וּךָ אַחֶ֔יךָ יָדְךָ֖ בְּעֹ֣רֶף אֹיְבֶ֑יךָ יִשְׁתַּחֲוּ֥וּ לְךָ֖ בְּנֵ֥י אָבִֽיךָ׃ גּ֤וּר אַרְיֵה֙
י יְהוּדָ֔ה מִטֶּ֖רֶף בְּנִ֣י עָלִ֑יתָ כָּרַ֨ע רָבַ֧ץ כְּאַרְיֵ֛ה וּכְלָבִ֖יא מִ֣י יְקִימֶֽנּוּ׃ לֹֽא־יָס֥וּר שֵׁ֙בֶט֙
יא מִֽיהוּדָ֔ה וּמְחֹקֵ֖ק מִבֵּ֣ין רַגְלָ֑יו עַ֚ד כִּֽי־יָבֹ֣א שִׁילֹ֔ה וְל֖וֹ יִקְּהַ֥ת עַמִּֽים׃ אֹסְרִ֤י לַגֶּ֙פֶן֙

THEMES | RELATIONSHIPS AND LOVE | LEADERSHIP | PROPHECY AND REVELATION

Episode 72: *Yaakov Blesses His Sons* – Bereshit 49:1–33

SUMMARY

Yaakov blesses his twelve sons amid discernible tension. His blessings to his oldest three sons, Reuven, Shimon, and Levi, read more like curses than blessings. Yet the fact is that he is blessing all twelve together in the same room at the same time, something we have not seen previously. There is no record of Avraham blessing either Yishmael or Yitzḥak, and Yitzḥak blesses Esav and Yaakov separately. The mere fact that Yaakov is able to gather his sons together is unprecedented and significant.

12 donkey's colt; he washes his clothes in wine, his robe in the blood of grapes.[5] His eyes are
darker than wine, and his teeth whiter than milk.[6]
13 Zevulun will live by the seashore; he will be a haven for ships. To Sidon his border will
reach.
14 Yissakhar is a strong-boned donkey, lying down among the sheep pens. Seeing how good
15 is his resting place, and how pleasant is the land, he will bend his shoulder to the load,
16 and work like a slave in harness. Dan will seek justice[7] for his people as one of
17 Israel's tribes. Dan: a snake by the roadside, a viper upon the path that bites the horse's
18 heel, so that its rider falls backward.[8] I wait for Your salvation, LORD. Gad will be
19
20 raided by raiders, but he then will raid at their heels.[9] From Asher will come rich
21 food, he will proffer the king's delights. Naftali is a deer set free, bearing loveliest
22 fawns. Yosef is a fruitful vine, a fruitful vine by a spring, whose branches spread
23 over a wall. Archers attacked him with bitterness, shot at him, harassed him. But his bow
24 stopped steady, and his arms held firm because of the hand of the Mighty One of Yaakov,
25 the Shepherd, Yisrael's Rock, because of the God of your father who will help you, because
of Shaddai who will bless you with blessings of heaven above, blessings of the deep that
26 lies under, blessings of breast and of womb. May your father's blessing surpass even the
blessings of my forebears – to the bounds of the everlasting hills. May they rest on the head
of Yosef, on the brow of the elect of his brothers.
27 Binyamin is a ravening wolf, devouring prey in the morning, and by evening dividing
28 the plunder." All these are the twelve tribes of Israel, and this is what their father said
29 to them when he blessed them, giving each his particular blessing. Then he gave
them instruction, saying, "I am about to be gathered to my people. Bury me with my
30 fathers in the cave in the field of Efron the Hittite, the cave in the field of Makhpela
near Mamre in Canaan, which Avraham bought, together with the field, from Efron
31 the Hittite as a burial place.[10] There Avraham and his wife Sara are buried, there
32 Yitzḥak and his wife Rivka are buried, and there I buried Leah. The field and the cave
33 in it were bought from the Hittites." There Yaakov finished instructing his sons. And
he drew his feet back onto the bed, breathed his last, and was gathered to his people.

---

5 | These images suggest luxuriant wealth.

6 | From the abundance of wine and milk.

7 | The word *yadin* ("seek justice") plays on the name Dan.

8 | This image suggests a type of military prowess.

9 | The phrase *gedud yegudenu* ("will be raided by raiders") and the word *yagud* ("will raid") play on the name Gad.

10 | See 23:16–18.

יב עִירֹה וְלַשֹּׂרֵקָה בְּנִי אֲתֹנוֹ כִּבֵּס בַּיַּיִן לְבֻשׁוֹ וּבְדַם־עֲנָבִים סוּתֹה׃ חַכְלִילִי עֵינַיִם
מִיָּיִן וּלְבֶן־שִׁנַּיִם מֵחָלָב׃
יג זְבוּלֻן לְחוֹף יַמִּים יִשְׁכֹּן וְהוּא לְחוֹף אֳנִיֹּת וְיַרְכָתוֹ עַל־צִידֹן׃
יד טו יִשָּׂשכָר חֲמֹר גָּרֶם רֹבֵץ בֵּין הַמִּשְׁפְּתָיִם׃ וַיַּרְא מְנֻחָה כִּי טוֹב וְאֶת־הָאָרֶץ כִּי
טז נָעֵמָה וַיֵּט שִׁכְמוֹ לִסְבֹּל וַיְהִי לְמַס־עֹבֵד׃ דָּן יָדִין עַמּוֹ כְּאַחַד שִׁבְטֵי
יז יִשְׂרָאֵל׃ יְהִי־דָן נָחָשׁ עֲלֵי־דֶרֶךְ שְׁפִיפֹן עֲלֵי־אֹרַח הַנֹּשֵׁךְ עִקְּבֵי־סוּס וַיִּפֹּל
יח יט רֹכְבוֹ אָחוֹר׃ לִישׁוּעָתְךָ קִוִּיתִי יְהוָה׃ גָּד גְּדוּד יְגוּדֶנּוּ וְהוּא יָגֻד חמישי
כ כא עָקֵב׃ מֵאָשֵׁר שְׁמֵנָה לַחְמוֹ וְהוּא יִתֵּן מַעֲדַנֵּי־מֶלֶךְ׃ נַפְתָּלִי
כב אַיָּלָה שְׁלֻחָה הַנֹּתֵן אִמְרֵי־שָׁפֶר׃ בֵּן פֹּרָת יוֹסֵף בֵּן פֹּרָת עֲלֵי־עָיִן בָּנוֹת
כג כד צָעֲדָה עֲלֵי־שׁוּר׃ וַיְמָרֲרֻהוּ וָרֹבּוּ וַיִּשְׂטְמֻהוּ בַּעֲלֵי חִצִּים׃ וַתֵּשֶׁב בְּאֵיתָן קַשְׁתּוֹ
כה וַיָּפֹזּוּ זְרֹעֵי יָדָיו מִידֵי אֲבִיר יַעֲקֹב מִשָּׁם רֹעֶה אֶבֶן יִשְׂרָאֵל׃ מֵאֵל אָבִיךָ וְיַעְזְרֶךָּ
וְאֵת שַׁדַּי וִיבָרְכֶךָּ בִּרְכֹת שָׁמַיִם מֵעָל בִּרְכֹת תְּהוֹם רֹבֶצֶת תָּחַת בִּרְכֹת שָׁדַיִם
כו וָרָחַם׃ בִּרְכֹת אָבִיךָ גָּבְרוּ עַל־בִּרְכֹת הוֹרַי עַד־תַּאֲוַת גִּבְעֹת עוֹלָם תִּהְיֶיןָ לְרֹאשׁ
יוֹסֵף וּלְקָדְקֹד נְזִיר אֶחָיו׃
כז כח בִּנְיָמִין זְאֵב יִטְרָף בַּבֹּקֶר יֹאכַל עַד וְלָעֶרֶב יְחַלֵּק שָׁלָל׃ כָּל־אֵלֶּה שִׁבְטֵי יִשְׂרָאֵל ששי
שְׁנֵים עָשָׂר וְזֹאת אֲשֶׁר־דִּבֶּר לָהֶם אֲבִיהֶם וַיְבָרֶךְ אוֹתָם אִישׁ אֲשֶׁר כְּבִרְכָתוֹ בֵּרַךְ
כט אֹתָם׃ וַיְצַו אוֹתָם וַיֹּאמֶר אֲלֵהֶם אֲנִי נֶאֱסָף אֶל־עַמִּי קִבְרוּ אֹתִי אֶל־אֲבֹתָי אֶל־
ל הַמְּעָרָה אֲשֶׁר בִּשְׂדֵה עֶפְרוֹן הַחִתִּי׃ בַּמְּעָרָה אֲשֶׁר בִּשְׂדֵה הַמַּכְפֵּלָה אֲשֶׁר־עַל־פְּנֵי
מַמְרֵא בְּאֶרֶץ כְּנָעַן אֲשֶׁר קָנָה אַבְרָהָם אֶת־הַשָּׂדֶה מֵאֵת עֶפְרֹן הַחִתִּי לַאֲחֻזַּת־
לא קָבֶר׃ שָׁמָּה קָבְרוּ אֶת־אַבְרָהָם וְאֵת שָׂרָה אִשְׁתּוֹ שָׁמָּה קָבְרוּ אֶת־יִצְחָק וְאֵת
לב רִבְקָה אִשְׁתּוֹ וְשָׁמָּה קָבַרְתִּי אֶת־לֵאָה׃ מִקְנֵה הַשָּׂדֶה וְהַמְּעָרָה אֲשֶׁר־בּוֹ מֵאֵת בְּנֵי־
לג חֵת׃ וַיְכַל יַעֲקֹב לְצַוֺּת אֶת־בָּנָיו וַיֶּאֱסֹף רַגְלָיו אֶל־הַמִּטָּה וַיִּגְוַע וַיֵּאָסֶף אֶל־עַמָּיו׃

THE ART OF MIDRASH

Blessings
Yoram Raanan (2013–2014)

Analysis

- Which elements of this image are directly mentioned in the text?
- Which elements of this image are not found in the text?
- What midrashic interpretation could be inferred from this image?

A QUESTION OF BIBLIODRAMA

TO YAAKOV

- What is your objective in giving these blessings?
- Why do you repeat to all your sons your wish to be buried in the cave of Makhpela after making Yosef take an oath to do this?
- Reflecting back on your life, have you achieved all that you hoped for?
- Would you do anything differently if you could live it again?

TO EACH SON

- What do you think of the blessing your father gave you on his deathbed?
- Will this in any way change your approach to life?

Astonishingly, given the many centuries of Jewish suffering, Biblical Hebrew has no word for tragedy. The word *ason* means a mishap, a disaster, a calamity, but not a tragedy in the classic sense. A tragedy is a drama with a sad outcome involving a hero destined to experience downfall or destruction through a character flaw or a conflict with an overpowering force, such as fate. Judaism has no word for this, because we do not believe in fate as something blind, inevitable, and inexorable. We are free. We can choose. As Isaac Bashevis Singer wittily said: "We *must* be free: we have no choice!"

There is a fundamental difference between a prophecy and a prediction. *If a prediction comes true, it has succeeded. If a prophecy comes true, it has failed.* A prophet delivers not a prediction but a warning. He or she does not simply say, "This will happen," but rather, "This will happen *unless* you change." The prophet speaks to human freedom, not to the inevitability of fate.

Do not believe that the future is written. It isn't. There is no fate we cannot change, no prediction we cannot defy. We are not predestined to fail; neither are we pre-ordained to succeed. We do not predict the future, because we make the future – by our choices, our willpower, our persistence, and our determination to survive.

The proof is the Jewish people itself. The first reference to Israel outside the Bible is engraved on the Merneptah stele, inscribed around 1225 BCE by Pharaoh Merneptah IV, Ramses II's successor. It reads: "Israel is laid waste; her seed is no more." It was, in short, an obituary. The Jewish people have been written off many times by their enemies, but they remain, after almost four millennia, still young and strong.

That is why, when Yaakov wanted to tell his children what would happen to them in the future, the divine spirit was taken away from him. Our children continue to surprise us, as we continue to surprise others. Made in the image of God, we are free. Sustained by the blessings of God, we can become greater than anyone, even ourselves, could foresee.

Rabbi Jonathan Sacks

Analysis

- What areas of understanding of human nature, society, and history do we have now that were unavailable to classical Jewish commentators? How can they aid our understanding of the text?
- What can we learn from this essay to help us understand the text?
- What further questions on the text do you have now that you have read this new take on the story?

INTEGRATING ḤOKHMA

Yaakov was on his deathbed. He summoned his children. He wanted to bless them before he died. But the text begins with a strange semi repetition: "Gather around so I can tell you what will happen to you in days to come. Assemble and listen, sons of Yaakov; listen to your father Israel" (Bereshit 49:1–2).

This seems to be saying the same thing twice, with one difference. In the first sentence, there is a reference to "what will happen to you in the days to come" (literally, "at the end of days"). This is missing from the second sentence.

Rashi, following the Talmud, says that "Yaakov wished to reveal what would happen in the future, but the Divine Presence was removed from him." He tried to foresee the future but found he could not.

This is no minor detail. It is a fundamental feature of Jewish spirituality. We believe that we cannot predict the future when it comes to human beings. We *make* the future by our choices. The script has not yet been written. The future is radically open.

This was a major difference between ancient Israel and ancient Greece. The Greeks believed in fate, *moira*, even blind fate, *ananke*. When the Delphic oracle told Laius that he would have a son who would kill him, he took every precaution to make sure it did not happen. When the child was born, Laius nailed him by his feet to a rock and left him to die. A passing shepherd found and saved him, and he was eventually raised by the king and queen of Corinth. Because his feet were permanently misshapen, he came to be known as Oedipus (the "swollen-footed").

The rest of the story is well known. Everything the oracle foresaw happened, and every act designed to avoid it actually helped bring it about. Once the oracle has been spoken and fate has been sealed, all attempts to avoid it are in vain. This cluster of ideas lies at the heart of one of the great Greek contributions to civilization: *tragedy*.

desperate effort. It is only when he has exhausted all avenues that he "draws his feet onto the bed" and dies (49:33), something we expected two chapters earlier.

Tragically, Yaakov dies without knowing if he is successful. And we, the readers, are held in suspense as well.

Rabbi Zvi Grumet

TAKING A LITERARY APPROACH

Even after his final message to Yosef, Yaakov remains unconvinced that Yosef will change his position. Yosef's oath to Yaakov does not pacify Yaakov's concerns, and the later encounter with Menashe and Efrayim confirms Yaakov's fears. Yaakov will not rest until he knows that he has exhausted every possibility. After blessing his sons individually, Yaakov instructs them all as a group, restating his burial wishes.

Yaakov has already sworn Yosef to this request. Why does he need to make the request of the rest of his sons? To be sure, one could argue that he wants them to feel included in the process, but it is just as likely that he still does not know if he can rely on Yosef to carry it through, and so he instructs them all – Yosef included – together.

A closer reading of Yaakov's request reveals a sharper focus on the issues he raised earlier with Yosef as well as some significant omissions. He refers twice to Avraham's purchase, twice to the fact that his ancestors were buried there, three times to the burial cave, and four times to the field. Missing from this speech is the explicit rejection of Egypt, which Yaakov mentions twice in his earlier request of Yosef.

Yaakov's reference to the place as a family burial plot with a three-generation history is designed to strengthen the bond with the past, building upon and sharpening the idea he raised briefly with Yosef. Similarly, the references to Avraham's purchase of the land are intended to deepen the bonds with that ancestral plot. He does not need to reject Egypt in front of his other sons, as they are foreigners in Egypt, but the rejection of Egypt is apparently replaced by a subtler, hidden polemic against Egyptian burial rites. At Makhpela there are no monuments and nothing above ground to catch the eye. Instead there is a field with a cave, an underground burial. Yaakov's message remains consistent even as his formulation has changed – the Egyptian way is not the way of his clan.

This is Yaakov's final attempt to secure the future of the covenant, and it concludes a lengthy narrative. We first hear of Yaakov's impending death in Bereshit 47:28: "Yaakov lived in Egypt for seventeen years; the total years of Yaakov's life were one hundred and forty-seven." When we read the parallel verse at the end of Avraham's life (25:7), it is followed immediately by Avraham's death. But Yaakov is not yet prepared to die. He summons Yosef, takes Yosef's sons as his own, blesses them with not-so-subtle messages about Canaan, blesses Yosef similarly, and finally instructs the remainder of his children regarding his burial. All of that is part of Yaakov's

50 1 Yosef fell on his father's face and wept over him and kissed him. Then Yosef instructed
2 his servants the physicians to embalm his father. So the physicians embalmed Yisrael. It
3 took them forty days; that was the time required for embalming. The Egyptians mourned
4 him for seventy days. When the period of mourning was over, Yosef spoke to Pharaoh's
court: "If I have found favor in your eyes, please speak to Pharaoh on my behalf. Tell him,
5 'My father made me swear an oath, saying, "I am about to die. Bury me in the grave I
prepared for myself in the land of Canaan." Now let me go up and bury my father; then I
6 will return.'" Pharaoh said, "Go and bury your father as he had you swear." So Yosef went
7 up to bury his father. With him went all Pharaoh's officials, the elders of his palace and
8 all the other elders of Egypt, together with all Yosef's household, his brothers, and his
father's household. They left only their children and flocks and herds in Goshen. With
9 them too went a chariot brigade and horsemen; it was a very large retinue. When they

UNLOCKING THE TEXT

- What is embalming? Why did Yosef choose this way to bury his father, and is it compatible with a Torah approach to death and burial?
- Why did the Egyptians mourn for Yaakov? Why for seventy days?
- Why did Yosef need to ask permission to bury his father in the land of Canaan?
- Why did Pharaoh's officials, with a chariot brigade and horsemen, accompany the family to Canaan to bury Yaakov?
- Why is it important to mention that they left their flocks and children in Goshen?
- What is the significance of the threshing floor of Atad, and why did they stop there to hold a mourning ritual?
- Did Yaakov really instruct his sons to tell Yosef to forgive them, or are they lying to protect themselves?
- If he did, why didn't the Torah report it, and why didn't he say it directly to Yosef?
- Why did Yosef weep when he heard their words?
- How does Yosef's response address the concerns of his brothers?

FINDING YOURSELF IN THE TEXT

- Have you ever had to ask permission to do something you need to do because you have promised someone else you would, or just because you know it is the right thing to do?
- Have you ever told a white lie for the greater good?
- Can you reflect back on a difficult time in your life and see that it was for the best and/or part of God's plan?

Consider using these questions as the basis for your own commentary or creative midrash.

How does reflecting on these firsthand experiences help you better understand the text?

נ א וַיִּפֹּל יוֹסֵף עַל־פְּנֵי אָבִיו וַיֵּבְךְּ עָלָיו וַיִּשַּׁק־לוֹ: ב וַיְצַו יוֹסֵף אֶת־עֲבָדָיו אֶת־הָרֹפְאִים
ג לַחֲנֹט אֶת־אָבִיו וַיַּחַנְטוּ הָרֹפְאִים אֶת־יִשְׂרָאֵל: וַיִּמְלְאוּ־לוֹ אַרְבָּעִים יוֹם כִּי כֵּן
ד יִמְלְאוּ יְמֵי הַחֲנֻטִים וַיִּבְכּוּ אֹתוֹ מִצְרַיִם שִׁבְעִים יוֹם: וַיַּעַבְרוּ יְמֵי בְכִיתוֹ וַיְדַבֵּר
יוֹסֵף אֶל־בֵּית פַּרְעֹה לֵאמֹר אִם־נָא מָצָאתִי חֵן בְּעֵינֵיכֶם דַּבְּרוּ־נָא בְּאָזְנֵי פַרְעֹה
ה לֵאמֹר: אָבִי הִשְׁבִּיעַנִי לֵאמֹר הִנֵּה אָנֹכִי מֵת בְּקִבְרִי אֲשֶׁר כָּרִיתִי לִי בְּאֶרֶץ
ו כְּנַעַן שָׁמָּה תִּקְבְּרֵנִי וְעַתָּה אֶעֱלֶה־וְאֶקְבְּרָה אֶת־אָבִי וְאָשׁוּבָה: וַיֹּאמֶר פַּרְעֹה
ז עֲלֵה וּקְבֹר אֶת־אָבִיךָ כַּאֲשֶׁר הִשְׁבִּיעֶךָ: וַיַּעַל יוֹסֵף לִקְבֹּר אֶת־אָבִיו וַיַּעֲלוּ אִתּוֹ
ח כָּל־עַבְדֵי פַרְעֹה זִקְנֵי בֵיתוֹ וְכֹל זִקְנֵי אֶרֶץ־מִצְרָיִם: וְכֹל בֵּית יוֹסֵף וְאֶחָיו וּבֵית
ט אָבִיו רַק טַפָּם וְצֹאנָם וּבְקָרָם עָזְבוּ בְּאֶרֶץ גֹּשֶׁן: וַיַּעַל עִמּוֹ גַּם־רֶכֶב גַּם־פָּרָשִׁים

THEMES	RELATIONSHIPS AND LOVE	LEADERSHIP	LAND OF ISRAEL

Episode 73: *Yaakov's Death and Burial* – Bereshit 50:1–21

SUMMARY

The death of Yaakov, the elderly patriarch of the family, is followed by several official mourning ceremonies and emotional responses. Even the Egyptians pay their final respects to Yosef's father. After Yaakov is embalmed and mourned in Egypt, the Egyptian nobility escort Yosef with chariots and horses to the threshing floor of Atad, where there is another seven-day eulogy and mourning period so large that the Canaanites call the place Avel Mitzrayim. Only after that do Yaakov's sons bring him to the cave of Makhpela and bury him there.

10 reached the threshing floor of Atad, beyond the Jordan, they held a great and solemn
lamentation, and Yosef observed a seven-day period of mourning for his father. When
11 the Canaanites who lived there saw the mourning at the threshing floor of Atad they said,
"Egypt is in deep mourning here"; that is why the place beyond the Jordan was called Avel
12 13 Mitzrayim.[11] So his sons did as he had instructed them. They carried him to Canaan and
buried him in the cave of the field of Makhpela, near Mamre, which Avraham had bought
14 as a burial site from Efron the Hittite. After burying his father, Yosef returned to Egypt
together with his brothers and all those who had accompanied him to his father's burial.
15 When Yosef's brothers knew that their father was dead, they said, "What if Yosef really
16 hates us and decides to pay us back for all the wrong we did to him?" So they sent word
17 to Yosef saying, "Your father gave these instructions before his death: 'This is what you
are to say to Yosef: "Please forgive the crime and sin of your brothers who inflicted such
harm upon you."' That being so, please forgive the crime of these servants of your father's
18 God." Yosef wept as they spoke to him. Then his brothers came and threw themselves
19 down before him and said, "We are your slaves." But Yosef said to them, "Do not be afraid.
20 Am I in place of God? You intended to harm me, but God intended it for good, to bring
21 about what is now being done: the saving of many lives. So, do not be afraid. I myself will
provide for you and your children." And he comforted them and spoke to their hearts.

11 | Meaning "mourning of Egypt."

THE ART OF MIDRASH

Analysis

- Which elements of this image are directly mentioned in the text?
- Which elements of this image are not found in the text?
- What midrashic interpretation could be inferred from this image?

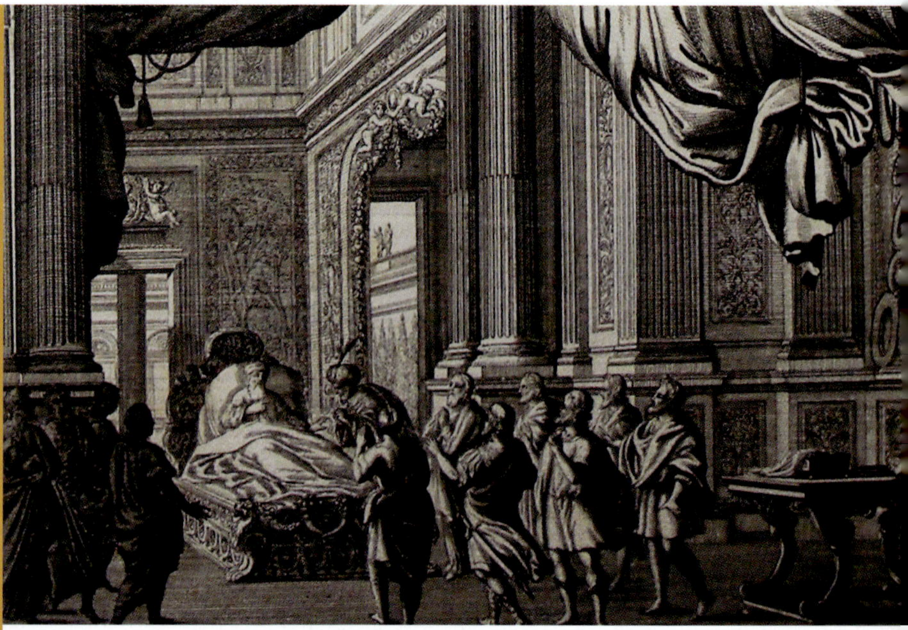

Death of Jacob
Adam Perelle (17th century)

י וַיְהִי הַמַּחֲנֶה כָּבֵד מְאֹד׃ וַיָּבֹאוּ עַד־גֹּרֶן הָאָטָד אֲשֶׁר בְּעֵבֶר הַיַּרְדֵּן וַיִּסְפְּדוּ־שָׁם
יא מִסְפֵּד גָּדוֹל וְכָבֵד מְאֹד וַיַּעַשׂ לְאָבִיו אֵבֶל שִׁבְעַת יָמִים׃ וַיַּרְא יוֹשֵׁב הָאָרֶץ
הַכְּנַעֲנִי אֶת־הָאֵבֶל בְּגֹרֶן הָאָטָד וַיֹּאמְרוּ אֵבֶל־כָּבֵד זֶה לְמִצְרָיִם עַל־כֵּן קָרָא
יב יג שְׁמָהּ אָבֵל מִצְרַיִם אֲשֶׁר בְּעֵבֶר הַיַּרְדֵּן׃ וַיַּעֲשׂוּ בָנָיו לוֹ כֵּן כַּאֲשֶׁר צִוָּם׃ וַיִּשְׂאוּ אֹתוֹ
בָנָיו אַרְצָה כְּנַעַן וַיִּקְבְּרוּ אֹתוֹ בִּמְעָרַת שְׂדֵה הַמַּכְפֵּלָה אֲשֶׁר קָנָה אַבְרָהָם אֶת־
יד הַשָּׂדֶה לַאֲחֻזַּת־קֶבֶר מֵאֵת עֶפְרֹן הַחִתִּי עַל־פְּנֵי מַמְרֵא׃ וַיָּשָׁב יוֹסֵף מִצְרַיְמָה הוּא
טו וְאֶחָיו וְכָל־הָעֹלִים אִתּוֹ לִקְבֹּר אֶת־אָבִיו אַחֲרֵי קָבְרוֹ אֶת־אָבִיו׃ וַיִּרְאוּ אֲחֵי־יוֹסֵף
כִּי־מֵת אֲבִיהֶם וַיֹּאמְרוּ לוּ יִשְׂטְמֵנוּ יוֹסֵף וְהָשֵׁב יָשִׁיב לָנוּ אֵת כָּל־הָרָעָה אֲשֶׁר
טז יז גָּמַלְנוּ אֹתוֹ׃ וַיְצַוּוּ אֶל־יוֹסֵף לֵאמֹר אָבִיךָ צִוָּה לִפְנֵי מוֹתוֹ לֵאמֹר׃ כֹּה־תֹאמְרוּ
לְיוֹסֵף אָנָּא שָׂא נָא פֶּשַׁע אַחֶיךָ וְחַטָּאתָם כִּי־רָעָה גְמָלוּךָ וְעַתָּה שָׂא נָא לְפֶשַׁע
יח עַבְדֵי אֱלֹהֵי אָבִיךָ וַיֵּבְךְּ יוֹסֵף בְּדַבְּרָם אֵלָיו׃ וַיֵּלְכוּ גַּם־אֶחָיו וַיִּפְּלוּ לְפָנָיו וַיֹּאמְרוּ
יט כ הִנֶּנּוּ לְךָ לַעֲבָדִים׃ וַיֹּאמֶר אֲלֵהֶם יוֹסֵף אַל־תִּירָאוּ כִּי הֲתַחַת אֱלֹהִים אָנִי׃ וְאַתֶּם
חֲשַׁבְתֶּם עָלַי רָעָה אֱלֹהִים חֲשָׁבָהּ לְטֹבָה לְמַעַן עֲשֹׂה כַּיּוֹם הַזֶּה לְהַחֲיֹת עַם־רָב׃
כא וְעַתָּה אַל־תִּירָאוּ אָנֹכִי אֲכַלְכֵּל אֶתְכֶם וְאֶת־טַפְּכֶם וַיְנַחֵם אוֹתָם וַיְדַבֵּר עַל־לִבָּם׃ שביעי

A QUESTION OF BIBLIODRAMA

TO YOSEF

- How did it feel to have a large and impressive entourage accompany your father on his final journey?
- Why did you weep when you heard what your brothers told you?
- Do you believe what you said to them, or did you say it just to comfort and reassure them?

TO THE BROTHERS

- What do you think of the Egyptian-style mourning and burial that Yosef arranged for your father?
- How did it feel to have a large and impressive entourage accompany your father on his final journey?
- Why did you lie to Yosef and tell him your father gave you a message for him? What were you afraid of?
- What do you think of his response? Was it what you had hoped for?

intended it for good to accomplish what is now being done, the saving of many lives" (50:19–20).

Yosef is helping his brothers to revise their memory of the past. In doing so, he is challenging one of our most fundamental assumptions about time, namely its asymmetry. We can change the future. We cannot change the past. But is that entirely true? What Yosef is doing for his brothers is what he has clearly done for himself: events have changed his and their understanding of the past.

Which means: We cannot fully understand what is happening to us now until we can look back in retrospect and see how it all turned out. This means that we are not held captive by the past. Things can happen to us, not as dramatically as to Yosef perhaps, but nonetheless benign, that can completely alter the way we look back and remember. *By action in the future, we can redeem the past.*

Professor Mordechai Rotenberg of the Hebrew University has argued that this kind of technique, of reinterpreting the past, could be used as a therapeutic technique in rehabilitating patients suffering from a crippling sense of guilt. If we cannot change the past, then it is always there holding us back like a ball and chain around our legs. We cannot change the past, but we can reinterpret it by integrating it into a new and larger narrative. That is what Yosef was doing, and having used this technique to help him survive a personal life of unparalleled ups and downs, he now uses it to help his brothers live without overpowering guilt.

It is by telling stories that we make sense of our lives and the life of our people. And it is by allowing the present to reshape our understanding of the past that we redeem history and make it live as a positive force in our lives.

Rabbi Jonathan Sacks

Analysis

- What areas of understanding of human nature and society do we now have that were unavailable to classical Jewish commentators? How can they aid our understanding of the text?
- What can we learn from this passage to help us understand the text?
- What further questions on the text do you have now that you have read this new take on the story?

INTEGRATING ḤOKHMA

In Bereshit 45, Yosef does something unusual. Revealing himself to his brothers, fully aware that they will suffer shock and then guilt as they remember how it is that their brother is in Egypt, he *reinterprets the past*.

Yosef described these events when he spoke to the chief butler in prison: "I was forcibly carried off from the land of the Hebrews, and even here I have done nothing to deserve being put in a dungeon" (40:15). Then, it was a story of kidnap and injustice.

Now, it has become a story of divine providence and redemption. It wasn't you, he tells his brothers, it was God. You didn't realize that you were part of a larger plan. And though it began badly, it has ended well. So don't hold yourselves guilty. And do not be afraid of any desire for revenge on my part. There is no such desire. I realize that we were all being directed by a force greater than ourselves, greater than we can fully understand.

Yosef does the same in Bereshit 50, when the brothers fear that he may take revenge after their father's death: "Don't be afraid. Am I in the place of God? *You intended to harm me, but God*

connection, hold far more value and importance than does power – both for the person himself and for all those around him. Ultimately, power finds expression in dependence. When all is said and done, who is dependent upon whom? Are Yosef's brothers dependent upon him – the master, the lord, the ruler, the viceroy – or is he perhaps dependent upon them, yearning for their acceptance, desiring their closeness?

Many years later, Yosef again faces the limits of power: "Yosef said to his brothers: I am dying" (50:24). In death, all power disappears as though it had never existed; everything is lost. He continues, "But God will surely remember you": You belong to the land of Israel; you belong to the Jewish faith; you belong to our father's household. You belong to him, you represent him, while I remain on the outside. "Bring me in," Yosef asks: "God will surely remember you, and you shall carry up my bones from here" (v. 25).

Who will bring up the bones of the brothers to the land of Israel? The text, it seems, has no need to address this question; someone will take care of it. However, there is no one who will willingly, of his own initiative, bring up the bones of Yosef; he must bind his brothers by an oath. Yosef remains attached to his mask, the mask of his life.

Here the secret is revealed. It is this that causes Yosef to weep in the beginning, and it is for the same reason that he cries in the end. He weeps over the weakness inherent in power, over the terrible price that he has paid for it. His dreams have indeed been realized, on some level, but the tragedy remains just as real. The torn shreds of the family have not been made completely whole.

When will the shreds be made whole? Only a few hundred years later, with someone who appears on the stage of Jewish history as an infant crying in a basket among the bulrushes. It is he who seeks the bones of Yosef and, in the midst of the exodus, takes the trouble to bring them up for burial in Israel. It is only when they leave Egypt, only when they leave the territory where Yosef had been lord and ruler, and only through renewed weeping, that Yosef succeeds – that history succeeds – in sewing the pieces back together.

The story of Yosef's weeping is a stirring tragedy, full of lessons, brimming with spiritual, psychological, and social significance. His weeping conveys the inner reality of a person who allows himself to lower all of the barriers with which a person tends to surround himself. By weeping, Yosef allows his inner self to break through and to rise up.

Rabbi Aharon Lichtenstein

TAKING A LITERARY APPROACH

Yosef's reunion with his brothers should have been his greatest hour; it is the realization of his dream. He has dreamt of having everyone dependent upon him – and now this dream has become reality! Yosef believes that at this encounter his brothers will be filled with joy. He removes the mask from his face – but he is suddenly taken aback. Instead of having his brothers plead before him, he pleads before them: "Please [*na*] come near me" (Bereshit 45:4). The word *na* always indicates pleading. What is he begging for? Is this moment not meant to be the high point of Yosef's life, the instant when all of his hopes and dreams are literally realized?

At this moment it becomes clear to Yosef the terrible price he has paid for his success, for his integration into Egyptian culture, for all of his restraint. Yosef stands alone. Even once he has decided to emerge from his isolation, to put an end to his alienation, those around him remain alienated from him. It is only now that Yosef discovers what he has sacrificed in exchange for the power that he has accumulated, for being the ruler over all of Egypt, for presuming to be the one to feed, nourish, command, and sustain.

This tone, so tragic for Yosef, finds further expression later on. After Yaakov's death, Yosef cries once more: "Yosef fell upon his father's face and wept upon him and kissed him" (50:1). Understandably, he is filled with sorrow over the death of his father, but why is he the only one weeping? Where are all of his brothers?

It seems that what separates Yosef at this point is not the grief over Yaakov's passing, but the guilt over his separation. It is not only the two decades of silence; even the seventeen years during which Yaakov lives in Goshen are years in which Yosef is preoccupied with matters of state. Apparently, his weeping with Binyamin does not put an end to his restraint. Admittedly, the center of gravity has shifted. The man who now cries is no longer Tzafenat Paneaḥ, viceroy of Egypt, with a tenuous tie to Jewish culture. Rather, it is Yosef, who stands firmly and squarely within Jewish culture. Still, the connection with Egypt prevails in his home; he is the master of Pharaoh's house. Yosef is still involved in Egyptian life and culture. It is this connection that finds expression later on, in Egypt's seventy days of weeping. Is the nation really so touched by the death of Yaakov? This is not an inner, genuine weeping, but rather an external show, part of an official ritual. In the first chapter of *The Waning of the Middle Ages*, historian Johan Huizinga describes medieval society as characterized by the need to weep the loudest, to spill the most tears. Egypt is no different.

It is after the burial that Yosef stands at the most difficult climax of the story. All of the fear that has accompanied him, the abyss that has opened between him and his brothers – all of this now confronts him in his final scene of weeping, when confronted with the imaginary story that his brothers concoct.

It is clear why Yosef cries: what more could he have done for them in order to gain their faith, their affection, and their trust? Yosef has removed his mask; he has returned to his roots. He has revealed himself, wept aloud, brought together the torn shreds of their fraternity. What else can he do? Despite all of this, Yosef's brothers continue to regard him with suspicion and fear that he will take revenge. Is this the level of brotherly love they award him? Admittedly, they have moved away from their starting point of "They hated him even more," but the same primal distrust remains.

At this moment, Yosef discovers the limits of raw power. He discovers the extent to which the human connection, the personal connection, the family

22 Yosef remained in Egypt together with his father's family, and he lived one hundred and ten
23 years. Yosef saw the third generation of Efrayim's children, and the children of Menashe's
24 son Makir were also born on Yosef's knees.[12] Yosef said to his brothers, "I am about to
die. But God will surely take note of you and bring you out of this land to the land He
25 promised to Avraham, Yitzḥak, and Yaakov." Then Yosef bound the children of Israel by
26 an oath: "When God takes note of you, carry my bones up from this place." Yosef died at
the age of one hundred and ten. He was embalmed and placed in a coffin there, in Egypt.

12 | That is, they were born during Yosef's lifetime.

UNLOCKING THE TEXT

- What does it mean that his grandchildren were "born on his knees"?
- Why did Yosef feel the need to remind his brothers of the covenantal promise to take them out of Egypt and return them to the land of Israel?
- Why did Yosef want to be buried in Israel?
- Where in Israel? Why not in the cave of Makhpela?
- Why did he make them swear an oath?
- Was this to be carried out immediately? Why was it not?

Consider using these questions as the basis for your own commentary or creative midrash.

FINDING YOURSELF IN THE TEXT

- Do you ever think about your future grandchildren and what they might be like?
- What would you write in your last will and testament?
- Are you a direct descendant of Avraham, Yitzḥak, and Yaakov? How does that feel?

How does reflecting on these firsthand experiences help you better understand the text?

כב וַיֵּ֤שֶׁב יוֹסֵף֙ בְּמִצְרַ֔יִם ה֖וּא וּבֵ֣ית אָבִ֑יו וַיְחִ֣י יוֹסֵ֔ף מֵאָ֥ה וָעֶ֖שֶׂר שָׁנִֽים׃ כג וַיַּ֤רְא יוֹסֵף֙ מפטיר
לְאֶפְרַ֔יִם בְּנֵ֖י שִׁלֵּשִׁ֑ים גַּ֗ם בְּנֵ֤י מָכִיר֙ בֶּן־מְנַשֶּׁ֔ה יֻלְּד֖וּ עַל־בִּרְכֵּ֥י יוֹסֵֽף׃ כד וַיֹּ֤אמֶר
יוֹסֵף֙ אֶל־אֶחָ֔יו אָנֹכִ֖י מֵ֑ת וֵֽאלֹהִ֞ים פָּקֹ֧ד יִפְקֹ֣ד אֶתְכֶ֗ם וְהֶעֱלָ֤ה אֶתְכֶם֙ מִן־
הָאָ֣רֶץ הַזֹּ֔את אֶל־הָאָ֕רֶץ אֲשֶׁ֥ר נִשְׁבַּ֛ע לְאַבְרָהָ֥ם לְיִצְחָ֖ק וּֽלְיַעֲקֹֽב׃ כה וַיַּשְׁבַּ֣ע
יוֹסֵ֔ף אֶת־בְּנֵ֥י יִשְׂרָאֵ֖ל לֵאמֹ֑ר פָּקֹ֨ד יִפְקֹ֤ד אֱלֹהִים֙ אֶתְכֶ֔ם וְהַעֲלִתֶ֥ם אֶת־עַצְמֹתַ֖י
מִזֶּֽה׃ כו וַיָּ֣מָת יוֹסֵ֔ף בֶּן־מֵאָ֥ה וָעֶ֖שֶׂר שָׁנִ֑ים וַיַּחַנְט֣וּ אֹת֔וֹ וַיִּ֥ישֶׂם בָּאָר֖וֹן בְּמִצְרָֽיִם׃

THEMES | RELATIONSHIPS AND LOVE | LEADERSHIP | LAND OF ISRAEL

Episode 74: *Yosef's Death* – Bereshit 50:22–26

SUMMARY

Yosef lives another fifty-four years, to the age of 110, and takes an active role in raising his grandchildren, great-grandchildren, and great-great-grandchildren. Before his passing, he reminds his brothers that the day will come when God will redeem them from Egypt and bring them to the land promised to Avraham, Yitzḥak, and Yaakov. He makes those assembled take an oath that, when that day comes, they will bring his bones from Egypt for burial in Canaan. Yosef dies, is embalmed, and his body is kept in Egypt.

THE ART OF MIDRASH

Joseph's Tomb in Shechem
Tom Miller (2014)

Analysis

- Which elements of this image are directly mentioned in the text?
- Which elements of this image are not found in the text?
- What midrashic interpretation could be inferred from this image?

A QUESTION OF BIBLIODRAMA

TO YOSEF

- Why is it important to you to be buried in the land of Israel?
- Do you have confidence that your brothers will fulfill this wish?
- When you reflect on your life, are you satisfied with what you have achieved?
- Are you concerned for the future of your people? Do you have faith in the covenant of your fathers?

INTEGRATING ḤOKHMA

BERESHIT

TIME PERIOD OF THE PATRIARCHS

Years according to Rashi

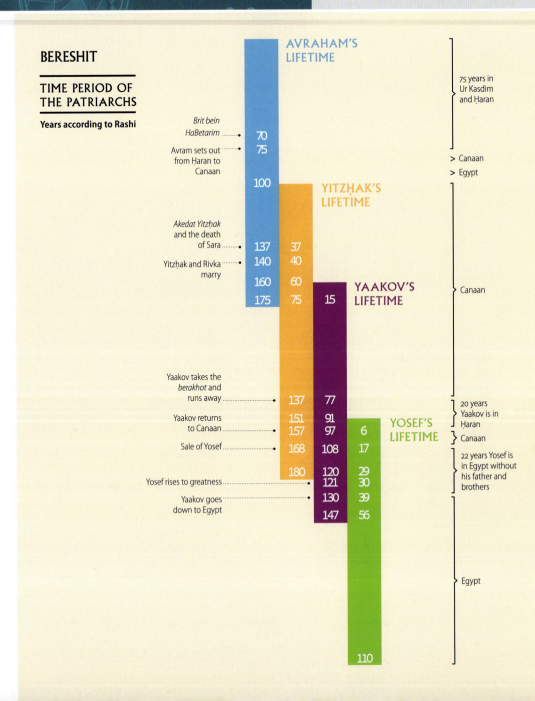

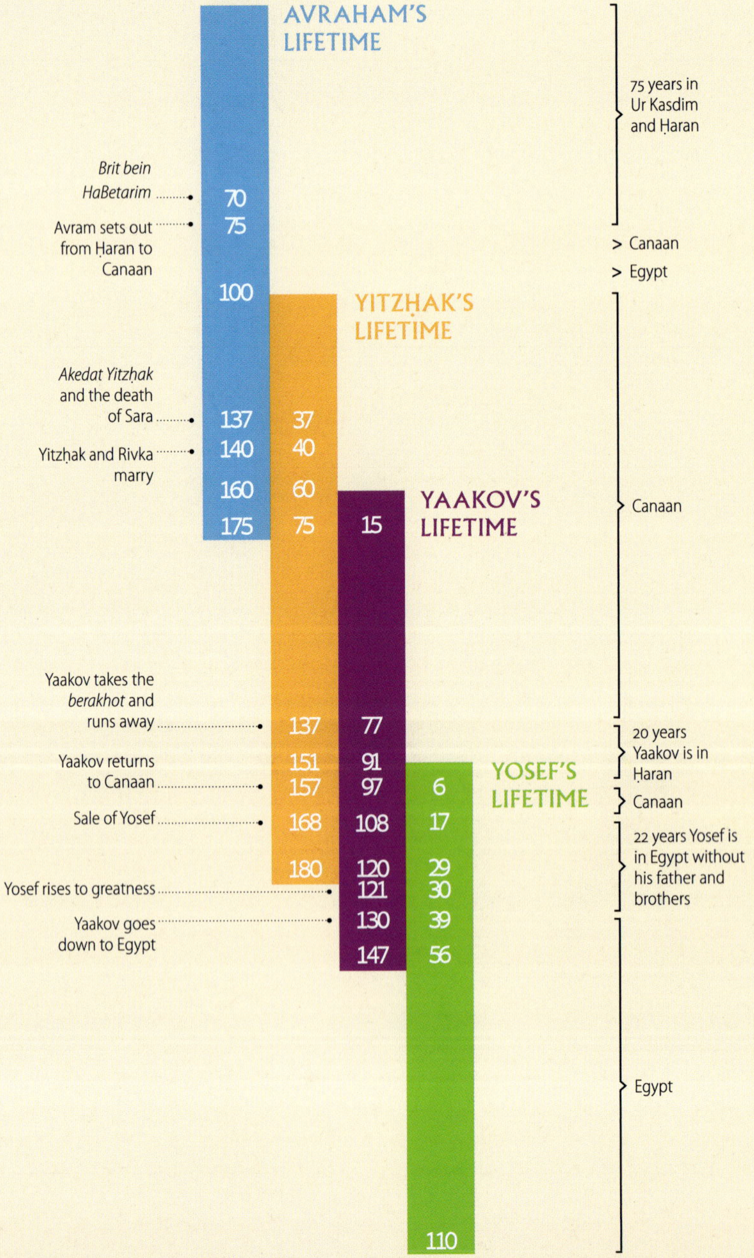

Timeline of the avot

TAKING A LITERARY APPROACH

Although the *parasha* gets its name from the opening word, *Vayeḥi* – denoting life – the *parasha* actually describes the death of two people: Yaakov and Yosef.

It begins with a description of Yaakov's preparations, knowing that he is about to die. He commands Yosef to bury him in Canaan; he declares that Efrayim and Menashe will have special status as sons deserving of an inheritance; he blesses all of his children and commands all of them to bury him in the cave of Makhpela. The text then describes his death, the mourning that follows, and the funeral procession. Then there is a conversation between Yosef and his brothers, straightening out the affairs between them. It then ends with Yosef's parting words to his brothers and his death.

If we compare the two descriptions of death – that of Yaakov and that of Yosef – we find a considerable degree of similarity. Admittedly, the description in Yaakov's case is far more detailed, but the same central elements appear in both:

Dwelling in Egypt:

Yaakov: "And Israel dwelled in the land of Egypt" (Bereshit 47:27).

Yosef: "And Yosef dwelled in Egypt – he and his father's household" (50:22).

Noting the length of life:

Yaakov: "And Yaakov's lifetime, the years of his life, were one hundred and forty-seven years" (47:25).

Yosef: "And Yosef lived one hundred and ten years" (50:22).

Mention of the redemption:

Yaakov: "And Israel said to Yosef: 'Behold, I am going to die, but God will be with you and restore you to the land of your forefathers'" (48:21).

Yosef: "And Yosef said to his brothers: 'I am going to die, but God will surely remember you and bring you up from this land to the land which He promised to Avraham, to Yitzḥak, and to Yaakov'" (50:24).

Command concerning burial in the land:

Yaakov: "'Place your hand under my thigh, and act toward me with kindness and truth: do not bury me in Egypt. Let me lie with my ancestors; you shall carry me from Egypt and bury me in their burial place.' And he said: 'Swear to me'; and he swore to him" (47:29–31).

"Bury me with my ancestors at the cave which is in the field of Efron, the Ḥittite" (49:29–32).

Yosef: "And Yosef caused *Benei Yisrael* to swear, saying…'And you shall take up my bones from here'" (50:25).

The death:

Yaakov: "And he gathered his legs to his bed, and he expired, and was gathered to his people" (49:33).

Yosef: "And Yosef died, aged one hundred and ten" (50:26).

Embalming:

Yaakov: "And the physicians embalmed Israel" (50:2).

Yosef: "And they embalmed him" (50:26).

Burial:

Yaakov: "And Yosef went up to bury his father…and his sons carried him to the land of Canaan, and they buried him in the cave of the field of Makhpela" (50:7–13).

Yosef: "And placed him in a casket in Egypt" (50:26).

Both Yaakov and Yosef know that there will be redemption from Egypt, and both command their descendants to bury them in Canaan. However, there are two important differences between them: Yaakov does not tell all of his sons that there will be redemption; he tells only Yosef. Yosef, on the other hand, tells all of his brothers. Second, Yaakov's body is brought to Canaan for burial, while Yosef's body remains, for the meantime, in a casket in Egypt.

Rabbanit Sharon Rimon

ב יוֹסֵף בְּמִצְרַיִם הוּא וּבֵית יְ
אֶפְרַיִם בְּנֵי שִׁלֵשִׁים גַּם בְּנֵי מָכִ
יוֹסֵף אֶל־אֶחָיו אָנֹכִי מֵת וֵאלֹהִים
הָאָרֶץ הַזֹּאת אֶל־הָאָרֶץ אֲשֶׁר נִ
סֵף אֶת־בְּנֵי יִשְׂרָאֵל לֵאמֹר פָּקֹד יְ
ה: וַיָּמָת יוֹסֵף בֶּן־מֵאָה וָעֶשֶׂ

הפטרות
Haftarot

HAFTARAT BERESHIT

On erev Rosh Ḥodesh Marḥeshvan, some read the haftara on page 664.

42 5 So says God, the Lord, who created the skies, who stretched them across and set down ISAIAH
the land and all her children, and gave humanity upon her breath, and spirit to those who
6 walk her. I, the Lord, call you forth in victory, and I will hold your hand; I shall form you
7 and make you a covenant people, make you a light unto nations, to open blinded eyes,
8 to bring prisoners out of captivity, and those who dwell in darkness from their jail. I am
the Lord; this is My name, and I share not My glory with others, My praise with idols.
9 What I said at the beginning: see, it has come, and I tell you now what will be afresh
10 before it pushes through the earth; you will hear it first from Me. Sing out to
the Lord a new song, His praise from the ends of the earth, You who go to sea, and all
11 that fill it, distant coastlands and you who live there. Desert and its towns, raise your
voices, Kedarites in their scattered camps; those who dwell in the rocks must sing out joy
12 from the mountaintops, shout and give the Lord His glory; His praise will be spoken in
13 the distant coastlands. The Lord sets out like a hero, rousing His passion like a man of
14 war; He gives the war cry, bellows the war cry, overthrows His enemies. Always
I held still and was silent, held back; I will bellow out like one giving birth, breathing
15 out, breathing in all together, will vanquish hills and mountains and will dry up all the
16 green; I shall turn the rivers into coastlands and desiccate the lakes, and lead the blind
along a way they know not, on paths unknown shall guide them; I shall turn darkness
to light before them, the treacherous road to open highway; these things I will perform,
17 and will not fail. Those who trust in idols will step back ashamed, those who say to
18 molded statuary, "You – you are our gods." All you deaf ones – listen, and you
19 who are blind – now see. Who is blind if not My servant, who deaf like the messenger I
send? Who could be blind like him – who is devoted, blind like this, the Lord's servant?
20 21 Many things seen, but you remember not, with open ears, hear nothing. Yet the Lord
has desired them, that His righteousness be known, to raise aloft His teachings, to confer
22 majesty. He is with this plundered, this torn-apart people, who are trapped away in pits, *Sepharadim end here*
hidden in prison, plunder with none to save them, given over to looters with none to
23 cry, "Give back!" Who among you will listen to this, will hear it and heed for the future?
24 Who was it who gave Yaakov up for looting, Israel for plunder – was it not the Lord?
Him against whom we sinned; whose ways they cared not to follow, whose Law they
25 did not heed. He poured out the fire of His rage against them, His terrible warfare, and
flames raged all around them, yet they did not know; they burned but still they took
43 1 it not to heart. And now, Yaakov, so says the Lord, your Creator, the One
2 who formed you, Israel: Do not fear: I redeem you; I name you: you are Mine. Though
you pass through waters – I am with you; through rivers – they will not wash you away.
Though you walk right through the fire, you will not be burned, and no flame will take
3 hold of you, for I am the Lord your God, the Holy One of Israel, your rescuer. I have

הפטרת בראשית

On ערב ראש חודש מרחשון *some read the* הפטרה *on page 665.*

מב ה כֹּה־אָמַר הָאֵל ׀ יהוה בּוֹרֵא הַשָּׁמַיִם וְנוֹטֵיהֶם רֹקַע הָאָרֶץ וְצֶאֱצָאֶיהָ נֹתֵן נְשָׁמָה ישעיה
ו לָעָם עָלֶיהָ וְרוּחַ לַהֹלְכִים בָּהּ: אֲנִי יהוה קְרָאתִיךָ בְצֶדֶק וְאַחְזֵק בְּיָדֶךָ וְאֶצָּרְךָ
ז וְאֶתֶּנְךָ לִבְרִית עָם לְאוֹר גּוֹיִם: לִפְקֹחַ עֵינַיִם עִוְרוֹת לְהוֹצִיא מִמַּסְגֵּר אַסִּיר
ח מִבֵּית כֶּלֶא יֹשְׁבֵי חֹשֶׁךְ: אֲנִי יהוה הוּא שְׁמִי וּכְבוֹדִי לְאַחֵר לֹא־אֶתֵּן וּתְהִלָּתִי
ט לַפְּסִילִים: הָרִאשֹׁנוֹת הִנֵּה־בָאוּ וַחֲדָשׁוֹת אֲנִי מַגִּיד בְּטֶרֶם תִּצְמַחְנָה אַשְׁמִיעַ
י אֶתְכֶם: שִׁירוּ לַיהוה שִׁיר חָדָשׁ תְּהִלָּתוֹ מִקְצֵה הָאָרֶץ יוֹרְדֵי הַיָּם וּמְלֹאוֹ
יא אִיִּים וְיֹשְׁבֵיהֶם: יִשְׂאוּ מִדְבָּר וְעָרָיו חֲצֵרִים תֵּשֵׁב קֵדָר יָרֹנּוּ יֹשְׁבֵי סֶלַע מֵרֹאשׁ הָרִים
יב יג יִצְוָחוּ: יָשִׂימוּ לַיהוה כָּבוֹד וּתְהִלָּתוֹ בָּאִיִּים יַגִּידוּ: יהוה כַּגִּבּוֹר יֵצֵא כְּאִישׁ מִלְחָמוֹת
יד יָעִיר קִנְאָה יָרִיעַ אַף־יַצְרִיחַ עַל־אֹיְבָיו יִתְגַּבָּר: הֶחֱשֵׁיתִי מֵעוֹלָם אַחֲרִישׁ
טו אֶתְאַפָּק כַּיּוֹלֵדָה אֶפְעֶה אֶשֹּׁם וְאֶשְׁאַף יָחַד: אַחֲרִיב הָרִים וּגְבָעוֹת וְכָל־עֶשְׂבָּם
טז אוֹבִישׁ וְשַׂמְתִּי נְהָרוֹת לָאִיִּים וַאֲגַמִּים אוֹבִישׁ: וְהוֹלַכְתִּי עִוְרִים בְּדֶרֶךְ לֹא יָדָעוּ
בִּנְתִיבוֹת לֹא־יָדְעוּ אַדְרִיכֵם אָשִׂים מַחְשָׁךְ לִפְנֵיהֶם לָאוֹר וּמַעֲקַשִּׁים לְמִישׁוֹר אֵלֶּה
יז הַדְּבָרִים עֲשִׂיתִם וְלֹא עֲזַבְתִּים: נָסֹגוּ אָחוֹר יֵבֹשׁוּ בֹשֶׁת הַבֹּטְחִים בַּפָּסֶל הָאֹמְרִים
יח לְמַסֵּכָה אַתֶּם אֱלֹהֵינוּ: הַחֵרְשִׁים שְׁמָעוּ וְהַעִוְרִים הַבִּיטוּ לִרְאוֹת:
יט מִי עִוֵּר כִּי אִם־עַבְדִּי וְחֵרֵשׁ כְּמַלְאָכִי אֶשְׁלָח מִי עִוֵּר כִּמְשֻׁלָּם וְעִוֵּר כְּעֶבֶד יהוה:
כ כא רָאִית רַבּוֹת וְלֹא תִשְׁמֹר פָּקוֹחַ אָזְנַיִם וְלֹא יִשְׁמָע: יהוה חָפֵץ לְמַעַן צִדְקוֹ יַגְדִּיל רָאוֹת
כב תּוֹרָה וְיַאְדִּיר:* וְהוּא עַם־בָּזוּז וְשָׁסוּי הָפֵחַ בַּחוּרִים כֻּלָּם וּבְבָתֵּי כְלָאִים הָחְבָּאוּ *Sepharadim end here*
כג הָיוּ לָבַז וְאֵין מַצִּיל מְשִׁסָּה וְאֵין־אֹמֵר הָשַׁב: מִי בָכֶם יַאֲזִין זֹאת יַקְשִׁב וְיִשְׁמַע
כד לְאָחוֹר: מִי־נָתַן למשוסה יַעֲקֹב וְיִשְׂרָאֵל לְבֹזְזִים הֲלוֹא יהוה זוּ חָטָאנוּ לוֹ וְלֹא־ לִמְשִׁסָּה
כה אָבוּ בִדְרָכָיו הָלוֹךְ וְלֹא שָׁמְעוּ בְּתוֹרָתוֹ: וַיִּשְׁפֹּךְ עָלָיו חֵמָה אַפּוֹ וֶעֱזוּז מִלְחָמָה
מג א וַתְּלַהֲטֵהוּ מִסָּבִיב וְלֹא יָדָע וַתִּבְעַר־בּוֹ וְלֹא־יָשִׂים עַל־לֵב: וְעַתָּה
כֹּה־אָמַר יהוה בֹּרַאֲךָ יַעֲקֹב וְיֹצֶרְךָ יִשְׂרָאֵל אַל־תִּירָא כִּי גְאַלְתִּיךָ קָרָאתִי בְשִׁמְךָ
ב לִי־אָתָּה: כִּי־תַעֲבֹר בַּמַּיִם אִתְּךָ־אָנִי וּבַנְּהָרוֹת לֹא יִשְׁטְפוּךָ כִּי־תֵלֵךְ בְּמוֹ־אֵשׁ לֹא
ג תִכָּוֶה וְלֶהָבָה לֹא תִבְעַר־בָּךְ: כִּי אֲנִי יהוה אֱלֹהֶיךָ קְדוֹשׁ יִשְׂרָאֵל מוֹשִׁיעֶךָ נָתַתִּי

4 paid Egypt as your ransom, Kush and Seva in your place. Because you are valued in My
eyes, you are honored. I love you enough to give up other men for you, whole nations
5 in your place. Do not fear, for I am with you. I will bring your children from the east,
6 will gather you back from the west. To the north I will say, "Give over"; to the south,
"Imprison no more." Bring My sons from far away, My daughters back from the ends
7 of the earth, all the people I called by My name, created for My glory; I formed them, I
8 made them. He brought out a people – blind though they have eyes, deaf though they
9 have ears. Were all the nations to gather, the peoples to come into session, who of them
could tell of this? Who could speak of this before? Let them bring their witnesses to
10 vindicate them, so that hearers may say, "This is truth." No – you are My witnesses, so
says the LORD, My servants whom I chose, so that you should know, and trust in Me and
understand that I am He; before Me, no god was made, and after Me – no other.

HAFTARAT NOAḤ

On Rosh Ḥodesh Marḥeshvan read the haftara on page 660.

ISAIAH

54 1 Barren woman, never a mother, rejoice; break out in joyful song though you have not
given birth, for the children of the forsaken woman will outnumber those of the wife,
2 so says the LORD. Broaden the site of your tent; stretch out your canvas home; do
3 not hold back; lengthen your tent cords, and strengthen its pegs: you shall overflow
rightward and left, your children possessing nations, and filling forsaken towns with
4 life. Do not fear – you will not be shamed; fear not, for none can disgrace you. You will
forget your youthful abjection; the debasement of your widowhood you will call no
5 more to mind, for your husband, He who made you – the LORD of Hosts is His name,
6 and your redeemer, Israel's Holy One – will be named God of all the world, for as a
woman abandoned, of sorrowful spirit, the LORD has called to you: Can the young
7 bride ever be rejected? says your God; for one small moment I left you; with infinite
8 care shall I gather you back; in the flash of My fury I hid My face from you for just a
moment, and in everlasting love will I care for you now. So speaks the LORD, your
9 redeemer. For these are the waters of Noaḥ to Me, and I swore that the waters
of Noaḥ would never sweep again over the earth. And so did I swear no more to be
10 furious with you, no more to rebuke you. For mountains may move, hills may crumble
away; but My love for you will not be moved, nor My pact of peace crumble. So speaks
11 the LORD, who cares for you. Oppressed and storm swept, never comforted;
Sepharadim end here
12 behold: I am paving your ground with garnet, lapis lazuli your foundations. I am fitting
your windows with rubies, your gates with glowing granite, marking your borders with
13 stones men covet. All your children will be students of the LORD, and great will be your
14 children's peace. On righteousness will you be founded; stay far from oppression; you
15 will not fear, and terror will never come near you. No strife can arise without My assent;

ד כָּפְרְךָ מִצְרַיִם כּוּשׁ וּסְבָא תַּחְתֶּיךָ: מֵאֲשֶׁר יָקַרְתָּ בְעֵינַי נִכְבַּדְתָּ וַאֲנִי אֲהַבְתִּיךָ
ה וְאֶתֵּן אָדָם תַּחְתֶּיךָ וּלְאֻמִּים תַּחַת נַפְשֶׁךָ: אַל־תִּירָא כִּי אִתְּךָ־אָנִי מִמִּזְרָח אָבִיא
ו זַרְעֶךָ וּמִמַּעֲרָב אֲקַבְּצֶךָּ: אֹמַר לַצָּפוֹן תֵּנִי וּלְתֵימָן אַל־תִּכְלָאִי הָבִיאִי בָנַי מֵרָחוֹק
ז וּבְנוֹתַי מִקְצֵה הָאָרֶץ: כֹּל הַנִּקְרָא בִשְׁמִי וְלִכְבוֹדִי בְּרָאתִיו יְצַרְתִּיו אַף־עֲשִׂיתִיו:
ח ט הוֹצִיא עַם־עִוֵּר וְעֵינַיִם יֵשׁ וְחֵרְשִׁים וְאָזְנַיִם לָמוֹ: כָּל־הַגּוֹיִם נִקְבְּצוּ יַחְדָּו וְיֵאָסְפוּ
לְאֻמִּים מִי בָהֶם יַגִּיד זֹאת וְרִאשֹׁנוֹת יַשְׁמִיעֻנוּ יִתְּנוּ עֵדֵיהֶם וְיִצְדָּקוּ וְיִשְׁמְעוּ וְיֹאמְרוּ
י אֱמֶת: אַתֶּם עֵדַי נְאֻם־יְהוָה וְעַבְדִּי אֲשֶׁר בָּחָרְתִּי לְמַעַן תֵּדְעוּ וְתַאֲמִינוּ לִי וְתָבִינוּ
כִּי־אֲנִי הוּא לְפָנַי לֹא־נוֹצַר אֵל וְאַחֲרַי לֹא יִהְיֶה:

הפטרת נח

On ראש חודש מרחשון *read the* הפטרה *on page 661.*

נד א רָנִּי עֲקָרָה לֹא יָלָדָה פִּצְחִי רִנָּה וְצַהֲלִי לֹא־חָלָה כִּי־רַבִּים בְּנֵי־שׁוֹמֵמָה מִבְּנֵי *ישעיה*
ב בְעוּלָה אָמַר יְהוָה: הַרְחִיבִי ׀ מְקוֹם אָהֳלֵךְ וִירִיעוֹת מִשְׁכְּנוֹתַיִךְ יַטּוּ אַל־תַּחְשֹׂכִי
ג הַאֲרִיכִי מֵיתָרַיִךְ וִיתֵדֹתַיִךְ חַזֵּקִי: כִּי־יָמִין וּשְׂמֹאול תִּפְרֹצִי וְזַרְעֵךְ גּוֹיִם יִירָשׁ
ד וְעָרִים נְשַׁמּוֹת יוֹשִׁיבוּ: אַל־תִּירְאִי כִּי־לֹא תֵבוֹשִׁי וְאַל־תִּכָּלְמִי כִּי לֹא תַחְפִּירִי
ה כִּי בֹשֶׁת עֲלוּמַיִךְ תִּשְׁכָּחִי וְחֶרְפַּת אַלְמְנוּתַיִךְ לֹא תִזְכְּרִי־עוֹד: כִּי בֹעֲלַיִךְ עֹשַׂיִךְ
ו יְהוָה צְבָאוֹת שְׁמוֹ וְגֹאֲלֵךְ קְדוֹשׁ יִשְׂרָאֵל אֱלֹהֵי כָל־הָאָרֶץ יִקָּרֵא: כִּי־כְאִשָּׁה
ז עֲזוּבָה וַעֲצוּבַת רוּחַ קְרָאָךְ יְהוָה וְאֵשֶׁת נְעוּרִים כִּי תִמָּאֵס אָמַר אֱלֹהָיִךְ: בְּרֶגַע
ח קָטֹן עֲזַבְתִּיךְ וּבְרַחֲמִים גְּדֹלִים אֲקַבְּצֵךְ: בְּשֶׁצֶף קֶצֶף הִסְתַּרְתִּי פָנַי רֶגַע מִמֵּךְ
ט וּבְחֶסֶד עוֹלָם רִחַמְתִּיךְ אָמַר גֹּאֲלֵךְ יְהוָה: כִּי־מֵי נֹחַ זֹאת לִי אֲשֶׁר
נִשְׁבַּעְתִּי מֵעֲבֹר מֵי־נֹחַ עוֹד עַל־הָאָרֶץ כֵּן נִשְׁבַּעְתִּי מִקְּצֹף עָלַיִךְ וּמִגְּעָר־בָּךְ:
י כִּי הֶהָרִים יָמוּשׁוּ וְהַגְּבָעוֹת תְּמוּטֶנָה וְחַסְדִּי מֵאִתֵּךְ לֹא־יָמוּשׁ וּבְרִית שְׁלוֹמִי
יא לֹא תָמוּט אָמַר מְרַחֲמֵךְ יְהוָה:* עֲנִיָּה סֹעֲרָה לֹא נֻחָמָה הִנֵּה אָנֹכִי *Sepharadim end here*
יב מַרְבִּיץ בַּפּוּךְ אֲבָנַיִךְ וִיסַדְתִּיךְ בַּסַּפִּירִים: וְשַׂמְתִּי כַּדְכֹד שִׁמְשֹׁתַיִךְ וּשְׁעָרַיִךְ לְאַבְנֵי
יג יד אֶקְדָּח וְכָל־גְּבוּלֵךְ לְאַבְנֵי־חֵפֶץ: וְכָל־בָּנַיִךְ לִמּוּדֵי יְהוָה וְרַב שְׁלוֹם בָּנָיִךְ: בִּצְדָקָה
טו תִּכּוֹנָנִי רַחֲקִי מֵעֹשֶׁק כִּי־לֹא תִירָאִי וּמִמְּחִתָּה כִּי לֹא־תִקְרַב אֵלָיִךְ: הֵן גּוֹר יָגוּר

16 who among you fears one who could come upon you? For I create the craftsman who
blows the charcoal fire and brings forth the tools of his trade; I create also the destroyer
17 to do harm. No weapon made to harm you can prevail; any tongue that calls you into
judgment, you will prove its fault. This is the birthright of the LORD's servants, for their
55 1 innocence is Mine; so says the LORD. You who are thirsty, all, come to water;
you who have no silver, come, take food and eat; come and take food without silver,
2 wine and milk without cost, for why should you weigh out your silver for no bread, your
labor bringing you no fullness? Listen – listen to Me: let goodness nourish you, and let
3 your souls delight in plenty. Turn your ear to Me and come; listen, that your souls may
4 live; let Me forge an everlasting covenant with you, like David's faithful promises, for I
5 make him a witness to nations, a leader, a ruler of nations; for you shall call out, call, to
a people you know not, and a people who know you not will come running out to you
for the sake of the LORD your God, the Holy One of Israel, your glory.

HAFTARAT LEKH LEKHA

40 27 Why do you say, Yaakov; Israel, why declare, "My way is hidden from the LORD; my ISAIAH
28 God overlooks my claim"? Do you not know this; have you not heard? The LORD is God
eternal, Creator of all horizons; He does not weary, does not tire; no one can plumb His
29 30 understanding. He gives the weary strength, the helpless, power: more and more. Youths
31 will tire, grow weary; young men will falter and fall, but those who wait for the LORD,
their strength will be renewed; they will rise on their wings like eagles, will run and never
41 1 grow weary, will walk on and never grow tired. Hush before Me, coastlands and
nations; renew your strength, and then come forward, speak, draw close; let us come
2 into judgment. Who roused the one from the eastand called victory to his feet? Who
herded nations before him, laid their kings low, and made his swords numerous as dust,
3 his bowshots like chaff in the wind? He pursued them and came through in peace on
4 paths that his feet never walked. Who was it who acted and did this, who called forth
generations long before? I, the LORD, am the first, and I shall be, I, with the last who
5 will be. Coastlands witness this and fear, earth's horizons witness, tremble, draw near,
6 come. Each man helps his fellow and tells his brother, "Be strong." 7"Strong," says the
wright to the goldsmith, the hammerman to him who beats. He says of the glue, "This
8 is good," and firms it up with nails, never to fall. And you, Israel, My servant,
9 Yaakov whom I chose, children of Avraham who loved Me, whom I lifted and brought
from the ends of the earth, calling you forth from its furthest corners, telling you: You
10 are My servant; You have I chosen, and I will not reject you; do not fear, for I am with
you; do not be afraid: I am your God; I strengthen you and help you, uphold you with
11 My right hand of righteousness. All who rage against you will be shamed, debased;
12 become like nothing, lost, all those who fight you. Look for them then – you will not

הַנֵּה ‏ ‏ ‏ ‏ ‏ ‏ ‏ אֶ֤פֶס מֵאוֹתַ֙י מִיגֻ֣ר אִתָּ֔ךְ עָלַ֣יִךְ יִפּ֑וֹל: הֵ֣ן אָנֹכִ֞י בָּרָ֣אתִי חָרָ֗שׁ נֹפֵ֙חַ֙ בְּאֵ֣שׁ פֶּחָ֔ם טז

וּמוֹצִ֥יא כְלִ֖י לְמַֽעֲשֵׂ֑הוּ וְאָֽנֹכִ֛י בָּרָ֥אתִי מַשְׁחִ֖ית לְחַבֵּֽל: כָּל־כְּלִ֞י יוּצַ֤ר עָלַ֙יִךְ֙ לֹ֣א יז

יִצְלָ֔ח וְכָל־לָשׁ֛וֹן תָּֽקוּם־אִתָּ֥ךְ לַמִּשְׁפָּ֖ט תַּרְשִׁ֑יעִי זֹ֡את נַֽחֲלַ֞ת עַבְדֵ֤י יהו֙ה וְצִדְקָתָ֣ם

מֵֽאִתִּ֖י נְאֻם־יהוֹה: ‏ ‏ ‏ ‏ ‏ ‏ הֽ֤וֹי כָּל־צָמֵ֙א֙ לְכ֣וּ לַמַּ֔יִם וַֽאֲשֶׁ֥ר אֵֽין־ל֖וֹ כָּ֑סֶף לְכ֤וּ נה א

שִׁבְר֣וּ וֶֽאֱכֹ֔לוּ וּלְכ֣וּ שִׁבְר֗וּ בְּלוֹא־כֶ֛סֶף וּבְל֥וֹא מְחִ֖יר יַ֥יִן וְחָלָֽב: לָ֤מָּה תִשְׁקְלוּ־כֶ֙סֶף֙ ב

בְּלוֹא־לֶ֔חֶם וִֽיגִֽיעֲכֶ֖ם בְּל֣וֹא לְשָׂבְעָ֑ה שִׁמְע֤וּ שָׁמ֙וֹעַ֙ אֵלַ֔י וְאִכְלוּ־ט֔וֹב וְתִתְעַנַּ֥ג

בַּדֶּ֖שֶׁן נַפְשְׁכֶֽם: הַטּ֤וּ אָזְנְכֶם֙ וּלְכ֣וּ אֵלַ֔י שִׁמְע֖וּ וּתְחִ֣י נַפְשְׁכֶ֑ם וְאֶכְרְתָ֤ה לָכֶם֙ בְּרִ֣ית ג

עוֹלָ֔ם חַסְדֵ֥י דָוִ֖ד הַנֶּֽאֱמָנִֽים: הֵ֛ן עֵ֥ד לְאוּמִּ֖ים נְתַתִּ֑יו נָגִ֥יד וּמְצַוֵּ֖ה לְאֻמִּֽים: הֵ֣ן גּ֤וֹי ד ה

לֹֽא־תֵדַע֙ תִּקְרָ֔א וְג֛וֹי לֹֽא־יְדָע֖וּךָ אֵלֶ֣יךָ יָר֑וּצוּ לְמַ֙עַן֙ יהו֣ה אֱלֹהֶ֔יךָ וְלִקְד֥וֹשׁ יִשְׂרָאֵ֖ל

כִּ֥י פֵֽאֲרָֽךְ:

הפטרת לך לך

‏ ‏ ‏ ‏ לָ֤מָּה תֹאמַר֙ יַֽעֲקֹ֔ב וּתְדַבֵּ֖ר יִשְׂרָאֵ֑ל נִסְתְּרָ֤ה דַרְכִּי֙ מֵֽיהו֔ה וּמֵֽאֱלֹהַ֖י מִשְׁפָּטִ֥י יַֽעֲבֽוֹר: מ כז

הֲל֨וֹא יָדַ֜עְתָּ אִם־לֹ֣א שָׁמַ֗עְתָּ אֱלֹהֵ֙י עוֹלָ֤ם ׀ יהוֹ֙ה בּוֹרֵא֙ קְצ֣וֹת הָאָ֔רֶץ לֹ֥א יִיעַ֖ף וְלֹ֣א כח

יִיגָ֑ע אֵ֥ין חֵ֖קֶר לִתְבֽוּנָתֽוֹ: נֹתֵ֥ן לַיָּעֵ֖ף כֹּ֑חַ וּלְאֵ֥ין אוֹנִ֖ים עָצְמָ֥ה יַרְבֶּֽה: וְיִֽעֲפ֥וּ נְעָרִ֖ים כט ל

וְיִגָ֑עוּ וּבַֽחוּרִ֖ים כָּשׁ֥וֹל יִכָּשֵֽׁלוּ: וְקוֹיֵ֤י יהוֹה֙ יַֽחֲלִ֣יפוּ כֹ֔חַ יַֽעֲל֥וּ אֵ֖בֶר כַּנְּשָׁרִ֑ים יָר֖וּצוּ וְלֹ֣א לא

יִיגָ֔עוּ יֵֽלְכ֖וּ וְלֹ֥א יִיעָֽפוּ: ‏ ‏ ‏ ‏ ‏ ‏ ‏ הַֽחֲרִ֤ישׁוּ אֵלַי֙ אִיִּ֔ים וּלְאֻמִּ֖ים יַֽחֲלִ֣יפוּ כֹ֑חַ יִגְּשׁוּ֙ אָ֣ז מא א

יְדַבֵּ֔רוּ יַחְדָּ֖ו לַמִּשְׁפָּ֥ט נִקְרָֽבָה: מִ֤י הֵעִיר֙ מִמִּזְרָ֔ח צֶ֖דֶק יִקְרָאֵ֣הוּ לְרַגְל֑וֹ יִתֵּ֣ן לְפָנָ֣יו ב

גּוֹיִ֗ם וּמְלָכִ֙ים֙ יַ֔רְדְּ יִתֵּ֤ן כֶּֽעָפָר֙ חַרְבּ֔וֹ כְּקַ֥שׁ נִדָּ֖ף קַשְׁתּֽוֹ: יִרְדְּפֵ֖ם יַֽעֲב֣וֹר שָׁל֑וֹם אֹ֥רַח ג

בְּרַגְלָ֖יו לֹ֥א יָבֽוֹא: מִֽי־פָעַ֣ל וְעָשָׂ֔ה קֹרֵ֥א הַדֹּר֖וֹת מֵרֹ֑אשׁ אֲנִ֤י יהוֹה֙ רִאשׁ֔וֹן וְאֶת־ ד

אַֽחֲרֹנִ֖ים אֲנִי־הֽוּא: רָא֤וּ אִיִּים֙ וְיִירָ֔אוּ קְצ֥וֹת הָאָ֖רֶץ יֶֽחֱרָ֑דוּ קָֽרְב֖וּ וַיֶּֽאֱתָיֽוּן: אִ֤ישׁ ה ו

אֶת־רֵעֵ֙הוּ֙ יַעְזֹ֔רוּ וּלְאָחִ֖יו יֹאמַ֥ר חֲזָֽק: וַיְחַזֵּ֤ק חָרָשׁ֙ אֶת־צֹרֵ֔ף מַֽחֲלִ֥יק פַּטִּ֖ישׁ אֶת־ ז

הוֹלֶ֣ם פָּ֑עַם אֹמֵ֤ר לַדֶּ֙בֶק֙ ט֣וֹב ה֔וּא וַיְחַזְּקֵ֥הוּ בְמַסְמְרִ֖ים לֹ֥א יִמּֽוֹט: ‏ ‏ ‏ ‏ ‏ וְאַתָּה֙ ח

יִשְׂרָאֵ֣ל עַבְדִּ֔י יַֽעֲקֹ֖ב אֲשֶׁ֣ר בְּחַרְתִּ֑יךָ זֶ֖רַע אַבְרָהָ֥ם אֹֽהֲבִֽי: אֲשֶׁ֤ר הֶֽחֱזַקְתִּ֙יךָ֙ מִקְצ֣וֹת ט

הָאָ֔רֶץ וּמֵֽאֲצִילֶ֖יהָ קְרָאתִ֑יךָ וָֽאֹ֤מַר לְךָ֙ עַבְדִּי־אַ֔תָּה בְּחַרְתִּ֖יךָ וְלֹ֥א מְאַסְתִּֽיךָ:

אַל־תִּירָא֙ כִּ֣י עִמְּךָ־אָ֔נִי אַל־תִּשְׁתָּ֖ע כִּֽי־אֲנִ֣י אֱלֹהֶ֑יךָ אִמַּצְתִּ֙יךָ֙ אַף־עֲזַרְתִּ֔יךָ אַ֨ף־ י

תְּמַכְתִּ֖יךָ בִּימִ֥ין צִדְקִֽי: הֵ֤ן יֵבֹ֙שׁוּ֙ וְיִכָּ֣לְמ֔וּ כֹּ֖ל הַנֶּֽחֱרִ֣ים בָּ֑ךְ יִֽהְי֥וּ כְאַ֖יִן וְיֹֽאבְד֖וּ יא

אַנְשֵׁ֥י רִיבֶֽךָ: תְּבַקְשֵׁם֙ וְלֹ֣א תִמְצָאֵ֔ם אַנְשֵׁ֖י מַצֻּתֶ֑ךָ יִֽהְי֥וּ כְאַ֛יִן וּכְאֶ֖פֶס אַנְשֵׁ֥י יב

13 find them – the men with whom you are wrestling, adversaries in war, like nothing, like
no more. For I am the LORD your God, holding your right hand, telling you: Do not fear,
14 for I am here: I help you. Yaakov: worm, men of Israel, do not fear; I will help
15 you, so speaks the LORD, the Holy One of Israel, your redeemer. You shall see: I have
made you a slotted threshing board, new and razor edged; you will thresh mountains,
16 turn them to powder, and hills into chaff. As you winnow, the wind will lift them, and
the storm will spread them far; you will rejoice in the LORD and will, through the Holy
One of Israel, be praised.

HAFTARAT VAYERA

II KINGS

4 1 A woman – the wife of one of the brotherhood of the prophets – cried out to Elisha,
"Your servant, my husband, is dead! You know that your servant always feared the LORD.
2 Now a creditor has come to take my two children away to be his slaves." "What can I
do for you?" said Elisha. "Tell me, what do you have in the house?" "Your servant has
3 nothing at all at home," she said, "except for a jar of oil." "Go out and borrow vessels from
4 all your neighbors," he said to her, "empty vessels – as many as you can. When you come
back in, close the door behind you and your sons. Then pour away into all those vessels,
5 setting them aside when they are full." And so she left him. When she closed the door
6 behind her and her sons, they kept bringing vessels to her while she kept pouring. When
the vessels were full, she said to her son, "Bring me another vessel," and he said to her,
7 "There are no more vessels" – and the oil stopped flowing. She came and told the man
of God, and he said, "Go, sell the oil and pay off your debt, and you and your sons can
8 live on the rest." One day, Elisha was passing through Shunem, and a wealthy
woman there urged him to have something to eat. So whenever he passed through, he
9 would stop there for some food. She said to her husband, "Look, I am sure that the
10 man who passes through here regularly is a holy man of God. Let us make him a small
enclosed upper chamber and provide him with a bed, table, chair, and lamp there, so that
11 whenever he comes to us, he can turn in there." One day, he came by; he turned in to the
12 upper chamber and lay down there. He said to Geḥazi, his servant, "Call the Shunamite
13 woman." He called her, and she stood before him. He said to him, "Please say to her,
'You have shown us so much concern. What can we do for you? Shall I speak to the king
on your behalf, or to the army commander?'" "I live among my own people," she said.
14 "Then what can be done for her?" he said. "Well, she is childless," said Geḥazi, "and her
15 16 husband is old." "Call her," he said, and he called her, and she stood in the entrance. "At
this time next year," he said, "you will be embracing a son." "No, my lord, man of God,"
17 she said. "Do not delude your servant." But the woman did conceive, and she bore a son

יג מִלְחַמְתֶּךָ: כִּי אֲנִי יְהוָה אֱלֹהֶיךָ מַחֲזִיק יְמִינֶךָ הָאֹמֵר לְךָ אַל־תִּירָא אֲנִי
יד עֲזַרְתִּיךָ: אַל־תִּירְאִי תּוֹלַעַת יַעֲקֹב מְתֵי יִשְׂרָאֵל אֲנִי עֲזַרְתִּיךְ
טו נְאֻם־יְהוָה וְגֹאֲלֵךְ קְדוֹשׁ יִשְׂרָאֵל: הִנֵּה שַׂמְתִּיךְ לְמוֹרַג חָרוּץ חָדָשׁ בַּעַל פִּיפִיּוֹת
טז תָּדוּשׁ הָרִים וְתָדֹק וּגְבָעוֹת כַּמֹּץ תָּשִׂים: תִּזְרֵם וְרוּחַ תִּשָּׂאֵם וּסְעָרָה תָּפִיץ אוֹתָם
וְאַתָּה תָּגִיל בַּיהוָה בִּקְדוֹשׁ יִשְׂרָאֵל תִּתְהַלָּל:

הפטרת וירא

ד א וְאִשָּׁה אַחַת מִנְּשֵׁי בְנֵי־הַנְּבִיאִים צָעֲקָה אֶל־אֱלִישָׁע לֵאמֹר עַבְדְּךָ אִישִׁי מֵת וְאַתָּה מלכים ב׳
יָדַעְתָּ כִּי עַבְדְּךָ הָיָה יָרֵא אֶת־יְהוָה וְהַנֹּשֶׁה בָּא לָקַחַת אֶת־שְׁנֵי יְלָדַי לוֹ לַעֲבָדִים:
ב וַיֹּאמֶר אֵלֶיהָ אֱלִישָׁע מָה אֶעֱשֶׂה־לָּךְ הַגִּידִי לִי מַה־יֶּשׁ־לכי בַּבָּיִת וַתֹּאמֶר אֵין לָךְ
ג לְשִׁפְחָתְךָ כֹל בַּבַּיִת כִּי אִם־אָסוּךְ שָׁמֶן: וַיֹּאמֶר לְכִי שַׁאֲלִי־לָךְ כֵּלִים מִן־הַחוּץ
ד מֵאֵת כָּל־שכניכי כֵּלִים רֵקִים אַל־תַּמְעִיטִי: וּבָאת וְסָגַרְתְּ הַדֶּלֶת בַּעֲדֵךְ וּבְעַד־בָּנַיִךְ שְׁכֵנָיִךְ
ה וְיָצַקְתְּ עַל כָּל־הַכֵּלִים הָאֵלֶּה וְהַמָּלֵא תַּסִּיעִי: וַתֵּלֶךְ מֵאִתּוֹ וַתִּסְגֹּר הַדֶּלֶת בַּעֲדָהּ
ו וּבְעַד בָּנֶיהָ הֵם מַגִּשִׁים אֵלֶיהָ וְהִיא מיצקת: וַיְהִי ׀ כִּמְלֹאת הַכֵּלִים וַתֹּאמֶר אֶל־ מוֹצָקֶת
ז בְּנָהּ הַגִּישָׁה אֵלַי עוֹד כֶּלִי וַיֹּאמֶר אֵלֶיהָ אֵין עוֹד כֶּלִי וַיַּעֲמֹד הַשָּׁמֶן: וַתָּבֹא וַתַּגֵּד
לְאִישׁ הָאֱלֹהִים וַיֹּאמֶר לְכִי מִכְרִי אֶת־הַשֶּׁמֶן וְשַׁלְּמִי אֶת־נשיכי וְאַתְּ בניכי תִּחְיִי נִשְׁיֵךְ | וּבָנַיִךְ
ח בַּנּוֹתָר: וַיְהִי הַיּוֹם וַיַּעֲבֹר אֱלִישָׁע אֶל־שׁוּנֵם וְשָׁם אִשָּׁה גְדוֹלָה וַתַּחֲזֶק־בּוֹ
ט לֶאֱכָל־לָחֶם וַיְהִי מִדֵּי עָבְרוֹ יָסֻר שָׁמָּה לֶאֱכָל־לָחֶם: וַתֹּאמֶר אֶל־אִישָׁהּ הִנֵּה־
י נָא יָדַעְתִּי כִּי אִישׁ אֱלֹהִים קָדוֹשׁ הוּא עֹבֵר עָלֵינוּ תָּמִיד: נַעֲשֶׂה־נָּא עֲלִיַּת־קִיר
קְטַנָּה וְנָשִׂים לוֹ שָׁם מִטָּה וְשֻׁלְחָן וְכִסֵּא וּמְנוֹרָה וְהָיָה בְּבֹאוֹ אֵלֵינוּ יָסוּר שָׁמָּה:
יא יב וַיְהִי הַיּוֹם וַיָּבֹא שָׁמָּה וַיָּסַר אֶל־הָעֲלִיָּה וַיִּשְׁכַּב־שָׁמָּה: וַיֹּאמֶר אֶל־גֵּיחֲזִי נַעֲרוֹ קְרָא
יג לַשּׁוּנַמִּית הַזֹּאת וַיִּקְרָא־לָהּ וַתַּעֲמֹד לְפָנָיו: וַיֹּאמֶר לוֹ אֱמָר־נָא אֵלֶיהָ הִנֵּה חָרַדְתְּ ׀
אֵלֵינוּ אֶת־כָּל־הַחֲרָדָה הַזֹּאת מֶה לַעֲשׂוֹת לָךְ הֲיֵשׁ לְדַבֶּר־לָךְ אֶל־הַמֶּלֶךְ אוֹ
יד אֶל־שַׂר הַצָּבָא וַתֹּאמֶר בְּתוֹךְ עַמִּי אָנֹכִי יֹשָׁבֶת: וַיֹּאמֶר וּמֶה לַעֲשׂוֹת לָהּ וַיֹּאמֶר
טו גֵּיחֲזִי אֲבָל בֵּן אֵין־לָהּ וְאִישָׁהּ זָקֵן: וַיֹּאמֶר קְרָא־לָהּ וַיִּקְרָא־לָהּ וַתַּעֲמֹד בַּפָּתַח:
טז וַיֹּאמֶר לַמּוֹעֵד הַזֶּה כָּעֵת חַיָּה אתי חֹבֶקֶת בֵּן וַתֹּאמֶר אַל־אֲדֹנִי אִישׁ הָאֱלֹהִים אַתְּ
יז אַל־תְּכַזֵּב בְּשִׁפְחָתֶךָ: וַתַּהַר הָאִשָּׁה וַתֵּלֶד בֵּן לַמּוֹעֵד הַזֶּה כָּעֵת חַיָּה אֲשֶׁר־דִּבֶּר

18 at that time during the following year, just as Elisha had promised her. The child grew
19 up. One day, he went out to his father, who was with the reapers. "My head! My head!"
20 he said to his father, who said to the servant, "Carry him to his mother." He carried him
over and brought him to his mother; he sat on her lap until noon, and then he died.
21 She went up and laid him on the man of God's bed, closed the door behind him, and
22 went out. Then she called to her husband. "Send me one of the servants and one of the
donkeys at once," she said. "I must rush over to the man of God and come right back."
23 "Why are you going to him today?" he said. "It is not the New Moon, nor the Sabbath."
24 "All is well," she said. She saddled the donkey and said to her servant, "Drive! Be off! Do *Sepharadim end here*
25 not stop riding on my account unless I tell you." She set out and reached the man of God
at Mount Carmel. When the man of God saw her in the distance, he said to Geḥazi, his
26 servant, "Look, there is that Shunamite woman. Run to meet her straightaway and say
to her, 'Are you well? Is your husband well? Is your child well?'" "All is well," she said.
27 But she came up to the man of God at the mountain and grasped his feet. Geḥazi came
forward to push her away, but the man of God said, "Leave her be, for she is bitter of
28 spirit, and the LORD has hidden this from me and did not tell me." "Did I ask my lord
29 for a son?" she said. "Did I not say, 'Do not lead me on?'" "Hitch up your tunic," Elisha
said to Geḥazi. "Take my staff in your hand, and set out. If you meet anyone, do not greet
them, and if anyone greets you, do not answer them. Place my staff on the boy's face."
30 "As the LORD lives, and by your own life," said the boy's mother, "I will not leave you."
31 So he followed straight behind her. Geḥazi went on ahead of them and placed the staff
on the boy's face, but there was no sound and no response. He went back to meet him
32 and told him, "The boy did not wake." Elisha entered the house, and there was the boy
33 laid out on his bed – dead. He entered and closed the door behind the two of them, and
34 he prayed to the LORD. Then he mounted the bed and lay on top of the boy; he placed
his mouth on his mouth and his eyes on his eyes and his palms on his palms, and he
35 bent down over him, and the child's body became warm. He went back down and paced
about the house, back and forth, then he climbed up and crouched down over him. And
36 the boy sneezed – seven times – and the boy opened his eyes. He called to Geḥazi and
said to him, "Call the Shunamite woman." He called her, and she came to him. "Pick up
37 your son," he said. And she came and fell at his feet and bowed to the ground. Then she
picked up her son and went out.

HAFTARAT ḤAYEI SARA

1 1 King David was old, advanced in years, and though they covered him with bedclothes, I KINGS
2 he never felt warm. His servants said to him, "Let a young virgin be sought out for our
lord the king, to wait upon the king and become his companion; when she lies in your

יח יט אֵלֶיהָ אֱלִישָׁע: וַיִּגְדַּל הַיָּלֶד וַיְהִי הַיּוֹם וַיֵּצֵא אֶל־אָבִיו אֶל־הַקֹּצְרִים: וַיֹּאמֶר אֶל־
כ אָבִיו רֹאשִׁי ׀ רֹאשִׁי וַיֹּאמֶר אֶל־הַנַּעַר שָׂאֵהוּ אֶל־אִמּוֹ: וַיִּשָּׂאֵהוּ וַיְבִיאֵהוּ אֶל־אִמּוֹ
כא וַיֵּשֶׁב עַל־בִּרְכֶּיהָ עַד־הַצָּהֳרַיִם וַיָּמֹת: וַתַּעַל וַתַּשְׁכִּבֵהוּ עַל־מִטַּת אִישׁ הָאֱלֹהִים
כב וַתִּסְגֹּר בַּעֲדוֹ וַתֵּצֵא: וַתִּקְרָא אֶל־אִישָׁהּ וַתֹּאמֶר שִׁלְחָה נָא לִי אֶחָד מִן־הַנְּעָרִים
כג וְאַחַת הָאֲתֹנוֹת וְאָרוּצָה עַד־אִישׁ הָאֱלֹהִים וְאָשׁוּבָה: וַיֹּאמֶר מַדּוּעַ אתי הלכתי אַתְּ הֹלֶכֶת
כד אֵלָיו הַיּוֹם לֹא־חֹדֶשׁ וְלֹא שַׁבָּת וַתֹּאמֶר שָׁלוֹם:* וַתַּחֲבֹשׁ הָאָתוֹן וַתֹּאמֶר אֶל־ *Sepharadim end here*
כה נַעֲרָהּ נְהַג וָלֵךְ אַל־תַּעֲצָר־לִי לִרְכֹּב כִּי אִם־אָמַרְתִּי לָךְ: וַתֵּלֶךְ וַתָּבוֹא אֶל־אִישׁ
הָאֱלֹהִים אֶל־הַר הַכַּרְמֶל וַיְהִי כִּרְאוֹת אִישׁ־הָאֱלֹהִים אֹתָהּ מִנֶּגֶד וַיֹּאמֶר אֶל־גֵּיחֲזִי
כו נַעֲרוֹ הִנֵּה הַשּׁוּנַמִּית הַלָּז: עַתָּה רוּץ־נָא לִקְרָאתָהּ וֶאֱמָר־לָהּ הֲשָׁלוֹם לָךְ הֲשָׁלוֹם
כז לְאִישֵׁךְ הֲשָׁלוֹם לַיָּלֶד וַתֹּאמֶר שָׁלוֹם: וַתָּבֹא אֶל־אִישׁ הָאֱלֹהִים אֶל־הָהָר וַתַּחֲזֵק
בְּרַגְלָיו וַיִּגַּשׁ גֵּיחֲזִי לְהָדְפָהּ וַיֹּאמֶר אִישׁ הָאֱלֹהִים הַרְפֵּה־לָהּ כִּי־נַפְשָׁהּ מָרָה־לָהּ
כח וַיהוָה הֶעְלִים מִמֶּנִּי וְלֹא הִגִּיד לִי: וַתֹּאמֶר הֲשָׁאַלְתִּי בֵן מֵאֵת אֲדֹנִי הֲלֹא אָמַרְתִּי
כט לֹא תַשְׁלֶה אֹתִי: וַיֹּאמֶר לְגֵיחֲזִי חֲגֹר מָתְנֶיךָ וְקַח מִשְׁעַנְתִּי בְיָדְךָ וָלֵךְ כִּי־תִמְצָא
אִישׁ לֹא תְבָרְכֶנּוּ וְכִי־יְבָרֶכְךָ אִישׁ לֹא תַעֲנֶנּוּ וְשַׂמְתָּ מִשְׁעַנְתִּי עַל־פְּנֵי הַנָּעַר:
ל לא וַתֹּאמֶר אֵם הַנַּעַר חַי־יְהוָה וְחֵי־נַפְשְׁךָ אִם־אֶעֶזְבֶךָּ וַיָּקָם וַיֵּלֶךְ אַחֲרֶיהָ: וְגֵחֲזִי עָבַר
לִפְנֵיהֶם וַיָּשֶׂם אֶת־הַמִּשְׁעֶנֶת עַל־פְּנֵי הַנַּעַר וְאֵין קוֹל וְאֵין קָשֶׁב וַיָּשָׁב לִקְרָאתוֹ
לב וַיַּגֶּד־לוֹ לֵאמֹר לֹא הֵקִיץ הַנָּעַר: וַיָּבֹא אֱלִישָׁע הַבָּיְתָה וְהִנֵּה הַנַּעַר מֵת מֻשְׁכָּב
לג לד עַל־מִטָּתוֹ: וַיָּבֹא וַיִּסְגֹּר הַדֶּלֶת בְּעַד שְׁנֵיהֶם וַיִּתְפַּלֵּל אֶל־יְהוָה: וַיַּעַל וַיִּשְׁכַּב
עַל־הַיֶּלֶד וַיָּשֶׂם פִּיו עַל־פִּיו וְעֵינָיו עַל־עֵינָיו וְכַפָּיו עַל־כַּפָּו וַיִּגְהַר עָלָיו וַיָּחָם בְּשַׂר
לה הַיָּלֶד: וַיָּשָׁב וַיֵּלֶךְ בַּבַּיִת אַחַת הֵנָּה וְאַחַת הֵנָּה וַיַּעַל וַיִּגְהַר עָלָיו וַיְזוֹרֵר הַנַּעַר עַד־
לו שֶׁבַע פְּעָמִים וַיִּפְקַח הַנַּעַר אֶת־עֵינָיו: וַיִּקְרָא אֶל־גֵּיחֲזִי וַיֹּאמֶר קְרָא אֶל־הַשֻּׁנַמִּית
לז הַזֹּאת וַיִּקְרָאֶהָ וַתָּבוֹא אֵלָיו וַיֹּאמֶר שְׂאִי בְנֵךְ: וַתָּבֹא וַתִּפֹּל עַל־רַגְלָיו וַתִּשְׁתַּחוּ
אָרְצָה וַתִּשָּׂא אֶת־בְּנָהּ וַתֵּצֵא:

הפטרת חיי שרה

מלכים א׳

א א ב וְהַמֶּלֶךְ דָּוִד זָקֵן בָּא בַּיָּמִים וַיְכַסֻּהוּ בַּבְּגָדִים וְלֹא יִחַם לוֹ: וַיֹּאמְרוּ לוֹ עֲבָדָיו
יְבַקְשׁוּ לַאדֹנִי הַמֶּלֶךְ נַעֲרָה בְתוּלָה וְעָמְדָה לִפְנֵי הַמֶּלֶךְ וּתְהִי־לוֹ סֹכֶנֶת וְשָׁכְבָה

3 embrace, our lord the king will feel warm." They searched throughout Israel's borders
4 for a beautiful girl, found Avishag the Shunamite, and brought her to the king. The girl
was most beautiful, and she became the king's companion and served him, but the
5 king was not intimate with her. Meanwhile, Adoniya son of Ḥagit promoted himself,
declaring, "I will become king," and he procured a chariot and riders and fifty men to
6 run before him. Now his father had never disciplined him, saying, "Why have you acted
7 like that?" He was born after Avshalom, and he too was devastatingly handsome. He
8 conspired with Yoav son of Tzeruya and Avyatar the priest, and they lent their support
to Adoniya. But Tzadok the priest, Benayahu son of Yehoyada, Natan the prophet,
9 Shimi and Rei, and David's warriors were not on Adoniyahu's side. Adoniyahu sacrificed
sheep, oxen, and fatlings by the Zoḥelet Stone near the Rogel Spring, and he invited all
10 his brothers – the king's sons – and all the men of Yehuda, the king's subjects. But he
11 did not invite the prophet Natan or Benayahu or the warriors, or his brother Shlomo.
And Natan said to Batsheva, Shlomo's mother, "Have you heard? Adoniyahu the son
12 of Ḥagit has become king without our lord David's knowledge. Come now, let me give
13 you advice – to save your own life and the life of your son Shlomo. Go to King David
at once and say to him, 'My lord the king, did you not swear to your handmaid, "Your
14 son Shlomo will rule after me, and he will sit on my throne"? Why, then, has Adoniyahu
become king?' And while you are still speaking there with the king, I will come in after
15 you and confirm your words." So Batsheva went to the king in the inner chamber – the
16 king had aged severely, and Avishag the Shunamite was tending to him – and Batsheva
17 bowed down low in homage to the king. "What is the matter?" asked the king. "My
lord," she said to him, "you swore by the Lord your God to your handmaid, 'Your son
18 Shlomo will rule after me, and he will sit on my throne.' But now, look – Adoniya has
19 become king – and you, my lord the king, did not even know! He has sacrificed a wealth
of oxen and fatlings and sheep and invited all the king's sons, the priest Avyatar, and the
20 army commander Yoav, but he did not invite your servant Shlomo. But all the eyes of
21 Israel look to you, my lord the king, to tell them who will succeed my lord the king on
his throne. Otherwise, when my lord the king lies with his ancestors, my son Shlomo
22 23 and I will be considered offenders." And as she was still speaking with the king, Natan
the prophet arrived. "Here is Natan the prophet," they announced to the king, and he
24 came before the king and bowed to him with his face to the ground. "My lord the king,"
25 said Natan, "Did you yourself say, 'Adoniyahu will be king after me, and he will sit on my
throne'? For he went down today and sacrificed a wealth of oxen, fatlings, and sheep and
invited all the king's sons, the army officers, and Avyatar the priest. And now they are
26 feasting before him and toasting him and declaring, 'Long live King Adoniyahu!' But
he did not invite me, your servant, or the priest Tzadok, or Benayahu son of Yehoyada,
27 or your servant Shlomo. Could it be that my lord the king has decided this without

ג בְחֵיקֶךָ וְחַם לַאדֹנִי הַמֶּלֶךְ: וַיְבַקְשׁוּ נַעֲרָה יָפָה בְּכֹל גְּבוּל יִשְׂרָאֵל וַיִּמְצְאוּ אֶת־
ד אֲבִישַׁג הַשּׁוּנַמִּית וַיָּבִאוּ אֹתָהּ לַמֶּלֶךְ: וְהַנַּעֲרָה יָפָה עַד־מְאֹד וַתְּהִי לַמֶּלֶךְ סֹכֶנֶת
ה וַתְּשָׁרְתֵהוּ וְהַמֶּלֶךְ לֹא יְדָעָהּ: וַאֲדֹנִיָּה בֶן־חַגִּית מִתְנַשֵּׂא לֵאמֹר אֲנִי אֶמְלֹךְ וַיַּעַשׂ
ו לוֹ רֶכֶב וּפָרָשִׁים וַחֲמִשִּׁים אִישׁ רָצִים לְפָנָיו: וְלֹא־עֲצָבוֹ אָבִיו מִיָּמָיו לֵאמֹר מַדּוּעַ
ז כָּכָה עָשִׂיתָ וְגַם־הוּא טוֹב־תֹּאַר מְאֹד וְאֹתוֹ יָלְדָה אַחֲרֵי אַבְשָׁלוֹם: וַיִּהְיוּ דְבָרָיו
ח עִם יוֹאָב בֶּן־צְרוּיָה וְעִם אֶבְיָתָר הַכֹּהֵן וַיַּעְזְרוּ אַחֲרֵי אֲדֹנִיָּה: וְצָדוֹק הַכֹּהֵן וּבְנָיָהוּ
בֶן־יְהוֹיָדָע וְנָתָן הַנָּבִיא וְשִׁמְעִי וְרֵעִי וְהַגִּבּוֹרִים אֲשֶׁר לְדָוִד לֹא הָיוּ עִם־אֲדֹנִיָּהוּ:
ט וַיִּזְבַּח אֲדֹנִיָּהוּ צֹאן וּבָקָר וּמְרִיא עִם אֶבֶן הַזֹּחֶלֶת אֲשֶׁר־אֵצֶל עֵין רֹגֵל וַיִּקְרָא אֶת־
י כָּל־אֶחָיו בְּנֵי הַמֶּלֶךְ וּלְכָל־אַנְשֵׁי יְהוּדָה עַבְדֵי הַמֶּלֶךְ: וְאֶת־נָתָן הַנָּבִיא וּבְנָיָהוּ
יא וְאֶת־הַגִּבּוֹרִים וְאֶת־שְׁלֹמֹה אָחִיו לֹא קָרָא: וַיֹּאמֶר נָתָן אֶל־בַּת־שֶׁבַע אֵם־שְׁלֹמֹה
יב לֵאמֹר הֲלוֹא שָׁמַעַתְּ כִּי מָלַךְ אֲדֹנִיָּהוּ בֶן־חַגִּית וַאֲדֹנֵינוּ דָוִד לֹא יָדָע: וְעַתָּה לְכִי
יג אִיעָצֵךְ נָא עֵצָה וּמַלְּטִי אֶת־נַפְשֵׁךְ וְאֶת־נֶפֶשׁ בְּנֵךְ שְׁלֹמֹה: לְכִי וּבֹאִי ׀ אֶל־הַמֶּלֶךְ
דָּוִד וְאָמַרְתְּ אֵלָיו הֲלֹא־אַתָּה אֲדֹנִי הַמֶּלֶךְ נִשְׁבַּעְתָּ לַאֲמָתְךָ לֵאמֹר כִּי־שְׁלֹמֹה
יד בְנֵךְ יִמְלֹךְ אַחֲרַי וְהוּא יֵשֵׁב עַל־כִּסְאִי וּמַדּוּעַ מָלַךְ אֲדֹנִיָּהוּ: הִנֵּה עוֹדָךְ מְדַבֶּרֶת
טו שָׁם עִם־הַמֶּלֶךְ וַאֲנִי אָבוֹא אַחֲרַיִךְ וּמִלֵּאתִי אֶת־דְּבָרָיִךְ: וַתָּבֹא בַת־שֶׁבַע אֶל־
טז הַמֶּלֶךְ הַחַדְרָה וְהַמֶּלֶךְ זָקֵן מְאֹד וַאֲבִישַׁג הַשּׁוּנַמִּית מְשָׁרַת אֶת־הַמֶּלֶךְ: וַתִּקֹּד
יז בַּת־שֶׁבַע וַתִּשְׁתַּחוּ לַמֶּלֶךְ וַיֹּאמֶר הַמֶּלֶךְ מַה־לָּךְ: וַתֹּאמֶר לוֹ אֲדֹנִי אַתָּה נִשְׁבַּעְתָּ
יח בַּיהוה אֱלֹהֶיךָ לַאֲמָתֶךָ כִּי־שְׁלֹמֹה בְנֵךְ יִמְלֹךְ אַחֲרָי וְהוּא יֵשֵׁב עַל־כִּסְאִי: וְעַתָּה
יט הִנֵּה אֲדֹנִיָּה מָלָךְ וְעַתָּה אֲדֹנִי הַמֶּלֶךְ לֹא יָדָעְתָּ: וַיִּזְבַּח שׁוֹר וּמְרִיא־וְצֹאן לָרֹב
וַיִּקְרָא לְכָל־בְּנֵי הַמֶּלֶךְ וּלְאֶבְיָתָר הַכֹּהֵן וּלְיֹאָב שַׂר הַצָּבָא וְלִשְׁלֹמֹה עַבְדְּךָ לֹא
כ קָרָא: וְאַתָּה אֲדֹנִי הַמֶּלֶךְ עֵינֵי כָל־יִשְׂרָאֵל עָלֶיךָ לְהַגִּיד לָהֶם מִי יֵשֵׁב עַל־כִּסֵּא
כא אֲדֹנִי־הַמֶּלֶךְ אַחֲרָיו: וְהָיָה כִּשְׁכַב אֲדֹנִי־הַמֶּלֶךְ עִם־אֲבֹתָיו וְהָיִיתִי אֲנִי וּבְנִי שְׁלֹמֹה
כב כג חַטָּאִים: וְהִנֵּה עוֹדֶנָּה מְדַבֶּרֶת עִם־הַמֶּלֶךְ וְנָתָן הַנָּבִיא בָּא: וַיַּגִּידוּ לַמֶּלֶךְ לֵאמֹר
כד הִנֵּה נָתָן הַנָּבִיא וַיָּבֹא לִפְנֵי הַמֶּלֶךְ וַיִּשְׁתַּחוּ לַמֶּלֶךְ עַל־אַפָּיו אָרְצָה: וַיֹּאמֶר נָתָן
כה אֲדֹנִי הַמֶּלֶךְ אַתָּה אָמַרְתָּ אֲדֹנִיָּהוּ יִמְלֹךְ אַחֲרָי וְהוּא יֵשֵׁב עַל־כִּסְאִי: כִּי ׀ יָרַד הַיּוֹם
וַיִּזְבַּח שׁוֹר וּמְרִיא־וְצֹאן לָרֹב וַיִּקְרָא לְכָל־בְּנֵי הַמֶּלֶךְ וּלְשָׂרֵי הַצָּבָא וּלְאֶבְיָתָר
כו הַכֹּהֵן וְהִנָּם אֹכְלִים וְשֹׁתִים לְפָנָיו וַיֹּאמְרוּ יְחִי הַמֶּלֶךְ אֲדֹנִיָּהוּ: וְלִי אֲנִי־עַבְדֶּךָ
כז וּלְצָדֹק הַכֹּהֵן וְלִבְנָיָהוּ בֶן־יְהוֹיָדָע וְלִשְׁלֹמֹה עַבְדְּךָ לֹא קָרָא: אִם מֵאֵת אֲדֹנִי
הַמֶּלֶךְ נִהְיָה הַדָּבָר הַזֶּה וְלֹא הוֹדַעְתָּ אֶת־עַבְדֶיךָ מִי יֵשֵׁב עַל־כִּסֵּא אֲדֹנִי־הַמֶּלֶךְ

עַבְדְּךָ

28 informing your servant who will succeed my lord the king on his throne?" "Summon
29 Batsheva to me," King David said in response, and she came before the king and stood in
the king's presence. And the king swore an oath. "As the Lord lives," he said, "who has
30 rescued me from every danger, what I swore to you by the Lord, God of Israel – that
Shlomo your son will rule after me, and that he will sit on my throne in my place – I
31 shall fulfill this very day." And Batsheva bowed her face to the ground in royal homage
and said, "May my lord, King David, live forever!"

HAFTARAT TOLEDOT

On erev Rosh Ḥodesh Kislev read the haftara on page 664.

1 1 2 An oracle: the word of the Lord to Israel through Malakhi. The Lord says, "I have MALACHI
loved you." But you say, "How have You loved us?" Is Esav not a brother to Yaakov? So
3 says the Lord: Yet I loved Yaakov and hated Esav, so I made his mountains desolate
4 and gave his inheritance over to desert jackals. Even should Edom say, "We have been
destroyed, but we will return and rebuild the ruins," says the Lord of Hosts, they will
build; I will destroy, and they will be called the territory of evil and the nation that
5 suffers the Lord's wrath forever. Your eyes will see this, and you will say, "The Lord is
6 great beyond the territory of Israel." A son honors his father, and a slave his master; if I
am a Father, where is My honor, and if I am the Master, where is My reverence? So says
the Lord of Hosts to you, the priests who scorn My name. Yet you say, "How have we
7 scorned Your name?" You offer defiled bread on My altar. Yet you say, "How have we
8 defiled You?" In saying the Lord's table is repugnant. When you offer a blind animal to
be sacrificed, is this no evil? And when you offer the lame and the sick, is this no evil?
Offer it if you will to your governor. Would he then accept you – let you lift your face to
9 him? So says the Lord of Hosts. Now, please, beseech God, and let Him be gracious to
us. This was in your hands – would He turn His face for any one of you? So says the Lord
10 of Hosts: O, who is there among you who would close the doors so that you might not
light My altar for naught? I have no desire for you, says the Lord of Hosts. I will accept
11 no offering from your hands. For from one end of the earth to the other, My name is
great among the nations. Incense is offered in My name, a pure offering everywhere,
12 for My name is great among the nations, says the Lord of Hosts. Yet you desecrate it
by saying that the Lord's table is defiled and its fruit too repugnant to be consumed.
13 You say, "O, how wearisome," and you snort at it says the Lord of Hosts. You bring
what is stolen, the Lord says, what is lame, what is ill; you bring this offering. Am I to
14 accept it from your hands? Cursed is the knave who has a ram in his flock but pledges
and sacrifices a damaged animal to the Lord. For I am a great King, says the Lord of
2 1 Hosts, and My name is revered among the nations. Now, this is your command, priests:
2 If you do not listen, if you do not take it to heart to honor My name, says the Lord of

כח אַחֲרָיו: וַיַּעַן הַמֶּלֶךְ דָּוִד וַיֹּאמֶר קִרְאוּ־לִי לְבַת־שָׁבַע וַתָּבֹא לִפְנֵי הַמֶּלֶךְ וַתַּעֲמֹד

כט לִפְנֵי הַמֶּלֶךְ: וַיִּשָּׁבַע הַמֶּלֶךְ וַיֹּאמַר חַי־יְהוָה אֲשֶׁר־פָּדָה אֶת־נַפְשִׁי מִכָּל־צָרָה:

ל כִּי כַּאֲשֶׁר נִשְׁבַּעְתִּי לָךְ בַּיהוָה אֱלֹהֵי יִשְׂרָאֵל לֵאמֹר כִּי־שְׁלֹמֹה בְנֵךְ יִמְלֹךְ אַחֲרַי

לא וְהוּא יֵשֵׁב עַל־כִּסְאִי תַּחְתָּי כִּי כֵּן אֶעֱשֶׂה הַיּוֹם הַזֶּה: וַתִּקֹּד בַּת־שֶׁבַע אַפַּיִם אֶרֶץ

וַתִּשְׁתַּחוּ לַמֶּלֶךְ וַתֹּאמֶר יְחִי אֲדֹנִי הַמֶּלֶךְ דָּוִד לְעֹלָם:

הפטרת תולדות

On ערב ראש חודש כסלו read the הפטרה on page 665.

א מַשָּׂא דְבַר־יְהוָה אֶל־יִשְׂרָאֵל בְּיַד מַלְאָכִי: אָהַבְתִּי אֶתְכֶם אָמַר יְהוָה וַאֲמַרְתֶּם   מלאכי
ב

ג בַּמָּה אֲהַבְתָּנוּ הֲלוֹא־אָח עֵשָׂו לְיַעֲקֹב נְאֻם־יְהוָה וָאֹהַב אֶת־יַעֲקֹב: וְאֶת־עֵשָׂו

ד שָׂנֵאתִי וָאָשִׂים אֶת־הָרָיו שְׁמָמָה וְאֶת־נַחֲלָתוֹ לְתַנּוֹת מִדְבָּר: כִּי־תֹאמַר אֱדוֹם

רֻשַּׁשְׁנוּ וְנָשׁוּב וְנִבְנֶה חֳרָבוֹת כֹּה אָמַר יְהוָה צְבָאוֹת הֵמָּה יִבְנוּ וַאֲנִי אֶהֱרוֹס וְקָרְאוּ

ה לָהֶם גְּבוּל רִשְׁעָה וְהָעָם אֲשֶׁר־זָעַם יְהוָה עַד־עוֹלָם: וְעֵינֵיכֶם תִּרְאֶינָה וְאַתֶּם

ו תֹּאמְרוּ יִגְדַּל יְהוָה מֵעַל לִגְבוּל יִשְׂרָאֵל: בֵּן יְכַבֵּד אָב וְעֶבֶד אֲדֹנָיו וְאִם־אָב אָנִי

אַיֵּה כְבוֹדִי וְאִם־אֲדוֹנִים אָנִי אַיֵּה מוֹרָאִי אָמַר ׀ יְהוָה צְבָאוֹת לָכֶם הַכֹּהֲנִים בּוֹזֵי

ז שְׁמִי וַאֲמַרְתֶּם בַּמֶּה בָזִינוּ אֶת־שְׁמֶךָ: מַגִּישִׁים עַל־מִזְבְּחִי לֶחֶם מְגֹאָל וַאֲמַרְתֶּם

ח בַּמֶּה גֵאַלְנוּךָ בֶּאֱמָרְכֶם שֻׁלְחַן יְהוָה נִבְזֶה הוּא: וְכִי־תַגִּשׁוּן עִוֵּר לִזְבֹּחַ אֵין רָע

וְכִי תַגִּישׁוּ פִּסֵּחַ וְחֹלֶה אֵין רָע הַקְרִיבֵהוּ נָא לְפֶחָתֶךָ הֲיִרְצְךָ אוֹ הֲיִשָּׂא פָנֶיךָ אָמַר

ט יְהוָה צְבָאוֹת: וְעַתָּה חַלּוּ־נָא פְנֵי־אֵל וִיחָנֵּנוּ מִיֶּדְכֶם הָיְתָה זֹּאת הֲיִשָּׂא מִכֶּם פָּנִים

י אָמַר יְהוָה צְבָאוֹת: מִי גַם־בָּכֶם וְיִסְגֹּר דְּלָתַיִם וְלֹא־תָאִירוּ מִזְבְּחִי חִנָּם אֵין־לִי

חֵפֶץ בָּכֶם אָמַר יְהוָה צְבָאוֹת וּמִנְחָה לֹא־אֶרְצֶה מִיֶּדְכֶם: כִּי מִמִּזְרַח־שֶׁמֶשׁ וְעַד־

יא מְבוֹאוֹ גָּדוֹל שְׁמִי בַּגּוֹיִם וּבְכָל־מָקוֹם מֻקְטָר מֻגָּשׁ לִשְׁמִי וּמִנְחָה טְהוֹרָה כִּי־גָדוֹל

יב שְׁמִי בַּגּוֹיִם אָמַר יְהוָה צְבָאוֹת: וְאַתֶּם מְחַלְּלִים אוֹתוֹ בֶּאֱמָרְכֶם שֻׁלְחַן אֲדֹנָי

יג מְגֹאָל הוּא וְנִיבוֹ נִבְזֶה אָכְלוֹ: וַאֲמַרְתֶּם הִנֵּה מַתְּלָאָה וְהִפַּחְתֶּם אוֹתוֹ אָמַר יְהוָה

צְבָאוֹת וַהֲבֵאתֶם גָּזוּל וְאֶת־הַפִּסֵּחַ וְאֶת־הַחוֹלֶה וַהֲבֵאתֶם אֶת־הַמִּנְחָה הַאֶרְצֶה

יד אוֹתָהּ מִיֶּדְכֶם אָמַר יְהוָה: וְאָרוּר נוֹכֵל וְיֵשׁ בְּעֶדְרוֹ זָכָר וְנֹדֵר וְזֹבֵחַ מָשְׁחָת לַאדֹנָי

ב א כִּי מֶלֶךְ גָּדוֹל אָנִי אָמַר יְהוָה צְבָאוֹת וּשְׁמִי נוֹרָא בַגּוֹיִם: וְעַתָּה אֲלֵיכֶם הַמִּצְוָה

ב הַזֹּאת הַכֹּהֲנִים: אִם־לֹא תִשְׁמְעוּ וְאִם־לֹא תָשִׂימוּ עַל־לֵב לָתֵת כָּבוֹד לִשְׁמִי אָמַר

Hosts, then I will set a curse on you, and I will curse your blessings – indeed, I have
3 cursed your blessing, for you do not take it to heart. I will drive away the crops because
of you, and I will scatter filth in your face, the filth of your holiday sacrifices, and you
4 will be carried away after it. And you will know that I sent you this command so that
5 My covenant may endure with Levi, says the Lord of Hosts. My covenant endures in
him – life and peace. I gave them to him so as to be revered. He revered Me and was in
6 awe of My name. True teaching was in his mouth, no sin from his lips; he walked with
7 Me in peace and uprightness and returned many from iniquity. For a priest's lips should
safeguard knowledge, and the people should seek teaching from his mouth, for he is a
messenger of the Lord of Hosts.

HAFTARAT VAYETZE

Sepharadim begin here

HOSEA

11 7 My people waver – whether to turn back to Me, although Israel is summoned upward,
8 they will not praise Him together. How can I relinquish you, Efrayim; hand you over,
Israel? How can I make you like Adma and treat you like Tzevoyim? My heart has turned
9 upon Me; My compassion has been kindled. No, I will not unleash My burning wrath,
I will not turn again to destroy Efrayim – for I am God, I am not a man; within you, My
10 holiness dwells; I will not enter the city with hatred. They will follow after the Lord;
11 He will roar like a lion. When He roars, His children will rush forth from the west. They
will be like a frightened bird coming out of Egypt, like a dove leaving the land of Assyria.
12 1 I will bring them to settle safely in their homes. So declares the Lord. Efrayim
besieges Me with lies, the House of Israel with deception, but Yehuda still walks with
2 God and remains faithful to the Holy One. Efrayim shepherds the wind; he chases the
east winds. Day and night he increases lies and ruin; he makes pacts with Assyria and
3 to Egypt bears oil. But also with Yehuda the Lord has a dispute: He will visit upon
4 Yaakov as he deserves, as befits his deeds – He will repay him. In the womb he grasped
5 his brother by the heel, and with all his strength he struggled with God. He struggled
with an angel and prevailed; he cried and pleaded with him; in Beit El He found him,
6 7 and there He spoke to us. But the Lord, God of Hosts, the Lord is His name. Now you,
too, return to your God, uphold compassion and justice, and long for your God forever
8 9 more. Still the merchant possesses false scales; he loves to exploit. Efrayim exclaims, "I
have become wealthy; I have found fortune from my own labors; in all the fruits of my
10 toil they will find neither sin nor iniquity." I am the Lord your God from the time you
11 were in the land of Egypt; once more I will settle you safely in tents as in days of old.I
have spoken by way of the prophets; I endowed them with many visions, and through
12 images I communicated with the prophets. As Gilad is rampant with iniquity, so too
they are empty and vain; in Gilgal they sacrifice oxen, and their altars too will become *Some end here*
13 like rocks piled high in furrows of the fields. Yaakov fled to the lands of Aram, and *Ashkenazim begin here*

יְהוָה צְבָאוֹת וְשִׁלַּחְתִּי בָכֶם אֶת־הַמְּאֵרָה וְאָרוֹתִי אֶת־בִּרְכוֹתֵיכֶם וְגַם אָרוֹתִיהָ
ג כִּי אֵינְכֶם שָׂמִים עַל־לֵב׃ הִנְנִי גֹעֵר לָכֶם אֶת־הַזֶּרַע וְזֵרִיתִי פֶרֶשׁ עַל־פְּנֵיכֶם פֶּרֶשׁ
ד חַגֵּיכֶם וְנָשָׂא אֶתְכֶם אֵלָיו׃ וִידַעְתֶּם כִּי שִׁלַּחְתִּי אֲלֵיכֶם אֵת הַמִּצְוָה הַזֹּאת לִהְיוֹת
ה בְּרִיתִי אֶת־לֵוִי אָמַר יְהוָה צְבָאוֹת׃ בְּרִיתִי ׀ הָיְתָה אִתּוֹ הַחַיִּים וְהַשָּׁלוֹם וָאֶתְּנֵם־לוֹ
ו מוֹרָא וַיִּירָאֵנִי וּמִפְּנֵי שְׁמִי נִחַת הוּא׃ תּוֹרַת אֱמֶת הָיְתָה בְּפִיהוּ וְעַוְלָה לֹא־נִמְצָא
ז בִשְׂפָתָיו בְּשָׁלוֹם וּבְמִישׁוֹר הָלַךְ אִתִּי וְרַבִּים הֵשִׁיב מֵעָוֺן׃ כִּי־שִׂפְתֵי כֹהֵן יִשְׁמְרוּ־
דַעַת וְתוֹרָה יְבַקְשׁוּ מִפִּיהוּ כִּי מַלְאַךְ יְהוָה־צְבָאוֹת הוּא׃

הפטרת ויצא

Sepharadim begin here
הושע

יא ז ח וְעַמִּי תְלוּאִים לִמְשׁוּבָתִי וְאֶל־עַל יִקְרָאֻהוּ יַחַד לֹא יְרוֹמֵם׃ אֵיךְ אֶתֶּנְךָ אֶפְרַיִם
אֲמַגֶּנְךָ יִשְׂרָאֵל אֵיךְ אֶתֶּנְךָ כְאַדְמָה אֲשִׂימְךָ כִּצְבֹאיִם נֶהְפַּךְ עָלַי לִבִּי יַחַד נִכְמְרוּ
ט נִחוּמָי׃ לֹא אֶעֱשֶׂה חֲרוֹן אַפִּי לֹא אָשׁוּב לְשַׁחֵת אֶפְרָיִם כִּי אֵל אָנֹכִי וְלֹא־אִישׁ
י בְּקִרְבְּךָ קָדוֹשׁ וְלֹא אָבוֹא בְּעִיר׃ אַחֲרֵי יְהוָה יֵלְכוּ כְּאַרְיֵה יִשְׁאָג כִּי־הוּא יִשְׁאַג
יא וְיֶחֶרְדוּ בָנִים מִיָּם׃ יֶחֶרְדוּ כְצִפּוֹר מִמִּצְרַיִם וּכְיוֹנָה מֵאֶרֶץ אַשּׁוּר וְהוֹשַׁבְתִּים
יב א עַל־בָּתֵּיהֶם נְאֻם־יְהוָה׃ סְבָבֻנִי בְכַחַשׁ אֶפְרַיִם וּבְמִרְמָה בֵּית יִשְׂרָאֵל
ב וִיהוּדָה עֹד רָד עִם־אֵל וְעִם־קְדוֹשִׁים נֶאֱמָן׃ אֶפְרַיִם רֹעֶה רוּחַ וְרֹדֵף קָדִים כָּל־
ג הַיּוֹם כָּזָב וָשֹׁד יַרְבֶּה וּבְרִית עִם־אַשּׁוּר יִכְרֹתוּ וְשֶׁמֶן לְמִצְרַיִם יוּבָל׃ וְרִיב לַיהוָה
ד עִם־יְהוּדָה וְלִפְקֹד עַל־יַעֲקֹב כִּדְרָכָיו כְּמַעֲלָלָיו יָשִׁיב לוֹ׃ בַּבֶּטֶן עָקַב אֶת־אָחִיו
ה וּבְאוֹנוֹ שָׂרָה אֶת־אֱלֹהִים׃ וַיָּשַׂר אֶל־מַלְאָךְ וַיֻּכָל בָּכָה וַיִּתְחַנֶּן־לוֹ בֵּית־אֵל
ו ז יִמְצָאֶנּוּ וְשָׁם יְדַבֵּר עִמָּנוּ׃ וַיהוָה אֱלֹהֵי הַצְּבָאוֹת יְהוָה זִכְרוֹ׃ וְאַתָּה בֵּאלֹהֶיךָ
ח תָשׁוּב חֶסֶד וּמִשְׁפָּט שְׁמֹר וְקַוֵּה אֶל־אֱלֹהֶיךָ תָּמִיד׃ כְּנַעַן בְּיָדוֹ מֹאזְנֵי מִרְמָה
ט לַעֲשֹׁק אָהֵב׃ וַיֹּאמֶר אֶפְרַיִם אַךְ עָשַׁרְתִּי מָצָאתִי אוֹן לִי כָּל־יְגִיעַי לֹא
י יִמְצְאוּ־לִי עָוֺן אֲשֶׁר־חֵטְא׃ וְאָנֹכִי יְהוָה אֱלֹהֶיךָ מֵאֶרֶץ מִצְרָיִם עֹד אוֹשִׁיבְךָ
יא בָאֳהָלִים כִּימֵי מוֹעֵד׃ וְדִבַּרְתִּי עַל־הַנְּבִיאִים וְאָנֹכִי חָזוֹן הִרְבֵּיתִי וּבְיַד הַנְּבִיאִים
יב אֲדַמֶּה׃ אִם־גִּלְעָד אָוֶן אַךְ־שָׁוְא הָיוּ בַּגִּלְגָּל שְׁוָרִים זִבֵּחוּ גַּם מִזְבְּחוֹתָם כְּגַלִּים
יג עַל תַּלְמֵי שָׂדָי׃ * וַיִּבְרַח יַעֲקֹב שְׂדֵה אֲרָם וַיַּעֲבֹד יִשְׂרָאֵל בְּאִשָּׁה וּבְאִשָּׁה שָׁמָר׃

Some end here
Ashkenazim begin here

14 Yisrael labored to acquire a bride; for a bride he kept sheep. With a prophet the LORD
15 brought Israel up out of Egypt, and with a prophet He kept watch over us. Efrayim has
provoked bitter anger; the guilt from the blood he shed will remain, and the Lord will
13 1 turn his scorn back upon him. So it was: when Efrayim spoke, they trembled in fear;
he was esteemed in Israel, but when found guilty of worshipping Baal, he was as dead.
2 Now their sinning goes on and on; they cast graven images from their silver, mold idols
as they understood, each entirely the craft of men; of them they say, "Men who offer
3 sacrifices must kiss calves." So they will dissolve like morning mist, like dew at daybreak
that swiftly fades. They will scatter like chaff from the threshing floor, like smoke from
4 the window. I am the LORD your God from the land of Egypt; you know no God other
5 than Me; no one can save you except for Me. I knew you, cared for you in the desert, in
6 the parched, bereft land. But when they grazed, they became sated and satisfied; their *Sepharadim end here*
7 hearts became haughty – then they forgot Me. Therefore l will be as a lion to them; as a
8 leopard I will watch, lurking on the path. I will fall upon them like a bear who mourns
her whelps and tear apart their sealed hearts; there I will consume them like a lion; wild
9 beasts will shred them to pieces. You have brought ruin upon yourself, Israel, for your
10 help is to be found in Me. I am your King, then who will save you in all your cities, and
11 what of your judges of whom you said, "Appoint me a king and officers"? In My rage I
12 gave you a king, and in My wrath I will take him away. The sinfulness of Efrayim
13 is tied together; his sins are stored away. Pangs of birth will overcome him, but he is not
14 a wise son, for when the moment of birth comes, he will break and not survive. I will
rescue them from Sheol; I will redeem them from the clutches of death. I shall be your
plague, O Death; I will be your destruction, O Sheol; any qualms will be concealed from
15 My eyes. For though he will flourish wildly among the reeds, an east wind will come; a
gust from the LORD will rise from the wilderness. His fountain will dry up; his spring
14 1 will parch; his enemy will plunder all of his treasures. Shomron will be held guilty, for
she has rebelled against her God; she will fall by the sword, her young smashed to pieces,
2 her women with child ripped apart. O Israel, return, go back to the LORD your
3 God, for you have stumbled in your own sinfulness. Take words of remorse with you and
return to the LORD; say to Him, "Forgive all of our sins; accept our goodness – instead
4 of calves we offer You our words of prayer. Assyria will not save us; no more will we ride
upon horses; never again will we say, 'You are our god' to the work of our hands, for only
5 in You will the orphan find mercy." I will mend their rebellion with gracious love, for I
6 have turned My anger away from them. I will be as dew to Israel; he will bloom like a
7 lily and set down roots as deep as the trees of Lebanon. His branches will spread wide;
8 his splendor will be as the olive tree, and his fragrance as the trees of Lebanon. They
who return will dwell beneath his shade; they will revive once again as grain and flower
9 like vines; their acclaim will linger as the scent of the wine of Lebanon. Efrayim will say,
"What need do I have of these idols?" And I will answer him; I will look after him. I will

יד וּבְנָבִ֗יא הֶעֱלָ֧ה יְהֹוָ֛ה אֶת־יִשְׂרָאֵ֖ל מִמִּצְרָ֑יִם וּבְנָבִ֖יא נִשְׁמָֽר׃ הִכְעִ֥יס אֶפְרַ֖יִם תַּמְרוּרִ֑ים

יג א וְדָמָיו֙ עָלָ֣יו יִטּ֔וֹשׁ וְחֶ֨רְפָּת֔וֹ יָשִׁ֥יב ל֖וֹ אֲדֹנָֽיו׃ כְּדַבֵּ֤ר אֶפְרַ֨יִם֙ רְתֵ֔ת נָשָׂ֥א ה֖וּא בְּיִשְׂרָאֵ֑ל

ב וַיֶּאְשַׁ֥ם בַּבַּ֖עַל וַיָּמֹֽת׃ וְעַתָּ֣ה ׀ יוֹסִ֣פוּ לַחֲטֹ֗א וַיַּֽעֲשׂ֣וּ לָהֶם֩ מַסֵּכָ֨ה מִכַּסְפָּ֜ם כִּתְבוּנָ֣ם

ג עֲצַבִּ֗ים מַעֲשֵׂ֤ה חָֽרָשִׁים֙ כֻּלֹּ֔ה לָהֶ֖ם הֵ֣ם אֹמְרִ֑ים זֹבְחֵ֣י אָדָ֔ם עֲגָלִ֖ים יִשָּׁקֽוּן׃ לָכֵ֗ן יִֽהְיוּ֙

ד כַּעֲנַן־בֹּ֔קֶר וְכַטַּ֖ל מַשְׁכִּ֣ים הֹלֵ֑ךְ כְּמֹץ֙ יְסֹעֵ֣ר מִגֹּ֔רֶן וּכְעָשָׁ֖ן מֵאֲרֻבָּֽה׃ וְאָנֹכִ֛י יְהֹוָ֥ה

ה אֱלֹהֶ֖יךָ מֵאֶ֣רֶץ מִצְרָ֑יִם וֵאלֹהִ֤ים זֽוּלָתִי֙ לֹ֣א תֵדָ֔ע וּמוֹשִׁ֖יעַ אַ֥יִן בִּלְתִּֽי׃ אֲנִ֥י יְדַעְתִּ֖יךָ

Sepharadim
end here

ו בַמִּדְבָּ֑ר בְּאֶ֖רֶץ תַּלְאֻבֽוֹת׃* כְּמַרְעִיתָם֙ וַיִּשְׂבָּ֔עוּ שָׂבְע֖וּ וַיָּ֣רׇם לִבָּ֑ם עַל־כֵּ֖ן שְׁכֵחֽוּנִי׃

ז וָאֱהִ֥י לָהֶ֖ם כְּמוֹ־שָׁ֑חַל כְּנָמֵ֖ר עַל־דֶּ֥רֶךְ אָשֽׁוּר׃ אֶפְגְּשֵׁם֙ כְּדֹ֣ב שַׁכּ֔וּל וְאֶקְרַ֖ע סְג֣וֹר

ח לִבָּ֑ם וְאֹכְלֵ֥ם שָׁם֙ כְּלָבִ֔יא חַיַּ֥ת הַשָּׂדֶ֖ה תְּבַקְּעֵֽם׃ שִֽׁחֶתְךָ֥ יִשְׂרָאֵ֖ל כִּי־בִ֥י בְעֶזְרֶֽךָ׃

ט אֱהִ֤י מַלְכְּךָ֙ אֵפ֔וֹא וְיוֹשִֽׁיעֲךָ֖ בְּכׇל־עָרֶ֑יךָ וְשֹׁ֣פְטֶ֔יךָ אֲשֶׁ֣ר אָמַ֔רְתָּ תְּנָה־לִּ֖י מֶ֥לֶךְ וְשָׂרִֽים׃

י אֶתֶּן־לְךָ֥ מֶ֙לֶךְ֙ בְּאַפִּ֔י וְאֶקַּ֖ח בְּעֶבְרָתִֽי׃ ‏‏‏‏‏‏‏‏‏ צָרוּר֙ עֲוֺ֣ן אֶפְרָ֔יִם צְפוּנָ֖ה חַטָּאתֽוֹ׃

יב יג חֶבְלֵ֥י יֽוֹלֵדָ֖ה יָבֹ֣אוּ ל֑וֹ הוּא־בֵן֙ לֹ֣א חָכָ֔ם כִּֽי־עֵ֥ת לֹֽא־יַעֲמֹ֖ד בְּמִשְׁבַּ֥ר בָּנִֽים׃ מִיַּ֤ד שְׁאוֹל֙

יד אֶפְדֵּ֔ם מִמָּ֖וֶת אֶגְאָלֵ֑ם אֱהִ֨י דְבָרֶ֜יךָ מָ֗וֶת אֱהִ֤י קׇֽטׇבְךָ֙ שְׁא֔וֹל נֹ֖חַם יִסָּתֵ֥ר מֵעֵינָֽי׃ כִּ֣י

טו ה֤וּא בֵּ֣ין אַחִים֙ יַפְרִ֔יא יָב֣וֹא קָדִ֗ים ר֤וּחַ יְהֹוָה֙ מִמִּדְבָּ֣ר עֹלֶ֔ה וְיֵב֣וֹשׁ מְקוֹר֔וֹ וְיֶחֱרַ֖ב

יד א מַעְיָנ֑וֹ ה֣וּא יִשְׁסֶ֔ה אוֹצַ֖ר כׇּל־כְּלִ֥י חֶמְדָּֽה׃ תֶּאְשַׁם֙ שֹׁ֣מְר֔וֹן כִּ֥י מָרְתָ֖ה בֵּאלֹהֶ֑יהָ בַּחֶ֣רֶב

ב יִפֹּ֔לוּ עֹלְלֵיהֶ֣ם יְרֻטָּ֔שׁוּ וְהָרִיּוֹתָ֖יו יְבֻקָּֽעוּ׃ ‏‏‏‏‏‏‏‏‏ שׁ֚וּבָה יִשְׂרָאֵ֔ל עַ֖ד יְהֹוָ֣ה אֱלֹהֶ֑יךָ

ג כִּ֥י כָשַׁ֖לְתָּ בַּעֲוֺנֶֽךָ׃ קְח֤וּ עִמָּכֶם֙ דְּבָרִ֔ים וְשׁ֖וּבוּ אֶל־יְהֹוָ֑ה אִמְר֣וּ אֵלָ֗יו כׇּל־תִּשָּׂ֤א

ד עָוֺן֙ וְקַח־ט֔וֹב וּֽנְשַׁלְּמָ֥ה פָרִ֖ים שְׂפָתֵֽינוּ׃ אַשּׁ֣וּר ׀ לֹ֣א יוֹשִׁיעֵ֗נוּ עַל־סוּס֙ לֹ֣א נִרְכָּ֔ב

ה וְלֹא־נֹ֧אמַר ע֛וֹד אֱלֹהֵ֖ינוּ לְמַעֲשֵׂ֣ה יָדֵ֑ינוּ אֲשֶׁר־בְּךָ֖ יְרֻחַ֥ם יָתֽוֹם׃ אֶרְפָּא֙ מְשׁ֣וּבָתָ֔ם

ו אֹהֲבֵ֖ם נְדָבָ֑ה כִּ֛י שָׁ֥ב אַפִּ֖י מִמֶּֽנּוּ׃ אֶהְיֶ֤ה כַטַּל֙ לְיִשְׂרָאֵ֔ל יִפְרַ֖ח כַּשּֽׁוֹשַׁנָּ֑ה וְיַ֥ךְ שׇׁרָשָׁ֖יו

ז כַּלְּבָנֽוֹן׃ יֵֽלְכוּ֙ יֹ֣נְקוֹתָ֔יו וִיהִ֥י כַזַּ֖יִת הוֹד֑וֹ וְרֵ֥יחַֽ ל֖וֹ כַּלְּבָנֽוֹן׃ יָשֻׁ֙בוּ֙ יֹשְׁבֵ֣י בְצִלּ֔וֹ יְחַיּ֥וּ דָגָ֖ן

ח וְיִפְרְח֣וּ כַגָּ֑פֶן זִכְר֖וֹ כְּיֵ֥ין לְבָנֽוֹן׃ אֶפְרַ֕יִם מַה־לִּ֥י ע֖וֹד לָעֲצַבִּ֑ים אֲנִ֥י עָנִ֖יתִי וַאֲשׁוּרֶ֑נּוּ

10 be as a cypress tree, lush and leafy; you will find in Me your source of fruit. He who is
wise will fathom these words; the insightful will grasp them, for the ways of the Lord
are just, and the righteous will walk in them, but sinners will stumble over them. *Some add*
2 26 You will eat, eat and be sated, and you will praise the name of the Lord, your God, JOEL
27 who has done wonders for you, for My nation will never be ashamed. You will know
that I am among Israel, and I am the Lord, your God; there is no other. My nation will
never be ashamed.

HAFTARAT VAYISHLAḤ

1 1 This is Ovadya's vision: So says the Lord God to Edom – we have heard tidings from OBADIAH
the Lord: and an envoy has been sent among the nations, "Come, let us rise up in battle
2 against her." Look, I have made you small among nations; you are utterly scorned. The
3 arrogance of your heart deceived you, you who dwell in the cliff's niches, your lofty
4 abode, saying in your heart, "Who could bring me down to earth?" But even if you rise
as high as an eagle, if you make your nest among the stars, I shall bring you down from
5 there, declares the Lord. If thieves come upon you, bandits in the night, do they not
6 take only their fill? If grape gatherers come upon you, do they not leave gleanings? Yet
7 how has Esav been ransacked, his hidden treasures laid bare. Your allies all have forced
you to the borders; those with whom you had made peace all deceived you, defeated
you. Those with whom you broke your bread laid a snare for you, bereft of awareness.
8 Behold, on that day, says the Lord, I will purge Edom of wise men, the mountains of
9 Esav of awareness. Your warriors will be frightened, Teiman, for the mountains of Esav
10 will be unmanned by slaughter. For the violence you wrought against your brother
11 Yaakov shame will cover you, and you will be cut off forever. The day you stood aside,
the day strangers took captive his forces, and foreigners entered his gates, casting lots for
12 Jerusalem – you too were like one of them. Do not gloat over the day of your brother's
destruction, the day he becomes a stranger. Do not rejoice over the children of Yehuda
13 on the day of their destruction. Do not open your mouth on the day of trouble. Do not
enter My people's gate on the day of their ruin. Do not gloat over its misfortune on the
14 day of its ruin. Do not extend your hands to take its wealth on the day of his ruin. Do
not stand at the crossroads to cut down his refugees. Do not surrender his survivors on
15 the day of trouble. For the day of the Lord draws near for all the nations. What you
have done shall be done to you; what you have wrought will return upon your head.
16 What you drank on My holy mountain, all the nations will always drink. They will drink
17 and they will swallow, and they will be as if they never were. There will be a remnant on
Mount Zion, and it will be holy, and the House of Yaakov will possess their inheritance.
18 The House of Yaakov will be fire, the House of Yosef, flame; the House of Esav, straw.

י אֲנִי כִּבְרוֹשׁ רַעֲנָן מִמֶּנִּי פֶּרְיְךָ נִמְצָא: מִי חָכָם וְיָבֵן אֵלֶּה נָבוֹן וְיֵדָעֵם כִּי־יְשָׁרִים
דַּרְכֵי יהוה וְצַדִּקִים יֵלְכוּ בָם וּפֹשְׁעִים יִכָּשְׁלוּ בָם:

Some add יואל

ב כו וַאֲכַלְתֶּם אָכוֹל וְשָׂבוֹעַ וְהִלַּלְתֶּם אֶת־שֵׁם יהוה אֱלֹהֵיכֶם אֲשֶׁר־עָשָׂה עִמָּכֶם
כז לְהַפְלִיא וְלֹא־יֵבֹשׁוּ עַמִּי לְעוֹלָם: וִידַעְתֶּם כִּי בְקֶרֶב יִשְׂרָאֵל אָנִי וַאֲנִי יהוה אֱלֹהֵיכֶם
וְאֵין עוֹד וְלֹא־יֵבֹשׁוּ עַמִּי לְעוֹלָם:

הפטרת וישלח

עובדיה

א א חֲזוֹן עֹבַדְיָה כֹּה־אָמַר אֲדֹנָי יֱהֹוִה לֶאֱדוֹם שְׁמוּעָה שָׁמַעְנוּ מֵאֵת יהוה וְצִיר בַּגּוֹיִם
ב שֻׁלָּח קוּמוּ וְנָקוּמָה עָלֶיהָ לַמִּלְחָמָה: הִנֵּה קָטֹן נְתַתִּיךָ בַּגּוֹיִם בָּזוּי אַתָּה מְאֹד:
ג זְדוֹן לִבְּךָ הִשִּׁיאֶךָ שֹׁכְנִי בְחַגְוֵי־סֶלַע מְרוֹם שִׁבְתּוֹ אֹמֵר בְּלִבּוֹ מִי יוֹרִדֵנִי אָרֶץ:
ד ה אִם־תַּגְבִּיהַּ כַּנֶּשֶׁר וְאִם־בֵּין כּוֹכָבִים שִׂים קִנֶּךָ מִשָּׁם אוֹרִידְךָ נְאֻם־יהוה: אִם־
גַּנָּבִים בָּאוּ־לְךָ אִם־שׁוֹדְדֵי לַיְלָה אֵיךְ נִדְמֵיתָה הֲלוֹא יִגְנְבוּ דַּיָּם אִם־בֹּצְרִים בָּאוּ
ו ז לָךְ הֲלוֹא יַשְׁאִירוּ עֹלֵלוֹת: אֵיךְ נֶחְפְּשׂוּ עֵשָׂו נִבְעוּ מַצְפֻּנָיו: עַד־הַגְּבוּל שִׁלְּחוּךָ
כֹּל אַנְשֵׁי בְרִיתֶךָ הִשִּׁיאוּךָ יָכְלוּ לְךָ אַנְשֵׁי שְׁלֹמֶךָ לַחְמְךָ יָשִׂימוּ מָזוֹר תַּחְתֶּיךָ אֵין
ח תְּבוּנָה בּוֹ: הֲלוֹא בַּיּוֹם הַהוּא נְאֻם־יהוה וְהַאֲבַדְתִּי חֲכָמִים מֵאֱדוֹם וּתְבוּנָה מֵהַר
ט י עֵשָׂו: וְחַתּוּ גִבּוֹרֶיךָ תֵּימָן לְמַעַן יִכָּרֶת־אִישׁ מֵהַר עֵשָׂו מִקָּטֶל: מֵחֲמַס אָחִיךָ יַעֲקֹב
יא תְּכַסְּךָ בוּשָׁה וְנִכְרַתָּ לְעוֹלָם: בְּיוֹם עֲמָדְךָ מִנֶּגֶד בְּיוֹם שְׁבוֹת זָרִים חֵילוֹ וְנָכְרִים
יב בָּאוּ שְׁעָרָו וְעַל־יְרוּשָׁלִַם יַדּוּ גוֹרָל גַּם־אַתָּה כְּאַחַד מֵהֶם: וְאַל־תֵּרֶא בְיוֹם־אָחִיךָ
בְּיוֹם נָכְרוֹ וְאַל־תִּשְׂמַח לִבְנֵי־יְהוּדָה בְּיוֹם אָבְדָם וְאַל־תַּגְדֵּל פִּיךָ בְּיוֹם צָרָה:
יג אַל־תָּבוֹא בְשַׁעַר־עַמִּי בְּיוֹם אֵידָם אַל־תֵּרֶא גַם־אַתָּה בְּרָעָתוֹ בְּיוֹם אֵידוֹ וְאַל־
יד תִּשְׁלַחְנָה בְחֵילוֹ בְּיוֹם אֵידוֹ: וְאַל־תַּעֲמֹד עַל־הַפֶּרֶק לְהַכְרִית אֶת־פְּלִיטָיו וְאַל־
טו תַּסְגֵּר שְׂרִידָיו בְּיוֹם צָרָה: כִּי־קָרוֹב יוֹם־יהוה עַל־כָּל־הַגּוֹיִם כַּאֲשֶׁר עָשִׂיתָ יֵעָשֶׂה
טז לָּךְ גְּמֻלְךָ יָשׁוּב בְּרֹאשֶׁךָ: כִּי כַּאֲשֶׁר שְׁתִיתֶם עַל־הַר קָדְשִׁי יִשְׁתּוּ כָל־הַגּוֹיִם תָּמִיד
יז וְשָׁתוּ וְלָעוּ וְהָיוּ כְּלוֹא הָיוּ: וּבְהַר צִיּוֹן תִּהְיֶה פְלֵיטָה וְהָיָה קֹדֶשׁ וְיָרְשׁוּ בֵּית יַעֲקֹב
יח אֵת מוֹרָשֵׁיהֶם: וְהָיָה בֵית־יַעֲקֹב אֵשׁ וּבֵית יוֹסֵף לֶהָבָה וּבֵית עֵשָׂו לְקַשׁ וְדָלְקוּ

They will blaze among them and consume them, and there will be no survivors of the
19 House of Esav, for the LORD has spoken. They will take possession of the Negev, along
with the mountains of Esav, and the Shefela, from the Philistines. And they will take
possession of the land of Efrayim and the land of Shomron; and Binyamin, along with
20 the Gilad – they, the exiled force of the children of Israel who are among the Canaanites
as far as Tzarfat and the exiled of Jerusalem who are in Sepharad will take possession of
21 the cities of the Negev. And saviors shall go up to Mount Zion to judge the mountains
of Esav, and dominion shall be the LORD's.

HAFTARAT VAYESHEV

On Ḥanukka read the haftara on page 674.

AMOS

2 6 So says the LORD: On account of Israel's three crimes and on account of the fourth, I
will not forgive them. They sold the righteous for silver and the poor for the price of
7 shoes. They are those who trample the dust of the earth atop the heads of the poor;
they turn the humble away from the path. A man and his father visit the same girl to
8 desecrate My holy name. They spread confiscated clothing beside every altar and drink
9 wine bought with fines in the house of their gods. But I had destroyed before them the
Amorite, whose height was as tall as cedars and whose strength was like that of oaks. Yet
10 I obliterated their fruit above and their roots below. I brought you up from the land of
11 Egypt and led you in the desert for forty years to inherit Amorite lands. I raised up into
prophets some of your sons and into nazirites some of your young men. Is this not so,
12 children of Israel? said the LORD. But you made the nazirites drink wine and ordered
13 the prophets not to prophesy. Behold, I will hold you back in your place, as a wagon
14 loaded with sheaves is held back. The swift will lose the ability to flee; the strong will
15 not gather their strength; the warrior will not escape with his life. The bowman will
not stand; the fleet of foot will not escape; the horse rider will not escape with his life.
16 He who considers himself strongest among warriors will flee naked on that day, says
3 1 the LORD. Hear this word, which the LORD has spoken about you, children
2 of Israel: About the whole family I brought up from the land of Egypt, it is only you
that I have known from among all the families on earth, so I will visit all your sins upon
3 4 you. Would two walk together if they had not met? Would a lion roar in the forest if it
had not caught prey? Would a young lion raise its voice from its den if it had not seized
5 prey? Would a bird plunge into a trap on the ground if it were not baited? Would the
6 trap spring up from the earth if it had not trapped quarry? Would a warning horn blow
in the city and the people not be afraid? Would disaster come upon the city were it not
7 an act of the LORD? The Lord GOD does not do anything without revealing His secret
8 to His servants, the prophets. A lion roars; who would not fear? The Lord GOD speaks;
who would not prophesy?

יט בָּהֶם וְאָכָלוּם וְלֹא־יִהְיֶה שָׂרִיד לְבֵית עֵשָׂו כִּי יְהוָה דִּבֵּר׃ וְיָרְשׁוּ הַנֶּגֶב אֶת־הַר עֵשָׂו
וְהַשְּׁפֵלָה אֶת־פְּלִשְׁתִּים וְיָרְשׁוּ אֶת־שְׂדֵה אֶפְרַיִם וְאֵת שְׂדֵה שֹׁמְרוֹן וּבִנְיָמִן אֶת־
כ הַגִּלְעָד׃ וְגָלֻת הַחֵל־הַזֶּה לִבְנֵי יִשְׂרָאֵל אֲשֶׁר־כְּנַעֲנִים עַד־צָרְפַת וְגָלֻת יְרוּשָׁלִַם
כא אֲשֶׁר בִּסְפָרַד יִרְשׁוּ אֵת עָרֵי הַנֶּגֶב׃ וְעָלוּ מוֹשִׁעִים בְּהַר צִיּוֹן לִשְׁפֹּט אֶת־הַר עֵשָׂו
וְהָיְתָה לַיהוָה הַמְּלוּכָה׃

הפטרת וישב

On חנוכה *read the* הפטרה *on page 675.*

עמוס

ב ו כֹּה אָמַר יְהוָה עַל־שְׁלֹשָׁה פִּשְׁעֵי יִשְׂרָאֵל וְעַל־אַרְבָּעָה לֹא אֲשִׁיבֶנּוּ עַל־מִכְרָם
ז בַכֶּסֶף צַדִּיק וְאֶבְיוֹן בַּעֲבוּר נַעֲלָיִם׃ הַשֹּׁאֲפִים עַל־עֲפַר־אֶרֶץ בְּרֹאשׁ דַּלִּים
וְדֶרֶךְ עֲנָוִים יַטּוּ וְאִישׁ וְאָבִיו יֵלְכוּ אֶל־הַנַּעֲרָה לְמַעַן חַלֵּל אֶת־שֵׁם קָדְשִׁי׃
ח ט וְעַל־בְּגָדִים חֲבֻלִים יַטּוּ אֵצֶל כָּל־מִזְבֵּחַ וְיֵין עֲנוּשִׁים יִשְׁתּוּ בֵּית אֱלֹהֵיהֶם׃ וְאָנֹכִי
הִשְׁמַדְתִּי אֶת־הָאֱמֹרִי מִפְּנֵיהֶם אֲשֶׁר כְּגֹבַהּ אֲרָזִים גָּבְהוֹ וְחָסֹן הוּא כָּאַלּוֹנִים
י וָאַשְׁמִיד פִּרְיוֹ מִמַּעַל וְשָׁרָשָׁיו מִתָּחַת׃ וְאָנֹכִי הֶעֱלֵיתִי אֶתְכֶם מֵאֶרֶץ מִצְרָיִם
יא וָאוֹלֵךְ אֶתְכֶם בַּמִּדְבָּר אַרְבָּעִים שָׁנָה לָרֶשֶׁת אֶת־אֶרֶץ הָאֱמֹרִי׃ וָאָקִים מִבְּנֵיכֶם
יב לִנְבִיאִים וּמִבַּחוּרֵיכֶם לִנְזִרִים הַאַף אֵין־זֹאת בְּנֵי יִשְׂרָאֵל נְאֻם־יְהוָה׃ וַתַּשְׁקוּ אֶת־
יג הַנְּזִרִים יָיִן וְעַל־הַנְּבִיאִים צִוִּיתֶם לֵאמֹר לֹא תִּנָּבְאוּ׃ הִנֵּה אָנֹכִי מֵעִיק תַּחְתֵּיכֶם
יד כַּאֲשֶׁר תָּעִיק הָעֲגָלָה הַמְלֵאָה לָהּ עָמִיר׃ וְאָבַד מָנוֹס מִקָּל וְחָזָק לֹא־יְאַמֵּץ
טו כֹּחוֹ וְגִבּוֹר לֹא־יְמַלֵּט נַפְשׁוֹ׃ וְתֹפֵשׂ הַקֶּשֶׁת לֹא יַעֲמֹד וְקַל בְּרַגְלָיו לֹא יְמַלֵּט
טז וְרֹכֵב הַסּוּס לֹא יְמַלֵּט נַפְשׁוֹ׃ וְאַמִּיץ לִבּוֹ בַּגִּבּוֹרִים עָרוֹם יָנוּס בַּיּוֹם־הַהוּא נְאֻם־
ג א יְהוָה׃ שִׁמְעוּ אֶת־הַדָּבָר הַזֶּה אֲשֶׁר דִּבֶּר יְהוָה עֲלֵיכֶם בְּנֵי יִשְׂרָאֵל
ב עַל כָּל־הַמִּשְׁפָּחָה אֲשֶׁר הֶעֱלֵיתִי מֵאֶרֶץ מִצְרַיִם לֵאמֹר׃ רַק אֶתְכֶם יָדַעְתִּי מִכֹּל
ג מִשְׁפְּחוֹת הָאֲדָמָה עַל־כֵּן אֶפְקֹד עֲלֵיכֶם אֵת כָּל־עֲוֺנֹתֵיכֶם׃ הֲיֵלְכוּ שְׁנַיִם יַחְדָּו בִּלְתִּי
ד אִם־נוֹעָדוּ׃ הֲיִשְׁאַג אַרְיֵה בַּיַּעַר וְטֶרֶף אֵין לוֹ הֲיִתֵּן כְּפִיר קוֹלוֹ מִמְּעֹנָתוֹ בִּלְתִּי אִם־
ה לָכָד׃ הֲתִפֹּל צִפּוֹר עַל־פַּח הָאָרֶץ וּמוֹקֵשׁ אֵין לָהּ הֲיַעֲלֶה־פַּח מִן־הָאֲדָמָה וְלָכוֹד
ו לֹא יִלְכּוֹד׃ אִם־יִתָּקַע שׁוֹפָר בְּעִיר וְעָם לֹא יֶחֱרָדוּ אִם־תִּהְיֶה רָעָה בְּעִיר וַיהוָה
ז לֹא עָשָׂה׃ כִּי לֹא יַעֲשֶׂה אֲדֹנָי יְהוִה דָּבָר כִּי אִם־גָּלָה סוֹדוֹ אֶל־עֲבָדָיו הַנְּבִיאִים׃
ח אַרְיֵה שָׁאָג מִי לֹא יִירָא אֲדֹנָי יְהוִה דִּבֶּר מִי לֹא יִנָּבֵא׃

HAFTARAT MIKETZ

On Ḥanukka read the haftara on page 674 (even on Rosh Ḥodesh or erev Rosh Ḥodesh Tevet).
On the second Shabbat of Ḥanukka read the haftara on page 676.

I KINGS

3 15 Then Shlomo awoke – it had all been a dream! When he came to Jerusalem, he stood
before the Ark of the Lord's Covenant and offered up burnt offerings and presented
16 peace offerings, and he held a feast for all his servants. Then two harlot women
17 came before the king and stood before him. "If you please, my lord," said the first woman,
18 "this woman and I live in one house, and I gave birth while she was in the house. On the
third day after I gave birth, this woman also gave birth. The two of us live together – there
19 was no one else in the house besides us, just the two of us in the house. The son of this
20 woman died in the night, for she lay on him. But she got up during the night and took
my own son from me while your handmaid was sleeping and lay down with him in her
21 embrace, and laid her own dead son in my embrace. I woke up in the morning to nurse
my son to find that he was dead! But when I looked at him closely in the morning,
22 why – it wasn't my own son, the one I had borne!" "No!" said the other woman. "My
son is the one who is alive, and your son is the one who died!" "No," she said, "your son
23 is dead, and my son is alive!" and they continued arguing before the king. "This one
says, 'This is my son, who is alive, and your son is dead,'" said the king, "and this one
24 says, 'No, your son is dead, and my son is alive.'" And the king said, "Fetch me
25 a sword," and they brought a sword before the king. "Cut the living child into two," the
26 king declared, "and give half to one and half to the other." But the woman whose son was
alive spoke up, for she burned with compassion for her son. "Please, my lord," she said,
"give her the living child; do anything but kill him!" while the other one said, "Neither
27 of us will have him – cut him up." And the king spoke up. "Give her the living child," he
28 said, "and make no move to kill him. She is his mother." When all of Israel heard about
the case that the king had judged, they held the king in awe, for they saw that divine
4 1 wisdom was within him to do justice. King Shlomo was king of all Israel.

HAFTARAT VAYIGASH

EZEKIEL

37 15 16 The word of the LORD came to me, saying: "And you, Man, take a branch and write on
it, 'For Yehuda and the children of Israel associated with him.' Then take one branch and
write on it, 'For Yosef – the branch of Efrayim – and all of the House of Israel associated
17 with him.' Bring them together to make one branch, so that they are one in your hand.
18 19 When your people say to you, 'Tell us, what do these mean to you?' say to them: So
says the Lord GOD: See, I am going to take the branch of Yosef, which is in the hand
of Efrayim, and the tribes of Israel who are associated with him, and join them with
him, with the branch of Yehuda; I will make them into one branch, and they will be

הפטרת מקץ

On חנוכה read the הפטרה on page 675 (even on ראש חודש טבת or ערב ראש חודש טבת).
On the second שבת of חנוכה read the הפטרה on page 677.

מלכים א׳

וַיִּקַץ שְׁלֹמֹה וְהִנֵּה חֲלוֹם וַיָּבוֹא יְרוּשָׁלַ͏ִם וַיַּעֲמֹד ׀ לִפְנֵי ׀ אֲרוֹן בְּרִית־אֲדֹנָי וַיַּעַל עֹלוֹת ﬞﬞ טו

וַיַּעַשׂ שְׁלָמִים וַיַּעַשׂ מִשְׁתֶּה לְכָל־עֲבָדָיו: אָז תָּבֹאנָה שְׁתַּיִם נָשִׁים טז

זֹנוֹת אֶל־הַמֶּלֶךְ וַתַּעֲמֹדְנָה לְפָנָיו: וַתֹּאמֶר הָאִשָּׁה הָאַחַת בִּי אֲדֹנִי אֲנִי וְהָאִשָּׁה יז

הַזֹּאת יֹשְׁבֹת בְּבַיִת אֶחָד וָאֵלֵד עִמָּהּ בַּבָּיִת: וַיְהִי בַּיּוֹם הַשְּׁלִישִׁי לְלִדְתִּי וַתֵּלֶד יח

גַּם־הָאִשָּׁה הַזֹּאת וַאֲנַחְנוּ יַחְדָּו אֵין־זָר אִתָּנוּ בַּבַּיִת זוּלָתִי שְׁתַּיִם־אֲנַחְנוּ בַּבָּיִת:

וַיָּמָת בֶּן־הָאִשָּׁה הַזֹּאת לָיְלָה אֲשֶׁר שָׁכְבָה עָלָיו: וַתָּקָם בְּתוֹךְ הַלַּיְלָה וַתִּקַּח אֶת־ יט
כ

בְּנִי מֵאֶצְלִי וַאֲמָתְךָ יְשֵׁנָה וַתַּשְׁכִּיבֵהוּ בְּחֵיקָהּ וְאֶת־בְּנָהּ הַמֵּת הִשְׁכִּיבָה בְחֵיקִי:

וָאָקֻם בַּבֹּקֶר לְהֵינִיק אֶת־בְּנִי וְהִנֵּה־מֵת וָאֶתְבּוֹנֵן אֵלָיו בַּבֹּקֶר וְהִנֵּה לֹא־הָיָה בְנִי כא

אֲשֶׁר יָלָדְתִּי: וַתֹּאמֶר הָאִשָּׁה הָאַחֶרֶת לֹא כִי בְּנִי הַחַי וּבְנֵךְ הַמֵּת וְזֹאת אֹמֶרֶת כב

לֹא כִי בְּנֵךְ הַמֵּת וּבְנִי הֶחָי וַתְּדַבֵּרְנָה לִפְנֵי הַמֶּלֶךְ: וַיֹּאמֶר הַמֶּלֶךְ זֹאת אֹמֶרֶת זֶה־ כג

בְּנִי הַחַי וּבְנֵךְ הַמֵּת וְזֹאת אֹמֶרֶת לֹא כִי בְּנֵךְ הַמֵּת וּבְנִי הֶחָי: וַיֹּאמֶר כד

הַמֶּלֶךְ קְחוּ לִי־חָרֶב וַיָּבִאוּ הַחֶרֶב לִפְנֵי הַמֶּלֶךְ: וַיֹּאמֶר הַמֶּלֶךְ גִּזְרוּ אֶת־הַיֶּלֶד הַחַי כה

לִשְׁנָיִם וּתְנוּ אֶת־הַחֲצִי לְאַחַת וְאֶת־הַחֲצִי לְאֶחָת: וַתֹּאמֶר הָאִשָּׁה אֲשֶׁר־בְּנָהּ הַחַי כו

אֶל־הַמֶּלֶךְ כִּי־נִכְמְרוּ רַחֲמֶיהָ עַל־בְּנָהּ וַתֹּאמֶר ׀ בִּי אֲדֹנִי תְּנוּ־לָהּ אֶת־הַיָּלוּד הַחַי

וְהָמֵת אַל־תְּמִיתֻהוּ וְזֹאת אֹמֶרֶת גַּם־לִי גַם־לָךְ לֹא יִהְיֶה גְּזֹרוּ: וַיַּעַן הַמֶּלֶךְ וַיֹּאמֶר כז

תְּנוּ־לָהּ אֶת־הַיָּלוּד הַחַי וְהָמֵת לֹא תְמִיתֻהוּ הִיא אִמּוֹ: וַיִּשְׁמְעוּ כָל־יִשְׂרָאֵל אֶת־ כח

הַמִּשְׁפָּט אֲשֶׁר שָׁפַט הַמֶּלֶךְ וַיִּרְאוּ מִפְּנֵי הַמֶּלֶךְ כִּי רָאוּ כִּי־חָכְמַת אֱלֹהִים בְּקִרְבּוֹ

לַעֲשׂוֹת מִשְׁפָּט: וַיְהִי הַמֶּלֶךְ שְׁלֹמֹה מֶלֶךְ עַל־כָּל־יִשְׂרָאֵל: ד א

הפטרת ויגש

יחזקאל

וַיְהִי דְבַר־יְהֹוָה אֵלַי לֵאמֹר: וְאַתָּה בֶן־אָדָם קַח־לְךָ עֵץ אֶחָד וּכְתֹב עָלָיו לִיהוּדָה לז טז

וְלִבְנֵי יִשְׂרָאֵל חֲבֵרָו וּלְקַח עֵץ אֶחָד וּכְתוֹב עָלָיו לְיוֹסֵף עֵץ אֶפְרַיִם וְכָל־בֵּית יִשְׂרָאֵל

חֲבֵרָו: וְקָרַב אֹתָם אֶחָד אֶל־אֶחָד לְךָ לְעֵץ אֶחָד וְהָיוּ לַאֲחָדִים בְּיָדֶךָ: וְכַאֲשֶׁר יז

יֹאמְרוּ אֵלֶיךָ בְּנֵי עַמְּךָ לֵאמֹר הֲלוֹא־תַגִּיד לָנוּ מָה־אֵלֶּה לָּךְ: דַּבֵּר אֲלֵהֶם כֹּה־ יח יט

אָמַר אֲדֹנָי יֱהֹוִה הִנֵּה אֲנִי לֹקֵחַ אֶת־עֵץ יוֹסֵף אֲשֶׁר בְּיַד־אֶפְרַיִם וְשִׁבְטֵי יִשְׂרָאֵל

חֲבֵרָו וְנָתַתִּי אוֹתָם עָלָיו אֶת־עֵץ יְהוּדָה וַעֲשִׂיתִם לְעֵץ אֶחָד וְהָיוּ אֶחָד בְּיָדִי:

20 one in My hand. Let these branches that you write upon be in your hand before their
21 eyes. Speak to them: So says the Lord God: See that I am taking the children of Israel
from among the nations that they went to; I will gather them from all around, and I will
22 bring them to their land. I will make them into one nation in the land, in the mountains
of Israel; one king will be king for all of them, and they will no longer be two nations;
23 they will no longer be split into two kingdoms. They will no longer be defiled by their
idols or by their detestable things and all their transgressions; I will deliver them from
all the dwelling places where they have sinned; I will purify them, and they will be My
24 people, and I will be their God. My servant David will be king over them; there shall
be one shepherd for all, and they will follow My laws, and they will keep My statutes
25 and perform them. They will live on the land that I gave to My servant Yaakov, where
your ancestors lived. They will live upon it, they and their children and their children's
26 children, for eternity, and David My servant will be their prince for eternity. I will make
a covenant of peace with them; it will be an everlasting covenant with them. I will place
them securely there, I will make them ever more numerous; I will place My Sanctuary
27 among them for eternity. My presence will be upon them; I will be their God, and they
28 will be My people. And the nations will know that I the Lord make Israel holy when
My Sanctuary is among them for all eternity."

HAFTARAT VAYḤI

I KINGS

2 1 2 The time of David's death was drawing near, and he gave instructions to his son Shlomo. "I
am going the way of all the earth," he said. "You must be strong and prove yourself a man.
3 You must keep the charge of the Lord your God, following His ways and keeping His
laws and commandments, His rulings and decrees, as written in the teaching of Moshe.
4 For then you will succeed in whatever you do, wherever you turn. For then, the Lord will
fulfill the promise He made to me, saying: If your sons keep to their path and walk before
Me truly, with all their heart and all their soul, then no one of your lineage will be cut off
5 from the throne of Israel. Now you know what Yoav son of Tzeruya did to me – how he
dealt with the two commanders of Israel's forces, Avner son of Ner and Amasa son of
Yeter. By killing them, he shed the blood of war in peacetime and tainted the belt around
6 his waist and the shoes upon his feet with the blood of war. Use your wisdom – do not
7 let his gray-haired head go down to Sheol in peace. As for the sons of Barzilai
the Gileadite, show them loyalty and let them dine at your table, for they befriended me
8 when I was fleeing from Avshalom your brother. Now, look – though Shimi son of Gera
the Benjaminite from Baḥurim is with you, he cursed me with a vehement curse on the
day I left Maḥanayim. When he came down to meet me by the Jordan, I swore to him
9 by the Lord that I would not put him to death by sword – but now, do not let him go

כ כא וְהָיוּ הָעֵצִים אֲשֶׁר־תִּכְתֹּב עֲלֵיהֶם בְּיָדְךָ לְעֵינֵיהֶם: וְדַבֵּר אֲלֵיהֶם כֹּה־אָמַר אֲדֹנָי
יֱהֹוִה הִנֵּה אֲנִי לֹקֵחַ אֶת־בְּנֵי יִשְׂרָאֵל מִבֵּין הַגּוֹיִם אֲשֶׁר הָלְכוּ־שָׁם וְקִבַּצְתִּי אֹתָם
כב מִסָּבִיב וְהֵבֵאתִי אוֹתָם אֶל־אַדְמָתָם: וְעָשִׂיתִי אֹתָם לְגוֹי אֶחָד בָּאָרֶץ בְּהָרֵי יִשְׂרָאֵל
וּמֶלֶךְ אֶחָד יִהְיֶה לְכֻלָּם לְמֶלֶךְ וְלֹא יהיה־עוֹד לִשְׁנֵי גוֹיִם וְלֹא יֵחָצוּ עוֹד לִשְׁתֵּי יִהְיוּ־
כג מַמְלָכוֹת עוֹד: וְלֹא יִטַּמְּאוּ עוֹד בְּגִלּוּלֵיהֶם וּבְשִׁקּוּצֵיהֶם וּבְכֹל פִּשְׁעֵיהֶם וְהוֹשַׁעְתִּי
אֹתָם מִכֹּל מוֹשְׁבֹתֵיהֶם אֲשֶׁר חָטְאוּ בָהֶם וְטִהַרְתִּי אוֹתָם וְהָיוּ־לִי לְעָם וַאֲנִי אֶהְיֶה
כד לָהֶם לֵאלֹהִים: וְעַבְדִּי דָוִד מֶלֶךְ עֲלֵיהֶם וְרוֹעֶה אֶחָד יִהְיֶה לְכֻלָּם וּבְמִשְׁפָּטַי יֵלֵכוּ
כה וְחֻקּוֹתַי יִשְׁמְרוּ וְעָשׂוּ אוֹתָם: וְיָשְׁבוּ עַל־הָאָרֶץ אֲשֶׁר נָתַתִּי לְעַבְדִּי לְיַעֲקֹב אֲשֶׁר
יָשְׁבוּ־בָהּ אֲבוֹתֵיכֶם וְיָשְׁבוּ עָלֶיהָ הֵמָּה וּבְנֵיהֶם וּבְנֵי בְנֵיהֶם עַד־עוֹלָם וְדָוִד עַבְדִּי
כו נָשִׂיא לָהֶם לְעוֹלָם: וְכָרַתִּי לָהֶם בְּרִית שָׁלוֹם בְּרִית עוֹלָם יִהְיֶה אוֹתָם וּנְתַתִּים
כז וְהִרְבֵּיתִי אוֹתָם וְנָתַתִּי אֶת־מִקְדָּשִׁי בְּתוֹכָם לְעוֹלָם: וְהָיָה מִשְׁכָּנִי עֲלֵיהֶם וְהָיִיתִי
כח לָהֶם לֵאלֹהִים וְהֵמָּה יִהְיוּ־לִי לְעָם: וְיָדְעוּ הַגּוֹיִם כִּי אֲנִי יְהֹוָה מְקַדֵּשׁ אֶת־יִשְׂרָאֵל
בִּהְיוֹת מִקְדָּשִׁי בְּתוֹכָם לְעוֹלָם:

הפטרת ויחי

ב א ב וַיִּקְרְבוּ יְמֵי־דָוִד לָמוּת וַיְצַו אֶת־שְׁלֹמֹה בְנוֹ לֵאמֹר: אָנֹכִי הֹלֵךְ בְּדֶרֶךְ כָּל־הָאָרֶץ מלכים א׳
ג וְחָזַקְתָּ וְהָיִיתָ לְאִישׁ: וְשָׁמַרְתָּ אֶת־מִשְׁמֶרֶת ׀ יְהֹוָה אֱלֹהֶיךָ לָלֶכֶת בִּדְרָכָיו לִשְׁמֹר
חֻקֹּתָיו מִצְוֹתָיו וּמִשְׁפָּטָיו וְעֵדְוֹתָיו כַּכָּתוּב בְּתוֹרַת מֹשֶׁה לְמַעַן תַּשְׂכִּיל אֵת כָּל־
ד אֲשֶׁר תַּעֲשֶׂה וְאֵת כָּל־אֲשֶׁר תִּפְנֶה שָׁם: לְמַעַן יָקִים יְהֹוָה אֶת־דְּבָרוֹ אֲשֶׁר דִּבֶּר
עָלַי לֵאמֹר אִם־יִשְׁמְרוּ בָנֶיךָ אֶת־דַּרְכָּם לָלֶכֶת לְפָנַי בֶּאֱמֶת בְּכָל־לְבָבָם וּבְכָל־
ה נַפְשָׁם לֵאמֹר לֹא־יִכָּרֵת לְךָ אִישׁ מֵעַל כִּסֵּא יִשְׂרָאֵל: וְגַם אַתָּה יָדַעְתָּ אֵת אֲשֶׁר־
עָשָׂה לִי יוֹאָב בֶּן־צְרוּיָה אֲשֶׁר עָשָׂה לִשְׁנֵי־שָׂרֵי צִבְאוֹת יִשְׂרָאֵל לְאַבְנֵר בֶּן־נֵר
וְלַעֲמָשָׂא בֶן־יֶתֶר וַיַּהַרְגֵם וַיָּשֶׂם דְּמֵי־מִלְחָמָה בְּשָׁלֹם וַיִּתֵּן דְּמֵי מִלְחָמָה בַּחֲגֹרָתוֹ
ו אֲשֶׁר בְּמָתְנָיו וּבְנַעֲלוֹ אֲשֶׁר בְּרַגְלָיו: וְעָשִׂיתָ כְּחָכְמָתֶךָ וְלֹא־תוֹרֵד שֵׂיבָתוֹ בְּשָׁלֹם
ז שְׁאֹל: וְלִבְנֵי בַרְזִלַּי הַגִּלְעָדִי תַּעֲשֶׂה־חֶסֶד וְהָיוּ בְּאֹכְלֵי שֻׁלְחָנֶךָ כִּי־כֵן
ח קָרְבוּ אֵלַי בְּבָרְחִי מִפְּנֵי אַבְשָׁלוֹם אָחִיךָ: וְהִנֵּה עִמְּךָ שִׁמְעִי בֶן־גֵּרָא בֶן־הַיְמִינִי
מִבַּחֻרִים וְהוּא קִלְלַנִי קְלָלָה נִמְרֶצֶת בְּיוֹם לֶכְתִּי מַחֲנָיִם וְהוּא־יָרַד לִקְרָאתִי
ט הַיַּרְדֵּן וָאֶשָּׁבַע לוֹ בַיהֹוָה לֵאמֹר אִם־אֲמִיתְךָ בֶּחָרֶב: וְעַתָּה אַל־תְּנַקֵּהוּ כִּי אִישׁ

free. You are a wise man, and you will know how to deal with him – bring his gray-haired
10 head down in blood to Sheol." And David slept with his ancestors and was buried in the
11 City of David. The length of time that David had reigned over Israel was forty
years; he reigned in Ḥevron for seven years, and he reigned in Jerusalem for thirty-three
12 years. Now Shlomo sat on his father David's throne, and his kingdom was firmly
established.

י חָכָ֣ם אָ֑תָּה וְיָֽדַעְתָּ֙ אֵ֣ת אֲשֶׁ֣ר תַּעֲשֶׂה־לּ֔וֹ וְהוֹרַדְתָּ֧ אֶת־שֵׂיבָת֛וֹ בְּדָ֖ם שְׁאֽוֹל׃ וַיִּשְׁכַּ֥ב
יא דָּוִ֖ד עִם־אֲבֹתָ֑יו וַיִּקָּבֵ֖ר בְּעִ֥יר דָּוִֽד׃ וְהַיָּמִ֗ים אֲשֶׁ֨ר מָלַ֤ךְ דָּוִד֙ עַל־יִשְׂרָאֵ֔ל
יב אַרְבָּעִ֖ים שָׁנָ֑ה בְּחֶבְר֤וֹן מָלַךְ֙ שֶׁ֣בַע שָׁנִ֔ים וּבִירוּשָׁלִַ֣ם מָלַ֔ךְ שְׁלֹשִׁ֥ים וְשָׁלֹ֖שׁ שָׁנִֽים׃
וּשְׁלֹמֹ֕ה יָשַׁ֕ב עַל־כִּסֵּ֖א דָּוִ֣ד אָבִ֑יו וַתִּכֹּ֥ן מַלְכֻת֖וֹ מְאֹֽד׃

READINGS AND HAFTAROT FOR SPECIAL SHABBATOT

MAFTIR FOR SHABBAT ROSH ḤODESH

NUMBERS

28 9 On the Sabbath day: two yearling lambs without blemish and two-tenths of a measure
10 of fine flour as a grain offering, mixed with oil, and its libation. This is the burnt offering
for every Sabbath, to be brought in addition to the regular daily burnt offering and its
libation.
11 On your New Moons you shall present a burnt offering to the LORD: two young bulls,
12 one ram, and seven yearling lambs, all without blemish. There shall be a grain offering
of three-tenths of a measure of fine flour mixed with oil for each bull, a grain offering of
13 two-tenths of fine flour mixed with oil for each ram, and a grain offering of one-tenth of
fine flour mixed with oil for each lamb. This shall be a burnt offering of pleasing aroma, a
14 fire offering to the LORD. Their libations shall be half a hin of wine for a bull, a third of a
hin of wine for a ram, and a quarter of a hin of wine for a lamb. This is the monthly burnt
15 offering for each New Moon of the year. One male goat shall be brought as a purification
offering to the LORD, in addition to the regular burnt offering and its libation.

HAFTARA FOR SHABBAT ROSH ḤODESH

ISAIAH

66 1 Thus speaks the LORD: The heavens are My throne; the world, My footstool. What
2 house, then, would You build for Me, where could I rest? All this – My own hands made,
all these are Mine, so says the LORD. And these are the ones I look toward: the poor, of
3 humbled spirit, who tremble at My words. While he, killing his ox is like a murderer of
men, the one who offers up a lamb might so well behead a dog; the offering brought
may just as well be pigs' blood; and his remembrance incense is a blessing of iniquity.
4 These men, they choose their paths, their souls desire their disgusting things, and so I
too will choose – will choose their torments, and bring to them what they most fear. I
called out – no one answered; I spoke, but none was listening. They did what was evil
5 in My sight, and chose what I never desired. You who tremble to hear His
word, listen to the LORD's word: Your brothers said, the ones who hated you, who cast
you out, "Because of my name, the LORD is honored." We will see your joy, and they
6 will be shamefaced. A voice roaring out from the city, a voice, out of the Sanctuary, a
7 voice – it is the LORD's, as He repays His enemies. Before she had writhed in labor she
8 gave birth; before the agonies took her she was delivered of a boy. Who ever heard of
anything like this? Who ever saw such happenings as these? Can the land give birth in

קריאות והפטרות לשבתות מיוחדות

מפטיר לשבת ראש חודש

במדבר

כח ט וּבְיוֹם֙ הַשַּׁבָּ֔ת שְׁנֵֽי־כְבָשִׂ֥ים בְּנֵֽי־שָׁנָ֖ה תְּמִימִ֑ם וּשְׁנֵ֣י עֶשְׂרֹנִ֗ים סֹ֛לֶת מִנְחָ֛ה בְּלוּלָ֥ה
י בַשֶּׁ֖מֶן וְנִסְכּֽוֹ׃ עֹלַ֥ת שַׁבַּ֖ת בְּשַׁבַּתּ֑וֹ עַל־עֹלַ֥ת הַתָּמִ֖יד וְנִסְכָּֽהּ׃
יא וּבְרָאשֵׁי֙ חָדְשֵׁיכֶ֔ם תַּקְרִ֥יבוּ עֹלָ֖ה לַֽיהוָ֑ה פָּרִ֨ים בְּנֵֽי־בָקָ֤ר שְׁנַ֙יִם֙ וְאַ֣יִל אֶחָ֔ד כְּבָשִׂ֧ים
יב בְּנֵי־שָׁנָ֛ה שִׁבְעָ֖ה תְּמִימִֽם׃ וּשְׁלֹשָׁ֣ה עֶשְׂרֹנִ֗ים סֹ֤לֶת מִנְחָה֙ בְּלוּלָ֣ה בַשֶּׁ֔מֶן לַפָּ֖ר
יג הָאֶחָ֑ד וּשְׁנֵ֣י עֶשְׂרֹנִ֗ים סֹ֤לֶת מִנְחָה֙ בְּלוּלָ֣ה בַשֶּׁ֔מֶן לָאַ֖יִל הָאֶחָֽד׃ וְעִשָּׂרֹ֣ן עִשָּׂר֗וֹן סֹ֤לֶת
יד מִנְחָה֙ בְּלוּלָ֣ה בַשֶּׁ֔מֶן לַכֶּ֖בֶשׂ הָאֶחָ֑ד עֹלָה֙ רֵ֣יחַ נִיחֹ֔חַ אִשֶּׁ֖ה לַֽיהוָֽה׃ וְנִסְכֵּיהֶ֗ם חֲצִ֣י
הַהִין֩ יִהְיֶ֨ה לַפָּ֜ר וּשְׁלִישִׁ֧ת הַהִ֣ין לָאַ֗יִל וּרְבִיעִ֥ת הַהִ֛ין לַכֶּ֖בֶשׂ יָ֑יִן זֹ֣את עֹלַ֥ת חֹ֙דֶשׁ֙
טו בְּחָדְשׁ֔וֹ לְחָדְשֵׁ֖י הַשָּׁנָֽה׃ וּשְׂעִ֨יר עִזִּ֥ים אֶחָ֛ד לְחַטָּ֖את לַֽיהוָ֑ה עַל־עֹלַ֨ת הַתָּמִ֜יד
יֵעָשֶׂ֖ה וְנִסְכּֽוֹ׃

הפטרת שבת ראש חודש

ישעיה

סו א כֹּ֚ה אָמַ֣ר יְהוָ֔ה הַשָּׁמַ֣יִם כִּסְאִ֔י וְהָאָ֖רֶץ הֲדֹ֣ם רַגְלָ֑י אֵי־זֶ֥ה בַ֙יִת֙ אֲשֶׁ֣ר תִּבְנוּ־לִ֔י וְאֵי־
ב זֶ֥ה מָק֖וֹם מְנוּחָתִֽי׃ וְאֶת־כָּל־אֵ֙לֶּה֙ יָדִ֣י עָשָׂ֔תָה וַיִּהְי֥וּ כָל־אֵ֖לֶּה נְאֻם־יְהוָ֑ה וְאֶל־זֶ֣ה
ג אַבִּ֔יט אֶל־עָנִי֙ וּנְכֵה־ר֔וּחַ וְחָרֵ֖ד עַל־דְּבָרִֽי׃ שׁוֹחֵ֨ט הַשּׁ֜וֹר מַכֵּה־אִ֗ישׁ זוֹבֵ֤חַ הַשֶּׂה֙
עֹ֣רֵֽף כֶּ֔לֶב מַעֲלֵ֤ה מִנְחָה֙ דַּם־חֲזִ֔יר מַזְכִּ֥יר לְבֹנָ֖ה מְבָ֣רֵֽךְ אָ֑וֶן גַּם־הֵ֗מָּה בָּֽחֲרוּ֙ בְּדַרְכֵיהֶ֔ם
ד וּבְשִׁקּוּצֵיהֶ֖ם נַפְשָׁ֥ם חָפֵֽצָה׃ גַּם־אֲנִ֞י אֶבְחַ֣ר בְּתַעֲלֻלֵיהֶ֗ם וּמְגֽוּרֹתָם֙ אָבִ֣יא לָהֶ֔ם
יַ֣עַן קָרָ֙אתִי֙ וְאֵ֣ין עוֹנֶ֔ה דִּבַּ֖רְתִּי וְלֹ֣א שָׁמֵ֑עוּ וַיַּעֲשׂ֤וּ הָרַע֙ בְּעֵינַ֔י וּבַאֲשֶׁ֥ר לֹֽא־חָפַ֖צְתִּי
ה בָּחָֽרוּ׃ שִׁמְעוּ֙ דְּבַר־יְהוָ֔ה הַחֲרֵדִ֖ים אֶל־דְּבָר֑וֹ אָֽמְרוּ֩ אֲחֵיכֶ֨ם שֹׂנְאֵיכֶ֜ם
ו מְנַדֵּיכֶ֗ם לְמַ֤עַן שְׁמִי֙ יִכְבַּ֣ד יְהוָ֔ה וְנִרְאֶ֥ה בְשִׂמְחַתְכֶ֖ם וְהֵ֥ם יֵבֹֽשׁוּ׃ ק֤וֹל שָׁאוֹן֙ מֵעִ֔יר ק֖וֹל
ז מֵֽהֵיכָ֑ל ק֣וֹל יְהוָ֔ה מְשַׁלֵּ֥ם גְּמ֖וּל לְאֹיְבָֽיו׃ בְּטֶ֥רֶם תָּחִ֖יל יָלָ֑דָה בְּטֶ֨רֶם יָב֥וֹא חֵ֛בֶל לָ֖הּ
ח וְהִמְלִ֥יטָה זָכָֽר׃ מִֽי־שָׁמַ֣ע כָּזֹ֗את מִ֤י רָאָה֙ כָּאֵ֔לֶּה הֲי֤וּחַל אֶ֙רֶץ֙ בְּי֣וֹם אֶחָ֔ד אִם־יִוָּ֥לֵד
ט גּ֖וֹי פַּ֣עַם אֶחָ֑ת כִּי־חָ֛לָה גַּם־יָלְדָ֥ה צִיּ֖וֹן אֶת־בָּנֶֽיהָ׃ הַאֲנִ֥י אַשְׁבִּ֛יר וְלֹ֥א אוֹלִ֖יד יֹאמַ֣ר

a day? Can a nation be born at a single step? Yet Zion has labored, and has birthed her
9 children. Would I bring on the labor and not deliver? So the Lord speaks: Would I who
10 fathered close the womb? So your God speaks. Bring Jerusalem joy, exult in
11 her, all of you who love her; celebrate her joy with her, all of you who mourned her. That
you may suck your fill from the bosom of her comforting; may suckle, take delight in
12 the brilliance of her glory. For thus says the Lord: See Me make peace flow
to her like a river, and the substance of nations – like a rushing brook – and you shall
13 suckle. You will be borne upon hips, playing upon loving laps; as a man is consoled by
14 his mother, just so shall I comfort you, and in Jerusalem, you shall be consoled. You shall
look on, your heart rejoicing, while your bones grow vigorous, like grass, and the hand
15 of the Lord becomes known to His servants, and His rage known to all His foes. For
see: the Lord is coming in fire, His chariots a storm wind, to slake His fury in rage, His
16 rebuke in flames of fire. For in fire, the Lord comes to judgment, and by the sword, to
17 all flesh, and many are those the Lord will execute. Those in the gardens, sanctifying
and cleansing themselves, one after the other in the midst of it, while eating the flesh of
pigs and pests and mice, they will all be gathered in together: so the Lord has spoken.
18 For I – I know their works, their thoughts; and time will come, to gather all nations
19 and tongues, and they will come, and look upon My glory. I shall place a sign among
them, send out survivors from them to all nations, to Tarshish, Pul, and Lud, to the
great archers, Tuval, Yavan, to the distant coastlands where none ever heard tell of Me
20 or saw My glory, and they will tell of My glory to the nations. And they will bring back
all your brothers from among all other nations, an offering to the Lord, on horseback
and on chariot, on camels, mules, dromedaries, to My holy mount, Jerusalem – so says
the Lord – just as the children of Israel would bring up their offerings in pure vessels,
21 to the Lord's House, and from among them also I shall take priests and Levites, so
22 says the Lord. For just as the new heavens, the new earth that I am now forming, will
stand forever before Me, so says the Lord, so will stand your children, your name.
23 And it will be – every New Moon, every Sabbath – all flesh will come to worship Me,
24 so says the Lord. Going out, they will see bodies of those people who sinned against
Me, for the worms will not die nor the fire be quenched, and they will be repugnant to
all flesh.

And it will be – every New Moon, every Sabbath – all flesh will come to worship Me, so says the Lord.

When a two-day Rosh Ḥodesh falls on Shabbat and Sunday, Sepharadim add the first and last verses of the haftara for erev Rosh Ḥodesh, *on the following page.*

י יְהוָה אִם־אֲנִי הַמּוֹלִיד וְעָצַרְתִּי אָמַר אֱלֹהָיִךְ׃ שִׂמְחוּ אֶת־יְרוּשָׁלַ͏ִם וְגִילוּ
יא בָהּ כָּל־אֹהֲבֶיהָ שִׂישׂוּ אִתָּהּ מָשׂוֹשׂ כָּל־הַמִּתְאַבְּלִים עָלֶיהָ׃ לְמַעַן תִּינְקוּ וּשְׂבַעְתֶּם
יב מִשֹּׁד תַּנְחֻמֶיהָ לְמַעַן תָּמֹצּוּ וְהִתְעַנַּגְתֶּם מִזִּיז כְּבוֹדָהּ׃ כִּי־כֹה ׀ אָמַר יְהוָה
הִנְנִי נֹטֶה־אֵלֶיהָ כְּנָהָר שָׁלוֹם וּכְנַחַל שׁוֹטֵף כְּבוֹד גּוֹיִם וִינַקְתֶּם עַל־צַד תִּנָּשֵׂאוּ
יג וְעַל־בִּרְכַּיִם תְּשָׁעֳשָׁעוּ׃ כְּאִישׁ אֲשֶׁר אִמּוֹ תְּנַחֲמֶנּוּ כֵּן אָנֹכִי אֲנַחֶמְכֶם וּבִירוּשָׁלַ͏ִם
יד תְּנֻחָמוּ׃ וּרְאִיתֶם וְשָׂשׂ לִבְּכֶם וְעַצְמוֹתֵיכֶם כַּדֶּשֶׁא תִפְרַחְנָה וְנוֹדְעָה יַד־יְהוָה
טו אֶת־עֲבָדָיו וְזָעַם אֶת־אֹיְבָיו׃ כִּי־הִנֵּה יְהוָה בָּאֵשׁ יָבוֹא וְכַסּוּפָה מַרְכְּבֹתָיו לְהָשִׁיב
טז בְּחֵמָה אַפּוֹ וְגַעֲרָתוֹ בְּלַהֲבֵי־אֵשׁ׃ כִּי בָאֵשׁ יְהוָה נִשְׁפָּט וּבְחַרְבּוֹ אֶת־כָּל־בָּשָׂר וְרַבּוּ
יז חַלְלֵי יְהוָה׃ הַמִּתְקַדְּשִׁים וְהַמִּטַּהֲרִים אֶל־הַגַּנּוֹת אַחַר אחד בַּתָּוֶךְ אֹכְלֵי בְּשַׂר אַחַת
יח הַחֲזִיר וְהַשֶּׁקֶץ וְהָעַכְבָּר יַחְדָּו יָסֻפוּ נְאֻם־יְהוָה׃ וְאָנֹכִי מַעֲשֵׂיהֶם וּמַחְשְׁבֹתֵיהֶם
יט בָּאָה לְקַבֵּץ אֶת־כָּל־הַגּוֹיִם וְהַלְּשֹׁנוֹת וּבָאוּ וְרָאוּ אֶת־כְּבוֹדִי׃ וְשַׂמְתִּי בָהֶם אוֹת
וְשִׁלַּחְתִּי מֵהֶם ׀ פְּלֵיטִים אֶל־הַגּוֹיִם תַּרְשִׁישׁ פּוּל וְלוּד מֹשְׁכֵי קֶשֶׁת תֻּבַל וְיָוָן הָאִיִּים
הָרְחֹקִים אֲשֶׁר לֹא־שָׁמְעוּ אֶת־שִׁמְעִי וְלֹא־רָאוּ אֶת־כְּבוֹדִי וְהִגִּידוּ אֶת־כְּבוֹדִי
כ בַּגּוֹיִם׃ וְהֵבִיאוּ אֶת־כָּל־אֲחֵיכֶם ׀ מִכָּל־הַגּוֹיִם ׀ מִנְחָה ׀ לַיהוָה בַּסּוּסִים וּבָרֶכֶב
וּבַצַּבִּים וּבַפְּרָדִים וּבַכִּרְכָּרוֹת עַל הַר קָדְשִׁי יְרוּשָׁלַ͏ִם אָמַר יְהוָה כַּאֲשֶׁר יָבִיאוּ בְנֵי
כא יִשְׂרָאֵל אֶת־הַמִּנְחָה בִּכְלִי טָהוֹר בֵּית יְהוָה׃ וְגַם־מֵהֶם אֶקַּח לַכֹּהֲנִים לַלְוִיִּם אָמַר
כב יְהוָה׃ כִּי כַאֲשֶׁר הַשָּׁמַיִם הַחֲדָשִׁים וְהָאָרֶץ הַחֲדָשָׁה אֲשֶׁר אֲנִי עֹשֶׂה עֹמְדִים לְפָנַי
כג נְאֻם־יְהוָה כֵּן יַעֲמֹד זַרְעֲכֶם וְשִׁמְכֶם׃ וְהָיָה מִדֵּי־חֹדֶשׁ בְּחָדְשׁוֹ וּמִדֵּי שַׁבָּת בְּשַׁבַּתּוֹ
כד יָבוֹא כָל־בָּשָׂר לְהִשְׁתַּחֲוֺת לְפָנַי אָמַר יְהוָה׃ וְיָצְאוּ וְרָאוּ בְּפִגְרֵי הָאֲנָשִׁים הַפֹּשְׁעִים
בִּי כִּי תוֹלַעְתָּם לֹא תָמוּת וְאִשָּׁם לֹא תִכְבֶּה וְהָיוּ דֵרָאוֹן לְכָל־בָּשָׂר׃

והיה מדי חדש בחדשו ומדי שבת בשבתו יבוא כל
בשר להשתחות לפני אמר יהוה

When a two-day ראש חודש *falls on* שבת *and Sunday,*
Sepharadim add the first and last verses of the הפטרה *for* ערב ראש חודש*,*
on the following page.

HAFTARA FOR SHABBAT EREV ROSH ḤODESH

20 18 Yehonatan then said to David, "Tomorrow is the New Month, and you shall be missed, I SAMUEL
19 for your seat will be empty. Now wait three days, then on the day people go back to work,
20 make your way swiftly down to your hiding place, and stay close to the Ezel Stone. As
21 for me – I will shoot three arrows to its side, as though aiming at a target. Now, when I
send the boy off to find the arrows, if I say to him, 'Look, the arrows are just past you,
come take them,' then come, for all is well with you, and there is nothing wrong – as
22 the Lord lives. But if I say to the boy, 'Look, the arrows are far past you,' then go, for
23 the Lord has sent you away. As for the matter we spoke of, you and I – the Lord is
24 between me and you forever." David hid out in the field. The New Month
25 came around, and the king sat down at the feast to eat. When the king sat in his usual seat
by the wall, Yehonatan rose, and Avner sat by Sha'ul's side while David's seat remained
26 empty. Sha'ul did not mention anything that day. "It must be by chance that he is not
27 clean," he thought; "he must be unclean." But the next day, on the second day
of the New Month, David's seat was still empty, and Sha'ul asked Yehonatan, his son,
28 "Why did the son of Yishai fail to come to the feast – both yesterday and today?" "David
29 urgently asked me for leave to Beit Leḥem," Yehonatan answered Sha'ul. "He said, 'Please
let me go, for we have a family feast in the city, and my brother has bid me – so now,
if I have gained your favor, please let me get away to see my brothers.' That is why he
30 has not come to the king's table." Sha'ul burst into a rage at Yehonatan. "Son
of a perverse, wayward woman!" he said. "Oh, I knew you would side with the son of
31 Yishai – to your own disgrace and the disgrace of your mother's nakedness! But as
long as the son of Yishai lives on this earth, you and your kingship will not endure – so
32 bring him to me now, for he is a dead man!" But Yehonatan answered Sha'ul,
33 his father. "Why should he be killed?" he said to him. "What has he done?" And Sha'ul
hurled the spear toward him to strike him down, and Yehonatan realized that his father
34 was determined to kill David. Furious, Yehonatan rose up from the table;
he ate no food on the second day of the New Month out of anguish for David, for his
35 father had humiliated him. In the morning, Yehonatan went out to the field
36 for the rendezvous with David, a young boy with him. He said to his boy, "Now, run and
find the arrows I am about to shoot." The boy ran off, and he shot the arrows past him.
37 When the boy reached the place where Yehonatan's arrows had fallen, Yehonatan called
out after the boy, "Oh – the arrows are far past you." Then Yehonatan called out after
38 the boy, "Quick – hurry, do not linger." When Yehonatan's boy gathered up the arrows
39 and came back to his master – the boy knew nothing; only Yehonatan and David knew
40 about the arrangement – Yehonatan gave his gear to his boy and said to him, "Go – bring
41 these back to town." When the boy had left, David emerged from the southern side of
the stone, flung his face to the ground, and bowed three times. And they kissed each

הפטרת שבת ערב ראש חודש

כ יח יט וַיֹּאמֶר־לוֹ יְהוֹנָתָן מָחָר חֹדֶשׁ וְנִפְקַדְתָּ כִּי יִפָּקֵד מוֹשָׁבֶךָ: וְשִׁלַּשְׁתָּ תֵּרֵד מְאֹד שמואל א׳
וּבָאתָ אֶל־הַמָּקוֹם אֲשֶׁר־נִסְתַּרְתָּ שָּׁם בְּיוֹם הַמַּעֲשֶׂה וְיָשַׁבְתָּ אֵצֶל הָאֶבֶן הָאָזֶל:
כ כא וַאֲנִי שְׁלֹשֶׁת הַחִצִּים צִדָּה אוֹרֶה לְשַׁלַּח־לִי לְמַטָּרָה: וְהִנֵּה אֶשְׁלַח אֶת־הַנַּעַר לֵךְ
מְצָא אֶת־הַחִצִּים אִם־אָמֹר אֹמַר לַנַּעַר הִנֵּה הַחִצִּים ׀ מִמְּךָ וָהֵנָּה קָחֶנּוּ וָבֹאָה כִּי־
כב שָׁלוֹם לְךָ וְאֵין דָּבָר חַי־יְהוָה: וְאִם־כֹּה אֹמַר לָעֶלֶם הִנֵּה הַחִצִּים מִמְּךָ וָהָלְאָה
כג לֵךְ כִּי שִׁלַּחֲךָ יְהוָה: וְהַדָּבָר אֲשֶׁר דִּבַּרְנוּ אֲנִי וָאָתָּה הִנֵּה יְהוָה בֵּינִי וּבֵינְךָ עַד־
כד עוֹלָם: וַיִּסָּתֵר דָּוִד בַּשָּׂדֶה וַיְהִי הַחֹדֶשׁ וַיֵּשֶׁב הַמֶּלֶךְ עַל־הַלֶּחֶם לֶאֱכוֹל: אֶל־
כה וַיֵּשֶׁב הַמֶּלֶךְ עַל־מוֹשָׁבוֹ כְּפַעַם ׀ בְּפַעַם אֶל־מוֹשַׁב הַקִּיר וַיָּקָם יְהוֹנָתָן וַיֵּשֶׁב אַבְנֵר
כו מִצַּד שָׁאוּל וַיִּפָּקֵד מְקוֹם דָּוִד: וְלֹא־דִבֶּר שָׁאוּל מְאוּמָה בַּיּוֹם הַהוּא כִּי אָמַר
כז מִקְרֶה הוּא בִּלְתִּי טָהוֹר הוּא כִּי־לֹא טָהוֹר: וַיְהִי מִמָּחֳרַת הַחֹדֶשׁ הַשֵּׁנִי
וַיִּפָּקֵד מְקוֹם דָּוִד וַיֹּאמֶר שָׁאוּל אֶל־יְהוֹנָתָן בְּנוֹ מַדּוּעַ לֹא־בָא בֶן־יִשַׁי גַּם־תְּמוֹל
כח גַּם־הַיּוֹם אֶל־הַלָּחֶם: וַיַּעַן יְהוֹנָתָן אֶת־שָׁאוּל נִשְׁאֹל נִשְׁאַל דָּוִד מֵעִמָּדִי עַד־בֵּית
כט לָחֶם: וַיֹּאמֶר שַׁלְּחֵנִי נָא כִּי זֶבַח מִשְׁפָּחָה לָנוּ בָּעִיר וְהוּא צִוָּה־לִי אָחִי וְעַתָּה
אִם־מָצָאתִי חֵן בְּעֵינֶיךָ אִמָּלְטָה נָּא וְאֶרְאֶה אֶת־אֶחָי עַל־כֵּן לֹא־בָא אֶל־שֻׁלְחַן
ל הַמֶּלֶךְ: וַיִּחַר־אַף שָׁאוּל בִּיהוֹנָתָן וַיֹּאמֶר לוֹ בֶּן־נַעֲוַת הַמַּרְדּוּת הֲלוֹא
לא יָדַעְתִּי כִּי־בֹחֵר אַתָּה לְבֶן־יִשַׁי לְבָשְׁתְּךָ וּלְבֹשֶׁת עֶרְוַת אִמֶּךָ: כִּי כָל־הַיָּמִים אֲשֶׁר
בֶּן־יִשַׁי חַי עַל־הָאֲדָמָה לֹא תִכּוֹן אַתָּה וּמַלְכוּתֶךָ וְעַתָּה שְׁלַח וְקַח אֹתוֹ אֵלַי כִּי
לב בֶן־מָוֶת הוּא: וַיַּעַן יְהוֹנָתָן אֶת־שָׁאוּל אָבִיו וַיֹּאמֶר אֵלָיו לָמָּה יוּמַת
לג מֶה עָשָׂה: וַיָּטֶל שָׁאוּל אֶת־הַחֲנִית עָלָיו לְהַכֹּתוֹ וַיֵּדַע יְהוֹנָתָן כִּי־כָלָה הִיא מֵעִם
לד אָבִיו לְהָמִית אֶת־דָּוִד: וַיָּקָם יְהוֹנָתָן מֵעִם הַשֻּׁלְחָן בָּחֳרִי־אָף וְלֹא־אָכַל
לה בְּיוֹם־הַחֹדֶשׁ הַשֵּׁנִי לֶחֶם כִּי נֶעְצַב אֶל־דָּוִד כִּי הִכְלִמוֹ אָבִיו: וַיְהִי בַבֹּקֶר
לו וַיֵּצֵא יְהוֹנָתָן הַשָּׂדֶה לְמוֹעֵד דָּוִד וְנַעַר קָטֹן עִמּוֹ: וַיֹּאמֶר לְנַעֲרוֹ רֻץ מְצָא־נָא
לז אֶת־הַחִצִּים אֲשֶׁר אָנֹכִי מוֹרֶה הַנַּעַר רָץ וְהוּא־יָרָה הַחֵצִי לְהַעֲבִרוֹ: וַיָּבֹא הַנַּעַר
עַד־מְקוֹם הַחֵצִי אֲשֶׁר יָרָה יְהוֹנָתָן וַיִּקְרָא יְהוֹנָתָן אַחֲרֵי הַנַּעַר וַיֹּאמֶר הֲלוֹא הַחֵצִי
לח מִמְּךָ וָהָלְאָה: וַיִּקְרָא יְהוֹנָתָן אַחֲרֵי הַנַּעַר מְהֵרָה חוּשָׁה אַל־תַּעֲמֹד וַיְלַקֵּט נַעַר
לט יְהוֹנָתָן אֶת־הַחִצִּי וַיָּבֹא אֶל־אֲדֹנָיו: וְהַנַּעַר לֹא־יָדַע מְאוּמָה אַךְ יְהוֹנָתָן וְדָוִד יָדְעוּ הַחִצִּים
מ אֶת־הַדָּבָר: וַיִּתֵּן יְהוֹנָתָן אֶת־כֵּלָיו אֶל־הַנַּעַר אֲשֶׁר־לוֹ וַיֹּאמֶר לוֹ לֵךְ הָבֵיא הָעִיר:

42 other and wept with each other until David's sobs reached a crescendo. "Go in peace,"
Yehonatan said to David, "for the two of us have sworn in the name of the Lord, 'May
the Lord be between me and you, and between my seed and your seed, forever.'"

READINGS FOR ḤANUKKA

On Shabbat that falls on any day of Ḥanukka, read the passage for the appropriate day as marked below. Afterward, read the haftara for the first or second Shabbat of Ḥanukka, as appropriate (pp. 675–677).

When Shabbat of Ḥanukka falls on Rosh Ḥodesh Tevet, three Torah scrolls are taken out. In the first, six aliyot are read from Parashat Miketz. In the second, the maftir for Shabbat Rosh Ḥodesh is read (p. 661). Then Half-Kaddish is recited, and the passage for the sixth day of Ḥanukka is read from the third Torah scroll (p. 669). Afterward, read the haftara on page 675.

For the first day Sepharadim begin here

NUMBERS

6 22 23 The Lord spoke to Moshe: "Tell Aharon and his sons: This is how you are to bless
24 the Israelites. Say to them: 'May the Lord bless you and watch over
25 you. May the Lord make His face shine upon you and
26 be gracious to you. May the Lord raise His face toward you and grant
27 you peace.' They shall set My name upon the Israelites, and I will bless
7 1 them." On the day when Moshe finished establishing the Tabernacle, he *Ashkenazim begin here*
anointed it and consecrated it. He anointed and consecrated the altar, too, and all its
2 utensils. And the princes of Israel, leaders of their ancestral houses, drew close. They
3 were the princes of the tribes, the ones who had directed the census. And they brought
their offerings before the Lord: six covered wagons and twelve oxen – a wagon for
every two leaders, and for each one an ox. They presented them before the Tabernacle.
4 5 The Lord said to Moshe, "Accept these from them and use them for service in the
6 Tent of Meeting. Give them to the Levites, to each according to his service." Moshe
7 took the wagons and the oxen, and he gave them to the Levites. He gave two wagons
8 and four oxen to the Gershonites as their service required. He gave four wagons and
eight oxen to the Merarites for their service under the supervision of Itamar son of
9 Aharon the priest. But to the Kohatites he gave none, for their responsibility was for
10 the sacred articles that had to be carried on their shoulders. The princes presented their
dedication offering for the altar at the time when it was anointed. The princes brought
11 their offerings before the altar. The Lord said to Moshe, "Each day one prince is to
12 bring close his offering for the dedication of the altar." The one who presented
his offering on the first day was Naḥshon son of Aminadav, from the tribe of Yehuda.
13 His offering was one silver bowl weighing one hundred and thirty shekel and one silver
basin weighing seventy shekel according to the Sanctuary weight, both filled with

מא   הַנַּ֗עַר בָּ֚א וְדָוִ֣ד קָ֣ם מֵאֵ֣צֶל הַנֶּ֔גֶב וַיִּפֹּ֨ל לְאַפָּ֥יו אַ֛רְצָה וַיִּשְׁתַּ֖חוּ שָׁלֹ֣שׁ פְּעָמִ֑ים וַֽיִּשְּׁק֣וּ ׀

מב   אִ֣ישׁ אֶת־רֵעֵ֗הוּ וַיִּבְכּוּ֙ אִ֣ישׁ אֶת־רֵעֵ֔הוּ עַד־דָּוִ֖ד הִגְדִּֽיל: וַיֹּ֧אמֶר יְהוֹנָתָ֛ן לְדָוִ֖ד לֵ֣ךְ לְשָׁל֑וֹם אֲשֶׁר֩ נִשְׁבַּ֨עְנוּ שְׁנֵ֜ינוּ אֲנַ֗חְנוּ בְּשֵׁ֤ם יְהוָה֙ לֵאמֹ֔ר יְהוָ֞ה יִֽהְיֶ֣ה ׀ בֵּינִ֣י וּבֵינֶ֗ךָ וּבֵ֥ין זַרְעִ֛י וּבֵ֥ין זַרְעֲךָ֖ עַד־עוֹלָֽם:

קריאה לחנוכה

On שבת *that falls on any day of* חנוכה, *read the passage for the appropriate day as marked below. Afterward, read the* הפטרה *for the first or second* שבת *of* חנוכה, *as appropriate (pp. 675–677).*

When שבת *of* חנוכה *falls on* ראש חודש טבת, *three Torah scrolls are taken out. In the first, six* עליות *are read from* פרשת מקץ. *In the second, the* מפטיר *for* שבת ראש חודש *is read (p. 661). Then* חצי קדיש *is recited, and the passage for the sixth day of* חנוכה *is read from the third Torah scroll (p. 669). Afterward, read the* הפטרה *on page 675.*

For the first day Sepharadim begin here
במדבר

ו   וַיְדַבֵּ֥ר יְהוָ֖ה אֶל־מֹשֶׁ֥ה לֵּאמֹֽר: דַּבֵּ֤ר אֶֽל־אַהֲרֹן֙ וְאֶל־בָּנָ֣יו לֵאמֹ֔ר כֹּ֥ה תְבָרֲכ֖וּ אֶת־בְּנֵ֣י

כג

כד   יִשְׂרָאֵ֑ל אָמ֖וֹר לָהֶֽם: יְבָרֶכְךָ֥ יְהוָ֖ה וְיִשְׁמְרֶֽךָ:   יָאֵ֨ר יְהוָ֧ה ׀ פָּנָ֛יו

כה

כו   אֵלֶ֖יךָ וִֽיחֻנֶּֽךָּ:   יִשָּׂ֨א יְהוָ֤ה ׀ פָּנָיו֙ אֵלֶ֔יךָ וְיָשֵׂ֥ם לְךָ֖ שָׁלֽוֹם: וְשָׂמ֥וּ

Ashkenazim begin here

ז   אֶת־שְׁמִ֖י עַל־בְּנֵ֣י יִשְׂרָאֵ֑ל וַאֲנִ֖י אֲבָרֲכֵֽם: ✶וַיְהִ֡י בְּיוֹם֩ כַּלּ֨וֹת מֹשֶׁ֜ה

א

ב   לְהָקִ֣ים אֶת־הַמִּשְׁכָּ֗ן וַיִּמְשַׁ֨ח אֹת֜וֹ וַיְקַדֵּ֤שׁ אֹתוֹ֙ וְאֶת־כָּל־כֵּלָ֔יו וְאֶת־הַמִּזְבֵּ֖חַ וְאֶת־כָּל־כֵּלָ֑יו וַיִּמְשָׁחֵ֖ם וַיְקַדֵּ֥שׁ אֹתָֽם: וַיַּקְרִ֨יבוּ֙ נְשִׂיאֵ֣י יִשְׂרָאֵ֔ל רָאשֵׁ֖י בֵּ֣ית אֲבֹתָ֑ם

ג   הֵ֚ם נְשִׂיאֵ֣י הַמַּטֹּ֔ת הֵ֥ם הָעֹמְדִ֖ים עַל־הַפְּקֻדִֽים: וַיָּבִ֣יאוּ אֶת־קָרְבָּנָ֞ם לִפְנֵ֣י יְהוָ֗ה שֵׁשׁ־עֶגְלֹ֥ת צָב֙ וּשְׁנֵ֣י עָשָׂ֣ר בָּקָ֔ר עֲגָלָ֛ה עַל־שְׁנֵ֥י הַנְּשִׂאִ֖ים וְשׁ֣וֹר לְאֶחָ֑ד וַיַּקְרִ֥יבוּ

ד   אוֹתָ֖ם לִפְנֵ֥י הַמִּשְׁכָּֽן: וַיֹּ֥אמֶר יְהוָ֖ה אֶל־מֹשֶׁ֥ה לֵּאמֹֽר: קַ֚ח מֵֽאִתָּ֔ם וְהָי֕וּ לַעֲבֹ֕ד

ה

ו   אֶת־עֲבֹדַ֖ת אֹ֣הֶל מוֹעֵ֑ד וְנָתַתָּ֤ה אוֹתָם֙ אֶל־הַלְוִיִּ֔ם אִ֖ישׁ כְּפִ֥י עֲבֹדָתֽוֹ: וַיִּקַּ֣ח מֹשֶׁ֔ה

ז   אֶת־הָעֲגָלֹ֖ת וְאֶת־הַבָּקָ֑ר וַיִּתֵּ֥ן אוֹתָ֖ם אֶל־הַלְוִיִּֽם: אֵ֣ת ׀ שְׁתֵּ֣י הָעֲגָלֹ֗ת וְאֵת֙

ח   אַרְבַּ֣עַת הַבָּקָ֔ר נָתַ֖ן לִבְנֵ֣י גֵרְשׁ֑וֹן כְּפִ֖י עֲבֹדָתָֽם: וְאֵ֣ת ׀ אַרְבַּ֣ע הָעֲגָלֹ֗ת וְאֵת֙ שְׁמֹנַ֣ת

ט   הַבָּקָ֔ר נָתַ֖ן לִבְנֵ֣י מְרָרִ֑י כְּפִי֙ עֲבֹ֣דָתָ֔ם בְּיַד֙ אִֽיתָמָ֔ר בֶּֽן־אַהֲרֹ֖ן הַכֹּהֵֽן: וְלִבְנֵ֥י קְהָ֖ת

י   לֹ֣א נָתָ֑ן כִּֽי־עֲבֹדַ֤ת הַקֹּ֙דֶשׁ֙ עֲלֵהֶ֔ם בַּכָּתֵ֖ף יִשָּֽׂאוּ: וַיַּקְרִ֣יבוּ הַנְּשִׂאִ֗ים אֵ֚ת חֲנֻכַּ֣ת

יא   הַמִּזְבֵּ֔חַ בְּי֖וֹם הִמָּשַׁ֣ח אֹת֑וֹ וַיַּקְרִ֧יבוּ הַנְּשִׂיאִ֛ם אֶת־קָרְבָּנָ֖ם לִפְנֵ֥י הַמִּזְבֵּֽחַ: וַיֹּ֥אמֶר יְהוָ֖ה אֶל־מֹשֶׁ֑ה נָשִׂ֨יא אֶחָ֜ד לַיּ֗וֹם נָשִׂ֤יא אֶחָד֙ לַיּ֔וֹם יַקְרִ֙יבוּ֙ אֶת־קָ֣רְבָּנָ֔ם לַחֲנֻכַּ֖ת

יב   הַמִּזְבֵּֽחַ:   וַיְהִ֗י הַמַּקְרִ֛יב בַּיּ֥וֹם הָרִאשׁ֖וֹן אֶת־קָרְבָּנ֑וֹ נַחְשׁ֖וֹן בֶּן־עַמִּינָדָ֑ב

יג   לְמַטֵּ֣ה יְהוּדָֽה: וְקָרְבָּנ֞וֹ קַֽעֲרַת־כֶּ֣סֶף אַחַ֗ת שְׁלֹשִׁ֣ים וּמֵאָה֮ מִשְׁקָלָהּ֒ מִזְרָ֤ק אֶחָד֙ כֶּ֔סֶף שִׁבְעִ֥ים שֶׁ֖קֶל בְּשֶׁ֣קֶל הַקֹּ֑דֶשׁ שְׁנֵיהֶ֣ם ׀ מְלֵאִ֗ים סֹ֛לֶת בְּלוּלָ֥ה בַשֶּׁ֖מֶן לְמִנְחָֽה:

14 fine flour mixed with oil for a grain offering; one golden spoon weighing ten shekel,
15 full of incense; one young bull, one ram, and one yearling sheep for a burnt offering;
16 17 one goat for a purification offering; and for the peace sacrifice two oxen, five rams,
five male goats, and five yearling sheep. This was the offering of Naḥshon son of
Aminadav.

18 19 On the second day Netanel son of Tzuar, prince of Yissakhar, presented his offering. He *For the second day*
presented as his offering one silver bowl weighing one hundred and thirty shekel and one
silver basin weighing seventy shekel according to the Sanctuary weight, both filled with
20 fine flour mixed with oil for a grain offering; one golden spoon weighing ten shekel, full
21 22 of incense; one young bull, one ram, and one yearling sheep for a burnt offering; one
23 goat for a purification offering; and for the peace sacrifice two oxen, five rams, five male
goats, and five yearling sheep. This was the offering of Netanel son of Tzuar.

24 25 On the third day came Eliav son of Ḥelon, prince of the Zebulunites: His offering was *For the third day*
one silver bowl weighing one hundred and thirty shekel and one silver basin weighing
seventy shekel according to the Sanctuary weight, both filled with fine flour mixed with
26 27 oil for a grain offering; one golden spoon weighing ten shekel, full of incense; one young
28 bull, one ram, and one yearling sheep for a burnt offering; one goat for a purification
29 offering; and for the peace sacrifice two oxen, five rams, five male goats, and five yearling
sheep. This was the offering of Eliav son of Ḥelon.

30 31 On the fourth day came Elitzur son of Shedeiur, prince of the Reubenites: His offering *For the fourth day*
was one silver bowl weighing one hundred and thirty shekel and one silver basin
weighing seventy shekel according to the Sanctuary weight, both filled with fine flour
32 mixed with oil for a grain offering; one golden spoon weighing ten shekel, full of incense;
33 34 one young bull, one ram, and one yearling sheep for a burnt offering; one goat for a
35 purification offering; and for the peace sacrifice two oxen, five rams, five male goats, and
five yearling sheep. This was the offering of Elitzur son of Shedeiur.

36 37 On the fifth day came Shelumiel son of Tzurishadai, prince of the Simeonites: His *For the fifth day*
offering was one silver bowl weighing one hundred and thirty shekel and one silver
basin weighing seventy shekel according to the Sanctuary weight, both filled with fine
38 flour mixed with oil for a grain offering; one golden spoon weighing ten shekel, full of
39 40 incense; one young bull, one ram, and one yearling sheep for a burnt offering; one goat
41 for a purification offering; and for the peace sacrifice two oxen, five rams, five male goats,
and five yearling sheep. This was the offering of Shelumiel son of Tzurishadai.

42 43 On the sixth day came Elyasaf son of Deuel, prince of the Gadites: His offering was *For the sixth day*
one silver bowl weighing one hundred and thirty shekel and one silver basin weighing
seventy shekel according to the Sanctuary weight, both filled with fine flour mixed with
44 45 oil for a grain offering; one golden spoon weighing ten shekel, full of incense; one young

יד טו כַּף אַחַת עֲשָׂרָה זָהָב מְלֵאָה קְטֹרֶת׃ פַּר אֶחָד בֶּן־בָּקָר אַיִל אֶחָד כֶּבֶשׂ־אֶחָד
טז יז בֶּן־שְׁנָתוֹ לְעֹלָה׃ שְׂעִיר־עִזִּים אֶחָד לְחַטָּאת׃ וּלְזֶבַח הַשְּׁלָמִים בָּקָר שְׁנַיִם
אֵילִם חֲמִשָּׁה עַתֻּדִים חֲמִשָּׁה כְּבָשִׂים בְּנֵי־שָׁנָה חֲמִשָּׁה זֶה קָרְבַּן נַחְשׁוֹן בֶּן־
עַמִּינָדָב׃

For the second day

יח יט בַּיּוֹם הַשֵּׁנִי הִקְרִיב נְתַנְאֵל בֶּן־צוּעָר נְשִׂיא יִשָּׂשכָר׃ הִקְרִב אֶת־קָרְבָּנוֹ קַעֲרַת־
כֶּסֶף אַחַת שְׁלֹשִׁים וּמֵאָה מִשְׁקָלָהּ מִזְרָק אֶחָד כֶּסֶף שִׁבְעִים שֶׁקֶל בְּשֶׁקֶל הַקֹּדֶשׁ
כ שְׁנֵיהֶם ׀ מְלֵאִים סֹלֶת בְּלוּלָה בַשֶּׁמֶן לְמִנְחָה׃ כַּף אַחַת עֲשָׂרָה זָהָב מְלֵאָה
כא כב קְטֹרֶת׃ פַּר אֶחָד בֶּן־בָּקָר אַיִל אֶחָד כֶּבֶשׂ־אֶחָד בֶּן־שְׁנָתוֹ לְעֹלָה׃ שְׂעִיר־עִזִּים
כג אֶחָד לְחַטָּאת׃ וּלְזֶבַח הַשְּׁלָמִים בָּקָר שְׁנַיִם אֵילִם חֲמִשָּׁה עַתֻּדִים חֲמִשָּׁה כְּבָשִׂים
בְּנֵי־שָׁנָה חֲמִשָּׁה זֶה קָרְבַּן נְתַנְאֵל בֶּן־צוּעָר׃

For the third day

כד כה בַּיּוֹם הַשְּׁלִישִׁי נָשִׂיא לִבְנֵי זְבוּלֻן אֱלִיאָב בֶּן־חֵלֹן׃ קָרְבָּנוֹ קַעֲרַת־כֶּסֶף אַחַת שְׁלֹשִׁים
וּמֵאָה מִשְׁקָלָהּ מִזְרָק אֶחָד כֶּסֶף שִׁבְעִים שֶׁקֶל בְּשֶׁקֶל הַקֹּדֶשׁ שְׁנֵיהֶם ׀ מְלֵאִים
כו כז סֹלֶת בְּלוּלָה בַשֶּׁמֶן לְמִנְחָה׃ כַּף אַחַת עֲשָׂרָה זָהָב מְלֵאָה קְטֹרֶת׃ פַּר אֶחָד בֶּן־
כח כט בָּקָר אַיִל אֶחָד כֶּבֶשׂ־אֶחָד בֶּן־שְׁנָתוֹ לְעֹלָה׃ שְׂעִיר־עִזִּים אֶחָד לְחַטָּאת׃ וּלְזֶבַח
הַשְּׁלָמִים בָּקָר שְׁנַיִם אֵילִם חֲמִשָּׁה עַתֻּדִים חֲמִשָּׁה כְּבָשִׂים בְּנֵי־שָׁנָה חֲמִשָּׁה זֶה
קָרְבַּן אֱלִיאָב בֶּן־חֵלֹן׃

For the fourth day

ל לא בַּיּוֹם הָרְבִיעִי נָשִׂיא לִבְנֵי רְאוּבֵן אֱלִיצוּר בֶּן־שְׁדֵיאוּר׃ קָרְבָּנוֹ קַעֲרַת־כֶּסֶף אַחַת
שְׁלֹשִׁים וּמֵאָה מִשְׁקָלָהּ מִזְרָק אֶחָד כֶּסֶף שִׁבְעִים שֶׁקֶל בְּשֶׁקֶל הַקֹּדֶשׁ שְׁנֵיהֶם ׀
לב לג מְלֵאִים סֹלֶת בְּלוּלָה בַשֶּׁמֶן לְמִנְחָה׃ כַּף אַחַת עֲשָׂרָה זָהָב מְלֵאָה קְטֹרֶת׃ פַּר
לד אֶחָד בֶּן־בָּקָר אַיִל אֶחָד כֶּבֶשׂ־אֶחָד בֶּן־שְׁנָתוֹ לְעֹלָה׃ שְׂעִיר־עִזִּים אֶחָד לְחַטָּאת׃
לה וּלְזֶבַח הַשְּׁלָמִים בָּקָר שְׁנַיִם אֵילִם חֲמִשָּׁה עַתֻּדִים חֲמִשָּׁה כְּבָשִׂים בְּנֵי־שָׁנָה חֲמִשָּׁה
זֶה קָרְבַּן אֱלִיצוּר בֶּן־שְׁדֵיאוּר׃

For the fifth day

לו לז בַּיּוֹם הַחֲמִישִׁי נָשִׂיא לִבְנֵי שִׁמְעוֹן שְׁלֻמִיאֵל בֶּן־צוּרִישַׁדָּי׃ קָרְבָּנוֹ קַעֲרַת־כֶּסֶף אַחַת
שְׁלֹשִׁים וּמֵאָה מִשְׁקָלָהּ מִזְרָק אֶחָד כֶּסֶף שִׁבְעִים שֶׁקֶל בְּשֶׁקֶל הַקֹּדֶשׁ שְׁנֵיהֶם ׀
לח לט מְלֵאִים סֹלֶת בְּלוּלָה בַשֶּׁמֶן לְמִנְחָה׃ כַּף אַחַת עֲשָׂרָה זָהָב מְלֵאָה קְטֹרֶת׃ פַּר
מ אֶחָד בֶּן־בָּקָר אַיִל אֶחָד כֶּבֶשׂ־אֶחָד בֶּן־שְׁנָתוֹ לְעֹלָה׃ שְׂעִיר־עִזִּים אֶחָד לְחַטָּאת׃
מא וּלְזֶבַח הַשְּׁלָמִים בָּקָר שְׁנַיִם אֵילִם חֲמִשָּׁה עַתֻּדִים חֲמִשָּׁה כְּבָשִׂים בְּנֵי־שָׁנָה חֲמִשָּׁה
זֶה קָרְבַּן שְׁלֻמִיאֵל בֶּן־צוּרִישַׁדָּי׃

For the sixth day

מב מג בַּיּוֹם הַשִּׁשִּׁי נָשִׂיא לִבְנֵי גָד אֶלְיָסָף בֶּן־דְּעוּאֵל׃ קָרְבָּנוֹ קַעֲרַת־כֶּסֶף אַחַת שְׁלֹשִׁים

46 bull, one ram, and one yearling sheep for a burnt offering; one goat for a purification
47 offering; and for the peace sacrifice two oxen, five rams, five male goats, and five yearling
sheep. This was the offering of Elyasaf son of Deuel.

For the seventh day

48 49 On the seventh day came Elishama son of Amihud, prince of the Efraimites: His
offering was one silver bowl weighing one hundred and thirty shekel and one silver
basin weighing seventy shekel according to the Sanctuary weight, both filled with fine
50 flour mixed with oil for a grain offering; one golden spoon weighing ten shekel, full of
51 52 incense; one young bull, one ram, and one yearling sheep for a burnt offering; one goat
53 for a purification offering; and for the peace sacrifice two oxen, five rams, five male goats,
and five yearling sheep. This was the offering of Elishama son of Amihud.

For the eighth day

54 55 On the eighth day came Gamliel son of Pedahtzur, prince of the Manassites: His
offering was one silver bowl weighing one hundred and thirty shekel and one silver
basin weighing seventy shekel according to the Sanctuary weight, both filled with fine
56 flour mixed with oil for a grain offering; one golden spoon weighing ten shekel, full of
57 58 incense; one young bull, one ram, and one yearling sheep for a burnt offering; one goat
59 for a purification offering; and for the peace sacrifice two oxen, five rams, five male goats,
and five yearling sheep. This was the offering of Gamliel son of Pedahtzur.

60 61 On the ninth day came Avidan son of Gidoni, prince of the Benjaminites: His offering
was one silver bowl weighing one hundred and thirty shekel and one silver basin
weighing seventy shekel according to the Sanctuary weight, both filled with fine flour
62 mixed with oil for a grain offering; one golden spoon weighing ten shekel, full of incense;
63 64 one young bull, one ram, and one yearling sheep for a burnt offering; one goat for a
65 purification offering; and for the peace sacrifice two oxen, five rams, five male goats, and
five yearling sheep. This was the offering of Avidan son of Gidoni.

66 67 On the tenth day came Aḥiezer son of Amishadai, prince of the Danites: His offering was
one silver bowl weighing one hundred and thirty shekel and one silver basin weighing
seventy shekel according to the Sanctuary weight, both filled with fine flour mixed with
68 69 oil for a grain offering; one golden spoon weighing ten shekel, full of incense; one young
70 bull, one ram, and one yearling sheep for a burnt offering; one goat for a purification
71 offering; and for the peace sacrifice two oxen, five rams, five male goats, and five yearling
sheep. This was the offering of Aḥiezer son of Amishadai.

72 73 On the eleventh day came Pagiel son of Okhran, prince of the Asherites: His offering
was one silver bowl weighing one hundred and thirty shekel and one silver basin
weighing seventy shekel according to the Sanctuary weight, both filled with fine flour
74 mixed with oil for a grain offering; one golden spoon weighing ten shekel, full of incense;
75 76 one young bull, one ram, and one yearling sheep for a burnt offering; one goat for a

וּמֵאָה מִשְׁקָלָהּ מִזְרָק אֶחָד כֶּסֶף שִׁבְעִים שֶׁקֶל בְּשֶׁקֶל הַקֹּדֶשׁ שְׁנֵיהֶם ׀ מְלֵאִים
מד מה סֹלֶת בְּלוּלָה בַשֶּׁמֶן לְמִנְחָה: כַּף אַחַת עֲשָׂרָה זָהָב מְלֵאָה קְטֹרֶת: פַּר אֶחָד בֶּן־
מו מז בָּקָר אַיִל אֶחָד כֶּבֶשׂ־אֶחָד בֶּן־שְׁנָתוֹ לְעֹלָה: שְׂעִיר־עִזִּים אֶחָד לְחַטָּאת: וּלְזֶבַח
הַשְּׁלָמִים בָּקָר שְׁנַיִם אֵילִם חֲמִשָּׁה עַתֻּדִים חֲמִשָּׁה כְּבָשִׂים בְּנֵי־שָׁנָה חֲמִשָּׁה זֶה
קָרְבַּן אֶלְיָסָף בֶּן־דְּעוּאֵל:

For the seventh day

מח מט בַּיּוֹם הַשְּׁבִיעִי נָשִׂיא לִבְנֵי אֶפְרָיִם אֱלִישָׁמָע בֶּן־עַמִּיהוּד: קָרְבָּנוֹ קַעֲרַת־כֶּסֶף אַחַת
שְׁלֹשִׁים וּמֵאָה מִשְׁקָלָהּ מִזְרָק אֶחָד כֶּסֶף שִׁבְעִים שֶׁקֶל בְּשֶׁקֶל הַקֹּדֶשׁ שְׁנֵיהֶם ׀
נ נא מְלֵאִים סֹלֶת בְּלוּלָה בַשֶּׁמֶן לְמִנְחָה: כַּף אַחַת עֲשָׂרָה זָהָב מְלֵאָה קְטֹרֶת: פַּר
נב אֶחָד בֶּן־בָּקָר אַיִל אֶחָד כֶּבֶשׂ־אֶחָד בֶּן־שְׁנָתוֹ לְעֹלָה: שְׂעִיר־עִזִּים אֶחָד לְחַטָּאת:
נג וּלְזֶבַח הַשְּׁלָמִים בָּקָר שְׁנַיִם אֵילִם חֲמִשָּׁה עַתֻּדִים חֲמִשָּׁה כְּבָשִׂים בְּנֵי־שָׁנָה חֲמִשָּׁה
זֶה קָרְבַּן אֱלִישָׁמָע בֶּן־עַמִּיהוּד:

For the eighth day

נד נה בַּיּוֹם הַשְּׁמִינִי נָשִׂיא לִבְנֵי מְנַשֶּׁה גַּמְלִיאֵל בֶּן־פְּדָהצוּר: קָרְבָּנוֹ קַעֲרַת־כֶּסֶף אַחַת
שְׁלֹשִׁים וּמֵאָה מִשְׁקָלָהּ מִזְרָק אֶחָד כֶּסֶף שִׁבְעִים שֶׁקֶל בְּשֶׁקֶל הַקֹּדֶשׁ שְׁנֵיהֶם ׀
נו נז מְלֵאִים סֹלֶת בְּלוּלָה בַשֶּׁמֶן לְמִנְחָה: כַּף אַחַת עֲשָׂרָה זָהָב מְלֵאָה קְטֹרֶת: פַּר
נח אֶחָד בֶּן־בָּקָר אַיִל אֶחָד כֶּבֶשׂ־אֶחָד בֶּן־שְׁנָתוֹ לְעֹלָה: שְׂעִיר־עִזִּים אֶחָד לְחַטָּאת:
נט וּלְזֶבַח הַשְּׁלָמִים בָּקָר שְׁנַיִם אֵילִם חֲמִשָּׁה עַתֻּדִים חֲמִשָּׁה כְּבָשִׂים בְּנֵי־שָׁנָה חֲמִשָּׁה
זֶה קָרְבַּן גַּמְלִיאֵל בֶּן־פְּדָהצוּר:

ס סא בַּיּוֹם הַתְּשִׁיעִי נָשִׂיא לִבְנֵי בִנְיָמִן אֲבִידָן בֶּן־גִּדְעֹנִי: קָרְבָּנוֹ קַעֲרַת־כֶּסֶף אַחַת שְׁלֹשִׁים
וּמֵאָה מִשְׁקָלָהּ מִזְרָק אֶחָד כֶּסֶף שִׁבְעִים שֶׁקֶל בְּשֶׁקֶל הַקֹּדֶשׁ שְׁנֵיהֶם ׀ מְלֵאִים
סב סג סֹלֶת בְּלוּלָה בַשֶּׁמֶן לְמִנְחָה: כַּף אַחַת עֲשָׂרָה זָהָב מְלֵאָה קְטֹרֶת: פַּר אֶחָד בֶּן־
סד סה בָּקָר אַיִל אֶחָד כֶּבֶשׂ־אֶחָד בֶּן־שְׁנָתוֹ לְעֹלָה: שְׂעִיר־עִזִּים אֶחָד לְחַטָּאת: וּלְזֶבַח
הַשְּׁלָמִים בָּקָר שְׁנַיִם אֵילִם חֲמִשָּׁה עַתֻּדִים חֲמִשָּׁה כְּבָשִׂים בְּנֵי־שָׁנָה חֲמִשָּׁה זֶה
קָרְבַּן אֲבִידָן בֶּן־גִּדְעֹנִי:

סו סז בַּיּוֹם הָעֲשִׂירִי נָשִׂיא לִבְנֵי דָן אֲחִיעֶזֶר בֶּן־עַמִּישַׁדָּי: קָרְבָּנוֹ קַעֲרַת־כֶּסֶף אַחַת
שְׁלֹשִׁים וּמֵאָה מִשְׁקָלָהּ מִזְרָק אֶחָד כֶּסֶף שִׁבְעִים שֶׁקֶל בְּשֶׁקֶל הַקֹּדֶשׁ שְׁנֵיהֶם ׀
סח סט מְלֵאִים סֹלֶת בְּלוּלָה בַשֶּׁמֶן לְמִנְחָה: כַּף אַחַת עֲשָׂרָה זָהָב מְלֵאָה קְטֹרֶת: פַּר
ע אֶחָד בֶּן־בָּקָר אַיִל אֶחָד כֶּבֶשׂ־אֶחָד בֶּן־שְׁנָתוֹ לְעֹלָה: שְׂעִיר־עִזִּים אֶחָד לְחַטָּאת:
עא וּלְזֶבַח הַשְּׁלָמִים בָּקָר שְׁנַיִם אֵילִם חֲמִשָּׁה עַתֻּדִים חֲמִשָּׁה כְּבָשִׂים בְּנֵי־שָׁנָה חֲמִשָּׁה
זֶה קָרְבַּן אֲחִיעֶזֶר בֶּן־עַמִּישַׁדָּי:

77 purification offering; and for the peace sacrifice two oxen, five rams, five male goats, and
five yearling sheep. This was the offering of Pagiel son of Okhran.
78 79 On the twelfth day came Aḥira son of Einan, prince of the Naftalites: His offering was
one silver bowl weighing one hundred and thirty shekel and one silver basin weighing
seventy shekel according to the Sanctuary weight, both filled with fine flour mixed with
80 81 oil for a grain offering; one golden spoon weighing ten shekel, full of incense; one young
82 bull, one ram, and one yearling sheep for a burnt offering; one goat for a purification
83 offering; and for the peace sacrifice two oxen, five rams, five male goats, and five yearling
sheep. This was the offering of Aḥira son of Einan.
84 All this was the dedication offering from the princes of Israel for the altar at the time it
was anointed: There were twelve silver bowls, twelve silver basins, and twelve golden
85 spoons, each silver bowl weighing one hundred and thirty shekel and each basin seventy
shekel – so all the silver in the utensils weighed two thousand four hundred shekel
86 according to the Sanctuary weight. There were twelve gold spoons full of incense
weighing ten shekel each according to the Sanctuary weight – so all the gold of the
87 spoons weighed one hundred and twenty shekel. The total number of the animals for
the burnt offerings was twelve bulls, twelve rams, and twelve yearling sheep, along with
88 their grain offerings. There were also twelve goats for the purification offerings. The total
number of all the animals for the peace sacrifices was twenty-four bulls, sixty rams, sixty
goats, and sixty yearling sheep. This was the dedication offering for the altar after it was
89 anointed. When Moshe entered the Tent of Meeting to speak with the LORD, he would
hear the Voice speaking to him from above the cover over the Ark of the Covenant, from
between the two cherubim. Thus did He speak to him.
8 1 2 And the LORD spoke to Moshe: "Speak to Aharon; say to him: When you raise up
3 the lamps, the seven lamps shall light the space in front of the candelabrum." Aharon
did so; he mounted the lamps toward the front of the candelabrum as the LORD
4 had commanded Moshe. This is how the lampstand was made: of hammered gold,
hammered from its base to its flowers. According to the vision that the LORD had shown
Moshe, so was the lampstand made.

עב עג בְּיוֹם עַשְׁתֵּי עָשָׂר יוֹם נָשִׂיא לִבְנֵי אָשֵׁר פַּגְעִיאֵל בֶּן־עָכְרָן׃ קָרְבָּנוֹ קַעֲרַת־כֶּסֶף אַחַת
שְׁלֹשִׁים וּמֵאָה מִשְׁקָלָהּ מִזְרָק אֶחָד כֶּסֶף שִׁבְעִים שֶׁקֶל בְּשֶׁקֶל הַקֹּדֶשׁ שְׁנֵיהֶם ׀
עד עה מְלֵאִים סֹלֶת בְּלוּלָה בַשֶּׁמֶן לְמִנְחָה׃ כַּף אַחַת עֲשָׂרָה זָהָב מְלֵאָה קְטֹרֶת׃ פַּר
עו אֶחָד בֶּן־בָּקָר אַיִל אֶחָד כֶּבֶשׂ־אֶחָד בֶּן־שְׁנָתוֹ לְעֹלָה׃ שְׂעִיר־עִזִּים אֶחָד לְחַטָּאת׃
עז וּלְזֶבַח הַשְּׁלָמִים בָּקָר שְׁנַיִם אֵילִם חֲמִשָּׁה עַתֻּדִים חֲמִשָּׁה כְּבָשִׂים בְּנֵי־שָׁנָה חֲמִשָּׁה
זֶה קָרְבַּן פַּגְעִיאֵל בֶּן־עָכְרָן׃
עח עט בְּיוֹם שְׁנֵים עָשָׂר יוֹם נָשִׂיא לִבְנֵי נַפְתָּלִי אֲחִירַע בֶּן־עֵינָן׃ קָרְבָּנוֹ קַעֲרַת־כֶּסֶף אַחַת
שְׁלֹשִׁים וּמֵאָה מִשְׁקָלָהּ מִזְרָק אֶחָד כֶּסֶף שִׁבְעִים שֶׁקֶל בְּשֶׁקֶל הַקֹּדֶשׁ שְׁנֵיהֶם ׀
פ פא מְלֵאִים סֹלֶת בְּלוּלָה בַשֶּׁמֶן לְמִנְחָה׃ כַּף אַחַת עֲשָׂרָה זָהָב מְלֵאָה קְטֹרֶת׃ פַּר
פב אֶחָד בֶּן־בָּקָר אַיִל אֶחָד כֶּבֶשׂ־אֶחָד בֶּן־שְׁנָתוֹ לְעֹלָה׃ שְׂעִיר־עִזִּים אֶחָד לְחַטָּאת׃
פג וּלְזֶבַח הַשְּׁלָמִים בָּקָר שְׁנַיִם אֵילִם חֲמִשָּׁה עַתֻּדִים חֲמִשָּׁה כְּבָשִׂים בְּנֵי־שָׁנָה חֲמִשָּׁה
זֶה קָרְבַּן אֲחִירַע בֶּן־עֵינָן׃
פד זֹאת ׀ חֲנֻכַּת הַמִּזְבֵּחַ בְּיוֹם הִמָּשַׁח אֹתוֹ מֵאֵת נְשִׂיאֵי יִשְׂרָאֵל קַעֲרֹת כֶּסֶף שְׁתֵּים
פה עֶשְׂרֵה מִזְרְקֵי־כֶסֶף שְׁנֵים עָשָׂר כַּפּוֹת זָהָב שְׁתֵּים עֶשְׂרֵה׃ שְׁלֹשִׁים וּמֵאָה הַקְּעָרָה
הָאַחַת כֶּסֶף וְשִׁבְעִים הַמִּזְרָק הָאֶחָד כֹּל כֶּסֶף הַכֵּלִים אַלְפַּיִם וְאַרְבַּע־מֵאוֹת בְּשֶׁקֶל
פו הַקֹּדֶשׁ׃ כַּפּוֹת זָהָב שְׁתֵּים־עֶשְׂרֵה מְלֵאֹת קְטֹרֶת עֲשָׂרָה עֲשָׂרָה הַכַּף בְּשֶׁקֶל הַקֹּדֶשׁ
פז כָּל־זְהַב הַכַּפּוֹת עֶשְׂרִים וּמֵאָה׃ כָּל־הַבָּקָר לָעֹלָה שְׁנֵים עָשָׂר פָּרִים אֵילִם שְׁנֵים־
עָשָׂר כְּבָשִׂים בְּנֵי־שָׁנָה שְׁנֵים עָשָׂר וּמִנְחָתָם וּשְׂעִירֵי עִזִּים שְׁנֵים עָשָׂר לְחַטָּאת׃
פח וְכֹל בְּקַר ׀ זֶבַח הַשְּׁלָמִים עֶשְׂרִים וְאַרְבָּעָה פָּרִים אֵילִם שִׁשִּׁים עַתֻּדִים שִׁשִּׁים
פט כְּבָשִׂים בְּנֵי־שָׁנָה שִׁשִּׁים זֹאת חֲנֻכַּת הַמִּזְבֵּחַ אַחֲרֵי הִמָּשַׁח אֹתוֹ׃ וּבְבֹא מֹשֶׁה
אֶל־אֹהֶל מוֹעֵד לְדַבֵּר אִתּוֹ וַיִּשְׁמַע אֶת־הַקּוֹל מִדַּבֵּר אֵלָיו מֵעַל הַכַּפֹּרֶת אֲשֶׁר
עַל־אֲרֹן הָעֵדֻת מִבֵּין שְׁנֵי הַכְּרֻבִים וַיְדַבֵּר אֵלָיו׃
ח א ב וַיְדַבֵּר יהוה אֶל־מֹשֶׁה לֵּאמֹר׃ דַּבֵּר אֶל־אַהֲרֹן וְאָמַרְתָּ אֵלָיו בְּהַעֲלֹתְךָ אֶת־
ג הַנֵּרֹת אֶל־מוּל פְּנֵי הַמְּנוֹרָה יָאִירוּ שִׁבְעַת הַנֵּרוֹת׃ וַיַּעַשׂ כֵּן אַהֲרֹן אֶל־מוּל פְּנֵי
ד הַמְּנוֹרָה הֶעֱלָה נֵרֹתֶיהָ כַּאֲשֶׁר צִוָּה יהוה אֶת־מֹשֶׁה׃ וְזֶה מַעֲשֵׂה הַמְּנֹרָה מִקְשָׁה
זָהָב עַד־יְרֵכָהּ עַד־פִּרְחָהּ מִקְשָׁה הִוא כַּמַּרְאֶה אֲשֶׁר הֶרְאָה יהוה אֶת־מֹשֶׁה כֵּן
עָשָׂה אֶת־הַמְּנֹרָה׃

HAFTARA FOR THE FIRST SHABBAT OF ḤANUKKA

ZECHARIAH

2 14 Shout out and be joyful, daughter Zion, for I am coming, and I will dwell in your
15 midst – the LORD has spoken. Many nations will join themselves to the LORD on that
day, and they will be My people. I will dwell in your midst, and you will know that the
16 LORD of Hosts sent me to you. The LORD will take possession of Yehuda as His portion
17 of holy ground, and He will choose Jerusalem once again. Hush, all flesh, before the
3 1 LORD, for He has stirred from His holy abode. Then He showed me Yehoshua
the High Priest standing before an angel of the LORD with the Adversary on his right
2 to oppose him. The LORD said to the Adversary: The LORD drives you away, Adversary.
The LORD, who has chosen Jerusalem, drives you away. Yes, this is a firebrand saved
3 from the fire. And Yehoshua, wearing filthy clothing, was standing before the angel,
4 who spoke and said to those standing before him, "Take those filthy clothes off him."
Then the angel said to him, "See, I have removed your guilt from you and dressed you
5 in finery." I said, "Place a pure turban on his head," and they placed a pure turban on his
6 head. They dressed him in clothing. The angel of the LORD remained standing. Then that
7 angel of the LORD testified regarding Yehoshua: "So says the LORD of Hosts: If you walk
in My ways, if you keep My watch, if you judge My House, and guard My courtyards,
8 then I will give you walkers among these who are standing. Listen, Yehoshua the High
Priest, you and your friends who sit before you, for they are men of wonders: Behold, I
9 am bringing My servant Tzemaḥ. Upon the stone that I set before Yehoshua, one stone
with seven eyes, I will engrave its inscription, and I will wipe away the guilt of this land
10 in one day. On that day – the LORD of Hosts has spoken – you will call one to another:
4 1 Come under the shade of the vine; come under the shade of the fig." Then the
angel with whom I had spoken returned and roused me like a man stirring from his sleep.
2 He said to me, "What do you see?" I said, "I see a candelabrum of pure gold, its bowl at
the top. It has seven lamps – seven – and seven indentations for the lamps, which are at
3 4 the top. Next to it are two olive trees, one to the right of the bowl and one to its left." I
5 spoke and said to the angel with whom I spoke, "What are these, my lord?" And the angel
with whom I spoke replied and said, "You know what these are." I said, "No, my lord."
6 Then he spoke and said to me, "This is the word of the LORD to Zerubavel: Not with
7 valor and not with strength, but with My spirit, says the LORD of Hosts. Who are you,
great mountain before Zerubavel? Surely it will become a level plain. He will remove
the re-foundation stone with clamor: Favor, favor to her!"

הפטרה לשבת ראשונה של חנוכה

ב יד טו רָנִּי וְשִׂמְחִי בַּת־צִיּוֹן כִּי הִנְנִי־בָא וְשָׁכַנְתִּי בְתוֹכֵךְ נְאֻם־יְהוָה׃ וְנִלְווּ גוֹיִם רַבִּים אֶל־ זכריה
יְהוָה בַּיּוֹם הַהוּא וְהָיוּ לִי לְעָם וְשָׁכַנְתִּי בְתוֹכֵךְ וְיָדַעַתְּ כִּי־יְהוָה צְבָאוֹת שְׁלָחַנִי
טז יז אֵלָיִךְ׃ וְנָחַל יְהוָה אֶת־יְהוּדָה חֶלְקוֹ עַל אַדְמַת הַקֹּדֶשׁ וּבָחַר עוֹד בִּירוּשָׁלִָם׃
ג א הַס כָּל־בָּשָׂר מִפְּנֵי יְהוָה כִּי נֵעוֹר מִמְּעוֹן קָדְשׁוֹ׃ וַיַּרְאֵנִי אֶת־יְהוֹשֻׁעַ
ב הַכֹּהֵן הַגָּדוֹל עֹמֵד לִפְנֵי מַלְאַךְ יְהוָה וְהַשָּׂטָן עֹמֵד עַל־יְמִינוֹ לְשִׂטְנוֹ׃ וַיֹּאמֶר
יְהוָה אֶל־הַשָּׂטָן יִגְעַר יְהוָה בְּךָ הַשָּׂטָן וְיִגְעַר יְהוָה בְּךָ הַבֹּחֵר בִּירוּשָׁלִָם הֲלוֹא
ג ד זֶה אוּד מֻצָּל מֵאֵשׁ׃ וִיהוֹשֻׁעַ הָיָה לָבֻשׁ בְּגָדִים צוֹאִים וְעֹמֵד לִפְנֵי הַמַּלְאָךְ׃ וַיַּעַן
וַיֹּאמֶר אֶל־הָעֹמְדִים לְפָנָיו לֵאמֹר הָסִירוּ הַבְּגָדִים הַצֹּאִים מֵעָלָיו וַיֹּאמֶר אֵלָיו
ה רְאֵה הֶעֱבַרְתִּי מֵעָלֶיךָ עֲוֺנֶךָ וְהַלְבֵּשׁ אֹתְךָ מַחֲלָצוֹת׃ וָאֹמַר יָשִׂימוּ צָנִיף טָהוֹר
עַל־רֹאשׁוֹ וַיָּשִׂימוּ הַצָּנִיף הַטָּהוֹר עַל־רֹאשׁוֹ וַיַּלְבִּשֻׁהוּ בְּגָדִים וּמַלְאַךְ יְהוָה עֹמֵד׃
ו ז וַיָּעַד מַלְאַךְ יְהוָה בִּיהוֹשֻׁעַ לֵאמֹר׃ כֹּה־אָמַר יְהוָה צְבָאוֹת אִם־בִּדְרָכַי תֵּלֵךְ
וְאִם אֶת־מִשְׁמַרְתִּי תִשְׁמֹר וְגַם־אַתָּה תָּדִין אֶת־בֵּיתִי וְגַם תִּשְׁמֹר אֶת־חֲצֵרָי
ח וְנָתַתִּי לְךָ מַהְלְכִים בֵּין הָעֹמְדִים הָאֵלֶּה׃ שְׁמַע־נָא יְהוֹשֻׁעַ ׀ הַכֹּהֵן הַגָּדוֹל אַתָּה
ט וְרֵעֶיךָ הַיֹּשְׁבִים לְפָנֶיךָ כִּי־אַנְשֵׁי מוֹפֵת הֵמָּה כִּי־הִנְנִי מֵבִיא אֶת־עַבְדִּי צֶמַח׃
כִּי ׀ הִנֵּה הָאֶבֶן אֲשֶׁר נָתַתִּי לִפְנֵי יְהוֹשֻׁעַ עַל־אֶבֶן אַחַת שִׁבְעָה עֵינָיִם הִנְנִי
י מְפַתֵּחַ פִּתֻּחָהּ נְאֻם יְהוָה צְבָאוֹת וּמַשְׁתִּי אֶת־עֲוֺן הָאָרֶץ־הַהִיא בְּיוֹם אֶחָד׃ בַּיּוֹם
הַהוּא נְאֻם יְהוָה צְבָאוֹת תִּקְרְאוּ אִישׁ לְרֵעֵהוּ אֶל־תַּחַת גֶּפֶן וְאֶל־תַּחַת
ד א תְּאֵנָה׃ וַיָּשָׁב הַמַּלְאָךְ הַדֹּבֵר בִּי וַיְעִירֵנִי כְּאִישׁ אֲשֶׁר־יֵעוֹר מִשְּׁנָתוֹ׃
ב וַיֹּאמֶר אֵלַי מָה אַתָּה רֹאֶה ויאמר רָאִיתִי וְהִנֵּה מְנוֹרַת זָהָב כֻּלָּהּ וְגֻלָּהּ עַל־רֹאשָׁהּ וָאֹמַר
ג וְשִׁבְעָה נֵרֹתֶיהָ עָלֶיהָ שִׁבְעָה וְשִׁבְעָה מוּצָקוֹת לַנֵּרוֹת אֲשֶׁר עַל־רֹאשָׁהּ׃ וּשְׁנַיִם
ד זֵיתִים עָלֶיהָ אֶחָד מִימִין הַגֻּלָּה וְאֶחָד עַל־שְׂמֹאלָהּ׃ וָאַעַן וָאֹמַר אֶל־הַמַּלְאָךְ
ה הַדֹּבֵר בִּי לֵאמֹר מָה־אֵלֶּה אֲדֹנִי׃ וַיַּעַן הַמַּלְאָךְ הַדֹּבֵר בִּי וַיֹּאמֶר אֵלַי הֲלוֹא יָדַעְתָּ
ו מָה־הֵמָּה אֵלֶּה וָאֹמַר לֹא אֲדֹנִי׃ וַיַּעַן וַיֹּאמֶר אֵלַי לֵאמֹר זֶה דְּבַר־יְהוָה אֶל־זְרֻבָּבֶל
ז לֵאמֹר לֹא בְחַיִל וְלֹא בְכֹחַ כִּי אִם־בְּרוּחִי אָמַר יְהוָה צְבָאוֹת׃ מִי־אַתָּה הַר־הַגָּדוֹל
לִפְנֵי זְרֻבָּבֶל לְמִישֹׁר וְהוֹצִיא אֶת־הָאֶבֶן הָרֹאשָׁה תְּשֻׁאוֹת חֵן ׀ חֵן לָהּ׃

HAFTARA FOR THE SECOND SHABBAT OF ḤANUKKA

I KINGS

7 40 Ḥiram crafted the lavers and the shovels and the basins. And so Ḥiram completed all
41 the work for the House of the Lord as commissioned by King Shlomo: two pillars
and two globe-shaped capitals for the pillar tops; two pieces of meshwork to cover
42 the two globe-shaped capitals for the pillar tops; four hundred pomegranates for
the two pieces of meshwork – two rows of pomegranates for each piece of meshwork,
43 which covered the two globe-shaped capitals on top of the pillars; ten stands and ten
44 45 lavers for the stands; one Sea with twelve oxen beneath the Sea; pots, shovels, and
basins. All these vessels, which Ḥiram crafted for King Shlomo, for the House of the
46 Lord, were of burnished bronze. The king had them cast in clay molds on the Jordan
47 plain between Sukkot and Tzartan. Due to their sheer abundance, Shlomo left all the
48 vessels out of account;the weight of the bronze was not determined. Shlomo made
all the vessels for the House of the Lord: the altar was of gold, and the table for the
49 showbread was of gold. The candelabra – five on the right and five on the left, in front
of the Inner Sanctuary – were of solid gold; the flowers, the lamps, and the tongs were
50 all of gold. The bowls, shears, basins, spoons, and firepans were of solid gold. The hinges
of the doors to the inner House, to the Holy of Holies, and of the doors of the House
to the Sanctuary, were of gold.

הפטרה לשבת שנייה של חנוכה

ז מ וַיַּעַשׂ חִירוֹם אֶת־הַכִּיֹּרוֹת וְאֶת־הַיָּעִים וְאֶת־הַמִּזְרָקוֹת וַיְכַל חִירָם לַעֲשׂוֹת מלכים א׳
מא אֶת־כָּל־הַמְּלָאכָה אֲשֶׁר עָשָׂה לַמֶּלֶךְ שְׁלֹמֹה בֵּית יְהוָה׃ עַמֻּדִים שְׁנַיִם וְגֻלֹּת
הַכֹּתָרֹת אֲשֶׁר־עַל־רֹאשׁ הָעַמּוּדִים שְׁתָּיִם וְהַשְּׂבָכוֹת שְׁתַּיִם לְכַסּוֹת אֶת־שְׁתֵּי
מב גֻּלֹּת הַכֹּתָרֹת אֲשֶׁר עַל־רֹאשׁ הָעַמּוּדִים׃ וְאֶת־הָרִמֹּנִים אַרְבַּע מֵאוֹת לִשְׁתֵּי
הַשְּׂבָכוֹת שְׁנֵי־טוּרִים רִמֹּנִים לַשְּׂבָכָה הָאֶחָת לְכַסּוֹת אֶת־שְׁתֵּי גֻּלֹּת הַכֹּתָרֹת אֲשֶׁר
מג מד עַל־פְּנֵי הָעַמּוּדִים׃ וְאֶת־הַמְּכֹנוֹת עָשֶׂר וְאֶת־הַכִּיֹּרֹת עֲשָׂרָה עַל־הַמְּכֹנוֹת׃
מה וְאֶת־הַיָּם הָאֶחָד וְאֶת־הַבָּקָר שְׁנֵים־עָשָׂר תַּחַת הַיָּם׃ וְאֶת־הַסִּירוֹת וְאֶת־הַיָּעִים
וְאֶת־הַמִּזְרָקוֹת וְאֵת כָּל־הַכֵּלִים האהל אֲשֶׁר עָשָׂה חִירָם לַמֶּלֶךְ שְׁלֹמֹה בֵּית יְהוָה הָאֵלֶּה
מו נְחֹשֶׁת מְמֹרָט׃ בְּכִכַּר הַיַּרְדֵּן יְצָקָם הַמֶּלֶךְ בְּמַעֲבֵה הָאֲדָמָה בֵּין סֻכּוֹת וּבֵין צָרְתָן׃
מז מח וַיַּנַּח שְׁלֹמֹה אֶת־כָּל־הַכֵּלִים מֵרֹב מְאֹד מְאֹד לֹא נֶחְקַר מִשְׁקַל הַנְּחֹשֶׁת׃ וַיַּעַשׂ
שְׁלֹמֹה אֵת כָּל־הַכֵּלִים אֲשֶׁר בֵּית יְהוָה אֵת מִזְבַּח הַזָּהָב וְאֶת־הַשֻּׁלְחָן אֲשֶׁר עָלָיו
מט לֶחֶם הַפָּנִים זָהָב׃ וְאֶת־הַמְּנֹרוֹת חָמֵשׁ מִיָּמִין וְחָמֵשׁ מִשְּׂמֹאול לִפְנֵי הַדְּבִיר זָהָב
נ סָגוּר וְהַפֶּרַח וְהַנֵּרֹת וְהַמֶּלְקַחַיִם זָהָב׃ וְהַסִּפּוֹת וְהַמְזַמְּרוֹת וְהַמִּזְרָקוֹת וְהַכַּפּוֹת
וְהַמַּחְתּוֹת זָהָב סָגוּר וְהַפֹּתוֹת לְדַלְתוֹת הַבַּיִת הַפְּנִימִי לְקֹדֶשׁ הַקֳּדָשִׁים לְדַלְתֵי
הַבַּיִת לַהֵיכָל זָהָב׃

Appendices

Contributors

Rabbi Yehuda Amital (1924–2010) was raised in pre-Holocaust Hungary, where he spent his youth immersed in yeshiva study. At the age of nineteen, he was deported to a Nazi labor camp and emerged as the sole survivor of his family. Upon his liberation, he made his way to the land of Israel. Fulfilling a promise that if he survived he would study Torah in Jerusalem, he attended Yeshivat Hevron for the next several years until he joined the Israel Defense Forces. After fighting in Israel's War of Independence, Rabbi Amital embarked on a remarkable career in Jewish education. In 1968, he founded Yeshivat Har Etzion and, alongside Rabbi Aharon Lichtenstein, built it into a world-renowned center of higher Torah learning and service to the Jewish people. From 1995–96, he served as a minister in the Israeli government in charge of religious-secular and Israel-Diaspora relations. After heading the largest *hesder* yeshiva for four decades and appointing his successors, Rabbi Amital retired in 2008. An exceptional public figure and religious teacher, Rabbi Amital lived a life of deep faith, humility, ethical responsibility, and commitment to individual and national vibrancy.

Rabbi Amnon Bazak serves as a *Ram* in Yeshivat Har Etzion and teaches Tanakh at Herzog College and at the SKA Beit Midrash for Women in Migdal Oz. He authored the two-volume *Nekudat Petiḥa* – short studies in *peshuto shel mikra*, and *Makbilot Nifgashot*, on literary parallels in the book of Shmuel.

Rabbi Yaakov Beasley graduated Yeshiva University with a degree in Tanakh and Jewish Education. He has taught Tanakh in schools and programs in and around Jerusalem for the past fifteen years. He is the Tanakh coordinator at Yeshivat Lev HaTorah and is completing a doctorate on the book of Mikha at Bar-Ilan University. He is the author of the volumes *Nahum, Habbakuk, and Zephaniah* and *Joel, Obadiah, and Micah* for the Maggid Studies in Tanakh series.

◂ Rabbi Ezra Bick

Rabbi Ezra Bick teaches Talmud and Jewish philosophy at Yeshivat Har Etzion, and is the director of the Israel Koschitzky Virtual Beit Midrash. He is the author of *In His Mercy: Understanding the Thirteen Midot* (Maggid Books).

Rabbi Yoel Bin-Nun studied at Yeshivat Merkaz HaRav and Yeshivat Har Etzion, where he was among the founders. He was Rosh Yeshiva at Yeshivat HaKibbutz HaDati, and currently teaches Bible and Jewish Philosophy at Herzog College.

Rabbi Mordechai Breuer (1921–2007) taught at Yeshivat Har Etzion for over thirty years, where he trained a generation of younger scholars. He was the originator of the method of biblical interpretation known as *shitat habeḥinot*. He authored two volumes of *Pirkei Moadot* (1986). Two volumes of his articles on Bereshit (*Pirkei Bereshit*) appeared after his death, as well as a volume on the book of Yeshaya.

Dr. Erica Brown is the Vice Provost for Values and Leadership at Yeshiva University and the founding director of its Rabbi Lord Jonathan Sacks-Herenstein Center for Values and Leadership. She was both a faculty member and a student of Rabbi Sacks at Jews' College, where Rabbi Sacks served as her Masters' thesis advisor. She earned a PhD from Baltimore Hebrew University, and previously served as the director of the Mayberg Center for Jewish Education and Leadership and an associate professor of curriculum and pedagogy at The George Washington University. Dr. Brown is the author of twelve books on leadership, the Hebrew Bible, and spirituality. She was a Jerusalem Fellow, is a faculty member of the Wexner Foundation, an Avi Chai Fellow, and the recipient of the 2009 Covenant Award for her work in education. She currently serves as a community scholar for Congregation Etz Chaim in Livingston, NJ.

Rabbanit Yafit Clymer received her BA from Hebrew University and her MA from Haifa University, and spent five years studying intensively at Beit Midrash Matan in Jerusalem. She continues to lecture at the various Matan campuses while also teaching in various other institutions in Israel. Rabbanit Clymer is on the steering committee of the Beit Hillel rabbinic organization and is involved with its Meshivat Nafesh initiative, bringing women's scholarship to modern questions of Jewish law and thought.

Michael A. Eisenberg is a co-founder and partner at Aleph, a venture capital fund focused on partnering with great Israeli entrepreneurs to build large, meaningful companies and impactful global brands. Mr. Eisenberg sits on the boards of Yeshivat Har Etzion and Hashomer HaChadash and lectures frequently on topics such as Israeli economics, the transition from Startup Nation to Scale-Up Nation and Israeli entrepreneurship. In the years 2016–17, he wrote *Ben Baruch*, an analysis of Tractate Brachot in the Jerusalem Talmud, *The Vanishing Jew: A*

◂ Wake-Up Call

Wake-Up Call From the Book of Esther, and *The Tree of Life and Prosperity :* 21st Century Business Principles from the Book of Genesis.

Rabbi Gad Eldad is a graduate of Yeshivat Har Etzion, Herzog College, and the Eretz Hemda Institute. He is a lecturer in Biblical and Oral Torah in the Beit Midrash for Rabbis in Rome, and the rabbi of the Beit Shmuel Synagogue in the city. He qualified to be a judge on behalf of the Chief Rabbinate of Israel, is a member of the court in Rome and Milan, and has published articles in a variety of journals in the fields of halakha, Bible, and philosophy.

Dr. Brachi Elitzur is the head of the women's campus of Herzog College, where she lectures on Bible studies and rabbinic literature in the undergraduate and graduate programs, conducts research on midrashic literature, and coordinates the Regev accelerated degree program for academically gifted students. As head of the women's campus, Dr. Elitzur advances special programs that expand the students' teaching skills, introduce students to diverse populations, and help students meet the changing needs of the education system. Dr. Elitzur holds a doctorate in Talmud from Bar-Ilan University. She lives in Ofra.

Rabbi Yitzchak Etshalom was born and raised in Los Angeles. He attended Yeshivat Kerem B'Yavneh, the Rabbi Isaac Elhanan Theological Seminary, and Yeshivat Har Etzion before receiving *semikha* from the Chief Rabbi of Yerushalayim, Rabbi Yitzhak Kolitz. Rabbi Etshalom has been a dynamic and exciting educator in the Los Angeles community since his return in 1985. He has authored two volumes of *Between the Lines of the Bible*, a methodological guide to the study of Tanakh.

Rabbi Tamir Granot studied at Yeshivat Har Etzion and earned a doctorate in Jewish Philosophy from Bar-Ilan University. He teaches Talmud and Jewish Philosophy at Herzog College and other colleges, and is the author of a Israel Koschitzky Virtual Beit Midrash series on Jewish thought and the Holocaust.

Rabbi Yonatan Grossman studied at Yeshivat Har Etzion and received a doctorate in Bible from Bar-Ilan University. He has taught at Yeshivat Har Etzion since 1998 and currently teaches Bible at Bar-Ilan University and Herzog College.

Rabbi Dr. Zvi Grumet is a master Bible teacher who lectures widely across the English-speaking world. Having earned his rabbinic ordination and Ed.D. at Yeshiva University, Rabbi Grumet dedicated the first eighteen years of his career to teaching Torah and leading educational institutions in the US. Today, he teaches at Yeshivat Eretz Hatzvi, the Pardes Institute of Jewish Studies, and Hebrew College in Boston. He is also a senior staff member at The Lookstein

Center for Jewish Education, where he is editor of *Jewish Educational Leadership* and generates initiatives to help advance Jewish education on four continents.

Rabbi Michael Hattin is a master teacher of Tanakh at the Pardes Institute of Jewish Studies in Jerusalem and serves as the Director of the Beit Midrash for the Pardes Center for Jewish Educators. He studied for rabbinic ordination at Yeshivat Har Etzion and holds a professional degree in architecture from the University of Toronto. Rabbi Hattin is the author of *Passages: Text and Transformation in the Parasha* (2012) and a number of series on the Israel Koschitzky Virtual Beit Midrash.

Rabbi Yair Kahn is head of the Overseas Students Program and has been a *Ram* at Yeshivat Har Etzion since 1987. Rabbi Kahn is the editor of the *Shiurei Hagrid* series.

Judy Klitsner is a senior lecturer at the Pardes Institute of Jewish Studies, where she has been teaching Bible and biblical exegesis for more than two decades. A disciple of the great Torah teacher Nehama Leibowitz, Ms. Klitsner has had a profound impact on a generation of students, of whom many now serve as teachers and heads of Jewish studies programs in the US, UK, and Israel. She lectures internationally at synagogues, campuses, and adult education programs that span the denominational spectrum, and she holds a visiting lectureship at the London School of Jewish Studies.

Yael Leibowitz has taught Tanakh at Ramaz, Yeshiva University's Stern College for Women, and the Drisha Institute for Jewish Education, and she has served as Resident Scholar at the Jewish Center of Manhattan. She earned her Master's degree in Judaic Studies from Columbia University. She currently teaches at Matan Women's Institute for Torah Learning and Pardes Institute of Jewish Studies.

Rabbi Menachem Leibtag was head of the program for overseas students at Yeshivat Har Etzion for over a decade. He initiated the Tanach Study Center, a comprehensive online program for the study of Tanakh. He teaches Tanakh at Yeshivat Har Etzion, Midreshet Lindenbaum, and Yeshivat Shaalvim.

Rabbi Dr. Aharon Lichtenstein (1933–2015) was born in Paris, France, and escaped the Nazi occupation with his family, arriving in the United States in 1941. After studying at Yeshivat Rabbi Chaim Berlin under Rabbi Yitzchok Hutner, he earned his rabbinic ordination at Yeshiva University and a PhD in English Literature at Harvard University. While at Yeshiva University, he became a close disciple of Rabbi Joseph B. Soloveitchik, who was later to become his father-in-law. After serving as a Rosh Yeshiva and Rosh Kollel at Yeshiva University for several years, Rabbi Lichtenstein made aliya to Israel in 1971 and joined Rabbi Yehuda Amital at the

◄ helm of Yeshivat

helm of Yeshivat Har Etzion in Alon Shevut. Committed to intensive and original Torah study, Rabbi Lichtenstein also articulated a bold Jewish worldview that embraced elements of modernity within the framework of a Torah life. In recognition of his outstanding scholarship and contributions, in 2014 Rabbi Lichtenstein was awarded the State of Israel's highest honor, the Israel Prize, in the category of Torah Literature. Alongside his genuine Torah greatness and the breadth and depth of his philosophy, he was renowned for his deep humility, nobility, and love of humanity.

Rabbi Mosheh Lichtenstein is Rosh Yeshiva at Yeshivat Har Etzion. He holds a degree in English Literature from Hebrew University, and is the author of *Moses: Envoy of God, Envoy of His People.*

Rabbi Yaakov Medan is Rosh Yeshiva at Yeshivat Har Etzion. He serves as a *Ram* for fourth-year students at the yeshiva, and teaches Tanakh and Jewish Thought at Herzog College.

Rabbanit Sharon Rimon holds a master's degree in Bible from Matan Institute and Baltimore University. She teaches Tanakh at the Women's Beit Midrash in Efrat.

Rabbi Yehuda Rock received his *semikha* from Rabbi Aharon Lichtenstein. He has taught in the Otniel *hesder* yeshiva, and was Rosh Kollel at the Boca Raton Community Kollel. He is the author of *Eved HaMelekh* on tzitzit and *tekhelet.*

Rabbi Lord Jonathan Sacks (1948–2020) was a global religious leader, respected moral voice, philosopher, and the author of more than thirty books. These include a new English translation and commentary for the Koren Sacks Siddur, the first new Orthodox siddur in a generation, and powerful commentaries for the Rosh HaShana, Yom Kippur, Sukkot, Pesaḥ, and Shavuot *maḥzorim.* Rabbi Sacks read Philosophy at Cambridge before pursuing postgraduate studies at New College, Oxford, and King's College, London. He served as Chief Rabbi of the United Hebrew Congregations of the Commonwealth from 1991 until 2013. He held eighteen honorary degrees and was awarded numerous prizes in recognition of his work, including the 2016 Templeton Prize in recognition of his "exceptional contributions to affirming life's spiritual dimension."

Rabbi Elchanan Samet has taught at Yeshivat Birkat Moshe (Maale Adumim) and currently is a senior lecturer at Herzog Teacher's College. He is the author of two series of studies in *parashat hashavua* as well as *Pirkei Eliyahu*, *Pirkei Elisha*, and *Yad LaRambam.*

Rabbi Dr. Mordechai Schiffman is an Assistant Professor at Yeshiva University's Azrieli Graduate School and an instructor at the Rabbi Isaac Elchanan Theological Seminary (RIETS), the Wurzweiler School of Social Work, and the Straus Center for Torah and Western Thought. He received his MS from Azrieli, rabbinic ordination from RIETS, and a doctorate in psychology from St. John's

University. Rabbi Dr. Schiffman has been on the rabbinic staff of Kingsway Jewish Center in Brooklyn, NY, since 2011 and practices as a licensed psychologist. He authored *Psyched for Torah*, and many of his articles and lectures are accessible on www.PsychedForTorah.com.

Dr. Gerald L. Schroeder earned his BSc, MSc, and PhD in Nuclear Physics and Earth and Planetary Sciences at the Massachusetts Institute of Technology, where he taught physics for seven years. He has served as a consultant to various governments worldwide and has been published in *Time*, *Newsweek*, and *Scientific American*. He is the author of *Genesis and the Big Bang*, *The Discovery of Harmony Between Modern Science and the Bible*, *The Science of God*, *The Hidden Face of God*, and *God According to God*.

Rabbanit Dr. Adina Sternberg has a BA in Bible from Hebrew University and a MA and PhD in Talmud from Bar-Ilan University. She studied at Midreshet Lindenbaum, Migdal Oz, Havruta, and the Advanced Talmud Institute at Matan. She currently teaches Bible and Talmud at Matan, and Efrata and Orot colleges. She lives in Adam (Geva Binyamin) with her family.

Rabbi Abraham J. Twerski (1930–2021) was a scion of the Chernobyl hasidic dynasty, and a world-renowned psychiatrist specializing in substance abuse. He was a prolific writer of books on a diverse array of Jewish topics, and often brought the world of Torah and psychiatry together in his writings. He was co-spiritual leader of Congregation Beth Jehudah in Milwaukee, WI.

Rabbi Chanoch Waxman received *semikha* from Yeshiva University and holds Master's degrees in Jewish and General Philosophy. He has taught at Matan in Jerusalem and been the Rosh Kollel of the Torah Mitzion Kollel in Chicago, IL. He currently teaches at Yeshivat Har Etzion.

Dr. Yael Ziegler is a lecturer in Tanakh at Herzog College and at Matan Jerusalem. A graduate of Stern College and Bar-Ilan University, she is the author of *Promises to Keep: The Oath in Biblical Narrative*, *Ruth: From Alienation to Monarchy*, and *Lamentations: Faith in a Turbulent World*.

Bibliography of Sources Cited

Eisenberg, M. A., *The Tree of Life and Prosperity: 21st Century Business Principles from the Book of Genesis* (Wicked Son, 2021).

Etshalom, Y., *Between the Lines of the Bible: Genesis* (Urim, 2015).

Grumet, Z., *Genesis: From Creation to Covenant* (Maggid Books, 2017).

Klitsner, J., *Subversive Sequels in the Bible* (Maggid Books, 2019).

Sacks, J., *Covenant & Conversation: A Weekly Reading of the Bible – Genesis: The Book of Beginnings* (Maggid Books, 2009).

Future Tense (Maggid Books, 2021).

Lessons on Leadership: A Weekly Reading of the Jewish Bible (Maggid Books, 2015).

Not in God's Name (Maggid Books, 2016).

Essays on Ethics: A Weekly Reading of the Jewish Bible (Maggid Books, 2016).

Judaism's Life-Changing Ideas: A Weekly Reading of the Jewish Bible (Maggid Books, 2020).

Studies in Spirituality: A Weekly Reading of the Jewish Bible (Maggid Books, 2021).

I Believe: A Weekly Reading of the Jewish Bible (Maggid Books, 2022).

Schiffman, M., *Psyched for Torah* (Kodesh Press, 2022).

Schroeder, G. L., *The Science of God* (Free Press, 1997).

Koren Tanakh LeMetayel (Koren, 2020).

Torah MiEtzion: New Readings in Tanach – Bereshit (Maggid Books, 2011).

Image credits

All maps and images are copyright Koren Publishers Jerusalem, except for:

BERESHIT

Page 6, *Day 7* © Yoram Raanan, yoramraanan.com; page 18, *Adam and Eve* © Michelle Levy; page 26, *Adam and Eve Driven Out of Eden* © Jan Arkesteijn, by Gustave Doré, self-scanned, public domain; page 33, *Cain & Abel* © Adi Nes, courtesy Jack Shainman Gallery, NY; page 42, *God Appears to Noah* © Dauster, public domain; page 48, *The World on Fire*, photo by Javier Miranda on Unsplash.

NOAḤ

Page 58, *Noah's Ark*, Philadelphia Museum of Art: Bequest of Lisa Norris Elkins, 1950, 1950-92-7 (public domain); page 61, *The Ark Encounter* © EUGENIO ROIG / Alamy Stock Photo; page 66, *The Deluge* © Heritage Image Partnership Ltd / Alamy Stock Photo; page 74, *The Dove Sent Forth from the Ark* © Elton Luz, public domain, by Gustave Doré; page 76, *The Mountains of Ararat*, Սէրուժ Ուրիշեան (Serouj Ourishian), own work, CC BY 4.0; *Map of Mountains of Ararat* © Steinsaltz Center; pages 82–83, *Rainbow Landscape* © Yoram Raanan, yoramraanan.com; page 88, *Noah Cursing Canaan*, Gustave Doré, public domain, via Wikimedia Commons; page 97, *Noah's Family Tree,* created by Tani Bayer; page 104, *The Tower of Babel,* by Pieter Brueghel the Elder, public domain; page 107, *Ancient Ziggurat in Iraq* © Akram Harby; page 112, *Abraham Journeying into the Land of Canaan*, engraving by H. Pisan after illustration by Gustave Doré, Héliodore-Joseph Pisan, public domain.

LEKH LEKHA

Page 118, *Lech Lecha* © Yoram Raanan, yoramraanan.com; page 124, *Abraham and Sarah at the Court of the Pharaohs*, Archivio fotografico del Museo Civico di Modena; page 134, *The Parting of Lot and Abraham*, public domain; page 137, *Dead Sea Valley at Sunrise*, public domain, Amykill26 CC BY-SA 4.0; page 142, *The Meeting of Abraham and Melchizedek*, public domain, by Dieric Bouts; page 150, *The Covenant of the Pieces*, courtesy of Moshe Castel Museum; pages 152–3, *heifer*, Udi Steinwell; *ram*, SuperJew CC BY-SA 3.0; *goat*, Raphael Melnick CC BY-SA 2.0; *turtledove*, Kev Chapman CC BY-SA 2.0; *pigeon*, Pixabay, scottslm; page 158, *Hagar and Ishmael* © Dikla Laor; page 160, aerial photo of the Desert of Shur, demonzak CC BY-SA 3.0; page 166, *Blessed Are You* © Zena Behrman (2013).

VAYERA

Page 176, *Les Hotes d'Abraham*, Abel Pann © Estate of the artist; page 188, *The Destruction of Sodom and Gomorrah*, public domain, by John Martin, via Wikimedia Commons; page 194, Marc Chagall, *Sarah and Abimelech* © ADAGP, Paris, 2023; page 200, *A Mother's Joy*, created by Tani Bayer with Freepik image; page 206, *Hagar and Ishmael in the Wilderness*, public domain, by Gustave Doré, via Wikimedia Commons; page 212, *Abraham and Abimelech*, public domain by Jan de Herdt, via Wikimedia Commons; page 215, *Excavations at Tel Be'er Sheva* © Daniel Baránek CC BY-SA 4.0; page 222, *Sacrifice of Isaac*, photograph © The State Hermitage, by Rembrandt van Rijn – Web Gallery of Art, public domain.

ḤAYEI SARA

Page 234, *Cave of the Patriarchs* © Yoram Raanan, yoramraanan.com; page 237, *Cave of Makhpela in Ḥevron*, Utilisateur:Djampa CC BY-SA 4.0; page 244, *Rebecca* © Dikla Laor; page 247, *Ancient ruins in Ḥaran*, Alen Ištoković CC BY-SA 3.0; page 254, *Isaac's Servant Tying the Bracelet on Rebecca's Arm*, public domain, by Benjamin West, via Wikimedia Commons; page 262, *The Meeting of Isaac and Rebecca*, public domain, by James Jacques Joseph Tissot, via Wikimedia Commons; page 270, *Family of Abraham*, public domain, by unknown author, via Wikimedia Commons; page 276, *Burial of Abraham*, Art World / Alamy Stock Photo; page 279, *Ein Ovdat*, Mboesch, CC BY-SA 4.0.

TOLEDOT

Page 284, *Jacob and Esau* © Adi Nes, courtesy Jack Shainman Gallery, NY; page 294, *The Jewish Bride*, DcoetzeeBot, public domain; page 304, *Isaac Blessing Jacob* © Yoram Raanan, yoramraanan.com; page 312, *The Eighth Commandment: "Thou shalt not steal"* © The Ratner Museum, courtesy of Yad LaBanim Beer Sheva; page 322, *Isaac Blessing Jacob*, public domain, by Gustave Doré, via Wikimedia Commons; page 325, *Foundations of the Cave of Makhpela in Ḥevron*, CyberCop, CC BY-SA 3.0.

VAYETZE

Page 332, Marc Chagall, *Jacob's Ladder* © ADAGP, Paris, 2023; page 342, *Jacob and Rachel at the Well*, public domain, by James Tissot, via Wikimedia Commons; page 352, *And God Remembered Rachel*, Abel Pann © Estate of the artist; page 360, *Jacob Leading the Flocks of Laban*, public domain, by Giovanni Benedetto, via Wikimedia Commons; page 366, *Jacob Persuades Leah and Rachel to Flee*, public domain, by Pieter Symonsz Potter – Mauritshuis, via Wikimedia Commons; page 376, Marc Chagall, *Rachel Hides Her Father's Household Gods* © ADAGP, Paris, 2023; page 378,

View of the mountains of Gilad and the Yabok Stream, Jim Greenhill, U.S. Army, public domain, via Wikimedia Commons.

VAYISHLAḤ

Page 386, *The Prayer of Jacob*, World History Archive / Alamy Stock Photo; page 394, *Jacob Wrestling with the Angel*, Rembrandt van Rijn, public domain, via Wikimedia Commons; pages 396–7, *Zarqa River*, Adeeb Atwan CC BY-SA 3.0; page 404, *The Meeting of Esau and Jacob*, photo by Javier Miranda on Unsplash; page 415, *Dina* © Dikla Laor; page 422, *Deborah, The Nurse of Rebecca* © Dikla Laor; pages 424–5, *Remains of a Canaanite cultic site at Tel Beit El*, Deror_avi CC BY SA 4.0; page 430, *Journey to Pray with Rachel* © Alex Levin; page 432, *The Tomb of Rahel in 1900 and today* © Israel Government Press Office © Michael Yakobson/Wikimedia; page 438, *The Families of Jacob* © The Ratner Museum; Courtesy of Yad LaBanim Beer Sheva.

VAYESHEV

Page 446, *Joseph Tells His Dreams to Jacob*, courtesy of Rijksmuseum, Amsterdam; page 456, *Joseph's Brothers Throw Him in the Pit*, © Lebrecht Music & Arts / Alamy Stock Photo; page 464, Marc Chagall, *Tamar, Daughter-in-Law of Judah* © ADAGP, Paris, 2023; pages 466–7, *View of Tel Batash*, Nizzan Zvi Coehn, CC BY-SA 4.0; page 473, *Joseph Accused by Potiphar's Wife*, public domain, by Workshop of Rembrandt; page 480, *Joseph in Prison*, by Gerbrand van den Eeckhout.

MIKETZ

Page 494, Marc Chagall, *Joseph Explains the Dreams of Pharaoh* © ADAGP, Paris, 2023; page 502, *Joseph Dwelt in Egypt*, James Tissot, public domain, via Wikimedia Commons; page 512, *Joseph And His Brothers In Egypt* © Salvador Dalí, Fundació Gala-Salvador Dalí, VEGAP, Tel Aviv, 2024; page 520, *Drought*, created by Tani Bayer; page 521, *Almond branch*, public domain; page 523, *Pistachio nuts*, Zeynel Cebeci CC BY-SA 4.0; *Pink rockrose*, SuperJew CC BY-SA 3.0; page 530, *The Banquet* © Yoram Raanan, yoramraanan.com; page 534, *The Silver Goblet Is Found in Benjamin's Sack*, Alexander Ivanov, public domain, via Wikimedia Commons.

VAYIGASH

Page 542, *Yehuda*, created by Tani Bayer; page 550, *Joseph Reveals Himself to His Brothers*, Gustave Doré, public domain, via Wikimedia Commons; page 552, *The Nile Delta*, NASA Goddard Space Flight Center from Greenbelt, MD, USA, CC BY 2.0; page 558, *The Land of Goshen*, Penta Springs

Limited / Alamy Stock Photo; page 568, *Jacob Goes to Egypt*, Gustave Doré, public domain, via Wikimedia Commons; page 574, *The Reunion* © Yoram Raanan, yoramraanan.com; page 582, *Joseph Selling Corn in Egypt*, Pieter Lastman, CC BY-SA 4.0.

VAYEḤI

Page 592, *Pilgrims by the Cave of Machpelah* © Alex Levin; page 602, *Jacob Blessing the Children of Joseph*, Rembrandt van Rijn, public domain, via Wikimedia Commons; page 610, *Blessings* © Yoram Raanan, yoramraanan.com; page 618, *Death of Jacob*, Philip De Vere, CC BY-SA 3.0; page 626, *Joseph's Tomb in Shechem*, Tom Miller, CC BY-SA 2.0.

KOREN